The Handbook of Stress

Wiley-Blackwell Handbooks of Behavioral Neuroscience

The rapidly expanding field of behavioral neuroscience examines neurobiological aspects of behavior, utilizing techniques from molecular biology, neuropsychology, and psychology. This series of handbooks provides a cutting-edge overview of classic research, current scholarship, and future trends in behavioral neuroscience. The series provides a survey of representative topics in this field, suggesting implications for basic research and clinical applications.

Series editor: David Mostofsky, Boston University

The Handbook of Stress: Neuropsychological Effects on the Brain
Edited by Cheryl D. Conrad

Forthcoming:

The Handbook of the Neuropsychology of Language (2 Volumes)
Edited by Miriam Faust

The Handbook of Alzheimer's Disease and Other Dementias
Edited by Neil W. Kowall and Andrew E. Budson

The Handbook of Stress

Neuropsychological Effects on the Brain

Edited by Cheryl D. Conrad

WILEY-BLACKWELL

A John Wiley & Sons, Ltd., Publication

This edition first published 2011
© 2011 Blackwell Publishing Ltd.

Blackwell Publishing was acquired by John Wiley & Sons in February 2007. Blackwell's publishing program
has been merged with Wiley's global Scientific, Technical, and Medical business to form Wiley-Blackwell.

Registered Office
John Wiley & Sons Ltd, The Atrium, Southern Gate, Chichester, West Sussex, PO19 8SQ, United Kingdom

Editorial Offices
350 Main Street, Malden, MA 02148-5020, USA
9600 Garsington Road, Oxford, OX4 2DQ, UK
The Atrium, Southern Gate, Chichester, West Sussex, PO19 8SQ, UK

For details of our global editorial offices, for customer services, and for information about how to apply for
permission to reuse the copyright material in this book please see our website at www.wiley.com/
wiley-blackwell.

The right of Cheryl D. Conrad to be identified as the author of the editorial material in this work has been
asserted in accordance with the UK Copyright, Designs and Patents Act 1988.

Library of Congress Cataloging-in-Publication Data

The handbook of stress : neuropsychological effects on the brain / edited by Cheryl D. Conrad.
   p. ; cm. – (Wiley-Blackwell handbooks of behavioral neuroscience)
   Includes bibliographical references and index.
   ISBN 978-1-4443-3023-6 (hardcover : alk. paper) – ISBN 978-1-118-07865-5 (ePDF) –
ISBN 978-1-118-08322-2 (Wiley online library) – ISBN 978-1-118-07871-6 (ePub) –
ISBN 978-1-118-08320-8 (mobi)
   1. Stress (Psychology)   2. Anxiety disorders.   3. Brain.   4. Neuropsychiatry.   I. Conrad, Cheryl
D.   II. Series: Wiley-Blackwell handbooks of behavioral neuroscience.
   [DNLM: 1. Stress, Psychological–complications.   2. Anxiety Disorders–complications.   3. Brain
Diseases–etiology.   4. Brain Diseases–physiopathology. WM 172]
   RC455.4.S87H36 2011
   616.9'8–dc22
                                           2011006755

A catalogue record for this book is available from the British Library.

This book is published in the following electronic formats: ePDFs 9781118078655; Wiley Online Library
9781118083222; ePub 9781118078716; mobi 9781118083208

Set in 10.5 on 13 pt Minion by Toppan Best-set Premedia Limited
Printed and bound in Singapore by Markono Print Media Pte Ltd

1   2011

To my son and husband, Ely and Stuart, for your understanding in allowing me the guiltless pleasure to pursue my passion.
You are the Yin to my Yang.

Contents

Contributors

D. Caroline Blanchard, Department of Psychology, Pacific Biosciences Research Center, University of Hawaii at Manoa, USA

Robert J. Blanchard, Department of Psychology, Pacific Biosciences Research Center, University of Hawaii at Manoa, USA

Erik B. Bloss, Fishberg Department of Neuroscience, Mount Sinai School of Medicine, New York, USA

J. Douglas Bremner, Departments of Psychiatry and Behavioral Sciences and Radiology, Emory University, School of Medicine, Atlanta, USA

Patrizia Campolongo, Department of Physiology and Pharmacology, University of Rome "La Sapienza," Italy

John A. Cidlowski, Laboratory of Signal Transduction, NIEHS/NIH/DHHS, Research Triangle Park, USA

Hagit Cohen, Beer-Sheva Mental Health Center, The State of Israel Ministry of Health, Anxiety and Stress Research Unit, Faculty of Health Sciences, Ben-Gurion University of the Negev, Beer-Sheva, Israel

Andrew Collins, Henry Wellcome Laboratories for Integrative Neuroscience and Endocrinology, University of Bristol, Bristol, UK

Cheryl D. Conrad, Department of Psychology and Division of Natural Sciences, College of Liberal Arts and Sciences, Arizona State University, USA

Jacek Dębiec, Department of Psychiatry, New York University School of Medicine – Bellevue Hospital Center, New York, USA

E. Ronald de Kloet, Division of Medical Pharmacology/LACDR-LUMC, University of Leiden, The Netherlands

Dominique J.-F. de Quervain, Department of Psychology, Division of Cognitive Neuroscience, and Psychiatric University Clinic, University of Basel, Switzerland

Roel H. DeRijk, Division of Medical Pharmacology/LACDR-LUMC, University of Leiden, The Netherlands

David M. Diamond, Medical Research Service, VA Hospital, Tampa, FL, Departments of Psychology and Molecular Pharmacology & Physiology, and Center for Preclinical & Clinical Research on PTSD, University of South Florida, Tampa, USA

Michael N. Dretsch, Cognitive Assessment and Diagnostics Branch, United States Army Aeromedical Research Laboratory (USAARL), Fort Rucker, USA

Gabriele Flügge, German Primate Center, Leibniz Institute for Primate Research, Göttingen, Germany

Eberhard Fuchs, German Primate Center, Leibniz Institute for Primate Research, Göttingen, Germany

Allison Jane Fulford, Centre for Comparative and Clinical Anatomy, School of Medical Sciences, University of Bristol, UK

Elizabeth Gould, Department of Psychology and Neuroscience Institute, Princeton University, USA

Femke Groeneweg, Department of Neuroscience & Pharmacology, Rudolf Magnus Institute of Neuroscience, UMC Utrecht, The Netherlands

María Gutièrrez-Mecinas, Henry Wellcome Laboratories for Integrative Neuroscience and Endocrinology, University of Bristol, UK

Michel Hamon, INSERM UMR S894, and UPMC Université Paris 06, France

James P. Herman, Department of Psychiatry and Behavioral Neuroscience, University of Cincinnati, USA

Marian Joëls, Department of Neuroscience & Pharmacology, Rudolf Magnus Institute of Neuroscience, UMC Utrecht, The Netherlands

Ilia N. Karatsoreos, Laboratory of Neuroendocrinology, Rockefeller University, New York, USA

Henk Karst, Department of Neuroscience & Pharmacology, Rudolf Magnus Institute of Neuroscience, UMC Utrecht, The Netherlands

Efthymia Kitraki, Department of Basic Sciences, School of Dentistry, University of Athens, Greece

Laurence Lanfumey, INSERM UMR S894, and UPMC Université Paris 06, France

François Laplante, Department of Psychiatry, McGill University, Montréal, Québec, Canada

Joseph E. LeDoux, Center for Neural Science, New York University, USA

Linda J. Luecken, Department of Psychology, Arizona State University, Tempe, USA

Victoria N. Luine, Hunter College of CUNY, Department of Psychology, New York, USA

Sonia J. Lupien, Centre for Studies on Human Stress, Fernand-Seguin Research Center, Louis-H. Lafontaine Hospital, Faculty of Medicine, Université de Montréal, Quebec, Canada

Marie-France Marin, Centre for Studies on Human Stress, Fernand-Seguin Research Center, Louis-H. Lafontaine Hospital, Faculty of Medicine, Université de Montréal, Quebec, Canada

Bruce S. McEwen, Laboratory of Neuroendocrinology, Rockefeller University, New York, USA

Onno C. Meijer, Division of Medical Pharmacology/LACDR-LUMC, University of Leiden, The Netherlands

Raymond Mongeau, INSERM UMR S894, and UPMC Université Paris 06, France

John H. Morrison, Fishberg Department of Neuroscience, Kastor Neurobiology of Aging Laboratories, Mount Sinai School of Medicine, New York, USA

Miranda Olff, Department of Psychiatry, Academic Medical Center, University of Amsterdam, The Netherlands

Collin R. Park, Medical Research Service, VA Hospital, Tampa, FL, and Department of Psychology and Center for Preclinical & Clinical Research on PTSD, University of South Florida, USA

Brandon L. Pearson, Department of Psychology, Pacific Biosciences Research Center, University of Hawaii at Manoa, USA

Catherine Purdom, Department of Psychology, Arizona State University, Tempe, USA

Johannes M. H. M. Reul, Henry Wellcome Laboratories for Integrative Neuroscience and Endocrinology, University of Bristol, Bristol, UK

Gal Richter-Levin, The Institute for the Study of Affective Neuroscience (ISAN), The Brain and Behavior Research Center, Department of Psychology & Department of Neurobiology and Ethology, University of Haifa, Israel

Russell D. Romeo, Department of Psychology and Neuroscience and Behavior Program, Barnard College of Columbia University, New York, USA

Benno Roozendaal, Department of Neuroscience, Section Anatomy, University Medical Center Groningen, University of Groningen, The Netherlands

Danielle S. Roubinov, Department of Psychology, Arizona State University, Tempe, USA

Carmen Sandi, Laboratory of Behavioral Genetics, Brain Mind Institute, Swiss Federal Institute of Technology (EPFL), Lausanne, Switzerland

Timothy J. Schoenfeld, Department of Psychology and Neuroscience Institute, Princeton University, USA

Alyson B. Scoltock, Laboratory of Signal Transductionk, NIEHS/NIH/DHHS, Research Triangle Park, USA

Ron M. Sullivan, Department of Psychiatry, McGill University, Montréal, Québec, Canada

Kenneth J. Thiel, Cognitive Assessment and Diagnostics Branch, United States Army Aeromedical Research Laboratory (USAARL), Fort Rucker, USA

Cara L. Wellman, Department of Psychological & Brain Sciences, Indiana University, Bloomington, USA

Oliver T. Wolf, Department of Cognitive Psychology, Ruhr-University Bochum, Germany

Joseph Zohar, The Chaim Sheba Medical Center, Sackler Medical School, Tel-Aviv University, Tel Hashomer, Israel

Phillip R. Zoladz, Department of Psychology and Sociology, Ohio Northern University, Ada, USA

Foreword

The superb book you hold in your hand concerns two domains of stress research. One domain is mechanistic in nature, with implications for understanding disease; the other domain is a remnant of a neurosis that plagued the field in its youth.

The mixed contribution first. Around the 1960s, stress physiology suffered a crisis of self-definition and self-confidence. From its start in the primordial ooze of Cannon and Selye, the field was just that—physiology. This was the era where the flashiest scientists obsessed over vaccines, microbes, and drug development. In contrast, the basic stress concept, the notion that generic "challenges" could result in generic "poor health," felt squishy—less scientific. Thus, the early stress physiologists had a strong incentive to study hard-nosed things like whether there was a linear relationship between the magnitude of hypotension and the magnitude of the stress-response. *Real* science.

But then, the trauma of the 1960s, as room had to be *made for psychologists and the fact that the magnitude of the stress-response could be modulated by things like whether an organism felt a sense of control over the stressor . . . by what the organism felt*!

Despite becoming more reductive, the physiological tradition of stress research has still had to accommodate the embarrassing and growing relevance of the imprecise world of affect and subjectivity and personality.

This timely book summarizes an emerging détente. Mothering style causes epigenetic changes in an infant; depression alters telomere length; anxiety modulates gene transcription. Psychobiological and molecular approaches are utterly intertwined.

This book is also an advance in a second domain, helping to resolve a seeming paradox: a) stressful events in life, beginning with fetal life, can have adverse consequences that are life-long, even multigenerational; b) numerous environmental interventions mitigate against those life-long effects. In other words, lots of stress and you're potentially screwed for a long, long time . . . but rarely irreparably. How to understand extremely persistent biological footprints that, nonetheless, can be erased? Understanding the biology of why humans develop with opposable thumbs but not antlers—easy. Understanding the biology of why muscle mass increases if you exercise—easy. But it's not easy to understand how stress can have consequences as persistent as the days we will spend without antlers, while those consequences can be lessened by the equivalents of doing push-ups regularly.

And what this book does is present the cutting-edge mechanisms that enable the simultaneity of persistence and reversibility. Phosphorylation and dephosphorylation. Up- and down-regulation of receptors. LTP and LTD, synapses that come and go, dendritic atrophy and sprouting. And of course the two most exciting realms of plasticity—epigenetics and adult neurogenesis.

It is the duty of every writer of book forewords to argue that this is an especially auspicious time for progress in their field, so I might as well do the same, arguing that what once seemed "squishy" with mixed recognition is now center stage. That is, the pathogenicity of sadness, anxiety, or social isolation is fast becoming as much a molecular phenomenon as is the pathogenicity of, say, clogged arteries. And the specific knowledge being gained emphasizes the imperative of environmental—individual and societal—interventions that can lessen the impact of stress.

Robert Sapolsky

Preface

The purpose of this book is to serve as a comprehensive and authoritative guide to the central issues and state-of-the-art research on the effects of stress on brain health. It fills a void in the literature, coalescing works from leading international scholars in the field of stress and brain function. Contributing scholars investigate stress actions in the brain at all levels of analysis, stemming from those who work at the level of the molecular stage, the cellular phase, systems interactions, and function using animal models and clinical settings. The breadth of the topics covered include the basics of the stress response (Part I) to introduce the reader to terms and concepts that are used throughout the book, which are followed by the variety of ways that stress can influence brain plasticity and cognition (Part II) and its actions across the life span (Part III). Subsequent chapters cover pathological outcomes such as anxiety, posttraumatic stress disorder (PTSD), and depression (Part IV). The final chapters (Part V) reveal that many factors contribute to brain plasticity and pathology in response to stress, called resilience, and these include coping strategies, predictability, and genetic factors such as gender. This book is unique because it focuses on both the beneficial and detrimental effects of stress on brain health. Readers will gain an appreciation for the brain's ability to adapt and respond to stress in ways that maximize brain function in a dynamic world, but will also come to understand that the brain has limits, with maladaptive outcomes occurring when exceeding these limits.

To conceptualize the theme of balance, the cover art of this book was chosen to visualize the integration of *stress* and the brain, to represent the universal theme of balance, or yin yang. Yin is characterized as soft, cold, wet, and tranquil. In contrast, Yang is hard, fast, edgy, and dry. These two forces are somewhat opposite, but they are not opposing: they balance each other. In a similar parallel, stress also has a balance: it is needed to produce energy and motivation so that an individual can survive challenges. However, persistent or unregulated stress can lead to maladaptive outcomes. The key is finding mechanisms that allow for harmony.

In Part I, Basics of the Stress Response, the fundamentals of the stress response are covered to allow readers the opportunity to become familiar with the terms and concepts that follow in the subsequent chapters. In Chapter 1 by Thiel and Dretsch, a historical context is presented before core themes in stress research are outlined. In Chapter 2, Herman presents the latest findings on the central nervous system regulation of the hypothalamic–pituitary–adrenal (HPA) axis. de Kloet, DeRijk, and Meijer (Chapter 3) discuss the role of the corticosteroid steroid receptors in endocrine regulation and behavioral balance. Joëls, Groeneweg, and Karst (Chapter 4), Reul, Collins, and Gutièrrez-Mecinas (Chapter 5), and Scoltock and Cidlowski (Chapter 6) present novel findings about nontraditional mechanisms for corticosteroid actions and processes by which the genome can be regulated through epigenetics; that is, the facilitation or hindrance of gene expression. Despite the introductory role of this section, the authors present some of the most novel and cutting-edge findings in the field of stress research today.

Part II is entitled Stress Influences on Brain Plasticity and Cognition. The effects of stress are discussed along many different levels of plasticity, from actions on hippocampal neurogenesis by Schoenfeld and Gould (Chapter 7) to actions on cognition, the latter of which falls along many dimensions. Zoladz, Park, and Diamond (Chapter 8) describe the neurobiological effects of stress on synaptic plasticity and memory in animal models. Campolongo and Roozendaal (Chapter 9) discuss how glucocorticoids influence memory as a function of arousal. Wellman (Chapter 10) introduces the consequences of chronic stress on limbic morphology and Sandi (Chapter 11) describes the consequences of chronic stress on memory. This section concludes with Marin and Lupien (Chapter 12) integrating the most recent studies on how stress and glucocorticoids influence learning and memory in humans.

The goal of Part III, Stress Effects Across the Life Span, is to demonstrate that stress has unique actions that depend upon the age of the subject. Sections were chosen to capture concepts across most developmental milestones and these include early life by Romeo and Karatsoreos (Chapter 13), Fulford (Chapter 14), and Luecken, Roubinov, and Purdom (Chapter 15). The effects of chronic stress on altering the brain, such as the hippocampus, are described by Conrad (Chapter 16) to emphasize that vulnerability to stress continues in adulthood. Finally, Bloss, Morrison, and McEwen (Chapter 17) conclude this section to highlight that stress and environment have a relationship that can increase or decrease pathology to disease.

Within the last decade, a huge number of research papers have shown connections between the stress system and pathology and these are showcased in Part IV, Stress Involvement in Anxiety, Posttraumatic Stress Disorder, and Depression. Pearson, Blanchard, and Blanchard (Chapter 18) summarize how social conflict and defeat can contribute to anxiety. Cohen, Richter-Levin, and Zohar (Chapter 19), Dębiec and LeDoux (Chapter 20), and de Quervain (Chapter 21) focus on parallels between stress and PTSD with unique niches: Cohen and colleagues use a unique model for a *behavioral cut-off* that allows for individual differences to be factored into outcome measures. Debiec and LeDoux present work with fear conditioning, a procedure that is simple with well described pathways and mediators. De Quervain offers insights for a glucocorticoid-mediated process in PTSD in humans. Bremner (Chapter 22) demonstrates changes in the human brain diagnosed with PTSD, based upon functional neuroimaging studies. The last three chapters focus on the connection between stress and depression. Despite depression being projected as the second leading cause of disability and disease burden throughout the world, according to the World Health Organization, little progress has been made in the last few decades to produce new antidepressant therapies. Fuchs and Flügge (Chapter 23) describe the latest findings on chronic stress and depression. Mongeau, Hamon, and Lanfumey (Chapter 24) draw parallels between chronic stress and depression through the serotonergic system. Last, Sullivan and Laplante (Chapter 25) discuss the link between stress and depression through lateralized alterations in the prefrontal cortex. These outcomes are not mutually exclusive and most likely demonstrate the numerous etiologies of stress-related pathology.

The last part, Part V on Stress, Coping, Predisposition, and Sex Differences, illustrates that the effects of stress on brain health occur with mitigating factors, as many variables contribute to brain plasticity, resilience, and pathology. These variables include sex/gender, which is described by Luine (Chapter 26) and Wolf (Chapter 27). Moreover, age of the subject is important as described by Luine (Chapter 26), as well as the type of diet consumed, as described by Kitraki (Chapter 28), and appraisal of the stressor and coping strategies employed as reported by Olff (Chapter 29). These reports highlight the importance in the multitude of variables that can significantly impact how stress influences the brain.

Cheryl D. Conrad
Tempe, Arizona

Acknowledgments

I give my heartfelt gratitude to David Mostofsky for initiating the process and inviting me to become the editor of this volume in the Wiley-Blackwell Handbooks of Behavioral Neuroscience series. This endeavor was the furthest from my mind when I was approached to embark on the project, but has evolved into one of the most gratifying intellectual experiences in my career. The process was not without its ups and downs, ironically reflecting a microchasm of the yin yang perspective. But as the project reaches its completion, I now reflect fondly upon the experience and am immensely proud of the final book. It is important to recognize that the book is a group effort, with every author deserving of my warmest appreciation and deepest respect. Each author showed a profound and dedicated work ethic toward the final goal, and each produced an outstanding chapter. I also want to recognize the help of my husband, Stuart Greenstein and my son, Ely Conrad Greenstein, for helping to conceptualize the cover art and allowing me time on weekends and late nights to work on the book, which has been long and reached nearly 2 years from its inception. Finally, this book could not have come to fruition without the enormous help from the Wiley-Blackwell publishing staff and freelance writers, which includes Christine Cardone, Constance Adler, Nicole Benevenia, Matthew Bennett, Nik Prowse, and Joanna Pyke.

Abbreviations

Aβ	amyloid-β
ACTH	adrenocorticotrophic hormone
AD	Alzheimer's disease
ADX	adrenalectomy
AF	activation function
AMPA	α-amino-3-hydroxy-5-methyl-4-isoxazole propionate
AP-1	activator protein 1
APP	amyloid precursor protein
Arc	activity-regulated cytoskeletal-associated protein
ASR	acoustic startle response
avBST	anteroventral bed nucleus of the stria terminalis
AVP	arginine vasopressin
B	basal nuclei of the amygdala
BDNF	brain-derived neurotrophic factor
BLA	basolateral amygdala
BNST	bed nucleus of the stria terminalis
BPD	borderline personality disorder
BrdU	bromodeoxyuridine
BRG-1	Brahma-related gene 1
BSA	bovine serum albumin
CA	cornu ammonis
CaMK	calcium/calmodulin-dependent protein kinase
cAMP	adenosine 3′,5′-cyclic monophosphate
CARM	coactivator-associated arginine methyltransferase
CB1R	cannabinoid type-1 receptor
CBG	corticosteroid-binding globulin (also known as transcortin)

CBP	CREB-binding protein
CDK	cyclin-dependent kinase
CE	central nuclei of the amygdala
CeA	central amygdaloid nucleus
ChIP	chromatin immunoprecepitation
ChIP-seq	chromatin immunoprecepitation/DNA sequencing
CNS	central nervous system
COMT	catechol-O-methyltransferase
CORT	cortisol and corticosterone
COX-2	cyclooxygenase 2
CPB	CREB-binding protein
CREB	cAMP-response-element binding protein
CRH	corticotropin-releasing hormone
CS	conditioned stimulus
CVS	chronic variable stress
DBD	DNA-binding domain
DCOC	differential contextual-odor conditioning
dlPFC	dorsolateral prefrontal cortex
DOI	1-(2,5-dimethoxy-4-iodophenyl)-2-aminopropane
DRIP	vitamin D receptor-interacting protein
DRN	dorsal raphe nucleus
EBR	extreme behavioral response
EEG	electroencephalographic
EGFR	epidermal growth factor receptor
Egr-1	early growth response factor 1
Elk-1	Ets-like protein 1
EPM	elevated-plus maze
ERα	estrogen receptor α
ERβ	estrogen receptor β
ERK	extracellular signal-regulated kinase
ESET	ERG-associated protein with SET domain
fMRI	functional magnetic resonance imaging
fPFC	frontopolar prefrontal cortex
GABA	γ-aminobutyric acid
GAS	General Adaptation Syndrome
GC	glucocorticoid
GFAP	glial fibrillary acid protein
GLP-1	glucagon-like peptide 1
GM-CSF	granulocyte macrophage colony-stimulating factor
GR	glucocorticoid receptor
GRE	glucocorticoid response element
GSK-3	glycogen synthase kinase 3
H3S10p/K14ac	histone H3 phosphorylated at serine 10 and acetylated at lysine 14

List of Abbreviations

HAT	histone acetyltransferase
HDAC	histone deacetylase
HFS	high-frequency stimulation
hGR	human glucocorticoid receptor
HPA	hypothalamic–pituitary–adrenal
5-HT	5-hydroxytryptamine (also known as serotonin)
5-HTT	5-hydroxytryptamine transporter
IGF-1	insulin-like growth factor 1
IL cortex	infralimbic cortex (of the medial prefrontal cortex)
IL-1	interleukin-1
iNOS	inducible nitric oxide synthase
IPC	interparental conflict
JAK	Janus kinase
JNK	c-Jun N-terminal kinases
LA	lateral nuclei of the amygdala
LBD	ligand-binding domain
LC	locus coerulus
LTP	long-term potentiation
MAPK	mitogen-activated protein kinase
MBR	minimal behavioral response
mCPP	m-chlorophenylpiperazine ($5\text{-}HT_{2C}$ receptor agonist)
MeA	medial amygdaloid nucleus
mEPSC	miniature excitatory postsynaptic current
MMP-1	matrix metalloprotease-1
MMTV	mouse mammary tumor virus
mPFC	medial prefrontal cortex
MR	mineralocorticoid receptor
MRI	magnetic resonance imaging
α-MSH	α-melanocortin-stimulating hormone
MSK	mitogen- and stress-activated kinase
NAA	N-acetyl-aspartate
NAcc	nucleus accumbens
NCAM	neural cell adhesion molecule
NCoR	nuclear receptor corepressor
NFAT	nuclear factor of activated T cells
NF-κB	nuclear factor κB
nGRE	negative glucocorticoid-response element
NMDA	N-methyl-D-aspartate
NMDAR	N-methyl-D-aspartate receptor (glutamate receptor)
NTD	N-terminal transactivation domain
NTS	nucleus of the solitary tract
OFC	orbitofrontal cortex
OFT	open field test
p300	adenovirus E1A-associated 300 kDa protein

p38MAPK	p38 mitogen-activated protein kinase
PBR	partial behavioral response
pBST	posterior bed nucleus of the stria terminalis
PCAF	p300/CBP-associated factor
pCREB	phosphorylated cAMP-response-element binding protein
pElk-1	phosphorylated Ets-like protein 1
pERK1/2	phosphorylated extracellular signal-regulated kinase types 1 and 2
PEST motif	peptide sequence enriched in proline, glutamic acid, serine, and threonine
PET	positron emission tomography
PFC	prefrontal cortex
PKA	protein kinase A
PKC	protein kinase C
pMSK1	phosphorylated mitogen- and stress-activated kinase 1
POMC	proopiomelanocortin
PPI	prepulse inhibition
PRMT1	protein arginine methyltransferase 1
pRSK1/2	phosphorylated ribosomal S6 kinase 1/2
PSS	predator scent stress
PTSD	posttraumatic stress disorder
PVN	paraventricular nucleus
qPCR	quantitative polymerase chain reaction
RIZ1	retinoblastoma protein-interacting zinc-finger gene 1
rTMS	repetitive transcardial magnetic stimulation
SAM	sympathetic–adrenal–medulla
SCP	small CTD phosphatase
SECPT	Socially Evaluated Cold Pressor Test
sEPSC	spontaneous excitatory postsynaptic current
SMCC	SRB-MED-containing complex
SMRT	silencing mediator for retinoid and thyroid hormone receptor
SNP	single-nucleotide polymorphism
SNS	sympathetic nervous system
SPECT	single-photon emission computed tomography
SRC-1	steroid receptor coactivator 1
SRE	serum response element
SSRI	selective serotonin-reuptake inhibitor
STAT	signal transducer and activator of transcription
SUMO-1	small ubiquitin-related modifier-1
SWI/SNF	switch/sucrose nonfermentable
TLR	Toll-like receptor
TNFα	tumor necrosis factor α
TRAP	thyroid receptor-associated protein

TSST	Trier Social Stress Test
TTP	tristetraprolin
US	unconditioned stimulus
VEGF	vascular endothelial growth factor
vSUB	ventral subiculum

Part I
Basics of the Stress Response

1

The Basics of the Stress Response
A Historical Context and Introduction
Kenneth J. Thiel and Michael N. Dretsch

An Introduction to Stress

Stress is a concept that everybody can identify with and yet, if asked to define stress, most people might indicate that it is synonymous with feeling overwhelmed, anxious, or under intense pressure. To this end, stress is typically thought about from the perspective of what causes it. However, an issue to consider when thinking about stress in terms of its source (i.e., the stressor) is the subjective dilemma that occurs when a stressful event or circumstance is not perceived the same way among different individuals. For example, riding a roller coaster may be a very pleasurable experience for one person while being an extremely unpleasant experience for another. It is unlikely the individual who enjoys the roller coaster would label it as a stressor. Nevertheless, that person's body undergoes similar internal physical reactions as the individual who perceives the roller-coaster ride negatively, highlighting the caveat that even fun and exciting experiences can be considered stressors based upon the objective methods of defining stress in terms of the neurobiological cascade of responses that underlie an arousing experience. However, a complex interplay between physiological, psychological, and behavioral processes that varies across situations precludes developing a singular definition of stress based solely on the physical response. Thus, both stressor and stress-response elements need to be taken into careful consideration when studying stress as a scientific construct. The goal of this chapter is to provide an introductory overview of these elements, including a brief historical perspective, and highlight the important relationship between stress, emotions, and neuropsychological health.

The Handbook of Stress: Neuropsychological Effects on the Brain, First Edition.
Edited by Cheryl D. Conrad.
© 2011 Blackwell Publishing Ltd. Published 2011 by Blackwell Publishing Ltd.

Although stress is often perceived in a negative light, it is actually a very useful and highly adaptive response. The body understands the importance of stress, but also the potential damage that it can cause, and is therefore equipped with central and peripheral systems that both promote and suppress it (Sapolsky et al., 2000). Activation of these systems (i.e., the stress response) represents an evolutionarily conserved ability of an organism to deal with circumstances that require vigilance, arousal, and/or action (Neese and Young, 2000). In addition to facilitating the perception and processing of stress, the stress response is also designed to restore balance. To this end, the various neurotransmitters, peptides, and hormones that are released in response to stress serve a protective function for an organism (McEwen, 2000b). Importantly, these neurochemical mediators stimulate tissues to respond in an appropriate and adaptive manner to the stressful circumstance at hand (McEwen and Seeman, 1999). The physiological component of the stress response can be further modified by psychological processes, such as coping and appraisal, which can aide in (or potentially hinder) the restoration of balance.

The experience of too much stress over time can have adverse consequences on health and behavior, but never experiencing any stress would result in inactivity, boredom, and an inability to adequately respond to internal/external demands. For instance, stress can be useful to motivate and prepare organisms to deal with situations such as writing a research paper or escaping from a predator. To appreciate the function of stress in a given situation, it is important to consider the stressor. There are a number of internal and external causes of stress, and these are generally characterized into two categories. Systemic (also referred to as *physiological*) stressors represent a physically based threat to an organism without requiring cognitive processing. Systemic stressors can include internal factors, such as inflammation or hemorrhage, and external factors, such as a burn or bite. Psychogenic stressors represent a more psychologically based disturbance that requires cognitive processing. As such, psychogenic stressors typically involve an anticipatory component along with real-time appraisal. In general, stress has been popularly conceptualized as any physical or psychological event, whether it be actual or imagined, that disrupts homeostatic processes within an organism. Therefore, a more precise definition of a stressor is anything that jeopardizes a state of balance, or homeostasis, within an organism.

The Road to Conceptualizing Stress

In the sections that follow, we will elaborate further on the details of the stress response and the different types of stressors and regulation mechanisms. However, it is important to first acknowledge a few of the seminal findings that have shaped our modern understanding of these concepts, and touch upon one of the current influential perspectives on how the field views stress (i.e., allostasis). The original studies on the physiology of the stress response by Walter Cannon and Hans Selye suggested initially that the body's reaction is nonspecific in nature, and thus that all stressors in general produce the same ends. For Cannon (1932) the focus was on exploring the sympathetic-adrenal (i.e., autonomic) response to an immediate stressor. His work established that an organism prepares itself to deal with a threat via release of epinephrine (also referred to as adrenaline) from the adrenal medulla, which subsequently activates the body's energy reserves by accelerating heart rate and blood pressure, mobilizing blood glucose levels, increasing respiration, and inhibiting unnecessary energy-utilizing processes such as digestion and reproduction. The ultimate result is to quickly prime an organism for a fight-or-flight (Cannon, 1929), or freeze, response (Bracha et al., 2004). Notably, Cannon helped develop the concept of homeostasis and stress by postulating that stress disturbs equilibrium, and that the autonomic response helps to restore one's internal processes (or milieu) to steady-state levels necessary for health and survival in the face of challenge (Cannon, 1932).

Selye (1956) expanded upon Cannon's work by investigating the other primary system involved in stress: the hypothalamic–pituitary–adrenal (HPA) axis (i.e., the endocrine system). Namely, Selye focused on the release of hormones (glucocorticoids, GCs) from the adrenal cortex and their role in the stress response. He coined the concept of a General Adaptation Syndrome (GAS), which represents a reliable pattern of physiological reactions that correspond to the body's attempt to mediate resistance to a threat. The GAS hypothesis consists of three stages: an alarm stage (i.e., physiological activation of the HPA axis and the sympathetic nervous system [SNS] in preparation to deal with the threat), a resistance stage (i.e., the period following the initial reaction to the threat whereby the body mediates ongoing stress and attempts to return to steady-state levels), and an exhaustion stage (i.e., when a prolonged stress response overexerts the body's defense systems, thus draining it of its reserve resources and leading to illness). GCs were thought to be the primary mediator of the GAS. Because a large variety of harmful, physically based stressors produced the GAS and consistently resulted in ulcers, enlarged adrenals, and a compromised immune system when administered chronically, Selye referred to the stress response as being nonspecific in nature. Thus, whereas Cannon viewed stress in terms of the stressor, Selye's approach was to view stress in terms of the components of the stress response. Although subsequent work would demonstrate that not all stressors result in the same physiological response (e.g., depending on factors such as type and source of stressor, duration, perception, and appraisal), Selye's invaluable contribution to the field was to pioneer the exploration of the relationship between GC physiology and stress.

Munck et al. (1984) proposed a novel way to think about the role of GCs in the stress response that countered Selye's general viewpoint that GCs direct the stress response. Selye's idea that chronic stress leads to the GAS going awry and causing pathology such as rheumatoid arthritis was not compatible with findings summarized by Munck that GCs produce anti-inflammatory effects and actually provide relief from symptoms of rheumatoid arthritis. Munck et al. (1984) therefore hypothesized that GCs work to suppress, rather than enhance, the normal defense

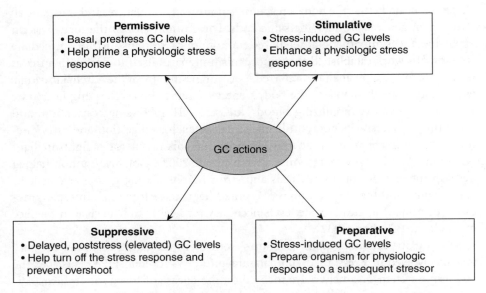

Figure 1.1 Overview of different types of GC actions with respect to the stress response. For a more detailed perspective refer to Table 1 in Sapolsky et al. (2000).

mechanisms that are activated by stress in order to prevent these systems from overshooting and seriously threatening homeostasis. In other words, GCs confer protection from the stress response. This hypothesis added to Selye's traditional view that the body is equipped to adapt to stressors, but had the added advantage of including a role of GCs that was in line with their actual physiological consequences. Sapolsky et al. (2000) updated Munck's view on GCs to include a more comprehensive set of preparative, simulative, permissive, and suppressive functions of GCs, depending on when examined with relation to the stressor, that further take into account the more rapid, as well as circadian, actions of GCs (see Figure 1.1 and Chapter 2 in this volume).

The predominately physiological-based concepts of homeostasis and the stress response were given a more psychologically based perspective through the works of John Mason and Richard Lazarus. For instance, Mason (1975) discovered that the GAS response could be modified based on situational and emotional factors, and that psychological interpretation of a stressor is necessary for the subsequent endocrine response to occur. Lazarus (1985) demonstrated that individual differences in various cognitive and motivational variables, such as appraisal and coping, can arbitrate the relationship between a stressor and the stress reaction. Thus, an evaluation of stressors determines their level of threat and their subsequent ability to elicit a stress response. Furthermore, Chrousos and Gold (1992) integrated the concept of individual differences based on genetic factors as an important consideration for measuring the stress response (see Chapters 26, 27, 28, and 29).

The body is designed to react in an efficient manner to the vast array of stressors it may experience. However, this reaction is clearly complicated, containing intricate physiological responses to restore homeostasis that are further modulated by environmental, behavioral, and psychological influences. There are instances (i.e., under intense or chronic conditions), though, when the demands that the stressors exert on the body outweigh the ability of the body to respond without a cost. Certainly over time there is an increasing price the body has to pay when continually trying to restabilize. To address this, a novel concept called *allostasis* was introduced to the stress field (McEwen, 1998). Allostasis refers to the ability of the body to achieve and maintain stability through change, and represents an adaptive coping mechanism in which various stress response processes are engaged during stress (McEwen, 2000a). Allostasis can be distinguished from homeostasis. In its purest sense, homeostasis refers to maintenance of processes that are essential for survival, and large divergences in these processes leads to death. Homeostasis by itself involves reaching a physiological equilibrium or set point in which adjustments carry no real price, whereas allostasis essentially refers to maintaining homeostasis through-out challenges and involves a network of mediators (e.g., behavioral, sympathetic, and neuroendocrine factors) that can exact a cost when the adjustments have to be maintained outside of their normal range for a period of time. The mediators of the stress response that fluctuate during a demand do not cause death, but rather, they maintain other homeostatic systems within the body, and can be stimulated even by the anticipation of a disturbance. To this end, the term allostasis is useful for illustrating the important distinction that adaptations are in place to promote and maintain survival mechanisms in the body, and that these adaptive responses are not confined to a critical range that implies death when breached. The cost (i.e., wear and tear) that these responses can exert over time, however, is referred to as *allostatic load* (McEwen, 2000a), and can result from either too much stress output (e.g., adrenal overactivity) or inefficient operation of the stress response system (e.g., inefficient shut-off or having an inadequate stress response to begin with). The key advantage of the allostatic concept is that it accounts for the ability of an organism to be adaptable and maintain its body in an altered state for a sustained period of time. The extent to which this occurs exacts a toll that could eventually manifest itself as a stress-related neuropsychological disorder (i.e., allostatic over-load; see Chapters 16 and 17).

Overview of Stress-response Physiology

A detailed outline of the integration and execution of the various components of the stress response is beyond the scope of this chapter, but what follows is an intro-duction to the fundamentals of the SNS and HPA axis in relation to stress. At the most basic level, the stress response involves a series of SNS and endocrine responses that aim to restore stability within the body and promote the ability of an organism to deal with a threat. A critical feature of these systems is to mobilize energy resources for instant use while simultaneously inhibiting body functions that are nonessential for immediate survival. Thus, heart rate, blood pressure, and blood glucose levels are elevated while digestive and reproductive processes are curtailed. Inflammation is reduced and pain perception is blunted. The immune response is immediately activated to promote defense, followed by processes put into place to prevent overshoot and the possibility of autoimmune damage. Components of the central nervous system (CNS) are activated, via neurotransmitter, neuropeptide, and hormonal messengers, to enhance learning and memory processes, and to further regulate maintenance of HPA output. Behavioral changes also occur, with organisms experiencing increased arousal and vigilance in order to identify and appraise threats within the environment.

At the core of an acute stress response is the initiation of the fight-or-flight response, which is characterized by its sympathetic-adrenal medullary components that serve as the *first response* to prepare the body for the energy resources it will require. Upon experiencing a threatening or stressful situation, the SNS is engaged and stimulates rapid release of catecholamine hormones (i.e., epinephrine and norepinephrine [or noradrenaline]) to direct autonomic processes. Norepinephrine is released from postganglionic fibers onto target organs, providing a local release of norepinephrine (see Figure 1.2). Sympathetic innervation of the adrenal medulla is cholinergic and arises from preganglionic fibers situated within the intermediolateral cell column of the spinal cord (Holgert et al., 1995). Upon activation, epinephrine and norepinephrine are released from the adrenal medulla into circulation. The collective result of SNS catecholamine release is a cascade of physiological effects including increased respiration rate, increased heart rate, dilation of skeletal muscle blood vessels, glycogen to glucose conversion, and vasoconstriction of digestive and reproductive organ blood vessels. These changes serve to selectively increase blood flow and oxygen/glucose availability to brain tissues and skeletal muscles that require energy to prepare for action (McCarty, 2000).

The hallmark neuroendocrine system response to stress involves activation of the HPA axis (see Figure 1.3). When a particular stressor is perceived, information is relayed to the parvocellular division of neurons located within the paraventricular nucleus (PVN) of the hypothalamus. It is from this brain control center that endocrine activity can be directed. Within the parvocellular neurons, the hypothalamic-releasing hormones known as corticotropin-releasing hormone (CRH; previously known as CRF) and arginine vasopressin (AVP) are synthesized. Upon PVN activation, the axons of these neurons projecting into the external zone of the median eminence release CRH and AVP into the portal blood system. This portal blood system feeds into the hypophysis (i.e., the pituitary gland), whereby CRH and AVP specifically target the synthesis and release of adrenocorticotrophic hormone (ACTH) from pituitary corticotrophs located specifically within the anterior pituitary. Although both CRH and AVP are ACTH secretagogues, CRH is considered to be more effective. Importantly, AVP synergistically potentiates CRH-elicited ACTH secretion, but by itself is actually a weak secretagogue (Rivier and Vale, 1983; Whitnall, 1993). As such, CRH is considered crucial for ACTH stimula-

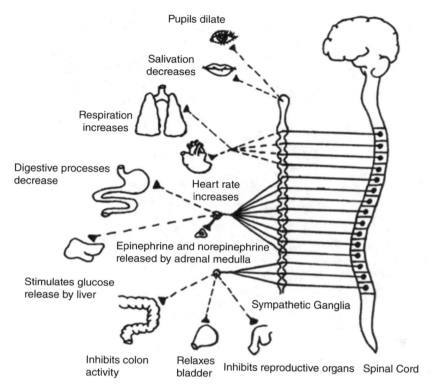

Pupils dilate

Salivation decreases

Respiration increases

Digestive processes decrease

Heart rate increases

Epinephrine and norepinephrine released by adrenal medulla

Stimulates glucose release by liver

Sympathetic Ganglia

Inhibits colon activity

Relaxes bladder

Inhibits reproductive organs   Spinal Cord

Figure 1.2   A basic representation of the SNS along with several of its targets. Activation of the SNS results in local release of catecholamines (i.e., norepinephrine) onto target organs, and stimulates additional catecholamine (i.e., both epinephrine and norepinephrine) release from the adrenal medulla. Solid lines represent preganglionic fibers and dashed lines represent postganglionic fibers.

tion during an acute stress response, whereas AVP is typically relegated to promoting maintenance of basal ACTH production (de Keyzer et al., 1997). However, during periods of chronic stress, AVP appears to play a more critical role in ACTH regulation. Indeed, under chronic stress conditions there is a marked shift in hypothalamic CRH/AVP signal in favor of AVP, as well as a downregulation of CRH receptors within the anterior pituitary, suggesting a dynamic role for AVP in mediating the stress axis (Scott and Dinan, 1998).

Stimulation of the anterior pituitary corticotroph cells via activation of a CRH/AVP receptor (i.e., CRH type 1 and V1b, respectively) results in a signal transduction cascade that leads to transcription and translation of the ACTH precursor protein, proopiomelanocortin (POMC), and subsequent cleavage of ACTH as one of its products. ACTH released into the circulating bloodstream travels to the adrenal gland, whereby it binds to cells located in the zona fasciculata of the adrenal cortex. The binding of ACTH to its receptor (i.e., melanocortin type 2) initiates a cascade

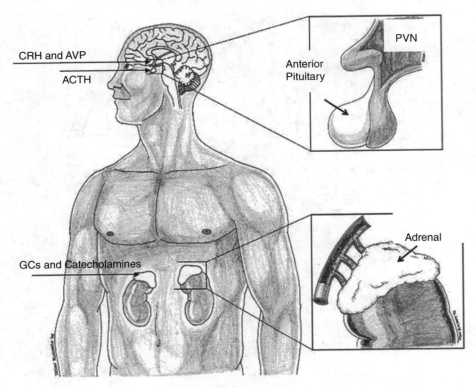

CRH and AVP

ACTH

PVN

Anterior
Pituitary

Adrenal

GCs and Catecholamines

Figure 1.3   An illustration of the primary components of the HPA axis. In response to stress, CRH and AVP are released from parvocellular neurons within the PVN of the hypothalamus into the hypophysial portal blood system. CRH and AVP then stimulate synthesis and release of ACTH from the anterior pituitary gland. ACTH travels through the bloodstream to the triangular adrenal glands located above the kidneys where it stimulates the synthesis and release of GCs from the adrenal cortex. Activation of the SNS in response to stress concurrently stimulates the release of catecholamines from the adrenal medulla. *Source:* Figure drawn by Jason Blaichman. Used with permission of Sonia Lupien.

of intracellular enzymatic events that converts free cholesterol into GCs via a steroidogenic pathway (Hall, 2001). Subsequently, GCs (referred to as corticosterone in rats and cortisol in humans) diffuse away from the cell and are released into circulation. Within the blood, the highly lipophilic GCs bind reversibly to corticosteroid-binding globulin (transcortin) and serum albumin where they remain inactive while transported throughout the body. GCs remain inactive while in this bound state, and thus these binding proteins, through up- or downregulation, can be used to regulate GC actions. It is important to note that although ACTH is the predominate regulator of GC synthesis and production from the adrenal cortex, there are extra-ACTH forms of adrenal cortex regulation, including hormonal signals from the adrenal medulla, cytokine stimulation from peripheral circulation, and direct neuronal control via SNS innervation of the adrenal cortex that also mediate GC release (Ehrhart-Bornstein et al., 2000; Ulrich-Lai and Engeland, 2005).

GCs act at two different receptor subtypes: mineralocorticoid receptors (MRs) and glucocorticoid receptors (GRs) (Reul and de Kloet, 1985; see also Chapter 3). Each receptor is characterized by a differential affinity profile for its endogenous ligands. MRs have a high and relatively equal affinity for both GCs and aldosterone. In contrast, GRs have a much lower affinity for GCs compared to MRs, but they are more selective for GCs over aldosterone (i.e., they are GC-preferring receptors). Given these differential receptor properties, it is generally believed that MRs are typically saturated under resting conditions, whereas GRs are predominately activated during periods of high GC levels (e.g., during a stress response). Moreover, GCs can be further regulated by enzymes 11β hydrosteroid dehydrogenase type 1 (11β-HSD1) or type 2 (11β-HSD2), which can activate or inactivate GCs, respectively (Funder et al., 1988; Seckl et al., 2005). The brain is nearly devoid of 11β-HSD2, which enables GCs to influence cells via both MRs and GRs. Traditional GRs are located within the cytoplasm of a cell and are translocated into the nucleus upon binding with a GC (which enters the cell via passive diffusion), where they subsequently function as transcription factors to regulate gene expression (Chrousos and Kino, 2009). GCs are able to produce faster actions, however, whereby they rapidly hyperpolarize and inhibit neuron firing within regions such as the hippocampus and hypothalamus, likely through an as-yet-unidentified cell membrane receptor subtype (Orchinik, 1998). Within the brain, MRs are more localized to sensory and limbic structure neurons (Reul et al., 2000) whereas GRs exhibit widespread distribution (Fuxe et al., 1985). Importantly, GR levels are high throughout limbic structures, the brainstem, the PVN, and the pituitary gland (de Kloet et al., 2005b).

GCs serve many important functions related to regulation of the stress response. In one respect, GCs play a permissive role in the stress response, such as stimulating gluconeogenesis, aiding the catabolic processes mediated by cathecholamines, priming neural regions involved in sensory processing, attention, and adaptive responding, and directing/regulating immune and inflammation response mediators (Dhabhar and McEwen, 1996; Buckingham, 2000; Sapolsky et al., 2000). On the other hand, GCs also play a suppressive/protective role via robust immunosuppressive and anti-inflammatory actions, as well as enhancing glucose transport to the CNS and cardiovascular tissues that require a high-energy demand (Buckingham, 2000; Sapolsky et al., 2000). Importantly, GCs also work within critical brain regions (e.g., hippocampus and amygdala) to facilitate learning and memory processes that promote adaptive behaviors in response to a particular stressor in the future (Korte, 2001; see also Chapters 8–12). Thus, GCs are essential in facilitating response to a pending or ongoing stressor and reducing the stress response once responding is no longer necessary, as well as preparing the organism for future threats. In general, the permissive actions of GCs are thought to be predominately mediated via MRs, given that these effects occur when GCs are at prestress basal levels in which the high-affinity MRs are saturated. The suppressive actions occur under conditions of high, stress-induced levels of GCs in which the GRs are sufficiently occupied (de Kloet et al., 1998).

Although Selye originally proposed that the stress response is nonspecific, it has since been established that not all stressors elicit an identical combination of responses (Pacak et al., 1998). Although there is a general conformity among stressors' ability to provoke eventual release of GCs and catecholamines, the arrangement of responses of these hormonal signals fluctuates depending on factors such as the type of stressor, the current physical state on the organism, arousal/appraisal, and the use of psychological/behavioral coping mechanisms (Goldstein and Kopin, 2007; see also Chapter 29). In addition, each type of stressor is proposed to have its own *neurochemcial identity*, such as variations in the ratio of CRH/AVP release or variations in interactions between GCs and other transcription factors during negative feedback, which result in an altered picture of the overall stress response depending on the type of stressor (Jessop, 1999).

Overview of Key Stress Response Mediators

One of the key regulators of the HPA axis stress response is the GC products themselves. Following the initial reactions to a stressor, GCs function to return the organism back to a balanced state via negative-feedback mechanisms to suppress further HPA activity. GC-mediated negative feedback occurs at multiple levels, thus presenting a redundancy in regulation to ensure the stress response effectively serves its purpose without being detrimental. The key sites of action include regulation at the level of the hippocampus, PVN, and pituitary gland. Hippocampal activation via GCs (likely mediated through GRs) results in enhanced inhibitory γ-aminobutyric acid (GABA)-ergic tone surrounding the PVN, thus inhibiting HPA function (Joëls and de Kloet, 1993). At the PVN and anterior pituitary, GCs exert negative feedback primarily via GR activation and subsequent transrepression whereby the GC–GR complex interacts with transcription factors, such as activator protein 1 (AP-1), Nurr77, and cAMP-response-element binding protein (CREB), to prevent transcription of *CRH* and *POMC* genes (Pearce and Yamamoto, 1993; Martens et al., 2005).

In line with the different locations and mechanisms of GC feedback, there is also a temporal characterization involved. Rapid GC feedback occurs within seconds to minutes of the stress response, and is characterized by the ability of GCs to inhibit CRH/ACTH release prior to alterations in genomic processing, likely via interactions with cell membrane receptor molecules on PVN parvocellular neurons and pituitary corticotrophs (Dallman, 2005). An intermediate time course for GC feedback, typically beginning around 30 min following a stress response and lasting for hours, is characterized by protein synthesis blockade as discussed above and serves to blunt HPA activity without completely abolishing it (Dallman, 2000). A slower form of negative feedback also occurs following chronic, high-level exposure to GCs over days or weeks, and is characterized by inhibited CRH/AVP and POMC mRNA expression throughout the PVN and anterior pituitary, resulting in lack of responsiveness to additional stressors (Keller-Wood and Dallman, 1984; Dallman, 2000). In addition to these mechanisms of GC feedback, local ACTH released from the anterior pituitary can also act at the level of the pituitary and the PVN to dampen release of itself and CRH/AVP via short-loop negative feedback (Sawchenko and Arias, 1995).

In addition to hormonal feedback, the HPA axis is regulated by a variety of CNS inputs, including the brainstem and corticolimbic structures. The nature of a stressor (i.e., a systemic stressor compared to a psychogenic) dictates the neural pathway that is utilized to activate/regulate the PVN (see Figure 1.4). For example, an internal

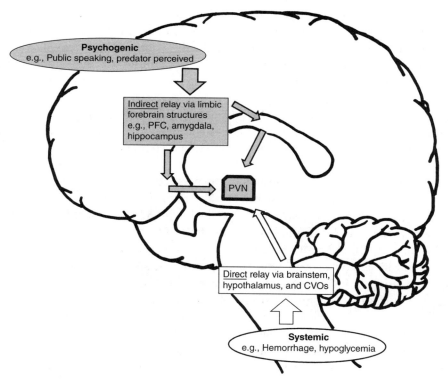

Figure 1.4 A basic overview of regional processing and input depending on type (psychogenic or systemic) of stressor. Psychogenic (psychological) stressors are relayed indirectly to the hypothalamic PVN via higher-level engagement of limbic forebrain structures that are involved in the anticipation and appraisal of potentially stressful circumstances. In contrast, systemic (physiological) stressors are relayed directly to the PVN via ascending input from brainstem structures, as well as other subnuclei of the hypothalamus and circumventricular organs (CVOs) containing osmoreceptors and additional homeostatic sensors. PFC, prefrontal cortex.

systemic stressor that possesses an immediate physiological threat, such as hemorrhaging, would likely be transmitted directly to the PVN via catecholaminergic projections arising from the nucleus tractus solitarus located in the brainstem (Herman and Cullinan, 1997). On the other hand, a psychogenic stressor that requires anticipation and evaluation, such as preparing to talk in front of a group, will primarily be processed by higher corticolimbic brain structures before being relayed indirectly to the PVN (Herman and Cullinan, 1997). Stressors that possess both a cognitive and physical component, such as restraint stress, will utilize both somatosensory processing in the brainstem nuclei and corticolimbic processing via regions such as the prefrontal cortex, hippocampus, and amygdala to stimulate the PVN (see Chapter 2 of this volume for further detail on psychogenic and systemic mechanisms).

The locus coerulus (LC)-noradrenergic system located within the pontine brainstem mediates the stress response by directing the processes of arousal and attention. In the face of a challenge, it is highly adaptive to experience-increased arousal and sensory processing in order to promote the detection and processing of a stressor while simultaneously ignoring nonessential features of the environment. Norepinephrine released from the brainstem serves as an alert signal that activates both the sympathetic and neuroendocrine legs of the stress response, as well as higher brain structures such as the prefrontal cortex (PFC), hippocampus, and amygdala involved in fear-related behaviors and memories (Chrousos, 2009). The PVN and LC share reciprocal connections, with CRH-containing neurons projecting to the LC and activating it via CRH type 1 receptors (Schulz et al., 1996). During a stress response, CRH increases tonic discharge of the LC and alters sensory responding by reducing overall signal-to-noise ratio (i.e., discharge in response to a novel stimulus is attenuated; Valentino and Foote, 1987). This pattern of LC firing is associated with a shift from focused attention to scanning attention (Valentino and Wehby, 1988), and allows an organism to stay alert and aroused within a dangerous or threatening environment. Furthermore, this attention pattern may facilitate acquisition of information related to a stressor, thereby giving an organism a better opportunity of forming a stress-related memory and retaining it for future retrieval. In general, norepinephrine release results in widespread increase in cortical and hippocampal electroencephalographic activation, further suggesting that CRH-elicited stimulation of the LC-noradrenergic system may increase arousal as well as additional behavioral/affective processes related to the stress response (Berridge, 2005).

Cytokines released during inflammation stress are also potent regulators of the HPA axis. Peripheral cytokines gain access to the hypothalamus (likely via openings in the blood–brain barrier, such as the median eminence, area postrema, and choroid plexus; Saper and Breder, 1994) and stimulate parvocellular CRH/AVP neurons (Habu et al., 1998). In addition, peripheral cytokines can be detected by sensory fibers that activate brainstem nuclei, which in turn send direct inputs to activate the PVN. Evidence also suggests that cytokine-mediated ACTH secretion can occur via a CRH-independent mechanism (Bethin et al., 2000). Indeed, cytokines can act directly at the level of the anterior pituitary gland to stimulate POMC expression and subsequent ACTH release (Pereda et al., 2000). By activating the HPA axis, and subsequently eliciting GC secretion, cytokines effectively can regulate (i.e., repress) their own inflammatory effects.

Overview of the Stress Response Following Chronic Stress

The stress response can be remarkably different depending on factors such as history and duration of stress experience. Much of what has been discussed thus far has centered on the stress response elicited by an acute stressor. To reiterate, the cascade of endocrine, sympathetic, and CNS events that occur in response to an acute stressor serve an adaptive function of regulating appropriate physiological and behavioral reactions to a threat while simultaneously maintaining balance and preventing system overshoot/damage. However, circumstances in which an organism is exposed to chronic stress result in an altered stress-response profile. Chronic exposure to a repeated daily stressor, such as restraint stress, is associated with a profile of elevated HPA activity (i.e., high plasma ACTH and GC levels) that persists for the first few days but eventually returns to normal levels, possibly reflecting diminished regulatory input into the HPA axis (Kant et al., 1983). For instance, the phenotypic profile of HPA inputs following chronic restraint stress includes hypertrophy within the amygdala, dendritic remodeling and reduced cell proliferation within the hippocampus, and downregulation of MR and GR expression throughout the limbic system (see Conrad, 2006; de Kloet et al., 2005a; Joëls, 2011; see also Chapters 7 and 10). Sustained chronic stressors, such as chronic inflammation, are characterized by lasting high levels of plasma GCs and ACTH that do not return to baseline, likely due to dysregulated negative-feedback mechanisms (Harbuz et al., 2003). Interestingly, parvocellular PVN CRH expression and release is diminished under these conditions while AVP expression and release is elevated, suggesting that AVP may mediate high HPA axis activity during sustained chronic stress (Aguilera et al., 2008).

It has been well documented that an acute stressor can elicit an altered stress response depending on an organism's history with either that particular stressor or other stressors in general. For example, an animal repeatedly exposed to restraint stress, compared to a naïve animal, will demonstrate a blunted ACTH and GC response upon an acute exposure to restraint. In this case, acute exposure to restraint stress is referred to as a homotypic stressor for the animals with a prior history of chronic restraint (Dallman et al., 2000). In contrast, compared to a naïve animal, an animal with a history of chronic restraint stress will demonstrate an exaggerated ACTH and GC response upon exposure to a different type of stressor (e.g., foot shock). An acute stressor that is novel compared to the chronic stressor is referred to as a heterotypic stressor (Dallman et al., 2000). An elevated stress response to a heterotypic stressor is not limited to HPA axis output, as rats repeatedly exposed to immobilization stress also display an exaggerated sympathoadrenal stress response to a heterotypic stressor compared to control (unstressed) animals (Dronjak et al., 2004). HPA axis modulation via amygdala input, which itself integrates information from the paraventricular thalamus and raphe nucleus while processing emotional and memory components of stressors, appears to be central in mediating an organism's habituation/adaptation to homotypic stressors and exacerbation to heterotypic stressors (Dallman et al., 2000).

Emotional Response to Stress

Humans typically interpret stress with an emotional response. In response to a stressor, SNS activation of visceral structures such as the heart, stomach, epidermis, and other organs generates physiological changes that may lead to a perception of an emotion (Heilman, 1994). This peripheral response is closely integrated with CNS components that are involved in the evaluation and regulation of emotion necessary for behavioral changes that allow an organism to adapt to the environment. For example, when confronted by a threatening individual in a dark alley, the arousal would elicit a physiological response (e.g., tachycardia and vasoconstriction) that not only prepares the individual to flee as a means of self-preservation, but also provides affective cues as a motivation strategy to immediately avoid a possibly harmful situation (Jelen and Zagrodzka, 2001). Learning (both implicit and explicit) as a result of prior exposure plays an important role in mediation of the stress response. In humans this includes imagination of rational or irrational events. For example, just imagining a negative stimulus or situation can elicit similar physiological responses and feelings as if in the actual presence of the elicitor (Behar et al., 2005).

Negative emotional responses can guide behaviors both subconsciously and consciously (Hermans et al., 2002), and influence the way an organism interacts with its environment. However, negative emotions elicited from a stressor are not always perceived as stressful. The experience of the emotion requires higher cognitive processes for evaluation of the organism's physiological state. Cognitive appraisal of stimuli (actual or imagined) can lead to positive or negative emotions. When the appraisal is of internally represented cognitive goals, interruption of attainment of these goals can also lead to negative emotions (e.g., anger) and subsequent stress (Damasio, 1999).

Stress and Cognition

GCs effect both memory consolidation and memory retrieval (Roozendaal, 2002; Chapters 8 and 9). The GC effect on memory consolidation depends primarily on noradrenergic activation of the basolateral complex of the amygdala and subsequent interactions with other brain regions (Roozendaal et al., 2004). For example, the human amygdala and hippocampus interact to encode emotional information for learning and memory (Phelps, 2004). Furthermore, evidence indicates that negative emotional events enhance accuracy in recalling details of long-term memories (Kensinger, 2007). Although stress may elicit emotions that enhance learning and memory-related processes, GCs have an inverse effect when it comes to retrieval processes under stressful conditions (Kuhlmann et al., 2005).

In the following sections we delineate the neuroanatomical substrates of emotional regulation and related behaviors, as well as the effects of chronic stress on both the neurobiology and function of these regions and neural networks observed in individuals suffering from psychiatric disorders.

Neuroanatomy of Emotional Regulation

The ability to regulate emotional responses to stressors can theoretically impact long-term health outcomes as well as aspects of neuropsychological functioning. Both endogenous and exogenous stimuli can elicit a stress-related physiological response (Knight et al., 2005). As mentioned above, a number of neuroanatomical substrates and neurochemicals are responsible for eliciting and mediating a stress response. Recently, cognitive neuroscientists have focused on cognitive processes involved in top-down regulation of emotions as well as the neural underpinnings that support these processes (Pecchinenda et al., 2006; Dretsch and Tipples, 2008; Knight et al., 2010). Studies using functional magnetic resonance imaging have shown that emotional regulation depends on interactions between cortical and subcortical regions (Knight et al., 2010). This mediation has been referred to as implementation of cognitive control on limbic regions. In particular, the PFC plays a paramount role.

A multitude of processes of the PFC are implicated in regulation of emotional responses (see Figure 1.5). The PFC comprises approximately one third of the entire cortex, and lies anterior to the premotor cortex and supplementary motor area. The PFC may be subdivided into three regions: the dorsolateral prefrontal cortex (dlPFC), the orbitofrontal cortex (OFC), and the frontopolar prefrontal cortex (fPFC) (Happaney et al., 2004). The dlPFC receives input from the parietal and inferior temporal visual cortex and is primarily known for its involvement in spatial and object working memory (Roberts et al., 2004). Evidence reveals that the dlPFC is implicated in top-down regulation of emotion through learning processes and control of attention (Knight et al., 2010; McRae et al., 2009). The OFC constitutes part of the reward-processing network and is an important region for emotional regulation (Rolls, 2004). The OFC is part of the frontostriatal dopaminergic circuit which has strong connections to the amygdala and other parts of the limbic system, including connections with the basal ganglia, somatosensory cortices, and insula (Krawczyk, 2002). The anatomical positioning of OFC is optimal for the integration of affective and nonaffective information, and the regulation of motivational responses and emotional processing (Rolls, 2004). The fPFC, the most anterior part of the frontal lobes, is implicated in subgoal processing, multitasking,

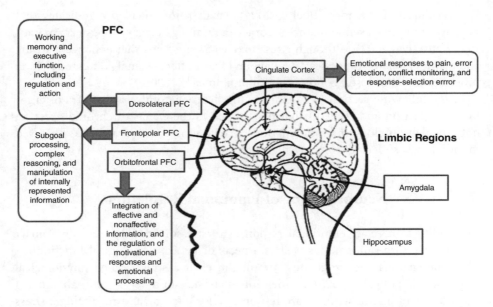

Figure 1.5   A depiction of specific regions of the PFC implicated in top-down regulation of emotional responses that rely on various limbic structures.

complex reasoning, and manipulation of mentally represented information (Krawczyk, 2002; Koechlin and Hyafil, 2007). The cingulate cortex, although not directly part of the PFC, has been shown to work closely with the dlPFC and OFC in regulatory processes that encompass the processing of pain, cognitive control, performance monitoring, error detection, conflict monitoring, and response selection (Carter et al., 1998; Shima and Tanji, 1998; Turken and Swick, 1999). More specifically, neuroimaging evidence suggests that the caudal anterior region of the cingulate is involved in pain processing (Bentley et al., 2003) and that the posterior cingulate is involved in self-reflecting on one's emotions (Ochsner et al., 2004). Although functionally there is some casual independence between regions and subareas of the PFC, there is considerable overlap in not only functionality, but also cortical layering, cellular density, and organization used for defining the cytoarchitecture of the frontal lobes. Most of these regions work in concert with midbrain structures as part of a neural network for regulating emotion, behavior, and motivation.

Stress Pathology: Brain Structure and Function

Much of the evidence supporting stress-related pathophysiological changes in various cortical and subcortical structures is derived from clinical studies. For example, for posttraumatic stress disorder (PTSD) the neurobiological changes that impact both functions and structure have been well documented (Lanius et al., 2006). Individuals with depression and PTSD often display neurocognitive deficits in attention and memory (Rokke et al., 2002; Vasterling et al., 2002; Dretsch et al., 2010). However, some evidence suggests that these neurocognitive deficits are not a product of stress-related neurobiological changes, but rather represent premorbid vulnerability to the development of PTSD (Breslau et al., 2006).

Reductions in cortex volume, histopathologic changes, and abnormal activation of subregions of the OFC, such as the medial prefrontal cortex (mPFC), are also implicated in the mediation of the stress response and emotional behaviors associated with mood disorders (Drevets, 2000). Reduced hippocampal volume has been linked with depression (Rao et al., 2010) and anxiety disorders such as PTSD (Karl et al., 2006). Brain-imaging techniques have shown that PTSD is associated with reduced overall white matter and smaller hippocampal volume (Villarreal et al., 2002) and abnormal functioning of the amygdala, cingulated cortex, and mPFC (Williams et al., 2006).

Stress Resilience: Genes, Endophenotype, and Neuropsychological Functioning

Individual resilience to stress can be studied at many levels (see Figure 1.6). The degree to which individuals respond physiologically and emotionally to stressors, the time that it takes to recover from the response, and the temporal frequency and duration of stressful events must all be taken into consideration when discussing resilience. The complex interplay of genetics with environmental factors, such as the serotonin transporter gene and traumatic experiences in early life, can modify capacity to cope with stressors and contribute to psychopathology (Feder et al., 2009). By comparing group differences characterized by the serotonin transporter allele, neuroimaging research suggests that the stress response is mediated by genetic variations in neurotransmitter modulation (Hariri et al., 2002; Heinz et al., 2007). Other evidence reveals that amygdala activation in response to stress is mediated by variations in neuropeptide Y haplotype (Zhou et al., 2008). Neuropeptide Y is abundantly expressed in regions of the limbic system that are induced by stress and arousal, and is implicated in the assignment of emotional valences to stimuli and memories (Heilig, 2004). Many other genetic haplotypes and polymorphisms, such as catechol-O-methyltransferase (also known as COMT) and brain-derived neurotrophic factor, have been implicated in resilience to stress (Feder et al., 2009). Although many gene–gene and gene–environment interactions that underpin individual systems (e.g., HPA axis) and neural circuitry (e.g., regulation of emotion and behavior) of resilience to stressors have been identified, there is a need for continued advancements in neuroscience techniques to further explore these interactions.

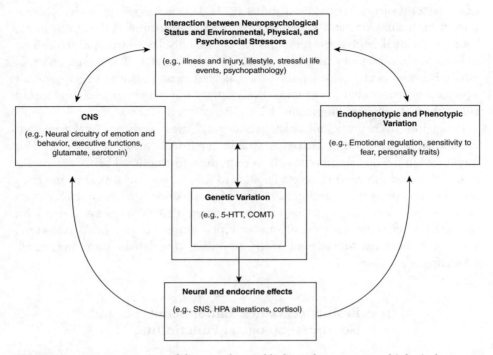

Figure 1.6 A representation of direct and causal linkages between neurobiological systems and environmental and psychosocial stressors. COMT, catechol-O-methyltransferase; 5-HTT, 5-hydroxytryptamine transporter.

Evidence also reveals that the genetic influence on stress response can be expressed outwardly, as observed with intermediary phenotypes (Krueger, 2000). For example, cognitive vulnerabilities, which are trait-like characteristics such as negative attributional style and rumination, are posited to contribute to both the development and maintenance of PTSD symptoms (Elwood et al., 2009). Twin studies have provided evidence which suggests that self-perceptions of coping with stress contribute to stress response, as indexed by endocrine markers (Wüst et al., 2000). Hence, personality trait differences influence the perception of acute and chronic stress and have been shown to mediate mental health outcomes (Lawrence and Fauerbach, 2003).

Given that resilience to stress is such a dynamic concept, the integrity of neuropsychological functioning may be one of the paramount predictors of stress resiliency. For example, executive functions moderate all of the stages of the stress response—exposure, reactivity, recovery, and restoration (Williams et al., 2009)—and have been associated with temperament, personality, and psychopathology (Hariri, 2009). Furthermore, persistent findings of impaired executive functioning in stress-related disorders, such as PTSD, provide some evidence of a vulnerability factor (Leskin and White, 2007). In fact, general intelligence (IQ) has been associated with decreased risk for the development of PTSD (Breslau et al., 2006). Resilience to stress requires many levels of investigation on genetic, endophenotypic, phenotypic, and psychosocial mediators of neural circuits that regulate fear, reward, emotion, and behavior. The concerted interactions of such systems underpin successful coping and resilience to stress.

Concluding Remarks

The stress response is an evolutionary mechanism that is essential for bioregulation to allow internal adaptation as well as to prepare an organism for manipulation of behavior and environment to maintain homeostasis. Across organisms there is a well-defined set of SNS and endocrine systems in place to stimulate and regulate the stress response. The CNS also plays an important role in further initiating, processing, and modifying components of the stress response.

The human stress response, although an adaptive process, is mediated by genes and moderated by higher neuropsychological processes, which can result in chronic and eventually deleterious effects on individual biological systems, including those that impact cardiovascular, metabolic, immunological, and neurological health. In the most complex organ in the body, the brain, neurobiological alterations in response to chronic stress are becoming better understood with advancements in the neurosciences. In particular, brain-imaging techniques have provided evidence of both structural and functional abnormalities associated with various stress-related psychopathologies such as PTSD and depression. Although some of the differences between healthy individuals and those suffering from a psychiatric condition, such as PTSD, may have etiologies that differ depending on interactions with the environment, evidence suggest that such differences reflect premorbid vulnerability factors. Even though strides have been taken to understand the gene–environment interplay that contributes to the development of stress-related psychopathology, much work still needs to be completed to understand how to increase resiliency, optimize interventions, and improve the efficacy of treatments for such conditions.

References

Aguilera, G., Subburaju, S., Young, S., & Chen, J. (2008). The parvocellular vasopressinergic system and responsiveness of the hypothalamic pituitary adrenal axis during chronic stress. *Progress in Brain Research*, *170*, 29–39.

Behar, E., Zuellig, A. R., & Borkovec, T. D. (2005). Thought and imaginal activity during worry and trauma recall. *Behavior Therapy*, *36*, 157–168.

Bentley, D. E., Derbyshire, S. W., Youell, P. D., & Jones, A. K. (2003). Caudal cingulate cortex involvement in pain processing: an inter-individual laser evoked potential source localisation study using realistic head models. *Pain*, *102*(3), 265–271.

Berridge, C. W. (2005). The locus-coeruleus-noradrenergic system and stress: modulation of arousal state and state-dependent behavioral processes. In T. Steckler, N. H. Kalin, & J. M. H. M. Reul (Eds.), *Handbook of stress and the brain* (pp. 437–464). Amsterdam: Elsevier.

Bethin, K. E., Vogt, S. K., & Muglia, L. J. (2000). Interleukin-6 is an essential, corticotropin-releasing hormone-independent stimulator of the adrenal axis during immune system activation. *Proceedings of the National Academy of Sciences USA, 97*(16), 9317–9322.

Bracha, H. S., Ralston, T. C., Matsukawa, J. M., Williams, A. E., & Bracha, A. S. (2004). Does "fight or flight" need updating? *Psychosomatics, 45*(5), 448–449.

Breslau, N., Lucia, V. C., & Alvarado, G. F. (2006). Intelligence and other predisposing factors in exposure to trauma and posttraumatic stress disorder: a follow-up study at age 17 years. *Archives of General Psychiatry, 63*(11), 1238–1245.

Buckingham, J. C. (2000). Glucocorticoids, role in stress. In G. Fink (Ed.), *Encyclopedia of stress* (pp. 261–269). New York: Academic Press.

Cannon, W. B. (1929). *Bodily changes in pain, hunger, fear, and rage.* New York: Appleton.

Cannon, W. B. (1932). *Wisdom of the body.* New York: Norton.

Carter, C. S., Braver, T. S., Barch, D. M., Botvinick, M. M., Noll, D., & Cohen, J. D. (1998). Anterior cingulate cortex, error detection, and the online monitoring of performance. *Science, 280*(5364), 747–749.

Chrousos, G. P. (2009). Stress and disorders of the stress system. *Nature Reviews. Endocrinology, 5*(7), 374–381.

Chrousos, G. P., & Gold, P. W. (1992). The concepts of stress and stress system disorders. Overview of physical and behavioral homeostasis. *Jama: the Journal of the American Medical Association, 267*(9), 1244–1252.

Chrousos, G. P., & Kino, T. (2009). Glucocorticoid signaling in the cell. Expanding clinical implications to complex human behavioral and somatic disorders. *Annals of the New York Academy of Sciences, 1179,* 153–166.

Conrad, C. D. (2006). What is the functional significance of chronic stress-induced CA3 dendritic retraction within the hippocampus? *Behavioral and Cognitive Neuroscience Reviews, 5*(1), 41–60.

Dallman, M. F. (2000). Glucocorticoid negative feedback. In G. Fink (Ed.), *Encyclopedia of stress* (pp. 224–228). New York: Academic Press.

Dallman, M. F. (2005). Fast glucocorticoid actions on brain: back to the future. *Frontiers in Neuroendocrinology, 26*(3–4), 103–108.

Dallman, M. F., Bhatnagar, S., & Viau, V. (2000). Hypothalamo-pituitary-adrenal axis. In G. Fink (Ed.), *Encyclopedia of stress* (pp. 468–477). New York: Academic Press.

Damasio, A. (1999). *The feeling of what happens: body and emotion in the making of consciousness.* New York: Harvest Book.

De Keyzer, Y., Rene, P., Lenne, F., Auzan, C., Clauser, E., & Bertagna, X. (1997). V3 vasopressin receptor and corticotropic phenotype in pituitary and nonpituitary tumors. *Hormone Research, 47*(4–6), 259–262.

de Kloet, E. R., Vreugdenhil, E., Oitzl, M. S., & Joëls, M. (1998). Brain corticosteroid receptor balance in health and disease. *Endocrine Reviews, 19*(3), 269–301.

de Kloet, E. R., Joëls, M., & Holsboer, F. (2005a). Stress and the brain: from adaptation to disease. *Nature Reviews. Neuroscience, 6*(6), 463–475.

de Kloet, E. R., Schmidt, M., & Meijer, O. C. (2005b). Corticosteroid receptors and HPA-axis regulation. In T. Steckler, N. H. Kalin, & J. M. H. M. Reul (Eds.), *Handbook of stress and the brain* (pp. 265–294). Amsterdam: Elsevier.

Dhabhar, F. S., & McEwen, B. S. (1996). Stress-induced enhancement of antigen-specific cell-mediated immunity. *Journal of Immunology, 156*(7), 2608–2615.

Dretsch, M. N., & Tipples, J. (2008). Working memory involved in predicting future outcomes based on past experiences. *Brain and Cognition, 66*(1), 83–90.

Dretsch, M. N., Prue-Owens, K., Salvatore, A., & Fjordbak, B. (2010). Mild traumatic brain injury moderates executive attention in soldiers with posttraumatic stress disorder. *Brain Injury, 24,* 368–369.

Drevets, W. C. (2000). Neuroimaging studies of mood disorders. *Biological Psychiatry, 48*(8), 813–829.

Dronjak, S., Jezova, D., & Kvetnansky, R. (2004). Different effects of novel stressors on sympathoadrenal system activation in rats exposed to long-term immobilization. *Annals of the New York Academy of Sciences, 1018,* 113–123.

Ehrhart-Bornstein, M., Haidan, A., Alesci, S., & Bornstein, S. R. (2000). Neurotransmitters and neuropeptides in the differential regulation of steroidogenesis in adrenocortical-chromaffin co-cultures. *Endocrine Research, 26*(4), 833–842.

Elwood, L. S., Hahn, K. S., Olatunji, B. O., & Williams, N. L. (2009). Cognitive vulnerabilities to the development of PTSD: a review of four vulnerabilities and the proposal of an integrative vulnerability model. *Clinical Psychology Review, 29*(1), 87–100.

Feder, A., Nestler, E. J., & Charney, D. S. (2009). Psychobiology and molecular genetics of resilience. *Nature Reviews. Neuroscience, 10*(6), 446–457.

Funder, J. W., Pearce, P. T., Smith, R., & Smith, A. I. (1988). Mineralocorticoid action: target tissue specificity is enzyme, not receptor, mediated. *Science, 242,* 583–585.

Fuxe, K., Wikstrom, A. C., Okret, S., Agnati, L. F., Harfstrand, A., Yu, Z. Y., Granholm, L., Zoli, M., Vale, W., & Gustafsson, J. A. (1985). Mapping of glucocorticoid receptor immunoreactive neurons in the rat tel- and diencephalon using a monoclonal antibody against rat liver glucocorticoid receptor. *Endocrinology, 117*(5), 1803–1812.

Goldstein, D. S., & Kopin, I. J. (2007). Evolution of concepts of stress. *Stress, 10*(2), 109–120.

Habu, S., Watanobe, H., Yasujima, M., & Suda, T. (1998). Different roles of brain interleukin 1 in the adrenocorticotropin response to central versus peripheral administration of lipopolysaccharide in the rat. *Cytokine, 10*(5), 390–394.

Hall, P. F. (2001). Actions of corticotropin on the adrenal cortex: biochemistry and cell biology. In B. S. McEwen (Ed.), *Handbook of physiology IV. Coping with the environment: neural and endocrine mechanisms* (pp. 61–101). New York: Oxford University Press.

Happaney, K., Zelazo, P. D., & Stuss, D. T. (2004). Development of orbitofrontal function: current themes and future directions. *Brain and Cognition, 55*(1), 1–10.

Harbuz, M. S., Chover-Gonzalez, A. J., & Jessop, D. S. (2003). Hypothalamo-pituitary-adrenal axis and chronic immune activation. *Annals of the New York Academy of Sciences, 992,* 99–106.

Hariri, A. R. (2009). The neurobiology of individual differences in complex behavioral traits. *Annual Review of Neuroscience, 32,* 225–247.

Hariri, A. R., Mattay, V. S., Tessitore, A., Kolachana, B., Fera, F., Goldman, D., Egan, M. F., & Weinberger, D. R. (2002). Serotonin transporter genetic variation and the response of the human amygdala. *Science, 297*(5580), 400–403.

Heilig, M. (2004). The NPY system in stress, anxiety and depression. *Neuropeptides, 38*(4), 213–224.

Heilman, K. M. (1994). Emotion and the brain: a distributed modular network mediating emotional experience. In D. W. Zaidel (Ed.), *Neuropsychology* (pp. 139–158). San Diego, CA: Academic Press.

Heinz, A., Smolka, M. N., Braus, D. F., Wrase, J., Beck, A., Flor, H., Mann, K., Schumann, G., Buchel, C., Hariri, A. R., & Weinberger, D. R. (2007). Serotonin transporter genotype (5-HTTLPR): effects of neutral and undefined conditions on amygdala activation. *Biological Psychiatry, 61*(8), 1011–1014.

Herman, J. P., & Cullinan, W. E. (1997). Neurocircuitry of stress: central control of the hypothalamo-pituitary-adrenocortical axis. *Trends in Neurosciences, 20*(2), 78–84.

Hermans, D., Vansteenwegen, D., Crombez, G., Baeyens, F., & Eelen, P. (2002). Expectancy-learning and evaluative learning in human classical conditioning: affective priming as an indirect and unobtrusive measure of conditioned stimulus valence. *Behaviour Research and Therapy, 40*(3), 217–234.

Holgert, H., Aman, K., Cozzari, C., Hartman, B. K., Brimijoin, S., Emson, P., Goldstein, M., & Hokfelt, T. (1995). The cholinergic innervation of the adrenal gland and its relation to enkephalin and nitric oxide synthase. *Neuroreport, 6*(18), 2576–2580.

Jelen, P., & Zagrodzka, J. (2001). Heart rate changes in partially restrained rats during behaviorally and pharmacologically evoked emotional states. *Acta Neurobiologiae Experimentalis, 61*(1), 53–67.

Jessop, D. S. (1999). Stimulatory and inhibitory regulators of the hypothalamo-pituitary-adrenocortical axis. *Bailliere's Best Practice & Research, 13*(4), 491–501.

Joëls, M. (2011) Impact of glucocorticoids on brain function: relevance for mood disorders. *Psychoneuroendocrinology*, in press.

Joëls, M., & de Kloet, E. R. (1993). Corticosteroid actions on amino acid-mediated transmission in rat CA1 hippocampal cells. *Journal of Neuroscience, 13*(9), 4082–4090.

Kant, G. J., Bunnell, B. N., Mougey, E. H., Pennington, L. L., & Meyerhoff, J. L. (1983). Effects of repeated stress on pituitary cyclic AMP, and plasma prolactin, corticosterone and growth hormone in male rats. *Pharmacology, Biochemistry, and Behavior, 18*(6), 967–971.

Karl, A., Schaefer, M., Malta, L. S., Dorfel, D., Rohleder, N., & Werner, A. (2006). A meta-analysis of structural brain abnormalities in PTSD. *Neuroscience and Biobehavioral Reviews, 30*(7), 1004–1031.

Keller-Wood, M. E., & Dallman, M. F. (1984). Corticosteroid inhibition of ACTH secretion. *Endocrine Reviews, 5*(1), 1–24.

Kensinger, E. A. (2007). Negative emotion enhances memory accuracy: behavioral and neuroimaging evidence. *Current Directions in Psychological Sciences, 16*, 213–218.

Knight, D. C., Nguyen, H. T., & Bandettini, P. A. (2005). The role of the human amygdala in the production of conditioned fear responses. *Neuroimage, 26*(4), 1193–1200.

Knight, D. C., Waters, N. S., King, M. K., & Bandettini, P. A. (2010). Learning-related diminution of unconditioned SCR and fMRI signal responses. *Neuroimage, 49*(1), 843–848.

Koechlin, E., & Hyafil, A. (2001). Anterior prefrontal function and the limits of human decision-making. *Science, 318*(5850), 594–598.

Korte, S. M. (2001). Corticosteroids in relation to fear, anxiety and psychopathology. *Neuroscience and Biobehavioral Reviews*, 25(2), 117–142.

Krawczyk, D. C. (2002). Contributions of the prefrontal cortex to the neural basis of human decision making. *Neuroscience and Biobehavioral Reviews*, 26(6), 631–664.

Krueger, R. F. (2000). Phenotypic, genetic, and nonshared environmental parallels in the structure of personality: a view from the multidimensional personality questionnaire. *Journal of Personality and Social Psychology*, 79(6), 1057–1067.

Kuhlmann, S., Piel, M., & Wolf, O. T. (2005). Impaired memory retrieval after psychosocial stress in healthy young men. *Journal of Neuroscience*, 25(11), 2977–2982.

Lanius, R. A., Bluhm, R., Lanius, U., & Pain, C. (2006). A review of neuroimaging studies in PTSD: heterogeneity of response to symptom provocation. *Journal of Psychiatric Research*, 40(8), 709–729.

Lawrence, J. W., & Fauerbach, J. A. (2003). Personality, coping, chronic stress, social support and PTSD symptoms among adult burn survivors: a path analysis. *Journal of Burn Care & Rehabilitation*, 24(1), 63–72; discussion 62.

Lazarus, R. S. (1985). The psychology of stress and coping. *Issues in Mental Health Nursing*, 7(1–4), 399–418.

Leskin, L. P., & White, P. M. (2007). Attentional networks reveal executive function deficits in posttraumatic stress disorder. *Neuropsychology*, 21(3), 275–284.

Martens, C., Bilodeau, S., Maira, M., Gauthier, Y., & Drouin, J. (2005). Protein-protein interactions and transcriptional antagonism between the subfamily of NGFI-B/Nur77 orphan nuclear receptors and glucocorticoid receptor. *Molecular Endocrinology*, 19(4), 885–897.

Mason, J. W. (1975). A historical view of the stress field. *Journal of Human Stress*, 1(1), 6–12.

McCarty, R. (2000). Fight-or-flight response. In G. Fink (Ed.), *Encyclopedia of stress* (pp. 143–145). New York: Academic Press.

McEwen, B. S. (1998). Stress, adaptation, and disease. Allostasis and allostatic load. *Annals of the New York Academy of Sciences*, 840, 33–44.

McEwen, B. S. (2000a). Allostasis and allostatic load: implications for neuropsychopharmacology. *Neuropsychopharmacology*, 22(2), 108–124.

McEwen, B. S. (2000b). The neurobiology of stress: from serendipity to clinical relevance. *Brain Research*, 886(1–2), 172–189.

McEwen, B. S., & Seeman, T. (1999). Protective and damaging effects of mediators of stress. Elaborating and testing the concepts of allostasis and allostatic load. *Annals of the New York Academy of Sciences*, 896, 30–47.

McRae, K., Hughes, B., Chopra, S., Gabrieli, J. D. E., Gross, J. J., & Ochsner, K. N. (2009). The neural bases of distraction and reappraisal. *Journal of Cognitive Neuroscience*, 22, 248–262.

Munck, A., Guyre, P. M., & Holbrook, N. J. (1984). Physiological functions of glucocorticoids in stress and their relation to pharmacological actions. *Endocrine Reviews*, 5(1), 25–44.

Neese, R. M., & Young, E. A. (2000). Evolutionary origins and functions of the stress response. In G. Fink (Ed.), *Encyclopedia of stress* (pp. 79–84). New York: Academic Press.

Ochsner, K. N., Knierim, K., Ludlow, D. H., Hanelin, J., Ramachandran, T., Glover, G., & Mackey, S. C. (2004). Reflecting upon feelings: an fMRI study of neural systems supporting the attribution of emotion to self and other. *Journal of Cognitive Neuroscience, 16*(10), 1746–1772.

Orchinik, M. (1998). Glucocorticoids, stress, and behavior: shifting the timeframe. *Hormones and Behavior, 34*(3), 320–327.

Pacak, K., Palkovits, M., Yadid, G., Kvetnansky, R., Kopin, I. J., & Goldstein, D. S. (1998). Heterogeneous neurochemical responses to different stressors: a test of Selye's doctrine of nonspecificity. *American Journal of Physiology Regulatory, Integrative and Comparative Physiology, 275*(4 Pt 2), R1247–R1255.

Pearce, D., & Yamamoto, K. R. (1993). Mineralocorticoid and glucocorticoid receptor activities distinguished by nonreceptor factors at a composite response element. *Science, 259*(5098), 1161–1165.

Pecchinenda, A., Dretsch, M., & Chapman, P. (2006). Working memory involvement in emotion-based processes underlying choosing advantageously. *Experimental Psychology, 53*(3), 191–197.

Pereda, M. P., Lohrer, P., Kovalovsky, D., Perez Castro, C., Goldberg, V., Losa, M., Chervin, A., Berner, S., Molina, H., Stalla, G. K., Renner, U., & Arzt, E. (2000). Interleukin-6 is inhibited by glucocorticoids and stimulates ACTH secretion and POMC expression in human corticotroph pituitary adenomas. *Experimental and Clinical Endocrinolology & Diabetes, 108*(3), 202–207.

Phelps, E. A. (2004). Human emotion and memory: interactions of the amygdala and hippocampal complex. *Current Opinion in Neurobiology, 14*(2), 198–202.

Rao, U., Chen, L. A., Bidesi, A. S., Shad, M. U., Thomas, M. A., & Hammen, C. L. (2010) Hippocampal changes associated with early-life adversity and vulnerability to depression. *Biological Psychiatry, 67*(4), 357–364.

Reul, J. M., & de Kloet, E. R. (1985). Two receptor systems for corticosterone in rat brain: microdistribution and differential occupation. *Endocrinology, 117*(6), 2505–2511.

Reul, J. M., Gesing, A., Droste, S., Stec, I. S., Weber, A., Bachmann, C., Bilang-Bleuel, A., Holsboer, F., & Linthorst, A. C. (2000). The brain mineralocorticoid receptor: greedy for ligand, mysterious in function. *European Journal of Pharmacology, 405*(1–3), 235–249.

Rivier, C., & Vale, W. (1983). Interaction of corticotropin-releasing factor and arginine vasopressin on adrenocorticotropin secretion in vivo. *Endocrinology, 113*(3), 939–942.

Roberts, N. A., Beer, J. S., Werner, K. H., Scabini, D., Levens, S. M., Knight, R. T., & Levenson, R. W. (2004). The impact of orbital prefrontal cortex damage on emotional activation to unanticipated and anticipated acoustic startle stimuli. *Cognitive, Affective & Behavioral Neuroscience, 4*(3), 307–316.

Rokke, P. D., Arnell, K. M., Koch, M. D., & Andrews, J. T. (2002). Dual-task attention deficits in dysphoric mood. *Journal of Abnormal Psychology, 111*(2), 370–379.

Rolls, E. T. (2004). The functions of the orbitofrontal cortex. *Brain and Cognition, 55*(1), 11–29.

Roozendaal, B. (2002). Stress and memory: opposing effects of glucocorticoids on memory consolidation and memory retrieval. *Neurobiology of Learning and Memory, 78*(3), 578–595.

Roozendaal, B., McReynolds, J. R., & McGaugh, J. L. (2004). The basolateral amygdala interacts with the medial prefrontal cortex in regulating glucocorticoid effects on working memory impairment. *Journal of Neuroscience, 24*(6), 1385–1392.

Saper, C. B., & Breder, C. D. (1994). The neurologic basis of fever. *New England Journal of Medicine, 330*(26), 1880–1886.

Sapolsky, R. M., Romero, L. M., & Munck, A. U. (2000). How do glucocorticoids influence stress responses? Integrating permissive, suppressive, stimulatory, and preparative actions. *Endocrine Reviews, 21*(1), 55–89.

Sawchenko, P. E., & Arias, C. (1995). Evidence for short-loop feedback effects of ACTH on CRF and vasopressin expression in parvocellular neurosecretory neurons. *Journal of Neuroendocrinology, 7*(9), 721–731.

Schulz, D. W., Mansbach, R. S., Sprouse, J., Braselton, J. P., Collins, J., Corman, M., Dunaiskis, A., Faraci, S., Schmidt, A. W., Seeger, T., Seymour, P., Tingley, 3rd, F. D., Winston, E. N., Chen, Y. L., & Heym, J. (1996). CP-154,526: a potent and selective nonpeptide antagonist of corticotropin releasing factor receptors. *Proceedings of the National Academy of Sciences USA, 93*(19), 10477–10482.

Scott, L. V., & Dinan, T. G. (1998). Vasopressin and the regulation of hypothalamic-pituitary-adrenal axis function: implications for the pathophysiology of depression. *Life Sciences, 62*(22), 1985–1998.

Seckl, J. R., Yau, J. L. W., & Homes, M. C. (2005). The role of 11b-hydroxysteroid dehydrogenases in the regulation of corticosteroid activity in the brain. In T. Steckler, N. H. Kalin, & J. M. H. M. Reul (Eds.), *Handbook of stress and the brain* (pp. 313–328). Amsterdam: Elsevier.

Selye, H. (1956). *The stress of life.* New York: McGraw-Hill.

Shima, K., & Tanji, J. (1998). Role for cingulate motor area cells in voluntary movement selection based on reward. *Science, 282*(5392), 1335–1338.

Turken, A. U., & Swick, D. (1999). Response selection in the human anterior cingulate cortex. *Nature Neuroscience, 2*(10), 920–924.

Ulrich-Lai, Y. M., & Engeland, W. C. (2005). Sympatho-adrenal activity and hypothalamic-pituitary-adrenal axis regulation. In T. Steckler, N. H. Kalin, & J. M. H. M. Reul (Eds.), *Handbook of stress and the brain* (pp. 419–435). Amsterdam: Elsevier.

Valentino, R. J., & Foote, S. L. (1987). Corticotropin-releasing factor disrupts sensory responses of brain noradrenergic neurons. *Neuroendocrinology, 45*(1), 28–36.

Valentino, R. J., & Wehby, R. G. (1988). Corticotropin-releasing factor: evidence for a neurotransmitter role in the locus ceruleus during hemodynamic stress. *Neuroendocrinology, 48*(6), 674–677.

Vasterling, J. J., Duke, L. M., Brailey, K., Constans. J. I., Allain, A. N. & Sutker, P. B. (2002). Attention, learning, and memory performances and intellectual resources in Vietnam Veterans: PTSD and no disorder comparisons. *Neuropsychology, 16*, 5–14.

Villarreal, G., Hamilton, D. A., Petropoulos, H., Driscoll, I., Rowland, L. M., Griego, J. A., Kodituwakku, P. W., Hart, B. L., Escalona, R., & Brooks, W. M. (2002). Reduced hippocampal volume and total white matter volume in posttraumatic stress disorder. *Biological Psychiatry, 52*(2), 119–125.

Whitnall, M. H. (1993). Regulation of the hypothalamic corticotropin-releasing hormone neurosecretory system. *Progress in Neurobiology, 40*(5), 573–629.

Williams, L. M., Kemp, A. H., Felmingham, K., Barton, M., Olivieri, G., Peduto, A., Gordon, E., & Bryant, R. A. (2006). Trauma modulates amygdala and medial prefrontal responses to consciously attended fear. *Neuroimage, 29*(2), 347–357.

Williams, P. G., Suchy, Y., & Rau, H. K. (2009). Individual differences in executive functioning: implications for stress regulation. *Annals of Behavioral Medicine, 37*(2), 126–140.

Wust, S., Federenko, I., Hellhammer, D. H., & Kirschbaum, C. (2000). Genetic factors, perceived chronic stress, and the free cortisol response to awakening.*Psychoneuroendoc rinology, 25*(7), 707–720.

Zhou, Z., Zhu, G., Hariri, A. R., Enoch, M. A., Scott, D., Sinha, R., Virkkunen, M., Mash, D. C., Lipsky, R. H., Hu, X. Z., Hodgkinson, C. A., Xu, K., Buzas, B., Yuan, Q., Shen, P. H., Ferrell, R. E., Manuck, S. B., Brown, S. M., Hauger, R. L., Stohler, C. S., Zubieta, J. K., & Goldman, D. (2008). Genetic variation in human NPY expression affects stress response and emotion. *Nature, 452*(7190), 997–1001.

2

Central Nervous System Regulation of the Hypothalamic–Pituitary–Adrenal Axis Stress Response

James P. Herman

The Problem of Stress

The concept of *stress* was first articulated by Hans Selye, based on a common constellation of physiological responses to a wide variety of noxious stimuli (Selye, 1936). Selye defined stress as "the non-specific response of the organism to any challenge" (Selye, 1976). The stress concept has undergone substantial revision over the ensuing decades, including challenge to the central tenet of nonspecificity (see Pacak et al., 1998). Moreover, the actual meaning of the word 'stress' has changed over time; whereas Selye used stress to denote the *response* itself, modern usage assumes stress to be an inferred state of the organism, and refers to indicators of this state as the *stress response*. The modern usage is firmly embedded in the field and the lay public, and will be used in the current chapter, with an apologetic nod to Selye's immense contribution to the field.

Although a number of definitions are proposed, current thinking generally holds that stress is a real or anticipated threat to homeostasis or an anticipated threat to well-being. Stressors can be characterized on the basis of response mechanism. Real homeostatic threats (e.g., hemorrhage) trigger reflexive responses that include engagement of the hypothalamic–pituitary–adrenal (HPA) axis and autonomic nervous system. However, a large proportion of stressors fall into the category of *anticipated* threats, wherein sensory stimuli are interpreted with respect to previous experience or innate (instinctual) predispositions (Herman et al., 2003; Ulrich-Lai and Herman, 2009). Responses to anticipated threat (termed *psychogenic* responses) are highly influenced by genetics and lifelong stress-exposure history, and is a very

The Handbook of Stress: Neuropsychological Effects on the Brain, First Edition.
Edited by Cheryl D. Conrad.
© 2011 Blackwell Publishing Ltd. Published 2011 by Blackwell Publishing Ltd.

James P. Herman

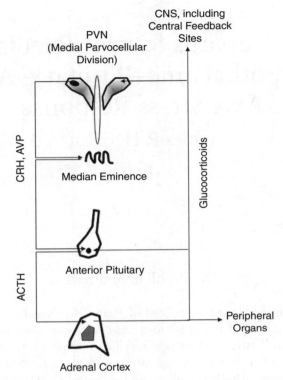

Figure 2.1 Organization of the HPA axis. Neurons located within the hypothalamic par-aventricular nucleus (PVN) drive pituitary corticotrophs via release of secretagogues (such as corticotropin-releasing hormone [CRH] and arginine vasopressin [AVP]) into the portal vasculature, stimulating adrenocorticotrophic hormone (ACTH). ACTH, in turn, mediates the synthesis and release of corticosteroids from the adrenal glands. Glucocorticoids then travel via the system circulation to a wide variety of organ systems, and provide feedback signals at the pituitary, PVN, and other sites of the central nervous system (CNS) to inhibit subsequent HPA activation.

important component of stress-related diseases, such as depression and posttrau-matic stress disorder (as well as many systemic diseases).

The HPA axis is one of several components of responding to stress. This system (Figure 2.1) introduces glucocorticoids into the systemic circulation, which act via genomic (as well as nongenomic) mechanisms in multiple organ systems in the body (see Chapters 3 and 4 in this volume). Responses are initiated by neural and humoral inputs onto corticotrophin-releasing hormone (CRH) neurons in the medial parvocellular zone of the hypothalamic paraventricular nucleus (PVN), which are responsible for excitation of adrenocorticotrophic hormone (ACTH) secretion at the level of the anterior pituitary. ACTH elicits release of glucocorticoids (cortisol and/or corticosterone depending on species) from the adrenal cortex (Herman, 2009). Glucocorticoids act at multiple organ systems to optimize survival in the face of adversity, for example, by enhancing plasma glucose levels (via hepatic glycogenolysis), maintaining vascular tone, holding inflammatory processes in check, and limiting activity in nonsurvival-related systems (growth, reproduction; see Munck et al., 1984). Glucocorticoids also feed back on brain circuits driving the HPA axis, providing a mechanism for efficient shut-off of the metabolically expensive stress response (see Keller-Wood and Dallman, 1984). The acute HPA axis stress response is invaluable to the organism and comprises a key component of adaptation. However, processes initiated and maintained by glucocorticoids can become maladaptive if prolonged in time, underscoring the survival value of feedback inhibition.

This chapter focuses on neurocircuits that regulate activity of the HPA axis following stress. The characteristics of acute and chronic HPA responsiveness vary widely, so mechanisms of acute and chronic HPA axis regulation will be considered separately, and factors that may underlie transition from acute to chronic response patterns are discussed in the final section.

Acute Stress Responses

Stimulation of the HPA axis is generally time-locked to stressor exposure, giving glucocorticoids a (perhaps erroneous) designation as *stress hormones*. Pathways responsible for stress activation generally take one of two routes: direct activation via circuits processing homeostatic information, and indirect activation via multisynaptic forebrain limbic pathways (see Figure 2.2).

Activation of the HPA axis: direct pathways

The *direct pathway* is rapidly recruited by physiological (so-called systemic) stressors and is thought to be part of a reflexive response of the HPA axis to adjust to homeostatic perturbations (Herman et al., 2003). Ascending norepinephrine (and/or epinephrine) neurons in the nucleus of the solitary tract (NTS) and, to a lesser extent, ventrolateral medulla play a substantial role in stimulation of CRH neurons (Plotsky et al., 1989; Cunningham and Sawchenko, 1988). In responses to physiological challenges such as hypovolemia, ether inhalation, and hypoglycemia, norepinephrine is released in the PVN (Pacak et al., 1995) and activates CRH neurons, promoting ACTH release and subsequent secretion of glucocorticoids (see Gaillet et al., 1991; Ritter et al., 2003). The importance of the NTS is likely related to its position as a brainstem viscerosensory relay site, providing a rapid (i.e., one-synapse) activation in responses to physiologic challenge.

Activation of the HPA axis is also mediated by monosynaptic input from homeostatic sensors in the hypothalamus and circumventricular organs. The mediobasal hypothalamus senses changes in circulating factors regulating energy balance, including insulin, leptin, glucose, and possibly ghrelin (Ahima et al., 2000; Levin,

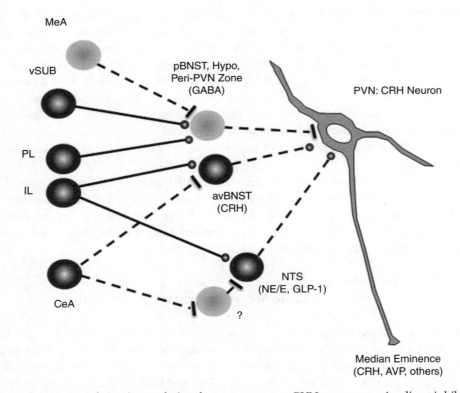

Figure 2.2 Neural circuits regulating the stress response. PVN neurons receive direct inhibitory (γ-aminobutyric acid [GABA]-containing) input (light-shaded circles) from neurons in the bed nucleus of the stria terminalis (BNST) and numerous hypothalamic nuclei (Hypo) and excitatory input (dark-shaded circles) from the brainstem, including neurons of the nucleus of the solitary tract (NTS; containing mutually exclusive populations of norepinephrine/epinephrine [NE/E] and glucagon-like peptide-1 [GLP-1]-containing neurons). These direct pathways are heavily influenced by input from limbic structures, which likely fuel psychogenic stress responses and underlie HPA pathology associated with affective disease or chronic stress. Inhibitory circuits receive excitatory input from regions such as the hippocampus (via the ventral subiculum [vSUB] and medial prefrontal cortex, or prelimbic [PL], regions), which results in a net inhibition of the stress response. In contrast, inhibitory PVN inputs receive GABAergic (i.e., inhibitory) input from the medial amygdaloid nucleus (MeA) and central amygdaloid nucleus (CeA), resulting in disinhibition at the level of the PVN (and thus activation of the HPA axis). PVN excitatory regions (such as the anteroventral BNST and NTS) receive direct innervation from glutamate neurons of the infralimbic (IL) region of the medial prefrontal cortex, which may enhance HPA activity; brainstem excitatory regions also receive input from the CeA, which may disinhibit brainstem neurons by way of local inhibitory interneurons. avBNST, anteroventral BNST; AVP, arginine vasopressin; pBNST, posterior BNST.

2002; Belgardt et al., 2009). Neurons of the arcuate nucleus integrate these signals, and a subpopulation of these cells project directly to the PVN, wherein *feeding peptides* can stimulate (neuropeptide Y; Haas and George, 1987; Wahlestedt et al., 1987) or inhibit (melanocortins; Cragnolini et al., 2004; Xiao et al., 2003) stress-induced activation of the HPA axis. The subfornical organ, a circumventricular organ that is blood–brain-barrier-deficient, sends angiotensin II projections to the PVN and promotes HPA activation (Lind et al., 1984; Plotsky et al., 1988; Krause et al., 2008), perhaps via processing of peripheral information on fluid and electrolyte balance and cardiovascular status. Finally, inflammatory signals appear to directly activate ascending norepinephrine neurons of the NTS and possibly the PVN itself via local vascular synthesis of prostaglandins and related molecules (Rivest, 2001; Schiltz and Sawchenko, 2003).

Homeostatic signals may also be relayed by multisynaptic sources. For example, there is evidence for a multisynaptic loop linking the mediobasal hypothalamus to the PVN, involving the ventromedial hypothalamus, dorsomedial hypothalamus, and PVN (ter Horst and Luiten, 1987). In addition, the NTS projects to numerous sites that in turn send projections to the PVN (ter Horst and Streefland, 1994). The multinode arrangement allows for integration of energy-balance signals from multiple sources, and may be important for coordination and adjustment of responses.

Activation of the HPA axis: indirect pathways

Regulation of responses to psychogenic (or psychological) stressors is a more complicated process that requires integration of multimodal sensory information with respect to memories or innate-response predispositions (Herman, 2009; Herman et al., 2003). This class of stress response differs from systemic responses in that the HPA axis is activated in anticipation of physiologic challenge. The psychogenic activation system essentially prepares the body to cope with adversity, rather than to react to a defined physiological stimulus. Given that periods of pronounced physiological challenge are generally rare, the psychogenic response likely represents the lion's share of the onus of stress on the organism.

Psychogenic responses are mediated by multisynaptic pathways, likely originating in limbic forebrain structures. Psychogenic activation is linked to the amygdala and the infralimbic division of the medial prefrontal cortex (see Herman, 2009). The amygdala is an extremely complex set of subnuclei. There is substantial cortical input to the lateral subnuclei of the amygdala, which then sends excitatory intra-amygdalar connections to key output nuclei (Swanson and Petrovich, 1998). Lesions to these key output subnuclei (central and medial nuclei) generally reduce the magnitude of the HPA axis response, consistent with an activational role of the structure as a whole (Herman et al., 2003). The importance of the central versus medial nuclei varies with stimulus modality, suggesting differential processing of stressful information in these subnuclei (Dayas and Day, 2002; Xu et al., 1999; Prewitt and Herman, 1997). For example, the central amygdaloid nucleus is critical for regulation of HPA axis responses to systemic but not psychogenic stressors, whereas the reverse is true for the medial amygdaloid nucleus (Dayas and Day, 2002; Xu et al., 1999; Prewitt and Herman, 1997). In addition, the role of amydgalar nuclei in stress regulation may relate to output pathways. The central nucleus is most clearly linked to autonomic responses, whereas the medial nucleus is more closely associated with HPA axis activation (see Herman, 2009). Importantly, the output of both the central and medial nuclei is primarily γ-aminobutyric acid (GABA)-ergic (Swanson and Petrovich, 1998).

There is evidence for infralimbic-cortex stimulation of psychogenic responses, in that lesions of this region decrease corticosterone responses to repeated restraint and reduce activation of (preautonomic) PVN neurons (Radley et al., 2006; Sullivan and Gratton, 1999). In addition, stimulation of the infralimbic cortex (in contrast with the overlying prelimbic cortex) enhances cardiovascular responses to stress (Frysztak and Neafsey, 1991; Resstel and Correa, 2006). The influence of the infra-limbic cortex appears to be lateralized, with the right infralimbic cortex being of most importance to stress stimulation (Sullivan and Gratton, 1999). As was the case for the central amygdaloid nucleus, the infralimbic cortex appears most tightly linked to regulation of autonomic responses.

Neither the amygdala nor the infralimbic cortex project directly to the PVN. Therefore, connections between these structures and HPA axis-regulatory PVN neurons are multisynaptic. Recent data strongly link HPA activation to amygdalar and prefrontal relays in the bed nucleus of the stria terminalis (BNST). The antero-ventral BNST, selectively targeted by central amygdala and infralimbic cortex, sends direct projections to the PVN (Dong et al., 2001). Lesions of this region reduce HPA axis activation and cardiovascular responses to stress (Choi et al., 2007; Crestani et al., 2009), consistent with a role for this area in stress excitation. Notably, this region contains CRH neurons that project directly to the PVN (Champagne et al., 1998), suggesting the intriguing possibility that forebrain activation of PVN CRH may be itself regulated by extrahypothalamic sources of CRH peptide. The infralimbic-BNST-PVN circuit is a logical means to confer transsynaptic excitation, as it involves sequential excitatory synaptic inputs. In addition, the anteroventral BNST also contains populations of GABAergic neurons that also project into the PVN (Dong et al., 2001). Given that the principal outflow of the central nucleus is GABAergic, it is possible that central amygdalar stimulation of the HPA axis is mediated by sequential GABAergic synapses, comprising transsynaptic disinhibi-tion. The synaptology of central nucleus versus infralimbic cortex input awaits definitive characterization.

It is also possible that at least part of forebrain-mediated stress excitation is medi-ated by interactions between the infralimbic cortex and central amygdaloid nucleus at the level of the brainstem, interacting with neurons involved in *reflexive* responses. Whereas NTS norepinephrine appears to be selectively involved in responses to systemic stressors (Ritter et al., 2003), other populations of NTS neurons appear to be important in integration of psychogenic responses. For example, neurons con-taining glucagon-like peptide 1 (GLP-1) are involved in generating responses to both homestatic challenge (visceral illness) and psychological stress (elevated platform exposure; Kinzig et al., 2003). These neurons do not coexpress norepinephrine (Larsen et al., 1997), indicating that regulatory classes of response may be cell- and/ or circuit-specific. Given that the NTS receives descending information from the infralimbic cortex and central amygdala, it is plausible that forebrain limbic structures may use selected reflexive pathways for control of the HPA axis.

Serotonin neurons (5-hydroxytryptamine or 5-HT) of the midbrain raphe nuclei also play a role in HPA axis stimulation (Herman et al., 2003). Current evidence suggests that 5-HT directly activates CRH neurons via resident 5-HT_{2A} receptors (Zhang et al., 2002). However, 5-HT innervation is present in and around the PVN (Sawchenko et al., 1983), a complicated arrangement that positions 5-HT for involvement in both direct activation and transsynaptic inhibition, the latter potentially mediated by neighboring peri-PVN neurons (Lowry, 2002). The raphe nuclei are innervated by numerous stress-relevant pathways, including the BNST, central amygdala, and limbic cortices, and 5-HT neurons appear to be responsive to CRH (Kirby et al., 2008). Thus, 5-HT neurons of the raphe appear to be an additional means of transsynaptic activation of the PVN. Given the known role for the raphe in regulation of mood and arousal it is plausible that regulation of the HPA axis represents a component of more global, integrated signals controlled by brain 5-HT.

Inhibition of the HPA axis: negative feedback

Glucocorticoid release causes significant redistribution of energy resources and is metabolically expensive. As a consequence, glucocorticoid balance is rigorously defended by the body, in large part by feedback inhibition of ACTH release by the hormones themselves. Feedback takes many forms, and is a regulated process at all nodes of the HPA axis. Rapid inhibition of glucocorticoid release is mediated by nongenomic mechanisms, working at the level of the pituitary and brain to rapidly limit CRH and ACTH release, respectively (Buckingham et al., 2006; Di et al., 2003). In the brain, fast feedback appears to be mediated primarily at the level of the PVN CRH neuron, and involves mobilization of local endocannabinoid synthesis and subsequent presynaptic inhibition of glutamate release (Di et al., 2003). In the pituitary, glucocorticoids cause rapid translocation of annexin 1 to the cell membrane of folliculostellate cells, which can then bind to receptors on corticotrophs and cause juxtacrine inhibition of ACTH release (Buckingham et al., 2006). The receptors involved in fast feedback have yet to be definitively determined.

The duration of the glucocorticoid response is regulated largely in brain. Inhibition of response duration requires the concerted action of the mineralocorticoid receptor (MR) and glucocorticoid receptor (GR), which are classical mediators of glucocorticoid-regulated gene transcription. The MR is a high-affinity receptor that is largely saturated at low resting levels of glucocorticoids, and is thought to be permissive for feedback inhibition (Reul and de Kloet, 1985; Bradbury et al., 1994; de Kloet et al., 1998). The GR has a lower affinity and is thus extensively bound only at high (i.e., stress) circulating levels of glucocorticoids (de Kloet et al., 1998; Reul and de Kloet, 1985). The GR is required for normal shut-off of the HPA axis after stress (see Boyle et al., 2005).

The GR and MR are localized to numerous stress-regulatory brain regions, including inhibitory regions such as the hippocampus and prefrontal cortex (Herman, 1993). Studies from site-specific GR-knockout mice reveal that the presence of GR in forebrain (e.g., hippocampus, cortex, and cortical amygdaloid nuclei) is required for normal shut-off of the HPA axis response to psychogenic stress (Boyle et al., 2005; Furay et al., 2008). However, responses to systemic stressors are maintained in forebrain-GR-knockout mice, indicating that feedback inhibition of the HPA axis is dependent on brain region and perhaps the nature of the stimulus (Furay et al., 2008).

Consistent with the knockout data, a number of studies implicate the ventral subiculum (principal outflow of the ventral hippocampus) and prelimbic cortex in inhibition of responses to psychogenic stressors. Damage to both regions causes prolonged glucocorticoid secretion after psychogenic but not systemic stressor exposure (Diorio et al., 1993; Herman et al., 1998). As was the case for the infralimbic cortex and amygdalar subnuclei there are few direct connections between the prelimbic cortex or ventral subiculum and PVN, indicating that inhibition is trans-synaptic. As the principal outflow of both regions is excitatory (glutamate) it is likely that HPA inhibition involves contact with an inhibitory relay neuron (Herman et al., 2003). In the case of the ventral subiculum putative inhibitory relays can be identified in regions such as the posterior BNST, medial preoptic area, and dorsomedial hypothalamus (Cullinan et al., 1993). In these regions ventral subiculum afferents directly contact PVN projecting neurons, the vast majority of which express the inhibitory neurotransmitter GABA (Cullinan et al., 1993). Notably, lesions to either the posterior BNST or medial preoptic area increase HPA axis stress responsiveness (Choi et al., 2007; Viau and Meaney, 1996), verifying that these regions are involved in inhibitory control of CRH neurons.

The PVN also receives heavy GABAergic innervation from a number of hypothalamic nuclei (Cullinan et al., 1993; Roland and Sawchenko, 1993), some (but not all) of which receive inputs from limbic forebrain structures. These GABA inputs provide significant tonic inhibit onto CRH neurons. Some inhibitory inputs are strategically placed to relay information on physiologic status (e.g., GABAergic afferents from the arcuate nucleus [energy balance] and preoptic area [temperature]).

Control of acute psychogenic stress responses

The information above notes that psychogenic HPA axis responses are controlled by both excitatory and inhibitory limbic structures. The amygdala and infralimbic cortex provide a *go* signal, perhaps in keeping with the role of these structures in processing emotional memory (Cardinal et al., 2002). It is logical that these structures are engaged in threatening situations and are involved in preparing the animal to cope, in a physiological sense, with a potential threat. The hippocampus and prelimbic cortex appear to generate a *no-go* signal, consistent their roles in spatial memory and executive function. The net outflow of these regions may signal safety; that is, that a prolonged physiological response is not necessary. Relay neurons in the BNST are well positioned to integrate both go and no-go signals, in that the nucleus receives input from both disinhibitory (e.g., amygdala) and inhibitory (e.g, hippocampus, prelimbic cortex) regions. Finally, both the limbic forebrain regions themselves and the BNST interface extensively with hypothalamic neurons that read physiological status and may therefore modulate the significance of limbic input with respect to ongoing homeostatic status.

Chronic Stress Responses

The acute stress response is geared to adapt the animal to new changes in the internal milieu or external environment. However, organisms are often confronted with prolonged challenges that require continuous adaptation. In this case, the brain is confronted with an interesting problem: how to adjust HPA axis function to cope with repeated stress while maintaining responsiveness to new potential threats. Successful adaptation appears to be attained by balancing processes of *habituation* and *sensitization* (Figure 2.3). Habituation occurs when an animal is repeatedly exposed to a single type or modality of stressor (i.e., *homotypic* stressors). If the

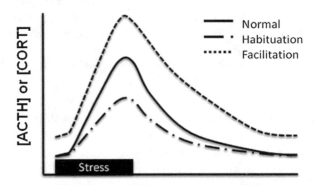

Figure 2.3   HPA axis habituation and facilitation after chronic stress. Upon repeated exposure to a given stressor, the magnitude of the ACTH and/or cortisosterone (CORT) response to the stressor undergoes substantial attenuation (habituation; compare solid and dashed/dotted lines). If the animal is then exposed to a novel stressor, the response to that stressor will be equivalent to or greater than that observed in unstressed animals (facilitation; compare solid and dashed lines), indicating that response capacity is maintained despite the history of heterotypic stress. In general, the more intense or unpredictable the chronic stress regimen, the greater the degree of sensitization.

repeated stressor is sufficiently benign, the HPA axis response will wane with repeated stimulation, and many of the more pronounced physiological changes seen with initial stress (e.g., anorexia) will be reversed (Dhabhar et al., 1997; Girotti et al., 2006). At the same time, the response to new stressors is maintained or even sensitized (Akana et al., 1992). Notably, the *maintained* or *sensitized* response often occurs against a backdrop of elevated glucocorticoids, and is thus considered an active process that overcomes feedback. The latter mechanism was extensively characterized by Dallman and colleagues, and is referred to as *facilitation* (Akana et al., 1992).

If stressors are sufficiently intense or unpredictable (as observed in stress regimens providing randomized exposure to *heterotypic* stressors), the animal is not able to successfully habituate. In these regimens, weight loss and HPA axis hyperactivity are maintained over time (Herman et al., 1995) and significant dysfunction encountered, as measured by both aberrant neural changes (McEwen, 1999) and development of depression-like behaviors (Willner, 2005). These types of regimen provide parallels to numerous human conditions and are used to model disease states and test potential palliative interventions.

Habituation of the HPA axis appears to involve circuits that are distinct from those that control acute stress responses. For example, lesions of paraventricular thalamus inhibit habituation of corticosterone responses to repeated restraint (Bhatnagar et al., 2002; however, see Fernandes et al., 2002), without affecting acute glucocorticoid responses. Notably, this region is also required for stress facilitation (Bhatnagar and Dallman, 1998), suggesting that it may be of general importance in integrating the chronicity of stress responses. The paraventricular thalamus receives heavy projections from the ventral subiculum and the prelimbic and infralimbic cortices (Canteras and Swanson, 1992; Cullinan et al., 1993; Hurley et al., 1991; Sesack et al., 1989) and projects heavily to the central amygdala and dorsomedial hypothalamus (Moga et al., 1995; Li and Kirouac, 2008). Accordingly, this region is well positioned to integrate inputs from limbic stress-inhibitory and stress-excitatory brain regions, and subsequently modulate PVN activity via oligosynaptic relays in regions such as the amygdala and hypothalamus.

Habituation and facilitation are differentially influenced by MR and GR. Habituation appears to require the neuronal MR, as MR antagonists block reductions in corticosterone responses seen with repeated restraint in rats (Cole et al., 2000). In contrast, chronic stress downregulates GR in key feedback targets (hippocampus, prefrontal cortex), a phenomenon that is thought to attenuate feedback inhibition of the HPA axis and thereby promote facilitation (Gomez et al., 1996; Herman et al., 1995; Mizoguchi et al., 2003). (However, the magnitude of HPA axis dysfunction and stress facilitation are not affected by forebrain GR deletion in mice [Furay et al., 2008], calling the generality of this finding into question.) In addition, chronic stress and glucocorticoids sensitize synthesis and release of CRH in the central amygdaloid nucleus (Cook, 2004; Cook, 2002; Makino et al., 1994, 1999), suggesting a GR-mediated recruitment of this putative stress-excitatory pathway.

Maladaptive HPA responses engendered by heterotypic (i.e., variable) or severe homotypic regimens are associated with a number of neural changes across multiple stress circuits. For example, neurons in the hippocampus and prefrontal cortex lose dendritic complexity with chronic stress (Cook and Wellman, 2004; Magarinos and McEwen, 1995; Wellman, 2001), whereas dendritic trees of amygdalar neurons expand (Vyas et al., 2002). In combination, the data suggest a shift in the balance toward amygdalar stress excitation. Chronic stress also causes marked reduction in hippocampal brain-derived neurotrophic factor expression (Smith et al., 1995), a phenomenon that is linked to depression-like behaviors. Finally, chronic stress drives numerous neuroplastic changes at the level of the PVN, including reductions in GR as well as GABA-A receptor subunit expression (Cullinan, 2000; Herman et al., 1995), enhanced expression of glutamate receptors (Ziegler et al., 2005), and increased noradrenergic and glutamatergic innervations of PVN CRH neurons (Flak et al., 2009). These PVN changes all bias the HPA axis toward hypersecretion, and may contribute to enhanced glucocorticoid release and associated pathologies.

Recent data suggest that the subgenual cingulate cortex of the human, the proposed human homolog of the rodent infralimbic cortex, appears hyperactive in depressed patients, suggesting that this region is a good candidate in chronic stress pathology (Mayberg et al., 2005). In addition, there are some very recent data suggesting that the rodent prefrontal cortex is important in stress habituation (Weinberg et al., 2010). Collectively, the data implicate the prefrontal system as a major node for processing the overall impact of repeated stress. Other regions involved in regulation of acute stress responses (locus coeruleus, medial amygdala, central amygdala, ventral subiculum) do not appear to be involved in the development or severity of HPA axis dysfunction pursuant to chronic stress (Ziegler et al., 1999; Prewitt and Herman, 1997; Solomon et al., 2010), suggesting that chronic stress processing may be primarily mediated by upstream cortical structures. Alternatively, the mechanism governing generation and maintenance of chronic stress-induced HPA axis hyperactivity/hyperresponsiveness may be associated with aggregate neuroplastic responses to numerous stress nodes, rather than by concerted actions of any single stress pathway.

Perspective: Stress, Chronic Stress, and Disease

Regulation of the HPA axis involves a hierarchical organization of brain circuits designed to integrate the significance of stressful information. Reflexive responses are required for adaptation to frank physiological perturbation and have a direct line to PVN neurons that initiate stress responses. Psychogenic responses require integration of multimodal sensory information, past experience, and ongoing physiological status, requiring multisynaptic interactions of forebrain limbic sites, the BNST, and the hypothalamus. In many cases, limbic forebrain actions on the HPA axis use circuitry that mediate reflexive responses, in essence co-opting systems that are engaged during physiological challenge to mount psychogenic responses. Given the potentially deleterious effects of prolonged glucocorticoid exposure, the HPA axis is tightly controlled by numerous feedback mechanisms, and generally shows substantial adaptation to even prolonged stress exposure, provided the challenge is not overly severe. However, high stressor intensity and/or unpredictability are able to place the system in a state of *overdrive*, which can override existing control mechanisms and place individuals in a state of glucocorticoid dyshomeostasis.

Control of the HPA axis stress response is of substantial health significance. Glucocorticoid hypersecretion has multiple deleterious somatic effects, ranging from metabolic disorders to cardiovascular disease. In addition, glucocorticoid dyshomeostasis is observed in human stress-related diseases, including depression (hypersecretion) and posttraumatic stress disorder (hyposecretion). Notably, chronic stress in animals and stress-related diseases in humans are associated with structural and functional alterations in forebrain stress-regulatory regions such as the prefrontal cortex, hippocampus, and amygdala, suggesting that hormonal dysfunction may be a symptom of inadequate control of limbic stress pathways. Amelioration of stress-related disease will clearly require additional understanding of the molecular and cellular events driving disorders of the anticipatory stress pathway.

References

Ahima, R. S., Saper, C. B., Flier, J. S., & Elmquist, J. K. (2000). Leptin regulation of neuroendocrine systems. *Frontiers in Neuroendocrinology, 21*, 263–307.

Akana, S. F., Dallman, M. F., Bradbury, M. J., Scribner, K. A., Strack, A. M., & Walker, C. D. (1992). Feedback and facilitation in the adrenocortical system: unmasking facilitation by partial inhibition of the glucocorticoid response to prior stress. *Endocrinology, 131*, 57–68.

Belgardt, B. F., Okamura, T., & Bruning, J. C. (2009). Hormone and glucose signalling in POMC and AgRP neurons. *Journal of Physiology, 587*, 5305–5314.

Bhatnagar, S., & Dallman, M. (1998). Neuroanatomical basis for facilitation of hypothalamic-pituitary-adrenal responses to a novel stressor after chronic stress. *Neuroscience, 84*, 1025–1039.

Bhatnagar, S., Huber, R., Nowak, N., & Trotter, P. (2002). Lesions of the posterior paraventricular thalamus block habituation of hypothalamic-pituitary-adrenal responses to repeated restraint. *Journal of Neuroendocrinology, 14*, 403–410.

Boyle, M. P., Brewer, J. A., Funatsu, M., Wozniak, D. F., Tsien, J. Z., Izumi, Y., & Muglia, L. J. (2005). Acquired deficit of forebrain glucocorticoid receptor produces depression-like changes in adrenal axis regulation and behavior. *Proceedings of the National Academy of Sciences USA, 102*, 473–478.

Bradbury, M. J., Akana, S. F., & Dallman, M. F. (1994). Roles of type I and type II corticosteroid receptors in regulation of basal activity in the HPA axis during the diurnal trough and the peak: evidence for a non-additive effect of combined receptor occupation. *Endocrinology, 134*, 1286–1296.

Buckingham, J. C., John, C. D., Solito, E., Tierney, T., Flower, R. J., Christian, H., & Morris, J. (2006). Annexin 1, glucocorticoids, and the neuroendocrine-immune interface. *Annals of the New York Academy of Sciences, 1088*, 396–409.

Canteras, N. S., & Swanson, L. W. (1992). Projections of the ventral subiculum to the amygdala, septum, and hypothalamus: a PHAL anterograde tract-tracing study in the rat. *Journal of Comparative Neurology, 324*, 180–194.

Cardinal, R. N., Parkinson, J. A., Hall, J., & Everitt, B. J. (2002). Emotion and motivation: the role of the amygdala, ventral striatum, and prefrontal cortex. *Neuroscience and Biobehavioral Reviews, 26*, 321–352.

Champagne, D., Beaulieu, J., & Drolet, G. (1998). CRFergic innervation of the paraventricular nucleus of the rat hypothalamus: a tract-tracing study. *Journal of Neuroendocrinology, 10*, 119–131.

Choi, D. C., Furay, A. R., Evanson, N. K., Ostrander, M. M., Ulrich-Lai, Y. M., & Herman, J. P. (2007). Bed nucleus of the stria terminalis subregions differentially regulate hypothalamic-pituitary-adrenal axis activity: implications for the integration of limbic inputs. *Journal of Neuroscience, 27*, 2025–2034.

Cole, M. A., Kalman, B. A., Pace, T. W., Topczewski, F., Lowrey, M. J., & Spencer, R. L. (2000). Selective blockade of the mineralocorticoid receptor impairs hypothalamic-pituitary-adrenal axis expression of habituation. *Journal of Neuroendocrinology, 12*, 1034–1042.

Cook, C. J. (2002). Glucocorticoid feedback increases the sensitivity of the limbic system to stress. *Physiology and Behavior, 75*, 455–464.

Cook, C. J. (2004). Stress induces CRF release in the paraventricular nucleus, and both CRF and GABA release in the amygdala. *Physiology and Behavior, 82*, 751–762.

Cook, S. C., & Wellman, C. L. (2004). Chronic stress alters dendritic morphology in rat medial prefrontal cortex. *Journal of Neurobiology, 60*, 236–248.

Cragnolini, A. B., Perello, M., Schioth, H. B., & Scimonelli, T. N. (2004). Alpha-MSH and gamma-MSH inhibit IL-1beta induced activation of the hypothalamic-pituitary-adrenal axis through central melanocortin receptors. *Regulatory Peptides, 122*, 185–190.

Crestani, C. C., Alves, F. H., Tavares, R. F., & Correa, F. M. (2009). Role of the bed nucleus of the stria terminalis in the cardiovascular responses to acute restraint stress in rats. *Stress, 12*, 268–278.

Cullinan, W. E. (2000). GABA(A) receptor subunit expression within hypophysiotropic CRH neurons: a dual hybridization histochemical study. *Journal of Comparative Neurology, 419*, 344–351.

Cullinan, W. E., Herman, J. P., & Watson, S. J. (1993). Ventral subicular interaction with the hypothalamic paraventricular nucleus: evidence for a relay in the bed nucleus of the stria terminalis. *Journal of Comparative Neurology, 332*, 1–20.

Cunningham, Jr, E. T., & Sawchenko, P. E. (1988). Anatomical specificity of noradrenergic inputs to the paraventricular and supraoptic nuclei of the rat hypothalamus. *Journal of Comparative Neurology, 274*, 60–76.

Dayas, C. V., & Day, T. A. (2002). Opposing roles for medial and central amygdala in the initiation of noradrenergic cell responses to a psychological stressor. *European Journal of Neuroscience, 15*, 1712–1718.

de Kloet, E. R., Vreugdenhil, E., Oitzl, M. S., & Joëls, M. (1998). Brain corticosteroid receptor balance in health and disease. *Endocrine Reviews, 19*, 269–301.

Dhabhar, F. S., McEwen, B. S., & Spencer, R. L. (1997). Adaptation to prolonged or repeated stress–comparison between rat strains showing intrinsic differences in reactivity to acute stress. *Neuroendocrinology, 65,* 360–368.

Di, S., Malcher-Lopes, R., Halmos, K. C., & Tasker, J. G. (2003). Nongenomic glucocorticoid inhibition via endocannabinoid release in the hypothalamus: a fast feedback mechanism. *Journal of Neuroscience, 23,* 4850–4857.

Diorio, D., Viau, V., & Meaney, M. J. (1993). The role of the medial prefrontal cortex (cingulate gyrus) in the regulation of hypothalamo-pituitary-adrenal responses to stress. *Journal of Neuroscience, 13,* 3839–3847.

Dong, H. W., Petrovich, G. D., Watts, A. G., & Swanson, L. W. (2001). Basic organization of projections from the oval and fusiform nuclei of the bed nuclei of the stria terminalis in adult rat brain. *Journal of Comparative Neurology, 436,* 430–455.

Fernandes, G. A., Perks, P., Cox, N. K., Lightman, S. L., Ingram, C. D., & Shanks, N. (2002). Habituation and cross-sensitization of stress-induced hypothalamic-pituitary-adrenal activity: effect of lesions in the paraventricular nucleus of the thalamus or bed nuclei of the stria terminalis. *Journal of Neuroendocrinology, 14,* 593–602.

Flak, J. N., Ostrander, M. M., Tasker, J. G., & Herman, J. P. (2009). Chronic stress-induced neurotransmitter plasticity in the PVN. *Journal of Comparative Neurology, 517,* 156–165.

Frysztak, R. J., & Neafsey, E. J. (1991). The effect of medial frontal cortex lesions on respiration, "freezing," and ultrasonic vocalizations during conditioned emotional responses in rats. *Cerebral Cortex, 1,* 418–425.

Furay, A. R., Bruestle, A. E., & Herman, J. P. (2008). The role of the forebrain glucocorticoid receptor in acute and chronic stress. *Endocrinology, 149,* 5482–5490.

Gaillet, S., Lachuer, J., Malaval, F., Assenmacher, I., & Szafarczyk, A. (1991). The involvement of noradrenergic ascending pathways in the stress-induced activation of ACTH and corticosterone secretions is dependent on the nature of stressors. *Experimental Brain Research, 87,* 173–180.

Girotti, M., Pace, T. W., Gaylord, R. I., Rubin, B. A., Herman, J. P., & Spencer, R. L. (2006). Habituation to repeated restraint stress is associated with lack of stress-induced c-fos expression in primary sensory processing areas of the rat brain. *Neuroscience, 138,* 1067–1081.

Gomez, F., Lahmame, A., de Kloet, E. R., & Armario, A. (1996). Hypothalamic-pituitary-adrenal response to chronic stress in five inbred rat strains: differential responses are mainly located at the adrenocortical level. *Neuroendocrinology, 63,* 327–337.

Haas, D. A., & George, S. R. (1987). Neuropeptide Y administration acutely increases hypothalamic corticotropin-releasing factor immunoreactivity: lack of effect in other rat brain regions. *Life Science, 41,* 2725–2731.

Herman, J. P. (1993) Regulation of adrenocorticosteroid receptor mRNA expression in the central nervous system. *Cellular and Molecular Neurobiology, 13,* 349–372.

Herman, J. P. (2009). Stress response: neural and feedback regulation of the HPA axis. In L. R. Squire (Ed.), *Encyclopedia of neuroscience* (pp. 505–510). Amsterdam: Elsevier.

Herman, J. P., Adams, D., & Prewitt, C. (1995). Regulatory changes in neuroendocrine stress-integrative circuitry produced by a variable stress paradigm. *Neuroendocrinology, 61,* 180–190.

Herman, J. P., Dolgas, C. M., & Carlson, S. L. (1998). Ventral subiculum regulates hypothalamo-pituitary-adrenocortical and behavioural responses to cognitive stressors. *Neuroscience, 86,* 449–459.

Herman, J. P., Figueiredo, H., Mueller, N. K., Ulrich-Lai, Y., Ostrander, M. M., Choi, D. C., & Cullinan, W. E. (2003). Central mechanisms of stress integration: hierarchical circuitry controlling hypothalamo-pituitary-adrenocortical responsiveness. *Frontiers in Neuroendocrinology, 24,* 151–180.

Hurley, K. M., Herbert, H., Moga, M. M., & Saper, C. B. (1991). Efferent projections of the infralimbic cortex of the rat. *Journal of Comparative Neurology, 308,* 249–276.

Keller-Wood, M., & Dallman, M. F. (1984). Corticosteroid inhibition of ACTH secretion. *Endocrine Reviews, 5,* 1–24.

Kinzig, K. P., D'alessio, D. A., Herman, J. P., Sakai, R. R., Vahl, T. P., Figueiredo, H. F., Murphy, E. K., & Seeley, R. J. (2003). CNS glucagon-like peptide-1 receptors mediate endocrine and anxiety responses to interoceptive and psychogenic stressors. *Journal of Neuroscience, 23,* 6163–6170.

Kirby, L. G., Freeman-Daniels, E., Lemos, J. C., Nunan, J. D., Lamy, C., Akanwa, A., & Beck, S. G. (2008). Corticotropin-releasing factor increases GABA synaptic activity and induces inward current in 5-hydroxytryptamine dorsal raphe neurons. *Journal of Neuroscience, 28,* 12927–12937.

Krause, E. G., Melhorn, S. J., Davis, J. F., Scott, K. A., Ma, L. Y., de Kloet, A. D., Benoit, S. C., Woods, S. C., & Sakai, R. R. (2008). Angiotensin type 1 receptors in the subfornical organ mediate the drinking and hypothalamic-pituitary-adrenal response to systemic isoproterenol. *Endocrinology, 149,* 6416–6424.

Larsen, P. J., Tang-Christensen, M., Holst, J. J., & Orskov, C. (1997). Distribution of glucagon-like peptide-1 and other preproglucagon-derived peptides in the rat hypothalamus and brainstem. *Neuroscience, 77,* 257–270.

Levin, B. E. (2002). Metabolic sensors: viewing glucosensing neurons from a broader perspective. *Physiology and Behavior, 76,* 397–401.

Li, S., & Kirouac, G. J. (2008). Projections from the paraventricular nucleus of the thalamus to the forebrain, with special emphasis on the extended amygdala. *Journal of Comparative Neurology, 506,* 263–287.

Lind, R. W., Swanson, L. W., & Ganten, D. (1984). Angiotensin II immunoreactive pathways in the central nervous system of the rat: evidence for a projection from the subfornical organ to the paraventricular nucleus of the hypothalamus. *Clinical and Experimental Hypertension [A], 6,* 1915–1920.

Lowry, C. A. (2002). Functional subsets of serotonergic neurones: implications for control of the hypothalamic-pituitary-adrenal axis. *Journal of Neuroendocrinology, 14,* 911–923.

Magarinos, A. M., & McEwen, B. S. (1995). Stress-induced atrophy of apical dendrites of hippocampal CA3c neurons: involvement of glucocorticoid secretion and excitatory amino acid receptors. *Neuroscience, 69,* 89–98.

Makino, S., Gold, P. W., & Schulkin, J. (1994). Corticosterone effects on corticotropin-releasing hormone mRNA in the central nucleus of the amygdala and the parvocellular region of the paraventricular nucleus of the hypothalamus. *Brain Research, 640,* 105–112.

Makino, S., Shibasaki, T., Yamauchi, N., Nishioka, T., Mimoto, T., Wakabayashi, I., Gold, P. W., & Hashimoto, K. (1999). Psychological stress increased corticotropin-releasing hormone mRNA and content in the central nucleus of the amygdala but not in the hypothalamic paraventricular nucleus in the rat. *Brain Research, 850,* 136–143.

Mayberg, H. S., Lozano, A. M., Voon, V., Mcneely, H. E., Seminowicz, D., Hamani, C., Schwalb, J. M., & Kennedy, S. H. (2005). Deep brain stimulation for treatment-resistant depression. *Neuron, 45,* 651–660.

McEwen, B. S. (1999). Stress and hippocampal plasticity. *Annual Review of Neuroscience, 22,* 105–122.

Mizoguchi, K., Ishige, A., Aburada, M., & Tabira, T. (2003). Chronic stress attenuates gluco-corticoid negative feedback: involvement of the prefrontal cortex and hippocampus. *Neuroscience, 119,* 887–897.

Moga, M. M., Weis, R. P., & Moore, R. Y. (1995). Efferent projections of the paraventricular thalamic nucleus in the rat. *Journal of Comparative Neurology, 359,* 221–238.

Munck, A., Guyre, P. M., & Holbrook, N. J. (1984). Physiological functions of glucocorticoids in stress and their relations to pharmacological actions. *Endocrine Reviews, 5,* 25–44.

Pacak, K., Palkovits, M., Kvetnansky, R., Yadid, G., Kopin, I. J., & Goldstein, D. S. (1995). Effects of various stressors on in vivo norepinephrine release in the hypothalamic par-aventricular nucleus and on the pituitary-adrenocortical axis. *Annals of the New York Academy of Sciences, 771,* 115–130.

Pacak, K., Palkovits, M., Yadid, G., Kvetnansky, R., Kopin, I. J., & Goldstein, D. S. (1998). Heterogeneous neurochemical responses to different stressors: a test of Selye's doctrine of nonspecificity. *American Journal of Physiology Regulatory, Integrative and Comparative Physiology, 275,* R1247–R1255.

Plotsky, P. M., Sutton, S. W., Bruhn, T. O., & Ferguson, A. V. (1988). Analysis of the role of angiotensin II in mediation of adrenocorticotropin secretion. *Endocrinology, 122,* 538–545.

Plotsky, P. M., Cunningham, E. T., Jr., & Widmaier, E. P. (1989). Catecholaminergic modula-tion of corticotropin-releasing factor and adrenocorticotropin secretion. *Endocrine Reviews, 10,* 437–458.

Prewitt, C. M., & Herman, J. P. (1997). Hypothalamo-pituitary-adrenocortical regulation following lesions of the central nucleus of the amygdala. *Stress, 1,* 263–280.

Radley, J. J., Arias, C. M., & Sawchenko, P. E. (2006). Regional differentiation of the medial prefrontal cortex in regulating adaptive responses to acute emotional stress. *Journal of Neuroscience, 26,* 12967–12976.

Resstel, L. B., & Correa, F. M. (2006). Involvement of the medial prefrontal cortex in central cardiovascular modulation in the rat. *Autonomic Neuroscience, 126–127,* 130–138.

Reul, J. M., & de Kloet, E. R. (1985). Two receptor systems for corticosterone in rat brain: microdistribution and differential occupation. *Endocrinology, 117,* 2505–2511.

Ritter, S., Watts, A. G., Dinh, T. T., Sanchez-Watts, G., & Pedrow, C. (2003). Immunotoxin lesion of hypothalamically projecting norepinephrine and epinephrine neurons dif-ferentially affects circadian and stressor-stimulated corticosterone secretion. *Endocrinology, 144,* 1357–1367.

Rivest, S. (2001). How circulating cytokines trigger the neural circuits that control the hypothalamic-pituitary-adrenal axis. *Psychoneuroendocrinology, 26,* 761–788.

Roland, B. L., & Sawchenko, P. E. (1993). Local origins of some GABAergic projections to the paraventricular and supraoptic nuclei of the hypothalamus of the rat. *Journal of Comparative Neurology, 332,* 123–143.

Sawchenko, P. E., Swanson, L. W., Steinbusch, H. W., & Verhofstad, A. A. (1983). The distribution and cells of origin of serotonergic inputs to the paraventricular and supraoptic nuclei of the rat. *Brain Research, 277*, 355–360.

Schiltz, J. C., & Sawchenko, P. E. (2003). Signaling the brain in systemic inflammation: the role of perivascular cells. *Frontiers in Bioscience, 8*, s1321–s1329.

Selye, H. (1936). A syndrome produced by diverse nocuous agents. *Nature, 138*, 32.

Selye, H. (1976). *The stress of life*, New York: McGraw-Hill.

Sesack, S. R., Deutch, A. Y., Roth, R. H., & Bunney, B. S. (1989). Topographical organization of the efferent projections of the medial prefrontal cortex in the rat: an anterograde tract-tracing study with *Phaseolus vulgaris* leucoagglutinin. *Journal of Comparative Neurology, 290*, 213–242.

Smith, M. A., Makino, S., Kvetnansky, R., & Post, R. M. (1995). Stress and glucocorticoids affect the expression of brain-derived neurotrophic factor and neurotrophin-3 mRNAs in the hippocampus. *Journal of Neuroscience, 15*, 1768–1777.

Solomon, M. B., Jones, K., Packard, B. A., & Herman, J. P. (2010). The medial amygdala modulates body weight but not neuroendocrine responses to chronic stress. *Journal of Neuroendocrinology, 22*, 13–23.

Sullivan, R. M., & Gratton, A. (1999) Lateralized effects of medial prefrontal cortex lesions on neuroendocrine and autonomic stress responses in rats. *Journal of Neuroscience, 19*, 2834–2840.

Swanson, L. W., & Petrovich, G. D. (1998). What is the amygdala? *Trends in Neuroscience, 21*, 323–331.

Ter Horst, G. J., & Luiten, P. G. M. (1987). *Phaseolus vulgaris* leuco-agglutinin tracing of intrahypothalamic connections of the lateral, ventromedial, dorsomedial and paraventricular hypothalamic nuclei in the rat. *Brain Research Bulletin, 18*, 191–203.

Ter Horst, G. J., & Streefland, C. (1994). Ascending projections of the solitary tract nuclei. In I. R. A. Barraco (Ed.), *Nucleus of the solitary tract*. Boca Raton, FL: CRC Press.

Ulrich-Lai, Y. M., & Herman, J. P. (2009). Neural regulation of endocrine and autonomic stress responses. *Nature Reviews Neuroscience, 10*, 397–409.

Viau, V., & Meaney, M. J. (1996). The inhibitory effect of testosterone on hypothalamo-pituitary-adrenal responses to stress is mediated by the medial preoptic area. *Journal of Neuroscience, 16*, 1866–1876.

Vyas, A., Mitra, R., Shankaranarayana Rao, B. S., & Chattarji, S. (2002). Chronic stress induces contrasting patterns of dendritic remodeling in hippocampal and amygdaloid neurons. *Journal of Neuroscience, 22*, 6810–6818.

Wahlestedt, C., Skagerberg, G., Ekman, R., Heilig, M., Sundler, F., & Hakanson, R. (1987). Neuropeptide Y (NPY) in the area of the hypothalamic paraventricular nucleus activates the pituitary-adrenocortical axis in the rat. *Brain Research, 417*, 33–38.

Weinberg, M. S., Johnson, D. C., Bhatt, A. P., & Spencer, R. L. (2010). Medial prefrontal cortex activity can disrupt the expression of stress response habituation. *Neuroscience, 168*, 744–756.

Wellman, C. L. (2001). Dendritic reorganization in pyramidal neurons in medial prefrontal cortex after chronic corticosterone administration. *Journal of Neurobiology, 49*, 245–253.

Willner, P. (2005). Chronic mild stress (CMS) revisited: consistency and behavioural-neurobiological concordance in the effects of CMS. *Neuropsychobiology, 52*, 90–110.

Xiao, E., Xia-Zhang, L., Vulliemoz, N. R., Ferin, M., & Wardlaw, S. L. (2003). Agouti-related protein stimulates the hypothalamic-pituitary-adrenal (HPA) axis and enhances the HPA response to interleukin-1 in the primate. *Endocrinology, 144*, 1736–1741.

Xu, Y., Day, T. A., & Buller, K. M. (1999). The central amygdala modulates hypothalamic-pituitary-adrenal axis responses to systemic interleukin-1beta administration. *Neuroscience, 94*, 175–183.

Zhang, Y., Damjanoska, K. J., Carrasco, G. A., Dudas, B., D'souza, D. N., Tetzlaff, J., Garcia, F., Hanley, N. R., Scripathirathan, K., Petersen, B. R., Gray, T. S., Battaglia, G., Muma, N. A., & Van De Kar, L. D. (2002). Evidence that 5-HT2A receptors in the hypothalamic paraventricular nucleus mediate neuroendocrine responses to (-)DOI. *Journal of Neuroscience, 22*, 9635–9642.

Ziegler, D. R., Cass, W. A., & Herman, J. P. (1999). Excitatory influence of the locus coeruleus in hypothalamic-pituitary-adrenocortical axis responses to stress. *Journal of Neuroendocrinology, 11*, 361–369.

Ziegler, D. R., Cullinan, W. E., & Herman, J. P. (2005). Organization and regulation of paraventricular nucleus glutamate signaling systems: N-methyl-D-aspartate receptors. *Journal of Comparative Neurology, 484*, 43–56.

3

Corticosteroid Receptor Involvement in the Stress Response

E. Ronald de Kloet, Roel H. DeRijk, and Onno C. Meijer

According to the pioneer in stress research Seymour Levine, *stress* can be defined as a composite, multidimensional construct, in which three components interact: the input (the stressor), the processing of the stressful information including the subjective experience, and the output (the stress response). The output is the spectrum of physiological and behavioral adaptations to restore homeostasis (the equilibrium). The three components interact via complex self-regulating feedback loops (Levine, 2005). The strongest stressor is a condition of no control, with no information to predict ongoing events, but with the uncertain anxious feeling of threat, either real or imagined. If coping with the stressor fails, stress becomes pathogenic. Coping is dependent on experience- and gene-related factors, and is affected by cognitive and environmental inputs. Coping resources rely in particular on the context of the stressful experience, which is determined by psychosocial factors such as, for example, social position, safety, and attachment. If any of these factors is disrupted— loss of control in a social environment, expulsion, homelessness, or deprivation of (maternal) care—the challenge may exceed the coping resources, resulting in strong emotional reactions, which can ultimately lead to a condition of chronic stress and enhanced vulnerability to disease (Lazarus, 2006).

To understand adaptation to stress better, it is essential to study how integrative communication systems operate to maintain homeostasis. This integration is managed by transmitter, neuropeptide, and hormonal signals which are organized in the autonomic nervous system and the hypothalamic–pituitary–adrenal (HPA) axis, both orchestrated by corticotropin-releasing hormone (CRH) released from the paraventricular neurons in the hypothalamus. The signals of these systems operate in concert to promote structural and functional neural plasticity with the

The Handbook of Stress: Neuropsychological Effects on the Brain, First Edition.
Edited by Cheryl D. Conrad.
© 2011 Blackwell Publishing Ltd. Published 2011 by Blackwell Publishing Ltd.

goal to adapt to a stressful environment and to store the experience in the memory in preparation for future demands (de Kloet et al., 2005).

Here the focus is on the HPA axis (see Chapter 2 in this volume), in particular on its endproducts cortisol and corticosterone (the latter for rodents only), corticosteroids, which are collectively called CORTs here. The actions of these CORTs in brain are mediated by two types of receptor: mineralocorticoid receptors (MRs) and glucocorticoid receptors (GR), which act intracellularly as gene transcription factors (see Chapter 6), while more recently rapid nongenomic actions were also firmly established for these very same receptor proteins (see Chapter 4).

CORTs acting through GRs have profound effects on energy metabolism. Via GRs, CORTs restrain psychological stress reactions, but also inflammatory and immune responses, as well as the response of the HPA axis to stress. The MR is aldosterone-selective in the kidney and other epithelial cells involved in the regulation of electrolyte balance. In brain this aldosterone selectivity is lost because the enzyme responsible for metabolic conversion of bioactive cortisol into inactive cortisone is absent in brain. Therefore the brain MR is responding to CORT as well as aldosterone, but MR predominantly *sees* CORT because of the much higher concentration of this steroid.

In this chapter we will address (1) the role of these receptors in the action of CORT under basal and stressful conditions in control of HPA axis activity and (2) the signaling mechanism these receptors operate in stress-regulating centers of the brain. We conclude the chapter with the thesis that imbalance in MR- and GR-mediated actions may lead to neuroendocrine dysregulation and behavioral impairments which after passing a certain threshold enhance the vulnerability to stress-related disorders for which the individual is predisposed.

Basal and Stress-induced Secretory Patterns

Until recently, textbooks conveniently depicted circadian changes in CORT secretion as smooth lines with peak levels of circulating hormone at the beginning of the activity period. However, CORT is secreted under basal conditions in approximately hourly pulses, which are produced within minutes and usually last about 20 min (Walker et al., 2010; see Figure 3.1). The ultradian rhythm occurs in humans, monkeys, and other mammals including rodents (Lightman et al., 2008). The pulses are thought to synchronize and coordinate daily and sleep-related events.

The synchrony between adrenocorticotrophic hormone (ACTH) and corticosteroid pulses is, however, poor and suggests that non-ACTH mechanisms are also involved. Indeed, removal of the splanchnic nerve input to the adrenal increases the number of CORT pulses during the diurnal trough by increasing the adrenal responsiveness to ACTH (Jasper and Engeland, 1997). Hence, the generator of the hourly ACTH pulses is thought to be in the brain, presumably at the suprachiasmatic nucleus, while at the adrenal level the action of these ACTH pulses can be amplified via spanchnic nerve input. The non-ACTH sensitizing mechanism of the

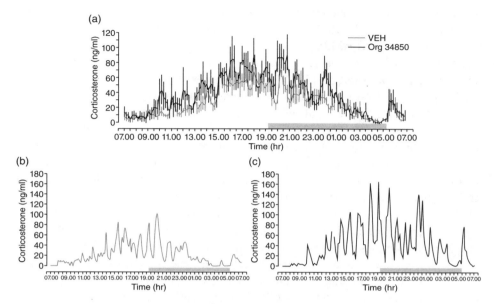

Figure 3.1 Effect of chronic antiglucocorticoid treatment on corticosterone diurnal rhythm. Data in (a) represent the mean±SEM of blood corticosterone levels of rats injected twice a day for 5 days with a GR antagonist (Org 34850; 10 mg/kg subcutaneously, $n = 7$) or vehicle (VEH). (b, c) Individual corticosterone levels of rats treated with either saline (b) or the GR antagonist (c). The dark phase was between 19.00 and 05.00 hr. *Source:* From Spiga et al. (2007). Reproduced with permission by John Wiley and Sons.

adrenal may become particularly prominent under conditions of metabolic crises. For instance, the hypercorticism occurring at the onset of diabetes is characterized by hypersecretion of CORT in the absence of a rise in ACTH (Revsin et al., 2008).

The detection of the ultradian rhythm requires repeated blood sampling every 10 min and deconvolution analysis of the data as a mathematical tool to quantitate secretion and clearance of the hormone (Carroll et al., 2007). Studies using such frequent blood sampling showed that CORT pulses increase in amplitude towards the activity period, which is the nighttime in rodents, and daytime in humans. Interestingly, the profound increase in CORT toward the activity period is uncoupled from ACTH, again suggesting an additional role for the splanchnic nerve input sensitizing the adrenal for ACTH at the circadian peak. Inflammatory disorders are characterized by increased frequency of the ultradian rhythm (Windle et al., 2001). During the aging process, the ACTH/CORT patterns become disorderly (Veldhuis et al., 2000). Accordingly, frequency encoding is an important mode of operation of the HPA axis, and variations in amplitude, frequency, and pattern may occur. As a result, the function of the HPA axis as the major integrative homeostatic control system in adaptation to change is largely dependent on its ultradian rhythmicity.

Using deconvolution analysis to quantitate 24-hr pulsatile secretions over 10-min intervals, Carroll et al. (2007) recently reevaluated established facts of the pathophysiology of hypercortisolism with a small number of inpatients suffering from depression. The hypercortisolemia was accounted for by increased amplitude rather than frequency of both ACTH and CORT pulses (see also Holsboer, 2000). Since CORT pulses with large amplitude also occurred at the nadir of the rhythm, this would explain the flattening of the circadian rhythm characteristic for depression. Moreover, these pulses occur independently of ACTH, again suggesting an additional role by, for example, splanchnic nerve input.

It is well established that excess CORT causes psychotic disorganization and emotional dysregulation in severe depression (Holsboer, 2000). It is thought that the negative feedback exerted by elevated CORT levels is inadequate to contain the HPA axis hyperdrive in severe depression. To further understand the pathophysiology of severe depression it is therefore essential to examine how excess CORT operates in the central CRH system (see section on MR, GR, and CRH, below).

CORT secretory bursts can be triggered by a stressor at any time and are superimposed on the ultradian and circadian rhythms; the phase of the rhythms in fact determines the magnitude of the CORT burst (Windle et al., 1998). Like basal circadian and ultradian patterns, the stress-induced CORT secretion pattern serves as a biomarker for breakdown of adaptation and stress-related disease. In the case of severe depression, for instance, stress-induced CORT is excessive and prolonged. Alternatively, CORT responses may be inadequate to contain initial stress reactions, as observed in individuals suffering from fibromyalgia (Griep et al., 1998) and in subjects at risk for posttraumatic stress disorder (Yehuda, 2006).

That the central drive to the pituitary is enhanced can be assessed by the effect of potent synthetic glucocorticoids. These steroids predominantly target the pituitary corticotrophs because of their poor penetration in the brain (De Kloet et al., 1975; Meijer et al., 1998). Escape from dexamethasone suppression (i.e., the dexamethasone-suppression test), enhanced by CRH (DEX-CRH test), is a hallmark for the hyperdrive in the HPA axis and hypercorticism during severe depression (Bardeleben and Holsboer, 1989). In contrast, posttraumatic stress disorder usually is characterized by enhanced dexamethasone suppression (Yehuda, 2006).

Interestingly, stress-induced ACTH and CORT release are different depending on the phase of the ultradian pulse. Post hoc analysis revealed that responsiveness to stressors is enhanced in the ascending phase, and attenuated if experienced during the descending slope of the pulse (Windle et al., 1998). In a recent study, we (Sarabdjitsingh et al., 2010b) modeled ultradian variations in stress responsiveness by artificially creating different patterns of CORT in adrenalectomized rats. As was the case in the post hoc analysis pulsatile administration of CORT facilitated a brisker response, which was markedly greater in the rising than in the falling phase of a CORT pulse. This differential phase-dependent effect was also seen in the behavioral response to noise, which was much greater in the rising phase. This finding raises the possibility that stress responsivity and coping resources show hourly oscillations.

In conclusion, frequency encoding by CORT is crucial for responsivity of the HPA axis to stress and is a determining factor in the control of tissue responsiveness to CORT. These new facts on the HPA axis and CORT pulsatility need to be incorporated into neuropsychological and psychiatric studies, which are currently still based mainly on saliva sampling for CORT measurement.

To summarize, the HPA axis displays hourly pulses, which are prominent at the adrenal level. This pulsatile CORT secretion can be generated by an ACTH and/or non-ACTH adrenocortical mechanism. Pulsatility synchronizes brain and body function. Stress responsivity varies over the hourly cycles of the ultradian rhythm. Moreover, CORT pulsatility is crucial for responsivity of its target tissues.

Receptor and Action Patterns

It is well established that traditionally MRs and GRs are nuclear receptors operating as transcription factors. The nuclear MR binds CORT with a very high affinity and is abundantly expressed in limbic structures involved in mood, affect, and memory processes. Nuclear GR has a 10-fold lower affinity and is expressed widely in neurons and glial cells with highest expression in centers involved in regulating the stress response, but in rodents it is very low after postnatal day 7 in the hippocampal CA3 (where CA means cornu ammonis, a subregion of the hippocampus) and the suprachiasmatic nucleus (Van Eekelen et al., 1988). There is some debate over GR expression in the primate hippocampus, but this issue was resolved when the proper antibodies were used (Patel et al., 2000; Sánchez et al., 2000). Thus, in limbic structures, such as the neuronal circuits of hippocampus (CA1, CA2, and the dentate gyrus), the amygdala nuclei, and areas of the prefrontal cortex, MR and GR are colocalized and expressed in large amounts. The properties and localization of the receptors have been the guiding principle for the design of stress experiments over the past few years.

The ultradian secretory pulses of CORT in blood are reflected in brain as derived from studies using microdialysis probes inserted in the brain (Droste et al., 2008). CORT released after stress, however, enters the brain with some delay and is cleared rapidly, upon which the rhythm resumes. Hence neural function is subject to coding by frequency and amplitude of the pulses. Why the pattern of CORT after stress is different may be because of modulating factors. Blood transcortin or corticosteroid-binding globulin determines bioavailability of CORT and can be rapidly induced (Droste et al., 2008). The entrance of synthetic glucocorticoids and cortisol, but not corticosterone, is hampered by multidrug resistance (mdr) P glycoproteins in the blood–brain barrier (Karssen et al., 2001; Meijer et al., 1998). Not only in rodents, in humans corticosterone is much better retained in the brain than cortisol (Karssen et al., 2001; Raubenheimer et al., 2006).

11β-Hydroxysteroid dehydrogenase (11β-HSD) type 2 confers prereceptor binding specificity in typical MR target tissues. The brain lacks this oxidase except for the aldosterone targets involved in regulation of salt homeostasis in periventricular brain regions. Instead the larger part of the brain contains the reductase isoform, 11β-HSD type 1, which generates CORT from the inactive 11-dehydroCORT precursor. This enzyme is present in the limbic brain and thus functions as a CORT trap (Seckl, 1997). Indeed, brain 11β-HSD type 1-overexpressing mice or knockout mouse mutants show signs of intraneuronal excess or lack of CORT, respectively (Yau et al., 2007).

Because of the high affinity of MR, the hourly pulses maintain occupancy of this receptor in the nucleus, whereas the lower affinity GRs follow in nuclear translocation the pulsatile changes in plasma and brain levels of the hormone under basal conditions (Conway-Campbell et al., 2007). Recently, it was demonstrated that ultradian hormone stimulation induces cyclic GR-mediated transcriptional regulation by pulsing receptor occupancy of glucocorticoid response elements (GREs). As a consequence gene pulsing is driven by rapid GR exchange with response elements and by GR recycling through the chaperone machinery, which promotes GR activation and reactivation in response to the ultradian hormone release (Stavreva et al., 2009). The implication is that these hourly GR-mediated pulses are sufficient to maintain the levels of mRNA and protein expression of target genes.

However, the history of GR activation does make a difference for subsequent responsiveness to stress-induced pulses. Target gene responses are attenuated under a regime of continuous glucocorticoid exposure as compared to genes operating during intermittent pulsatile exposure (Sarabdjitsingh et al., 2010a). Accordingly, the GR signaling pathway is tuned for a prompt and timely response to fluctuations in hormone levels, indicating that a resilient biologically accurate regulation of gene targets by GR requires an ultradian mode of hormone stimulation (Sarabdjitsingh et al., 2010a; Stavreva et al., 2009).

Since the high-affinity MR is always substantially occupied by pulsatile exposure to endogenous CORT, changes in receptor activity seem to be the rate-limiting factor. How this selective regulation of MR activity occurs is not known. MR recruits distinctly different coregulator patterns than GR, and their properties are differently affected by sumoylation and proteasomal activity (Meijer et al., 2006; Tirard et al., 2007). Although receptor kinetics and dynamics are very different for GR and MR, they both are capable of binding to the same GREs as dimers, affecting the transcription machinery to achieve transactivation in a complementary fashion (Datson et al., 2008). However, GR, but not MR, can act as a monomer: GR monomers bind to other transcription factors that are activated by intracellular signaling pathways triggered by the initial stressor, and hence attenuate gene transcription by transrepression.

What is the significance of each receptor type in the regulation of HPA axis pulsatility and stress responsiveness? Analysis of the receptors has revealed their involvement in a number of aspects of the stress system: control of basal HPA axis activity, control over the initial response to stress, and recovery and adapation to stress. The basic principle underlying these effects is that the HPA axis coordinates behavior and experience with the secretion and action of CORT. In its basal pulsatile pattern this function relates to the coordination and synchronization of daily- and sleep-related events. The pulse generator is possibly in the brain, although pulsatility may already be an intrinsic property of any system operating with delays in feed-forward and feedback modes (Veldhuis et al., 2000; Walker et al., 2010). Therefore brain, pituitary, and adrenal may all contribute to the oscillatory pattern.

During the stress response, the HPA axis mediates the ability to cope. Although the secretion of CORT for that purpose may not seem to be very economical at first glance one should remember that CORT is a hormone. The primary function of the hormone—together with the other hormones of the HPA axis—is to facilitate communication and coordination between body and brain during coping with and adaptation to the stressor. If the trigger is an inflammatory response, CORT feeds back on the inflammatory process to restrain it. In brain, CORT targets circuits that underlie perception and appraisal of the initial trigger of the stress response. It coordinates the stress response by modulating emotional and cognitive processes in parallel, as well as metabolism.

For a further indepth analysis, one should realize that the two receptor systems, MR and GR, operate in a complementary fashion. CORT can boost the initial stress reaction, a concept underpinned with the discovery of membrane receptors for the hormone in the hippocampus that enhanced excitatory neurotransmission (Di et al., 2003; Joëls et al., 2008; Karst et al., 2005). CORT promotes motivation, arousal, and cognitive performance. Subsequently, at a later stage, CORT dampens the initial stress (defence) reactions to the stressor, and prevents them from overshooting (Sapolsky et al., 2000). This action is as diverse as the wealth of stressors. For example, after tissue damage CORT limits inflammatory reactions, and during infection it suppresses the immune response. In the brain it curtails neurochemical reactions in specific circuits mediating the processing of (psychosocial) stressors (de Kloet et al., 2005; McEwen, 2007). In parallel with these activating and suppressing actions of CORT on the stress response the hormone also promotes energy metabolism. For that purpose it coordinates appetite, nutrient choice, and food intake with energy disposition to the challenged tissues (Peters et al., 2007).

With these new data on the ultradian rhythm at hand, it is noteworthy to mention that most clinical studies use saliva as a source of CORT measures. This method provides free bioavailable CORT levels rather than estimates of CORT secretion rate from the adrenals and its clearance from the blood. Hence, saliva measurements of CORT, a method currently in vogue with neuropsychologists and psychiatrists, are inadequate for conclusions on the role of the HPA axis in human studies, unless a careful time course is made allowing for the measurement of pulsatility or the outcome of a stressful or pharmacological challenge. While subject to debate, and depending on the actual paradigm, two prechallenge samples at a 20-min interval and four postchallenge samples at 15-min intervals (as used in the cortisol awakening response) seem a reasonable starting point for experiments.

In conclusion, CORT is secreted as an endproduct of the HPA axis and enhances via the MR the initial stress reaction, which is then terminated via GR. To exert these actions variants of the traditional nuclear MRs and GRs appear to mediate rapid nongenomic actions. Collectively these genomic and nongenomic actions promote cognitive and emotional processes underlying the behavioral adaptation to stress.

To summarize, CORT is essential for health and wellbeing and a healthy resilient organism is characterized by a rapid activation of the CORT as long as it is also turned off efficiently. However, if CORT action is excessive and prolonged or inadequate the hormone causes damage and disease. To understand how CORT can switch from protective to damaging, it is crucial to know how MRs and GRs operate. The span of control of CORT mediated by these two complementary receptor systems is enormous, a fact that was emphasized with the recent discovery that CORT also can bind with lower affinity to the membrane versions of the very same nuclear MRs and GRs.

Brain MRs

The studies leading to the above generalization on brain MR functions can be summarized as follows. Ratka et al. (1989) showed that the MR antagonist RU28318 injected into the ventricles (intracerebroventricular [icv] route) in a bolus dose of 100 ng/1 μl during basal trough levels (in rodents; morning) caused a transient rise in circulating CORT level. The MR antagonist icv also enhanced the evening rise in ACTH and CORT secretion (Oitzl et al., 1995) in the ventricular system (100 ng) or in the dorsal hippocampus (10 ng) (van Haarst et al., 1997). MR blockade also facilitates the CORT response to a novelty stressor (Ratka et al., 1989). Likewise, morning intracerebroventricular infusion of MR antisense DNA sequence increased circulating CORT levels (Reul et al., 1997). Chronic RU28318 (100 ng/hr, icv) administered via an Alzet minipump gave an initial rise in ACTH and CORT in the evening phase of the first infusion day. Subsequently, HPA activity normalized but adrenal sensitivity to ACTH was increased twofold (Reul et al., 1997; van Haarst et al., 1996). Under these conditions the animals have impaired spatial memory (Yau et al., 1999).

Systemic administration of a 1000-fold higher dose of the MR antagonist was needed (50 mg/kg) to trigger a morning CORT response (Spencer et al., 1998). In experiments using an automatic blood-sampling system allowing sampling every 5 min an intravenous bolus of the MR antagonist spironolactone enhanced the hourly pulses of ACTH and CORT under basal morning conditions, while a rapid suppressive effect was observed by the agonist aldosterone on the ultradian rhythm (Atkinson et al., 2008).

In humans, in contrast to rodents, basal HPA axis activity is high in the morning, and diminishes toward the afternoon. In humans, the MR antagonists spironolactone (Young et al., 1998) or canrenoate (Dodt et al., 1993; Grottoli et al., 2002) in large amounts orally (200 mg) induced a rise in evening CORT. In some cases the antagonists activated HPA axis activity after an injection in the morning (Kellner et al., 2002; Young et al., 2003), and in others in the evening during the quiescent phase of the circadian rhythm (Berardelli et al., 2010; Grottoli et al., 2002; Mattsson et al., 2009), a finding that was in line with the suppressive effects by agonist aldosterone under the same conditions (Buckley et al., 2007). Repeated daily injections of spironolactone over 2 days (Young et al., 1998) or 8 days (Heuser et al., 2000) increased CORT levels but not ACTH, which points to adaptive changes resulting in enhanced adrenal sensitivity. Twenty eight days of spironolactone treatment of young women further amplifies spontaneous and CRH-induced CORT secretion (Berardelli et al., 2010).

The effect of spironolactone on CORT was further enhanced during aging (Heuser et al., 2000). Otte et al. (2003a) depleted MRs by treating humans with metyrapone, and subsequently demonstrated suppression of the enhanced HPA axis activity by the MR agonist fludrocortisone; the effect of the agonist was attenuated during aging, which is in line with a reduced MR function at senescence (Otte et al., 2003b). The MR antagonist also has been tested in psychiatric disorders. In depressed patients the basal and CRH-induced ACTH and CORT levels were elevated by spironolactone (Deuschle et al., 1998; Grottoli et al., 2002; Kellner et al., 2002; Young et al., 2003). In patients suffering from posttraumatic stress syndrome the response to MR antagonist was not different from controls (Kellner et al., 2002).

Mouse lines carrying targeted mutations of the MR have been studied in basal and stress-induced HPA axis activity. MR-knockout mice rescued by saline in the drinking water have enhanced activity of the renin–angiotensin and HPA axis (Gass et al., 2000). Conditional forebrain-knockout animals with MR deletion from postnatal day 12 have normal basal CORT levels and an enhanced CORT secretion during fear conditioning (Berger et al., 2006; Brinks et al., 2009). Mice with conditional forebrain overexpression show normal basal HPA axis activity (ultradian rhythm not investigated), but an attenuated CORT response to stressors (Lai et al., 2007; Rozeboom et al., 2007). MR overexpression in the forebrain decreases anxiety-like behavior and modifies GR and 5-hydroxytryptamine ($5HT_{1A}$) receptor expression in the hippocampus (Lai et al., 2007). In contrast, forebrain MR-calcium/calmodulin-dependent protein kinase (CaMK)-Cre-knockout mice that have the MR inactivated using the Cre/LoxP-recombination system enhances emotional arousal after stress. Their fear acquisition and contextual fear memory are also enhanced. These mice show impaired behavioral and endocrine adaptation to stressors.

In conclusion, pharmacological and genetic manipulations of the MR in animal studies have uncovered that this receptor in its membrane form enhances excitatory transmission which, when activated in the hippocampus, enhances negative-feedback inhibition over the HPA axis, a finding supported by human studies. Current research aims to further unravel the membrane and nuclear function of this receptor that is crucial for electrolyte metabolism in epithelial cells, but which allows it to function as a high-affinity CORT receptor in nonepithelial cells in the limbic brain involved in cognitive and emotional processes modulating the HPA axis response to stress.

To summarize, MR function, notably in limbic structures, controls HPA tone. Acute blockade of central MR disinhibits HPA axis driven CORT during the ultradian and circadian rhythm and after a stressor related to hippocampus or amygdala function; that is, exposure to novelty or a fear conditioning procedure. Chronic MR blockade leads to slow HPA axis adaptations, ultimately producing enhanced adrenocortical responsiveness to ACTH. The current transgenic animal models with forebrain-specific knockout or overexpression largely agree with this MR phenotype, but numerous as yet poorly understood adaptations have occurred in the mutants.

Brain GRs

Below, an overview is given of studies directed to understand the function of the GR in neuroendocrine regulation, by either blocking or genetic manipulation of this receptor in brain. The GR (and progesterone) antagonist mifepristone (RU486) does not activate the HPA axis when administered acutely under basal morning resting conditions in the rat, neither 1 hr nor 24 hr after systemic, intracerebroventricular, or intrahippocampal injection. In the evening phase (toward the peak of circadian activity) mifepristone administered intracerebroventricularly or near the paraventricular nucleus (PVN) enhanced the circadian rise in ACTH and CORT release 1 hr post intracerebroventricular injection, but suppressed it if injected in the hippocampus (De Kloet et al., 1988; Ratka et al., 1989; van Haarst et al., 1996, 1997). The explanation is that GR occupancy is too low for blockade during nadir, because the circulating CORT levels are too low. Similar data were obtained with frequent blood sampling after systemic administration of mifepristone; an acute injection did not exert immediate effects on the pulsatile pattern of CORT at nadir but during the circadian peak (Spiga et al., 2007).

A condition of chronic central GR blockade was evoked by chronic intracerebroventricular infusion of the antiglucocorticoid mifepristone through Alzet minipumps (100 ng/hr) over a period of 14 days. The experiments occurred in parallel with the MR antagonist infusion mentioned in the previous section. Controls received the vehicle intracerebroventricularly. On the first day mifepristone administration triggered an enhanced evening rise in both ACTH and CORT. On the following days the HPA response, including CRH mRNA expression, was not different from controls, but on day 4 the enhanced evening CORT surge reappeared. In addition, adrenal weight and sensitivity to ACTH were markedly enhanced (van Haarst et al., 1996).

The above findings indicate that the HPA axis slowly adapts to the condition of central GR blockade induced by chronic mifepristone with an increased CORT output during the circadian peak. Since basal trough levels are not affected, the result of chronic central GR blockade is an enhanced circadian amplitude in CORT. An altered pattern of CORT secretion was also observed with frequent blood sampling. After a treatment for 5 days twice a day with a systemic antiglucocorticoid, the pulse amplitude at the circadian peak was increased (Spiga et al., 2007). This finding is of interest because it demonstrates that by chronic blockade of the GR the negative feedback is impaired and as a consequence the oscillations in HPA axis activity and CORT secretion are enhanced.

The response to stressors was also affected differentially by mifepristone treatment. One hour after morning GR antagonist administration the initial CORT response to novelty was suppressed, an effect opposite to that of MR antagonist (Ratka et al., 1989). The duration of the CORT response was prolonged after both the MR and the GR antagonist, but the underlying reason is different. The GR antagonist interferes with negative feedback after the novel stressor, but the MR antagonist produces higher peak values and, therefore, the response lasts longer. However, 24 hr after the single administration of mifepristone novelty-induced ACTH and CORT responses were enhanced, but there was no interference with negative feedback. Yet, chronic intracerebroventricular infusion resulting in the actual presence of the antagonist at the time of the novel stressor interfered again with negative feedback and as a consequence the response to the novel stressor then remained elevated for prolonged periods of time. These effects exerted by the antagonist centrally may be stressor-specific, since an HPA axis response induced by noise stress was not affected by the antiglucocorticoid (Spiga et al., 2007). The underlying mechanism probably is that novelty and noise stressors are processed in different brain circuits (novelty in hippocampus and noise in amygdale) with different sensitivity to the antiglucocortocoid.

Mifepristone also was applied as a therapeutic agent in humans. Several years ago, mifepristone appeared to ameliorate the depressive and psychotic symptoms in patients with Cushing syndrome in a fast and effective manner (van der Lely et al., 1991). More recently, patients suffering from psychotic depression also rapidly improved (Belanoff et al., 2002; DeBattista and Belanoff, 2006). In these patients mifepristone enhanced the amplitude of the flattened CORT rhythm (Belanoff et al., 2001), a result reminiscent to the effect of chronic treatment of rats, as mentioned in the previous paragraph. Mattsson et al. (2009) demonstrated that MR and GR antagonist each individually had modest effects on CORT in lean and obese men, but if given together a profound synergizing effect inducing basal CORT levels was observed. Other researchers (for review see Wolkowitz et al., 2001) also reported positive results in affect and cognitive performance. Although mifepristone is a mixed glucocorticoid and progesterone antagonist, its effect on cognition, mood, affect, and HPA regulation in animals and humans are due to blockade of the GR.

Mice carrying a targeted mutation of the GR all have in common that the HPA axis is disinhibited. This includes the antisense GR-knockdown mice (Barden et al., 1997); the GR-knockout animals developed by Cole et al. (1995) that still had a truncated GR variant expressing minimal amounts of GR, rescuing about 10% of the animals; and finally, complete GR-knockout heterozygotes showing impaired feedback in the dexamethasone-suppression test (Ridder et al., 2005). The GR$^{dim/dim}$ mice—in which dimerization of the GR was prevented—had elevated basal ACTH and CORT, demonstrating direct transcriptional control at the pituitary level while stress-activated signaling pathways are suppressed by transrepression (Oitzl et al., 2001; Reichardt et al., 1998). The brain-GR-knockout mice (GR^{NesCre}) of Tronche et al. (1999) also showed increased HPA axis activity, as did forebrain-specific GR mutants (Boyle et al., 2005). GR overexpression transgenic mice showed no differences in circadian changes of HPA axis activity, but enhanced suppression in the dexamethasone-suppression test (Ridder et al., 2005; Wei et al., 2004). None of these models were investigated for ultradian rhythmicity.

In conclusion, CORT action via GRs restrains stress reactions that are boosted via MRs in the brain. Under basal conditions, blockade of GRs enhances the ultradian and circadian oscillations of CORT and the HPA axis. This action exerted by the antagonists could well be fundamental for its therapeutic efficacy in stress-related mental disorders because increased oscillations also enhance responsiveness (resilience) of the target tissues.

To summarize, glucocorticoid feedback resistance induced by chronic central GR blockade produces a sequelae of adaptations ultimately resulting in an enhanced HPA reactivity, as exemplified by a larger ultradian CORT amplitude and enhanced stress responsiveness. GRs mediate, in response to stressors, negative feedback action in pituitary corticotrophs and in particular in the hypothalamic PVN. The feedback action in the other brain areas is ambiguous and seems to be context- and state-dependent, modulating the activity of the CRH-expressing neurons of the PVN.

MR and GR Polymorphisms

There is an abundance of genetic variation in the human genome, ranging from 1 bp to loss of parts of a chromosome. Single-nucleotide polymorphisms (SNPs) are probably the most widespread type of variation in the human genome. Besides direct effects on the primary amino acid sequence, as often seen in overt *mutations*, SNPs can influence gene expression by affecting promoter activity, transcription efficiency, gene splicing, or mRNA stability, and effects on translation efficacy have also been described (Kimchi-Sarfaty et al., 2007). Moreover, these SNPs often appear in specific combinations, designated haplotypes.

Several genetic variants have been described in both the MR and GR genes, showing associations with different levels of HPA axis reactivity (DeRijk and de Kloet, 2008) (see Figure 3.2). The structures of the genes for MR (chromosome 4q31.1) and GR (chromosome 5q31–32) are comparable, with the coding region of the genes formed by exons 2–9 and the 5′ promoter region, with several versions of exon 1. Considering the importance of the CORT receptors in the regulation of the HPA axis, it is expected that common funtional genetic variants will modulate HPA axis reactivity.

Currently, two *MR* gene variants are the subject of study in relation to HPA axis reactivity. At position −2, two nucleotides before the first ATG start codon, a G/C

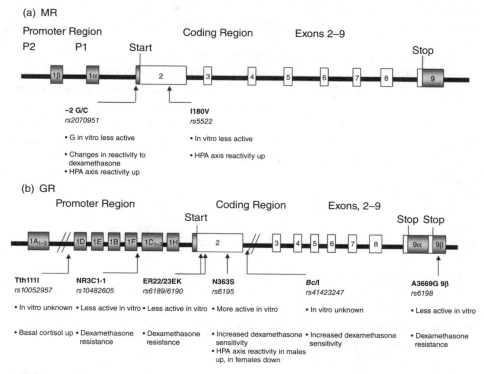

Figure 3.2 An overview of the common genetic variants in the human *MR* and *GR* genes, and their effects on HPA axis (re)activity.

SNP (rs2070951; frequency approximately 50%) change in vitro transactivational activity (van Leeuwen et al., 2010a), probably mediated by increased expression of the MR protein (van Leeuwen et al., 2011). Furthermore, in exon 2 of the human *MR* gene, at codon 180, the GTT-to-ATT variation results in an isoleucine-to-valine change (rs5522; frequency approximately 11%). This MR 180V shows loss of function in vitro using cortisol as a ligand (DeRijk et al., 2006).

The −2 C variant was associated with lower basal cortisol levels (Kuningas et al., 2007) and also modulated morning cortisol levels following administration of 0.5 mg dexamethasone on the previous day (van Leeuwen et al., 2010b). Using a psychosocial challenge, the so-called Trier Social Stress Test (TSST), both these *MR* gene variants were found to associate with changes in plasma ACTH, plasma cortisol, and saliva cortisol levels (DeRijk et al., 2006). In addition, heart-beat frequency was modulated by these two SNPs, indicative of effects on the autonomic nervous system.

For the *GR* gene several SNPs have been tested in vitro for functionality with increased or decreased activity in different cell types or systems. Just as in the *MR* gene, genetic variants of the *GR* gene are expected to modulate several levels of HPA axis control. With respect to *basal* nonmodulated levels of cortisol, the GR TthIIII mutation was found to associate with higher basal cortisol secretion in men (Rosmond et al., 2000). No associations with other SNPs have been found or tested.

Using the dexamethasone-suppression test, predominantly targeting the GR at the level of the pituitary gland, effects of all tested *GR* gene variants were uncovered. The GR N363S mutation and the *Bcl*I restriction site were found to associate with lower morning cortisol levels following 0.25 mg dexamethasone (Huizenga et al., 1998; Stevens et al., 2004). This is in line with the in vitro data, suggesting increased corticosteroid sensitivity induced by this N363S GR variant. In contrast, variants NR3C1-1 (in linkage with the GR A3669G variant), ER22/23EK, and A3669G displayed decreased sensitivity to dexamethasone, seen as higher postdexamethasone plasma ACTH and cortisol levels in males. The decreased activity in vitro of these *GR* gene variants fits with these findings, suggesting a relative CORT resistance in vivo. However, in females the NR3C1-1/A3669G variants associated with lower levels of ACTH/cortisol, indicating an important influence of sex hormones.

In the TSST, highest levels of ACTH were observed in carriers of the NR3C1-1 and the A3669G variants (in linkage disequilibrium), but not for cortisol. Heterozygotes of the *Bcl*I variant showed increased responses of cortisol whereas, unexpectedly, homozygotes displayed lower levels. In particular, male carriers of N363S had high levels of cortisol. Importantly, in a recent follow-up study including both males and females (Kumsta et al., 2007), males showed typically similar effects, with N363S carriers having the highest responses. Of note, none of the *GR* gene variants affected heart-beat responses, suggesting little effect on autonomic regulation during the TSST.

The data show that *MR* and *GR* gene variants affect different aspects of HPA axis regulation with strong gender effects appearing. Moreover, the MR I180V variant also modifies autonomic function during stress, with effects appearing within minutes. With the in vitro information at hand it was anticipated that increased GR activity would result in less vigorous cortisol responses and vice versa. However, this was not found to be the case. Also an increased expression of the MR (as determined in vitro) was found to associate with increased cortisol responsiveness. These seemingly contradictory findings indicate that in vitro data, obtained from artificial models, do not necessarily reflect observations made in vivo, although the in vitro data do indicate functionality. Furthermore, the stress response is regulated in several subregions (limbic structures, hypothalamus, pituitary) with their own dynamics and context-dependent regulation. Moreover, the strong gender-dependent effects indicate the involvement of other (sex) hormones, which might interact with MR and GR variants in their own specific manner.

In conclusion, *MR* and *GR* gene variants modulate the stress response. The MR variants generally affect the initial response to the stressor, whereas GR variants affect the termination of the stress response. These SNPs or haplotypes affect receptor synthesis, affinity for the ligand, or binding of other partners, or are important for the stability of the receptor. With the identification of MR and GR variants an important step forward has been made toward understanding the mechanism underlying individual variation in stress adaptation in humans.

To summarize, genetic variants in MRs and GRs occur, some of them with high frequency, which can affect stress responsiveness and adaptation. Studies are beginning to identify the functional implications of these variants with promising perspectives as biomarkers for vulnerability and resilience to psychopathology.

MR, GR, and CRH

The genomic response to CORT shows enormous diversity. Whereas a few genes, such as the *gilz* gene, seem to be ubiquitously responsive to CORT (van der Laan et al., 2008b), transcriptional effects mediated by MR and GR show a substantial degree of dependence on cell type and cellular state. The high degree of cellular specificity is exemplified by the gene coding for CRH, which can be activated and repressed via GR depending on the brain area, such as amygdala or PVN (Makino et al., 1994). Such cell-type-dependent effects of CORT may be due to receptor diversity; either MR/GR stoichiometry, or isoforms of the receptors (see previous section, on MR and GR Polymorphisms). In the periphery, GR-mediated effects can be clearly state-dependent. For example, the induction of gluconeogenic enzymes can depend strongly on feeding state and insulin levels (Phuc Le et al., 2005). In brain cells, state-dependent transcriptional effects have not been explored in great detail.

However, CORT action on the *CRH* gene in PVN and amygdala is mediated by the same GR, which clearly indicates that other cellular factors play a role in the opposite outcomes in the two brain regions. One obvious category of factors is represented by proteins like nuclear factor κB (NF-κB), activator protein 1 (AP-1), and signal transducer and activator of transcription (STAT) 5: inducible transcription factors that can interact with the steroid receptors, independent of actual DNA binding by the latter (Göttlicher et al., 1998; Stoecklin et al., 1999). The stoichiometry of such crosstalk partners can determine to what extent CORT represses via GR, and even MR, as was shown for the regulation of the 5-HT_{1A} receptor promoter (Meijer et al., 2000).

In addition, there can be considerable diversity in the actual signal transduction of MR and GR once they are bound to DNA: the effects on transcription of these nuclear receptors are in fact mediated via recruitment of *coregulator proteins*. These coregulators may modify histone structure and/or the transcription machinery, and may act as either coactivator or corepressor. Which coregulators are recruited depends on the configuration of the receptor, which is in turn dependent on the exact DNA sequence (Meijsing et al., 2009), or on binding of other transcription factors in the vicinity (Diamond et al., 1990). MR and GR function depend on a spectrum of coregulators that are partly overlapping and partly receptor-specific.

The expression levels and activity of proteins that interact with MR and GR can vary considerably with brain region, and may therefore be an important

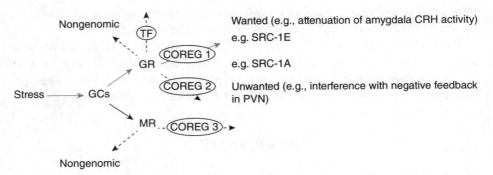

Figure 3.3 Glucocorticoids (GCs) affect different processes in the brain via two receptor types (MRs and GRs), and multiple receptor mechanisms: both receptors can act in a non-genomic manner, and as transcription factors (TFs). Genomic actions take place via interactions with TFs and coregulators (COREGs), each responsible for a subset of effects. Mechanisms can be selectively targeted by novel types of drugs, as illustrated by the pathway of action for a hypothetical dissociating GR ligand with agonism in PVN but antagonism in the central amygdala (gray arrows).

determinant of the outcome of MR/GR activation. The immediate early gene c-*fos*, for example, is a constituent of the GR crosstalk partner AP-1, its expression differs as a function of neuronal state (Ceccatelli et al., 1989), and it is highly expressed in, for example, the stressed PVN. Stress has indeed been shown to affect AP-1/GR signaling in rat hypothalamus, suggesting in vivo relevance of AP-1–GR interactions in negative feedback of CORT on stress-induced HPA axis activation (Kovács et al., 2000). Thus, GR would repress transcription in activated PVN neurons, but at the same time be less efficient in transactivation. In addition, both coregulators and receptors are subject to posttranslational modifications that can markedly influence the efficacy of GR function, such as phosphorylation (Beck et al., 2009; Han et al., 2009).

The diversity of GR- and MR-mediated actions may actually present an opportunity for selective targeting of effector pathways (Figure 3.3). It has become clear that some ligands can induce conformations of the receptors that allow some, but prohibit other, interactions with crosstalk partners and coregulators. Analogous to the quest in peripheral CORT biology to achieve immune suppression without inducing Cushing-like features, such *selective receptor modulators* or *dissociating ligands* could be used to achieve a greater selectivity than the common endogenous and synthetic agonists.

In the core of the HPA axis there are two clear targets for CORT negative feedback through transcription: the proopiomelanocortin (*POMC*) gene in the anterior pituitary, from which ACTH is derived, and the *CRH* gene in the parvocellular part of the PVN. Regulation of these two genes via GR is discussed below. Studies in conditional or site-specific transgenic animals have provided strong evidence for direct regulation of these genes, but also emphasize the importance of regulation beyond secretagogue synthesis, for example at the level of actual release of hormones.

To summarize, it is clear that CORT does not act in a uniform manner in all cells and tissues, and that various receptor mechanisms play a role. Also the history of the cells may determine how neurons respond to glucocorticoids. The molecular biology of CORT-receptor-mediated actions in negative feedback in PVN and the pituitary has been elucidated to a considerable extent with respect to regulation of expression of the arginine vasopressin (*AVP*), *CRH*, and *POMC* genes. Which CORT mechanism modulates the afferent pathways to the PVN remains to be resolved. In future these diverse mechanisms may be pharmacologically targeted in a selective manner, in experimental and perhaps clinical settings.

POMC expression and ACTH release

Strong evidence for a direct repression of the stress-induced *POMC* gene by GR is provided by pituitary-specific GR-knockout mice, in which POMC levels are much elevated (Schmidt et al., 2009). Insights into putative mechanisms come from the AtT-20 cells (Gumbiner and Kelly, 1981), which can synthesize and release ACTH. The POMC promoter is driven by, for example, AP-1 and cAMP-response-element binding protein (CREB), which are activated by stimulation with CRH (Boutillier et al., 1995) and suppressed by GR via protein–protein interactions. Also, the CRH-driven transcription factor Nurr77 is a target for a transrepression mechanism that involves the GR DNA-binding domain, but no direct DNA binding of GR (Martens et al., 2005). In addition, the *POMC* gene may have ways to *escape* from CORT negative feedback under some conditions (Bousquet et al., 2000), depending on the particular factors other than CRH driving POMC expression (Latchoumanin et al., 2007) and the intracellular presence of corticosteroid-binding-globulin-like molecules protecting the gene from CORT exposure (de Kloet et al., 1984).

Negative regulation of this promoter also may occur via a negative glucocorticoid response element (GRE) (Drouin et al., 1993). The role of this *negative GRE* mechanism seems to be strengthened by the involvement of a nuclear receptor coregulator steroid receptor coactivator 1 (SRC-1). SRC-1 can have both coactivator and corepressor effects on GR (van der Laan et al., 2008a), and is indispensible for repression of stress-induced POMC expression by CORT in vivo (Lachize et al., 2009; Winnay et al., 2006), suggesting a negative-GRE-GR-SRC-1 pathway.

A substantial increase in corticotroph POMC expression is observed in mouse mutants incapable of GR dimerization and DNA binding (Reichardt et al., 1998). However, ACTH levels are not markedly elevated in *dim/dim* mice (Reichardt et al., 1998). Furthermore, whereas GR-mediated negative feedback occurs also in isolated pituitary cells, CORT effects on the cells surrounding the corticotrophs seem to play an important additional role through juxtacellular mechanisms involving the protein annexin-1 (John et al., 2008). Interestingly, arginine vasopressin (AVP), which strongly potentiates the effect of CRH on ACTH release, reduces the sensitivity to CORT feedback in isolated corticotropes. This may explain why (chronic) stress conditions with a strong AVPergic drive to the pituitary are relatively stress-resistant (Lim et al., 2002). MR is also present in the pituitary (Spencer et al., 1993), but the role of these receptors in gene regulation of for example POMC is not clear.

CRH and AVP in the PVN

CRH and AVP in the PVN are also subject to negative feedback by CORT (Swanson and Simmons, 1989). Similar to the POMC/ACTH system, GR-mediated action can suppress secretagogue synthesis and secretion in various ways. These include both direct actions of CORT on PVN as well as on (transsynaptic) afferents involving various mechanisms (Kretz et al., 1999; Shepard et al., 2005; Watts, 2005). Like the POMC gene, the CRH gene harbors several elements that can mediate suppression via GR in cell lines; that is, a negative GRE where GR may bind directly to the DNA and a CREB-binding site at which GR may act via protein–protein interactions (Guardiola-Diaz et al., 1996; Malkoski and Dorin, 1999). Recently, a TORC-2 pathway has been demonstrated that acts in concert with CREB on CRH gene expression (Liu et al., 2010). In addition to CRH, AVP can also activate ACTH release. The CRH and AVP genes are responsive to particular physiological situations. For example, whereas CRH expression is already repressed via GR under basal conditions, repression of the AVP gene depends on active synaptic input (Kuwahara et al., 2003).

Recent progress has also been made in relation to postreceptor mechanisms that play a role in CRH repression. We recently found that like POMC, the CRH gene is resistant to dexamethasone-induced downregulation in mice lacking the coactivator SRC-1 (Lachize et al., 2009). This is likely due the particular splice variant SRC-1A, which has a repression domain and is able to potentiate repression of forskolin-induced activation of the CRH promoter in cultured cells (van der Laan et al., 2008a). Thus, it appears that for GR-mediated repression of the two core secretagogues in the HPA axis similar mechanisms play a role.

Extrahypothalamic mechanisms
Extrahypothalamic MR- and GR-mediated genomic actions can influence the HPA axis through (transsynaptic) afferents. These genomic actions exerted by CORT are now being identified in laser-dissected brain nuclei using deep sequencing and microarray approaches, followed by advanced pathways analysis (Datson et al., 2008). Moreover, the application of the genomewide chromatin immunoprecipitation technique can show where MR and GR bind to the genome, and in which combinations with other transcription factors.

Comprehensive analysis of the different modes of action of GR and MR in the brain is a topic for future studies, but different signaling modes do occur. In the

GR$^{dim/dim}$ mice, DNA-binding-dependent and -independent mechanisms could be dissociated. Also, in knockout mice for SRC-1, regulation of the *CRH* gene by CORT was impaired both in PVN and in the amygdala, whereas induction of other target genes was preserved. Apparently, GRE-dependent transactivation effects can be subdivided based on signaling factors like SRC-1.

In conclusion, MR and GR mediate powerful effects on gene expression in the core of the HPA axis and elsewhere in the stress system, to control its response capacity and its responsiveness. Regulation of secretagogue genes (*POMC* and *CRH*) is well studied, but is only part of the adaptive process within the HPA axis. MR and GR can use several mechanisms, mostly specific for each receptor type, which are dependent on the cellular context. The latter emphasizes the importance of—relatively scarce—studies on molecular mechanisms that are conducted in the context of particular stressors and the relevant brain regions activated by those stressors. Quantifying MR and GR expression levels has limited value in interpreting actual glucocorticoid responsiveness, compared to measuring actual responses to glucocorticoids.

Future Directions

In the brain CORT action regulates about 20% of the genome. These approximately 6000 responsive genes display differential responsivity to CORT in the context of varying environmental, emotional, and cognitive inputs. The responsive genes are expressed in the core of the HPA axis and in neural afferents to the PVN involved in processing of stressful information. These actions exerted by CORT on the stress circuitry require coordination of energy metabolism, plasticity, and other processes that ultimately promote adaptation to stress. How these apparent disparate actions of the steroid are coordinated is not known and evidence explaining this high-order control is lacking. One approach to resolve this issue will be to use genomewide chromatin immunoprecepitation/DNA sequencing (ChIP-seq) approaches in the specific physiological conditions to delineate the actual genomic sites of action, and the consequences of MR and GR signaling on these sites.

CORT action is mediated by two closely related but complementary receptor systems: MR and GR. MRs appear implicated in the initial stress reaction, which is opposed and terminated via GR-mediated actions (Figure 3.4) These actions of CORT mediated by MR and GR operate with the other HPA signals to maintain homeostasis and health. What becomes apparent however is that imbalance in MR-/ GR-mediated actions destabilizes the stress circuitry, causing neuroendocrine dys-regulation and impairment of behavioral adaptation. If the adverse condition persists and a certain threshold is passed susceptibility to stress-related diseases is increased (de Kloet et al., 1998).

Important determinants in responsiveness to stress are genetic and experience-related factors. These factors may alter the ultradian rhythm and the altered pattern

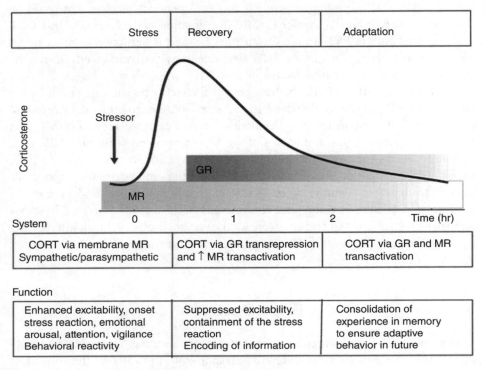

Stress	Recovery	Adaptation

Corticosterone

Stressor

GR

MR

System

| 0 | 1 | 2 | Time (hr) |

CORT via membrane MR Sympathetic/parasympathetic	CORT via GR transrepression and ↑ MR transactivation	CORT via GR and MR transactivation

Function

Enhanced excitability, onset stress reaction, emotional arousal, attention, vigilance Behavioral reactivity	Suppressed excitability, containment of the stress reaction Encoding of information	Consolidation of experience in memory to ensure adaptive behavior in future

Figure 3.4 Complementary actions mediated by MR and GR.

of pulsatile CORT exposure may modulate responsiveness to stress-induced CORT. Variants of MR and GR were found to affect this basal pulsatility, but also the processing of stressful information reflected in altered activity of the HPA axis. Experience-related factors can change the components of the HPA axis, including MR and GR, by epigenetic modification. Hence, for understanding the function of the HPA axis in adaptation to stress, both ultradian and stress-responsive patterns of CORT need to be taken into account.

The diverse signaling modes of the receptors, using different transrepression partners or specific coregulator pathways, holds a dual promise. On the one hand, these mechanisms may be specifically targeted by transgenic approaches or dissociating ligands. This will allow us to study functional domains of the stress-response pathways that depend on particular signaling modes, and relate these to other pathways that converge on the downstream proteins. On the other hand, dissociating ligands may actually be used in stress-related disorders, for example by blocking anxiety-related effects in the amygdala without disrupting endocrine negative feedback in the core of the HPA axis. Surely, the advancing molecular insights in receptor function will translate into better understanding of the impact of stress on the brain, and open up important opportunities for therapeutic intervention.

Acknowledgment

Support by the Royal Netherlands Academy of Sciences, North American Alliance for Research on Schizophrenia and Depression (through a van Ameringen Investigator award), and Center of Medical Systems Biology is gratefully acknowledged.

References

Atkinson, H. C., Wood, S. A., Castrique, E. S., Kershaw, Y. M., Wiles, C. C., & Lightman, S. L. (2008). Corticosteroids mediate fast feedback of the rat hypothalamic-pituitary-adrenal axis via the mineralocorticoid receptor. *American Journal of Physiology Endocrinology and Metabolism, 294*(6), E1011–E1022.

Bardeleben, U., & Holsboer, F. (1989). Cortisol response to a combined dexamethasone-human corticotrophin-releasing hormone challenge in patients with depression. *Journal of Neuroendocrinology, 1*(6), 485–488.

Barden, N., Stec, I. S., Montkowski, A., Holsboer, F., & Reul, J. M. (1997). Endocrine profile and neuroendocrine challenge tests in transgenic mice expressing antisense RNA against the glucocorticoid receptor. *Neuroendocrinology, 66*(3), 212–220.

Beck, I. M., Vanden Berghe, W., Vermeulen, L., Yamamoto, K. R., Haegeman, G., & De Bosscher, K. (2009). Crosstalk in inflammation: the interplay of glucocorticoid receptor-based mechanisms and kinases and phosphatases. *Endocrine Reviews, 30*(7), 830–882.

Belanoff, J. K., Flores, B. H., Kalezhan, M., Sund, B., & Schatzberg, A. F. (2001). Rapid reversal of psychotic depression using mifepristone. *Journal of Clinical Psychopharmacology, 21*(5), 516–521.

Belanoff, J. K., Rothschild, A. J., Cassidy, F., DeBattista, C., Baulieu, E. E., Schold, C., & Schatzberg, A. F. (2002). An open label trial of C-1073 (mifepristone) for psychotic major depression. *Biological Psychiatry, 52*(5), 386–392.

Berardelli, R., Karamouzis, I., Marinazzo, E., Prats, E., Picu, A., Giordano, R., Ghigo, E., & Arvat, E. (2010). Effect of acute and prolonged mineralocorticoid receptor blockade on spontaneous and stimulated hypothalamus-pituitary-adrenal (HPA) axis in humans. *European Journal of Endocrinology, 162*(6), 1067–1074.

Berger, S., Wolfer, D. P., Selbach, O., Alter, H., Erdmann, G., Reichardt, H. M., Chepkova, A. N., Welzl, H., Haas, H. L., Lipp, H. P., & Schütz, G. (2006). Loss of the limbic mineralocorticoid receptor impairs behavioral plasticity. *Proceedings of the National Academy of Sciences USA, 103*(1), 195–200.

Bousquet, C., Zatelli, M. C., & Melmed, S. (2000). Direct regulation of pituitary proopiomelanocortin by STAT3 provides a novel mechanism for immuno-neuroendocrine interfacing. *Journal of Clinical Investigation, 106*(11), 1417–1425.

Boutillier, A. L., Monnier, D., Lorang, D., Lundblad, J. R., Roberts, J. L., & Loeffler, J. P. (1995). Corticotropin-releasing hormone stimulates proopiomelanocortin transcription by cFos-dependent and -independent pathways: characterization of an AP1 site in exon 1. *Molecular Endocrinology (Baltimore, Md.), 9*(6), 745–755.

Boyle, M. P., Brewer, J. A., Funatsu, M., Wozniak, D. F., Tsien, J. Z., Izumi, Y., & Muglia, L. J. (2005). Acquired deficit of forebrain glucocorticoid receptor produces depression-like changes in adrenal axis regulation and behavior. *Proceedings of the National Academy of Sciences USA, 102*(2), 473–478.

Brinks, V., Berger, S., Gass, P., de Kloet, E. R., & Oitzl, M. S. (2009). Mineralocorticoid receptors in control of emotional arousal and fear memory. *Hormones and Behavior, 56*(2), 232–238.

Buckley, T. M., Mullen, B. C., & Schatzberg, A. F. (2007). The acute effects of a mineralocorticoid receptor (MR) agonist on nocturnal hypothalamic-adrenal-pituitary (HPA) axis activity in healthy controls. *Psychoneuroendocrinology, 32*(8–10), 859–864.

Carroll, B. J., Cassidy, F., Naftolowitz, D., Tatham, N. E., Wilson, W. H., Iranmanesh, A., Liu, P. Y., & Veldhuis, J. D. (2007). Pathophysiology of hypercortisolism in depression. *Acta Psychiatrica Scandinavica Supplementum, 433*, 90–103.

Ceccatelli, S., Villar, M. J., Goldstein, M., & Hökfelt, T. (1989). Expression of c-Fos immunoreactivity in transmitter-characterized neurons after stress. *Proceedings of the National Academy of Sciences USA, 86*(23), 9569–9573.

Cole, T. J., Blendy, J. A., Monaghan, A. P., Schmid, W., Aguzzi, A., & Schütz, G. (1995). Molecular genetic analysis of glucocorticoid signaling during mouse development. *Steroids, 60*(1), 93–96.

Conway-Campbell, B. L., McKenna, M. A., Wiles, C. C., Atkinson, H. C., de Kloet, E. R., & Lightman, S. L. (2007). Proteasome-dependent down-regulation of activated nuclear hippocampal glucocorticoid receptors determines dynamic responses to corticosterone. *Endocrinology, 148*(11), 5470–5477.

Datson, N. A., Morsink, M. C., Meijer, O. C., & de Kloet, E. R. (2008). Central corticosteroid actions: Search for gene targets. *European Journal of Pharmacology, 583*(2–3), 272–289.

DeBattista, C., & Belanoff, J. (2006). The use of mifepristone in the treatment of neuropsychiatric disorders. *Trends in Endocrinology and Metabolism, 17*(3), 117–121.

de Kloet, E. R., Voorhuis, T. A., Leunissen, J. L., & Koch, B. (1984). Intracellular CBG-like molecules in the rat pituitary. *Journal of Steroid Biochemistry, 20*(1), 367–371.

de Kloet, E. R., De Kock, S., Schild, V., & Veldhuis, H. D. (1988). Antiglucocorticoid RU 38486 attenuates retention of a behaviour and disinhibits the hypothalamic-pituitary adrenal axis at different brain sites. *Neuroendocrinology, 47*(2), 109–115.

de Kloet, E. R., Vreugdenhil, E., Oitzl, M. S., & Joëls, M. (1998). Brain corticosteroid receptor balance in health and disease. *Endocrine Reviews, 19*(3), 269–301.

de Kloet, E. R., Joëls, M., & Holsboer, F. (2005). Stress and the brain: from adaptation to disease. *Nature Reviews Neuroscience, 6*(6), 463–475.

de Kloet, R., Wallach, G., & McEwen, B. S. (1975). Differences in corticosterone and dexamethasone binding to rat brain and pituitary. *Endocrinology, 96*(3), 598–609.

DeRijk, R. H., & de Kloet, E. R. (2008). Corticosteroid receptor polymorphisms: determinants of vulnerability and resilience. *European Journal of Pharmacology, 583*(2–3), 303–311.

DeRijk, R. H., Wüst, S., Meijer, O. C., Zennaro, M. C., Federenko, I. S., Hellhammer, D. H., Giacchetti, G., Vreugdenhil, E., Zitman, F. G., & de Kloet, E. R. (2006). A common polymorphism in the mineralocorticoid receptor modulates stress responsiveness. *Journal of Clinical Endocrinology and Metabolism, 91*(12), 5083–5089.

Deuschle, M., Weber, B., Colla, M., Müller, M., Kniest, A., & Heuser, I. (1998). Mineralocorticoid receptor also modulates basal activity of hypothalamus-pituitary-adrenocortical system in humans. *Neuroendocrinology, 68*(5), 355–360.

Di, S., Malcher-Lopes, R., Halmos, K. C., & Tasker, J. G. (2003). Nongenomic glucocorticoid inhibition via endocannabinoid release in the hypothalamus: a fast feedback mechanism. *Journal of Neuroscience, 23*(12), 4850–4857.

Diamond, M. I., Miner, J. N., Yoshinaga, S. K., & Yamamoto, K. R. (1990). Transcription factor interactions: selectors of positive or negative regulation from a single DNA element. *Science, 249*(4974), 1266–1272.

Dodt, C., Kern, W., Fehm, H. L., & Born, J. (1993). Antimineralocorticoid canrenoate enhances secretory activity of the hypothalamus-pituitary-adrenocortical (HPA) axis in humans. *Neuroendocrinology, 58*(5), 570–574.

Droste, S. K., de Groote, L., Atkinson, H. C., Lightman, S. L., Reul, J. M., & Linthorst, A. C. (2008). Corticosterone levels in the brain show a distinct ultradian rhythm but a delayed response to forced swim stress. *Endocrinology, 149*(7), 3244–3253.

Drouin, J., Sun, Y. L., Chamberland, M., Gauthier, Y., De Léan, A., Nemer, M., & Schmidt, T. J. (1993). Novel glucocorticoid receptor complex with DNA element of the hormone-repressed POMC gene. *EMBO Journal, 12*(1), 145–156.

Gass, P., Kretz, O., Wolfer, D. P., Berger, S., Tronche, F., Reichardt, H. M., Kellendonk, C., Lipp, H. P., Schmid, W., & Schütz, G. (2000). Genetic disruption of mineralocorticoid receptor leads to impaired neurogenesis and granule cell degeneration in the hippocampus of adult mice. *EMBO Reports, 1*(5), 447–451.

Göttlicher, M., Heck, S., & Herrlich, P. (1998). Transcriptional cross-talk, the second mode of steroid hormone receptor action. *Journal of Molecular Medicine (Berlin), 76*(7), 480–489.

Griep, E. N., Boersma, J. W., Lentjes, E. G., Prins, A. P., van der Korst, J. K., & de Kloet, E. R. (1998). Function of the hypothalamic-pituitary-adrenal axis in patients with fibromyalgia and low back pain. *Journal of Rheumatology, 25*(7), 1374–1381.

Grottoli, S., Giordano, R., Maccagno, B., Pellegrino, M., Ghigo, E., & Arvat, E. (2002). The stimulatory effect of canrenoate, a mineralocorticoid antagonist, on the activity of the hypothalamus-pituitary-adrenal axis is abolished by alprazolam, a benzodiazepine, in humans. *Journal of Clinical Endocrinology and Metabolism, 87*(10), 4616–4620.

Guardiola-Diaz, H. M., Kolinske, J. S., Gates, L. H., & Seasholtz, A. F. (1996). Negative glucocorticoid regulation of cyclic adenosine 3′,5′-monophosphate-stimulated corticotropin-releasing hormone-reporter expression in AtT-20 cells. *Molecular Endocrinology (Baltimore, Md.), 10*(3), 317–329.

Gumbiner, B., & Kelly, R. B. (1981). Secretory granules of an anterior pituitary cell line, AtT-20, contain only mature forms of corticotropin and beta-lipotropin. *Proceedings of the National Academy of Sciences USA, 78*(1), 318–322.

Han, S. J., Lonard, D. M., & O'Malley, B. W. (2009). Multi-modulation of nuclear receptor coactivators through posttranslational modifications. *Trends in Endocrinology and Metabolism, 20*(1), 8–15.

Heuser, I., Deuschle, M., Weber, A., Kniest, A., Ziegler, C., Weber, B., & Colla, M. (2000). The role of mineralocorticoid receptors in the circadian activity of the human hypothalamus-pituitary-adrenal system: effect of age. *Neurobiology of Aging, 21*(4), 585–589.

Holsboer, F. (2000). The corticosteroid receptor hypothesis of depression. *Neuropsychopharmacology, 23*(5), 477–501.

Huizenga, N. A., Koper, J. W., De Lange, P., Pols, H. A., Stolk, R. P., Burger, H., Grobbee, D. E., Brinkmann, A. O., De Jong, F. H., & Lamberts, S. W. (1998). A polymorphism in the glucocorticoid receptor gene may be associated with and increased sensitivity to glucocorticoids in vivo. *Journal of Clinical Endocrinology and Metabolism, 83*(1), 144–151.

Jasper, M. S., & Engeland, W. C. (1997). Splanchnicotomy increases adrenal sensitivity to ACTH in nonstressed rats. *American Journal of Physiology Endocrinology and Metabolism, 273*(2 Pt 1), E363–E368.

Joëls, M., Karst, H., DeRijk, R., & de Kloet, E. R. (2008). The coming out of the brain mineralocorticoid receptor. *Trends in Neurosciences, 31*(1), 1–7.

John, C. D., Gavins, F. N., Buss, N. A., Cover, P. O., & Buckingham, J. C. (2008). Annexin A1 and the formyl peptide receptor family: neuroendocrine and metabolic aspects. *Current Opinion in Pharmacology, 8*(6), 765–776.

Karssen, A. M., Meijer, O. C., van der Sandt, I. C., Lucassen, P. J., de Lange, E. C., de Boer, A. G., & de Kloet, E. R. (2001). Multidrug resistance P-glycoprotein hampers the access of cortisol but not of corticosterone to mouse and human brain. *Endocrinology, 142*(6), 2686–2694.

Karst, H., Berger, S., Turiault, M., Tronche, F., Schütz, G., & Joëls, M. (2005). Mineralocorticoid receptors are indispensable for nongenomic modulation of hippocampal glutamate transmission by corticosterone. *Proceedings of the National Academy of Sciences USA, 102*(52), 19204–19207.

Kellner, M., Baker, D. G., Yassouridis, A., Bettinger, S., Otte, C., Naber, D., & Wiedemann, K. (2002). Mineralocorticoid receptor function in patients with posttraumatic stress disorder. *American Journal of Psychiatry, 159*(11), 1938–1940.

Kimchi-Sarfaty, C., Oh, J. M., Kim, I. W., Sauna, Z. E., Calcagno, A. M., Ambudkar, S. V., & Gottesman, M. M. (2007). A "silent" polymorphism in the MDR1 gene changes substrate specificity. *Science, 315*(5811), 525–528.

Kovács, K. J., Földes, A., & Sawchenko, P. E. (2000). Glucocorticoid negative feedback selectively targets vasopressin transcription in parvocellular neurosecretory neurons. *Journal of Neuroscience, 20*(10), 3843–3852.

Kretz, O., Reichardt, H. M., Schütz, G., & Bock, R. (1999). Corticotropin-releasing hormone expression is the major target for glucocorticoid feedback-control at the hypothalamic level. *Brain Research, 818*(2), 488–491.

Kumsta, R., Entringer, S., Koper, J. W., van Rossum, E. F., Hellhammer, D. H., & Wüst, S. (2007). Sex specific associations between common glucocorticoid receptor gene variants and hypothalamus-pituitary-adrenal axis responses to psychosocial stress. *Biological Psychiatry, 62*(8), 863–869.

Kuningas, M., de Rijk, R. H., Westendorp, R. G., Jolles, J., Slagboom, P. E., & van Heemst, D. (2007). Mental performance in old age dependent on cortisol and genetic variance in the mineralocorticoid and glucocorticoid receptors. *Neuropsychopharmacology, 32*(6), 1295–1301.

Kuwahara, S., Arima, H., Banno, R., Sato, I., Kondo, N., & Oiso, Y. (2003). Regulation of vasopressin gene expression by cAMP and glucocorticoids in parvocellular neurons of the paraventricular nucleus in rat hypothalamic organotypic cultures. *Journal of Neuroscience, 23*(32), 10231–10237.

Lachize, S., Apostolakis, E. M., van der Laan, S., Tijssen, A. M., Xu, J., de Kloet, E. R., & Meijer, O. C. (2009). Steroid receptor coactivator-1 is necessary for regulation of corticotropin-releasing hormone by chronic stress and glucocorticoids. *Proceedings of the National Academy of Sciences USA, 106*(19), 8038–8042.

Lai, M., Horsburgh, K., Bae, S. E., Carter, R. N., Stenvers, D. J., Fowler, J. H., Yau, J. L., Gomez-Sanchez, C. E., Holmes, M. C., Kenyon, C. J., Seckl, J. R., & Macleod, M. R. (2007). Forebrain mineralocorticoid receptor overexpression enhances memory, reduces anxiety and attenuates neuronal loss in cerebral ischaemia. *European Journal of Neuroscience, 25*(6), 1832–1842.

Latchoumanin, O., Mynard, V., Devin-Leclerc, J., Dugué, M. A., Bertagna, X., & Catelli, M. G. (2007). Reversal of glucocorticoids-dependent proopiomelanocortin gene inhibition by leukemia inhibitory factor. *Endocrinology, 148*(1), 422–432.

Lazarus, R. S. (2006). Emotions and interpersonal relationships: toward a person-centered conceptualization of emotions and coping. *Journal of Personality, 74*(1), 9–46.

Levine, S. (2005). Developmental determinants of sensitivity and resistance to stress. *Psychoneuroendocrinology, 30*(10), 939–946.

Lightman, S. L., Wiles, C. C., Atkinson, H. C., Henley, D. E., Russell, G. M., Leendertz, J. A., McKenna, M. A., Spiga, F., Wood, S. A., & Conway-Campbell, B. L. (2008). The significance of glucocorticoid pulsatility. *European Journal of Pharmacology, 583*(2–3), 255–262.

Lim, M. C., Shipston, M. J., & Antoni, F. A. (2002). Posttranslational modulation of glucocorticoid feedback inhibition at the pituitary level. *Endocrinology, 143*(10), 3796–3801.

Liu, Y., Coello, A. G., Grinevich, V., & Aguilera, G. (2010). Involvement of transducer of regulated cAMP response element-binding protein activity on corticotropin releasing hormone transcription. *Endocrinology, 151*(3), 1109–1118.

Makino, S., Gold, P. W., & Schulkin, J. (1994). Effects of corticosterone on CRH mRNA and content in the bed nucleus of the stria terminalis; comparison with the effects in the central nucleus of the amygdala and the paraventricular nucleus of the hypothalamus. *Brain Research, 657*(1–2), 141–149.

Malkoski, S. P., & Dorin, R. I. (1999). Composite glucocorticoid regulation at a functionally defined negative glucocorticoid response element of the human corticotropin-releasing hormone gene. *Molecular Endocrinology (Baltimore, Md.), 13*(10), 1629–1644.

Martens, C., Bilodeau, S., Maira, M., Gauthier, Y., & Drouin, J. (2005). Protein-protein interactions and transcriptional antagonism between the subfamily of NGFI-B/Nur77 orphan nuclear receptors and glucocorticoid receptor. *Molecular Endocrinology (Baltimore, Md.), 19*(4), 885–897.

Mattsson, C., Reynolds, R. M., Simonyte, K., Olsson, T., & Walker, B. R. (2009). Combined receptor antagonist stimulation of the hypothalamic-pituitary-adrenal axis test identifies impaired negative feedback sensitivity to cortisol in obese men. *Journal of Clinical Endocrinology and Metabolism, 94*(4), 1347–1352.

McEwen, B. S. (2007). Physiology and neurobiology of stress and adaptation: central role of the brain. *Physiological Reviews, 87*(3), 873–904.

Meijer, O. C., de Lange, E. C., Breimer, D. D., de Boer, A. G., Workel, J. O., & de Kloet, E. R. (1998). Penetration of dexamethasone into brain glucocorticoid targets is enhanced in mdr1A P-glycoprotein knockout mice. *Endocrinology, 139*(4), 1789–1793.

Meijer, O. C., Williamson, A., Dallman, M. F., & Pearce, D. (2000). Transcriptional repression of the 5-HT1A receptor promoter by corticosterone via mineralocorticoid receptors depends on the cellular context. *Journal of Neuroendocrinology, 12*(3), 245–254.

Meijer, O. C., van der Laan, S., Lachize, S., Steenbergen, P. J., & de Kloet, E. R. (2006). Steroid receptor coregulator diversity: what can it mean for the stressed brain? *Neuroscience, 138*(3), 891–899.

Meijsing, S. H., Pufall, M. A., So, A. Y., Bates, D. L., Chen, L., & Yamamoto, K. R. (2009). DNA binding site sequence directs glucocorticoid receptor structure and activity. *Science, 324*(5925), 407–410.

Oitzl, M. S., van Haarst, A. D., Sutanto, W., & de Kloet, E. R. (1995). Corticosterone, brain mineralocorticoid receptors (MRs) and the activity of the hypothalamic-pituitary-adrenal (HPA) axis: the Lewis rat as an example of increased central MR capacity and a hyporesponsive HPA axis. *Psychoneuroendocrinology, 20*(6), 655–675.

Oitzl, M. S., Reichardt, H. M., Joëls, M., & de Kloet, E. R. (2001). Point mutation in the mouse glucocorticoid receptor preventing DNA binding impairs spatial memory. *Proceedings of the National Academy of Sciences USA, 98*(22), 12790–12795.

Otte, C., Jahn, H., Yassouridis, A., Arlt, J., Stober, N., Maass, P., Wiedemann, K., & Kellner, M. (2003a). The mineralocorticoid receptor agonist, fludrocortisone, inhibits pituitary-adrenal activity in humans after pre-treatment with metyrapone. *Life Sciences, 73*(14), 1835–1845.

Otte, C., Yassouridis, A., Jahn, H., Maass, P., Stober, N., Wiedemann, K., & Kellner, M. (2003b). Mineralocorticoid receptor-mediated inhibition of the hypothalamic-pituitary-adrenal axis in aged humans. *Journals of Gerontology. Series A, Biological Sciences and Medical Sciences, 58*(10), B900–B905.

Patel, P. D., Lopez, J. F., Lyons, D. M., Burke, S., Wallace, M., & Schatzberg, A. F. (2000). Glucocorticoid and mineralocorticoid receptor mRNA expression in squirrel monkey brain. *Journal of Psychiatric Research, 34*(6), 383–392.

Peters, A., Pellerin, L., Dallman, M. F., Oltmanns, K. M., Schweiger, U., Born, J., & Fehm, H. L. (2007). Causes of obesity: looking beyond the hypothalamus. *Progress in Neurobiology, 81*(2), 61–88.

Phuc Le, P., Friedman, J. R., Schug, J., Brestelli, J. E., Parker, J. B., Bochkis, I. M., & Kaestner, K. H. (2005). Glucocorticoid receptor-dependent gene regulatory networks. *PLoS Genetics, 1*(2), p. e16.

Ratka, A., Sutanto, W., Bloemers, M., & de Kloet, E. R. (1989). On the role of brain mineralocorticoid (type I) and glucocorticoid (type II) receptors in neuroendocrine regulation. *Neuroendocrinology, 50*(2), 117–123.

Raubenheimer, P. J., Young, E. A., Andrew, R., & Seckl, J. R. (2006). The role of corticosterone in human hypothalamic-pituitary-adrenal axis feedback. *Clinical Endocrinology, 65*(1), 22–26.

Reichardt, H. M., Kaestner, K. H., Tuckermann, J., Kretz, O., Wessely, O., Bock, R., Gass, P., Schmid, W., Herrlich, P., Angel, P., & Schütz, G. (1998). DNA binding of the glucocorticoid receptor is not essential for survival. *Cell, 93*(4), 531–541.

Reul, J. M., Probst, J. C., Skutella, T., Hirschmann, M., Stec, I. S., Montkowski, A., Landgraf, R., & Holsboer, F. (1997). Increased stress-induced adrenocorticotropin response after long-term intracerebroventricular treatment of rats with antisense mineralocorticoid receptor oligodeoxynucleotides. *Neuroendocrinology, 65*(3), 189–199.

Revsin, Y., van Wijk, D., Saravia, F. E., Oitzl, M. S., De Nicola, A. F., & de Kloet, E. R. (2008). Adrenal hypersensitivity precedes chronic hypercorticism in streptozotocin-induced diabetes mice. *Endocrinology, 149*(7), 3531–3539.

Ridder, S., Chourbaji, S., Hellweg, R., Urani, A., Zacher, C., Schmid, W., Zink, M., Hörtnagl, H., Flor, H., Henn, F. A., Schütz, G., & Gass, P. (2005). Mice with genetically altered glucocorticoid receptor expression show altered sensitivity for stress-induced depressive reactions. *Journal of Neuroscience, 25*(26), 6243–6250.

Rosmond, R., Chagnon, Y. C., Chagnon, M., Pérusse, L., Bouchard, C., & Björntorp, P. (2000). A polymorphism of the 5'-flanking region of the glucocorticoid receptor gene locus is associated with basal cortisol secretion in men. *Metabolism: Clinical and Experimental, 49*(9), 1197–1199.

Rozeboom, A. M., Akil, H., & Seasholtz, A. F. (2007). Mineralocorticoid receptor overexpression in forebrain decreases anxiety-like behavior and alters the stress response in mice. *Proceedings of the National Academy of Sciences USA, 104*(11), 4688–4693.

Sánchez, M. M., Young, L. J., Plotsky, P. M., & Insel, T. R. (2000). Distribution of corticosteroid receptors in the rhesus brain: relative absence of glucocorticoid receptors in the hippocampal formation. *Journal of Neuroscience, 20*(12), 4657–4668.

Sapolsky, R. M., Romero, L. M., & Munck, A. U. (2000). How do glucocorticoids influence stress responses? Integrating permissive, suppressive, stimulatory, and preparative actions. *Endocrine Reviews, 21*(1), 55–89.

Sarabdjitsingh, R. A., Isenia, S., Polman, A., Mijalkovic, J., Lachize, S., Datson, N., de Kloet, E. R., & Meijer, O. C. (2010a). Disrupted corticosterone pulsatile patterns attenuate responsiveness to glucocorticoid signaling in rat brain. *Endocrinology, 151*(3), 1177–1186.

Sarabdjitsingh, R. A., Conway-Campbell, B. L., Leggett, J. D., Waite, E. J., Meijer, O. C., de Kloet, E. R., & Lightman, S. L. (2010b). Stress responsiveness varies over the ultradian glucocorticoid cycle in a brain-region-specific manner. *Endocrinology, 151*(11), 5369–5379.

Schmidt, M. V., Sterlemann, V., Wagner, K., Niederleitner, B., Ganea, K., Liebl, C., Deussing, J. M., Berger, S., Schütz, G., Holsboer, F., & Müller, M. B. (2009). Postnatal glucocorticoid excess due to pituitary glucocorticoid receptor deficiency: differential short- and long-term consequences. *Endocrinology, 150*(6), 2709–2716.

Seckl, J. R. (1997). 11beta-Hydroxysteroid dehydrogenase in the brain: a novel regulator of glucocorticoid action? *Frontiers in Neuroendocrinology, 18*(1), 49–99.

Shepard, J. D., Liu, Y., Sassone-Corsi, P., & Aguilera, G. (2005). Role of glucocorticoids and cAMP-mediated repression in limiting corticotropin-releasing hormone transcription during stress. *Journal of Neuroscience, 25*(16), 4073–4081.

Spencer, R. L., Miller, A. H., Moday, H., Stein, M., & McEwen, B. S. (1993). Diurnal differences in basal and acute stress levels of type I and type II adrenal steroid receptor activation in neural and immune tissues, *Endocrinology, 133*(5), 1941–1950.

Spencer, R. L., Kim, P. J., Kalman, B. A., & Cole, M. A. (1998). Evidence for mineralocorticoid receptor facilitation of glucocorticoid receptor-dependent regulation of hypothalamic-pituitary-adrenal axis activity. *Endocrinology, 139*(6), 2718–2726.

Spiga, F., Harrison, L. R., Wood, S. A., Atkinson, H. C., MacSweeney, C. P., Thomson, F., Craighead, M., Grassie, M., & Lightman, S. L. (2007). Effect of the glucocorticoid receptor antagonist Org 34850 on basal and stress-induced corticosterone secretion. *Journal of Neuroendocrinology, 19*(11), 891–900.

Stavreva, D. A., Wiench, M., John, S., Conway-Campbell, B. L., McKenna, M. A., Pooley, J. R., Johnson, T. A., Voss, T. C., Lightman, S. L., & Hager, G. L. (2009). Ultradian hormone stimulation induces glucocorticoid receptor-mediated pulses of gene transcription. *Nature Cell Biology, 11*(9), 1093–1102.

Stevens, A., Ray, D. W., Zeggini, E., John, S., Richards, H. L., Griffiths, C. E., & Donn, R. (2004). Glucocorticoid sensitivity is determined by a specific glucocorticoid receptor haplotype. *Journal of Clinical Endocrinology and Metabolism, 89*(2), 892–897.

Stoecklin, E., Wissler, M., Schaetzle, D., Pfitzner, E., & Groner, B. (1999). Interactions in the transcriptional regulation exerted by Stat5 and by members of the steroid hormone receptor family, *The Journal of Steroid Biochemistry and Molecular Biology, 69*(1–6), 195–204.

Swanson, L. W., & Simmons, D. M. (1989). Differential steroid hormone and neural influences on peptide mRNA levels in CRH cells of the paraventricular nucleus: a hybridization histochemical study in the rat. *Journal of Comparative Neurology, 285*(4), 413–435.

Tirard, M., Almeida, O. F., Hutzler, P., Melchior, F., & Michaelidis, T. M. (2007). Sumoylation and proteasomal activity determine the transactivation properties of the mineralocorticoid receptor. *Molecular and Cellular Endocrinology, 268*(1–2), 20–29.

Tronche, F., Kellendonk, C., Kretz, O., Gass, P., Anlag, K., Orban, P. C., Bock, R., Klein, R., & Schütz, G. (1999). Disruption of the glucocorticoid receptor gene in the nervous system results in reduced anxiety, *Nature Genetics, 23*(1), 99–103.

van der Laan, S., Lachize, S. B., Vreugdenhil, E., de Kloet, E. R., & Meijer, O. C. (2008a). Nuclear receptor coregulators differentially modulate induction and glucocorticoid receptor-mediated repression of the corticotropin-releasing hormone gene. *Endocrinology, 149*(2), 725–732.

van der Laan, S., Sarabdjitsingh, R. A., Van Batenburg, M. F., Lachize, S. B., Li, H., Dijkmans, T. F., Vreugdenhil, E., de Kloet, E. R., & Meijer, O. C. (2008b). Chromatin immunoprecipitation scanning identifies glucocorticoid receptor binding regions in the proximal promoter of a ubiquitously expressed glucocorticoid target gene in brain. *Journal of Neurochemistry, 106*(6), 2515–2523.

van der Lely, A. J., Foeken, K., van der Mast, R. C., & Lamberts, S. W. (1991). Rapid reversal of acute psychosis in the Cushing syndrome with the cortisol-receptor antagonist mifepristone (RU 486). *Annals of Internal Medicine, 114*(2), 143–144.

Van Eekelen, J. A., Jiang, W., De Kloet, E. R., & Bohn, M. C. (1988). Distribution of the mineralocorticoid and the glucocorticoid receptor mRNAs in the rat hippocampus. *Journal of Neuroscience Research, 21*(1), 88–94.

van Haarst, A. D., Oitzl, M. S., Workel, J. O., & de Kloet, E. R. (1996). Chronic brain glucocorticoid receptor blockade enhances the rise in circadian and stress-induced pituitary-adrenal activity. *Endocrinology, 137*(11), 4935–4943.

van Haarst, A. D., Oitzl, M. S., & de Kloet, E. R. (1997). Facilitation of feedback inhibition through blockade of glucocorticoid receptors in the hippocampus. *Neurochemical Research, 22*(11), 1323–1328.

van Leeuwen, N., Kumsta, R., Entringer, S., de Kloet, E. R., Zitman, F. G., de Rijk, R. H., & Wüst, S. (2010a). Functional mineralocorticoid receptor (MR) gene variation influences the cortisol awakening response after dexamethasone. *Psychoneuroendocrinology, 35*(3), 339–349.

van Leeuwen, N., Kumsta, R., Entringer, S., de Kloet, E. R., Zitman, F. G., DeRijk, R. H., & Wüst, S. (2010b). Functional mineralocorticoid receptor (MR) gene variation influences the cortisol awakening response after dexamethasone. *Psychoneuroendocrinology, 35*(3), 339–349.

van Leeuwen, N., Bellingrath, S., de Kloet, E. R., Zitman, F. G., DeRijk, R. H., Kudielka, B. M., & Wüst, S. (2011) Human mineralocorticoid receptor (MR) gene haplotypes modulate MR expression and transactivation: implication for the stress response. *Psychoneuroendocrinology, 36*, 699–709.

Veldhuis, J. D., Iranmanesh, A., Godschalk, M., & Mulligan, T. (2000). Older men manifest multifold synchrony disruption of reproductive neurohormone outflow. *Journal of Clinical Endocrinology and Metabolism, 85*(4), 1477–1486.

Walker, J. J., Terry, J. R., & Lightman, S. L. (2010). Origin of ultradian pulsatility in the hypothalamic-pituitary-adrenal axis. *Proceedings of the Royal Society Series B Biological Sciences, 277*(1688), 1627–1633.

Watts, A. G. (2005). Glucocorticoid regulation of peptide genes in neuroendocrine CRH neurons: a complexity beyond negative feedback. *Frontiers in Neuroendocrinology, 26*(3–4), 109–130.

Wei, Q., Lu, X. Y., Liu, L., Schafer, G., Shieh, K. R., Burke, S., Robinson, T. E., Watson, S. J., Seasholtz, A. F., & Akil, H. (2004). Glucocorticoid receptor overexpression in forebrain: a mouse model of increased emotional lability. *Proceedings of the National Academy of Sciences USA, 101*(32), 11851–11856.

Windle, R. J., Wood, S. A., Lightman, S. L., & Ingram, C. D. (1998). The pulsatile characteristics of hypothalamo-pituitary-adrenal activity in female Lewis and Fischer 344 rats and its relationship to differential stress responses. *Endocrinology, 139*(10), 4044–4052.

Windle, R. J., Wood, S. A., Kershaw, Y. M., Lightman, S. L., Ingram, C. D., & Harbuz, M. S. (2001). Increased corticosterone pulse frequency during adjuvant-induced arthritis and its relationship to alterations in stress responsiveness. *Journal of Neuroendocrinology, 13*(10), 905–911.

Winnay, J. N., Xu, J., O'Malley, B. W., & Hammer, G. D. (2006). Steroid receptor coactivator-1-deficient mice exhibit altered hypothalamic-pituitary-adrenal axis function. *Endocrinology, 147*(3), 1322–1332.

Wolkowitz, O. M., Epel, E. S., & Reus, V. I. (2001). Stress hormone-related psychopathology: pathophysiological and treatment implications. *World Journal of Biological Psychiatry, 2*(3), 115–143.

Yau, J. L., Noble, J., & Seckl, J. R. (1999). Continuous blockade of brain mineralocorticoid receptors impairs spatial learning in rats. *Neuroscience Letters, 277*(1), 45–48.

Yau, J. L., McNair, K. M., Noble, J., Brownstein, D., Hibberd, C., Morton, N., Mullins, J. J., Morris, R. G., Cobb, S., & Seckl, J. R. (2007). Enhanced hippocampal long-term potentiation and spatial learning in aged 11beta-hydroxysteroid dehydrogenase type 1 knockout mice. *Journal of Neuroscience, 27*(39), 10487–10496.

Yehuda, R. (2006). Advances in understanding neuroendocrine alterations in PTSD and their therapeutic implications. *Annals of the New York Academy of Sciences 1071*, 137–166.

Young, E. A., Lopez, J. F., Murphy-Weinberg, V., Watson, S. J., & Akil, H. (1998). The role of mineralocorticoid receptors in hypothalamic-pituitary-adrenal axis regulation in humans. *Journal of Clinical Endocrinology and Metabolism, 83*(9), 3339–3345.

Young, E. A., Lopez, J. F., Murphy-Weinberg, V., Watson, S. J., & Akil, H. (2003). Mineralocorticoid receptor function in major depression. *Archives of General Psychiatry, 60*(1), 24–28.

4

Nongenomic Cellular Actions of Corticosteroids in the Brain

Marian Joëls, Femke Groeneweg, and Henk Karst

Introduction

Shortly after stress, high amounts of glucocorticoids (mostly cortisol in humans and corticosterone in rodents) are released from the adrenal gland. This surge of corticosteroid release comes on top of the circadian and ultradian release pattern (Lightman et al., 2008). The hormones reach all organs, including the brain. The latter is well protected by the blood–brain barrier but glucocorticoids easily pass this barrier due to their lipophilic character (Pariante, 2008).

Brain cells can express two main types of corticosteroid receptor (for review see de Kloet et al., 2005; see also Chapter 1 in this volume): the mineralocorticoid receptor (MR) and the glucocorticoid receptor (GR). Splice variants and differences in the transcription-initiation site cause some diversity in these two molecules (Revollo and Cidlowski, 2009). The two main receptor types belong to the family of nuclear receptors and either bind directly to recognition sites in gene-promoter sequences or engage in protein–protein interactions with other transcription factors. Through both pathways they exert a slow and long-lasting transcriptional control over a subset of genes expressed in the brain (for review see Datson et al., 2008; see also Chapter 6).

MRs display a very high affinity for the endogenous glucocorticoid, both in humans and in rodents (de Kloet et al., 2005; Chapter 3). Even with basal levels of the hormone—that is, during the circadian trough and the nadir of the ultradian pulses—these MRs are already substantially occupied. MR expression is quite restricted, with very high levels in neurons of the hippocampus, lateral septum, and

The Handbook of Stress: Neuropsychological Effects on the Brain, First Edition.
Edited by Cheryl D. Conrad.
© 2011 Blackwell Publishing Ltd. Published 2011 by Blackwell Publishing Ltd.

some motor nuclei in the brainstem, and lower expression levels in, for example, the amygdala, hypothalamus, and neocortex. By contrast, the expression of GRs is quite widespread, in neurons and glial cells. Very high expression levels are encountered in the CA1 hippocampal subfield (where CA means cornu ammonis, a subregion of the hippocampus), the dentate gyrus, and the paraventricular nucleus (PVN) of the hypothalamus, the main site for negative feedback in the stress axis. GR affinity is lower than that of MRs, so that GRs are only extensively activated when hormone levels peak, for example after stress.

Over the past few decades, many glucocorticoid effects on brain cells (particularly in the hippocampus, which expresses high amounts of MR as well as GR) have been reported. In nearly all cases the effects were slow in onset, persistent, and dependent on gene transcription and/or protein synthesis, consistent with the genomic signaling pathway of MRs and GRs (see Joëls et al., 2007 for review). In the first section of this chapter these slow, gene-mediated effects of glucocorticoids on neuronal function are summarized. In general, these actions depend on GR activation and serve to normalize stress-induced changes in neuronal activity and prepare the organism for future events.

However, it has been known for many years that glucocorticoids can exert very rapid effects. A clear example was provided in the amphibian brain (Orchinik et al., 1991). Some of the rapid effects were visible within minutes (e.g., Dubrovsky et al., 1993), whereas other effects peak after approximately 20–30 min (Pfaff et al., 1971; Vidal et al., 1986; Joëls and de Kloet, 1993). The very rapid effects in particular are incompatible with a gene-mediated signaling pathway. For many years these effects were noted but remained ill understood. Advanced electrophysiological methods, though, allowing precise recordings in reduced preparations, indisputably demonstrated glucocorticoid effects that develop over the course of minutes and which are independent of gene transcription (Di et al., 2003, 2005, 2009; Karst et al., 2005; Olijslagers et al., 2008). These recent electrophysiological studies are reviewed in the section on rapid, nongenomic effects of glucocorticoids.

While it is now clear that rapid nongenomic glucocorticoid actions take place in various parts of the rodent brain, many actions still remain unresolved. For instance, in nearly all cases the responsible receptor seems to be located near to or even in the plasma membrane. In those cases where the involvement of MRs or GRs was made plausible, it is unclear why or how these receptor molecules—normally residing in the cytoplasm—move to the plasma membrane instead of the nucleus. Interestingly, membrane receptors for estrogens have been recognized for some time now (for review see Kelly and Rønnekleiv, 2009). In the section entitled Putative Mechanism of Action we speculate that signaling pathways involved in nongenomic glucocorticoid actions might resemble those involved in rapid effects of estradiol. We conclude by formulating a number of questions which may help to focus research into explaining how nongenomic glucocorticoid actions in brain are accomplished and what their significance could be for the function of limbic cells.

Slow, Gene-mediated Effects of Glucocorticoids

For many years it was thought that glucocorticoids affect limbic cell function primarily via gene-mediated pathways. Indeed, exposure in vitro of tissue to a pulse of corticosterone causes slow-onset changes in cellular properties. By and large, two different classes of endpoint have been studied: effects of corticosteroids on ion conductances and on parameters involved in neurotransmission.

Ion conductances

Early on, it became apparent that conditions associated with predominant activation of MRs (e.g., tissue from nonstressed animals, prepared at the trough of the circadian rhythm) result in relatively small calcium conductances in CA1 cells (Karst et al., 1994). However, when animals were stressed or when GRs were activated in vitro, the amplitude of calcium currents slowly increased (Kerr et al., 1992; Karst et al., 1994, 2000), particularly of L-type calcium currents (Kerr et al., 1992; Chameau et al., 2007). Follow-up studies revealed that GRs may target calcium channel β4 subunits (see Figure 4.1), which could enhance surface expression of the pore-forming subunits of L-type calcium channels (Chameau et al., 2007). Delayed increases in calcium influx were also observed for CA3 pyramidal neurons (Kole et al., 2001) and pyramidal-like neurons in the basolateral amygdala (BLA; Karst et al., 2002), but not for granule cells in the dentate gyrus (Van Gemert et al., 2009). The latter cells did respond to GR activation with transcriptional regulation of β4 subunits, but at the protein level neither β4 nor pore-forming α subunits were altered by corticosteroid application. This lack of GR effect in the dentate gyrus is presently unexplained; however, it underlines that a surge of corticosterone may reach many brain cells but will not change cell function uniformly.

Enhanced calcium influx into CA1 pyramidal cells is coupled to a GR-dependent reduction in calcium efflux (Bhargava et al., 2002). Consequently, a stress-induced surge in corticosteroids will slowly enhance the intracellular calcium concentration in these (and possibly other) cells. One of the immediate consequences could be that calcium-dependent phenomena are also boosted by GR activation. This is indeed the case for a small potassium conductance that is strongly calcium dependent (Joëls and de Kloet, 1989; Kerr et al., 1989). This potassium conductance is responsible for slowing down the rate of action potentials during steady depolarization of pyramidal neurons, so that the transfer of excitatory information is attenuated (Figure 4.2). Application of glucocorticoids was indeed shown to reduce firing frequency in CA1 and CA3 neurons (Joëls and de Kloet, 1989; Kerr et al., 1989; Kole et al., 2001), although not in principal cells of the BLA (Duvarci and Paré, 2007; Liebmann et al., 2008), again stressing the regional differences in responses to glucocorticoids. All of these effects (as far as they have been examined) were slow in onset, long-lasting, dependent on protein synthesis, and mediated by GRs.

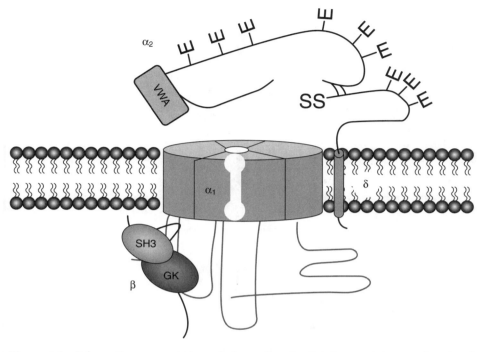

Figure 4.1 Schematic representation of the main subunits that constitute a functional calcium channel. Four α_1 subunits form the pore of the channel, through which calcium ions flow across the membrane. In addition, the channel contains auxiliary β and $\alpha_2\delta$ subunits, which add to the gating and voltage-dependent properties of the channel, but are also involved in trafficking of channels to the plasma membrane, each in a different way. Thus, β subunits are thought to enhance the trafficking of the channels to the plasma membrane by binding via their SH3-guanylate kinase (GK)-like domain to the α interaction domain, whereas $\alpha_2\delta$ subunits promote trafficking of the calcium channel complex by a mechanism that involves their von Willebrand factor-A (VWA) domain. *Source:* From Dolphin (2009). With permission from Elsevier.

Of all ion conductances examined, calcium currents were found to be most sensitive to corticosteroids; this also indirectly affects the (small) calcium-dependent potassium conductance. Direct effects on a number of potassium currents (I_A, delayed rectifier, Ih) were more subtle or absent (for review see Joëls et al., 2007). Similarly, glucocorticoids did not strongly alter properties of the voltage-dependent sodium current.

All in all, glucocorticoids affect particularly L-type voltage-dependent calcium currents in limbic neurons. Over the course of several hours this gradually attenuates information transfer through the CA1 area. By this delayed attenuation, CA1 hippocampal activity is slowly normalized after stress, back to prestress levels. This phenomenon of normalization seems less prominent in the dentate gyrus and

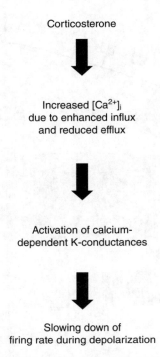

Corticosterone

Increased [Ca^{2+}]$_i$
due to enhanced influx
and reduced efflux

Activation of calcium-
dependent K-conductances

Slowing down of
firing rate during depolarization

Figure 4.2 Corticosterone slowly enhances the influx of calcium ions through L-type calcium channels in CA1 neurons, as well as reducing the efflux of calcium ions, by repressing plasma membrane Ca^{2+}-ATPase 1. Consequently, the intracellular concentration of calcium is enhanced some hours after exposure to the hormone. This can give rise to activation of a particular class of calcium-dependent potassium channels, which will eventually reduce the firing rate of hippocampal cells. [Ca^{2+}]$_i$, intracellular calcium concentration.

certainly in the BLA. The latter may explain why situations related to extensive amygdalar activity (i.e., strongly emotional situations) are less constrained and hence may give rise to inordinately strong memories (e.g., see Buchanan and Lovallo, 2001). For all regions it seems to hold that if glucocorticoid exposure is prolonged or coupled to prolonged depolarization (e.g., during an epileptic insult), intracellular calcium levels become extremely high. In such circumstances glucocorticoid exposure could impose an increased risk on delayed cell death (Sapolsky, 1994).

Neurotransmitter responses

Shortly after stress not only the corticosteroid level but also the concentration of various neurotransmitters is increased, most notably of monoamines. For instance, norepinephrine (noradrenaline) levels are temporarily enhanced in important limbic regions such as the amygdala (McIntyre et al., 2002). Depending on the receptor subtypes expressed, norepinephrine can exert excitatory or inhibitory actions (e.g., Ferry et al., 1997). Behavioral studies have shown that in particular effects via the β-adrenoceptor play an important role in the effects of stress on cognitive function (Quirarte et al., 1997). This instigated a series of electrophysiological studies which focused on the interactions between corticosteroids and the β-adrenoceptor. These studies demonstrated that in CA1, dentate, and BLA neurons corticosterone gradually suppresses excitatory effects induced via the β-adrenoceptor (Joëls and de Kloet, 1989; Pu et al., 2007, 2009). The delayed suppressive action is in line with the view that arousing effects shortly after stress are slowly normalized via glucocorticoids. Interestingly, in the dentate gyrus (but not amygdala) corticosterone was found to facilitate β-adrenoceptor-mediated actions in a rapid (presumably nongenomic) manner (Pu et al., 2007), implying that when these two hormones are present at the same location and at the same time they can act synergistically.

A second neurotransmitter that is clearly modulated by corticosteroid hormones is serotonin (5-hydroxytryptamine, 5-HT). Activation of GRs causes a gene-dependent enhancement of responses via the 5-HT$_{1A}$ receptor (Karst et al., 2000). The underlying mechanism has not been resolved, since neither 5-HT$_{1A}$ receptor expression (Karten et al., 1999) nor levels of the G-proteins (Okuhara et al., 1997), regulating proteins (e.g., RGS4; Van Gemert et al., 2006), or potassium channels involved in the 5-HT$_{1A}$ receptor signaling pathway (Muma and Beck, 1999) seem to be a target for glucocorticoids.

Until recently, glucocorticoid effects on the main excitatory neurotransmitter—glutamate—were only examined in terms of synaptically evoked responses. These studies did not demonstrate marked gene-mediated actions by corticosteroid; rather, corticosterone seemed to exert nonspecific, relatively fast effects, generally suppressing excitatory transmission (e.g., Vidal et al., 1986; Joëls and de Kloet, 1993). However, it has now become clear that corticosterone does affect glutamate-mediated transmission in a more subtle way, which nevertheless may have consequences for network function. Thus, in the CA1 hippocampal area miniature excitatory postsynaptic currents (mEPSCs) were enhanced in amplitude by glucocorticoid treatment (Karst and Joëls, 2005; Martin et al., 2009). The enhanced amplitude of mEPSCs was paralleled by a GR-dependent increase in surface expression of GluR2-subunit containing α-amino-3-hydroxy-5-methyl-4-isoxazole propionate (AMPA) receptors (Groc et al., 2008; Martin et al., 2009). Interestingly, long-term potentiation (LTP), chemically induced in hippocampal cell cultures, was no longer possible in conditions associated with enhanced GluR2-subunit surface expression (Groc et al., 2008), hinting at the possibility that LTP and GR-mediated effects on glutamate transmission share essential aspects, so that establishment of the one occludes induction of the other. This may be one explanation for the consistent finding that GR activation slowly reduces the possibility to induce LTP in the CA1 area (review by Kim and Diamond, 2002). Combined with the earlier described effects of corticosterone on calcium homeostasis, the picture emerges that, several hours after stress, transfer of information and synaptic strengthening in the CA1 region is attenuated. This may serve to restore activity after stress and protect earlier encoded information from retrograde interference.

Rapid, Nongenomic Effects of Glucocorticoids

More recently, electrophysiological experiments have shown that neuronal properties are also affected by corticosteroids at a much faster rate, thus elaborating on
earlier (usually extracellularly recorded) observations. The first study (Di et al.,
2003) in this new line reported rapid inhibition of spontaneous miniature EPSC
(mEPSC) frequency by corticosterone in parvocellular neurons of the hypothalamic
PVN; mEPSCs each represent the postsynaptic response to a neurotransmitter-
containing vesicle which fuses with the presynaptic membrane due to spontaneous
activity; that is, in the absence of the stimulation of presynaptic fibers. The effect
in the PVN was proposed to be due to a membrane-located GR which, via retro-
gradely transported endocannabinoids, inhibits presynaptic release of glutamate.
Corticosteroids similarly inhibited mEPSC frequency in magnocellular neurons of
the PVN, while at the same time enhancing spontaneous inhibitory input via a different (nonendocannabinoid) pathway (Di et al., 2005, 2009). Based on this research,
Tasker and colleagues (2006) proposed that corticosterone exerts rapid inhibitory
effects on PVN neurons, a process that may underlie the phenomenon of rapid
negative feedback in the hypothalamic–pituitary–adrenal (HPA) axis.

   Around that time we also reported rapid effects of corticosterone in the CA1
hippocampal area. Administration of corticosterone to CA1 pyramidal neurons
rapidly and reversibly increased the frequency but not amplitude of mEPSCs
(Karst et al., 2005; Figure 4.3). Paired pulse stimulation results supported the
hypothesis that corticosterone actually enhances the probability that glutamate-
containing vesicles are being released, rather than increasing the number of synaptic
contacts. Follow-up studies revealed that this involves an extracellular signal-
regulated kinase (ERK) 1/2 intracellular signaling pathway (Olijslagers et al., 2008).
We found no evidence for involvement of known retrograde messengers, for example
nitric oxide or substances acting on endocannabinoid receptors (Olijslagers et al.,
2008). CA1 neurons also displayed at least two *post*synaptic nongenomic effects of
the hormone. First, electrophysiological experiments demonstrated a rapid reduction in the amplitude of the transient K-conductance I_A, via a G-protein-dependent
pathway (Olijslagers et al., 2008). Secondly, corticosterone was shown to rapidly
promote lateral diffusion of GluR2 subunits in the plasma membrane of cultured
hippocampal cells (Groc et al., 2008).

   To induce these effects relatively high doses of corticosterone were necessary
(10 nM or higher). Despite the fact that this value is close to the K_d value of the GR,
pharmacological as well as genetic interventions proved that the rapid corticosteroid
effects in the CA1 hippocampal area do in fact critically depend on MRs (Karst
et al., 2005). This points to a new role for the MR (Joëls et al., 2008). Up until
recently, MRs were always regarded as rather dull, because they are already substantially activated even with very low (nonstress) levels of corticosteroids, so that they
can hardly play a role in the stress response. However, if indeed MRs inserted into

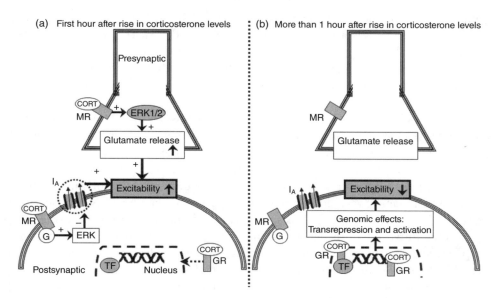

Figure 4.3 Rapid and delayed effects of corticosterone in the CA1 hippocampal area. (a) Shortly after stress, while corticosteroid levels are high, corticosterone (CORT) presumably binds to MRs inserted into the presynaptic membrane. Via an extracellular signal-regulated kinase (ERK) 1/2-dependent pathway this leads to an increased release probability of glutamate-containing vesicles. There is also evidence that MRs are inserted into the postsynaptic membrane. This involves a G-protein-coupled pathway (shown by a circled G) which inhibits the K-conductance I_A. Both effects potentially increase the excitability of CA1 neurons. (b) Some time later, when hormone levels have normalized, gene-mediated effects of corticosterone become apparent. These involve GR homodimers binding to the DNA or GR monomers which form protein–protein interactions with other transcription factors (TFs). The gene-mediated corticosteroid effects cause a delayed attenuation of CA1 neuron excitability, thus restoring local activity to prestress levels.

the membrane display an apparent 10-fold lower affinity, this fraction of the receptor pool could be very important in the initial phase of the stress response, causing rapid activation of limbic cells, in close association with other stress hormones like catecholamines.

It is not known currently to what extent these rapid corticosteroid effects show regional differentiation, like the slow gene-mediated effects. Recent evidence, though, suggests that nongenomic effects of corticosterone cannot be evoked in all limbic cells; nor do responding cells show exactly the same response. Thus, principal neurons in the central amygdala do not show rapid changes in mEPSC frequency or amplitude (Karst et al., 2010). By contrast, BLA neurons do respond to corticosterone with enhanced mEPSC frequency, via an MR-dependent process. However, these effects are not rapidly reversible. Rather, they evolve via a gene-mediated pathway in a long-lasting enhancement of mEPSC frequency; the slowly developing and lasting component of the response requires GRs. The lasting enhancement of mEPSC frequency was also seen in animals subjected to stress prior to the slice preparation. These long-lasting effects of corticosterone further contribute to the extended window of enhanced activity after stress in the BLA, thus possibly allowing preferential encoding of emotional (as compared with neutral) aspects of the stressful event.

Given these lasting responses one could wonder how these cells will respond to a new pulse of corticosterone: will cells show a further enhancement of mEPSC frequency or become refractory? As it turns out, neither is the case (Karst et al., 2010). Instead, cells with raised mEPSC frequency due to earlier stress exposure respond to renewed corticosterone application with a *reduction* of mEPSC frequency, in a manner very similar to what has been described for PVN neurons, for example involving GRs and CB1 receptors. This underlines that rapid corticosteroid effects can differ in nature, depending on the recent stress history of the organism, a phenomenon which we dubbed the *metaplasticity of the stress response* (Karst et al., 2010; see Figure 4.4), in analogy with metaplastic changes described for synaptic potentiation (Abraham and Bear, 1996). The rapid GR-dependent reduction of local excitability in the BLA seems to be the prime mechanism by which stress hormones can shut down activity in this region.

Putative Mechanism of Action

Many issues regarding nongenomic corticosteroid effects remain unanswered. For instance, the presence of MRs at the plasma membrane has not yet been demonstrated, and nor do we understand how the MR is integrated into the membrane. How is a subpopulation of MRs and GRs targeted to the membrane? How big is this population and how is the process regulated? And how are rapid nongenomic effects integrated with genomic actions? Below we present some thoughts, mostly derived from the literature on (1) rapid corticosteroid effects in cell lines and (2) rapid actions via other nuclear (e.g., estrogen) receptors, for which the current evidence regarding membrane localization is much stronger and the insight more advanced (for recent reviews see Foradori et al., 2008; Haller et al., 2008; Levin, 2008; Lösel and Wehling, 2008; Michels and Hoppe, 2008; Vasudevan and Pfaff, 2008; Grossmann and Gekle, 2009; Micevych and Dominguez, 2009; Prager and Johnson, 2009).

How can steroid receptors be incorporated in the membrane?

Steroid receptors do not have a transmembrane domain, so how can they be incorporated into or close to the membrane? One approach to investigating the regulation of membrane translocation is to determine which domain(s) of the receptor is required for membrane localization. This was first established for the estrogen

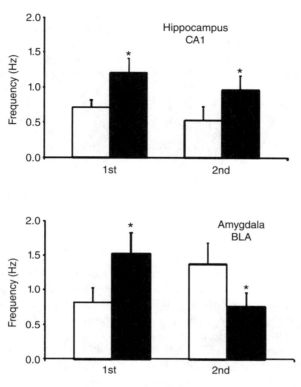

Figure 4.4 Corticosterone (black bar, top left) transiently increases the mEPSC frequency of CA1 hippocampal neurons compared to the baseline frequency observed before hormone application in vitro (open bar, top left). In response to a second application of corticosterone (top right), hippocampal neurons display a highly comparable increase in mEPSC frequency. This is different for principal neurons of the BLA (bottom graph). Thus, similar to the hippocampus, neurons in the BLA respond to a first pulse of corticosterone with an increase in mEPSC frequency. However, this increase is long lasting so that prior to a second application of corticosterone some hours later the mEPSC frequency is still high. In response to this second application of the hormone, BLA neurons now show a *decrease* in mEPSC frequency, quickly bringing the frequency back to the original value before the first hormonal treatment. Asterisks show statistical significance. Based on Karst et al. (2010).

receptor α (ERα). Transfection of an ERα transcript with only the E and F domains (ligand-binding domains) still resulted in membrane localization of the gene product (Razandi et al., 2003). Also, treatment with estradiol caused rapid signaling in cells expressing this transcript. The EF domains also determine membrane localization of the MR. A recent paper showed that transfection of either the full length or only the EF domains of the MR activates rapid signaling after aldosterone treatment (Grossmann et al., 2008), in the absence of any transactivation.

Follow-up studies with site-directed mutagenesis of ERα identified two main sequences in the EF domains that determine membrane translocation (Figure 4.5).

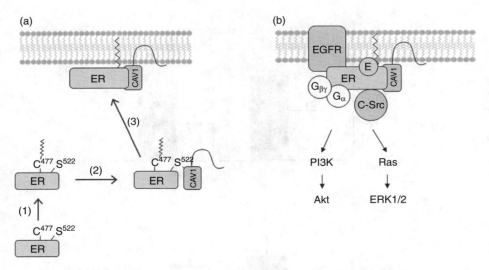

Figure 4.5 Overview of estrogen receptor (ER) membrane translocation and signaling. (a) The three essential steps in ER membrane translocation: (1) the ER is palmitoylated on cysteine[477], (2) through serine[522], the palmitoylated receptor associates with caveolin-1 (CAV1), and (3) the receptor–caveolin-1 complex translocates to the plasma membrane. Whether the ER is integrated in the inner or outer layer of the membrane is still under debate. (b) A simplified schematic of rapid estradiol signaling. Binding of the hormone (estradiol, E) activates the ER. The activated receptor binds to G_α, $G_{\beta\gamma}$, c-Src, and the epidermal growth factor receptor (EGFR). This complex activates, among others, the Ras-ERK and the phosphoinositide-3-kinase (PI3K)-Akt pathways.

The first essential amino acid is serine[522]. A S522A mutant of the ER_α showed a reduction of membrane localization by approximately 60% (Razandi et al., 2003). Importantly, this sequence was found to determine binding of the ER to caveolin-1. Caveolin-1 is a scaffolding protein that transports proteins to the membrane and is the major component of specialized membrane rafts termed caveolae (Anderson, 1998). Caveolae are characterized by an increased concentration of signaling molecules, for example kinases. The ER can bind to caveolin-1 and has been identified in caveolae (Razandi et al., 2002). The S522A mutation reduced the interaction of ER and caveolin-1 by 60%, which explains the reduced membrane localization and signaling of this ER mutant. Relevant to observations with corticosterone, GR was found to bind to caveolin-1 (Matthews et al., 2008) and downregulation of caveolin-1 prevented rapid signaling of the GR ligand dexamethasone (Matthews et al., 2008).

A second amino acid residue essential for membrane translocation of the ER is cysteine 477 (Acconcia et al., 2005). This cysteine serves as a substrate for palmitoylation of the receptor. Palmitoylation is a posttranscriptional modification often seen in membrane proteins; a palmitate tail is covalently coupled to the molecule, rendering insertion in the plasma membrane possible. First it was established that

ER$_\alpha$ is palmitoylated and that inhibition of palmitoylation prevents rapid signaling of estradiol (Pedram et al., 2007). The C447A mutant of the ER$_\alpha$ is not palmitoylated. This mutant no longer associates with caveolin-1 and membrane localization is severely diminished (Acconcia et al., 2005). Interestingly, the cysteine[447] residue was found to be part of a nine-amino acid motif required for palmitoylation (Pedram et al., 2007). This motif is present in many other steroid receptors, including the GR, the estrogen receptor β (ERβ), the androgen receptor, and the progesterone receptor. A breakthrough in the field was reached when the group of Levin established that mutation of key amino acids in this motif disrupts membrane localization and functioning of all steroid receptors investigated (Pedram et al., 2007).

Interestingly, both the GR and the MR show a similar conserved motif. The motif of the GR contains all essential groups and would be predicted to be a palmitoylation site (although the GR was not tested in the original study). The MR, by contrast, lacks the essential cysteine residue. As this cysteine provides the thiol group to which the palmitate tail is transferred, this raises the question of whether or not the MR can be palmitoylated at this or perhaps another motif.

Why do some receptors translocate to the plasma membrane?

Why does only part of the receptor population translocate to the membrane while the bulk remains in cytoplasm and nucleus, and what determines the proportion of these pools? For the ER$_\alpha$, most studies estimate that approximately 5–10% of the receptor population is localized at or in the membrane, with 90–95% of the population in the cytoplasm and nucleus (Chambliss et al., 2000). As yet it is unknown which processes contribute to this ratio, although it has been proposed that the rate-limiting step in membrane localization is the palmitoylation process, as that seems to be the initial step.

It is known that ligand binding affects membrane translocation. Most studies show that treatment with (high concentrations of) ligands reduces palmitoylation, association with caveolin-1, and membrane expression (Razandi et al., 2002; Acconcia et al., 2005; Micevych and Dominguez, 2009). In contrast, other studies report an increased membrane translocation with steroid treatment (Razandi et al., 2002; Gorosito et al., 2008). Clearly, the timing, concentration, and duration of ligand exposure will influence these effects.

Part of the reduction of membrane-localized receptor upon stimulation could be explained by internalization of ligand-bound receptors. For example, treatment of cells with fluorescent bovine serum albumin (BSA)–estradiol resulted in internalization of the BSA–estradiol (Dominguez et al., 2009; Micevych and Dominguez, 2009). The internalized complex was seen in association with mitochondria and endosomes. The ligand-bound receptor is apparently internalized, presumably in vesicles, carrying the membrane-impermeable BSA–estradiol along. It is still unknown whether the receptors are then recycled back to the membrane or degraded.

Localization studies of several classical steroid receptors by electron microscopy, immunofluorescence, or other techniques confirm membrane localization and provide further clues to special regulation. For example, expression of GR at the membrane has been shown in amygdalar neurons with electron microscopy (Johnson et al., 2005). In this area, GR localized mostly at the presynaptic density, and at dendrites and spines. This indicates that the GR might be localized only at specialized fractions of the membrane.

Signaling pathways downstream of the membrane receptor

Although steroids can be involved in very different physiological processes, ranging from stress and sexual behavior to electrolyte homeostasis, their rapid signaling pathways are actually almost identical. In general, all steroids appear to activate growth hormone pathways, most importantly the Ras-ERK pathway and the phosphoinositide-3-kinase (PI3K)-Akt pathway. For example, enhanced phosphorylation and hence activation of ERK1/2 is found for effectively all steroids tested (Pedram et al., 2007; Grossmann et al., 2008; Levin, 2008). Often these effects on phosphorylation require the expression of the corresponding (classical) receptor for the steroid. For example, treatment with aldosterone in a cell line without MR expression does not induce ERK activation, whereas a clear activation is seen after transfection of the cells with the MR transcript (Grossmann et al., 2008). The initial steps in the signaling cascades involve a physical interaction of the steroid receptors with various G-proteins and c-Src. In addition, interactions with other membrane receptors are also implicated, either with G-protein-coupled receptors or receptor tyrosine kinases. Thus, rapid aldosterone signaling through the MR in peripheral tissues activates the epidermal growth factor receptor (EGFR) (Grossmann et al., 2005). Indeed, it has been suggested that the main action of membrane-localized steroid signaling may be to initiate signaling of other receptors, such as growth factor receptors or metabotropic glutamate receptors (Boulware et al., 2005; Micevych and Dominguez, 2009).

Integration of nongenomic and genomic signaling

As described in the above sections, one hormone (corticosterone) can successively activate hippocampal cells via nongenomic pathways and subsequently dampen this activity via the genomic route. The fact that these two different actions are orchestrated by the same hormone already emphasizes that nongenomic and genomic signaling are tightly linked. This pattern is common for steroid receptors. For example, pretreatment with BSA–estradiol, which forces the steroid to exert its actions via the membrane because it cannot pass through the cellular membrane, potentiates the effects of a second pulse of *free* estradiol on both transcription and sexual behavior in female rats (Kow and Pfaff, 2004; Vasudevan et al., 2005). This potentiating effect of BSA–estradiol on lordosis can be mimicked with pharmaco-logical activation of protein kinases C or A (Kow and Pfaff, 2004). How the rapid signaling integrates with the nuclear receptor is yet unclear. Possibly, ERK and protein kinase C can phosphorylate the ER, thereby changing its nuclear function. Another possible pathway for this integration is through activation of other tran-scription factors, such as cAMP-response-element binding protein (CREB). Similar integrations might well be true for the rapid and genomic phases of the stress response.

Concluding Remarks

Although rapid corticosteroid actions in brain, at a timescale precluding genomic pathways, have been described for decades, evidence over the past few years has firmly established that such effects indeed occur. Classic receptors seem required to express these nongenomic actions, although it cannot be excluded that other mol-ecules are also involved in nongenomic effects of corticosteroids (Towle and Sze, 1983). Some aspects of receptor localization and downstream signaling pathways have been elucidated, but many more aspects are still unresolved. Dedicated studies visualizing the receptor in the membrane or during its transport, and molecular studies determining receptor properties essential for such transport as well as down-stream signaling, will be necessary to come to a better understanding of the process.

A final unresolved issue regards the functional relevance of rapid nongenomic corticosteroid actions in brain. In general these actions seem to enhance neurotrans-mitter release and local excitability during the early phase of a stress response, but this is region-dependent and also modulated by the recent stress history of the organism. More importantly, the consequences for firing rate and connectivity between brain areas in vivo still need to be addressed. These rapid actions certainly cannot be studied without taking rapid effects exerted by other stress hormones into account. Eventually, it is the collective and interactive effect of all of these hormones which determines how the brain quickly responds to stress. The fact, however, that corticosteroids do contribute to this quick response of the brain is novel and adds to the power of corticosteroid actions in the brain.

References

Abraham, W. C., & Bear, M. F. (1996). Metaplasticity: the plasticity of synaptic plasticity. *Trends in Neuroscience, 19*, 126–130.

Acconcia, F., Ascenzi, P., Bocedi, A., Spisni, E., Tomasi, V., Trentalance, A., Visca, P., & Marino, M. (2005). Palmitoylation-dependent estrogen receptor alpha membrane localization: regulation by 17beta-estradiol. *Molecular Biology of the Cell, 16*, 231–237.

Anderson, R. G. (1998). The caveolae membrane system. *Annual Review of Biochemistry, 67*, 199–225.

Bhargava, A., Mathias, R. S., McCormick, J. A., Dallman, M. F., & Pearce, D. (2002). Glucocorticoids prolong Ca(2+) transients in hippocampal-derived H19-7 neurons by repressing the plasma membrane Ca(2+)-ATPase-1. *Molecular Endocrinology*, *16*, 1629–1637.

Boulware, M. I., Weick, J. P., Becklund, B. R., Kuo, S. P., Groth, R. D., & Mermelstein, P. G. (2005). Estradiol activates group I and II metabotropic glutamate receptor signaling, leading to opposing influences on cAMP response element-binding protein. *Journal of Neuroscience*, *25*, 5066–5078.

Buchanan, T. W., & Lovallo, W. R. (2001). Enhanced memory for emotional material following stress-level cortisol treatment in humans. *Psychoneuroendocrinology*, *26*, 307–317.

Chambliss, K. L., Yuhanna, I. S., Mineo, C., Liu, P., German, Z., Sherman, T. S., Mendelsohn, M. E., Anderson, R. G., & Shaul, P. W. (2000). Estrogen receptor alpha and endothelial nitric oxide synthase are organized into a functional signaling module in caveolae. *Circulation Research*, *87*, E44–E52.

Chameau, P., Qin, Y., Spijker, S., Smit, G., & Joëls, M. (2007). Glucocorticoids specifically enhance L-type calcium current amplitude and affect calcium channel subunit expression in the mouse hippocampus. *Journal of Neurophysiology*, *97*, 5–14.

Datson, N. A., Morsink, M. C., Meijer, O. C., & de Kloet, E. R. (2008). Central corticosteroid actions: search for gene targets. *European Journal of Pharmacology*, *583*, 272–289.

de Kloet, E. R., Joëls, M., & Holsboer, F. (2005). Stress and the brain: from adaptation to disease. *Nature Reviews Neuroscience*, *6*, 463–475.

Di, S., Malcher-Lopes, R., Halmos, K. C., & Tasker, J. G. (2003). Nongenomic glucocorticoid inhibition via endocannabinoid release in the hypothalamus: a fast feedback mechanism. *Journal of Neuroscience*, *23*, 4850–4857.

Di, S., Malcher-Lopes, R., Marcheselli, V. L., Bazan, N. G., & Tasker, J. G. (2005). Rapid glucocorticoid-mediated endocannabinoid release and opposing regulation of glutamate and gamma-aminobutyric acid inputs to hypothalamic magnocellular neurons. *Endocrinology*, *146*, 4292–4301.

Di, S., Maxson, M. M., Franco, A., & Tasker, J. G. (2009). Glucocorticoids regulate glutamate and GABA synapse-specific retrograde transmission via divergent nongenomic signaling pathways. *Journal of Neuroscience*, *29*, 393–401.

Dolphin, A. C. (2009). Calcium channel diversity: multiple roles of calcium channel subunits. *Current Opinion in Neurobiology*, *19*, 237–244.

Dominguez, R., Hu, E., Zhou, M., & Baudry, M. (2009). 17beta-Estradiol-mediated neuroprotection and ERK activation require a pertussis toxin-sensitive mechanism involving GRK2 and beta-arrestin-1. *Journal of Neuroscience*, *29*, 4228–4238.

Dubrovsky, B., Gijsbers, K., Filipini, D., & Birmingham, M. K. (1993). Effects of adrenocortical steroids on long-term potentiation in the limbic system: basic mechanisms and behavioral consequences. *Cellular and Molecular Neurobiology*, *13*, 399–414.

Duvarci, S., & Paré, D. (2007). Glucocorticoids enhance the excitability of principal basolateral amygdala neurons. *Journal of Neuroscience*, *27*, 4482–4491.

Ferry, B., Magistretti, P. J., & Pralong, E. (1997). Noradrenaline modulates glutamate-mediated neurotransmission in the rat basolateral amygdala in vitro. *European Journal of Neuroscience*, *9*, 1356–1364.

Foradori, C. D., Weiser, M. J., & Handa, R. J. (2008). Non-genomic actions of androgens. *Frontiers in Neuroendocrinology*, *29*, 169–181.

Gorosito, S. V., Lorenzo, A. G., & Cambiasso, M. J. (2008). Estrogen receptor alpha is expressed on the cell-surface of embryonic hypothalamic neurons. *Neuroscience, 154,* 1173–1177.

Groc, L., Choquet, D., & Chaouloff, F. (2008). The stress hormone corticosterone conditions AMPAR surface trafficking and synaptic potentiation. *Nature Neuroscience, 11,* 868–870.

Grossmann, C., & Gekle, M. (2009). New aspects of rapid aldosterone signaling. *Molecular and Cellular Endocrinology, 308,* 53–62.

Grossmann, C., Benesic, A., Krug, A. W., Freudinger, R., Mildenberger, S., Gassner, B., & Gekle, M. (2005). Human mineralocorticoid receptor expression renders cells responsive for nongenotropic aldosterone actions. *Molecular Endocrinology, 19,* 1697–1710.

Grossmann, C., Freudinger, R., Mildenberger, S., Husse, B., & Gekle, M. (2008). EF domains are sufficient for nongenomic mineralocorticoid receptor actions. *Journal of Biological Chemistry, 283,* 7109–7116.

Haller, J., Mikics, E., & Makara, G. B. (2008). The effects of non-genomic glucocorticoid mechanisms on bodily functions and the central neural system. A critical evaluation of findings. *Frontiers in Neuroendocrinology, 29,* 273–291.

Joëls, M., & de Kloet, E. R. (1989). Effects of glucocorticoids and norepinephrine on the excitability in the hippocampus. *Science, 245,* 1502–1505.

Joëls, M., & de Kloet, E. R. (1993). Corticosteroid actions on amino acid-mediated transmission in rat CA1 hippocampal cells. *Journal of Neuroscience, 13,* 4082–4090.

Joëls, M., Karst, H., Krugers, H. J., & Lucassen, P. J. (2007). Chronic stress: implications for neuronal morphology, function and neurogenesis. *Frontiers in Neuroendocrinology, 28,* 72–96.

Joëls, M., Karst, H., DeRijk, R., & de Kloet, E. R. (2008). The coming out of the brain mineralocorticoid receptor. *Trends in Neuroscience, 31,* 1–7.

Johnson, L. R., Farb, C., Morrison, J. H., McEwen, B. S., & LeDoux, J. E. (2005). Localization of glucocorticoid receptors at postsynaptic membranes in the lateral amygdala. *Neuroscience, 136,* 289–299.

Karst, H., & Joëls, M. (2005). Corticosterone slowly enhances miniature excitatory postsynaptic current amplitude in mice CA1 hippocampal cells. *Journal of Neurophysiology, 94,* 3479–3486.

Karst, H., Wadman, W. J., & Joëls, M. (1994). Corticosteroid receptor-dependent modulation of calcium currents in rat hippocampal CA1 neurons. *Brain Research, 649,* 234–242.

Karst, H., Karten, Y. J., Reichardt, H. M., de Kloet, E. R., Schütz, G., & Joëls, M. (2000). Corticosteroid actions in hippocampus require DNA binding of glucocorticoid receptor homodimers. *Nature Neuroscience, 3,* 977–978.

Karst, H., Nair, S., Velzing, E., Rumpff-van Essen, L., Slagter, E., Shinnick-Gallagher, P., & Joëls, M. (2002). Glucocorticoids alter calcium conductances and calcium channel subunit expression in basolateral amygdala neurons. *European Journal of Neuroscience, 16,* 1083–1089.

Karst, H., Berger, S., Turiault, M., Tronche, F., Schütz, G., & Joëls, M. (2005). Mineralocorticoid receptors are indispensable for nongenomic modulation of hippocampal glutamate transmission by corticosterone. *Proceedings of the National Academy of Sciences USA, 102,* 19204–19207.

Karst, H., Berger, S., Erdmann, G., Schütz, G., & Joëls, M. (2010). Metaplasticity of amygdalar responses to the stress hormone corticosterone. *Proceedings of the National Academy of Sciences USA, 107,* 14449–14454.

Karten, Y. J., Nair, S. M., van Essen, L., Sibug, R., & Joëls, M. (1999). Long-term exposure to high corticosterone levels attenuates serotonin responses in rat hippocampal CA1 neurons. *Proceedings of the National Academy of Sciences USA, 96,* 13456–13461.

Kelly, M. J., & Rønnekleiv, O. K. (2009). Control of CNS neuronal excitability by estrogens via membrane-initiated signaling. *Molecular and Cellular Endocrinology, 308,* 17–25.

Kerr, D. S., Campbell, L. W., Hao, S. Y., & Landfield, P. W. (1989). Corticosteroid modulation of hippocampal potentials: increased effect with aging. *Science, 245,* 1505–1509.

Kerr, D. S., Campbell, L. W., Thibault, O., & Landfield, P. W. (1992). Hippocampal glucocorticoid receptor activation enhances voltage-dependent Ca2+ conductances: relevance to brain aging. *Proceedings of the National Academy of Sciences USA, 89,* 8527–8531.

Kim, J. J., & Diamond, D. M. (2002). The stressed hippocampus, synaptic plasticity and lost memories. *Nature Reviews Neuroscience, 3,* 453–462.

Kole, M. H., Koolhaas, J. M., Luiten, P. G., & Fuchs, E. (2001). High-voltage-activated Ca2+ currents and the excitability of pyramidal neurons in the hippocampal CA3 subfield in rats depend on corticosterone and time of day. *Neuroscience Letters, 307,* 53–56.

Kow, L. M., & Pfaff, D. W. (2004). The membrane actions of estrogens can potentiate their lordosis behavior-facilitating genomic actions. *Proceedings of the National Academy of Sciences USA, 101,* 12354–12357.

Levin, E. R. (2008). Rapid signaling by steroid receptors. *American Journal of Physiology Regulatory, Integrative and Comparative Physiology, 295,* R1425–R1430.

Liebmann, L., Karst, H., Sidiropoulou, K., van Gemert, N., Meijer, O. C., Poirazi, P., & Joëls, M. (2008). Differential effects of corticosterone on the slow afterhyperpolarization in the basolateral amygdala and CA1 region: possible role of calcium channel subunits. *Journal of Neurophysiology, 99,* 958–968.

Lightman, S. L., Wiles, C. C., Atkinson, H. C., Henley, D. E., Russell, G. M., Leendertz, J. A., McKenna, M. A., Spiga, F., Wood, S. A., & Conway-Campbell, B. L. (2008). The significance of glucocorticoid pulsatility. *European Journal of Pharmacology, 583,* 255–262.

Lösel, R. M., & Wehling, M. (2008). Classic versus non-classic receptors for nongenomic mineralocorticoid responses: emerging evidence. *Frontiers in Neuroendocrinology, 29,* 258–267.

Martin, S., Henley, J. M., Holman, D., Zhou, M., Wiegert, O., van Spronsen, M., Joëls, M., Hoogenraad, C. C., & Krugers, H. J. (2009). Corticosterone alters AMPAR mobility and facilitates bidirectional synaptic plasticity. *PLoS One, 4,* e4714.

Matthews, L., Berry, A., Ohanian, V., Ohanian, J., Garside, H., & Ray, D. (2008). Caveolin mediates rapid glucocorticoid effects and couples glucocorticoid action to the antiproliferative program. *Molecular Endocrinology, 22,* 1320–1330.

McIntyre, C. K., Hatfield, T., & McGaugh, J. L. (2002). Amygdala norepinephrine levels after training predict inhibitory avoidance retention performance in rats. *European Journal of Neuroscience, 16,* 1223–1226.

Micevych, P., & Dominguez, R. (2009). Membrane estradiol signaling in the brain. *Frontiers in Neuroendocrinology, 30,* 315–327.

Michels, G., & Hoppe, U. C. (2008). Rapid actions of androgens. *Frontiers in Neuroendocrinology, 29,* 182–198.

Muma, N. A., & Beck, S. G. (1999). Corticosteroids alter G protein inwardly rectifying potassium channels protein levels in hippocampal subfields. *Brain Research, 839,* 331–335.

Okuhara, D. Y., Beck, S. G., & Muma, N. A. (1997). Corticosterone alters G protein alphasubunit levels in the rat hippocampus. *Brain Research, 745,* 144–151.

Olijslagers, J. E., de Kloet, E. R., Elgersma, Y., van Woerden, G. M., Joëls, M., & Karst, H. (2008). Rapid changes in hippocampal CA1 pyramidal cell function via pre- as well as postsynaptic membrane mineralocorticoid receptors. *European Journal of Neuroscience, 27,* 2542–2550.

Orchinik, M., Murray, T. F., & Moore, F. L. (1991). A corticosteroid receptor in neuronal membranes. *Science, 252,* 1848–1851.

Pariante, C. M. (2008). The role of multi-drug resistance p-glycoprotein in glucocorticoid function: studies in animals and relevance in humans. *European Journal of Pharmacology, 583,* 263–271.

Pedram, A., Razandi, M., Sainson, R. C., Kim, J. K., Hughes, C. C., & Levin, E. R. (2007). A conserved mechanism for steroid receptor translocation to the plasma membrane. *Journal of Biological Chemistry, 282,* 22278–22288.

Pfaff, D. W., Silva, M. T., & Weiss, J. M. (1971). Telemetered recording of hormone effects on hippocampal neurons. *Science, 172,* 394–395.

Prager, E. M., & Johnson, L. R. (2009). Stress at the synapse: signal transduction mechanisms of adrenal steroids at neuronal membranes. *Science Signaling, 2,* re5.

Pu, Z., Krugers, H. J., & Joëls, M. (2007). Corticosterone time-dependently modulates beta-adrenergic effects on long-term potentiation in the hippocampal dentate gyrus. *Learning and Memory, 14,* 359–367.

Pu, Z., Krugers, H. J., & Joëls, M. (2009). Beta-adrenergic facilitation of synaptic plasticity in the rat basolateral amygdala in vitro is gradually reversed by corticosterone. *Learning and Memory, 16,* 155–160.

Quirarte, G. L., Roozendaal, B., & McGaugh, J. L. (1997). Glucocorticoid enhancement of memory storage involves noradrenergic activation in the basolateral amygdala. *Proceedings of the National Academy of Sciences USA, 94,* 14048–14053.

Razandi, M., Oh, P., Pedram, A., Schnitzer, J., & Levin, E. R. (2002). ERs associate with and regulate the production of caveolin: implications for signaling and cellular actions. *Molecular Endocrinology, 16,* 100–115.

Razandi, M., Alton, G., Pedram, A., Ghonshani, S., Webb, P., & Levin, E. R. (2003). Identification of a structural determinant necessary for the localization and function of estrogen receptor alpha at the plasma membrane. *Molecular and Cellular Biology, 23,* 1633–1646.

Revollo, J. R., & Cidlowski, J. A. (2009). Mechanisms generating diversity in glucocorticoid receptor signaling. *Annals of the New York Academy of Sciences, 1179,* 167–178.

Sapolsky, R. M. (1994). The physiological relevance of glucocorticoid endangerment of the hippocampus. *Annals of the New York Academy of Sciences, 746,* 294–304.

Tasker, J. G., Di, S., & Malcher-Lopes, R. (2006). Minireview: rapid glucocorticoid signaling via membrane-associated receptors. *Endocrinology, 147,* 5549–5556.

Towle, A. C., & Sze, P. Y. (1983). Steroid binding to synaptic plasma membrane: differential binding of glucocorticoids and gonadal steroids. *Journal of Steroid Biochemistry, 18,* 135–143.

Van Gemert, N. G., Meijer, O. C., Morsink, M. C., & Joëls, M. (2006) Effect of brief corticosterone administration on SGK1 and RGS4 mRNA expression in rat hippocampus. *Stress, 9,* 165–170.

Van Gemert, N. G., Carvalho, D. M., Karst, H., van der Laan, S., Zhang, M., Meijer, O. C., Hell, J. W., & Joëls, M. (2009). Dissociation between rat hippocampal CA1 and dentate gyrus cells in their response to corticosterone: effects on calcium channel protein and current. *Endocrinology, 150,* 4615–4624.

Vasudevan, N., & Pfaff, D. W. (2008). Non-genomic actions of estrogens and their interactions with genomic actions in the brain. *Frontiers in Neuroendocrinology, 29,* 238–257.

Vasudevan, N., Kow, L. M., & Pfaff, D. (2005). Integration of steroid hormone initiated membrane action to genomic function in the brain. *Steroids, 70,* 388–396.

Vidal, C., Jordan, W., & Zieglgänsberger, W. (1986). Corticosterone reduces the excitability of hippocampal pyramidal cells in vitro. *Brain Research, 383,* 54–59.

5

Stress Effects on the Brain
Intracellular Signaling Cascades, Epigenetic
Mechanisms, and Implications for Behavior

Johannes M. H. M. Reul, Andrew Collins, and
María Gutièrrez-Mecinas

Introduction

The response of mammalian organisms to a stressful event is highly complex and manifold. In people, examples of psychologically or emotionally stressful events would be situations of domestic dispute, assault, or being fired from a job, whereas in (other) animals an attack by a predator would be an example. The so-called stress response to such events involves autonomic and neuroendocrine changes which are aimed to accommodate the immediate physiological needs and to support adaptive behavioral responses of the organism. The overall aim of these responses is to cope with the threat and to prepare the organism for future recurrences. Both the acute and long-term adaptations are vital for survival and to stay healthy. The brain plays a major role in the coordination of these responses to a stressful event. Furthermore, as an important means to be prepared if events reoccur in the future, the brain engages in the formation of episodic memories of the endured event. It is a long-standing observation that memories of emotionally stressful events are strong and often last for a life time. Such memories are established by a complex interplay between parts of the limbic system (e.g., amygdala, hippocampus) and regions of the neocortex. The amygdala processes the emotional aspects of the event, whereas the hippocampus is involved in the storage of episodic (contextual) memories of the event. Both limbic structures play major roles in the organization of the stress response. Glucocorticoid hormones which are released as part of the neuroendocrine response to the stressful event play a critical role in enhancing the formation of such memories. Thus, glucocorticoids exert actions not only during and shortly

The Handbook of Stress: Neuropsychological Effects on the Brain, First Edition.
Edited by Cheryl D. Conrad.
© 2011 Blackwell Publishing Ltd. Published 2011 by Blackwell Publishing Ltd.

after stressful events but they are also greatly involved in long-term cognitive adaptations related to the events.

The Inter-relationship of Stress and Cognition

Particularly when investigating the effects of psychological or emotional stress it is important to consider the cognitive implications of such events. Such stressors involve sensory and associative processing by higher limbic brain structures such as the amygdala and hippocampus, and the neocortex. Hence, as a consequence various aspects (e.g., context) of the event will be stored in memory which will impact upon not only the behavioral responses but also on the physiological responses if a similar event reoccurs in the future. Conversely, behavioral tests that are commonly regarded as learning and memory paradigms may present markedly stressful situations. For instance, the Morris water-maze test, which is generally considered as a paradigm for spatial memory formation, is very stressful because forcing rodents such as rats and mice to swim is regarded as aversive. There is an obvious similarity here with the forced-swim test. Consequently, during the learning trials substantial amounts of glucocorticoid hormones are secreted and, moreover, these hormones have been shown to be of critical importance for the process of memory consolidation (Oitzl and de Kloet, 1992; Sandi et al., 1997; Beylin and Shors, 2003; Roozendaal et al., 2006; Bilang-Bleuel et al., 2005; Reul and Chandramohan, 2007; Reul et al., 2009). Thus, behavioral tests, particularly in rodents, inherently present a stressful situation for the subject. Given that glucocorticoid hormones strongly facilitate the formation of memories of the experienced event, the hormone effect may be regarded as a physiological mechanism to give salience to the endured event.

The forced-swim test has been for many years the subject of considerable controversy. This test is also called the Porsolt forced-swim test (Porsolt et al., 1977). In this test, rodents like rats or mice are placed in a tank filled with water (usually 25°C; Linthorst et al., 2008) from which they can neither escape nor touch the bottom. Mostly, the test consists of a 15-min exposure on the first day and a second exposure (i.e., the retest) of 5 min on the next day. In the first test, in an attempt to escape from the water the animal will initially try to climb against the wall of the beaker (also called struggling) and swim. Later, that is after several minutes, the animal will mainly show immobility or floating behavior whereby the animal hardly moves except for an occasional paw movement to keep the head above the water. In the retest, after a short episode of struggling and swimming the animal will show mainly immobility behavior—that is, about 75% of the 5-min period—which is much more than the time spent on this behavior during the first 5 min of the initial test (approximately 20%). The controversy lies in the interpretation of the immobility response. Some researchers interpret immobility behavior as an indication that the animal has given up, thus showing helpless or *depressive* behavior (Porsolt et al., 1977; Lucki, 1997). This interpretation is strengthened by the observation that many, but not all, antidepressant drugs decrease immobility behavior (Porsolt et al.,

1977; Lucki, 1997). However, the drug-treatment regimen usually consists of three injections (i.e., one immediately after the initial test, and two injections, 5 hr and 1 hr, before the retest). Thus, reflected by the difference in treatment regimens, the *antidepressant* behavioral effect of antidepressant drugs in the forced-swim test is in stark contrast with the clinical effects of these drugs which take at least 4–6 weeks of chronic treatment to develop.

Other researchers interpret the behavioral immobility response in the retest as an adaptive behavioral strategy (De Pablo et al., 1989; Korte, 2001; Bilang-Bleuel et al., 2005; West, 1990). They regard this behavioral response as a learned response because in the retest the animal will remember that it has been in this inescapable situation before and, importantly, was saved from it. Therefore, it is likely that the animal will recall the experience of the previous day and show more immobility behavior to conserve energy. This notion implies that the animal forms memories of the endured forced-swim event and the increased immobility behavior in the retest would be a reflection of the recollection of such memories. One may argue that 1-day-old memories can hardly be called long-term memories. Recently, however, we found that if rats were retested 4 weeks after the initial test they indeed showed the learned behavioral immobility response. This suggests that the memories of the first forced-swim event had lasted for at least 4 weeks (M. Gutièrrez-Mecinas, A. Collins, and J.M.H.M. Reul, unpublished observations).

In terms of underlying signaling mechanisms regarding the learned immobility response, a long-standing observation is the critical requirement of elevated glucocorticoid hormone levels during the consolidation phase after the initial forced-swim session (Veldhuis et al., 1985; de Kloet et al., 1988). In a series of studies it was shown that glucocorticoid receptor (GR) activation was required, in terms of time, immediately after the initial test and, in terms of neuroanatomical localization, specifically in the dentate gyrus of the hippocampus to obtain a normal expression of behavioral immobility in the retest. Although substantial work still needs to be done to harmonize experimental designs and neuroanatomical targets, the dependence of the forced-swim test of glucocorticoid hormones corresponds with the hormone requirements seen in the Morris water maze and contextual fear-conditioning paradigms (Oitzl and de Kloet, 1992; Sandi et al., 1997; Revest et al., 2005). Moreover, in recent years evidence has been accumulating that the learned immobility response in the forced-swim test, contextual fear conditioning, and Morris water-maze learning share a critical involvement of the *N*-methyl-D-aspartate (NMDA)/extracellular signal-regulated kinase (ERK) mitogen-activated protein kinase (MAPK) signaling pathway and downstream epigenetic mechanisms affecting gene expression (Reul and Chandramohan, 2007; Chandramohan et al., 2008; Reul et al., 2009; Sweatt, 2001; Chwang et al., 2006, 2007; Revest et al., 2005). Below an account is given regarding the neurotransmitters, signaling pathways, and epigenetic mechanisms, taking place in the hippocampus, that play a major role in stress-related learning and memory in behavioral models such as the forced-swim test, Morris water-maze paradigm, and contextual fear conditioning. These pathways and mechanisms will be addressed within their cellular context.

NMDA Receptor-mediated Signaling and Neuroplasticity

A role of the neurotransmitter glutamate in neuroplasticity processes underlying (stress-related) learning and memory has been in the focus of research for many years. Particularly with regard to neuroplasticity processes, the glutamate-binding NMDA receptor has received much attention. Upon ligand binding and concomitant membrane depolarization, NMDA receptors act as Na^+-/Ca^{2+}-permeable cation channels resulting in a rise of intracellular calcium concentrations, leading to the activation of calcium/calmodulin-dependent protein kinase II (CaMKII), protein kinase C (PKC), protein kinase A (PKA; via calcium-mediated activation of adenylate cyclases 1 and 8), and the ERK MAPK signaling cascade (Impey et al., 1999). ERK MAPK signaling is critical for synaptic plasticity (e.g., dendritic spine formation; Sweatt, 2001, 2004; Impey et al., 1999), long-term potentiation (LTP; Impey et al., 1999), and learning and memory (Impey et al., 1999). A number of downstream transcription factors and immediate-early gene products, such as cAMP-response-element binding protein (CREB), early growth response factor 1 (Egr-1; also named zif268, krox24, NGFI-A, TIS8, or ZENK), c-Fos, and Arc, can be activated or induced by these signaling pathways and are thought via modulation of gene transcription to play a significant role in these neuroplasticity processes and memory formation.

Epigenetic Mechanisms in Gene Transcription

During the last decade it has become clear that gene transcription is highly controlled by epigenetic mechanisms at the chromatin level (Figure 5.1; Spencer and Davie, 2000; Jaskelioff and Peterson, 2003). Chromatin consists of DNA–histone protein complexes building together a so-called nucleosomal structure. Nucleosomes are the basic building blocks of chromatin. Epigenetic mechanisms affect the chromatin structure and function without changing the DNA code. They include the covalent modifications (i.e., involving strong chemical bonds) of histone molecules and the methylation of DNA. In this chapter we will focus on the role of histone modifications. Histone proteins such as histone H3 have evolutionarily highly conserved N-terminal tails which stand out from the nucleosome and can be subjected to covalent modifications such as acetylation, phosphorylation, methylation, and others (Figure 5.1; Strahl and Allis, 2000). These histone modifications, and more importantly the combination of various histone modifications, determine the functional state of the chromatin. The acetylation of lysine amino acids in histone H3 and H4 is seen in open, transcriptionally active chromatin (Strahl and Allis, 2000). Some immediate-early genes such as c-*fos* and c-*jun* (Clayton et al., 2000), and other genes (e.g., matrix metalloprotease-1, MMP-1; Martens et al., 2003) require the phosphorylation of serine 10 (S10p) combined with the acetylation of lysine 14 (K14ac) for induction of gene expression. The specific combination of histone H3

(a)

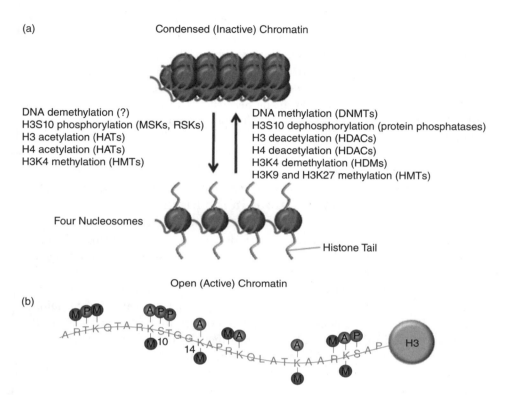

Condensed (Inactive) Chromatin

DNA demethylation (?)
H3S10 phosphorylation (MSKs, RSKs)
H3 acetylation (HATs)
H4 acetylation (HATs)
H3K4 methylation (HMTs)

DNA methylation (DNMTs)
H3S10 dephosphorylation (protein phosphatases)
H3 deacetylation (HDACs)
H4 deacetylation (HDACs)
H3K4 demethylation (HDMs)
H3K9 and H3K27 methylation (HMTs)

Four Nucleosomes

Histone Tail

Open (Active) Chromatin

(b)

Figure 5.1 Basically, the chromatin can be in two distinct functional states. It is either in a condensed, inactive state in which it is transcriptionally inactive or in an open, active state in which it can be transcriptionally active (a). In the open state the chromatin is accessible for transcription factors whereas in the condensed state it isn't. The different states are associated with DNA (de)methylation and various covalent modifications of amino acids in the N-terminal tails of histone molecules. It is thought that the various modifications do not evoke chromatin remodeling themselves but rather if these modifications occur they result in the recruitment of chromatin remodeling or silencing factors, as appropriate. The involved enzymes are given in parentheses. The enzyme responsible for DNA demethylation has not been discovered yet, hence the question mark. (b) Part of the N-terminal tail of histone H3 and some of the potential modifications (i.e., phosphorylation, acetylation, methylation) of amino acids in this histone tail. DNMT, DNA methyltransferase; HAT, histone acetyltransferase; HDAC, histone deacetylase; HDM, histone demethylase; HMT, histone methyl transferase; MSK, mitogen- and stress-activated kinase; RSK, ribosomal S6 kinase.

modifications (or *marks*) may be required for the recruitment of specific nuclear factors to the chromatin to allow induction of transcription. The methylation of histone H3 tails is associated with transcriptional activation as well as gene silencing. Methylation of the H3K4 mark results in gene activation whereas H3K9 and H3K27 methylation leads to gene silencing (Akbarian and Huang, 2009). The combination of the H3K9 methylation and H3S10 phosphorylation marks is associated with gene silencing (Sabbattini et al., 2007). As the combinatorial H3S10p/K14ac marks are thought to play a role in the local opening of condensed, inactive chromatin these histone modifications may be crucial for the transcriptional activation of dormant genes (Cheung et al., 2000; Clayton et al., 2000). However, whether the H3S10p/K14ac marks are required for any gene located in condensed heterochromatin still needs to be firmly established. Even the necessity of these histone marks for the induction of c-Fos may depend on the cell type or tissue under investigation (see below).

Emotional Challenges Result in Transcription-related Histone Modifications in the Brain

Ten years ago we made the serendipitous finding of neurons expressing H3S10p in the rat and mouse brain (Bilang-Bleuel et al., 2000). Using an antibody against H3S10p (also recognizing H3S10p acetylated at lysine-14, i.e., H3S10p/K14ac; Chandramohan et al., 2007; Y. Chandramohan and J.M.H.M. Reul, unpublished observations) neurons were found showing a speckled nuclear immunostaining pattern. H3S10p-positive neurons were mainly located in the dentate gyrus of the hippocampus and there were only a few neurons scattered in the amygdala, neo-cortex, and striatum (Bilang-Bleuel et al., 2005; Chandramohan et al., 2007). Our studies indicated that if phosphorylated at serine 10 histone H3 will be acetylated at lysine 14, thus forming H3S10p/K14ac (Chandramohan et al., 2007). As we were interested in how animals adapt to and learn from psychologically stressful events we studied whether such challenges would affect the number of neurons expressing H3S10p/K14ac. Confronting rats or mice with forced swimming, a predator or a novel environment, resulted in a marked rise in the number of H3S10p/K14ac-positive neurons specifically in the dentate gyrus (Bilang-Bleuel et al., 2005; Chandramohan et al., 2007, 2008). The increase peaked at 1–2 hr after the challenge and returned to baseline levels after approximately 4 hr (Chandramohan et al., 2007, 2008). Thus, the response was relatively fast and transient showing that epi-genetic changes underlying gene expression can be highly dynamic. Morris water-maze learning (Y. Chandramohan and J.M.H.M. Reul, unpublished observations; Chwang et al., 2007) and fear conditioning (Y. Chandramohan, B. Sacchetti, P. Strata, and J.M.H.M. Reul, unpublished observations; Chwang et al., 2007) also resulted in increases in the number of H3S10p/K14ac-expressing neurons in the dentate gyrus. The question arose of why the combinatorial H3S10p/K14ac mark in dentate neurons responded similarly to such different stimuli. The response pattern of H3S10p/K14ac-positive neurons in the dentate gyrus indeed does not give clues about the challenge the animal has been confronted with (see for instance Bilang-Bleuel et al., 2005; Chandramohan et al., 2007, 2008). These findings none-theless correspond with the role of the dentate gyrus in learning and memory processes.

The Dentate Gyrus Shows Sparse Epigenetic Responses

The dentate gyrus is a part of the hippocampus which is one of the principal structures of the limbic system. It plays a major role in learning and memory processes.
As the main neuroanatomical gate of the hippocampus, the dentate gyrus receives
inputs from the entorhinal cortex, the principal neocortical region that feeds integrated sensory and other information into the limbic system (Witter, 2007). After
processing, the dentate neurons pass this information on to pyramidal neurons in
the other hippocampal cell fields (mainly CA3; where CA means cornu ammonis,
a subregion of the hippocampus) where the information is integrated with other,
stimulus-specific information for further processing to yield appropriate physiological and behavioral responses and, ultimately, formation of memories formation
of the endured event (Rolls and Kesner, 2006; Treves and Rolls, 1994). Thus, when
animals are challenged, as a result of the sensory information flow, granule neurons
in the dentate gyrus are activated. γ-Aminobutyric acid (GABA)ergic interneurons
exert a high-tonic inhibitory control on dentate granule neurons and therefore only
relatively few granule cells (fewer than 5%) become activated. Such sparse activation
occurs irrespective of the stimulus (e.g., novelty, forced swimming, Morris water-
maze learning; in contrast, strong depolarizing agents, such as kainate or electroconvulsive shocks, evoke a widespread activation; Rolls and Kesner, 2006;
Bilang-Bleuel et al., 2005; Chandramohan et al., 2007, 2008; Chawla et al., 2005).
Indeed, recently we found that GABA is an important controller of baseline and
novelty-evoked H3S10p/K14ac and c-Fos in dentate neurons (Papadopoulos et al.,
2008, 2011; see below). Thus, the neuronal activation pattern in the dentate gyrus
seems to be a reflection of the degree to which salience is given to afferent sensory
stimuli. It appears that the enhanced H3S10p/K14ac expression in dentate granule
neurons after such stimuli is part of the sparse activation response of this hippocampal region.

Despite the abundance of evidence favoring a role of the H3S10p/K14ac marks
in gene activation, until now surprisingly few genes have been identified the expression of which depends on these epigenetic marks. Clayton et al. (2000) demonstrated in cell culture experiments in vitro that phosphoacetylated histone H3 is
associated with the induction of the immediate-early genes c-*fos* and c-*jun*. Later
studies of Martens and colleagues (2003) showed that H3S10p is involved in MMP-1
induction. We showed for the first time in vivo that the H3S10p/K14ac marks in
rat and mouse dentate granule neurons are associated with c-Fos induction
(Chandramohan et al., 2007, 2008; Gutièrrez-Mecinas et al., 2009). A first indication
was based on the strictly parallel changes in H3S10p/K14ac-positive and c-Fos-
positive neurons after various experimental manipulations and the colocalization
of the epigenetic mark and gene product in the same dentate neurons based on
immunofluorescence analyses (Chandramohan et al., 2007, 2008). Recently, we
showed using chromatin immunoprecipitation (ChIP) and quantitative polymerase

chain reaction that forced swimming indeed evoked the combinatorial histone marks in the c-*fos* promoter region in dentate neurons (Gutièrrez-Mecinas et al., 2009). Moreover, forced swimming also resulted in histone H4 hyperacetylation, but not H3 hyperacetylation, in this promoter (Gutièrrez-Mecinas et al., 2009). A similar pattern of histone modification marks has been reported for the hippocampal c-*fos* promoter after electroconvulsive shock treatment, which is known to elicit a full-blown c-Fos induction in the hippocampus including the dentate gyrus (Tsankova et al., 2004). In contrast, the neocortex which is also known to induce c-Fos after forced swimming (Bilang-Bleuel et al., 2002) presented a different pattern of epigenetic marks at the c-*fos* promoter. ChIP revealed hyperacetylation of H4 in the c-*fos* promoter after forced swimming but no changes in H3S10p/K14ac and acetylated H3 (Gutièrrez-Mecinas et al., 2009). Presently, studies on elucidating which other genes are associated with the H3S10p/K14ac mark in hippocampus and other brain regions are underway.

These observations confirm earlier findings that the rise in H3S10p/K14ac observed after stressful challenges such as forced swimming and novelty is exclusively occurring in the dentate gyrus and is not seen elsewhere in the brain (Bilang-Bleuel et al., 2005; Chandramohan et al., 2007, 2008). Thus, in different neuronal populations in the brain expression of the same gene may be driven by epigenetically diverse mechanisms. Furthermore, in different neurons epigenetic mechanisms controlling expression of the gene may be steered by distinct signaling pathways.

Integration of Extracellular and Intracellular Pathways Signaling to the Chromatin

Requirement of concomitant signaling through the NMDA receptor and GR

For survival, an organism needs to adapt to and learn from challenges imposed by its environment. Evidence has been accumulating that the cognitive processing of environmental challenges involves epigenetic and gene expression changes in the brain. The environment impacts on the brain through activation of various signaling pathways. It is however still unclear how signaling molecules affect epigenetic mechanisms in neurons. Recently we reported that the neurotransmitter glutamate and the glucocorticoid hormone corticosterone (acting through the NMDA receptor and the GR, respectively) are both required for the forced-swimming- and novelty-induced histone H3 phosphoacetylation and c-Fos induction in dentate neurons (Bilang-Bleuel et al., 2005; Chandramohan et al., 2007, 2008). The requirement for activation of both pathways was supported by the finding that the sole injection of rats with a GR-occupying dose of corticosterone was ineffective (Chandramohan et al., 2007). The mineralocorticoid receptor and the gaseous messenger nitric oxide were not involved (Chandramohan et al., 2007, 2008), suggesting there is specificity regarding the participating signaling molecules.

Epigenetic responses in the dentate gyrus are under GABAergic control

It is thought that based on electrophysiological and computational studies the encoding of sensory information within the dentate gyrus is conducted orthogonally by sparsely distributed granule neurons (Rolls and Kesner, 2006). The sparse neuronal activation pattern is required for appropriate information processing (Rolls and Kesner, 2006; Leutgeb et al., 2007) and involves an important role of the strong tonic inhibitory control exerted by local GABAergic interneurons (Rolls and Kesner, 2006; Treves and Rolls, 1994). Thus, granule neurons seem to only become excited if the stimulus is strong enough to overcome the GABAergic inhibitory tone. The excitation is brought about by glutamate acting via NMDA receptors (Collingridge and Singer, 1990; Richter-Levin et al., 1995; McHugh et al., 2007; Treves and Rolls, 1994).

As psychological challenges evoke a sparse pattern of H3S10p/K14ac and c-Fos in dentate granule neurons GABA may be an important modulator of such epigenetic responses. Indeed, the benzodiazepine lorazepam, an indirect GABA-A receptor agonist, dose-dependently blocked the effect of a novel cage challenge on histone H3 phosphoacetylation and c-Fos induction in dentate neurons of rats (Papadopoulos et al., 2008, 2011). The dose of the benzodiazepine at which this inhibition was accomplished was found to be anxiolytic but not sedative. Conversely, the partial inverse GABA-A agonist FG-7142, a drug that is known to attenuate the GABAergic inhibition of dentate granule neurons, profoundly enhanced baseline levels as well as novelty-induced increases in the number of H3S10p/K14ac- and c-Fos-positive dentate neurons (Papadopoulos et al., 2008, 2011). Corresponding with previous reports, after FG-7142 the rats showed anxiety-like behavior and hypervigilance in the novel cage. Furthermore, the FG-7142-evoked enhancements in epigenetic and gene-xpression responses were found to be completely blocked by the NMDA receptor antagonist MK-801, which underscores the critical importance of this glutamate receptor in dentate granule neuron activation (Papadopoulos et al., 2008, 2011).

These observations confirm that GABA is as a major modulator of dentate granule neuron activity. This function precipitates at least in part through its control of epigenetic and gene-expression responses in the granule neurons. Thus, regulators of GABA activity in the dentate gyrus may modulate the extent to which salience is given to incoming sensory information.

ERK-activated MSK phosphorylates serine 10 in histone H3

At present, relatively little is known about the signaling mechanisms involved in the activation or inhibition of histone-modifying enzymes. The signaling cascade mediating the phosphorylation and acetylation of histone H3 has, however, been rather well established. Pharmacological and mutant mouse studies provided the first indications for an involvement of the extracellular signal-regulated kinases ERK1/2 and the mitogen- and stress-activated kinases MSK1/2 in the forced-swimming-induced epigenetic and gene-expression effects (Chandramohan et al., 2008). ERK1/2 has been shown to be activated by phosphorylation via the MAPK pathway after NMDA receptor stimulation (Sweatt, 2004). Phospho-ERK1/2 (pERK1/2; as well as p38MAPK) can phosphorylate MSK1 at serine 360, threonine 581, and threonine 700, after which MSK1 autophosphorylates itself at multiple sites resulting in full catalytic—H3S10 kinase—activity (Hauge and Frodin, 2006; Arthur, 2008). Dentate gyrus neurons are known to express NMDA receptors, ERK1/2, and MSK1 but it has never been demonstrated whether pERK1/2, phospho-MSK1 (pMSK1), H3S10p/ K14ac, and c-Fos would actually become activated or expressed in the same neurons after a psychological challenge. The often-practiced Western blot analysis of course does not provide the necessary neuroanatomical resolution in this regard. Recently, in a series of immunohistochemical and immunofluorescence studies we showed for the first time that forced swimming indeed evokes ERK1/2 phosphorylation (see Plate 1) and MSK1 phosphorylation in dentate granule neurons (Gutièrrez-Mecinas et al., 2009). Moreover, we could show that pERK1/2, pMSK1, and H3S10p/K14ac are expressed in the same dentate neurons after a forced-swim challenge, thus providing clear evidence that H3S10 phosphorylation is the result of NMDA/ERK1/2/ MSK1 signaling in these neurons (Gutièrrez-Mecinas et al., 2009; Figure 5.2). In addition, neither expression of another MSK kinase—that is, phospho-p38MAPK, nor expression of the MSK-related kinase, phosphorylated ribosomal S6 kinase 1/2 (pRSK1/2)—was found in dentate granule neurons (Gutièrrez-Mecinas et al., 2009). Thus, there is specificity in the signaling mechanisms recruited to convey environmental challenges to the neuronal chromatin.

Mechanisms involved in lysine-14 acetylation of H3S10p resulting in the combinatorial H3S10p/K14ac marks

Some time ago, we proposed on the basis of the following observations that pCREB/ CREB-binding protein (CBP) may be responsible for the lysine-14 acetylation in H3S10p (Reul and Chandramohan, 2007; Chandramohan et al., 2008; Reul et al., 2009). First, psychological challenges such as forced swimming result in a strongly increased phosphorylation of the transcription factor CREB in dentate gyrus neurons (Bilang-Bleuel et al., 2002). Second, MSK is, in addition to a H3S10 kinase, also a CREB kinase (Arthur and Cohen, 2000). Third, the *c-fos* gene promoter contains a cAMP-response-element site. Finally, pCREB is able to recruit CREB-binding protein (CBP/p300, proteins with histone acetyltransferase [HAT] activity) to the promoter (Schiltz et al., 1999). However, after forced swimming phosphorylation of CREB takes place in virtually all dentate gyrus neurons (Bilang-Bleuel et al., 2002), which is in stark contrast to the sparse H3S10p/K14ac and c-Fos induction. Therefore, although a role of pCREB/CBP cannot be entirely excluded (Figure 5.2), pCREB may be playing a more general, neuroprotective role (Papadia et al., 2005) in the dentate gyrus after a psychological challenge. Recently, we discovered that challenges like forced swimming and novelty result in the phosphorylation of the E twenty-six (ETS)-domain protein ETS-like protein 1 (Elk-1; Sharrocks,

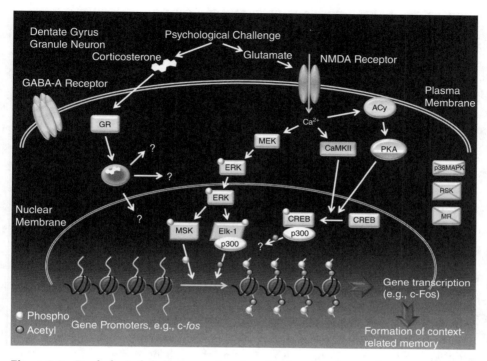

Figure 5.2 Psychological challenges such as forced swimming, fear conditioning, or Morris water-maze learning impact on epigenetic mechanisms and memory formation through convergent activation of the GR and NMDA/ERK-driven MSK1 and Ets-like protein 1 (Elk-1) signaling pathways. Activation of these pathways leads to serine 10 phosphorylation and lysine 14 acetylation of histone H3, hyperacetylation of histone H4, transcriptional induction of c-Fos (and other genes) in a distinct population of mature dentate granule neurons (Bilang-Bleuel et al., 2005; Chandramohan et al., 2007, 2008; Gutièrrez-Mecinas et al., 2009), and the encoding of contextual memory of the endured event. These epigenetic processes are modulated by GABA-A receptor function. Such psychological challenges also lead to, albeit nonsparse, CREB phosphorylation in dentate granule neurons. Formation of phospho-CREB, through recruitment of histone acetyltransferases like p300, could potentially contribute to histone acetylation in these neurons (see text for further discussion). Furthermore, our research has shown that factors such as the MSK kinase p38MAPK, the MSK-related kinase ribosomal S6 kinase (RSK), and the glucocorticoid-binding mineralocorticoid receptor (MR) are not involved in the observed epigenetic, gene-expression, and cognitive phenomena. ACy, adenylate cyclase; MEK, MAPK kinase. *Source:* From Reul et al. (2009). Reproduced with permission by Kimberly Mitchell of Landes Bioscience.

2001; Yordy and Muise-Helmericks, 2000; Shaw and Saxton, 2003) specifically in pERK1/2/pMSK1/H3S10p/K14ac/c-Fos-positive neurons of the dentate gyrus (Gutièrrez-Mecinas et al., 2009). According to studies performed in vitro, Elk-1 can be activated through ERK MAPK signaling (Yang et al., 2003a, 2003b). Moreover, phosphorylated Elk1 (pElk-1) bound to the Elk-1-binding site within the serum response element (SRE) of the *c-fos* promoter recruits HATs like p300 to the promoter that subsequently acetylate histone molecules in adjacent nucleosomes (Li et al., 2003a; O'Donnell et al., 2008). Thus, ERK1/2-driven Elk-1 phosphorylation in dentate neurons may drive the acetylation of H3S10p (and H4) in the c-*fos* promoter (Figure 5.2). This notion is supported by our recent immunofluorescence data showing the colocalization of pElk-1 with pERK1/2, pMSK1, H3S10p/K14ac and c-Fos (Gutièrrez-Mecinas et al., 2009).

Histone H3 phosphoacetylation and c-*fos* gene expression in dentate gyrus neurons require GR activation

In a series of studies we demonstrated that GR plays a major role in the establishment of the combinatorial H3S10p/K14ac marks and consequent c-Fos induction in dentate gyrus neurons, in addition to signaling through the NMDA/ERK1/2/ MSK1 and Elk-1 pathway (Bilang-Bleuel et al., 2005; Chandramohan et al., 2007, 2008). Presently, however, it is unclear at which level(s) the distinct signaling pathways are interacting (Figure 5.2). Classically, GRs act as ligand-dependent transcription factors altering gene expression through interaction with glucocorticoid response elements in promoter regions of glucocorticoid-responsive genes. As H3 phosphoacetylation after a challenge such as forced swimming is rather quick (significant increases within 15 min), a role for a glucocorticoid-induced gene product is unlikely. However, GRs may also be acting through nongenomic mechanisms. GRs can interact with different signaling pathways among which the ERK MAPK signaling pathway (Revest et al., 2005). Similar to the demonstrated interaction of the progesterone receptor with ERK1/2 to produce MSK activation (Vicent et al., 2006), we propose, based on the strong similarity between the GR and the progesterone receptor, that the GR may be required for the full activation of MSK1. Alternatively, GRs have been shown to recruit chromatin-remodeling proteins such as ATP-dependent chromatin-remodeling complexes and histone-modifying enzymes such as HATs (e.g., p300/CBP-associated factor, PCAF), thereby promoting chromatin decondensation, histone acetylation, and transcriptional activation (Li et al., 2003b; Hebbar and Archer, 2003; Kinyamu and Archer, 2004). Thus, GRs interact with signaling pathways and the chromatin in a highly complex manner and clearly more research is required. Nevertheless, it seems that activated GRs are of crucial importance in the facilitation of NMDA/ERK/MSK and Elk-1 signaling to the chromatin.

Significance of H3S10p/K14ac-associated Gene Expression in Dentate Gyrus Granule Neurons in Hippocampus-related Memory Formation

Using well-characterized primary antibodies and immunofluorescence analysis it is now possible to demonstrate epigenetic mechanisms linked to specific gene-expression events (e.g., c-Fos induction) in single cells in the brain. Moreover, intracellular molecules (e.g., pERK1/2, pMSK1, pElk-1) can be traced signaling to the chromatin, thereby affecting gene expression. Over the last decade an impressive collection of data has been accumulating that strongly support a role of the combinatorial H3S10p/K14ac epigenetic marks and associated gene expression in hippocampus-associated learning and memory processes. Behavioral tests for hippocampus-associated (episodic) memory formation include the forced-swim test, Morris water-maze learning, and contextual fear conditioning. In view of its role in sensory information processing and encoding the dentate gyrus is critically involved in memory formation in these tests (Treves and Rolls, 1994; Rolls and Kesner, 2006). With regard to the learned behavioral immobility response in the forced-swim test a strict requirement was the generation of H3S10p/K14ac and c-Fos in dentate granule neurons after the initial test, thus during the acquisition and consolidation phase of memory formation. If the generation of H3S10p/K14ac and c-Fos in these neurons was disrupted due to NMDA receptor or GR blockade, MAPK kinase (MEK) inhibition (thereby preventing of ERK activation), or MSK1/2 gene deletion, the learned immobility response normally seen in the retest was greatly impaired (Reul and Chandramohan, 2007; Chandramohan et al., 2007, 2008; Reul et al., 2009). Correspondingly, antagonism of the mineralocorticoid receptor (another glucocorticoid-binding receptor in the brain; Reul and de Kloet, 1985) neither affected memory formation of forced-swim experience (as shown before; Veldhuis et al., 1985) nor H3S10p/K14ac and c-Fos in the dentate gyrus (Chandramohan et al., 2008).

There is preliminary evidence that Morris water-maze learning involves H3S10p/K14ac and c-Fos induction in dentate neurons (Y. Chandramohan and J.M.H.M. Reul, unpublished observations). Indeed, using whole hippocampus extracts and Western analysis, Chwang et al. (2007) observed a role of H3S10p in memory formation in the Morris water maze and contextual fear conditioning requiring signaling through ERK1/2 and MSK1. Presently, a role of histone H3 and H4 methylation is emerging, which is complex as lysine residues can carry up to three methyl groups and the degree of methylation has implications for chromatin structure and transcriptional activity. Mono-, di-, and trimethyl H3K4 are all associated with transcriptional activation (Akbarian and Huang, 2009). However, the monomethylation marks of lysines 9 and 27 of H3 and lysine 20 of H4 are linked with gene activation whereas the di- and trimethylation marks of these residues are associated with gene repression (Akbarian and Huang, 2009). It should be emphasized that these findings are based on studies in vitro and until now only few reports exist on histone methylation-associated changes in neuronal gene expression in vivo (e.g., Huang et al., 2007; Schaefer et al., 2009). We found preliminary evidence for increased H3K4 methylation of the c-*fos* promoter in the hippocampus after forced swimming (S.A. Hesketh and J.M.H.M. Reul, unpublished observations). Hunter and colleagues (2009) recently reported changes in overall levels of H3K4, H3K9, and H3K27 methylation in the brain of acutely and chronically (restraint-) stressed rats. Conditional mutagenesis of H3K9 methyltransferase complex G9a-like protein/G9a in mice resulted in altered exploratory, locomotor, and cognitive behaviors (Schaefer et al., 2009). Gupta et al. (2010) demonstrated that H3K4 methylation is involved in the establishment of contextual fear memories. It seems we are at the very start of beginning to understand how major life events impact on epigenetic mechanisms in neurons participating in the formation of memories of such events.

Concluding Remarks

There is now ample evidence that emotionally stressful challenges impact on distinct extracellular and intracellular signaling and gene-expression-modulating epigenetic pathways in the brain. Furthermore, evidence is gathering that these pathways play a decisive role in the formation of contextual and spatial (episodic) memories of the endured event. We described in this chapter a principal role of the NMDA/ERK1/2/MSK1 and Elk-1 signaling cascade in the serine-10 phosphorylation and lysine-14 acetylation of histone H3, the hyperacetylation of H4, and subsequently induction of c-Fos in dentate granule neurons in response to stressful learning paradigms such as forced swimming, fear conditioning, and Morris water-maze learning. A role of the NMDA/ERK MAPK signaling pathway in learning and memory processes has been amply described. However, although a facilitatory role of glucocorticoid hormones on such cognitive processes has often been described as well, until now the molecular mechanism underlying this hormone action has remained elusive. We have found evidence that glucocorticoids facilitate learning and memory processes through a—nongenomic—interaction of GRs with the ERK/MSK1 and Elk-1 signaling cascade, resulting in enhanced downstream epigenetic and gene-expression responses in dentate granule neurons. This interaction provides the first evidence for a molecular basis of the emotion/cognition interface in stress-related learning and memory. Other histone modifications such methylation and demethylation events may be playing important roles as well but these require further characterization. Finally, in addition to glutamate and glucocorticoid hormones, GABA was identified as a major controller of emotional stress-induced epigenetic and gene-expression responses in dentate granule neurons. Thus, it may be considered that through afferent modulation of GABA the impact of events can be epigenetically and cognitively boosted or attenuated. Follow-up studies on these signaling, epigenetic and gene-expression mechanisms should increase our insight into the etiology of stress-related psychiatric disorders such major depression and anxiety-related disorders (e.g., posttraumatic stress disorder; Reul and Nutt, 2008).

References

Akbarian, S., & Huang, H. S. (2009). Epigenetic regulation in human brain-focus on histone lysine methylation. *Biological Psychiatry, 65*, 198–203.

Arthur, J. S. (2008). MSK activation and physiological roles. *Frontiers in Bioscience, 13*, 5866–5879.

Arthur, J. S., & Cohen, P. (2000). MSK1 is required for CREB phosphorylation in response to mitogens in mouse embryonic stem cells. *FEBS Letters, 482*, 44–48.

Beylin, A. V., & Shors, T. J. (2003). Glucocorticoids are necessary for enhancing the acquisition of associative memories after acute stressful experience. *Hormones and Behavior, 43*, 124–131.

Bilang-Bleuel, A., Droste, S., Gesing, A., Rech, J., Linthorst, A. C. E., & Reul, J. M. H. M. (2000). *Impact of stress and voluntary exercise on neurogenesis in the adult hippocampus: quantitative analysis by detection of Ki-67.* Program no. 571.13. 2000 Neuroscience Meeting Planner. Society for Neuroscience, New Orleans, LA.

Bilang-Bleuel, A., Rech, J., Holsboer, F., & Reul, J. M. H. M. (2002). Forced swimming evokes a biphasic response in CREB phosphorylation in extrahypothalamic limbic and neocortical brain structures. *European Journal of Neuroscience, 15*, 1048–1060.

Bilang-Bleuel, A., Ulbricht, S., Chandramohan, Y., De Carli, S., Droste, S. K., & Reul, J. M. H. M. (2005). Psychological stress increases histone H3 phosphorylation in adult dentate gyrus granule neurons: involvement in a glucocorticoid receptor-dependent behavioural response. *European Journal of Neuroscience, 22*, 1691–1700.

Chandramohan, Y., Droste, S. K., & Reul, J. M. H. M. (2007). Novelty stress induces phospho-acetylation of histone H3 in rat dentate gyrus granule neurons through coincident signalling via the N-methyl-d-aspartate receptor and the glucocorticoid receptor: relevance for c-fos induction. *Journal of Neurochemistry, 101*, 815–828.

Chandramohan, Y., Droste, S. K., Arthur, J. S., & Reul, J. M. H. M. (2008). The forced swimming-induced behavioural immobility response involves histone H3 phospho-acetylation and c-Fos induction in dentate gyrus granule neurons via activation of the N-methyl-D-aspartate/extracellular signal-regulated kinase/mitogen- and stress-activated kinase signalling pathway. *European Journal of Neuroscience, 27*, 2701–2713.

Chawla, M. K., Guzowski, J. F., Ramirez-Amaya, V., Lipa, P., Hoffman, K. L., Marriott, L. K., Worley, P. F., McNaughton, B. L., & Barnes, C. A. (2005). Sparse, environmentally selective expression of Arc RNA in the upper blade of the rodent fascia dentata by brief spatial experience. *Hippocampus, 15*, 579–586.

Cheung, P., Tanner, K. G., Cheung, W. L., Sassone-Corsi, P., Denu, J. M., & Allis, C. D. (2000). Synergistic coupling of histone H3 phosphorylation and acetylation in response to epidermal growth factor stimulation. *Molecular Cell, 5*, 905–915.

Chwang, W. B., O'Riordan, K. J., Levenson, J. M., & Sweatt, J. D. (2006). ERK/MAPK regulates hippocampal histone phosphorylation following contextual fear conditioning. *Learning and Memory, 13*, 322–328.

Chwang, W. B., Arthur, J. S., Schumacher, A., & Sweatt, J. D. (2007). The nuclear kinase mitogen- and stress-activated protein kinase 1 regulates hippocampal chromatin remodeling in memory formation. *Journal of Neuroscience, 27*, 12732–12742.

Clayton, A. L., Rose, S., Barratt, M. J., & Mahadevan, L. C. (2000). Phosphoacetylation of histone H3 on *c-fos*-and *c-jun*-associated nucleosomes upon gene activation. *EMBO Journal, 19*, 3714–3726.

Collingridge, G. L., Singer, W. (1990). Excitatory amino acid receptors and synaptic plasticity. *Trends in Pharmacological Sciences, 11*, 290–296.

de Kloet, E. R., De Kock, S., Schild, V., & Veldhuis, H. D. (1988). Antiglucocorticoid, R. U. 38486 attenuates retention of a behaviour and disinhibits the hypothalamic-pituitary adrenal axis at different brain sites. *Neuroendocrinology, 47,* 109–115.

De Pablo, J. M., Parra, A., Segovia, S., & Guillamón, A. (1989). Learned immobility explains the behavior of rats in the forced swim test. *Physiology & Behavior, 46,* 229–237.

Gupta, S., Kim, S. Y., Artis, S., Molfese, D. L., Schumacher, A., Sweatt, J. D., Paylor, R. E., & Lubin, F. D. (2010). Histone methylation regulates memory formation. *Journal of Neuroscience, 30,* 3589–3599.

Gutièrrez-Mecinas, M., Collins, A., Qian, X., Hesketh, S. A., & Reul, J. M. H. M. (2009). *Forced swimming-evoked histone H3 phospho-acetylation and c-Fos induction in dentate gyrus granule neurons involves ERK1/2-mediated MSK1 and Elk-1 phosphorylation.* Program no. 777.17. 2009 Neuroscience Meeting Planner. Society for Neuroscience, Chicago, IL.

Hauge, C., & Frodin, M. (2006). RSK and MSK in MAP kinase signalling. *Journal of Cell Science, 119,* 3021–3023.

Hebbar, P. B., & Archer, T. K. (2003). Chromatin remodeling by nuclear receptors. *Chromosoma, 111,* 495–504.

Huang, H. S., Matevossian, A., Whittle, C., Kim, S. Y., Schumacher, A., Baker, S. P., & Akbarian, S. (2007). Prefrontal dysfunction in schizophrenia involves mixed-lineage leukemia 1-regulated histone methylation at GABAergic gene promoters. *Journal of Neuroscience, 27,* 11254–11262.

Hunter, R. G., McCarthy, K. J., Milne, T. A., Pfaff, D. W., & McEwen, B. S. (2009). Regulation of hippocampal H3 histone methylation by acute and chronic stress. *Proceedings of the National Academy of Sciences USA, 106,* 20912–20917.

Impey, S., Obrietan, K., & Storm, D. R. (1999). Making new connections: role of ERK/MAP kinase signaling in neuronal plasticity. *Neuron, 23,* 11–14.

Jaskelioff, M., & Peterson, C. L. (2003). Chromatin and transcription: histones continue to make their marks. *Nature Cell Biology, 5,* 395–399.

Kinyamu, H. K., & Archer, T. K. (2004). Modifying chromatin to permit steroid hormone receptor-dependent transcription. *Biochimica Biophysica Acta, 1677,* 30–45.

Korte, S. M. (2001). Corticosteroids in relation to fear, anxiety and psychopathology. *Neuroscience and Biobehavioral Reviews, 25,* 117–142.

Leutgeb, J. K., Leutgeb, S., Moser, M. B., & Moser, E. I. (2007). Pattern separation in the dentate gyrus and CA3 of the hippocampus. *Science, 315,* 961–966.

Li, Q-J., Yang, S. H., Maeda, Y., Sladek, F. M., Sharrocks, A. D., & Martins-Green, M. (2003a). MAP kinase phosphorylation-dependent activation of Elk-1 leads to activation of the co-activator p300. *EMBO Journal, 22,* 281–291.

Li, X., Wong, J., Tsai, S. Y., Tsai, M. J., & O'Malley, B. W. (2003b). Progesterone and glucocorticoid receptors recruit distinct coactivator complexes and promote distinct patterns of local chromatin modification. *Molecular and Cellular Biology, 23,* 3763–3773.

Linthorst, A. C., Flachskamm, C., & Reul, J. M. H. M. (2008). Water temperature determines neurochemical and behavioural responses to forced swim stress: an in vivo microdialysis and biotelemetry study in rats. *Stress, 11,* 88–100.

Lucki, I. (1997). The forced swimming test as a model for core and component behavioral effects of antidepressant drugs. *Behavioral Pharmacology, 8,* 523–532.

Martens, J. H., Verlaan, M., Kalkhoven, E., & Zantema, A. (2003). Cascade of distinct histone modifications during collagenase gene activation. *Molecular and Cellular Biology, 23,* 1808–1816.

McHugh, T. J., Jones, M. W., Quinn, J. J., Balthasar, N., Coppari, R., Elmquist, J. K., Lowell, B. B., Fanselow, M. S., Wilson, M. A., & Tonegawa, S. (2007). Dentate gyrus NMDA receptors mediate rapid pattern separation in the hippocampal network. *Science, 317,* 94–99.

O'Donnell, A., Yang, S. H., & Sharrocks, A. D. (2008). MAP kinase-mediated c-fos regulation relies on a histone acetylation relay switch. *Molecular Cell, 29,* 780–785.

Oitzl, M. S., & de Kloet, E. R. (1992). Selective corticosteroid antagonists modulate specific aspects of spatial orientation learning. *Behavioral Neuroscience, 106,* 62–71.

Papadia, S., Stevenson, P., Hardingham, N. R., Bading, H., & Hardingham, G. E. (2005). Nuclear Ca2+ and the cAMP response element-binding protein family mediate a late phase of activity-dependent neuroprotection. *Journal of Neuroscience, 25,* 4279–4287.

Papadopoulos, A., Chandramohan, Y., Collins, A., Droste, S. K., Nutt, D. J., & Reul, J. M. H. M. (2008). GABAergic control of stress-responsive epigenetic and gene expression mechanisms in the dentate gyrus. *European Neuropsychopharmacology, 18,* S211–S212.

Papadopoulos, A., Chandramohan, Y., Collins, A., Droste, S. K., Nutt, D. J., & Reul, J. M. H. M. (2011). GABAergic control of stress-responsive epigenetic and gene expression mechanisms in the dentate gyrus. *European Neuropsychopharmacology, 21*(4), 316–324.

Porsolt, R. D., Le Pichon, M., & Jalfre, M. (1977). Depression: a new animal model sensitive to antidepressant treatments. *Nature, 266,* 730–732.

Reul, J. M. H. M., & de Kloet, E. R. (1985). Two receptor systems for corticosterone in rat brain: microdistribution and differential occupation. *Endocrinology, 117,* 2505–2512.

Reul, J. M. H. M., & Chandramohan, Y. (2007). Epigenetic mechanisms in stress-related memory formation. *Psychoneuroendocrinology, 32*(Suppl. 1), S21–S25.

Reul, J. M. H. M., & Nutt, D. J. (2008). Glutamate and cortisol–a critical confluence in PTSD? *Journal of Psychopharmacology, 22,* 469–472.

Reul, J. M. H. M., Hesketh, S. A., Collins, A., & Gutièrrez-Mecinas, M. (2009). Epigenetic mechanisms in the dentate gyrus act as a molecular switch in hippocampus-associated memory function. *Epigenetics, 4,* 434–439.

Revest, J. M., Di, B. F., Kitchener, P., Rouge-Pont, F., Desmedt, A., Turiault, M., Tronche, F., & Piazza, P. V. (2005). The MAPK pathway and Egr-1 mediate stress-related behavioral effects of glucocorticoids. *Nature Neuroscience, 8,* 664–672.

Richter-Levin, G., Canevari, L., & Bliss, T. V. (1995). Long-term potentiation and glutamate release in the dentate gyrus: links to spatial learning. *Behavioral Brain Research, 66,* 37–40.

Rolls, E. T., & Kesner, R. P. (2006). A computational theory of hippocampal function, and empirical tests of the theory. *Progress in Neurobiology, 79,* 1–48.

Roozendaal, B., Hui, G. K., Hui, I. R., Berlau, D. J., Mcgaugh, J. L., & Weinberger, N. M. (2006). Basolateral amygdala noradrenergic activity mediates corticosterone-induced enhancement of auditory fear conditioning. *Neurobiology of Learning and Memory, 86,* 249–255.

Sabbattini, P., Canzonetta, C., Sjoberg, M., Nikic, S., Georgiou, A., Kemball-Cook, G., Auner, H. W., & Dillon, N. (2007). A novel role for the Aurora B kinase in epigenetic marking of silent chromatin in differentiated postmitotic cells. *EMBO Journal, 26,* 4657–4669.

Sandi, C., Loscertales, M., & Guaza, C. (1997). Experience-dependent facilitating effect of corticosterone on spatial memory formation in the water maze. *European Journal of Neuroscience, 9,* 637–642.

Schaefer, A., Sampath, S. C., Intrator, A., Min, A., Gertler, T. S., Surmeier, D. J., Tarakhovsky, A., & Greengard, P. (2009). Control of cognition and adaptive behavior by the GLP/G9a epigenetic suppressor complex. *Neuron, 64,* 678–691.

Schiltz, R. L., Mizzen, C. A., Vassilev, A., Cook, R. G., Allis, C. D., & Nakatani, Y. (1999). Overlapping but distinct patterns of histone acetylation by the human coactivators p300 and PCAF within nucleosomal substrates. *Journal of Biological Chemistry, 274,* 1189–1192.

Sharrocks, A. D. (2001). The ETS-domain transcription factor family. *Nature Reviews Molecular Cell Biology, 2,* 827–837.

Shaw, P. E., & Saxton, J. (2003). Ternary complex factors: prime nuclear targets for mitogen-activated protein kinases. *International Journal of Biochemistry and Cell Biology, 35,* 1210–1226.

Spencer, V. A., & Davie, J. R. (2000). Signal transduction pathways and chromatin structure in cancer cells. *Journal of Cellular Biochemistry Supplement, 35,* 27–35.

Strahl, B. D., & Allis, C. D. (2000). The language of covalent histone modifications. *Nature, 403,* 41–45.

Sweatt, J. D. (2001). The neuronal MAP kinase cascade: a biochemical signal integration system subserving synaptic plasticity and memory. *Journal of Neurochemistry, 76,* 1–10.

Sweatt, J. D. (2004). Mitogen-activated protein kinases in synaptic plasticity and memory. *Current Opinion in Neurobiology, 14,* 1–7.

Treves, A., & Rolls, E. T. (1994). Computational analysis of the role of the hippocampus in memory. *Hippocampus, 4,* 374–391.

Tsankova, N. M., Kumar, A., & Nestler, E. J. (2004). Histone modifications at gene promoter regions in rat hippocampus after acute and chronic electroconvulsive seizures. *Journal of Neuroscience, 24,* 5603–5610.

Veldhuis, H. D., De Korte, C. C. M. M., & de Kloet, E. R. (1985). Glucocorticoids facilitate the retention of acquired immobility during forced swimming. *European Journal of Pharmacology, 115,* 211–217.

Vicent, G. P., Ballare, C., Silvina Nacht, A., Clausell, J., Subtil-Rodriquez, A., Quiles, I., Jordan, A., & Beato, M. (2006). Induction of progesterone target genes requires activation of Erk and Msk kinases and phosphorylation of histone H3. *Molecular Cell, 24,* 367–381.

West, A. P. (1990). Neurobehavioral studies of forced swimming: the role of learning and memory in the forced swim test. *Progress in Neuro-psychopharmacology & Biological Psychiatry, 14,* 863–877.

Witter, M. P. (2007). The perforant path: projections from the entorhinal cortex to the dentate gyrus. *Progress in Brain Research, 163,* 43–61.

Yang, S. H., Jaffray, E., Hay, R. T., & Sharrocks, A. D. (2003a). Dynamic interplay of the SUMO and ERK pathways in regulating Elk-1 transcriptional activity. *Molecular Cell, 12,* 63–74.

Yang, S. H., Sharrocks, A. D., & Whitmarsh, A. J. (2003b). Transcriptional regulation by the MAP kinase signaling cascades. *Gene, 320,* 3–21.

Yordy, J. S., & Muise-Helmericks, R. C. (2000). Signal transduction and the Ets family of transcription factors. *Oncogene, 19,* 6503–6513.

6

Mechanisms of Glucocorticoid Receptor Regulation of Gene Expression

Alyson B. Scoltock and John A. Cidlowski

Introduction

Living organisms have evolved complex mechanisms to maintain homeostasis in the face of the ongoing stress of survival. In humans and other mammals the system that coordinates our response to stress is the hypothalamic–pituitary–adrenal (HPA) axis. Stressful stimuli, both physical (such as pain, toxins, inflammation, trauma) and perceived (fear, anxiety), activate the hypothalamus to release corticotropin-releasing hormone (CRH), which in turn causes the pituitary to release adrenocorticotrophic hormone (ACTH). ACTH in turn stimulates the release of the glucocorticoid hormones from the adrenal glands which ultimately feed back to negatively regulate the HPA axis. Once released into the bloodstream, these steroid hormones help the organism to adapt and survive by regulating many tissue- and organ-specific functions such as glucose homeostasis, carbohydrate metabolism, blood pressure, and the inflammatory response. Via their effects on the central nervous system they are also involved in the regulation of arousal, cognition, mood, and sleep. Glucocorticoids are also essential for proper embryogenesis and development. Due to their well-known anti-inflammatory actions, synthetic gluco-corticoids are widely prescribed drugs used in the treatment of asthma, rheumatoid arthritis, transplant rejection, ulcerative colitis, and other immune diseases. Additionally, glucocorticoids are effective chemotherapeutic agents in the treatment of cancers of hematological origin (Barnes, 1998; Rhen and Cidlowski, 2005).

Glucocorticoids exert the majority of their effects via the glucocorticoid receptor (GR), an intracellular protein that is expressed in almost all tissues of the body. Surprisingly the pleiotropic effects of glucocorticoid hormones are dependent on a

The Handbook of Stress: Neuropsychological Effects on the Brain, First Edition.
Edited by Cheryl D. Conrad.
© 2011 Blackwell Publishing Ltd. Published 2011 by Blackwell Publishing Ltd.

single gene. Current understanding of the mechanism of transcriptional regulation mediated by the glucocorticoid receptor is explored in the following sections.

GR: gene and protein

The GR (NR3C1) is a member of the nuclear receptor superfamily, which is a large family of ligand-activated transcription factors. Members of this superfamily are characterized by the presence of three distinct domains: the C-terminal ligand-binding domain (LBD), the internal zinc-finger DNA-binding domain (DBD), and the N-terminal transactivation domain (NTD; Laudet et al., 1992; Escriva et al., 2004). Current nomenclature accepted by the scientific community lists six groups of receptor subfamilies based on evolutionary classification (Germain et al., 2006). The steroid receptors for estrogen, androgen, progesterone, mineralocorticoid, and glucocorticoid are in subfamily three. These receptors are typically sequestered in complexes with chaperone proteins in the absence of ligand whereas receptors such as thyroid, vitamin D, and retinoid receptors constitutively bind to DNA regardless of ligand (Dennis and O'Malley, 2005).

There has been only one *GR* gene identified in every mammalian species examined to date. The human *GR* (*hGR*) gene is located on chromosome 5q31–32 and comprises over 140 kb of nucleotides, fewer than 2% of which are exons. There are nine exons in the *hGR* gene: exon 1 represents the 5′-untranslated region whereas exons 2–9 are protein coding (Duma et al., 2006). Exon 2 encodes the N-terminal domain that contains the first activation function (AF-1) domain (amino acids 77–262), which interacts with the basal transcription machinery to induce transcription (Wright et al., 1993). The central DBD (amino acids 418–488) is encoded by exons 3–4 and consists of two conserved zinc fingers. The region between the two zinc fingers houses a nuclear export signal (Miesfeld et al., 1987; Black et al., 2001). A hinge region adjacent to the DBD contains a nuclear localization signal at amino acids 491–498 (Freedman and Yamamoto, 2004). Finally, exons 5–9 encode the C-terminal LBD (amino acids 526–777). This region is responsible for ligand binding and also contains the second activation function (AF-2) domain (Dahlman-Wright et al., 1992; Schaaf and Cidlowski, 2002) (Figure 6.1a).

Exon 9 contains coding sequences for the two alternative C-termini (9α and 9β) of the LBD of the receptor. Through alternative splicing 2 isoforms of the receptor protein can be generated, termed hGR-α and hGR-β (Figure 6.1a). The hGR-α isoform binds glucocorticoids, is ubiquitously expressed and is considered to be the predominant functional isoform (Hollenberg et al., 1985; Weinberger et al., 1985; Giguere et al., 1986). The hGR-β isoform, though not as widely expressed and not binding glucocorticoid hormone, appears to be an inhibitor of hGR-α function (Bamberger et al., 1995; Oakley et al., 1996, 1997) and possibly contributes to glucocorticoid resistance. For example, increased hGR-β levels have been reported in T cells in the airway, peripheral blood mononuclear cells, and tuberculin-induced inflammatory lesions in glucocorticoid-insensitive asthmatics (Barnes, 1998; Hamid et al., 1999; Sousa et al., 2000). Therefore, an imbalance in the relative levels of hGR-α and hGR-β may contribute to clinical conditions associated with glucocorticoid resistance, such as rheumatoid arthritis, systemic lupus erythematosus, or ulcerative colitis (Chrousos, 1995).

Other splice variants of the GR—GR-γ, GR-P, and GR-A—have been described (Figure 6.1a). The GR-γ splice variant harbors an additional three-base insertion in the DBD, resulting in the insertion of an arginine residue between the two zinc fingers of the DBD, thus reducing its transactivation capacity by as much as 50% (Ray et al., 1996). The GR-γ isoform is expressed in lymphocytes (3.8–8.7% of total GR mRNA) (Rivers et al., 1999) and has been detected in acute childhood lymphoblastic leukemia (Beger et al., 2003). The GR-A splice variant lacks exons 5–7, resulting in a truncated LBD and impaired transactivation activity. Finally, the GR-P splice variant lacks exons 8 and 9, also resulting in a truncated LBD lacking the ability to bind glucocorticoids (Moalli et al., 1993). These variants have been detected at high levels in glucocorticoid-resistant myeloma patients and implicated in glucocorticoid resistance (Lu and Cidlowski, 2004).

Recently other functional isoforms of the receptor protein have been reported. Our laboratory has shown that hGR-α mRNA is translated from at least eight alternative initiation sites into multiple GR-α isoforms (Yudt and Cidlowski, 2001; Lu and Cidlowski, 2005). The translation of a single hGR-α mRNA into multiple receptor proteins can occur by use of alternative start codons in the GR mRNA, leading to the production of progressively shorter proteins. There are two mechanisms that account for the use of these alternate start sites. The first is ribosomal leaky scanning, and in this mechanism a suboptimal nucleotide context in the region of the first AUG start codon causes weak ribosomal binding, allowing other ribosomes to scan downstream for binding sites for alternative translation-initiation sites located in exon 2. An additional mechanism is ribosomal shunting. In this process the ribosome complex is assembled at the 5′ cap sequence of the mRNA. Due to the formation of hairpin structures in the RNA, ribosomes can bypass or *shunt* across internal sections of the RNA and initiate transcription at alternative initiation sites. All known alternative initiation sites for the GR mRNA are in the NTD. Therefore both of these mechanisms result in proteins with identical DNA and LBDs but differing in the length of their transactivation domains (Figure 6.1b).

Receptor subcellular localization

When unbound to hormone the GR protein resides primarily in the cytoplasm in a multiprotein complex containing chaperones such as heat-shock proteins 90 and 70, stabilizing protein p23, and the chaperone protein FK506-binding protein 52 (Pratt et al., 2004; Grad and Picard, 2007). Other cochaperones and their functional characteristics are listed in Table 6.1. This complex presumably maintains the receptor in a nonactivated state but in a conformation that binds ligand with high affinity. Glucocorticoid hormones, due to their lipophilic nature, passively diffuse through

(a)

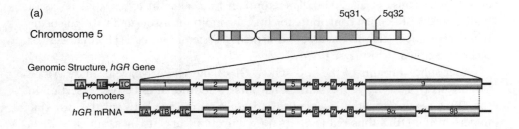

Chromosome 5

Genomic Structure, *hGR* Gene

Promoters

hGR mRNA

Alternative Splicing

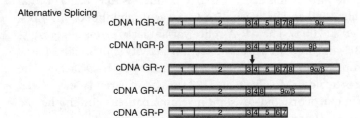

cDNA hGR-α

cDNA hGR-β

cDNA GR-γ

cDNA GR-A

cDNA GR-P

(b)

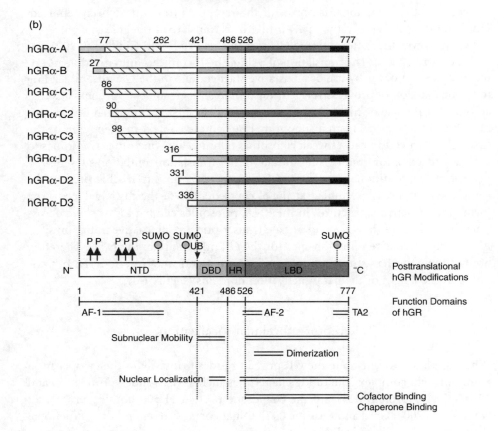

hGRα-A

hGRα-B

hGRα-C1

hGRα-C2

hGRα-C3

hGRα-D1

hGRα-D2

hGRα-D3

Posttranslational hGR Modifications

Function Domains of hGR

AF-1   AF-2   TA2

Subnuclear Mobility

Dimerization

Nuclear Localization

Cofactor Binding
Chaperone Binding

Figure 6.1 (a) Genomic localization, organization of hGR, and diversity of cDNA. The hGR is the product of one gene (located in chromosome 5) that contains 10 exons (numbering in boxes). The promoter region/5′-flanking region contains three transcription-initiation sites (promoters 1A, 1B, and 1C), each of which produce an alternative first exon that is fused to a common exon 2 after splicing. Alternative splicing of exon 9 results in two mRNAs coding for hGR-α and hGR-β. Alternative splicing of the other exons can also result in insertion of an additional arginine codon between exons 3 and 4 (arrow; GR-γ), in skipping of exons 5–7 (GR-A), or in deletion of exons 8 and 9 (GR-P). (b) Multiple hGR-α isoforms: alternative translation-initiation sites, protein structure, and functional domains. Generation of multiple hGR protein isoforms is a result of alternative translation initiation. Translation can be initiated in each of the AUG codons corresponding to the positions 1, 27, 86, 90, 98, 316, 331, and 336 of the hGR-α NTD, resulting in a set of hGR isoforms with different lengths, sizes, and functional domains. Residues in the functional domain of hGR are subjected to posttranslational modifications by phosphorylation, SUMOylation, and ubiquitination. TA2, additional transactivation activity; HR, hinge region; P, phosphorylation site; SUMO, SUMOylation sites; UB, ubiquitination sites.

←

Table 6.1 Binding partners of the GR cytoplasmic complex. Unbound to ligand, the GR is part of a multisubunit complex in the cytoplasm. This table presents examples of some of the better studied binding partners along with their functional characteristics. *Source:* Found in Grad and Picard (2007); copyright 2007 with permission from Elsevier.

Full name	*Abbreviation*	*Characteristics*
Heat-shock protein 90	Hsp90	Molecular chaperone involved in protein activation
Heat-shock protein 70	Hsp70	Molecular chaperone involved in protein folding
Heat-shock protein 40	Hsp40	Cochaperone of Hsp70, activates ATPase activity
Hsp70-Hsp90-organizing protein	Hop, p60	Links Hsp70 and Hsp90
Hsp70-interacting protein	Hip, p48	Cochaperone of Hsp70, prolongs interaction with GR
Bcl2-associated athanogene-1	Bag-1	Cochaperone of Hsp90, stimulates GR release
Hsp90 cochaperone p23	p23	Stabilizes GR binding
Activator of heat-shock protein 90 ATPase	Aha1	Cochaperone of Hsp90, stimulates Hsp90 ATPase
FK506-binding proteins 51 and 52	FKBP51 and FKBP52	Cochaperones of Hsp90

the cell membrane and bind to the receptor, causing a conformational change that releases the receptor from the chaperone complex (Freedman and Yamamoto, 2004; Hager et al., 2004). This change exposes the nuclear localization signals on the receptor that are recognized by nuclear translocation proteins (Okamoto et al., 1993). These proteins actively shuttle the receptor to the nucleus where it regulates the transcription of genes by a wide variety of mechanisms.

Mechanisms of Glucocorticoid-regulated Gene Expression

Direct DNA binding

Once in the nucleus the GR pairs with another GR molecule in a process called homodimerization (Freedman and Yamamoto, 2004; Hager et al., 2004). These receptor homodimers can then bind to specific sequences on DNA called glucocorticoid-response elements or GREs (Figure 6.2). The first proposed mechanism for glucocorticoid regulation of gene transcription was a GR homodimer binding to a GRE in the promoter of a glucocorticoid-responsive gene (Zaret and Yamamoto, 1984; Beato et al., 1989), thus enabling the AF domains to interact with the basal transcription machinery to induce the expression of that gene. The consensus GRE is described as a palindromic sequence (since it is binding to a receptor dimer) of AGAACANNNTGTTCT and there are many well-characterized genes regulated by this mechanism such as tyrosine aminotransferase (Grange et al., 1989; Beato et al., 1989). However, as many as 40% of known GR-responsive genes do not contain a classic GRE palindromic sequence but rather have combinations of half-sites (Merkulov and Merkulova, 2009) or no element resembling a GRE.

It has been shown that genes the expression of which is repressed by glucocorticoids (this includes the *CRH* gene) contain a negative GRE or nGRE in their promoters, regulated by direct DNA binding of GR homodimers (Figure 6.2). Negative GREs contribute to the regulation of the HPA axis (by regulating proopiomelanocortin [POMC] and CRH), bone (osteocalcin) and skin (keratins) function, inflammation (interleukin-1β), angiogenesis (proliferin), and lactation (prolactin; Nakai et al., 1991; Dostert and Heinzel, 2004). However, unlike the GRE there has been no consensus sequence defined for the nGRE.

Transcriptional coregulators

Binding of the GR to DNA causes a conformational change that promotes the recruitment of proteins known as coactivators and corepressors. These proteins can affect the rate of transcription by interacting with the general transcription machinery and remodeling chromatin, and thereby fine tune a cell's response to glucocorticoids. The suggestion that these factors existed came from observing a phenomenon known as *squelching*, where transcriptional interference occurs between two

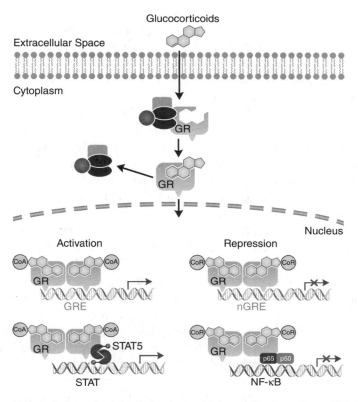

Figure 6.2 GR regulation of transcription by multiple mechanisms. Ligand binding to the GR leads to the dissociation of a cytoplasmic cochaperone complex interacting with GR. Ligand-bound GR rapidly translocates into the nucleus and forms homodimers. GR homodimers can recruit either coactivators (CoA) or corepressors (CoR). The GR can activate gene expression by directly binding to GREs in the DNA, or associate with transcription factors such as signal transducer and activator of transcription 5 (STAT5). GR can also promote gene silencing by directly interacting with negative GREs (nGREs) in the DNA, or by protein–protein interactions with transcription factors such as nuclear factor κB (NF-κB).

activated nuclear receptors presumably competing for a limited pool of enhancers (Meyer et al., 1989; Tora et al., 1989). This mechanism has been intensively studied in the past decade, especially as it pertains to nuclear receptor signaling. Research shows there are many multisubunit coregulator complexes that need to be recruited to correctly express a specific gene. These complexes exhibit different enzymatic activities that can act to change the nucleosome to a state either more or less accessible to the transcriptional machinery. The following paragraphs will give a review of some of the different classes of coregulators but it is by no means exhaustive. An excellent review article of coregulators and the transcriptional machinery can be found in *Genes & Development* (Rosenfeld et al., 2006).

Proteins that enhance transcription are known as coactivators. Coactivators include steroid receptor coactivator (SRC) 1, 2, and 3 of the SRC family, cAMP-response-element binding protein (CREB)-binding protein (CBP), adenovirus E1A-associated 300 kDa protein (p300), and p300/CBP-associated factor (PCAF). Several of these proteins (CBP and p300) also act as enhancers for many other transcription factors besides steroid receptors, such as CREB, signal transducer and activator of transcription (STAT) 2, and p53. To obtain specificity for regulating GR transcription these proteins have other factors that associate with them, forming a coactivator complex. Coactivator proteins can be divided into several groups. Some, such as the SRCs, have acetyltransferase activity, posttranslationally modifying lysine residues in the N-terminal tail of histones. Others have methylase activity, such as protein arginine methyltransferase 1 (PRMT1) and coactivator-associated arginine methyltransferase (CARM). Histone acetylation and methylation have been proposed to neutralize the electrostatic interaction between positively charged amino acids in histones and the negatively charged phosphate backbone of DNA, consequently loosening the association between the two. Another group is represented by multiprotein complexes able to bridge nuclear receptors to the basal transcriptional machinery such as thyroid receptor-associated protein (TRAP; Fondell et al., 1996), vitamin D receptor-interacting protein (DRIP; Rachez et al., 1998), and SRB-MED-containing complex (SMCC; Gu et al., 1999). The third type of coactivator is the ATP-dependent chromatin-remodeling complexes such as SWI/SNF (switch/sucrose nonfermentable). These complexes do not induce covalent modifications of histones but rather introduce a superhelical torsion into chromatin and change the topology of the nucleosome, including causing nucleosome sliding that makes the chromatin more accessible to the general transcription machinery. The SWI/SNF complex was originally discovered in yeast but has mammalian homologues such as Brahma-related gene 1 (BRG-1), which has been shown to interact with the GR in a ligand-dependent manner (Fryer and Archer, 1998; John et al., 2008). Current evidence suggests that coactivator complexes do not all descend on the promoter at the same time but rather are sequentially recruited. The mechanism for this regulation has not been fully elucidated but may involve posttranslational modifications, such as ubiquitination that target the proteins for degradation by the proteosome.

Proteins interacting with transcription factors and DNA that keep the compact structure of the nucleosome intact and less accessible to the transcriptional machinery are known as corepressors. Silencing mediator for retinoid and thyroid hormone receptor (SMRT) and nuclear receptor corepressor (NCoR) are two well-studied corepressors that act on nuclear receptors through association with and recruitment of chromatin-condensing histone deacetylases (HDACs, such as HDAC1 and 2). These repressors also associate with histone methyltransferases such as retinoblastoma protein-interacting zinc-finger gene 1 (RIZ1) and ERG-associated protein with SET domain (ESET), both of which can promote association of proteins important for maintaining heterochromatin and silenced regions of DNA (Yoon et al., 2003). Repressors can act directly on the transcription machinery such as the

Table 6.2 Examples of transcriptional coregulators and their actions. Transcription factors such as the GR are regulated by proteins that modify chromatin structure or provide links to the transcriptional machinery. Coactivators enhance, while corepressors reduce, transcriptional activity of the GR.

Coregulator	Actions
Coactivator	
SRC-1, SRC-2 (GRIP1), SRC-3, CBP, PCAF, p300	Histone acetyltransferase activity, recruiting other coactivators
PRMT1, CARM	Arginine methyltransferase activity
TRAP, DRIP	Bridge to transcriptional machinery
BRG-1, SWI/SNF	ATP-dependent chromatin remodeling
Corepressor	
NCoR, SMRT	Recruiting histone deacetylases and other corepressors
RIZ1, ESET	Histone methyltransferase activity
SCP-1	Protein phosphatase activity
HDAC-1, HDAC-2	Histone deacetylase activity

phosphatase small CTD phosphatase 1 (SCP-1), which dephosphorylates RNA polymerase II. NCoR and SMRT were originally described as corepressors associated with receptors that can reside on their response elements in an unliganded state (such as retinoic acid receptor and thyroid receptor). But these proteins have also been reported to bind to the GR (Wang and Simons, 2005) and GR bound to the antagonist, RU486 (Frego and Davidson, 2006). Interestingly, the GR-β isoform, which doesn't bind hormone and resides primarily in the nucleus, has recently been reported to recruit HDACs and inhibit the expression of cytokine genes (Bowen et al., 2008). A summary of types of coregulators and examples of each can be found in Table 6.2.

Indirect (non-DNA-binding) mechanisms: binding to other transcription factors

The fact that glucocorticoids suppress inflammatory responses emphasized the repressive role of GR on proinflammatory genes. However, very few if any glucocorticoid-regulated inflammatory genes are reported to utilize nGREs. The failure to discover nGREs in the promoters of these genes and the study of possible interactions of the GR with other proteins that regulate transcription led to the discovery that GR can bind and interact with transcription factors important for the induction of cytokines without itself directly binding DNA. Indeed, GR-mediated inhibition of proinflammatory transcription factors such as activator protein (AP-1), STATs, nuclear factor of activated T cells (NFAT), and nuclear factor κB (NF-κB) leads to repression of the production of a number of cytokines including tumor necrosis factor α (TNFα), granulocyte macrophage colony-stimulating factor (GM-CSF), interleukins 1β, 2, 3, 6, 8, and 11, and other enzymes associated with the synthesis of inflammatory mediators such as inducible nitric oxide synthase (iNOS) and cyclooxygenase 2 (COX-2; Almawi and Melemedjian, 2002).

The mechanism of repression by protein–protein interaction has been widely studied and characterized, especially for NF-κB and AP-1. The GR can physically interact with p65, one of the subunits of NF-κB, and repress its transcriptional activity (Figure 6.2). Reciprocally, NF-κB has also been shown to negatively regulate GR-mediated transcription (McKay and Cidlowski, 2000; Tao et al., 2001). Multiple mechanisms have been proposed to account for this antagonism. For example, the physical interaction of GR with NF-κB may sequester both in the cytoplasm and thus inhibits translocation to the nucleus. Additionally GR can interact with DNA-bound NF-κB to inhibit activation of the basal transcriptional machinery. Another proposed mechanism is competition for mutual cofactors such as CBP and SRC-1, which are needed for the maximal transcriptional activity of both GR and NF-κB. GR has also been shown to obstruct p65-mediated histone acetyltransferase activity while promoting the recruitment of HDAC-2 to NF-κB target genes (Ito et al., 2000, 2006).

GR can also directly interact with the AP-1 subunit, c-Jun. The mechanisms of GR transcriptional repression of AP-1 are thought to be much the same as for NF-κB (Jonat et al., 1990). Although SRC-1 and CBP are required for maximal transcriptional activity of AP-1 as well as GR and NF-κB, competition for coactivators does not seem to be one of the mechanisms of GR repression of AP-1 (De Bosscher et al., 2001).

Interestingly, GR modulation of STAT transcription factors is more variable, with both inhibition and enhancement of transcription depending on the particular STAT involved. Many cytokines utilize the Janus kinase (JAK)/STAT signaling pathway to regulate gene transcription. The STATs themselves are induced by cytokines such as interleukins 4, 6, and 10. Since the STATs are responsible for increased inflammatory signaling it was assumed that glucocorticoid would repress these proinflammatory transcription factors, much like AP-1 and NF-κB discussed previously. For example, STAT1 induction of interferon-γ is repressed by GR. Thus it was surprising when a study reported that GR could synergize the prolactin induction of the β-casein gene through interaction with STAT5. The β-casein promoter contains no identifiable GREs and the DBD of the GR is not necessary for the synergy. GR can directly interact with STAT5 as shown by coimmunoprecipitation and gel-shift assays (Stoecklin et al., 1997). It has been proposed that GR acts like a coactivator in conjunction with STAT5 binding to its regulatory element (Figure 6.2). Another important family of proinflammatory genes are the Toll-like receptors (TLRs), which can be induced by bacterial lipoprotein and peptidoglycan and are components of the innate immune system. Interestingly the *TLR2* gene can be activated by GR as well as its more classical inducer, TNFα, in several cell types. Moreover, a combination of glucocorticoid and TNFα shows cooperative induction of TLR2 that depends on the presence of STAT5 (Hermoso et al., 2004). Finally, another example of *STAT* gene regulation that is enhanced by GR is interleukin-6/ STAT3 induction of γ-fibrinogen and α-2-macroglobulin. Although direct STAT3-GR binding has been demonstrated by coimmunoprecipitation this does not seem to be the mechanism in all cases.

In addition to the mechanisms described above recent studies have revealed secondary actions of glucocorticoids which can also affect gene expression; one example of this is the glucocorticoid regulation of tristetraprolin (TTP). Rather than antagonizing a transcription factor responsible for induction of a cytokine, the zinc-finger protein TTP destabilizes several proinflammatory cytokine mRNAs by binding to the AU-rich elements within their 3′ untranslated regions, targeting them for degradation. One of the prime examples of a cytokine targeted by TTP is TNFα. The synthetic glucocorticoid dexamethasone can induce TTP in a direct manner, which in turn represses TNFα mRNA in A549 cells and rat tissues (Smoak and Cidlowski, 2006). This provides a posttranscriptional mechanism of repression of inflammation mediated by the GR.

Translation and posttranslational modification of the GR

The GR protein, as stated above, can exist in multiple isoforms generated by alternative splicing and alternative translation initiation (Yudt and Cidlowski, 2001; Lu and Cidlowski, 2004). Interestingly, although these isoforms can bind hormone with relatively equal affinity, microarray analysis of single isoforms stably transfected into U-2 OS cells shows they can regulate different subsets of glucocorticoid-responsive genes. One potential explanation for these results is differential recruitment of coregulators by the individual isoform homodimers. Additionally, different GR isoforms could heterodimerize, providing yet another layer of complexity of transcriptional control by the GR. Another potential explanation for isoform-specific gene regulation could be subcellular localization of the receptor. For example, most of the isoforms, like GR-α, reside in the cytoplasm and translocate to the nucleus upon binding hormone; however, the GRα-D isoform is located primarily in nucleus even in the absence of ligand. In spite of this, the D isoform regulates the least number of genes and exhibits weak transactivational activity on reporter genes (Lu and Cidlowski, 2006). Finally, each GR isoform may be subject to isoform-specific posttranslational modifications including phosphorylation, ubiquitination, and SUMOylation. These modifications play important roles in the receptor's subcellular distribution, protein turnover, and transcriptional activities.

Phosphorylation

Among the nuclear receptor superfamily, GR was one of the earliest proteins evaluated for potential phosphorylation. The major kinases postulated to be responsible for the receptor phosphorylation include the mitogen-activated protein kinases (MAPKs), cyclin-dependent kinases (CDKs; Krstic et al., 1997), and c-Jun N-terminal kinases (JNKs; Itoh et al., 2002). The GR is constitutively phosphorylated under physiological conditions, but also undergoes agonist-induced and cell-cycle-dependent hyperphosphorylation on many sites (Orti et al., 1989; Bodwell et al., 1995). Early studies with synchronized cells showed that cell lines are sensitive to glucocorticoids in the DNA-replication phase of the cell cycle (late G_1 and S phase), but become resistant during the mitotic phase (G_2, M, and early G_1). Cells in S phase have low basal phosphorylation of GR whereas cells in G_2/M have hyperphosphorylated GR. This suggests a differential response to glucocorticoids depending on cell cycle and phosphorylation status of the receptor (Griffin and Ber, 1969; Bodwell et al., 1998). Phosphorylation of GR can alter its transcriptional activity, but the mechanism is complex. Surprisingly substitution of all serine/threonine residues thought to be phosphorylated in mouse GR had very little effect on transcriptional activity of a mouse mammary tumor virus (MMTV) promoter in a transfected receptor/COS-1 system (Mason and Housley, 1993; Webster et al., 1997). Mutations of all sites in the hGR produced a similar effect with a reporter carrying an MMTV promoter. However, with a minimal promoter containing two copies of a GRE the mutant receptors showed a significant downregulation of transcription, indicating that promoter context is important (Webster et al., 1997). Analysis of individual phosphorylation sites yielded some interesting results correlating intracellular localization, phosphorylation status as well as transactivational activity of GR. When phosphorylated on serine 203 or 211 hGR showed an increase in transcription in stably transfected and endogenous systems. Additionally serine 211 seemed to be important for ligand-induced translocation to the nucleus (Wang et al., 2002). However other studies have found no effect on translocation (Webster et al., 1997). Phosphorylation of GR at serine 404 was shown to be carried out by glycogen synthase kinase 3β (GSK-3β) and was hormone-dependent. Interestingly, cells harboring a receptor incapable of being phosphorylated by GSK-3β showed a redirection of the overall transcriptional response as assessed by whole-genome expression analysis. This was partially due to differences in recruitment of cofactors such as CBP (Galliher-Beckley et al., 2008). The phosphorylation of a particular site could create a steric hindrance, thereby altering the ability of the receptor to recruit specific cofactors. Phosphorylation of the GR may also affect the stability of the protein. In COS-1 cells phosphorylated mouse GR had a half-life of 8–9 hr in the presence of hormone. However, the mutation of multiple phosphorylation sites increased its half-life to 32 hr (Webster et al., 1997). Interestingly, phosphorylation has been shown to act as a signal for protein recognition by the ubiquitin-degradation pathway and this could be one explanation for the existence of multiple phosphorylation sites on the GR.

Ubiquitination and proteosomal degradation

Another posttranslational modification of the GR is the covalent attachment of ubiquitin, marking it for degradation by the 26 S proteosome. Ubiquitin-ligase enzymes E2 and E3 add ubiquitin molecules to the targeted protein. Polyubiquitination allows the protein to be recognized by the proteosome which degrades it into small peptides and amino acids (Skowyra et al., 1999). A simple model for including the degradation machinery in GR transcriptional regulation is downregulating transcription by destroying the ligand-bound receptor. Indeed, both the GR message and protein undergo homologous downregulation upon ligand binding. At the RNA level studies have shown that glucocorticoid treatment decreases GR mRNA levels by 50–80% in different tissues (Burnstein et al., 1994). Additionally ligand binding of GR led to a reduction in receptor protein levels (Dong et al., 1988; Hoeck et al., 1989). Studies examining the half-life of the protein have shown that ligand occupation of the receptor significantly decreases the half-life from 18 to 9 hr. As mentioned in the previous section, phosphorylation status is also an important determinant of GR protein stability. Phosphorylation is thought to be a signal that allows substrate recognition by enzymes in the ubiquitination pathway. The recognition site for E2 and E3, termed a PEST motif (that is, a peptide sequence enriched in proline, glutamic acid, serine, and threonine), has been identified in mouse, rat, and human *GR* genes (Rogers et al., 1986; Rechsteiner and Rogers, 1996). Use of the proteosomal inhibitor MG132 can block ligand-dependent downregulation of GR protein. Additionally glucocorticoid-induced transcriptional activity was increased when treated with MG132 (Wallace and Cidlowski, 2001). Interestingly, serine 412 located in a PEST motif of the mouse GR is also a target for phosphorylation, again linking phosphorylation status and protein degradation.

Another possible model of transcriptional regulation by the proteosome would be the targeting and degradation of coregulators, and indeed there is evidence that this occurs. Coactivators such as SRCs and CBP exhibit greater coactivator activity in the presence of MG132 (Lonard et al., 2000). The coactivator p300 has been shown to be degraded by the 26 S proteosome through kinase signaling pathways (Chen et al., 2004). The corepressors SMRT and NCoR are also targets of the proteosome (Zhang et al., 1998; Yan et al., 2003). This level of modulation would allow for increases (by degrading a repressor) as well as decreases in transcriptional activity.

SUMOylation

GR function can also be regulated by another posttranslational mechanism, which is the addition of a small ubiquitin-related modifier-1 (SUMO-1). Many proteins that are involved in gene regulation are targets for SUMO, including transcription factors, coregulators, and chromatin-remodeling proteins (Le Drean et al., 2002). Unlike ubiquitination, the linking of a SUMO-1 to a target protein does not lead to proteosomal degradation but rather regulates protein stability, localization, and activity of transcriptional regulators (Gill, 2005). There are three consensus SUMO-attachment sites on the GR, at lysines 277, 293, and 703; the first two are located in the NTD and the third is in the LBD. This suggests that modification by SUMOylation is important in GR regulation. The evidence so far supports SUMOylation of GR having an overall repressive effect on transcription but the mechanism underlying this effect is not clear. Studies with transfected constructs of GR showed that SUMOylation could cause a repression or no change in transcription depending on promoter context. A transcriptional corepressor, Daxx, is recruited to SUMOylated sites on the GR and interference with this binding relieves transcriptional repression (Lin et al., 2006).

Other possible mechanisms of action

The GR can be involved in what is termed rapid action or nongenomic signaling by glucocorticoids. This signaling can be independent of the receptor itself and is carried out by members of the chaperone complex released upon ligand binding to GR (Croxtall et al., 2000), or possibly dependent on membrane-bound GRs (Gametchu et al., 1999; Bartholome et al., 2004).

Other members of the nuclear receptor superfamily can affect transcription independently of ligand. This has been well defined for type II receptors, which are generally not sequestered in the cytoplasm, such as the thyroid receptor, which can occupy their response elements in an unliganded state (Glass and Rosenfeld, 2000). Promoters bound by heterodimers of thyroid receptor and the retinoid X receptor are repressed in the absence of thyroid hormone and activated by its presence (Lazar, 2003). There is evidence, however, that type I receptors such as the estrogen receptor, androgen receptor, and progesterone receptor can also affect transcription in the absence of ligand. For example unliganded estrogen receptor-α can bind to the promoter of the *E-cadherin* gene via a partial estrogen-response element and induce transcription in breast cancer cells (Cardamone et al., 2009). Additionally, androgen receptor can be activated and signal in the absence of androgens, possibly a fundamental step in the development of androgen-independent prostate cancer (Taplin and Balk, 2004). Progesterone receptor can regulate the expression of COX-2 and aromatase in the presence and absence of progesterone (Hardy et al., 2008). Although there is currently no direct evidence for ligand-independent GR-α signaling, it is not hard to imagine that such a mechanism exists for this receptor as well. Although the majority of GR-α resides in the cytoplasm there is the possibility of unliganded receptor in the nucleus. As stated above one of the GR-α isoforms generated by different transcription start sites (GR-D) is primarily located in the nucleus even in the absence of hormone (Lu and Cidlowski, 2005). Additionally, hGR-β, which does not bind glucocorticoid at all, is also located in the nucleus and can affect transcription by repressing cytokine genes (Bowen et al., 2008).

Concluding Remarks

The importance of maintaining homeostasis in the face of numerous environmental insults is reflected in the highly regulated functioning of glucocorticoids via the transcription factor, the GR. Glucocorticoids are present in almost all physiologic, cellular, and molecular networks and are fundamental in the behavioral and physical response to stress. This includes the inflammatory response, as well as the processes of sleep, growth, and reproduction. Disturbed regulation of this system leads to a wide variety of pathologies, such as Cushing syndrome, Addison's disease, chronic inflammation, and psychiatric disorders such as depression (Chrousos et al., 1993; McEwen, 1998). Given the overall importance of these hormones to the life of an organism it is fascinating to realize that the majority of signaling is through the GR, the product of only a single gene. Initially it was thought that there was one major functional form of this protein, GR-α. We now know that there are multiple splice variants and isoforms giving rise to unexpected receptor heterogeneity, as described in this chapter. The transcriptional activity of the GR was also initially thought to be accomplished by only direct binding of ligand-activated receptor to response elements in the promoters of glucocorticoid-regulated genes. Subsequently researchers discovered that glucocorticoid actions can be due to protein–protein interactions with other transcription factors. With the discovery and description of multiple transcriptional coregulator proteins another layer of complexity was added to the possible mechanisms of transcriptional regulation. Finally, posttranslational modification and proteosomal degradation contribute further diversity of transcriptional control mechanisms to achieve organ, tissue, and cell specificity of glucocorticoid actions.

References

Almawi, W. Y., & Melemedjian, O. K. (2002). Molecular mechanisms of glucocorticoid antiproliferative effects: antagonism of transcription factor activity by glucocorticoid receptor. *Journal of Leukocyte Biology, 71*(1), 9–15.

Bamberger, C. M., Bamberger, A. M., de Castro, M., & Chrousos, G. P. (1995). Glucocorticoid receptor beta, a potential endogenous inhibitor of glucocorticoid action in humans. *Journal of Clinical Investigation, 95*(6), 2435–2441.

Barnes, P. J. (1998). Anti-inflammatory actions of glucocorticoids: molecular mechanisms. *Clinical Science (London), 94*(6), 557–572.

Bartholome, B., Spies, C. M., Gaber, T., Schuchmann, S., Berki, T., Kunkel, D., Bienert, M., Radbruch, A., Burmester, G. R., Lauster, R., Scheffold, A., & Buttgereit, F. (2004). Membrane glucocorticoid receptors (mGCR) are expressed in normal human peripheral blood mononuclear cells and up-regulated after in vitro stimulation and in patients with rheumatoid arthritis. *FASEB Journal, 18*(1), 70–80.

Beato, M., Chalepakis, G., Schauer, M., & Slater, E. P. (1989). DNA regulatory elements for steroid hormones. *Journal of Steroid Biochemistry, 32*(5), 737–747.

Beger, C., Gerdes, K., Lauten, M., Tissing, W. J., Fernandez-Munoz, I., Schrappe, M., & Welte, K. (2003). Expression and structural analysis of glucocorticoid receptor isoform gamma in human leukaemia cells using an isoform-specific real-time polymerase chain reaction approach. *British Journal of Haematology, 122*(2), 245–252.

Black, B. E., Holaska, J. M., Rastinejad, F., & Paschal, B. M. (2001). DNA binding domains in diverse nuclear receptors function as nuclear export signals. *Current Biology, 11*(22), 1749–1758.

Bodwell, J. E., Hu, J. M., Orti, E., & Munck, A. (1995). Hormone-induced hyperphosphoryla-tion of specific phosphorylated sites in the mouse glucocorticoid receptor. *Journal of Steroid Biochemistry and Molecular Biology, 52*(2), 135–140.

Bodwell, J. E., Webster, J. C., Jewell, C. M., Cidlowski, J. A., Hu, J.-M., & Munck, A. (1998). Glucocorticoid receptor phosphorylation: overview, function and cell cycle-dependence. *Journal of Steroid Biochemistry and Molecular Biology, 65*, 91–99.

Bowen, H., Kelly, A., Lee, T., & Lavender, P. (2008). Control of cytokine gene transcription in Th1 and Th2 cells. *Clinical and Experimental Allergy, 38*(9), 1422–1431.

Burnstein, K. L., Jewell, C. M., Sar, M., & Cidlowski, J. A. (1994). Intragenic sequences of the human glucocorticoid receptor complementary DNA mediate hormone-inducible receptor messenger RNA down-regulation through multiple mechanisms. *Molecular Endocrinology, 8*(12), 1764–1773.

Cardamone, M. D., Bardella, C., Gutierrez, A., Di Croce, L., Rosenfeld, M. G., Di Renzo, M. F., & De Bortoli, M. (2009). ERalpha as ligand-independent activator of CDH-1 regu-lates determination and maintenance of epithelial morphology in breast cancer cells. *Proceedings of the National Academy of Sciences USA 106*(18), 7420–7425.

Chen, J., Halappanavar, S. S., St-Germain, J. R., Tsang, B. K., & Li, Q. (2004). Role of Akt/ protein kinase B in the activity of transcriptional coactivator p300. *Cellular and Molecular Life Sciences, 61*(13), 1675–1683.

Chrousos, G. P. (1995). The hypothalamic-pituitary-adrenal axis and immune-mediated inflammation. *New England Journal of Medicine, 332*(20), 1351–1362.

Chrousos, G. P., Detera-Wadleigh, S. D., & Karl, M. (1993). Syndromes of glucocorticoid resistance. *Annals of Internal Medicine, 119*(11), 1113–1124.

Croxtall, J. D., Choudhury, Q., & Flower, R. J. (2000). Glucocorticoids act within minutes to inhibit recruitment of signalling factors to activated EGF receptors through a receptor-dependent, transcription-independent mechanism. *British Journal of Pharmacology, 130*(2), 289–298.

Dahlman-Wright, K., Wright, A. P., & Gustafsson, J. A. (1992). Determinants of high-affinity DNA binding by the glucocorticoid receptor: evaluation of receptor domains outside the DNA-binding domain. *Biochemistry, 31*(37), 9040–9044.

De Bosscher, K., Vanden Berghe, W., & Haegeman, G. (2001). Glucocorticoid repression of AP-1 is not mediated by competition for nuclear coactivators. *Molecular Endocrinology, 15*(2), 219–227.

Dennis, A. P., & O'Malley, B. W. (2005). Rush hour at the promoter: how the ubiquitin-proteasome pathway polices the traffic flow of nuclear receptor-dependent transcrip-tion. *Journal of Steroid Biochemistry and Molecular Biology, 93*(2–5), 139–151.

Dong, Y., Poellinger, L., Gustafsson, J. A., & Okret, S. (1988). Regulation of glucocorticoid receptor expression: evidence for transcriptional and posttranslational mechanisms. *Molecular Endocrinology, 2*(12), 1256–1264.

Dostert, A., & Heinzel, T. (2004). Negative glucocorticoid receptor response elements and their role in glucocorticoid action. *Current Pharmaceutical Design, 10*(23), 2807–2816.

Duma, D., Jewell, C. M., & Cidlowski, J. A. (2006). Multiple glucocorticoid receptor isoforms and mechanisms of post-translational modification. *Journal of Steroid Biochemistry and Molecular Biology, 102*(1–5), 11–21.

Escriva, H., Bertrand, S., & Laudet, V. (2004). The evolution of the nuclear receptor super-family. *Essays in Biochemistry, 40*, 11–26.

Fondell, J. D., Ge, H., & Roeder, R. G. (1996). Ligand induction of a transcriptionally active thyroid hormone receptor coactivator complex. *Proceedings of the National Academy of Sciences USA 93*(16), 8329–8333.

Freedman, N. D., & Yamamoto, K. R. (2004). Importin 7 and importin alpha/importin beta are nuclear import receptors for the glucocorticoid receptor. *Molecular Biology of the Cell, 15*(5), 2276–2286.

Frego, L., & Davidson, W. (2006). Conformational changes of the glucocorticoid receptor ligand binding domain induced by ligand and cofactor binding, and the location of cofactor binding sites determined by hydrogen/deuterium exchange mass spectrometry. *Protein Science, 15*(4), 722–730.

Fryer, C. J., & Archer, T. K. (1998). Chromatin remodelling by the glucocorticoid receptor requires the BRG1 complex. *Nature, 393*(6680), 88–91.

Galliher-Beckley, A. J., Williams, J. G., Collins, J. B., & Cidlowski, J. A. (2008). Glycogen synthase kinase 3beta-mediated serine phosphorylation of the human glucocorticoid receptor redirects gene expression profiles. *Molecular and Cellular Biology, 28*(24), 7309–7322.

Gametchu, B., Chen, F., Sackey, F., Powell, C., & Watson, C. S. (1999). Plasma membrane-resident glucocorticoid receptors in rodent lymphoma and human leukemia models. *Steroids, 64*(1–2), 107–119.

Germain, P., Staels, B., Dacquet, C., Spedding, M., & Laudet, V. (2006). Overview of nomenclature of nuclear receptors. *Pharmacological Reviews, 58*(4), 685–704.

Giguere, V., Hollenberg, S. M., Rosenfeld, M. G., & Evans, R. M. (1986). Functional domains of the human glucocorticoid receptor. *Cell, 46*(5), 645–652.

Gill, G. (2005). Something about SUMO inhibits transcription. *Current Opinion in Genetics & Development, 15*(5), 536–541.

Glass, C. K., & Rosenfeld, M. G. (2000). The coregulator exchange in transcriptional functions of nuclear receptors. *Genes & Development, 14*(2), 121–141.

Grad, I., & Picard, D. (2007). The glucocorticoid responses are shaped by molecular chaperones. *Molecular and Cellular Endocrinology, 275*(1–2), 2–12.

Grange, T., Roux, J., Rigaud, G., & Pictet, R. (1989). Two remote glucocorticoid responsive units interact cooperatively to promote glucocorticoid induction of rat tyrosine aminotransferase gene expression. *Nucleic Acids Research, 17*(21), 8695–8709.

Griffin, M. J., & Ber, R. (1969). Cell cycle events in the hydrocortisone regulation of alkaline phosphatase in HeLa S3 cells. *Journal of Cell Biology, 40*(2), 297–304.

Gu, W., Malik, S., Ito, M., Yuan, C. X., Fondell, J. D., Zhang, X., & Roeder, R. G. (1999). A novel human SRB/MED-containing cofactor complex, SMCC, involved in transcription regulation. *Molecular Cell, 3*(1), 97–108.

Hager, G. L., Nagaich, A. K., Johnson, T. A., Walker, D. A., & John, S. (2004). Dynamics of nuclear receptor movement and transcription. *Biochimica et Biophysica Acta, 1677*(1–3), 46–51.

Hamid, Q. A., Wenzel, S. E., Hauk, P. J., Tsicopoulos, A., Wallaert, B., Lafitte, J. J., & Leung, D. Y. (1999). Increased glucocorticoid receptor beta in airway cells of glucocorticoid-insensitive asthma. *American Journal of Respiratory and Critical Care Medicine, 159*(5 Pt 1), 1600–1604.

Hardy, D. B., Janowski, B. A., Chen, C. C., & Mendelson, C. R. (2008). Progesterone receptor inhibits aromatase and inflammatory response pathways in breast cancer cells via ligand-dependent and ligand-independent mechanisms. *Molecular Endocrinology*, *22*(8), 1812–1824.

Hermoso, M. A., Matsuguchi, T., Smoak, K., & Cidlowski, J. A. (2004). Glucocorticoids and tumor necrosis factor alpha cooperatively regulate toll-like receptor 2 gene expression. *Molecular and Cellular Biology*, *24*(11), 4743–4756.

Hoeck, W., Rusconi, S., & Groner, B. (1989). Down-regulation and phosphorylation of glu-cocorticoid receptors in cultured cells. Investigations with a monospecific antiserum against a bacterially expressed receptor fragment. *Journal of Biology Chemistry*, *264*(24), 14396–14402.

Hollenberg, S. M., Weinberger, C., Ong, E. S., Cerelli, G., Oro, A., Lebo, R., & Evans, R. M. (1985). Primary structure and expression of a functional human glucocorticoid recep-tor cDNA. *Nature*, *318*(6047), 635–641.

Ito, K., Barnes, P. J., & Adcock, I. M. (2000). Glucocorticoid receptor recruitment of histone deacetylase 2 inhibits interleukin-1beta-induced histone H4 acetylation on lysines 8 and 12. *Molecular and Cellular Biology*, *20*(18), 6891–6903.

Ito, K., Yamamura, S., Essilfie-Quaye, S., Cosio, B., Ito, M., Barnes, P. J., & Adcock, I. M. (2006). Histone deacetylase 2-mediated deacetylation of the glucocorticoid receptor enables NF-kappaB suppression. *Journal of Experimental Medicine*, *203*(1), 7–13.

Itoh, M., Adachi, M., Yasui, H., Takekawa, M., Tanaka, H., & Imai, K. (2002). Nuclear export of glucocorticoid receptor is enhanced by c-Jun N-terminal kinase-mediated phospho-rylation. *Molecular Endocrinology*, *16*(10), 2382–2392.

John, S., Sabo, P. J., Johnson, T. A., Sung, M. H., Biddie, S. C., Lightman, S. L., Voss, T. C., Davis, S. R., Meltzer, P. S., Stamatoyannopoulos, J. A., & Hager, G. L. (2008). Interaction of the glucocorticoid receptor with the chromatin landscape. *Molecular Cell*, *29*(5), 611–624.

Jonat, C., Rahmsdorf, H. J., Park, K. K., Cato, A. C., Gebel, S., Ponta, H., & Herrlich, P. (1990). Antitumor promotion and antiinflammation: down-modulation of AP-1 (Fos/Jun) activity by glucocorticoid hormone. *Cell*, *62*(6), 1189–1204.

Krstic, M. D., Rogatsky, I., Yamamoto, K. R., & Garabedian, M. J. (1997). Mitogen-activated and cyclin-dependent protein kinases selectively and differentially modulate transcrip-tional enhancement by the glucocorticoid receptor. *Molecular and Cellular Biology*, *17*(7), 3947–3954.

Laudet, V., Hanni, C., Coll, J., Catzeflis, F., & Stehelin, D. (1992). Evolution of the nuclear receptor gene superfamily. *EMBO Journal*, *11*(3), 1003–1013.

Lazar, M. A. (2003). Thyroid hormone action: a binding contract. *Journal of Clinical Investigation*, *112*(4), 497–499.

Le Drean, Y., Mincheneau, N., Le Goff, P., & Michel, D. (2002). Potentiation of glucocorticoid receptor transcriptional activity by sumoylation. *Endocrinology*, *143*(9), 3482–3489.

Lin, D. Y., Huang, Y. S., Jeng, J. C., Kuo, H. Y., Chang, C. C., Chao, T. T., & Shih, H. M. (2006). Role of SUMO-interacting motif in Daxx SUMO modification, subnuclear localization, and repression of sumoylated transcription factors. *Molecular Cell*, *24*(3), 341–354.

Lonard, D. M., Nawaz, Z., Smith, C. L., & O'Malley, B. W. (2000). The 26S proteasome is required for estrogen receptor-alpha and coactivator turnover and for efficient estrogen receptor-alpha transactivation. *Molecular Cell*, *5*(6), 939–948.

Lu, N. Z., & Cidlowski, J. A. (2004). The origin and functions of multiple human glucocor-ticoid receptor isoforms. *Annals of the New York Academy of Sciences*, *1024*, 102–123.

Lu, N. Z., & Cidlowski, J. A. (2005). Translational regulatory mechanisms generate N-terminal glucocorticoid receptor isoforms with unique transcriptional target genes. *Molecular Cell*, *18*(3), 331–342.

Lu, N. Z., & Cidlowski, J. A. (2006). Glucocorticoid receptor isoforms generate transcription specificity. *Trends in Cell Biology*, *16*(6), 301–307.

Mason, S. A., & Housley, P. R. (1993). Site-directed mutagenesis of the phosphorylation sites in the mouse glucocorticoid receptor. *Journal of Biology Chemistry*, *268*(29), 21501–21504.

McEwen, B. S. (1998). Protective and damaging effects of stress mediators. *New England Journal of Medicine*, *338*(3), 171–179.

McKay, L. I., & Cidlowski, J. A. (2000). CBP (CREB binding protein) integrates NF-kappaB (nuclear factor-kappaB) and glucocorticoid receptor physical interactions and antagonism. *Molecular Endocrinology*, *14*(8), 1222–1234.

Merkulov, V. M., & Merkulova, T. I. (2009). Structural variants of glucocorticoid receptor binding sites and different versions of positive glucocorticoid responsive elements: Analysis of GR-TRRD database. *Journal of Steroid Biochemistry and Molecular Biology*, *115*(1–2), 1–8.

Meyer, M. E., Gronemeyer, H., Turcotte, B., Bocquel, M. T., Tasset, D., & Chambon, P. (1989). Steroid hormone receptors compete for factors that mediate their enhancer function. *Cell*, *57*(3), 433–442.

Miesfeld, R., Godowski, P. J., Maler, B. A., & Yamamoto, K. R. (1987). Glucocorticoid receptor mutants that define a small region sufficient for enhancer activation. *Science*, *236*(4800), 423–427.

Moalli, P. A., Pillay, S., Krett, N. L., & Rosen, S. T. (1993). Alternatively spliced glucocorticoid receptor messenger RNAs in glucocorticoid-resistant human multiple myeloma cells. *Cancer Research*, *53*(17), 3877–3879.

Nakai, Y., Usui, T., Tsukada, T., Takahashi, H., Fukata, J., Fukushima, M., & Imura, H. (1991). Molecular mechanisms of glucocorticoid inhibition of human proopiomelanocortin gene transcription. *Journal of Steroid Biochemistry and Molecular Biology*, *40*(1–3), 301–306.

Oakley, R. H., Sar, M., & Cidlowski, J. A. (1996). The human glucocorticoid receptor beta isoform. Expression, biochemical properties, and putative function. *Journal of Biology Chemistry*, *271*(16), 9550–9559.

Oakley, R. H., Webster, J. C., Sar, M., Parker, C. R., Jr., & Cidlowski, J. A. (1997). Expression and subcellular distribution of the beta-isoform of the human glucocorticoid receptor. *Endocrinology*, *138*(11), 5028–5038.

Okamoto, K., Hirano, H., & Isohashi, F. (1993). Molecular cloning of rat liver glucocorticoid-receptor translocation promoter. *Biochemical and Biophysical Research Communications*, *193*(3), 848–854.

Orti, E., Mendel, D. B., Smith, L. I., & Munck, A. (1989). Agonist-dependent phosphorylation and nuclear dephosphorylation of glucocorticoid receptors in intact cells. *Journal of Biology Chemistry*, *264*(17), 9728–9731.

Pratt, W. B., Galigniana, M. D., Morishima, Y., & Murphy, P. J. (2004). Role of molecular chaperones in steroid receptor action. *Essays in Biochemistry*, *40*, 41–58.

Rachez, C., Suldan, Z., Ward, J., Chang, C. P., Burakov, D., Erdjument-Bromage, H., Tempst, P., & Freedman, L. P. (1998). A novel protein complex that interacts with the vitamin D3 receptor in a ligand-dependent manner and enhances VDR transactivation in a cell-free system. *Genes & Development*, *12*(12), 1787–1800.

Ray, D. W., Davis, J. R., White, A., & Clark, A. J. (1996). Glucocorticoid receptor structure and function in glucocorticoid-resistant small cell lung carcinoma cells. *Cancer Research*, *56*(14), 3276–3280.

Rechsteiner, M., & Rogers, S. W. (1996). PEST sequences and regulation by proteolysis. *Trends in Biochemical Science, 21*(7), 267–271.

Rhen, T., & Cidlowski, J. A. (2005). Antiinflammatory action of glucocorticoids–new mechanisms for old drugs. *New England Journal of Medicine, 353*(16), 1711–1723.

Rivers, C., Levy, A., Hancock, J., Lightman, S., & Norman, M. (1999). Insertion of an amino acid in the DNA-binding domain of the glucocorticoid receptor as a result of alternative splicing. *Journal of Clinical Endocrinology and Metabolism, 84*(11), 4283–4286.

Rogers, S., Wells, R., & Rechsteiner, M. (1986). Amino acid sequences common to rapidly degraded proteins: the PEST hypothesis. *Science, 234*(4774), 364–368.

Rosenfeld, M. G., Lunyak, V. V., & Glass, C. K. (2006). Sensors and signals: a coactivator/corepressor/epigenetic code for integrating signal-dependent programs of transcriptional response. *Genes & Development, 20*(11), 1405–1428.

Schaaf, M. J., & Cidlowski, J. A. (2002). Molecular mechanisms of glucocorticoid action and resistance. *Journal of Steroid Biochemistry and Molecular Biology, 83*(1–5), 37–48.

Skowyra, D., Koepp, D. M., Kamura, T., Conrad, M. N., Conaway, R. C., Conaway, J. W., & Harper, J. W. (1999). Reconstitution of G1 cyclin ubiquitination with complexes containing SCFGrr1 and Rbx1. *Science, 284*(5414), 662–665.

Smoak, K., & Cidlowski, J. A. (2006). Glucocorticoids regulate tristetraprolin synthesis and posttranscriptionally regulate tumor necrosis factor alpha inflammatory signaling. *Molecular and Cellular Biology, 26*(23), 9126–9135.

Sousa, A. R., Lane, S. J., Cidlowski, J. A., Staynov, D. Z., & Lee, T. H. (2000). Glucocorticoid resistance in asthma is associated with elevated in vivo expression of the glucocorticoid receptor beta-isoform. *Journal of Allergy and Clinical Immunology, 105*(5), 943–950.

Stoecklin, E., Wissler, M., Moriggl, R., & Groner, B. (1997). Specific DNA binding of Stat5, but not of glucocorticoid receptor, is required for their functional cooperation in the regulation of gene transcription. *Molecular and Cellular Biology, 17*(11), 6708–6716.

Tao, Y., Williams-Skipp, C., & Scheinman, R. I. (2001). Mapping of glucocorticoid receptor DNA binding domain surfaces contributing to transrepression of NF-kappa B and induction of apoptosis. *Journal of Biology Chemistry, 276*(4), 2329–2332.

Taplin, M. E., & Balk, S. P. (2004). Androgen receptor: a key molecule in the progression of prostate cancer to hormone independence. *Journal of Cellular Biochemistry, 91*(3), 483–490.

Tora, L., White, J., Brou, C., Tasset, D., Webster, N., Scheer, E., & Chambon, P. (1989). The human estrogen receptor has two independent nonacidic transcriptional activation functions. *Cell, 59*(3), 477–487.

Wallace, A. D., & Cidlowski, J. A. (2001). Proteasome-mediated glucocorticoid receptor degradation restricts transcriptional signaling by glucocorticoids. *Journal of Biology Chemistry, 276*(46), 42714–42721.

Wang, D., & Simons, Jr, S. S. (2005). Corepressor binding to progesterone and glucocorticoid receptors involves the activation function-1 domain and is inhibited by molybdate. *Molecular Endocrinology, 19*(6), 1483–1500.

Wang, Z., Frederick, J., & Garabedian, M. J. (2002). Deciphering the phosphorylation "code" of the glucocorticoid receptor in vivo. *Journal of Biology Chemistry, 277*(29), 26573–26580.

Webster, J. C., Jewell, C. M., Bodwell, J. E., Munck, A., Sar, M., & Cidlowski, J. A. (1997). Mouse glucocorticoid receptor phosphorylation status influences multiple functions of the receptor protein. *Journal of Biology Chemistry, 272*(14), 9287–9293.

Weinberger, C., Hollenberg, S. M., Ong, E. S., Harmon, J. M., Brower, S. T., Cidlowski, J., & Evans, R. M. (1985). Identification of human glucocorticoid receptor complementary DNA clones by epitope selection. *Science, 228*(4700), 740–742.

Wright, A. P., Zilliacus, J., McEwan, I. J., Dahlman-Wright, K., Almlof, T., Carlstedt-Duke, J., & Gustafsson, J. A. (1993). Structure and function of the glucocorticoid receptor. *Journal of Steroid Biochemistry and Molecular Biology, 47*(1–6), 11–19.

Yan, F., Gao, X., Lonard, D. M., & Nawaz, Z. (2003). Specific ubiquitin-conjugating enzymes promote degradation of specific nuclear receptor coactivators. *Molecular Endocrinology, 17*(7), 1315–1331.

Yoon, H. G., Chan, D. W., Reynolds, A. B., Qin, J., & Wong, J. (2003). N-CoR mediates DNA methylation-dependent repression through a methyl CpG binding protein Kaiso. *Molecular Cell, 12*(3), 723–734.

Yudt, M. R., & Cidlowski, J. A. (2001). Molecular identification and characterization of a and b forms of the glucocorticoid receptor. *Molecular Endocrinology, 15*(7), 1093–1103.

Zaret, K. S., & Yamamoto, K. R. (1984). Reversible and persistent changes in chromatin structure accompany activation of a glucocorticoid-dependent enhancer element. *Cell, 38*(1), 29–38.

Zhang, J., Guenther, M. G., Carthew, R. W., & Lazar, M. A. (1998). Proteasomal regulation of nuclear receptor corepressor-mediated repression. *Genes & Development, 12*(12), 1775–1780.

Part II

Stress Influences on Brain Plasticity and Cognition

7

Stress and Adult Neurogenesis

Timothy J. Schoenfeld and Elizabeth Gould

The seminal studies of McEwen and colleagues (1968) showed that the hippocampus is enriched with adrenal steroid receptors. Glucocorticoids play an important role in the stress response: increased levels of circulating glucocorticoids help mobilize energy, particularly under low-glucose conditions, presumably to cope with an immediate threat. One of the functions of adrenal steroid receptors in the hippocampus is to respond to elevated glucocorticoid levels and participate in returning the hypothalamic–pituitary–adrenal (HPA) axis to baseline. Indeed, studies have shown that lesion of the ventral hippocampus impairs the HPA axis shut off response (Jacobson and Sapolsky, 1991; Herman et al., 1995). Because glucocorticoids are catabolic hormones and the hippocampus exhibits a high degree of structural plasticity, including the ongoing production of new neurons throughout life, the concentration of glucocorticoid receptors in this brain region renders it potentially vulnerable to growth inhibition.

Studies have shown that glucocorticoids can alter structural plasticity in the hippocampus in various ways. High levels of glucocorticoids applied chronically can decrease dendritic arborization in the CA3 region of the hippocampus (where CA means cornu ammonis; Woolley et al., 1990; McEwen, 1999; see also Figure 7.1). Glucocorticoids can also diminish the rates of cell proliferation and adult neurogenesis in the dentate gyrus (Cameron and Gould, 1994; McEwen, 1999; Mirescu and Gould, 2006). Furthermore, glucocorticoids decrease blood flow to the hippocampus, potentially producing neuronal damage (Endo et al., 1997). The effects of glucocorticoids in the hippocampus do not just result from exogenous administration of hormones: stress-induced elevations in circulating glucocorticoids exert similar effects on hippocampal structure (Watanabe et al., 1992; McEwen, 1999;

The Handbook of Stress: Neuropsychological Effects on the Brain, First Edition.
Edited by Cheryl D. Conrad.
© 2011 Blackwell Publishing Ltd. Published 2011 by Blackwell Publishing Ltd.

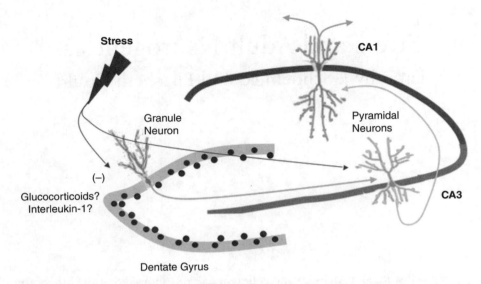

Figure 7.1   Principal cell types in the hippocampus and some effects of stress. Schematic diagram showing the three principal cell types in the hippocampus—granule cells of the dentate gyrus, pyramidal cells of the CA3 region, and pyramidal cells of the CA1 region—as well as their main axonal projection patterns. The dentate gyrus undergoes adult neurogenesis (new neurons are shown as black dots), a process that is inhibited by stress, through elevated glucocorticoid levels and, potentially, interleukin-1. Stress also influences pyramidal neurons in the CA3 region by inducing atrophy of apical dendrites. In addition to these changes, stress alters many other processes, such as blood flow, gliogenesis, and dendritic spine number, size, and shape throughout the hippocampus.

Tanapat et al., 2001; Mirescu and Gould, 2006). This chapter will focus on how stressful experiences can alter adult neurogenesis in the dentate gyrus of the hippocampus. We will review research conducted over the past decade examining the effects of different stressors, the putative mechanisms that underlie stress effects on neurogenesis, and the possible role of adult neurogenesis in hippocampal function.

Adult Neurogenesis in the Dentate Gyrus

The traditional view of brain development is that neuron production, or neurogenesis, stops shortly after birth. In the 1960s, Altman and colleagues discovered newly generated neurons in the dentate gyrus of the adult rat, cat, and guinea pig (Altman, 1963; Altman and Das, 1965; Altman and Das, 1967). Although this work was detailed and thorough, it did not alter the traditional view of brain development. In the 1970s and 1980s, Michael Kaplan used electron microscopy to further characterize new cells in the adult rat brain as neurons (Kaplan and Hinds, 1977; Kaplan and Bell, 1984). Like Altman's work, these findings were not well received by the scientific community and did little to convince skeptics that neurogenesis in the brain may persist beyond development. In the 1980s, Nottebohm showed that neurons were produced in the brains of adult song birds and that the new neurons received synaptic input, extended axons into target regions, and responded to auditory stimuli with the generation of action potentials (Nottebohm, 1985). Because these studies were carried out in birds and not mammals, however, the phenomenon of adult neurogenesis was believed to be restricted to nonmammals.

It was not until the late 1990s, when the technique of bromodeoxyuridine (BrdU) labeling was applied to the question, that adult neurogenesis was rediscovered in the dentate gyrus of mammals. BrdU is a synthetic thymidine analogue that, when exogenously applied, is incorporated into the DNA of dividing cells. BrdU labeling does not require autoradiography, which involves radioactivity and underestimates the number of new cells in a thick tissue section, and can be combined with neuron-specific markers to discriminate new neurons from glia (Kuhn et al., 1996). This latter point is particularly important because glial cells and other nonneuronal cells are known to divide in adulthood. Using this method, adult neurogenesis in the dentate gyrus has now been demonstrated in a variety of mammalian species, including the mouse (Kempermann et al., 1997), rat (Kuhn et al., 1996; Cameron and McKay, 2001), guinea pig (Guidi et al., 2005), marsupial (Harman et al., 2003), tree shrew (Gould et al., 1997), marmoset (Gould et al., 1998), macaque (Gould et al., 1999a), and even human (Eriksson et al., 1998). Thus, it took four decades to overturn the traditional view that neurogenesis only occurs during development; work from many laboratories strongly supports the view that neurogenesis is a robust feature of the dentate gyrus throughout life. It should be noted that adult neurogenesis is also a robust phenomenon in the olfactory bulb and has been reported in a large number of other brain regions, including the striatum, amygdala, hypothalamus, and neocortex, but consensus in the field has only been reached for the dentate gyrus and olfactory bulb (see Gould, 2007 for review).

The process of adult neurogenesis can be divided into three stages: cell proliferation, differentiation, and survival. Cell proliferation refers to the creation of new cells by the asymmetric division of progenitor cells located in the subgranular zone, the region between the hilus and the granule cell layer (Plate 2). Progenitor cells exhibit radial glia-like morphology (Seri et al., 2001) and express the astroglial marker glial fibrillary acid protein (GFAP). These progenitor cells give rise to transient amplifying neuroblasts (Kempermann et al., 2004). Differentiation occurs after cell division when molecular factors seal the fate of a daughter cell into a neuron or glia. Glial differentiation produces morphological changes as the cell continues to express GFAP, while neuronal differentiation downregulates GFAP expression and induces expression of doublecortin and polysialated neuronal cell adhesion molecule, markers for immature neurons. Postmitotic immature neurons then migrate the short distance into the granule cell layer and become granule cells (van Praag et al., 2002). Mature neurons express the neuronal markers NeuN and calbindin, among others. Over the course of a few weeks following cell division, new neurons develop dendritic arbors characteristic of granule cells (Ribak et al., 2004), extend axons into the CA3 region of the hippocampus (Hastings and Gould, 1999; Zhao et al., 2006), generate action potentials (van Praag et al., 2002), and exhibit synaptic plasticity (Snyder et al., 2001; Ge et al., 2007; see Figure 7.1). It is worth noting that for a few weeks after their production new neurons cannot be inhibited by γ-aminobutyric acid (GABA), the main inhibitory neurotransmitter of mature granule cells, and instead respond to GABA with depolarization. During this time as well, new neurons exhibit enhanced synaptic plasticity (Snyder et al., 2001; Ge et al., 2007). These characteristics—lack of synaptic inhibition and enhanced plasticity—make new neurons ideal candidates for influencing hippocampal function. Thus, although small in number relative to developmentally generated granule cells, granule cells produced in adulthood are likely to have a large effect on hippocampal circuitry.

Effects of Aversive Experience on Adult Neurogenesis

A large number of studies have focused on the effects of exposure to aversive experience on adult neurogenesis in the dentate gyrus (reviewed in Mirescu and Gould, 2006). In examining the larger literature on the subject, the overall picture is that stress has a suppressive effect on adult neurogenesis, causing a reduction in the production of new neurons (Table 7.1). However, some studies suggest that stress

Table 7.1 Effects of different stressors on cell proliferation, differentiation, and survival.

Stressor		Cell proliferation	Cell differentiation	Cell survival
Restraint	Acute	No change (rat) Increase (mouse)	NA	NA
	Chronic	Decrease (rat)	NA	Decrease (rat)
Psychosocial	Acute	Decrease (marmoset, tree shrew, mouse) No change (rat)	NA	NA
	Chronic	Decrease (tree shrew, rat)	NA	Decrease (tree shrew, rat)
Inescapable shock	Acute	Decrease (rat)	NA	NA
	Chronic	Decrease (rat)	Decrease (rat)	NA
Predator odor		Decrease or no change (rat)	NA	NA
Maternal separation		Decrease (rat)	Decrease (rat)	No change (rat)
Postpartum experience		Decrease (rat)	Decrease (rat)	No change (rat)
Difficult learning paradigm		Decrease (rat)	NA	Decrease (rat)
Chronic mild stress		Decrease (rat)	Decrease (rat)	Decrease (rat)
Running		Increase (rat, mouse)	Increase (rat, mouse)	Increase (rat, mouse)
Environmental enrichment		Increase (rat, mouse)	Increase (rat, mouse)	Increase (rat, mouse)

affects different stages of neurogenesis and no effects or stimulatory effects have also been demonstrated. One possible explanation for these differences may lie in the various stressors used and the different hormonal and neural mechanisms these experiences may engage.

Social stressors

When placed with a larger, more aggressive conspecific, a rodent typically experiences a stress reaction. The influence of social stress on the hippocampus has been investigated in several mammalian species; in all cases, the effects of social stress appear to be detrimental. Tree shrews establish strong dominant/subordinate relationships that are particularly stressful for the subordinate animal. Acute exposure to a dominant tree shrew is sufficient to decrease cell proliferation in the dentate gyrus of subordinate tree shrews (Gould et al., 1997). Similar effects have been reported in adult marmosets, New World monkeys, when exposed to a resident/intruder model of social stress (Gould et al., 1998). In tree shrews, chronic social stress has a similar effect to acute social stress: a decrease in cell proliferation in the dentate gyrus (Czeh et al., 2001, 2002; Simon et al., 2005). Moreover, chronic social stress decreases the survival of new neurons in the dentate gyrus (Czeh et al., 2002). Similar effects have been observed for social stress in rodents. In mice exposed to chronic social stress, subordinate behavior is correlated negatively with rates of cell proliferation (Mitra et al., 2006). In rats, acute psychosocial stress does not affect cell proliferation, but decreases both short-term (10 days) and long-term (4 weeks) survival of new neurons in subordinate animals (Thomas et al., 2007). However, in this latter experiment the new cells were labeled before the stress so a direct test of stress effects on cell proliferation was not made. Chronic psychosocial stress decreases both cell proliferation and survival of new cells in the dentate gyrus of subordinate rats (Czeh et al., 2007). Taken together, these results strongly suggest that social stress decreases the production of new neurons by reducing the proliferation of progenitor cells and the survival of new neurons.

Predator odor exposure

Because rodents rely heavily on olfactory cues to detect danger, it is not surprising that odors of natural predators, such as foxes or weasels, elicit a stress reaction. Exposure to predator odor activates the HPA axis and produces defensive and anxiety-like behavior in rats. Acute exposure to trimethylthiazoline, a main component of fox feces, decreases cell proliferation and the production of immature neurons in the dentate gyrus of adult male rats (Tanapat et al., 2001; Mirescu et al., 2004; Hill et al., 2006; Kambo and Galea, 2006). This effect seems to be related to the stressful nature of the stimulus, as opposed to any novelty or enrichment effect, in that other novel odors, such as peppermint, did not reduce cell proliferation in the dentate gyrus. Moreover, the inhibitory effects of trimethylthiazoline exposure on cell proliferation were blocked by normalizing corticosterone levels (through adrenalectomy followed by replacement with low-dose corticosterone in the drinking water) (Tanapat et al., 2001). Although the inhibitory effect of fox odor exposure on cell proliferation appears to be robust in male rats, it does not occur in females, suggesting a sex difference in the mechanisms that control adult neurogenesis (Falconer and Galea, 2003). It should be noted that one study failed to demonstrate a decrease in cell proliferation with predator odor exposure (Thomas et al., 2006) despite an increase in glucocorticoid levels, but this study labeled the new cells during, instead of following, stressor exposure. Thus it was not an adequate test of the effects of stress on cell proliferation.

Restraint

Exposure to restraint is a commonly used stressor for evaluation of effects on the hippocampus. The effects of restraint on adult neurogenesis, however, are complicated and do not directly correspond to the effects of social stress and predator odor exposure. In addition, the effects of restraint on adult neurogenesis are contradictory. Several studies have shown that acute restraint lasting between 2 and 6 hr has no effect on cell proliferation in the dentate gyrus of adult rats (Pham et al., 2003; Kee et al., 2002; Rosenbrock et al., 2005). By contrast, Bain and colleagues (2004) reported that 3 hr of restraint decreases cell proliferation in the dentate gyrus of adult rats. Chronic restraint has been shown to significantly reduce the proliferation of new cells in the dentate gyrus of adult rats in one study (Rosenbrock et al., 2005), with another showing no such effect on cell proliferation but instead reduced survival of new cells (Pham et al., 2003). A more recent report suggests a temporary but beneficial effect of restraint stress on the survival of new neurons in the dentate gyrus (Snyder et al., 2009b). Buynitsky and Mostofsky (2009) recently suggested that comparisons between studies of different methodological approaches to restraint are difficult because changes in the intensity, duration, and frequency of restraint involve complex changes within the rodent brain. Although the reasons for these discrepancies remain unknown, the opposite restraint stress effect (increase in cell proliferation) has been observed in mice (Bain et al., 2004), suggesting that species and possibly strain differences could be responsible for some differential outcomes in the response to restraint.

Electric shock

Shock to the tail or foot is known to activate the HPA axis and induce anxiety-like behavior. Inescapable foot shock or acute exposure to shock-avoidance testing results in decreases in cell proliferation in the dentate gyrus of the adult rat (Malberg and Duman, 2003). Chronic foot shock also decreases cell proliferation and differentiation of new neurons (Dagyte et al., 2009). However, cell proliferation does not change directly following foot-shock trials, instead showing a delayed decrease in cell proliferation 7 days after foot-shock trials (Fornal et al., 2007). As with social stress and restraint, the differential effects of stress across studies may be dependent on the timing of stress exposure relative to cell labeling as well as the strain or species used.

Maternal separation and postpartum experience

Pups that are maternally separated exhibit increased anxiety-like behavior later in life (Sánchez et al., 2001). Prolonged maternal separation decreases cell proliferation and differentiation of new neurons in the dentate gyrus (Mirescu et al., 2004; Oomen et al., 2010). Additional stressors, such as exposure to predator odor, in adulthood do not further suppress cell proliferation in maternally separated rats despite producing a seemingly normal activation of the HPA axis (Mirescu et al., 2004). As observed with fox odor exposure in adult rats, the inhibitory effects of maternal separation on adult neurogenesis of offspring are dependent on glucocorticoids; normalization of corticosterone levels prevents the effects (Mirescu et al., 2004). The postpartum period is also associated with elevated glucocorticoids in the mother (Leuner et al., 2007). Similar to other stressful experiences, cell proliferation and differentiation of new neurons are decreased in the postpartum period of mother rats, with no effect on neuronal survival (Leuner et al., 2007). As observed with other experiences that elevate glucocorticoid levels, the reduction in cell proliferation during the postpartum period is dependent on pup-induced increases in corticosterone levels. Preventing the rise in glucocorticoids in mother rats eliminates the reduction in cell proliferation in the dentate gyrus (Leuner et al., 2007).

Training on intensive learning tasks

Although many studies show increases in the number of new neurons in the dentate gyrus of animals trained on learning tasks (Gould et al., 1999b; Leuner et al., 2004, 2006), some evidence suggests that learning can have an inhibitory effect on adult neurogenesis when the experience is difficult and stressful (Aztiria et al., 2007). Ehninger and Kempermann (2006) suggest that stress related to a novel testing environment may decrease cell proliferation, despite learning. Increasing the difficulty of a testing paradigm does not alter cell proliferation in the dentate gyrus of adult rats, but stepwise increases in task difficulty sequentially decrease short-term survival (2 weeks) of new neurons in the dentate gyrus of adult rats (Epp et al., 2010).

Multiple mild stressors

Chronic mild stress is a paradigm often used as an animal model of depression, in which an animal is consistently exposed to unpredictable mild stressors over the course of multiple days. Repeated exposure to varying mild stressors can eventually lead to the development of learned helplessness. Mild stressors can include food- and water-deprivation, damp cage bedding, cold-water swim, tilted cage, chronic illumination, immobilization, tail pinch, social isolation, foot shock, shaker stress, restraint, and exposure to white noise, although usually not all. Chronic mild stress reduces cell proliferation in the dentate gyrus immediately after stressor exposure (Xu et al., 2007). Chronic mild stress does not appear to have a lasting effect on cell proliferation but it does seem to inhibit the differentiation (Oomen et al., 2007) and survival (Lee et al., 2006) of new neurons born prior to stress exposure. The extent to which differences in adult neurogenesis contribute to symptoms of learned helplessness remains unknown.

Age, Species, and Sex Differences

Numerous studies have reported age-related decline in adult neurogenesis in the hippocampus (Cameron and McKay, 1999; Leuner et al., 2006), raising the possibility that stress effects on neurogenesis may be affected by age. Some evidence suggests this is the case. Middle-aged tree shrews exhibit a greater decrease in cell proliferation in the dentate gyrus in response to stress than young adult tree shrews (Simon et al., 2006). In rats, recovery from chronic mild stress seems to occur in young adults (these animals show increased neuronal differentiation) but not in older adults (Toth et al., 2008).

Although adult neurogenesis seems to be a common feature of most mammalian species, there are differences in its rate and magnitude. A clear example of this can be seen comparing rats to mice (Snyder et al., 2009a): rats produce more new neurons and these neurons differentiate more rapidly and play a greater role in hippocampal function than those observed in mice. Baseline differences in adult neurogenesis may contribute to species differences in stress effects; as described above, restraint stress has been shown to decrease adult neurogenesis in rats and increase adult neurogenesis in mice (Bain et al., 2004).

Sex differences in baseline adult neurogenesis in the dentate gyrus, if they exist, are not robust. However, some evidence suggests that adult neurogenesis in the dentate gyrus of males responds to stress differently than in females. Chronic foot shock decreases short-term survival (2 weeks) of new neurons in adult male rats but increases short-term survival of new neurons in adult female rats. These sex differences appear to be dependent on social housing conditions and only emerge when animals are housed in isolation: group housing rats eliminates the difference between males and females (Westenbroek et al., 2004). Prenatal stress decreased survival of new neurons in adult male rats, but appears to have no effect on adult female rats (Zuena et al., 2008). Early weaning has a more pronounced detrimental effect on cell proliferation and survival of new neurons in adult male mice than adult female mice (Kikusui et al., 2009). Taken together, these findings raise the possibility that differences across the life span, across species, and between sexes exist in the response of adult neurogenesis to stress. These differences may underlie some of the contradictory findings in the literature on stress effects and may further point to different mechanisms that control neuron production.

Stress Effects on Adult Neurogenesis: a Role for Glucocorticoids?

Increased corticosterone levels decrease cell proliferation in the dentate gyrus of adult rats (Cameron and Gould, 1994). Corticosterone injection also decreases the survival of new neurons and differentiation of new cells into neurons in the dentate gyrus of adult rats (Wong and Herbert, 2006). Removal of circulating adrenal steroid hormones can be accomplished through adrenalectomy. Adrenalectomy increases cell proliferation in the adult rat dentate gyrus (Gould et al., 1992) and neuron-specific proliferation in the adult rat dentate gyrus (Cameron and Gould, 1994), and even restores the rate of cell proliferation in the dentate gyrus of the aged rat (Cameron and McKay, 1999). Adrenal steroid hormones act on two different receptors in the hippocampus: mineralocorticoid receptors (MRs) and glucocorticoid receptors (GRs) (Beato et al., 1995). Dexamethasone, a GR agonist, inhibits cell proliferation in the dentate gyrus of adult rats (Kim et al., 2004), which may work through inducing hypoactivity of MRs (Hassan et al., 1996). Likewise, MR$^{-/-}$ mutant mice lacking MRs show decreased proliferation rate in the dentate gyrus, whereas GR$^{-/-}$ mutant mice lacking GRs show normal levels of cell proliferation (Gass et al., 2000). Compared to wild-type mice, GR$^{+/-}$ mutant mice show 50% of the protein expression for GRs. Although GR$^{+/-}$ mice do not show differences in baseline cell proliferation rates in the dentate gyrus, adults have more potent decreases in cell proliferation in the dentate gyrus after restraint stress (Kronenberg et al., 2009). Also, treatment with mifepristone, a GR antagonist, restores cell proliferation to normal levels in the dentate gyrus of chronically stressed adult rats (Oomen et al., 2007). Therefore, GRs may respond to elevated corticosterone levels during stressful experiences by decreasing activity in MRs, leading to decreased cell proliferation and survival of new neurons in the dentate gyrus. Taken together, these results raise the possibility that elevated corticosterone is responsible for the stress-induced reductions in adult neurogenesis in the dentate gyrus. Some evidence, described above, directly supports this possibility. Diminished cell proliferation observed with fox odor exposure, maternal separation, and the postpartum period can be prevented by normalizing glucocorticoid levels. However, the extent to which glucocorticoids participate in stress-induced reductions in neuronal differentiation and survival remain unknown.

A Role for Interleukin-1?

Interleukin-1 (IL-1) is a proinflammatory cytokine, an immune factor that signals inflammation to the central nervous system, which activates the pituitary to stimulate glucocorticoid release by the adrenal glands (Bernton et al., 1987). Inflammation decreases cell proliferation and neuronal survival in the dentate gyrus of the adult rat (Ekdahl et al., 2003). Administration of IL-1β through subcutaneous injections decreases hippocampal neurogenesis (Goshen et al., 2008; Koo and Duman, 2008). Removing IL-1 receptor activity through knockout mice or antagonist overexpression abolishes the depressive-like behavioral effect of chronic mild stress, as mice still show normal spatial exploration and sucrose preference (Goshen et al., 2008). Studies in vitro suggest that hippocampal progenitors have IL-1 receptors and activation of these receptors decreases proliferation (Koo and Duman, 2008). IL-1 receptor antagonists block the decrease of cell proliferation in the dentate gyrus associated with chronic isolation (Ben Menachem-Zidon et al., 2008). These findings raise the possibility that stress effects on adult neurogenesis involve interleukin (Figure 7.1). The extent to which interleukin plays a role remains unknown.

Paradoxical Effects of Stress on Adult Neurogenesis

Contrary to evidence that glucocorticoid elevations, applied either exogenously or via exposure to aversive experience, inhibit hippocampal neurogenesis, some data suggest that activation of the HPA axis can be associated with enhanced hippocampal neurogenesis. For example, running activates the HPA axis and increases the levels of circulating glucocorticoids (Makatsori et al., 2003; Droste et al., 2003; Stranahan et al., 2006). Running also increases cell proliferation, neuronal differentiation, and survival of new neurons in the dentate gyrus of the adult mouse (van Praag et al., 1999; Klaus et al., 2009) and rat (Stranahan et al., 2006; Yi et al., 2009). Running also reverses the alcohol-induced decrease in hippocampal progenitor cell proliferation (Crews et al., 2004). These finding suggest that running must engage mechanisms that prevent elevated glucocorticoids from reducing cell proliferation. The same protective mechanisms may promote neuronal growth or additional processes may be responsible for those actions.

Like running, exposure to an enriched environment can elevate glucocorticoid levels (Benaroya-Milshtein et al., 2004) and increase adrenal gland size (Moncek et al., 2004). Environmental enrichment also increases differentiation and survival of new neurons in the dentate gyrus of the adult mouse (van Praag et al., 1999), even rescuing the age-related decline in neurogenesis (Kempermann et al., 2002). Environmental enrichment also ameliorates the decrease in both cell proliferation (Veena et al., 2009a) and the differentiation and survival of new neurons (Veena et al., 2009b) in the dentate gyrus of chronically stressed adult rats. Learning can increase circulating corticosterone levels (Leuner et al., 2004), and has been shown in multiple studies to increase adult neurogenesis in the dentate gyrus (Leuner et al., 2006).

How can experiences that activate the HPA axis and increase glucocorticoid levels also promote adult neurogenesis in the hippocampus? First, there are a number of growth factors that may be activated with running and environmental enrichment. Brain-derived neurotrophic factor (BDNF) has been implicated in the long-term survival of new neurons in the dentate gyrus of the adult mouse (Sairanen et al., 2005). Running increases BDNF expression (Ying et al., 2005), so BDNF may be a candidate for increasing survival of new neurons in the dentate gyrus. BDNF is also required for the effect of environmental enrichment, as BDNF-knockout mice fail to increase cell proliferation in response to enriched environment (Rossi et al., 2006). Decreased BDNF can also diminish the differentiation of new neurons in the adult mouse dentate gyrus, suggesting that it is required for normal adult neurogenesis as well (Taliaz et al., 2010). Vascular endothelial growth factor (VEGF) stimulates cell proliferation in the adult rat (Jin et al., 2002). VEGF mediates increases in adult neurogenesis from both running (Fabel et al., 2003) and environmental enrichment (Cao et al., 2004). Chronic stress decreases VEGF expression (Heine et al., 2005), whereas antidepressants increase VEGF expression (Warner-Schmidt and Duman, 2007). Therefore, VEGF is another good candidate for proliferative effects of some stressors. Insulin-like growth factor 1 (IGF-1) increases cell proliferation (Aberg et al., 2000). The proliferative effects of running are mediated by IGF-1 (Carro et al., 2000), and IGF-1 is upregulated following antidepressant treatment (Khawaja et al., 2004). IGF-1 may also be a key to the proliferative effects of some stressors. Taken together, these results strongly suggest that elevated glucocorticoids are not the only deciding factor in determining the rate of adult neurogenesis. It is only under certain conditions, such as those of aversive stress, that elevated glucocorticoids exert growth inhibition.

Social factors are also important for the proliferative effects of running on hippocampal neurogenesis. Socially isolated rats do not show short-term running-induced increases in cell proliferation in the dentate gyrus of adult males (Stranahan et al., 2006) and females (Leasure and Decker, 2009). Some studies have suggested that running either has no effect on cell proliferation in the dentate gyrus of the adult mouse (Hauser et al., 2009) or that increases in neuronal differentiation in the dentate gyrus of adult mice due to running have a detrimental effect on the stress response (Fuss et al., 2009). However, in both of these studies the experimental animals were housed in isolation, so the results may be difficult to interpret.

Potential Functions of Adult Neurogenesis

The influence of stress on adult neurogenesis raises questions about what the functional impact of these changes might be. Although we are far from providing a definitive answer to these questions, some evidence suggests that new neurons may participate in hippocampal functions, such as learning, modulation of the HPA axis, and anxiety regulation (Leuner and Gould, 2010). Snyder et al. (2010) used trans-genic mice specifically lacking adult neurogenesis in the dentate gyrus and measured how the HPA axis would respond to a mild stressor. After brief exposure to stress circulating corticosterone levels were significantly higher than controls in mice lacking adult neurogenesis, suggesting that ablation of hippocampal neurogenesis increased activation of the HPA axis. These results suggest that new neurons in the dentate gyrus may play an inhibitory role in the stress response. Eadie et al. (2009) used Fmr1-knockout mice, an animal model of fragile X syndrome, to explore the relationship between hippocampal neurogenesis and anxiety regulation in the ventral hippocampus. The hippocampus can be divided axially in the rodent into dorsal and ventral sections (Fanselow and Dong, 2010). The dorsal hippocampus seems to be more important for spatial navigation learning, while the ventral hip-pocampus is more important for regulation of anxiety-like behavior. Fmr1-knockout mice show increased anxiety responses and no differences in hippocampal-dependent learning paradigms, such as the Morris water maze. When examining hippocampal neurogenesis, the researchers found no differences in cell proliferation or differentiation of new neurons in the dorsal or ventral dentate gyrus of adult mice compared to controls. However, they did find significant decreases in the survival of new neurons in the ventral dentate gyrus specifically. The results indi-rectly suggest that new neurons in the ventral hippocampus are involved in inhibi-tory control over anxiety-like behavior.

In addition to the purported influence of new neurons in the hippocampus over anxiety and stress regulation, a larger literature suggests a link between adult neu-rogenesis and learning (see Leuner et al., 2006 for review). Methods for reducing adult neurogenesis, such as by use of antiproliferative agents, irradiation, and trans-genic models, have reported a diverse array of changes in learning and memory capabilities (Shors et al., 2001; Snyder et al., 2005, 2009a; Winocur et al., 2006; Clelland et al., 2009) although much of this work is contradictory. Although the precise role that new neurons play in learning and memory is unknown, the pos-sibility that stress-induced changes in cognitive function occur through actions on new neuron production exists. For example, chronic stress reduces adult neurogen-esis in the dentate gyrus and impairs hippocampal-dependent place learning (Ferragud et al., 2010). However, stress affects many systems in the brain, including dendritic architecture and synaptic plasticity in the hippocampus, so it may seem overly simplistic to claim that changes in adult hippocampal neurogenesis are solely responsible for changes in learning and memory. More likely, stress-related decreases in hippocampal neurogenesis are just one of the many contributors to cognitive function with chronic stress.

Summary

Neural progenitor cells in the subgranular zone of the dentate gyrus divide to create immature postmitotic cells that differentiate into mature granule cells. These granule cells integrate into functional networks in the hippocampus, receiving input from afferents and sending axons to the CA3 region of Ammon's horn. Adult neurogenesis in the hippocampus is susceptible to stress, and aversive stressful experiences have been shown to decrease the rate of cell proliferation, neuronal differentiation, and survival in the dentate gyrus. Pathways including glucocorticoids and IL-1 are potential mechanisms for the suppressive effects of stress on hippocampal neurogenesis. Although most experiences that activate the HPA axis are considered aversive stressors, there are some that both activate the HPA axis and increase hippocampal neurogenesis, most notably running and environmental enrichment. The beneficial effects of running and environmental enrichment may be mediated by the growth factors BDNF, VEGF, and IGF-1. Recent evidence has suggested that adult neurogenesis in the ventral dentate gyrus has a particular function as an inhibitory control over the HPA axis in response to stress and anxiety regulation. Further studies are needed to determine how new neurons are functionally integrated in circuits and the long-term effects of stress-induced changes in new neuron number.

References

Aberg, M. A., Aberg, N. D., Hedbacker, H., Oscarsson, J., & Eriksson, P. S. (2000). Peripheral infusion of IGF-1 selectively induces neurogenesis in the adult rat hippocampus. *Journal of Neuroscience, 20*, 2896–2903.

Altman, J. (1963). Autoradiographic investigation of cell proliferation in the brains of rats and cats. *Anatomical Record, 145*, 573–591.

Altman, J., & Das, G. D. (1965). Autoradiographic and histological evidence of postnatal hippocampal neurogenesis in rats. *Journal of Comparative Neurology, 124*, 319–335.

Altman, J., & Das, G. D. (1967). Postnatal neurogenesis in the guinea-pig. *Nature, 214*, 1098–1101.

Aztiria, E., Capodieci, G., Arancio, L., & Leanza, G. (2007). Extensive training in a maze task reduces neurogenesis in the adult rat dentate gyrus probably as a result of stress. *Neuroscience Letters, 416*, 133–137.

Bain, M. J., Dwyer, S. M., & Rusak, B. (2004). Restraint stress affects hippocampal cell proliferation differently in rats and mice. *Neuroscience Letters, 368*, 7–10.

Beato, M., Herrlich, P., & Schutz, G. (1995). Steroid hormone receptors: many actors in search of a plot. *Cell, 83*, 851–857.

Benaroya-Milshtein, N., Hollander, N., Apter, A., Kukulansky, T., Raz, N., Wilf, A., Yaniv, I., & Pick, C. G. (2004). Environmental enrichment in mice decreases anxiety, attenuates stress responses and enhances natural killer cell activity. *European Journal of Neuroscience, 20*, 1341–1347.

Ben Menachem-Zidon, O., Goshen, I., Kreisel, T., Ben Menahem, Y., Reinhartz, E., Ben Hur, T., & Yirmiya, R. (2008). Intrahippocampal transplantation of transgenic neural precursor cells overexpressing interleukin-1 antagonist blocks chronic isolation-induced impairment in memory and neurogenesis. *Neuropsychopharmacology, 33*, 2251–2262.

Bernton, E. W., Beach, J. E., Holaday, J. W., Smallridge, R. C., & Fein, H. G. (1987). Release of multiple hormones by a direct action of interleukin-1 on pituitary cells. *Science, 238*, 519–521.

Buynitsky, T., & Mostofsky, D. I. (2009). Restraint stress in biobehavioral research: Recent developments. *Neuroscience and Biobehavioral Reviews, 33*, 1089–1098.

Cameron, H. A., & Gould, E. (1994). Adult neurogenesis is regulated by adrenal steroids in the dentate gyrus. *Neuroscience, 61*, 203–209.

Cameron, H. A., & McKay, R. D. (1999). Restoring production of hippocampal neurons in old age. *Nature Neuroscience, 2*, 894–897.

Cameron, H. A., & McKay, R. D. (2001). Adult neurogenesis produces a large pool of new granule cells in the dentate gyrus. *Journal of Comparative Neurology, 435*, 406–417.

Cao, L., Jiao, X., Zuzga, D. S., Liu, Y., Fong, D. M., Young, D., & During, M. J. (2004). VEGF links hippocampal activity with neurogenesis, learning, and memory. *Nature Genetics, 36*, 827–835.

Carro, E., Nunez, A., Busiguina, S., & Torres-Aleman, I. (2000). Circulating insulin-like growth factor I mediates effects of exercise on the brain. *Journal of Neuroscience, 20*, 2926–2933.

Clelland, C. D., Choi, M., Romberg, C., Clemenson, Jr, G. D., Fragniere, A., Tyers, P., Jessberger, S., Saksida, L. M., Barker, R. A., Gage, F. H., & Bussey, T. J. (2009). A functional role for adult hippocampal neurogenesis in spatial pattern separation. *Science, 325*, 210–3.

Crews, F. T., Nixon, K., & Wilkie, M. E. (2004). Exercise reverses ethanol inhibition of neural stem cell proliferation. *Alcohol, 33*, 63–71.

Czeh, B., Michaelis, T., Watanabe, T., Frahm, J., de Biurrun, G., van Kampen, M., Bartolomucci, A., & Fuchs, E. (2001). Stress-induced changes in cerebral metabolites, hippocampal volume, and cell proliferation are prevented by antidepressant treatment with tianeptine. *Proceedings of the National Academy of Sciences USA, 98*, 12796–12801.

Czeh, B., Welt, T., Fischer, A. K., Erhardt, A., Schmitt, W., Müller, M. B., Toschi, N., Fuchs, E., & Keck, M. E. (2002). Chronic psychosocial stress and concomitant repetitive transcranial magnetic stimulation: effects on stress hormone levels and adult hippocampal neurogenesis. *Biological Psychiatry, 52*, 1057–1065.

Czeh, B., Muller-Keuker, J. I., Rygula, R., Abumaria, N., Hiemke, C., Domenici, E., & Fuchs, E. (2007). Chronic social stress inhbits cell proliferation in the adult medial prefrontal cortex: hemispheric asymmetry and reversal by fluoxetine treatment. *Neuropsychopharmacology, 32*, 1490–1503.

Dagyte, G., Van der Zee, E. A., Postema, F., Luiten, P. G., Den Boer, J. A., Trentani, A., & Meerlo, P. (2009). Chronic but not acute foot-shock stress leads to temporary suppression of cell proliferation in rat hippocampus. *Neuroscience, 162*, 904–913.

Droste, S. K., Gesing, A., Ulbricht, S., Muller, M. B., Linthorst, A. C., & Reul, J. M. (2003). Effects of long-term voluntary exercise on the mouse hypothalamic-pituitary-adrenocortical axis. *Endocrinology, 144*, 3012–3023.

Eadie, B. D., Zhang, W. N., Boehme, G., Gil-Mohapel, J., Kainer, L., Simpson, J. M., & Christie, B. R. (2009). Fmr1 knockout mice show reduced anxiety and alterations in neurogenesis that are specific to the ventral dentate gyrus. *Neurobiology of Disease, 36*, 361–373.

Ehninger, D., & Kempermann, G. (2006). Paradoxical effects of learning the Morris water maze on adult hippocampal neurogenesis in mice may be explained by a combination of stress and physical activity. *Genes, Brain, and Behavior, 5*, 29–39.

Ekdahl, C. T., Claasen, J. H., Bonde, S., Kokaia, Z., & Lindvall, O. (2003). Inflammation is detrimental for neurogenesis in adult brain. *Proceedings of the National Academy of Sciences USA, 100*, 13632–13637.

Endo, Y., Nishimura, J. I., Kobayashi, S., & Kimura, F. (1997). Long-term glucocorticoid treatments decrease local cerebral blood flow in the rat hippocampus, in association with histological damage. *Neuroscience, 79*, 745–752.

Epp, J. R., Haack, A. K., & Galea, L. A. (2010). Task difficulty in the Morris water task influences the survival of new neurons in the dentate gyrus. *Hippocampus, 20*, 866–876.

Eriksson, P. S., Perfilieva, E., Bjork-Eriksson, T., Alborn, A. M., Nordborg, C., Peterson, D. A., & Gage, F. H. (1998). Neurogenesis in the adult human hippocampus. *Nature Medicine, 4*, 1313–1317.

Fabel, K., Fabel, K., Tam, B., Kaufer, D., Baiker, A., Simmons, N., Kuo, C. J., & Palmer, T. D. (2003). VEGF is necessary for exercise-induced adult hippocampal neurogenesis. *European Journal of Neuroscience, 18*, 2803–2812.

Falconer, E. M., & Galea, L. A. (2003). Sex differences in cell proliferation, cell death and defensive behavior following acute predator odor stress in adult rats. *Brain Research, 975*, 22–36.

Fanselow, M. S., & Dong, H. W. (2010). Are the dorsal and ventral hippocampus functionally distinct structures? *Neuron, 65*, 7–19.

Ferragud, A., Haro, A., Sylvain, A., Velazquez-Sanchez, C., Hernandez-Rabaza, V., & Canales, J. J. (2010). Enhanced habit-based learning and decreased neurogenesis in the adult hippocampus in a murine model of chronic social stress. *Behavioral Brain Research, 210*, 134–139.

Fornal, C. A., Stevens, J., Barson, J. R., Blakley, G. G., Patterson-Buckendahl, P., & Jacobs, B. L. (2007). Delayed suppression of hippocampal cell proliferation in rats following inescapable shocks. *Brain Research, 1130*, 48–53.

Fuss, J., Ben Abdallah, N. M., Vogt, M. A., Touma, C., Pacifici, P. G., Palme, R., Witzemann, V., Hellweg, R., & Gass, P. (2009). Voluntary exercise induces anxiety-like behavior in adult C57BL/6J mice correlating with hippocampal neurogenesis. *Hippocampus, 20*, 364–376.

Gass, P., Kretz, O., Wolfer, D. P., Berger, S., Tronche, F., Reichardt, H. M., Kellendonk, C., Lipp, H. P., Schmid, W., & Schütz, G. (2000). Genetic disruption of mineralocorticoid receptor leads to impaired neurogenesis and granule cell degeneration in the hippocampus of adult mice. *EMBO Reports, 1*, 447–451.

Ge, S., Yang, C. H., Hsu, K. S., Ming, G. L., & Song, H. (2007). A critical period for enhanced synaptic plasticity in newly generated neurons of the adult brain. *Neuron, 54*, 559–566.

Goshen, I., Kreisel, T., Ben-Menachem-Zidon, O., Licht, T., Weidenfeld, J., Ben-Hur, T., & Yirmiya, R. (2008). Brain interleukin-1 mediates chronic stress-induced depression in mice via adrenocortical activation and hippocampal neurogenesis suppression. *Molecular Psychiatry, 13*, 717–728.

Gould, E. (2007). How widespread is adult neurogenesis in mammals? *Nature Reviews Neuroscience, 8*, 481–488.

Gould, E., Cameron, H. A., Daniels, D. C., Woolley, C. S., & McEwen, B. S. (1992). Adrenal hormones suppress cell division in the adult rat dentate gyrus. *Journal of Neuroscience, 12*, 3642–3650.

Gould, E., McEwen, B. S., Tanapat, P., Galea, L. A., & Fuchs, E. (1997). Neurogenesis in the dentate gyrus of the adult tree shrew is regulated by psychosocial stress and NMDA receptor activation. *Journal of Neuroscience, 17*, 2492–2498.

Gould, E., Tanapat, P., McEwen, B. S., Flugge, G., & Fuchs, E. (1998). Proliferation of granule cell precursors in the dentate gyrus of adult monkeys is diminished by stress. *Proceedings of the National Academy of Sciences USA, 95*, 3168–3171.

Gould, E., Reeves, A. J., Fallah, M., Tanapat, P., Gross, C. G., & Fuchs, E. (1999a). Hippocampal neurogenesis in adult Old World primates. *Proceedings of the National Academy of Sciences USA, 96,* 5263–5267.

Gould, E., Tanapat, P., Hastings, N. B., & Shors, T. J. (1999b). Neurogenesis in adulthood: a possible role in learning. *Trends in Cognative Science, 3,* 186–192.

Guidi, S., Ciani, E., Severi, S., Contestabile, A., & Bartesaghi, R. (2005). Postnatal neurogenesis in the dentate gyrus of the guinea pig. *Hippocampus, 15,* 285–301.

Harman, A., Meyer, P., & Ahmat, A. (2003). Neurogenesis in the hippocampus of an adult marsupial. *Brain, Behavior and Evolution, 62,* 1–12.

Hassan, A. H., van Rosenstiel, P., Patchev, V. K., Holsboer, F., & Almeida, O. F. (1996). Exacerbation of apoptosis in the dentate gyrus of the aged rat by dexamethasone and the protective role of corticosterone. *Experimental Neurology, 140,* 43–52.

Hastings, N. B., & Gould, E. (1999). Rapid extension of axons into the CA3 region by adult-generated granule cells. *Journal of Comparative Neurology, 413,* 146–154.

Hauser, T., Klaus, F., Lipp, H. P., & Amrein, I. (2009). No effect of running and laboratory housing on adult hippocampal neurogenesis in wild caught long-tailed wood mouse. *BMC Neuroscience, 10,* 43.

Heine, V. M., Zareno, J., Maslam, S., Joels, M., & Lucassen, P. J. (2005). Chronic stress in the adult dentate gyrus reduces cell proliferation near the vasculature and VEGF and Flk-1 protein expression. *European Journal of Neuroscience, 21,* 1304–1314.

Herman, J. P., Cullinan, W. E., Morano, M. I., Akil, H., & Watson, S. J. (1995). Contribution of the ventral subiculum to inhibitory regulation of the hypothalamo-pituitary-adrenocortical axis. *Neuroendocrinology, 7,* 475–482.

Hill, M. N., Kambo, J. S., Sun, J. C., Gorzalka, B. B., & Galea, L. A. (2006). Endocannabinoids modulate stress-induced suppression of hippocampal cell proliferation and activation of defensive behaviours. *European Journal of Neuroscience, 24,* 1845–1849.

Jacobson, L., & Sapolsky, R. (1991). The role of hippocampus in feedback regulation of the hypothalamic-pituitary-adrenocortical axis. *Endocrine Reviews 12,* 118–134.

Jin, K., Zhu, Y., Sun, Y., Mao, X. O., Xie, L., & Greenberg, D. A. (2002). Vascular endothelial growth factor (VEGF) stimulates neurogenesis in vitro and in vivo. *Proceedings of the National Academy of Sciences USA, 99,* 11946–11950.

Kambo, J. S., & Galea, L. A. (2006). Activation levels of androgens influence risk assessment behaviour but do not influence stress-induced suppression in hippocampal cell proliferation in adult male rats. *Behavioral Brain Research, 175,* 263–270.

Kaplan, M. S., & Bell, D. H. (1984). Mitotic neuroblasts in the 9-day-old and 11-month-old rodent hippocampus. *Journal of Neuroscience, 4,* 1429–1441.

Kaplan, M. S., & Hinds, J. W. (1977). Neurogenesis in the adult rat: electron microscope analysis of light radioautographs. *Science, 197,* 1092–1094.

Kee, N., Sivalingam, S., Boonstra, R., & Wojtowicz, J. M. (2002). The utility of Ki-67 and BrdU as proliferative markers of adult neurogenesis. *Journal of Neuroscience Methods, 115,* 97–105.

Kempermann, G., Kuhn, H. G., & Gage, F. H. (1997). More hippocampal neurons in adult mice living in an enriched environment. *Nature, 386,* 493–495.

Kempermann, G., Gast, D., & Gage, F. H. (2002). Neuroplasticity in old age: sustained fivefold induction of hippomcampal neurogenesis by long-term environmental enrichment. *Annals of Neurology, 52,* 135–143.

Kempermann, G., Jessberger, S., Steiner, B., & Kronenberg, G. (2004). Milestones of neuronal development in the adult hippocampus. *Trends in Neuroscience, 27,* 447–452.

Khawaja, X., Xu, J., Liang, J. J., & Barrett, J. E. (2004). Proteomic analysis of protein changes developing in rat hippocampus after chronic antidepressant treatment: implications for depressive disorders and future therapies. *Journal of Neuroscience Research, 75,* 451–460.

Kikusui, T., Ichikawa, S., & Mori, Y. (2009). Maternal deprivation by early weaning increases corticosterone and decreases hippocampal BDNF and neurogenesis in mice. *Psychoneuroendocrinology, 34,* 762–772.

Kim, J. B., Ju, J. Y., Kim, J. H., Kim, T. Y., Yang, B. H., Lee, Y. S., & Son, H. (2004). Dexamethasone inhibits proliferation of adult hippocampal neurogenesis in vivo and in vitro. *Brain Research, 1027,* 1–10.

Klaus, F., Hauser, T., Slomianka, L., Lipp, H. P., & Amrein, I. (2009). A reward increases running-wheel performance without changing cell proliferation, neuronal differentiation or cell death in the dentate gyrus of C57BL/6 mice. *Brain Research, 204,* 175–181.

Koo, J. W., & Duman, R. S. (2008). IL-1beta is an essential mediator of the antineurogenic and anhedonic effects of stress. *Proceedings of the National Academy of Sciences USA, 105,* 751–756.

Kronenberg, G., Kirste, I., Inta, D., Chourbaji, S., Heuser, I., Endres, M., & Gass, P. (2009). Reduced hippocampal neurogenesis in the GR(+/−) genetic model of depression. *European Archives of Psychiatry and Clinical Neuroscience, 259,* 499–504.

Kuhn, H. G., Dickinson-Anson, H., & Gage, F. H. (1996). Neurogenesis in the dentate gyrus of the adult rat: age-related decrease of neuronal progenitor proliferation. *Journal of Neuroscience, 16,* 2027–2033.

Leasure, J. L., & Decker, L. (2009). Social isolation prevents exercise-induced proliferation of hippocampal progenitor cells in female rats. *Hippocampus, 19,* 907–912.

Lee, K. J., Kim, S. J., Kim, S. W., Shin, Y. C., Park, S. H., Moon, B. H., Cho, E., Lee, M. S., Choi, S. H., Chun, B. G., & Shin, K. H. (2006). Chronic mild stress decreases survival, but not proliferation, of new-born cells in adult rat hippocampus. *Experimental & Molecular Medicine, 38,* 44–54.

Leuner, B., & Gould, E. (2010). Structural plasticity and hippocampal function. *Annual Review of Psychology, 61,* 111–140.

Leuner, B., Mendolia-Loffredo, S., Kozorovitskiy, Y., Samburg, D., Gould, E., & Shors, T. J. (2004). Learning enhances the survival of new neurons beyond the time when the hippocampus is required for memory. *Journal of Neuroscience, 24,* 7477–7481.

Leuner, B., Gould, E., & Shors, T. J. (2006). Is there a link between adult neurogenesis and learning? *Hippocampus, 16,* 216–224.

Leuner, B., Mirescu, C., Noiman, L., & Gould, E. (2007). Maternal experience inhibits the production of immature neurons in the hippocampus during the postpartum period through elevations in adrenal steroids. *Hippocampus, 17,* 434–442.

Makatsori, A., Duncko, R., Schwendt, M., Moncek, F., Johansson, B. B., & Jezova, D. (2003). Voluntary wheel running modulates glutamate receptor subunit gene expression and stress hormone release in Lewis rats. *Psychoneuroendocrinology, 28,* 702–714.

Malberg, J. E., & Duman, R. S. (2003). Cell proliferation in adult hippocampus is decreased by inescapable stress: reversal by fluoxetine treatment. *Neuropsychopharmacology, 28,* 1562–1571.

McEwen, B. S. (1999). Stress and hippocampal plasticity. *Annual Review of Neuroscience, 22,* 105–122.

McEwen B.S., Weiss, J. M., & Schwartz, L. S. (1968). Selective retention of corticosterone by limbic structures in rat brain. *Nature, 220,* 911–912.

Mirescu, C., & Gould, E. (2006). Stress and adult neurogenesis. *Hippocampus, 16,* 233–238.

Mirescu, C., Peters, J. D., & Gould, E. (2004). Early life experience alters response of adult neurogenesis to stress. *Nature Neuroscience, 7,* 841–846.

Mitra, R., Sundlass, K., Parker, K. J., Schatzberg, A. F., & Lyons, D. M. (2006). Social stress-related behavior affects hippocampal cell proliferation in mice. *Physiology & Behavior, 89,* 123–127.

Moncek, F., Duncko, R., Johansson, B. B., & Jezova, D. (2004). Effect of environmental enrichment on stress related systems in rats. *Journal of Neuroendocrinology, 16,* 423–431.

Nottebohm, F. (1985). Neuronal replacement in adulthood. *Annals of the New York Academy of Sciences, 457,* 143–161.

Oomen, C. A., Mayer, J. L., de Kloet, E. R., Joels, M., & Lucassen, P. J. (2007). Brief treatment with the glucocorticoid receptor antagonist mifepristone normalizes the reduction in neurogenesis after chronic stress. *European Journal of Neuroscience, 26,* 3395–3401.

Oomen, C. A., Soeters, H., Audureau, N., Vermunt, L., van Hasselt, F. N., Manders, E. M., Joëls, M., Lucassen, P. J., & Krugers, H. (2010). Severe early life stress hampers spatial learning and neurogenesis, but improves hippocampal synaptic plasticity and emotional learning under high-stress conditions in adulthood. *Journal of Neuroscience, 30,* 6635–6645.

Pham, K., Nacher, J., Hof, P. R., & McEwen, B. S. (2003). Repeated restraint stress suppresses neurogenesis and induces biphasic PSA-NCAM expression in the adult rat dentate gyrus. *European Journal of Neuroscience, 17,* 879–886.

Ribak, C. E., Korn, M. J., Shan, Z., & Obenaus, A. (2004). Dendritic growth cones and recurrent basal dendrites are typical features of newly generated dentate granule cells in the adult hippocampus. *Brain Research, 1000,* 195–199.

Rosenbrock, H., Koros, E., Bloching, A., Podhorna, J., & Borsini, F. (2005). Effect of chronic intermittent restraint stress on hippocampal expression of marker proteins for synaptic plasticity and progenitor cell proliferation in rats. *Brain Research, 1040,* 55–63.

Rossi, C., Angelucci, A., Costantin, L., Braschi, C., Mazzantini, M., Babbini, F., Fabbri, M. E., Tessarollo, L., Maffei, L., Berardi, N., & Caleo, M. (2006). Brain-derived neurotrophic factor (BDNF) is required for the enhancement of hippocampal neurogenesis following environmental enrichment. *European Journal of Neuroscience, 24,* 1850–1856.

Sairanen, M., Lucas, G., Ernfors, P., Castren, M., & Castren, E. (2005). Brain-derived neurotrophic factor and antidepressant drugs have different but coordinated effects on neuronal turnover, proliferation, and survival in the adult dentate gyrus. *Journal of Neuroscience, 25,* 1089–1094.

Sánchez, M. M., Ladd, C. O., & Plotsky, P. M. (2001). Early adverse experience as a developmental risk factor for later psychopathology: evidence from rodent and primate models. *Development and Psychopathology, 13,* 419–449.

Seri, B., Garcia-Verdugo, J. M., McEwen, B. S., & Alvarez-Buylla, A. (2001). Astrocytes give rise to new neurons in the adult mammalian hippocampus. *Journal of Neuroscience, 21,* 7153–7160.

Simon, M., Czeh, B., & Fuchs, E. (2005). Age-dependent susceptibility of adult hippocampal cell proliferation to chronic psychosocial stress. *Brain Research, 1049,* 244–248.

Snyder, J. S., Brewer, M., Glover, L., Sanzone, K., & Cameron, H. (2010). Adult hippocampal neurogenesis regulates the response to stress. *Soc. Neurosci. Abstr.*

Snyder, J. S., Kee, N., & Wojtowicz, J. M. (2001). Effects of adult neurogenesis on synaptic plasticity in the rat dentate gyrus. *Journal of Neurophysiology, 85*, 2423–2431.

Snyder, J. S., Hong, N. S., McDonald, R. J., & Wojtowicz, J. M. (2005). A role for adult neurogenesis in spatial long-term memory. *Neuroscience, 130*, 843–852.

Snyder, J. S., Choe, J. S., Clifford, M. A., Jeurling, S. I., Hurley, P., Brown, A., Kamhi, J. F., & Cameron, H. A. (2009a). Adult-born hippocampal neurons are more numerous, faster maturing, and more involved in behavior in rats than in mice. *Journal of Neuroscience, 29*, 14484–14495.

Snyder, J. S., Glover, L. R., Sanzone, K. M., Kamhi, J. F., & Cameron, H. A. (2009b). The effects of exercise and stress on the survival and maturation of adult-generated granule cells. *Hippocampus, 19*, 898–906.

Stranahan, A. M., Khalil, D., & Gould, E. (2006). Social isolation delays the positive effects of running on adult neurogenesis. *Nature Neuroscience, 9*, 526–533.

Taliaz, D., Stall, N., Dar, D. E., & Zangen, A. (2010). Knockdown of brain-derived neurotrophic factor in specific brain sites precipitates behaviors associated with depression and reduces neurogenesis. *Molecular Psychiatry, 15*, 80–92.

Tanapat, P., Hastings, N. B., Rydel, T. A., Galea, L. A., & Gould, E. (2001). Exposure to fox odor inhibits cell proliferation in the hippocampus of adult rats via an adrenal hormone-dependent mechanism. *Journal of Comparative Neurology, 437*, 496–504.

Thomas, R. M., Urban, J. H., & Peterson, D. A. (2006). Acute exposure to predator odor elicits a robust increase in corticosterone and a decrease in activity without altering proliferation in the adult rat hippocampus. *Experimental Neurology, 201*, 308–315.

Thomas, R. M., Hotsenpiller, G., & Peterson, D. A. (2007). Acute psychosocial stress reduces cell survival in adult hippocampal neurogenesis without altering proliferation. *Journal of Neuroscience, 27*, 2734–2743.

Toth, E., Gersner, R., Wilf-Yarkoni, A., Raizel, H., Dar, D. E., Richter-Levin, G., Levit, O., & Zangen, A. (2008). Age-dependent effects of chronic stress on brain plasticity and depressive behavior. *Journal of Neurochemistry, 107*, 522–532.

van Praag, H., Kempermann, G., & Gage, F. H. (1999). Running increases cell proliferation and neurogenesis in the adult mouse dentate gyrus. *Nature Neuroscience, 2*, 266–270.

van Praag, H., Schinder, A. F., Christie, B. R., Toni, N., Palmer, T. D., & Gage, F. H. (2002). Functional neurogenesis in the adult hippocampus. *Nature, 415*, 1030–1034.

Veena, J., Srikumar, B. N., Mahati, K., Bhagya, V., Raju, T. R., & Shankaranarayana Rao, B. S. (2009a). Enriched environment restores hippocampal cell proliferation and ameliorates cognitive deficits in chronically stressed rats. *Journal of Neuroscience Research, 87*, 831–843.

Veena, J., Srikumar, B. N., Raju, T. R., & Shankaranarayana Rao, B. S. (2009b). Exposure to enriched environment restores the survival and differentiation of new born cells in the hippocampus and ameliorates depressive symptoms in chronically stressed rats. *Neuroscience Letters, 455*, 178–182.

Warner-Schmidt, J. L., & Duman, R. S. (2007). VEGF is an essential mediator of the neurogenic and behavioral actions of antidepressants. *Proceedings of the National Academy of Sciences USA, 104*, 4647–4652.

Watanabe, Y., Gould, E., & McEwen, B. S. (1992). Stress induces atrophy of apical dendrites of hippocampal CA3 pyramidal neurons. *Brain Research, 588*, 341–345.

Westenbroek, C., Den Boer, J. A., Veenhuis, M., & Ter Horst, G. J. (2004). Chronic stress and social housing differentially affect neurogenesis in male and female rats. *Brain Research Bulletin, 64,* 303–308.

Winocur, G., Wojtowicz, J. M., Sekeres, M., Snyder, J. S., & Wang, S. (2006). Inhibition of neurogenesis interferes with hippocampus-dependent memory function. *Hippocampus, 16,* 296–304.

Wong, E. Y., & Herbert, J. (2006). Raised circulating corticosterone inhibits neuronal differentiation of progenitor cells in the adult hippocampus. *Neuroscience, 137,* 83–92.

Woolley, C. S., Gould, E., & McEwen, B. S. (1990). Exposure to excess glucocorticoids alters dendritic morphology of adult hippocampal pyramidal neurons. *Brain Research, 531,* 225–231.

Xu, Y., Ku, B., Cui, L., Li, X., Barish, P. A., Foster, T. C., & Ogle, W. O. (2007). Curcumin reverses impaired hippocampal neurogenesis and increases serotonin receptor 1A mRNA and brain-derived neurotrophic factor expression in chronically stressed rats. *Brain Research, 1162,* 9–18.

Yi, S. S., Hwang, I. K., Yoo K.Y., Park, O. K., Yu, J., Yan, B., Kim, I. Y., Kim, Y. N., Pai, T., Song, W., Lee, I. S., Won, M. H., Seong, J. K., & Yoon, Y. S. (2009). Effects of treadmill exercise on cell proliferation and differentiation in the subgranular zone of the dentate gyrus in a rat model of type II diabetes. *Neurochemical Research, 34,* 1039–1046.

Ying, Z., Roy, R. R., Edgerton, V. R., & Gomez-Pinilla, F. (2005). Exercise restores levels of neurotrophins and synaptic plasticity following spinal cord injury. *Experimental Neurology, 193,* 411–419.

Zhao, C., Teng, E. M., Summers, Jr, R. G., Ming, G. L., & Gage, F. H. (2006). Distinct morphological stages of dentate granule neuron maturation in the adult mouse hippocampus. *Journal of Neuroscience, 26,* 3–11.

Zuena, A. R., Mairesse, J., Casolini, P., Cinque, C., Alemá, G. S., Morley-Fletcher, S., Chiodi, V., Spagnoli, L. G., Gradini, R., Catalani, A., Nicoletti, F., & Maccari, S. (2008). Prenatal restraint stress generates two distinct behavioral and neurochemical profiles in male and female rats. *PLoS ONE, 3,* e2170.

8

Neurobiological Basis of the Complex Effects of Stress on Memory and Synaptic Plasticity

Phillip R. Zoladz, Collin R. Park, and David M. Diamond

Progress in the Study of Stress, Memory, and Brain Function

The past two decades have been witness to extensive research providing considerable insight into the neurobiological basis of stress–memory interactions. For some time, there was a tendency for researchers to view stress as exerting a global impairment of hippocampal function, perhaps via increased levels of glucocorticoids (Metcalfe and Jacobs, 1998; Metcalfe and Mischel, 1999; Nadel and Jacobs, 1998). However, this view has slowly been replaced with a significant body of work which has shown that the effects of stress on hippocampal function, as well as memory in general, are much more complex. Numerous studies have shown that acute stress can enhance, impair, or have no effect on learning and memory, depending on several factors related to the stressor, the learning experience, and the subjects under investigation (Akirav and Richter-Levin, 2006; Joels et al., 2006; Joels and Baram, 2009; Sandi and Pinelo-Nava, 2007; Schwabe et al., 2010). Moreover, stress or corticosteroid administration have been shown to enhance, as well as to impair, hippocampus-dependent memory and synaptic plasticity (Ahmed et al., 2006; Almaguer-Melian et al., 2005; Bangasser and Shors, 2010; Davis et al., 2004; Frey, 2001; Joels et al., 2006, 2009; Joels and Baram, 2009; Kim and Diamond, 2002; Li et al., 2003; Schwabe et al., 2010; Seidenbecher et al., 1997; Smeets et al., 2009; Straube et al., 2003; Uzakov et al., 2005). Thus, a major challenge for behavioral neuroscientists is to develop an understanding of the conditions by which stress enhances or impairs learning and memory and to identify the cellular and molecular mechanisms that mediate these effects.

The Handbook of Stress: Neuropsychological Effects on the Brain, First Edition.
Edited by Cheryl D. Conrad.
© 2011 Blackwell Publishing Ltd. Published 2011 by Blackwell Publishing Ltd.

We approach the issue of how stress affects brain memory systems from an evolutionary perspective. In our theorizing, we have assumed that each component of the stress response has contributed to processes which have enhanced the survival of organisms in times of extreme stress, such as a threat to an animal's life. Thus, we interpret all shifts in learning and memory capacity and changes in brain processing that occur during life-threatening situations as adaptive processes. This assumption holds true even if the stress appears to have an adverse or inhibitory effect on brain function, including a suppression of brain plasticity or an impairment of memory. Our task, therefore, is to understand the adaptive significance of positive, as well as seemingly negative, changes in brain function and memory in response to stress.

We have focused on the idea that stress activates physiological mechanisms that promote, and give greatest priority to, the storage of information that is related directly to the stress experience. The enhancement of storage processes restricted to stress-relevant information, however, may interfere with the processing of recently acquired information unrelated to the stress experience. Hence, the processing of information with great survival value would take priority over the consolidation and retrieval processes involved in other memories, even if the other memories are important. For example, the perceived threat to one's life is given priority by brain memory systems, but, in the process, the stress may cause someone to forget other items of importance, such as the location of one's keys when they are left in a new location each day.

The purpose of the present chapter is to address the cognitive, neurobiological, and neuroendocrine factors which mediate the competition for memory storage and retrieval processes that take place during times of stress. We discuss the neurobiological and neuroendocrine mechanisms that underlie the influence of stress on learning and memory, with a particular emphasis on stress–synaptic plasticity interactions in the hippocampus, amygdala, and prefrontal cortex (PFC). This chapter is an extension of recent developments on this topic which have been reviewed by our group (Diamond et al., 2004, 2005, 2007; Kim and Diamond, 2002) and by others (Akirav and Richter-Levin, 2006; Bangasser and Shors, 2010; Conrad, 2010; Joels et al., 2006; Joels and Baram, 2009; Sandi and Pinelo-Nava, 2007; Schwabe et al., 2010).

Stress Effects on Memory Consolidation and Retrieval

In the present chapter, we have focused on how stress affects *hippocampus-dependent* learning and memory, which includes declarative (fact- or event-based) as well as spatial learning and memory (Burgess et al., 2002; Eichenbaum, 2001; Konkel and Cohen, 2009; Mizuno and Giese, 2005). In humans, this type of learning and memory is often tested by having participants learn and subsequently recall/recognize a list of words or pictures. In rodents, hippocampus-dependent learning and memory is frequently assessed by having rats or mice learn the location of a hidden platform in a water maze or recognize a place (i.e., context) to which they have previously been exposed. Hippocampus-independent learning and memory, on the other hand, includes procedural/skill learning, nonassociative learning (e.g., habituation, sensitization), perceptual learning, and priming (Baddeley, 1982; Poldrack et al., 1999; Poldrack and Packard, 2003; Schacter, 1997; White and McDonald, 2002). These latter forms of learning depend largely on structures outside the hippocampus, such as the striatum, neocortex, amygdala, and cerebellum.

Extensive work has shown that stress differentially affects memory consolidation and retrieval (Joels et al., 2006; Joels and Baram, 2009; Roozendaal, 2003; Sandi and Pinelo-Nava, 2007; Schwabe et al., 2010). Numerous factors appear to influence how stress affects memory consolidation, but stress typically exerts deleterious effects on the retrieval of recently acquired information that is unrelated to the stressor (de Quervain et al., 2009). For example, we have shown in a series of studies that exposing a rat to a cat interferes with the rat's retrieval of the memory of the location of a hidden platform in a water maze (Campbell et al., 2008; Conboy et al., 2009; Diamond et al., 1999, 2006; Diamond and Park, 2000; Park et al., 2008; Sandi et al., 2005; Woodson et al., 2003; Zoladz et al., 2008). Cat exposure, being outside of the explicit learning experience, interferes with retrieval of hippocampus-dependent information, just as stress may interfere with a person's ability to remember information outside of the stress experience, such as a word list (Wolf, 2009).

With regards to memory consolidation, studies on humans and rodents have consistently reported that postlearning stress enhances long-term memory, oftentimes primarily for information that is emotional in nature (Cahill et al., 2003; Hui et al., 2006; Smeets et al., 2008; Zorawski et al., 2006). Prelearning stress, on the other hand, has been shown to enhance, impair or have no effect on the storage of information. For instance, brief stress (e.g., 2 min) administered to rats immediately before learning enhanced 24-hr spatial memory, but 30 min of stress administered immediately before learning impaired 24-hr spatial memory (Diamond et al., 2007), and suppressed the morphological (dendritic spine) plasticity that was associated with successful memory retrieval (Diamond et al., 2006).

Influence of Extrinsic and Intrinsic Stress on Memory

Researchers have differentiated between the effects of *extrinsic* stressors and *intrinsic* stressors on learning (Bisaz et al., 2009; de Kloet et al., 1999). Extrinsic stressors are stressors that occur outside the context of the explicit learning experience that is tested in the experiment, while intrinsic stressors are a component of the explicit learning experience itself. Intrinsic stressors tend to be beneficial for learning and could be discussed in the context of traumatic memory production. For example, exposure to electric shock can be considered a traumatic experience to an animal, with greater shock intensities producing greater evidence of fear memory for the explicit learning experience (the shock context) (Cordero et al., 2002). In a similar manner, an individual who experiences intense stress during natural disasters or wartime combat may have vivid and durable memories that underlie the memory component of posttraumatic stress disorder (Kitayama et al., 2000; Mehlum et al., 2006); the event producing the trauma does itself form an intrinsic component of the traumatic memory. Indeed, the intrinsic component of the traumatic memory is so deeply entrenched in memory and is so readily retrieved that, as William James (1890) wrote over a century ago, it is as if a traumatic memory can leave "a scar on the cerebral tissues."

In rodent work, investigators have manipulated water temperature in water mazes to examine the influence of intrinsic stress on spatial learning. The results of these manipulations have shown that rats trained in relatively cold (i.e., 19°C) water exhibit greater corticosteroid levels (suggestive of a greater stress response) and better memory than rats trained in warmer (i.e., 25°C) water (Sandi et al., 1997). However, rats trained in *extremely* cold water (12°C) demonstrated impaired memory (Selden et al., 1990), suggesting an overall inverted U-shaped relationship between the intrinsic stressfulness of the task and spatial memory. Thus, although intrinsic stress can be beneficial to learning, at extremely high levels, it can have adverse effects on memory-related processes (Yerkes and Dodson, 1908).

Joels and colleagues (2006) proposed that extrinsic stressors can enhance memory as long as the stressor is in close temporal and spatial proximity to the learning experience. In practice, this conjunction of time and space in an emotional memory would enable an animal to remember where it was when it was attacked by a predator, or people would remember incidental information when they learned of a national tragedy, such as where they were when they heard about the terrorist attacks in the USA on September 11, 2001 (Curci and Luminet, 2006). Thus, under normal conditions, otherwise neutral information would be incorporated into the memory of the stress experience because the neutral information overlays in time and space with the emotionally evocative stimuli.

We have tested the hypothesis that the memory of extrinsic information would be enhanced only if the nonstress information occurred in the same time and space as the stress-related information. In a recent study, we exposed rats to a cat for a brief (2-min) period of time in one environment (the cat-housing room), and then immediately gave them water-maze training in another room. Thus, while cat exposure and water-maze training occurred close in time, the two experiences occurred in very different locations. We found that brief cat exposure enhanced long-term (24-hr) water-maze memory in rats (Diamond et al., 2007). Thus, the temporal, but not spatial, component was the crucial factor in the stress-induced enhancement of memory. This finding indicated that the brief stress experience needed to occur close in time with, but not in the same context as, the learning experience to enhance memory consolidation.

Recent work by Schwabe and Wolf (2010) empirically assessed the effects of stress at the time of learning on long-term memory in humans. These investigators had participants learn a list of words while experiencing a Socially Evaluated Cold Pressor Test (SECPT). During the SECPT, participants immersed their right hands in ice water (0–2°C) for 3 min while being videotaped and closely watched by an unsociable experimenter. The SECPT experience *impaired*, rather than enhanced, free recall and recognition of the words 24 hr later. Such a finding appeared to contrast with the notion that stress occurring during a learning experience enhances long-term memory for that experience. However, the authors contended that perhaps stress enhances learning only when that learning would facilitate an individual's ability to cope with the stress. That is, if learning a list of words would assist an individual in coping with the SECPT, then this learning would potentially be enhanced. On the other hand, the learning of fact-based information that is unrelated to the stress experience would not be of much benefit to the individual's coping response, which may explain why that memory was impaired in this study.

The notion that stress would enhance the acquisition of information which may be beneficial to coping with the stress fits well with the findings discussed above regarding the relationship between water temperature and spatial learning in the water maze. Specifically, enhanced learning and memory of the location of a hidden platform in a water maze with relatively cold (i.e., 19°C) water would allow the rat to more rapidly escape (possibly better cope with) the aversive environment. On the other hand, if this hypothesis is correct, why is it that exposing a rat to even colder (i.e., 12°C) water has been shown to impair spatial learning (Selden et al., 1990), especially since in this case it may be even more important for proper coping with the stress? These findings, in conjunction with those of Schwabe and Wolf (2010), are consistent with the seminal work of Yerkes and Dodson (1908) demonstrating a task-specific impairment of performance only with high levels of stress. Thus, a stress-induced impairment in how the PFC interacts with the hippocampus would contribute to the impairment of memory performance in more cognitively-demanding tasks. The challenge is to understand how the hippocampus, amygdala, and PFC generate a representation of arousing events, as well as how the incidental components of the context in which those arousing events occurred are either remembered very well or forgotten.

Stress-induced Modulation of Synaptic Plasticity

Long-term potentiation (LTP) is a well-studied physiological model of memory in which an enhancement of synaptic transmission is produced by high-frequency stimulation (HFS) of afferent fibers. LTP is considered a physiological model of learning because it occurs rapidly, demonstrates longevity, is strengthened by repetition, and exhibits associativity and input specificity (Lynch, 2004). We emphasize here, as we have discussed previously (Diamond et al., 2004, 2005, 2007), that one great value of LTP is that its induction serves as a diagnostic tool to assess the functional state of a brain structure. That is, if stress impairs the induction of LTP in one compared with another brain region, we would contend that this finding indicates that stress selectively interferes with the functional capabilities of the brain structure exhibiting impaired LTP.

Extensive work has shown that acute stress impairs the induction of LTP in the hippocampus and PFC. The first evidence for a stress-induced impairment of synaptic plasticity was provided in 1987 when Thompson and coworkers reported that exposing rats to 30 min of restraint or restraint combined with tail shock blocked the induction of LTP in the CA1 region (where CA means cornu ammonis) of the rat hippocampus in vitro (Foy et al., 1987). Around this time, Diamond and colleagues showed that acute stress (exposure to a novel environment) blocked the induction of primed-burst potentiation, a low-threshold form of LTP, in the CA1 region of the behaving rat (Diamond et al., 1990, 1994). Since then, investigators have reported that exposing rodents to a variety of stressors, including predators, predator scent, restraint, tail shock, elevated platform stress, and a novel environment, impair the induction of hippocampal LTP and primed-burst potentiation in vitro and in vivo, primarily in the CA1 region (reviewed in Diamond et al., 2007; Kim and Diamond, 2002). Other researchers have extended the findings of stress effects in the hippocampus with the demonstration that stress impairs the induction of LTP in the PFC as well (Maroun and Richter-Levin, 2003; Qi et al., 2009; Rocher et al., 2004).

Importantly, the effects of acute stress on synaptic plasticity in the hippocampus depend on the amount of stress and the temporal relationship between the stressor and the application of HFS. In studies reporting a stress-induced impairment of hippocampal LTP, the animals were typically exposed to a relatively long (e.g., 30–60-min) stress experience before electrical stimulation was applied to the hippocampus (e.g., Mesches et al., 1999). However, when a brief stressor is applied around the time of HFS application the induction of LTP is frequently enhanced (reviewed in Diamond et al., 2007). These electrophysiological findings ultimately could explain whether stress enhances or impairs the consolidation of recently acquired information.

Stress, Memory, Synaptic Plasticity, and Corticosteroids

Stress exerts powerful effects on learning and memory, in large part, because it has dramatic effects on hippocampal functioning. Over four decades ago, Bruce McEwen and colleagues reported that the hippocampus contains a greater density of corticosteroid receptors than other brain regions, thereby rendering it highly sensitive to stress (McEwen et al., 1968, 1969). Subsequent work on stress–memory interactions extended these findings to suggest an involvement of corticosteroids in the stress-induced impairment of memory by revealing an association between endogenous levels of corticosteroids and memory impairment on hippocampus-dependent tasks. For example, de Quervain and colleagues reported that exposing rats to foot shock 30 min, but not 2 min or 4 hr, before a spatial memory test impaired rat memory for the location of a hidden platform in the Morris water maze (de Quervain et al., 1998). This finding led to the hypothesis that corticosteroids were responsible for the memory impairment because peak levels of this hormone are not achieved until approximately 30 min following stress exposure. De Quervain and colleagues (1998) provided further support for this hypothesis by demonstrating that prevention of the stress-induced increase in corticosteroid levels, via administration of the corticosteroid synthesis inhibitor metyrapone, blocked the stress-induced impairment of spatial memory.

Many studies in humans and rodents have provided evidence for corticosteroid involvement in the stress-induced modulation of learning and memory. Corticosteroids are not only involved in the stress-induced *impairment* of learning and memory, they also contribute to the stress-induced *enhancement* of learning and memory. Indeed, several studies reporting enhanced long-term memory following prelearning or postlearning stress have provided evidence for an association between corticosteroid levels and memory performance, as well as a blockade of the adverse effects of stress on memory by pharmacological agents that prevent stress-induced increases in corticosteroid levels (Conrad, 2005; Roozendaal et al., 2006).

Comparable electrophysiological studies have provided strong evidence of an involvement of corticosteroids in the stress-induced alteration of LTP. For example, when Foy et al. (1987) reported that acute stress impaired hippocampal synaptic plasticity they noted a significant negative relationship between corticosteroid levels and the magnitude of LTP. Since then, several studies have reported that both abnormally low and abnormally high levels of corticosteroids impair hippocampus-dependent learning and synaptic plasticity, suggesting an inverted U-shaped dose–response relationship between corticosteroid levels and hippocampal function. Diamond and colleagues found that at low levels of circulating corticosteroids (i.e., 0–20 μg/dL) there was a positive relationship between corticosteroids and hippocampal primed-burst potentiation, whereas at elevated levels (i.e. stress levels, or >20 μg/dL) this relationship was negative (Bennett et al., 1991; Diamond et al., 1992). These investigators also reported that extremely high levels of corticosteroids (i.e., >60 μg/dL) promoted synaptic depression. Such findings suggested that there was a hormetic (i.e., low doses enhance, while high doses impair), rather than a simple inverted U-shaped, dose–response relationship between corticosteroids and hippocampal function (Diamond, 2008; Zoladz and Diamond, 2008).

The hormetic function between synaptic plasticity and corticosteroids appears to be based, in part, on the two types of corticosteroid receptors both of which are widely distributed throughout the hippocampus. One type is the mineralocorticoid receptor (MR), which has a high affinity for corticosteroids and is almost fully saturated under baseline physiological conditions. The second type is the glucocorticoid receptor (GR), which has one-tenth the affinity for corticosteroids as the MR and becomes extensively occupied only when there is a large increase in circulating levels of corticosteroids, as occurs during stress (Joels, 2008). Most MRs and GRs are located intracellularly, and when bound by corticosteroids, they act slowly through classical steroid receptor actions to synthesize proteins via gene activation. Some research has indicated that corticosteroids can also bind to membrane-bound receptors and exert nongenomic effects on cellular activity (Orchinik et al., 1991). The nongenomic effects have become increasingly important in contributing to our understanding of the cellular and molecular mechanisms by which stress affects learning and memory (Joels, 2008).

The effects of stress on hippocampus-dependent learning and synaptic plasticity are mediated, in part, by the differential activation of the two corticosteroid receptor subtypes. For example, whereas MR agonists facilitate the induction of hippocampal LTP, GR agonists impair its production (Pavlides et al., 1995a, 1995b). These findings suggest that MR activation is responsible for stress- and corticosteroid-induced enhancements of hippocampal function, whereas GR activation is responsible for stress- and corticosteroid-induced impairments of hippocampal function (Conrad et al., 1999). Mechanistically, these effects may involve an alteration of the neural membrane potential, as low levels of circulating corticosteroids (i.e., MR saturation) decrease the amplitude of postburst afterhyperpolization and enhance LTP induction, whereas high levels of circulating corticosteroids (i.e., activation of GRs) have been shown to increase postburst afterhyperpolization and consequentially lead to LTP impairment (Joels, 2008).

The traditional view of corticosteroid action is that it exerts its effects on cells in a delayed manner by first binding to intracellular receptors which enter the nucleus and act as transcription factors to modulate gene expression and produce proteins, which then slowly affect cell function. However, the effects of stress and corticosteroid administration on hippocampal function are now known to have rapid actions as well. Corticosteroids can bind to membrane-bound receptors and then exert rapid, nongenomic effects on neuronal transmission. Systemic administration of corticosterone in rats rapidly (e.g., <15 min) increases glutamatergic activity in the CA1 region of the hippocampus, an effect that can still be observed following the administration of selective intracellular corticosteroid receptor antagonists (Joels et al., 2009; Joels and Baram, 2009).

Complementary findings from this group has shown that within 5–10 min of bath application of corticosteroids there is an enhancement of the frequency of miniature excitatory postsynaptic currents in CA1 hippocampal neurons (Karst et al., 2005). This effect was shown to be mediated by an MR-dependent increase in glutamate transmission, although membrane-bound GRs have been reported in various brain regions as well. Interestingly, the threshold corticosteroid concentration for the rapid nongenomic effects is 10- to 20-fold greater than in vitro effects observed on intracellular MRs, which could explain how stress can have an immediate excitatory effect on hippocampal synaptic plasticity and learning and memory.

Despite the well-established involvement of corticosteroids in the stress-induced modulation of learning and memory, it is important to note that an increase in corticosteroid levels is neither necessary nor sufficient to impair hippocampal function. Previous work from our laboratory has shown that the administration of corticosteroids prior to memory retrieval, to otherwise unstressed animals, resulted in stress levels of serum corticosteroids, but had no effect on recall (Park et al., 2006). Other work has shown that manipulations, such as lesions of the amygdala, inactivation of the amygdala, or the administration of pharmacological agents, can prevent the effects of stress on hippocampus-dependent learning and synaptic plasticity, while leaving the stress-induced increase in serum corticosteroid levels unaffected (Campbell et al., 2008; Kim et al., 2005). Along the same lines, we have reported that stress impaired spatial memory in adrenalectomized rats, which indicates that a stress-induced increase in corticosteroids is not essential for stress to impair memory (Zoladz et al., 2008). In addition, our laboratory has shown that exposing male rats to a sexually receptive female rat had no effect on their spatial memory retrieval, despite the fact that the female-exposed rats exhibited increased serum corticosteroid levels which were equivalent to those observed in cat-exposed, memory-impaired rats (Woodson et al., 2003). Thus, multiple levels of analysis have revealed that corticosteroids serve as an indicator of a heightened stress state and are clearly involved in the modulation of hippocampal function, but other factors, such as direct effects of stress on glutamatergic transmission and amygdala activity, are more directly involved in the acute stress-induced modulation of hippocampus-dependent learning and synaptic plasticity.

The effects of stress and corticosteroids on hippocampal synaptic plasticity have been shown to be dependent on β-adrenergic receptor activity in the amygdala. Indeed, studies have shown that administration of β-adrenergic receptor antagonists either systemically or directly into the basolateral amygdala (BLA) prevents the stress- or corticosteroid-induced modulation of hippocampus-dependent learning and synaptic plasticity (Roozendaal et al., 2006). The necessary involvement of the amygdala in the stress-induced modulation of hippocampal function has been addressed in studies revealing that inactivation or lesioning of the BLA prevents the stress-induced impairment of hippocampus-dependent learning and synaptic plasticity (Kim et al., 2005). In recent work, we have confirmed that amygdala activation is a necessary component of the adverse effects of stress on spatial memory. We have found that muscimol-induced inactivation of the BLA blocked the adverse effects of predator stress on spatial memory (Figure 8.1).

Overall, these studies are consistent with extensive evidence of the central role of the amygdala in orchestrating how the brain processes emotional memories. A more global perspective on emotional memory processing is that positive, as well as negative, effects of stress on memory involve complex interactions among several brain structures, including the hippocampus, PFC, and amygdala, and neuromodulators, including corticosterone, epinephrine (adrenaline), and norepinephrine (noradrenaline). In the following section, we discuss how these different brain memory systems appear to interact under stress, compared with emotionally neutral conditions.

Stress and Multiple Brain Memory Systems

Extensive research has shown that stress or corticosteroid administration can enhance or impair declarative and/or spatial memory consolidation and retrieval, while leaving procedural and reference memory intact. For example, in one study, we gave rats water-maze training in which the hidden platform was in the same location on every trial over the course of many days (Woodson et al., 2003). This

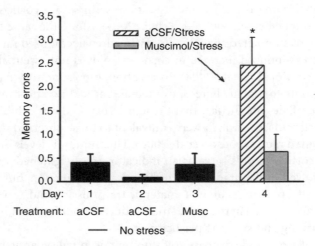

Figure 8.1 Application of muscimol to the BLA blocked the predator stress-induced impairment of spatial memory. Isoflurane-anesthetized rats were implanted with a cannula at histologically confirmed placements in the BLA. One week after cannula implantation, all rats were trained to locate a hidden platform in the radial-arm water maze. All infusions took place 4 hr before daily training began (at 08.00). On each day of training, the rats were given an acquisition phase (eight trials), followed by a 30-min delay period, which terminated with a memory test trial, as described in previous work (Park et al., 2008; Sandi et al., 2005). The hidden platform was always in a different location on each of the 4 days of training. The first 3 days of training served as control (no-stress) tests in which rats spent the delay period in their home cages. On days 1 and 2, artificial cerebrospinal fluid (aCSF) was infused into the BLA; on day 3, muscimol (Musc) was infused into the BLA. Day 4 was the stress day of testing, with all rats exposed to a cat during the 30-min delay, as described previously (Diamond et al., 2006; Park et al., 2008; Sandi et al., 2005; Woodson et al., 2003); half of the rats received an infusion of aCSF into the BLA, and the other half received an infusion of muscimol into the BLA. Infusion of muscimol under control (no-stress) conditions had no effect on learning and memory, as demonstrated by the lack of a drug effect on day 3. Rats infused with aCSF and exposed to the cat on day 4 exhibited a significant impairment of spatial memory. By contrast, rats infused with muscimol and exposed to the cat on day 4 exhibited intact spatial memory (*$P < 0.01$ relative to Muscimol/Stress, Student's t test). Therefore, inactivation of the BLA with muscimol blocked the amnestic effects of stress on hippocampus-dependent spatial memory.

form of overtraining would be expected to produce a spatial memory which could be retrieved independent of hippocampal integrity (i.e., reference memory). Indeed, when rats that had been overtrained were exposed to a cat, the predator stress had no effect on their spatial memory retrieval. We reported similar findings in a study in which exposure of rats to the stress of a novel environment impaired newly acquired, but not long-term, spatial memory for food locations (Diamond et al., 1996). Overall, these findings are consistent with the notion that stress exerts a greater effect on the retrieval of more recently formed memories that are dependent upon hippocampal function than on memories that are more thoroughly consolidated and, therefore, can be retrieved independent of the hippocampus.

Related work has provided an extensive assessment of multiple brain memory systems and how they interact. Most of this research has focused on the differential involvement of a hippocampus-based spatial/cognitive system and a neostriatum-based habit/response system in the acquisition of various tasks (Metcalfe and Jacobs, 1998; Packard, 2009; White and McDonald, 2002). These two systems have often been found to be dissociated in individuals with anterograde amnesia. For instance, the well-known amnesiac H.M. underwent a temporal lobectomy to control his problems with epilepsy. This surgery left him with severe anterograde amnesia for explicit, or declarative, learning, but had no effect on his abilities to acquire habit-based, procedural knowledge (Squire, 1992).

Research has addressed how these memory systems interact when animals learn a task that could be acquired by using either spatial/cognitive or habit/response strategies. Interestingly, these studies have shown that on such tasks, animals initially adopt a hippocampus-based, spatial/cognitive strategy, but over time (or as learning continues), they switch to a habit/response-based approach (Packard and McGaugh, 1996). Recent work has examined how stress affects the use of these strategies to acquire such tasks. These studies have demonstrated that stress biases a rodent (Dias-Ferreira et al., 2009; Packard, 2009) or person (Schwabe and Wolf, 2009) toward using a habit/response learning strategy, rather than the more hippocampus-based, spatial/cognitive strategy. This observation is consistent with the view that brain memory systems compete against each other; in the low-emotion state, the hippocampus dominates the dorsal striatum, whereas in the stress state, the reverse appears to occur (Metcalfe and Jacobs, 1998; Packard, 2009).

Temporal Dynamics Model of the Stress-induced Modulation of Memory

We recently summarized an extensive body of research demonstrating that stress produces different temporal activation profiles in different brain regions, which potentially addresses the basis of the complexity of stress effects on learning and memory (Diamond et al., 2007). We proposed that acute stress produces a rapid enhancement of hippocampal synaptic plasticity that facilitates the storage of information; however, as the stress persists, the hippocampus descends into a refractory state for producing new plasticity, and therefore, the threshold for the induction of hippocampal plasticity increases. While the hippocampus is in this poststress refractory state, the storage of new information, and thereby new memory formation, would be impaired. This perspective on time-dependent shifts in hippocampal functioning following the onset of stress is illustrated in Figure 8.2.

We also speculated that stress immediately impairs the functioning of the PFC, which would explain why stress rapidly impairs problem-solving and decision-making abilities (Figure 8.2). Our model provided a neurobiological basis for the

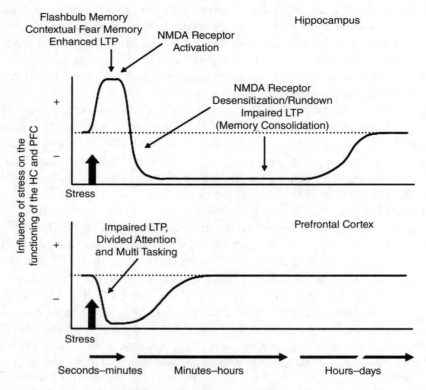

Figure 8.2 Temporal dynamics model of how stress affects memory-related processing in the hippocampus (HC) and PFC. The onset of a strong emotional experience produces a rapid, but brief, enhancement of hippocampal functioning, as illustrated by the positive component of the curve in the top graph. Within minutes of the activation of the hippocampus, it descends into a refractory state, as indicated by the downward component of the top graph. The refractory state is driven, in part, by the reduction in the sensitivity of *N*-methyl-ᴅ-aspartate (NMDA) receptors, which addresses why stress blocks the induction of hippocampal LTP. The lower graph illustrates a summary of research which indicates that the PFC, in contrast to the hippocampus, is only inhibited by stress; the timing of the recovery from the suppression of functioning of the PFC would depend on the nature and intensity of the stressor, interacting with the ability of the individual to cope with the experience.

finding that stress commonly exerts greater effects on cognitive tasks that depend on greater attentional resources (i.e., PFC-dependent processing). This observation is consistent with Easterbrook's cue-utilization hypothesis, which proposed that under conditions of high emotionality, such as those that occur during stress, the range of cues that an individual can process declines substantially (Easterbrook, 1959). The alterations in PFC functioning likely explain, at least in part, why stress exerts deleterious effects on complex cognitive tasks.

Our temporal dynamics hypothesis was inspired, in part, by research demonstrating a biphasic modulation of hippocampal plasticity by amygdala activation. Akirav and Richter-Levin (1999) found that electrical stimulation of the BLA 1 hr prior to HFS of the perforant pathway impaired LTP in the dentate gyrus, while stimulating the BLA immediately before HFS enhanced dentate gyrus LTP. The time-dependent effects of amygdala activation on the hippocampus may be mediated, in part, by the rapid (excitatory) versus delayed (inhibitory) effects of corticosterone on hippocampal excitability and plasticity (Wiegert et al., 2006). The adverse influence of prolonged stress on LTP appears to be specific to CA1 of the hippocampus, as related work demonstrated that prolonged (1-hr) predator stress enhanced LTP in the BLA, but impaired LTP in the CA1 region of the rat hippocampus (Mesches et al., 1999; Vouimba et al., 2004).

Taken together, these findings suggest that at the onset of a stress experience the amygdala is rapidly activated, which, in addition to activating the hypothalamus–pituitary–adrenal (HPA) axis, would stimulate and enhance hippocampal memory functioning. The rapid enhancement of hippocampal functioning would be fueled by a dramatic increase in levels of numerous excitatory neuromodulators (e.g., glutamate, acetylcholine, corticotropin-releasing hormone, norepinephrine, dopamine), all of which would, in theory, activate endogenous forms of neuroplasticity in the hippocampus and thereby facilitate memory storage (Joels and Baram, 2009). The effects of corticosterone on the hippocampus would not be observed immediately, as there is a delay of at least several minutes from the onset of stress to the release of corticosteroids from the adrenal cortex. Nevertheless, endogenously circulating corticosteroids that are already present in the hippocampus at the time of the stress onset could facilitate the rapid enhancement of hippocampal plasticity by the amygdala and neuromodulators. When the newly synthesized corticosteroids reached the hippocampus, they would exert an immediate nongenomic, MR-dependent, excitatory effect on synaptic plasticity by enhancing glutamate transmission and facilitating N-methyl-D-aspartate (NMDA) receptor-dependent synaptic plasticity (Joels, 2008). We therefore hypothesize that the rapid stress-induced enhancement of glutamate-based plasticity links the hippocampus with the amygdala to generate flashbulb memories of events occurring with the onset of the stress experience (Ehlers et al., 2002; Van der Kolk and Fisler, 1995).

Extending the Temporal Dynamics Model to Address Stress Effects on Retrieval

Our temporal dynamics model focused on addressing inconsistencies in the literature regarding stress–LTP–memory interactions. We noted that an enhancement of the magnitude, and particularly the duration, of hippocampal LTP has been shown to occur when tetanizing electrical stimulation occurred in conjunction with the onset of an arousing experience (Diamond et al., 2007). We interpreted this finding as an indication that the hippocampus is maximally activated to store information for events occurring at the onset of a stressful event. By contrast, LTP tended to be inhibited in studies in which tetanizing stimulation was delivered 30 min or more after the onset of the stress. We hypothesized that following a relatively brief period of stress-induced activation, the hippocampus descends into a prolonged refractory state of plasticity.

The temporal dynamics model, therefore, addressed the processes involved in the acquisition of new information occurring either at the onset of a stress experience or after the stress experience began. One extension of the model is to address how stress affects memory retrieval. We suggest that the same process that rapidly activates the hippocampus with the onset of stress to store new information will interfere with the ability of the hippocampus to retrieve recently stored memories. This process is adaptive since it enables individuals to generate a representation of the events occurring at a time when a situation escalates from one that is emotionally neutral to one that is emotionally strong (and therefore potentially life-threatening). Thus, events occurring with this dramatic shift in emotional state gain greater access to resources in the hippocampus and amygdala involved in memory-related plasticity. The processing of the new stressful experience transiently dominates hippocampal plasticity underlying the storage of a new flashbulb memory, but at the same time, the induction of stressor-related plasticity interferes with the retrieval of recently stored, stress-irrelevant information.

Summary and Speculation on the Neural Basis of Traumatic Memory Processing

It is a great challenge to develop a comprehensive analysis of the complex effects of stress on cognitive processes. Arousing experiences can have paradoxical and opposing effects on different aspects of learning, memory, and attention; over a century of research has demonstrated an enhancement, impairment, or no effect of strong arousal on each of these processes. In this chapter, we have summarized progress toward understanding systematic features of how stress affects memory consolidation and retrieval. We have focused on issues related to stress and memory processing from an evolutionary perspective. That is, we view every aspect of the stress response as a means with which to promote an individual's survival in response to a life-threatening event, even if the process involves suppressing aspects of brain functioning.

We have discussed endocrine and cognitive processes which are coactivated with the onset of a stressor. Thus, in parallel with the activation of the HPA-axis stress response is the almost immediate activation of the hippocampus/amygdala-based flashbulb memory system. We have proposed that these two structures, working in conjunction, would generate a representation which is restricted to events occurring in the first few seconds to minutes after the onset of an arousing experience. This perspective on emotional memory processing is different from the consensus view of enhanced functioning of the amygdala, but not hippocampus, in response to traumatic stress (Kim and Diamond, 2002; Layton and Krikorian, 2002; Metcalfe and Jacobs, 1998; Metcalfe and Mischel, 1999; Nadel and Jacobs, 1998).

Our hypothesis that there is conjoint activation of the hippocampus and amygdala at the onset of stress is consistent with Ehlers et al. (2002), theorizing that traumatic memories tend to emphasize the processing of cues that occur at the onset, or with the escalation, of emotionality during a traumatic experience. This temporally-restricted period of intense activation of hippocampal and amygdaloid plasticity may provide the neural basis of the finding that memories of trauma tend to be time-restricted fragments of the experience (Van der Kolk and Fisler, 1995). The neural basis of fragmented memories of trauma would be the relatively brief, time-restricted period in which there is a dramatic increase in hippocampal and amygdaloid glutamate levels, resulting in an increase in NMDA receptor-mediated LTP-like processes in these two structures.

We have also speculated as to how the initial activation of the hippocampus and amygdala by stress could be relevant to impaired retrieval processes. There is extensive evidence that one of the most commonly observed effects of stress is the impairment of the retrieval of recently stored memories. For example, we have shown that rats exposed to a cat exhibited impaired memory for the location of the hidden platform in a water maze at 30 min, as well as 24 hr, after learning (Campbell et al., 2008; Conboy et al., 2009; Diamond et al., 1999, 2006; Diamond and Park, 2000; Park et al., 2008; Sandi et al., 2005; Woodson et al., 2003; Zoladz et al., 2008). Similarly, stress interferes with declarative (hippocampus-dependent) memory in people as well (Payne et al., 2002; Wolf, 2009). We have proposed that the onset of stress has a constructive effect, by which there is a saturation of hippocampal synaptic plasticity devoted to the processing of new flashbulb memories; this same plasticity, however, prevents the hippocampus from retrieving recently stored information.

Finally, one feature of posttraumatic stress disorder is that memories of the trauma tend to be intrusive and can be activated with even subtle reminders of the original experience. Within our schema of the neurobiology of flashbulb memory processing, each reactivation of the traumatic memory would produce a relatively brief period of activation of the hippocampus and prolonged activation of the amygdala, in conjunction with increases in levels of neuroendocrine modulators, including catecholamines and glucocorticoids, in each of these structures. There would be two consequences of the repeated reactivation of the hippocampal-amygdaloid circuit in a traumatized person. First, the reactivation of the traumatic memory would intensify the plasticity underlying the circuitry of the traumatic memory, thereby interfering with therapeutic attempts at extinguishing the conditioned fear memories. Second, the repeated reactivation of intrusive memories, and therefore repeated reactivation of the hippocampus, would interfere with the involvement of the hippocampus in the processing of new fact-based information. The detrimental effects of the constant activation of the hippocampus by intrusive memories may underlie the cognitive deficits which are commonly reported in people with posttraumatic stress disorder (Bremner, 2006).

In recent work, we have modeled the phenomenon of intrusive memory in rats (Diamond et al., 2004; Zoladz et al., 2010). In one study (Zoladz et al., 2010), rats were given shock-avoidance conditioning, and at different ensuing time points (1 day to 1 year), they were given a single day of water-maze training, followed 30 min later by a spatial memory test. The most compelling finding was that reactivation of the 1-year-old memory of the shock experience produced a potent inhibitory effect on new memory retrieval. That is, when rats were reexposed to the shock environment, they exhibited intact fear memory for the shock experience, but following the reactivation of their fear memory, they were impaired at retrieving their newly formed memory of the location of the hidden platform in the water maze. These findings may provide insight into the processes by which the repeated activation of a traumatic memory and attempts to suppress intrusive memories can interfere with ongoing cognition in people (Levy and Anderson, 2008).

In summary, we have emphasized that the initiation of a stressful experience triggers a multitude of dynamic processes, each of which can enhance, as well as impair, different features of memory processing. Understanding how different brain structures process stress-relevant, as well as stress-irrelevant, information at different times after stress onset is an important direction to follow in research addressing the complexity of stress–memory–brain interactions.

Acknowledgment

Support for the authors during the preparation of this chapter was provided by Research Career Scientist and Merit Review Awards from the Department of Veterans Affairs to DMD.

References

Ahmed, T., Frey, J. U., & Korz, V. (2006). Long-term effects of brief acute stress on cellular signaling and hippocampal LTP. *Journal of Neuroscience, 26,* 3951–3958.

Akirav, I., & Richter-Levin, G. (1999). Biphasic modulation of hippocampal plasticity by behavioral stress and basolateral amygdala stimulation in the rat. *Journal of Neuroscience, 19,* 10530–10535.

Akirav, I., & Richter-Levin, G. (2006). *Factors* that determine the non-linear amygdala influence on hippocampus-dependent memory. *Dose-Response, 4,* 22–37.

Almaguer-Melian, W., Cruz-Aguado, R., Riva, C. L., Kendrick, K. M., Frey, J. U., & Bergado, J. (2005). Effect of LTP-reinforcing paradigms on neurotransmitter release in the dentate gyrus of young and aged rats. *Biochemical and Biophysical Research Communications, 327,* 877–883.

Baddeley, A. D. (1982). Implications of neuropsychological evidence for theories of normal memory. *Philosophical Transactions of the Royal Society of London. Series B, Biological Sciences, 298*, 59–72.

Bangasser, D. A., & Shors, T. J. (2010). Critical brain circuits at the intersection between stress and learning. *Neuroscience and Biobehavioral Reviews, 34*, 1223–1233.

Bennett, M. C., Diamond, D. M., Fleshner, M., & Rose, G. M. (1991). Serum corticosterone level predicts the magnitude of hippocampal primed burst potentiation and depression in urethane-anesthetized rats. *Psychobiology, 19*, 301–307.

Bisaz, R., Conboy, L., & Sandi, C. (2009). Learning under stress: a role for the neural cell adhesion molecule NCAM. *Neurobiology of Learning and Memory, 91*, 333–342.

Bremner, J. D. (2006). The relationship between cognitive and brain changes in posttraumatic stress disorder. *Annals of the New York Academy of Sciences, 1071*, 80–86.

Burgess, N., Maguire, E. A., & O'Keefe, J. (2002). The human hippocampus and spatial and episodic memory. *Neuron, 35*, 625–641.

Cahill, L., Gorski, L., & Le, K. (2003). Enhanced human memory consolidation with post-learning stress: interaction with the degree of arousal at encoding. *Learning & Memory, 10*, 270–274.

Campbell, A. M., Park, C. R., Zoladz, P. R., Munoz, C., Fleshner, M., & Diamond, D. M. (2008). Pre-training administration of tianeptine, but not propranolol, protects hippocampus-dependent memory from being impaired by predator stress. *European Neuropsychopharmacology, 18*, 87–98.

Conboy, L., Tanrikut, C., Zoladz, P. R., Campbell, A. M., Park, C. R., Gabriel, C., Mocaer, E., Sandi, C., & Diamond, D. M. (2009). The antidepressant agomelatine blocks the adverse effects of stress on memory and enables spatial learning to rapidly increase neural cell adhesion molecule (NCAM) expression in the hippocampus of rats. *International Journal of Neuropsychopharmacology, 12*, 329–341.

Conrad, C. D. (2005). The nonlinear effects of acute glucocorticoid activity on hippocampal function. *Non-Linear Relationships in Biology, Toxicology and Medicine, 3*, 57–78.

Conrad, C. D. (2010). A critical review of chronic stress effects on spatial learning and memory. *Progress in Neuro-psychopharmacology & Biological Psychiatry, 34*, 742–755.

Conrad, C. D., Lupien, S. J., & McEwen, B. S. (1999). Support for a bimodal role for Type II adrenal steroid receptors in spatial memory. *Neurobiology of Learning and Memory, 72*, 39–46.

Cordero, M. I., Kruyt, N. D., Merino, J. J., & Sandi, C. (2002). Glucocorticoid involvement in memory formation in a rat model for traumatic memory. *Stress, 5*, 73–79.

Curci, A., & Luminet, O. (2006). Follow-up of a cross-national comparison on flashbulb and event memory for the September 11th attacks. *Memory, 14*, 329–344.

Davis, C. D., Jones, F. L., & Derrick, B. E. (2004). Novel environments enhance the induction and maintenance of long-term potentiation in the dentate gyrus. *Journal of Neuroscience, 24*, 6497–6506.

de Kloet, E. R., Oitzl, M. S., & Joels, M. (1999). Stress and cognition: are corticosteroids good or bad guys? *Trends in Neurosciences, 22*, 422–426.

de Quervain, D. J., Roozendaal, B., & McGaugh, J. L. (1998). Stress and glucocorticoids impair retrieval of long-term spatial memory. *Nature, 394*, 787–790.

de Quervain, D. J., Aerni, A., Schelling, G., & Roozendaal, B. (2009). Glucocorticoids and the regulation of memory in health and disease. *Frontiers in Neuroendocrinology, 30*, 358–370.

Diamond, D. M. (2008). The search for hormesis in the nervous system. *Critical Reviews in Toxicology, 38,* 619–622.

Diamond, D. M., & Park, C. R. (2000). Predator exposure produces retrograde amnesia and blocks synaptic plasticity. Progress toward understanding how the hippocampus is affected by stress. *Annals of the New York Academy of Sciences, 911,* 453–455.

Diamond, D. M., Bennett, M. C., Stevens, K. E., Wilson, R. L., & Rose, G. M. (1990). Exposure to a novel environment interferes with the induction of hippocampal primed burst potentiation in the behaving rat. *Psychobiology, 18,* 273–281.

Diamond, D. M., Bennett, M. C., Fleshner, M., & Rose, G. M. (1992). Inverted-U relationship between the level of peripheral corticosterone and the magnitude of hippocampal primed burst potentiation. *Hippocampus, 2,* 421–430.

Diamond, D. M., Fleshner, M., & Rose, G. M. (1994). Psychological stress repeatedly blocks hippocampal primed burst potentiation in behaving rats. *Behavioural Brain Research, 62,* 1–9.

Diamond, D. M., Fleshner, M., Ingersoll, N., & Rose, G. M. (1996). Psychological stress impairs spatial working memory: relevance to electrophysiological studies of hippocampal function. *Behavioral Neuroscience, 110,* 661–672.

Diamond, D. M., Park, C. R., Heman, K. L., & Rose, G. M. (1999). Exposing rats to a predator impairs spatial working memory in the radial arm water maze. *Hippocampus, 9,* 542–552.

Diamond, D. M., Park, C. R., & Woodson, J. C. (2004). Stress generates emotional memories and retrograde amnesia by inducing an endogenous form of hippocampal LTP. *Hippocampus, 14,* 281–291.

Diamond, D. M., Park, C. R., Campbell, A. M., & Woodson, J. C. (2005). Competitive interactions between endogenous LTD and LTP in the hippocampus underlie the storage of emotional memories and stress-induced amnesia. *Hippocampus, 15,* 1006–1025.

Diamond, D. M., Campbell, A. M., Park, C. R., Woodson, J. C., Conrad, C. D., Bachstetter, A. D., & Mervis, R. F. (2006). Influence of predator stress on the consolidation versus retrieval of long-term spatial memory and hippocampal spinogenesis. *Hippocampus, 16,* 571–576.

Diamond, D. M., Campbell, A. M., Park, C. R., Halonen, J., & Zoladz, P. R. (2007). The temporal dynamics model of emotional memory processing: a synthesis on the neurobiological basis of stress-induced amnesia, flashbulb and traumatic memories, and the Yerkes-Dodson Law. *Neural Plasticity,* 60803.

Dias-Ferreira, E., Sousa, J. C., Melo, I., Morgado, P., Mesquita, A. R., Cerqueira, J. J., Costa, R. M., & Sousa, N. (2009). Chronic stress causes frontostriatal reorganization and affects decision-making. *Science, 325,* 621–625.

Easterbrook, J. A. (1959). The effect of emotion on the utilisation and the organisation of behavior. *Psychological Review, 66,* 183–201.

Ehlers, A., Hackmann, A., Steil, R., Clohessy, S., Wenninger, K., & Winter, H. (2002). The nature of intrusive memories after trauma: the warning signal hypothesis. *Behaviour Research and Therapy, 40,* 995–1002.

Eichenbaum, H. (2001). The hippocampus and declarative memory: cognitive mechanisms and neural codes. *Behavioural Brain Research, 127,* 199–207.

Foy, M. R., Stanton, M. E., Levine, S., & Thompson, R. F. (1987). Behavioral stress impairs long-term potentiation in rodent hippocampus. *Behavioral and Neural Biology, 48,* 138–149.

Frey, J. U. (2001). Long-lasting hippocampal plasticity: cellular model for memory consolidation? *Results and Problems in Cell Differentiation, 34*, 27–40.

Hui, I. R., Hui, G. K., Roozendaal, B., McGaugh, J. L., & Weinberger, N. M. (2006). Posttraining handling facilitates memory for auditory-cue fear conditioning in rats. *Neurobiology of Learning and Memory, 86*, 160–163.

James, W. (1890). *Principles of Psychology.* New York: Holt and Company.

Joels, M. (2008). Functional actions of corticosteroids in the hippocampus. *European Journal of Pharmacology, 583*, 312–321.

Joels, M., & Baram, T. Z. (2009). The neuro-symphony of stress. *Nature Reviews Neuroscience, 10*, 459–466.

Joels, M., Pu, Z., Wiegert, O., Oitzl, M. S., & Krugers, H. J. (2006). Learning under stress: how does it work? *Trends in Cognitive Sciences, 10*, 152–158.

Joels, M., Krugers, H. J., Lucassen, P. J., & Karst, H. (2009). Corticosteroid effects on cellular physiology of limbic cells. *Brain Research, 1293*, 91–100.

Karst, H., Berger, S., Turiault, M., Tronche, F., Schutz, G., & Joels, M. (2005). Mineralocorticoid receptors are indispensable for nongenomic modulation of hippocampal glutamate transmission by corticosterone. *Proceedings of the National Academy of Sciences USA, 102*, 19204–19207.

Kim, J. J., & Diamond, D. M. (2002). The stressed hippocampus, synaptic plasticity and lost memories. *Nature Reviews Neuroscience, 3*, 453–462.

Kim, J. J., Koo, J. W., Lee, H. J., & Han, J. S. (2005). Amygdalar inactivation blocks stress-induced impairments in hippocampal long-term potentiation and spatial memory. *Journal of Neuroscience, 25*, 1532–1539.

Kitayama, S., Okada, Y., Takumi, T., Takada, S., Inagaki, Y., & Nakamura, H. (2000). Psychological and physical reactions on children after the Hanshin-Awaji earthquake disaster. *Kobe Journal of Medical Sciences, 46*, 189–200.

Konkel, A., & Cohen, N. J. (2009). Relational memory and the hippocampus: representations and methods. *Frontiers in Neuroscience, 3*, 166–174.

Layton, B., & Krikorian, R. (2002). Memory mechanisms in posttraumatic stress disorder. *Journal of Neuropsychiatry and Clinical Neurosciences, 14*, 254–261.

Levy, B. J., & Anderson, M. C. (2008). Individual differences in the suppression of unwanted memories: the executive deficit hypothesis. *Acta Psychologica, 127*, 623–635.

Li, S., Cullen, W. K., Anwyl, R., & Rowan, M. J. (2003). Dopamine-dependent facilitation of LTP induction in hippocampal CA1 by exposure to spatial novelty. *Nature Neuroscience, 6*, 526–531.

Lynch, M. A. (2004). Long-term potentiation and memory. *Physiological Review, 84*, 87–136.

Maroun, M., & Richter-Levin, G. (2003). Exposure to acute stress blocks the induction of long-term potentiation of the amygdala-prefrontal cortex pathway in vivo. *Journal of Neuroscience, 23*, 4406–4409.

McEwen, B. S., Weiss, J. M., & Schwartz, L. S. (1968). Selective retention of corticosterone by limbic structures in rat brain. *Nature, 220*, 911–912.

McEwen, B. S., Weiss, J. M., & Schwartz, L. S. (1969). Uptake of corticosterone by rat brain and its concentration by certain limbic structures. *Brain Research, 16*, 227–241.

Mehlum, L., Koldsland, B. O., & Loeb, M. E. (2006). Risk factors for long-term posttraumatic stress reactions in unarmed UN military observers: a four-year follow-up study. *Journal of Nervous and Mental Disease, 194*, 800–804.

Mesches, M. H., Fleshner, M., Heman, K. L., Rose, G. M., & Diamond, D. M. (1999). Exposing rats to a predator blocks primed burst potentiation in the hippocampus in vitro. *Journal of Neuroscience, 19,* RC18.

Metcalfe, J., & Jacobs, W. J. (1998). Emotional memory: The effects of stress on "cool" and "hot" memory systems. *Psychology of Learning and Motivation, 38,* 187–222.

Metcalfe, J., & Mischel, W. (1999). A hot/cool-system analysis of delay of gratification: Dynamics of willpower. *Psychological Review, 106,* 3–19.

Mizuno, K., & Giese, K. P. (2005). Hippocampus-dependent memory formation: do memory type-specific mechanisms exist? *Journal of Pharmacological Sciences, 98,* 191–197.

Nadel, L., & Jacobs, W. J. (1998). Traumatic memory is special. *Current Directions in Psychological Science, 7,* 154–157.

Orchinik, M., Murray, T. F., & Moore, F. L. (1991). A corticosteroid receptor in neuronal membranes. *Science, 252,* 1848–1851.

Packard, M. G. (2009). Anxiety, cognition, and habit: a multiple memory systems perspective. *Brain Research, 1293,* 121–128.

Packard, M. G., & McGaugh, J. L. (1996). Inactivation of hippocampus or caudate nucleus with lidocaine differentially affects expression of place and response learning. *Neurobiology of Learning and Memory, 65,* 65–72.

Park, C. R., Campbell, A. M., Woodson, J. C., Smith, T. P., Fleshner, M., & Diamond, D. M. (2006). Permissive influence of stress in the expression of a U-shaped relationship between serum corticosterone levels and spatial memory errors in rats. *Dose-Response, 4,* 55–74.

Park, C. R., Zoladz, P. R., Conrad, C. D., Fleshner, M., & Diamond, D. M. (2008). Acute predator stress impairs the consolidation and retrieval of hippocampus-dependent memory in male and female rats. *Learning & Memory, 15,* 271–280.

Pavlides, C., Kimura, A., Magarinos, A. M., & McEwen, B. S. (1995a). Hippocampal homosynaptic long-term depression/depotentiation induced by adrenal steroids. *Neuroscience, 68,* 379–385.

Pavlides, C., Watanabe, Y., Magarinos, A. M., & McEwen, B. S. (1995b). Opposing roles of type I and type II adrenal steroid receptors in hippocampal long-term potentiation. *Neuroscience, 68,* 387–394.

Payne, J. D., Nadel, L., Allen, J. J., Thomas, K. G., & Jacobs, W. J. (2002). The effects of experimentally induced stress on false recognition. *Memory, 10,* 1–6.

Poldrack, R. A., & Packard, M. G. (2003). Competition among multiple memory systems: converging evidence from animal and human brain studies. *Neuropsychologia, 41,* 245–251.

Poldrack, R. A., Prabhakaran, V., Seger, C. A., & Gabrieli, J. D. (1999). Striatal activation during acquisition of a cognitive skill. *Neuropsychology, 13,* 564–574.

Qi, H., Mailliet, F., Spedding, M., Rocher, C., Zhang, X., Delagrange, P., McEwen, B., Jay, T. M., & Svenningsson, P. (2009). Antidepressants reverse the attenuation of the neurotrophic MEK/MAPK cascade in frontal cortex by elevated platform stress; reversal of effects on LTP is associated with GluA1 phosphorylation. *Neuropharmacology, 56,* 37–46.

Rocher, C., Spedding, M., Munoz, C., & Jay, T. M. (2004). Acute stress-induced changes in hippocampal/prefrontal circuits in rats: effects of antidepressants. *Cerebral Cortex, 14,* 224–229.

Roozendaal, B. (2003). Systems mediating acute glucocorticoid effects on memory consolidation and retrieval. *Progress in Neuro-psychopharmacology & Biological Psychiatry, 27,* 1213–1223.

Roozendaal, B., Okuda, S., de Quervain, D. J., & McGaugh, J. L. (2006). Glucocorticoids interact with emotion-induced noradrenergic activation in influencing different memory functions. *Neuroscience, 138,* 901–910.

Sandi, C., & Pinelo-Nava, M. T. (2007). Stress and memory: behavioral effects and neurobiological mechanisms. *Neural Plasticity,* 78970.

Sandi, C., Loscertales, M., & Guaza, C. (1997). Experience-dependent facilitating effect of corticosterone on spatial memory formation in the water maze. *European Journal of Neuroscience, 9,* 637–642.

Sandi, C., Woodson, J. C., Haynes, V. F., Park, C. R., Touyarot, K., Lopez-Fernandez, M. A., Venero, C., & Diamond, D. M. (2005). Acute stress-induced impairment of spatial memory is associated with decreased expression of neural cell adhesion molecule in the hippocampus and prefrontal cortex. *Biological Psychiatry, 57,* 856–864.

Schacter, D. L. (1997). The cognitive neuroscience of memory: perspectives from neuroimaging research. *Philosophical Transactions of the Royal Society of London. Series B, Biological Sciences, 352,* 1689–1695.

Schwabe, L., & Wolf, O. T. (2009). Stress prompts habit behavior in humans. *Journal of Neuroscience, 29,* 7191–7198.

Schwabe, L., & Wolf, O. T. (2010). Learning under stress impairs memory formation. *Neurobiology of Learning and Memory, 93,* 183–188.

Schwabe, L., Wolf, O. T., & Oitzl, M. S. (2010). Memory formation under stress: quantity and quality. *Neuroscience and Biobehavioral Reviews, 34,* 584–591.

Seidenbecher, T., Reymann, K. G., & Balschun, D. (1997). A post-tetanic time window for the reinforcement of long-term potentiation by appetitive and aversive stimuli. *Proceedings of the National Academy of Sciences USA, 94,* 1494–1499.

Selden, N. R., Cole, B. J., Everitt, B. J., & Robbins, T. W. (1990). Damage to ceruleo-cortical noradrenergic projections impairs locally cued but enhances spatially cued water maze acquisition. *Behavioural Brain Research, 39,* 29–51.

Smeets, T., Otgaar, H., Candel, I., & Wolf, O. T. (2008). True or false? Memory is differentially affected by stress-induced cortisol elevations and sympathetic activity at consolidation and retrieval. *Psychoneuroendocrinology, 33,* 1378–1386.

Smeets, T., Wolf, O. T., Giesbrecht, T., Sijstermans, K., Telgen, S., & Joels, M. (2009). Stress selectively and lastingly promotes learning of context-related high arousing information. *Psychoneuroendocrinology, 34,* 1152–1161.

Squire, L. R. (1992). Memory and the hippocampus: a synthesis from findings with rats, monkeys, and humans. *Psychological Review, 99,* 195–231.

Straube, T., Korz, V., & Frey, J. U. (2003). Bidirectional modulation of long-term potentiation by novelty-exploration in rat dentate gyrus. *Neuroscience Letters, 344,* 5–8.

Uzakov, S., Frey, J. U., & Korz, V. (2005). Reinforcement of rat hippocampal LTP by holeboard training. *Learning & Memory, 12,* 165–171.

Van der Kolk, B. A., & Fisler, R. (1995). Dissociation and the fragmentary nature of traumatic memories: overview and exploratory study. *Journal of Trauma and Stress, 8,* 505–525.

Vouimba, R. M., Yaniv, D., Diamond, D., & Richter-Levin, G. (2004). Effects of inescapable stress on LTP in the amygdala versus the dentate gyrus of freely behaving rats. *European Journal of Neuroscience, 19,* 1887–1894.

White, N. M., & McDonald, R. J. (2002). Multiple parallel memory systems in the brain of the rat. *Neurobiology of Learning and Memory, 77,* 125–184.

Wiegert, O., Joels, M., & Krugers, H. (2006). Timing is essential for rapid effects of corticosterone on synaptic potentiation in the mouse hippocampus. *Learning & Memory, 13,* 110–113.

Wolf, O. T. (2009). Stress and memory in humans: twelve years of progress? *Brain Research, 1293,* 142–154.

Woodson, J. C., Macintosh, D., Fleshner, M., & Diamond, D. M. (2003). Emotion-induced amnesia in rats: working memory-specific impairment, corticosterone-memory correlation, and fear versus arousal effects on memory. *Learning & Memory, 10,* 326–336.

Yerkes, R. M., & Dodson, J. D. (1908). The relation of strength of stimulus to rapidity of habit-formation. *Journal of Comparative Neurology and Psychology, 18,* 459–482.

Zoladz, P. R., & Diamond, D. M. (2008). Linear and non-linear dose-response functions reveal a hormetic relationship between stress and learning. *Dose-Response, 7,* 132–148.

Zoladz, P. R., Park, C. R., Munoz, C., Fleshner, M., & Diamond, D. M. (2008). Tianeptine: an antidepressant with memory-protective properties. *Current Neuropharmacology, 6,* 311–321.

Zoladz, P. R., Woodson, J. C., Haynes, V. F., & Diamond, D. M. (2010). Activation of a remote (1-year old) emotional memory interferes with the retrieval of a newly formed hippocampus-dependent memory in rats. *Stress: The International Journal on the Biology of Stress, 13,* 36–52.

Zorawski, M., Blanding, N. Q., Kuhn, C. M., & LaBar, K. S. (2006). Effects of stress and sex on acquisition and consolidation of human fear conditioning. *Learning & Memory, 13,* 441–450.

9

Acute Glucocorticoids Interact with Arousal State in Regulating Long-term Memory Formation

Patrizia Campolongo and Benno Roozendaal

Introduction

Stress leads to an activation of the sympathetic nervous system and the hypothalamic–pituitary–adrenal (HPA) axis, culminating in the release of catecholamines and glucocorticoids from the adrenal medulla and cortex, respectively (McCarty and Gold, 1981; de Boer et al., 1990; Roozendaal et al., 1996a; see also Chapter 1 in this volume). These hormones are known to influence the organism's ability to cope with stress, influencing target systems in the periphery but also inducing a myriad of effects on the brain. In addition to preparing an individual for the acute consequences of dangerous or threatening situations and the return to homeostasis, an important function of stress is to induce long-term adaptive responses (McEwen, 1998). Emotionally significant experiences typically leave lasting and vivid memories, and it certainly seems highly adaptive that we record and retain lasting memories of our significant experiences. However, intensely emotional experiences such as automobile accidents, fires, muggings, rapes, wartime battles, or terrorist bombings can also create maladaptive traumatic memories and result in the development of anxiety disorders such as posttraumatic stress disorder (de Quervain et al., 2009; see also Part IV of this volume).

The scope of this chapter is to summarize recent findings on some novel mechanisms underlying the acute effects of glucocorticoid hormones on memory. Extensive evidence from both animal and human studies has indicated that adrenal stress hormones, together with many other stress-activated systems, strengthen the consolidation of memory of many different training experiences (Gold and Van Buskirk, 1975; Oitzl and de Kloet, 1992; Sandi and Rose, 1994; de Kloet et al., 1998;

The Handbook of Stress: Neuropsychological Effects on the Brain, First Edition.
Edited by Cheryl D. Conrad.
© 2011 Blackwell Publishing Ltd. Published 2011 by Blackwell Publishing Ltd.

Roozendaal, 2000). However, glucocorticoids do not enhance memory of all training experiences. Recent findings indicate that these hormones interact with arousal-induced activation of noradrenergic transmission within the basolateral amygdala (BLA) as well as several other brain regions to selectively modulate the consolidation of memory of emotionally arousing training experiences. Moreover, such interactions between glucocorticoids and the noradrenergic system do not appear to be mediated through the classic genomic action of glucocorticoids, but to involve rapid effects through an activation of membrane-associated steroid receptors and increased endocannabinoid signaling (Tasker et al., 2006; Campolongo et al., 2009).

Acute Glucocorticoid Effects on Memory Consolidation

Over the past decades considerable evidence has accumulated indicating that glucocorticoids (cortisol in humans, corticosterone in rodents) are crucially involved in memory processing. Early reports on both enhancing and impairing properties of glucocorticoids on memory (Bohus and Lissak, 1968; Flood et al., 1978; Beckwith et al., 1986; Luine et al., 1993; Arbel et al., 1994) indicate that these hormones have complex effects on cognitive functions. However, more recent studies investigating glucocorticoid effects on distinct memory phases helped to disentangle the multi-faceted actions of these stress hormones. Specifically, glucocorticoids have been shown to enhance the consolidation of memory of emotionally arousing experiences, but to impair memory retrieval and working memory during emotionally arousing test situations (de Quervain et al., 1998; Roozendaal, 2000; Roozendaal et al., 2004; Conrad, 2005; de Quervain et al., 2009). There is now extensive evidence from animal studies that glucocorticoids are critically involved in regulating the consolidation of memory processes (Flood et al., 1978; de Kloet, 2000; Roozendaal, 2000; McGaugh and Roozendaal, 2002). Acute systemic administration of corticosterone or synthetic glucocorticoid ligands typically enhances long-term memory consolidation when given either before or immediately after a training experience (Flood et al., 1978; Sandi and Rose, 1994; Pugh et al., 1997; Roozendaal et al., 1999b; Cordero et al., 2002). In contrast, a blockade of glucocorticoid production with the synthesis inhibitor metyrapone impairs memory consolidation (Roozendaal et al., 1996a; Maheu et al., 2004) and prevents stress- and epinephrine (adrenaline)-induced memory enhancement (Roozendaal et al., 1996b; Liu et al., 1999). Such glucocorticoid effects on memory consolidation follow an inverted U-shape dose–response relationship: Moderate doses enhance memory, whereas higher doses are typically less effective or may even impair memory consolidation (Roozendaal et al., 1999b). A similar inverted-U relationship has been reported between circulating corticosterone levels and neural plasticity and several other cellular functions within the hippocampus (Diamond et al., 1992; Joëls, 2006). Such biphasic effects of glucocorticoids on memory consolidation have been observed in many different kinds of learning tasks, including inhibitory avoidance, contextual and cued fear conditioning, water-maze spatial and cued training, object recognition, and conditioned taste aversion (Roozendaal et al., 2006a). These findings indicate that, in animals, glucocorticoids do not only enhance memory of training on hippocampus-dependent tasks that have a strong spatial/contextual component, but also memory of recognition and procedural training that are known to depend on other brain systems (Miranda et al., 2008; Quirarte et al., 2009). In humans, glucocorticoid effects on memory consolidation have been investigated mostly with respect to hippocampus-dependent declarative tasks (de Quervain et al., 2009), and beneficial effects on memory consolidation were found in several studies, even though the findings are not always consistent.

Recent findings indicate that glucocorticoids in moderate levels enhance memory consolidation of emotionally arousing training experiences but do not affect memory consolidation of emotionally neutral information. Learning tasks in animal experiments are usually emotionally arousing because of the motivational stimulation necessary to elicit changes in behavior. In a recent study, we investigated the importance of emotional arousal in mediating glucocorticoid effects on memory consolidation in rats trained on an object-recognition task (Okuda et al., 2004). Although no rewarding or aversive stimulation is used during object-recognition training, such training induces modest novelty-induced stress or arousal (de Boer et al., 1990). However, extensive habituation of rats to the experimental context (in the absence of any objects) reduces the arousal level during the training. We found that corticosterone, administered systemically immediately after training, enhanced 24-hr retention performance of rats that were not previously habituated to the experimental context (i.e., emotionally aroused rats). In contrast, posttraining corticosterone did not affect 24-hr retention in rats that had received extensive prior habituation to the experimental context and thus had decreased novelty-induced emotional arousal during training (Okuda et al., 2004). Human studies support the hypothesis that learning-associated arousal is a prerequisite for the enhancing effects of glucocorticoids on memory consolidation (Abercrombie et al., 2006; Wolf, 2008; de Quervain et al., 2009; van Stegeren et al., 2010).

Fast and Slow Glucocorticoid Actions

Naturally occurring glucocorticoids freely enter the brain and bind to two distinct intracellular receptors: mineralocorticoid receptors (MRs) and glucocorticoid receptors (GRs) (Reul and de Kloet, 1985; de Kloet et al., 1998). GRs have a low affinity for corticosterone and become occupied only during stress and at the circadian peak, when levels of glucocorticoids are high. In contrast, MRs have a high affinity for corticosterone and are almost saturated under basal conditions (Reul and de Kloet, 1985). To examine whether the memory-enhancing effects of glucocorticoids depend on GR or MR activation, rats were given intracerebroventricular

infusions of specific antagonists for either GRs or MRs. Both pretraining or immediate posttraining infusions of a GR antagonist, but not an MR antagonist, impaired
spatial memory in a water maze (Oitzl and de Kloet, 1992; Roozendaal et al., 1996c).
Additionally, posttraining infusions of a GR antagonist impaired memory
consolidation for avoidance training in chicks and blocked the enhancing effects of
posttraining corticosterone (Sandi and Rose, 1994). Another study revealed that
the level of GR occupancy was significantly correlated with spatial memory performance following an inverted-U shape curve, whereas the level of MR occupancy
was not (Conrad et al., 1999). GR-knockout mice also show impaired memory
function (Oitzl et al., 1997). Together, these findings clearly indicate that the GR,
and not the MR, is involved in regulating glucocorticoid effects on memory
consolidation.

Delayed glucocorticoid effects are mediated by classical steroid mechanisms
involving transcriptional regulation. GRs can influence transcription through DNA-
binding-dependent and -independent mechanisms. To assess the importance of
these two modes of action in modulating memory, Oitzl et al. (2001) used GR$^{dim/dim}$
mutant mice in which homodimerization and DNA binding of the GR is largely
prevented while protein–protein interactions with other transcription factors still
take place. As these mice showed impaired spatial memory in the water maze, the
findings demonstrate that the facilitating effects of corticosterone on memory
depend on the DNA-binding capacity of the GR.

However, more recent evidence indicates that glucocorticoids also mediate physiological and behavioral effects that occur too fast to be mediated through a genomic
action. Orchinik and colleagues (e.g., Orchinik et al., 1991; Rose et al., 1993) provided the first evidence that glucocorticoids can exert rapid, nongenomically mediated effects by binding to a receptor on neuronal membranes. More recently, Karst
et al. (2005) demonstrated that corticosterone enhances the frequency of miniature
excitatory postsynaptic potentials in CA1 pyramidal neurons (where CA means
cornu ammonis, a subregion of the hippocampus) of rat hippocampus and reduces
paired-pulse facilitation, pointing to a hormone-dependent enhancement of
glutamate-release probability. This rapid effect of corticosterone on increased glutamate release was accomplished through a nongenomic pathway involving a putative
membrane-located MR. Interestingly, Johnson and coworkers (2005) used electron
microscopy to show that GRs are not only found in the cytosol or nucleus of rat
lateral amygdala neurons, but are also localized to nongenomic sites such as glia
processes, presynaptic terminals, neuronal dendrites, and dendritic spines, including spine organelles and postsynaptic membrane densities. In very recent work these
authors also showed the existence of an MR on the cell surface (Prager and Johnson,
2009). As will be shown below, the rapid effects of glucocorticoids, mediated by the
activation of one or more membrane-associated G-protein-coupled receptors, cause
the activation of downstream signaling cascades and several neurotransmitters (e.g.,
norepinephrine [noradrenaline] and endocannabinoids) which are normally activated during emotionally arousal experiences (Tasker, 2006; Tasker et al., 2006; Di
and Tasker, 2008; Roozendaal et al., 2010; see also Chapter 4).

Role of the Amygdala in Mediating Glucocorticoid Effects on Memory Consolidation

Stress and emotional arousal are known to activate the amygdala. Extensive evidence indicates that the BLA is involved in mediating stress and emotional arousal effects on memory consoliation (McGaugh, 2000; McGaugh, 2002; Paré, 2003). In particular, converging findings provide evidence that the BLA is critically involved in enabling us to acquire and retain lasting memories of emotional experiences (McGaugh, 2000; LeDoux, 2007). Glucocorticoids, secreted from the adrenal cortex following arousing or stressful stimulation, readily enter the brain and bind directly to adrenal steroid receptors in the BLA and other brain regions (Reul and de Kloet, 1985). Extensive evidence indicates that the BLA is critically involved in mediating glucocorticoid effects on memory consolidation. Selective lesions of the BLA block the memory-enhancing effects of systemic administration of the synthetic glucocorticoid dexamethasone (Roozendaal and McGaugh, 1996), whereas posttraining intra-BLA infusions of the GR agonist RU28362 enhance memory consolidation for inhibitory avoidance training (Roozendaal and McGaugh, 1997b). In contrast, lesions of the adjacent central amygdala or infusions of a GR agonist into the central amygdala do not affect inhibitory avoidance memory. Selective BLA lesions also block memory impairment induced by an intracerebroventricular administration of the GR antagonist RU38486 or after removing the main source of glucocorticoids via adrenalectomy (Roozendaal et al., 1996c). Furthermore, intra-BLA infusions of a GR antagonist impair retention performance in a water-maze spatial task (Roozendaal and McGaugh, 1997b). These findings indicate, therefore, that the BLA is a critical locus of action of glucocorticoids in modulating memory processing.

Although evidence suggests that the BLA might be a critical site involved in the encoding, storage, and expression of fear-related memories (LeDoux, 2007), an involvement of the BLA in modulating long-term memory formation has been obtained in experiments using many different kinds of training task, including contextual fear conditioning, cued fear conditioning, inhibitory avoidance, Y-maze discrimination training, change in reward magnitude, conditioned place preference, radial-arm maze appetitive training, water-maze spatial and cued training, conditioned taste aversion, olfactory training, object recognition, extinction of contextual fear conditioning, and extinction of conditioned reward (McGaugh and Roozendaal, 2009). As these different training experiences are known to engage different brain systems (Quillfeldt et al., 1996; Izquierdo et al., 1997; Packard and Knowlton, 2002; McGaugh, 2002; Packard et al., 1994), the BLA-induced modulation no doubt involves influences on processing occurring in these brain regions (McGaugh and Roozendaal, 2002). The BLA is known to interact with the hippocampus in regulating emotional arousal effects on spatial and/or contextual memory (McGaugh et al., 1996; Roozendaal et al., 1996c; Roozendaal and McGaugh, 1997a; Huff and Rudy, 2004; McIntyre et al., 2005) and with the dorsal striatum and cortical brain regions in regulating emotional arousal effects on other aspects of memory and cognition (Packard et al., 1994; Malin and McGaugh, 2006). In one study (Roozendaal and McGaugh, 1997a) the GR agonist RU28362 was administered into the dorsal hippocampus immediately after inhibitory avoidance training. Such GR agonist administration enhanced later retention. However, and most importantly, neuro-chemical lesions of the BLA blocked the memory enhancement induced by intra-hippocampal administration of the GR agonist. BLA lesions also blocked the impairing effect of a GR antagonist infused into the hippocampus on spatial memory in a water maze (Roozendaal and McGaugh, 1997a). Consistent with these findings, electrolytic lesions of the amygdala before exposure to uncontrollable restraint/tail-shock stress prevented stress-induced impairment of hippocampal long-term potentiation and spatial memory in rats (Kim et al., 2001). Findings from electrophysiological studies also indicate that BLA activity influences stress-induced or perforant-path-stimulation-induced long-term potentiation in the hippocampus (Frey et al., 2001; Akirav and Richter-Levin, 2002; Nakao et al., 2004). Moreover, norepinephrine and corticosterone both influence the effects of BLA stimulation on synaptic plasticity in the dentate gyrus (Akirav and Richter-Levin, 2002; Vouimba et al., 2007) and recent findings indicate that BLA activity is required for enabling corticosterone-induced expression of the synaptic-plasticity-related protein Arc in the hippocampus (McReynolds et al., 2010).

The BLA also interacts with the medial prefrontal cortex (mPFC) in mediating glucocorticoid effects on memory consolidation. However, the findings suggest that this interaction may serve quite a different role in memory than that described between the BLA and hippocampus. A growing body of evidence indicates that BLA neuronal activity is closely regulated by the mPFC, a brain region involved in higher-order cognitive and affective processing as well as executive function (Davidson, 2002; Quirk and Gehlert, 2003). We recently found that the memory-enhancing effect of an immediate posttraining infusion of the GR agonist RU28362 administered into the mPFC depends on a rapid increase in the phosphorylation of extracellular signal-regulated kinase 1/2 (pERK1/2) in the BLA, and, conversely, that the memory enhancement induced by intra-BLA administration of RU28362 requires elevated pERK1/2 levels in the mPFC (Roozendaal et al., 2009b). Thus, these findings strongly suggest that these two brain regions function as a bidirectional circuit in influencing memory consolidation in other brain regions. Several studies indicate that such interactions between the mPFC and BLA exert cognitive and emotional control of brain activity, essential for an adaptive regulation of affect and memory (Amat et al., 2005; Burgos-Robles et al., 2007; Mueller et al., 2008).

Human studies are consistent with these findings from animal experiments and have provided evidence that glucocorticoid effects on enhancing declarative memory for emotionally arousing experiences require amygdala activity. Declarative memory for emotionally arousing material is not enhanced in human subjects with selective bilateral damage to the amygdala, as it is in normal subjects (Cahill et al., 1995; Adolphs et al., 1997). Studies using brain positron emission tomography and functional magnetic resonance imaging techniques have provided evidence that amygdala activity during viewing of emotionally arousing pictures or scenes correlates strongly with the subjects' recall of the material assessed weeks later (Cahill et al., 1996; Hamann et al., 1999; Canli et al., 2000). Furthermore, the relationship between amygdala activity during encoding and subsequent memory was greatest for the material rated as being the most emotionally intense (Cahill et al., 1996; Hamann et al., 1999; Canli et al., 2000). Moreover, a recent study revealed that amygdala activity during viewing of emotionally arousing pictures was greatest for those subjects who responded with a large increase in endogenous cortisol (van Stegeren et al., 2007). And, importantly, in accordance with the animal studies described below, a β-adrenoceptor antagonist blocked the increase in amygdala activity and enhanced retention induced by either emotional arousal or endogenous cortisol (Cahill et al., 1994; Strange and Dolan, 2004; van Stegeren et al., 2005).

Glucocorticoid Interactions with Noradrenergic Mechanisms in the BLA

The enhancing effects of glucocorticoids on memory consolidation depend on the integrity of the amygdala noradrenergic system (Roozendaal et al., 1999a, 2009a; McGaugh, 2000; Roozendaal, 2000; McGaugh and Roozendaal, 2002). Intra-BLA infusions of a β-adrenoceptor antagonist block the memory-enhancing effects of systemic injections of dexamethasone or corticosterone as well as the effect of the GR agonist RU28362 infused into the BLA concurrently (Quirarte et al., 1997; Roozendaal et al., 2002, 2006a, 2006b). Studies using in vivo microdialysis and high-performance liquid chromatography (HPLC) have shown that emotional arousal such as that produced by foot shock induces the release of norepinephrine in the amygdala (Galvez et al., 1996; Quirarte et al., 1998). Furthermore, amygdala norepinephrine levels assessed following aversively motivated inhibitory avoidance training correlate with retention latencies tested 24 hr later (McIntyre et al., 2002), whereas posttraining infusions of norepinephrine or β-adrenoceptor agonists into the amygdala (or selectively into the BLA) produce dose-dependent enhancement of memory consolidation (Liang et al., 1986; Ferry et al., 1999b; Hatfield and McGaugh, 1999; LaLumiere et al., 2003; Roozendaal et al., 2008a). Furthermore, posttraining intra-amygdala infusions of β-adrenoceptor antagonists impair retention of inhibitory avoidance and block the memory-enhancing effect of coadministered norepinephrine (Liang et al., 1986, 1995). In addition to β-adrenoceptor influences, α-adrenoceptor activation in the BLA also modulates memory consolidation. Intra-BLA infusions of the α_1-adrenoceptor antagonist prazosin impair inhibitory avoidance memory (Ferry et al., 1999a) whereas infusions of the α_1-adrenoceptor agonist cirazoline enhance retention of this training (Roozendaal et al., 2008b). The α_1-adrenoceptor-induced memory enhancement most likely involves an interaction with β-adrenoceptors, as posttraining intra-BLA infusions of the β-adrenoceptor antagonist atenolol block inhibitory avoidance memory enhancement produced by activation of α_1-adrenoceptors. The finding that posttraining intra-BLA infusions of the synthetic adenosine 3',5'-cyclic monophosphate (cAMP) analogue 8-bromo-cAMP enhance retention (Liang et al., 1995) is consistent with the hypothesis that activation of β-adrenoceptors modulates memory via a direct coupling to adenylate cyclase (Daly et al., 1981). Thus, the finding that intra-BLA infusions of the α_1-adrenoceptor antagonist prazosin did not prevent the memory enhancement induced by concurrently infused 8-bromo-cAMP suggests that the memory-enhancing effects of α_1-adrenoceptor activation are mediated by an interaction with β-adrenoceptors upstream from cAMP, probably at the G-protein level (Ferry et al., 1999b).

Based on the evidence summarized above, it may be hypothesized that emotional arousal-induced increases in noradrenergic activity within the BLA are essential for enabling glucocorticoid effects on memory consolidation. Such a mechanism may then provide a direct explanation of the finding that glucocorticoids selectively enhance memory consolidation of emotionally arousing experiences. We recently investigated this issue in rats trained on an object-recognition task. As is discussed above, corticosterone enhances memory of object-recognition training when administered to naïve rats, but is ineffective in rats that have reduced training-associated emotional arousal because of prior habituation to the experimental context (Okuda et al., 2004). We found that in nonhabituated (i.e., emotionally aroused) rats the β-adrenoceptor antagonist propranolol, when administered, systemically blocked corticosterone-induced memory enhancement (Roozendaal et al., 2006a). Propranolol infused directly into the BLA also blocked the enhancing effects of corticosterone on object-recognition memory. To determine whether the failure of corticosterone to enhance memory consolidation under low-arousing conditions is due to insufficient training-induced noradrenergic activation, low doses of the α_2-adrenoceptor antagonist yohimbine, which increases norepinephrine levels in the brain, were coadministered with the corticosterone to well-habituated rats immediately after object-recognition training. The critical finding of this study was that such an augmented noradrenergic tone was sufficient to mimic the effects of emotional arousal in that simultaneously administered corticosterone now enhanced memory consolidation (Roozendaal et al., 2006a). Further, in habituated rats, corticosterone activated BLA neurons, as assessed by phosphorylated cAMP-response-element binding protein (pCREB) immunoreactivity levels, but only in animals also given yohimbine. Such observations strongly suggest that because glucocorticoid effects on memory consolidation require noradrenergic activation within the BLA they only modulate memory under emotionally arousing conditions that induce the release of norepinephrine.

Findings of studies investigating the mechanism of glucocorticoid interactions with the noradrenergic system suggest that activation of GRs in the BLA may facilitate memory consolidation by potentiating the norepinephrine-signaling cascade through an interaction with G-protein-mediated effects (Roozendaal et al., 2002). Posttraining intra-BLA infusions of the β-adrenoceptor agonist clenbuterol or the cAMP analogue 8-bromo-cAMP enhance memory consolidation in a dose-dependent fashion (Introini-Collison et al., 1991; Liang et al., 1995; Ferry et al., 1999b). The GR antagonist RU38486 infused into the BLA shortly before training shifts the dose–response effects of clenbuterol such that a much higher dose of clenbuterol is required to induce comparable memory enhancement (Roozendaal et al., 2002). In contrast, the GR antagonist did not modify the dose–response effects of 8-bromo-cAMP, indicating that cAMP acts in the BLA downstream from the locus of interaction of glucocorticoids with the β-adrenoceptor-cAMP/cAMP-dependent kinase (protein kinase A, PKA) pathway. These findings strongly suggest that glucocorticoids enhance memory consolidation, in a permissive fashion, by potentiating β-adrenoceptor-cAMP/PKA efficacy in the BLA (Roozendaal et al., 2002). We showed that GRs may influence β-adrenoceptor-cAMP/PKA efficacy in the BLA via a coupling with postsynaptic $α_1$-adrenoceptors (Roozendaal et al., 2002). Moreover, recent findings indicate that the memory-modulating effects of the neuropeptide corticotropin-releasing hormone (CRH), which is released in the amygdala after stress, also depend on interactions with the β-adrenoceptor-cAMP cascade in the BLA (Roozendaal et al., 2008b). And, consistent with the evidence that glucocorticoids enhance memory consolidation via a similar interaction with the β-adrenoceptor-cAMP cascade, we further found that the CRH and glucocorticoid systems within the BLA interact in influencing β-adrenoceptor-cAMP effects on memory consolidation: a GR antagonist infused into the BLA blocked the enhancing effect of CRH on memory consolidation.

In addition to such postsynaptic actions, glucocorticoid administration may increase the availability of norepinephrine in the BLA via an activation of GRs located in brainstem noradrenergic cell groups. The nucleus of the solitary tract and the locus coeruleus are known to send noradrenergic projections to forebrain regions involved in memory consolidation, including the amygdala. Posttraining infusions of the GR agonist RU28362 into the nucleus of the solitary tract dose-dependently enhance memory consolidation of inhibitory avoidance training and the memory enhancement is blocked by intra-BLA infusions of a β-adrenoceptor antagonist (Roozendaal et al., 1999b). The findings of a recent in vivo microdialysis experiment support the view that glucocorticoids may facilitate the training-induced release of norepinephrine in the amygdala (McReynolds et al., 2010). Corticosterone administered immediately after inhibitory avoidance training increased amygdala norepinephrine levels whereas corticosterone administered to nonaroused control animals did not affect norepinephrine levels in the amygdala. Interestingly, as norepinephrine levels in the amygdala were elevated within 15 min after the corticosterone administration, these effects are compatible with rapid nongenomic effect of glucocorticoids. Figure 9.1 summarizes the interactions of glucocorticoids with the noradrenergic system in the BLA that are involved in regulating memory consolidation.

On the whole, the abovementioned behavioral studies suggest that, shortly after stress, norepinephrine and corticosterone interact to enhance the function of BLA neurons in regulating memory for emotionally arousing experiences. Liebmann and coworkers (2009) have tested, with an elegant electrophysiological approach at the single-cell level, to what extent α-amino-3-hydroxy-5-methyl-4-isoxazole propionate (AMPA) and N-methyl-D-aspartate (NMDA) receptor-mediated synaptic responses of identified BLA neurons are affected by relatively low concentrations of the β-adrenoceptor agonist isoproterenol, how this is influenced by concomitant application of corticosterone, and how isoproterenol effects are influenced by

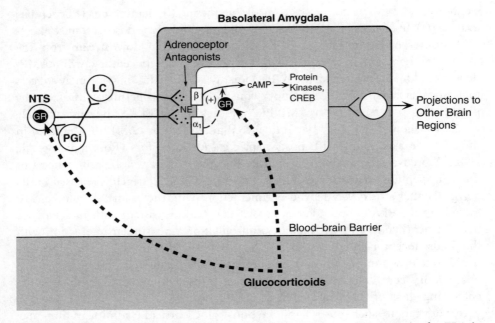

Figure 9.1   Interactions of glucocorticoids with the noradrenergic system in the BLA in modulating memory consolidation. Glucocorticoids freely enter the brain and bind to GRs in brainstem noradrenergic neurons to potentiate norepinephrine release in the BLA, as well as postsynaptically in BLA neurons to facilitate the norepinephrine signaling cascade. Glucocorticoids may influence the β-adrenoceptor-cAMP system via a coupling with α_1-adrenoceptors. These stress-hormone effects on noradrenergic activation in the BLA are required for regulating memory consolidation in other brain regions. α_1, α_1-Adrenoceptor; β, β-adrenoceptor; LC, locus coerulus; NTS, nucleus of the solitary tract; PGi, nucleus para-gigantocellularis. *Source:* From Roozendaal (2000). With permission from Elsevier.

corticosterone given several hours in advance. They observed that isoproterenol enhances AMPA-receptor-mediated, but not NMDA-receptor-mediated, responses and that corticosterone alone did not affect AMPA- and NMDA-mediated responses. If corticosterone was coapplied with isoproterenol, facilitation of AMPA-mediated responses was comparable to that seen with isoproterenol alone. However, if the corticosterone was applied several hours in advance of the β-adrenoceptor agonist, the effect of isoproterenol on AMPA-mediated responses was reduced. This supports the notion that, in the BLA, isoproterenol facilitates synaptic transmission, a process that can be suppressed by corticosterone in a slow manner. Overall, the data are consistent with the *temporal dynamics model* of Diamond et al. (2007; and see Chapter 8, this volume). These authors proposed that after an initial activational period, corticosterone and noradrenergic stimulation exerts a normalizing action on local activity of the BLA as well as several other brain regions, during which the induction of new plasticity is suppressed. Both the period of activation and suppression may be required for the facilitation of memory consolidation processes.

Recent findings indicate that the BLA is not the only brain region mediating glucocorticoid interactions with the noradrenergic system in regulating memory consolidation. As indicated above, infusions of the GR agonist RU28362 into the mPFC also enhance memory consolidation of inhibitory avoidance training (Roozendaal et al., 2009b). Highly comparable to the effects found in the BLA, infusions of a β-adrenoceptor antagonist or PKA inhibitor into the mPFC prevented the memory enhancement of the GR agonist administered concurrently (A. Barsegyan et al., 2010). Moreover, corticosterone administered systemically immediately after inhibitory avoidance training increased PKA activity in the mPFC within 30 min, further supporting the view that glucocorticoid effects on noradrenergic signaling are mediated via rapid, nongenomic actions. Glucocorticoids also interact with the noradrenergic system in the insular cortex in regulating memory consolidation. In one study (Roozendaal et al., 2010) corticosterone conjugated to a bovine serum albumin molecule (i.e., cort:BSA) was infused into the insular cortex immediately after object-recognition training, a brain region critically involved in object-recognition memory (Bermudez-Rattoni et al., 2005). This conjugate does not cross the cell membrane and thus selectively activates adrenal steroid receptors on the cell surface (Chiyo et al., 2003). This corticosterone conjugate enhanced memory consolidation of this training, and the effect was blocked by coadministration of a GR antagonist, but not an MR antagonist, thus providing further support for the view that GRs on the cell surface are implicated in mediating glucocorticoid effects on memory consolidation. Moreover, consistent with the view that glucocorticoids interact with the norepinephrine signaling pathway, a selective PKA inhibitor blocked the cort:BSA-induced memory enhancement. Immunocytochemistry revealed that cort:BSA infusions after object-recognition training increased PKA-dependent pCREB levels in insular cortex neurons.

In an entirely new line of research, we found that glucocorticoid effects on norepinephrine signaling and pCREB activation enhance the consolidation of object-recognition memory via chromatin modification in the insular cortex (Roozendaal et al., 2010). Systemic corticosterone increased histone acetylation, a form of chromatin modification, in the insular cortex as assessed 1 hr after training on an object-recognition task. Furthermore, infusion of the histone deacetylase (HDAC) inhibitor sodium butyrate administered into the insular cortex immediately after object-recognition training enhanced memory consolidation of this training. Inducing a histone hyperacetylated state via HDAC inhibition appears to facilitate transcription by relaxing chromatin structure, resulting in enhanced synaptic plasticity and long-term memory processes (Barrett and Wood, 2008). However, the effect of the HDAC inhibitor on memory enhancement was completely abolished by blocking GR activity, but not by blocking MR activity. Additionally, a PKA inhibitor also blocked the ability of HDAC inhibition to enhance memory in the insular cortex. Thus, these findings indicate that inducing a histone-hyperacetylated state via HDAC inhibition is not sufficient to enhance long-term memory. It is still necessary to have upstream signaling via GR and PKA activity. Presumably, these signaling events are triggering steps necessary to activate transcription factors and coactivators such as CREB and CREB-binding protein (CBP).

Rapid Glucocorticoid Interactions with Endocannabinoid Mechanisms

As mentioned, glucocorticoids are thought to modulate neurophysiology and behavior through both genomic and nongenomic pathways (de Kloet, 2000; Dallman, 2005; see also Chapters 3 and 4 in this volume). Although the ability of steroids to regulate gene transcription is a well-characterized process of direct binding of homodimers or heterodimers of GRs to nuclear DNA, or through protein–protein interactions with transcription factors (de Kloet, 2000), the nongenomic mechanisms of glucocorticoid action are poorly understood (Dallman, 2005). However, as emphasized in this chapter, accumulating evidence demonstrates that glucocorticoid hormones enhance long-term consolidation of emotionally arousing experiences involving rapid actions on intracellular signaling cascades in the BLA (Roozendaal, 2000; McGaugh and Roozendaal, 2002). In the previous section we described that glucocorticoids, via an activation of membrane-bound GRs, influence norepinephrine signaling in regulating memory consolidation. The question arises as to whether there are additional, or cooperating, downstream mechanisms by which glucocorticoids exert their rapid actions. In search of an answer, Di and coworkers (2003) used in vitro electrophysiological recording of parvocellular neurons in the paraventricular nucleus of the hypothalamus of the rat to demonstrate that glucocorticoids rapidly suppressed glutamate release through a mechanism that involved postsynaptic activation of membrane-bound GRs. Activation of this receptor launched a G-protein signaling cascade that induced the synthesis of endocannabinoid ligands, which in turn traversed back across the synapse where they bind to presynaptic cannabinoid type-1 receptors (CB1Rs) localized on glutamatergic terminals and inhibit subsequent glutamate release. Coddington and coworkers (2007) then took this model to their newt preparation and demonstrated that the ability of glucocorticoids to inhibit sensory-evoked stimulation of medullary neurons and courtship clasping is mediated by an endocannabinoid intermediary. Collectively, these studies revealed a novel mechanism of glucocorticoid activation via a membrane-bound G-protein-coupled receptor, which induces endocannabinoid synthesis. The endocannabinoids then diffuse to local neuronal populations and inhibit neurotransmitter release (Hill and McEwen, 2009). It is important to note that this mechanism of rapid glucocorticoid effects via membrane-associated GRs and endocannabinoid release appears to coexist with another recently described model of rapid glucocorticoid effects involving the activation of MRs located on presynaptic membranes (see Chapter 4). These latter effects do not appear to depend on endocannabinoid signaling.

Endogenous ligands for cannabinoid receptors, endocannabinoids, serve as retrograde messengers at central synapses. Endocannabinoids are produced on demand in an activity-dependent manner and are released from postsynaptic neurons. The released endocannabinoids travel backward across the synapse, activate presynaptic CB1Rs, and modulate presynaptic functions. Retrograde endocannabinoid signaling is crucial for certain forms of short-term and long-term synaptic plasticity at excitatory or inhibitory synapses in many brain regions, and thereby contributes to various aspects of brain function, including learning and memory (Hashimotodani et al., 2007). Animal studies suggest that cannabinoid treatment affects memory encoding and consolidation processes (Riedel and Davies, 2005; Clarke et al., 2008; Robinson et al., 2008). Cannabinoid receptors are highly expressed in the BLA, where they modulate synaptic transmission (Katona et al., 2001) and neuronal firing (Pistis et al., 2004). Such modulating influences within the BLA may contribute to the emotionally relevant behavioral effects of cannabinoid drugs. It has been demonstrated that endocannabinoids within the amygdala facilitate memory consolidation of fear learning (Marsicano et al., 2002) as well as extinction of aversive memories (Bucherelli et al., 2006). In view of the evidence described above, we investigated whether the endocannabinoid system in the BLA influences memory consolidation and whether glucocorticoids interact with this system. As is shown in Figure 9.2 we found that intra-BLA infusion of a CB1R agonist or

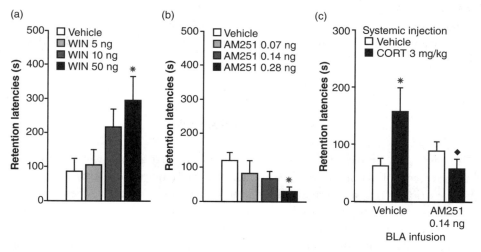

Figure 9.2 Endocannabinoids in the BLA enhance memory consolidation and enable glucocorticoid modulation of memory. (a) Immediately posttraining bilateral intra-BLA infusions of the CB1R agonist WIN55,212-2 (WIN; 5, 10, and 50 ng in 0.2 μl) enhance inhibitory avoidance retention. (b) Immediate posttraining intra-BLA infusions of the CB1R antagonist AM251 (0.07, 0.14, and 0.28 ng in 0.2 μl) impair inhibitory avoidance retention. (c) Immediate posttraining bilateral infusions of AM251 (0.14 ng in 0.2 μl) into the BLA block retention enhancement induced by subcutaneously injections of corticosterone (CORT; 3.0 mg/kg, subcutaneous). Data represent step-through latencies (mean + SEM) in seconds on the 48-hr inhibitory avoidance-retention test. *$P < 0.05$ compared with the corresponding vehicle group; ◆, $P < 0.05$ compared with the corresponding corticosterone group. *Source:* From Campolongo et al. (2009).

antagonist immediately after inhibitory avoidance training dose-dependently enhanced or impaired emotional memory consolidation, respectively (Campolongo et al., 2009). These findings indicate that cannabinoids in the BLA are involved in the regulation of memory consolidation. Importantly, intra-BLA administration of a CB1R antagonist blocked the ability of systemically administered corticosterone to facilitate aversive memory consolidation (Campolongo et al., 2009). Moreover, Hill et al. (2010) showed that an acute administration of corticosterone increased endocannabinoid levels in the amygdala. These findings (Campolongo et al., 2009) add to the Tasker model (Di et al., 2003, 2005; Tasker, 2006; Tasker et al., 2006; Di and Tasker, 2008) by demonstrating that glucocorticoids modulate memory consolidation of emotionally arousing experiences through an induction of endocannabinoid signaling in the BLA, providing the first in vivo evidence in mammals of the existence of this pathway (Hill and McEwen, 2009). In addition, these data might help us to understand the neuronal mechanisms by which glucocorticoids induce noradrenergic activation and modulate emotional memory consolidation. In this model, glucocorticoids bind to membrane-bound receptors that activate a G-protein-coupled signaling cascade that induces endocannabinoid synthesis. The ensuing release of endocannabinoid ligands that follows might diffuse to local γ-aminobutyric acid (GABA)-ergic terminals and inhibit GABAergic release onto noradrenergic terminals. The end result of this process would be an increase of norepinephrine release into the BLA, and subsequently an enhancement of emotional memory consolidation (Hill and McEwen, 2009).

Concluding Remarks

The evidence summarized in this chapter indicates that glucocorticoids enhance memory consolidation in various animal and human memory tasks. Although glucocorticoids may act in many different brain regions to modulate these memory processes, the effects appear to depend critically on arousal-induced BLA activation and noradrenergic neurotransmission within the BLA. These findings may help to explain why glucocorticoids do not uniformly modulate memory for all kinds of information but, rather, preferentially influence the consolidation of emotionally arousing information. Furthermore, the findings indicate that glucocorticoids not only modulate memory consolidation via their classically recognized genomic actions, but that glucocorticoid interactions with the noradrenergic arousal system depend critically on rapid, nongenomic actions via an activation of membrane-bound GRs, increased endocannabinoid signaling, and chromatin modification. Future studies will have to determine whether and how such rapid glucocorticoid effects on arousal mechanisms might cooperate with the slow actions in influencing gene transcription and the formation of strong and stabile memories of emotionally significant experiences.

References

Abercrombie, H. C., Speck, N. S., & Monticelli, R. M. (2006). Endogenous cortisol elevations are related to memory facilitation only in individuals who are emotionally aroused. *Psychoneuroendocrinology, 31*, 187–196.

Adolphs, R., Cahill, L., Schul, R., & Babinsky, R. (1997). Impaired declarative memory for emotional material following bilateral amygdala damage in humans. *Learning & Memory, 4*, 291–300.

Akirav, I., & Richter-Levin, G. (2002). Mechanisms of amygdala modulation of hippocampal plasticity. *Journal of Neuroscience, 22*, 9912–9921.

Amat, J., Baratta, M. W., Paul, E., Bland, S. T., Watkins, L. R., & Maier, S. F. (2005). Medial prefrontal cortex determines how stressor controllability affects behavior and dorsal raphe nucleus. *Nature Neuroscience, 8*, 365–371.

Arbel, I., Kadar, T., Silbermann, M., & Levy, A. (1994). The effects of long-term corticosterone administration on hippocampal morphology and cognitive performance of middle-aged rats. *Brain Research, 657*, 227–235.

Barrett, R. M., & Wood, M. A. (2008). Beyond transcription factors: the role of chromatin modifying enzymes in regulating transcription required for memory. *Learning & Memory, 15*, 460–467.

Barsegyan, A., Mackenzie, S. M., Kurose, B. D., McGaugh, J. L., & Roozendaal, B. (2010). Glucocorticoids in the prefrontal cortex enhance memory consolidation and impair working memory by a common neural mechanism. *Proceedings of the National Academy of Sciences USA, 107*, 16655–16660.

Beckwith, B. E., Petros, T. V., Scaglione, C., & Nelson, J. (1986). Dose-dependent effects of hydrocortisone on memory in human males. *Physiology & Behavior, 36*, 283–286.

Bermudez-Rattoni, F., Okuda, S., Roozendaal, B., & McGaugh, J. L. (2005). Insular cortex is involved in consolidation of object recognition memory. *Learning & Memory, 12*, 447–449.

Bohus, B., & Lissak, K. (1968). Adrenocortical hormones and avoidance behaviour of rats. *International Journal of Neuropharmacology, 7*, 301–306.

Bucherelli, C., Baldi, E., Mariottini, C., Passani, M. B., & Blandina, P. (2006). Aversive memory reactivation engages in the amygdala only some neurotransmitters involved in consolidation. *Learning & Memory, 13*, 426–430.

Burgos-Robles, A., Vidal-Gonzalez, I., Satini, E., & Quirk, G. J. (2007). Consolidation of fear extinction requires NMDA receptor-dependent bursting in the ventromedial prefrontal cortex. *Neuron, 53*, 871–880.

Cahill, L., Prins, B., Weber, M., & McGaugh, J. L. (1994). Beta-adrenergic activation and memory for emotional events. *Nature, 371*, 702–704.

Cahill, L., Babinsky, R., Markowitsch, H. J., & McGaugh, J. L. (1995). The amygdala and emotional memory. *Nature, 377*, 295–296.

Cahill, L., Haier, R. J., Fallon, J., Alkire, M. T., Tang, C., Keator, D., Wu, J., & McGaugh, J. L. (1996). Amygdala activity at encoding correlated with long-term, free recall of emtional information. *Proceedings of the National Academy of Sciences USA, 93*, 8016–8021.

Campolongo, P., Roozendaal, B., Trezza, V., Hauer, D., Schelling, G., McGaugh, J. L., & Cuomo, V. (2009). Endocannabinoids in the rat basolateral amygdala enhance memory consolidation and enable glucocorticoid modulation of memory. *Proceedings of the National Academy of Sciences USA, 106*, 4888–4893.

Canli, T., Zhao, Z., Brewer, J., Gabrieli, J. D., & Cahill, L. (2000). Event-related activation in the human amygdala associates with later memory for individual emotional experience. *Journal of Neuroscience, 20,* RC99.

Chiyo, T., Yamazaki, T., Aoshika, K., Kominami, S., & Ohta, Y. (2003). Corticosterone enhances adrenocorticotropin-induced calcium signals in bovine adrenocortical cells. *Endocrinology, 144,* 3376–3381.

Clarke, J. R., Rossato, J. I., Monteiro, S., Bevilaqua, L. R., Izquierdo, I., & Cammarota, M. (2008). Posttraining activation of CB1 cannabinoid receptors in the CA1 region of the dorsal hippocampus impairs object recognition long-term memory. *Neurobiology of Learning and Memory, 90,* 374–381.

Coddington, E., Lewis, C., Rose, J. D., & Moore, F. L. (2007). Endocannabinoids mediate the effects of acute stress and corticosterone on sex behavior. *Endocrinology, 148,* 493–500.

Conrad, C. D. (2005). The relationship between acute glucocorticoid levels and hippocampal function depends upon task aversiveness and memory processing stage. *Nonlinearity in Biology, Toxicology and Medicine, 3,* 57–78.

Conrad, C. D., Lupien, S. J., & McEwen, B. S. (1999). Support for a bimodal role for type II adrenal steroid receptors in spatial memory. *Neurobiology of Learning and Memory, 72,* 39–46.

Cordero, M. I., Kruyt, N. D., Merino, J. J., & Sandi, C. (2002). Glucocorticoid involvement in memory formation in a rat model for traumatic memory. *Stress, 5,* 73–79.

Dallman, M. F. (2005). Fast glucocorticoid actions on brain: back to the future. *Frontiers in Neuroendocrinology, 26,* 103–108.

Daly, J. W., Bruns, R. F., & Snyder, S. H. (1981). Adenosine receptors in the central nervous system: relationship to the central actions of methylxanthines. *Life Science, 28,* 2083–2097.

Davidson, R. J. (2002). Anxiety and affective style: role of prefrontal cortex and amygdala. *Biological Psychiatry, 51,* 68–80.

de Boer, S. F., Koopmans, S. J., Slangen, J. L., & Van der Gugten, J. (1990). Plasma catecholamine, corticosterone and glucose responses to repeated stress in rats: effect of interstressor interval length. *Physiology & Behavior, 47,* 1117–1124.

de Kloet, E. R. (2000). Stress in the brain. *European Journal of Pharmacology, 405,* 187–198.

de Kloet, E. R., Vreugdenhil, E., Oitzl, M. S., & Joels, M. (1998). Brain corticosteroid receptor balance in health and disease. *Endocrine Reviews, 19,* 269–301.

de Quervain, D. J., Roozendaal, B., & McGaugh, J. L. (1998). Stress and glucocorticoids impair retrieval of long-term spatial memory. *Nature, 394,* 787–790.

de Quervain, D. J., Aerni, A., Schelling, G., & Roozendaal, B. (2009). Glucocorticoids and the regulation of memory in health and disease. *Frontiers in Neuroendocrinology, 30,* 358–370.

Di, S., & Tasker, J. G. (2008). Rapid synapse-specific regulation of hypothalamic magnocellular neurons by glucocorticoids. *Progress in Brain Research, 170,* 379–388.

Di, S., Malcher-Lopes, R., Halmos, K. C., & Tasker, J. G. (2003). Nongenomic glucocorticoid inhibition via endocannabinoid release in the hypothalamus: a fast feedback mechanism. *Journal of Neuroscience, 23,* 4850–4857.

Di, S., Malcher-Lopes, R., Marcheselli, V. L., Bazan, N. G., & Tasker, J. G. (2005). Rapid glucocorticoid-mediated endocannabinoid release and opposing regulation of glutamate and gamma-aminobutyric acid inputs to hypothalamic magnocellular neurons. *Endocrinology, 146,* 4292–4301.

Diamond, D. M., Bennett M. C., Fleshner, M., & Rose, G. M. (1992). Inverted-U relationship between the level of peripheral corticosterone and the magnitude of hippocampal primed burst potentiation. *Hippocampus, 2,* 421–430.

Diamond, D. M., Campbell, A. M., Park, C. R., Halonen, J., & Zoladz, P. R. (2007). The temporal dynamics model of emotional memory processing: a synthesis on the neurobiological basis of stress-induced amnesia, flashbulb and traumatic memories, and the Yerkes-Dodson law. *Neural Plasticity, 60803.*

Ferry, B., Roozendaal, B., & McGaugh, J. L. (1999a). Involvement of alpha1-adrenoceptors in the basolateral amygdala in modulation of memory storage. *European Journal of Pharmacology, 372,* 9–16.

Ferry, B., Roozendaal, B., & McGaugh, J. L. (1999b). Basolateral amygdala noradrenergic influences on memory storage are mediated by an interaction between beta- and alpha$_1$-adrenoceptors. *Journal of Neuroscience, 19,* 5119–5123.

Flood, J. F., Vidal, D., Bennett, E. L., Orme, A. E., Vasquez, S., & Jarvik, M. E. (1978). Memory facilitating and anti-amnesic effects of corticosteroids. *Pharmacology, Biochemistry, and Behavior, 8,* 81–87.

Frey, S., Bergado-Rosado, J., Seidenbecher, T., Pape, H. C., & Frey, J. U. (2001). Reinforcement of early long-term potentiation (early-LTP) in dentate gyrus by stimulation of the basolateral amygdala: heterosynaptic induction mechanisms of late-LTP. *Journal of Neuroscience, 21,* 3697–3703.

Galvez, R., Mesches, M. H., & McGaugh, J. L. (1996). Norepinephrine release in the amygdala in response to footshock stimulation. *Neurobiology of Learning and Memory, 66,* 253–257.

Gold, P. E., & Van Buskirk, R. B. (1975). Facilitation of time-dependent memory processes with posttrial epinephrine injections. *Behavioral Biology, 13,* 145–153.

Hamann, S. B., Ely, T. D., Grafton, S. T., & Kilts, C. D. (1999). Amygdala activity related to enhanced memory for pleasant and aversive stimuli. *Nature Neuroscience, 2,* 289–293.

Hashimotodani, Y., Ohno-Shosaku, T., & Kano, M. (2007). Endocannabinoids and synaptic function in the CNS. *Neuroscientist, 13,* 127–137.

Hatfield, T., & McGaugh, J. L. (1999). Norepinephrine infused into the basolateral amygdala posttraining enhances retention in a spatial water maze task. *Neurobiology of Learning and Memory, 91,* 232–239.

Hill, M. N., & McEwen, B. S. (2009). Endocannabinoids: the silent partner of glucocorticoids in the synapse. *Proceedings of the National Academy of Sciences USA, 106,* 4579–4580.

Hill, M. N., Karatsoreos, I. N., Hillard, C., & McEwen, B. S. (2010). Rapid induction of limbic endocannabinoid signaling by glucocorticoid hormones in vivo. *Psychoneuroendocrinology, 35,* 1333–1338.

Huff, N. C., & Rudy, J. W. (2004). The amygdala modulates hippocampus-dependent context memory formation and stores cue-shock associations. *Behavioral Neuroscience, 118,* 53–62.

Introini-Collison, I. B., Miyazaki, B., & McGaugh, J. L. (1991). Involvement of the amygdala in the memory-enhancing effects of clenbuterol. *Psychopharmacology 104,* 541–544.

Izquierdo, I., Quillfeldt, J. A., Zanatta, M. S., Quevedo, J., Schaeffer, E., Schmitz, P. K., & Medina, J. H. (1997). Sequential role of hippocampus and amygdala, entorhinal cortex and parietal cortex in formation and retrieval of memory for inhibitory avoidance in rats. *European Journal of Neuroscience, 9,* 786–793.

Joëls, M. (2006). Corticosteroid effects in the brain: U-shape it. *Trends in Pharmacological Sciences, 27,* 244–250.

Johnson, L. R., Farb, C., Morrison, J. H., McEwen, B. S., & LeDoux, J. E. (2005). Localization of glucocorticoid receptors at postsynaptic membranes in the lateral amygdala. *Neuroscience, 136*, 289–299.

Karst, H., Berger, S., Turiault, M., Tronche, F., Schutz, G., & Joels, M. (2005). Mineralocorticoid receptors are indispensable for nongenomic modulation of hippocampal glutamate transmission by corticosterone. *Proceedings of the National Academy of Sciences USA, 102*, 19204–19207.

Katona, I., Rancz, E. A., Acsady, L., Ledent, C., Mackie, K., Hajos, N., & Freund, T. F. (2001). Distribution of CB1 cannabinoid receptors in the amygdala and their role in the control of GABAergic transmission. *Journal of Neuroscience, 21*, 9506–9518.

Kim, J. J., Lee, H. J., Han, J. S., & Packard, M. G. (2001). Amygdala is critical for stress-induced modulation of hippocampal long-term potentiation and learning. *Journal of Neuroscience, 21*, 5222–5228.

LaLumiere, R. T., Buen, T. V., & McGaugh, J. L. (2003). Post-training intra-basolateral amygdala infusions of norepinephrine enhance consolidation of memory for contextual fear conditioning. *Journal of Neuroscience, 23*, 6754–6758.

LeDoux, J. E. (2007) The amygdala. *Current Biology, 17*, R868–R874.

Liang, K. C., Juler, R. G., & McGaugh, J. L. (1986). Modulating effects of posttraining epinephrine on memory: involvement of the amygdala noradrenergic system. *Brain Research, 368*, 125–133.

Liang, K. C., Chen, L. L., & Huang, T. E. (1995). The role of amygdala norepinephrine in memory formation: involvement in the memory enhancing effect of peripheral epinephrine. *Chinese Journal of Physiology, 38*, 81–91.

Liebmann, L., Karst, H., & Joels, M. (2009). Effects of corticosterone and the beta-agonist isoproterenol on glutamate receptor-mediated synaptic currents in the rat basolateral amygdala. *European Journal of Neuroscience, 30*, 800–807.

Liu, L., Tsuji, M., Takeda, H., Takada, K., & Matsumiya, T. (1999). Adrenocortical suppression blocks the enhancement of memory storage produced by exposure to psychological stress in rats. *Brain Research, 821*, 134–140.

Luine, V. N., Spencer, R. L., & McEwen, B. S. (1993). Effects of chronic corticosterone ingestion on spatial memory performance and hippocampal serotonergic function. *Brain Research, 616*, 65–70.

Maheu, F. S., Joober, R., Beaulieu, S., & Lupien, S. J. (2004). Differential effects of adrenergic and corticosteroid hormonal systems on human short- and long-term declarative memory for emotionally arousing material. *Behavioral Neuroscience, 118*, 420–428.

Malin, E. L., & McGaugh, J. L. (2006). Differential involvement of the hippocampus, anterior cingulate cortex, and basolateral amygdala in memory for context and footshock. *Proceedings of the National Academy of Sciences USA, 103*, 1959–1963.

Marsicano, G., Wotjak, C. T., Azad, S. C., Bisogno, T., Rammes, G., Cascio, M. G., Hermann, H., Tang, J., Hofmann, C., Zieglgansberger, W., Di Marzo, V., & Lutz, B. (2002). The endogenous cannabinoid system controls extinction of aversive memories. *Nature, 418*, 530–534.

McCarty, R., & Gold, P. E. (1981). Plasma catecholamines: effects of footshock level and hormonal modulators of memory storage. *Hormones and Behavior, 15*, 168–182.

McEwen, B. S. (1998). Stress, adaptation, and disease. Allostasis and allostatic load. *Annals of the New York Academy of Sciences, 840*, 33–44.

McGaugh, J. L. (2000). Memory–a century of consolidation. *Science, 287*, 248–251.

McGaugh, J. L. (2002). Memory consolidation and the amygdala: a systems perspective. *Trends in Neuroscience, 25,* 456.

McGaugh, J. L., & Roozendaal, B. (2002). Role of adrenal stress hormones in forming lasting memories in the brain. *Current Opinions in Neurobiology, 12,* 205–210.

McGaugh, J. L., & Roozendaal, B. (2009). Memory modulation In J. H. Byrne (Ed.), *Concise learning and memory: The editor's selection* (pp. 571–603). London: Academic Press.

McGaugh, J. L., Cahill, L., & Roozendaal, B. (1996). Involvement of the amygdala in memory storage: interaction with other brain systems. *Proceedings of the National Academy of Sciences USA, 93,* 13508–13514.

McIntyre, C. K., Hatfield, T., & McGaugh, J. L. (2002). Amygdala norepinephrine levels after training predict inhibitory avoidance retention performance in rats. *European Journal of Neuroscience, 16,* 1223–1226.

McIntyre, C. K., Miyashita, T., Setlow, B., Marjon, K. D., Steward, O., Guzowski, J. F., & McGaugh, J. L. (2005). Memory-influencing intra-basolateral amygdala drug infusions modulate expression of Arc protein in the hippocampus. *Proceedings of the National Academy of Sciences USA, 102,* 10718–10723.

McReynolds, J. R., Donowho, K., Abdi, A., McGaugh, J. L., Roozendaal, B., & McIntyre, C. K. (2010). Memory-enhancing corticosterone treatment increases amygdala norepinephrine and Arc protein expression in hippocampal synaptic fractions. *Neurobiology of Learning and Memory, 93,* 312–321.

Miranda, M. I., Quirarte, G. L., Rodriguez-Garcia, G., McGaugh, J. L., & Roozendaal, B. (2008). Glucocorticoids enhance taste aversion memory via actions in the insular cortex and basolateral amygdala. *Learning & Memory, 15,* 468–476.

Mueller, D., Porter, J. T., & Quirk, G. J. (2008) Noradrenergic signaing in infralimbic cortex increases cell excitability and strengthens memory for fear extinction. *Journal of Neuroscience, 28,* 369–375.

Nakao, K., Matsuyama, K., Matsuki, N., & Ikegaya, Y. (2004). Amygdala stimulation modulates hippocampal synaptic plasticity. *Proceedings of the National Academy of Sciences USA, 101,* 14270–14275.

Oitzl, M. S., & de Kloet, E. R. (1992). Selective corticosteroid antagonists modulate specific aspects of spatial orientation learning. *Behavioral Neuroscience, 106,* 62–71.

Oitzl, M. S., de Kloet, E. R., Joels, M., Schmid, W., & Cole, T. J. (1997). Spatial learning deficits in mice with a targeted glucocorticoid receptor gene disruption. *European Journal of Neuroscience, 9,* 2284–2296.

Oitzl, M. S., Reichardt, H. M., Joels, M., & de Kloet, E. R. (2001). Point mutation in the mouse glucocorticoid receptor preventing DNA binding impairs spatial memory. *Proceedings of the National Academy of Sciences USA, 98,* 12790–12795.

Okuda, S., Roozendaal, B., & McGaugh, J. L. (2004). Glucocorticoid effects on object recognition memory require training-associated emotional arousal. *Proceedings of the National Academy of Sciences USA, 101,* 853–858.

Orchinik, M., Murray, T. F., & Moore, F. L. (1991). A corticosteroid receptor in neuronal membranes. *Science, 252,* 1848–1851.

Packard, M. G., & Knowlton, B. J. (2002). Learning and memory functions of the basal ganglia. *Annual Review of Neuroscience, 25,* 563–593.

Packard, M. G., Cahill, L., & McGaugh, J. L. (1994). Amygdala modulation of hippocampal-dependent and caudate nucleus-dependent memory processes. *Proceedings of the National Academy of Sciences USA, 91,* 8477–8481.

Paré, D. (2003). Role of the basolateral amygdala in memory consolidation. *Progress in Neurobiology, 70,* 409–420.

Pistis, M., Perra, S., Pillolla, G., Melis, M., Gessa, G. L., & Muntoni, A. L. (2004). Cannabinoids modulate neuronal firing in the rat basolateral amygdala: evidence for CB1- and non-CB1-mediated actions. *Neuropharmacology, 46,* 115–125.

Prager, E. M., & Johnson, L. R. (2009). Stress at the synapse: signal transduction mechanisms of adrenal steroids at neuronal membranes. *Science Signaling, 2,* re5.

Pugh, C. R., Tremblay, D., Fleshner, M., & Rudy, J. W. (1997). A selective role for corticosterone in contextual-fear conditioning. *Behavioral Neuroscience, 111,* 503–511.

Quillfeldt, J. A., Zanatta, M. S., Schmitz, P. K., Quevedo, J., Schaeffer, E., Lima, J. B., Medina, J. H., & Izquierdo, I. (1996). Different brain areas are involved in memory expression at different times from training. *Neurobiology of Learning and Memory, 66,* 97–102.

Quirarte, G. L., Roozendaal, B., & McGaugh, J. L. (1997). Glucocorticoid enhancement of memory storage involves noradrenergic activation in the basolateral amygdala. *Proceedings of the National Academy of Sciences USA, 94,* 14048–14053.

Quirarte, G. L., Galvez, R., Roozendaal, B., & McGaugh, J. L. (1998). Norepinephrine release in the amygdala in response to footshock and opioid peptidergic drugs. *Brain Research, 808,* 134–140.

Quirarte, G. L., de la Teja, I. S., Casillas, M., Serafín, N., Prado-Alcalá, R. A., & Roozendaal, B. (2009). Corticosterone infused into the dorsal striatum selectively enhances memory consolidation of cued water-maze training. *Learning & Memory, 16,* 586–589.

Quirk, G. J., & Gehlert, D. R. (2003). Inhibition of the amygdala: key to pathological states? *Annals of the New York Academy of Sciences, 985,* 263–272.

Reul, J. M., & de Kloet, E. R. (1985). Two receptor systems for corticosterone in rat brain: microdistribution and differential occupation. *Endocrinology, 117,* 2505–2511.

Riedel, G., & Davies, S. N. (2005). Cannabinoid function in learning, memory and plasticity. *Handbook of Experimental Pharmacology,* 445–477.

Robinson, L., McKillop-Smith, S., Ross, N. L., Pertwee, R. G., Hampson, R. E., Platt, B., & Riedel, G. (2008). Hippocampal endocannabinoids inhibit spatial learning and limit spatial memory in rats. *Psychopharmacology, 198,* 551–563.

Roozendaal, B. (2000). 1999 Curt P. Richter award. Glucocorticoids and the regulation of memory consolidation. *Psychoneuroendocrinology, 25,* 213–238.

Roozendaal, B., & McGaugh, J. L. (1996). Amygdaloid nuclei lesions differentially affect glucocorticoid-induced memory enhancement in an inhibitory avoidance task. *Neurobiology of Learning and Memory, 65,* 1–8.

Roozendaal, B., & McGaugh, J. L. (1997a). Basolateral amygdala lesions block the memory-enhancing effect of glucocorticoid administration in the dorsal hippocampus of rats. *European Journal of Neuroscience, 9,* 76–83.

Roozendaal, B., & McGaugh, J. L. (1997b). Glucocorticoid receptor agonist and antagonist administration into the basolateral but not central amygdala modulates memory storage. *Neurobiology of Learning and Memory, 67,* 176–179.

Roozendaal, B., Bohus, B., & McGaugh, J. L. (1996a). Dose-dependent suppression of adrenocortical activity with metyrapone: effects on emotion and memory. *Psychoneuroendocrinology, 21,* 681–693.

Roozendaal, B., Carmi, O., & McGaugh, J. L. (1996b). Adrenocortical suppression blocks the memory-enhancing effects of amphetamine and epinephrine. *Proceedings of the National Academy of Sciences USA, 93,* 1429–1433.

Roozendaal, B., Portillo-Marquez, G., & McGaugh, J. L. (1996c). Basolateral amygdala lesions block glucocorticoid-induced modulation of memory for spatial learning. *Behavioral Neuroscience, 110*, 1074–1083.

Roozendaal, B., Nguyen, B. T., Power, A. E., & McGaugh, J. L. (1999a). Basolateral amygdala noradrenergic influence enables enhancement of memory consolidation induced by hippocampal glucocorticoid receptor activation. *Proceedings of the National Academy of Sciences USA, 96*, 11642–11647.

Roozendaal, B., Williams, C. L., & McGaugh, J. L. (1999b). Glucocorticoid receptor activation in the rat nucleus of the solitary tract facilitates memory consolidation: involvement of the basolateral amygdala. *European Journal of Neuroscience, 11*, 1317–1323.

Roozendaal, B., Quirarte, G. L., & McGaugh, J. L. (2002). Glucocorticoids interact with the basolateral amygdala beta-adrenoceptor–cAMP/PKA system in influencing memory consolidation. *European Journal of Neuroscience, 15*, 553–560.

Roozendaal, B., Hahn, E. L., Nathan, S. V., de Quervain, D. J., & McGaugh, J. L. (2004). Glucocorticoid effects on memory retrieval require concurrent noradrenergic activity in the hippocampus and basolateral amygdala. *Journal of Neuroscience, 24*, 8161–8169.

Roozendaal, B., Okuda, S., de Quervain, D. J., & McGaugh, J. L. (2006a). Glucocorticoids interact with emotion-induced noradrenergic activation in influencing different memory functions. *Neuroscience, 138*, 901–910.

Roozendaal, B., Okuda, S., Van der Zee, E. A., & McGaugh, J. L. (2006b). Glucocorticoid enhancement of memory requires arousal-induced noradrenergic activation in the basolateral amygdala. *Proceedings of the National Academy of Sciences USA, 103*, 6741–6746.

Roozendaal, B., Castello, N., Vedana, G., Barsegyan, A., & McGaugh, J. L. (2008a). Noradrenergic activation of the basolateral amygdala modulates consolidation of object recognition memory. *Neurobiology of Learning and Memory, 90*, 576–579.

Roozendaal, B., Schelling, G., & McGaugh, J. L. (2008b). Corticotropin-releasing factor in the basolateral amygdala enhances memory consolidation via an interaction with the beta-adrenoceptor-cAMP pathway: dependence on glucocorticoid receptor activation. *Journal of Neuroscience, 28*, 6642–6651.

Roozendaal, B., McEwen, B. S., & Chattarji, S. (2009a). Stress, memory and the amygdala. *Nature Reviews Neuroscience, 10*, 423–433.

Roozendaal, B., McReynolds, J. R., Van der Zee, E. A., Lee, S., McGaugh, J. L., & McIntyre, C. K. (2009b). Glucocorticoid effects on memory consolidation depend on functional interactions between the medial prefrontal cortex and basolateral amygdala. *Journal of Neuroscience, 29*, 14299–14308.

Roozendaal, B., Hernandez, A., Cabrera, S. M., Hagewoud, R., Malvaez, M., Stefanko, D. P., Haettig, J., & Wood, M. A. (2010). Membrane-associated glucocorticoid activity is necessary for modulation of long-term memory via chromatin modification. *Journal of Neuroscience, 30*, 5037–5046.

Rose, J. D., Moore, F. L., & Orchinik, M. (1993). Rapid neurophysiological effects of corticosterone on medullary neurons: relationship to stress-induced suppression of courtship clasping in an amphibian. *Neuroendocrinology, 57*, 815–824.

Sandi, C., & Rose, S. P. (1994). Corticosterone enhances long-term retention in one-day-old chicks trained in a weak passive avoidance learning paradigm. *Brain Research, 647*, 106–112.

Strange, B. A., & Dolan, R. J. (2004). Beta-adrenergic modulation of emotional memory-evoked human amygdala and hippocampal responses. *Proceedings of the National Academy of Sciences USA, 101,* 11454–11458.

Tasker, J. G. (2006). Rapid glucocorticoid actions in the hypothalamus as a mechanism of homeostatic integration. *Obesity (Silver Spring, Md.), 14 Suppl, 5,* 259S–265S.

Tasker, J. G., Di, S., & Malcher-Lopes, R. (2006). Minireview: rapid glucocorticoid signaling via membrane-associated receptors. *Endocrinology, 147,* 5549–5556.

van Stegeren, A. H., Goekoop, R., Everaerd, W., Scheltens, P., Barkhof, F., Kuijer, J. P., & Rombouts, S. A. (2005). Noradrenaline mediates amygdala activation in men and women during encoding of emotional material. *Neuroimage, 24,* 898–909.

van Stegeren, A. H., Wolf, O. T., Everaerd, W., Scheltens, P., Barkhof, F., & Rombouts, S. A. (2007). Endogenous cortisol level interacts with noradrenergic activation in the human amygdala. *Neurobiology of Learning and Memory, 87,* 57–66.

van Stegeren, A. H., Roozendaal, B., Kindt, M., Wolf, O. T., & Joëls, M. (2010) Interacting noradrenergic and corticosteroid systems shift human brain activation patterns during encoding. *Neurobiology of Learning and Memory, 93,* 56–65.

Vouimba, R. M., Yaniv, D., & Richter-Levin, G. (2007). Glucocorticoid receptors and beta-adrenoceptors in basolateral amygdala modulate synaptic plasticity in hippocampal dentate gyrus, but not in area CA1. *Neuropharmacology, 52,* 244–252.

Wolf, O. T. (2008). The influence of stress hormones on emotional memory: relevance for psychopathology. *Acta Psychologica, 127,* 513–531.

10

Chronic Stress Effects on Corticolimbic Morphology

Cara L. Wellman

Introduction

Stress, either acute or chronic, can precipitate or exacerbate many psychological disorders, most notably depression, schizophrenia, and posttraumatic stress disorder, and can also disrupt cognitive and emotional behavior. A variety of studies have documented its association with the development of psychological disorders such as depression (Brown and Harris, 1989) and schizophrenia (Ventura et al., 1989) and changes in cognition (Lupien and Lepage, 2001). Animal studies have also demonstrated detrimental effects of stress on many behaviors. For instance, several studies have demonstrated stress-induced deficits on a variety of cognitive tasks, including fear conditioning and retrieval of extinction, attentional set-shifting, spatial learning and recognition, and working memory (reviewed in Quirk and Mueller, 2007; Holmes and Wellman, 2009; McLaughlin et al., 2009).

Corticolimbic structures such as the hippocampus, amygdala, and prefrontal cortex are all targets of stress-related neurochemicals and hormones (e.g., Herman et al., 2003), contribute to many of the behaviors influenced by both stress and glucocorticoids (e.g., Maren and Quirk, 2004; Holmes and Wellman, 2009; McLaughlin et al., 2009), and have been implicated in many stress-related psychopathologies (e.g., Phillips et al., 2003; Haldane and Frangou, 2006; Hajek et al., 2008). Thus, stress-induced changes in these structures may be responsible for the changes in behavior, and understanding how stress influences corticolimbic structure and function may elucidate mechanisms underlying disorders such as depression, schizophrenia, and posttraumatic stress disorder. This chapter provides an overview of the effects of chronic stress on the morphology of hippocampus,

The Handbook of Stress: Neuropsychological Effects on the Brain, First Edition.
Edited by Cheryl D. Conrad.
© 2011 Blackwell Publishing Ltd. Published 2011 by Blackwell Publishing Ltd.

amygdala, striatum, and prefrontal cortex; mechanisms that may mediate these effects; and functional implications of these stress-induced changes. As sex differences in stress effects are reviewed in other chapters in this volume, this chapter will focus exclusively on chronic stress effects in males. Likewise, the growing body of literature documenting stress effects on neurogenesis in dentate gyrus is reviewed elsewhere in this volume (Chapter 7). Thus, this chapter will focus on dendritic morphology and spine density and morphology (see Table 10.1).

A hallmark of the stress response is hypothalamic–pituitary–adrenal (HPA) axis activation and consequent increases in release of the adrenal glucocorticoids cortisol (in most mammals) and corticosterone (in rodents; for review see Chapter 1 in this volume). Many of the effects of chronic stress are mediated at least in part by stress-induced increases in circulating levels of glucocorticoids (see below). Further, chronic elevations of circulating glucocorticoids have been shown to produce a variety of cognitive alterations (Sandi and Pinelo-Nava, 2007), and HPA axis dysfunction is associated with psychological disorders such as depression and post-traumatic stress disorder (e.g., Appelhof et al., 2006; Yehuda and LeDoux, 2007). Thus, the discussion in this chapter will include morphological changes arising from direct manipulations of glucocorticoids.

Hippocampus

The hippocampus has been implicated in stress-related disorders such as depression and posttraumatic stress disorder (e.g., Vermetten and Bremner, 2002) and plays a critical role in several behaviors influenced by stress, including contextual fear conditioning (Maren, 2001) and spatial learning and memory (Eichenbaum, 2004). The hippocampus is a complicated structure; however, the basic excitatory circuitry includes mossy fiber projections from dentate gyrus granule cells to CA3 pyramidal neurons (where CA means cornu ammonis, a subregion of the hippocampus); CA3 pyramidal neurons project via the Shaffer collaterals to CA1 pyramidal neurons. The effects of stress on these hippocampal subregions are summarized below.

Dentate gyrus

The bulk of work examining the effects of chronic stress on neuroplasticity in dentate gyrus has focused on stress-induced alterations in neurogenesis, reviewed elsewhere in this volume. However, several studies have demonstrated stress-induced alterations in dentate gyrus-to-CA3 projections. For instance, qualitative observations suggested that prolonged, severe stress decreased numbers of mossy fiber terminals in CA3 (Uno et al., 1989), although quantitative stereological analyses indicated that a less severe and prolonged stressor does not alter mossy fiber terminal number here (Magariños et al., 1997). Nonetheless, Magariños and colleagues (1997) found that in mossy fiber terminals in stratum lucidum of CA3 in rats

Table 10.1 Summary of chronic stress effects on several measures of corticolimbic morphology, reversibility of stress effects on dendritic arborization, and whether dendritic changes are associated with functional changes in each structure. While much research has been accomplished, many questions remain. AC, anterior cingulate cortex; BLA, basolateral amygdala; CA, cornu ammonis; DG, dentate gyrus; DL, dorsal lateral; IL cortex, infralimbic cortex; MA, medial amygdala; NAcc, nucleus accumbens; OFC, orbitofrontal cortex; PL, prelimbic cortex; ↑, increase; ↓, decrease; ●, mixed results; ?, unknown.

Region	Hippocampus			Prefrontal cortex			Amygdala		Striatum	
Dependent measure	DG	CA1	CA3	AC/PL	IL cortex	OFC	BLA	MA	NAcc	DL striatum
Dendritic length and/or branch number	●	●	↓	↓	↓	↑	↑	?	↑ Proximal, ↓ Distal	↑
Reversibility (days to recover)	?	?	≤10	≤21	>21?	?	>21?	?	?	?
Functional correlate	?	?	Yes	Yes	Yes	No	Yes	?	?	Yes
Altered axonal morphology	●	Rare	Rare	?	?	?	?	?	?	?
Spine density	↓	●	●	↓	↓	?	↑	↓	↓	?
Altered spine morphology	?	Yes	?	Yes	?	?	?	?	?	?
Cell death	No	No	No	No	No	?	?	?	?	?

subjected to 21 days of restraint stress (6 hr/day), synaptic vesicles were increased in number and more likely to be clustered at active zones; in addition, mitochondria were increased in the mossy fiber terminals of these animals. These changes might increase the excitatory influence of the dentate gyrus granule cells on CA3 pyramidal neurons, potentially leading to abnormal excitation of, or compensatory changes in, CA3 pyramidal neurons (see Conrad, 2008).

The data on stress-induced dendritic changes in dentate gyrus are limited and mixed. Woolley and colleagues (1990) showed that 3 weeks of daily corticosterone administration did not alter granule cell dendritic morphology. In contrast, others have shown that 1 month of chronic variable stress, including injection of hypertonic saline, overcrowding, restraint, and placement on a vibrating/rocking platform, reduced dendritic extent in granule cells (Sousa et al., 2000), as well as the number, volume, and surface area of mossy fiber terminals. This effect was reversible, as animals allowed 1 month of recovery did not show this significant decrease relative to controls. Thus, the direction of changes in dentate gyrus granule cell morphology may depend on the chronicity or intensity of the stressor. Note, however, that Magariños and colleagues examined Sprague–Dawley rats, while the Sousa group employed Wistar rats. Given the well-documented strain differences in neurotransmitter systems critical to the stress response (Tejani-Butt et al., 1994; Pare and Tejani-Butt, 1996) and behavioral responses to stress (Pare and Tejani-Butt, 1996; Zafar et al., 1997), the discrepancy between these studies could reflect strain differences in stress responsivity rather than differences in the stressors employed.

CA3

Behavioral stressors typically do not directly produce neuronal death in hippocampal areas CA1 and CA3 (e.g., Fuchs et al., 1995; Vollmann-Honsdorf et al., 1997; Sousa et al., 1998). Indeed, in tree shrews, 28 days of psychosocial stress actually decreased rates of apoptosis (programmed cell death) in CA3 (Lucassen et al., 2001). However, chronic exposure to the glucocorticoids involved in the stress response appears to potentiate the neurotoxic effects of other processes such as those occurring in aging (Kerr et al., 1991; but see Sousa, 1998) or excitotoxicity (Conrad et al., 2004, 2007).

In addition, early reports suggested a variety of neurodegenerative changes in hippocampus of vervet monkeys experiencing prolonged, severe, social stress, including shrunken somata of pyramidal neurons, decreased synaptic vesicle number, and dystrophic dendrites with reduced numbers of neurotubules. These changes were most pronounced in area CA3 (Uno et al., 1989), but also present to a lesser extent in CA1 and CA4.

Pyramidal cell dendrites in area CA3 seem to be especially responsive to chronic stress, with consistent reductions in apical dendritic length and branch number reported as a result of a variety of stress manipulations (Figure 10.1). For instance, in the original demonstration of the potential for chronic stress-induced dendritic

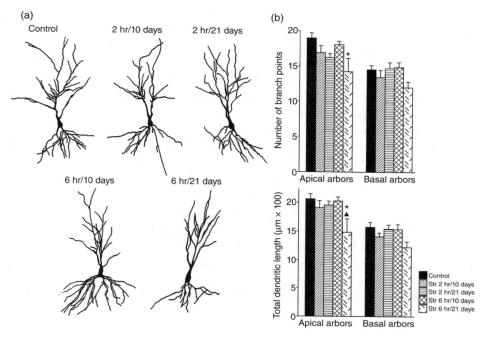

Figure 10.1 Chronic stress effects on dendritic morphology in hippocampal area CA3 in male Sprague–Dawley rats. (a) Reconstructions of Golgi-stained CA3 pyramidal neurons in male rats exposed to either 2 or 6 hr of restraint stress daily for either 10 or 21 days. (b) Average branch number (top) and length (bottom) in control rats and rats exposed to restraint stress (Str) for 2 hr per day for 10 or 21 days, or 6 hr per day for 10 or 21 days. Apical dendritic branch number and length were decreased only in rats exposed to 6 hr of restraint per day for 21 days. *Significant difference relative to control; triangle indicates significant difference relative to all other groups. *Source:* From McLaughlin et al. (2007). With permission from Elsevier.

remodeling, McEwen and colleagues showed that 3 weeks of daily administration of high-stress levels of corticosterone results in extensive retraction and debranching of apical dendrites of pyramidal neurons in hippocampal area CA3 in rats (Woolley et al., 1990; Watanabe et al., 1992a). Three weeks of daily restraint (6 hr/ day) produces a similar pattern of apical dendritic retraction in rats (Magariños and McEwen, 1995; Conrad et al., 1999; Magariños et al., 1999), as does chronic psychosocial stress (28 days of daily social defeat) in tree shrews (Magariños et al., 1996; Kole et al., 2004b) and rats (Kole et al., 2004a). This dendritic retraction appears to be induced specifically by long-term daily stressors. In a heroic parametric study, McLaughlin et al. (2007) found that rats exposed to 6 hr of daily restraint for 3 weeks demonstrated pronounced retraction of CA3 apical dendrites, whereas 6 hr of daily restraint for 10 days did not produce this effect. Likewise, the intensity of the daily stressor also appears to be critical: 2 hr of restraint per day for either 10 days or 3 weeks also failed to produce CA3 dendritic retraction (McLaughlin et al.,

2007; but see Kole et al., 2004a). On the other hand, more intense daily stressors may produce dendritic remodeling after a shorter duration. For instance, using immobilization in plastic bags (2 h/day), which is generally considered to be a more intense stressor than restraint in either wire mesh or commercially available hard-plastic restrainers (Vyas et al., 2002; Miracle et al., 2006; McLaughlin et al., 2007), Vyas and colleagues (2002) found dendritic retraction in CA3 apical dendrites after only 10 days. Finally, Kole and colleagues (2004a) compared the effects of social defeat every other day for 21 days to the effects of two consecutive days of social defeat followed by single housing for 21 days in Wistar rats. They found that the 21-day social-defeat regimen produced apical dendritic retraction in CA3 similar to that seen after 21 days of restraint stress. Further, they found similar but less pronounced apical retraction in the group that experienced only two social defeats followed by 21 days of single housing. Interestingly, this group also showed proliferation of basilar dendrites in area CA3, suggesting that a brief psychosocial stressor either produces a different and relatively long-lasting pattern of dendritic changes than that seen after a more prolonged chronic stress exposure, or that remodeling of basilar dendrites occurs in the 3 weeks following the cessation of a brief stressor. Alternatively, given that rats are social animals, it may be that single housing is a mild stressor, as evidenced by the comparable increases in adrenal-to-body-weight ratio in both groups relative to controls. Thus, the dendritic alterations in the brief social defeat group may reflect the effects of brief social defeat along with 21 days of mild stress.

Chronic stress-induced alterations in hippocampal dendritic morphology are not limited to branch length and number: a number of studies have demonstrated stress-induced alterations in spine density and morphology in area CA3. However, the direction of the effect varies quite a bit across studies. For instance, Sunanda and colleagues (1995) reported that chronic restraint stress (6 hr/day, 21 days) produced small but significant increases in spine density on apical and basilar branches of CA3 pyramidal neurons. On the other hand, Sandi and colleagues (2003) demonstrated that this same manipulation reduced the density of asymmetric axo-spinous synapses in stratum lucidum (and thus proximal apical dendrites) in CA3. Whereas dendritic morphology in area CA3 appears to respond relatively slowly to stress, dendritic spines may be more sensitive. For instance, using electron microscopy and stereological methods to estimate total spiny synapses, Hajszan et al. (2009) found that a single exposure to an intense and inescapable stressor (60, 0.85 mA foot shocks over approximately 1 hr, each averaging 15 s in duration) produced dramatic reductions in axospinous synapses in CA1, CA3, and dentate gyrus. Interestingly, the effect in CA3 and dentate gyrus was reversed with a week of desipramine treatment, whereas the effect in CA1 was more persistent.

CA1

There is some evidence that CA1 dendritic morphology may be less susceptible to the effects of chronic stress. For instance, 3 weeks of daily corticosterone administration does not significantly alter CA1 dendritic morphology (Woolley et al., 1990). Nonetheless, a few studies have reported stress-induced dendritic remodeling in area CA1. For instance, Sousa and colleagues (2000) showed that terminal branches of apical dendrites of CA1 pyramidal cells in rats undergo retraction and debranching as a result of exposure to 1 month of chronic unpredictable stress, suggesting that stress may produce more subtle alterations in area CA1. Lambert and colleagues (1998) employed an unusual *activity-stress* paradigm in which rats were exposed to voluntary wheel-running and food restriction, and consequently underwent dramatic weight loss. They demonstrated that just 6 days of this procedure, which dramatically increases plasma corticosterone levels, produced retraction of apical dendrites of both CA1 and CA3 pyramidal cells. Similarly, another intense stressor, chronic immobilization (2 h day/10 days), produced apical dendritic retraction and debranching in areas CA1 and CA3 (Christian et al., 2011). Thus, whereas CA1 dendritic morphology may be less sensitive to chronic stress compared to CA3, more intense stressors or longer durations of chronic stress may result in more obvious dendritic remodeling in CA1. Alternatively, the nature of the stressor (physical or psychosocial stress) or strain differences may also have contributed to these differential CA1 effects. For instance, activity stress or immobilization might be considered physical stressors, whereas restraint or social defeat are considered psychosocial stressors (see McLaughlin et al., 2007). Likewise, although the majority of the studies demonstrating effects of chronic stress in CA3 but not CA1 used Sprague–Dawley rats, Sousa and colleagues employed Wistar rats, and Lambert and colleagues examined Long–Evans rats. Again, this suggests the possibility of strain differences. Collectively, these results are difficult to interpret, and will likely remain so until the effects of individual stressors—at, for instance, multiple durations and intensities—are assessed across several hippocampal structures in a single study.

Evidence for stress-induced alterations in CA1 spines is also mixed. An acute intense stressor, inescapable tail shock, increased spine density on apical and basilar dendrites in CA1, assessed 24 hr later in Golgi-stained tissue (Shors et al., 2001). In addition, Horner and colleagues (1991) showed that 22 days of daily intraperitoneal saline injections increased spine density on apical and basilar branches of CA1 neurons visualized using the Golgi technique, which suggests that a long-term but relatively mild stressor can produce similar alterations in spine density in this region. On the other hand, a very small (10%) but significant reduction in apical spine density in area CA1 of mice after 21 days of daily restraint has been reported (Pawlak et al., 2005). Finally, Donohue et al. (2006) used electron microscopy and unbiased stereological techniques to assess potential changes in axospinous synapse number and morphology in stratum lacunosum-moleculare in CA1 following chronic restraint stress (6 hr/day, 21 days) in rats. They reported no changes in overall spine density or estimates of total axospinous synapse number in this layer. Thus, it is unclear whether spine density is altered after acute but not chronic stress, or whether spine density is altered after chronic stress, but only in specific dendritic compartments. On the other hand, Donohue and colleagues (2006) did find changes in the morphology of stratum lacunosum-moleculare axospinous synapses, including increases in synapse size as well as the ratio of postsynaptic-density surface area to spine surface area specific to non-macular spines.

Reversibility

Stress-induced changes in area CA3 apical dendritic morphology are not permanent: Conrad et al. (1999) demonstrated that CA3 apical dendritic length was restored to control levels within 10 days after cessation of chronic restraint stress (6 hr/day, 21 days). Interestingly, a recent study demonstrated continued CA3 apical dendritic retraction in Wistar rats up to 17 days after cessation of the same stressor (Ramkumar et al., 2008). This discrepancy again suggests the possibility of strain differences. Alternatively, the latter study restricted analyses to short-shaft pyramidal neurons; thus the difference in these two may reflect more persistent alterations in one neuronal subpopulation. Stewart and colleagues (2005) demonstrated that chronic restraint stress (6 hr/day, 21 days) reduces thorny excrescences on CA3 apical dendrites, which perhaps might be described as short apical dendrites located proximal to the soma and bearing many dendritic spines. Interestingly, this effect was reversed by water-maze training. It is interesting to speculate whether this reversal was an effect of physical or cognitive activity (swimming or spatial learning) or instead controllability: learning that a stressor—placement in the water maze—is controllable as they find the escape platform.

Amygdala

The amygdala has also been implicated in stress-related disorders, most notably increased activity in posttraumatic stress disorder (Bremner et al., 2008), and is a critical site of plasticity in fear conditioning (Maren, 2001), a behavior influenced by stress (Conrad et al., 1999). The basolateral nucleus of the amygdala appears to be especially critical for fear conditioning (Maren, 2001), and thus has received special attention in terms of chronic stress effects.

Several recent studies have begun to assess stress-induced changes in dendritic morphology in the amygdala. Interestingly, chronic stress produces a very different pattern of changes in basolateral amygdala compared to hippocampal CA3. Chattarji and colleagues found that as little as 10 days of immobilization stress (2 hr/day) increased both length and number of dendritic branches of pyramidal and stellate neurons in the basolateral amygdala in rats (Vyas et al., 2002, 2004, 2006; Mitra et al., 2005; Govindarajan et al., 2006). Similar changes in dendritic length are seen after chronic restraint stress in mice (6 hr/day for 21 days; Johnson et al., 2009). These changes in dendritic morphology are paralleled by increases in spine density in both rats and mice (Mitra et al., 2005; Govindarajan et al., 2006; Vyas et al., 2006).

Regional specificity and reversibility

Potential stress-induced alterations in dendritic length and branch number have not been assessed across multiple subregions of the amygdala. However, stress-induced changes in dendritic spine density have been shown to vary across amygdaloid nuclei. For instance, in the medial amygdaloid nucleus of mice, chronic restraint stress (6 hr/day for 3 weeks) decreased spine density on stellate neurons, whereas the same manipulation increased spine density in basolateral amygdala (Bennur et al., 2007).

Interestingly, whereas stress-induced changes in dendritic morphology in hippocampus have been demonstrated to be reversible within 10 days (Conrad et al., 1999), the effects of stress on amygdaloid morphology may be more persistent. Vyas and colleagues (2004) demonstrated that the dendritic hypertrophy in basolateral amygdala resulting from chronic immobilization (2 h/day, 10 days) persists at least 21 days after the cessation of stress.

Striatum

Stress is an important trigger of relapse to drug abuse in patients who have achieved abstinence, and projections from prefrontal cortex—specifically, prelimbic cortex—to nucleus accumbens and dorsal striatum have been implicated in both the establishment of addictions and relapse to drug-seeking (Koob et al., 2004). Recent studies demonstrate morphological changes in the nucleus accumbens resulting from either chronic stress or corticosterone administration. For instance, 3 weeks of daily corticosterone injections resulted in a dramatic reduction of spine density on medium spiny neurons (Morales-Medina et al., 2009). This was accompanied by a remodeling of dendrites, with increases in dendritic material proximal to the soma—in first- and second-order branches—and decreases in dendritic material distal to the soma—in fifth-order branches (Morales-Medina et al., 2009). This reorganization, with dendritic proliferation proximally and retraction distally, is reminiscent of the effect of this same regimen of corticosterone administration on dendritic morphology in medial prefrontal cortex (Wellman, 2001). Further, 3 weeks of chronic unpredictable stress also produced dendritic reorganization in dorsal striatum, with contrasting patterns of changes seen in medial versus lateral regions. In dorsolateral striatum, chronic unpredictable stress markedly increased dendritic length of medium spiny neurons, whereas in mediodorsal striatum a nonsignificant tendency towards reduced dendritic material was seen (Dias-Ferreira et al., 2009).

Prefrontal Cortex

As in primates, prefrontal cortex in rodents can be subdivided into several major subregions. Medial prefrontal cortex includes anterior cingulate, prelimbic, and infralimbic cortex. This region is functionally homologous to the primate dorsolateral and ventromedial prefrontal cortices, and plays a role in autonomic and HPA-axis regulation, emotion regulation (e.g., prelimbic cortex plays a role in expression of conditioned fear, while infralimbic cortex plays a role in retrieval of extinction; see Sotres-Bayon and Quirk, 2010), and working memory. Orbitofrontal cortex, which includes the medial, ventral, and lateral orbitofrontal subregions, is functionally homologous to primate orbitofrontal cortex and appears to play a role in modulating behavioral responses based on changing incentive values of reward-related stimuli (Holmes and Wellman, 2009).

Prefrontal cortex has been implicated in myriad stress-related psychological disorders (Phillips et al., 2003), and prefrontal cortex contributes to many of the cognitive processes influenced by stress, including working memory, attentional set-shifting, and memory for fear extinction (reviewed in Holmes and Wellman, 2009). A summary of stress-induced changes in dendritic morphology across various prefrontal subregions follows.

Medial prefrontal cortex

Chronic administration of corticosterone decreases volume of anterior cingulate, prelimbic, and infralimbic cortex but does not decrease neuron number in any of these subregions (Cerqueira et al., 2005a, 2005b, 2007b). These changes in volume are likely due to dendritic alterations. In the first demonstration that pyramidal neurons in medial prefrontal cortex exhibit morphological changes in response to stress, 3 weeks of corticosterone administration reorganized dendrites of pyramidal neurons in layer II–III of prelimbic and anterior cingulate cortex (Wellman, 2001). In a follow-up study, a marked reduction in apical dendritic material in this area was seen following chronic restraint stress (3 h/21 days; Cook and Wellman, 2004). In both studies, dendritic remodeling was specific to the apical dendrites, with the most dramatic reductions in branch number and length occurring in terminal branches relatively distal to the soma. This effect was subsequently replicated by a number of laboratories (Radley et al., 2004, 2005; Liston et al., 2006; Cerqueira et al., 2007a; Liu and Aghajanian, 2008; Dias-Ferreira et al., 2009), and has been demonstrated in layer V of infralimbic cortex as well (Goldwater et al., 2009). Stress-induced retraction of apical dendrites is associated with a significant decrease in the density of dendritic spines (Radley et al., 2006, 2008; Michelsen et al., 2007). Changes in spine morphology have also been documented, with chronic restraint stress (6 hr/21 days) decreasing spine volume and surface area and shifting the distribution of spines from larger to smaller (Radley et al., 2008). This alteration in morphology may indicate a failure of spines to mature and stabilize (Radley et al., 2008), which could have important functional implications.

Surprisingly, in the initial demonstration of the effect of daily corticosterone administration on morphology of prefrontal cortex, rats receiving subcutaneous vehicle injections also showed dendritic remodeling relative to unhandled controls, although to a lesser extent (Wellman, 2001). In contrast, the same regimen of vehicle injections did not alter dendritic morphology in hippocampal CA3 pyramidal neurons (Woolley et al., 1990). This suggested that pyramidal neurons in medial prefrontal cortex might be more sensitive to stress than neurons in the hippocampus. Subsequent studies support this hypothesis. For example, daily brief restraint (10 min/day) for just 1 week causes significant but less pronounced dendritic retraction in anterior cingulate and prelimbic cortex (Brown et al., 2005), as does 20 min of immobilization per day for 1 week (Liu and Aghajanian, 2008). Further, a single 10-min forced swim followed by tone-shock fear conditioning produced apical dendritic retraction in infralimbic cortex of mice (Izquierdo et al., 2006). Thus, dendritic morphology of pyramidal neurons in medial prefrontal cortex appears to be exquisitely sensitive to stress (see Figure 10.2).

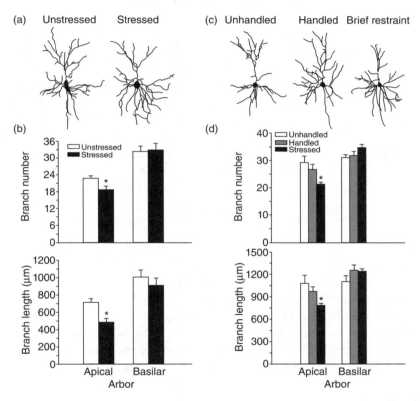

Figure 10.2 Chronic stress effects on dendritic morphology in medial prefrontal cortex in male Sprague–Dawley rats. (a) Reconstructions of Golgi-stained pyramidal neurons in layer II–III of medial prefrontal cortex in unstressed and stressed rats. Three weeks of daily restraint stress resulted in significant retraction of apical dendrites. *Source:* From Cook and Wellman (2004). Reproduced with permission of John Wiley and Sons. (b) Mean number and length of apical and basilar branches in unstressed and stressed rats. *Significant difference relative to unstressed rats. (c) Just 1 week of brief daily restraint stress resulted in significant retraction of apical dendrites of pyramidal neurons in medial prefrontal cortex. (d) Mean number and length of apical and basilar branches in unstressed, handled, and stressed rats. *Significant difference relative to unstressed and handled rats. *Source:* From Brown et al. (2005). By permission of Oxford University Press.

While chronic stress appears to produce similar alterations across subregions of medial prefrontal cortex, recent work from Fuchs and colleagues suggests hemispheric specificity of these changes, with chronic restraint stress (6 hr/3 weeks) producing differential effects in the left and right hemispheres of medial prefrontal cortex (Czéh et al., 2008; Perez-Cruz et al., 2009). Indeed, this finding is consistent with data demonstrating differential contributions of left and right ventral medial prefrontal cortex to HPA-axis regulation (e.g., Sullivan and Gratton, 1999; Sullivan, 2004; see also Chapter 25 in this volume).

Orbitofrontal cortex

Whereas chronic stress via a variety of manipulations results in apical dendritic retraction in medial prefrontal cortex, changes in orbitofrontal cortex are quite different: a chronic restraint procedure (6 hr/21 days) that produces dendritic retraction in anterior cingulate and prelimbic cortex increases dendritic material in lateral orbitofrontal cortex in rats (Liston et al., 2006), as does 3 weeks of chronic unpredictable stress (Dias-Ferreira et al., 2009). Thus, just as stress differentially alters dendritic morphology across hippocampal subregions, amygdaloid nuclei, and striatal regions, stress produces opposite effects on the morphology of pyramidal neurons in medial prefrontal and orbitofrontal cortices.

Reversibility

Chronic restraint stress-induced dendritic retraction in dorsal medial prefrontal cortex is no longer evident 3 weeks after stress (Radley et al., 2005), and substantial recovery of dendritic morphology in infralimbic cortex occurs by this time as well (Goldwater et al., 2009). Given that morphology of CA3 neurons recovers within 10 days after the cessation of chronic stress, a study of the time course of recovery in prefrontal cortex would be useful. Regardless, the finding that stress effects on both hippocampal CA3 and prefrontal dendritic morphology are reversible demonstrates that these neurons are quite plastic, and suggests the possibility that the mechanisms mediating this plasticity can be identified and targeted therapeutically.

Mechanisms of Stress-induced Dendritic Remodeling

Many corticolimbic neurotransmitter systems and molecular signaling pathways are altered by stress and could contribute to stress-induced dendritic alterations. These systems and pathways include the monoaminergic neurotransmitters serotonin (Robbins, 2005; Maier et al., 2006; Holmes, 2008; Lapiz-Bluhm et al., 2009), dopamine (Murphy et al., 1996a, 1996b; Mizoguchi et al., 2000, 2004; Pani et al., 2000), and norepinephrine (Ramos and Arnsten, 2007); the glutamatergic system

(Brann, 1995; Moghaddam, 2002; Moghaddam and Jackson, 2004), neurotrophic factors such as brain-derived neurotrophic factor (BDNF; Duman and Monteggia, 2006), and glucocorticoids (Liu and Aghajanian, 2008). This section will focus on three of these possibilities: glucocorticoids, the glutamatergic system, and BDNF.

Hippocampus

Because stress-induced alterations in hippocampal dendritic morphology have most consistently been documented in area CA3, investigations of mechanisms have largely focused on this subregion. Administration of corticosterone mimicked stress-induced dendritic changes in area CA3 (Woolley et al., 1990), suggesting a potential role for corticosterone in stress-induced dendritic remodeling in area CA3. Indeed, administration of the 3-β-hydroxysteroid dehydrogenase blocker cyanoketone, which blocks stress-induced increases in corticosterone, prevented the stress-induced retraction and debranching of CA3 apical dendrites (Magariños and McEwen, 1995).

Corticosterone may exert its effects on CA3 dendritic morphology in parallel or in concert with the glutamatergic and serotonergic systems. Corticosterone modulates N-methyl-D-aspartate (NMDA) receptor-mediated influx of calcium ions in cultured hippocampal neurons (Takahashi et al., 2002) and NMDA-dependent long-term potentiation (LTP; Shors et al., 1989), and these effects are mediated by glucocorticoid receptors (Xu et al., 1998; Yang et al., 2004). Moreover, hippocampal NMDA receptors are altered by chronic stress. Chronic restraint stress (6 hr/21 days) decreased expression of the NR1, NR2A, and NR2B subunits of the NMDA receptor in CA1, CA3, and dentate gyrus in mice (Pawlak et al., 2005) and increased NMDA receptor-mediated excitatory currents at mossy fiber-to-CA3 synapses in rats (Kole et al., 2002). Further, systemic administration of the competitive NMDA receptor antagonist CGP 43487 prevented the dendritic atrophy of CA3 apical dendrites resulting from either chronic restraint stress or corticosterone administration (Magariños and McEwen, 1995), providing direct evidence for a role for NMDA receptors. The critical site of action for NMDA's role is likely in area CA3: mice with selective post-adolescent genetic ablation of CA3 NMDA receptors failed to show the retraction of CA3 apical dendrites seen in wild-type mice after 10 days of immobilization stress (2 h/day; Christian et al., 2011). Administration of the serotonin-reuptake facilitator tianeptine during chronic restraint also prevented stress-induced dendritic retraction in CA3 (Watanabe et al., 1992b), while administration of tianeptine for 2 weeks following chronic restraint or corticosterone administration reversed the dendritic retraction (Watanabe et al., 1992b). Interestingly, this effect may also be NMDA receptor-mediated: tianeptine administration during chronic restraint stress prevents the stress-induced alteration of NMDA receptor excitatory postsynaptic currents (Kole et al., 2002).

BDNF plays a well-documented role in dendritic plasticity (reviewed in Horch, 2004) and is a target of many pharmacological treatments for stress-related disorders such as depression (reviewed in Duman and Monteggia, 2006). Both acute and chronic stress decrease BDNF mRNA and protein in several brain regions including the hippocampus and medial prefrontal cortex (reviewed in Duman and Monteggia, 2006). For instance, acute immobilization stress dramatically decreased hippocampal BDNF expression, an effect mediated by corticosterone (Adlard and Cotman, 2004). Chronic daily immobilization (45 min/7 days) also decreases hippocampal *BDNF* mRNA (Smith et al., 1995). Thus, stress-induced alterations in BDNF could contribute to dendritic remodeling in CA3. One more recent study provides support for this hypothesis: whereas chronic immobilization stress (2 h/10 days) produced retraction of CA3 apical dendrites in wild-type mice, transgenic mice engineered to overexpress BDNF did not show significant stress-induced changes in CA3 apical dendritic morphology (Govindarajan et al., 2006).

Amygdala

Very little is known about the mechanisms underlying stress-induced dendritic remodeling in the amygdala. Given the opposite effects of chronic stress on dendritic morphology in CA3 versus basolateral amygdala, one could hypothesize that different mechanisms mediate these effects. However, one intriguing study suggests a shared pathway with stress-induced dendritic changes in the hippocampus: BDNF overexpression increased dendritic extent in basolateral amygdala of unstressed mice and occluded the stress-induced increase in dendritic length and spine density seen in wild-type mice (Govindarajan et al., 2006). This pattern of results suggests that whereas stress-induced decreases in hippocampal BDNF may contribute to CA3 dendritic retraction, stress-induced increases in amygaloid BDNF may contribute to the opposite pattern of effects seen in this structure.

Prefrontal cortex

Chronic corticosterone administration mimics the regression of distal apical dendrites in medial prefrontal cortex seen after chronic restraint stress (Wellman, 2001; Cerqueira et al., 2007a), and systemic administration of the glucocorticoid receptor blocker RU38486 prevents the apical dendritic retraction resulting from 10 days of daily restraint (Liu and Aghajanian, 2008). Thus, as in hippocampal CA3, stress-induced increases in corticosterone contribute to stress-induced dendritic retraction.

As in the hippocampus, stress-induced elevations of corticosterone may alter prefrontal morphology and physiology via interactions between glucocorticoid receptors and NMDA receptors. Glutamate release in medial prefrontal cortex is increased during acute stress (Moghaddam, 1993). Thus, glutamatergic transmission at NMDA receptors may play a role in stress-induced dendritic reorganization in medial prefrontal cortex. Consistent with this hypothesis, chronic administration of the stress hormone corticosterone downregulates expression of the NR2B subunit of the NMDA receptor in medial prefrontal cortex (Gourley et al., 2008). Further, systemic administration of the NMDA receptor blocker CPP during daily restraint

(3 h/day for 1 week) prevented stress-induced dendritic retraction in medial prefrontal cortex, suggesting that NDMA receptor activation during stress does indeed contribute to stress-induced dendritic remodeling here (Martin and Wellman, 2011).

Finally, BDNF has been implicated in both hippocampal and amygdalar stress-induced dendritic remodeling. Although a direct test of the role of BDNF in stress-induced dendritic remodeling has not yet occurred, current evidence for a role of BDNF is not strong. For instance, whereas Lee and colleagues (2006) showed that acute immobilization stress upregulates *BDNF* mRNA in medial prefrontal cortex, Lin and colleagues (2009) found no change in BDNF protein in prelimbic cortex following either acute or chronic foot-shock stress.

Functional Implications of Stress-induced Dendritic Remodeling

Dendrites are a major site of synaptic connectivity, with adult pyramidal neurons receiving approximately 15,000 synaptic inputs (Huttenlocher, 1994). The geometry of the dendritic arbor (e.g., dendritic branching patterns, distribution, and overall shape) determines many functional properties of neurons (e.g., Rall et al., 1992; Mainen and Sejnowksi, 1996; Koch and Segev, 2000; Lu et al., 2001; Grudt and Perl, 2002), and alterations in neuronal excitability are associated with changes in dendritic morphology (e.g., Gazzaley et al., 2002; Monfils et al., 2004; Monfils and Teskey, 2004; Muller et al, 2000). For instance, repeated high-frequency stimulation of callosal fibers in behaving rats results in increases in both dendritic length and potentiation of excitability of cortical pyramidal cells (Monfils et al., 2004), while repeated low-frequency stimulation produces dendritic retraction and concomitant decreases in the excitability of cortical pyramidal cells (Monfils and Teskey, 2004). Thus, stress-induced dendritic alterations could result in altered excitability of these neurons, thus impairing behavior. Further, given evidence for a relationship between dendritic spine morphology and dynamics of neuronal processing such as calcium signaling (e.g., Alvarez and Sabatini, 2007), such morphological changes may have important implications for the functional properties of these neurons, and hence may contribute to stress-induced cognitive changes.

Hippocampus

Administration of both corticosterone and chronic stress alter hippocampal excitability (Foy et al., 1987, 1990; Joëls and de Kloet, 1989; Kole et al., 2004a). For instance, either brief or more chronic psychosocial stress altered intrinsic excitability of CA3 pyramidal neurons, decreasing onset latencies of excitatory postsynaptic potentials and increasing input resistance. In addition, these stress manipulations impaired LTP induction at commissural-associational collaterals, and changes in the physiological properties of these neurons were correlated with dendritic retraction (Kole et al., 2004a).

Such functional alterations may contribute to stress-induced deficits on hippocampally mediated tasks. An extensive literature documents the effects of chronic stress on hippocampally mediated tasks such as spatial recognition memory, spatial learning in the Morris water maze, and contextual fear conditioning (reviewed in Luine et al., 2007; Sandi and Pinelo-Nava, 2007; Conrad, 2010). Several studies suggest a relationship between stress-induced dendritic changes in CA3 and deficits on hippocampal tasks. For instance, chronic restraint stress (6 hr/21 days) resulted in both CA3 dendritic retraction and deficits in spatial recognition assessed on the Y maze. Importantly, 10 days after the last day of restraint, both dendritic morphology and spatial recognition performance were normalized. In addition, tianeptine treatment during restraint prevented both the stress-induced dendritic retraction and the spatial recognition deficit (Conrad et al., 1996). Similarly, 1 month of chronic unpredictable stress decreased CA3 volume and apical dendritic extent and produced deficits in spatial learning as assessed in the Morris water maze; both morphological and behavioral deficits were gone 1 month after the final day of stress (Sousa et al., 2000).

Amygdala

Studies have shown chronic stress effects on amygdala-mediated behaviors, including enhancement of fear conditioning (Conrad et al., 1999; Farrell et al., 2010; Sanders et al., 2010) and increases in measures of anxiety and risk assessment, as investigated using the elevated-plus maze (Vyas et al., 2002, 2004). No studies to date have directly assessed the relationship between dendritic hypertrophy in the basolateral amygdala and fear conditioning. However, Conrad and colleagues (1999) demonstrated enhanced cued and contextual fear conditioning and decreased open-field exploration after chronic restraint (6 hr/21 days). Interestingly, treatment with tianeptine during the stress manipulation prevented stress-induced dendritic retraction in hippocampal area CA3, but failed to prevent the stress-induced alterations in fear conditioning and open-field exploration (Conrad et al., 1999), suggesting that dendritic retraction in CA3 was not responsible for the increased emotionality. Vyas and colleagues (2004) demonstrated that dendritic hypertrophy and increased spine density on basolateral amygdala pyramidal neurons continued 21 days after the cessation of immobilization stress (2 hr/10 days), and that this persistent hypertrophy was associated with continued increases in anxiety. Thus, it is interesting to speculate that dendritic hypertrophy in the basolateral amygdala may contribute to the potentiation of fear conditioning after chronic stress.

Striatum

Given the relative recency of the finding of stress-induced alterations in striatal morphology it is not surprising that little is known of potential behavioral correlates. However, Dias-Ferreira and colleagues (2009) demonstrated that the same chronic unpredictable stressor that resulted in dendritic proliferation in lateral dorsal striatum also produced deficits in operant tasks that depend on using expected outcomes to guide behavior; instead, the stressed rats showed a bias for habitual behaviors. Given the important role of dorsolateral striatum in habit learning this outcome is consistent with the hypothesis that the dendritic proliferation here may have resulted in hyperactivity of this structure.

Prefrontal cortex

Stress alters synaptic plasticity of medial prefrontal cortex neurons. In rats, a single 30-min bout of elevated platform stress impaired the induction of LTP in prelimbic cortex in response to theta-burst stimulation of afferents from the basolateral amygdala (Maroun and Richter-Levin, 2003) and in the hippocampus-to-medial prefrontal cortex pathway (Jay et al., 2004; Rocher et al., 2004; Dupin et al., 2006; Mailliet et al., 2008; Qi et al., 2009). Chronic stress produces similar physiological alterations. For instance, chronic immobilization (20 min/10 days) produced apical dendritic retraction in prelimbic pyramidal neurons and reduced excitatory postsynaptic potentials evoked by 5-hydroxytryptamine (5-HT) application. Importantly, the very strong correlation between apical dendritic length and 5-HT-evoked responses in unstressed rats was completely eliminated in stressed rats (Liu and Aghajanian, 2008). Chronic restraint stress impaired hippocampus-to-medial prefrontal cortex LTP induction (Cerqueira et al., 2007b). Further, conditioned fear potentiates hippocampus-to-medial prefrontal cortex field potentials (Farinelli et al., 2006), and prior exposure to 3 weeks of chronic unpredictable mild stress attenuated this potentiation (Garcia et al., 2008). Likewise, prior exposure to 1 week of daily restraint stress inhibits conditioned-stimulus-related firing in infralimbic cortex during retrieval of extinction of conditioned fear (Wilber et al., 2011).

Chronic stress has been shown to alter a variety of prefrontally mediated behaviors, including spatial and nonspatial working memory, attentional set-shifting, reversal learning, and retrieval of extinction of conditioned fear (reviewed in Holmes and Wellman, 2009). While very few studies have examined the relationship between stress-induced morphological changes and alterations in prefrontal behaviors, results are intriguing. For instance, chronic corticosterone treatment impaired spatial reversal learning, and this impairment was correlated with reductions in the volume of medial prefrontal cortex (Cerqueira et al., 2005b, 2007b). Chronic unpredictable stress (1 hr/4 weeks) resulted in deficits in spatial working memory assessed in the water maze, and this deficit paralleled reductions in the volume of medial prefrontal cortex (Cerqueira et al., 2007b). Repeated swim stress (10 min/3 days) produced deficits in retrieval of extinction of conditioned fear, a behavior mediated by infralimbic cortex, and concomitant apical dendritic retraction in that region (Izquierdo et al., 2006). Finally, chronic restraint stress (6 hr/3 weeks) impaired attentional set-shifting, a task mediated by medial prefrontal cortex. This deficit correlated quite strongly with the extent of dendritic retraction in anterior cingulate cortex (Liston et al., 2006).

Future Directions

Comparisons of stressor type, intensity, and chronicity across corticolimbic structures

As described above, the available evidence suggests differential vulnerability to chronic stress, across both corticolimbic structures and particular regions within those structures. However, that conclusion is often based in large part on comparisons across different rodent strains and even species, and across numerous stressors, both psychosocial (e.g., social defeat or restraint stress) and physical (e.g., activity stress or tail shock). However, stress is a complex variable (not all stressors are the same), and as such might be expected to have different impacts and mechanisms. As has been suggested previously (McLaughlin et al., 2007), documented differences in stress effects across various structures, or discrepancies in stress effects within a structure may reflect differences in strain, species, or stressor type. The literature would benefit enormously from more parametric studies (e.g., McLaughlin et al., 2007) carefully evaluating potential differential effects of one stressor of varying intensity or duration across various structures, or directly comparing qualitatively different stressors within the same study.

Structure–function relationships in stress effects

Although several studies demonstrate an association between stress-induced morphological changes in corticolimbic structures and alterations in behaviors mediated by them, a causal relationship has not yet been directly demonstrated. A direct test of the causal hypothesis awaits the development of tools that will allow us to either prevent or induce only the dendritic changes that result from chronic stress. Further, deficits in spatial recognition occur in concert with stress-induced apical retraction in CA3 and are ameliorated by manipulations that restore or prevent dendritic retraction (Conrad et al., 1996). Nonetheless, corticosterone synthesis blockade at the time of testing can ameliorate the spatial recognition deficit, despite the presence of dendritic retraction, suggesting that the dendritic changes may set the stage for behavioral deficits, but are not solely responsible (Wright et al., 2006). Characterizing how dendritic changes may interact with other factors to produce behavioral deficits is an important area for future investigation.

Mechanisms of stress effects on corticolimbic morphology

Although several studies have identified potential neurochemical mechanisms for stress-induced dendritic retraction in corticolimbic structures, much work remains to be done, both at the level of neurochemical mechanisms and localization of these mechanisms to specific structures. For instance, glucocorticoid receptors are plentiful in both the hippocampus and medial prefrontal cortex (reviewed in Herman et al., 2005), and have been implicated in stress-induced dendritic retraction in both (Magariños and McEwen, 1995; Liu and Aghajanian, 2008). However, it is not known whether glucocorticoid receptors contribute to stress-induced dendritic retraction via direct actions in target structures. For instance, hippocampal areas CA1 and CA3 both project directly to medial prefrontal cortex (Swanson and Cowan, 1977; Swanson, 1981). Similarly, basolateral amygdala provides projections to medial prefrontal cortex (McDonald, 1991; Verwer et al., 1996), which in turn provides projections to the amygdala (Gabbott et al., 2005). Thus, it is possible that stress-induced dendritic retraction in medial prefrontal cortex could be a response to alterations in inputs from the hippocampus.

Circuit-level contributions to stress effects

Finally, as described above, the corticolimbic structures on which this chapter focuses are interconnected and often contribute to the same behaviors. For instance, lesion or inactivation of either hippocampus or prelimbic cortex produces deficits on a spatial working memory task (e.g., Wolf et al., 1987; Steele and Morris, 1999) that is impaired after chronic stress (Cerqueira et al., 2007b). Likewise, basolateral amygdala is a critical site of plasticity in fear conditioning (Maren, 2001), prelimbic cortex may play a role in expression of conditioned fear (Burgos-Robles et al., 2009), projections from the hippocampus to prefrontal cortex may be important in consolidation of extinction (Garcia et al., 2008), and infralimbic cortex appears to play a role in retrieval of extinction (Quirk et al., 2006), all of which are influenced by chronic stress (e.g., Conrad et al., 1999; Izquierdo et al., 2006; Miracle et al., 2006). Thus, delineating the differential contributions of these corticolimbic structures to stress-induced alterations in behaviors mediated by them is critical. Studies employing temporary inactivation of specific corticolimbic structures during stress or subsequent behavioral testing, administering, for instance glucocorticoid receptor blockers into specific corticolimbic structures, or conditional or viral inactivation of specific genes or gene products within these structures, could tease apart the contribution of each of these interconnected structures to both stress-induced dendritic alterations and their contributions to stress-induced changes in behaviors mediated by these structures.

References

Adlard, P. A., & Cotman, C. W. (2004). Voluntary exercise protects against stress-induced decreases in brain-derived neurotrophic factor protein expression. *Neuroscience, 124,* 985–992.

Alvarez, V. A., & Sabatini, B. L. (2007). Anatomical and physiological plasticity of dendritic spines. *Annual Review of Neuroscience, 30*, 79–97.

Appelhof, B. C., Huyser, J., Verweij, M., Brouwer, J. P., van Dyck, R., Fliers, E., Hoogendijk, W. J. G., Tijssen, J. G. P., Wiersinga, W. M., & Schene, A. H. (2006). Glucocorticoids and relapse of major depression (dexamethasone/corticotropin-releasing hormone test in relation to relapse of major depression). *Biological Psychiatry, 59*, 696–701.

Bennur, S., Shankaranarayana Rao, B. S., Pawlak, R., Strickland, S., McEwen, B. S., & Chattarji, S. (2007). Stress-induced spine loss in the medial amygdala is mediated by tissue-plasminogen activator. *Neuroscience, 144*, 8–16.

Brann, D. W. (1995). Glutamate: a major excitatory transmitter in neuroendocrine regulation. *Neuroendocrinology, 61*, 213–225.

Bremner, J. D., Elzinga, B., Schmahl, C., & Vermetten, E. (2008). Structural and functional plasticity of the human brain in posttraumatic stress disorder. In *Stress hormones and post traumatic stress disorder: Basic studies and clinical perspectives* (pp. 171–186). Boston, MA: Elsevier.

Brown, G. W., & Harris, T. O. (1989). Depression. In G. W. Brown & T. O. Harris (Eds.), *Life events and illness* (pp. 49–93). New York: Guilford.

Brown, S. M., Henning, S., & Wellman, C. L. (2005). Short-term, mild stress alters dendritic morphology in rat medial prefrontal cortex. *Cerebral Cortex, 15*, 1714–1722.

Burgos-Robles, A., Vidal-Gonzalez, I., & Quirk, G. J. (2009). Sustained conditioned responses in prelimbic prefrontal neurons are correlated with fear expression and extinction failure. *Journal of Neuroscience, 29*, 8474–8482.

Cerqueira, J., Taipa, R., Uylings, H. B. M., Almeida, O. F. X., & Sousa, N. (2007a). Specific configuration of dendritic degeneration in pyramidal neurons of the medial prefrontal cortex induced by differing corticosteroid regimens. *Cerebral Cortex, 17*, 1998–2006.

Cerqueira, J. J., Catania, C., Sotiropoulos, I., Schubert, M., Kalisch, R., Almeida, O. F., Auer, D. P., & Sousa, N. (2005a). Corticosteroid status influences the volume of the rat cingulate cortex-a magnetic resonance imaging study. *Journal of Psychiatric Research, 39*, 451–460.

Cerqueira, J. J., Pego, J. M., Taipa, R., Bessa, J. M., Almeida, O. F. X., & Sousa, N. (2005b). Morphological correlates of corticosteroid-induced changes in prefrontal cortex-dependent behaviors. *Journal of Neuroscience, 25*, 7792–7800.

Cerqueira, J. J., Mailliet, F., Almeida, O. F. X., Jay, T. M., & Sousa, N. (2007a). The prefrontal cortex as a key target of the maladaptive response to stress. *Journal of Neuroscience, 27*, 2781–2787.

Christian, K. M., Miracle, A. D., Wellman, C. L., & Nakazawa, K. (2011). Chronic stress-induced hippocampal dendritic retraction requires CA3 NMDA receptors. *Neuroscience, 174*, 26–36.

Conrad, C. D. (2008). Chronic stress-induced hippocampal vulnerability: the glucocorticoid vulnerability hypothesis. *Reviews in Neurosciences, 19*, 395–411.

Conrad, C. D. (2010). A critical review of chronic stress effects on spatial learning and memory. *Progress in Neuro-psychopharmacology & Biological Psychiatry, 34*, 742–755.

Conrad, C. D., Galea, L. A., Kuroda, Y., & McEwen, B. S. (1996). Chronic stress impairs rat spatial memory on the Y maze, and this effect is blocked by tianeptine pretreatment. *Behavioral Neuroscience, 110*, 1321–1334.

Conrad, C. D., LeDoux, J. E., Magariños, A. M., & McEwen, B. S. (1999). Repeated restraint stress facilitates fear conditioning independently of causing hippocampal CA3 dendritic atrophy. *Behavioral Neuroscience, 113*, 902–913.

Conrad, C. D., Jackson, J. L., & Wise, L. S. (2004). Chronic stress enhances ibotenic acid-induced damage selectively within the hippocampal CA3 region of male, but not female rats. *Neuroscience, 125*, 759–767.

Conrad, C. D., McLaughlin, K. J., Harman, J. S., Foltz, C., Wieczorek, L., Lightner, E., & Wright, R. L. (2007). Chronic glucocorticoids increase hippocampal vulnerability to neurotoxicity under conditions that produce CA3 dendritic retraction but fail to impair spatial recognition memory. *Journal of Neuroscience, 27*, 8278–8285.

Cook, S. C., & Wellman, C. L. (2004). Chronic stress alters dendritic morphology in rat medial prefrontal cortex. *Journal of Neurobiology, 60*, 236–248.

Czéh, B., Perez-Cruz, C., Fuchs, E., & Flügge, G. (2008). Chronic stress-induced cellular changes in the medial prefrontal cortex and their potential clinical implications: Does hemisphere location matter? *Behavioral Brain Research, 190*, 1–13.

Dias-Ferreira, E., Sousa, J. C., Melo, I., Morgado, P., Mesquita, A. R., Cerqueira, J. J., Costa, R. M., & Sousa, N. (2009). Chronic stress causes frontostriatal reorganization and affects decision-making. *Science, 325*, 621–625.

Donohue, H. S., Gabbott, P. L. A., Davies, H. A., Rodríguez, J. J., Cordero, M. I., Sandi, C., Medvedev, N. I., Popov, V. I., Colyer, F. M., Peddie, C. J., & Stewart, M. G. (2006). Chronic restraint stress induces changes in synapse morphology in stratum lacunosum-moleculare CA1 rat hippocampus: a stereological and three-dimensional ultrastructural study. *Neuroscience, 140*, 597–606.

Duman, R. S., & Monteggia, L. M. (2006). A neurotrophic model for stress-related mood disorders. *Biological Psychiatry, 59*, 1116–1127.

Dupin, N., Mailliet, F., Rocher, C., Kessal, K., Spedding, M., & Jay, T. M. (2006). Common efficacy of psychotropic drugs in restoring stress-induced impairment of prefrontal plasticity. *Neurotoxicity Research, 10*, 193–198.

Eichenbaum, H. (2004). Hippocampus: cognitive processes and neural representations that underlie declarative memory. *Neuron, 44*, 109–120.

Farinelli, M., Deschaux, O., Hugues, S., Thevenet, A., & Garcia, R. (2006). Hippocampal train stimulation modulates recall of fear extinction independently of prefrontal cortex synaptic plasticity and lesions. *Learning & Memory, 13*, 329–334.

Farrell, M. R., Sayed, J. A., Underwood, A. R., & Wellman, C. L. (2010). Lesion of infralimbic cortex occludes stress effects on retrieval of extinction but not fear conditioning. *Neurobiology of Learning and Memory, 94*, 240–246.

Foy, M. R., Stanton, M. E., Levine, S., & Thompson, R. F. (1987). Behavioral stress impairs long-term potentiation in rodent hippocampus. *Behavioral and Neural Biology, 48*, 138–149.

Foy, M. R., Foy, J. G., Levine, S., & Thompson, R. F. (1990). Manipulation of pituitary-adrenal activity affects neural plasticity in rodent hippocampus. *Psychological Science, 1*, 201–204.

Fuchs, E., Uno, H., & Flugge, G. (1995). Chronic psychosocial stress induces morphological alterations in hippocampal pyramidal neurons of the tree shrew. *Brain Research, 673*, 275–282.

Gabbott, P. L. A., Warner, T. A., Jays, P. R. L., Salway, P., & Busby, S. J. (2005). Prefrontal cortex in the rat: Projections to subcortical autonomic, motor, and limbic centers. *Journal of Comparative Neurology, 492*, 145–177.

Garcia, R., Spennato, G., Nilsson-Todd, L., Moreau, J.-L., & Deschaux, O. (2008). Hippocampal low-frequency stimulation and chronic mild stress similarly disrupt fear extinction memory in rats. *Neurobiology of Learning and Memory, 89*, 560–566.

Gazzaley, A., Kay, S., & Benson, D. L. (2002). Dendritic spine plasticity in hippocampus. *Neuroscience, 111*, 853–862.

Goldwater, D. S., Pavlides, C., Hunter, R. G., Bloss, E. B., Hof, P. R., McEwen, B. S., & Morrison, J. H. (2009). Structural and functional alterations to rat medial prefrontal cortex following chronic restraint stress and recovery. *Neuroscience, 164*, 798–808.

Gourley, S. L., Kedves, A. T., Olausson, P., & Taylor, J. R. (2008). A history of corticosterone exposure regulates fear extinction and cortical NR2B, GluR2/3, and BDNF. *Neuropsychopharmacology, 34*, 707–716.

Govindarajan, A., Rao, B. S., Nair, D., Trinh, M., Mawjee, N., Tonegawa, S., & Chattarji, S. (2006). Transgenic brain-derived neurotrophic factor expression causes both anxiogenic and antidepressant effects. *Proceedings of the National Academy of Sciences USA, 103*, 13208–13213.

Grudt, T. J., & Perl, E. R. (2002). Correlations between neuronal morphology and electrophysiology features in the rodent superficial dorsal horn. *Journal of Physiology, 540*, 189–207.

Hajek, T., Kozeny, J., Kopecek, M., Alda, M., & Hoschl, C. (2008). Reduced subgenual cingulate volumes in mood disorders: a meta-analysis. *Journal of Psychiatry & Neuroscience, 33*, 91–99.

Hajszan, T., Dow, A., Warner-Schmidt, J. L., Szigeti-Buck, K., Sallam, N. L., Parducz, A., Leranth, C., & Duman, R. S. (2009). Remodeling of Hippocampal Spine Synapses in the Rat Learned Helplessness Model of Depression. *Biological Psychiatry, 65*, 392–400.

Haldane, M., & Frangou, S. (2006). Functional neuroimaging studies in mood disorders. *Acta Neuropsychiatrica, 18*, 88–99.

Herman, J. P., Figueiredo, H., Mueller, N. K., Ulrich-Lai, Y., Ostrander, M. M., Choi, D. C., & Cullinan, W. E. (2003). Central mechanisms of stress integration: hierarchical circuitry controlling hypothalamo-pituitary-adrenocortical responsiveness. *Frontiers in Neuroendocrinology, 24*, 151–180.

Herman, J. P., Ostrander, M. M., Mueller, N. K., & Figueiredo, H. (2005). Limbic system mechanisms of stress regulation: hypothalamo-pituitary-adrenocortical axis. *Progress in Neuro-psychopharmacology & Biological Psychiatry, 29*, 1201–1213.

Holmes, A. (2008). Genetic variation in cortico-amygdala serotonin function and risk for stress-related disease. *Neuroscience and Biobehavioral Reviews, 32*, 1293–1314.

Holmes, A., & Wellman, C. L. (2009). Stress-induced prefrontal reorganization and executive dysfunction in rodents. *Neuroscience and Biobehavioral Reviews, 33*, 773–783.

Horch, H. W. (2004). Local effects of BDNF on dendritic growth. *Reviews in the Neurosciences, 15*, 117–129.

Horner, C. H., O'Regan, M., & Arbuthnott, E. (1991). Neural plasticity of the hippocampal (CA1) pyramidal cell–quantitative changes in spine density following handling and injection for drug testing. *Journal of Anatomy, 174*, 229–238.

Huttenlocher, P. R. (1994). Synaptogenesis in human cerebral cortex. In G. Dawson & K. W. Fischer (Eds.), *Human behavior and the developing brain* (pp. 137–152). New York: Guilford Press.

Izquierdo, A., Wellman, C. L., & Holmes, A. (2006). Rapid dendritic retraction in medial prefrontal neurons and impaired fear extinction following exposure to uncontrollable stress. *Journal of Neuroscience, 26*, 5733–5738.

Jay, T. M., Rocher, C., Hotte, M., Naudon, L., Gurden, H., & Spedding, M. (2004). Plasticity at hippocampal to prefrontal cortex synapses is impaired by loss of dopamine and stress: importance for psychiatric diseases. *Neurotoxicity Research, 6*, 233–244.

Joëls, M., & de Kloet, R. (1989). Effects of glucocorticoids and norepinephrine on the excitability in the hippocampus. *Science, 245*, 1502–1505.

Johnson, S. A., Wang, J. F., Sun, X., McEwen, B. S., Chattarji, S., & Young, L. T. (2009). Lithium treatment prevents stress-induced dendritic remodeling in the rodent amygdala. *Neuroscience, 163*, 34–39.

Kerr, D. S., Campbell, L. W., Applegate, M. D., Brodish, A., & Landfield, P. W. (1991). Chronic stress-induced acceleration of electrophysiologic and morphometric biomarkers of hippocampal aging. *Journal of Neuroscience, 11*, 1316–1324.

Koch, C., & Segev, I. (2000). The role of single neurons in information processing. *Nature Neuroscience, 3*, 1171–1177.

Kole, M. H. P., Swan, L., & Fuchs, E. (2002). The antidepressant tianeptine persistently modulates glutamate receptor currents of the hippocampal CA3 commissural associational synapse in chronically stressed rats. *European Journal of Neuroscience, 16*, 807–816.

Kole, M. H. P., Costoli, T., Koolhaas, J. M., & Fuchs, E. (2004a). Bidirectional shift in the cornu ammonis 3 pyramidal dendritic organization following brief stress. *Neuroscience, 125*, 337–347.

Kole, M. H. P., Czeh, B., & Fuchs, E. (2004b). Homeostatic maintenance in excitability of tree shrew hippocampal CA3 pyramidal neurons after chronic stress. *Hippocampus, 14*, 742–751.

Koob, G. F., Ahmed, S. H., Boutrel, B., Chen, S. A., Kenny, P. J., Markou, A., O'Dell, L. E., Parsons, L. H., & Sanna, P. P. (2004). Neurobiological mechanisms in the transition from drug use to drug dependence. *Neuroscience and Biobehavioral Reviews, 27*, 739–749.

Lambert, K. G., Buckelew, S. K., Staffiso-Sandoz, G., Gaffga, S., Carpenter, W., Fisher, J., & Kinsley, C. H. (1998). Activity-stress induces atrophy of apical dendrites of hippocampal pyramidal neurons in male rats. *Physiological Behavior, 65*, 43–49.

Lapiz-Bluhm, M. D., Soto-Pina, A. E., Hensler, J. G., & Morilak, D. A. (2009). Chronic intermittent cold stress and serotonin depletion induce deficits of reversal learning in an attentional set-shifting test in rats. *Psychopharmacology, 202*, 329–341.

Lee, Y., Duman, R. S., & Marek, G. J. (2006). The mGlu2/3 receptor agonist LY354740 suppresses immobilization stress-induced increase in rat prefrontal cortical BDNF mRNA expression. *Neuroscience Letters, 398*, 328–332.

Lin, Y., Ter Horst, G. J., Wichmann, R., Bakker, P., Liu, A. H., Li, X. J., & Westenbroek, C. (2009). Sex differences in the effects of acute and chronic stress and recovery after long-term stress on stress-related brain regions of rats. *Cerebral Cortex, 19*, 1978–1989.

Liston, C., Miller, M. M., Goldwater, D. S., Radley, J. J., Rocher, A. B., Hof, P. R., Morrison, J. H., & McEwen, B. S. (2006). Stress-induced alterations in prefrontal cortical dendritic morphology predict selective impairments in perceptual attentional set-shifting. *Journal of Neuroscience, 26*, 7870–7874.

Liu, R.-J., & Aghajanian, G. K. (2008). Stress blunts serotonin- and hypocretin-evoked EPSCs in prefrontal cortex: Role of corticosterone-mediated apical dendritic atrophy. *Proceedings of the National Academy of Sciences USA, 105*, 359–364.

Lu, Y., Inokuchi, H., McLachlan, E. M., Li, J.-S., & Higashi, H. (2001). Correlation between electrophysiology and morphology of three groups of neurons in the dorsal commissural nucleus of lumbosacral spinal cord of mature rats studied in vitro. *Journal of Comparative Neurology, 437*, 156–169.

Lucassen, P. J., Vollmann-Honsdorf, G. K., Gleisberg, M., Czéh, B., de Kloet, E. R., & Fuchs, E. (2001). Chronic psychosocial stress differentially affects apoptosis in hippocampal subregions and cortex of the adult tree shrew. *European Journal of Neuroscience, 14,* 161–166.

Luine, V. N., Beck, K. D., Bowman, R. E., Frankfurt, M., & MacLusky, N. J. (2007). Chronic stress and neural function: accounting for sex and age. *Journal of Neuroendocrinology, 19,* 743–751.

Lupien, S. J., & Lepage, M. (2001). Stress, memory, and the hippocampus: can't live with it, can't live without it. *Behavioral Brain Research, 127,* 137–158.

Magariños, A. M., & McEwen, B. S. (1995). Stress-induced atrophy of apical dendrites of hippocampal CA3c neurons: involvement of glucocorticoid secretion and excitatory amino acid receptors. *Neuroscience, 69,* 89–98.

Magariños, A. M., McEwen, B. S., Flugge, G., & Fuchs, E. (1996). Chronic psychosocial stress causes apical dendritic atrophy of hippocampal CA3 pyramidal neurons in subordinate tree shrews. *Journal of Neuroscience, 16,* 3534–3540.

Magariños, A. M., Verdugo, J. M. G., & McEwen, B. S. (1997). Chronic stress alters synaptic terminal structure in hippocampus. *Proceedings of the National Academy of Sciences USA, 94,* 14002–14008.

Magariños, A. M., Deslandes, A., & McEwen, B. S. (1999). Effects of antidepressants and benzodiazepine treatments on the dendritic structure of CA3 pyramidal neurons after chronic stress. *European Journal of Pharmacology, 371,* 113–122.

Maier, S. F., Amat, J., Baratta, M. W., Paul, E., & Watkins, L. R. (2006). Behavioral control, the medial prefrontal cortex, and resilience. *Dialogues in Clinical Neuroscience, 8,* 397–406.

Mailliet, F., Qi H, Rocher, C., Spedding, M., Svenningsson, P., & Jay, T. M. (2008). Protection of stress-induced impairment of hippocampal/prefrontal LTP through blockade of glucocorticoid receptors: implication of MEK signaling. *Experimental Neurology, 211,* 593–596.

Mainen, Z. F., & Sejnowksi, T. J. (1996). Influence of dendritic structure on firing pattern in model neocortical neurons. *Nature, 382,* 363–366.

Maren, S. (2001). Neurobiology of pavlovian fear conditioning. *Annual Review of Neuroscience, 24,* 897–931.

Maren, S., & Quirk, G. J. (2004). Neuronal signalling of fear memory. *Nature Reviews Neuroscience, 5,* 844–852.

Maroun, M., & Richter-Levin, G. (2003). Exposure to acute stress blocks the induction of long-term potentiation of the amygdala-prefrontal cortex pathway in vivo. *Journal of Neuroscience, 23,* 4406–4409.

Martin, K. P., & Wellman, C. L. (2011). NMDA receptor blockade alters stress-induced dendritic remodeling in medial prefrontal cortex. *Cerebral Cortex,* doi: 10.1093/cercor/ bhr02.

McDonald, A. J. (1991). Organization of amygdaloid projections to the prefrontal cortex and associated striatum in the rat. *Neuroscience, 44,* 1–14.

McLaughlin, K., Baran, S., & Conrad, C. (2009). Chronic stress- and sex-specific neuromorphological and functional changes in limbic structures. *Molecular Neurobiology, 40,* 166–182.

McLaughlin, K. J., Gomez, J. L., Baran, S. E., & Conrad, C. D. (2007). The effects of chronic stress on hippocampal morphology and function: An evaluation of chronic restraint paradigms. *Brain Research, 1161,* 56–64.

Michelsen, K. A., van den Hove, D. L. A., Schmitz, C., Segers, O., Prickaerts, J., & Steinbusch, H. W. M. (2007). Prenatal stress and subsequent exposure to chronic mild stress influence dendritic spine density and morphology in the rat medial prefrontal cortex. *BMC Neuroscience, 8*, 107.

Miracle, A. D., Brace, M. F., Huyck, K. D., Singler, S. A., & Wellman, C. L. (2006). Chronic stress impairs recall of extinction of conditioned fear. *Neurobiology of Learning and Memory, 85*, 213–218.

Mitra, R., Jadhav, S., McEwen, B. S., Vyas, A., & Chattarji, S. (2005). Stress duration modulates the spatiotemporal patterns of spine formation in the basolateral amygdala. *Proceedings of the National Academy of Sciences USA, 102*, 9371–9376.

Mizoguchi, K., Yuzurihara, M., Ishige, A., Sasaki, H., Chui, D. H., & Tabira, T. (2000). Chronic stress induces impairment of spatial working memory because of prefrontal dopaminergic dysfunction. *Journal of Neuroscience, 20*, 1568–1574.

Mizoguchi, K., Ishige, A., Takeda, S., Aburada, M., & Tabira, T. (2004). Endogenous glucocorticoids are essential for maintaining prefrontal cortical cognitive function. *Journal of Neuroscience, 24*, 5492–5499.

Moghaddam, B. (1993). Stress preferentially increases extraneuronal levels of excitatory amino acids in the prefrontal cortex: comparison to hippocampus and basal ganglia. *Journal of Neurochemistry, 60*, 1650–1657.

Moghaddam, B. (2002). Stress activation of glutamate neurotransmission in the prefrontal cortex: implications for dopamine-associated psychiatric disorders. *Biological Psychiatry, 51*, 775–787.

Moghaddam, B., & Jackson, M. (2004). Effect of stress on prefrontal cortex function. *Neurotoxicity Research, 6*, 73–78.

Monfils, M. H., & Teskey, G. C. (2004). Induction of long-term depression is associated with decreased dendritic length and spine density in layers II and V of sensorimotor neocortex. *Synapse, 53*, 114–121.

Monfils, M. H., VandenBerg, P. M., & Kleim, J. A. (2004). Long-term potentiation induces expanded movement representation and dendritic hypertrophy in layer V of rat sensorimotor neocortex. *Cerebral Cortex, 14*, 586–593.

Morales-Medina, J. C., Sanchez, F., Flores, G., Dumont, Y., & Quirion, R. (2009). Morphological reorganization after repeated corticosterone administration in the hippocampus, nucleus accumbens, and amygdala in the rat. *Journal of Chemical Neuroanatomy, 38*, 266–272.

Muller, D., Toni, N., & Buchs, P.-A. (2000). Spine changes associated with long-term potentiation. *Hippocampus, 10*, 596–604.

Murphy, B. L., Arnsten, A. F., Goldman-Rakic, P. S., & Roth, R. H. (1996a). Increased dopamine turnover in the prefrontal cortex impairs spatial working memory performance in rats and monkeys. *Proceedings of the National Academy of Sciences USA, 93*, 1325–1329.

Murphy, B. L., Arnsten, A. F., Jentsch, J. D., & Roth, R. H. (1996b). Dopamine and spatial working memory in rats and monkeys: pharmacological reversal of stress-induced impairment. *Journal of Neuroscience, 16*, 7768–7775.

Pani, L., Porcella, A., & Gessa, G. L. (2000). The role of stress in the pathophysiology of the dopaminergic system. *Molecular Psychiatry, 5*, 14–21.

Pare, W. P., & Tejani-Butt, S. M. (1996). Effect of stress on the behavior and 5-HT system in Sprague-Dawley and Wistar Kyoto rat strains. *Integrative Physiological and Behavioral Science, 31*, 112.

Pawlak, R., Rao, B. S. S., Melchor, J. P., Chattarji, S., McEwen, B., & Strickland, S. (2005). Tissue plasminogen activator and plasminogen mediate stress-induced decline of neuronal and cognitive functions in the mouse hippocampus. *Proceedings of the National Academy of Sciences USA, 102,* 18201–18206.

Perez-Cruz, C., Simon, M., Czéh, B., Flügge, G., & Fuchs, E. (2009). Hemispheric differences in basilar dendrites and spines of pyramidal neurons in the rat prelimbic cortex: activity- and stress-induced changes. *European Journal of Neuroscience, 29,* 738–747.

Phillips, M. L., Drevets, W. C., Rauch, S. L., & Lane, R. (2003). Neurobiology of emotion perception II: implications for major psychiatric disorders. *Biological Psychiatry, 54,* 515–528.

Qi, H., Mailliet, F., Spedding, M., Rocher, C., Zhang, X., Delagrange, P., McEwen, B., Jay, T. M., & Svenningsson, P. (2009). Antidepressants reverse the attenuation of the neurotrophic MEK/MAPK cascade in frontal cortex by elevated platform stress; reversal of effects on LTP is associated with GluA1 phosphorylation. *Neuropharmacology, 56,* 37–46.

Quirk, G. J., & Mueller, D. (2007). Neural mechanisms of extinction learning and retrieval. *Neuropsychopharmacology, 33,* 56–72.

Quirk, G. J., Garcia, R., & Gonzalez-Lima, F. (2006). Prefrontal mechanisms in extinction of conditioned fear. *Biological Psychiatry, 60,* 337–343.

Radley, J. J., Sisti, H. M., Hao, J., Rocher, A. B., McCall, T., Hof, P. R., McEwen, B. S., & Morrison, J. H. (2004). Chronic behavioral stress induces apical dendritic reorganization in pyramidal neurons of the medial prefrontal cortex. *Neuroscience, 125,* 1–6.

Radley, J. J., Rocher, A. B., Janssen, W. G. M., Hof, P. R., McEwen, B. S., & Morrison, J. H. (2005). Reversibility of apical dendritic retraction in the rat medial prefrontal cortex following repeated stress. *Experimental Neurology, 196,* 199–203.

Radley, J. J., Rocher, A. B., Miller, M., Janssen, W. G. M., Liston, C., Hof, P. R., McEwen, B. S., & Morrison, J. H. (2006). Repeated stress induces dendritic spine loss in the rat medial prefrontal cortex. *Cerebral Cortex, 16,* 313–320.

Radley, J. J., Rocher, A. B., Rodriguez, A., Ehlenberger, D. B., Dammann, M., McEwen, B. S., Morrison, J. H., Wearne, S. L., & Hof, P. R. (2008). Repeated stress alters dendritic spine morphology in the rat medial prefrontal cortex. *Journal of Comparative Neurology, 507,* 1141–1150.

Rall, W., Burke, R. E., Holmes, W. R., Jack, J. J., Redman, S. J., & Segev, I. (1992). Matching dendritic neuron models of experimental data. *Physiological Review, 72,* S159–S186.

Ramkumar, K., Srikumar, B., Shankaranarayana Rao, B., & Raju, T. (2008). Self-stimulation rewarding experience restores stress-induced CA3 dendritic atrophy, spatial memory deficits and alterations in the levels of neurotransmitters in the hippocampus. *Neurochemical Research, 33,* 1651–1662.

Ramos, B. P., & Arnsten, A. F. (2007). Adrenergic pharmacology and cognition: focus on the prefrontal cortex. *Pharmacology & Therapeutics, 113,* 523–536.

Robbins, T. W. (2005). Chemistry of the mind: neurochemical modulation of prefrontal cortical function. *Journal of Comparative Neurology, 493,* 140–146.

Rocher, C., Spedding, M., Munoz, C., & Jay, T. M. (2004). Acute stress-induced changes in hippocampal/prefrontal circuits in rats: effects of antidepressants. *Cerebral Cortex, 14,* 224–229.

Sanders, M. J., Stevens, S., & Boeh, H. (2010). Stress enhancement of fear learning in mice is dependent upon stressor type: Effects of sex and ovarian hormones. *Neurobiology of Learning and Memory, 94,* 254–262.

Sandi, C., & Pinelo-Nava, M. T. (2007). Stress and memory: behavioral effects and neuro-biological mechanisms. *Neural Plasticity*, 78970.

Sandi, C., Davies, H. A., Cordero, M. I., Rodriguez, J. J., Popov, V. I., & Stewart, M. G. (2003). Rapid reversal of stress induced loss of synapses in CA3 of rat hippocampus following water maze training. *European Journal of Neuroscience, 17*, 2447–2456.

Shors, T. J., Seib, T. B., Levine, S., & Thompson, R. F. (1989). Inescapable versus escapable shock modulates long-term potentiation in the rat hippocampus. *Science, 244*, 224–226.

Shors, T. J., Chua, C., & Falduto, J. (2001). Sex differences and opposite effects of stress on dendritic spine density in the male versus female hippocampus. *Journal of Neuroscience, 27*, 6292–6297.

Smith, M. A., Makino, S., Kvetnansky, R., & Post, R. M. (1995). Stress alters the expression of brain-derived neurotrophic factor and neurotrophin-3 mRNAs in the hippocampus. *Journal of Neuroscience, 15*, 1768–1777.

Sotres-Bayon, F., & Quirk, G. J. (2010). Prefrontal control of fear: more than just extinction. *Current Opinions in Neurobiology, 20*, 231–235.

Sousa, N., Almeida, O. F. X., Holsboer, F., Paula-Barbosa, M. M., & Madeira, M. D. (1998). Maintenance of hippocampal cell numbers in young and aged rats submitted to chronic unpredictable stress. Comparison with the effects of corticosterone treatment. *Stress, 2*, 237–250.

Sousa, N., Lukoyanov, N. V., Madeira, M. D., Almeida, O. F. X., & Paula-Barbosa, M. M. (2000). Reorganization of the morphology of hippocampal neurites and synapses after stress-induced damage correlates with behavioral improvement. *Neuroscience, 97*, 253–266.

Steele, R. J., & Morris, R. G. M. (1999). Delay-dependent impairment of a matching-to-place task with chronic and intrahippocampal infusion of the NMDA-antagonist D-AP5. *Hippocampus, 9*, 118–136.

Stewart, M. G., Davies, H. A., Sandi, C., Kraev, I. V., Rogachevsky, V. V., Peddie, C. J., Rodriguez, J. J., Cordero, M. I., Donohue, H. S., Gabbott, P. L. A., & Popov, V. I. (2005). Stress suppresses and learning induces plasticity in CA3 of rat hippocampus: a three-dimensional ultrastructural study of thorny excrescences and their postsynaptic densities. *Neuroscience, 131*, 43–54.

Sullivan, R. M. (2004). Hemispheric asymmetry in stress processing in rat prefrontal cortex and the role of mesocortical dopamine. *Stress, 7*, 131–143.

Sullivan, R. M., & Gratton, A. (1999). Lateralized effects of medial prefrontal cortex lesions on neuroendocrine and autonomic stress responses in rats. *Journal of Neuroscience, 19*, 2834–2840.

Sunanda, M. S., Rao, S., & Raju, T. R. (1995). Effect of chronic restraint stress on dendritic spines and excrescences of hippocampal CA3 pyramidal neurons–a quantitative study. *Brain Research, 694*, 312–317.

Swanson, L. W. (1981). A direct projection from Ammon's horn to prefrontal cortex in the rat. *Brain Research, 217*, 150–154.

Swanson, L. W., & Cowan, W. M. (1977). An autoradiographic study of the organization of the efferent connections of the hippocampal formation in the rat. *Journal of Comparative Neurology, 172*, 49–84.

Takahashi, T., Kimoto, T., Tanabe, N., Hattori, T., Yasumatsu, N., & Kawato, S. (2002). Corticosterone acutely prolonged N-methyl-D-aspartate receptor-mediated Ca2+

elevation in cultured rat hippocampal neurons. *Journal of Neurochemistry, 83,* 1441–1451.

Tejani-Butt, S. M., Paré, W. P., & Yang, J. (1994). Effect of repeated novel stressors on depressive behavior and brain norepinephrine receptor system in Sprague-Dawley and Wistar Kyoto (WKY) rats. *Brain Research, 649,* 27–35.

Uno, H., Tarara, R., Else, J. G., Suleman, M. A., & Sapolsky, R. M. (1989). Hippocampal damage associated with prolonged and fatal stress in primates. *Journal of Neuroscience, 9,* 1705–1711.

Ventura, J., Neuchterlein, K. H., Lukoff, D., & Hardesty, J. D. (1989). A prospective study of stressful life events and schizophrenic relapse. *Journal of Abnormal Psychology, 98,* 407–411.

Vermetten, E., & Bremner, J. D. (2002). Circuits and systems in stress. II. Applications to neurobiology and treatment in posttraumatic stress disorder. *Depression and Anxiety, 16,* 14–38.

Verwer, R. W., Van Vulpen, E. H., & Van Uum, J. F. (1996). Postnatal development of amygdaloid projections to the prefrontal cortex in the rat studied with retrograde and anterograde tracers. *Journal of Comparative Neurology, 376,* 75–96.

Vollmann-Honsdorf, G. K., Flügge, G., & Fuchs, E. (1997). Chronic psychosocial stress does not affect the number of pyramidal neurons in tree shrew hippocampus. *Neuroscience Letters, 233,* 121–124.

Vyas, A., Mitra, R., Shankaranarayana Rao, B. S., & Chattarji, S. (2002). Chronic stress induces contrasting patterns of dendritic remodeling in hippocampal and amygdaloid neurons. *Journal of Neuroscience, 22,* 6810–6818.

Vyas, A., Pillai, A. G., & Chattarji, S. (2004). Recovery after chronic stress fails to reverse amygdaloid neuronal hypertrophy and enhanced anxiety-like behavior. *Neuroscience, 128,* 667–673.

Vyas, A., Jadhav, S., & Chattarji, S. (2006). Prolonged behavioral stress enhances synaptic connectivity in the basolateral amygdala. *Neuroscience, 143,* 387–393.

Watanabe, Y., Gould, E., Cameron, H., Daniels, D. C., & McEwen, B. S. (1992a). Phenytoin prevents stress- and corticosterone-induced atrophy of CA3 pyramidal neurons. *Hippocampus, 2,* 431–436.

Watanabe, Y., Gould, E., Daniels, D. C., Cameron, H., & McEwen, B. S. (1992b). Tianeptine attenuates stress-induced morphological changes in the hippocampus. *European Journal of Pharmacology, 222,* 157–162.

Wellman, C. L. (2001). Dendritic reorganization in pyramidal neurons in medial prefrontal cortex after chronic corticosterone administration. *Journal of Neurobiology, 49,* 245–253.

Wilber, A. A., Walker, A. G., Southwood, C. J., Farrell, M. R., Lin, G. L., Rebec, G. V., & Wellman, C. L. (2011). Chronic stress alters neural activity in medial prefrontal cortex during retrieval of extinction. *Neuroscience, 174,* 115–131.

Wolf, C., Waksman, D., Finger, S., & Almli, C. R. (1987). Large and small medial frontal cortex lesions and spatial performance of the rat. *Brain Research Bulletin, 18,* 1–5.

Woolley, C., Gould, E., & McEwen, B. S. (1990). Exposure to excess glucocorticoids alters dendritic morphology of adult hippocampal pyramidal neurons. *Brain Research, 531,* 225–231.

Wright, R. L., Lightner, E. N., Harman, J. S., Meijer, O. C., & Conrad, C. D. (2006). Attenuating corticosterone levels on the day of memory assessment prevents chronic stress-induced impairments in spatial memory. *European Journal of Neuroscience, 24,* 595–605.

Xu L, Holscher, C., Anwyl, R., & Rowan, M. J. (1998). Glucocorticoid receptor and protein/ RNA synthesis-dependent mechanisms underlie the control of synaptic plasticity by stress. *Proceedings of the National Academy of Sciences USA, 95,* 3204–3208.

Yang, C.-H., Huang, C.-C., & Hsu, K.-S. (2004). Behavioral stress modifies hippocampal synaptic plasticity through corticosterone-induced sustained extracellular signal-regulated kinase/mitogen-activated protein kinase activation. *Journal of Neuroscience, 24,* 11029–11034.

Yehuda, R., & LeDoux, J. (2007). Response variation following trauma: a translational neuroscience approach to understanding PTSD. *Neuron, 56,* 19–32.

Zafar, H. M., Pare, W. P., & Tejani-Butt, S. M. (1997). Effect of acute or repeated stress on behavior and brain norepinephrine system in Wistar-Kyoto (WKY) rats. *Brain Research Bulletin, 44,* 289–295.

11

Effects of Chronic Stress on Memory and Neuroplasticity: Animal Studies

Carmen Sandi

Cognitive function can be profoundly affected by stress. In particular, stress has proved to be a major modulator of memory processes. Whereas moderate, acute stress experienced during learning can facilitate information storage, experiencing either excessive stress acutely or moderate to high stress chronically is generally regarded as highly detrimental to memory function (Sandi and Pinelo-Nava, 2007). Although the cognitive effects of chronic stress are considered detrimental, not all cognitive functions are impaired. Instead, the specific effect induced by chronic stress depends on the particular learning type. Moreover, not all individuals are equally affected in their cognitive capabilities when exposed to repeated stress. Individual factors such as gender, personality traits, and age are strongly related to the cognitive consequences of stress.

In this chapter, the main findings described on male rodents in the field of chronic stress during the past three decades will be summarized. Gender effects are critical (see Chapters 26 and 27 in this volume, which cover sex-related differences of stress actions on cognition). Because structural effects of chronic stress differ depending on the brain area analyzed and the reported differences match with divergent behavioral effects of stress on tasks depending on the respective brain regions, I organize the behavioral information by grouping effects on cognitive tasks according to the main brain area on which they rely. I refer to the modulatory role of individual differences and illustrate the factors related to different cognitive outcomes of stress and introduce the concept of vulnerability linked to different life span periods. Finally, I analyze some of the neurobiological mechanisms implicated in the cognitive impact of chronic stress by focusing on the synapse-enriched proteins in the cell membrane known as neuronal cell adhesion molecules.

The Handbook of Stress: Neuropsychological Effects on the Brain, First Edition.
Edited by Cheryl D. Conrad.
© 2011 Blackwell Publishing Ltd. Published 2011 by Blackwell Publishing Ltd.

However, before reviewing the effects of stress on memory function it is important to note that chronic stress can affect a number of noncognitive processes that can eventually affect performance in memory tasks. Chronic stress reduces exploratory activity (Wood et al., 2004), enhances anxiety-like (Vyas and Chattarji, 2004) and depression-like (Wilner, 2005) behaviors, and increases intermale aggression (Wood et al., 2003). Because performance in the different phases and processes involved in memory function (i.e., from acquisition to consolidation and retrieval of information) can hypothetically be modulated by these *emotional* effects of stress, it is important to keep this information in mind when interpreting data obtained in learning tasks. Therefore, a critical view will be incorporated when relevant in presenting stress effects on specific learning tasks by taking the potential contribution of these additional processes into account.

Hippocampus-related Learning Processes: Spatial Learning

Traditionally, research aimed at understanding the effects of stress on cognitive function has focused, to a large extent, on tests and tasks related to hippocampal function. This research was originally motivated by the early discovery that the stress hormones, glucocorticoids, bind with particularly high affinity in the hippocampus (McEwen et al., 1986). Subsequently, chronic stress was found to affect different features of hippocampal morphology, from the pioneering findings of dendritic atrophy in hippocampal CA3 pyramidal neurons (where CA means cornu ammonis; Watanabe et al., 1992; Magariños and McEwen, 1995) to a full range of structural alterations in all hippocampal subregions (McEwen, 2001; Joëls et al., 2004).

These findings stimulated intensive research investigating whether these structural alterations would be accompanied by deficits in behaviors dependent on the hippocampus. Because learning, memory, and spatial learning require intact hippocampal functioning (Eichenbaum et al., 1992), researchers expected to find impaired spatial learning following chronic stress. Initial evidence was reported by Luine et al. (1994) in which chronically restrained rats (6 hr/day for 21 days) tested in an eight-arm radial maze showed impairment during acquisition. The impairment was reversible and temporally limited, and paralleled by a reversible stress-induced atrophy of dendrites in hippocampal CA3 neurons. While these findings indicated impairment in hippocampus-dependent learning capabilities in parallel with stress-induced structural alterations, the test used to assess spatial learning had a food reward as the motivation to perform. Given that chronic stress can induce anhedonic (Willner, 2005) and anorexic (Solomon et al., 2010) effects, the specificity of the observed effects to the cognitive domain should be questioned to some extent.

Subsequent studies included motivation to learn the spatial environment in other types of animals. Conrad et al. (1996) exploited a rat's natural tendency to explore new environments using the Y maze. In this test, animals are initially allowed to explore two arms (start and other) of the maze for 15 min while one arm (novel) is blocked. Four hours later, rats are placed in the start arm and allowed to explore all arms for 5 min. The authors first performed lesion experiments to show that the natural tendency of control animals to explore the novel arm during the test session was dependent on hippocampal function. They next showed that chronic restraint stress impairs spatial memory performance on the Y maze when rats are tested the day after the last stress session and that the antidepressant tianeptine prevents stress-induced impairment of spatial memory. These findings provide important support for a functional/behavioral translation of the chronic stress-induced alterations in hippocampal structure. However, a note of caution should be added when interpreting these results due to the fact that chronic stress increases anxiety-like behavior in rodents (Pawlack et al., 2003) and memory in the Y maze is assessed by exploration of a novel arm that could be perceived as anxiogenic by stressed individuals. However, the anxiogenic component in this test is somehow mitigated by the narrow walls of the maze that allow rats to use thigmotaxic behavior (in fact, crossings or total entries to the different arms are classically similar between control and chronically stressed rats).

Other authors have used negative reinforcement to evaluate potential hippocampal-dependent learning and memory deficits following chronic stress exposure in rodents. For this purpose, the radial six-arm water maze is a valuable set-up because animals are motivated to escape from the water and find a hidden platform by following a well-structured maze that allows the assessment of errors in spatial orientation. Moreover, hippocampal lesions impair learning in this maze (Diamond et al., 1999). In a series of elegant experiments, Park et al. (2001) showed that rats exposed to a cat for 5 weeks (psychosocial stress) had impaired learning and memory, as well as impaired habituation to a novel environment and heightened anxiety. Other studies using a variety of stress protocols have shown impaired learning in the Morris water maze, in which animals have to find a hidden platform in a circular pool 1–2 m in diameter (Venero et al., 2002; Sandi et al., 2003; Song et al., 2006). However, it is important to mention that the effects on learning acquisition were frequently of small magnitude and only appeared sporadically in scattered trials over the training procedure. This result could be interpreted as a drawback to the view that stress-induced structural changes have functional consequences in behavioral terms. However, one should bear in mind that the morphological alterations described to this point (dendritic and spine retraction in CA3, reduced neurogenesis in the dentate gyrus, decreased synaptic density in CA1 and CA3; Sandi, 2004) are far from challenging the flow of information in hippocampal circuitry to the same extent as lesion approaches do. Therefore, the mild deficits observed in spatial learning in the water maze could, in fact, reflect the underlying neurobiological modifications found in the hippocampus after repeated exposure to stress.

An important factor for the impairing effect of chronic stress on spatial learning is the duration of the chronic-stress protocols. Whereas 3–6 weeks of chronic stress generally leads to the impairing effects described above, results from studies using shorter periods of stress exposure are less consistent. For example, Luine et al.

(1996), using the eight-arm radial maze and chronic restraint stress given for 13 instead of 21 days in Sprague–Dawley rats, found improved learning. Improved learning and memory in the Morris water maze was also found in Sprague–Dawley rats after exposure to chronic unpredictable stress for 10 days (Gouirand and Matuszewich, 2005). On the contrary, immobilization stress for 7 days in Long–Evans rats impairs subsequent performance in the Morris water maze that is associated with attenuated long-term potentiation in hippocampal slices (Radecki et al., 2005). Thus, in addition to the importance of stress duration and the type of stress-induction protocol, these studies raise the potential relevance of individual differences in the vulnerability to cognitive alterations following chronic stress. There is a section on the issue of individual differences later in this chapter.

Although these results support the view that the hippocampal-related structural alterations are partially responsible for the functional impairments observed after chronic stress, a few studies question this interpretation. Roozendaal et al. (2001) suggested that chronic stress produces spatial-memory deficits by inducing a dysregulation of the hypothalamic–pituitary–adrenal (HPA) axis instead of by altering hippocampal morphology. These authors presented evidence that attenuation of CA3-lesion-induced increases in circulating corticosterone levels using the synthesis inhibitor metyrapone administered shortly before a retention session in the water maze blocks the impairing effects of the lesion on memory retrieval. These findings suggested that elevated adrenocortical activity is critical in directly mediating memory-retrieval deficits induced by hippocampal damage. Consequently, Roozendaal (2002) hypothesized that chronic stress might gradually elevate baseline corticosterone levels, which would be a key factor in the observed chronic-stress-induced impairments to spatial memory. Wright et al. (2006) presented further evidence that spatial-memory deficits induced by chronic stress may be mediated by HPA axis dysregulation. More specifically, their findings suggested that corticosterone elevations and reductions in hippocampal glucocorticoid receptor expression at the time of behavioral assessment are involved in memory deficits. In any case, it is important to note that glucocorticoids have, in fact, been implicated in chronic-stress-induced alterations in hippocampal structure. Treatment of chronically stressed rats with the steroid synthesis blocker cyanoketone prevents stress-induced dendritic atrophy in CA3 (Magariños and McEwen, 1995).

Amygdala-related Learning: Fear Conditioning

Three weeks of chronic restraint stress did not impair contextual fear conditioning but in fact resulted in the opposite, facilitating, effect (Conrad et al., 1999; Sandi et al., 2001). This result was surprising because fear conditioning is known to be dependent on hippocampal function (Phillips and LeDoux, 1992; Kim and Fanselow, 1992). In this task, animals learn to fear a context (the conditioned stimulus) that is paired with aversive foot shocks (the unconditioned stimulus) and develop a conditioned freezing response when reexposed to the same context in the future in the absence of further aversive stimulation (Blanchard and Blanchard, 1969). Chronically stressed animals are not impaired in forming a memory for the context, but show increased freezing in the test session (Conrad et al., 1999; Sandi et al., 2001). Evidence excluding the possibility that stress-induced hippocampal alterations are involved in this enhancement of fear conditioning was provided by a series of elegant experiments showing that stress facilitation of fear conditioning is also observed in rats in which hippocampal atrophy is prevented with the antidepressant tianeptine (Conrad et al., 1999).

An alternative possibility is that hippocampal damage has no deleterious impact on the learning involved in contextual fear conditioning and that there are stress actions in other brain areas that participate in the improved learning reported in this task. It should be noted that cued fear conditioning consisting of the pairing of a tone (conditioned stimulus) with foot shocks (unconditioned stimulus) is hippocampus-independent, but both contextual and cued fear conditioning are impaired following amygdala lesions (Phillips and LeDoux, 1992; Kim and Fanselow, 1992). In addition to facilitating conditioning to context, chronic stress also facilitates freezing to cued fear conditioning (Conrad et al., 1999). These observations fit well with the view that the facilitation of amygdala function by chronic stress exposure might underlie stress effects in fear conditioning. They also fit with morphological observations indicating that stress induces synaptic remodeling and growth in dendritic branching in the basolateral and medial amygdala that are accompanied by increases in anxiety (Roozendaal et al., 2009). Strikingly, only those chronic stress protocols that lead to dendritic growth in the basolateral amygdala lead to higher anxiety-like behavior (Vyas et al., 2002; Vyas and Chattarji, 2004), raising the issue of the specificity of the stress-induced enhancement of fear conditioning to the cognitive domain. Indeed, increased anxiety in these animals might lead to enhanced emotional responsiveness to environmental stimuli that could overlap with enhanced fear learning. This interpretation is supported by enhanced freezing responses observed following shock delivery during the fear conditioning session in chronically stressed animals (Sandi et al., 2001; Cordero et al., 2003a; Bisaz and Sandi, 2010).

As indicated previously for hippocampal-related functions, glucocorticoids are involved in the effects of chronic stress in fear conditioning. Conrad et al. (2001) suggested that increased emotionality and enhanced fear conditioning exhibited by chronically stressed rats is due to endogenous corticosterone secretion at the time of fear-conditioned training. In fact, both fear responses (Corodimas et al., 1994) and amygdala activity (Thompson et al., 2004) are potentiated by corticosterone. A single exposure to restraint stress enhances contextual fear conditioning 2 days after stress in an experimental set-up in which stressed animals display higher posttraining corticosterone levels (Cordero et al., 2003b). Although these studies suggest that glucocorticoids participate in the facilitation of fear conditioning by stress, they do not discard the involvement of the described structural changes in the amygdala (spinogenesis, dendritic hypertrophy). Both a single stress session and elevated glucocorticoid levels can result in dendritic hypertrophy in the basolateral amygdala and heightened anxiety, as measured on an elevated-plus maze (Mitra and Sapolsky, 2008), even if the structural changes induced by chronic stress are more robust (for a review see Roozendaal et al., 2009).

Learning Tasks Related to Prefrontal Cortical Function

The prefrontal cortex (PFC) comprises areas in the anterior part of the frontal lobes that play key roles in the processing and regulation of emotional stimuli and responses, in the control of behaviors and actions, and in the organization of complex cognitive operations (Robbins and Arnstern, 2009). More specifically, the PFC orchestrates a series of higher-order *executive functions* that coordinate attention and information processing leading to the planning and control of behavior under both stable and changing conditions. Working memory is a typical function of the PFC. Deficits in PFC function associated with alterations in executive functions underlie different psychopathological conditions (Holmes and Wellman, 2009).

The PFC is particularly sensitive to the effects of stress. Increasing evidence indicates that the PFC experiences marked morphological changes (diminished spine density and spine loss) after stress exposure earlier than the hippocampus in association with deficits in behaviors related to PFC function (Holmes and Wellman, 2009; Arnsten, 2009). In fact, the sensitivity of PFC to stress, in terms of both structural and behavioral outcomes, is evident even after acute intense stress. At the cognitive level, chronic stress impairs behaviors that require cognitive operations related to PFC function such as attentional set-shifting in rats, working memory, and cognitive flexibility, as well as emotional dysregulation in the form of impaired fear extinction. Thus, attentional shifting is impaired by chronic stress (Liston et al., 2006). After 21 days of repeated restraint stress, rats were tested on a perceptual attentional set-shifting task that yields dissociable measures of reversal learning and attentional set-shifting, functions that are mediated by the orbitofrontal cortex and the medial PFC (mPFC), respectively. Chronic stress induced a selective impairment in attentional set-shifting with a corresponding retraction (20%) of apical dendritic arbors in the mPFC. In stressed rats, but not in control rats, decreased dendritic arborization in the mPFC predicted impaired attentional set-shifting performance. In contrast, stress did not adversely affect reversal learning or dendritic morphology in the lateral orbitofrontal cortex. Instead, apical dendritic arborization in the orbitofrontal cortex was increased by 43%. This study provided the first evidence that dendritic remodeling in the PFC may underlie the functional deficits in attentional control that are symptomatic of stress-related mental illnesses. A similar finding was subsequently reported in humans exposed to 1 month of psychosocial stress (Liston et al., 2009).

Working memory is also impaired by chronic stress. Pioneer work was performed in a spatial delayed alternation task in a T maze. This task requires working memory as well as behavioral inhibition and the ability to overcome distraction, and requires an intact mPFC function in rats (Dalley et al., 2004). Mizoguchi et al. (2000) showed that rats submitted to chronic stress (water immersion and restraint) for 4 weeks and allowed to recover during 10 days presented a working memory impairment caused by reduced dopamine transmission, and mediated by the D1 receptor, in the PFC. Hains et al. (2009) also tested chronically stressed rats (21 days of restraint stress) in a similar task in the T maze, but animals had been previously trained before stress exposure. Exposure to stress induced a marked and progressive loss of delayed alternation performance that increased with stress exposure. Importantly, impaired performance of working memory was associated with an increase in perseveration, which was indexed by consecutive errors within the same session. Perseveration is induced by PFC dysfunction (Collins et al., 1998). Importantly, chronic stress did not affect a spatial discrimination task in the same T maze (Hains et al., 2009), which does not require an intact PFC. In the same study, a correlation was found between apical dendritic spine density in layer II–III pyramidal neurons and cognitive performance toward the end of the repeated stress procedure.

Using the Morris water maze, Cerqueira et al. (2007) found that 4 weeks of chronic unpredictable stress impaired working memory (the requirement for this task was to learn a new platform position each day, and performance is checked in a series of four consecutive trials; the cognitive challenge is to keep the newly acquired information online within each training session) and behavioral flexibility in the reversal learning task (after prior learning in the reference memory task and acquisition of a stable learning for a given platform location, the requirement for the reversal learning task was to learn a new platform location, when the platform had been moved to the opposite quadrant; the cognitive challenge is to simultaneously inhibit a previously acquired spatial navigation strategy and to develop a new strategy). Behavioral flexibility is related to the ability to adapt behavior to changes in environmental conditions. Chronic administration of corticosterone impairs reversal learning in this task, without affecting working memory (Cerqueira et al., 2005). Interestingly, Cerqueira et al. (2007) also showed that the experimental conditions leading to this behavioral alteration were accompanied by impaired synaptic plasticity (i.e., reduced induction of long-term potentiation) in the hippocampal–PFC connection and morphological atrophy in the PFC (more precisely, a selective reduction in the volume of the upper prefrontal layers, I and II). However, it should be noted that some studies did not find alterations in working-memory function (hippocampal-independent maze navigation with a 1-min delay in the Y maze) after repeated restraint stress (Kleen et al., 2006). A possible explanation for this discrepancy could be that instead of dealing with working-memory processes (that require maintaining the information online during a certain period), the latter study relied upon the assumption that animals will spontaneously explore novel environments. Cognitive processes other than working memory (e.g., recognition memory, familiarity, or novelty detection) are probably implicated in performance on this task.

Extinction of fear conditioning consists of repeatedly presenting a tone-conditioned stimulus previously paired with a foot shock in the absence of foot shock, causing fear responses to diminish. Strong evidence has implicated the mPFC in memory circuits for fear extinction (Quirk and Mueller, 2008). Chronic stress studies showed that 1 week (Miracle et al., 2006) and 3 weeks (Baran et al., 2009) of stress impaired recall of extinction training.

Interestingly, the emerging view is that exposure to high stress levels might impair performance of tasks that require complex, flexible reasoning while improving performance of simpler and/or well-rehearsed tasks. This would fit with the impairments observed in cognitive tasks that rely on PFC operations and with simultaneous sparing or enhancement of habits that rely on basal ganglia circuits (Arnsten, 2009; Luksys et al., 2009). A recent study in rats has provided behavioral and morphological evidence in support of the view that chronic stress biases decision-making strategies, affecting the ability of stressed animals to perform actions on the basis of their consequences. Dias-Ferreira et al. (2009) investigated decision-making in chronically stressed rats. They were interested in exploring whether stress would affect the selection of the appropriate actions on the basis of their consequences and decision-making under changing situations. Using two different operant tasks they showed that, in making choices, rats subjected to chronic stress became insensitive to changes in outcome value and resistant to changes in action-outcome contingency. The insensitivity to changes in outcome value were observed after devaluating the outcome provided in initial training: while control animals became highly sensitive to sensory-specific satiety, diminishing their responses, stressed rats were insensitive to the expected value of the outcome, as indicated by a lack of a devaluation effect. The resistance to changes in action-outcome contingency was detected by training animals in a task involving two actions (i.e., pressing either the left or the right lever), each leading to a particular outcome (i.e., either pellets or sucrose). Once the task was acquired, the contingency between one of the actions and the respective outcome was degraded (i.e., to get that particular outcome, the animals no longer needed to press the lever), a procedure that in control animals led to a specific reduction in their responses on the degraded lever. Interestingly, stressed animals pressed both levers similarly, which suggests that they failed to choose the action that was necessary to obtain the outcome and that their behavior was habitual. Simultaneously, this study showed that chronic stress caused opposing structural changes in the associative and sensorimotor corticostriatal circuits underlying these different behavioral strategies with atrophy of mPFC and the associative striatum and hypertrophy of the sensorimotor striatum. The authors suggested that the relative advantage of circuits coursing through sensorimotor striatum observed after chronic stress leads to a bias in behavioral strategies toward habit. These results are consistent with a recent study performed in mice and humans in parallel, showing that chronic stress shifts cognitive performance toward more rigid stimulus-response learning (Schwabe et al., 2008). In this study, mice that had been repeatedly exposed to rats (*rat stress*) used a stimulus-response strategy in a circular hole-board task significantly more often than did control mice (33 compared with 0%, respectively). Similarly, humans who had experienced high levels of chronic stress before being tested used a stimulus-response strategy more often (94%) than participants in a group with low chronic stress (52%). Interestingly, glucocorticoids promoted the transition from spatial to stimulus-response memory systems (Schwabe et al., 2010).

Individual Differences

Although the topic of individual differences in the cognitive outcome of chronic stress has not been systematically addressed, evidence from the animal and human literature indicates the existence of considerable variability in the vulnerability of individuals to display cognitive changes when exposed to stress. Whereas some individuals are particularly _vulnerable_, others are quite _resistant_ to the effects of stress. These differences could be due to predisposing factors, previous life experiences or, more likely, both.

In the case of chronic stress, the most typical examples are given by studies in which responses from different mouse strains are compared (Pothion et al., 2004; Palumbo et al., 2009). For example, chronic mild stress was shown to impair learning in the passive avoidance task in BALB/c mice, but not C57Bl/6 mice, suggesting that BALB/c mice are more vulnerable to stress than C57BL/6 mice (Palumbo et al., 2009). Because BALB/c mice display considerably more anxiety-like behaviors than C57Bl/6 mice, indicative of a personality-like bias toward anxiety trait, this finding supports the possibility that anxiety plays a key role in the cognitive impact of chronic stress (Sandi and Richter-Levin, 2009). Importantly, attention toward salient stressful stimuli in mice is associated with their susceptibility to chronic stress (Ducottet et al., 2004) and mouse strains high in anxiety traits are more prone to develop depression-like behaviors than less anxious strains when submitted to a subchronic stress procedure (Ducottet and Belzung, 2005). In this connection, genetic variation in molecules involved in the regulation of pathways involved in anxiety have been hypothesized to have a major influence on individual differences in the stress response and risk for stress-related disease (Holmes, 2008).

Using the outbred rat strain Sprague–Dawley, animals with a high anxiety trait were found to show a particular vulnerability to altered amygdala responsiveness to corticotropin-releasing factor after exposure to chronic unpredictable stress (Sandi et al., 2008). An interesting study showed that peripubertal anxiety levels can be predictive of the detrimental effects of chronic stress on hippocampal-dependent spatial memory (Bellani et al., 2006). In fact, the high anxiety trait has been highlighted as a risk factor for the development of stress-related neuropsychiatric disorders, such as depression in humans (Sandi and Richter-Levin, 2009).

In addition to the anxiety trait, animal studies have also highlighted the behavioral trait of novelty reactivity as a vulnerability factor for the development of stress-related cognitive alterations. In rats, this behavioral trait of novelty reactivity resembles some of the features of high-sensation seekers in humans. The first evidence that this trait could be related to stress vulnerability was provided by a life span study in rats. Dellu et al. (1996) classified young adult rats as either high or low responders to novelty, according to the locomotor activity displayed in a novel environment, and found that corticosterone secretion was higher and showed a quicker increase with age in the high responders. Subsequent studies showed that after exposure to psychosocial stress for 3 weeks in adulthood high, but not low, responders displayed a marked deficit in spatial learning in the water maze (Touyarot et al., 2004), supporting the view that the novelty reactivity trait is related to susceptibility to display stress-induced impairments in hippocampus-dependent learning tasks. Interestingly, this susceptibility is linked to the development of cognitive deficits during early aging. In a study in which high- and low-reactive animals were exposed to chronic stress at midlife (12 months old) and tested in the Morris water maze during early aging (18 months old), impaired performance was observed in stressed high-reactive rats compared with unstressed high- and low-reactive rats (Sandi and Touyarot, 2006).

Other factors that can account for individual differences on the cognitive impact of chronic stress are social factors (Bartolomucci et al., 2005), gender (Shors, 2004; Luine et al., 2007; McLaughlin et al., 2009; Baran et al., 2009), and age (Bodnoff et al., 1995; Fenoglio et al., 2006; Luine et al., 2007).

Latent Vulnerability to Stress across the Life span

Variability in the degree of cognitive decline in later life is a central aspect of aging and increasing evidence supports the view that chronic stress experienced at specific periods during the life span can contribute to age-related cognitive decline (McEwen, 2002).

Early life experiences are known to exert profound influences in stress reactivity in adulthood and cognitive aging (Meaney et al., 1988; Heim and Nemeroff, 1999). Pioneering work by the group of Tallie Baram has shown in rodents that chronic stress experienced during the early postnatal period has an impact on cognitive function (spatial learning and novel object recognition) when evaluated in middle age, but not in young adulthood (Brunson et al., 2005), suggesting that the impact of early stress can remain latent until the individual undergoes a life period of vulnerability. Adolescence has also been highlighted as a period when stress can lead to latent vulnerability, as indicated by a study in male mice that were exposed to chronic social stress during adolescence. When these mice were tested 12 months after the end of the stress period they showed impaired spatial learning along with a concomitant impairment in induction of long-term potentiation in CA1 neurons (Stelermann et al., 2009).

As mentioned previously, midlife can also be a period of latent vulnerability in certain individuals. When high- and low-reactive rats were exposed to chronic stress at midlife (12 months old) and tested for their spatial learning abilities in the water maze during the early senescence period (18 months old), highly reactive rats showed impaired learning (Sandi and Touyarot, 2006). That midlife was a period of particular sensitivity to the effects of stress had been originally suggested by a study in which a chronic corticosterone treatment for 3 months was given to either young adult or middle-aged rats (Bodnoff et al., 1995). When tested in the Morris water maze 2 weeks after the termination of the treatment, no effect was observed in young rats but middle-aged rats showed a clear learning impairment. The authors then examined the effect of social stress for 6 months in middle-aged rats and found that this treatment also resulted in significant spatial learning impairments in the water maze. These effects were absent in socially stressed animals that had been previously adrenalectomized and supplemented with low-level corticosterone levels, suggesting that elevated glucocorticoid levels mediate the effects of stress on spatial memory in older animals.

Stress Effects on Neuroplasticity Mediating the Behavioral Effects: a Focus on the Neural Cell Adhesion Molecule

As indicated above and in other chapters of this book, chronic stress produces profound changes in neuronal morphology in different brain areas. There is a great interest in identifying key molecular players whereby stress alters neuronal circuitry and associated behavioral changes. A large number of molecules have been identified as critical targets of stress, including various neurotransmitters, signal transduction pathways, neurotrophic factors, and epigenetic modulators (McEwen, 2001; Castrén et al., 2007; Surget et al., 2008; Krishnan and Nestler, 2008). However, a critical issue is to establish whether there is a direct link between the molecular changes associated with the neuronal remodeling and the behavioral alterations observed after chronic stress.

One of the molecules that has been particularly investigated in this connection is the neural cell adhesion molecule (NCAM), because early work showed that chronic stress diminishes hippocampal NCAM expression (Sandi et al., 2001; Sandi and Touyarot, 2006; Venero et al., 2002). NCAM is an abundant cell adhesion macromolecule that participates in cell–cell homophilic and heterophilic binding as well as in activity-dependent synaptic rearrangements (Sandi, 2004). Manipulations interfering with NCAM function lead to learning and memory deficits in a variety of cognitive tasks (Conboy et al., 2010). NCAM also acts in neuronal remodeling and can simultaneously interact with cytoskeletal elements, neurotrophic signals, and intracellular signaling cascades. Because all of these cellular processes have been implicated in the deleterious effects of stress in the brain (McEwen, 2002; Kuipers et al., 2003; Duman and Monteggia, 2006) and NCAM is reduced after chronic stress, it was hypothesized that NCAM might play a key role in stress-induced behavioral alterations (Sandi, 2004; Sandi and Bisaz, 2007).

Recent studies have addressed this question using conditional NCAM-deficient mice in which NCAM is ablated under the control of the α-calcium/calmodulin-dependent protein kinase II (αCaMKII) promoter in hippocampal neurons postnatally (Bukalo et al., 2004). Bisaz et al. (2011) first validated that the effects of chronic stress described in rats are generalized to mice and described that, indeed, there is less hippocampal NCAM in C57BL/6 wild-type mice exposed to chronic unpredictable stress and deficits in their learning and reversal learning abilities in the water maze. These authors then showed that, in adulthood, forebrain-specific conditional NCAM-deficient mice (NCAM-floxed mice that express the Cre recombinase under the control of the promoter of the α subunit of CaMKII) show a marked reduction of NCAM in the hippocampus and PFC and display poor performance in the water maze that was comparable to that of stressed wild-type mice. These deficits could not be attributed to increased anxiety, which was less pronounced in these mice when compared to their wild-type littermates, or to altered hormonal stress responses as their corticosterone levels were comparable to those of wild-type mice. Interestingly, the performance of both NCAM-deficient and wild-type chronically stressed mice in the water maze improved after posttraining injections of the NCAM mimetic peptide termed fibroblast growth loop (FGL; that mimics NCAM activation of the fibroblast growth factor receptor). These findings have provided strong support for a key role of NCAM in the stress-induced deficits in cognitive performance.

Interestingly, the opposite pattern of NCAM regulation (i.e., an increase as opposed to the decrease found in the hippocampus) by chronic stress was found in the amygdala (Bisaz and Sandi, 2010), which fits with the opposite morphological changes in dendritic processes described for the effects of chronic stress in the hippocampus (i.e., structural atrophy) and the amygdala (i.e., dendritic hypertrophy). In an attempt to evaluate whether these changes in NCAM expression in the amygdala are related to stress-induced enhancement of auditory fear conditioning and anxiety-like behavior, the forebrain-specific conditional NCAM-deficient mice, in which amygdala NCAM expression levels were reduced, were tested (Bisaz and Sandi, 2010). These mice displayed impaired auditory fear conditioning that was not altered following chronic stress exposure. Likewise, these results have highlighted increased NCAM expression in the amygdala among the mechanisms whereby stress facilitates fear-conditioning processes.

Conclusions

I have summarized a growing field of research that shows how cognitive operations that rely on the functioning of specific brain areas are affected by chronic stress exposure and clearly illustrated that repeated stress does not always lead to cognitive deficits (as is typical for hippocampus- and PFC-related functions) but typically potentiate amygdala-related fear-conditioning processes. I have also indicated a number of factors that define a differential vulnerability to cognitive alterations following prolonged stress exposure and introduced the concept of latent vulnerability when stress is experienced at specific periods over the life span. Finally, I have summarized work identifying molecular targets of stress, linking its neural and behavioral alterations, highlighting NCAMs as key molecules in the translation of stress effects on behavioral changes, and showing that drugs targeting these molecules can prevent some cognitive deficits. In my view these studies open new avenues for the development of potential treatments for stress-induced psychopathological alterations associated with cognitive disturbances.

References

Arnsten, A. F. T. (2009). Stress signaling pathways that impair prefrontal cortex structure and function. *Nature Reviews Neuroscience, 10,* 410–422.

Baran, S. E., Armstrong, C. E., Niren, D. C., Hanna, J. J., & Conrad, C. D. (2009). Chronic stress and sex differences on the recall of fear conditioning and extinction. *Neurobiology of Learning and Memory, 91,* 323–332.

Bartolomucci, A., Palanza, P., Sacerdote, P., Panerai, A. E., Sgoifo, A., Dantzer, R., & Parmigiani, S. (2005). Social factors and individual vulnerability to chronic stress exposure. *Neuroscience and Biobehavioral Reviews, 29,* 67–81.

Bellani, R., Luecken, L. J., & Conrad, C. D. (2006). Peripubertal anxiety profile can predict predisposition to spatial memory impairments following chronic stress. *Behavioral Brain Research, 166,* 263–270.

Bisaz, R., & Sandi, C. (2010). The role of NCAM in auditory fear conditioning and its modulation by stress: a focus on the amygdala. *Genes, Brain, and Behavior, 9,* 353–364.

Bisaz, R., Schachner, M., & Sandi, C. (2011). Causal evidence for the involvement of the neural cell adhesion molecule, NCAM, in chronic stress-induced cognitive impairments. *Hippocampus, 21,* 56–71.

Blanchard, R. J., & Blanchard, D. C. (1969). Crouching as an index of fear. *Journal of Comparative and Physiological Psychology, 67,* 370–375.

Bodnoff, S. R., Humphreys, A. G., Lehman, J. C., Diamond, D. M., Rose, G. M., & Meaney M.J. (1995). Enduring effects of chronic corticosterone treatment on spatial learning, synaptic plasticity, and hippocampal neuropathology in young and mid-aged rats. *Journal of Neuroscience, 15,* 61–69.

Bukalo, O., Fentrop, N., Lee, A. Y., Salmen, B., Law, J. W., Wotjak, C. T., Schweizer, M., Dityatev, A., & Schachner, M. (2004). Conditional ablation of the neural cell adhesion molecule reduces precision of spatial learning, long-term potentiation, and depression in the CA1 subfield of mouse hippocampus. *Journal of Neuroscience, 24,* 1565–1577.

Castrén, E., Võikar, V., & Rantamäki, T. (2007). Role of neurotrophic factors in depression. *Current Opinions in Pharmacology, 7,* 18–21.

Cerqueira, J. J., Pêgo, J. M., Taipa, R., Bessa, J. M., Almeida, O. F., & Sousa, N. (2005). Morphological correlates of corticosteroid-induced changes in prefrontal cortex-dependent behaviors. *Journal of Neuroscience, 25,* 7792–7800.

Cerqueira, J. J., Mailliet, F., Almeida, O. F., Jay, T. M., & Sousa, N. (2007). The prefrontal cortex as a key target of the maladaptive response to stress. *Journal of Neuroscience, 27,* 2781–2787.

Collins, P., Roberts, A. C., Dias, R., Everitt, B. J., & Robbins, T. W. (1998). Perseveration and strategy in a novel spatial self-ordered sequencing task for nonhuman primates: effects of excitotoxic lesions and dopamine depletions of the prefrontal cortex. *Journal of Cognitive Neuroscience, 10,* 332–354.

Conboy, L., Bisaz, R., Markram, K., & Sandi, C. (2010). Role of NCAM in emotion and learning. *Advances in Experimental Medicine and Biology, 663,* 271–296.

Conrad, C. D., Galea, L. A., Kuroda, Y., & McEwen, B. S. (1996). Chronic stress impairs rat spatial memory on the Y maze, and this effect is blocked by tianeptine pretreatment. *Behavioral Neuroscience, 110*, 1321–1334.

Conrad, C. D., LeDoux, J. E., Magariños A. M., & McEwen, B. S. (1999). Repeated restraint stress facilitates fear conditioning independently of causing hippocampal CA3 dendritic atrophy. *Behavioral Neuroscience, 113*, 902–913.

Conrad, C. D., Mauldin-Jourdain, M. L., & Hobbs, R. J. (2001). Metyrapone reveals that previous chronic stress differentially impairs hippocampal-dependent memory. *Stress, 4*, 305–318.

Cordero, M. I., Kruyt, N. D., & Sandi, C. (2003a). Modulation of contextual fear conditioning by chronic stress in rats is related to individual differences in behavioral reactivity to novelty. *Brain Research, 970*, 242–245.

Cordero, M. I., Venero, C., Kruyt, N. D., & Sandi, C. (2003b). Prior exposure to a single stress session facilitates subsequent contextual fear conditioning in rats. Evidence for a role of corticosterone. *Hormones and Behavior, 44*, 338–345.

Corodimas, K. P., LeDoux, J. E., Gold, P. W., & Schulkin, J. (1994). Corticosterone potentiation of conditioned fear in rats. *Annals of the New York Academy of Sciences, 746*, 392–393.

Dalley, J. W., Cardinal, R. N., & Robbins T.W. (2004). Prefrontal executive and cognitive functions in rodents: neural and neurochemical substrates. *Neuroscience and Biobehavioral Reviews, 28*, 771–784.

Dellu, F., Mayo, W., Vallée, M., Maccari, S., Piazza, P. V., Le Moal, M., & Simon, H. (1996). Behavioral reactivity to novelty during youth as a predictive factor of stress-induced corticosterone secretion in the elderly–a life-span study in rats. *Psychoneuroendocrinology, 21*, 441–453.

Diamond, D. M., Park, C. R., Heman, K. L., & Rose, G. M. (1999). Exposing rats to a predator impairs spatial working memory in the radial arm water maze. *Hippocampus, 9*, 542–552.

Dias-Ferreira, E., Sousa, J. C., Melo, I., Morgado, P., Mesquita, A. R., Cerqueira, J. J., Costa, R. M., & Sousa, N. (2009). Chronic stress causes frontostriatal reorganization and affects decision-making. *Science, 325*, 621–625.

Ducottet, C., & Belzung, C. (2005). Correlations between behaviours in the elevated plus-maze and sensitivity to unpredictable subchronic mild stress: evidence from inbred strains of mice. *Behavioral Brain Research, 156*, 153–162.

Ducottet, C., Aubert, A., & Belzung, C. (2004). Susceptibility to subchronic unpredictable stress is related to individual reactivity to threat stimuli in mice. *Behavioral Brain Research, 155*, 291–299.

Duman, R. S., & Monteggia, L. M. (2006). A neurotrophic model for stress-related mood disorders. *Biological Psychiatry, 59*, 1116–1127.

Eichenbaum, H., Otto, T., Cohen, N. J. (1992). The hippocampus—what does it do? *Behavioral and Neural Biology, 57*, 2–36.

Fenoglio, K. A., Brunson, K. L., & Baram, T. Z. (2006). Hippocampal neuroplasticity induced by early-life stress: functional and molecular aspects. *Frontiers in Neuroendocrinology, 27*, 180–192.

Gouirand, A. M., & Matuszewich, L. (2005). The effects of chronic unpredictable stress on male rats in the water maze. *Physiology & Behavior, 86*, 21–31.

Hains, A. B., Vu, M. A., Maciejewski, P.K., van Dyck, C. H., Gottron, M., & Arnsten, A. F. (2009). Inhibition of protein kinase C signaling protects prefrontal cortex dendritic spines and cognition from the effects of chronic stress. *Proceedings of the National Academy of Sciences USA, 106,* 17957–17962.

Heim, C., & Nemeroff, C. B. (1999). The impact of early adverse experiences on brain systems involved in the pathophysiology of anxiety and affective disorders. *Biological Psychiatry, 46,* 1509–1522.

Holmes, A. (2008). Genetic variation in cortico-amygdala serotonin function and risk for stress-related disease. *Neuroscience and Biobehavioral Reviews, 32,* 1293–1314.

Holmes, A., & Wellman, C. L. (2009). Stress-induced prefrontal reorganization and executive dysfunction in rodents. *Neuroscience and Biobehavioral Reviews, 33,* 773–783.

Joëls, M., Karst, H., Alfarez, D., Heine, V. M., Qin, Y., van Riel, E., Verkuyl, M., Lucassen, P. J., & Krugers, H. J. (2004). Effects of chronic stress on structure and cell function in rat hippocampus and hypothalamus. *Stress, 7,* 221–231.

Kim, J. J., & Fanselow, M. S. (1992). Modality-specific retrograde amnesia of fear. *Science, 256,* 675–677.

Kleen, J. K., Sitomer, M. T., Killeen, P. R., & Conrad, C. D. (2006). Chronic stress impairs spatial memory and motivation for reward without disrupting motor ability and motivation to explore. *Behavioral Neuroscience, 120,* 842–851.

Krishnan, V., & Nestler, E. J. (2008). The molecular neurobiology of depression. *Nature, 455,* 894–902.

Kuipers, S. D., Trentani, A., Den Boer, J. A., & Ter Horst, G. J. (2003). Molecular correlates of impaired prefrontal plasticity in response to chronic stress. *Journal of Neurochemistry, 85,* 1312–1323.

Liston, C., Miller, M. M., Goldwater, D. S., Radley, J.J., Rocher, A. B., Hof, P. R., Morrison, J. H., & McEwen, B. S. (2006). Stress-induced alterations in prefrontal cortical dendritic morphology predict selective impairments in perceptual attentional set-shifting. *Journal of Neuroscience, 26,* 7870–7874.

Liston, C., McEwen, B. S., & Casey, B. J. (2009). Psychosocial stress reversibly disrupts prefrontal processing and attentional control. *Proceedings of the National Academy of Sciences USA, 106,* 912–917.

Luine, V., Villegas, M., Martinez, C., & McEwen, B. S. (1994). Repeated stress causes reversible impairments of spatial memory performance. *Brain Research, 639,* 167–170.

Luine, V., Martinez, C., Villegas, M., Magariños, A. M., & McEwen, B. S. (1996). Restraint stress reversibly enhances spatial memory performance. *Physiology & Behavior, 59,* 27–32.

Luine, V. N., Beck, K. D., Bowman, R. E., Frankfurt, M., & Maclusky, N. J. (2007). Chronic stress and neural function: accounting for sex and age. *Journal of Neuroendocrinology, 19,* 743–751.

Luksys, G., Gerstner, W., & Sandi, C. (2009). Stress, genotype and norepinephrine in the prediction of mouse behavior using reinforcement learning. *Nature Neuroscience, 12,* 1180–1186.

Magariños, A. M., & McEwen, B. S. (1995). Stress-induced atrophy of apical dendrites of hippocampal CA3c neurons: involvement of glucocorticoid secretion and excitatory amino acid receptors. *Neuroscience, 69,* 89–98.

McEwen, B. S. (2001). Plasticity of the hippocampus: adaptation to chronic stress and allostatic load. *Annals of the New York Academy of Sciences, 933,* 265–277.

McEwen, B. S. (2002). Sex, stress and the hippocampus: allostasis, allostatic load and the aging process. *Neurobiology of Aging, 23,* 921–939.

McEwen, B. S., De Kloet, E. R., & Rostene, W. (1986). Adrenal steroid receptors and actions in the nervous system. *Physiological Review*, 66, 1121–1188.

McLaughlin, K. J., Baran, S. E., & Conrad, C. D. (2009). Chronic stress- and sex-specific neuromorphological and functional changes in limbic structures. *Molecular Neurobiology*, 40, 166–182.

Meaney, M. J., Aitken, D., Berkel, H., Bhatnager, S., & Sapolsky, R. M. (1988). Effect of neo-natal handling on age-related impairments associated with the hippocampus. *Science*, 239, 766–768.

Miracle, A. D., Brace, M. F., Huyck, K. D., Singler, S. A., & Wellman, C. L. (2006). Chronic stress impairs recall of extinction of conditioned fear. *Neurobiology of Learning and Memory*, 85, 213–218.

Mitra, R., & Sapolsky, R. M. (2008). Acute corticosterone treatment is sufficient to induce anxiety and amygdaloid dendritic hypertrophy. *Proceedings of the National Academy of Sciences USA*, 105, 5573–5578.

Mizoguchi, K., Yuzurihara, M., Ishige, A., Sasaki, H., Chui, D. H., & Tabira, T. (2000). Chronic stress induces impairment of spatial working memory because of prefrontal dopamin-ergic dysfunction. *Journal of Neuroscience*, 20, 1568–1574.

Palumbo, M. L., Zorrilla Zubilete, M. A., Cremaschi, G. A., & Genaro, A. M. (2009). Different effect of chronic stress on learning and memory in BALB/c and C57BL/6 inbred mice: Involvement of hippocampal NO production and PKC activity. *Stress*, 12, 350–361.

Park, C. R., Campbell, A. M., & Diamond, D. M. (2001). Chronic psychosocial stress impairs learning and memory and increases sensitivity to yohimbine in adult rats. *Biological Psychiatry*, 50, 994–1004.

Pawlak, R., Magariños, A. M., Melchor, J., McEwen, B., & Strickland, S. (2003). Tissue plas-minogen activator in the amygdala is critical for stress-induced anxiety-like behavior. *Nature Neuroscience*, 6, 168–174.

Phillips, R. G., & LeDoux, J. E. (1992). Differential contribution of amygdala and hippoc-ampus to cued and contextual fear conditioning. *Behavioral Neuroscience*, 106, 274–285.

Pothion, S., Bizot, J. C., Trovero, F., & Belzung, C. (2004). Strain differences in sucrose prefer-ence and in the consequences of unpredictable chronic mild stress. *Behavioral Brain Research*, 155, 135–146.

Quirk, G. J., & Mueller, D. (2008). Neural mechanisms of extinction learning and retrieval. *Neuropsychopharmacology*, 33, 56–72.

Radecki, D. T., Brown, L. M., Martinez, J., & Teyler, T. J. (2005). BDNF protects against stress-induced impairments in spatial learning and memory and LTP. *Hippocampus*, 15, 246–253.

Robbins, T. W., & Arnsten, A. F. (2009). The neuropsychopharmacology of fronto-executive function: monoaminergic modulation. *Annual Review of Neuroscience*, 32, 267–287.

Roozendaal, B. (2002). Stress and memory: opposing effects of glucocorticoids on memory consolidation and memory retrieval. *Neurobiology of Learning and Memory*, 78, 578–595.

Roozendaal, B., McEwen, B. S., & Chattarji, S. (2009). Stress, memory and the amygdala. *Nature Reviews Neuroscience*, 10, 423–433.

Roozendaal, B., Phillips, R. G., Power, A. E., Brooke, S. M., Sapolsky, R. M., & McGaugh, J. L. (2001). Memory retrieval impairment induced by hippocampal CA3 lesions is blocked by adrenocortical suppression. *Nature Neuroscience*, 4, 1169–1171.

Sandi, C. (2004). Stress, cognitive impairment and cell adhesion molecules. *Nature Reviews Neuroscience, 5*, 917–930.

Sandi, C., & Touyarot, K. (2006). Mid-life stress and cognitive deficits during early aging in rats: individual differences and hippocampal correlates. *Neurobiology of Aging, 27*, 128–140.

Sandi, C., & Bisaz, R. (2007). A model for the involvement of neural cell adhesion molecules in stress-related mood disorders. *Neuroendocrinology, 85*, 158–176.

Sandi, C., & Pinelo-Nava, M. T. (2007). Stress and memory: behavioral effects and neuro-biological mechanisms. *Neural Plasticity, 78970.*

Sandi, C., & Richter-Levin. G. (2009). From high anxiety trait to depression: a neurocognitive hypothesis. *Trends in Neuroscience, 32*, 312–320.

Sandi, C., Merino, J. J., Cordero, M. I., Touyarot, K., & Venero, C. (2001). Effects of chronic stress on contextual fear conditioning and the hippocampal expression of the neural cell adhesion molecule, its polysialylation, and L1. *Neuroscience, 102*, 329–339.

Sandi, C., Davies, H. A., Cordero, M. I., Rodriguez, J. J., Popov, V. I., & Stewart, M. G. (2003). Rapid reversal of stress induced loss of synapses in CA3 of rat hippocampus following water maze training. *European Journal of Neuroscience, 17*, 2447–2456.

Sandi, C., Cordero, M. I., Ugolini, A., Varea, E., Caberlotto, L., & Large, C. H. (2008). Chronic stress-induced alterations in amygdala responsiveness and behavior-modulation by trait anxiety and corticotropin-releasing factor systems. *European Journal of Neuroscience, 28*, 1836–1848.

Schwabe, L., Dalm, S., Schächinger, H., & Oitzl, M. S. (2008). Chronic stress modulates the use of spatial and stimulus-response learning strategies in mice and man. *Neurobiology of Learning and Memory, 90*, 495–503.

Schwabe, L., Schächinger, H., de Kloet, E. R., & Oitzl, M. S. (2010). Corticosteroids operate as a switch between memory systems. *Journal of Cognitive Neuroscience, 22*, 1362–1372.

Shors, T. J. (2004). Learning during stressful times. *Learning & Memory, 11*, 137–144.

Solomon, M. B., Jones, K., Packard, B. A., & Herman, J. P. (2010). The medial amygdala modulates body weight but not neuroendocrine responses to chronic stress. *Journal of Neuroendocrinology, 22*, 13–23.

Song, L., Che, W., Min-Wei, W., Murakami, Y., & Matsumoto, K. (2006). Impairment of the spatial learning and memory induced by learned helplessness and chronic mild stress. *Pharmacology, Biochemistry, and Behavior, 83*, 186–193.

Sterlemann, V., Rammes, G., Wolf, M., Liebl, C., Ganea, K., Müller, M. B., & Schmidt, M. V. (2009). Chronic social stress during adolescence induces cognitive impairment in aged mice. *Hippocampus, 20*, 540–549.

Surget, A., Saxe, M., Leman, S., Ibarguen-Vargas, Y., Chalon, S., Griebel, G., Hen, R., & Belzung, C. (2008). Drug-dependent requirement of hippocampal neurogenesis in a model of depression and of antidepressant reversal. *Biological Psychiatry, 64*, 293–301.

Thompson, B. L., Erickson, K., Schulkin, J., & Rosen, J. B. (2004). Corticosterone facilitates retention of contextually conditioned fear and increases CRH mRNA expression in the amygdala. *Behavioral Brain Research, 149*, 209–215.

Touyarot, K., Venero, C., & Sandi, C. (2004). Spatial learning impairment induced by chronic stress is related to individual differences in novelty reactivity: search for neurobiological correlates. *Psychoneuroendocrinology, 29*, 290–305.

Venero, C., Tilling, T., Hermans-Borgmeyer, I., Schmidt, R., Schachner, M., & Sandi, C. (2002). Chronic stress induces opposite changes in the mRNA expression of the cell adhesion molecules NCAM and L1. *Neuroscience, 115,* 1211–1219.

Vyas, A., & Chattarji, S. (2004). Modulation of different states of anxiety-like behavior by chronic stress. *Behavioral Neuroscience, 118,* 1450–1454.

Vyas, A., Mitra, R., Shankaranarayana Rao, B. S., & Chattarji, S. (2002). Chronic stress induces contrasting patterns of dendritic remodeling in hippocampal and amygdaloid neurons. *Journal of Neuroscience, 22,* 6810–6818.

Watanabe, Y., Gould, E., Cameron, H. A., Daniels, D. C., & McEwen, B. S. (1992). Phenytoin prevents stress- and corticosterone-induced atrophy of CA3 pyramidal neurons. *Hippocampus, 2,* 431–435.

Willner, P. (2005). Chronic mild stress (CMS) revisited: consistency and behavioural-neurobiological concordance in the effects of CMS. *Neuropsychobiology, 52,* 90–110.

Wood, G. E., Young, L. T., Reagan, L. P., & McEwen, B. S. (2003). Acute and chronic restraint stress alter the incidence of social conflict in male rats. *Hormones and Behavior, 43,* 205–213.

Wood, G. E., Young, L. T., Reagan, L. P., Chen, B., & McEwen, B. S. (2004). Stress-induced structural remodeling in hippocampus: prevention by lithium treatment. *Proceedings of the National Academy of Sciences USA, 101,* 3973–3978.

Wright, R. L., Lightner, E. N., Harman, J. S., Meijer, O. C., & Conrad, C. D. (2006). Attenuating corticosterone levels on the day of memory assessment prevents chronic stress-induced impairments in spatial memory. *European Journal of Neuroscience, 24,* 595–605.

12

Stress and Glucocorticoid Effects on Learning and Memory
Human Studies
Marie-France Marin and Sonia J. Lupien

History and Definitions of Stress

The term *stress* was borrowed by Dr Hans Selye from the engineers who were using it to illustrate the phenomenon that a certain level of strain can be put on a metal until it reaches a specific point where it can break like glass. As a medical doctor, Selye used the term stress response to represent the cluster of nonspecific symptoms that were manifested when the body's equilibrium was threatened in any way. Moreover, Selye thought that the determinants of the stress response were nonspecific (Selye, 1998). Importantly, Selye's career was mostly devoted to the study of physical stressors (e.g., extreme cold, hemorrhage) using animals. Eventually, some people disagreed with Selye's view, especially on the notion that the determinants of a stress response were nonspecific. One of the main reasons explaining these divergent opinions was Selye's focus on physical stressors and the emergence of the notion that some stressors were psychological (e.g., public speaking). John Mason, a psychologist, was convinced that there were some specific characteristics that would make the body react. By carrying out different experiments, he came up with three specific characteristics that, when present in a situation, would provoke a physiological stress response. These are novelty, unpredictability, and a low sense of control (Mason, 1968). Since then, a fourth component—threat to the ego—has been recognized (Dickerson and Kemeny, 2004). These four components are known to be independent and additive in such a way that only one characteristic is necessary to induce a stress response but the more characteristics there are the more important the magnitude of the stress response is likely to be.

The Handbook of Stress: Neuropsychological Effects on the Brain, First Edition.
Edited by Cheryl D. Conrad.
© 2011 Blackwell Publishing Ltd. Published 2011 by Blackwell Publishing Ltd.

Thus, a stressor could be seen as a threat to the psychological or physical integrity of an individual. Moreover, stressors could be dichotomized in two main categories: absolute (e.g., a natural disaster) and relative (e.g., public speaking) (Lupien et al., 2006). These could be differentiated on the basis of the likelihood of a response by a group of individuals. For example, everyone will have a stress response when facing an absolute stressor and this could easily be explained from an evolutionary perspective. On the contrary, not everyone will have a stress response when having to do an oral presentation. The reason for this difference is very simple. The individual will react only if novelty, unpredictability, a decreased sense of control, and/ or a threat to the ego are perceived in the situation. Consequently, the stressor is relative given that only a portion of individuals will have a stress response and the determinants inducing this response might even differ between two individuals. This is where the notion of individual differences comes into play and it is necessary to keep this in mind when studying the notion of stress. Nowadays, in Western societies, absolute stressors are rare but relative stressors are much more frequent. Consequently, this chapter will focus mostly on relative psychological stressors. Another notion that is important to keep in mind when studying the effects of stress hormones on cognition is the chronicity of exposure to stressors or to elevated levels of stress hormones. As it will be discussed, an acute stress reponse will affect cognitive processes differently than chronically elevated stress hormone levels.

The Stress Response: Catecholamines and Glucocorticoids

Upon perception of a stressor, the sympathetic–adrenal–medulla (SAM) and the hypothalamic–pituitary–adrenal (HPA) axes are activated. The SAM axis is controlled by the central nervous system with the ultimate hormonal outcome involving the quick release of catecholamines (epinephrine [adrenaline] and norepinephrine [noradrenaline]) from the medullar part of the adrenal glands that sit on top of the kidneys. The catecholamines have many actions that allow an organism to respond quickly to a challenge, such as dilating the pupils and increasing the heart rate (see Chapter 1 in this volume for more information). Moreover, the catecholamines can also influence the brain, albeit indirectly due to their lipophobic nature that blocks brain entry. Nonetheless, catecholamines can activate β-adrenoceptors on vagal afferents ending in the nucleus of the solitary tract. The noradrenergic cells in the nucleus of the solitary tract project either directly to the amydgala or indirectly by the locus coeruleus to further regulate brain function and the stress response (Fallon and Ciofi, 1992). The HPA axis is activated by the secretion of corticotropin-releasing hormone from the paraventricular nucleus of the hypothalamus. Corticotropin-releasing hormone then binds to its receptors at the level of the anterior pituitary gland and adrenocorticotrophic hormone is released in the bloodstream until it binds to its receptors that are located, notably, on the adrenal glands. Glucocorticoids (GCs), the end product of the HPA axis, are then released from the cortex of the adrenal glands. GCs have many targets to help sustain a stress response, such as by facilitating energy levels in the blood (see Chapter 1). Notably, GCs are liposoluble and can readily access the brain to influence brain functions, as well as to exert negative feedback at multiple levels (see Chapters 1 and 2) to maintain homeostasis (Brown, 1999). Importantly, under basal nonstressful conditions, GCs exhibit a circadian rhythm, where high levels are found in the morning and lower levels in the afternoon and the evening (Nelson, 2000).

GC receptors

The brain has a high density of GC receptors and these could be subdivided in two types: the mineralocorticoid receptors (MRs, or Type I) and the GC receptors (GRs, or Type II). These two categories of receptor differ with regards to their affinity and their distribution throughout the brain. First of all, MRs bind to GCs with an affinity that is about six to ten times higher than that of GRs (Reul and de Kloet, 1985). Thus, during the circadian trough, the endogenous hormone occupies more than 90% of MRs, but only 10% of GRs. However, during a stress response and/or the circadian peak of GC secretion, MRs become saturated and there is approximately a 67–74% occupation of GRs (de Kloet et al., 1999). The two categories of GC receptors also differ with regards to their distribution in the brain. In fact, the MR is exclusively present in the limbic system, with a preferential distribution in the hippocampus, parahippocampal gyrus, and entorhinal and insular cortices. On the other hand, the GR is widely present in subcortical (paraventricular nucleus and other hypothalamic nuclei, the hippocampus and parahippocampal gyrus) and cortical structures, with a preferential distribution in the prefrontal cortex (Diorio et al., 1993; McEwen et al., 1968, 1986; Meaney et al., 1985; Sarrieau et al., 1988; Sanchez et al., 2000).

The high density of GC receptors in the hippocampus, the amygdala, and the prefrontal cortex convinced the scientists to further investigate the role of stress hormones on the cognitive functions subserved by these different brain structures. Notably, the amygdala is involved in the processing of emotional information. It is particularly important for threat detection. The prefrontal cortex plays an important role in executive functions such as planning, reasoning, and selective attention. On the other hand, the hippocampus is involved in learning and memory (Scoville and Milner, 1957). It is especially important for episodic memories as well as spatial navigation.

Stress Methodology

Given that this chapter is devoted to documenting the effects of GCs on memory in humans, it is first important to review the different methods used in the laboratory to induce a variation of GC levels and to briefly discuss their respective advantages and disadvantages. There are two main categories of technique used to induce a variation in GC levels: exogenous and endogenous means. The exogenous method relies on pharmacological protocols. To increase the levels of GCs, synthetic cortisol is mostly used; to decrease the levels of GCs, then antagonists of GCs receptors (Tytherleigh et al., 2004) or metyrapone—an inhibitor of cortisol synthesis—are used. Moreover, dexamethasone is sometimes used to test the functioning of the HPA axis. In individuals having a normally functioning HPA axis, dexamethasone, a synthetic steroid that passes poorly through the blood–brain barrier, binds mainly at the level of the anterior pituitary to promote negative feedback and inhibit the release of GCs.

On the other hand, the endogenous methods refer to psychological or physical stressors that are validated for their capacity to increase GC levels. In humans, the Cold Pressor Test is the most used physical stressor. In this paradigm the subject places an arm in very cold water, which will consequently increase noradrenergic activity and for some individuals the GC system as well. Other researchers prefer to use a psychological stressor and the most known and validated one to date is the Trier Social Stress Test (Kirschbaum et al., 1993). It is a psychologically challenging task known to increase the levels of cortisol. The task contains an anticipation phase and a test phase. This latter portion is divided in a speech section and a mental arithmetic section. The task is performed in front of a panel of confederates who pretend to be experts in behavioral analysis. The socioevaluative threat that the confederates represent is the key to increasing GC levels. Other paradigms are emerging in the literature, notably the Yales Interpersonal Stressor (Stroud et al., 2000), which consists of an interaction between the participant and two confederates. The group is given a topic to discuss and gradually the two confederates exclude the participant using verbal (e.g., disagreeing and criticizing the participant's opinion) and nonverbal (e.g., switching body position away from the participant) methods. Interestingly, women seem to be more sensitive to this paradigm whereas men are more sensitive to the Trier Social Stress Test. This underlies the importance of taking into account sex when examining the effects of stress hormones on different cognitive functions.

When using exogenous methods it is important to keep in mind some basic rules. First, the peak concentrations of the drug will be reached at different rates depending on the method of administration (e.g., oral administration or intravenous injection). Second, depending on the question being asked, a decision needs to be taken to establish whether the dose will be the same for all individuals or if it will be tailored to their metabolism (usually based on their weight). Third, if the method of administration requires a needle, this in itself could induce an endogenous stress response in some individuals and thus could result in a less rigorous protocol, especially if looking at a dose–response effect. However, one of the major advantages of the exogenous method is that it is the only way to study the effects of very low levels of GCs (e.g., metyrapone administration). On the other hand, one of the main advantages of using psychosocial stressors is that it closely resembles everyday life situations. Moreover, it allows the researcher to further investigate the moderating factors that influence the reactivity of an individual to a stressful situation. In contrast, the psychological stressor will not only act on the stress system (by increasing noradrenergic and GC activity), but will also carry an important psychological component. This psychological load could have some impact on different cognitive processes (e.g., negative mood following a stressor could bias the perception of different stimuli). Moreover, despite this potential confounding effect of psychological load, the endogenous methods will activate the HPA and SAM axes, which means that any effects observed cannot be disentangled with regards to a specific class of stress hormones. The exogenous method allows targeting specifically one stress axis. Another important thing to consider with regards to endogenous methods is that the nature of the stressor is not always clear. For example, the Cold Pressor Test is thought to be a physical stressor but there could also be a psychological component to it and it is hard to know whether the physical nature or the psychological nature of the stressor has contributed to any potential effect.

Emotions: an Important Modulator of Human Memory

The difference between stress response and emotion

Emotions often modulate how stress hormones influence memory, but stress and emotion are not interchangeable terms. Stressful experiences always trigger emotions, whereas emotions do not always trigger a stress response. Moreover, there are important differences in terms of how these two entities (stress response and emotion) are induced in a laboratory setting. Generally, the emotion will be triggered by the learning material (e.g., a sad movie) whereas a physical or a psychological stressor that is not related to the learning material will induce the stress response. Nonetheless, emotions and stressors share some features, which include being capable of elevating arousal, catecholamines, and GCs (for a review see Lupien and Brière, 2000).

Characteristics of emotional memories

It is well known that emotional memories are usually better remembered than neutral memories (Cahill and McGaugh, 1995; Heuer and Reisberg, 1990). The amygdala is a key player in explaining this phenomenon, since it has the capacity to modulate emotional memories. Once released, the catecholamines activate the amygdala which modulates the hippocampus' activity and, as a result, influences the strength of the emotional memory trace. It seems that coactivation of these structures allows the potentiation of the memory trace (Roozendaal et al., 2006). In fact, it has been demonstrated that patients with bilateral amygdala lesions do not show the usual perception bias towards emotional material (Anderson and Phelps, 2001). This strongly supports the amygdala as essential for the processing of emotions and for enhancing this information in memory.

Apart from the fact that they are better remembered, emotional memories differ from neutral ones in two other major respects. Notably, people working in the field of law enforcement report that witnesses of crimes demonstrate a weapon-focus phenomenon, such that the weapon captures most of the victim's attention, resulting in a reduced ability to recall other details of the scene and to recognize the assailant at a later time. This phenomenon was replicated in a laboratory. In fact, Christianson and Loftus (1991) showed subjects a series of slides in which the emotional valence of one critical slide was varied. In the neutral version, the critical slide depicted a woman riding a bicycle. In the emotional version, the same woman was seen lying injured on the street near the bicycle. In both versions, a peripheral car was seen in the distant background. The results showed that the central information (woman and bicycle) was well retained in the emotional condition, while the peripheral information (car in background) was better retained in the neutral condition. Furthermore, memory for central information is less susceptible to the effects of misleading information than is memory for peripheral details (Roebers and Schneider, 2000).

Another aspect that differentiates emotional memories from neutral ones is with regards to retention interval. Studies in humans show that emotional and/or traumatic information is better recalled after a certain period of time compared to immediately after encoding. Memory for neutral events, on the other hand, decreases over longer intervals. This is well illustrated in a study by Kleinsmith and Kaplan (1963). The authors asked participants to learn pairs of words where some were neutral and others were emotionally negative. Memory of the word pairs was tested 2 min or 1 week after encoding. Immediate memory for the emotional material was inhibited but the pattern was reversed on testing 1 week later. These results have been replicated many times and the majority of studies have shown enhanced memory for emotionally arousing material when it is tested after a certain time period. In terms of mechanism that could explain this phenomenon, a recent review by Diamond and colleagues (2007) proposes a temporal model for the formation of emotional memories by taking into account how a stress response could modulate the functioning of the hippocampus, the amygdala, and the prefrontal cortex in a dynamic manner depending on time.

Acute Effects of GCs on Memory

When studying the effects of stress hormones on memory, it is of crucial importance to take into account the different memory processes. In fact, stress hormones have been shown to have differential effects on memory and this has to do, at least in part, with the memory process under investigation.

Effects of GCs on working memory

For many years the field has been particularly interested in the effects of GCs on declarative memory given the known presence of GC receptors in the hippocampus.

However, in 2000, a study on primates demonstrated the presence of GC receptors in the prefrontal cortex (mainly Type II receptors). This led researchers to hypothesize that an increase in GC levels could have an impact on cognitive functions that are dependent on the frontal lobe. Multiple neuropsychological studies were suggesting that the prefrontal cortex was involved in working memory, a process that allows an individual to maintain a limited amount of information online for a limited period of time. In fact, scientists noted working memory deficits in patients with prefrontal cortex lesions.

With this in mind, the effects of GCs on working memory have been investigated in different studies. For example, it was demonstrated that hydrocortisone administration had detrimental effects on working memory in young healthy adults (Lupien et al., 1999). Moreover, in that same study the authors also measured declarative memory and reported no impairment. This suggests that working memory is more sensitive than declarative memory to an elevation of GC levels.

Other studies have used a psychosocial stressor instead of a hydrocortisone administration. They also found that elevated levels of GCs had detrimental effects on working memory functions (Oei et al., 2006; Schoofs et al., 2008). There are still only a few studies on the effects of stress hormones on the cognitive functions that are subserved by the prefrontal cortex. So far, they all point towards the same results but more studies are needed to better understand the mechanisms. For example, could stress hormones have different effects on working memory if the material has emotional content?

Effects of GCs on memory consolidation

When people experience a new event, a certain part of it will be retained and thus made available later for retrieval. The newly acquired information is first in a fragile and unstable state and dependent on the hippocampus. The process by which unstable memories stabilize in the brain has been termed memory consolidation. It has been suggested that new information is first dependent on the short-term memory system and is then transferred through consolidation into the long-term memory system in a more stable form (McGaugh, 2000).

Many studies have demonstrated that it is possible to impair or enhance this consolidation process, arguing for the unstable nature of the memory trace at the beginning of the consolidation process. Stress hormones are candidates that have been investigated for their modulatory role on the consolidation process. In terms of methodology, the variation in GC levels should occur very close to the time of encoding if one wants to impact the consolidation process. If the treatment is administered just before encoding, there will be an impact on memory consolidation, but the attention/encoding part will also be affected. To make sure that only memory consolidation is targeted, the modulation in GC levels should occur after encoding.

In general, an elevation in GC levels enhances memory consolidation (Beckner et al., 2006; Buchanan and Lovallo, 2001; Cahill et al., 2003; Kuhlmann and Wolf, 2006; Payne et al., 2007; Schwabe et al., 2008). Importantly, some studies have reported an inverted-U relationship between the levels of GCs and memory consolidation (Abercrombie et al., 2003; Andreano and Cahill, 2006). Altogether, these results suggest that moderate increases in GC levels would promote an optimal consolidation process. Important factors need to be considered, one of them being the valence of the to-be-remembered material.

For example, in humans, psychosocial stress following encoding of a neutral movie has been shown to enhance memory consolidation, suggesting a facilitating effect of GCs on consolidation of neutral information (Beckner et al., 2006). Another group exposed participants to a psychosocial stressor before encoding neutral and emotional information. One week later participants who were exposed to the stressor had higher emotional memories but worse neutral memories compared to the participants who were not exposed to the stressor (Payne et al., 2007). Thus, the results of this study suggest a facilitating effect of GCs on memory consolidation of emotional material and an impairing effect of GCs on memory consolidation of neutral material. Administration of exogenous cortisol (20 mg) before encoding of the stimulus enhances the long-term memory for the emotional stimuli compared to the neutral ones, suggesting that higher levels of GCs at the time of encoding allows a better consolidation of the emotional material (Buchanan and Lovallo, 2001). Another study administered exogenous cortisol (30 mg) shortly before encoding and reported enhanced memory consolidation for emotional memory (Kuhlmann and Wolf, 2006). Although these results seem contradictory, it is important to keep in mind that in some cases only neutral or emotional material was presented whereas in other cases both emotional and neutral material were presented. It is possible to hypothesize that GCs first promote the consolidation of emotional memory. In stressful situations one function of GC release is to allow remembering. Consequently, it is possible that GCs will favor consolidation of emotional memories (that is, probably relevant in times of stress) at the detriment of consolidating neutral memories. However, if the increase in GCs is paired with neutral material only then the system will promote the consolidation of this information by default.

Importantly, the studies described above focused on the role of GCs on memory consolidation, in some cases contrasting emotional and neutral memories. However, as discussed at the beginning of this chapter, a stress response involves not only the release of GCs but also the release of catecholamines. Given the importance of the amygdala in potentiating the emotional memory trace, there was a debate in the literature to determine whether GCs or norepinephrine are responsible for consolidation of emotional memories. To answer this question an interesting study exposed participants to neutral and emotionally arousing material. Their short-term and long-term memories were assessed following either blockade of norepinephrine (administration of propanolol) or inhibition of GCs (administration of metyrapone). Results demonstrated that short-term and long-term memories for emotionally arousing material were impaired following blockade of norepinephrine whereas long-term memory for both emotionally arousing and neutral material was impaired following inhibition of GCs (Maheu et al., 2004). This suggests that norepinephrine is involved in the immediate organization of the emotional memory trace and that GCs are necessary for the transfer of both neutral and emotional memories in the long-term memory system.

Effects of GCs on memory retrieval

Although GCs promote the consolidation of memories, their impact on memory retrieval is quite different. Retrieval refers to the notion of remembering the memory trace that is already consolidated. Typically, studies investigating the impact of GCs on memory retrieval allow at least a delay of 24 hr for the memory trace to consolidate under normal conditions (no manipulation at the time of consolidation). Then, variations in GC levels occur before the retrieval and the main challenge here is to make sure that the methods chosen to increase or decrease GC levels will have an optimal effect when participants are asked to recall the previously consolidated information. In general, studies have reported detrimental effects of GCs on memory retrieval (Buchanan and Tranel, 2008; Buchanan et al., 2006; de Quervain, 2006; de Quervain et al., 1998, 2000; Kuhlmann et al., 2005a, 2005b; Tollenaar et al., 2009; Het et al., 2005). In other words, when GC levels are elevated, the capacity of the participants to retrieve an already consolidated memory trace is reduced (Het et al., 2005).

Moreover, some of these studies suggest that these effects are particularly pronounced for emotional memories. For example, a study exposed participants to a psychosocial stressor prior to the retrieval of a list of words learned 24 hr before. They found an impairing effect on memory retrieval for the group exposed to the stressor. However, when looking more closely at the results, the authors noted that positive and negative words were the ones affected whereas retrieval of neutral words was not impacted on (Kuhlmann et al., 2005b). This suggests that emotional stimuli (both negative and positive) may be more sensitive to the effects of stress hormones. This study also highlights the importance of studying emotionally positive stimuli. In fact, the focus so far has been mostly on neutral and negative stimuli.

However, it would be wrong to assume that the relationship between GCs and memory retrieval is linear. Studies have demonstrated that metyrapone administration, which considerably decreases GC levels by inhibiting its synthesis, is also detrimental for delayed memory recall (Lupien et al., 2002). These findings fall in line with the proposed inverted-U shape relationship between circulating levels of GCs and memory performance (Lupien and McEwen, 1997). This hypothesis states that both very low and very high levels of GCs are detrimental for memory performance whereas moderate levels will result in an optimal performance.

Importantly, these studies on GCs and memory retrieval were conducted with the idea that the effects of GCs on memory would be transient. In other words, scientists thought that the effects on retrieval would only last for the time that GC levels were modulated. It was thought that memory performance would be back to normal levels when GC levels were not manipulated anymore. Given that the memory trace is already consolidated, an elevation in GC levels was thought to temporarily block access to the memory trace, thus explaining a transient effect of GC levels on memory retrieval.

Effects of GCs on memory reconsolidation

However, studies in the field of cognitive neurosciences have demonstrated that the process of memory retrieval serves as a reactivation mechanism whereby the memory trace that is reactivated during the retrieval process is once again sensitive to modifications by pharmacological or environmental manipulations (Misanin et al., 1968; Nader et al., 2000). This means that immediately after being reactivated a memory trace could be modulated by different conditions, and this effect could potentially persist over time. By combining this knowledge and the data on GCs and retrieval, the field is now moving one step further in trying to document the long-term effects of GCs on memory retrieval.

This is a new field of study and very few data have been published on this topic to this date. In humans, Tollenaar and colleagues (2009) have reported an impairing effect of cortisol administration on the retrieval (reactivation) of neutral and emotional words and the effect was still present after a washout period of 1 week. This suggests that the increase in GC levels at the time of retrieval (reactivation) is not only blocking access to the memory trace in a temporary manner but is modulating this memory trace in a long-lasting fashion.

When information is encoded, it first goes into the short-term memory system and is in an unstable state. With time, this information will stabilize in the long-term memory system (consolidation). Once in the long-term memory system, the information is accessible for retrieval. New theories suggest that, upon retrieval, the memory trace becomes unstable once again in the short-term memory system and needs to undergo a second round of consolidation to be restabilized in the long-term memory system again (reconsolidation; see Figure 12.1). Modulation of GC levels will have different effects depending on the timing of the modulation. For

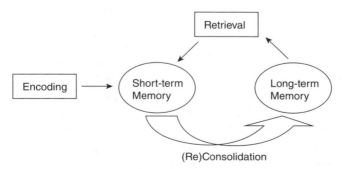

Figure 12.1   Dynamics of the different memory processes.

example, modulation of GC levels either immediately before or after encoding will affect memory consolidation. Once the consolidation process is over, if GC levels are manipulated immediately before the participant recalls the material then the retrieval process will be affected. On the other hand, it is also possible to retrieve the memory and then modulate GC levels, which will probably have an effect on the reconsolidation process.

Is That the End of the Story?

As mentioned at the beginning of this chapter, the notion of chronicity is important to consider when testing the effects of GCs on memory. So far, the literature that has been reviewed related to acute variations in GC levels and how this could modulate memory processes. It is common to hear that an acute stress response is beneficial and can save one's life. In fact, an acute stress response serves adaptation purposes and this explains, at least in part, why it could promote the consolidation of emotional memories. However, when exposure to stressors and/or to high levels of GCs is chronic, the effects on cognition are not necessarily beneficial. It is thus very important to differentiate between the effects of acute and chronic stress on memory.

Chronic effects of stress and GCs on memory

It is important to note that what led the field of research into the investigation of acute effects of GCs on different cognitive functions was the observation that chronic exposure to high levels of GCs had detrimental effects on behavior. In the 1940s, GCs were recognized for their anti-inflammatory functions. Keep in mind that the effects of GCs were thought to be in periphery given that the localization of GC receptors in the brain was still unknown. Consequently, some people were prescribed major doses of GCs to treat different health conditions such as asthma. Different affective and cognitive manifestations were noted following chronic use of these medications. This has led researchers to further examine this phenomenon.

With this notion in mind, older adults were a particularly interesting population to study. In fact, cognitive decline was thought to be a normal consequence of aging. However, at some point, the field started to realize that some older adults had intact cognitive functions and thus scientists became more and more interested in understanding the various factors that could lead to this differential aging phenomenon. If chronic exposure to high levels of GCs can lead to severe mental disturbances, then could chronic exposure to stressors and/or to high levels of GCs during life explain different cognitive outcomes in older adults?

This is exactly what Lupien and colleagues decided to investigate in a longitudinal study with 51 healthy individuals aged between 60 and 87 years of age. For a period ranging between 3 and 6 years, 24-hr collection of blood samples was obtained from these individuals on an annual basis. This method made it possible to have a measure of cortisol variation during those years. Three different patterns of cortisol detection were observed in this population. First, 37.9% of these older adults had an increase of cortisol and reached relatively high levels (*increased/high levels* group). Another subgroup (46.7%) also had an increase, but their levels of cortisol were moderate (*increased/moderate levels* group) and, finally, a third subgroup (15.3%) had decreasing levels of cortisol (*decreased/moderate levels* group) (Lupien et al., 1996).

Based on animal findings that reported memory deficits and smaller hippocampal volume in rats that were secreting high levels of GCs, Lupien and colleagues investigated whether these three subgroups of older adults were different in terms of memory performance. Participants from the increased/high levels group had a significantly lower memory performance than the two other groups. Importantly, the deficit was only observed in declarative memory tasks. In fact, when tested on nondeclarative tasks, the three groups had similar memory performance (Lupien et al., 1994). This underlies the importance of the hippocampus in declarative memory and the sensitivity of this structure to increased levels of GCs. Moreover, the increased/high levels group had a hippocampal volume 14% smaller than the decreased/moderate levels group. A strong negative correlation was observed between the hippocampal volume and the degree of cortisol elevation throughout years (Lupien et al., 1998). Importantly, one cannot draw conclusions about causal effects of GCs on hippocampal volume given that the results were based on correlations (Lupien et al., 2007).

This is just one example of how chronic exposure to high levels of GCs is known to have negative effects on cognition. In humans, we could also study different populations suffering from stress-related disorders or disorders requiring them to take GCs as a medication. By looking at their cortisol secretion profile, their hippocampal volumes, and their cognitive performance it was possible to learn more about chronic exposure to high levels of GCs and its brain correlates. Notably, depression has been associated with hypercortisolism in some studies (Holsboer, 2000; Nemeroff, 1996; Pariante and Miller, 2001). Moreover, studies revealed that depressed individuals have deficits in simple and complex attentional tasks as well as verbal and visual memory tasks (Beats et al., 1996; Roy-Byrne et al., 1986; Schatzberg et al., 2000; Tancer et al., 1990). Similar deficits have been observed in individuals with steroid-induced psychosis (induced by the long-term steroid use) (Varney et al., 1984). Thus, overall, extended elevations in GCs appear to be detrimental to several cognitive processes. Moreover, many studies have documented the relationship between hippocampal volume and different stress-related disorders. Notably, smaller hippocampal volumes have been detected in patients suffering from depression (Bremner et al., 2000), posttraumatic stress disorder (PTSD) (Bremner et al., 1995; Gurvits et al., 1996), and schizophrenia (Nelson et al., 1998).

At first, these results led multiple scientists to affirm that chronic exposure to high levels of GCs was causing hippocampal atrophy. This is known as the neurotoxicity hypothesis. However, other studies that were performed later led to the birth of the vulnerability hypothesis. This hypothesis suggests that a smaller hippocampal volume can render an individual more at risk for developing stress-related disorders. A very convincing study by Gilbertson and colleagues (2002) illustrates this idea well. The authors reported smaller hippocampal volume in war veterans who were diagnosed with PTSD compared to other veterans who did not develop the psychiatric condition. Intuitively, this seems to confirm the neurotoxicity hypothesis. However, the authors also studied the homozygote twin brothers of those veterans who never went to war. They reported that the twins of those who developed PTSD also had smaller hippocampal volume when compared to the twins of the group who did not develop PTSD. Consequently, the smaller hippocampal volume seems to be a preexisting condition that increases vulnerability to PTSD upon exposure to trauma rather than the pure consequence of this traumatic event. Importantly, the hypotheses (neurotoxicity or vulnerability) are not necessarily exclusive to each other. In fact, what determines the hippocampal volume in the first place remains to be fully documented. Genetics seem to account for 40% of the variance whereas experiential factors seem to be responsible for 60% of the variance (Sullivan et al., 2001). Within this wide category of experiential factors, early adversity has received considerable attention. It has been shown to have an impact on the development of different brain structures, notably the hippocampus, the amygdala, and the prefrontal cortex. As demonstrated recently in a review, these chronic stressors could affect different brain structures depending on when they occur during the development of the individual. This new model is called the Life-Cycle Model of Stress (Lupien et al., 2009). Thus, the timing will have an influence on certain brain structures and this will, in turn, render the individual more or less at risk of developing certain mental health conditions. Moreover, it has recently been proposed that a history of chronic exposure to elevated levels of GCs might render the hippocampus more vulnerable to future neurotoxic or metabolic challenges. This model has been called the glucocorticoids vulnerability hypothesis (Conrad, 2008). These new models are good examples of how the two different theories (neurotoxicity and vulnerability) are not necessarily exclusive and could be well integrated in a common framework.

Conclusion

Over the years, the global understanding of stress has progressed considerably. By building on animal studies and by taking into account the distribution of GC receptors throughout the brain, the field has advanced one step further in its understanding of the mechanisms by which stress hormones exert their effects, either acutely or chronically, on the brain and on diverse cognitive functions.

References

Abercrombie, H. C., Kalin, N. H., Thurow, M. E., Rosenkranz, M. A., & Davidson, R. J. (2003). Cortisol variation in humans affects memory for emotionally laden and neutral information. *Behavioral Neuroscience, 117,* 505–516.

Anderson, A. K., & Phelps, E. A. (2001). Lesions of the human amygdala impair enhanced perception of emotionally salient events. *Nature, 411,* 305–309.

Andreano, J. M., & Cahill, L. (2006). Glucocorticoid release and memory consolidation in men and women. *Psychological Science, 17,* 466–470.

Beats, B. C., Sahakian, B. J., & Levy, R. (1996). Cognitive performance in tests sensitive to frontal lobe dysfunction in the elderly depressed. *Psychological Medicine, 26,* 591–603.

Beckner, V. E., Tucker, D. M., Delville, Y., & Mohr, D. C. (2006). Stress facilitates consolidation of verbal memory for a film but does not affect retrieval. *Behavioral Neuroscience, 120,* 518–527.

Bremner, J. D., Randall, P., Scott, T. M., Bronen, R. A., Seibyl, J. P., Southwick, S. M., Delaney, R. C., McCarthy, G., Charney, D. S., & Innis, R. B. (1995). MRI-based measurement of hippocampal volume in patients with combat-related posttraumatic stress disorder. *American Journal of Psychiatry, 152,* 973–981.

Bremner, J. D., Narayan, M., Anderson, E. R., Staib, L. H., Miller, H. L., & Charney, D. S. (2000). Hippocampal volume reduction in major depression. *American Journal of Psychiatry, 157,* 115–118.

Brown, R. E. (1999). *An introduction to neuroendocrinology.* Cambridge: Cambridge University Press.

Buchanan, T. W., & Lovallo, W. R. (2001). Enhanced memory for emotional material following stress-level cortisol treatment in humans. *Psychoneuroendocrinology, 26,* 307–317.

Buchanan, T. W., & Tranel, D. (2008). Stress and emotional memory retrieval: effects of sex and cortisol response. *Neurobiology of Learning and Memory, 89,* 134–141.

Buchanan, T. W., Tranel, D., & Adolphs, R. (2006). Impaired memory retrieval correlates with individual differences in cortisol response but not autonomic response. *Learning & Memory, 13,* 382–387.

Cahill, L., & McGaugh, J. L. (1995). A novel demonstration of enhanced memory associated with emotional arousal. *Conscious Cognition, 4,* 410–421.

Cahill, L., Gorski, L., & Le, K. (2003). Enhanced human memory consolidation with post-learning stress: interaction with the degree of arousal at encoding. *Learning & Memory, 10,* 270–274.

Christianson, S. A., & Loftus, E. F. (1991). Remembering emotional events: the fate of detailed information. *Cognition & Emotion, 5,* 81–108.

Conrad, C. D. (2008). Chronic stress-induced hippocampal vulnerability: the glucocorticoid vulnerability hypothesis. *Reviews in the Neurosciences, 19,* 395–411.

de Kloet, E. R., Oitzl, M. S., & Joëls, M. (1999). Stress and cognition: are corticosteroids good or bad guys? *Trends in Neuroscience, 22,* 422–426.

de Quervain, D. J. (2006). Glucocorticoid-induced inhibition of memory retrieval: implications for posttraumatic stress disorder. *Annals of the New York Academy of Sciences, 1071,* 216–220.

de Quervain, D. J., Roozendaal, B., & McGaugh, J. L. (1998). Stress and glucocorticoids impair retrieval of long-term spatial memory. *Nature, 394,* 787–790.

de Quervain, D. J., Roozendaal, B., Nitsch, R. M., McGaugh, J. L., & Hock, C. (2000). Acute cortisone administration impairs retrieval of long-term declarative memory in humans. *Nature Neuroscience, 3*, 313–314.

Diamond, D. M., Campbell, A. M., Park, C. R., Halonen, J., & Zoladz, P. R. (2007). The temporal dynamics model of emotional memory processing: a synthesis on the neurobiological basis of stress-induced amnesia, flashbulb and traumatic memories, and the Yerkes-Dodson law. *Neural Plasticity*, 60803.

Dickerson, S. S., & Kemeny, M. E. (2004). Acute stressors and cortisol responses: a theoretical integration and synthesis of laboratory research. *Psychological Bulletin, 130*, 355–391.

Diorio, D., Viau, V., & Meaney, M. J. (1993). The role of the medial prefrontal cortex (cingulate gyrus) in the regulation of hypothalamic-pituitary-adrenal responses to stress. *Journal of Neuroscience, 13*, 3839–3847.

Fallon, J. L., & Ciofi, P. (1992). Distribution of monoamines within the amygdala. In J. Aggleton (Ed.), *The amygdala: Neurobiological aspects of emotion, memory, and mental dysfunction.* New York: Wiley-Liss.

Gilbertson, M. W., Shenton, M. E., Ciszewski, A., Kasai, K., Lasko, N. B., Orr, S. P., & Pitman, R. K. (2002). Smaller hippocampal volume predicts pathologic vulnerability to psychological trauma. *Nature Neuroscience, 5*, 1242–1247.

Gurvits, T. V., Shenton, M. E., Hokama, H., Ohta, H., Lasko, N. B., Gilbertson, M. W., Orr, S. P., Kikinis, R., Jolesz, F. A., McCarley, R. W., & Pitman, R. K. (1996). Magnetic resonance imaging study of hippocampal volume in chronic, combat-related posttraumatic stress disorder. *Biological Psychiatry, 40*, 1091–1099.

Het, S., Ramlow, G., & Wolf, O. T. (2005). A meta-analytic review of the effects of acute cortisol administration on human memory. *Psychoneuroendocrinology, 30*, 771–784.

Heuer, F., & Reisberg, D. (1990). Vivid memories of emotional events: the accuracy of remembered minutiae. *Memory & Cognition, 18*, 496–506.

Holsboer, F. (2000). The corticosteroid receptor hypothesis of depression. *Neuropsychopharmacology, 23*, 477–501.

Kirschbaum, C., Pirke, K. M., & Hellhammer, D. H. (1993). The "Trier Social Stress Test"—a tool for investigating psychobiological stress responses in a laboratory setting. *Neuropsychobiology, 28*, 76–81.

Kleinsmith, L. J., & Kaplan, S. (1963). Paired-associate learning as a function of arousal and interpolated interval. *Journal of Experimental Psychology, 65*, 190–193.

Kuhlmann, S., Kirschbaum, C., & Wolf, O. T. (2005a). Effects of oral cortisol treatment in healthy young women on memory retrieval of negative and neutral words. *Neurobiology of Learning and Memory, 83*, 158–162.

Kuhlmann, S., Piel, M., & Wolf, O. T. (2005b). Impaired memory retrieval after psychosocial stress in healthy young men. *Journal of Neuroscience, 25*, 2977–2982.

Kuhlmann, S., & Wolf, O. T. (2006). Arousal and cortisol interact in modulating memory consolidation in healthy young men. *Behavioral Neuroscience, 120*, 217–223.

Lupien, S. J., & McEwen, B. S. (1997). The acute effects of corticosteroids on cognition: integration of animal and human model studies. *Brain Research Brain Research Reviews, 24*, 1–27.

Lupien, S. J., & Brière, S. (2000). Memory and stress. In G. Fink (Ed.), *The encyclopedia of stress* (pp. 721–728). San Diego, CA: Academic Press.

Lupien, S., Lecours, A. R., Lussier, I., Schwartz, G., Nair, N. P., & Meaney, M. J. (1994). Basal cortisol levels and cognitive deficits in human aging. *Journal of Neuroscience, 14,* 2893–2903.

Lupien, S., Lecours, A. R., Schwartz, G., Sharma, S., Hauger, R. L., Meaney, M. J., & Nair, N. P. (1996). Longitudinal study of basal cortisol levels in healthy elderly subjects: evidence for subgroups. *Neurobiology of Aging, 17,* 95–105.

Lupien, S. J., de Leon, M., de Santi, S., Convit, A., Tarshish, C., Nair, N. P., Thakur, M., McEwen, B. S., Hauger, R. L., & Meaney, M. J. (1998). Cortisol levels during human aging predict hippocampal atrophy and memory deficits. *Nature Neuroscience, 1,* 69–73.

Lupien, S. J., Gillin, C. J., & Hauger, R. L. (1999). Working memory is more sensitive than declarative memory to the acute effects of corticosteroids: a dose-response study in humans. *Behavioral Neuroscience, 113,* 420–430.

Lupien, S. J., Wilkinson, C. W., Briere, S., Menard, C., Ng Ying Kin, N. M., & Nair, N. P. (2002). The modulatory effects of corticosteroids on cognition: studies in young human populations. *Psychoneuroendocrinology, 27,* 401–416.

Lupien, S. J., Ouellet-Morin, I., Hupbach, A., Walker, D., Tu, M. T., Buss, C., Pruessner, J. C., & McEwen, B. S. (2006). Beyond the stress concept: allostatic load—a developmental biological and cognitive perspective. In D. Cicchetti, & D. J. Cohen (Eds.), *Developmental psychopathology volume 2: Developmental neuroscience* (pp. 578–628). New York: Wiley.

Lupien, S. J., Evans, A., Lord, C., Miles, J., Pruessner, M., Pike, B., & Pruessner, J. C. (2007). Hippocampal volume is as variable in young as in older adults: implications for the notion of hippocampal atrophy in humans. *Neuroimage, 34,* 479–485.

Lupien, S. J., McEwen, B. S., Gunnar, M. R., & Heim, C. (2009). Effects of stress throughout the lifespan on the brain, behaviour and cognition. *Nature Reviews Neuroscience, 10,* 434–445.

Maheu, F. S., Joober, R., Beaulieu, S., & Lupien, S. J. (2004). Differential effects of adrenergic and corticosteroid hormonal systems on human short- and long-term declarative memory for emotionally arousing material. *Behavioral Neuroscience, 118,* 420–428.

Mason, J. W. (1968). A review of psychoendocrine research on the sympathetic-adrenal medullary system. *Psychosomatic Medicine, 30,* Suppl, 631–653.

McEwen, B. S., Weiss, J. M., & Schwartz, L. S. (1968). Selective retention of corticosterone by limbic structures in rat brain. *Nature, 220,* 911–912.

McEwen, B. S., De Kloet, E. R., & Rostene, W. (1986). Adrenal steroid receptors and actions in the nervous system. *Physiological Reviews, 66,* 1121–1188.

McGaugh, J. L. (2000). Memory–a century of consolidation. *Science, 287,* 248–251.

Meaney, M. J., Sapolsky, R. M., & McEwen, B. S. (1985). The development of the glucocorticoid receptor system in the rat limbic brain. II. An autoradiographic study. *Brain Research, 350,* 165–168.

Misanin, J. R., Miller, R. R., & Lewis, D. J. (1968). Retrograde amnesia produced by electroconvulsive shock after reactivation of a consolidated memory trace. *Science, 160,* 554–555.

Nader, K., Schafe, G. E., & LeDoux, J. E. (2000). Fear memories require protein synthesis in the amygdala for reconsolidation after retrieval. *Nature, 406,* 722–726.

Nelson, M. D., Saykin, A. J., Flashman, L. A., & Riordan, H. J. (1998). Hippocampal volume reduction in schizophrenia as assessed by magnetic resonance imaging: a meta-analytic study. *Archives of General Psychiatry, 55,* 433–440.

Nelson, R. J. (2000). *An introduction to behavioral endocrinology*. Sunderland, MA: Sinauer Associates.

Nemeroff, C. B. (1996). The corticotropin-releasing factor (CRF) hypothesis of depression: new findings and new directions. *Molecular Psychiatry*, 1, 336–342.

Oei, N. Y., Everaerd, W. T., Elzinga, B. M., van Well, S., & Bermond, B. (2006). Psychosocial stress impairs working memory at high loads: an association with cortisol levels and memory retrieval. *Stress*, 9, 133–141.

Pariante, C. M., & Miller, A. H. (2001). Glucocorticoid receptors in major depression: relevance to pathophysiology and treatment. *Biological Psychiatry*, 49, 391–404.

Payne, J. D., Jackson, E. D., Hoscheidt, S., Ryan, L., Jacobs, W. J., & Nadel, L. (2007). Stress administered prior to encoding impairs neutral but enhances emotional long-term episodic memories. *Learning & Memory*, 14, 861–868.

Reul, J. M., & de Kloet, E. R. (1985). Two receptor systems for corticosterone in rat brain: microdistribution and differential occupation. *Endocrinology*, 117, 2505–2511.

Roebers, C. M., & Schneider, W. (2000). The impact of misleading questions on eyewitness memory in children and adults. *Applied Cognitive Psychology*, 14, 509–526.

Roozendaal, B., Okuda, S., de Quervain, D. J., & McGaugh, J. L. (2006). Glucocorticoids interact with emotion-induced noradrenergic activation in influencing different memory functions. *Neuroscience*, 138, 901–910.

Roy-Byrne, P. P., Weingartner, H., Bierer, L. M., Thompson, K., & Post, R. M. (1986). Effortful and automatic cognitive processes in depression. *Archives of General Psychiatry*, 43, 265–267.

Sanchez, M. M., Young, L. J., Plotsky, P. M., & Insel, T. R. (2000). Distribution of corticosteroid receptors in the rhesus brain: relative absence of glucocorticoid receptors in the hippocampal formation. *Journal of Neuroscience*, 20, 4657–4668.

Sarrieau, A., Dussaillant, M., Sapolsky, R. M., Aitken, D. H., Olivier, A., Lal, S., Rostene, W. H., Quirion, R., & Meaney, M. J. (1988). Glucocorticoid binding sites in human temporal cortex. *Brain Research*, 442, 157–160.

Schatzberg, A. F., Posener, J. A., DeBattista, C., Kalehzan, B. M., Rothschild, A. J., & Shear, P. K. (2000). Neuropsychological deficits in psychotic versus nonpsychotic major depression and no mental illness. *American Journal of Psychiatry*, 157, 1095–1100.

Schoofs, D., Preuss, D., & Wolf, O. T. (2008). Psychosocial stress induces working memory impairments in an n-back paradigm. *Psychoneuroendocrinology*, 33, 643–653.

Schwabe, L., Bohringer, A., Chatterjee, M., & Schachinger, H. (2008). Effects of pre-learning stress on memory for neutral, positive and negative words: Different roles of cortisol and autonomic arousal. *Neurobiology of Learning and Memory*, 90, 44–53.

Scoville, W. B., & Milner, B. (1957). Loss of recent memory after bilateral hippocampal lesions. *Journal of Neurology, Neurosurgery, and Psychiatry*, 20, 11–21.

Selye, H. (1998). A syndrome produced by diverse nocuous agents. 1936. *Journal of Neuropsychiatry and Clinical Neurosciences*, 10, 230–231.

Stroud, L. R., Tanofsky-Kraff, M., Wilfley, D. E., & Salovey, P. (2000). The Yale Interpersonal Stressor (YIPS): affective, physiological, and behavioral responses to a novel interpersonal rejection paradigm. *Annals of Behavioral Medicine*, 22, 204–213.

Sullivan, E. V., Pfefferbaum, A., Swan, G. E., & Carmelli, D. (2001). Heritability of hippocampal size in elderly twin men: equivalent influence from genes and environment. *Hippocampus*, 11, 754–762.

Tancer, M. E., Brown, T. M., Evans, D. L., Ekstrom, D., Haggerty, J. J., Jr., Pedersen, C., & Golden, R. N. (1990). Impaired effortful cognition in depression. *Psychiatry Research, 31*, 161–168.

Tollenaar, M. S., Elzinga, B. M., Spinhoven, P., & Everaerd, W. (2009). Immediate and prolonged effects of cortisol, but not propranolol, on memory retrieval in healthy young men. *Neurobiology of Learning and Memory, 91*, 23–31.

Tytherleigh, M. Y., Vedhara, K., & Lightman, S. L. (2004). Mineralocorticoid and glucocorticoid receptors and their differential effects on memory performance in people with Addison's disease. *Psychoneuroendocrinology, 29*, 712–723.

Varney, N. R., Alexander, B., & MacIndoe, J. H. (1984). Reversible steroid dementia in patients without steroid psychosis. *American Journal of Psychiatry, 141*, 369–372.

Part III

Stress Effects Across the Life Span

13

Adolescence and Stress
From Hypothalamic–Pituitary–Adrenal Function to Brain Development

Russell D. Romeo and Ilia N. Karatsoreos

Introduction

Adolescent maturation is marked by major gains in both physiological and neuropsychological function (Spear, 2000, 2010; Steinberg, 2008). Yet, despite these developmental gains, adolescence is also associated with many neurobehavioral vulnerabilities (Andersen, 2003; Dahl, 2004), including depression, anxiety, and drug abuse (Conger and Petersen, 1984; Masten, 1987; Spear, 2000; Costello et al., 2003; Patton and Viner, 2007; Spear, 2010). Although it is presently unclear what mediates the pubertal increase in these dysfunctions, recent studies in adolescent boys and girls point to adolescent exposure to stress as a particularly important factor that contributes to these vulnerabilities (Ge et al., 1994, 2001; Seiffge-Krenke, 2000; Goodyer, 2002; Grant et al., 2003, 2004; Turner and Lloyd, 2004).

A growing body of literature from both human and animal studies indicates that many cortical and limbic brain regions implicated in cognitive and emotional function continue to mature well into the adolescent stage of maturation (Giedd, 2004, 2008; Juraska and Markham, 2004; Spear, 2010). For instance, frontal gray-matter volume decreases during adolescence (Giedd et al., 1999; Gogtay et al., 2004), while hippocampal and amygdalar volumes increase (Giedd et al., 1996; Giedd, 2008). Although these structural changes in the adolescent brain appear to be part of normal development, it is noteworthy that the regions demonstrating this substantial postpubertal maturation are also exquisitely sensitive to the glucocorticoids (McEwen, 2005; McEwen, 2007). Thus, exposure to stressors during adolescence may perturb the normal developmental trajectory of neural circuits imperative in modulating cognitive processes and emotionality.

The Handbook of Stress: Neuropsychological Effects on the Brain, First Edition.
Edited by Cheryl D. Conrad.
© 2011 Blackwell Publishing Ltd. Published 2011 by Blackwell Publishing Ltd.

The purpose of this chapter is to highlight research examining the interaction of stress and adolescent brain maturation. To these ends, two overlapping areas of investigation will be discussed. The first will describe the maturation of the hypothalamic–pituitary–adrenal (HPA) axis from the juvenile to adult transition and the role that stressful experiences play during adolescence in shaping the responsiveness of this axis. The second will cover the relatively nascent area of research demonstrating the effects of stress on brain regions that continue to mature during adolescence and that are important in cognitive and emotional function, namely the hippocampal formation and prefrontal cortex (PFC). However, prior to discussing these two related topics and to providing a temporal framework for the data reviewed in this chapter, we define and delineate some of the key stages of development through which an organism progresses to reach adulthood. As this chapter will focus largely on data derived from animal studies, the next section briefly describes the terminology and approximate age ranges often used in the context of laboratory rodent development, particularly that of rats and mice.

Stages of Development

Prenatal development in rats and mice occurs over a 3-week gestational period. However, as these species are born in an altricial state, parturition is followed by a relatively long and intense period of parental care lasting 14–21 days, often referred to as the neonatal or preweaning stage of maturation. In most laboratories animals are weaned from their mothers between 21 and 25 days of age and enter the prepubertal or postweaning stage, which is then closely followed by puberty and adolescence. Though puberty and adolescence are often used interchangeably, and have some chronological overlap, these terms have separate meanings (Sisk and Foster, 2004). Specifically, puberty is a relatively discrete physiological event marked by dramatic hormonal and somatic changes, while adolescence is more protracted stage of development beginning with puberty and ending when the animal attains sexual maturity and neurobehavioral characteristics associated with the adult of the species. Although the exact age span that encompasses adolescence is not clear, rats and mice undergo various behavioral and neurobiological changes between 30 and 60 days of age akin to adolescent-related changes observed in many other species, including humans. Such changes include decreases in play and risk-taking behaviors and increases in mating and aggressive behaviors, as well as changes in the volumes of gray and white matter (Spear, 2000, 2010; Romeo et al., 2002; Gogtay et al., 2004; Juraska and Markham, 2004; Markham et al., 2007). Finally, we will use the term *juvenile* to refer to the period of maturation that encapsulates the neonatal, prepubertal, and pubertal stages of development. Figure 13.1 provides a schematic of these developmental stages and their associated ages.

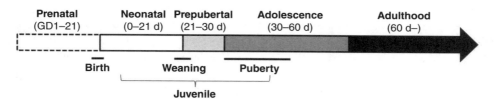

Figure 13.1 A time line of key developmental stages and their approximate age ranges in rats and mice. GD, gestational day; d, day.

Maturation of HPA Axis during the Juvenile to Adult Transition

As introduced throughout this volume, the HPA axis is the primary neuroendocrine axis that regulates the secretion of adrenal hormones into the bloodstream. This axis comprises both neural and endocrine components. In the brain, the paraventricular nucleus (PVN) of the hypothalamus is a central structure in the regulation of the hormonal stress response. Importantly, this brain region receives inputs from various cortical, limbic, hypothalamic, and hindbrain structures, which can initiate and modulate the stress response (Herman and Cullinan, 1997; Ulrigh-Lai and Herman, 2009; see also Chapter 2 in this volume). Neurosecretory cells of the PVN release corticotropin-releasing hormone into the hypothalamo-hypophyseal portal system and stimulate the anterior pituitary to release adrenocorticotropic hormone (ACTH). ACTH then stimulates the adrenal cortex to synthesize and release the glucocorticoids, such as cortisol in primates and corticosterone in many rodent species (see Chapter 1).

Under normal homeostatic conditions, a circadian (i.e., daily) rhythm of circulating corticosteroids is observed in most adult animals, and is driven by the master circadian clock in the suprachiasmatic nucleus of the hypothalamus (Moore and Eichler, 1972; Abe et al., 1979). The circadian rhythmicity in corticosteroid secretion is mediated in part by the suprachiasmatic nucleus modulating the inhibitory inputs to the PVN (Saeb-Parsy et al., 2000; Cui et al., 2001). However, under physically and/or psychologically stressful conditions, inputs from the amygdala, brainstem, and other regions of the hypothalamus stimulate the PVN to induce a surge in corticosteroids (and other factors) that prepare the organism to cope with physiological and behavioral demands imposed by the stressful event (Sapolsky et al., 2000; McEwen, 2007). Importantly, both the rhythmicity and the stress-induced release of glucocorticoid are significantly affected by adolescent development.

As indicated above, plasma corticosteroids display a circadian rhythm such that in adults of most species corticosteroids begin to rise just before waking, peaking at around the time of the beginning of daily activity, and gradually dropping through the reminder of the active phase. During early development there are changes in the rhythm of corticosterone secretion, transitioning from the prepubertal pattern to an adult pattern over the span of 7–8 days (Ramaley, 1978). More specifically, prepubertal rats at 22 days of age show a biphasic pattern, with two peaks (one in the middle of the light cycle and one after lights-off), gradually changing by 24 days of age to a monophasic peak just after lights-off, and then acquiring an appropriately timed *adult-like* peak (just before lights-off) by 26 days of age (Ramaley, 1978). Similar results have been demonstrated in humans, in that there is a correlation between the timing of the peak of salivary cortisol and the pubertal stage of development (Kiess et al., 1995), although not all studies have shown this association (Knutsson et al., 1997).

In addition to these developmental changes in rhythmic hormone secretion, stress-evoked ACTH and corticosterone responses are dramatically different in animals before and after adolescent maturation. Specifically, prepubertal rats exposed to an acute stressor, such as an intermittent foot shock, ether inhalation, or restraint, show a protracted ACTH and corticosterone (total and free) response compared to that of adults (Goldman et al., 1973; Vazquez and Akil, 1993; Romeo et al., 2004a; see also Figure 13.2a). Whereas this prolonged hormonal response in prepubertal rats has been observed in both males and females (Romeo et al., 2004a, 2004b), in different strains (Goldman et al., 1973; Vazquez and Akil, 1993), and in the light and dark phases of the light/dark cycle (Romeo et al., 2006b), it is still unclear what mediates this differential responsiveness of the developing HPA axis, or what the physiological and behavioral implications are.

Given the integral role of the hypothalamus in initiating the hormonal stress response, we investigated whether the prepubertal and adult PVN exhibited

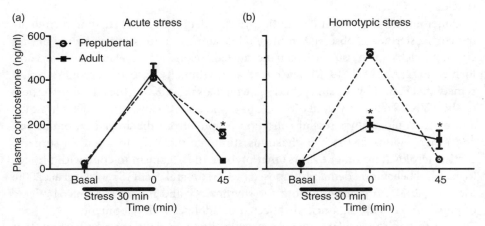

Figure 13.2 Mean (±SEM) plasma corticosterone concentrations in prepubertal (28 days of age) and adult (77 days of age) male rats exposed to a single (acute stress; a) or a daily 30-min session of restraint stress for 7 days (homotypic stress; b) Asterisks indicate significant differences between ages. Black bars underneath the *x* axes indicate 30 min of restraint stress. Adapted from Romeo et al. (2006a).

differential activation following an acute stressor. Interestingly, we found greater activation of corticotropin-releasing hormone cells in the prepubertal PVN following 30 min of restraint compared to adults (Romeo et al., 2006a). Moreover, previous research has shown that the synthetic glucocorticoid, dexamethasone, is less effective at blunting a stress-induced corticosterone response in prepubertal compared to adult males, suggesting reduced negative feedback in adolescent animals (Goldman et al., 1973). Therefore, changes in both central drive from the PVN and pubertal-related shifts in negative feedback may underlie these developmental changes in hormonal responsiveness following an acute stressor.

The effect of experience on the plasticity of HPA function is also different depending on developmental stage. For instance, in response to repeated restraint stress (e.g., homotypic stress), adult animals show an attenuated response such that stress-induced ACTH and corticosterone levels are lower compared to adults exposed to a single (e.g., acute) session of restraint (Magariños and McEwen, 1995b; Bhatnagar et al., 2002; Fernandes et al., 2002; Girotti et al., 2006). Intriguingly, prepubertal animals exposed to repeated restraint do not show this attenuated response. Instead, ACTH and corticosterone levels are significantly higher in prepubertal animals experiencing homotypic stress compared to prepubertal animals experiencing acute stress or adults exposed to either acute or homotypic stress (Romeo et al., 2006a; Figure 13.2b). These data indicate that age and stress history interact to shape HPA responsiveness, but the mechanisms that mediate these differential shifts in stress reactivity before and after adolescence remain elusive.

In addition to pubertal-related changes in stress responsiveness, experiments have demonstrated that chronic exposure to physical or social stress during adolescence can influence how the individual responds to stressors later in life (Isgor et al., 2004; McCormick and Mathews, 2007; McCormick et al., 2010). For example, Isgor et al. (2004) reported that rats exposed to chronic variable stress (CVS) during adolescence (i.e., 28–56 days of age) display a heightened stress-induced corticosterone response in adulthood compared to adult animals not exposed to CVS during adolescence. This study also showed that glucocorticoid receptor mRNA levels in the hippocampus were significantly lower in the animals that experienced CVS during adolescence, suggesting that reduced hippocampal glucocorticoid-dependent negative feedback may play a role in their greater stress reactivity (Isgor et al., 2004). It is also interesting to note that chronic stress during adolescence can disrupt the circadian peak and trough of corticosterone secretion in rats and mice, such that the usual increase in corticosterone observed in the dark phase of the light/dark cycle is reduced 1–2 weeks following the exposure to chronic stress during adolescence (Schmidt et al., 2007; Toth et al., 2008).

The studies reviewed above clearly indicate that HPA function is significantly affected by adolescent maturation. Specifically, this stage of development is marked by changes in both basal and stress-induced secretion of ACTH and corticosterone. Moreover, similar to the long-term effects of stress experienced during the perinatal period of development (Meaney, 2001; Maccari et al., 2003), chronic stress exposure during adolescence leads to heightened HPA responsiveness in adulthood. Although the glucocorticoids are known to be potent modulators of neurobiological activity (de Kloet et al., 2005), the physiological and neurobehavioral implications of these pubertal shifts in HPA function are not well understood. A growing body of evidence indicates that the adolescent and adult nervous system may be differentially sensitive to the glucocorticoids, including corticosterone (Lee et al., 2003; Lupien et al., 2009). Thus, pubertal-related changes in HPA output may have significant ramifications for the structure and function of the developing adolescent brain. The next section will highlight some recent studies on how stress and stress-related hormones influence key regions in the adolescent brain involved in cognitive processes and emotionality, particularly the hippocampal formation and PFC.

Stress and the Hippocampal Formation

The hippocampal formation is imperative for the learning and formation of episodic and declarative memories (Squire, 1992; Eichenbaum, 1997). In addition, the ventral aspect of the hippocampus also plays an important role in regulating emotionality (Bannerman et al., 2002, 2004; Kjelstrup et al., 2002; Degroot and Treit, 2004; Fanselow and Dong, 2010). The effects of stress on the structure and function of the adult hippocampal formation have been well studied (reviewed in Sapolsky, 2003; de Kloet et al., 2005; McEwen, 2007; McEwen and Milner, 2007). However, there is a paucity of studies on how stress affects the adolescent hippocampus. In an effort to place the few experiments that have examined stress and the adolescent hippocampal formation in perspective, we will first highlight some of the literature that describes the effects of stress on the adult hippocampus.

Magnetic resonance imaging studies in adult humans have demonstrated that individuals reporting high levels of perceived chronic stress show reduced hippocampal volumes (Gianaros et al., 2007). Moreover, individuals afflicted with major depressive disorder or pituitary and adrenal tumors associated with Cushing's syndrome show significantly reduced hippocampal volumes compared to healthy controls (Sheline et al., 1996; Starkman et al., 1999; Campbell et al., 2004; Videbech and Ravnkilde, 2004). As these disorders are marked by hyperfunction of the HPA axis (Arborelius et al., 1999; Starkman et al., 1999), such data suggest that increased exposure to glucocorticoids can lead to hippocampal atrophy in humans.

Studies using animal models have been able to show a direct relationship between stress and stress-related hormones and changes in hippocampal structure and function. In adult male rats, chronic restraint and variable physical and/or social stress significantly reduce branching of the apical dendrites of the CA3 pyramidal cells (where CA means cornu ammonis, a subregion of the hippocampus), and to a lesser extent the CA1 pyramidal cells and granule cells of the dentate gyrus (Watanabe et al., 1992; Magariños and McEwen, 1995a, 1995b; McEwen, 1999; McKittrick et al., 2000; Sousa et al., 2000; Vyas et al., 2002). This stress-induced remodeling of the hippocampal formation is dependent on corticosterone because administration of cyanoketone, an inhibitor of corticosterone synthesis, blocks the stress-induced atrophy of hippocampal dendrites (Magariños and McEwen, 1995b), while chronic injections of corticosterone mimic the stress-induced atrophy (Woolley et al., 1990).

Such stress-induced structural changes in the hippocampus likely underlie, at least in part, the compromised performance on hippocampal-dependent memory tasks (Conrad et al., 1996), as well as the changes in emotionality observed after periods of chronic stress in adults (McEwen, 2005). While the effects of stress on the adult hippocampus and hippocampal-dependent behaviors are profound, they are remarkably reversible. For instance, 10 days after cessation of stress, dendritic branching patterns return to those prior to stress exposure (Conrad et al., 1999; Conrad, 2010).

Although the hippocampus continues to mature well into adolescence (Meyer et al., 1978; Giedd et al., 1996; Heine et al., 2004), only a single animal study has assessed the effects of chronic stress during adolescence on the structure and developmental trajectory of this key brain area (Isgor et al., 2004). In this study it was demonstrated that exposure to CVS from 28 to 56 days of age resulted in a significantly smaller hippocampal volume in adulthood compared to nonstressed controls (Isgor et al., 2004). Moreover, animals exposed to CVS during adolescence showed impairments on the hippocampal-dependent Morris water-maze task. Intriguingly, these differences were apparent 30 days after the termination of the CVS paradigm, suggesting that alterations induced by chronic stress during adolescence may be longer lasting compared to the more transient stress-induced changes in adulthood (Conrad et al., 1999).

While structural remodeling of existing neurons in the hippocampal circuit is one example of the plasticity exhibited by the hippocampal formation, another aspect is the ability of the dentate gyrus to produce new neurons throughout an organism's life span (van Praag et al., 2002; Gould, 2007; see also Chapter 7 in this volume). The rate of hippocampal neurogenesis changes throughout adolescent development with a decline in neurogenesis observed through the juvenile-to-adult transition (Heine et al., 2004; Kim et al., 2004; Crews et al., 2007; He and Crews, 2007; Cowen et al., 2008). In adulthood it is well established that neurogenesis is influenced by chronic restraint and social stress (Gould et al., 1997; Pham et al., 2003; Dranovsky and Hen, 2006). Interestingly, in adolescent rats the effects of chronic stress on hippocampal neurogenesis were found to be opposite to those in adults, in that stress led to a decrease in neurogenesis in adulthood, but an increase during adolescence (Toth et al., 2008).

In addition to stress it appears the hippocampal formation is also differentially sensitive to corticosterone before and after pubertal development. In adrenalectomized prepubertal and adult animals treated with a corticosterone implant, only the prepubertal animals showed a significant increase in mRNA expression for a hippocampal N-methyl-D-aspartate (NMDA)-receptor subunit (Lee et al., 2003). As the implants resulted in equivalent circulating plasma corticosterone levels between the prepubertal and adult animals, these data suggest that corticosterone regulates hippocampal gene expression differently before and after pubertal development.

Together, the studies reviewed above indicate that the adolescent and adult hippocampal formation is differentially sensitive to stress and stress hormones. Although many questions remain unanswered, these data suggest that stressful life events occurring during adolescence may shape the developmental trajectory of the hippocampal formation in ways that contribute to increases in stress-related vulnerabilities observed during this stage of development (Ge et al., 1994, 2001; Seiffge-Krenke, 2000; Goodyer, 2002; Grant et al., 2003, 2004; Turner and Lloyd, 2004). However the hippocampal formation is not the only structure that shows continued maturation during puberty and sensitivity to stress, and which plays an important role in cognitive and emotional function. We next turn to the PFC, and briefly discuss how stress may alter its structure and function during adolescence.

Stress and the PFC

The PFC is involved in the regulation of emotional behaviors, executive function, and fear extinction (Sotres-Bayon et al., 2006). Similar to the hippocampal formation, the adult PFC shows remarkable morphological plasticity in response to stress (Shansky and Morrison, 2009, Chapter 10). For instance, animal studies have shown that adults exposed to chronic restraint stress (i.e., 6 hr of restraint stress per day for 21 days) show a significant reduction in the dendritic complexity of the pyramidal neurons of the medial prefrontal cortex (mPFC; Cook and Wellman, 2004; Radley et al., 2004, 2006; Liston et al., 2006). As an earlier study reported, that chronic injections of corticosterone also resulted in decreased dendritic branching of mPFC neurons, the dendritic remodeling observed following chronic stress is likely mediated by the stress-induced release of corticosterone (Wellman, 2001). It is important to note that the dendritic remodeling in the mPFC following chronic stress is reversible. Animals given a 21-day recovery period after the exposure to chronic stress show dendritic branching similar to unstressed controls (Radley et al., 2005).

The stress-induced remodeling in the rodent PFC is correlated with impairment of attention set-shifting (Liston et al., 2006), a task of cognitive flexibility that is also impaired by lesions of the mPFC (Birrell and Brown, 2000). Interestingly, chronic psychosocial stress in humans has been reported to disrupt attentional control as well as the functional connectivity of prefrontal circuitry that plays a role in modulating attention (Liston et al., 2009). Similar to the animal studies, following a 30-day recovery period these human subjects showed attentional control and prefrontal processing at levels similar to low-stress controls (Liston et al., 2009). Taken together, these data show that stress and stress-related hormones alter the structure of the PFC and may underlie the changes in emotional behavior observed after prolonged exposure to stress (McEwen, 2005).

Surprisingly few studies have investigated the effects of chronic stress on the structure of the adolescent PFC, even though this structure demonstrates considerable maturation during adolescence in humans and animals (Huttenlocher, 1979; Gogtay et al., 2004; Juraska and Markham, 2004; Markham et al., 2007; Giedd, 2008), and is critically important in modulating changes in emotionality observed during adolescence (Yurgelun-Todd, 2007). A neuroimaging study in young women with a history of childhood sexual abuse reported little change in frontal-cortex gray-matter volume (Andersen et al., 2008). However, an animal study in male rats reported that the synaptic marker synaptophysin was reduced in the mPFC in young adulthood following social-isolation stress during adolescence (Leussis et al., 2008). As these changes were noted up to 25 days after cessation of the isolation stress, these data suggest more protracted effects of stress on the adolescent compared to the adult mPFC (Leussis et al., 2008). Although it is currently unknown whether stress-induced reductions in mPFC synaptophysin levels are permanent, these results imply that structural alterations of the mPFC may exist following chronic stress during adolescence. Given the clear association between stress burden during adolescence and later emotional dysfunction (Conger and Petersen, 1984; Masten, 1987; Spear, 2000, 2010; Costello et al., 2003; Patton and Viner, 2007) it will be imperative for future studies to further investigate the role of stress on PFC function and development during adolescence.

Conclusions

Adolescent development is marked by both continued brain maturation and significant changes in stress reactivity. As stress and stress-related hormones are potent modulators of neurobiological function (Sapolsky et al., 2000; de Kloet et al., 2005; McEwen, 2007) the interaction of stress and the development of the adolescent brain may contribute to the myriad vulnerabilities associated with adolescence. Although some progress has been made in our understanding regarding how stress affects the adolescent brain, many voids in this understanding remain. Moreover, the neurobiological mechanisms that mediate the differential stress-induced hormonal response in pubertal and adult organisms await elucidation. Future research will need to address these gaps in our understanding to shed light on how exposure to stressful life events during this crucial stage of maturation may result in negative consequences in adolescent mental health, and what this means for normal development.

References

Abe, K., Kroning, J., Greer, M. A., & Critchlow, V. (1979). Effects of destruction of the suprachiasmatic nuclei on the circadian rhytms in plasma corticosterone, body temperature, feeding and plasma thyrotropin. *Neuroendocrinology, 29*, 119–131.

Andersen, S. L. (2003). Trajectories of brain development: point of vulnerability or window of opportunity. *Neuroscience and Biobehavioral Reviews, 27*, 3–18.

Andersen, S. L., Tomada, A., Vincow, E. S., Valente, E., Polcari, A., & Teicher, M. H. (2008). Perliminary evidence for sensitive periods in the effect of childhood sexual abuse on regional brain development. *Journal of Neuropsychiatry and Clinical Neurosciences, 20*, 292–301.

Arborelius, L., Owens, M. J., Plotsky, P. M., & Nemeroff, C. B. (1999). The role of corticotropin-releasing factor in depression and anxiety disorders. *Journal of Endocrinology, 160*, 1–12.

Bannerman, D. M., Deacon, R. M., Offen, S., Friswell, J., Grubb, M., & Rawlins, J. N. (2002). Double dissociation of function within the hippocampus: spatial memory and hypo-neophagia. *Behavioral Neuroscience, 116*, 884–901.

Bannerman, D. M., Rawlins, J. N. P., McHugh, S. B., Deacon, R. M. J., Yee, B. K., Bast, T., Zhang, W.-N., Pothuizen, H. H. J., & Feldon, J. (2004). Regional dissocations within the hippocampus-memory and anxiety. *Neuroscience and Biobehavioral Reviews, 28*, 273–283.

Bhatnagar, S., Huber, R., Nowak, N., & Trotter, P. (2002). Lesions of the posterior paraventricular thalamus block habituation of hypothalamic-pituitary-adrenal responses to repeated restraint. *Journal of Neuroendocrinology, 14*, 403–410.

Birrell, J. M., & Brown, V. J. (2000). Medial frontal cortex mediates perceptual attentional set shifting in the rat. *Journal of Neuroscience, 20*, 4320–4324.

Campbell, S., Marriott, M., Nahmias, C., & MacQueen, G. M. (2004). Lower hippocampal volume in patients suffering from depression: a meta-analysis. *American Journal of Psychiatry, 161*, 598–607.

Conger, J., & Petersen, A. (1984). *Adolescence and Youth: Psychological Development in a Changing World*. New York: Harper and Row.

Conrad, C. D. (2010). A critical review of chronic stress effects on spatial learning and memory. *Progress in Neuro-Psychopharmacology & Biological Psychiatry, 34*, 742–755.

Conrad, C. D., Galea, L. A., Kuroda, Y., & McEwen, B. S. (1996). Chronic stress impairs rat spatial memory on the Y maze, and this effect is blocked by tianeptine pretreatment. *Behavioral Neuroscience, 110*, 1321–1334.

Conrad, C. D., Magariños, A. M., LeDoux, J. E., & McEwen, B. S. (1999). Repeated restraint stress facilitates fear conditioning independently of causing hippocampal CA3 dendritic atrophy. *Behavioral Neuroscience, 113*, 902–913.

Cook, S. C., & Wellman, C. L. (2004). Chronic stress alters dendritic morphology in rat medial prefrontal cortex. *Journal of Neurobiology, 60*, 263–248.

Costello, E. J., Mustillo, S., Erkanli, A., Keeler, G., & Angold, A. (2003). Prevalence and development of psychiatric disorders in childhood and adolescence. *Archives of General Psychiatry, 60*, 837–844.

Cowen, D. S., Takase, L. F., Fornal, C. A., & Jacobs, B. L. (2008). Age-dependent decline in hippocampal neurogenesis is not altered by chronic treatment with fluoxetine. *Brain Research, 1228*, 14–19.

Crews, F. T., He, J., & Hodge, C. (2007). Adolescent cortical development: a critical period of vulnerability for addiction. *Pharmacology, Biochemistry, and Behavior, 86*, 189–199.

Cui, L. N., Coderre, E., & Renaud, L. P. (2001). Glutamate and GABA mediate suprachiasmatic nucleus inputs to spinal-projecting paraventricular neurons. *American Journal of Physiology, 281*, R1283–R1289.

Dahl, R. E. (2004). Adolescent brain development: a period of vulnerabilities and opportunities. *Annals of the New York Academy of Sciences, 1021*, 1–22.

Degroot, A., & Treit, D. (2004). Anxiety is functionally segregated within the septo-hippocampal system. *Brain Research, 1001*, 60–71.

de Kloet, E. R., Joels, M., & Holsboer, F. (2005). Stress and the brain: from adaptation to disease. *Nature Reviews Neuroscience, 6*, 463–475.

Dranovsky, A., & Hen, R. (2006). Hippocampal neurogenesis: regulation by stress and antidepressants. *Biological Psychiatry, 59*, 1136–1143.

Eichenbaum, H. (1997). Declarative memory: insights from cognitive neurobiology. *Annual Review of Neuroscience, 48*, 547–572.

Fanselow, M. S., & Dong, H.-W. (2010). Are the dorsal and ventral hippocampus functionally distinct structures? *Neuron, 65*, 7–19.

Fernandes, G. A., Perks, P., Cox, N. K. M., Lightman, S. L., Ingram, C. D., & Shanks, N. (2002). Habituation and cross-sensitization of stress-induced hypothalamic-pituitary-adrenal activity: effect of lesions in the paraventricular nucleus of the thalamus or bed nuclei of the stria terminalis. *Journal of Neuroendocrinology, 14*, 593–602.

Ge, X., Lorenz, F. O., Conger, R. D., Elder, G. H., & Simons, R. L. (1994). Trajectories of stressful life events and depressive symptoms during adolescence. *Developmental Psychology, 30*, 467–483.

Ge, X., Conger, R. D., & Elder, G. H. (2001). Pubertal transition, stressful life events, and the emergence of gender differences in adolescent depressive symptoms. *Developmental Psychology, 37*, 404–417.

Gianaros, P. J., Jennings, J. R., Sheu, L. K., Greer, P. J., Kuller, L. H., & Matthews, K. A. (2007). Prospective reports of chronic life stress predict decreased grey matter volume in the hippocampus. *NeuroImage, 35*, 795–803.

Giedd, J. N. (2004). Structural magnetic resonance imaging of the adolescent brain. *Annals of the New York Academy of Sciences, 1021*, 77–85.

Giedd, J. N. (2008). The teen brain: insights from neuroimaging. *Journal of Adolescent Health, 42*, 335–343.

Giedd, J. N., Vaituzis, A. C., Hamburger, S. D., Lange, N., Rajapakse, J. C., Kaysen, D., Vauss, Y. C., & Rapoport, J. L. (1996). Quantitative MRI of the temporal lobe, amygdala, and hippocampus in normal human development: ages 4–18 years. *Journal of Comparative Neurology, 366*, 223–230.

Giedd, J. N., Blumenthal, J., Jeffries, N. O., Castellanos, F. X., Liu, H., Zijdenbos, A., Paus, T., Evans, A. C., & Rapoport, J. L. (1999). Brain development during childhood and adolescence: a longitudinal MRI study. *Nature Neuroscience, 2*, 861–863.

Girotti, M., Pace, T. W., Gaylord, R. I., Rubin, B. A., Herman, J. P., & Spencer, R. L. (2006). Habituation to repeated restraint stress is associated with lack of stress-induced c-fos expression in primary sensory processing areas of the rat brain. *Neuroscience, 138*, 1067–1081.

Gogtay, N., Giedd, J. N., Lusk, L., Hayashi, K. M., Greenstein, D., Vaituzis, A. C., Nugent, T. F., Herman, D. H., Clasen, L. S., Toga, A. W., Rappoport, J. L., & Thompson, P. M. (2004). Dynamic mapping of human cortical development during childhood through early adulthood. *Proceedings of the National Academy of Sciences USA, 101*, 8174–8179.

Goldman, L., Winget, C., Hollingshead, G. W., & Levine, S. (1973). Postweaning development of negative feedback in the pituitary-adrenal system of the rat. *Neuroendocrinology, 12*, 199–211.

Goodyer, I. M. (2002). Social adversity and mental functions in adolescents at high risk of psychopathology. *British Journal of Psychiatry, 181,* 383–386.

Gould, E. (2007). How widespread is adult neurogenesis in mammals. *Nature Reviews Neuroscience, 8,* 481–488.

Gould, E., McEwen, B. S., Tanapat, P., Galea, L. A., & Fuchs, E. (1997). Neurogenesis in the dentate gyrus of the adult tree shrew is regulated by psychosocial stress and NMDA receptor activation. *Journal of Neuroscience, 17,* 2492–2498.

Grant, K. E., Compas, B. E., Stuchlmacher, A. F., Thurn, A. E., McMahon, S. D., & Halpert, J. A. (2003). Stressors and child and adolescent psychopathology: moving from markers to mechanisms of risk. *Psychological Bulletin, 129,* 447–466.

Grant, K. E., Compas, B. E., Thurn, A. E., McMahon, S. D., & Gipson, P. Y. (2004). Stressors and child and adolescent psychopathology: measurement issues and prospective effects. *Journal of Clinical Child and Adolescent Psychology, 33,* 412–425.

He, J., & Crews, F. T. (2007). Neurogenesis decreases during brain maturation from adolescence to adulthood. *Pharmacology, Biochemistry, and Behavior, 86,* 327–333.

Heine, V. M., Maslam, S., Joels, M., & Lucassen, P. J. (2004). Prominent decline of newborn cell proliferation, differentiation, and apoptosis in the aging dentate gyrus, in absence of an age-related hypothalamic-pituitary-adrenal axis activation. *Neurobiology of Aging, 25,* 361–375.

Herman, J. P., & Cullinan, W. E. (1997). Neurocircuitry of stress: central control of the hypothalamo-pituitary-adrenocortical axis. *Trends in Neuroscience, 20,* 78–84.

Huttenlocher, P. R. (1979). Synaptic density in human frontal cortex—developmental changes and effects of aging. *Brain Research, 163,* 195–205.

Isgor, C., Kabbaj, M., Akil, H., & Watson, S. J. (2004). Delayed effects of chronic variable stress during peripubertal-juvenile period of hippocampal morphology and on cognitive and stress axis function in rats. *Hippocampus, 14,* 636–648.

Juraska, J. M., & Markham, J. A. (2004). The cellular basis for volume changes in the rat cortex during puberty: white and gray matter. *Annals of the New York Academy of Sciences, 1021,* 431–435.

Kiess, W., Meidert, A., Dressendorfer, R. A., Schriever, K., Kessler, U., Konig, A., Schwarz, H. P., & Strasburger, C. J. (1995). Salivary cortisol levels throughout childhood and adolescence: relation with age, pubertal stage, and weight. *Pediatric Research, 37,* 502–506.

Kim, Y.-P., Kim, H., Shin, M.-S., Chang, H.-K., Jang, M.-H., Shin, M.-C., Lee, S.-J., Lee, H.-H., Yoon, J.-H., Jeong, I.-G., & Kim, C.-J. (2004). Age-dependence of the effect of treadmill exercise on cell proliferation in the dentate gyrus of rats. *Neuroscience Letters, 355,* 152–154.

Kjelstrup, K. G., Tuvnes, F. A., Steffenach, H.-A., Murison, R., Moser, E. I., & Moser, M.-B. (2002). Reduced fear expression after lesions of the ventral hippocampus. *Proceedings of the National Academy of Sciences USA, 99,* 10825–10830.

Knutsson, U., Dahlgren, U., Marcus, C., Roseberg, S., Bronnegard, M., Stierna, P., & Albertsson-Wikland, K. (1997). Circadian cortisol rhythms in healthy boys and girls: relationship with age, growth, body composition, and pubertal development. *Journal of Clinical Endocrinology and Metabolism, 82,* 536–540.

Lee, P. R., Brandy, D., & Koenig, J. I. (2003). Corticosterone alters N-methyl-D-aspartate receptor subunit mRNA expression before puberty. *Molecular Brain Research, 115,* 55–62.

Leussis, M. P., Lawson, K., Stone, K., & Andersen, S. L. (2008). The enduring effects of an adolescent social stressor on synaptic density, part II: poststress reversal of synaptic loss in the cortex by adinazolam and MK-801. *Synapse, 62,* 185–192.

Liston, C., Miller, M. M., Goldwater, D. S., Radley, J. J., Rocher, A. B., Hof, P. R., Morrison, J. H., & McEwen, B. S. (2006). Stress-induced alterations in frontal cortical dendritic morphology predict selective impairments in perceptual attentional set-shifting. *Journal of Neuroscience, 26,* 7870–7874.

Liston, C., McEwen, B. S., & Casey, B. J. (2009). Psychosocial stress reversibly disrupts prefrontal processing and attentional control. *Proceedings of the National Academy of Sciences USA, 106,* 912–917.

Lupien, S. J., McEwen, B. S., Gunnar, M. R., & Heim, C. (2009). Effects of stress throughout the lifespan on the brain, behaviour and cognition. *Nature Reviews Neuroscience, 10,* 434–445.

Maccari, S., Darnaudery, M., Morley-Fletcher, S., Zuena, A. R., Cinque, C., & Van Reeth, O. (2003). Prenatal stress and long-term consequences: implications of glucocorticoid hormones. *Neuroscience and Biobehavioral Reviews, 27,* 119–127.

Magariños, A. M., & McEwen, B. S. (1995a). Stress-induced atrophy of apical dendrites of hippocampal CA3c neurons: comparison of stressors. *Neuroscience, 69,* 83–88.

Magariños, A. M., & McEwen, B. S. (1995b). Stress-induced atrophy of apical dendrites of hippocampal CA3c neurons: involvement of glucocorticoid secretion and excitatory amino acid receptors. *Neuroscience, 69,* 89–98.

Markham, J. A., Morris, J. R., & Juraska, J. M. (2007). Neuron number decreases in the rat ventral, but not dorsal, medial prefrontal cortex between adolescence and adulthood. *Neuroscience, 144,* 961–968.

Masten, A. (1987). Toward a developmental psychopathology of early adolescence. In M. Levin, & E. McArnarny (Eds.), *Early adolescent transitions* (pp. 261–278). Lexington, MA: DC Heath.

McCormick, C. M., & Mathews, I. Z. (2007). HPA function in adolescence: role of sex hormones in its regulation and the enduring consequences of exposure to stressors. *Pharmacology, Biochemistry, and Behavior, 86,* 220–233.

McCormick, C. M., Mathews, I. Z., Thomas, C., & Waters, P. (2010). Investigations of HPA function and the enduring consequences of stressors in adolescence in animal models. *Brain and Cognition, 72,* 73–85.

McEwen, B. S. (1999). Stress and hippocampal synaptic plasticity. *Annual Review of Neuroscience, 22,* 105–122.

McEwen, B. S. (2005). Glucocorticoids, depression, and mood disorders: structural remodeling in the brain. *Metabolism Clinical and Experimental, 54,* 20–23.

McEwen, B. S. (2007). Physiology and neurobiology of stress and adaptation: central role of the brain. *Physiological Reviews, 87,* 873–904.

McEwen, B. S., & Milner, T. A. (2007). Hippocampal formation: shedding light on the influence of sex and stress on the brain. *Brain Research Reviews, 55,* 343–355.

McKittrick, C. R., Magariños, A. M., Blanchard, D. C., Blanchard, R. J., McEwen, B. S., & Sakai, R. R. (2000). Chronic social stress reduces dendritic arbors in CA3 hippocampus and decreases binding to serotonin transporter sites. *Synapse, 36,* 85–94.

Meaney, M. J. (2001). Maternal care, gene expression, and the transmission of individual differences in stress reactivity across generations. *Annual Review of Neuroscience, 24,* 1161–1192.

Meyer, G., Ferres-Torres, R., & Mas, M. (1978). The effects of puberty and castration on hippocampal dendritic spines of mice. A Golgi study. *Brain Research, 155,* 108–112.

Moore, R. Y., & Eichler, V. B. (1972). Loss of a circadian adrenal corticosterone rhythm following suprachiasmatic lesions in the rat. *Brain Research, 42,* 201–206.

Patton, G. C., & Viner, R. (2007). Pubertal transitions in health. *The Lancet, 369,* 1130–1139.

Pham, K., Nacher, J., Hof, P. R., & McEwen, B. S. (2003). Repeated restraint stress suppresses neurogenesis and induces biphasic PSA-NCAM expression in adult rat dentate gyrus. *European Journal of Neuroscience, 17,* 879–886.

Radley, J. J., Sisti, H. M., Hao, J., Rocher, A. B., McCall, T., Hof, P. R., McEwen, B. S., & Morrison, J. H. (2004). Chronic behavioral stress induces apical dendritic reorganization of pyramidal neurons of the medial prefrontal cortex. *Neuroscience, 125,* 1–6.

Radley, J. J., Rocher, A. B., Janssen, W. G. M., Hof, P. R., McEwen, B. S., & Morrison, J. H. (2005). Reversibility of apical dendritic retraction in the rat medial prefrontal cortex following repeated stress. *Experimental Neurology, 196,* 199–203.

Radley, J. J., Rocher, A. B., Miller, M., Janssen, W. G. M., Liston, C., Hof, P. R., McEwen, B. S., & Morrison, J. H. (2006). Repeated stress induces dendritic spine loss in the rat medial prefrontal cortex. *Cerebral Cortex, 16,* 313–320.

Ramaley, J. A. (1978). The adrenal rhythm and puberty onset in the female rat. *Life Sciences, 23,* 2079–2087.

Romeo, R. D., Richardson, H. N., & Sisk, C. L. (2002). Puberty and the maturation of the male brain and sexual behavior: recasting a behavioral potential. *Neuroscience and Biobehavioral Reviews, 26,* 379–389.

Romeo, R. D., Lee, S. J., Chhua, N., McPherson, C. R., & McEwen, B. S. (2004a). Testosterone cannot activate an adult-like stress response in prepubertal male rats. *Neuroendocrinology, 79,* 125–132.

Romeo, R. D., Lee, S. J., & McEwen, B. S. (2004b). Differential stress reactivity in intact and ovariectomized prepubertal and adult female rats. *Neuroendocrinology, 80,* 387–393.

Romeo, R. D., Bellani, R., Karatsoreos, I. N., Chhua, N., Vernov, M., Conrad, C. D., & McEwen, B. S. (2006a). Stress history and pubertal development interact to shape hypothalamic pituitary adrenal axis plasticity. *Endocrinology, 147,* 1664–1674.

Romeo, R. D., Karatsoreos, I. N., & McEwen, B. S. (2006b). Pubertal maturation and time of day differentially affect behavioral and neuroendocrine responses following an acute stressor. *Hormones & Behavior, 50,* 463–468.

Saeb-Parsy, K., Lombardelli, S., Khna, F. Z., McDowall, K., Au-Yong, I. T., & Dyball, R. E. (2000). Neural connections of hypothalamic neuroendocrine nuclei in the rat. *Journal of Neuroendocrinology, 12,* 635–648.

Sapolsky, R. M. (2003). Stress and plasticity in the limbic system. *Neurochemical Research, 28,* 1735–1742.

Sapolsky, R. M., Romero, L. M., & Munck, A. U. (2000). How do glucocorticoids influence stress responses? Integrating permissive, suppressive, stimulatory, and preparative actions. *Endocrine Reviews, 21,* 55–89.

Schmidt, M. V., Sterlemann, V., Ganea, K., Liebl, C., Alam, D., Harbich, D., Greetfled, M., Uhr, M., Holsboer, F., & Muller, M. B. (2007). Persistent neuroendocrine and behavioral effects of a novel, etiologically relevant mouse paradigm for chronic social stress during adolescence. *Psychoneuroendocrinology, 32,* 417–429.

Seiffge-Krenke, I. (2000). Causal links between stressful events, coping style, and adolescent symptomatology. *Journal of Adolescence, 23,* 675–691.

Shansky, R. M., & Morrison, J. H. (2009). Stress-induced dendritic remodeling in the medial prefrontal cortex: effects of circuit, hormones and rest. *Brain Research, 1293,* 108–113.

Sheline, Y. I., Wang, P. W., Gado, M. H., Csernansky, J. G., & Vannier, M. W. (1996). Hippocampal atrophy in recurrent major depression. *Proceedings of the National Academy of Sciences USA, 93,* 3908–3913.

Sisk, C. L., & Foster, D. L. (2004). The neural basis of puberty and adolescence. *Nature Neuroscience, 7,* 1040–1047.

Sotres-Bayon, F., Cain, C. K., & LeDoux, J. E. (2006). Brain mechanisms of fear extinction: historical perspectives on the contribution of prefrontal cortex. *Biological Psychiatry, 60,* 329–336.

Sousa, N., Lukoyanov, N. V., Madeira, M. D., Almeida, O. F., & Paula-Barbosa, M. M. (2000). Reorganization of the morphology of hippocampal neurites and synapses after stress-induced damage correlates with behavioral improvement. *Neuroscience, 97,* 253–266.

Spear, L. (2010). *The behavioral neuroscience of adolescence.* New York: Norton.

Spear, L. P. (2000). The adolescent brain and age-related behavioral manifestations. *Neuroscience and Biobehavioral Reviews, 24,* 417–463.

Squire, L. R. (1992). Memory and the hippocampus: a synthesis from findings with rats, monkeys, and humans. *Psychological Reviews, 99,* 195–231.

Starkman, M. N., Gebarski, S. S., Berent, S., & Schteingart, D. E. (1999). Hippocampal formation volume, memory dysfunction, and cortisol levels in patients with Cushing's syndrome. *Biological Psychiatry, 32,* 756–765.

Steinberg, L. (2008). *Adolescence.* New York: McGraw-Hill.

Toth, E., Gersner, R., Wilf-Yarkoni, A., Raizel, H., Dar, D. E., Richter-Levin, G., Levit, O., & Zangen, A. (2008). Age-dependent effects of chronic stress on brain plasticity and depressive behavior. *Journal of Neurochemistry, 107,* 522–532.

Turner, R. J., & Lloyd, D. A. (2004). Stress burden and the lifetime incidence of psychiatric disorder in young adults. *Archives of General Psychiatry, 61,* 481–488.

Ulrigh-Lai, Y. M., & Herman, J. P. (2009). Neural regulation of endocrine and autonomic stress responses. *Nature Reviews Neuroscience, 10,* 397–409.

van Praag, H., Schinder, A. F., Christie, B. R., Toni, N., Palmer, T. D., & Gage, F. H. (2002). Functional neurogenesis in the adult hippocampus. *Nature, 415,* 1030–1034.

Vazquez, D. M., & Akil, H. (1993). Pituitary-adrenal response to ether vapor in the weanling animal: characterization of the inhibitory effect of glucocorticoids on adrenocorticotropin secretion. *Pediatric Research, 34,* 646–653.

Videbech, P., & Ravnkilde, B. (2004). Hippocampal volume and depression: a meta-analysis of MRI studies. *American Journal of Psychiatry, 161,* 1957–1966.

Vyas, A., Mitra, R., Rao, B. S. S., & Chattarji, S. (2002). Chronic stress induces contrasting patterns of dendritic remodeling in hippocampus and amygdala neurons. *Journal of Neuroscience, 22,* 6810–6818.

Watanabe, Y., Gould, E., & McEwen, B. S. (1992). Stress induces atrophy of apical dendrites of hippocampal CA3 pyramidal neurons. *Brain Research, 588,* 341–345.

Wellman, C. L. (2001). Dendritic reorganization in pyramidal neurons in medial prefrontal cortex after chronic corticosterone administration. *Journal of Neurobiology, 49,* 245–253.

Woolley, C. S., Gould, E., & McEwen, B. S. (1990). Exposure to excess glucocorticoids alters dendritic morphology of adult hippocampal pyramidal neurons. *Brain Research, 531,* 225–231.

Yurgelun-Todd, D. (2007). Emotional and cognitive changes during adolescence. *Current Opinion in Neurobiology, 17,* 251–257.

14

Effect of Early Environment and Separation Animal Models on Neurobiological Development

Allison Jane Fulford

Shaping Brain and Behavior Through Experience

At the very beginning of the twentieth century, Gates (1904) published his hypothesis on *brain building*. He proposed that structural changes in the brain affecting overall volume could be induced by environmental manipulation. Hebb later observed that pet rats performed better than laboratory rats when learning a simple maze test (Hebb, 1947), leading to the premise that early experiential deprivation could produce intellectual deficits. Since such seminal work there has been a storm of interest in the concept that early environment can influence brain functions over the course of a lifetime. The consequences of social deprivation are obviously more significant in species that are by nature *social animals*. Thus, the effects of isolation are marked in the rat but quite different in the mouse, which is more territorial. The young rat engages in social play; behavior which is not seen, to such an extent, in other rodents (Einon et al., 1980). Thus, if isolation-rearing is introduced at a young age, exclusion of social play is quite detrimental to rat development, resulting in permanent deficits in behavior (Morgan, 1973; Einon and Morgan, 1977; Einon et al., 1980). Rhesus monkeys isolated during the first year of life also develop aberrant behaviors including stereotypy, hyperlocomotion, fearfulness, social withdrawal, learning deficits, and self-mutilation (Kraemer et al., 1984; Sanchez et al., 1998a, 1998b).

Models associated with aberrant neurodevelopment have been subject to intensive research. Understanding of the effects of adverse early environment has been impeded by discrepancies and variability in the literature. Such disparity involves variability in experimental parameters employed, including sex, strain, and species

The Handbook of Stress: Neuropsychological Effects on the Brain, First Edition.
Edited by Cheryl D. Conrad.
© 2011 Blackwell Publishing Ltd. Published 2011 by Blackwell Publishing Ltd.

of animal used, the age at induction of the adverse environment and its subsequent duration. It is important to standardize as many variables as possible, including source of animals (bred *in house* or bought commercially) and parameters like group size, housing density, and cage design (wire mesh or opaque plastic). These variables ultimately shape the impact of adversity in terms of behavioral and neurobiological effects, or *sequelae*. Studies that have compared males with females have identified some differences in terms of the sensitivity to environmental manipulation; however, most employ males. The importance of female gender has begun to receive greater attention and this is particularly important in the context of higher prevalence of certain neuropsychiatric disorders in women.

Behavioral Effects of Social Isolation Rearing in Rodents

It is generally agreed that the influence of social isolation on behavior and neurobiology is more dramatic if isolation is introduced at a young age, during early postnatal development (weeks 3–4 of life), rather than at maturity. In general, most animals used in isolation-rearing studies are physically separated from their conspecifics so they maintain visual, olfactory, and auditory contact with peers. The effects of stimulus deprivation appear to be negatively correlated with the age at which deprivation is introduced, in addition to its duration. The consequences of isolation housing have involved studies of the effects of postnatal isolation introduced at preweaning (before day 21 in the rat), at postweaning (begun on day 21/22), and in adulthood (after approximately 12 weeks of age). Of these the overwhelming majority of studies have examined effects of postweaning isolation continued for 4–8 weeks. As most published data relates to these animals, I will focus attention of the effects of postweaning social isolation. One of the most robust characteristics of postweaning isolation is locomotor hyperactivity (compared to group-reared controls) when exposed to a novel environment (Sahakian et al., 1975; Einon and Morgan, 1978; Gentsch et al., 1981), recorded in photocell cages (Wright et al., 1991a, 1991b), and tested 4–8 weeks postweaning. Isolation-induced hyperactivity is seen in a number of species, including mice, monkeys, cats, and dogs. Typically, isolation-reared rats are slower to habituate to a novel environment (Sahakian et al., 1975; Gentsch et al., 1981).

Isolation-induced changes in behavior are generally reflective of defects in corticolimbic-striatal function. Isolation-rearing induces changes in responsiveness to alcohol and psychomotor stimulants (Schenk et al., 1987; Kraemer and McKinney, 1985), which is suggestive of alterations in underlying limbic reward pathways. A comprehensive study by Schenk et al., (1990) demonstrated that rats reared in isolation for 12 weeks from weaning resulted in increased preference for alcohol and greater alcohol intake. Isolation-reared rats also acquire cocaine self-administration faster (Boyle et al., 1991) and show enhanced cocaine responsiveness (Fowler et al., 1993). Evidently, isolation-rearing disturbs the maturation of systems involved in drug reinforcement, and these are likely to involve dopaminergic, noradrenergic, and serotonergic systems. Although isolation-reared rats do not alter the amount of amphetamine self-administered they show an increase in the intensity of stereotyped responses to amphetamine and similarly, to the dopamine agonist apomorphine (Sahakian et al., 1975; Einon and Sahakian, 1979; Jones et al., 1992).

Deficits in learning and memory that target the hippocampus have been reported for postweaning isolates (Juraska et al., 1984). Isolation-reared rats perform less well in maze tests, for example the eight-arm radial maze (Einon, 1980) and Morris water maze (Lu et al., 2003), which are hippocampus-dependent spatial tasks. Performance deficits may not result in impairments in memory function per se, but reflect attentional or emotional bias. Some consider that isolation-induced hyperactivity underlies the poor maze performance owing to cue inattention. As isolation-reared rats are experientially deprived, this could also account for poor performance in spatial working-memory tasks involving maze learning. However, it is important to note that there are also other reports of enhanced performance in water-maze learning in postweaning isolation-reared rats compared to controls (Wongwitdecha and Marsden, 1996). Attenuated hippocampal neurogenesis and long-term potentiation in isolates could be relevant to learning and memory function. Interestingly, resocialization of postweaning isolation-reared rats is able to attenuate deficits in task performance, dentate gyrus neurogenesis, and hippocampal long-term potentiation (Lu et al., 2003). Postweaning isolation-reared rats also display deficits in recognition memory that has been associated with hippocampal cytoskeletal protein stabilization (Bianchi et al., 2006). Taken together, evidence indicates reliable effects on several hippocampal functions following postweaning isolation.

Postweaning isolation-reared rats make more anticipatory errors in schedules of differential reinforcement requiring low rates of responding. In such conditioning tasks rats are food-deprived, thus differences in incentive motivation may be relevant (Morgan et al., 1975; Jones et al., 1990). As isolation-induced perseveration is seen in tasks not involving an appetitive component, it suggests deficits in behavioral inhibition exist. Although postweaning isolation-reared rats are not impaired in the acquisition of visual cues, they show impairments in serial reversal learning (Jones et al., 1991). Monkeys reared in isolation demonstrate similar deficits in reversal learning and behavioral rigidity and isolation-reared chimpanzees display perseveration during oddity learning (Davenport et al., 1973). A number of performance deficits are consistent with schizophrenic symptoms. Postweaning isolation-reared rats exhibit less prepulse inhibition (PPI) of acoustic startle compared to group-reared rats (Geyer et al., 1993; Varty et al., 1999; Cilia et al., 2005a), a sensorimotor gating deficit typical of schizophrenia (Braff et al., 1992). PPI deficits can be replicated by augmented mesolimbic dopamine substrates. Indeed, dopamine receptor antagonist raclopride reverses isolation PPI deficits (Geyer et al., 1993), as do $\alpha 7$ nicotinic receptor agonists (Cilia et al., 2005b).

Enhanced emotionality and stress responsiveness of isolates has stimulated interest in the model. Isolated rats overreact to novelty, showing longer latencies to emerge into an open field, reflecting enhanced neophobia, but reduced neophobia to novel foods and drink (Gentsch et al., 1981). Enhanced responsiveness to novelty may result from restricted experience, heightened arousal, or deficits in behavioral inhibition. Interestingly, hyperactivity of isolates can be reduced with acute antidepressants and hyperactivity accompanies some subtypes of depressive illness (Willner, 1984). Efficacy of antidepressants in attenuating signs of the postweaning isolation syndrome is consistent with the presence of deficits in underlying monoaminergic neurotransmitter regulation. Postweaning isolation-reared rats demonstrate anxiogenesis in the elevated-plus maze (Wright et al., 1991a, 1991b) and in social interaction tests (Lukkes et al., 2009b), and display lower rearing and exploration (Molina-Hernandez et al., 2001). As anxiogenesis is not altered by resocialization (Wright et al., 1991b) it could be a trait effect. Benzodiazepine and nonbenzodiazepine anxiolytics reverse anxiogenesis in isolates (Parker and Morinan, 1986), supporting model validity. In other tests, including open field, postweaning isolates do not reliably show high anxiety and defecate less than grouped controls (Hall, 1998). Changes in fear conditioning would be expected in postweaning isolates, involving heightened conditioned freezing, although this has not been clearly demonstrated (Fulford and Marsden, 1998a, 1998b, 2007; Lukkes et al., 2009a). Indeed, a recent study in isolation-reared mice found that context-conditioned freezing is reduced (Gresack et al., 2010).

Neuroanatomical Correlates of Social Isolation-rearing

In terms of the neural basis of the postweaning isolation syndrome, most interest has focused on telencephalic regions including the hippocampus, amygdala, medial prefrontal cortex (mPFC), and nucleus accumbens (NAcc), which are closely anatomically and functionally connected. The amygdala mediates acquisition of fear associations and expression of behavioral, autonomic, and endocrine responses. The mPFC is vital for extinction and context-specific fear, including freezing. The ventral, limbically innervated striatum, or NAcc, is a common output from basolateral amygdala, hippocampus, and mPFC, and is implicated in gateway control of emotional and motivated behaviors.

With respect to neurodevelopment, full synaptic density is not completed until postweaning and in some structures, such as the hippocampus, maturation is not completed until postnatal days 35–40 in the rat (Lanier and Issacson, 1977). In dentate gyrus about 85% of granule cells are formed postnatally, with greatest cell proliferation seen between postnatal days 20 and 30. Isolates display a generalized reduction in neuronal and nuclear size, a reduction in glial cell density, and a decrease in dendritic morphology involving spine number and branches. Isolation-induced differences in dendritic arborization may be gender-dependent (Juraska et al., 1985; Ferdman et al., 2007). Postweaning isolation also reduces dendritic spine density of the pyramidal neurons of the mPFC (Silva-Gomez et al., 2003) and calcium-binding protein (calbindin-D28-K) immunoreactivity in layer II/III pyramidal neurons (Pascual et al., 2007). The latter is consistent with a functional loss of γ-aminobutyric acid- (GABA-)ergic mPFC neurons (Pascual et al., 2007) that may be critical for behavioral inhibition. Restructuring of dendrites in response to environment appears to be dependent on whether isolation is introduced around postnatal day 21 (as consistent with most isolation studies) versus late weaning at postnatal day 30. When cortical regions are closely examined, apical dendritic branching in anterior cingulate pyramidal neurons is apparently longer in postnatal day 21 postweaning male isolates, although apical dendritic arborization is lower in orbitofrontal cortex (Bock et al., 2008).

Magnetic resonance imaging and volumetry have refined our understanding of subregional remodeling in isolates. Isolation-induced changes in prefrontal cortical volume were confirmed; specifically, there were modest volume reductions (5%) of both right- and left-hemispheric mPFC, despite no differences between anterior cingulate, retrosplenial cortex, or hippocampal formation (Schubert et al., 2009). No striking relationship between cortical volume and behavioral effects including magnitude of PPI or locomotor activity were noted, although there was a positive correlation between hippocampal volume and PPI in controls, but not isolates. Structural modifications may be related to expression profiles in mPFC of isolation-reared rats who display decreased expression of immediate-early genes c-*fos*, *Arc*, and *Jun-B* compared with controls (Levine et al., 2007). Apoptosis-related genes are also downregulated in mPFC of isolates (Levine et al., 2007). Such remarkable changes in prefrontal cortical morphology and molecular characteristics would be expected to influence control of subcortical neurocircuits including amygdala, known for its prominent role in anxiety and fear. Clearly, further research into precise subnuclei and cytoarchitecture following early deprivation will be critical to explaining the reorganization of synaptic connectivity and behavior.

Numerous studies have highlighted robust functional changes in NAcc of postweaning isolation-reared rats. This region is important for limbic regulation of emotionality given that NAcc integrates inputs from mPFC and extended amygdala (see Levita et al., 2002). Structural changes involving the accumbens have been identified, with retraction and reduction in density of accumbal neuronal dendrites of postweaning isolates (Alquicer et al., 2008). Although interesting, this raises questions concerning the relationship between dendritic remodeling and enhanced presynaptic monoamine neurotransmission of NAcc in isolates (Jones et al., 1992; Fulford and Marsden, 1998a, 1998b).

Similarities between the effects of isolation and hippocampectomy are also revealing. Isolation-reared and hippocampectomized rats both share deficits in reversal learning and in acquisition and performance of maze tasks. Closer inspection of the hippocampus from differentially reared rats reveals important changes. In postweaning isolates, synaptophysin immunoreactivity (marker of synaptic density) in dentate gyrus molecular layer is reduced (Varty et al., 1999). Dendritic length and spine density of CA1 pyramidal neurons (where CA means cornu ammonis, a subregion of the hippocampus) are reduced following isolation-rearing (Silva-Gomez et al., 2003), as is the expression of hippocampal microtubule-associated protein-2 (MAP-2), a marker of dendritic development (Bianchi et al., 2006). Such remodeling would be likely to impact on synaptic connectivity in hippocampal networks and neuroplasticity, and have implications for hippocampal-dependent behavior. Hippocampal regions are sensitive to changes in circulating stress hormones such as plasma glucocorticoids; however, isolation-induced changes in hypothalamic–pituitary–adrenal (HPA) axis activity have not been robustly demonstrated (Lyons et al., 2007). Interestingly, rats housed in *enriched* conditions have enhanced synaptic density of the medial hippocampus compared to isolation rats. Fiala et al (1978) showed that there was a greater degree of lower-order dendritic branching in the dentate gyrus of rats reared in a complex environment compared to isolation. Recent evidence suggests that environmental enrichment can attenuate the impact of isolation-rearing during early postnatal development, and that this may involve oxytocinergic mechanisms (Vitalo et al., 2009). Importantly, socially deprived monkeys also have structural changes involving basal ganglia, cerebral cortex, hippocampus, and corpus callosum (Martin et al., 1991; Siegel et al., 1993; Sanchez et al., 1998a).

Postweaning Social Isolation and Central Neurotransmitter Function

At birth in the rat, levels of major transmitters such as norepinephrine (noradrenaline), dopamine, and 5-hydroxytryptamine (5-HT) are only 20, 25, and 50% of adult levels, with the peak of biosynthesis being reached at around weaning age (postnatal day 21). On the basis of the remarkable isolation syndrome, attention has focused on these monoaminergic transmitters. Isolation-reared rats show an altered time course of hyperactivity in response to D-amphetamine (Jones et al., 1992) and enhanced sedative effects of apomorphine (Jones et al., 1992). Postweaning isolation-reared rats have augmented presynaptic dopamine function in the caudate putamen and in response to cocaine (Howes et al., 2000). Increased locomotor response to D-amphetamine in isolates reflects enhanced presynaptic function of the NAcc (Jones et al., 1992). Presynaptic dopamine efflux, measured using microdialysis, is enhanced in the NAcc of isolation-reared rats in response to D-amphetamine (Jones et al., 1992), an aversive stimulus (mild foot shock), and context-conditioned emotional response (Fulford and Marsden, 1998a). Dopamine depletion of the accumbens successfully attenuates isolation-induced PPI deficits (Powell et al., 2003) and isolation-reared monkeys display similarly enhanced sensitivity to D-amphetamine (Kraemer et al., 1984). Isolation-rearing modifies other behaviors reliant upon striatal dopamine including tail pinch evoked oral behaviors and schedule-induced drinking (Jones et al., 1989). Increased incentive motivation for food may be a manifestation of mesolimbic dopamine and conditioned reinforcement also depends on presynaptic dopamine in amygdala and hippocampus. Rat dopamine type 2 receptors (D2 receptors) are sensitive to postweaning environment as mature levels are not established until postnatal day 28. Furthermore, isolation disrupts firing of prefrontal cortical pyramidal neurons in response to stimulation of the ventral tegmental area (Peters and O'Donnell, 2005) and dopamine turnover is reduced in prefrontal cortex of isolates (Jones et al., 1992; Heidbreder et al., 2000). Elevated mesocortical dopamine may subserve drug adminstration behaviors including enhanced cocaine self-administration and deficits in PPI (Geyer et al., 1993; Weiss and Feldon, 2001).

In addition to changes in presynaptic dopamine, changes in presynaptic serotonergic function in isolates exist. Reports are consistent with suppressed central 5-HT function (Bickerdike et al., 1993; Whitaker-Azmitia et al., 2000; Muchimapura et al., 2002). There is a sizeable reduction (50%) in hippocampal 5-HT turnover in isolates, consistent with reports that activity of the rate-limiting biosynthetic enzyme, tryptophan hydroxylase, is reduced following postweaning isolation-rearing and stress-induced deficits in hippocampal 5-HT function exist (Muchimapura et al., 2002). Pre- and postsynaptic 5-HT_{1A} receptor function is altered in isolation, and binding studies reveal there to be sex differences in 5-HT receptors in raphe and limbic regions (Wright et al., 1991a; Schiller et al., 2006). mRNA transcripts for postsynaptic 5-HT receptors are reduced in isolation mPFC and 5-HT_{1B}, 5-HT_{2A}, and 5-HT_{2C} receptor mRNAs are reduced in hypothalamus and midbrain, although 5-HT transporter levels are unchanged (Bibancos et al., 2007). Serotonergic neuronal firing rates are also lower in socially isolated rats (Oehler et al., 1987). Studies of 5-HT release in vivo have been useful in providing more detail regarding the site-specific changes in 5-HT systems. Isolation-rearing blunts serotonergic function in the frontal cortex and hippocampus (Bickerdike et al., 1993; Dalley et al., 2002; Muchimapura et al., 2002), consistent with isolation anxiogenesis. Interestingly, antidepressants that inhibit 5-HT reuptake successfully ameliorate the hyperactivity and aggression of isolates.

Serotonergic interactions with striatal dopamine function may account for some effects of 5-HT reuptake inhibition. Isolated rats have reduced 5-hydroxyindole acetic acid/5-HT ratio (5-hydroxyindole acetic acid is a serotonin metabolite) in the dopamine-rich NAcc (Jones et al., 1992); however, in response to foot shock and context-conditioned emotional response there is evidence for enhanced accumbal 5-HT release (Fulford and Marsden, 1998b). Presynaptic 5-HT function in the NAcc is dependent on presynaptic dopamine function (Fulford and Marsden, 2007), confirming that changes in serotonergic terminals do not reflect a primary isolation change. Hyperactivity may manifest by imbalance between 5-HT and dopamine in the NAcc. In addition, isolation-induced deficits in impulsivity are a sign of 5-HT and dopamine imbalance in the accumbens and prefrontal cortex (Dalley et al., 2002). Both monoamines are associated with impulsive behavior (Winstanley et al., 2005) and close appositions between dopamine neurons and 5-HT terminals in NAcc exist (Van Bockstaele and Pickel, 1993). Clearly the extent of neurotransmitter interactions at the circuit level is critical to explaining the behavioral sequelae of isolation. During postweaning neurodevelopment differential maturation of ventral striatal innervation occurs in isolates (Gos et al., 2006) and functional segregation of subcircuits in the NAcc (Schultz, 2007; McCittrick and Abercrombie, 2007) provides a new basis for studying isolation-altered NAcc function.

A number of behavioral characteristics of isolates are consistent with changes in presynaptic noradrenergic control including attentional deficits, hyperactivity, and enhanced emotionality. Isolation-reared rats show greater immobility in the forced-swim test; an effect that is reversed with chronic desipramine (Heritch et al., 1990). Isolation-rearing also reduces norepinephrine turnover in cingulate cortex, hippocampus, amygdala, caudate nucleus, and paraventricular nucleus. Evidence from nonhuman primates show that isolation reduces norepinephrine levels in cerebral spinal fluid (Kraemer et al., 1989). Research strongly suggests that upregulation of α_2-autoreceptor function occurs in isolation-reared rats and this is responsible for blunted stress-evoked norepinephrine efflux (Fulford et al., 1994; Fulford and Marsden, 1997a, 1997b). Furthermore, isolation-induced aggression may be associated with attenuated norepinephrine release. Low doses of yohimbine (α_2-antagonist) reduce nervousness and increase so-called *normal* behaviors like self-grooming (Coplan et al., 1992). To fully appreciate the phenotype of isolation-reared animals in the context of stress-related behaviors one must necessarily consider the numerous other neurotransmitter mediators of emotionality. To a large extent there is still much to be learnt in respect of early environmental influences on neurotransmission and behavior.

Neuroendocrine Adaptations and Importance of Early-life Environment

The impact of early social environment on adult HPA axis activity is dependent on the nature of adversity and its coincidence with a maximally sensitive period of neurodevelopment, involving the early preweaning or postweaning period. Diathesis–stress models highlight dual influences of early environment and genetics in programming individual stress vulnerability and predisposition to mental health disorders. Thus, a nurturing environment during early life can ameliorate stress reactions and attenuates anxiety in adulthood. Interestingly, postweaning isolation syndrome is not convincingly associated with chronic corticosterone hypersecretion or enhanced HPA axis reactivity to stressors. Isolation-rearing may increase (Gamallo et al., 1986; Heidbreder et al., 2000; Van den Berg et al., 1999), decrease (Sanchez et al., 1998a, 1998b; Miachon et al., 1993), or not change (Holson et al., 1991; Jones et al., 1989; Weiss et al., 2004; Lukkes et al., 2009a) HPA activity. Basal plasma corticosterone is elevated in isolated rats at 6 weeks but not 12 weeks after weaning (Gentsch et al., 1981). Some suggest that postweaning isolates have enhanced HPA axis responses to acute stressors (Serra et al., 2007), whereas others find attenuated acute stress responses. Isolation-rearing does not reliably alter the normal response of the HPA axis to acute restraint (Lukkes et al., 2009a); however, the corticosterone response to 15 min immobilization is attenuated (Sanchez et al., 1998b). Nevertheless it is clear that given the profound effect of early isolation on limbic-striatal circuits, isolation-induced changes are likely to impact on integrated neuroendocrine function and behavior. Isolation-rearing paradigms may provide a valuable model for studying the effects of early experience on behavioral and neuroendocrine adaptations, given that features of the isolation syndrome correlate with the sequelae of maternal deprivation.

Neuropeptide Neuromodulation and Early Social Environment

Given that central peptide transmitters serve major roles in the neuromodulation of stress and anxiety, memory, and behavior, their study in regard to early-life environment has been somewhat limited. Postweaning isolation-reared rats appear to be less sensitive to the anxiolytic effect of cholecystokinin A receptor antagonists (Bickerdike et al., 1994) for example. Oxytocin is another peptide that functions as a neuromodulator in circuits involved in altered anxiety states. Oxytocin acts on receptors that are predominantly located within the limbic system, especially the bed nucleus of the stria terminalis and amygdala. Oxytocin is linked to suppression of anxiety and neophobia (Uvnäs-Moberg et al., 1994) and facilitation of the milk-ejection reflex (Jiang and Wakerley, 1997). Appropriate maternal care may operate through central oxytocinergic mechanisms or the monoaminergic pathways with which they interact. Evidence that rearing can exert long-term effects on oxytocinergic systems was obtained by Meaney and colleagues (Champagne et al., 2001) who found that individual variability in maternal behavior is correlated with differences in levels of oxytocin receptors in bed nucleus of the stria terminalis and preoptic regions. Oxytocin receptors in the amygdala are modulated by dopamine (Bale et al., 2001), thereby limbic dopamine changes in early isolation could influence adult oxytocinergic system. Ontogenic studies also reveal that central oxytocinergic pathways are evident around postnatal day 4 and developmental expression of oxytocin transcript is relatively late, with only 40% adult hypothalamic levels expressed by postnatal day 28 (Almazan et al., 1989). Clearly, maturation of central oxytocinergic neurons may be sensitive to early social experience and this is a focus of interest in my own laboratory. Both oxytocin and the related neurohormone vasopressin are important in modulation of characteristic behaviors during weaning (Kavushansky and Leshem, 2004). Aggressive interactions in developing hamsters also lead to permanent changes in the vasopressinergic innervation of the septum (Ferris, 2000). We have also demonstrated robust isolation-induced changes in vasopressin innervation of the limbic system, and this contributes to isolation-induced fear and aggression (see Figure 14.1). Significantly, there is also emerging evidence for an isolation-induced increase in corticotropin-releasing hormone (CRH) fiber staining of the median eminence, although there is no change in paraventricular nucleus CRH immunoreactivity (Sanchez et al., 1998b). Despite this, CRH 1 receptors may be involved in enhanced fear behavior in isolated mice (Gresack et al., 2010), CRH 2 receptors evoke 5-HT release in the NAcc (Lukkes et al., 2009c) and CRH receptor antagonist infusion into the rat dorsal raphe attenuates isolation-induced anxiety in the social interaction test (Lukkes et al., 2009b). Clearly further research is

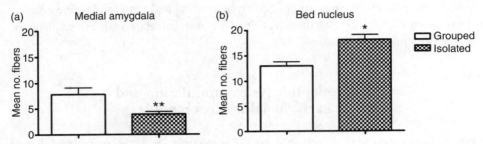

Figure 14.1 Histograms showing impact of early postweaning isolation in male Lister hooded rats on vasopressin-like immunoreactivity of limbic regions (a) medial amygdala and (b) bed nucleus. Rats were weaned at postnatal day 21 and conditions (isolation or grouped four per cage) were continued for 6–8 weeks (six rats per condition). Rats housed in isolation had reduced vasopressin fiber density of the medial amygdala but enhanced innervation of the bed nucleus. This suggests that isolation-induced disruption of vasopressinergic pathways involves imbalance between extended amygdala circuits that may contribute to heightened emotionality and aggression of male rats.

warranted to understand the relevance of neuropeptide function to the isolation syndrome and to close gaps in understanding of the integration of peptidergic and monoaminergic dysfunction in limbic circuits.

Other Paradigms involving Early-environment Manipulation

Research has revealed the *pre*weaning period (i.e. before day 21/22 in the rat) to be a most sensitive period in the development of stress-responsive brain circuits and endocrine systems. Interest has focused on the effect of handling early postnatal rat pups on subsequent development and anxiety (Levine, 1957; Levine and Mullins, 1968). Mild handling is considered to have a stimulatory effect on pup development with the appearance of modest and attenuated anxiety and stress responsiveness in adulthood. At adulthood postnatal-handled rats have comparatively low defecation scores and reduced emotionality. In paradigms of early postnatal handling, rat or mouse pups are typically removed from the cage and physically isolated for 3 or 15 min per day during the first three postnatal weeks. Such mild early postnatal handling and brief separation elicits greater exploratory activity in the novel environment when adult and is associated with less defecation than unhandled controls. In a number of respects the effects of postnatal handling appear opposite to those of adverse forms of early environmental manipulation, such as social isolation. It should be emphasized, though, that effects of such manipulations are dependent on parameters employed and laboratory conditions, such that interlaboratory differences can exert a large influence. Responses are largely dependent on gender, strain, or species of animal (Kosten et al., 2007). Effects appear to be more consistent when handling is initiated during neonatal week 1, rather than begun during the subsequent week or fortnight. This suggests that the intervention may be superimposed upon a critical window of development, or that another external factor may be important, such as temperature fluctations during short bouts of maternal separation. Stimulation of exploratory behavior following mild handling is entirely consistent with stimulation effects on other maturation parameters such as hair development and eye opening.

A major consideration when one attempts to explain the influence of early postnatal interventions during the preweaning period is the impact on mother–pup bonding. Physical removal of the mother for short periods compared with physical removal of pups from the nest for short bouts of separation have inherently differential impacts. Under normal circumstances the dam would be foraging for food and so leave the warm nest for short periods at a time. Physical removal of pups from the nest is an unwelcome nest intrusion and will undoubtedly interrupt natural maternal behavior and contribute to the overall *handling* manipulation. Such brief mother/pup separations have been known to stimulate the dam's pup-licking behavior once reunited. This enhanced maternal attentiveness has been associated with lower emotionality in pups when they reach adulthood. Given the complex regulation of hormonal systems during the early postnatal period, it is widely acknowledged that the ability of early environment to influence behavior may also program changes in adult neuroendocrine systems. Young pups experience a striking transitional inhibitory phase early postnatally, which is characterized as the *stress hyporesponsive period*, occurring between postnatal day 4 and 14 in the rat. During this phase of development the HPA axis is largely resistant to applied stressors, compared to when these are experienced during adulthood. The influence of appropriate maternal care in suppressing corticosterone responses of the young is considered to be a vital adaptation that helps facilitate optimal neurodevelopment, organization, and maturation of neural pathways (Cirulli et al., 2003). In contrast to the mild stimulatory effect of early postnatal handling, prolonged maternal separation has pronounced adverse impact on development of brain, and endocrine and behavioral responses when the stress hyporesponsive period is disrupted (Hall, 1998; Ladd et al., 2000; Litvin et al., 2010). Long-term repeated maternal separation (180 min per day), compared with maternal separation (15 min per day) or normal group housing of pups from postnatal day 2 to 14, elicits robust behavioral and endocrine changes encompassing lower locomotor activity, enhanced acoustic startle response, impaired acquisition of cue-conditioned fear, enhanced stereotypy, and heightened anxiety when tested in maturity (Plotsky and Meaney, 1993; Lippmann et al., 2007; Stevenson et al., 2009). Prolonged maternal separation results in elevated basal HPA activity involving increased CRH levels, enhanced adrenocorticotrophic hormone, and corticosterone responses to acute stressful stimuli, such as air puff or novel environment, that may constitute a model for *early-life stress* with relevance to human depression (Plotsky and Meaney, 1993; Biagini et al., 1998; Kalinichev et al., 2002). Changes in hippocampal neurotrophins may be relevant to reports of attenuated mossy fiber density in prolonged maternally separated rats (Huot et al., 2002). As chronic maternal separation blunts expression of neurotrophins in the striatum and hippocampus, including brain-derived neuro-trophic factor, this is likely to impact on cognitive functions in these animals (Schable et al., 2007; Aisa et al., 2009). Furthermore, such hippocampus-dependent changes provide additional support for this particular model as a paradigm of depression (Duman and Monteggia, 2006).

Conclusions

Manipulation of the early-life environment has proven to be a fertile area of neuro-biological research. Both postnatal isolation-rearing and maternal separation provide powerful models for the behaviorist with demonstrable validity for study-ing signs of human neuropsychiatric disorders. The discovery of enduring deficits in neuronal architecture, central neurotransmitter systems, and behaviors provides a compelling illustration of how manipulation of the early social environment can directly affect the plasticity and maturation of the central nervous system. The complex interactions between transmitter systems and neuronal pathways remain incompletely understood and better understanding of these will enable elucidation of the critical substrates of animal behavior. To this extent, the wide employment of nonpharmacologic, nonlesion models for studying aberrant neurodevelopment will undoubtedly continue to substantiate knowledge in this field.

Acknowledgment

I thank Dr Jon Wakerley (Bristol) for his collaboration with isolation studies of oxytocin and vasopressin peptide systems.

References

Aisa, B., Gil-Bea, F., Marcos, B., Tordera, R., Lasheras, B., Del Rio, J., & Ramirez, M. J. (2009). Neonatal stress affects vulnerability of cholinergic neurons and cognition in the rat: involvement of the HPA axis. *Psychoneuroendocrinology, 34,* 1495–1505.

Almazan, G., Lefebvre, D., & Zingg, H. (1989). Ontogeny of hypothalamic vasopressin, oxy-tocin and somatostatin gene expression. *Developmental Brain Research, 45,* 69–75.

Alquicer, G., Morales-Medina, J. C., Quirion, R., & Flores, G. (2008). Postweaning social isolation enhances morphological changes in the neonatal ventral hippocampal lesion rat model of psychosis. *Journal of Chemical Neuroanatomy, 35,* 179–187.

Bale, T. L., Davis, A. M., Auger, A. P., Dorsa, D. M., & McCarthy, M. M. (2001). CNS region-specific oxytocin receptor expression: importance in regulation of anxiety and sex behavior. *Journal of Neuroscience, 21,* 2546–2552.

Biagini, G., Pich, E., Carani, C., Marrama, P., & Agnati, L. F. (1998). Postnatal maternal sepa-ration during the stress hyporesponsive period enhances the adrenocortical response to novelty in adult rats by affecting feedback regulation in the CA1 hippocampal field. *International Journal of Developmental Neuroscience, 16*, 187–197.

Bianchi, M., Fone, K. C., Azmi, N., Heidbreder, C. A., Hagan, J., & Marsden, C. A. (2006). Isolation rearing induces recognition memory deficits accompanied by cytoskeletal alterations in rat hippocampus. *European Journal of Neuroscience, 24*, 2894–2902.

Bibancos, T., Jardin, D. L., Aneas, I., & Chiavegatto, S. (2007). Social isolation and expression of serotonergic neurotransmission-related genes in several brain areas of mice. *Genes, Brain, and Behavior, 6*, 529–539.

Bickerdike, M. J., Wright, I. K., & Marsden, C. A. (1993). Social isolation attenuates rat fore-brain 5-HT release induced by KCl stimulation and exposure to a novel environment. *Behavioral Pharmacology, 4*, 421–426.

Bickerdike, M. J., Marsden, C. A., Dourish, C. T., & Fletcher, A. (1994). The influence of 5-hydroxytryptamine re-uptake blockade on CCK receptor antagonist effects in the rat elevated zero-maze. *European Journal of Pharmacology, 271*, 403–411.

Bock, J., Murmu, R. P., Ferdman, N., Leshem, M., & Braun, K. (2008). Refinement of den-dritic and synaptic networks in the rodent anterior cingulate and orbitofrontal cortex: critical impact of early and late social experience. *Developmental Neurobiology, 68*, 685–695.

Boyle, A. E., Gill, K., Smith, B. R., & Amit, Z. (1991). Differential effects of an early housing manipulation on cocaine-induced activity and self-administration in laboratory rats. *Pharmacology, Biochemistry, and Behavior, 39*, 269–274.

Braff, D., Grillon, C., & Geyer, M. (1992). Gating and habituation of the startle reflex in schizophrenic patients. *Archives of General Psychiatry, 49*, 206–215.

Champagne, F., Diorio, S., Sharma, M. J., & Meaney, M. (2001). Variations in maternal care in the rat are associated with differences in estrogen-related changes in oxytocin recep-tor levels. *Proceedings of the National Academy of Sciences USA, 98*, 25026–25031.

Cilia, J., Hatcher, P. D., Reavill, C., & Jones, D. N. (2005a). Long-term evaluation of isolation-rearing induced prepulse inhibition deficits in rats: an update. *Psychopharmacology, 180*, 57–62.

Cilia, J., Cluderay, J. E., Robbins, M. J., Reavill, C., Southam, E., Kew, J. N., & Jones, D. N. (2005b). Reversal of isolation-rearing induced PPI deficits by an alpha7 nicotinic recep-tor agonist. *Psychopharmacology, 182*, 214–219.

Cirulli, F., Berry, A., & Alleva, E. (2003). Early disruption of the mother-infant relationship: effects on brain plasticity and implications for psychopathology. *Neuroscience and Biobehavioral Reviews, 27*, 73–82.

Coplan, J. D., Rosenblum, L. A., Friedman, S., Bassoff, T. B., & Gorman, J. M. (1992). Behavioural effects of oral yohimbine in differentially-reared non-human primates. *Neuropsychopharmacology, 6*, 21–37.

Dalley, J. W., Theobald, D. E., Pereira, E. A., Li, P. M., & Robbins, T. W. (2002). Specific abnormalities in serotonin release in the prefrontal cortex of isolation-reared rats meas-ured during behavioural performance of a task assessing visuospatial attention and impulsivity. *Psychopharmacology, 164*, 329–340.

Davenport, R. K., Rogers, C., & Rumbaugh, D. (1973). Long-term cognitive deficits in chim-panzees associated with early impoverished learning. *Developmental Psychology, 9*, 313–347.

Duman, R. S., & Monteggia, L. M. (2006). A neurotrophic model for stress-related mood disorders. *Biological Psychiatry, 59*, 1116–1127.

Einon, D. F. (1980). Spatial memory and response strategies in rats: age, sex and rearing differences in performance. *Quarterly Journal of Experimental Psychology*, *32*, 473–489.

Einon D. F., & Morgan, M. J. (1977). A critical period for social isolation in the rat. *Developmental Psychobiology*, *10*, 123–132.

Einon, D. F., & Morgan, M. J. (1978). Early social isolation produces enduring hyperactivity in the rat, but no effect upon spontaneous alternation. *Quarterly Journal of Experimental Psychology*, *30*, 151–156.

Einon, D. F., & Sahakian, B. J. (1979). Environmentally-induced differences in susceptibility of rats to CNS stimulatnts and CNS depressants: evidence against a unitary explanation. *Psychopharmacology*, *61*, 299–307.

Einon, D. F., Humphreys, A. P., Chivers, S. M., Field, S., & Naylor, V. (1980). Isolation has permanent effects upon the behaviour of the rat, but not the mouse, gerbil or guinea pig. *Developmental Psychobiology*, *14*, 343–355.

Ferdman, N., Murmu, R. P., Bock, J., Braun, K., & Leshem, M. (2007). Weaning age, social isolation, and gender, interact to determine adult explorative and social behaviour, and dendritic and spine morphology in prefrontal cortex of rats. *Behavioral Brain Research*, *180*, 174–182.

Ferris, C. F. (2000). Adolescent stress and neural plasticity in hamsters: a vasopressin-serotonin model of inappropriate aggressive behaviour. *Experimental Physiology*, *85S1*, 125S–130S.

Fiala, B., Joyce, C., & Greenough, W. (1978). Environmental complexity modulates growth of granule cell dendrites in developing but not adult hippocampus of rats. *Experimental Neurology*, *59*, 372–383.

Fowler, S. C., Johnson, J. S., Kallman, M. J., Lion, J.-R., Wilson, M. C., & Hikal, A. H. (1993). In a drug discrimination procedure, isolation-reared rats generalise to lower doses of cocaine and amphetamine than rats reared in an enriched environment. *Psychopharmacology*, *110*, 115–118.

Fulford, A. J., & Marsden, C. A. (1997a). Effect of isolation-rearing on noradrenaline release in the rat hypothalamus and hippocampus *in vitro*. *Brain Research*, *748*, 93–99.

Fulford, A. J., & Marsden, C. A. (1997b). Social isolation in the rat enhances α_2-autoreceptor function in the hippocampus *in vivo*. *Neuroscience*, *77*, 57–64.

Fulford, A. J., & Marsden, C. A. (1998a). Effect of isolation-rearing on conditioned dopamine release *in vivo* in the nucleus accumbens following isolation-rearing in the rat. *Journal of Neurochemistry*, *70*, 384–390.

Fulford, A. J., & Marsden, C. A. (1998b). Conditioned release of 5-hydroxytryptamine *in vivo* in the nucleus accumbens following isolation-rearing in the rat. *Neuroscience*, *83*, 481–487.

Fulford, A. J., & Marsden, C. A. (2007). An intact dopaminergic system is required for context-conditioned release of 5-HT in the nucleus accumbens of postweaning isolation-reared rats. *Neuroscience*, *149*, 392–400.

Fulford, A. J., Butler, S., Heal, D. J., Kendall, D. A., & Marsden, C. A. (1994). Evidence for altered α_2-adrenoceptor function in the isolation-reared rat. *Psychopharmacology*, *116*, 183–190.

Gamallo, A., Villanua, A., Trancho, G., & Fraile A.(1986). Stress adaptation and adrenal activity in isolated and crowded rats. *Physiology & Behavior*, *55*, 615–620.

Gates, E. (1904). *The relations and development of the mind and brain*. New York: Theosophical Society.

Gentsch, C., Lichtsteiner, M., & Feer, H. (1981). Locomotor activity, defaecation score and corticosterone levels during an open field exposure: a comparison among individually and group-housed rats, and genetically selected rat lines. *Physiology & Behavior, 27,* 183–186.

Geyer, M. A., Wilkinson, L. S., Humby, T., & Robbins, T. W. (1993). Isolation-rearing of rats produces a deficit in prepulse inhibition of acoustic startle similar to that in schizophrenia. *Biological Psychiatry, 34,* 361–372.

Gos, T., Becker, K., Bock, J., Malecki, U., Roberts, B., Poeggel, G., & Braun, K. (2006). Early neonatal and postweaning social emotional deprivation interferes with the maturation of serotonergic and tyrosine-hydroxylase immunoreactive afferent fibre systems in the rodent nucleus accumbens, hippocampus and amygdala. *Neuroscience, 140,* 811–821.

Gresack, J. E., Risbrough, V., Scott, C., Coste, S., Stenzel-Poore, M., Geyer, M., & Powell, S. B. (2010). Isolation-rearing-induced deficits in contextual fear learning do not require CRF2 receptors. *Behavioral Brain Research, 209,* 80–84.

Hall, F. S. (1998). Social deprivation of neonatal, adolescent and adult rats has distinct neurochemical and behavioral consequences. *Critical Reviews in Neurobiology, 12,* 129–162.

Hebb, D. O. (1947). The effects of early experience on problem solving at maturity. *American Psychologist, 2,* 306–307.

Heidbreder, C. A., Weiss, I., Domeney, A. M., Pryce, C., Homberg, J., Hedou, G., Feldon, J., Moran, M. C., & Nelson, P. (2000). Behavioural, neurochemical and endocrinological characterisation of the early social isolation syndrome. *Neuroscience, 100,* 749–768.

Heritch, A. J., Henderson, K., & Westfall, T. (1990). Effects of social isolation on brain catecholamines and forced swimming in rats: prevention by antidepressant treatment. *Journal of Psychiatric Research, 24,* 251–258.

Holson, R. R., Scallet, A. C., Ali, S., & Turner, B. B. (1991). "Isolation stress" revisited: isolation-rearing effects depend on animal care methods. *Physiology & Behavior, 49,* 1107–1118.

Howes, S. R., Dalley, J. W., Morrison, C. H., Robbins, T. W., & Everitt, B. J. (2000). Leftward shift in the acquisition of cocaine self-administration in isolation-reared rats: relationship to extracellular levels of dopamine, serotonin and glutamate in the nucleus accumbens and amygdala-striatal FOS expression. *Psychopharmacology, 151,* 55–63.

Huot, R. L., Plotsky, P., Lenox, R. H., & McNamara, R. (2002). Neonatal maternal separation reduces hippocampal mossy fibre density in Long Evans rats. *Brain Research, 950,* 52–63.

Jiang, Q. B., & Wakerley, J. B. (1997). The milk-ejection reflex in the peri-partum rat: effects of oestradiol and progesterone on basal milk-ejection frequency and the facilitatory response to central oxytocin. *Journal of Neuroendocrinology, 9,* 9–16.

Jones, G. H., Robbins, T. W., & Marsden, C. A. (1989). Isolation-rearing retards the acquisition of schedule-induced polydipsia in rats. *Physiology & Behavior, 45,* 71–77.

Jones, G. H., Marsden, C. A., & Robbins, T. W. (1990). Increased sensitivity to amphetamine and reward-related stimuli following social isolation in rats. *Psychopharmacology, 102,* 364–372.

Jones, G. H., Marsden, C. A., & Robbins, T. W. (1991). Behavioural rigidity and rule-learning deficits following isolation-rearing in the rat: neurochemical correlates. *Behavioral Brain Research, 43,* 35–50.

Jones, G. H., Hernandez, T. D., Kendall, D. A., Marsden, C. A., & Robbins, T. W. (1992). Dopaminergic and serotonergic function following isolation-rearing in rats: study of behavioural responses and postmortem and *in vivo* neurochemistry. *Pharmacology, Biochemistry, and Behavior, 43*, 17–35.

Juraska J. M., Henderson, C., & Muller, J. (1984). Differential rearing, experience, gender and radial maze performance. *Developmental Psychobiology, 17*, 209–215.

Juraska, J. M., Fitch, J. M., Henderson, C., & Rivers, N. (1985). Sex differences in the dendritic branching of dentate granule cells following differential experience. *Brain Research, 333*, 73–80.

Kalinichev, M., Easterling, K., Plotsky, P., & Holtzman, S. (2002). Long-lasting changes in stress-mediated corticosterone response and anxiety-like behaviors as a consequence of neonatal maternal separation in Long Evans rats. *Pharmacology, Biochemistry, and Behavior, 73*, 131–140.

Kavushansky, A., & Leshem, M. (2004). Role of oxytocin and vasopressin in the transitions of weaning in the rat. *Developmental Psychobiology, 45*, 231–238.

Kosten, T., Lee, H., & Kim, J. (2007). Neonatal handling alters learning in adult male and female rats in a task specific manner. *Brain Research, 1154*, 144–153.

Kraemer, G. W., & McKinney, W. T. (1985). Social separation increases alcohol consumption in rhesus monkeys. *Psychopharmacology, 86*, 182–189.

Kraemer, G. W., Ebert, M., Lake, C., & McKinney, W. T. (1984). Hypersensitivity to d-amphetamine several years after early social deprivation in rhesus monkeys. *Psychopharmacology, 82*, 266–271.

Kraemer, G. W., Ebert, M., Schmidt, D., & McKinney, W. T. (1989). A longitudinal study of the effect of different social rearing conditions on cerebrospinal norepinephrine and biogenic amine metabolites in rhesus monkeys. *Neuropsychopharmacology, 2*, 175–189.

Ladd, C. O., Huot, R. L., Thrivikraman, K. V., Nemeroff, C., Meaney, M., & Plotsky, P. (2000). Long-term behavioral and neuroendocrine adaptations to adverse early experience. *Progress in Brain Research, 122*, 81–103.

Lanier, L. P., & Issacson, R. L. (1977). Early developmental changes in the locomotor response to amphetamine and their relation to hippocampal function. *Brain Research, 126*, 567–575.

Levine, S. (1957). Infantile experience and resistance to physiological stress. *Science, 126*, 405–406.

Levine, J. B., Youngs, R. M., MacDonald, M. L., Chu, M., Leeder, A. D., Berthiaume, F., & Konradi, C. (2007). Isolation-rearing and hyperlocomotion are associated with reduced immediate early gene expression levels in the medial prefrontal cortex. *Neuroscience, 145*, 42–55.

Levine, S., & Mullins, R. F. (1968). Hormones in infancy. In G. Newton & S. Levine (Eds.), *Early experience and behaviour* (pp. 168–197). Springfield, IL: Charles Thomas.

Levita, L., Dalley, J., & Robbins, T. W. (2002). Nucleus accumbens dopamine and learned fear revisited: a review and some new findings. *Behavioral Brain Research, 137*, 115–127.

Lippman, M., Bress, A., Nemeroff, C., Plotsky, P., & Monteggia, L. (2007). Long-term behavioural and molecular alterations associated with maternal separation in rats. *European Journal of Neuroscience, 25*, 3091–3098.

Litvin, Y., Tovote, P., Pentkowski, N., Zeyda, T., King, L., Vasconcellos, A., Dunlap, C., Spiess, J., Blanchard, D. C., & Blanchard, R. J. (2010). Maternal separation modulates short-term behavioural and physiological indices of the stress response. *Hormones and Behavior, 58*, 241–249.

Lu, L., Bao, G., Chen, H., Xia, P., Fan, X., Zhang, J., Pei, G., & Ma, L. (2003). Modification of hippocampal neurogenesis and neuroplasticity by social environments. *Experimental Neurology, 183,* 600–609.

Lukkes, J. L., Mokin, M. V., Scholl, J. L., & Forster, G. L. (2009a). Adult rats exposed to early-life social isolation exhibit increased anxiety and conditioned fear behavior, and altered hormonal stress responses. *Hormones and Behavior, 55,* 248–256.

Lukkes, J. L., Vuong, S., Scholl, J., Oliver, H., & Forster, G. (2009b). Corticotropin-releasing factor receptor antagonism within the dorsal raphe nucleus reduces social anxiety-like behaviour after early social isolation. *Journal of Neuroscience, 29,* 9955–9960.

Lukkes, J. L., Summers, C. H., Scholl, J. L., Renner, K. J., & Forster, G. L. (2009c). Early life social isolation alters corticotropin-releasing factor responses in adult rats. *Neuroscience, 158,* 845–855.

Lyons, D. M., Parker, K. J., Zeitzer, J. M., Buckmaster, C. L., & Schatzberg, A. F. (2007). Preliminary evidence that hippocampal volumes in monkeys predict stress levels of adrenocorticotrophic hormone. *Biological Psychiatry, 62,* 1171–1174.

Martin, L., Spicer, D., Lewis, M., Gluck, J., & Cork, L. (1991). Social deprivation in infant rhesus monkeys alters the chemoarchitecture of the brain. *Journal of Neuroscience, 11,* 3344–3358.

McCittrick, C. R., & Abercrombie, E. D. (2007). Catecholamine mapping within nucleus accumbens: differences in basal and amphetamine-stimulated efflux of norepinephrine and dopamine in shell and core. *Journal of Neurochemistry, 100,* 1247–1256.

Miachon, S., Rochet, T., Matthian, B., Barbagli, B., & Claustrat, B. (1993). Long-term isolation of Wistar rats after brain monoamine turnover, blood corticosterone, and ACTH. *Brain Research Bulletin, 32,* 611–614.

Molina-Hernandez, M., Tellez-Alcantara, P., & Perez-Garcia, J. (2001). Isolation-rearing induced fear-like behavior without affecting learning abilities of Wistar rats. *Progress in Neuro-Psychopharmacology & Biological Psychiatry, 25,* 1111–1113.

Morgan, M. J. (1973). Effects of postweaning environment on learning in the rat. *Animal Behavior, 21,* 429–442.

Morgan, M. J., Einon, D., & Nicholas, D. (1975). The effect of isolation-rearing on behavioural inhibition in the rat. *Quarterly Journal of Experimental Psychology, 27,* 615–634.

Muchimapura, S., Fulford, A., Mason, R., & Marsden, C. A. (2002). Isolation-rearing in the rat disrupts the hippocampal response to stress. *Neuroscience, 112,* 697–705.

Oehler, J., Jahkel, M., & Schmidt, J. (1987). Neuronal transmitter sensitivity after social isolation in rats. *Physioloy and Behavior, 41,* 187–191.

Parker, V., & Morinan, A. (1986). The socially-isolated rat as a model for anxiety. *Neuropharmacology, 25,* 663–664.

Pascual, R., Zamora-Leon, P., Catalan-Ahumada, M., & Valero-Cabre, A. (2007). Early social isolation decreases the expression of calbindin D-28K and dendritic branching in the medial prefrontal cortex. *International Journal of Neuroscience, 117,* 465–476.

Peters, Y. M., & O'Donnell, O. (2005). Social isolation rearing affects prefrontal cortical response to ventral tegmental area stimulation. *Biological Psychiatry, 57,* 1205–1208.

Plotsky, P., & Meaney, M. (1993). Early postnatal experience alters hypothalamic corticotrophin-releasing factor (CRF). mRNA, median eminence CRF content and stress-induced release in adult rats. *Brain Research Molecular Brain Research*, *18*, 195–200.

Powell, S. B., Geyer, M., Preece, M., Pitcher, L. K., Reynolds, G., & Swedlow, N. R. (2003). Dopamine depletion of the nucleus accumbens reverses isolation-induced deficits in prepulse inhibition in rats. *Neuroscience*, *119*, 233–240.

Sahakian, B. J., Robbins, T. W., Morgan, M. J., & Iversen, S. D. (1975). The effects of psycho-motor stimulants on stereotypy and locomotor activity in socially deprived and control rats. *Brain Research*, *84*, 195–205.

Sanchez, M. M., Hearn, E. F., Do, D., Rilling, J. K., & Herndon, J. G. (1998a). Differential rearing affects corpus callosum size and cognitive function of rhesus monkeys. *Brain Research*, *812*, 38–49.

Sanchez, M. M., Aguado, F., Sanchez-Toscano, F., & Saphier, D. (1998b). Neuroendocrine and immunocytochemical demonstrations of decreased hypothalamo-pituitary-adrenal axis responsiveness to restraint stress after long-term social isolation. *Endocrinology*, *139*, 579–587.

Schable, S., Poeggel, G., Braun, K., & Gruss, M. (2007). Long-term consequences of early experience on adult avoidance learning in female rats: role of the dopaminergic system. *Neurobiology of Learning and Memory*, *87*, 109–122.

Schenk, S., Lacelle, G., Gorman, K., & Amit, Z. (1987). Cocaine self-adminstration in rats influenced by environmental conditions. *Neuroscience Letters*, *81*, 227–231.

Schenk, S., Gorman, K., & Amit, Z. (1990). Age-dependent effects of isolation housing on the self-administration of ethanol in laboratory rats. *Alcohol*, *7*, 321–326.

Schiller, L., Jahkel, M., & Oehler, J. (2006). The influence of sex and social isolation housing on pre- and postsynaptic 5-HT1A receptors. *Brain Research*, *1103*, 76–87.

Schubert, M. I., Porkess, M. V., Dashdor, J. N., Fone, K. C., & Auer, D. P. (2009). Effects of social isolation rearing on the limbic brain: a combined behavioral and magnetic reso-nance imaging volumetry study in rats. *Neuroscience*, *159*, 21–30.

Schultz, W. (2007). Mutliple dopamine functions at different time-courses. *Annual Review of Neuroscience*, *30*, 259–288.

Serra, M., Sanna, E., Mostallino, M. C., & Biggio, G. (2007). Social isolation stress and neuro-active steroids. *European Neuropsychopharmacology*, *17*, 1–11.

Siegel, S., Ginsberg, S., Hof, P., Foote, S., Young, W., Kraemer, G..W., McKinney, W. T., & Morrison, J. H. (1993). Effects of social deprivation in prepubescent rhesus monkeys: immunohistochemical analysis of the neurofilament protein triplet in the hippocampal formation. *Brain Research*, *619*, 299–305.

Silva-Gomez, A. B., Rojas, D., Juarez, I., & Flores, G. (2003). Decreased dendritic spine density on prefrontal cortical and hippocampal neurons in postweaning social isolation rats. *Brain Research*, *983*, 128–136.

Stevenson, C. W., Spicer, C. H., Mason, R., & Marsden, C. A. (2009). Early life programming of fear conditioning and extinction in adult male rats. *Behavioral Brain Research*, *205*, 505–510.

Uvnäs-Moberg, K., Ahlenius, S., Hillegaart, V., & Alster, P. (1994). High doses of oxytocin cause sedation and low doses cause an anxiolytic-like effect in male rats. *Pharmacology, Biochemistry, and Behavior*, *49*, 101–106.

Van Bockstaele, E. J., & Pickel, V. M. (1993). Ultrastructure of serotonin immunoreactive terminals in the core and shell of the rat nucleus accumbens: cellular substrates for interactions with catecholamine afferents. *Journal of Comparative Neurology*, *334*, 603–617.

Van den Berg, C. L., Hol, T., Van Ree, J. M., Spruijt, B. M., Everts, H., & Koolhaas J.M.(1999). Play is indispensable for an adequate development of coping with social challenges in the rat. *Developmental Psychobiology, 34,* 129–138.

Varty, G. B., Marsden, C. A., & Higgins, G. A. (1999). Reduced synaptophysin immunoreactivity in the dentate gyrus of prepulse inhibition-impaired isolation-reared rats. *Brain Research, 824,* 197–203.

Vitalo, A., Fricchione, J., Casali, M., Berdichevsky, Y., Hoge, E. A., Rauch, S. L., Berthiaume, F., Yarmush, M. L., Benson, H., Fricchione, G. L., & Levine, J. B. (2009). Nest making and oxytocin comparably promote wound healing in isolation reared rats. *PLoS One, 4*(5), e5523.

Weiss, I. C., & Feldon, J. (2001). Environmental models for sensorimotor gating deficits in schizophrenia: a review. *Psychopharmacology, 156,* 305–326.

Weiss, I. C., Pryce, C. R., Jongen-Rêlo, A. L., Nanz-Bahr, N. I., & Feldon, J. (2004). Effect of social isolation on stress-related behavioural and neuroendocrine state in the rat. *Behavioral Brain Research 152,* 279–295.

Whitaker-Azmitia, P., Zhou, F., & Borella, A. (2000). Isolation-rearing of rats produces deficits as adults in the serotonergic innervation of hippocampus. *Peptides, 21,* 1755–1759.

Willner, P. (1984). The validity of animal models of depression. *Psychopharmacology, 83,* 1–16.

Winstanley, C. A., Theobald, D. E., Dalley, J. W., & Robbins, T. W. (2005). Interactions between serotonin and dopamine in the control of impulsive choice in rats: therapeutic implications for impulse control disorders. *Neuropsychopharmacology, 30,* 669–682.

Wongwitdecha, N., & Marsden, C. A. (1996). Effects of social isolation rearing on learning in the Morris water maze. *Brain Research, 715*(1–2), 119–124.

Wright, I. K., Ismail, H., Upton, N., & Marsden, C. A. (1991a). Effect of isolation-rearing on 5-HT agonist-induced responses in the rat. *Psychopharmacology, 105,* 259–263.

Wright, I. K., Upton, N., & Marsden, C. A. (1991b). Resocialisation of isolation-reared rats does not alter their anxiogenic profile on the elevated plus maze model of anxiety. *Physiology & Behavior, 50,* 1129–1132.

15

Clinical Implications of Childhood Stress

Linda J. Luecken, Danielle S. Roubinov, and Catherine Purdom

Introduction

Childhood is a formative period that sets the stage for who and *how* we will be as adults. We are shaped emotionally, cognitively, and biologically by both positive and negative early-life experiences. The focus of this chapter is on the developmental influence of stress exposure early in life. A representative survey of over 8,000 households in the United States estimated that 74.4% of children experienced at least one significant adversity, including natural or humanmade disasters, accidents, witnessing a traumatic episode, crime victimization, or family adversities such as parental death, child abuse, or domestic violence (Kessler et al., 1997). Although the traumatic nature of these events may vary in magnitude, it is clear that the majority of children will encounter some form of adversity during development. Further, significant clustering was noted such that many children are exposed to multiple adversities (Kessler et al., 1997; Dong et al., 2003).

The family environment merits special consideration in studies of early-life stress, and is the focus of this chapter. Although normal maturation proceeds within a variety of contexts (e.g., schools, neighborhoods, peer groups, etc.), the family assumes greatest responsibility for facilitating the child's progression through developmental stages (Bronfenbrenner, 1986). Family-related stressors, in turn, exert particularly profound effects on developmental trajectories and outcomes. This chapter begins with a discussion of the prevalence and clinical impact of stressors in the childhood family environment. A number of mediating pathways have been identified (e.g., genetic, neurobiological, behavioral, psychosocial, cognitive) that may link early family experiences to clinical outcomes. These pathways have been

The Handbook of Stress: Neuropsychological Effects on the Brain, First Edition.
Edited by Cheryl D. Conrad.
© 2011 Blackwell Publishing Ltd. Published 2011 by Blackwell Publishing Ltd.

the subject of a number of reviews (Anda et al., 2006; DeBellis, 2002; Repetti et al., 2002; Tarullo and Gunnar, 2006) and are beyond the scope of this chapter. Instead, the focus will be on the impact of family stress on the development of emotion regulation. Below, we describe how the development of an adaptive capacity for emotion regulation is heavily influenced by the childhood family environment, and has significant implications for mental health. To illustrate, we then review four forms of childhood adversity for which a sufficiently developed research literature exists: child maltreatment, parental depression, parental death, and interparental conflict. For each we describe research on their prevalence, potential clinical impact, and evidence for emotion regulation as a mediating or moderating factor.

Finally, while the preponderance of evidence clearly demonstrates that significant childhood stress increases the risk of poor psychological health, most children who experience stressful events mature into healthy, productive adults. This chapter ends by considering emerging theory that suggests that, in some contexts, stress exposure may *enhance* long-term mental health, potentially via improved emotion regulation. Variously described as *stress inoculation*, *steeling*, *hardiness*, *adversarial growth*, or *toughening*, this theory suggests that some types of early-life stress may build a capacity for more positive adaptation to future stress than would be developed in a highly protective environment.

Family Environment Stressors

Epidemiologic studies have evaluated the prevalence of stressors in the childhood family environment, including physical, sexual, and emotional abuse, neglect, exposure to family conflict and domestic violence, parental loss (separation, divorce, or death), parent psychopathology, and/or problematic parent–child relationships (Copeland et al., 2009; Felitti et al., 1998; Finkelhor et al., 2005; Kessler et al., 1997; Menard et al., 2004). The percentage of adults reporting exposure to at least one childhood stressor has ranged from approximately half (Felitti et al., 1998) to over three-quarters (Menard et al., 2004) of community samples.

Studies linking stress in the family context to children's negative psychological outcomes are numerous and span a range of developmental periods. Family stressors have been associated with internalizing and externalizing problems during early childhood (Shaw et al., 1994), maladjustment during middle childhood (Rae-Grant et al., 1989), and depressive symptoms during adolescence (Matjasko et al, 2007). Among a large representative sample of U.S. adults, stressful childhood environments (including parental death, divorce, and psychopathology) remained significant risk factors for the development of subsequent mood disorders, substance abuse, and conduct disorders years after the stressor occurred (Kessler et al., 1997). A recent 45-year epidemiological study found that psychopathological consequences of childhood family adversity can persist through young adulthood and into middle age (Clark et al., 2010)

Emotion Regulation

Although there may be multiple pathways linking childhood adversity to psychological distress, children's experiences of emotion and their capacity to regulate those experiences provide a unique perspective for understanding pathways of adaptive or maladaptive development following adversity. Most researchers note a *biologically prepared* function for emotion that allows individuals to evaluate experiences and respond in an evolutionarily adaptive manner (Cole et al., 2004). Although strong negative emotions may inspire adaptive behavioral responses in the short term, they can become maladaptive if they are a poor fit for environmental demands over time. Hypervigilance to threat, for example, may be initially adaptive for children raised in unsafe family environments; however, when repeated and generalized to other (often nonthreatening or ambiguous) situations, it may strain the psychological resources necessary for sustained emotion regulation (Maughan and Cicchetti, 2002).

Most definitions of emotion regulation concern the ability to initiate, maintain, or alter emotional experience or expression. Thompson (1994) defines emotion regulation as "extrinsic and intrinsic processes responsible for monitoring, evaluating, and modifying emotional reactions, especially their intensive and temporal features, to accomplish one's goals." Internal processes for the regulation of negative emotion may include shifting attention towards or away from distressing stimuli, use of active coping skills, or modulating physiological arousal (Thompson, 1994). For children, external processes may include the direct management of emotion experiences by parental actions, important at early ages before children develop the capacity for self-management. *Emotion regulation* and *coping* are related but distinct constructs, and indeed coping strategies can be utilized in the process of regulating emotions. However, emotion regulation focuses on the expression and modulation of both positive and negative emotions at both conscious and unconscious levels, while coping more broadly includes voluntary actions taken to achieve both emotional and nonemotional goals (Gross, 1998).

Difficulty regulating negative emotions is linked to a variety of emotional, social, and behavioral problems in childhood (Eisenberg et al., 2005; Sheffield Morris et al., 2007; Valiente et al., 2006), and may increase risk for later maladaptation, psychological disorder, and impaired social and romantic relationships (John and Gross, 2007; Laurent and Powers, 2007; Lopes et al., 2005). High levels of negative emotion and poor emotion regulation are prominent features of a number of anxiety and mood disorders (Armstadter, 2008; Campbell-Sills and Barlow, 2007).

The family environment is the primary context in which children develop the capacity for appropriate expression and regulation of emotion. Although infants experience and display emotions, they have limited capacity for self-regulation of emotions and are reliant on caregivers as external regulators (e.g., by soothing an upset infant). As children grow, the socialization of emotion regulation by caregivers promotes children's capacity for self-management of emotion. Parents directly influence children's development of emotion regulation by their reactions to displays of emotion, parental discussion of emotions, coaching in emotion regulation, and modeling of emotional expression and regulation (Eisenberg et al., 1998; Sheffield Morris et al., 2007). Positive parenting styles, characterized by parental affection, acceptance, consistent discipline, and support are associated with the development of adaptive emotion regulation (Beauchaine et al., 2007; Eisenberg et al., 2005; Valiente et al., 2006). Negative parenting styles, such as hostility, excessive psychological or behavioral control, neglect, or lack of sensitivity, are linked to maladaptive emotion regulation (Sheffield Morris et al., 2007).

Common Family Stressors

Family stress can come in many forms, and the consequences for child emotional regulation and mental health are widespread and vary in magnitude. For illustration, we describe four common forms of family adversity for which a substantial literature documents clinical risks. For each, emotion regulation is theorized to represent one potential pathway linking exposure to clinical outcomes.

Child maltreatment

Childhood maltreatment includes the experience of physical abuse, emotional abuse, sexual abuse, and neglect. Family members are the most common perpetrators of these crimes (Finkelhor et al., 2005). In 2007, 3.5 million allegations of child maltreatment were documented in the United States (U.S. Department of Health and Human Services, 2009). Children are often grouped into a single maltreatment designation; however, victimization by multiple subtypes of maltreatment is more common (Manly et al., 2001).

Of the various types of adversity children may face, maltreatment may be "one of the most severe risk factors" for deleterious consequences across a variety of developmental outcomes (Alink et al., 2009, p. 831). Displays of physical aggression, a risk factor for later externalizing problems and antisocial behavior, are commonly observed among physically abused, elementary-age children (Shields and Cicchetti, 1998; Manly et al., 2001). Internalizing behaviors have also been associated with physical abuse among offspring in early, (Maughan and Cicchetti, 2002), and midchildhood (Shields and Cicchetti, 1998), as well as among emotionally abused and neglected young adults (Wright et al., 2009). Sexual abuse has been linked to externalizing problems (Manly et al., 2001), internalizing problems (Kendall-Tackett et al., 1993), posttraumatic stress disorder (PTSD; Kingston and Raghavan, 2009), and attention-deficit hyperactivity disorder (Merry and Andrews, 1994) across a range of age groups. The preschool period has been implicated as a particularly detrimental developmental stage for first maltreatment experiences to occur (Manly et al., 2001), whereas among older children maltreatment experiences specific to adolescence or persisting from childhood have been found to result in more adverse outcomes than those occurring in childhood alone (Thornberry et al., 2001). Schoedl and colleagues (2010) reported significantly elevated rates of PTSD if sexual abuse occurred after the age of 12, while rates of major depression were elevated if the abuse occurred before age 12, suggesting that age of exposure may predict unique clinical outcomes. Stage of development may also interact with maltreatment subtype to produce unique patterns of adjustment (Thornberry et al., 2001).

Emotion regulation merits serious consideration when modeling the effects of child maltreatment. Maughan and Cicchetti (2002) found that emotional under-regulation mediated the relation between maltreatment and children's internalizing symptoms. Emotion dysregulation, inferred from volatile, inflexible, and socially inappropriate emotional expressions, partially explained the extent to which physically abused children evidenced aggressive and disruptive behavior (Teisl and Cicchetti, 2008). Emotion dysregulation operationalized as poor emotion understanding/recognition mediated the relation of maltreatment to behavior problems and peer rejection (Rogosch et al., 1995). Emotion regulation is particularly important as a mediator between maltreatment and psychopathology among insecurely attached children (Alink et al., 2009).

Maltreatment may hinder the development of adaptive emotion regulation skills in several ways. Parental modeling of adaptive emotion regulation is significantly diminished, if not nonexistent, in cases of maltreatment, where the majority of parent–child interactions are characterized by negativity, harshness, and invalidation of children's emotional expression (Morris et al., 2007). Two contributors to the development of children's emotion regulation skills, validation of children's emotion and emotion coaching, occur significantly less among maltreating mothers, compared to nonmaltreating mothers (Shipman et al., 2007). Neglected children are more likely to conceal negative emotion (Shipman et al., 2005), which limits opportunities to learn and practice socially acceptable patterns of emotional expression.

Parental depression

Parental depression represents another form of early adversity with significant consequences for short- and long-term psychological adjustment. Large surveys outside of the U.S. report that between 12 and 15% of children are raised by a parent with a mental illness (Bassani et al., 2009; Vostanis et al., 2006). In the United States, approximately 17% of adults report being raised in a household with a mentally ill individual (Anda et al., 2009). Postpartum maternal depression is estimated to affect 10–15% of mothers (Centers for Disease Control and Prevention, 2007).

Young children of depressed parents are at elevated risk of major depression and other internalizing problems (Bayer et al., 2006). Among older children and adolescents, parental depression has been associated with social phobia (Lieb et al., 2000), conduct problems (Kopp and Beauchaine, 2007), and poor academic performance (Anderson and Hammen, 1993). Importantly, negative consequences of parental depression are also evident among children exposed to subclinical levels of parental depressive symptoms (West and Newman, 2003). Children continue to be at risk after the depression has remitted (Alpern and Lyons-Ruth, 1993) and into adulthood (Weissman et al, 2006). Although depression occurring in the early postnatal period may pose a profound risk for infants' developing self-regulatory capacities (Ashman and Dawson, 2002), research suggests that severity and chronicity factors may exert greater influence on child outcomes than the age at which children are first exposed (Brennan et al., 2000; Sohr-Preston and Scaramella, 2006). Hammen and Brennan (2003), for example, observed greater risk of depression among adolescents exposed to mothers' short-term major depression or long-term mild depression, regardless of the timing of onset.

In a longitudinal study, Maughan et al. (2007) found support for a mediational role of emotion regulation in the relation between maternal depression and children's social functioning. The extent to which children exhibited patterns of over- or undercontrolled emotions at 4 years old significantly explained the association between maternal depression when the child was 18 months old and children's social competence at 5 years old. Support for emotion regulation as a moderator of the relation between parental depression and children's psychological health has also been observed. Among 4- to 7-year-old children, maternal depression was positively associated with internalizing symptoms, a relation which was heightened among children unable to maintain or *upregulate* positive emotions during a frustrating task (Silk et al., 2006).

Parental depression may function similarly to other types of childhood adversity in the manner by which it compromises children's emotion regulation. Depressed caregivers may model poor emotion regulation or be incapable of coaching children on adaptive expression and modulation of negative emotion (Gross and Muñoz, 1995). Depressed mothers, for example, are less adept at providing their children with appropriate levels of support and guidance as they encounter challenging situations, which has been shown to negatively affect children's self-regulatory capacities (Hoffman et al., 2006). In interactions with their children, depressed mothers are less sensitive and responsive to their child's emotional states, more likely to display irritability, intrusion, and negative affect, and less likely to display positive affect than nondepressed mothers (Goodman and Gotlib, 1999; Lim et al., 2008). Depressed parents are also more likely to vacillate between harsh punitive and overly permissive discipline (Goodman and Gotlib, 1999). Lastly, children of depressed parents may inherit genetic risk for emotion regulation deficits that typify depressive disorders (Goodman, 2007).

Parental death

The early death of a parent, experienced by approximately 3–5% of children, is one of the most stressful events that can happen to a child (Yamamoto et al., 1998).

Parental death places children at higher short-term risk of major depression, anxiety disorder, PTSD, conduct problems, and impaired academic and social competence (for a review, see Luecken, 2008). In the long term, childhood parental death has been most commonly linked to major depression and anxiety and depressive disorders in adulthood. Epidemiological studies suggest that parental death during childhood serves as an independent predictor of the development of psychiatric disorders in middle-aged and older adults (Agid et al., 1999; Kendler, et al., 2002, 2006; Kivela et al., 1998). However, some studies fail to find direct links from childhood parental death to clinical disorder in adulthood, suggesting that other factors, such as the quality of caregiving following the loss, influence long-term vulnerability.

Maladaptive development of emotion regulation is proposed as a mechanism linking aspects of the postdeath environment to poor long-term adjustment. The early death of a caregiver presents a tremendous emotion regulatory challenge for children as well as surviving caregivers and may disrupt critical processes that promote children's adaptive development of emotion regulation. Two primary mechanisms may be involved in this disruption: caregiver depression and impaired parenting. The death of a spouse increases the risk of depression in bereaved surviving parents (Stroebe and Stroebe, 1993), compromising children's development of adaptive emotion regulation (as described above), and increasing the risk of maladjustment in the bereaved child (Kalter et al., 2002). Further, depression in surviving parents has been linked to a decrease in positive parenting, which in turn has been linked to impaired emotion regulation and mental health problems of bereaved children (Kwok et al., 2005).

Interparental conflict

Mild parental disputes and disagreements may be considered a normative and nondestructive part of family life (Cummings et al., 2001). Although the rates of children's exposure to elevated interparental conflict (IPC) are difficult to estimate, an extensive body of research documents the negative impact on children's psychological health. Children exposed to high levels of IPC are at particular risk for developing internalizing and externalizing disorders such as aggression (Marcus et al. 2001), opposition problems (Mann and MacKenzie, 1996), and depression and anxiety (Turner and Kopiec, 2006). Cummings and Davies (1994) found that such children are two to four times more likely to display behavior problems at the clinical level compared to children from low-conflict homes. Further, early exposure to heightened levels of IPC in childhood has been linked to poor coping in adolescents (Shelton and Harold, 2008) and decreased relationship efficacy in young adults (Cui et al., 2008).

The specific emotions theory (Crockenberg and Langrock, 2001) and the emotional security hypothesis (Davies and Cummings, 1994) may help explain the role of emotion regulation in the psychological adjustment of children exposed to high levels of IPC. According to the specific emotions theory (Crockenberg and Langrock, 2001), children's goal-related interpretations of marital conflict are thought to lead to specific emotional reactions and behavioral responses. With repeated IPC exposure, children develop *emotion schemas* that become automatic over time and alter the child's emotion regulation capacities across situations. Davies and Cummings (1994) argue that children's responses to IPC are motivated to maintain emotional security in their relationships to caregivers. Repeated exposure to IPC may threaten children's emotional security, leading to observable "patterns of emotional, cognitive, and behavioral self-regulation in response" to such exposure (Cummings and Keller, 2006). Within both theoretical models, children use maladaptive emotional reactions when future stressors are encountered, contributing to long-term maladjustment.

Support has been found for emotion regulation as both a mediator and moderator of the impact of IPC. Shelton and Harold (2008) found that children's use of venting negative emotions mediated the impact of IPC on children's adjustment problems. In a longitudinal study, Schermerhorn et al. (2007) found that children's negative emotional reactivity mediated the relationship between IPC exposure and children's engagement in dysregulated behavior following exposure to IPC. Children with well-regulated emotional reactivity do not appear to develop the adjustment problems seen in children with less-regulated emotional reactivity when exposed to IPC (Davies and Windle, 2001; El-Sheikh et al., 2001). David and Murphy (2004) found evidence that higher emotional functioning buffered youth exposed to intense IPC during childhood from sensitization to conflict exposure in young adulthood.

Stress Inoculation

An expansive literature on *resilience* describes the process by which individuals overcome adversity and regain a positive level of functioning through the use of individual, social, and environmental protective resources. The concept of *stress inoculation* is related to that of resilience, but focuses on a process by which repeated stress exposure (typically mild or moderate in magnitude) may facilitate adaptive responses to future stressors. That is, in some contexts exposure to adversity early in life may be associated with *better* adjustment in the face of later stressors relative to individuals raised in highly protective environments. Khoshaba and Maddi (1999) present evidence that adult men were better able to cope with current life stressors if they had successfully navigated a significant childhood stressor, typically in the context of a protective family environment. Similarly, Forest et al. (1996) found that the experience of an early-life stressor (e.g., death of loved one, divorce, or serious illness) reduced symptoms of depression in response to a current life stressor.

The bulk of research on stress inoculation comes from studies of rodents and nonhuman primates exposed to repeated mild stressors (predominately intermittent maternal separations). In general, rodent models demonstrate that stress inoculation due to intermittent maternal separation is mediated by increases in positive maternal behaviors (e.g., increases in licking, grooming, arched-back nursing) (Meany, 2001). Nonhuman primate models have been particularly beneficial in demonstrating the beneficial impact of mild/moderate stressors during early development on physiological and behavioral stress responses later in development (see Lyons and Parker, 2007 for a review). In addition to preserving a high degree of experimental integrity, primate models are more applicable to humans than rodent models, particularly concerning developmental processes (Lyons and Parker, 2007; Sanchez, 2006). In a series of studies with primates, Parker and colleagues (2006) tested the maternal mediation hypothesis and found that stress inoculation occurred regardless of maternal behaviors.

While conceptualizations of the impact of early stress typically evaluate linear relations to developmental outcomes, such experiences may be better represented by curvilinear influences. Boyce and Ellis (2005) suggest that environments extreme in either high or low levels of stress result in heightened stress reactivity, whereas environments with moderate levels of stress promote lower reactivity. Boyce and Ellis further argue that low reactivity may be particularly adaptive, as it may aid in "buffering individuals against the chronic stressors encountered in a world that is neither highly threatening nor consistently safe" (Ellis and Boyce, 2008, p. 185). Ellis et al. (2005) evaluated the curvilinear relationship between family environment and stress reactivity in studies involving cross-sectional and prospective designs. Overall, the studies supported the stress inoculation hypothesis, with children from households characterized by moderate stress having the lowest reactivity in both samples.

The Boyce and Ellis model suggests that a low–moderate magnitude of stress within the family should elicit a stress inoculation response, whereas a high-magnitude stressor would not. In experimental paradigms, set points can be determined (e.g., duration or frequency of separation); however, such clarity is not possible when evaluating the magnitude of stress within the naturally occurring family environment. While it is difficult to specify the magnitude of family stress required to elicit stress inoculation, cumulative evidence merits the claim that the stress has to be sufficient in magnitude to elicit negative emotions but not enough to cause dysfunction. For example, severe childhood abuse *increases* the risk of PTSD later in life (e.g., Goldberg and Garno, 2005), and would not be expected to promote stress inoculation.

Existing literature on stress inoculation has not specifically addressed emotion regulation; however, mild or manageable forms of childhood adversity are theorized to promote the development of adaptive skills for coping with stress (Rudolph and Flynn, 2007; Chorpita and Barlow, 1998). Huether (1996, 1998) argues that the alternation of controllable and uncontrollable stressors reorganizes neuronal networks, cementing effective patterns of appraisals and coping, and extinguishing maladaptive patterns. The presentation of mild stressors may improve basic cognitive functions critical for effective emotion regulation, including working memory, memory encoding, and retrieval (see review by Lupien et al., 2007; Yerkes and

Dodson, 1908). Successful navigation of the emotional challenges associated with stress may promote emotion regulation skills that enable the child to manage later-life stress in a more adaptive manner. For example, positive parenting following parental death can provide a supportive atmosphere for learning skills for the adaptive expression and modulation of strong negative emotions. Luecken (2000) and Luecken et al. (2009) found that young adults who lost a parent in childhood and reported a warm relationship with their surviving parent had higher social support and smaller stress-related increases in negative emotion during daily life stressors than nonbereaved adults who reported similarly caring relationships during childhood.

Methodological Considerations

A wide range of family stressors can potentially direct child development onto a risky trajectory. The preceding review highlights four types of family adversity for the purposes of illustrating emotion regulation as a pathway linking child stress to clinical outcomes. However, epidemiological studies demonstrate that different types of childhood adversity co-occur with high frequency, suggesting that it may not be appropriate to attempt to isolate the impact of individual stressors. Further, adverse childhood experiences differ in severity and potential traumatic impact. The magnitude of risk exposure has clear implications for clinical outcomes (Schilling et al., 2008) as well as the possibility of stress inoculation.

Emotion regulation is theorized to be one mediating pathway linking childhood adversity to clinical outcomes, yet a number of methodological issues limit the conclusions that can be drawn at this stage. Challenges defining emotion, emotion regulation, and emotion *dys*regulation, and distinguishing between them, have plagued researchers in this area (Cole et al., 2004; Campos et al., 2004). Within the context of a stressful family environment, the fit of the emotion regulation strategy to the environment becomes a critical consideration. A particular emotion regulation strategy may be adaptive in a one context but maladaptive in the long term or in other contexts. Cultural context is an important consideration as cultures differ widely on what is considered an appropriate level of emotion experience and expression.

Current research has typically taken a narrow approach, implying that positive emotions are *good* and negative emotions are *bad* (Bridges et al., 2004), yet it is evident that negative emotions can serve an important role in highlighting threat and guiding adaptive responses, a role that is particularly beneficial for children in high-stress environments. Reciprocal influences likely exist between family stress and child dysregulation. Child temperamental characteristics further complicate efforts to disentangle the direction of effects, and may even confound relations between family adversity, emotion regulation, and child psychopathology.

Related to the study of stress inoculation, major questions concern which types of stressors may promote inoculation, and in what contexts. Qualities of the caregiver–child relationship may help distinguish stressors that can promote stress inoculation from those that lead towards pathology. The magnitude of the stress is also an important factor to be considered. Stressors that are significant but not overwhelming may promote the development of skills for effectively managing subsequent stressors (Fergus and Zimmerman, 2005). Shonkoff et al. (2009) distinguish between "tolerable stress" during childhood, which is time-limited and occurs within the context of protective relationships, and "toxic stress," which is strong and/or prolonged and occurs in the absence of a supportive caregiver. However, it is methodologically difficult to quantitatively identify the magnitude of stress exposure, as it depends on chronicity, severity, context, emotional and biological reactions, prior experience, co-occurring stressors, appraisals, and consequences, among others. The limited empirical findings to date may imply that the types of family adversity described above exceed the magnitude of stress that could promote stress inoculation. Alternatively, studies focusing only on short-term or pathological outcomes may fail to evaluate enhanced long-term abilities to manage stress. Just as the detrimental effects of childhood adversity may not be evident for many years after exposure (Lupien et al., 2009), long-term studies may be necessary to uncover beneficial outcomes.

Animal models of early adversity often describe a "critical period" in development during which the stress must occur in order to impact stress physiology. For example, in rodents, noxious stimuli during the first 2 weeks of life have minimal effects on glucocorticoid response (the stress hyporesponsive period; Sapolsky and Meaney, 1986). Although not clearly delineated in nonhuman primates, evidence suggests a critical period for some biological consequences within the first 6 months of life. For human children, a hyporesponsive period may occur throughout childhood, supported by parental regulation of the stress response (Lupien et al., 2009). Thus, stressors related to inadequate parental care may elicit a stress response even during a stress hyporesponsive period. In short, the existence of critical periods in the developmental impact of family adversity is unclear. Overall, empirical studies suggest that traumatic experiences at any developmental stage can have long-lasting effects, but the specific outcome may depend on the type and timing of exposure.

Future Research

Existing research on the direct relation of early-life stress to mental health is vast; however, opportunities exist for more finely tuned examination of the underlying processes. We suggest the development of emotion regulation as one direction for future research. Much remains to be determined, including clarification of the causal role of emotion regulation in the development of psychopathology for at risk youth. Longitudinal studies will be an important step in this direction (Yap et al., 2007). A number of future directions for research on emotion regulation more broadly have been identified. These are beyond the scope of this chapter, but the interested reader is referred to Cole et al. (2004) and Eisenberg et al. (2007).

Although the current chapter focused on emotional responses to stress, emotion regulation involves responding at biological, behavioral, emotional, and cognitive levels. The integration of multiple levels of analyses, including physiological indices of emotion regulation (e.g., vagal tone, stress reactivity) represents an important advance in the field. However, there is debate as to whether such indices are an outcome of adverse early-life experiences, or individual risk/protective factors that moderate risk from negative family environments. The concurrent evaluation of multiple systems provides a more nuanced understanding of the integrated ability to respond adaptively to the environment. For example, El-Sheikh and colleagues (2009) demonstrated that opposing activation of the sympathetic and parasympathetic nervous systems increased the risk of externalizing disorders among boys exposed to IPC. Research into the processes by which adversity affects multiple levels of emotion regulation may identify areas of early intervention to improve the psychological health of children exposed to significant stress.

A critical research direction concerns the malleability of the effects of adverse childhood experiences. Although some research suggests that early adversity can lead to permanent neurobiological alterations, there is emerging evidence that early intervention may be capable of minimizing or reversing the long-term negative consequences, suggesting a degree of malleability in the impact of adversity. For example, children adopted into British families after experiencing severe deprivation in Romanian orphanages have been reported to demonstrate "a remarkable degree of recovery after restoration of normal family rearing" (Rutter and O'Connor, 2004, p. 89).

Most studies of childhood adversity focus on the presence or absence of pathology, failing to consider the possibility of enhanced competencies and positive well-being. Intriguing findings from animal studies outline plausible neurological alterations associated with early-life stress that may heighten later abilities to overcome challenge (Lyons et al., 2009). However, at this point the literature on stress inoculation exists more as a theoretical possibility than an empirically demonstrated outcome. Exploration of the processes that might not only protect children from psychopathology, but possibly even enhance abilities to conquer future challenges is an exciting direction for future research.

Concluding Comments

Although stress during any life period can negatively impact psychological adjustment, childhood represents a highly sensitive developmental period, during which the future capacity to respond in an adaptive manner to stressful experiences can be profoundly affected by an adverse environment. In particular, experiences within the family of origin influence the development of emotion regulation, theorized to represent a critical pathway linking childhood adversity to clinical outcomes. One bright spot in this literature rests in the intriguing possibility that successful navigation of early-life adversity, in the context of protective resources, may improve the ability to respond to future stressors. Although prevalent in folk literature and beliefs (e.g., fictional heroes are often orphaned in childhood; "what doesn't kill you makes you stronger"), limited empirical research has examined this possibility. Given the striking prevalence of childhood exposure to major stressful experiences, an understanding of the processes by which early-life stress directs a child onto a positive or negative life course has clear and immediate individual and public health significance.

References

Agid, O., Shapira, B., Zislin, J., Ritsner, M., Hanin, B., Murad, H., Troudart, T., Bloch, M., Heresco-Levy, U., & Lerer, B. (1999). Environment and vulnerability to major psychiatric illness: a case control study of early parental loss in major depression, bipolar disorder, and schizophrenia. *Molecular Psychiatry, 4*, 163–172.

Alink, L. R. A., Cicchetti, D., Kim, J., & Rogosch, F. A. (2009). Mediating and moderating processes in the relation between maltreatment and psychopathology: Mother-child relationship quality and emotion regulation. *Journal of Abnormal Child Psychology, 37*, 831–843.

Alpern, L., & Lyons-Ruth, K. (1993). Preschool children at social risk: Chronicity and timing of maternal depressive symptoms and child behavior problems at school and at home. *Development and Psychopathology, 5*, 371–387.

Anda, R. F., Felitti, V. J., Bremner, J. D., Walker, J. D., Whitfield, C., Perry, B. D., Dube, S. R., & Giles, W. H. (2006). The enduring effects of abuse and related adverse experiences in childhood: a convergence of evidence from neurobiology and epidemiology. *European Archives of Psychiatry and Clinical Neuroscience, 256*, 174–186.

Anda, R. F., Dong, M., Brown, D. W., Felitti, V. J., Giles, W. H., Perry, G. S., Valerie, E. J., & Dube, S. R. (2009). The relationship of adverse childhood experiences to a history of premature death of family members. *BMC Public Health, 9*(106).

Anderson, C. A., & Hammen, C. L. (1993). Psychosocial outcomes of children of unipolar depressed, bipolar, medically ill, and normal women: a longitudinal study. *Journal of Consulting and Clinical Psychology, 61*, 448–454.

Armstadter, A. (2008). Emotion regulation and anxiety disorders. *Journal of Anxiety Disorders, 22*, 211–221.

Ashman, S. B., & Dawson, G. (2002). Maternal depression, infant psychobiological development, and risk for depression. In S. H. Goodman & I. H. Gotlib (Eds.), *Children of depressed parents* (pp. 37–58). Washington DC: American Psychological Association.

Bassani, D. G., Padoin, C. V., Philipp, D., & Veldhuizen, S. (2009). Estimating the number of children exposed to parental psychiatric disorders through a national health survey. *Child and Adolescent Psychiatry and Mental Health, 3*(6).

Bayer, J. K., Sanson, A. V., & Hemphill, S. A. (2006). Parent influences on early childhood internalizing difficulties. *Journal of Applied Developmental Psychology, 27*, 542–559.

Beauchaine, T. P., Gatze-Kopp, L., & Mead, H. K. (2007). Polyvagal theory and developmental psychopathology: Emotion dysregulation and conduct problems from preschool to adolescence. *Biological Psychology, 74*, 174–184.

Boyce, W. T., & Ellis, B. J. (2005). Biological sensitivity to context: I. An evolutionary-developmental theory of the origins and functions of stress reactivity. *Development and Psychopathology, 17*, 271–301.

Brennan, P. A., Hammen, C., Andersen, M. J., Bor, W., Najman, J. M., & Williams, G. M. (2000). Chronicity, severity, and timing of maternal depressive symptoms: relationship with child outcomes at age 5. *Developmental Psychology, 36*(6), 759–766.

Bridges, L. J., Denham, S. A., & Ganiban, J. M. (2004). Definitional issues in emotion regulation research. *Child Development, 75*, 340–345.

Bronfenbrenner, U. (1986). Ecology of the family as a context for human development: Research prospectives. *Developmental Psychology, 22*, 723–742.

Campbell-Sills, L., & Barlow, D. H. (2007). Incorporating emotion regulation into conceptualizations and treatments of anxiety and mood disorders. In J. J. Gross (Ed.), *Handbook of emotion regulation* (pp. 542–559). New York: Guilford Press.

Campos, J. J., Frankel, C. B., & Camras, L. (2004). On the nature of emotion regulation. *Child Development, 75*, 377–394.

Centers for Disease Control and Prevention (2007). *Maternal and Infant Health.* Retrieved from http://www.cdc.gov/reproductivehealth/MaternalInfantHealth/.

Chorpita, B. F., & Barlow, D. H. (1998). The development of anxiety: The role of control in the early environment. *Psychological Bulletin, 124*, 3–21.

Clark, C. Caldwell, T., Power, C., & Stansfeld, S. (2010). Does the influence of childhood adversity on psychopathology persist across the lifecourse? A 45-year prospective epidemiologic study. *Annals of Epidemiology, 20*, 385–394.

Cole, P. M., Martin, S. E., & Dennis, T. A. (2004). Emotion regulation as a scientific construct: Methodological challenges and directions for child development research. *Child Development, 75*, 317–333.

Copeland, W., Shanahan, L., Costello, E. J., & Angold, A. (2009). Configurations of common childhood psychosocial risk factors. *Journal of Child Psychology and Psychiatry, 50*, 451–459.

Crockenberg, S., & Langrock, A. (2001). The role of specific emotions in children's responses to interparental conflict: a test of the model. *Journal of Family Psychology, 15*, 163–182.

Cui, M., Fincham, F. D., & Pasley, B. K. (2008). Young adult romantic relationships: the role of parent's marital problems and relationship efficacy. *Personality and Social Psychology Bulletin, 34*, 1226–1235.

Cummings, E. M., & Davies, P. T. (1994). *Children and marital conflict: The impact of family dispute and resolution.* New York: Guilford Press.

Cummings, E. M., & Keller, P. S. (2006). Marital discord and children's emotion regulation. In D. K. Snyder, J. Simpson, & J. N. Hughes (Eds.), *Emotion regulation in couples and families: Pathways to dysfunction and health* (pp. 163–168). Washington DC: American Psychological Association.

Cummings, E. M., Goeke-Morey, M. C., & Papp, L. M. (2001). Couple conflict, children, and families: It's not just you and me, babe. In A. Booth, A. C. Crouter, & M. Clements (Eds.), *Couples in conflict* (pp. 117–147). Hillsdale, NJ: Lawrence Erlbaum Associates Publishers.

David, K. M., & Murphy, B. C. (2004). Interparental conflict and late adolescents' sensitization to conflict: The moderating effects of emotional functioning and gender. *Journal of Youth and Adolescence, 33*, 187–200.

Davies, P. T., & Cummings, E. M. (1994). Marital conflict and child adjustment: An emotional security hypothesis. *Psychological Bulletin, 116*(3), 387–411.

Davies, P. T., & Windle, M. (2001). Interparental discord and adolescent adjustment trajectories: The potentiating and protective role of intrapersonal attributes. *Child Development, 72*, 1163–1178.

DeBellis, M. D. (2002). Developmental traumatology: a contributory mechanism for alcohol and substance use disorders. *Psychoneuroendocrinology, 27*, 155–170.

Dong, M., Anda, R. F., Dube, S. R., Giles, W. H., & Felitti, V. J. (2003). The relationship of exposure to childhood sexual abuse to other forms of abuse, neglect, and household dysfunction during childhood. *Child Abuse and Neglect, 27*, 625–639.

Eisenberg, N., Cumberland, A., & Spinrad, T. (1998). Parental socialization of emotion. *Psychological Inquiry, 9*, 241–273.

Eisenberg, N., Zhou, Q., Spinrad, T. L., Valiente, C., Fabes, R. A., & Liew, J. (2005). Relations among positive parenting, children's effortful control, and externalizing problems: A three-wave longitudinal study. *Child Development, 76*(5), 1055–1071.

Eisenberg, N., Hofer, C., & Vaughan, J. (2007). Effortful control and its socioemotional consequences. In J. J. Gross (Ed.), *Handbook of emotion regulation* (pp. 287–306). New York: Guilford Press.

Ellis, B. J., & Boyce, W. T. (2008). Biological sensitivity to context. *Current Directions in Psychological Science, 17*, 183–187.

Ellis, B. J., Essex, M. J., & Boyce, W. T. (2005). Biological sensitivity to context: II. Empirical explorations of an evolutionary-developmental theory. *Development and Psychopathology, 17*(2), 303–328.

El-Sheikh, M., Harger, J., & Whitson, S. M. (2001). Exposure to interparental conflict and children's adjustment and physical health. The moderating role of vagal tone. *Child Development, 72*, 1617–1636.

El-Sheikh, M., Kouros, C. D., Erath, S., Cummings, E. M., Keller, P., & Staton, L. (2009). Marital conflict and children's externalizing behavior: interactions between parasympathetic and sympathetic nervous system activity. *Monographs from the Society for Research on Child Development, 74*(1), 1–79.

Felitti, V. J., Anda, R. F., Nordenberg, D., Williamson, D. F., Spitz, A. M., Edwards, V., Koss, M. P., & Marks, J. S. (1998). Relationship of childhood abuse and household dysfunction to many of the leading causes of death in adults. *American Journal of Preventive Medicine, 14*, 245–258.

Fergus, S., & Zimmerman, M. A. (2005). Adolescent resilience: A framework for understanding healthy development in the face of risk. *Annual Reviews of Public Health, 26*, 399–419.

Finkelhor, D., Ormrod, R., Turner, H., & Hamby, S. L. (2005). The victimization of children and youth: A comprehensive, national survey. *Child Maltreatment, 10*, 5–25.

Forest, K. B., Moen, P., & Dempster-McClain, D. (1996). The effects of childhood family stress on women's depressive symptoms: A life course approach. *Psychology of Women Quarterly, 20*, 81–100.

Goldberg, J. F., & Garno, J. L. (2005). Development of posttraumatic stress disorder in adult bipolar patients with histories of severe childhood abuse. *Journal of Psychiatric Research, 39*, 595–601.

Goodman, S. H. (2007). Depression in mothers. *Annual Review of Clinical Psychology, 3*, 107–135.

Goodman, S. H., & Gotlib, I. H. (1999). Risk for psychopathology in the children of depressed mothers: A developmental model for understanding mechanisms of transmission. *Psychological Review, 106,* 458–490.

Gross, J. J. (1998). The emerging field of emotion regulation: An integrative review. *Review of General Psychology, 2,* 271–299.

Gross, J. J., & Muñoz, R. F. (1995). Emotion regulation and mental health. *Clinical Psychology: Science and Practice, 2,* 151–164.

Hammen, C., & Brennan, P. A. (2003). Severity, chronicity, and timing of maternal depression and risk for adolescent offspring diagnoses in a community sample. *Archives of General Psychiatry, 60,* 253–258.

Hoffman, C., Crnic, K. A., & Baker, J. K. (2006). Maternal depression and parenting: Implications for children's emergent emotion regulation and behavioral functioning. *Parenting: Science and Practice, 6,* 271–295.

Huether, G. (1996). The central adaptation syndrome: Psychosocial stress as a trigger for adaptive modifications of brain structure and brain function. *Progress in Neurobiology, 48,* 569–612.

Huether, G. (1998). Stress and the adaptive self-organization of neuronal connectivity during early childhood. *International Journal of Developmental Neuroscience, 16,* 297–306.

John, O. P., & Gross, J. J. (2007). Individual differences in emotion regulation. In J. J. Gross (Ed.), *Handbook of emotion regulation* (pp. 351–372). New York: Guilford Press.

Kalter, N., Lohnes, K. L., Chasin, J., Cain, A. C., Dunning, S., & Rowan, J. (2002). The adjustment of parentally bereaved children: Factors associated with short-term adjustment. *Omega: Journal of Death and Dying, 46,* 15–34.

Kendall-Tackett, K. A., Williams, L. M., & Finkelhor, D. (1993). Impact of sexual abuse on children: A review and synthesis of recent empirical studies. *Psychological Bulletin, 113,* 164–180.

Kendler, K. S., Gardner, C. O., & Prescott, C. A. (2002). Toward a comprehensive developmental model for major depression in women. *American Journal of Psychiatry, 159,* 1133–1145.

Kendler, K. S., Gardner, C. O., & Prescott, C. A. (2006). Toward a comprehensive developmental model for major depression in men. *American Journal of Psychiatry, 163,* 115–124.

Kessler, R. C., Davis, C. G., & Kendler, K. S. (1997). Childhood adversity and adult psychiatric disorder in the U.S. National Comorbidity Survey. *Psychological Medicine, 27,* 1101–1119.

Khoshaba, D. M., & Maddi, S. R. (1999). Early experiences in hardiness development. *Consulting Psychology Journal, 51,* 106–116.

Kingston, S., & Raghavan, C. (2009). The relationship of sexual abuse, early initiation of substance use, and adolescent trauma to PTSD. *Journal of Traumatic Stress, 22*(1), 65–68.

Kivela, S., Luukinen, H., Koski, K., Viramo, P., & Kimmo, P. (1998). Early loss of mother or father predicts depression in old age. *International Journal of Geriatric Psychiatry, 13,* 527–530.

Kopp, L. M., & Beauchaine, T. P. (2007). Patterns of psychopathology in the families of children with conduct problems, depression, and both psychiatric conditions. *Journal of Abnormal Child Psychology, 35,* 301–312.

Kwok, O. M, Haine, R., Sandler, I. N., Ayers, T. S., & Wolchik, S. A. (2005). Positive parenting as a mediator of the relations between parental psychological distress and mental health problems of parentally-bereaved children. *Journal of Clinical Child and Adolescent Psychology, 34*, 261–272.

Laurent, H., & Powers, S. (2007). Emotion regulation in emerging adult couples: temperament, attachment, and HPA response to conflict. *Biological Psychology, 76*, 61–71.

Lieb, R., Wittchen, H., Höfler, M., Fuetsch, M., Stein, M. B., & Merikangas, K. R. (2000). Parental psychopathology, parenting styles, and the risk of social phobia in offspring. *Archives of General Psychiatry, 57*, 859–866.

Lim, J., Wood, B. L., & Miller, B. D. (2008). Maternal depression and parenting in relation to child internalizing symptoms and asthma disease activity. *Journal of Family Psychology, 22*, 264–273.

Lopes, P. N., Salovey, P., Coté, S., & Beers, M. (2005). Emotion regulation abilities and the quality of social interaction. *Emotion, 5*(1),113–8.

Luecken, L. J. (2000). Attachment and loss experiences during childhood are associated with adult hostility, depression, and social support. *Journal of Psychosomatic Research, 49*(1), 85–91.

Luecken, L. J. (2008). Long-term consequences of parental death in childhood: Psychological and physiological manifestations. In M. S. Stroebe, R. O. Hansson, H. Schut, W. Stroebe & E. Van den Blink (Eds.), *Handbook of bereavement research and practice: Advances in theory and intervention* (pp. 397–416). Washington DC: American Psychological Association.

Luecken, L. J., Kraft, A., Appelhans, B. M., & Enders, C. (2009). Emotional and cardiovascular sensitization to daily stress following childhood parental loss. *Developmental Psychology, 45*(1), 296–302.

Lupien, S. J., Maheu, F., Tu, M., Fiocco, A., & Schramek, T. E. (2007). The effects of stress and stress hormones on human cognition: Implications for the field of brain and cognition. *Brain and Cognition, 65*, 209–237.

Lupien, S. J., McEwen, B. S., Gunnar, M. R., & Heim, C. (2009). Effects of stress throughout the lifespan on the brain, behaviour, and cognition. *Nature reviews. Neuroscience, 10*, 434–445.

Lyons, D. M., & Parker, K. J. (2007). Stress inoculation-induced indications of resilience in monkeys. *Journal of Traumatic Stress, 20*(4), 423–433.

Lyons, D. M., Parker, K. J., Katz, M., & Schatzberg, A. F. (2009). Developmental cascades linking stress inoculation, arousal regulation, and resilience. *Frontiers in Behavioral Neuroscience, 3*, 32.

Manly, J. T., Kim, J. E., Rogosch, F. A., & Cicchetti, D. (2001). Dimensions of child maltreatment and children's adjustment: Contributions of developmental timing and subtype. *Development and Psychopathology, 13*, 759–782.

Mann, B. J., & MacKenzie, E. P. (1996). Pathways among marital functioning, parental behaviors, and child behavior problems in school-age boys. *Journal of Clinical Child Psychology, 25*, 183–191.

Marcus, N. E., Lindahl, K. M., & Malik, N. M. (2001). Interparental conflict, children's social cognitions, and child aggression: A test of a mediational model. *Journal of Family Psychology, 15*, 315–333.

Matjasko, J. L., Grunden, L. N., & Ernst, J. L. (2007). Structural and dynamic process family risk factors: Consequences for holistic adolescent functioning. *Journal of Marriage and Family, 69*, 654–674.

Maughan, A., & Cicchetti, D. (2002). Impact of child maltreatment and interadult violence on children's emotion regulation abilities and socioemotional adjustment. *Child Development, 73*, 1525–1542.

Maughan, A., Cicchetti, D., Toth, S. L., & Rogosch, F. A. (2007). Early-occurring maternal depression and maternal negativity in predicting young children's emotion regulation and socioemotional difficulties. *Journal of Abnormal Child Psychology, 35*, 685–703.

Meaney, M. J. (2001). Maternal care, gene expression, and the transmission of individual differences in stress reactivity across generations. *Annual Review of Neuroscience, 24*, 1161–1192.

Menard, C., Bandeen-Roche, K. J., & Chilcoat, H. D. (2004). Epidemiology of multiple childhood traumatic events: Child abuse, parental psychopathology, and other family-level stressors. *Social Psychiatry and Psychiatric Epidemiology, 39*, 857–865.

Merry, S. N., & Andrews, L. K. (1994). Psychiatric status of sexually abused children 12 months after disclosure of abuse. *Journal of the American Academy of Child and Adolescent Psychiatry, 33*, 939–944.

Morris, A. S., Silk, J. S., Steinberg, L., Myers, S. S., & Robinson, L. R. (2007). The role of the family context in the development of emotion regulation. *Social Development, 16*, 361–388.

Parker, K. J., Buckmaster, C. L., Sundlass, K., Schatzberg, A. F., & Lyons, D. M. (2006). Maternal mediation, stress inoculation, and the development of neuroendocrine stress resistance in primates. *Proceedings of the National Academy of Sciences USA, 103*, 3000–3005.

Rae-Grant, N., Thomas, B. H., Offord, D. R., & Boyle, M. H. (1989). Risk, protective factors, and the prevalence of behavioral and emotional disorders in children and adolescents. *Journal of the American Academy of Child and Adolescent Psychiatry, 28*, 262–268.

Repetti, R. L., Taylor, S. E., & Seeman, T. E. (2002). Risky families: Family social environments and the mental and physical health of offspring. *Psychological Bulletin, 128*(2), 330–366.

Rogosch, F. A., Cicchetti, D., & Abner, J. L. (1995). The role of child maltreatment in early deviations in cognitive and affective processing abilities and later peer relationship problems. *Development and Psychopathology, 7*, 591–609.

Rudolph, K. D., & Flynn, M. (2007). Childhood adversity and youth depression: Influence of gender and pubertal status. *Development and Psychopathology, 19*, 497–521.

Rutter, M., & O'Connor, T. G. (2004). Are there biological programming effects for psychological development? Findings from a study of Romanian adoptees. *Developmental Psychology, 40*(1), 81–94.

Sanchez, M. M. (2006). The impact of early adverse care of HPA axis development: Nonhuman primate models. *Hormones and Behavior, 50*, 623–631.

Sapolsky, R. M., & Meaney, M. J. (1986). Maturation of the adrenocortical stress response: neuroendocrine control mechanisms and the stress hyporesponsive period. *Brain Research, 396*, 64–76.

Schermerhorn, A. C., Cummings, E. M., DeCarlo, C. A., & Davies, P. T. (2007). Children's influence in the marital relationship. *Journal of Family Psychology, 21*, 259–269.

Schilling, E. A., Aseltine, R. H., & Gore, S. (2008). The impact of cumulative childhood adversity on young adult mental health: measures, models, and interpretations. *Social Science and Medicine, 66*(5), 1140–51.

Schoedl, A. F., Costa, M. C., Mari, J. J., Mello, M. F., Tyrka, A. R., Carpenter, L. L., & Price, L. H. (2010). The clinical correlates of reported childhood sexual abuse: an association between age at trauma onset and severity of depression and PTSD in adults. *Journal of Child Sexual Abuse, 19,* 156–70.

Shaw, D. S., Vondra, J. I., Hommerding, K. D., Keenan, K., & Dunn, M. (1994). Chronic family adversity and early child behavior problems: A longitudinal study of low income families. *Journal of Child Psychology and Psychiatry, 35,* 1109–1122.

Sheffield Morris, A., Silk, J. S., Steinberg, L., Myers, S. S., & Robinson, L. R. (2007). The role of the family context in the development of emotion regulation. *Social Development, 16,* 361–388.

Shelton, K. H., & Harold, G. T. (2008). Pathways between interparental conflict and adolescent psychological adjustment: Bridging links through children's cognitive appraisals and coping strategies. *Journal of Early Adolescence, 28,* 555–582.

Shields, A., & Cicchetti, D. (1998). Reactive aggression among maltreated children: The contributions of attention and emotion regulation. *Journal of Child Clinical Psychology, 27,* 381–395.

Shipman, K., Edwards, A., Brown, A., Swisher, L, & Jennings, E. (2005). Managing emotion in a maltreating context: A pilot study examining child neglect. *Child Abuse & Neglect, 29,* 1015–1029.

Shipman, K. L., Schneider, R., Fitzgerald, M. M., Sims, C., Swisher, L., & Edwards, A. (2007). Maternal emotion socialization in maltreating and non-maltreating families: Implications for children's emotion regulation. *Social Development, 16,* 268–285.

Shonkoff, J. P., Boyce, W. T., & McEwen, B. S. (2009). Neuroscience, molecular biology, and the childhood roots of health disparities: building a new framework for health promotion and disease prevention. *Jama: the Journal of the American Medical Association, 301*(21), 2252–2259.

Silk, J. S., Shaw, D. S., Forbes, E. E., Lane, T. L., & Kovacs, M. (2006). Maternal depression and child internalizing: The moderating role of child emotion regulation. *Journal of Clinical Child and Adolescent Psychology, 29,* 116–126.

Sohr-Preston, S. L., & Scaramella, L. V. (2006). Implications of timing of maternal depressive symptoms and early cognitive and language development. *Clinical Child and Family Psychology Review, 9*(1), 65–83.

Stroebe, W., & Stroebe, M. (1993). Determinants of adjustment to bereavement in younger widows and widowers. In M. Stroebe, W. Stroebe, & R. Hansson (Eds.), *Handbook of bereavement: Theory, research, and intervention* (pp. 208–226). New York: Cambridge University Press.

Tarullo, A. R., & Gunnar, M. R. (2006). Child maltreatment and the developing HPA axis. *Hormones and Behavior, 50,* 632–639.

Teisl, M., & Cicchetti, D. (2008). Physical abuse, cognitive, and emotional processes, and aggressive/disruptive behavior problems. *Social Development, 17,* 1–23.

Thompson, R. A. (1994). Emotion regulation: A theme in search of a definition. In N.A. Fox (Ed.), *Monographs of the Society for Research in Child Development* (serial no. 240, vol. 59), Chicago, IL: University of Chicago Press.

Thornberry, T. P., Ireland, T. O., & Smith, C. A. (2001). The importance of timing: The varying impact of childhood and adolescent maltreatment on multiple problem outcomes. *Development and Psychopathology, 13,* 957–979.

Turner, H. A., & Kopiec, K. (2006). Exposure to interparental conflict and psychological disorder among young adults. *Journal of Family Issues, 27*(2), 131–158.

U.S. Department of Health and Human Services, Administration on Children Youth and Families (2009): *Child Maltreatment 2007*. Washington, DC: US Government Printing Office. Retrieved from http://www.acf.hhs.gov/programs/cb/pubs/cm07/index.htm.

Valiente, C., Eisenberg, N., Spinrad, T. L., Reiser, M., Cumberland, A., Losoya, S. H., & Liew, J. (2006). Relations among mothers' expressivity, children's effortful control, and their problem behaviors: A four-year longitudinal study. *Emotion, 6*(3), 459–472.

Vostanis, P., Graves, A., Meltzer, H., Goodman, R., Jenkins, R., & Brugha, T. (2006). Relationship between parental psychopathology, parenting strategies, and child mental health. *Social Psychology and Psychiatric Epidemiology, 41*, 509–514.

Weissman, M. M., Wickramarante, P., Nomura, Y., Warner, V., Pilowsky, D., & Verdeli, H. (2006). Offspring of depressed parents: 20 years later. *American Journal of Psychiatry, 163*, 1001–1008.

West, A. E., & Newman, D. L. (2003). Worried and blue: Mild parental anxiety and depression in relation to the development of young children's temperament and behavior problems. *Parenting: Science and Practice, 3*, 133–154.

Wright, M. O., Crawford, E., & Del Castillo, D. (2009). Childhood emotional maltreatment and later psychological distress among college students: The mediating role of maladaptive schemas. *Child Abuse & Neglect, 33*, 59–68.

Yamamoto, K., Whittaker, J., & Davis, Jr, O. L. (1998). Stressful events in the lives of U.K. children: A glimpse. *Educational Studies, 24*, 305–314.

Yap, M. B. H., Allen, N. B., & Sheeber, L. (2007). Using an emotion regulation framework to understand the role of temperament and family processes in risk for adolescent depressive disorders. *Clinical Child and Family Psychology, 10*, 180–196.

Yerkes, R. M., & Dodson, J. D. (1908). The relation of strength of stimulus to rapidity of habit formation. *Journal of Comparative Neurology and Psychology, 18*, 459–482.

16

Chronic Stress and Hippocampus Vulnerability to Functional Changes and Health in the Adult

Cheryl D. Conrad

Introduction

A misconception regarding the natural progression of cognitive function is that it declines with age. Part of this perception is driven by epidemiological data for many neurodegenerative disorders, especially those with dementia, showing that age increases the risk of cognitive dysfunction (see Bishop et al., 2010). However, age influences various types of memory differently (Tulving and Craik, 2000; Erickson and Barnes, 2003). Some forms of memory are relatively unperturbed by age, such as how to drive a car or bike, which represent procedural or nondeclarative memory (Owens, 1953; Erickson and Barnes, 2003). Other types of memory require conscious recall and are referred to as declarative memory and can be subcategorized further. Recalling facts, such as the government capital and national anthem, are forms of semantic declarative memory. Remembering details about personal experiences, such as who visited during Sunday brunch and what type of meal was served, represent episodic declarative memory. Semantic memory is less affected by age-associated decline than is episodic memory (Balota et al., 2000; Erickson and Barnes, 2003), while vocabulary actually improves with age (Erickson and Barnes, 2003). Therefore, age influences the different types of memory unequally, with episodic declarative memory being especially vulnerable to aging.

Critical neural substrates underlying episodic memory are the hippocampus and neocortex. The hippocampus helps with episodic memory formation by integrating the various sensory and environmental cues to form a relationship among them (O'Keefe and Nadel, 1978; Eichenbaum, 2000), a concept supported by the identification of *place cells* in the hippocampus (O'Keefe and Dostrovsky, 1971; Ekstrom

The Handbook of Stress: Neuropsychological Effects on the Brain, First Edition.
Edited by Cheryl D. Conrad.
© 2011 Blackwell Publishing Ltd. Published 2011 by Blackwell Publishing Ltd.

et al., 2003). Hippocampal place cells respond only when an animal is located within a particular spatial location (O'Keefe and Dostrovsky, 1971; Ekstrom et al., 2003). The hippocampus helps form relationships among environmental features, which allows one to navigate from one location to the next, even when embarking from a new starting point. This type of navigation has been referred to as a *cognitive* or *spatial* map (Tolman, 1948; O'Keefe and Nadel, 1978) and is an especially useful construct when assessing hippocampal function in rodents (Morris et al., 1982; Paul et al., 2009). The neocortex is thought to be responsible for the long-term storage of the information about these relationships (Eichenbaum, 2000). Notably, both the hippocampus and the frontal cortex are particularly vulnerable to age-related changes (Winocur and Gagnon, 1998; Burke and Barnes, 2006).

The progression of age-related decline in hippocampal-dependent spatial function involves many components and one that has received much attention is stress and the stress hormones, glucocorticoids, which include cortisol in humans and corticosterone in rodents. How stress and glucocorticoids may contribute to hippocampal aging was described in a seminal hypothesis called the glucocorticoid cascade hypothesis (Sapolsky et al., 1986). This hypothesis proposed that glucocorticoids secreted during periods of stress desensitize the hippocampus to further glucocorticoid exposure by downregulating glucocorticoid receptors (GRs), a process involving protein expression to detect glucocorticoids that is self-correcting and therefore reversible. However, during the period when the GRs within the hippocampus are downregulated, the hypersecretion of glucocorticoids continues and, at some point, hippocampal cell loss occurs. The loss of neurons is irreversible and this permanent hippocampal damage was proposed to make the hippocampus forever insensitive to further glucorticoid elevations, creating a feed-forward cycle of elevated glucocorticoids and continued hippocampal destruction as an individual ages (Figure 16.1). While elegant, the glucocorticoid cascade hypothesis had some inconsistencies, such as that the hypothalamic–pituitary–adrenal (HPA) axis does not always break down with age (see Swanwick et al., 1998; Angelucci, 2000). More recently, new findings have contributed to a modified hypothesis called the glucocorticoid vulnerability hypothesis, which states that cumulative stress, which includes repeated elevation of glucocorticoids, may make the hippocampus vulnerable to disruption. For example, chronic stress may impair hippocampal function, such as spatial learning and memory. Moreover, the hippocampus may be less able to handle a metabolic or neurotoxic challenge. Metabolic challenges refer to events that compromise energy use, such as hypoxia, ischemia, or hypoglycemia (Sapolsky, 1992). Neurotoxic challenges include kainic acid and ibotenic acid and these also compromise energy use by overstimulating neurons (Keilhoff et al., 1990), which eventually hinders energy use. This period of when the hippocampus is vulnerable spans beyond the duration of when glucocorticoids are elevated to permit a broad window by which these potential effects on function and structure could occur (Conrad, 2008). It is important to recognize that hippocampal damage does not necessarily result from chronic stress, but that chronic stress repeated over a lifetime will increase the risk for hippocampal disruption. This chapter will describe the

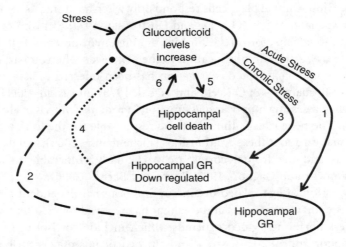

Figure 16.1   A schematic interpretation of the glucocorticoid cascade hypothesis (Sapolsky et al., 1986). Stress produces a milieu of responses, with the HPA axis and the release of glucocorticoids being one component of the stress response. (1) In response to acute stress, the glucocorticoids target many brain structures containing GRs. Hippocampal GRs bind to glucocorticoids and inhibit the subsequent release of glucocorticoids (2), which is illustrated by the long-dashed line ending with a filled circle. (3) With chronic stress and prolonged glucocorticoid release, the hippocampus downregulates GRs, a process that is reversible. During the downregulation, the hippocampus cannot effectively inhibit the HPA axis and the subsequent release of glucocorticoids (4), which is illustrated by the negative feedback being broken down (small dotted line). At some point, this glucocorticoid hypersecretion endangers the hippocampus and eventually kills hippocampal neurons (5), and with them even more GRs are removed and hence permanent insensitivity to glucocorticoids may develop (6). The difference between the outer loops reflected by 1–4 and the inner loop reflected by 5 and 6 is that the former processes are reversible, whereas the latter are permanent.

work that led up to the updated hypothesis, the glucocorticoid vulnerability hypothesis (Conrad, 2008; Conrad and Bimonte-Nelson, 2010). A critical difference between the glucococorticoid cascade hypothesis and the current glucocorticoid vulnerability hypothesis is that glucocorticoids need not be elevated at the time of a metabolic/neurotoxic challenge to compromise the hippocampus.

Glucocorticoid Cascade Hypothesis and Recent Developments

A wealth of information converged to support a role for the hippocampus in the glucocorticoid cascade hypothesis. Glucocorticoids directly influence the hippocampus, as the hippocampus contains a high density of the two receptor subtypes, the mineralocorticoid receptor (MR) and the GR (Reul and de Kloet, 1985; de Kloet et al., 1998). Hippocampal GRs decrease in a site-specific manner with stress and age (Sapolsky et al., 1983, 1984a). Moreover, the hippocampus influences glucocorticoid levels, as the hippocampus provides negative feedback to the HPA axis to reduce glucocorticoid secretion (Wilson et al., 1980; Sapolsky et al., 1984b; Herman et al., 1989). Finally, a wealth of data shows that glucocorticoids exacerbate hippocampal damage caused by neurochemical or metabolic challenges (Sapolsky, 1985a, 1985b, 1986; Sapolsky and Pulsinelli, 1985; Stein and Sapolsky, 1988; Tombaugh et al., 1992; Smith-Swintosky et al., 1996). Collectively, these studies show that acute glucocorticoid elevations exacerbate hippocampal damage when glucocorticoid elevations coincide with the neurotoxic or metabolic challenges (Sapolsky, 1992).

A core feature of the glucocorticoid cascade hypothesis is a shift from reversible GR downregulation in the hippocampus to permanent hippocampal cell death. The problem is whether this transition from hippocampal GR downregulation to hippocampal cell death occurs. Some studies suggest that GRs may not be particularly concentrated in the primate hippocampus (Sánchez et al., 2000), as found in the rodent (Reul and de Kloet, 1985), and hence the human hippocampus may not be sensitive to glucocorticoids. However, the issue may be methodological (see Chapter 3 in this volume): high levels of GRs and/or MRs are found within the hippocampus of many primates, including the squirrel monkey (Orchinik et al., 2001), macaque (Brooke et al., 1994), marmoset (Johnson et al., 1996), and even human (Sarrieau et al., 1988). A second concern is whether the HPA axis breaks down with age, which can be tested using a synthetic glucocorticoid, dexamethasone. Dexamethasone should inhibit the HPA axis via negative feedback, thereby reducing the subsequent release of endogenous glucocorticoids and thus identifying individuals with a compromised HPA-axis-feedback system. However, patients with Alzheimer's disease, a condition with progressive hippocampal degeneration, exhibited responses in a dexamethasone test that were comparable to healthy, age-matched adults (Franceschi et al., 1991; Swanwick et al., 1998). In another example, men in their sixties were found to show similar HPA-axis response patterns as men in their twenties (Kudielka et al., 2000). Finally, hippocampal cell loss is not always observed with prolonged exposure to glucocorticoids (Bodnoff et al., 1995; Vollmann-Honsdorf et al., 1997; Sousa et al., 1998; Leverenz et al., 1999; Fuchs et al., 2001; Müller et al., 2001; Coburn-Litvak et al., 2004; Tata et al., 2006) or with age (West et al., 1994; Sullivan et al., 2005; Terry, 2006). Therefore, elevated glucocorticoids do not necessarily confer hippocampal cell loss that becomes pronounced with age.

Investigating Hippocampal Structural Changes Beyond Neuronal Loss

Evidence presented so far clearly shows that glucocorticoids may not be necessary for hippocampal cell loss, but this section will reveal that glucocorticoids could still influence the hippocampus through other means, which is consistent with the general vision of the susceptibility of the hippocampus to glucocorticoids (Landfield et al., 1978, 1981; Sapolsky et al., 1986).

One important variable is that the methodology used to quantify cell loss has improved over the years. Many older reports showed that glucocorticoid or stress exposure contributed to hippocampal cell loss (Landfield et al., 1981; Sapolsky et al., 1985; Uno et al., 1989; Mizoguchi et al., 1992; Clark et al., 1995; Dachir et al., 1997), but these procedures were performed prior to the acceptance of rigorous stereological counting procedures (Sterio, 1983; West et al., 1991; West, 1993), which allow for the unbiased assessment of cell counts. If stress and glucocorticoids change the hippocampus, such as by shrinking the cell body, then cells could be counted less often because they have a lower probability of lying within the section (see Tata and Anderson, 2010). For studies that have implemented unbiased counting methods, stress and corticosterone fail to produce cell loss, even when glucocorticoid levels are very high and/or stress persists for months (Vollmann-Honsdorf et al., 1997; Sousa et al., 1998, 1999; Leverenz et al., 1999; Tata et al., 2006). Therefore, chronic stress via glucocorticoids is unlikely to alter the hippocampus by reducing cell counts.

An alternative to cell loss is for stress and glucocorticoids to alter the hippocampal neuropil, a region containing dendritic, synaptic, and glial processes (Tata and Anderson, 2010). The volume of the hippocampal neuropil is approximately 93% compared to the remaining 7% containing cell bodies (Tata et al., 2006). Consequently, marked changes in the neuropil could have dramatic consequences for hippocampal volume and hence function. One particular change in the neuropil that has been repeatedly documented following chronic stress or glucocorticoid elevations is dendritic retraction in the CA3 region of the hippocampus (where CA means cornu ammonis, a subregion of the hippocampus; Conrad, 2006), with the dendritic arbors in other hippocampal regions (CA1, dentate gyrus) expressing atrophy as stress continues or intensifies (Fuchs et al., 1995; Lambert et al., 1998; Sousa et al., 2000). Dendritic retraction refers to the pruning of the dendritic arbors by reducing the number of dendritic bifurcations and shortening of the total dendritic length (Figure 16.2). Such changes, including chronic stress-induced synapse loss (Tata et al., 2006), would render the hippocampus less sensitive to converging information. Moreover, these changes in the neuropil could produce the reduction in hippocampal volume that is detected following chronic stress (Lee et al., 2009). Therefore, the region with potential for dramatic alterations in volume without cell loss is the neuropil, which corresponds to the location containing the dendritic arbors that undergoes pruning following chronic stress.

Chronic-stress-induced CA3 dendritic retraction is also dynamic, being slow to develop and with the potential to recover, a feature that is consistent with volumetric changes in the hippocampus from patients with glucocorticoid hypersecretion. Using repeated restraint, chronic stress was observed to produce hippocampal dendritic retraction in the CA3 region after restraint was given for 6 hr each day for 21 days, but not after a shorter daily restraint session (2 hr/day for 10 days or 21 days), nor after 6 hr of restraint for fewer days (10 or 14 days; Luine et al., 1996; McLaughlin

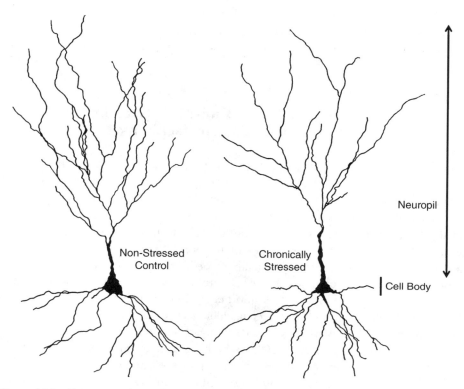

Figure 16.2   Representations of Golgi-stained hippocampal CA3 neurons that were traced using a camera lucida drawing tube (320×) attached to an Olympus BX51 microscope. Chronic stress using wire-mesh restraint for 6 hr/day for 21 days produces robust dendritic retraction in apical dendritic arbors of CA3 hippocampal neurons, a region that is the predominate component of the neuropil. The number of bifurcations and/or total dendritic length can determine reduced dendritic complexity. Apical CA3 dendritic arbors typically manifest dendritic retraction before the basal CA3 dendritic arbors and other hippocampal regions. *Source:* From McLaughlin et al. (2010). Reproduced with permission of John Wiley and Sons.

et al., 2007). Chronic glucocorticoid administration for 21 days produces CA3 dendritic retraction too (Woolley et al., 1990; Watanabe et al., 1992a) and blocking glucocorticoid secretion blocks stress-induced CA3 dendritic retraction (Magariños and McEwen, 1995a). Moreover, CA3 dendritic retraction reflects a highly dynamic and reversible process, with recovery detected around 10 or 30 days after chronic stress has ended (Conrad et al., 1999b; Sousa et al., 2000; Vyas et al., 2004). In patients with Cushing's disease, a rare disorder with glucocorticoid hypersecretion, hippocampal volume inversely correlates with glucocorticoid levels (Starkman et al., 1992) and hippocampal volumes increase by nearly 10% after glucocorticoid levels are normalized (Starkman et al., 1999; Bourdeau et al., 2005; Hook et al., 2007). Therefore, chronic stress most likely mediates its effects on the hippocampus through dynamic processe(s), such as observed with CA3 dendritic retraction, as opposed to producing irreversible cell loss, and these flexible responses are consistent with the volumetric alterations in the human hippocampus after prolonged exposure to glucocorticoids.

Hippocampal CA3 Dendritic Retraction: Consequences on Spatial Ability

The majority of studies show that the consequence of chronic stress on hippocampal function includes spatial learning and memory impairment (for review, Conrad, 2010). Chronic exposure to the same (homotypic) predictable stressor over many days to months impairs spatial learning and memory (Luine et al., 1994; Conrad et al., 1996; Nishimura et al., 1999; Sunanda et al., 2000; Venero et al., 2002; Kitraki et al., 2004; Radecki et al., 2005; Manikandan et al., 2006; Moosavi et al., 2007; Wright and Conrad, 2008). Chronic unpredictable types of stressors, or other forms of heterotypic stressors that include psychosocial stress, also reveal detrimental outcomes on spatial learning and memory (Bodnoff et al., 1995; Krugers et al., 1997; Ohl and Fuchs, 1999; Ohl et al., 2000; Sousa et al., 2000; Park et al., 2001; Gerges et al., 2004; Touyarot et al., 2004; Aleisa et al., 2006; Song et al., 2006; Cerqueira et al., 2007; Orsetti et al., 2007; Zoladz et al., 2008; Alzoubi et al., 2009; Srivareerat et al., 2009). Moreover, chronic stress conditions that produce CA3 dendritic retraction correspond to poor spatial ability: chronic restraint stress impaired spatial memory and produced CA3 dendritic retraction in the same subjects when restraint was given for 6 hr/day for 21 days, but neither impaired spatial memory nor altered CA3 dendritic arbors when restraint or number of days were shorter (2 hr/day for 21 days or 6 hr/day for 10 days; McLaughlin et al., 2007). These findings are consistent with functional spatial ability being expressed (Luine et al., 1994; Conrad et al., 1996) under conditions, such as with administration of phenytoin (an antiepileptic that reduces glutaminergic neurotransmission) or antidepressants, that blocked stress-induced CA3 dendritic retraction (Watanabe et al., 1992a, 1992b; Magariños and McEwen, 1995a; Luo and Tan, 2001) or when animals had time to recover from chronic stress (Luine et al., 1994). Therefore, chronic stress impairs spatial memory during periods that hippocampal CA3 dendritic retraction exists.

The aforementioned studies suggest that hippocampal CA3 dendritic retraction may be the underlying mechanism by which chronic stress impairs spatial ability; however, additional studies suggest a more complex role than whether CA3 dendritic retraction is present. Early attempts to investigate chronic glucocorticoid treatment on spatial ability in adults have reported mixed outcomes, with some documenting deficits (Dachir et al., 1993; Luine et al., 1993; Bardgett et al., 1994; Endo et al., 1996; McLay et al., 1998; Coburn-Litvak et al., 2003) and others finding no significant effect (Bodnoff et al., 1995; Clark et al., 1995; Coburn-Litvak et al., 2003). One interpretation is that structural alterations within the hippocampus are undetectable and so perhaps spatial memory may be unaffected unless glucocorticoids are administered for durations longer than 3 or 4 weeks (Coburn-Litvak et al., 2003). This explanation is plausible as many of the previous studies investigated changes in hippocampal cell number, a construct that may not reflect the structural changes in the hippocampus produced by chronic glucocorticoid exposure. Nonetheless, a recent study found that chronic glucocorticoid treatment failed to impair spatial memory despite confirmation from the same rats that CA3 dendritic retraction occurred (Conrad et al., 2007). Therefore, the presence of CA3 dendritic retraction does not necessarily indicate that hippocampal function, as measured by spatial navigation, will be impaired.

In another series of studies, chronically stressed subjects with a compromised hippocampus were found to be capable of exhibiting spatial learning and memory. Rats that were chronically stressed by restraint for 6 hr/day for 21 days, a procedure and time frame that reliably produces hippocampal CA3 dendritic retraction (Conrad, 2006; McLaughlin et al., 2007), also showed spatial memory deficits as expected (Wright et al., 2006). However, chronically stressed rats that were injected once on the day of spatial assessment with metyrapone, to attenuate stress levels of glucocorticoids, showed functional spatial abilities despite conditions that produced hippocampal CA3 dendritic retraction (Wright et al., 2006). Another report found that rats with chemical lesions targeting the CA3 region also showed spatial deficits that were prevented with a single injection of metyrapone to reduce glucocorticoid elevations on the day of memory assessment (Roozendaal et al., 2001). Moreover these spatial memory deficits were reinstated with a single corticosterone injection (Roozendaal et al., 2001). These studies reveal that manipulations compromising the CA3 region of the hippocampus can negatively impact spatial ability, but that a compromised CA3 region alone is not sufficient because spatial ability can be reinstated by attenuating glucocorticoid levels during spatial learning and/or recall.

Clearly, glucocorticoids can influence spatial memory, but this relationship is more complex than determining whether glucocorticoids are simply elevated (for review, Conrad, 2005). Generally speaking, the HPA axis has a nonlinear relationship with hippocampal-dependent spatial learning, with very low or high glucocorticoid levels impairing spatial learning and moderate glucocorticoid levels being optimal. On one extreme, the removal of glucocorticoids via adrenalectomy impairs spatial learning and memory (Oitzl and de Kloet, 1992; Conrad and Roy, 1993; Roozendaal et al., 1996; Conrad et al., 1997, 1999a). On the other end of the spectrum, stress levels of glucocorticoids or GR agonists also impair spatial learning and memory (Conrad et al., 1997, 1999a). For glucocorticoid ranges that facilitate spatial memory, basal (2 µg/dl) to low (approximately 10 µg/dl) corticosterone levels in blood serum positively correlate with spatial learning (Yau et al., 1995). Similarly, exogenously manipulating glucocorticoid levels produces an inverted U-shaped function for glucocorticoid levels and spatial memory (Mateo, 2008). Importantly, the context by which stress or glucocorticoids influence spatial learning and memory is critical (Yang et al., 2003). Specifically, glucocorticoid elevations in response to predator exposure impair spatial memory, whereas similar elevations of glucocorticoids in response to mating do not (Woodson et al., 2003).

Moreover, glucocorticoid elevations significantly correlate with spatial deficits only for the situation involving predator exposure and not for glucocorticoid elevations that follow mating behavior (Woodson et al., 2003). Therefore, glucocorticoids have a nonlinear relationship with spatial memory, with the context by which glucocorticoids are elevated being important too.

The previous paragraphs have already discussed how chronic stress produces structural changes in the hippocampus to influence spatial ability, but, importantly, changes in HPA axis are relevant too. A consistent finding in the literature is that chronic stress potentiates glucocorticoid release in response to a novel, heterotypic stressor compared to a familiar, homotypic stressor (Dallman, 2000, 2007; Bhatnagar et al., 2002; Herman et al., 2005). During spatial navigation, chronically stressed rats release higher levels of glucocorticoids than do controls, even when rats are tested on a relatively benign task, such as the Y maze (Wright et al., 2006; for review see Conrad, 2006). These data suggest that spatial navigation in the Y maze is analogous to a novel heterotypic stressor, which potentiates glucocorticoid levels from chronically stressed rats (Wright et al., 2006). However, elevated glucocorticoid levels alone cannot completely explain the poor spatial memory of chronically stressed rats: glucocorticoid levels that allow for optimal spatial memory in nonstressed controls impair spatial memory in chronically stressed rats (Wright et al., 2006). Moreover, biologically available glucocorticoids (i.e., unbound to corticosteroid-binding globulin) are similar between controls and chronically stressed rats (Wright et al., 2006). That circulating glucocorticoid levels did not differ among groups, while performance in a spatial maze did, supports the hypothesis that changes in brain sensitivity to glucocorticoids contribute to the spatial ability outcomes in chronically stressed rats.

Model for Chronic Stress and CA3 Dendritic Retraction in Spatial Ability

Under conditions of chronic stress that produce CA3 dendritic retraction we hypothesize that the hippocampus is susceptible to spatial-memory deficits following chronic glucocorticoid elevations at levels that are not typically disruptive in nonstressed controls. Chronically stressed subjects respond to a novel spatial memory paradigm with slightly potentiated glucocorticoid levels. Under these conditions that are combined with a compromised hippocampus expressing CA3 dendritic retraction these chronically stressed subjects will express spatial learning and memory impairments under conditions that would normally facilitate optimal spatial abilities in nonstressed controls (Figure 16.3). This hypothesis assumes that the spatial navigation paradigm is not overtly arousing or aversive, as would be found in fear conditioning or water-maze paradigms, conditions that activate the amygdalar regions and can mask hippocampal function (Conrad, 2006; McLaughlin et al., 2009), perhaps by shifting to well-learned behaviors (Dias-Ferreira et al., 2009). However, when subjects are navigating in a spatial environment under

(a) Acute *Heterotypic* Stress on Spatial Ability in Normal Controls

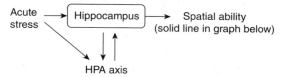

(b) Acute *Heterotypic* Stress on Spatial Ability after Chronic Stress

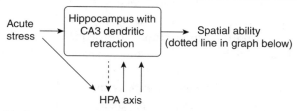

(c) Nonlinear Function for Glucocorticoids and Spatial Ability

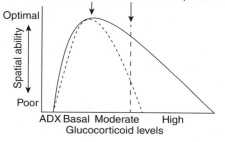

Figure 16.3 Model for chronic-stress actions via elevated glucocorticoids influencing spatial ability. (a) Without a history of chronic stress, an acute stressor triggers the HPA axis and elevates glucocorticoids, which could feed back to influence the hippocampus and its functions, such as spatial ability. The hippocampus also provides negative feedback on the HPA axis. The vertical arrows illustrate the reciprocal relationship between the hippocampus and the HPA axis. Under these conditions, glucocorticoids influence spatial ability by the inverted U-shaped function, as illustrated by the solid curve in the graph (panel c). (b) Following chronic stress, the hippocampus is compromised and exhibits CA dendritic retraction, along with other neurochemical and neuromorphological changes. Consequently, the hippocampus has poor regulation of the HPA axis, indicated by the dashed arrow, whereas the HPA axis and adrenals are overactive, indicated by the two large upward-pointing arrows, creating an imbalance. Under these chronic stress conditions, a change in the sensitivity of the hippocampus to novel stress and glucocorticoids is hypothesized to narrow the inverted U-shaped function, as illustrated by the dotted curve in the graph (panel c). (c) Consequently, glucocorticoid elevations that optimize spatial ability in nonstressed animals will impair spatial ability in those following chronic stress: compare the curves at the vertical dashed line. The thick arrowhead illustrates that, at low glucocorticoid levels, functional spatial ability is possible following chronic stress. ADX, adrenalectomy, or the removal of the endogenous source of glucocorticoids and a majority of catecholamines. *Source:* From Conrad & Bimonte-Nelson (2010). With permission from Elsevier.

nonthreatening conditions, then spatial abilities are hypothesized to differ between controls and chronically stressed subjects expressing hippocampal CA3 dendritic retraction.

How the hippocampus and the HPA axis contribute to spatial ability following chronic stress is illustrated in Figure 16.3. The hippocampus expressing CA3 dendritic retraction is compromised because it is unable to regulate the HPA axis effectively in response to heterotypic stressors (i.e., the novel environment) and is illustrated by the downward dotted arrow (Figure 16.3b). Moreover, the hippocampus is susceptible to glucocorticoid elevations, which is indicated by two solid upward arrows targeting the hippocampus. Consequently, the influence between the hippocampus and the HPA axis is no longer balanced, which we hypothesize is revealed by a change in the way the hippocampus responds to novel stress and glucocorticoid elevations. The consequence is that levels of glucocorticoids that optimize spatial ability in controls lead to impaired spatial ability in chronically stressed rats. Specifically, chronic stress is hypothesized to narrow the inverted U-shaped function for glucocorticoid effects on spatial ability, by shifting the descending right limb of the inverted U-shaped function to the left (Figure 16.3c). Consequently, moderate levels of glucocorticoids that do not impair spatial ability in controls are predicted to do so following chronic stress conditions that produce CA3 dendritic retraction.

Hippocampal CA3 Dendritic Retraction: Consequences on Hippocampal Health

Other ways that chronic stress influences the hippocampus are to alter the hippocampus' ability to respond to potential threats. Past work demonstrated that neurotoxic and metabolic challenges that damaged the hippocampus were even more damaging when these challenges occurred during periods that glucocorticoids were simultaneously elevated (Sapolsky, 1992). This work is extended to show that conditions surrounding chronic stress- or glucocorticoid-induced CA3 dendritic retraction are revealed to compromise hippocampal health, even when glucocorticoids are no longer elevated.

In the following studies, the neurotoxic challenges were presented to the hippocampus after chronic stress or glucocorticoids had subsided. When rats were chronically stressed by restraint at a duration that produces CA3 dendritic retraction, the CA3 region of the hippocampus showed exacerbated cell loss following an ibotenic acid challenge (Conrad et al., 2004). The ibotenic acid challenge occurred a few days after chronic stress ended, but within the time frame that CA3 dendritic retraction should exist (Conrad et al., 1999b). Moreover, rats exposed to one restraint session that was too brief to produce CA3 dendritic retraction (Magariños and McEwen, 1995b; McLaughlin et al., 2007) failed to exacerbate hippocampal damage following the ibotenic acid challenge (Conrad et al., 2004). Therefore, acute glucocorticoid elevations from restraint were unlikely to have exacerbated ibotenic acid-induced CA3 damage and emphasize that the history of chronic stress was critical for hippocampal susceptibility to a neurotoxin challenge.

In a final series of studies, the conditions surrounding hippocampal dendritic retraction were determined to be important. When rats were chronically stressed by restraint at a duration that does not yet produce CA1 dendritic retraction (compare Magariños and McEwen, 1995b; Sousa et al., 2000), ibotenic acid infusion into the CA1 region failed to result in exacerbated CA1 damage (Conrad et al., 2004). A similar outcome was found in the CA3 region: when dendritic retraction caused by chronic glucocorticoid exposure was blocked with phenytoin, an antiepileptic that reduces glutaminergic neurotransmission, ibotenic acid infusion into the CA3 region failed to cause further damage than observed in nonstressed controls (Conrad et al., 2007). Finally, the likelihood of the infusion procedure creating a potentiated stress response was excluded. Specifically, chronic restraint stress changes the HPA axis response, with the HPA axis becoming hyper-responsive to a novel, heterotypic stressor (Dallman et al., 2000; Dallman, 2007; see also Chapters 1 and 2 in this volume). Perhaps infusing ibotenic acid under surgical anesthesia may have caused a potentiated HPA axis response in chronically stressed subjects. Consequently, another cohort of rats were implanted with cannulae targeting the CA3 region and then after recovery, exposed to chronic glucocorticoids. A few days after the glucocorticoid treatment ended, rats were gently infused with ibotenic acid while alert (Conrad et al., 2007). Chronic glucocorticoid treatment exacerbated CA3 damage from the ibotenic acid challenge without significantly changing the glucocorticoid levels from the nonstressed controls (Conrad et al., 2007). These findings are significant because they show that chronic restraint stress via glucocorticoids leaves an *imprint* on the hippocampus that extends the window of time during which the hippocampus is vulnerable to damage. Previous studies showed that hippocampal damage caused by neurotoxic/metabolic challenges occurred when glucocorticoids were concurrently elevated. These recent studies demonstrate that the chronically stressed hippocampus is vulnerable to potential injury for a longer period of time than previously thought.

Glucocorticoid Vulnerability Hypothesis and Implications

A history of chronic stress through glucocorticoid elevations is proposed to alter the hippocampus, which extends the window of time during which the hippocampus is susceptible to damage from a neurotoxin/metabolic insult. In these experiments with chronic stress the hippocampus was challenged with the neurotoxin, ibotenic acid, which acts on glutamate receptors to kill neurons by overstimulation (Keilhoff et al., 1990). However, these outcomes may be extrapolated to situations involving metabolic challenges. For example, in the acute glucocorticoid model the presence of high glucocorticoid levels exacerbated hippocampal damage following exposure to a neurotoxin (Sapolsky, 1985a, 1985b) or to metabolic challenges of ischemia, hypoxia, or hypoglycemia (Sapolsky and Pulsinelli, 1985; Tombaugh et al., 1992). A critical difference between the glucocorticoid cascade hypothesis and the current glucocorticoid vulnerability hypothesis is that glucocorticoids need not be elevated at the time of a metabolic challenge. A history of chronic stress is proposed to leave an imprint on the hippocampus, which corresponds to the time when hippocampal dendritic retraction exists, making the hippocampus vulnerable for a longer duration to a potential metabolic challenge than when glucocorticoids would be elevated. Moreover, the dynamic nature of hippocampal dendritic retraction permits opportunities for improvement or recovery when chronic stress has subsided (Conrad et al., 1999b; Sousa et al., 2000; Vyas et al., 2004). Consequently, a hippocampus can be restored to the nonstressed/glucocorticoid condition when a metabolic or neurotoxic incident fails to occur. To summarize, chronic stress and glucocorticoids do not directly damage the hippocampus, but they play a critical role in priming the hippocampus for being susceptible to subsequent insults.

It is important to recognize that once cell death occurs the neurons in the majority of the hippocampus are irreplaceable and hippocampal regulation of the HPA axis becomes less effective, leading to ever-increasing glucocorticoid levels. Subsequent glucocorticoid elevations can become even more common, as the stress response to each single stressful event becomes prolonged due to faulty the negative feedback, causing glucocorticoids to stay elevated longer in an individual with hippocampal damage. Therefore, a damaged hippocampus makes itself even more susceptible to a metabolic challenge than a healthy hippocampus, creating a downward spiral of increased likelihood of potentiated hippocampal damage with each metabolic episode and this risk increases with age.

Other chapters in this volume describe potential connections between the stress responses and depression (see Chapters 23–25), but the link between reversible alterations in the hippocampus with depression and stress will be briefly described here. Individuals suffering from depression show decreased volumes in the hippocampus (Sheline et al., 1996, 1999, 2003; Bremner et al., 2000; Janssen et al., 2004; Neumeister et al., 2005; Saylam et al., 2006; Feldmann et al., 2007; MacMaster et al., 2008). Although neuron death within the hippocampus may underlie some causes of depression (Rajkowska, 2000; Sapolsky, 2000), not all structural changes within the hippocampus can be explained by cell loss. For example, postmortem hippocampal tissue from depressed patients shows alterations in neuropil without neuron loss (Stockmeier et al., 2004). Moreover, imaging studies reveal changes in the hippocampus that reflect dynamic and reversible processes that are unlikely with irreversible cell loss. For example, antidepressant treatment increases the volume of the hippocampus (Sheline, 2003; Sheline et al., 2003; Vermetten et al., 2003; Neumeister et al., 2005), and hippocampal volumes increase in depressed patients who are in remission (Frodl et al., 2008). Indeed, patients on long-term antidepressant treatment may be protected against decreases in hippocampal volume from cumulative depressive episodes (Sheline et al., 2003). Consequently, some structural changes occurring in depression most likely include reversible and/or dynamic processes without necessarily involving neuronal loss.

Whether individuals can successfully age and retain their hippocampal cognitive functions may be related to lifetime exposure to stress and glucocorticoids (McEwen,

1999; Pardon and Rattray, 2008). This concept has been described as *allostatic load*, and refers to the price the body pays for adapting to adverse situations (McEwen, 2000a, 2000b, 2001; Stewart, 2006). Essentially, the body alters itself to compensate for the immediate threat, but with some potentially debilitating long-term ramifications. A recent study suggests that aged animals may be less able to respond to repeated stress than young, in terms of corticosterone responses and anxiety profile (Shoji and Mizoguchi, 2010). Perhaps, hippocampal CA3 dendritic retraction may represent one such allostatic load measure. While hippocampal dendritic retraction may hinder the process of forming spatial memories, the advantage may be to shift strategies to habit-based programs. In other words, when a novel environment is uncertain under chronically stressful situations, then it may be better to default to a habit-based system that worked before (Dias-Ferreira et al., 2009; Sadowski et al., 2009; Schwabe et al., 2009). At another level, hippocampal dendritic retraction may reduce the likelihood for glutamate neurotoxicity, but at the risk for a potentially debilitating neurotoxic/metabolic event. Stress increases hippocampal glutamate levels (Stein-Behrens et al., 1994; Abrahám et al., 1998), making glutamate regulation paramount to safeguard neurons. Since, glutamate exposure is certain, then adjusting to the glutamate onslaught may be less risky than making adjustments for a metabolic event that is less certain. In most cases, the chronic stress duration ends and recovery occurs. However, when chronic stress is overlaid upon the individual's genetic predisposition and other mitigating factors, such as cardiovascular status (Raz et al., 2005), caloric intake and/or nutrition (Baran et al., 2005; Joseph et al., 2009), immune function (Segerstrom and Miller, 2004), aerobic activity (Cotman et al., 2007), and environmental enrichment (Wright and Conrad, 2008), then recovery could be modified. These lifelong experiences may contribute to why the aging population is so diverse in cognitive function (Barnes, 1979; Gage et al., 1984; Gallagher and Pelleymounter, 1988; Ingram, 1988; Moss et al., 1988; Markowska et al., 1989; Issa et al., 1990; Luine et al., 1990; Fischer et al., 1992; Rapp and Amaral, 1992; Geinisman et al., 1995; Matzel et al., 2008). Understanding why some individuals are able to successfully retain their cognitive abilities with age, whereas others are not, will be essential for facilitating healthy aging.

Acknowledgment

The insightful feedback by Ann N. Hoffman is gratefully appreciated. This work was funded by NIMH 64727 and the Arizona Biomedical Research Commission.

References

Abrahám, I., Juhász, G., Kékesi, K. A., & Kovács, K. J. (1998). Corticosterone peak is responsible for stress-induced elevation of glutamate in the hippocampus. *Stress, 2,* 171–181.

Aleisa, A. M., Alzoubi, K. H., Gerges, N. Z., & Alkadhi, K. A. (2006). Nicotine blocks stress-induced impairment of spatial memory and long-term potentiation of the hippocampal CA1 region. *International Journal of Neuropsychopharmacology, 9*(4), 417–426.

Alzoubi, K. H., Abdul-Razzak, K. K., Khabour, O. F., Al-Tuweiq, G. M., Alzubi, M. A., & Alkadhi, K. A. (2009). Adverse effect of combination of chronic psychosocial stress and high fat diet on hippocampus-dependent memory in rats. *Behavioral Brain Research*, *204*(1), 117–123.

Angelucci, L. (2000). The glucocorticoid hormone: From pedestal to dust and back. *European Journal of Pharmacology*, *405*, 139–147.

Balota, D. A., Dolan, P. O., & Duchek, J. M. (2000). Memory changes in healthy young and older adults. In E. Tulving, & F. I. M. Craik (Eds.), *Handbook of memory* (pp. 395–410). Oxford: Oxford University Press.

Baran, S. E., Campbell, A. M., Kleen, J. K., Foltz, C. H., Wright, R. L., Diamond, D. M., & Conrad, C. D. (2005). Synergy between high fat diet and chronic stress retracts apical dendrites in CA3. *NeuroReport*, *16*(1), 39–43.

Bardgett, M. E., Taylor, G. T., Csernansky, J. G., Newcomer, J. W., & Nock, B. (1994). Chronic corticosterone treatment impairs spontaneous alternation behavior in rats. *Behavioral and Neural Biology*, *61*, 186–190.

Barnes, C. A. (1979). Memory deficits associated with senescence: a neurophysiological and behavioral study in the rat. *Journal of Comparative and Physiological Psychology*, *93*(1), 74–104.

Bhatnagar, S., Huber, R., Nowak, N., & Trotter, P. (2002). Lesions of the posterior paraventricular thalamus block habituation of hypothalamic-pituitary-adrenal responses to repeated restraint. *Journal of Neuroendocrinology*, *14*(5), 403–410.

Bishop, N. A., Lu, T., & Yankner, B. A. (2010). Neural mechanisms of ageing and cognitive decline. *Nature*, *464*(7288), 529–535.

Bodnoff, S. R., Humphreys, A. G., Lehman, J. C., Diamond, D. M., Rose, G. M., & Meaney, M. J. (1995). Enduring effects of chronic corticosterone treatment on spatial learning, synaptic plasticity, and hippocampal neuropathology in young and mid-aged rats. *Journal of Neuroscience*, *15*(1), 61–69.

Bourdeau, I., Bard, C., Forget, H., Boulanger, Y., Cohen, H., & Lacroix, A. (2005). Cognitive function and cerebral assessment in patients who have Cushing's syndrome. *Endocrinology and Metabolism Clinics of North America*, *34*(2), 357–369.

Bremner, J. D., Narayan, M., Anderson, E. R., Staib, L. H., Miller, H. L., & Charney, D. S. (2000). Hippocampal volume reduction in major depression. *American Journal of Psychiatry*, *157*(1), 115–117.

Brooke, S. M., de Haas-Johnson, A. M., Kaplan, J. R., & Sapolsky, R. M. (1994). Characterization of mineralocorticoid and glucocorticoid receptors in primate brain. *Brain Research*, *637*(1–2), 303–307.

Burke, S. N., & Barnes, C. A. (2006). Neural plasticity in the ageing brain. *Nature Reviews Neuroscience*, *7*(1), 30–40.

Cerqueira, J. J., Mailliet, F., Almeida, O. F., Jay, T. M., & Sousa, N. (2007). The prefrontal cortex as a key target of the maladaptive response to stress. *Journal of Neuroscience*, *27*(11), 2781–2787.

Clark, A. S., Mitre, M. C., & Brinck-Johnsen, T. (1995). Anabolic-androgenic steroid and adrenal steroid effects on hippocampal plasticity. *Brain Research*, *679*, 64–71.

Coburn-Litvak, P. S., Pothakos, K., Tata, D. A., McCloskey, D. P., & Anderson, B. J. (2003). Chronic administration of corticosterone impairs spatial reference memory before spatial working memory in rats. *Neurobiology of Learning and Memory*, *80*, 11–23.

Coburn-Litvak, P. S., Tata, D. A., Gorby, H. E., McCloskey, D. P., Richardson, G., & Anderson, B. J. (2004). Chronic corticosterone affects brain weight, and mitochondrial, but not glial volume fraction in hippocampal area CA3. *Neuroscience, 124,* 429–438.

Conrad, C. D. (2005). The relationship between acute glucocorticoid levels and hippocampal function depends upon task aversiveness and memory processing stage. *Nonlinearity in Biology, Toxicology and Medicine, 3*(1), 57–78.

Conrad, C. D. (2006). What is the functional significance of chronic stress-induced CA3 dendritic retraction within the hippocampus? *Behavioral and Cognitive Neuroscience Reviews, 5*(1), 41–60.

Conrad, C. D. (2008). Chronic stress-induced hippocampal vulnerability: The glucocorticoid vulnerability hypothesis. *Reviews in the Neurosciences, 19*(6), 395–412.

Conrad, C. D. (2010). A critical review of chronic stress effects on spatial learning and memory. *Progress in Neuro-Psychopharmacology & Biological Psychiatry, 34,* 742–755.

Conrad, C. D., & Roy, E. J. (1993). Selective loss of hippocampal granule cells following adrenalectomy: Implications for spatial memory. *Journal of Neuroscience, 13*(6), 2582–2590.

Conrad, C. D., & Bimonte-Nelson, H. (2010). Impact of the hypothalamic-pituitary/gonadal axes on trajectory of age-related cognitive decline. In L. Martini (Ed.), *Progress in brain research* (vol. 182, pp. 31–76). New York: Elsevier.

Conrad, C. D., Galea, L. A. M., Kuroda, Y., & McEwen, B. S. (1996). Chronic stress impairs rat spatial memory on the Y-Maze, and this effect is blocked by tianeptine pretreatment. *Behavioral Neuroscience, 110*(6), 1321–1334.

Conrad, C. D., Lupien, S. J., Thanasoulis, L. C., & McEwen, B. S. (1997). The effects of Type I and Type II corticosteroid receptor agonists on exploratory behavior and spatial memory in the Y-Maze. *Brain Research, 759,* 76–83.

Conrad, C. D., Lupien, S. J., & McEwen, B. S. (1999a). Support for a bimodal role for Type II adrenal steroid receptors in spatial memory. *Neurobiology of Learning and Memory, 72*(1), 39–46.

Conrad, C. D., Magariños, A. M., LeDoux, J. E., & McEwen, B. S. (1999b). Repeated restraint stress facilitates fear conditioning independently of causing hippocampal CA3 dendritic atrophy. *Behavioral Neuroscience, 113*(5), 902–913.

Conrad, C. D., Jackson, J. L., & Wise, L. (2004). Chronic stress enhances ibotenic acid-induced damage selectively within the hippocampal CA3 region of male, but not female rats. *Neuroscience, 125*(3), 759–767.

Conrad, C. D., McLaughlin, K. J., Harman, J. S., Foltz, C., Wieczorek, L., Lightner, E., & Wright, R. L. (2007). Chronic glucocorticoids increase hippocampal vulnerability to neurotoxicity under conditions that produce CA3 dendritic retraction but fail to impair spatial recognition memory. *Journal of Neuroscience, 27*(31), 8278–8285.

Cotman, C. W., Berchtold, N. C., & Christie, L. A. (2007). Exercise builds brain health: key roles of growth factor cascades and inflammation. *Trends in the Neurosciences, 30*(9), 464–472.

Dachir, S., Kadar, T., Robinzon, B., & Levy, A. (1993). Cognitive deficits induced in young rats by long-term corticosterone administration. *Behavioral and Neural Biology, 60,* 103–109.

Dachir, S., Kadar, T., Robinzon, B., & Levy, A. (1997). Nimodipine's protection against corticosterone-induced morphological changes in the hippocampus of young rats. *Brain Research, 748*(1–2), 175–183.

Dallman, M. F. (2000). Glucocorticoid negative feedback. In G. Fink (Ed.), *Encyclopedia of stress* (vol. 2, pp. 224–228). San Diego, CA: Academic Press.

Dallman, M. F. (2007). Modulation of stress responses: How we cope with excess glucocorticoids. *Experimental Neurology, 206*(2), 179–182.

Dallman, M. F., Bhatnagar, S., & Viau, V. (2000). Hypothalamo-pituitary-adrenal axis. In G. Fink (Ed.), *Encyclopedia of stress* (vol. 2, pp. 468–477). New York: Academic Press.

de Kloet, E. R., Vreugdenhil, E., Oitzl, M. S., & Joëls, M. (1998). Brain corticosteroid receptor balance in health and disease. *Endocrine Reviews, 19*, 269–301.

Dias-Ferreira, E., Sousa, J. C., Melo, I., Morgado, P., Mesquita, A. R., Cerqueira, J. J., Costa, R. M., & Sousa, N. (2009). Chronic stress causes frontostriatal reorganization and affects decision-making. *Science, 325*(5940), 621–625.

Eichenbaum, H. (2000). A cortical-hippocampal system for declarative memory. *Nature Reviews Neuroscience, 1*(1), 41–50.

Ekstrom, A. D., Kahana, M. J., Caplan, J. B., Fields, T. A., Isham, E. A., Newman, E. L., & Fried, I. (2003). Cellular networks underlying human spatial navigation. *Nature, 425*(6954), 184–188.

Endo, Y., Nishimura, J., & Kimura, F. (1996). Impairment of maze learning in rats following long-term glucocorticoid treatments. *Neuroscience Letters, 203*, 199–202.

Erickson, C. A., & Barnes, C. A. (2003). The neurobiology of memory changes in normal aging. *Experimental Gerontology, 38*(1–2), 61–69.

Feldmann, Jr, R. E., Sawa, A., & Seidler, G. H. (2007). Causality of stem cell based neurogenesis and depression—to be or not to be, is that the question? *Journal of Psychiatric Research, 41*(9), 713–723.

Fischer, W., Chen, K. S., Gage, F. H., & Björklund, A. (1992). Progressive decline in spatial learning and integrity of forebrain cholinergic neurons in rats during aging. *Neurobiology of Aging, 13*(1), 9–23.

Franceschi, M., Airaghi, L., Gramigna, C., Truci, G., Manfredi, M. G., Canal, N., & Catania, A. (1991). ACTH and cortisol secretion in patients with Alzheimer's disease. *Journal of Neurology, Neurosurgery, and Psychiatry, 54*(9), 836–837.

Frodl, T. S., Koutsouleris, N., Bottlender, R., Born, C., Jager, M., Scupin, I., Reiser, M., Moller, H. J., & Meisenzahl, E. M. (2008). Depression-related variation in brain morphology over 3 years: effects of stress? *Archives of General Psychiatry, 65*(10), 1156–1165.

Fuchs, E., Uno, H., & Flügge, G. (1995). Chronic psychosocial stress induces morphological alterations in hippocampal pyramidal neurons of the tree shrew. *Brain Research, 673*(2), 275–282.

Fuchs, E., Flügge, G., Ohl, F., Lucassen, P., Vollmann-Honsdorf, G. K., & Michaelis, T. (2001). Psychosocial stress, glucocorticoids, and structural alterations in the tree shrew hippocampus. *Physiology & Behavior, 73*, 285–291.

Gage, F. H., Kelly, P. A. T., & Bjorklund, A. (1984). Regional changes in brain glucose metabolism reflect cognitive impairments in aged rats. *Journal of Neuroscience, 4*, 2856–2865.

Gallagher, M., & Pelleymounter, M. A. (1988). An age-related spatial learning deficit: Choline uptake distinquishes "Impaired" and "Unimpaired" rats. *Neurobiology of Aging, 9*, 363–369.

Geinisman, Y., Detoledo-Morrell, L., Morrell, F., & Heller, R. E. (1995). Hippocampal markers of age-related memory dysfunction: behavioral, electrophysiological and morphological perspectives. *Progress in Neurobiology, 45*(3), 223–252.

Gerges, N. Z., Alzoubi, K. H., Park, C. R., Diamond, D. M., & Alkadhi, K. A. (2004). Adverse effect of the combination of hypothyroidism and chronic psychosocial stress on hippocampus-dependent memory in rats. *Behavioural Brain Research, 155*(1), 77–84.

Herman, J. P., Schäfer, M. K.-H., Young, E. A., Thompson, R., Douglass, J., Akil, H., & Watson, S. J. (1989). Evidence for hippocampal regulation of neuroendocrine neurons of the hypothalamo-pituitary-adrenocortial axis. *Journal of Neuroscience, 9*(9), 3072–3082.

Herman, J. P., Ostrander, M. M., Mueller, N. K., & Figueiredo, H. (2005). Limbic system mechanisms of stress regulation: hypothalamo-pituitary-adrenocortical axis. *Progress in Neuropsychopharmacology and Biological Psychiatry, 29*(8), 1201–1213.

Hook, J. N., Giordani, B., Schteingart, D. E., Guire, K., Giles, J., Ryan, K., Gebarski, S. S., Lagenecker, S. A., & Starkman, M. N. (2007). Patterns of cognitive change over time and relationship to age following successful treatment of Cushing's disease. *Journal of International Neuropsychologcial Society, 13*, 21–29.

Ingram, D. K. (1988). Complex maze learning in rodents as a model of age-related memory impairment. *Neurobiology of Aging, 9*(5–6), 475–485.

Issa, A. M., Rowe, W., Gauthier, S., & Meaney, M. J. (1990). Hypothalamic-pituitary-adrenal activity in aged, cognitively impaired and cognitively unimpaired rats. *Journal of Neuroscience, 10*(10), 3247–3254.

Janssen, J., Hulshoff Pol, H. E., Lampe, I. K., Schnack, H. G., de Leeuw, F. E., Kahn, R. S., & Heeren, T. J. (2004). Hippocampal changes and white matter lesions in early-onset depression. *Biological Psychiatry, 56*(11), 825–831.

Johnson, E. O., Brady, L., Gold, P. W., & Chrousos, G. P. (1996). Distribution of hippocampal mineralocorticoid and glucocorticoid receptor mRNA in a glucocorticoid resistant nonhuman primate. *Steroids, 61*(2), 69–73.

Joseph, J., Cole, G., Head, E., & Ingram, D. (2009). Nutrition, brain aging, and neurodegeneration. *Journal of Neuroscience, 29*(41), 12795–12801.

Keilhoff, G., Wolf, G., Stastny, F., & Schmidt, W. (1990). Quinolinate neurotoxicity and glutamatergic structures. *Neuroscience, 34*, 235–242.

Kitraki, E., Kremmyda, O., Youlatos, D., Alexis, M., & Kittas, C. (2004). Spatial performance and corticosteroid receptor status in the 21-day restraint stress paradigm. *Annals of the New York Academy of Sciences, 1018*, 323–327.

Krugers, H. J., Douma, B. R. K., Andringa, G., Bohus, B., Korf, J., & Luiten, P. G. M. (1997). Exposure to chronic psychosocial stress and corticosterone in the rat: Effects on spatial discrimination learning and hippocampal protein kinase Cg immunoreactivity. *Hippocampus, 7*, 427–436.

Kudielka, B. M., Schmidt-Reinwald, A. K., Hellhammer, D. H., Schürmeyer, T., & Kirschbaum, C. (2000). Psychosocial stress and HPA functioning: No evidence for a reduced resilience in healthy elderly men. *Stress, 3*, 229–240.

Lambert, K. G., Buckelew, S. K., Staffiso-Sandoz, G., Gaffga, S., Carpenter, W., Fisher, J., & Kinsely, C. H. (1998). Activity-stress induces atrophy of apical dendrites of hippocampal pyramidal neurons in male rats. *Physiology & Behavior, 65*, 43–49.

Landfield, P. W., Waymire, J. C., & Lynch, G. (1978). Hippocampal aging and adrenocorticoids: Quantitative correlations. *Science, 202*(4372), 1098–1102.

Landfield, P. W., Baskin, R. K., & Pitler, T. A. (1981). Brain aging correlates: Retardation by hormonal-pharmacological treatments. *Science, 214*(4520), 581–584.

Lee, T., Jarome, T., Li, S. J., Kim, J. J., & Helmstetter, F. J. (2009). Chronic stress selectively reduces hippocampal volume in rats: a longitudinal magnetic resonance imaging study. *NeuroReport, 20*(17), 1554–1558.

Leverenz, J. B., Wilkinson, C. W., Wamble, M., Corbin, S., Grabber, J. E., Raskind, M. A., & Peskind, E. R. (1999). Effect of chronic high-dose exogenous cortisol on hippocampal neuronal number in aged nonhuman primates. *Journal of Neuroscience, 19*(6), 2356–2361.

Luine, V., Bowling, D., & Hearns, M. (1990). Spatial memory deficits in aged rats: contributions of monoaminergic systems. *Brain Research, 537*(1–2), 271–278.

Luine, V., Villegas, M., Martinez, C., & McEwen, B. S. (1994). Repeated stress causes reversible impairments of spatial memory performance. *Brain Research, 639*, 167–170.

Luine, V., Martinez, C., Villegas, M., Magariños, A. M., & McEwen, B. S. (1996). Restraint stress reversibly enhances spatial memory performance. *Physiology & Behavior, 59*(1), 27–32.

Luine, V. N., Spencer, R. L., & McEwen, B. S. (1993). Effects of chronic corticosterone ingestion on spatial memory performance and hippocampal serotonergic function. *Brain Research, 616*, 65–70.

Luo, L., & Tan, R. X. (2001). Fluoxetine inhibits dendrite atrophy of hippocampal neurons by decreasing nitric oxide synthase expression in rat depression model. *Acta Pharmacologica Sinica, 22*(10), 865–870.

MacMaster, F. P., Mirza, Y., Szeszko, P. R., Kmiecik, L. E., Easter, P. C., Taormina, S. P., Lynch, M., Rose, M., Moore, G. J., & Rosenberg, D. R. (2008). Amygdala and hippocampal volumes in familial early onset major depressive disorder. *Biological Psychiatry, 63*(4), 385–390.

Magariños, A. M., & McEwen, B. S. (1995a). Stress-induced atrophy of apical dendrites of hippocampal CA3c neurons: Involvement of glucocorticoid secretion and excitatory amino acid receptors. *Neuroscience, 69*(1), 89–98.

Magariños, A. M., & McEwen, B. S. (1995b). Stress-induced atrophy of apical dendrites of hippocampal CA3c neurons: Comparison of stressors. *Neuroscience, 69*(1), 83–88.

Manikandan, S., Padma, M. K., Srikumar, R., Jeya Parthasarathy, N., Muthuvel, A., & Sheela Devi, R. (2006). Effects of chronic noise stress on spatial memory of rats in relation to neuronal dendritic alteration and free radical-imbalance in hippocampus and medial prefrontal cortex. *Neuroscience Letters, 399*(1–2), 17–22.

Markowska, A. L., Stone, W. S., Ingram, D. K., Reynolds, J., Gold, P. E., Conti, L. H., Pontecorvo, M. J., Wenk, G. L., & Olton, D. S. (1989). Individual differences in aging: behavioral and neurobiological correlates. *Neurobiology of Aging, 10*(1), 31–43.

Mateo, J. M. (2008). Inverted-U shape relationship between cortisol and learning in ground squirrels. *Neurobiology of Learning and Memory, 89*(4), 582–590.

Matzel, L. D., Grossman, H., Light, K., Townsend, D., & Kolata, S. (2008). Age-related declines in general cognitive abilities of Balb/C mice are associated with disparities in working memory, body weight, and general activity. *Learning & Memory, 15*(10), 733–746.

McEwen, B. S. (1999). Stress and the aging hippocampus. *Frontiers in Neuroendocrinology, 20*, 49–70.

McEwen, B. S. (2000a). Allostasis and allostatic load: Implications for neuropsychopharmacology. *Neuropsychopharmacology, 22*(2), 108–124.

McEwen, B. S. (2000b). Allostasis, allostatic load, and the aging nervous system: role of excitatory amino acids and excitotoxicity. *Neurochemical Research, 25*(9–10), 1219–1231.

McEwen, B. S. (2001). Plasticity of the hippocampus: Adaptation to chronic stress and allostatic load. *Annals New York Academy of Sciences, 933*, 265–277.

McLaughlin, K. J., Gomez, J. L., Baran, S. E., & Conrad, C. D. (2007). The effects of chronic stress on hippocampal morphology and function: an evaluation of chronic restraint paradigms. *Brain Research, 1161*, 56–64.

McLaughlin, K. J., Baran, S. E., & Conrad, C. D. (2009). Chronic stress- and sex-specific neuromorphological and functional changes in limbic structures. *Molecular Neurobiology, 40*(2), 166–182.

McLaughlin, K. J., Wilson, J. O., Harman, J., Wright, R. L., Wieczorek, L., Gomez, J., Korol, D. L., & Conrad, C. D. (2010). Chronic 17B-estradiol or cholesterol prevents stress-induced hippocampal CA3 dendritic retraction in ovariectomized femal rats: Possible correspondence between CA1 spine properties and spatial acquisition. *Hippocampus*, 768–786.

McLay, R. N., Freeman, S. M., & Zadina, J. E. (1998). Chronic corticosterone impairs memory performance in the Barnes maze. *Physiology & Behavior, 63*, 933–937.

Mizoguchi, K., Kunishita, T., Chui, D.-H., & Tabira, T. (1992). Stress induces neuronal death in the hippocampus of castrated rats. *Neuroscience Letters, 138*, 157–160.

Moosavi, M., Naghdi, N., Maghsoudi, N., & Zahedi Asl, S. (2007). Insulin protects against stress-induced impairments in water maze performance. *Behavioral Brain Research, 176*(2), 230–236.

Morris, R. G. M., Garrud, P., Rawlins, J. N. P., & O'Keefe, J. (1982). Place navigation impaired in rats with hippocampal lesions. *Nature, 297*(5868), 681–683.

Moss, M. B., Rosene, D. L., & Peters, A. (1988). Effects of aging on visual recognition memory in the rhesus monkey. *Neurobiology of Aging, 9*(5–6), 495–502.

Müller, M. B., Lucassen, P. J., Yassouridis, A., Hoogendijk, W. J. G., Holsboer, F., & Swaab, D. F. (2001). Neither major depression nor glucocorticoid treatment affects the cellular integrity of the human hippocampus. *European Journal of Neuroscience, 14*, 1603–1612.

Neumeister, A., Wood, S., Bonne, O., Nugent, A. C., Luckenbaugh, D. A., Young, T., Bain, E. E., Charney, D. S., & Drevets, W. C. (2005). Reduced hippocampal volume in unmedicated, remitted patients with major depression versus control subjects. *Biological Psychiatry, 57*(8), 935–937.

Nishimura, J.-I., Endo, Y., Endo, Y., & Kimura, F. (1999). A long-term stress exposure impairs maze learning performance in rats. *Neuroscience Letters, 273*, 125–128.

Ohl, F., & Fuchs, E. (1999). Differential effects of chronic stress on memory processes in the tree shrew. *Cognitive Brain Research, 7*, 379–387.

Ohl, F., Michaelis, T., Vollmann-Honsdorf, G. K., Kirschbaum, C., & Fuchs, E. (2000). Effect of chronic psychosocial stress and long-term cortisol treatment on hippocampus-mediated memory and hippocampal volume: a pilot-study in tree shrews. *Psychoneuroendocrinology, 25*(4), 357–363.

Oitzl, M. S., & de Kloet, E. R. (1992). Selective corticosteroid antagonists modulate specific aspects of spatial orientation learning. *Behavioral Neuroscience, 106*(1), 62–71.

O'Keefe, J., & Dostrovsky, J. (1971). The hippocampus as a spatial map. Preliminary evidence from unit activity in the freely-moving rat. *Brain Research, 34*(1), 171–175.

O'Keefe, J., & Nadel, L. (1978). *The hippocampus as a cognitive map*. Oxford: Clarendon Press.

Orchinik, M., Carroll, S. S., Li, Y.-H., McEwen, B. S., & Weiland, N. G. (2001). Heterogeneity of hippocampal GABA$_A$ receptors: Regulation by corticosterone. *Journal of Neuroscience, 21*, 330–339.

Orsetti, M., Colella, L., Dellarole, A., Canonico, P. L., & Ghi, P. (2007). Modification of spatial recognition memory and object discrimination after chronic administration of haloperidol, amitriptyline, sodium valproate or olanzapine in normal and anhedonic rats. *International Journal of Neuropsychopharmacology*, *10*(3), 345–357.

Owens, J. W. A. (1953). Age and mental abilities: A longitudinal study. *Genetic Psychology Monographs*, *48*, 3–54.

Pardon, M. C., & Rattray, I. (2008). What do we know about the long-term consequences of stress on ageing and the progression of age-related neurodegenerative disorders? *Neuroscience and Biobehavioral Reviews*, *32*(6), 1103–1120.

Park, C. R., Campbell, A. M., & Diamond, D. M. (2001). Chronic psychosocial stress impairs learning and memory and increases sensitivity to yohimbine in rats. *Biological Psychiatry*, *50*, 994–1004.

Paul, C.-M., Magda, G., & Abel, S. (2009). Spatial memory: Theoretical basis and comparative review on experimental methods in rodents. *Behavioral Brain Research*, *203*(2), 151–164.

Radecki, D. T., Brown, L. M., Martinez, J., & Teyler, T. J. (2005). BDNF protects against stress-induced impairments in spatial learning and memory and LTP. *Hippocampus*, *15*(2), 246–253.

Rajkowska, G. (2000). Postmortem studies in mood disorders indicate altered numbers of neurons and glial cells. *Biological Psychiatry*, *48*(8), 766–777.

Rapp, P. R., & Amaral, D. G. (1992). Individual differences in the cognitive and neurobiological consequences of normal aging. *Trends in Neuroscience*, *15*(9), 340–345.

Raz, N., Lindenberger, U., Rodrigue, K. M., Kennedy, K. M., Head, D., Williamson, A., Dahle, C., Gerstorf, D., & Acker, J. D. (2005). Regional brain changes in aging healthy adults: general trends, individual differences and modifiers. *Cerebral Cortex*, *15*(11), 1676–80169.

Reul, J. M. H. M., & de Kloet, E. R. (1985). Two receptor systems for corticosterone in rat brain: Microdistribution and differential occupation. *Endocrinology*, *117*(6), 2505–2511.

Roozendaal, B., Portillo-Marquez, G., & McGaugh, J. L. (1996). Basolateral amygdala lesions block glucocorticoid-induced modulation of memory for spatial learning. *Behavioral Neuroscience*, *110*(5), 1074–1083.

Roozendaal, B., Phillips, R. G., Power, A. E., Brooke, S. M., Sapolsky, R. M., & McGaugh, J. L. (2001). Memory retrieval impairment induced by hippocampal CA3 lesions is blocked by adrenocortical suppression. *Nature Neuroscience*, *4*(12), 1169–1171.

Sadowski, R. N., Jackson, G. R., Wieczorek, L., & Gold, P. E. (2009). Effects of stress, corticosterone, and epinephrine administration on learning in place and response tasks. *Behavioral Brain Research*, *205*, 19–25.

Sánchez, M. M., Young, L. J., Plotsky, P. M., & Insel, T. R. (2000). Distribution of corticosteroid receptors in the rhesus brain: Relative absence of glucocorticoid receptors in the hippocampal formation. *Journal of Neuroscience*, *20*(12), 4657–4668.

Sapolsky, R. M. (1985a). A mechanism for glucocorticoid toxicity in the hippocampus: Increased neuronal vulnerability to metabolic insults. *Journal of Neuroscience*, *5*(5), 1228–1232.

Sapolsky, R. M. (1985b). Glucocorticoid toxicity in the hippocampus: Temporal aspects of neuronal vulnerability. *Brain Research*, *359*, 300–305.

Sapolsky, R. M. (1986). Glucocorticoid toxicity in the hippocampus: Reversal by supplementation with brain fuels. *Journal of Neuroscience, 6*(8), 2240–2244.

Sapolsky, R. M. (1992). *Stress, the aging brain, and the mechanisms of neuron death.* Cambridge, MA: MIT Press.

Sapolsky, R. M. (2000). Glucocorticoids and hippocampal atrophy in neuropsychiatric disorders. *Archives of General Psychiatry, 57,* 925–935.

Sapolsky, R. M., & Pulsinelli, W. A. (1985). Glucocorticoids potentiate ischemic injury to neurons: Therapeutic implications. *Science, 229*(4720), 1397–1399.

Sapolsky, R. M., Krey, L. C., & McEwen, B. S. (1983). Corticosterone receptors decline in a site-specific manner in the aged-rat brain. *Brain Research, 289,* 235–240.

Sapolsky, R. M., Krey, L. C., & McEwen, B. S. (1984a). Stress down-regulates corticosterone receptors in a site-specific manner in the brain. *Endocrinology, 114,* 287–292.

Sapolsky, R. M., Krey, L. C., & McEwen, B. S. (1984b). Glucocorticoid-sensitive hippocampal neurons are involved in terminating the adrenocortical stress response. *Proceedings of the National Academy of Sciences USA, 81,* 6174–6177.

Sapolsky, R. M., Krey, L. C., & McEwen, B. S. (1985). Prolonged glucocorticoid exposure reduces hippocampal neuron number: Implications for aging. *Journal of Neuroscience, 5*(5), 1222–1227.

Sapolsky, R. M., Krey, L. C., & McEwen, B. S. (1986). The neuroendocrinology of stress and aging: The glucocorticoid cascade hypothesis. *Endocrine Reviews, 7*(8), 284–301.

Sarrieau, A., Dussaillant, M., Sapolsky, R. M., Aitken, D. H., Olivier, A., Lal, S., Rostene, W. H., Quirion, R., & Meaney, M. J. (1988). Glucocorticoid binding sites in human temporal cortex. *Brain Research, 442*(1), 157–160.

Saylam, C., Ucerler, H., Kitis, O., Ozand, E., & Gonul, A. S. (2006). Reduced hippocampal volume in drug-free depressed patients. *Surgical and Radiologic Anatomy, 28*(1), 82–87.

Schwabe, L., Oitzl, M. S., Richter, S., & Schachinger, H. (2009). Modulation of spatial and stimulus-response learning strategies by exogenous cortisol in healthy young women. *Psychoneuroendocrinology, 34*(3), 358–366.

Segerstrom, S. C., & Miller, G. E. (2004). Psychological stress and the human immune system: a meta-analytic study of 30 years of inquiry. *Psychological Bulletin, 130*(4), 601–630.

Sheline, Y. I. (2003). Neuroimaging studies of mood disorder effects on the brain. *Biological Psychiatry, 54*(3), 338–352.

Sheline, Y. I., Wang, P. W., Gado, M. H., Csernansky, J. C., & Vannier, M. W. (1996). Hippocampal atrophy in recurrent major depression. *Proceedings of the National Academy of Sciences USA, 93,* 3908–3913.

Sheline, Y. I., Sanghavi, M., Mintun, M. A., & Gado, M. H. (1999). Depression duration but not age predicts hippocampal volume loss in medically healthy women with recurrent major depression. *Journal of Neuroscience, 19*(12), 5034–5043.

Sheline, Y. I., Gado, M. H., & Kraemer, H. C. (2003). Untreated depression and hippocampal volume loss. *American Journal of Psychiatry, 160*(8), 1516–1518.

Shoji, H., & Mizoguchi, K. (2010). Acute and repeated stress differentially regulates behavioral, endocrine, neural parameters relevant to emotional and stress response in young and aged rats. *Behavioral Brain Research, 211*(2), 169–177.

Smith-Swintosky, V. L., Pettigrew, L. C., Sapolsky, R. M., Phares, C., Craddock, S. D., Brooke, S. M., & Mattson, M. P. (1996). Metyrapone, an inhibitor of glucocorticoid production, reduces brain injury induced by focal and global ischemia and seizures. *Journal of Cerebral Blood Flow and Metabolism, 16,* 585–598.

Song, L., Che, W., Min-Wei, W., Murakami, Y., & Matsumoto, K. (2006). Impairment of the spatial learning and memory induced by learned helplessness and chronic mild stress. *Pharmacology Biochemistry and Behavior, 83*(2), 186–193.

Sousa, N., Madeira, M. D., & Paula-Barbosa, M. M. (1998). Effects of corticosterone treatment and rehabilitation on the hippocampal formation of neonatal and adult rats. An unbiased stereological study. *Brain Research, 794,* 199–210.

Sousa, N., Madeira, M. D., & Paula-Barbosa, M. M. (1999). Corticosterone replacement restores normal morphological features to the hippocampal dendrites, axons and synapses of adrenalectomized rats. *Journal of Neurocytology, 28*(7), 541–558.

Sousa, N., Lukoyanov, N. V., Madeira, M. D., Almeida, O. F. X., & Paula-Barbosa, M. M. (2000). Reorganization of the morphology of hippocampal neurites and synapses after stress-induced damage correlates with behavioral improvement. *Neuroscience, 97,* 253–266.

Srivareerat, M., Tran, T. T., Alzoubi, K. H., & Alkadhi, K. A. (2009). Chronic psychosocial stress exacerbates impairment of cognition and long-term potentiation in beta-amyloid rat model of Alzheimer's disease. *Biological Psychiatry, 65*(11), 918–926.

Starkman, M. N., Gebarski, S. S., Berent, S., & Schteingart, D. E. (1992). Hippocampal formation volume, memory dysfunction, and cortisol levels in patients with Cushing's syndrome. *Biological Psychiatry, 32,* 756–765.

Starkman, M. N., Giordani, B., Gebarski, S. S., Berent, S., Schork, M. A., & Schteingart, D. E. (1999). Decrease in cortisol reverses human hippocampal atrophy following treatment of Cushing's disease. *Biological Psychiatry, 46,* 1595–1602.

Stein, B. A., & Sapolsky, R. M. (1988). Chemical adrenalectomy reduces hippocampal damage induced by kainic acid. *Brain Research, 473,* 175–180.

Stein-Behrens, B. A., Lin, W. J., & Sapolsky, R. M. (1994). Physiological elevations of glucocorticoids potentiate glutamate accumulation in the hippocampus. *Journal of Neurochemistry, 63,* 596–602.

Sterio, D. C. (1983). The unbiased estimation of number and sizes of arbitrary particles using the disector. *Journal of Microscopy, 134*(2), 127–136.

Stewart, J. A. (2006). The detrimental effects of allostasis: allostatic load as a measure of cumulative stress. *Journal of Physiological Anthropology, 25*(1), 133–145.

Stockmeier, C. A., Mahajan, G. J., Konick, L. C., Overholser, J. C., Jurjus, G. J., Meltzer, H. Y., Uylings, H. B., Friedman, L., & Rajkowska, G. (2004). Cellular changes in the postmortem hippocampus in major depression. *Biological Psychiatry, 56*(9), 640–650.

Sullivan, E. V., Marsh, L., & Pfefferbaum, A. (2005). Preservation of hippocampal volume throughout adulthood in healthy men and women. *Neurobiology of Aging, 26*(7), 1093–1098.

Sunanda, Shankaranarayana Rao, B. S., & Raju, T. R. (2000). Chronic restraint stress impairs acquisition and retention of spatial memory task in rats. *Current Science, 79,* 1581–1584.

Swanwick, G. R., Kirby, M., Bruce, I., Buggy, F., Coen, R. F., Coakley, D., & Lawlor, B. A. (1998). Hypothalamic-pituitary-adrenal axis dysfunction in Alzheimer's disease: lack of association between longitudinal and cross-sectional findings. *American Journal of Psychiatry, 155*(2), 286–289.

Tata, D. A., & Anderson, B. J. (2010). The effects of chronic glucocorticoid exposure on dendritic length, synapse numbers and glial volume in animal models: Implications for hippocampal volume reductions in depression. *Physiology & Behavior, 99*(2), 186–193.

Tata, D. A., Marciano, V. A., & Anderson, B. J. (2006). Synapse loss from chronically elevated glucocorticoids: relationship to neuropil volume and cell number in hippocampal area CA3. *Journal of Comparative Neurology, 498*(3), 363–374.

Terry, R. D. (2006). Alzheimer's disease and the aging brain. *Journal of Geriatric Psychiatry and Neurology, 19*(3), 125–128.

Tolman, E. C. (1948). Cognitive maps in rats and men. *Psychological Review, 55*(4), 189–208.

Tombaugh, G. C., Yang, S. H., Swanson, R. A., & Sapolsky, R. M. (1992). Glucocorticoids exacerbate hypoxic and hypoglycemic hippocampal injury in vitro: Biochemical correlates and a role for astrocytes. *Journal of Neurochemistry, 59*, 137–146.

Touyarot, K., Venero, C., & Sandi, C. (2004). Spatial learning impairment induced by chronic stress is related to individual differences in novelty reactivity: Search for neurobiological correlates. *Psychoneuroendocrinology, 29*(2), 290–305.

Tulving, E., & Craik, F. I. (2000). *The Oxford handbook of memory.* New York: Oxford University Press.

Uno, H., Tarara, R., Else, J. G., Suleman, M. A., & Sapolsky, R. M. (1989). Hippocampal damage associated with prolonged and fatal stress in primates. *Journal of Neuroscience, 9*(5), 1705–1711.

Venero, C., Tilling, T., Hermans-Borgmeyer, I., Schmidt, R., Schachner, M., & Sandi, C. (2002). Chronic stress induces opposite changes in the mRNA expression of the cell adhesion molecules NCAM and L1. *Neuroscience, 115*(4), 1211–1219.

Vermetten, E., Vythilingam, M., Southwick, S. M., Charney, D. S., & Bremner, J. D. (2003). Long-term treatment with paroxetine increases verbal declarative memory and hippocampal volume in posttraumatic stress disorder. *Biological Psychiatry, 54*(7), 693–702.

Vollmann-Honsdorf, G. K., Flugge, G., & Fuchs, E. (1997). Chronic psychosocial stress does not affect the number of pyramidal neurons in tree shrew hippocampus. *Neuroscience Letters, 233*(2–3), 121–124.

Vyas, A., Pillai, A. G., & Chattarji, S. (2004). Recovery after chronic stress fails to reverse amygdaloid neuronal hypertrophy and enhanced anxiety-like behavior. *Neuroscience, 128*(4), 667–673.

Watanabe, Y., Gould, E., Cameron, H. A., Daniels, D. C., & McEwen, B. S. (1992a). Phenytoin prevents stress- and corticosterone-induced atrophy of CA3 pyramidal neurons. *Hippocampus, 2*(4), 431–436.

Watanabe, Y., Gould, E., Daniels, D. C., Cameron, H., & McEwen, B. S. (1992b). Tianeptine attenuates stress-induced morphological changes in the hippocampus. *European Journal of Pharmacology, 222*, 157–162.

West, M. J. (1993). New stereological methods for counting neurons. *Neurobiology of Aging, 14*, 275–285.

West, M. J., Slomianka, L., & Gundersen, H. J. G. (1991). Unbiased stereological estimation of the total number of neurons in the subdivisions of the rat hippocampus using the optical fractionator. *Anatomical Record, 231*, 482–497.

West, M. J., Coleman, P. D., Flood, D. G., & Troncoso, J. C. (1994). Differences in the pattern of hippocampal neuronal loss in normal ageing and Alzheimer's disease. *The Lancet, 344*(8925), 769–772.

Wilson, M., Greer, M., & Roberts, L. (1980). Hippocampal inhibition of pituitary-adrenocortical function in female rats. *Brain Research, 197*, 433–441.

Winocur, G., & Gagnon, S. (1998). Glucose treatment attenuates spatial learning and memory deficits of aged rats on tests of hippocampal function. *Neurobiology of Aging, 19*(3), 233–241.

Woodson, J. C., Macintosh, D., Fleshner, M., & Diamond, D. M. (2003). Emotion-induced amnesia in rats: Working memory-specific impairment, corticosterone-memory correlation, and fear versus arousal effects on memory. *Learning & Memory, 10*(5), 326–336.

Woolley, C. S., Gould, E., & McEwen, B. S. (1990). Exposure to excess glucocorticoids alters dendritic morphology of adult hippocampal pyramidal neurons. *Brain Research, 531*(1–2), 225–231.

Wright, R. L., & Conrad, C. D. (2008). Enriched environment prevents chronic stress-induced spatial learning and memory deficits. *Behavioural Brain Research, 187*(1), 41–47.

Wright, R. L., Lightner, E. N., Harman, J. S., Meijer, O. C., & Conrad, C. D. (2006). Attenuating corticosterone levels on the day of memory assessment prevents chronic stress-induced impairments in spatial memory. *European Journal of Neuroscience, 24*(2), 595–605.

Yang, Y., Cao, J., Xiong, W., Zhang, J., Zhou, Q., Wei, H., Liang, C., Deng, J., Li, T., Yang, S., & Xu, L. (2003). Both stress experience and age determine the impairment or enhancement effect of stress on spatial memory retrieval. *Journal of Endocrinology, 178*, 45–54.

Yau, J. L. W., Olsson, T., Morris, R. G. M., Meaney, M. J., & Seckl, J. R. (1995). Glucocorticoids, hippocampal corticosteroid receptor gene expression and antidepressant treatment: Relationship with spatial learning in young and aged rats. *Neuroscience, 66*(3), 571–581.

Zoladz, P. R., Conrad, C. D., Fleshner, M., & Diamond, D. M. (2008). Acute episodes of predator exposure in conjunction with chronic social instability as an animal model of post-traumatic stress disorder. *Stress, 11*(4), 259–281.

17

Stress and Aging

A Question of Resilience with Implications for Disease

Erik B. Bloss, John H. Morrison, and Bruce S. McEwen

Introduction

Aging is associated with a selective loss of mental capabilities and an elevated risk for the development of numerous neurodegenerative diseases. On one end of the spectrum, the risk of Alzheimer's disease (AD), a form of dementia characterized by a progressive and debilitating loss of mental ability, increases exponentially between the ages of 65 and 95 (Brookmeyer et al., 1998). On the other end, there is evidence that a subpopulation of elderly age quite successfully, retaining short- and long-term memory functions (Depp and Jeste, 2006). In between, many will experience a more moderate loss of cognition that falls short of disease. Thus, while aging may be thought of as a risk factor that increases vulnerability towards cognitive decline and neurodegenerative disease, the deterioration of mental function during the aging process is by no means inevitable for all.

The neurobiological mechanisms that mediate age-related vulnerability or resilience in the brain are poorly understood. Whereas we know of several candidate genes that are associated with development of neurodegenerative disease, our understanding how environmental and lifestyle factors interact with these genes in the context of aging and disease remains incomplete. Animal models, in which environment and experience can be tightly controlled, mimic many aspects of human aging including compromised executive functions, short- and long-term memory functions, and individual variability in cognitive decline (Gallagher and Rapp, 1997). In addition, transgenic mouse models have been engineered to accurately mirror some of the hallmark behavioral impairments and brain pathology in

The Handbook of Stress: Neuropsychological Effects on the Brain, First Edition.
Edited by Cheryl D. Conrad.

AD patients, and these models have been useful in the study of how environmental factors can increase or decrease pathology in the brain.

Studies using these strategies have provided evidence that the hypothalamic–pituitary–adrenal (HPA) axis can show abnormalities during aging and in disease. The HPA axis constitutes a major part of the neuroendocrine system and regulates many bodily processes such as energy balance, reproduction, immune system function, and cognition. Activation of the HPA axis is adaptive in times of stress, but chronic exposure to HPA mediators may be deleterious, particularly in the aging brain where susceptibility to maladaptive responses may be increased. Animal and human studies have demonstrated that dysfunction of the HPA axis is related to age-related cognitive decline and can exacerbate symptoms of neurodegenerative disease (Nichols et al., 2001). As the brain controls HPA-axis activity and a major target of HPA output, understanding how stress and stress hormones interact with brain aging is critical (McEwen, 2006). At the cellular level, animal research has suggested that stress exposure mimics the effects of age on multiple neurobiological measures of neuronal structure and function. Taken together, these data suggest stress exposure could be a prominent lifestyle factor that predisposes one to age-related cognitive dysfunction or to disease (see Figure 17.1).

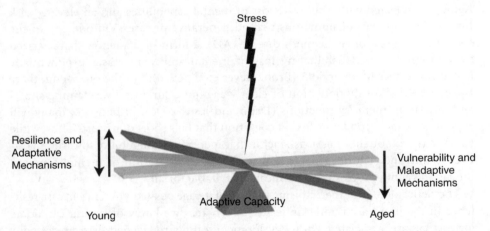

Figure 17.1 Stress, aging, and resilience. Although young subjects are not impervious to stress (seen by the movement of the plank on the left side of the seesaw), there is much evidence that suggests resilience mechanisms allow for successful adaptation over time. These resilience mechanisms include normalization of behavioral performance and reversible cellular plasticity mechanisms. Thus, the dark plank on the left represents normalization of behavioral and cellular measures with recovery from stress exposure in young subjects. In contrast, the aging process is marked by heightened vulnerability to maladaptive responses and failures of cellular resilience when faced with chronic stressors of various types. Evidence has documented stress and aging interactions on the development of hippocampal-dependent cognitive decline, reductions in cellular plasticity mechanisms, and exacerbation of neurodegenerative disease. Therefore, the dark plank on the right represents a failure to normalize behavioral and cellular measures with recovery from stress exposure in the aged subject.

How might stressful experience over the life span lead to a failure of resilience mechanisms and ultimately to heightened vulnerability to disease? A large focus of today's research are the cellular and molecular mechanisms of stress or aging; much less, however, has been done to integrate the two. Our focus here will be to review the neuroendocrine and neurobiological interactions between stress and aging, and to outline potential manipulations that may aid against stress-induced vulnerability in aging populations.

Neuroendocrine Mechanisms and Aging in Resilience and Vulnerability

Glucocorticoids modulate adaptive responses to stress

Activation of the HPA axis occurs in a predictable circadian rhythm that allows for adrenal glucocorticoids (GCs; cortisol in primates and corticosterone in most rodent species) to mobilize energy for expenditure at the time of waking. In addition, there is a rapid activation of the HPA axis by stress. The physiological importance of GCs is seen in patients with Addison's disease, whose failure to produce adequate GCs in response to a stressor can lead to cardiovascular complications.

The adaptive role of GCs has been studied for decades. Stress-induced GCs serve complex roles and can permit, enhance, or suppress other aspects of the neuroendocrine stress response in a way that focuses on immediate needs such as energy and minimizes long-term functions such as reproduction (Sapolsky et al., 2000; see also Chapter 1 in this volume). As GCs are catabolic in nature their release is kept in tight control by negative-feedback loops at the pituitary gland, hypothalamus, hippocampus, and prefrontal cortex (Herman et al., 2003; see also Chapter 2).

The role of GCs in modulating cognitive aging: rodent studies

A number of studies have demonstrated age-related increases in basal GC levels in rodents (Sapolsky, 1992a). These effects are not uniform across all aging animals, but rather occur in a subpopulation of aged rats (Issa et al., 1990). Aged rats also have prolonged GC responses to various stressors as compared to young animals (Sapolsky et al., 1983a). These data suggest that the efficiency of the negative-feedback system, both in the circadian GC rhythm and in response to stressors, is reduced with aging (Sapolsky et al., 1986). The pioneering studies by Landfield and colleagues were among the first to report an association between brain aging and excess HPA activity, and that reduction of GCs by adrenalectomy could reduce cognitive impairments and cellular markers of brain aging (Landfield et al., 1978, 1981).

Individual variability in age-related HPA axis dysfunction has been linked with vulnerability to cognitive decline in rat studies. Issa and colleagues found that aged rats that were impaired in a hippocampal-dependent spatial memory task showed basal elevations of plasma GCs, whereas age-matched rats that were unimpaired in the task did not (Issa et al., 1990). Using a similar paradigm to separate age-impaired from aged-unimpaired rats, Bizon and colleagues found that only aged-impaired rats showed a prolonged GC response to restraint stress, whereas young and aged-unimpaired rats were indistinguishable (Bizon et al., 2001).

In addition to changes in plasma GCs, the enzymatic machinery that controls tissue-specific levels of GCs has also been implicated in age-related cognitive decline. 11β Hydroxysteroid dehydrogenase type 1 (11β-HSD1), an intracellular enzyme that regenerates bioactive GCs from an inactive metabolite, is expressed in the hippocampus. Aged mice in which the *11β-HSD1* gene has been disrupted show enhanced behavioral performance in a hippocampus-dependent task relative to aged wild-type mice (Yau et al., 2007). Furthermore, the aged *11β-HSD1*-knockout mice had similar performance to young wild-type mice despite elevated plasma GCs, suggesting that tissue-specific control may be more important than plasma levels (Yau et al., 2007).

The role of GCs in modulating cognitive aging: human studies

As in rodents, individual variability in HPA axis function has been reported in aging humans and has been linked to compromised memory processes that depend on hippocampal function (Lupien et al., 1996). A large-scale, 5-year longitudinal study by Lupien and colleagues provided evidence that individual variability in age-related decline in hippocampal declarative memory is inversely associated with elevations in cortisol levels (Lupien et al., 1996). When subjects who had steadily increasing cortisol levels over 5 years and high cortisol levels at the time of the performance testing (increasing/high) were compared to those who had increasing cortisol with only moderate levels (increasing/moderate) or decreasing cortisol with moderate levels (decreasing/moderate), only those in the increasing/high group reported impairments in declarative memory (Lupien et al., 1994, 1996). A follow-up study comparing the two extreme groups, increasing/high and decreasing/moderate, showed that the increasing/high group had impaired performance on several tasks dependent on the hippocampus and a 14% reduction in hippocampal volume. Remarkably, the cortisol slope over time and current levels predict hippocampal volume (Lupien et al., 1998). Another set of studies employed cross-sectional and longitudinal designs to test the hypothesis that elevations in cortisol are associated with cognitive impairments. In both study designs, the adverse effects of elevated urinary cortisol on cognitive performance were found in aging women only (Seeman et al., 1997), suggesting that women may be particularly susceptible to the adverse effects of stress or elevated GCs (Becker et al., 2007). As in rodent studies, there is evidence for a role in tissue-specific levels of GCs; pharmacological inhibition of the 11β-HSD1 enzyme in aging humans also improves cognitive performance (Sandeep et al., 2004).

An emerging literature suggests that dysfunction of the HPA axis in humans may be a result of lifetime hardships such as low socioeconomic status, job dissatisfaction, and inadequate social networks. Nonhuman primate observational studies indicate that social rank is a powerful predictor of neuroendocrine status (Sapolsky, 1992b, 2005). Human longitudinal studies have observed similar phenomena, namely that flattened cortisol rhythms can be linked with poor health, poor sleep behaviors, and financial insecurity (Kumari et al., 2010; Seeman et al., 2010). Longitudinal studies by the McArthur Foundation have provided evidence that the cumulative wear and tear of adaptation is a powerful predictor of age-related cognitive decline (Karlamangla et al., 2002). These data provide compelling evidence that chronic stressors can modulate aging through a pathway that includes GC action; they further suggest that decisions to enhance healthy living (e.g., healthy diet, physical activity, a sense of optimism) might be a powerful way to increase resilience during aging (see below).

The role of corticosteroid receptor plasticity in age-related cognitive decline

In addition to GCs, age-related changes in GC receptors are also associated with cognitive decline. GCs exert their actions through two receptor types: the high-affinity mineralocorticoid receptor (MR), and the low-affinity glucocorticoid receptor (GR) (de Kloet et al., 1998; see also Chapter 3). Since there is enough free GC in the plasma at basal levels to saturate the MR, it is assumed these receptors are tonically occupied and mediate many of the permissive actions of GCs; in contrast, expression of the GR allows for a differential tissue response across basal or elevated GC levels. With repeated elevations in GCs, the expression of both MR and GR decrease in the hypothalamus, hippocampus, and prefrontal cortex; in contrast, adrenalectomy results in the increased expression of MR and GR (de Kloet et al., 1998). Thus GR expression is plastic and adaptive in response to changes in the availability of GCs.

Studies aimed at understanding how age may affect corticosteroid receptor systems have demonstrated that aged animals have impairments in multiple aspects of GR function. Aged rodent models in general show decreased GR expression, which may contribute to the impaired GC negative feedback seen in aging animals or be a compensatory response to chronic elevations of GCs (Sapolsky et al., 1983b). Aged rats also have reductions in corticosteroid receptor plasticity as judged by the ability to upregulate GR binding after adrenalectomy (Eldridge et al., 1989). Functional aspects of GR signaling are also disrupted with age; for example, the ability of GCs to translocate from the cytoplasm to the nucleus upon exposure to synthetic GCs is impaired in the prefrontal cortex and hippocampus of aged rats (Mizoguchi et al., 2009), and GR is impaired in its ability to bind its consensus DNA sequence in aged animals (Murphy et al., 2002). In a study by Bizon and colleagues (2001), decreased hippocampal GR mRNA was reported to correlate with learning ability in aging rats. Transgenic mouse models have also established that alterations in GR expression can lead to cognitive impairments. Heterozygous and homozygous *GR*-knockout mice are impaired in the Morris water maze task, which suggests GR signaling is necessary for hippocampal function (Oitzl et al., 1997). On the other hand, mice that overexpress the *GR* gene also show impairments in GC negative feedback and spatial memory performance, phenotypes that are similar to those observed in aging mice (Wei et al., 2007). Taken together, these experiments suggest that age-related changes in GR expression and signaling can compromise hippocampal function and contribute to cognitive decline.

A role for GCs in age-related neurodegenerative diseases such as AD

A life history of high stress exposure is a known risk factor for the development and progression of AD (Wilson et al., 2006, 2007). There is evidence that a large percentage of AD patients also present with hypercortisolemia (Davis et al., 1986; Elgh et al., 2006). However, only recently have animal studies addressed how stress or GCs could influence AD pathogenesis. The main pathological features of AD are the presence of senile plaques containing amyloid-β (Aβ) peptide, and neurofibrillary tangles composed of the hyperphosphoryated microtubule-associated protein tau. Two main strategies have been employed in animal models of AD: (1) transgenic mouse models in which genes that contribute to AD (i.e., presenilin 1, amyloid precursor protein [APP], and microtubule-associated protein tau) are mutated and (2) injections of Aβ peptides into brain.

In transgenic mice with mutations in the *APP* gene, immobilization stress can accelerate learning and memory impairments (Jeong et al., 2006). In triple transgenic mice (i.e., mice that harbor mutations in the *presenilin 1*, *APP*, and *tau* genes), stress-level GCs increase the cleavage of APP into the neurotoxic Aβ1-40 and Aβ1-42 peptides (Green et al., 2006). Administration of the synthetic GC dexamethasone to these mice increases Aβ and hyperphosphorylated tau protein immunoreactivity in the hippocampus, providing evidence that stress can exacerbate both pathological hallmarks of human AD (Green et al., 2006). In rat models of AD, exposure to stress preceding infusions of Aβ peptide causes greater deficits in a radial-arm-maze performance, exacerbated impairments in hippocampal synaptic transmission, and reductions in the activation of signaling molecules than animals subjected to stress or Aβ infusions alone (Srivareerat et al., 2009). In a novel *at-risk* paradigm, low doses of intracerebroventricular Aβ peptides which have minimal effects alone cause greater impairments in radial-arm-maze performance when combined with a stress paradigm than compared to either Aβ infusion or stress alone (Tran et al., 2011). As in the mouse studies, it has been demonstrated that both stress and GC administration can influence the natural metabolism of APP in rats in such a way that leads to increased formation of the C-terminal fragment, which in turn can generate amyloidogenic peptides that adversely affect behavior (Catania et al., 2009). These rodent data suggest that stress interacts with neurobiological mechanisms of disease progression and may hasten the onset of disease symptoms.

Since most of the effects of stress in these rodent models can be reproduced with GC administration, it is likely that stress exerts its effects through elevation of GC levels and increased GC signaling in the brain. As mentioned above, human studies have repeatedly found alterations in HPA axis function in a subset AD patients. Clinical evidence has shown that elevated levels of basal cortisol may predict a more rapid progression of AD, such that cortisol levels were inversely correlated with performance in a mini-mental state examination as well as hippocampal volume (Huang et al., 2009). In addition, a rare single-nucleotide polymorphism in the regulatory region of the *11β-HSD1* gene has been reported to cause a sixfold increase in the risk of developing sporadic AD (de Quervain et al., 2004), furthering the evidence that local tissue levels of GCs may be a major factor in disease risk.

In summary, the HPA axis is important for adaptation and survival. Alterations in HPA axis activity in aged subjects are associated with natural cognitive decline, increased risk for development of AD, and a more rapid progression of the disease. GC receptors and enzymes that control local GC levels also play critical roles in these processes. On the other hand, it should be emphasized that maintenance of GC sensitivity during aging might be neuroprotective, as rodent and human studies have shown that successful aging is associated with neuroendocrine responses similar to younger subjects.

Role of Cellular Plasticity Mechanisms in Stress and Aging

Stress impairs cellular neuroplasticity mechanisms

Studies investigating the cellular changes in the nervous system with exposure to stress or in aging have found stress-induced changes in cellular proliferation, neuronal structure, and synaptic plasticity. The subgranular zone of the dentate gyrus is one of the few places where new neurons are continuously born throughout the life span. Resident progenitor cells give rise to granule neurons that migrate into the granule cell layer and integrate themselves into hippocampal circuitry in a process that can take weeks in vivo (Zhao et al., 2006). The rate of neurogenesis is highly sensitive to stress exposure and is modified by stress through a mechanism involving both GCs and N-methyl-D-aspartate receptors (NMDARs; glutamate receptors) (Cameron et al., 1998; see also Chapter 7). Stress-induced reductions in neurogenesis are associated with deficits in hippocampal-dependent memory (Gould and Tanapat, 1999). Chronic stress has also been shown to affect neuronal dendritic morphology in several brain regions including the hippocampus, prefrontal cortex, and amygdala (Radley and Morrison, 2005; see also Chapter 10). In young rodents stress causes a loss of dendritic complexity and spine density in hippocampal CA3 and medial prefrontal cortical pyramidal neurons, while it increases complexity and spine density in basolateral amygdalar neurons (Watanabe et al., 1992; Vyas et al., 2002; Radley et al., 2004, 2006). Like neurogenesis, these changes in the hippocampus are also mediated in part though the interaction of GCs and NMDARs (Magarinos and McEwen, 1995). Furthermore, dendritic atrophy induced by stress in the medial prefrontal cortex and hippocampus is associated with a loss of cognitive flexibility (Liston et al., 2006) and spatial memory (Conrad et al., 1996), respectively, whereas dendritic hypertrophy in the basolateral amygdala is associated with increased anxiety behavior (Vyas et al., 2002). Lastly, it is established that stress also causes electrophysiological changes in these neuron populations (Joëls and Krugers, 2007). For example, in rat hippocampus and prefrontal cortex stress impairs long-term potentiation (LTP), a form of synaptic plasticity that has been proposed to be the cellular correlate of memory (Pavlides et al., 1993; Alfarez et al., 2003; Maroun and Richter-Levin, 2003).

The effects of stress mimic reductions in plasticity seen in aging and disease

Whereas the cellular mechanisms downstream of stress have been well studied, their interaction with age-related vulnerability to cognitive decline and disease remains unclear. Because stress and aging have similar adverse effects on hippocampal and prefrontal-dependent tasks, there is reason to suggest stress and aging may be targeting overlapping neuron populations (Dellu et al., 1992; Conrad et al., 1996; Barense et al., 2002; Liston et al., 2006). Aging is associated with reductions in the rate of cell proliferation in the dentate gyrus, and there is evidence that this process may be dependent on age-related GC elevations and reversible with manipulations such as adrenalectomy (Cameron and McKay, 1999; Montaron et al., 2006). Age-related alterations in the rate of neurogenesis have been found to correlate with age-related impairments in hippocampal-dependent memory (Bizon et al., 2004), and interestingly the effects of stress on dentate gyrus cellular proliferation have been reported to be long-lasting in animal models (Lemaire et al., 2006). Studies have also found reductions in neuronal complexity in aging hippocampal and cortical pyramidal neurons (Dickstein et al., 2007). In macaque monkeys, aging decreases synapse density in the dorsolateral prefrontal cortex, which correlates with age-related cognitive impairments (Peters et al., 2008). Furthermore, aging causes a reduction primarily in small, highly plastic dendritic spines in the dorsolateral prefrontal cortex, and estrogen therapy that reduces this age effect also reduces age-related impairments in cognition (Hao et al., 2007). These data suggest that neuronal morphological plasticity is highly sensitive to aging, and alterations may be considered a physical substrate for functional impairments. Aging is associated with a loss of synaptic plasticity in various electrophysiological paradigms (Burke and Barnes, 2006). For example, studies have demonstrated faster decay and reduced levels of LTP in aged rats, providing further evidence that synapses in the aging brain may be less plastic than those in younger subjects (Barnes, 2003).

Similar yet distinct mechanisms of cellular degeneration have been implicated in the progression of AD. Whereas neurons are not lost in the aging brain in the absence of disease, studies have demonstrated progressive neuron loss in the entorhinal cortex, hippocampus, and frontal cortex in AD patients (Morrison and Hof, 1997). There is some evidence that prolonged stress or GCs can lead to neuron death in vivo (Sapolsky et al., 1985), although it remains controversial (Sousa et al., 1998). Less controversial is the idea that stress or GCs leaves neurons highly vulnerable to metabolic insult or injury (Conrad, 2008), including mechanisms that may be at play in AD, such as Aβ deposition or formation of neurofibrillary tangles. Mouse models of AD have found losses in spine density and neuronal architecture that *precede* neuron loss and relate to impairments in hippocampal-dependent tasks (Jacobsen et al., 2006). Thus the prevailing view in AD is that changes in neuroarchitecture including synapse loss and dendritic reorganization occur prior to neuron death and may cause the initial symptoms of cognitive dysfunction in AD patients (Hof and Morrison, 2004). As mentioned above, the role of stress in AD progression is speculative, but animal models have provided some of the best evidence that stress interacts with neuronal vulnerability during the aging process.

Investigations aimed at elucidating further the molecular mechanisms of stress and age interactions, and how they affect adaptive capacity of a cell, network, or organism, should be a rich area for future research. An important mechanistic focus should be on the interaction between aging, stress-induced GCs, and excitotoxic mechanisms, in particular glutamate-NMDAR signaling and intracellular control of calcium levels (Conrad, 2008). Stress causes a robust release of glutamate in the hippocampus and prefrontal cortex, an effect mediated by GCs (Moghaddam et al., 1994). Furthermore, GCs potentiate cell death in response to neurotoxins through an NMDAR-dependent manner (Armanini et al., 1990), and stress/GCs also potentiate calcium channel currents while upregulating calcium-channel subunits (Chameau et al., 2007). These mechanisms have clear implications for aging and vulnerability to disease, as studies have found protracted GC and glutamate responses in the aging brain (Sapolsky et al., 1983a; Lowy et al., 1995), and there is evidence that aging neurons are highly vulnerable to excitotoxicity (Mattson and Magnus, 2006; Mattson, 2007).

Evidence has been reported that demonstrates age–stress interactions at the cellular level. For example, while it is known the effects of stress on hippocampal and prefrontal morphology are reversible (Conrad et al., 1999; Radley et al., 2005), we have recently determined that aging blunts the capacity for recovery-related remodeling in the aging rat prefrontal cortical neurons (Bloss et al., 2010). Similarly, studies of neuronal physiology also suggest that stress could modulate age-related vulnerability to impairments in synaptic plasticity mechanisms. In young rats, dopamine-receptor-mediated maintenance of LTP in the prefrontal cortex is altered by stress in a reversible manner (Goldwater et al., 2009). Based on the evidence that cortical catecholamine systems are vulnerable to aging (Arnsten, 1993), and the demonstration that resilience is reduced in the aging prefrontal cortex, these data would suggest that an interaction might exist between stress and aging catecholamine mechanisms of synaptic plasticity. Clearly more research is needed in this area to identify how stress and aging interact at the cellular and molecular levels, and to what extent these changes can be targeted by therapeutic strategies.

Potential Interventions that Might Increase Resilience to Stress and Aging: Caloric Restriction and Exercise

The first of the Baby Boomer generation (e.g., post-World War II) will reach the age of 65 in 2011. As we prepare for an unprecedented growth in the aging population, it is critical to focus on therapeutics that can prevent or delay the onset of age-related vulnerability in the brain. As it stands, the majority of current therapeutics for AD are only marginally effective (Kumar and Calache, 1991), although there are novel drugs in development aimed at improving memory function in the aged (Lynch, 2006; Bloss et al., 2008). An alternative approach is to investigate lifestyle interventions that may increase adaptive plasticity in the brain and increase the rate of successful cognitive aging. An obvious benefit of this approach is that these types of strategies would be available to all elements of the population, regardless of healthcare plan, socioeconomic status, or geography.

Some of the most exciting ongoing work in gerontology is pointing towards interventions such as caloric restriction and voluntary exercise. Most protocols for caloric restriction generally call for a daily reduction of 30% of daily intake or intermittent fasting (i.e., every other day). Research in invertebrate model systems from yeast to flies have demonstrated conserved mechanisms in response to caloric restriction that mediate increased longevity and resistance to disease (Bishop and Guarente, 2007). In mammalian species, caloric restriction protocols can provide a host of benefits to the aging organism including decreased adiposity, improved glucose tolerance, and increased life span (Hunt et al., 2006). Furthermore, there is evidence that protective actions of caloric restriction may extend to cognitive function and markers of brain aging (Martin et al., 2006). Caloric restriction moderately improves performance in hippocampal-dependent behavioral tasks in rodents (Martin et al., 2007) and reduces the adverse effects of AD transgenes in mouse models (Halagappa et al., 2007). The available data suggest that the cognitive benefits of caloric restriction might apply to humans as well (Witte et al., 2009). Similarly, voluntary exercise has been shown to exhibit neuroprotective actions in disease models (Nichol et al., 2007) and improve cognition in rodents and humans (Kramer et al., 2006; van Praag, 2008). Whereas it will be tough to get a large proportion of the aging population to adhere to caloric restriction regimens, convincing older adults to remain physically active is far more realistic. Furthermore, it appears exercise regimens can have rapid effects even in older people. For example, a recent study used longitudinal and cross-sectional designs to demonstrate that exercise increased cortical plasticity and improved executive function in a set of older adults; most interesting is that these protective effects were apparent after a short (i.e. only 6 months) mild exercise regimen (Colcombe et al., 2004).

Interestingly, both caloric restriction and exercise in general increase GC levels, but the protective actions of the manipulations appear to persist despite these elevations (Sapolsky, 1995; Patel and Finch, 2002). These beneficial actions of caloric restriction and exercise may be mediated through several mechanisms including increased resilience towards oxidative stress and neurotrophin signaling (Ang and Gomez-Pinilla, 2007; Fontan-Lozano et al., 2008; Llorens-Martin et al., 2008); furthermore, there is evidence that the downstream actions of caloric restriction may be dependent on the transcriptional coactivator cAMP-response-element binding protein (CREB)-binding protein (CBP) (Zhang et al., 2009). Oxidative stress is defined as toxic anion radicals (e.g., superoxide and hydrogen peroxide) that can result from normal mitochondrial respiration and from synaptic activity (Mattson, 1998). Accumulation of oxidatively modified proteins, nucleic acids, and lipid membranes has been implicated as a factor that might underlie cellular aging (Mattson, 2007). There is evidence that activation of CREB/CBP transcriptional complexes may be protective in excitotoxic models (Mabuchi et al., 2001), and *CBP* gene knockdown can increase sensitivity to oxidative stress (Zhang et al., 2009). Neurotrophins, on the other hand, are prosurvival peptides that were originally discovered to enhance axonal and dendritic growth, but are considered major targets for pharmacotherapies for a host of degenerative diseases (Thoenen and Sendtner, 2002). It is now known that brain-derived neurotrophic factor (BDNF) can regulate neuronal excitability and synapse development, and have downstream effects on gene transcription by several signaling cascades (Huang and Reichardt, 2001). Direct evidence for a protective effect of exercise on stress-induced decreases in hippocampal BDNF has been demonstrated (Adlard and Cotman, 2004), and it has been shown that BDNF may be a target of (Tao et al., 1998) and signal through (Finkbeiner et al., 1997) CREB/CBP transcriptional complexes. Taken together, it appears caloric restriction and exercise cause similar cellular adaptations, including resistance against oxidative stress and the activation of neurotrophin signaling pathways that mediate its protective action in the brain. These pathways may be downstream of CREB/CBP transcriptional complexes, although more work is needed and many questions still remain unanswered.

Conclusions and Summary

In conclusion, while some individuals age quite successfully others develop age-related cognitive impairments or are devastated by neurodegenerative disease. Abnormal HPA-axis reactivity and stress exposure are modulators of the aging process, and may increase vulnerability to maladaptive responses in the aging brain; conversely, successful cognitive aging is associated with HPA-axis reactivity similar to that seen in younger subjects. Both GC receptors and enzymes that control local tissue levels of GCs have been implicated in cognitive aging and disease. Interventions such as caloric restriction and exercise have demonstrated the ability to reduce cognitive and cellular markers of aging in animal models. Preclinical data in human studies have corroborated some of these benefits. Although pharmacological therapeutics that target the aging process have not yet been fully realized, recent studies reveal that signaling pathways activated by caloric restriction may provide novel targets. Future elucidation of the mechanisms by which caloric restriction and exercise may exert their protective actions against stress and decrease vulnerability in the aging brain will have important implications for our aging population and society as a whole.

References

Adlard, P. A., & Cotman, C. W. (2004). Voluntary exercise protects against stress-induced decreases in brain-derived neurotrophic factor protein expression. *Neuroscience, 124,* 985–992.

Alfarez, D. N., Joëls, M., & Krugers, H. J. (2003). Chronic unpredictable stress impairs long-term potentiation in rat hippocampal CA1 area and dentate gyrus in vitro. *European Journal of Neuroscience, 17,* 1928–1934.

Ang, E. T., & Gomez-Pinilla, F. (2007). Potential therapeutic effects of exercise to the brain. *Current Medicinal Chemistry, 14,* 2564–2571.

Armanini, M. P., Hutchins, C., Stein, B. A., & Sapolsky, R. M. (1990). Glucocorticoid endangerment of hippocampal neurons is NMDA-receptor dependent. *Brain Research, 532,* 7–12.

Arnsten, A. F. (1993). Catecholamine mechanisms in age-related cognitive decline. *Neurobiology of Aging, 14,* 639–641.

Barense, M. D., Fox, M. T., & Baxter, M. G. (2002). Aged rats are impaired on an attentional set-shifting task sensitive to medial frontal cortex damage in young rats. *Learning and Memory, 9,* 191–201.

Barnes, C. A. (2003). Long-term potentiation and the ageing brain. *Philosophical Transactions of the Royal Society of London Series B Biological Sciences, 358,* 765–772.

Becker, J. B., Monteggia, L. M., Perrot-Sinal, T. S., Romeo, R. D., Taylor, J. R., Yehuda, R., & Bale, T. L. (2007). Stress and disease: is being female a predisposing factor? *Journal of Neuroscience, 27,* 11851–11855.

Bishop, N. A., & Guarente, L. (2007). Genetic links between diet and lifespan: shared mechanisms from yeast to humans. *Nature Reviews Genetics, 8,* 835–844.

Bizon, J. L., Helm, K. A., Han, J. S., Chun, H. J., Pucilowska, J., Lund, P. K., & Gallagher, M. (2001). Hypothalamic-pituitary-adrenal axis function and corticosterone receptor expression in behaviourally characterized young and aged Long-Evans rats. *European Journal of Neuroscience, 14,* 1739–1751.

Bizon, J. L., Lee, H. J., & Gallagher, M. (2004). Neurogenesis in a rat model of age-related cognitive decline. *Aging Cell, 3,* 227–234.

Bloss, E. B., Hunter, R. G., Waters, E. M., Munoz, C., Bernard, K., & McEwen, B. S. (2008). Behavioral and biological effects of chronic S18986, a positive AMPA receptor modulator, during aging. *Experimental Neurology, 210,* 109–117.

Bloss, E. B., Janssen, W. G., McEwen, B. S., & Morrison, J. H. (2010). Interactive effects of stress and aging on structural plasticity in prefrontal cortex. *Journal of Neuroscience, 30,* 6726–6731.

Brookmeyer, R., Gray, S., & Kawas, C. (1998). Projections of Alzheimer's disease in the United States and the public health impact of delaying disease onset. *American Journal of Public Health, 88,* 1337–1342.

Burke, S. N., & Barnes, C. A. (2006). Neural plasticity in the ageing brain. *Nature Reviews Neuroscience, 7,* 30–40.

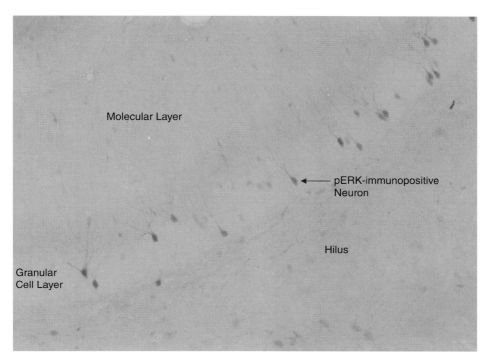

Plate 1 Sparse pERK expression in rat dentate gyrus granule neurons after forced swimming. Phospho-ERK immunostaining is clearly visible in the nuclear and cytoplasmic compartments of the granule neurons; note the staining in the dendritic trees reaching out into the molecular layer. Within the dentate gyrus pERK-immunopositive neurons were predominantly found in the middle and superficial aspects of the granular cell layer. Hardly any pERK-immunostained granule neurons were found in rats killed under baseline conditions (not shown).

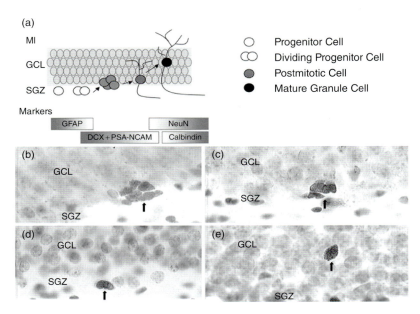

Plate 2 Stages of adult neurogenesis in the dentate gyrus. (a) Progenitor cells in the subgranular zone (SGZ) give rise to postmitotic daughter cells (cell proliferation). These cells express the glial marker GFAP. Postmitotic cells differentiate into immature neurons in the granule cell layer (GCL). Immature neurons express doublecortin (DCX) and polysialated neuronal cell adhesion molecule (PSA-NCAM) as they elaborate axons and develop dendritic trees which extend into the molecular layer (ML). Immature granule cells transition into mature granule cells when they express neuronal markers like NeuN and calbindin. Studies have shown that continued development occurs for several weeks as new neurons receive synaptic input and mature electrophysiological responses emerge. Photomicrographs represent different stages of adult neurogenesis. Proliferating progenitor cells located in the subgranular zone express endogenous markers of cell proliferation, such as Ki67 (b) and BrdU at a 2-hr post-BrdU injection time point (c). New neurons are seen in the granule cell layer labeled with BrdU at 1-week (d) and 3-week (e) post-BrdU injection time points.

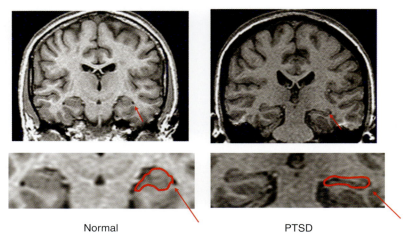

Normal   PTSD

Plate 3 Normal and PTSD brain scans. *Source:* From Bremner (2005). Used by permission of W.W. Norton and Company, Inc.

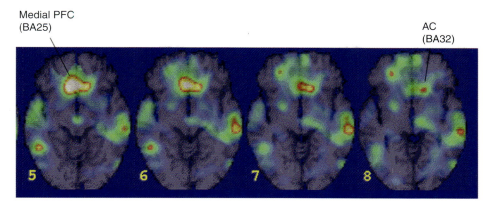

Plate 4 Medial prefrontal cortex (PFC) brain scan. AC, anterior cingulate; BA, Brodmann's area. *Source:* From Bremner (2005). Used by permission of W.W. Norton and Company, Inc.

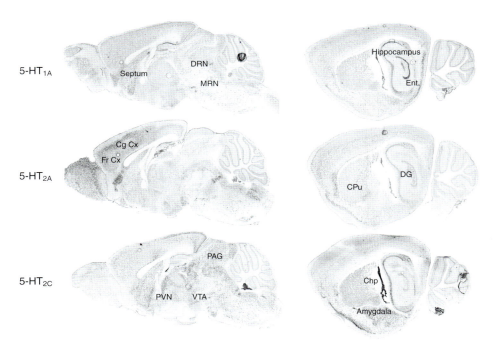

Plate 5 Distribution of 5-HT$_{1A}$, 5-HT$_{2A}$, and 5-HT$_{2C}$ receptor mRNA in various brain areas involved in the regulation of emotion and the stress response. ChP, choroid plexus; Cg Cx, cingulate cortex; CPu, caudate putamen; DG, dentate gyrus; DRN, dorsal raphe nucleus; Ent., entorhinal cortex; Fr Cx, frontal cortex; PAG, periaqueductal gray; PVN, paraventricular nucleus of the hypothalamus; MRN, median raphe nucleus; VTA, ventral tegmental area. *Source:* Modified *in situ* hybridization images from 18-month-old animals in Allen Developing Mouse Brain Atlas [internet]. Reference atlas developed by Luis Puellas, Ph.D. Seattle (WA): Allen Institute for Brain Science. © 2009. Available from: http://developing-mouse.brain-map.org

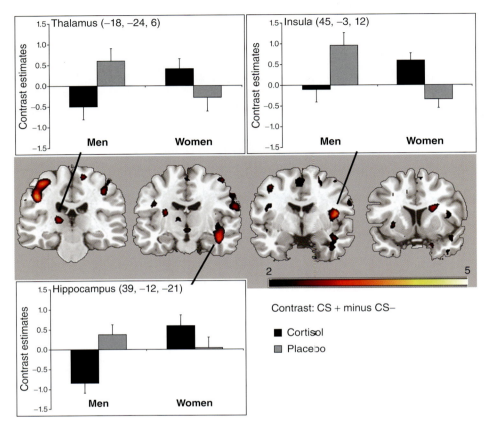

Plate 6 Neural activations for sex by cortisol interactions in the contrast CS+ minus CS− in a series of selected brain slices. This contrast is an index of emotional learning. Mean (and SEM) contrast estimates of the contrast CS+ minus CS− for women and men in the cortisol and placebo group in the insula, hippocampus, and thalamus in the respective peak voxels are illustrated in the bar graphs. All coordinates (*x*, *y*, *z*) are given in Montreal Neurological Institute (MNI) space. *Source:* Reprinted from Merz et al (2010). With permission from Elsevier.

Cameron, H. A., & McKay, R. D. (1999). Restoring production of hippocampal neurons in old age. *Nature Neuroscience, 2,* 894–897.

Cameron, H. A., Tanapat, P., & Gould, E. (1998). Adrenal steroids and N-methyl-D-aspartate receptor activation regulate neurogenesis in the dentate gyrus of adult rats through a common pathway. *Neuroscience, 82,* 349–354.

Catania, C., Sotiropoulos, I., Silva, R., Onofri, C., Breen, K. C., Sousa, N., & Almeida, O. F. (2009). The amyloidogenic potential and behavioral correlates of stress. *Molecular Psychiatry, 14,* 95–105.

Chameau, P., Qin, Y., Spijker, S., Smit, G., & Joëls, M. (2007). Glucocorticoids specifically enhance L-type calcium current amplitude and affect calcium channel subunit expression in the mouse hippocampus. *Journal of Neurophysiology, 97,* 5–14.

Colcombe, S. J., Kramer, A. F., Erickson, K. I., Scalf, P., McAuley, E., Cohen, N. J., Webb, A., Jerome, G. J., Marquez, D. X., & Elavsky, S. (2004). Cardiovascular fitness, cortical plasticity, and aging. *Proceedings of the National Academy of Sciences USA, 101,* 3316–3321.

Conrad, C. D. (2008). Chronic stress-induced hippocampal vulnerability: the glucocorticoid vulnerability hypothesis. *Reviews in the Neurosciences, 19,* 395–411.

Conrad, C. D., Galea, L. A., Kuroda, Y., & McEwen, B. S. (1996). Chronic stress impairs rat spatial memory on the Y maze, and this effect is blocked by tianeptine pretreatment. *Behavioral Neuroscience, 110,* 1321–1334.

Conrad, C. D., LeDoux, J. E., Magarinos, A. M., & McEwen, B. S. (1999). Repeated restraint stress facilitates fear conditioning independently of causing hippocampal CA3 dendritic atrophy. *Behavioral Neuroscience, 113,* 902–913.

Davis, K. L., Davis, B. M., Greenwald, B. S., Mohs, R. C., Mathe, A. A., Johns, C. A., & Horvath, T. B. (1986). Cortisol and Alzheimer's disease, I: Basal studies. *American Journal of Psychiatry, 143,* 300–305.

de Kloet, E. R., Vreugdenhil, E., Oitzl, M. S., & Joëls, M. (1998). Brain corticosteroid receptor balance in health and disease. *Endocrine Reviews, 19,* 269–301.

Dellu, F., Mayo, W., Cherkaoui, J., Le Moal, M., & Simon, H. (1992). A two-trial memory task with automated recording: study in young and aged rats. *Brain Research, 588,* 132–139.

Depp, C. A., & Jeste, D. V. (2006). Definitions and predictors of successful aging: a comprehensive review of larger quantitative studies. *American Journal of Geriatric Psychiatry, 14,* 6–20.

de Quervain, D. J., Poirier, R., Wollmer, M. A., Grimaldi, L. M., Tsolaki, M., Streffer, J. R., Hock, C., Nitsch, R. M., Mohajeri, M. H., & Papassotiropoulos, A. (2004). Glucocorticoid-related genetic susceptibility for Alzheimer's disease. *Human Molecular Genetics, 13,* 47–52.

Dickstein, D. L., Kabaso, D., Rocher, A. B., Luebke, J. I., Wearne, S. L., & Hof, P. R. (2007). Changes in the structural complexity of the aged brain. *Aging Cell, 6,* 275–284.

Eldridge, J. C., Fleenor, D. G., Kerr, D. S., & Landfield, P. W. (1989). Impaired up-regulation of type II corticosteroid receptors in hippocampus of aged rats. *Brain Research, 478,* 248–256.

Elgh, E., Lindqvist Astot, A., Fagerlund, M., Eriksson, S., Olsson, T., & Nasman, B. (2006). Cognitive dysfunction, hippocampal atrophy and glucocorticoid feedback in Alzheimer's disease. *Biological Psychiatry, 59,* 155–161.

Finkbeiner, S., Tavazoie, S. F., Maloratsky, A., Jacobs, K. M., Harris, K. M., & Greenberg, M. E. (1997). CREB: a major mediator of neuronal neurotrophin responses. *Neuron, 19,* 1031–1047.

Fontan-Lozano, A., Lopez-Lluch, G., Delgado-Garcia, J. M., Navas, P., & Carrion, A. M. (2008). Molecular bases of caloric restriction regulation of neuronal synaptic plasticity. *Molecular Neurobiology, 38,* 167–177.

Gallagher, M., & Rapp, P. R. (1997). The use of animal models to study the effects of aging on cognition. *Annual Review of Psychology, 48,* 339–370.

Goldwater, D. S., Pavlides, C., Hunter, R. G., Bloss, E. B., Hof, P. R., McEwen, B. S., & Morrison, J. H. (2009). Structural and functional alterations to rat medial prefrontal cortex following chronic restraint stress and recovery. *Neuroscience, 164,* 798–808.

Gould, E., & Tanapat, P. (1999). Stress and hippocampal neurogenesis. *Biological Psychiatry, 46,* 1472–1479.

Green, K. N., Billings, L. M., Roozendaal, B., McGaugh, J. L., & LaFerla, F. M. (2006). Glucocorticoids increase amyloid-beta and tau pathology in a mouse model of Alzheimer's disease. *Journal of Neuroscience, 26,* 9047–9056.

Halagappa, V. K., Guo, Z., Pearson, M., Matsuoka, Y., Cutler, R. G., Laferla, F. M., & Mattson, M. P. (2007). Intermittent fasting and caloric restriction ameliorate age-related behavioral deficits in the triple-transgenic mouse model of Alzheimer's disease. *Neurobiology of Disease, 26,* 212–220.

Hao, J., Rapp, P. R., Janssen, W. G., Lou, W., Lasley, B. L., Hof, P. R., & Morrison, J. H. (2007). Interactive effects of age and estrogen on cognition and pyramidal neurons in monkey prefrontal cortex. *Proceedings of the National Academy of Sciences USA, 104,* 11465–11470.

Herman, J. P., Figueiredo, H., Mueller, N. K., Ulrich-Lai, Y., Ostrander, M. M., Choi, D. C., & Cullinan, W. E. (2003). Central mechanisms of stress integration: hierarchical circuitry controlling hypothalamo-pituitary-adrenocortical responsiveness. *Frontiers in Neuroendocrinology, 24,* 151–180.

Hof, P. R., & Morrison, J. H. (2004). The aging brain: morphomolecular senescence of cortical circuits. *Trends in Neuroscience, 27,* 607–613.

Huang, C. W., Lui, C. C., Chang, W. N., Lu, C. H., Wang, Y. L., & Chang, C. C. (2009). Elevated basal cortisol level predicts lower hippocampal volume and cognitive decline in Alzheimer's disease. *Journal of Clinical Neuroscience, 16,* 1283–1286.

Huang, E. J., & Reichardt, L. F. (2001). Neurotrophins: roles in neuronal development and function. *Annual Review of Neuroscience, 24,* 677–736.

Hunt, N. D., Hyun, D. H., Allard, J. S., Minor, R. K., Mattson, M. P., Ingram, D. K., & de Cabo, R. (2006). Bioenergetics of aging and calorie restriction. *Ageing Research Reviews, 5,* 125–143.

Issa, A. M., Rowe, W., Gauthier, S., & Meaney, M. J. (1990). Hypothalamic-pituitary-adrenal activity in aged, cognitively impaired and cognitively unimpaired rats. *Journal of Neuroscience, 10,* 3247–3254.

Jacobsen, J. S., Wu, C. C., Redwine, J. M., Comery, T. A., Arias, R., Bowlby, M., Martone, R., Morrison, J. H., Pangalos, M. N., Reinhart, P. H., & Bloom, F. E. (2006). Early-onset behavioral and synaptic deficits in a mouse model of Alzheimer's disease. *Proceedings of the National Academy of Sciences USA, 103,* 5161–5166.

Jeong, Y. H., Park, C. H., Yoo, J., Shin, K. Y., Ahn, S. M., Kim, H. S., Lee, S. H., Emson, P. C., & Suh, Y. H. (2006). Chronic stress accelerates learning and memory impairments and increases amyloid deposition in APPV717I-CT100 transgenic mice, an Alzheimer's disease model. *FASEB Journal, 20,* 729–731.

Joëls, M., & Krugers, H. J. (2007). LTP after stress: up or down? *Neural Plasticity,* 93202.

Karlamangla, A. S., Singer, B. H., McEwen, B. S., Rowe, J. W., & Seeman, T. E. (2002). Allostatic load as a predictor of functional decline. MacArthur studies of successful aging. *Journal of Clinical Epidemiology*, *55*, 696–710.

Kramer, A. F., Erickson, K. I., & Colcombe, S. J. (2006). Exercise, cognition, and the aging brain. *Journal of Applied Physiology*, *101*, 1237–1242.

Kumar, V., & Calache, M. (1991). Treatment of Alzheimer's disease with cholinergic drugs. *International Journal of Clinical Pharmacology, Therapy and Toxicology*, *29*, 23–37.

Kumari, M., Badrick, E., Chandola, T., Adler, N. E., Epel, E., Seeman, T., Kirschbaum, C., & Marmot, M. G. (2010). Measures of social position and cortisol secretion in an aging population: findings from the Whitehall II study. *Psychosomatic Medicine*, *72*, 27–34.

Landfield, P. W., Waymire, J. C., & Lynch, G. (1978). Hippocampal aging and adrenocorticoids: quantitative correlations. *Science*, *202*, 1098–1102.

Landfield, P. W., Baskin, R. K., & Pitler, T. A. (1981). Brain aging correlates: retardation by hormonal-pharmacological treatments. *Science*, *214*, 581–584.

Lemaire, V., Lamarque, S., Le Moal, M., Piazza, P. V., & Abrous, D. N. (2006). Postnatal stimulation of the pups counteracts prenatal stress-induced deficits in hippocampal neurogenesis. *Biological Psychiatry*, *59*, 786–792.

Liston, C., Miller, M. M., Goldwater, D. S., Radley, J. J., Rocher, A. B., Hof, P. R., Morrison, J. H., & McEwen, B. S. (2006). Stress-induced alterations in prefrontal cortical dendritic morphology predict selective impairments in perceptual attentional set-shifting. *Journal of Neuroscience*, *26*, 7870–7874.

Llorens-Martin, M., Torres-Aleman, I., & Trejo, J. L. (2008). Growth factors as mediators of exercise actions on the brain. *Neuromolecular Medicine*, *10*, 99–107.

Lowy, M. T., Wittenberg, L., & Yamamoto, B. K. (1995). Effect of acute stress on hippocampal glutamate levels and spectrin proteolysis in young and aged rats. *Journal of Neurochemistry*, *65*, 268–274.

Lupien, S., Lecours, A. R., Lussier, I., Schwartz, G., Nair, N. P., & Meaney, M. J. (1994). Basal cortisol levels and cognitive deficits in human aging. *Journal of Neuroscience*, *14*, 2893–2903.

Lupien, S., Lecours, A. R., Schwartz, G., Sharma, S., Hauger, R. L., Meaney, M. J., & Nair, N. P. (1996). Longitudinal study of basal cortisol levels in healthy elderly subjects: evidence for subgroups. *Neurobiology of Aging*, *17*, 95–105.

Lupien, S. J., de Leon, M., de Santi, S., Convit, A., Tarshish, C., Nair, N. P., Thakur, M., McEwen, B. S., Hauger, R. L., & Meaney, M. J. (1998). Cortisol levels during human aging predict hippocampal atrophy and memory deficits. *Nature Neuroscience*, *1*, 69–73.

Lynch, G. (2006). Glutamate-based therapeutic approaches: ampakines. *Current Opinions in Pharmacology*, *6*, 82–88.

Mabuchi, T., Kitagawa, K., Kuwabara, K., Takasawa, K., Ohtsuki, T., Xia, Z., Storm, D., Yanagihara, T., Hori, M., & Matsumoto, M. (2001). Phosphorylation of cAMP response element-binding protein in hippocampal neurons as a protective response after exposure to glutamate in vitro and ischemia in vivo. *Journal of Neuroscience*, *21*, 9204–9213.

Magarinos, A. M., & McEwen, B. S. (1995). Stress-induced atrophy of apical dendrites of hippocampal CA3c neurons: involvement of glucocorticoid secretion and excitatory amino acid receptors. *Neuroscience*, *69*, 89–98.

Maroun, M., & Richter-Levin, G. (2003). Exposure to acute stress blocks the induction of long-term potentiation of the amygdala-prefrontal cortex pathway in vivo. *Journal of Neuroscience, 23,* 4406–4409.

Martin, B., Mattson, M. P., & Maudsley, S. (2006). Caloric restriction and intermittent fasting: two potential diets for successful brain aging. *Ageing Research Reviews, 5,* 332–353.

Martin, B., Pearson, M., Kebejian, L., Golden, E., Keselman, A., Bender, M., Carlson, O., Egan, J., Ladenheim, B., Cadet, J. L., Becker, K. G., Wood, W., Duffy, K., Vinayakumar, P., Maudsley, S., & Mattson, M. P. (2007). Sex-dependent metabolic, neuroendocrine, and cognitive responses to dietary energy restriction and excess. *Endocrinology, 148,* 4318–4333.

Mattson, M. P. (1998). Modification of ion homeostasis by lipid peroxidation: roles in neuronal degeneration and adaptive plasticity. *Trends in Neuroscience, 21,* 53–57.

Mattson, M. P. (2007). Calcium and neurodegeneration. *Aging Cell, 6,* 337–350.

Mattson, M. P., & Magnus, T. (2006). Ageing and neuronal vulnerability. *Nature Reviews Neuroscience, 7,* 278–294.

McEwen, B. S. (2006). Protective and damaging effects of stress mediators: central role of the brain. *Dialogues in Clinical Neuroscience, 8,* 367–381.

Mizoguchi, K., Ikeda, R., Shoji, H., Tanaka, Y., Maruyama, W., & Tabira, T. (2009). Aging attenuates glucocorticoid negative feedback in rat brain. *Neuroscience, 159,* 259–270.

Moghaddam, B., Bolinao, M. L., Stein-Behrens, B., & Sapolsky, R. (1994). Glucocorticoids mediate the stress-induced extracellular accumulation of glutamate. *Brain Research, 655,* 251–254.

Montaron, M. F., Drapeau, E., Dupret, D., Kitchener, P., Aurousseau, C., Le Moal, M., Piazza, P. V., & Abrous, D. N. (2006). Lifelong corticosterone level determines age-related decline in neurogenesis and memory. *Neurobiology of Aging, 27,* 645–654.

Morrison, J. H., & Hof, P. R. (1997). Life and death of neurons in the aging brain. *Science, 278,* 412–419.

Murphy, E. K., Spencer, R. L., Sipe, K. J., & Herman, J. P. (2002). Decrements in nuclear glucocorticoid receptor (GR) protein levels and DNA binding in aged rat hippocampus. *Endocrinology, 143,* 1362–1370.

Nichol, K. E., Parachikova, A. I., & Cotman, C. W. (2007). Three weeks of running wheel exposure improves cognitive performance in the aged Tg2576 mouse. *Behavioural Brain Research, 184,* 124–132.

Nichols, N. R., Zieba, M., & Bye, N. (2001). Do glucocorticoids contribute to brain aging? *Brain Research Brain Research Reviews, 37,* 273–286.

Oitzl, M. S., de Kloet, E. R., Joëls, M., Schmid, W., & Cole, T. J. (1997). Spatial learning deficits in mice with a targeted glucocorticoid receptor gene disruption. *European Journal of Neuroscience, 9,* 2284–2296.

Patel, N. V., & Finch, C. E. (2002). The glucocorticoid paradox of caloric restriction in slowing brain aging. *Neurobiology of Aging, 23,* 707–717.

Pavlides, C., Watanabe, Y., & McEwen, B. S. (1993). Effects of glucocorticoids on hippocampal long-term potentiation. *Hippocampus, 3,* 183–192.

Peters, A., Sethares, C., & Luebke, J. I. (2008). Synapses are lost during aging in the primate prefrontal cortex. *Neuroscience, 152,* 970–981.

Radley, J. J., & Morrison, J. H. (2005). Repeated stress and structural plasticity in the brain. *Ageing Research Reviews, 4,* 271–287.

Radley, J. J., Sisti, H. M., Hao, J., Rocher, A. B., McCall, T., Hof, P. R., McEwen, B. S., & Morrison, J. H. (2004). Chronic behavioral stress induces apical dendritic reorganization in pyramidal neurons of the medial prefrontal cortex. *Neuroscience, 125,* 1–6.

Radley, J. J., Rocher, A. B., Janssen, W. G., Hof, P. R., McEwen, B. S., & Morrison, J. H. (2005). Reversibility of apical dendritic retraction in the rat medial prefrontal cortex following repeated stress. *Experimental Neurology, 196,* 199–203.

Radley, J. J., Rocher, A. B., Miller, M., Janssen, W. G., Liston, C., Hof, P. R., McEwen, B. S., & Morrison, J. H. (2006). Repeated stress induces dendritic spine loss in the rat medial prefrontal cortex. *Cerebral Cortex, 16,* 313–320.

Sandeep, T. C., Yau, J. L., MacLullich, A. M., Noble, J., Deary, I. J., Walker, B. R., & Seckl, J. R. (2004). 11Beta-hydroxysteroid dehydrogenase inhibition improves cognitive function in healthy elderly men and type 2 diabetics. *Proceedings of the National Academy of Sciences USA, 101,* 6734–6739.

Sapolsky, R. M. (1992a). Do glucocorticoid concentrations rise with age in the rat? *Neurobiology of Aging, 13,* 171–174.

Sapolsky, R. M. (1992b). Cortisol concentrations and the social significance of rank instability among wild baboons. *Psychoneuroendocrinology, 17,* 701–709.

Sapolsky, R. M. (1995). Do the salutary effects of food restriction occur because of or despite of the accompanying hyperadrenocorticism? *Neurobiology of Aging, 16,* 849–850.

Sapolsky, R. M. (2005). The influence of social hierarchy on primate health. *Science, 308,* 648–652.

Sapolsky, R. M., Krey, L. C., & McEwen, B. S. (1983a). The adrenocortical stress-response in the aged male rat: impairment of recovery from stress. *Experimental Gerontology, 18,* 55–64.

Sapolsky, R. M., Krey, L. C., & McEwen, B. S. (1983b). Corticosterone receptors decline in a site-specific manner in the aged rat brain. *Brain Research, 289,* 235–240.

Sapolsky, R. M., Krey, L. C., & McEwen, B. S. (1985). Prolonged glucocorticoid exposure reduces hippocampal neuron number: implications for aging. *Journal of Neuroscience, 5,* 1222–1227.

Sapolsky, R. M., Krey, L. C., & McEwen, B. S. (1986). The adrenocortical axis in the aged rat: impaired sensitivity to both fast and delayed feedback inhibition. *Neurobiology of Aging, 7,* 331–335.

Sapolsky, R. M., Romero, L. M., & Munck, A. U. (2000). How do glucocorticoids influence stress responses? Integrating permissive, suppressive, stimulatory, and preparative actions. *Endocrine Reviews, 21,* 55–89.

Seeman, T., Epel, E., Gruenewald, T., Karlamangla, A., & McEwen, B. S. (2010). Socioeconomic differentials in peripheral biology: cumulative allostatic load. *Annals of the New York Academy of Science, 1186,* 223–239.

Seeman, T. E., McEwen, B. S., Singer, B. H., Albert, M. S., & Rowe, J. W. (1997). Increase in urinary cortisol excretion and memory declines: MacArthur studies of successful aging. *Journal of Clinical Endocrinology and Metabolism, 82,* 2458–2465.

Sousa, N., Almeida, O. F., Holsboer, F., Paula-Barbosa, M. M., & Madeira, M. D. (1998). Maintenance of hippocampal cell numbers in young and aged rats submitted to chronic unpredictable stress. Comparison with the effects of corticosterone treatment. *Stress, 2,* 237–249.

Srivareerat, M., Tran, T. T., Alzoubi, K. H., & Alkadhi, K. A. (2009). Chronic psychosocial stress exacerbates impairment of cognition and long-term potentiation in beta-amyloid rat model of Alzheimer's disease. *Biological Psychiatry, 65,* 918–926.

Tao, X., Finkbeiner, S., Arnold, D. B., Shaywitz, A. J., & Greenberg, M. E. (1998). Ca2+ influx regulates BDNF transcription by a CREB family transcription factor-dependent mechanism. *Neuron, 20,* 709–726.

Thoenen, H., & Sendtner, M. (2002). Neurotrophins: from enthusiastic expectations through sobering experiences to rational therapeutic approaches. *Nature Neuroscience 5* Suppl, 1046–1050.

Tran, T. T., Srivareerat, M., & Alkadhi, K. A. (2011). Chronic psychosocial stress triggers cognitive impairment in a novel at-risk model of Alzheimer's disease. *Neurobiology of Disease, 37,* 756–763.

van Praag, H. (2008). Neurogenesis and exercise: past and future directions. *Neuromolecular Medicine, 10,* 128–140.

Vyas, A., Mitra, R., Shankaranarayana Rao, B. S., & Chattarji, S. (2002). Chronic stress induces contrasting patterns of dendritic remodeling in hippocampal and amygdaloid neurons. *Journal of Neuroscience, 22,* 6810–6818.

Watanabe, Y., Gould, E., & McEwen, B. S. (1992). Stress induces atrophy of apical dendrites of hippocampal CA3 pyramidal neurons. *Brain Research, 588,* 341–345.

Wei, Q., Hebda-Bauer, E. K., Pletsch, A., Luo, J., Hoversten, M. T., Osetek, A. J., Evans, S. J., Watson, S. J., Seasholtz, A. F., & Akil, H. (2007). Overexpressing the glucocorticoid receptor in forebrain causes an aging-like neuroendocrine phenotype and mild cognitive dysfunction. *Journal of Neuroscience, 27,* 8836–8844.

Wilson, R. S., Arnold, S. E., Schneider, J. A., Kelly, J. F., Tang, Y., & Bennett, D. A. (2006). Chronic psychological distress and risk of Alzheimer's disease in old age. *Neuroepidemiology, 27,* 143–153.

Wilson, R. S., Arnold, S. E., Schneider, J. A., Li, Y., & Bennett, D. A. (2007). Chronic distress, age-related neuropathology, and late-life dementia. *Psychosomatic Medicine, 69,* 47–53.

Witte, A. V., Fobker, M., Gellner, R., Knecht, S., & Floel, A. (2009). Caloric restriction improves memory in elderly humans. *Proceedings of the National Academy of Sciences USA, 106,* 1255–1260.

Yau, J. L., McNair, K. M., Noble, J., Brownstein, D., Hibberd, C., Morton, N., Mullins, J. J., Morris, R. G., Cobb, S., & Seckl, J. R. (2007). Enhanced hippocampal long-term potentiation and spatial learning in aged 11beta-hydroxysteroid dehydrogenase type 1 knockout mice. *Journal of Neuroscience, 27,* 10487–10496.

Zhang, M., Poplawski, M., Yen, K., Cheng, H., Bloss, E., Zhu, X., Patel, H., & Mobbs, C. V. (2009). Role of CBP and SATB-1 in aging, dietary restriction, and insulin-like signaling. *PLoS Biology, 7,* e1000245.

Zhao, C., Teng, E. M., Summers, Jr, R. G., Ming, G. L., & Gage, F. H. (2006). Distinct morphological stages of dentate granule neuron maturation in the adult mouse hippocampus. *Journal of Neuroscience, 26,* 3–11.

Part IV

Stress Involvement in Anxiety, Posttraumatic Stress Disorder, and Depression

18

Social Stress Effects on Defensive Behavior and Anxiety

Brandon L. Pearson, D. Caroline Blanchard, and Robert J. Blanchard

Introduction

Social stress has typically been defined in terms of three constructs: (1) social stressors, agonistic or winner–loser interactions involving conspecifics, or severe perturbations in the typical social structure for an animal of that species; (2) behavioral stress responses, behaviors characteristic of responses to threat, or longer-term changes in behavior that are considered to provide indices of emotional perturbation such as anxiety, elicited by social stressors; (3) physiological indices such as activation of the hypothalamic–pituitary–adrenal (HPA) axis or the sympathetic nervous system. Of the two physiological indices, HPA axis activation, typically measured as an increase in circulating glucocorticoids—corticosterone for most rodent species, cortisol for most other mammalian species—is cited more commonly in this role. Here the focus will be on the first two of these, stressors and behavioral responses, with a latter, brief, consideration of glucocorticoid levels as indices of social stress.

This approach, focusing on both immediate threat-elicited behaviors and longer-term and more general emotional changes to social stressors, suggests that one important aspect of stress is that it tends to have an impact that is to some degree *portable*, that it becomes a feature of the stressed animal and changes its behaviors in a variety of situations rather than only those closely tied to the original stressful stimulus. This is in contradistinction to a simple aversive response, whether conditioned or not, that occurs only in the immediate presence of the stressor. The distinction may be seen in an early study by Yahr (1977), who found that after being attacked several times by a resident conspecific, Mongolian gerbils showed reduced

The Handbook of Stress: Neuropsychological Effects on the Brain, First Edition.
Edited by Cheryl D. Conrad.
© 2011 Blackwell Publishing Ltd. Published 2011 by Blackwell Publishing Ltd.

scent marking to the resident's area, although they freely marked other sites, including those scented with the resident's bedding odors. They also showed suppressed marking to an area visually similar to the one in which they were defeated, but without conspecific odors. This pattern indicates that marking was not generally reduced by the defeat experience, although the specific area associated with defeat did serve to inhibit marking. Insofar as the initial encounter elicited defensive behaviors in the intruder, this would be considered a social stress, but one that appears to have had less impact on behavior in other, albeit similar, situations than might be expected.

Resource Conflict as a Focal Feature of Social Stress

Social stress is an occasional, intermittent, recurring, or sometimes even chronic event in the life of virtually every vertebrate animal. A core evolutionary factor in the ubiquity of this form of stress is that all members of the same species utilize many of the same specific resources, leading to disputes that directly or indirectly impact access to these resources. Many crucial resources, such as food and shelter, are utilized by both sexes such that competition for these resources, and the stresses this competition engenders, may be common to both males and females. However, two groups of resources are typically sex-specific. Contested breeding access provides a motive that is seen, in most species, most strongly in males, whereas prolonged maternal involvement with young, particularly in mammals, serves as another sex-differentiated motive.

Given the central role of resource conflict as a factor in the evolution of social systems, it is logical that agonistic interactions have been strongly featured in the experimental analysis of social-stress effects, in species ranging from fish (e.g., Larson et al., 2004), reptiles (e.g., Korzan and Summers, 2007), and birds (Carere et al., 2001) through a variety of mammals (albeit with an emphasis on rodents) to primates including humans (reviewed in Björkqvist, 2001; Honess and Marin, 2006). Social defeat models range from acute experiences, typically involving an intruder into the territory of a conspecific resident (Miczek and O'Donnell, 1978), to long-term group-housing studies in which dominant and subordinate animals are identified and their behaviors/physiological changes analyzed (e.g., Barnett, 1978; Blanchard et al., 1993). Somewhere along an implicit continuum from acute to chronic social-stress experience may be variations in which conspecific pairs are maintained with a barrier between them that permits all sensory modalities except those based on contact (Kudryavtseva, 1991). This barrier can be removed at intervals and winner/loser or dominant/subordinate determinations made on the basis of agonistic interactions in those intervals. Models involving a trained or selected resident have the advantage that intruders are virtually always defeated, such that defeat is not associated with individual differences that might cloud the interpretation of defeat effects, whereas the longer-term grouping situations tend to provide a more consistent and prolonged social stress.

Although most models of social stress involving dominance/subordination relationships involve at least some actual agonistic contact, this may not be required; very subtle social manipulations can also constitute effective stressors. Dominant NMRI outbred mice exposed to the sight and sound of their own individual subordinate consorting with a female in an adjacent compartment, 30 min per day for 9 days, showed a significant reduction in sexual activity when placed with a female (D'Amato et al., 2001). This interesting effect occurred without any notable changes in the dominance status of the two males when they were placed together.

Social Stress from the Lack of Social Interaction

In contrast to social stress deriving from agonistic interactions, another stressor may be the lack of a social experience that is typical for that species. Severe social isolation can produce behavioral changes in some species regardless of age. For example, isolation of mice produces effects in anxiety models based on exploratory behavior (Crawley, 1985), suggesting that the isolated mouse, while consistently shown to be more aggressive (Valzelli, 1973) is nonetheless also more stressed. Golden hamsters also appear to be stressed by isolation, with specific effects mediated by higher levels of cortisol (Wommack and Delville, 2003). For male rats, isolation appears to be less stressful than grouping, presumably reflecting that groups of male rats do fight among themselves, even when females are not present, whereas for females grouping is less stressful than isolation (Palanza, 2001). This is consonant with findings that in rats social defeat was found to be more stressful for males whereas social instability (alternating crowding with mixed-sex crowding phases) was more stressful for females (Haller et al., 1999). When social defeat was followed by isolation, anxiety-like behaviors were heightened for a substantially longer period than when the defeated animal was housed with familiar conspecifics (Ruis et al., 1999). These isolation effects were not seen in groups not subjected to social defeat (Nakayasu and Ishii, 2008), in accord with suggestions that agonistic behavior during grouping of male rats is an important factor in reduced anxiety-like behaviors for isolated males.

Given the intense social nature of most primates, it is unsurprising that isolation effects are particularly robust in this group, including humans. In the latter, isolation effects are especially damaging when experienced by adolescents (Sebastian et al., 2010), and the elderly are another especially vulnerable group, because their risk of isolation and loneliness appears to be higher than for other ages (Luanaigh and Lawlor, 2008). The group most vulnerable to the effects of social isolation, however, is likely to be the infant. The well-known studies of Harlow and his collaborators (e.g., Harlow et al., 1965; Young et al., 1973) outlined a number of severe behavioral abnormalities in infant primates reared in social deprivation, and lesser degrees of social isolation (i.e., insensitive or inadequate mothering), have since been shown to interact with particular genetic conditions to produce behavioral abnormalities (Suomi, 1997, 2006). Such effects have also been extensively documented in rodents (Anisman et al., 1998; Meaney, 2001; Millstein and Holmes, 2007). There are indications, however, from both clinical and preclinical literature, that early social deprivation is likely to produce a wider array of behavioral deficits than those associated with social defeat alone (Arborelius et al., 1999; Sánchez et al., 2001). In addition, some extensive and well-done studies of early social deprivation in rodents have failed to find evidence of anxiety enhancement (Millstein and Holmes, 2007). As the topics of early maternal deprivation and social isolation are the foci of other entries in this volume, they will not be further examined here, except to note that their behavioral consequences may not be identical to those of social defeat and related social-stress models, and that these consequences may correspond more to behavioral changes commonly grouped under the rubric of depression, than anxiety.

Defensive Behaviors and Anxiety

The first indication that a specific social event may be a stressor is that it elicits some type of immediate response that suggests aversion. In recent years a particular group of defensive behaviors has emerged as the typical response to threat, particularly animate threat (Blanchard et al., 1997). These behaviors include flight/avoidance, hiding, freezing, defensive threat, defensive attack, and others such as defensive burying or startle. The *choice* of these behaviors is determined by characteristics of the threat stimulus, including distance between the threat and the subject, and by expediting or enabling features of the situation in which the threat is encountered. These features are analyzed, and defense choices made, in a process labeled *risk assessment* (Blanchard et al., 2011).

In response to social threat, especially in highly social species, a class of submissive behaviors may be included under defense. Submissive behaviors do not do anything to remove the subject from the threat situation or to physically protect it. Instead they appear to inhibit or otherwise reduce the attack propensities of a conspecific threatener, an inhibition that is much more pronounced when the combatants are members of a highly social species in which individuals have been selected for the development of such social signals. Stereotyped submissive signals in nonhuman primates, such as nonthreatening teeth displays and rear-end presentation (Chadwick-Jones, 1989; Maestripieri, 1996), or the familiar abdominal presentation noted in canids (Schenkel, 1967), are prominent inhibitors of agonistic attack. A related category of *appeasement signals* are emitted under circumstances where social conflict is imminent or more likely to occur (Judge and DeWaal, 1997). Why the attacking animal has evolved to heed these signals relates to why the species is social in the first place: there is some evolutionarily adaptive advantage in not killing or driving off conspecifics that is greater than the resource-conflict disadvantages of having them remain in the group.

In contrast to analyses of defense, indices of anxiety have typically been developed to serve as models for preclinical testing of potentially anxiolytic drugs (Litvin et al., 2008). The core requirement for a model of anxiety is that it respond appropriately to drugs that are known to be effective against anxiety in a clinical setting. Bidirectional responses, with an opposite response to anxiety-enhancing drugs, are also good, as are clear dose–response relationships. However, because of their role in preclinical research, anxiety tests are also evaluated on the basis of additional characteristics, such as ease, speed, and simplicity of testing, with the result that in recent years there has been a movement toward the use of situations that elicit unconditioned aversive responses. The most extensively used *anxiety tasks*, such as the elevated-plus maze (EPM), open field test (OFT), and light/dark box, provide environmental features that are potentially threatening for fossorial rodents— elevated, open, or well-lit areas—and they focus on measures of avoidance or escape from these threatening stimuli. Other *anxiety* measures include inhibition of contextually high-probability behaviors such as aggression or bar-pressing for an incentive, as in a variety of conditioned inhibition tasks.

Defensive Behaviors and Anxiety Measures Following Social Stress

Tables 18.1 and 18.2 present a representative survey of studies providing defensive behaviors and anxiety measures, respectively, during or following social stress, in rats, mice, and hamsters. These social-stress studies are restricted to those in which some degree of conspecific agonistic behavior is allowed, and refer to the behavior of the defeated animal. In studies using the visible burrow system, this involved chronic cohabitation of males with females, while the mouse colonies of Reber and Neumann (2008) were all males. In all colony studies a number of fighting episodes occurred. All other defeat studies involved a resident/intruder situation with single or repeated defeats by a trained aggressor in its home cage or in the home cage of the subordinate. As noted on Table 18.1, defensive behaviors were nearly always measured either during the social-stress event itself, or 24 hr later. All defensive behaviors were measured in the context of conspecific attack or threat, and most studies in which defensive behaviors were measured after the initial social-stress event involved a new attacker.

The defensive behavior studies presented very consistent effects. Defeated animals and subordinate colony males showed a variety of defensive behaviors such as reductions in ongoing behaviors including aggression; flight, escape, evasion, and avoidance of the attacker and features associated with the attacker such as a barrier between the two; use of situational features that provided partial concealment or protection ("guarding" in Walker et al., 2009); specific postures that protected especially vulnerable sites on the defender's body from biting attack (supine, upright, sideways defense), and, for rats, ultrasonic vocalizations in the 22-kHz range that are specifically associated with aversive events and have been interpreted as alarm cries (Blanchard et al., 1991). The behavior pattern that is described as *submission* varies from species to species, and sometimes within species. In hamster studies it

Table 18.1 Social stress effects on laboratory rodent defense in the defeated animal.

Stressor	Increases in	Decreases in	When measured re: stress	Biological system	Reference(s)
Rat					
VBS subordination	–	Aggression	During	↑5-HIAA/5-HT ratio, ↓testes weight	Blanchard et al. (1993)
	Flight, on the back (supine), boxing	–	During	–	Blanchard et al. (1995)
Repeated defeat	Boxing, supine, and flight	Aggression	During	↓Testosterone	Nguyen et al. (2007)
	Upright	–	During	Associated with hyperthermia and tachycardia	Tornatzky and Miczek (1993)
	Supine, USV	–	During	Adrenergic agents bidirectionally modify	Tornatzky and Miczek (1994)
	–	Aggression	24 hr	–	Albonetti and Farabollini (1994)
	Risk assessment	Rearing	1, 8, 14, 21 days	↑ACTH, corticosterone, ↓testosterone	Razzoli et al. (2006, 2007)*
	Avoidance of barrier associated with aggressor	–	1, 21 days	–	Razzoli et al. (2009)
Single defeat	USV	–	During	Morphine in PAG reduces USV	Vivian and Miczek (1998, 1999)
	Immobility	Exploration, locomotion	24 hr	Melatonin antagonist reduces immobility	Tuma et al. (2005)*
	USV	–	During	↑CRH and GR mRNA	Marini et al. (2006)
	Active coping, guarding	–	During	Defense correlated negatively with acute corticosterone response	Walker et al. (2009)

Mouse

Repeated defeat	Avoidance, risk assessment	—	24hr	Reduced by diazepam	Lumley et al. (2000)
	Evade, upright, sideways defense	—	24hr	↑Mesolimbic DOPAC corresponds to defense	Cabib et al. (2000)
	Upright, escape	—	During	Altered with NET knockout	Haller et al. (2002)
	Defensive crouch, escape	—	24hr	Defensiveness reduced by CRH1 antagonist	Robison et al. (2004)
	Immobility, stretch attend posture	—	9, 23 days	↑ Immunosuppression, fluoxetine reduces immobility	Beitia et al. (2005)*
	Flight, upright	—	During	↑Defense inversely associated with hippocampal cell proliferation	Mitra et al. (2006)

Hamster

Repeated defeat	Submission, defense	—	24hr	Submissive behavior attenuated with nonselective CRH antagonist	Jasnow et al. (2004)
Single defeat	Submission, defense	—	24hr	Bi-directionally modulated by 5-HT$_{1A}$ receptor	Cooper et al. (2008)

5-HT, 5-hydroxytryptamine; 5-HIAA/5-HT, serotonin metabolite/5-hydroxytryptamine ratio; ACTH, adrenocorticotrophic hormone; CRH, corticotropin-releasing hormone; DOPAC, 3,4-dihydroxiphenilacetic acid (a dopamine metabolite); GR, glucocorticoid receptor; NET, norepinephrine transporter; PAG, periaqueductal gray; USV, ultrasonic vocalizations; VBS, visible burrow system.

*Studies utilizing the same social-threat stimuli during the criterion tests as during the initial stress periods, but treating changes in behavior to these stimuli under the rubric of *anxiety* or *anxiety-like* behaviors. See text for further discussion.

Table 18.2 Social stress effects on laboratory rodent anxiety.

Stressor	Increases in	Decreases in	When measured re: stress	Biological system	Reference(s)
Rat					
VBS subordination	—	Activity in OFT	During	—	Blanchard et al. (2001)
Repeated defeat	EPM open-arm time, risk assessment	Exploration	21 days	↑NE and 5-HT in the vDG, ↓DA in the mPFC and NE in dRN	Watt et al. (2009)
	Acoustic startle reflex	—	10 days	—	Pulliam et al. (2010)
	—	EPM open-arm time	Immediate	Reduced by pretreatment with CRH antisense oligodeoxynucleotide	Skutella et al. (1994); Liebsch et al. (1995)
Single defeat	—	EPM open-arm time	14–17 hr	Fluoxetine pretreatment prevents	Berton et al. (1999)
	—	EPM open-arm time	24 hr	Attenuated by GR antagonist	Calfa et al. (2006)
	—	EPM open-arm time	24 hr	↑c-Fos in dorsal and ventral hippocampus; inactivation of ventral hippocampus prevents EPM anxiety with defeat	Calfa et al. (2007)
	—	OFT center time	14 days	—	Nakayasu and Ishii (2008)

Mouse

Chronic colony subordination	–	EPM open-arm time, LDB open area time	24 hr	↓Vasopressin expression in hypothalamus	Reber and Neumann (2008)
Repeated defeat	–	EPM open-arm time	2 days	5-HT$_{1A}$ antagonist increases open-arm time	Avgustanovich et al. (2003)
	–	EPM open-arm time, LDB open area time	1, 6, 14 days	↑IL-6 and TNF in socially stressed cultured splenocytes	Kinsey et al. (2007)
	–	Pre-pulse inhibition, OFT center time	10 weeks	–	Adamcio et al. (2009)
	–	Correct self-grooming transitions	1 hr	-	Denmark et al. (2010)
	–	Locomotion, exploration	2 days	Attenuated by CRH1 antagonist	Erhardt et al. (2009)
Single defeat	–	EPM open-arm time	Immediate	Ameliorated by AVPR1b antagonist and diazepam	Griebel et al. (2002a)
	–	EPM open-arm time	Immediate	Ameliorated by CRH1 antagonist and diazepam	Griebel et al. (2002b)

5-HT, 5-hydroxytryptamine; AVPR1b, arginine vasopressin receptor 1b; CRH, corticotropin-releasing hormone; DA, dopamine; dRN, dorsal raphe nucleus; EPM, elevated-plus maze; GR, glucocorticoid receptor; IL-6, interleukin 6; LDB, light/dark box; mPFC, medial prefrontal cortex; NE, norepinephrine; OFT, open field test; TNF, tumor necrosis factor; vDG, ventral dentate gyrus.

can involve a tail-up, lordosis-like posture (Johnston, 1985) or an upright stance facing the opponent and with arms extended in a *push-off* position. In rats it means lying supine or on the back, and in mice it is an upright posture with head pushed back and forelimbs widely splayed (Beitia et al., 2005). Such submissive behaviors are often used as a specific index of defeat, and may be associated with reductions in the incidence of attack, either serving as a signal that the animal is no longer offering a challenge to the attack, or concealing particular bodily targets of attack from the attacker.

In Table 18.1, measures taken during a particular defeat experience reflect the expression of defensive behaviors during that event. Measures taken following a defeat experience reflect changes in specific behaviors for the defeated animal compared to a previously undefeated animal, either the same animal prior to its initial defeat experience or an undefeated control. These data indicate that much of the same defensive behaviors that occur during the initial defeat experience tend to be exhibited in subsequent conspecific attack situations, regardless of whether the attacker is the same or different (note, the attacker is different in all but four studies: see below). There do appear to be some species-typical effects, in that defeated hamsters show a particularly pronounced and persistent submissive behavior in subsequent agonistic situations, or that only rats, the most social of these three species, show a specific vocalization in this context. However, the general consistency of defensive behaviors across rodent species is notable, as is the finding that previous defeat can strongly enhance defensiveness generally, or submissive behaviors in particular, in subsequent encounters.

Four studies (Razzoli et al., 2006, 2007; Tuma et al., 2005; Beitia et al., 2005) utilize the same social-threat stimuli during the criterion tests as during the initial stress periods, but treat changes in behavior to these stimuli under the rubric of *anxiety* or *anxiety-like* behaviors. Nonetheless, at least some of the behaviors they report are typical defensive, rather than anxiety-like behaviors. They (indicated in the table with asterisks in the references column) tend to report enhancement of *passive* defenses such as risk assessment, stretch attend, or immobility, with reductions in more active defenses such as flight.

Such results aside, defensive behaviors and anxiety-like behaviors are usually differentiated in terms of the situations in which measurements are taken, and on specifics of the behaviors that are measured. None of the anxiety tests utilized in the studies described in Table 18.1 involve social stimuli, although the initial stressors were social. Nonetheless, comparison of the two tables, listing effects of social defeat on defensive behaviors in Table 18.1, and on anxiety-like behaviors in anxiety tests in Table 18.2 such as the EPM or the OFT, suggest a substantial relationship between the two sets of measures. Social defeat or subordination situations that increase defensive behaviors also tend to increase anxiety-like behaviors in standard anxiety tests. Specifically, social-stress experience has been reported to reduce activity and center time in the OFT, decrease open-arm time in the EPM, and increase the acoustic startle reflex. These results are extremely, but not totally, consistent: eight studies found reductions in EPM open-arm time following social defeat, whereas one (Watt et al., 2009) reported an increase in EPM open-arm time. However, the Watt et al. (2009) study was run 3 weeks after the last defeat whereas all the other social-defeat studies were run following a considerably shorter post-defeat interval, suggesting the possibility of some type of rebound effect. Nonetheless, it is notable that social-stress effects are durable, lasting up to 23 days after the last defeat in some of the colony studies.

Additional insights into the relationship between defensive behaviors and measures of anxiety can be found in attempts to evaluate the effects of anxiolytic drugs on specific defenses. In a Mouse Defense Test Battery designed to elicit a range of defensive behaviors to predator stimuli, drugs effective against generalized anxiety disorder had a very consistent effect in reducing risk assessment, defensive threat or attack, and contextual anxiety to a situation in which a predator had previously been encountered (Blanchard et al., 2001, 2003). Also, flight tended to be more consistently responsive to drugs effective against panic disorder, raising the possibility that defensive behaviors are not only involved in anxiety; they also may provide some biological differentiation for the different symptoms, and specificity of drug response, for different types of anxiety disorder.

Social Stress and Glucocorticoids

It might be thought that the approach taken in this treatment, emphasizing social-stress stimuli and behavioral stress responses, tends to denigrate the role of physiological stress responses. In fact, it is more our aim to emphasize the complexity of the HPA-axis system in particular, and to suggest that while this complexity may make the HPA system beautifully positioned to both respond to stress and to facilitate its resolution, the release of glucocorticoids may not be the most precise way to determine whether a conspecific agonistic event is a stressor.

There are a number of reasons for this view, some of them detailed in McKittrick et al. (2008). As one example, corticosteroid-binding globulin (CBG; also known as transcortin) binds these elements and prevents them from reaching their intracellular receptors. As CBG normally binds a very high proportion of total plasma glucocorticoids, a reduction in CBG can have a dramatic effect on free glucocorticoid levels. Social stress can reduce CBG as well as—or without—enhancing total glucocorticoid levels. Subordinate male rats in a visible burrow system showed, in addition to enhanced total corticosterone levels, reductions in CBG that may have raised free corticosterone levels by an order of magnitude (Blanchard et al., 1993). Subordinates also showed fewer available splenic type II corticosterone receptors, reflecting these higher levels of free corticosterone (Spencer et al., 1996). Reduced CBG levels after social stress, presumably resulting in enhanced levels of free corticosterone, have also been reported in the absence of changes in total corticosterone (Stefanski, 2000). Similarly, late-pregnancy maternal stress reduced CBG in piglets without altering plasma cortisol levels (Otten et al., 2010). Dissociation between behavioral stress indicators and cortisol in nonhuman primates further admonish the reliance upon a standard dependent variable for the effects of social stress (Elder and Menzel, 2001; Higham et al., 2009). It is not clear whether such findings might be involved in occasional reports of a failure to find glucocorticoid level differences between dominants and subordinates (e.g., Bartolomucci et al., 2001) but they serve as a caution against accepting such a lack of difference as indicative of noninvolvement of the HPA axis in the dominant/subordinate distinction.

Another complexity is that species and sex differences, and their interactions may strongly impact the relationship between social stress, glucocorticoid release, and submissive or defensive behaviors (Huhman et al., 2003). Testosterone and estrogen strongly impact CBG levels (Viau and Meaney, 2004; Qureshi et al., 2007) and may impact basal HPA axis functioning in an interactive relationship that adds to the complexity of analysis of both systems (Viau, 2002). Dominance/subordination relationships in females of many species can be based on agonistic behaviors but may also involve reproductive suppression of subordinates with little overt agonistic behavior. Moreover, female subordinates may show no change in glucocorticoids (cotton-topped tamarins, Ziegler et al., 1995), reduced glucocorticoids (marmosets, Saltzman et al., 1998), increased glucocorticoids (cynomolgous monkeys, Shively, 1998), or a more complex pattern (in primates, Abbott et al., 2003; in hyenas, Goymann et al., 2001) that does not appear to directly reflect the degree of agonistic behavior in the dominant/subordinate relationship (Creel, 2001). Other social interactions that are not typically regarded as stressful, such as copulation (Norrby et al., 2007), can also enhance glucocorticoid release.

The point here is definitely not that the HPA axis is uninvolved in social stress; but that an increase in total glucocorticoid levels in response to a given social event involving agonistic behaviors or dominance/subordination relationships may not be the best criterion for determining whether that event was stressful. As an analogy, while behavioral responses do provide indices of stress, it is likely a poor idea to use differences in EPM scores as the focal stress criterion. Increased understanding of the dynamics of the HPA axis response in relation to stress is an extremely important goal, but over-reliance on a single aspect of this as the *gatekeeper* for stress may be counterproductive in the case of agonism-based social-stress events.

Summary

Animal studies of social stress suggest a potentially important differentiation between social stress based on agonistic behavior—that is, conspecific fighting, winning/losing, dominant/subordinate situations—and social stress based on significant deprivation, particularly during critical periods, of the types of social contact that are normal for that species. The former are seen, in one form or another, in virtually all higher species, whereas the latter are particularly important in species, including all mammals, in which interactive social relationships are crucial in at least some life stages. Here, only the first of these, stress deriving from agonistic interactions, is treated in any depth, but the suggestion is made that the outcomes of the two types of social stress may be somewhat different, with a greater focus on defensive or anxiety-like behaviors following agonism-based social stressors while those involving severe deprivation of social contacts during critical periods may be more linked to depression-like symptoms. The effects of social stress based on agonistic interactions appear to be very similar to the effects of exposure to other animate dangers such as predators, in that they involve a range of defensive behaviors responsive to features of both the threat stimulus and the situation in which it is encountered. These defensive behaviors, or variants of them, may also be hyperexpressed in other situations containing some element of potential danger. In terms of this analysis, *anxiety measures* largely represent defenses applied to situations of potential danger, reflecting also that these situations (e.g., EPM, OFT) are typically simplified to the point where they support only a few functional defenses, such as avoidance or immobility.

Nonetheless, models of social stress may provide information that is different from those involving other stressors, particularly insofar as there may be individual differences in responsivity to social as opposed to other stress stimuli. As one example, a genetic mouse model of autism-like deficiencies in social responding might well show differences in response to social stressors, but not differences of similar magnitude in response to an EPM (Blanchard laboratory, unpublished results). In addition, isolation or grouping at any age may have species- and sex-differentiated stress-enhancing or stress-reducing effects that interact with other stress-induced behaviors. In highly social groups such as primates, these additional grouping effects may provide an important mechanism for modulation of stress effects.

References

Abbott, D. H., Keverne, E. B., Bercovich, F. B., Shively, C. A., Mendoza, S. P., Saltzman, W., Snowdon, C. T., Ziegler, T. E., Banjevic, M., Garland, Jr, T., & Sapolsky, R. M. (2003). Are subordinates always stressed? a comparative analysis of rank differences in cortisol levels among primates. *Hormones and Behavior*, 43(1), 67–82.

Adamcio, B., Havemann-Reinecke, U., & Ehrenreich, H. (2009). Chronic psychosocial stress in the absence of social support induces pathological pre-pulse inhibition in mice. *Behavioural Brain Research*, 204(1), 246–249.

Albonetti, M. E., & Farabollini, F. (1994). Social stress by repeated defeat: effects on social behaviour and emotionality. *Behavioural Brain Research*, 62(2), 187–193.

Anisman, H., Zaharia, M. D., Meaney, M. J., & Merali, Z. (1998). Do early-life events permanently alter behavioral and hormonal responses to stressors? *International Journal of Developmental Neuroscience*, 16(3–4), 149–164.

Arborelius, L., Owens, M. J., Plotsky, P. M., & Nemeroff, C. B. (1999). The role of corticotrophin-releasing factor in depression and anxiety disorders. *Journal of Endocrinology*, 160(1), 1–12.

Avgustinovich, D. F., Alekseyenko, O. V., & Koryakina, L. A. (2003). Effects of chronic treatment with ipsapirone and buspirone on the C57BL/6J strain mice under social stress. *Life Sciences*, 72(13), 1437–1444.

Barnett, S. A., Dickson, R. G., Marples, T. G., & Radha, E. (1978). Sequences of feeding, sampling and exploration by wild and laboratory rats. *Behavioural Processes*, *3*(1), 29–43.

Bartolomucci, A., Palanza, P., Gaspani, L., Limiroli, E., Panerei, A. E., Ceresini, G., Poli, M. D., & Parmigiani, S. (2001). Social status in mice: behavioral, endocrine and immune changes are context dependent. *Physiology & Behavior*, *73*(3), 401–410.

Beitia, G., Garmendia, L., Azpiroz, A., Vegas, O., Brain, P. F., & Arregi, A. (2005). Time-dependent behavioral, neurochemical, and immune consequences of repeated experiences of social defeat stress in male mice and the ameliorative effects of fluoxetine. *Brain Behavior and Immunity*, *19*(6), 530–539.

Berton, O., Durand, M., Aguerre, S., Mormède, P., & Chaouloff, F. (1999). Behavioral, neuroendocrine and serotonergic consequences of single social defeat and repeated fluoxetine pretreatment in the Lewis rat strain. *Neuroscience*, *92*(1), 327–341.

Björkqvist, K. (2001). Social defeat as a stressor in humans. *Physiology & Behavior*, *73*(3), 435–442.

Blanchard, R. J., Blanchard, D. C., Agullana, R., & Weiss, S. M. (1991). Twenty-two kHz alarm cries to presentation of a predator, by laboratory rats living in visible burrow systems. *Physiology & Behavior*, *50*(5), 967–972.

Blanchard, D. C., Sakai, R. R., McEwen, B., Weiss, S. M., & Blanchard, R. J. (1993). Subordination stress: behavioral, brain, and neuroendocrine correlates. *Behavioural Brain Research*, *58*(1–2), 113–121.

Blanchard, D. C., Spencer, R. L., Weiss, S. M., Blanchard, R. J., McEwen, B., & Sakai, R. R. (1995). Visible burrow system as a model of chronic social stress: behavioral and neuroendocrine correlates. *Psychoneuroendocrinology*, *20*(2), 117–134.

Blanchard, R. J., Griebel, G., Henrie, J. A., & Blanchard, D. C. (1997). Differentiation of anxiolytic and panicolytic drugs by effects on rat and mouse defense test batteries. *Neuroscience and Biobehavioral Reviews*, *21*(6), 783–789.

Blanchard, R. J., McKittrick, C. R., & Blanchard, D. C. (2001). Animal models of social stress: effects on behavior and brain neurochemical systems. *Physiology & Behavior*, *73*(3), 261–271.

Blanchard, D. C., Griebel, G., & Blanchard, R. J. (2003). The mouse defense test battery: pharmacological and behavioral assays for anxiety and panic. *European Journal of Psychology*, *463*, 97–116.

Blanchard, D. C., Griebel, G., Pobbe, R., & Blanchard, R. J. (2011). Risk assessment as an evolved threat detection process. *Neuroscience and Biobehavioral Reviews*, *35*(4), 991–998.

Cabib, S., D'Amato, F. R., Puglisi-Allegra, S., & Maestripieri, D. (2000). Behavioral and mesocorticolimbic dopamine responses to non aggressive social interactions depend on previous social experiences and on the opponent's sex. *Behavioural Brain Research*, *112*(1–2), 13–22.

Calfa, G., Volosin, M., & Molina, V. A. (2006). Glucocorticoid receptors in lateral septum are involved in the modulation of the emotional sequelae induced by social defeat. *Behavioural Brain Research*, *172*(2), 324–332.

Calfa, G., Bussolino, D., & Molina, V. A. (2007). Involvement of the lateral septum and the ventral hippocampus in the emotional sequelae induced by social defeat: role of glucocorticoid receptors. *Behavioural Brain Research*, *181*(1), 23–34.

Carere, C., Welink, D., Drent, P. J., Koolhaas, J. M., & Groothuis, T. G. G. (2001). Effect of social defeat in a territorial bird (Parus major) selected for different coping styles. *Physiology & Behavior*, *73*(3), 427–433.

Chadwick-Jones, J. K. (1989). Presenting and mounting in non-human primates: theoretical developments. *Journal of Social and Biological Systems, 12*(4), 319–333.

Cooper, M. A., McIntyre, K. E., & Huhman, K. L. (2008). Activation of 5-HT1A autoreceptors in the dorsal raphe nucleus reduces the behavioral consequences of social defeat. *Psychoneuroendocrinology, 33*(9), 1236–1247.

Crawley, J. N. (1985). Exploratory behavior models of anxiety in mice. *Neuroscience and Biobehavioral Reviews, 9*(1), 37–44.

Creel, S. (2001). Social dominance and stress hormones. *Trends in Ecology & Evolution, 16*(9), 491–497.

D'Amato, F. R., Rizzi, R., & Moles, A. (2001). A model of social stress in dominant mice: effects on sociosexual behavior. *Physiology & Behavior, 73*(3), 421–426.

Denmark, A., Tien, D., Wong, K., Chung, A., Cachat, J., Goodspeed, J., Grimes, C., Elegante, M., Suciu, C., Elkhayat, S., Bartels, B., Jackson, A., Rosenberg, M., Chung, K. M., Badani, H., Kadri, F., Roy, S., Tan, J., Gaikwad, S., Stewart, A., Zapolsky, I., Gilder, T., & Kalueff, A. V. (2010). The effects of chronic social defeat stress on mouse self-grooming behavior and its patterning. *Behavioural Brain Research, 208*(2), 553–559.

Elder, C. M., & Menzel, C. R. (2001). Dissociation of cortisol and behavioral indicators of stress in an orangutan (*Pongo pygmaeus*) during a computerized task. *Primates, 42*(4), 345–357.

Erhardt, A., Müller, M. B., Rödel, A., Welt, T., Ohl, F., Holsboer, F., & Keck, M. E. (2009). Consequences of chronic social stress on behaviour and vasopressin gene expression in the PVN of DBA/2OlaHsd mice–influence of treatment with the CRHR1-antagonist R121919/NBI 30775. *Journal of Psychopharmacology, 23*(1), 31–39.

Goymann, W., East, M. L., Wachter, B., Höner, O., Möstl, E., Van't Holf, T. J., & Hofer, H. (2001). Social, state-dependent and environmental modulation of faecal corticosteroid levels in free-ranging female spotted hyenas. *Proceedings of the Royal Society of London Series B Biological Sciences, 268*(1484), 2453–2459.

Griebel, G., Simiand, J., Serradeil-Le Gal, C., Wagnon, J., Pascal, M., Scatton, B., Maffrand, J. P., & Soubrié, P. (2002a). Anxiolytic- and antidepressant-like effects of the non-peptide vasopressin V1b receptor antagonist, SSR149415, suggest an innovative approach for the treatment of stress-related disorders. *Proceedings of the National Academy of Sciences USA, 99*(9), 6370–6375.

Griebel, G., Simiand, J., Steinberg, R., Jung, M., Gully, D., Roger, P., Geslin, M., Scatton, B., Maffrand, J. P., & Soubrié, P. (2002b). 4-(2-Chloro-4-methoxy-5-methylphenyl)-N-[(1S)-2-cyclopropyl-1-(3-fluoro-4-methylphenyl)ethyl]5-methyl-N-(2-propynyl)-1, 3-thiazol-2-amine hydrochloride (SSR125543A), a potent and selective corticotrophin-releasing factor(1) receptor antagonist. II. Characterization in rodent models of stress-related disorders. *Journal of Pharmacology and Experimental Therapeutics, 301*(1), 333–345.

Haller, J., Fuchs, E., Halász, J., & Makara, G. B. (1999). Defeat is a major stressor in males while social instability is stressful mainly in females: towards the development of a social stress model in female rats. *Brain Research Bulletin, 50*(1), 33–39.

Haller, J., Bakos, N., Rodriguiz, R. M., Caron, M. G., Wetsel, W. C., & Liposits, Z. (2002). Behavioral responses to social stress in noradrenaline transporter knockout mice: effects on social behavior and depression. *Brain Research Bulletin, 58*(3), 279–284.

Harlow, H. F., Dodsworth, R. O., & Harlow, M. K. (1965). Total social isolation in monkeys. *Proceedings of the National Academy of Sciences USA, 54*(1), 90–97.

Higham, J. P., MacLarnon, A. M., Heistermann, M., Ross, C., & Semple, S. (2009). Rates of self-directed behaviour and faecal glucocorticoid leves are not correlated in wild female olive baboons (*Papio hamadryas anubis*). *Stress, 12*(6), 526–532.

Honess, P. E., & Marin, C. M. (2006). Behavioural and physiological aspects of stress and aggression in nonhuman primates. *Neuroscience and Biobehavioral Reviews, 30*(3), 390–412.

Huhman, K. L., Solomon, M. B., Janicki, M., Harmon, A. C., Lin, S. M., Israel, J. E., & Jasnow, A. M. (2003). Conditioned defeat in male and female Syrian hamsters. *Hormones and Behavior, 44*(3), 293–299.

Jasnow, A. M., Davis, M., & Huhman, K. L. (2004). Involvement of central amygdalar and bed nucleus of the stria terminalis corticotropin-releasing factor in behavioral responses to social defeat. *Behavioral Neuroscience, 118*(5), 1052–1061.

Johnston, R. E. (1985). Communication. In H. I. Siegel (Ed.), *The hamster* (pp. 121–154). New York: Plenum.

Judge, P. G., & de Waal, F. B. M. (1997). Rhesus monkey behaviour under diverse population densities: Coping with long-term crowding. *Animal Behaviour, 54*(3), 643–662.

Kinsey, S. G., Bailey, M. T., Sheridan, J. F., Padgett, D. A., & Avitsur, R. (2007). Repeated social defeat causes increased anxiety-like behavior and alters splenocyte function in C57BL/6 and CD-1 mice. *Brain Behavior and Immunity, 21*(4), 458–466.

Korzan, W. J., & Summers, C. H. (2007). Behavioral diversity and neurochemical plasticity: selection of stress coping strategies that define social status. *Brain Behavior and Evolution, 70*(4), 257–266.

Kudryavtseva, N. N. (1991). The sensory contact model for the study of aggressive and submissive behaviors in male mice. *Aggressive Behavior, 17*(5), 285–291.

Larson, E. T., Winberg, S., Mayer, I., Lepage, O., Summers, C. H., & Øverli, Ø. (2004). Social stress affects circulating melatonin levels in rainbow trout. *General and Comparative Endocrinology, 136*(3), 322–327.

Liebsch, G., Landgraf, R., Gerstberger, R., Probst, J. C., Wotjak, C. T., Engelmann, M., Holsboer, F., & Montkowski, A. (1995). Chronic infusion of a CRH1 receptor antisense oligodeoxynucleotide into the central nucleus of the amygdala reduced anxiety-related behavior in socially defeated rats. *Regulatory Peptides, 59*(2), 229–239.

Litvin, Y., Pentkowski, N. S., Pobbe, R. L., Blanchard, D. C., & Blanchard, R. J. (2008). Unconditioned models of fear and anxiety. In R. J. Blanchard, D. C. Blanchard, G. Griebel, & D. Nutt (Eds.), *Handbook of anxiety and fear* (pp. 81–102). Amsterdam: Elsevier.

Luanaigh, C. Ó., & Lawlor, B. A. (2008). Loneliness and the health of older people. *International Journal of Geriatric Psychiatry, 23*(12), 1213–1221.

Lumley, L. A., Charles, R. F., Charles, R. C., Hebert, M. A., Morton, D. M., & Meyerhoff, J. L. (2000). Effects of social defeat and of diazepam on behavior in a resident-intruder test in male DBA/2 mice. *Pharmacology Biochemistry and Behavior, 67*(3), 433–447.

Maestripieri, D. (1996). Primate cognition and the bared-teeth display: A reevaluation of the concept of formal dominance. *Journal of Comparative Psychology, 110*(4), 402–405.

Marini, F., Pozzato, C., Andreetta, V., Jansson, B., Arban, R., Domenici, E., & Carboni, L. (2006). Single exposure to social defeat increases corticotropin-releasing factor and glucocorticoid receptor mRNA expression in rat hippocampus. *Brain Research, 1067*(1), 25–35.

McKittrick, C. R., Blanchard, D. C., Hardy, M. P., & Blanchard, R. J. (2008). Social stress effects on hormones, brain and behavior. In D. Pfaff, A. Arnold, A. Etgen, S. Fahrbach,

& R. Rubin (Eds.), Hormones and behavior (2nd ed., pp. 333–365). San Diego, CA: Academic Press.

Meaney, M. J. (2001). Maternal care, gene expression, and the transmission of individual differences in stress reactivity across generations. *Annual Review of Neuroscience, 24,* 1161–1192.

Miczek, K. A., & O'Donnell, J. (1978). Intruder-evoked aggression in isolated and nonisolated mice: effects of psychomotor stimulants and L-Dopa. *Psychopharmacology, 57*(1), 47–55.

Millstein, R. A., & Holmes, A. (2007). Effects of repeated maternal separation on anxiety- and depression-related phenotypes in difference mouse strains. *Neuroscience and Biobehavioral Reviews, 31*(1), 3–17.

Mitra, R., Sundlass, K., Parker, K. J., Schatzberg, A. F., & Lyons, D. M. (2006). Social stress-related behavior affects hippocampal cell proliferation in mice. *Physiology & Behavior, 89*(2), 123–127.

Nakayasu, T., & Ishii, K. (2008). Effects of pair-housing after social defeat experience on elevated plus-maze behavior in rats. *Behavioural Processes, 78*(3), 477–480.

Nguyen, M. M., Tamashiro, K. L., Melhorn, S. J., Ma, L.Y., Gardner, S. R., & Sakai, R. R. (2007). Androgenic influences on behavior, body weight, and body composition in a model of chronic social stress. *Endocrinology, 148*(12), 6145–6156.

Norrby, M., Madsen, M. T., Alexandersen, C. B., Kindahl, H., & Madej, A. (2007). Plasma concentrations of cortisol and PGF2 metabolite in Danish sows during mating, and intrauterine and conventional insemination. *Acta Veterinaria Scandinavica, 49*(1), 36.

Otten, W., Kanitz, E., Couret, D., Veissier, I., Prunier, A., & Merlot, E. (2010). Maternal social stress during late pregnancy affects hypothalamic-pituitary-adrenal function and brain neurotransmitter systems in pig offspring. *Domestic Animal Endocrinology, 38*(3), 146–156.

Palanza, P. (2001). Animal models of anxiety and depression: how are females different? *Neuroscience and Biobehavioral Reviews, 25*(3), 219–233.

Pulliam, J. V., Dawaghreh, A. M., Alema-Mensah, E., & Plotsky, P. M. (2010). Social defeat stress produces prolonged alterations in acoustic startle and body weight gain in male Long Evans rats. *Journal of Psychiatric Research, 44*(2), 106–111.

Qureshi, A. C., Bahri, A., Breen, L. A., Barnes, S. C., Powrie, J. K., Thomas, S. M., & Carroll, P. V. (2007). The influence of the route of oestrogen administration on serum levels of cortisol-binding globulin and total cortisol. *Clinical Endocrinology, 66*(5), 632–635.

Razzoli, M., Roncari, E., Guidi, A., Carboni, L., Arban, R., Gerrard, P., & Bacchi, F. (2006). Conditioning properties of social subordination in rats: behavioral and biochemical correlates of anxiety. *Hormones and Behavior, 50*(2), 245–251.

Razzoli, M., Carboni, L., Guidi, A., Gerrard, P., & Arban, R. (2007). Social defeat-induced contextual conditioning differentially imprints behavioral and adrenal reactivity: a time-course study in the rat. *Physiology & Behavior, 92*(4), 734–740.

Razzoli, M., Carboni, L., & Arban, R. (2009). Alterations of behavioral and endocrinological reactivity induced by 3 brief social defeats in rats: relevance to human psychopathology. *Psychoneuroendocrinology, 34*(9), 1405–1416.

Reber, S. O., & Neumann I. D. (2008). Defensive behavioral strategies and enhanced state anxiety during chronic subordinate colony housing are accompanied by reduced hypothalamic vasopressin, but not oxytocin, expression. *Annals of the New York Academy of Sciences, 1148,* 184–195.

Robison, C. L., Meyerhoff, J. L., Saviolakis, G. A., Chen, W. K., Rice, K. C., & Lumley, L. A. (2004). A CRH1 antagonist into the amygdala of mice prevents defeat-induced defensive behavior. *Annals of the New York Academy of Sciences, 1032*, 324–327.

Ruis, M. A., te Brake, J. H., Buwalda, B., De Boer, S. F., Meerlo, P., Korte, S. M., Blokhuis, H. J., & Koolhaas, J. M. (1999). Housing familiar male wildtype rats together reduces the long-term adverse behavioural and physiological effects of social defeat. *Psychoneuroendocrinology, 24*(3), 285–300.

Saltzman, W., Schultz-Darken, N. J., Wegner, F. H., Wittwer, D. J., & Abbott, D. H. (1998). Suppression of cortisol levels in subordinate female marmosets: reproductive and social contributions. *Hormones and Behavior, 33*(1), 58–74.

Sánchez M.M., Ladd C.O., & Plotsky P.M. (2001). Early adverse experience as a developmental risk factor for later psychopathology: evidence from rodent and primate models. *Development and Psychopathology, 13*(3), 419–449.

Schenkel, R. (1967). Submission: its features and function in the wolf and dog. *American Zoologist, 7*(2), 319–329.

Sebastian, C., Viding, E., Williams, K. D., & Blakemore, S. (2010). Social brain development and the affective consequences of ostracism in adolescence. *Brain and Cognition, 72*(1), 134–145.

Shively, C. A. (1998). Social subordination stress, behavior, and central monoaminergic function in female cynomolgus monkeys. *Biological Psychiatry, 44*(9), 882–891.

Skutella, T., Montkowski, A., Stöhr, T., Probst, J. C., Landgraf, R., Holsboer, F., & Jirikowski, G. F. (1994). Corticotropin-releasing hormone (CRH) antisense oligodeoxynucleotide treatment attenuates social defeat-induced anxiety in rats. *Cellular and Molecular Neurobiology, 14*(5), 579–588.

Spencer, R. L., Miller, A. H., Moday, H., McEwan, B. S., Blanchard, R. J., Blanchard, D. C., & Sakai, R. R. (1996). Chronic social stress produces reductions in available splenic type II corticosteroid receptor binding and plasma corticosteroid binding globulin levels. *Psychoneuroendocrinology, 21*(1), 95–109.

Stefanski, V. (2000). Social stress in laboratory rats: hormonal responses and immune cell distribution. *Psychoneuroendocrinology, 25*(4), 389–406.

Suomi, S. J. (1997). Early determinants of behavior: evidence from primate studies. *British Medical Bulletin, 53*(1), 170–184.

Suomi, S. J. (2006). Risk, resilience, and gene x environment interactions in rhesus monkeys. *Annals of the New York Academy of Sciences, 1094*, 52–62.

Tornatzky, W., & Miczek, K. A. (1993). Long-term impairment of autonomic circadian rhythms after brief intermittent social stress. *Physiology & Behavior, 53*(5), 983–993.

Tornatzky, W., & Miczek, K. A. (1994). Behavioral and autonomic responses to intermittent social stress: differential protection by clonidine and metoprolol. *Psychopharmacology, 116*(3), 346–356.

Tuma, J., Strubbe, J. H., Mocaër, E., & Koolhaas, J. M. (2005). Anxiolytic-like action of the antidepressant agomelatine (S 20098) after a social defeat requires the integrity of the SCN. *European Neuropsychopharmacology, 15*(5), 545–555.

Valzelli, L. (1973). The "isolation syndrome" in mice. *Psychopharmacology, 31*(4), 302–320.

Viau, V. (2002). Functional cross-talk between the hypothalamic-pituitary-gonadal and -adrenal axes. *Journal of Neuroendocrinology, 14*(6), 506–513.

Viau, V., & Meaney, M. J. (2004). Testosterone-dependent variation in plasma and intrapituitary corticosteroid binding globulin and stress hypothalamic-pituitary-adrenal activity in the male rat. *Journal of Endocrinology, 181*, 223–231.

Vivian, J. A., & Miczek, K. A. (1998). Effects of mu and delta opioid agonists and antagonists on affective vocal and reflexive pain responses during social stress in rats. *Psychopharmacology, 139*(4), 364–375.

Vivian, J. A., & Miczek, K. A. (1999). Interactions between social stress and morphine in the periaqueductal gray: effects on affective vocal and reflexive pain responses in rats. *Psychopharmacology, 146*(2), 153–161.

Walker, F. R., Masters, L. M., Dielenberg, R. A., & Day, T. A. (2009). Coping with defeat: acute glucocorticoid and forebrain responses to social defeat vary with defeat episode behaviour. *Neuroscience, 162*(2), 244–253.

Watt, M. J., Burke, A. R., Renner, K. J., & Forster, G. L. (2009). Adolescent male rats exposed to social defeat exhibit altered anxiety behavior and limbic monoamines as adults. *Behavioral Neuroscience, 123*(3), 564–576.

Wommack, J. C., & Delville, Y. (2003). Repeated social stress and the development of agonistic behavior: individual differences in coping responses in male golden hamsters. *Physiology & Behavior, 80*(2–3), 303–308.

Yahr, P. (1977). Social subordination and scent-marking in male Mongolian gerbils (Meriones unguiculatus). *Animal Behaviour, 25*(2), 292–297.

Young, L. D., Suomi, S. S., Harlow, H. F., & McKinney, W. T. (1973). Early stress and later response to separation in rhesus monkeys. *American Journal of Psychiatry, 130*(4), 400–405.

Ziegler, T. E., Scheffler, G., & Snowdon, C. (1995). The relationship of cortisol levels to social environment and reproductive functioning in female cotton-top tamarins, *Saguinus oedipus. Hormones and Behavior, 29*(3), 407–424.

19

Stress and Animal Models of Posttraumatic Stress Disorder

Hagit Cohen, Gal Richter-Levin, and Joseph Zohar

The response of an individual to stress is characterized by emotional and physical manifestations, involving the activation of various physiological systems (McEwen, 2002). The consequences of this *stress response* are generally adaptive in the short run, representing a homeostatic reaction, but in the long run can cause dysregulation of the complex cascade of mechanisms responsible for maintenance of homeostasis (allostasis) (McEwen, 2002). When the dysregulation is not overcome by the organism to reestablish and maintain homeostasis long-term changes can occur and lead to a state of chronic dysregulation and psychophysiological imbalance. In humans these states include acute stress disorder and posttraumatic stress disorder (PTSD), in keeping with the time span they occupy (American Psychiatric Association, 1994). In the first hours to days following the experience, the vast majority of individuals exposed to an extreme event will demonstrate, to a varying degree, symptoms such as intense fear, helplessness, or horror followed by anxiety, depression, agitation, shock, or dissociation, and may have trouble functioning in their usual manner for a while (Bryant, 2006; Davidson, 2006; Shalev, 2002).

Retrospective and prospective epidemiological studies indicate that most individuals affected by a potential traumatic experience will adapt within a period of 1–4 weeks following exposure (Bryant, 2006; Foa et al., 2006), and only a small proportion will develop long-term psychopathology (Bryant, 2006; Foa et al., 2006). In the United States, studies report that the rate of lifetime exposure to at least one *serious* traumatic event (excluding grief and mourning) is quite high; a conservative estimate reported 61% among men and 51% among women (Breslau et al., 1998). Other studies have found similar rates (Breslau et al., 1991; Helzer et al., 1987;

The Handbook of Stress: Neuropsychological Effects on the Brain, First Edition.
Edited by Cheryl D. Conrad.
© 2011 Blackwell Publishing Ltd. Published 2011 by Blackwell Publishing Ltd.

Resnick et al., 1995; Shore et al., 1989). The lifetime prevalence of PTSD in the general population reaches about 7% overall (Fairbank et al., 1995), suggesting that about 20–30% of individuals exposed to severe stressors will develop PTSD (Breslau et al., 1991). This figure varies depending on the type of trauma studied, where male rape victims suffer very high rates and populations exposed to natural disasters significantly less (Peri et al., 2000). The discrepancy between the proportion of the general population exposed to potentially traumatic experience and those who eventually fulfill criteria for the disorder suggests qualitative differences in vulnerability and/or resilience.

After extensive study over the past two decades, PTSD was established as a disorder and listed in the *Diagnostic and Statistic Manual* (American Psychiatric Association, 1994). A diagnosis of PTSD is made if the required symptoms are present 1 month or more after exposure to a triggering event: (1) intrusive reexperiencing of the traumatic event in the form of nightmares and flashbacks, with an exaggerated response to trauma-related reminders/cues; (2) persistent avoidance of stimuli associated with the trauma and emotional numbing; and (3) persistent symptoms of exaggerated startle response, increased physiological arousal, and sustained preparedness for an instant alarm response (American Psychiatric Association, 1994).

PTSD has severe effects on widespread areas of the individual's functioning, severely compromising quality of life, affecting the workplace, the family, and social life. Moreover, PTSD is also often comorbid with other disorders such as depressive and anxiety disorders, drug and alcohol abuse, cognitive and memory impairments, and sexual dysfunction (American Psychiatric Association, 1994). The development of PTSD is often a gradual process and extends over time through a series of stages ranging from relatively contained distress to severe disability (Solomon et al., 2005). As the disorder evolves over time, pathological changes and debilitating comorbidity may become fixed and irreversible. Unlike processes in which exposure to repeated stimuli induces a process of learning or conditioning, implying increased efficiency in processing of data to produce the required response, the psychopathology underlying PTSD produces a paradoxical vulnerability to negative sequelae upon subsequent stress exposure (Solomon et al., 2005).

The sequelae of exposure to a traumatizing stressor are subject to extensive clinical study. Clinical research often gives rise to important questions or hypotheses as to the pathogenesis, clinical course, and outcomes of such events. Among the issues raised are those relating to factors that may confer risk or resilience for the development of more severe stress-induced clinical outcomes, such as PTSD. By their nature, clinical studies raise issues concerning premorbid factors largely by means of extrapolating retrospectively. Prospective studies are near-impossible to conceive and would most probably be prohibitively expensive to put into practice.

An animal model can give a good approximation of certain aspects of the complex clinical disorder, enabling the study of questions raised in clinical research in a prospective study design and under far more controllable conditions. Animal models of psychiatric disorders offer a complementary research modality that supports clinical research. To achieve a satisfactory degree of validity and reliability, animal models of complex and intricate psychiatric disorders must fulfill certain criteria. For example, the behavioral responses must be observable and measurable, and must reliably reflect clinical symptomatology, and pharmacological agents that are known to affect symptoms in human subjects should correct, with equal efficacy, measurable parameters that model symptoms of the disorder.

Developing an animal model for PTSD is not a trivial issue. Diagnosis in human patients relies heavily on personal reports of thoughts, dreams, and images, which cannot be studied in rats. Furthermore, several of the typical symptoms of PTSD may be unique to humans and thus not be found in rats. For example, intrusive memories of the traumatic event, one of the core symptoms for PTSD in humans, cannot be translated in animal behavioral models. Likewise, an important factor of the trauma in humans is the perception of the life-threatening potential of the situation. It is not clear whether rats can make this judgment or which stressors will be most effective for rats. In addition, there is as yet no clearly effective pharmacological treatment for PTSD. It is thus difficult to test a potential rodent model for its pharmacological predictability in relation to PTSD or other traumatic stress-related disorders.

Nevertheless, using animals to study PTSD holds advantages for several reasons. First, unlike many other mental disorders, the diagnostic criteria for PTSD specify an etiological factor, which is an exposure to a life threatening, traumatic event (Nutt and Davidson, 2000). In a model for PTSD, variables such as the quality and intensity of the stressor and the degree of exposure to it can be carefully controlled, and the behavioral and concomitant physiological responses to a (valid) threatening stimulus can be studied. Second, little is known about pretrauma etiological aspects of the disorder, since, naturally, the studies so far have focused on retrospective assessments of the patients after the onset of PTSD. An animal model enables a prospective follow-up design, in which the disorder is triggered at a specified time and in a uniform manner, in controllable and statistically sound population samples, and enables the assessment of behavioral and gross physiological parameters. Moreover, unlike studies in human subjects, animal model studies enable the assessment of concomitant biomolecular changes in dissected brain areas, and experimentation with pharmacological agents with potential therapeutic effects.

This chapter will present and discuss findings from various animal models of PTSD, which differ from one another in the rational for their development. These models use different paradigms but show a range of behavioral and physiological manifestations seen in PTSD patients. Moreover, we will present findings from a series of studies employing a model of individual behavioral response classification. A brief introduction to the standard stress paradigm, the standard behavioral methods, and the definition of the cut-off behavioral criteria (CBC) employed for classification will precede this.

Animal Models of PTSD

Trauma/stress-based models

Stress paradigms in animal studies aim to model criterion A of the *Diagnostic and Statistic Manual* diagnostic criteria (American Psychiatric Association, 1994). They thus use extremely stressful experiences aimed at engendering a sense of threat and helplessness in the animal. Some of these have focused more on the intensity of the experience, whereas others have combined intensity with an attempt to design an ethologically valid experience, one which an animal might encounter in its natural environment.

Exposure of rodents to predator stimuli (cat, cat odor, fox odor, or trimethylthi-azoline, a synthetic compound isolated from fox feces) is fear-provoking and stress-ful and produces long-lasting behavioral and physiological responses. Blanchard et al. (1990, 1998), Adamec (Adamec, 1997; Adamec and Shallow, 1993), and others (Cohen et al., 1996, 1999, 2000; Diamond et al., 2006; File et al., 1993; Griebel et al., 1995) have established the validity of this paradigm, in which adult rodents are exposed to feline predators for 5–10 min in a closed environment (i.e., inescap-able exposure). The resultant freezing response mode is ethologically adaptive for animals in situations where both *fight* and *flight* options are ineffective. Predator stress has ecological validity in that it mimics brief, intense, threatening experiences with lasting affective consequences (Adamec et al., 2006b, 2006c). The predator stress paradigm has proven to be effective in inducing the expected range of behav-ioral and physiological responses (Adamec et al., 2006a, 2006b, 2007; Nutt and Davidson, 2000). These include freezing, avoidance, increased secretion of stress hormones, and changes in transmission from the hippocampus via the ventral angular bundle to the basolateral amygdala, and from the central amygdala to the lateral column of the periaqueductal gray (Adamec et al., 2006a, 2007; Apfelbach et al., 2005; Blanchard et al., 2003; Blundell et al., 2005; Cohen et al., 1996, 1999, 2000; Diamond et al., 2006; Endres et al., 2005; File et al., 1993; Kozlovsky et al., 2007a, 2007b; Mazor et al., 2009; Roseboom et al., 2007; Sullivan and Gratton, 1998; Takahashi et al., 2005). These pathways are of interest because neuroplastic changes within them are associated with aversive learning. The potency of predator stimuli is comparable to that of a variety of paradigms in which the threat is more tangible and immediate, such as paradigms based on inescapable pain or electric shock, swimming and near-drowning, a small raised platform, and even direct proximity to a kitten or a cat (separated by a mesh divide or a solid divide with an opening large enough for the rodent to slip through).

Richter-Levin (1998) has developed an interesting stress model, the underwater trauma. Although rats naturally swim well and are able to dive and to cope with exposure to water, brief (30–45 s), uncontrollable restraint under water establishes an ethologically relevant traumatic experience. Exposure of rats to underwater trauma results in long-lasting, heightened anxiety and context-specific spatial memory deficits (Cohen et al., 2004; Richter-Levin, 1998); underwater trauma in a different (out-of-context) water container has no effects on the ability of rats to perform a spatial memory task in the water maze. These results may explain the lack of effect of inescapable tail-shock procedure on spatial performance reported by others (Warren et al., 1991), because in their study the stressor was not associated with the context of the maze. Moreover, underwater trauma results in both behavioral and electrophysiological aversive effects. Twenty minutes after the trauma the traumatized rats performed poorly in the spatial memory task in the water maze, and 40 min after the tetanic stimulation (100 min after the underwater trauma) they showed a reduced level of long-term potentiation. Thus, the underwater trauma induces electrophysiological alterations, which resemble those observed in other models of stress (Diamond and Rose, 1994). In addition, the impaired performance in the water maze was significantly correlated with the reduced ability to induce long-term potentiation. These findings of a strong correlation between long-term potentiation and spatial learning suggest that these two phenomena are related. However, it is possible that the trauma impairs performance not by affecting memory but by affecting memory-related processes such as attention. It was suggested that the underwater trauma could provide an important and potentially powerful model for understanding the mechanisms underlying the relationships among stress, cognition, and learning.

Mechanism-based models

Another approach in developing animal models of PTSD has been to consider potential brain mechanisms that may underlie the disorder and to develop behavioral protocols that would mimic the activation of such mechanisms.

Enhanced fear conditioning

The persistence of the psychological and biological fear responses could not be satisfactorily explained by the stress theory, leading some to suggest that fear conditioning might underlie the phenomenon (Yehuda and LeDoux, 2007). In certain respects, fear conditioning resembles PTSD (Milad et al., 2006). During Pavlovian fear conditioning, a neutral conditioned stimulus (CS; usually a tone or light) is repeatedly paired with an unconditioned stressful stimulus (US; usually a foot shock). Once the CS/US association has been formed, the CS produces a conditioned fear response—such as freezing (or movement arrest), enhancement of musculature (startle) reflexes, autonomic changes, analgesia, and behavioral response suppression—in anticipation of the US (Dunsmoor et al., 2007; LeDoux, 1996). A conditioned response is also evoked when the animal is placed in the environment in which the experiment took place. Translating to PTSD, the traumatic event (US) triggers an unconditioned response, which is characterized by strong arousal and intense fear. This unconditioned response becomes associated with cues, such as smells, voices, or sights (CSs) that were present during the traumatic event. As a result of this pairing, these cues can trigger similar responses (conditioned responses) even in the absence of the US (Blechert et al., 2007). Thus, given the association between traumatic recall and seemingly unrelated stimuli and the ensuing fearful response, the mechanism of enhanced fear conditioning has often been suggested as a model for the reexperiencing phenomena in PTSD (Foa and Kozak, 1986; LeDoux, 2000; Maren, 2001).

Impaired extinction

Conditioned fear responses can be extinguished by repeatedly presenting the CS without the US (Milad et al., 2006). Pavlov, in his classic investigation of appetitive conditioning in dogs, observed that extinguished responses spontaneously recovered with the passage of time (Milad et al., 2006). This suggested that extinction suppresses, rather than erases, the original CS/US association. Thus, extinction is an important behavioral phenomenon that allows the organism to adapt its behavior to a changing environment (Bouton, 2004). Moreover, experimental extinction is a behavioral technique leading to suppression of the acquired fear; that is, a decrease in the amplitude and frequency of a conditioned response as function of nonreinforced CS presentations (Akirav and Maroun, 2007). More recently, impaired extinction learning has been proposed as an alternative mechanism for the formation of PTSD symptoms (Maren and Chang, 2006; Myers and Davis, 2002).

Recently, a prominent role for medial prefrontal cortex–amygdala–hippocampus circuits has been suggested in the contextual modulation of the extinction of fear memory. The current neurocircuitry model for PTSD hypothesizes hyperresponsivity within the amygdala to threat-related stimuli, with inadequate top-down governance over the amygdala by ventromedial prefrontal cortex (encompassing the rostral anterior cingulated cortex, subcallosal cortex, and anterior cingulated cortex), orbitofrontal cortex, and the hippocampus (Rauch et al., 2006). The decreased medial prefrontal cortex inhibition of the amygdala prevents retention of extinction learning, thus allowing reinstatement of the conditioned fear response. Interestingly, neuroimaging data support the current neurocircuitry model of PTSD and provide evidence for heightened responsivity of the amygdala, diminished responsivity of the medial prefrontal cortex, diminished hippocampal volumes and integrity, and impaired hippocampal function in PTSD (De Bellis et al., 2002; Etkin and Wager, 2007; Liberzon and Sripada, 2008; Rauch et al., 2006).

Impaired contextualization

A different mechanism that may contribute to the development of PTSD symptoms is the inability to appropriately *contextualize* the traumatic events in autobiographic memory. Clinically, PTSD patients relive their traumatic experiences repeatedly, unable to assimilate them as time- and context-limited events without negative implications for their future. For example, for a combat veteran, the sound of a passing helicopter in the current, objectively safe environment can evoke the traumatic experience of combat that took place years earlier. Deficient embedding or contextualization of the traumatic events in autobiographic memory is thought to be one of the main problems in PTSD (Ehlers and Clark, 2000).

We have recently developed a novel experimental paradigm, differential contextual-odor conditioning (DCOC), to examine an animal's abilities to discriminate between the significance of an odor cue acquired in either safe or dangerous contextual environments when encountered in a novel, neutral environment. The odor cue consists of a cinnamon smell that could signal either reward or punishment (safety or threat signal) depending on the contextual cues that are present. Each of the conditions was learned in a different chamber. Animals were tested in a third, new chamber, so all other contextual cues were controlled for and the only previously encountered cue that was present was the cinnamon odor (Cohen et al., 2009). Our findings demonstrate that in this novel experimental paradigm animals trained in the DCOC paradigm acquired the ability to discriminate between contextual cues signaling safe and those signaling dangerous contextual environments, validating the DCOC paradigm for the assessment of contextualization. Exposure to severe traumatic stress (predator scent stress, PSS) interfered with processes related to subsequent adequate and flexible application of contextualization. Traumatized animals were unable to acquire the ability to accurately evaluate the contextual relevance of an odor stimulus or lost this ability after having effectively acquired it. Thus, the DCOC paradigm is suggested as an effective animal model that would enable the study of the neurobiology of contextualization and of related pathology (Cohen et al., 2009).

Individual differences in response to an exposure to a traumatic experience

Researchers who work with animals have long been aware that individual study subjects tend to display a varying range of responses to stimuli, certainly where stress paradigms are concerned. This heterogeneity in responses was accepted for many years and regarded as unavoidable. Since humans clearly do not respond homogeneously to potentially traumatic experience, the heterogeneity in animal responses might be regarded as confirming the validity of animal studies, rather than as a problem. It stands to reason that a model of diagnostic criteria for psychiatric disorders could be applied to animal responses to augment the validity of study data, as long as the criteria for classification are clearly defined, are reliably reproducible, and yield results that conform to findings in human subjects. Of course, different study paradigms may give rise to different sets of criteria.

Behavioral assessments

A variety of mazes and open environments have been employed to assess changes in exploratory behavior resulting from stress exposure. These test environments assess behaviors whose disruption indicates anxiety-like fearful behaviors and behaviors reflecting avoidance. Various learning and memory tasks are employed in which both exploration and learned task performance can be assessed. Some studies have investigated social behavior in home cages and in challenge situations. The startle response, which characterizes many PTSD patients, has been employed as one of the more definitively measurable parameters for the hypervigilant/hyperalert component of the behavioral responses (File et al., 1993). In the studies presented below exploratory behavior on the elevated-plus maze (EPM) serves as the main platform for the assessment of overall behavior, and the acoustic startle response (ASR) paradigm provides a precise quantification of hyperalertness, in terms of magnitude of response and habituation to the stimulus. For details regarding these tests, see Cohen et al. (2003, 2004) and Cohen and Zohar (2004).

As to the timing of behavioral assessments, a large number of studies performed in a range of research centers indicate quite clearly that behavioral changes that are observed in rodents at Day 7 after stress exposure are unlikely to change significantly over the next 30 days (Cohen et al., 2004). The average life expectancy for the domestic rat is between 2.5 and 3 years. Hence, behavioral patterns observed at Day 7 can reliably be taken to represent PTSD-like responses (i.e., *translating* a week for a rat to a month for a human).

Classification according to cut-off behavioral criteria

Data from a large series of studies had previously shown that 7 days after a single 10-min predator scent exposure the overall exposed population displayed significantly decreased time spent in the open arms and increased time in the closed arms of the EPM (which is translated to *avoidant* and *anxiety-like behavior*), and higher mean startle responses as compared to control rats (Figure 19.1). It is important to note that the rats' behavior was not uniformly disturbed, but rather demonstrated a broad range of variation in response severity. The pooled data were reexamined for definable behavioral criteria and revealed a group of animals whose behavioral response patterns clearly demonstrated no significant difference from unexposed control animals, and a second group whose responses to both test paradigms were equally significantly at the extreme end on all measures. Each of these groups was significantly distinct from animals whose behavior lay between the extremes.

The behavioral measures for each of these groups on the EPM and ASR tests were employed to define the basic CBCs. Since clinical diagnostic criteria require a sufficient number of symptoms from three symptom clusters in order to achieve satisfactory diagnostic specificity, the CBC response classification process requires that a given rat fulfill all criteria on both tests, performed in series. The standard algorithm for the CBC classification model also requires that, prior to classification, a significant overall effect be demonstrated (Figure 19.2).

The CBCs enable us to clearly classify a given rat as displaying extreme behavioral response (EBR) or minimal behavioral response (MBR)—that is, extreme responses on both EPM and ASR tests lead to classification as EBR, whereas minimal responses

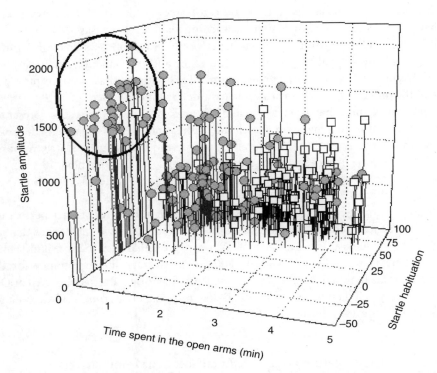

Figure 19.1 The effect of single PSS exposure versus unexposed control on rat anxiety-like behavior and acoustic startle response. Three-dimensional parameters: the x-axis represents time spent in the open arms (min), the y-axis represents acoustic startle amplitude, and the z-axis shows startle habituation. Squares represent the unexposed control group. Circles represent the exposed group. Within the PSS-exposed population a broad range of variation in behavioral response was observed and several subgroups were identifiable. In the exposed group 38 rats (25.3%) fulfilled criteria for extreme behavioral response (EBR), whereas 37 rats (24.7%) were characterized as minimal behavioral responders (MBR). All other rats fell between the CBCs for the extreme groups, and were defined as subthreshold. In the control group only two rats (1.33%) fulfilled criteria for EBR whereas the majority (120 rats, 80.0%) were well adapted (MBR).

are defined as MBR—both of which have been validated in a large series of studies. The remaining rats display clearly disrupted behavior patterns compared to controls, but the extent of the disruption does not cross the threshold for EBR. These are labeled partial behavioral responders (PBR) and have as yet not been further subclassified (Cohen and Zohar, 2004).

The pooled behavioral data for entire PSS-exposed populations were reexamined according to the CBCs, revealing that the overall prevalence rate for EBR rats was approximately 25%, as compared to 1.3% in unexposed control populations. The prevalence of MBR rats in the PSS-exposed groups was 24.7% as compared to 80.0% in the control groups.

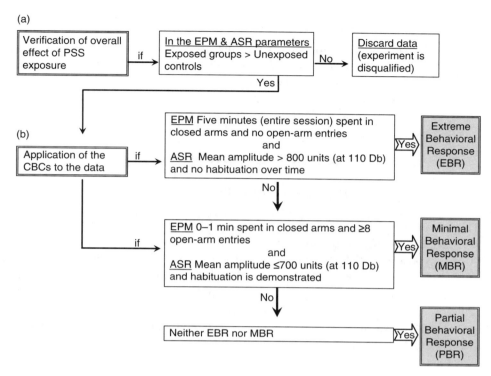

Figure 19.2 The CBC algorithm. In order to approximate the approach to understanding animal behavioral models more closely to contemporary clinical conceptions of PTSD, we use an approach that enables the classification of study animals into groups according to degree of response to the stressor; that is, the degree to which individual behavior is altered or disrupted. To achieve this, behavioral criteria were defined and then complemented by the definition of cut-off criteria reflecting severity of response; this parallels inclusion and exclusion criteria applied in clinical research. The procedure requires the following steps. (a) Verification of global effect: the data must demonstrate that the stressor had a significant effect on the overall behavior of exposed versus unexposed populations at the time of assessment. (b) Application of the CBCs to the data: to maximize the resolution and minimize false-positive results, extreme responses to both EPM and ASR paradigms, performed in sequence, were required for *inclusion* into the EBR group, whereas a negligible degree of response to both was required for inclusion in the MBR group.

The implication of this initial finding was that all prior study analyses must have included a significant proportion of animals whose behavior had not been affected by the stressor (MBR) and many animals whose response was of uncertain significance (PBR), alongside those whose response was unequivocally one of severely disrupted behavioral patterns (EBR). Hence, the method offered a feasible means for classifying animal response patterns to trauma, thereby increasing the conceptual accuracy of the data.

It is of interest to note that the proportion of the entire exposed population fulfilling criteria for extreme responses (EBR) was compatible with epidemiological data for PTSD among trauma-exposed human populations (Breslau et al., 1991), which report that between 15 and 35% fulfill criteria for PTSD and that approximately 20–30% display partial or subsymptomatic clinical pictures (Breslau et al., 1998; Resnick et al., 1995). This compatibility further supports the concept of criterion-based classification in terms of face validity.

Selected CBC-based Studies

Behavioral response patterns versus time

Time is an integral factor in traumatic stress-induced disorders. The prevalence rates of EBR rats were assessed among PSS-exposed rats on days 1, 3, 5, 7, 30, and 90 after exposure. Initially (Day 1), almost all animals displayed extreme disruptions of behavior (EBR = 90%). The proportion of EBR animals dropped rapidly over Days 1 and 3 and between Days 3 and 5 to about 25% at Day 7. This proportion remained stable until Day 30, dropping to about 15% by Day 90. The resulting time curve of EBR prevalence rates parallels the rates of stress-related symptoms in humans, culminating in acute and chronic traumatic stress disorders (Cohen et al., 2004).

Gender differences

Traditionally, women have been considered to be significantly more vulnerable to stress-related psychopathology, especially PTSD, than men (Olff et al., 2007). However, epidemiological data regarding gender differences in the prevalence of PTSD following traumatic experiences are contradictory (Breslau et al., 1999; Brewin et al., 2000; Freedman et al., 2002; Robin et al., 1997). Few animal models of PTSD have taken gender differences into account and have typically used male subjects. To explore gender-related PTSD-like stress-responses more thoroughly, we applied an animal model that focuses selectively on individual patterns of behavioral responses. The analysis of individual patterns of behavioral response to PSS exposure revealed that, although the global data for the entire populations appeared to indicate that males and females responded differently, in fact the prevalence rate of severely affected animals was not significantly affected by gender. Although baseline levels of stress were higher for females and their peak levels (expressing magnitude of response) were lower, the overall incidence of PTSD-like behavioral responses was the same for both genders (Mazor et al., 2009).

Physiological correlates

Physiological data were correlated with behavioral classification in a series of studies, including the hypothalamic–pituitary–adrenal (HPA) axis (circulating corticosterone, dehydroepiandrosterone and its sulphate derivative dehydroepiandrosterone-sulphate levels), autonomic nervous system (heart rate and heart-rate variability) (Cohen et al., 2003, 2007a), and immune system (Cohen et al., 2006b). Although the gross population data had shown that the parameters in each study displayed significant responses to the stressor, CBC classification revealed that animals whose behavior conformed to EBR criteria were characterized by significantly more disturbances on all measures, whereas MBR rats displayed almost none.

Strain/genetic studies

The CBC classification model was applied to genetically manipulated rodent strains to examine two aspects of PTSD. One study assessed the HPA-axis response in rat strains inbred to have either deficient or excessive HPA-axis responsiveness, compared to outbred rats. The other examined the heritability of vulnerability versus resilience factors using inbred (near-isogenic) mouse strains exposed to PSS and classified according to the CBC method.

HPA-axis response in Lewis and Fischer rats

PTSD has been associated with disordered levels of circulating cortisol, an integral component of the stress response (increased levels according to some studies, and decreased in others; Bremner et al., 1997; Delahanty et al., 2000; Mason et al., 1986; Pitman and Orr, 1990; Rasmusson et al., 2001; Yehuda, 2005; Yehuda et al., 2007). The study (Cohen et al., 2006c) examined whether low basal cortisol levels represent a consequence of traumatic exposure (i.e., possible neurotoxic effects of trauma) or a predisposing trait for pathological stress reactions in populations of inbred Lewis and Fischer rats compared to outbred Sprague–Dawley rats (controls). Lewis rats exhibit a reduced synthesis and secretion of corticotropin-releasing hormone, leading to reduced plasma adrenocorticotropic hormone, and reduced corticosterone release from the adrenal cortex, whereas Fischer rats possess a hyper-responsive HPA axis. After PSS exposure, prevalence rates of EBR individuals were significantly higher in Lewis (50%) than in Fischer rats (10%), or controls (25%) (Cohen et al., 2006c). However, exogenous administration of cortisol to Lewis rats before applying the stressor decreased the prevalence of EBR significantly (to 8%). These results suggest that a blunted HPA-axis response to stress may play a role in the susceptibility to experimentally induced PTSD-like behavioral changes, especially as these effects were reversed by preexposure administration of corticosterone (Cohen et al., 2006c).

Stress-induced behavioral responses in inbred mouse strains

Twin and family studies of PTSD patients raise questions as to a possible genetic predisposition to PTSD, although the relative contributions of genotype and environment to endophenotypic expression are unclear. Six inbred strains of mice frequently employed in transgenic research were assessed at baseline and 7 days after PSS exposure (Cohen et al., 2007b). Inbred strains are expected to demonstrate approximately 97.5% homozygosity of loci, as the result of at least 20 generations of sibling matings. The results, however, revealed an unexpectedly high degree of within-strain individual heterogeneity at baseline and a high degree of heterogeneity in response to stress. This within-strain phenotypic heterogeneity might imply that environmental factors play a significant role in characterizing individual responses, in spite of the significant strain-related (i.e., genetic) underpinnings. This study suggests that heritable factors may be involved only in part of the endophenotypes associated with the PTSD-like behavioral phenotype and may be influenced indirectly by interactions with environmental variables (Caspi and Moffitt, 2006).

Molecular neurobiological correlates

Selected brain areas, especially hippocampal substructures and frontal cortex, of rats classified according to the CBC procedure have been studied in correlation to both their behavioral and physiological response patterns. The studies have examined the expression of genes and gene products for key intracellular and intercellular biomolecules associated with neuromodulation, synaptic plasticity, and receptor systems. In some studies these data have also been correlated to individual performance on memory-related tasks.

The development of an extreme behavioral response has been shown to be associated with a distinct pattern of long-term and persistent downregulation of brain-derived neurotrophic factor (mRNA and protein levels) and synaptophysin, and an upregulation of glucocorticoid receptor protein levels and tyrosine kinase receptor mRNA in the CA1 subregion of the hippocampus (where CA means cornu ammonis, a subregion of the hippocampus), compared to PBR and MBR animals and to unexposed controls (Kozlovsky et al., 2007b, 2009). Moreover, EBR individuals selectively displayed significant downregulation of growth-associated protein 43, signal-regulated kinase mitogen-activated protein kinase (extracellular signal-regulated kinase 1/2; ERK1/2) and phospho-ERK1/2, p38 and phospho-38 and upregulation of postsynaptic density-95 in the hippocampus, compared to MBR, PBR, and unexposed controls (Kozlovsky et al., unpublished results). The persistently higher levels of glucocorticoids are associated with attenuation of brain-derived neurotrophic factor and synaptophysin, and expression of zif/268 and immediate early genes such as activity-regulated cytoskeletal-associated protein (Arc) in the EBR individuals; this suggests that glucocorticoids reflect or mediate the characteristic changes in neural plasticity and synaptic functioning underlying chronic, stress-induced behavioral disruption (Kozlovsky et al., 2007a). Taken together, decreased hippocampal expression of these genes may have physiological consequences, for example, inducing damage to hippocampal neurons.

Drug studies and molecular neurobiology

Selective serotonin-reuptake inhibitors (SSRIs) and other antidepressant drugs have been found to reinforce synaptic strength in mood-related brain regions in a manner akin to that achieved in experimental models of synaptic plasticity (Duman, 2002; Manji et al., 2001). Pei et al (2003) reported that repeated administration of the monoamine-reuptake inhibitors paroxetine, venlafaxine, or desipramine induces region-specific increases in *Arc* mRNA (in the frontal and parietal cortices and hippocampal CA1 area). Thus, whereas downregulation of *Arc* mRNA has been shown to promote stress-induced psychopathology in synaptic networks, long-term administration of SSRIs, etc., might prevent or reverse this effect. Taken together, SSRIs might, therefore, be able to protect and/or to rescue the functional integrity of neuronal circuitry from the effects of stress (Kozlovsky et al., 2007a).

Pharmacotherapeutic interventions

Acute-phase pharmacotherapeutic interventions that effectively alleviate symptoms and possess potential preventive effects on the development of PTSD and that are founded on large-scale, double-blind, controlled, prospective clinical trials are lacking. The CBC classification model affords distinct advantages for the prospective study of the therapeutic and preventive potential of medications. The model enables the prospective study of associations between the behavioral efficacy of the drug in question, in a quantifiable manner over specific periods of time, and the biomolecular and physiological correlates of these behavioral effects. The CBC model has been applied to the study of a number of drugs: an SSRI (sertraline), corticosteroids, and a benzodiazepine (alprazolam).

Early intervention with an SSRI (sertraline)
Based on the rationale that the acute phase in rodents is represented by the first 7 days following stress exposure (see subsection on the behavioral response patterns versus time), rats were randomly allocated to 7 days of treatment either immediately following exposure or as of Day 7, and compared to saline treatment. Behavioral and biomolecular assessments performed at Day 7 (or Day 14) demonstrated the following: brief immediate postexposure intervention with sertraline had an observable short-term effect on stress-induced behavioral changes compared to the later treatment regimen, and compared to the saline-treated control group (Matar et al., 2006). Seven days of treatment with sertraline immediately after PSS exposure elicited a statistically significant reduction (14%) in prevalence rates of EBR and an increase of 5% in prevalence rates of minimal response (MBR) compared to the placebo-control group. These finding suggest that SSRI drugs represent potential agents for secondary intervention in the acute aftermath of traumatic stress exposure and are thus worthy of further investigation.

Early intervention with corticosterone
Since corticosteroid treatment is clinically indicated only in cases in which there is significant physical illness or polytrauma, recurrent clinical reports of a significant

preventive effect in terms of the incidence of concomitant PTSD are difficult to interpret, despite their relative frequency and impressive results (Schelling et al., 2004). The CBC model was employed to examine the effect of a single high-dose intervention with the adrenocorticoid stress hormone corticosterone given imme-diately after exposure. This regimen was compared to lower doses, later treatment, and saline. Stress-induced behavioral responses were assessed at Day 30 and trauma cue-triggered freezing response was assessed on Day 31.

The results clearly showed that a single 25 mg/kg dose of corticosterone admin-istered immediately after exposure to the scent of predator urine resulted in a statistically significant reduction of 13.2% in the prevalence rates of EBR individuals at 30 days, with a concomitant increase of 12.4% in the prevalence of MBR indi-viduals, as compared to saline-controls; that is, a significant shift towards less extreme behavioral disruption ensuing from traumatic stress (Cohen et al., 2008). Rats in the high-dose corticosterone group responded markedly less extremely to exposure to the trauma cue (24% of time freezing) than the saline-control group (80% of time freezing). This pattern of response suggests that the single high-dose corticosterone treatment confers some degree of resilience to future trauma-related stress exposure (Cohen et al., 2008). Lower doses of corticosterone (0.1–5.0 mg/kg) were ineffective in attenuating behavioral disruptions, significantly increased the prevalence of EBR at Day 30 and significantly increased vulnerability to the trauma cue as compared to placebo.

The marked attenuation of the response of treated individuals to the trauma cue 31 days after exposure is of significance. The time frame in which corticosterone was administered (1 hr after stress exposure) conforms to the time frame within which the memory-consolidation process takes place at the cellular level (3–6 hr after initiation of data acquisition). The time at which the effect was assessed was sufficiently distant from the initial exposure as to suggest that the effect was medi-ated by memory-related processes. Furthermore, the same pattern was observed in another study, where the protein-synthesis inhibitor anisomycin was effective when administrated within an hour after exposure, but not when administered later on (after reactivation of the trauma by a trauma cue; Cohen et al., 2006a). This may suggest that the single high-dose corticosterone treatment interfered similarly, by disrupting consolidation of short-term memory to long-term memory (Cohen et al., 2008).

Early intervention with benzodiazepine (alprazolam)

Benzodiazepines are commonly used to relieve distress. Since it has been claimed that they impede adequate processing of acute grief, their effects on the processing of acute stress were examined. The CBC model was employed to examine the short-term efficacy and the long-term potential of brief, early postexposure admin-istration of a commonly prescribed benzodiazepine (alprazolam) for the prevention of subsequent PTSD-like behavioral changes and to examine its effects on subse-quent vulnerability to stress, compared to later treatment and placebo. As expected, the results demonstrated short-term efficacy, but no preventive potential. The finding that caused particular concern was that rats treated immediately after the initial exposure were rendered significantly more vulnerable to the trauma cue and by far more vulnerable to reexposure to PSS than control groups. Treatment initiated after 1 week did not affect vulnerability (Matar et al., 2009). It will be important to establish whether this finding is replicable and whether it is related to specific benzodiazepines and/or a certain time frame, in both animal and clinical studies. One possible mechanism might be related to the effect of alprazolam on cortisol secretion. The marked suppression of corticosterone activity during alprazolam treatment and the sharp rebound after its cessation may well be key factors in the pathogenesis of the different behavioral responses observed in the study subjects when treatment was initiated immediately. Since corticosterone plays a major role in the regulation of responses to stress, alterations in timing, and polarity of plasma corticosterone levels may be of great pathogenetic significance, especially in the earliest phases (Matar et al., 2009).

The results of studies such as those on early corticosterone administration, early SSRI administration, and others might shed some light on the intriguing question of whether PTSD be prevented.

Can PTSD Be Prevented?

After a trauma, certain medical sequelae can be ameliorated or even prevented if intervention occurs within a particular window of opportunity. This window of time has been given the euphemism *the golden hour(s)*, as intervention in that time is particularly effective. Several examples of this are well established. For example, in thrombotic cerebular vascular accident, there is a 3-hr window from the onset in which clot-busting drugs can be administered to relieve the thrombosis. In heart attack, reperfusion of the infarct-related artery in the first hour significantly reduces mortality rates. The principle is that immediate intervention is given to prevent or decrease the impending (usually devastating) sequelae of those events, which often trigger a chain of pathological processes. If the right intervention is given during the window of opportunity, it might dramatically improve outcome (Zohar et al., 2009).

Is there a golden hour in psychiatry? Can intervention right after exposure to traumatic events attenuate the pathological response that we refer to as PTSD? Ultimately, PTSD prevention, via either pharmacological or psychological mechanisms or a combination of both, may require the identification of a broader range of factors, including genetic or epigenetic modifications that underlie failure of reinstatement of physiological homeostasis. Potential targets for future intervention may be neurogenesis, the HPA axis, and other factors that enhance resilience, whether through decreasing the impact of the traumatic memory or via other, yet to be explored, mechanisms. In any event, it seems that the type of intervention in the golden hours in PTSD might be a key element in the odyssey to find out how PTSD can be prevented.

Conclusions

Animal models may complement clinical research and enable modalities that are difficult to attain in clinical studies. The animal model presented here, which is a combination of exposure to a predator and a focus on setting apart the affected based on behavioral cut-off criteria, has demonstrated high face validity, construct validity, and predictive validity. The cumulative results of our studies indicate that the contribution of animal models can be further enhanced by classifying individual animal study subjects according to their response patterns. This approach enables researchers to test interventions that might be impossible (e.g., anisomycin) or difficult (e.g., benzodiazepine, SSRI, cortisol) to do in a clinical setting without any proper preclinical basis. The animal model also enables the researcher to go one step further and correlate specific anatomic biomolecular and physiological parameters with the degree and pattern of individual behavioral response.

References

Adamec, R. (1997). Transmitter systems involved in neural plasticity underlying increased anxiety and defense–implications for understanding anxiety following traumatic stress. *Neuroscience and Biobehavioral Reviews, 21*, 755–765.

Adamec, R. E., & Shallow, T. (1993). Lasting effects on rodent anxiety of a single exposure to a cat. *Physiology & Behavior, 54*, 101–109.

Adamec, R., Head, D., Blundell, J., Burton, P., & Berton, O. (2006a). Lasting anxiogenic effects of feline predator stress in mice: sex differences in vulnerability to stress and predicting severity of anxiogenic response from the stress experience. *Physiology & Behavior, 88*, 12–29.

Adamec, R., Strasser, K., Blundell, J., Burton, P., & Mckay, D. W. (2006b). Protein synthesis and the mechanisms of lasting change in anxiety induced by severe stress. *Behavioral Brain Research, 167*, 270–286.

Adamec, R. E., Blundell, J., & Burton, P. (2006c). Relationship of the predatory attack experience to neural plasticity, pCREB expression and neuroendocrine response. *Neuroscience and Biobehavioral Reviews, 30*, 356–375.

Adamec, R., Muir, C., Grimes, M., & Pearcey, K. (2007). Involvement of noradrenergic and corticoid receptors in the consolidation of the lasting anxiogenic effects of predator stress. *Behavioral Brain Research, 179*, 192–207.

Akirav, I., & Maroun, M. (2007). The role of the medial prefrontal cortex-amygdala circuit in stress effects on the extinction of fear. *Neural Plasticity*, 30873.

American Psychiatric Association (1994). *Diagnostic and statistical manual of mental disorders* (4th ed.). Washington, DC: American Psychiatric Association.

Apfelbach, R., Blanchard, C. D., Blanchard, R. J., Hayes, R. A., & Mcgregor, I. S. (2005). The effects of predator odors in mammalian prey species: a review of field and laboratory studies. *Neuroscience and Biobehavioral Reviews, 29*, 1123–1144.

Blanchard, D. C., Griebel, G., & Blanchard, R. J. (2003). Conditioning and residual emotionality effects of predator stimuli: some reflections on stress and emotion. *Progress in Neuropsychopharmacol Biological Psychiatry, 27*, 1177–1185.

Blanchard, R. J., Blanchard, D. C., Rodgers, J., & Weiss, S. M. (1990). The characterization and modelling of antipredator defensive behavior. *Neuroscience and Biobehavioral Reviews, 14*, 463–472.

Blanchard, R. J., Nikulina, J. N., Sakai, R. R., Mckittrick, C., McEwen, B., & Blanchard, D. C. (1998). Behavioral and endocrine change following chronic predatory stress. *Physiology & Behavior, 63*, 561–569.

Blechert, J., Michael, T., Vriends, N., Margraf, J., & Wilhelm, F. H. (2007). Fear conditioning in posttraumatic stress disorder: evidence for delayed extinction of autonomic, experiential, and behavioural responses. *Behaviour Research and Therapy, 45*, 2019–2033.

Blundell, J., Adamec, R., & Burton, P. (2005). Role of NMDA receptors in the syndrome of behavioral changes produced by predator stress. *Physiology & Behavior, 86*, 233–243.

Bouton, M. E. (2004). Context and behavioral processes in extinction. *Learning and Memory, 11*, 485–494.

Bremner, J. D., Licinio, J., Darnell, A., Krystal, J. H., Owens, M. J., Southwick, S. M., Nemeroff, C. B., & Charney, D. S. (1997). Elevated CSF corticotropin-releasing factor concentrations in posttraumatic stress disorder. *American Journal of Psychiatry, 154*, 624–629.

Breslau, N., Davis, G. C., Andreski, P., & Peterson, E. (1991). Traumatic events and posttraumatic stress disorder in an urban population of young adults. *Archives of General Psychiatry, 48*, 216–222.

Breslau, N., Kessler, R. C., Chilcoat, H. D., Schultz, L. R., Davis, G. C., & Andreski, P. (1998). Trauma and posttraumatic stress disorder in the community: the 1996 Detroit Area Survey of Trauma. *Archives of General Psychiatry, 55*, 626–632.

Breslau, N., Chilcoat, H., Kessler, R., Peterson, E., & Lucia, V. (1999). Vulnerability to assaultive violence: further specification of the sex difference in post-traumatic stress disorder. *Psychological Medicine, 29*, 813–821.

Brewin, C., Andrews, B., & Valentine, J. (2000). Meta-analysis of risk factors for posttraumatic stress disorder in trauma-exposed adults. *Journal of Consulting and Clinical Psychology, 68*, 748–766.

Bryant, R. A. (2006). Recovery after the tsunami: timeline for rehabilitation. *Journal of Clinical Psychiatry, 67*, 50–55.

Caspi, A., & Moffitt, T. (2006). Gene-environment interactions in psychiatry: joining forces with neuroscience. *Nature Reviews Neuroscience, 7*, 583–590.

Cohen, H., & Zohar, J. (2004). Animal models of post traumatic stress disorder: The use of cut off behavioral criteria. *Annals of the New York Academy of Sciences, 1032*, 167–178.

Cohen, H., Friedberg, S., Michael, M., Kotler, M., & Zeev, K. (1996). Interaction of CCK-4 induced anxiety and post-cat exposure anxiety in rats. *Depression and Anxiety, 4*, 144–145.

Cohen, H., Kaplan, Z., & Kotler, M. (1999). CCK-antagonists in a rat exposed to acute stress: implication for anxiety associated with post-traumatic stress disorder. *Depression and Anxiety, 10*, 8–17.

Cohen, H., Benjamin, J., Kaplan, Z., & Kotler, M. (2000). Administration of high-dose ketoconazole, an inhibitor of steroid synthesis, prevents posttraumatic anxiety in an animal model. *European Neuropsychopharmacology, 10*, 429–435.

Cohen, H., Joseph, Z., & Matar, M. (2003). The relevance of differential response to trauma in an animal model of post-traumatic stress disorder. *Biological Psychiatry, 53*, 463–473.

Cohen, H., Zohar, J., Matar, M. A., Zeev, K., Loewenthal, U., & Richter-Levin, G. (2004). Setting apart the affected: the use of behavioral criteria in animal models of post traumatic stress disorder. *Neuropsychopharmacology, 29*, 1962–1970.

Cohen, H., Kaplan, Z., Matar, M., Loewenthal, U., Kozlovsky, N., & Zohar, J. (2006a). Anisomycin, a protein synthesis inhibitor, disrupts traumatic memory consolidation and attenuates post traumatic stress response in rats. *Biological Psychiatry, 60*(7), 767–776.

Cohen, H., Ziv, Y., Cardon, M., Kaplan, Z., Matar, M. A., Gidron, Y., Schwartz, M., & Kipnis, J. (2006b). Maladaptation to mental stress mitigated by the adaptive immune system via depletion of naturally occurring regulatory CD4+CD25+ cells. *Journal of Neurobiology, 66*, 552–563.

Cohen, H., Zohar, J., Gidron, Y., Matar, M. A., Belkind, D., Loewenthal, U., Kozlovsky, N., & Kaplan, Z. (2006c). Blunted HPA axis response to stress influences susceptibility to posttraumatic stress response in rats. *Biological Psychiatry, 59*, 1208–1218.

Cohen, H., Maayan, R., Touati-Werner, D., Kaplan, Z., Matar, M., Loewenthal, U., Kozlovsky, N., & Weizman, R. (2007a). Decreased circulatory levels of neuroactive steroids in behaviorally more extremely affected rats subsequent to exposure to a potentially traumatic experience. *International Journal of Neuropsychopharmacology, 10*, 203–209.

Cohen, H., Zohar, J., Matar, M., Loewenthal, U., & Kaplan, Z. (2007b). Post-traumatic stress behavioural responses in inbred mouse strains: can genetic predisposition explain phenotypic vulnerability? *International Journal of Neuropsychopharmacology, 11*, 331–349.

Cohen, H., Matar, M., Buskila, D., Kaplan, Z., & Zohar, J. (2008). Early post-stressor intervention with high dose corticosterone attenuates post traumatic stress response in an animal model of PTSD. *Biological Psychiatry, 15*, 708–717.

Cohen, H., Liberzon, I., & Richter-Levin, G. (2009). Exposure to extreme stress impairs contextual odor discrimination in an animal model of PTSD. *International Journal of Neuropsychopharmacology, 12*, 291–303.

Davidson, J. R. (2006). Pharmacologic treatment of acute and chronic stress following trauma: 2006. *Journal of Clinical Psychiatry, 67* (Suppl 2), 34–39.

De Bellis, M. D., Keshavan, M. S., Shifflett, H., Iyengar, S., Beers, S. R., Hall, J., & Moritz, G. (2002). Brain structures in pediatric maltreatment-related posttraumatic stress disorder: a sociodemographically matched study. *Biological Psychiatry, 52*, 1066–1078.

Delahanty, D., Raimonde, A., & Spoonster, E. (2000). Initial posttraumatic urinary cortisol levels predict subsequent PTSD symptoms in motor vehicle accident victims. *Biological Psychiatry 48*, 940–947.

Diamond, D. M., & Rose, G. M. (1994). Stress impairs LTP and hippocampal-dependent memory. *Annals of the New York Academy of Sciences, 746*, 411–414.

Diamond, D. M., Campbell, A. M., Park, C. R., Woodson, J. C., Conrad, C. D., Bachstetter, A. D., & Mervis, R. F. (2006). Influence of predator stress on the consolidation versus retrieval of long-term spatial memory and hippocampal spinogenesis. *Hippocampus, 16*, 571–576.

Duman, R. (2002). Synaptic plasticity and mood disorders. *Molecular Psychiatry, 7*, 29–34.

Dunsmoor, J. E., Bandettini, P. A., & Knight, D. C. (2007). Neural correlates of unconditioned response diminution during Pavlovian conditioning. *Neuroimage, 40*(2), 811–817.

Ehlers, A., & Clark, D. M. (2000). A cognitive model of posttraumatic stress disorder. *Behaviour Research and Therapy, 38*, 319–345.

Endres, T., Apfelbach, R., & Fendt, M. (2005). Behavioral changes induced in rats by exposure to trimethylthiazoline, a component of fox odor. *Behavioral Neuroscience, 119*, 1004–1010.

Etkin, A., & Wager, T. D. (2007). Functional neuroimaging of anxiety: A meta-analysis of emotional processing in PTSD, social anxiety disorder, and specific phobia. *American Journal of Psychiatry, 164*, 1476–1488.

Fairbank, J. A., Schlenger, W. E., Saigh, P. A., & Davidson, J. R. T. (1995). An epidemiologic profile of post-traumatic stress disorder: prevalence, comorbidity, and risk factors. In D. S. Charney, M. J. Friedman, & A. Y. Deutch (Eds.), *Neurobiological and clinical consequences of stress: from normal adaptation to PTSD* (pp. 415–427). Philadelphia, PA: Lippincott-Raven.

File, S. E., Zangrossi, Jr, H., Sanders, F. L., & Mabbutt, P. S. (1993). Dissociation between behavioral and corticosterone responses on repeated exposures to cat odor. *Physiology & Behavior, 54*, 1109–1111.

Foa, E. B., & Kozak, M. J. (1986). Emotional processing of fear: exposure to corrective information. *Psychological Bulletin, 99*, 20–35.

Foa, E. B., Stein, D. J., & Mcfarlane, A. C. (2006). Symptomatology and psychopathology of mental health problems after disaster. *Journal of Clinical Psychiatry, 67*, 15–25.

Freedman, S., Gluck, N., Tuval-Mashiach, R., Brandes, D., Peri, T., & Shalev, A. (2002). Gender differences in responses to traumatic events: a prospective study. *Journal of Traumatic Stress, 15*, 407–413.

Griebel, G., Blanchard, D. C., Jung, A., Lee, J. C., Masuda, C. K., & Blanchard, R. J. (1995). Further evidence that the mouse defense test battery is useful for screening anxiolytic and panicolytic drugs: effects of acute and chronic treatment with alprazolam. *Neuropharmacology, 34*, 1625–1633.

Helzer, J., Robins, L., & Mcevoy, L. (1987). Post-traumatic stress disorder in the general population. Findings of the epidemiologic catchment area survey. *New England Journal of Medicine, 317*, 1630–1634.

Kozlovsky, N., Matar, M. A., Kaplan, Z., Kotler, M., Zohar, J., & Cohen, H. (2007a). The immediate early gene Arc is associated with behavioral resilience to stress exposure in an animal model of posttraumatic stress disorder. *European Neuropsychopharmacology, 18*, 107–116.

Kozlovsky, N., Matar, M. A., Kaplan, Z., Kotler, M., Zohar, J., & Cohen, H. (2007b). Long-term down-regulation of BDNF mRNA in rat hippocampal CA1 subregion correlates with PTSD-like behavioural stress response. *International Journal of Neuropsychopharmacology, 10*(6), 1–18.

Kozlovsky, N., Matar, M. A., Kaplan, Z., Zohar, J., & Cohen, H. (2009). A distinct pattern of intracellular glucocorticoid-related responses is associated with extreme behavioral response to stress in an animal model of post-traumatic stress disorder. *European Neuropsychopharmacology, 19*, 759–771.

LeDoux, J. (1996). Emotional networks and motor control: a fearful view. *Progress in Brain Research, 107*, 437–446.

LeDoux, J. E. (2000). Emotion circuits in the brain. *Annual Review of Neuroscience, 23*, 155–184.

Liberzon, I., & Sripada, C. S. (2008). The functional neuroanatomy of PTSD: a critical review. *Progress in Brain Research, 167*, 151–169.

Manji, H., Drevets, W., & Charney, D. (2001). The cellular neurobiology of depression. *Nature Medicine, 7*, 541–547.

Maren, S. (2001). Neurobiology of Pavlovian fear conditioning. *Annual Review of Neuroscience*, *24*, 897–931.

Maren, S., & Chang, C. H. (2006). Recent fear is resistant to extinction. *Proceedings of the National Academy of Sciences USA*, *103*, 18020–18025.

Mason, J. W., Giller, E. L., Kosten, T. A., Ostroff, R. B., & Podd, L. (1986). Urinary free-cortisol levels in posttraumatic stress disorder patients. *Journal of Nervous and Mental Disease*, *174*, 145–149.

Matar, M. A., Cohen, H., Kaplan, Z., & Zohar, J. (2006). The effect of early poststressor intervention with sertraline on behavioral responses in an animal model of post-traumatic stress disorder. *Neuropsychopharmacology*, *31*, 2610–2618.

Matar, M., Zohar, J., Kaplan, Z., & Cohen, H. (2009). Alprazolam treatment immediately after stress exposure interferes with the normal HPA-stress response and increases vulnerability to subsequent stress in an animal model of PTSD. *European Neuropsychopharmacology 19*, 283–295.

Mazor, A., Matar, M., Kozlovsky, N., Zohar, J., Kaplan, Z., & Cohen, H. (2009). Gender-related qualitative differences in baseline and post stress anxiety responses are not reflected in the incidence of criterion-based PTSD-like behavior patterns. *World Journal of Biological Psychiatry*, *10*, 856–869.

McEwen, B. S. (2002). The neurobiology and neuroendocrinology of stress. Implications for post-traumatic stress disorder from a basic science perspective. *Psychiatric Clinics of North America*, *25*, 469–494.

Milad, M. R., Rauch, S. L., Pitman, R. K., & Quirk, G. J. (2006). Fear extinction in rats: implications for human brain imaging and anxiety disorders. *Biological Psychology*, *73*, 61–71.

Myers, K. M., & Davis, M. (2002). Behavioral and neural analysis of extinction. *Neuron*, *36*, 567–584.

Nutt, D., & Davidson, J. (2000). *Post-traumatic stress disorder diagnosis, management and treatment*. London: Taylor & Francis.

Olff, M., Langeland, W., Draijer, N., & Gersons, B. (2007). Gender differences in posttraumatic stress disorder. *Psychological Bulletin*, *133*, 183–204.

Pei, Q., Zetterstrom, T., Sprakes, M., Tordera, R., & Sharp, T. (2003). Antidepressant drug treatment induces Arc gene expression in the rat brain. *Neuroscience*, *121*, 975–982.

Peri, T., Ben-Shakhar, G., Orr, S. P., & Shalev, A. Y. (2000). Psychophysiologic assessment of aversive conditioning in posttraumatic stress disorder. *Biological Psychiatry*, *47*, 512–519.

Pitman, R., & Orr, S. (1990). Twenty-four hour urinary cortisol and catecholamine excretion in combat-related posttraumatic stress disorder. *Biological Psychiatry*, *27*, 245–247.

Rasmusson, A. M., Lipschitz, D. S., Wang, S., Hu, S., Vojvoda, D., Bremner, J. D., Southwick, S. M., & Charney, D. S. (2001). Increased pituitary and adrenal reactivity in premenopausal women with posttraumatic stress disorder. *Biological Psychiatry*, *50*, 965–977.

Rauch, S. L., Shin, L. M., & Phelps, E. A. (2006). Neurocircuitry models of posttraumatic stress disorder and extinction: human neuroimaging research–past, present, and future. *Biological Psychiatry*, *60*, 376–382.

Resnick, H., Yehuda, R., Pitman, R., & Foy, D. (1995). Effect of previous trauma on acute plasma cortisol level following rape. *American Journal of Psychiatry*, *152*, 1675–1677.

Richter-Levin, G. (1998). Acute and long-term behavioral correlates of underwater trauma–potential relevance to stress and post-stress syndromes. *Psychiatry Research*, *79*, 73–83.

Robin, R., Chester, B., Rasmussen, J., Jaranson, J., & Goldman, D. (1997). Prevalence and characteristics of trauma and posttraumatic stress disorder in a southwestern American Indian community. *American Journal of Psychiatry, 154,* 1582–1588.

Roseboom, P. H., Nanda, S. A., Bakshi, V. P., Trentani, A., Newman, S. M., & Kalin, N. H. (2007). Predator threat induces behavioral inhibition, pituitary-adrenal activation and changes in amygdala CRF-binding protein gene expression. *Psychoneuroendocrinology, 32,* 44–55.

Schelling, G., Kilger, E., Roozendaal, B., de Quervain, D. J., Briegel, J., Dagge, A., Rothenhausler, H. B., Krauseneck, T., Nollert, G., & Kapfhammer, H. P. (2004). Stress doses of hydrocortisone, traumatic memories, and symptoms of posttraumatic stress disorder in patients after cardiac surgery: a randomized study. *Biological Psychiatry, 55,* 627–633.

Shalev, A. Y. (2002). Acute stress reactions in adults. *Biological Psychiatry, 51,* 532–543.

Shore, J., Vollmer, W., & Tatum, E. (1989). Community patterns of posttraumatic stress disorders. *Journal of Nervous and Mental Disease, 177,* 681–685.

Solomon, Z., Shklar, R., & Mikulincer, M. (2005). Frontline treatment of combat stress reaction: a 20-year longitudinal evaluation study. *American Journal of Psychiatry, 162,* 2309–2314.

Sullivan, M., & Gratton, A. (1998). Relationships between stress-induced increases in medial prefrontal cortical dopamine and plasma corticosterone levels in rats: role of cerebral laterality. *Neuroscience, 83,* 81–91.

Takahashi, L. K., Nakashima, B. R., Hong, H., & Watanabe, K. (2005). The smell of danger: a behavioral and neural analysis of predator odor-induced fear. *Neuroscience and Biobehavioral Reviews, 29,* 1157–1167.

Warren, D. A., Castro, C. A., Rudy, J. W., & Maier, S. F. (1991). No spatial learning impairment following exposure to inescapable shock. *Psychobiology, 19,* 127–134.

Yehuda, R. (2005). Neuroendocrine aspects of PTSD. *Handbook of Experimental Pharmacology, 169,* 371–403.

Yehuda, R., & LeDoux, J. (2007). Response variation following trauma: a translational neuroscience approach to understanding PTSD. *Neuron, 56,* 19–32.

Yehuda, R., Morris, A., Labinsky, E., Zemelman, S., & Schmeidler, J. (2007). Ten-year follow-up study of cortisol levels in aging holocaust survivors with and without PTSD. *Journal of Traumatic Stress, 20,* 757–761.

Zohar, J., Sonnino, R., Juven-Wetzler, A., & Cohen, H. (2009). Can posttraumatic stress disorder be prevented? *CNS Spectrums, 14,* 44–51.

20

What Can Fear Conditioning Tell Us About Posttraumatic Stress Disorder?

Jacek Dębiec and Joseph E. LeDoux

Introduction

Posttraumatic stress disorder (PTSD) develops following an exposure to a severe psychological trauma. It is a common and debilitating condition with lifetime prevalence in general population around 10% (Kessler et al., 1995; Resnick et al., 1993). Adversities, such as war, increase the prevalence of PTSD up to around 30% (Farhood et al., 2006; Shalev et al., 2006; Seino et al., 2008). PTSD is characterized by three clusters of symptoms: reexperiencing of the trauma, avoidance of stimuli associated with the traumatic event, and increased arousal (American Psychiatric Association, 1994). PTSD is manifested by complex cognitive, emotional, and behavioral alterations, and many of these symptoms are unique for humans. Nevertheless, animal studies have played an essential role in better understanding of posttraumatic stress and other anxiety disorders (Sullivan et al., 2009). Much evidence indicates that learning mechanisms are involved in the development of pathological fear and anxiety (Rosen and Schulkin, 1998), and animal models have been especially useful in localizing neural circuits, as well as elucidating biochemical pathways and synaptic changes that mediate the physiological and behavioral responses of fear and anxiety (Sullivan et al., 2009).

One the most commonly used experimental models of fear learning is fear conditioning. In fear conditioning, a neutral stimulus (conditioned stimulus, CS) is paired with an aversive event (unconditioned stimulus, US), often a mild electric shock (LeDoux, 2000; Fanselow and Poulos, 2005). In rodent studies, auditory fear conditioning is most common and involves the pairing of an auditory CS, a tone, with a mild electric shock to the foot pads serving as the US (Figure 20.1).

The Handbook of Stress: Neuropsychological Effects on the Brain, First Edition.
Edited by Cheryl D. Conrad.
© 2011 Blackwell Publishing Ltd. Published 2011 by Blackwell Publishing Ltd.

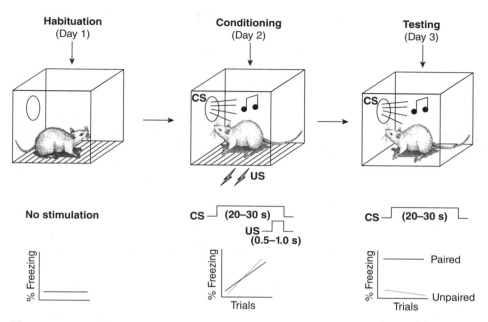

Figure 20.1 Auditory fear conditioning. In auditory fear conditioning a neutral stimulus (tone) known as conditioned stimulus (CS) is paired with an aversive stimulus (unconditioned stimulus, US), a mild electric shock to the foot pads. As a result of these pairings, subsequent exposures to the CS alone trigger fear responses, such as immobility or freezing. *Source:* From LeDoux (2008). Created: December 18, 2006; reviewed: November 7, 2007; accepted: April 10, 2008. http://www.scholarpedia.org/article/Amygdala

Prior to conditioning, the CS elicits only mild and transient responses, such as altering or orientation. After occurring with the US, though, the CS elicits hardwired and stereotyped patterns of defensive behavior, such as freezing, autonomic nervous system responses (changes in heart rate, blood pressure, and respiration), and the release of stress hormones (cortisol and epinephrine [adrenaline]) (e.g., Fanselow and Poulos, 2005; Sullivan et al., 2009). The autonomic and hormonal responses support the performance and maintenance of the metabolically demanding defensive behavior. In addition, hypoalgesia occurs (Helmstetter, 1992), and certain reflexes, such as eye blink and startle, are potentiated (Lang and Davis, 2006).

Conditioned fear associations may be also established through its variants: second-order fear conditioning and observational fear conditioning. Second-order fear conditioning begins with a standard (first-order) fear conditioning procedure in which a CS (now called first-order conditioned stimulus or CS1) is paired with a US (Gewirtz and Davis, 2000). Subsequently, a second distinct CS (second-order conditioned stimulus or CS2) is paired with CS1 in the absence of the US. In consequence, the CS2 is endowed with the ability to trigger fear responses. Recent studies demonstrate that animals can acquire conditioned fear responses through observing fearful reactions in their conspecifics. This type of learning is called observational fear conditioning. Observational fear conditioning has been shown in rodents (Jeon et al., 2010), monkeys (Mineka and Cook, 1993), and humans (Olsson and Phelps, 2004).

In summary, fear conditioning is a useful behavioral model for exploring fear learning. Fear conditioning is not a model of PTSD, but is relevant to PTSD in two ways. First, it allows an exploration of the brain mechanisms of fear, alterations of which may contribute to those aspects or symptoms of fear that occur in PTSD. Second, given that fear conditioning is an excellent tool for studying amygdala structure and function, and that amygdala structure and function are altered in several psychiatric conditions, including PTSD, studies of fear conditioning can be thought of as a way to study this important part of the brain. The fact that fear conditioning can be studied using very similar methods in humans and laboratory animals further amplifies these points.

The Neurocircuitry of Fear Conditioning

Although several brain sites are important for processing fear, it is well established that a key structure responsible for acquisition and expression of fear conditioning in vertebrate species is the amygdala (Davis, 1992; LeDoux, 2000; Maren, 2005; Fanselow and Poulos, 2005). The amygdala is a locus where information about the CS and the US converge, and from where the efferent pathways controlling downstream fear responses project (LeDoux, 2007). The amygdala, however, is not a homogenous structure but is composed of several structurally and functionally distinct nuclei. The most relevant to fear conditioning are the lateral (LA), basal (B), and central (CE) nuclei of the amygdala, as well as a subgroup of neurons known as intercalated cells (LeDoux, 2000, 2007; Pare et al., 2004; Fanselow and Poulos, 2005; Maren, 2005; Lang and Davis, 2006).

In auditory fear conditioning, the information about the tone CS enters the brain via the sensory apparatus of the ear and is then relayed through brainstem to the auditory part of the thalamus (LeDoux, 2007; Sigurdsson et al., 2007) (Figure 20.2). The auditory thalamus sends two independent projections, both terminating on neurons in LA nuclei: the rapid, direct monosynaptic *low road* and the slower, indirect *high road*, which is routed throughout the auditory neocortex (LeDoux, 1996). The low road provides the amygdala with a rapid but imprecise signal, while the high road delivers a more complex and detailed representation, albeit one that takes more processing time, from auditory association areas. In humans, the low road is believed to be responsible for immediate, unconscious responses to danger, whereas the high road is believed to be involved in processing of threats that can become conscious (LeDoux, 1996, 2008). Indeed, recent human brain-imaging studies demonstrate that the amygdala may be activated by the stimuli that are not consciously perceived (Vuilleumier et al., 2001; Phelps, 2006) and the subcortical route appears to be primarily involved in fast amygdala responses (Luo et al., 2010). The two-roads model of signal transmission explains how responses to danger can be initiated before we are able to consciously appreciate the stimulus (LeDoux, 1996; LeDoux, 2008).

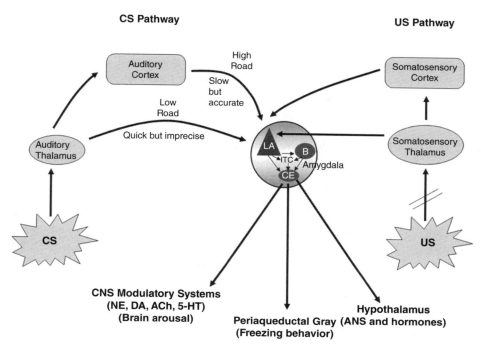

Figure 20.2 Amygdala inputs, outputs, and internal connections. The amygdala consists of a group of nuclei of which the most relevant to fear conditioning are the lateral (LA), basal (B), and central (CE) nuclei of the amygdala, as well as the distinct group of neurons known as intercalated cells (ITC). The LA is the main sensory input area. It receives projections from the thalamus and the cortex. The LA is a site where the information about the conditioned stimulus (CS) and unconditioned stimulus (US) converge. The information about the CS reaches the LA from the auditory thalamus through two independent projections: the rapid, direct monosynaptic *low road* and the slower, indirect *high road*. The low road delivers a rapid but imprecise signal, whereas the high road provides the amygdala with a detailed representation of the stimulus. The B nuclei receive projections from the hippocampus, enthorhinal, and polymodal associative cortices, areas that provide information about the environmental context in which the fearful event is occurring. The CE is the common output area controlling expression of behavioral, autonomic (autonomic nervous system, ANS), and endocrine responses. It also activates modulatory systems that further affect fear learning. These modulators include norepinephrine (NE), dopamine (DA), acetylcholine (ACh), serotonin (5-hydroxytryptamine, 5-HT), and others. The LA nuclei are connected with the CE in direct and indirect (via the basal nucleus and the intercalated cells) ways. The ITC have inhibitory control over the CE nuclei.

The information about the US enters the organism through sensory and pain receptors in the periphery, and is then relayed through spinothalamic tract to the thalamus (LeDoux, 2000). The thalamus sends it outputs conveying the information about the US to the LA nuclei. Studies of fear conditioning suggest that like CS information US information converges on the LA nuclei from thalamic and cortical routes (Shi and Davis, 1999; Lanuza et al., 2004, 2008).

Whereas the LA nuclei are believed to be the main sensory gateway, the CE nuclei are considered to be the major output region (Davis, 1992; LeDoux, 2007). The CE nuclei send projections to brain-stem areas and through these pathways control expression of fear responses, including autonomic, endocrine, and behavioral responses. In addition to managing reactions to threat, the CE nuclei are responsible for activating amine modulatory systems, such as adrenergic, dopaminergic, cholinergic, and serotonergic systems (LeDoux, 2000, 2007; Lang and Davis, 2006).

The LA and the CE nuclei are connected through direct and indirect routes (LeDoux, 2007; Pitkänen, 2000). The indirect routes are believed to be major communication pathways between the LA and CE nuclei and involve connections from the lateral to the basal nuclei, as well to the intercalated cells, both of which project to CE nuclei. The basal nucleus also receives fibers from the hippocampus and entorhinal and associate cortices and is believed to deliver information about the environmental context in which the threat is occurring (Maren, 2005; LeDoux, 2007). In addition to outputs to the CE nuclei, the B nuclei also project to ventral striatal areas. Some evidence suggests that these projections are involved in controlling instrumental behaviors (LeDoux, 2007; Everitt et al., 1999; Balleine and Killcross, 2006). Because of their proximity, the LA and B nuclei are sometimes referred to as lateral and basal nuclei of the amygdala (LBA) or the basolateral complex (BLA). However, this terminology, which lacks anatomical specificity, should be avoided when possible.

The intercalated cells consist of clusters of γ-aminobutyric acid (GABA) or GABAergic neurons that by way of forward inhibition control the flow of activity from the LA and B nuclei to the CE nuclei (Pare et al., 2003; Likhtik et al., 2008).

A part of the so-called extended amygdala is the bed nucleus of stria terminalis (BNST). BNST and the amygdala (mostly CE nuclei) are connected through reciprocal projections (Pitkänen, 2000). The BNST plays an important role in the regulation of the hypothalamic–pituitary–adrenal (HPA) axis during stress (Sullivan et al., 2004; Duvarci et al., 2009), but also in context conditioning (Sullivan et al., 2004). BNST has also been proposed as being involved in anxiety, as opposed to fear (Davis et al., 2010). Studies implicating the BNST in anxiety though are mostly based on elicitation of fear responses by contextual stimuli. Whether the BNST is thus truly involved in anxiety depends on whether context fear is truly a measure of anxiety.

The amygdala has also been implicated in appetitive conditioning (Holland and Gallagher, 2004; Balleine and Killcross, 2006; Everitt et al., 1999, 2003). Some authors have proposed that the LA nuclei and basal amygdala, the so-called basolateral complex, and the CE nuclei, operate in parallel (Balleine and Killcross, 2006). The main difference with the view above is not whether the amygdala processes information in series or parallel, but instead whether the inputs to the LA and CE nuclei are separate. Studies of aversive conditioning strongly suggest that the LA nuclei are the sensory gateway to the amygdala, whereas the view from appetitive conditioning proposes that under some conditions CE nuclei process CS information without the involvement of LA nuclei. Within the amygdala both models propose that extensive parallel processing takes place.

Biochemical Pathways and Synaptic Changes Underlying Fear Learning

Processes leading to the establishment of a memory are often referred to as memory consolidation (McGaugh, 2000). Behavioral and electrophysiological preparations, as well as pharmacological manipulations, indicate that consolidation of fear conditioning is mediated by alterations in the strength of synaptic signaling in the amygdala (Gale et al., 2004; Dityatev and Bolshakov, 2005; Fanselow and Poulos, 2005; Maren, 2005; Schafe et al., 2001; Rodrigues et al., 2004; Sigurdsson et al., 2007). Most of the fibers projecting onto the amygdala are excitatory and release glutamate, which binds to *N*-methyl-D-aspartate (NMDA) and α-amino-3-hydroxy-5-methyl-4-isoxazole propionate (AMPA) receptors which are localized on principal neurons.

Before fear conditioning, an exposure to a neutral tone produces only weak depolarization in LA nuclei which is insufficient to trigger defensive responses. However, pairing the tone and shock in time results in strong depolarization of LA neurons which in turn excites downstream brain areas mediating expression of fear responses. It has been proposed that activation of postsynaptic NMDA receptors in LA neurons in the context of the strong depolarization by the US inputs initiates calcium influx (Blair et al., 2001). This in turn triggers cascades of intracellular processes involving second messengers and protein kinases, which lead to activation of transcription factors, gene expression, new protein synthesis, and synaptic alterations (Rodrigues et al., 2004; Maren, 2005; LeDoux, 2007). Newly synthesized proteins, either structural or functional, are believed to strengthen synaptic connections. For example, recent study demonstrates that fear conditioning activates trafficking of AMPA receptors to synapses in LA nuclei (Rumpel et al., 2005). This insertion of new glutamatergic receptors potentiates the postsynaptic response elicited by presynaptic glutamatergic inputs. As a consequence, presenting a CS alone (which was previously paired with the US) results in a stronger depolarization of LA neurons and leads to the activation of brain areas involved in defensive responses.

Various neuromodulatory systems are involved in regulation of fear conditioning in the amygdala by influencing either principal neurons or GABAergic interneurons. These neuromodulators include glucocorticoids (Johnson et al., 2005; Duvarci and Pare, 2007), norepinephrine (noradrenaline; Dębiec and LeDoux, 2004; Tuly et al., 2007; Hu et al., 2007), dopamine (Guarraci et al., 2000; Kroner et al., 2005), brain-derived neurotrophic factor (Monfils et al., 2007), endocannabinoids (Azad et al., 2004), neuropeptide Y (Krysiak et al., 2000), nitric oxide (Schafe et al., 2005; Overeem et al., 2010), and others. Of special interest is the role of glucocorticoids and epinephrine in regulating fear conditioning, as these neuromodulators have been also implied in PTSD (Pitman, 1989; Bremner, 2006).

Stress Hormones and Fear Conditioning

There has been recently an increased interest in the study of the influence of stress and stress hormones on fear learning and memory (Ferry and McGaugh, 2000;

Prager and Johnson, 2009; Rodrigues et al., 2010). Ample data demonstrate that both acute and chronic stress enhance consolidation of fear conditioning (Conrad et al., 1999; Rau et al., 2005; Rodrigues et al., 2010). Major endocrine mediators of stress are glucocorticoids and catecholamines: epinephrine and norepinephrine. Stressful events activate the HPA axis, resulting in the release of glucocorticoids from the adrenal cortex and a release of epinephrine (mostly) and norepinephrine from the adrenal medulla and sympathetic nerves. In the brain, the major source of norepinephrine is the locus coerulus which projects to various sites including the amygdala, the hippocampus, and the neocortex. Stress increases norepinephrine release in these projection sites.

Glucocorticoid receptor activation in the LA nuclei and basal amygdala enhances (Conrad et al., 2004), whereas glucocorticoid receptor blockade in the same site impairs (Jin et al., 2007) consolidation of auditory fear conditioning. Manipulations of the glucocorticoid receptors in the LA also affect other forms of fear learning, such as contextual fear conditioning (Donley et al., 2005) and inhibitory avoidance (Roozendaal and McGaugh, 1997).

The role of the noradrenergic transmission in the amygdala in auditory fear conditioning has not yet been understood. Recent study shows that intra-LA β-noradrenergic receptor blockade impairs auditory fear conditioning (Bush et al., 2010), while the same manipulation administered immediately following training has no effect on auditory fear conditioning (Dębiec and LeDoux, 2004; Bush et al., 2010). This pattern of results suggests that β-adrenergic receptors in the amygdala are involved in the acquisition of auditory fear conditioning. Little is known about the role of α-adrenergic receptors in auditory fear conditioning. Lazzaro and colleagues (2010) have recently shown that intra-LA α-adrenergic blockade before conditioning enhances consolidation, while the same treatment delivered after conditioning has no effect on cue conditioned fear.

In addition, one published study suggests that noradrenergic activity in the LA may have an influence on the augmenting effects of glucocorticoids on auditory fear conditioning (Roozendaal et al., 2006). Noradrenergic transmission in the LA has been also implied in contextual fear conditioning (LaLumiere et al., 2003) and avoidance learning (Ferry and McGaugh, 1999).

Clinical studies demonstrate increased noradrenergic activity (Geracioti et al., 2001), as well as dysregulation of glucocorticoid signaling in PTSD (Yehuda et al., 1996; Meewisse et al., 2007). Two pilot studies show that oral administration of the β-adrenergic receptor antagonist propranolol following trauma lowers the risk of PTSD (Pitman et al., 2002; Vaiva et al., 2003). Further studies of stress hormones and their influence on fear learning will provide new insights into the pathophysiology of PTSD and may help to develop new treatments of traumatic stress.

Extinction and Reconsolidation of Conditioned Fear

Fear learning occurs very quickly. In fear conditioning, usually a single pairing of the CS with the US is sufficient to produce a memory. Once conditioned fear responses are acquired and consolidated, they may last throughout the lifetime of an animal (LeDoux, 2000). For long it was thought that following consolidation the memory is immune to interferences (McGaugh, 2000). Even if conditioned fear responses may be extinguished through multiple presentations of an unreinforced CS (memory extinction), they typically reappear either spontaneously or through behavioral manipulations (Bouton, 2004). Therefore, fear memory extinction is commonly conceptualized as a new learning experience in which an animal is trained that a previously fear-conditioned CS is safe (Bouton, 2004; Myers and Davis, 2007). Extinction of fear memories depends on the interaction of the amygdala, medial prefrontal cortex, and the hippocampus (Morgan et al., 1993; Milad and Quirk, 2002; Sotres-Bayon et al., 2007, 2009; Corcoran and Quirk, 2007; Ji and Maren, 2007). Rodent studies demonstrate that extinction of conditioned fear depends on the neuronal activation in the prefrontal cortex and the hippocampus (Milad and Quirk, 2002; Corcoran and Quirk, 2007; Burgos-Robles et al., 2009). These data are highly relevant to traumatic stress in humans as brain-imaging studies show diminished responsivity and smaller volume of the hippocampus and the prefrontal cortex in PTSD patients (Shin et al., 2006). Furthermore, extinction of conditioned fear as a form of learning depends on similar molecular mechanisms as fear conditioning. Recent studies show that intra-amygdala administration of the NMDA receptor agonist D-cycloserine facilitates extinction of fear-potentiated startle (Walker et al., 2002) and systemic injections of D-cycloserine augment extinction of auditory fear conditioning (Lee et al., 2006). Indeed, pilot clinical studies suggest that D-cycloserine may be useful in potentiating effects of exposure therapy in anxiety disorders (Ressler et al., 2004; Norberg et al., 2008).

However, despite the evidence of a lasting character of conditioned fear, recent studies show that the maintenance of fear memory depends on active mechanisms which are contingent on the use of this memory (Sara, 2000; Nader, 2003; Dudai, 2006). Reactivation of a memory through a presentation of a learning cue (CS) triggers synaptic processes which resemble consolidation, a phenomenon referred to as memory reconsolidation (Sara, 2000; Nader, 2003; Dudai, 2006). Reconsolidation mechanisms allow modification of the memory in the face of new experience (Lee, 2009). It has been shown that reconsolidation of auditory fear conditioning in the LA nuclei involves NMDA receptor activation (Lee et al., 2006; Ben Mamou et al., 2006), protein kinases (Duvarci et al., 2005; Tronson et al., 2006; Doyere et al., 2007), gene expression (Lee et al., 2005), new RNA and protein synthesis (Nader et al., 2000; Duvarci and Nader, 2004; Dębiec et al., 2006, 2010; Duvarci et al., 2008), as well as active actin rearrangements (Rehberg et al., 2010). It has also been demonstrated that reconsolidation of auditory fear conditioning in the LA nuclei is modulated by noradrenergic signaling (Dębiec and LeDoux, 2004, 2006; Dębiec et al., 2011). Thus, interference with reconsolidation processes at any stage may lead to attenuation or augmentation of conditioned fear responses. Indeed, recent study shows that postreactivation administration of β-adrenergic receptor antagonist propranolol impairs conditioned fear in healthy human subjects (Kindt et al., 2009). Pilot data suggest that propranolol following a controlled recall of psychological trauma may attenuate physiologic responses in patients with PTSD (Brunet et al., 2008).

Of special significance are interactions between extinction and reconsolidation processes. Recent studies in rats (Monfils et al., 2009) and in humans (Schiller et al., 2010) demonstrate that combining reconsolidation and extinction paradigms by applying extinction training after reconsolidation processes have been activated may provide an effective way of lastingly eliminating conditioned fear responses.

Conclusion

Fear conditioning is a model of fear and anxiety. Animal studies using fear conditioning significantly advanced our knowledge about the neurocircuitry and cellular and molecular mechanisms of fear learning. Brain regions of special relevance to fear conditioning are the amygdala, the hippocampus, and the prefrontal cortex. These regions have been also implicated in a variety of anxiety disorders, including PTSD. Investigating fear conditioning in animals allowed identification of cellular, molecular, and synaptic mechanisms of fear and anxiety. Some of these advancements have guided human research and have been successfully applied in translational and clinical studies. Future research will hopefully allow breaking new grounds in prevention, diagnosis, and treatment of PTSD and other anxiety disorders. However, in emphasizing research on fear conditioning and its implications for stress disorders in humans we do not mean to imply that fear conditioning can reveal all that needs to be known about the neurobiology of fear and anxiety and their relation to stress. Fear conditioning is an excellent model for understanding how simple associations can trigger fear and stress responses, but is less useful in understanding the cognitive processes that ultimately come to be layered over these simple associations and that also exert powerful control over decision-making and behavioral control. By uncovering the simple basic mechanisms we can learn important things about the fundamental processes that initiate and maintain fear in the short run. This is very significant because in some if not many cases long-lasting fear often begins as simple fear response.

References

American Psychiatric Association (1994). *Diagnostic and statistical manual of mental disorders* (4th ed.). Washington, DC: American Psychiatric Association.
Azad, S. C., Monory, K., Marsicano, G., Cravatt, B. F., Lutz, B., Zieglgansberger, W., & Rammes, G. (2004). Circuitry for associative plasticity in the amygdala involves endocannabinoid signaling. *Journal of Neuroscience, 24,* 9953–9961.
Balleine, B. W., & Killcross, S. (2006). Parallel incentive processing: an integrated view of amygdala function. *Trends in Neuroscience, 29,* 272–279.

Ben Mamou, C., Gamache, K., & Nader, K. (2006). NMDA receptors are critical for unleashing consolidated auditory fear memories. *Nature Neuroscience, 9,* 1237–1239.

Blair, H. T., Schafe, G. E., Bauer, E. P., Rodrigues, S. M., & LeDoux, J. E. (2001). Synaptic plasticity in the lateral amygdala: a cellular hypothesis of fear conditioning. *Learning and Memory, 8,* 229–242.

Bouton, M. E. (2004). Context and behavioral processes in extinction. *Learning and Memory, 11,* 485–494.

Bremner, J. D. (2006). Traumatic stress: effects on the brain. *Dialogues in Clinical Neuroscience, 8,* 445–461.

Brunet, A., Orr, S. P., Tremblay, J., Robertson, K., Nader, K., & Pitman, R. K. (2008). Effect of post-retrieval propranolol on psychophysiologic responding during subsequent script-driven traumatic imagery in post-traumatic stress disorder. *Journal of Psychiatric Research, 42,* 503–506.

Burgos-Robles, A., Vidal-Gonzalez, I., & Quirk, G. J. (2009). Sustained conditioned responses in prelimbic prefrontal neurons are correlated with fear expression and extinction failure. *Journal of Neuroscience, 29,* 8474–8482.

Bush, D. E. A., Caparosa, E. M., Gekker, A., & LeDoux, J. E. (2010). Beta-adrenergic receptors in the lateral nucleus of the amygdala contribute to the acquisition but not the consolidation of auditory fear conditioning. *Frontiers in Behavioral Neuroscience, 4,* 154.

Conrad, C. D., LeDoux, J. E., Magarinos, A. M., & McEwen, B. S. (1999). Repeated restraint stress facilitates fear conditioning independently of causing hippocampal CA3 dendritic atrophy. *Behavioral Neuroscience, 113,* 902–913.

Conrad, C. D., Macmillan, 2nd, D. D., Tsekhanov, S., Wright, R. L., Baran, S. E., & Fuchs, R. A. (2004). Influence of chronic corticosterone and glucocorticoid receptor antagonism in the amygdala on fear conditioning. *Neurobiology of Learning and Memory, 81,* 185–199.

Corcoran, K. A., & Quirk, G. J. (2007). Recalling safety: cooperative functions of the ventromedial prefrontal cortex and the hippocampus in extinction. *CNS Spectrums, 12,* 200–206.

Davis, M. (1992). The role of the amygdala in fear and anxiety. *Annual Review of Neuroscience, 15,* 353–375.

Davis, M., Walker, D. L., Miles, L., & Grillon, C. (2010). Phasic vs sustained fear in rats and humans: role of the extended amygdala in fear vs anxiety. *Neuropsychopharmacology, 35,* 105–135.

Dębiec, J., & LeDoux, J. E. (2004). Disruption of reconsolidation but not consolidation of auditory fear conditioning by noradrenergic blockade in the amygdala. *Neuroscience, 129,* 267–272.

Dębiec, J., & LeDoux, J. E. (2006). Noradrenergic signaling in the amygdala contributes to the reconsolidation of fear memory: treatment implications for PTSD. *Annals of the New York Academy of Sciences, 1071,* 521–524.

Dębiec, J., Doyere, V., Nader, K., & LeDoux, J. E. (2006). Directly reactivated, but not indirectly reactivated, memories undergo reconsolidation in the amygdala. *Proceedings of the National Academy of Sciences USA, 103,* 3428–3433.

Dębiec, J., Diaz-Mataix, L., Bush, D. E., Doyere, V., & LeDoux, J. E. (2010). The amygdala encodes specific sensory features of an aversive reinforcer. *Nature Neuroscience, 13,* 536–537.

Dębiec, J., Bush, D. E. A., & LeDoux, J. E. (2011). Noradrenergic enhancement of reconsolidation in the amygdale impairs extinction of conditioned fear in rats – a possible mechanism for the persistence of traumatic memories in PTSD. *Depression and Anxiety*, *28*, 186–193.

Dityatev, A. E., & Bolshakov, V. Y. (2005). Amygdala, long-term potentiation, and fear conditioning. *Neuroscientist*, *11*, 75–88.

Donley, M. P., Schulkin, J., & Rosen, J. B. (2005). Glucocorticoid receptor antagonism in the basolateral amygdala and ventral hippocampus interferes with long-term memory of contextual fear. *Behavioral Brain Research*, *164*, 197–205.

Doyere, V., Dębiec, J., Monfils, M. H., Schafe, G. E., & LeDoux, J. E. (2007). Synapse-specific reconsolidation of distinct fear memories in the lateral amygdala. *Nature Neuroscience*, *10*, 414–416.

Dudai, Y. (2006). Reconsolidation: the advantage of being refocused. *Current Opinions in Neurobiology*, *16*, 174–178.

Duvarci, S., & Nader, K. (2004). Characterization of fear memory reconsolidation. *Journal of Neuroscience*, *24*, 9269–9275.

Duvarci, S., & Pare, D. (2007). Glucocorticoids enhance the excitability of principal basolateral amygdala neurons. *Journal of Neuroscience*, *27*, 4482–4491.

Duvarci, S., Nader, K., & LeDoux, J. E. (2005). Activation of extracellular signal-regulated kinase- mitogen-activated protein kinase cascade in the amygdala is required for memory reconsolidation of auditory fear conditioning. *European Journal of Neuroscience*, *21*, 283–289.

Duvarci, S., Nader, K., & LeDoux, J. E. (2008). De novo mRNA synthesis is required for both consolidation and reconsolidation of fear memories in the amygdala. *Learning and Memory*, *15*, 747–755.

Duvarci, S., Bauer, E. P., & Pare, D. (2009). The bed nucleus of the stria terminalis mediates inter-individual variations in anxiety and fear. *Journal of Neuroscience*, *29*, 10357–10361.

Everitt, B. J., Parkinson, J. A., Olmstead, M. C., Arroyo, M., Robledo, P., & Robbins, T. W. (1999). Associative processes in addiction and reward. The role of amygdala-ventral striatal subsystems. *Annals of the New York Academy of Sciences*, *877*, 412–438.

Everitt, B. J., Cardinal, R. N., Parkinson, J. A., & Robbins, T. W. (2003). Appetitive behavior: impact of amygdala-dependent mechanisms of emotional learning. *Annals of the New York Academy of Sciences*, *985*, 233–250.

Fanselow, M. S., & Poulos, A. M. (2005). The neuroscience of mammalian associative learning. *Annual Review of Psychology*, *56*, 207–234.

Farhood, L., Dimassi, H., & Lehtinen, T. (2006). Exposure to war-related traumatic events, prevalence of PTSD, and general psychiatric morbidity in a civilian population from Southern Lebanon. *Journal of Transcultural Nursing*, *17*, 333–340.

Ferry, B., & McGaugh, J. L. (1999). Clenbuterol administration into the basolateral amygdala post-training enhances retention in an inhibitory avoidance task. *Neurobiology of Learning and Memory*, *72*, 8–12.

Ferry, B., & McGaugh, J. L. (2000). Role of amygdala norepinephrine in mediating stress hormone regulation of memory storage. *Acta Pharmacologica Sinica*, *21*, 481–493.

Gale, G. D., Anagnostaras, S. G., Godsil, B. P., Mitchell, S., Nozawa, T., Sage, J. R., Wiltgen, B., & Fanselow, M. S. (2004). Role of the basolateral amygdala in the storage of fear memories across the adult lifetime of rats. *Journal of Neuroscience*, *24*, 3810–3815.

Geracioti, Jr, T. D., Baker, D. G., Ekhator, N. N., West, S. A., Hill, K. K., Bruce, A. B., Schmidt, D., Rounds-Kugler, B., Yehuda, R., Keck, Jr, P. E., & Kasckow, J. W. (2001). CSF norepinephrine concentrations in posttraumatic stress disorder. *American Journal of Psychiatry*, *158*, 1227–1230.

Gewirtz, J. C., & Davis, M. (2000). Using pavlovian higher-order conditioning paradigms to investigate the neural substrates of emotional learning and memory. *Learning and Memory, 7*, 257–266.

Guarraci, F. A., Frohardt, R. J., Falls, W. A., & Kapp, B. S. (2000). The effects of intra-amygdaloid infusions of a D2 dopamine receptor antagonist on Pavlovian fear conditioning. *Behavioral Neuroscience, 114*, 647–651.

Helmstetter, F. J. (1992). The amygdala is essential for the expression of conditioned hypoalgesia. *Behavioral Neuroscience, 106*(3): 518–528.

Holland, P. C., & Gallagher, M. (2004). Amygdala-frontal interactions and reward expectancy. *Current Opinions in Neurobiology, 14*, 148–155.

Hu, H., Real, E., Takamiya, K., Kang, M. G., LeDoux, J., Huganir, R. L., & Malinow, R. (2007). Emotion enhances learning via norepinephrine regulation of AMPA-receptor trafficking. *Cell, 131*, 160–173.

Jeon, D., Kim, S., Chetana, M., Jo, D., Ruley, H. E., Lin, S. Y., Rabah, D., Kinet, J. P., & Shin, H. S. (2010). Observational fear learning involves affective pain system and Ca(v)1.2 Ca2+ channels in ACC. *Nature Neuroscience, 13*, 482–488.

Ji, J., & Maren, S. (2007). Hippocampal involvement in contextual modulation of fear extinction. *Hippocampus, 17*, 749–758.

Jin, X. C., Lu, Y. F., Yang, X. F., Ma, L., & Li, B. M. (2007). Glucocorticoid receptors in the basolateral nucleus of amygdala are required for postreactivation reconsolidation of auditory fear memory. *European Journal of Neuroscience, 25*, 3702–3712.

Johnson, L. R., Farb, C., Morrison, J. H., McEwen, B. S., & LeDoux, J. E. (2005). Localization of glucocorticoid receptors at postsynaptic membranes in the lateral amygdala. *Neuroscience, 136*, 289–299.

Kessler, R. C., Sonnega, A., Bromet, E., Hughes, M., & Nelson, C. B. (1995). Posttraumatic stress disorder in the National Comorbidity Survey. *Archives of General Psychiatry, 52*, 1048–1060.

Kindt, M., Soeter, M., & Vervliet, B. (2009). Beyond extinction: erasing human fear responses and preventing the return of fear. *Nature Neuroscience, 12*, 256–258.

Kroner, S., Rosenkranz, J. A., Grace, A. A., & Barrionuevo, G. (2005). Dopamine modulates excitability of basolateral amygdala neurons in vitro. *Journal of Neurophysiology, 93*, 1598–1610.

Krysiak, R., Obuchowicz, E., & Herman, Z. S. (2000). Conditioned fear-induced changes in neuropeptide Y-like immunoreactivity in rats: the effect of diazepam and buspirone. *Neuropeptides, 34*, 148–157.

Lalumiere, R. T., Buen, T. V., & McGaugh, J. L. (2003). Post-training intra-basolateral amygdala infusions of norepinephrine enhance consolidation of memory for contextual fear conditioning. *Journal of Neuroscience, 23*, 6754–6758.

Lang, P. J., & Davis, M. (2006). Emotion, motivation, and the brain: reflex foundations in animal and human research. *Progress in Brain Research, 156*, 3–29.

Lanuza, E., Nader, K., & LeDoux, J. E. (2004). Unconditioned stimulus pathways to the amygdala: effects of posterior thalamic and cortical lesions on fear conditioning. *Neuroscience, 125*, 305–315.

Lanuza, E., Moncho-Bogani, J., & LeDoux, J. E. (2008). Unconditioned stimulus pathways to the amygdala: effects of lesions of the posterior intralaminar thalamus on foot-shock-induced c-Fos expression in the subdivisions of the lateral amygdala. *Neuroscience, 155*, 959–968.

Lazzaro, S. C., Hou, M., Cunha, C., LeDoux, J. E., & Cain, C.K. (2010). Antagonism of lateral amygdala alpha1-adrenergic receptors facilitates fear conditioning and long-term potentiation. *Learning and Memory, 17*(10), 489–493.

LeDoux, J. E. (1996). *The emotional brain.* New York: Simon and Schuster.

LeDoux, J. E. (2000). Emotion circuits in the brain. *Annual Review of Neuroscience, 23,* 155–184.

LeDoux, J. (2007). The amygdala. *Current Biology, 17,* R868–R874.

LeDoux, J. (2008). Amygdala. *Scholarpedia, 3*(4), 2698.

LeDoux, J. (2008). Emotional colouration of consciousness: how feelings come about. In L. Wesikrnatz, & M. Davies (Eds.), *Frontiers of consciousness* (pp. 69–168). Oxford: Oxford University Press.

Lee, J. L. (2009). Reconsolidation: maintaining memory relevance. *Trends in Neuroscience, 32,* 413–420.

Lee, J. L., di Ciano, P., Thomas, K. L., & Everitt, B. J. (2005). Disrupting reconsolidation of drug memories reduces cocaine-seeking behavior. *Neuron, 47,* 795–801.

Lee, J. L., Milton, A. L., & Everitt, B. J. (2006). Reconsolidation and extinction of conditioned fear: inhibition and potentiation. *Journal of Neuroscience, 26,* 10051–10056.

Likhtik, E., Popa, D., Apergis-Schoute, J., Fidacaro, G. A., & Pare, D. (2008). Amygdala inter-calated neurons are required for expression of fear extinction. *Nature, 454,* 642–645.

Luo, Q., Holroyd, T., Majestic, C., Cheng, X., Schechter, J., & Blair, R. J. (2010). Emotional automaticity is a matter of timing. *Journal of Neuroscience, 30,* 5825–5829.

Maren, S. (2005). Synaptic mechanisms of associative memory in the amygdala. *Neuron, 47,* 783–786.

McGaugh, J. L. (2000). Memory–a century of consolidation. *Science, 287,* 248–251.

Meewisse, M. L., Reitsma, J. B., De Vries, G. J., Gersons, B. P., & Olff, M. (2007). Cortisol and post-traumatic stress disorder in adults: systematic review and meta-analysis. *British Journal of Psychiatry, 191,* 387–392.

Milad, M. R., & Quirk, G. J. (2002). Neurons in medial prefrontal cortex signal memory for fear extinction. *Nature, 420,* 70–74.

Mineka, S., & Cook, M. (1993). Mechanisms involved in the observational conditioning of fear. *Journal of Experimental Psychology. General, 122,* 23–38.

Monfils, M. H., Cowansage, K. K., & LeDoux, J. E. (2007). Brain-derived neurotrophic factor: linking fear learning to memory consolidation. *Molecular Pharmacology, 72,* 235–237.

Monfils, M. H., Cowansage, K. K., Klann, E., & LeDoux, J. E. (2009). Extinction-reconsolidation boundaries: key to persistent attenuation of fear memories. *Science, 324,* 951–955.

Morgan, M. A., Romanski, L. M., & LeDoux, J. E. (1993). Extinction of emotional learning: contribution of medial prefrontal cortex. *Neuroscience Letters, 163,* 109–113.

Myers, K. M., & Davis, M. (2007). Mechanisms of fear extinction. *Molecular Psychiatry, 12,* 120–150.

Nader, K. (2003). Memory traces unbound. *Trends in Neuroscience, 26,* 65–72.

Nader, K., Schafe, G. E., & LeDoux, J. E. (2000). Fear memories require protein synthesis in the amygdala for reconsolidation after retrieval. *Nature, 406,* 722–726.

Norberg, M. M., Krystal, J. H., & Tolin, D. F. (2008). A meta-analysis of D-cycloserine and the facilitation of fear extinction and exposure therapy. *Biological Psychiatry, 63,* 1118–1126.

Olsson, A., & Phelps, E. A. (2004). Learned fear of "unseen" faces after Pavlovian, observa-tional, and instructed fear. *Psychological Science, 15,* 822–828.

Overeem, K. A., Ota, K. T., Monsey, M. S., Ploski, J. E., & Schafe, G. E. (2010). A role for nitric oxide-driven retrograde signaling in the consolidation of a fear memory. *Frontiers in Behavioral Neuroscience*, 4, 2.

Pare, D., Royer, S., Smith, Y., & Lang, E. J. (2003). Contextual inhibitory gating of impulse traffic in the intra-amygdaloid network. *Annals of the New York Academy of Sciences*, 985, 78–91.

Pare, D., Quirk, G. J., & LeDoux, J. E. (2004). New vistas on amygdala networks in conditioned fear. *Journal of Neurophysiology*, 92, 1–9.

Phelps, E. A. (2006). Emotion and cognition: insights from studies of the human amygdala. *Annual Review of Psychology*, 57, 27–53.

Pitkänen A. (2000). Connectivity of the rat amygdaloid complex. In J. P. Aggleton (Ed.), *The amygdala. A functional analysis* (2nd ed., pp. 31–117). New York: Oxford University Press.

Pitman, R. K. (1989). Post-traumatic stress disorder, hormones, and memory. *Biological Psychiatry*, 26, 221–223.

Pitman, R. K., Sanders, K. M., Zusman, R. M., Healy, A. R., Cheema, F., Lasko, N. B., Cahill, L., & Orr, S. P. (2002). Pilot study of secondary prevention of posttraumatic stress disorder with propranolol. *Biological Psychiatry*, 51, 189–192.

Prager, E. M., & Johnson, L. R. (2009). Stress at the synapse: signal transduction mechanisms of adrenal steroids at neuronal membranes. *Science Signaling*, 2, re5.

Rau, V., Decola, J. P., & Fanselow, M. S. (2005). Stress-induced enhancement of fear learning: an animal model of posttraumatic stress disorder. *Neuroscience and Biobehavioral Reviews*, 29, 1207–1223.

Rehberg, K., Bergado-Acosta, J. R., Koch, J. C., & Stork, O. (2010). Disruption of fear memory consolidation and reconsolidation by actin filament arrest in the basolateral amygdala. *Neurobiology of Learning and Memory*, 94(2), 117–126.

Resnick, H. S., Kilpatrick, D. G., Dansky, B. S., Saunders, B. E., & Best, C. L. (1993). Prevalence of civilian trauma and posttraumatic stress disorder in a representative national sample of women. *Journal of Consulting and Clinical Psychology*, 61, 984–991.

Ressler, K. J., Rothbaum, B. O., Tannenbaum, L., Anderson, P., Graap, K., Zimand, E., Hodges, L., & Davis, M. (2004). Cognitive enhancers as adjuncts to psychotherapy: use of D-cycloserine in phobic individuals to facilitate extinction of fear. *Archives of General Psychiatry*, 61, 1136–1144.

Rodrigues, S. M., Schafe, G. E., & LeDoux, J. E. (2004). Molecular mechanisms underlying emotional learning and memory in the lateral amygdala. *Neuron*, 44, 75–91.

Rodrigues, S. M., LeDoux, J. E., & Sapolsky, R. M. (2010). The influence of stress hormones on fear circuitry. *Annual Review of Neuroscience*, 32, 289–313.

Roozendaal, B., & McGaugh, J. L. (1997). Glucocorticoid receptor agonist and antagonist administration into the basolateral but not central amygdala modulates memory storage. *Neurobiology of Learning and Memory*, 67, 176–179.

Roozendaal, B., Hui, G. K., Hui, I. R., Berlau, D. J., McGaugh, J. L., & Weinberger, N. M. (2006). Basolateral amygdala noradrenergic activity mediates corticosterone-induced enhancement of auditory fear conditioning. *Neurobiology of Learning and Memory*, 86, 249–255.

Rosen, J. B., & Schulkin, J. (1998). From normal fear to pathological anxiety. *Psychological Review*, 105, 325–350.

Rumpel, S., LeDoux, J., Zador, A., & Malinow, R. (2005). Postsynaptic receptor trafficking underlying a form of associative learning. *Science*, 308, 83–88.

Sara, S. J. (2000). Retrieval and reconsolidation: toward a neurobiology of remembering. *Learning and Memory, 7*, 73–84.

Schafe, G. E., Nader, K., Blair, H. T., & LeDoux, J. E. (2001). Memory consolidation of Pavlovian fear conditioning: a cellular and molecular perspective. *Trends in Neuroscience, 24*(9), 540–546.

Schafe, G. E., Bauer, E. P., Rosis, S., Farb, C. R., Rodrigues, S. M., & LeDoux, J. E. (2005). Memory consolidation of Pavlovian fear conditioning requires nitric oxide signaling in the lateral amygdala. *European Journal of Neuroscience, 22*, 201–211.

Schiller, D., Monfils, M. H., Raio, C. M., Johnson, D. C., LeDoux, J. E., & Phelps, E. A. (2010). Preventing the return of fear in humans using reconsolidation update mechanisms. *Nature, 463*, 49–53.

Seino, K., Takano, T., Mashal, T., Hemat, S., & Nakamura, K. (2008). Prevalence of and factors influencing posttraumatic stress disorder among mothers of children under five in Kabul, Afghanistan, after decades of armed conflicts. *Health and Quality of Life Outcomes, 6*, 29.

Shalev, A. Y., Tuval, R., Frenkiel-Fishman, S., Hadar, H., & Eth, S. (2006). Psychological responses to continuous terror: a study of two communities in Israel. *American Journal of Psychiatry, 163*, 667–673.

Shi, C., & Davis, M. (1999). Pain pathways involved in fear conditioning measured with fear-potentiated startle: lesion studies. *Journal of Neuroscience, 19*, 420–430.

Shin, L. M., Rauch, S. L., & Pitman, R. K. (2006). Amygdala, medial prefrontal cortex, and hippocampal function in PTSD. *Annals of the New York Academy of Sciences, 1071*, 67–79.

Sigurdsson, T., Doyere, V., Cain, C. K., & LeDoux, J. E. (2007). Long-term potentiation in the amygdala: a cellular mechanism of fear learning and memory. *Neuropharmacology, 52*, 215–227.

Sotres-Bayon, F., Bush, D. E., & LeDoux, J. E. (2007). Acquisition of fear extinction requires activation of NR2B-containing NMDA receptors in the lateral amygdala. *Neuropsychopharmacology, 32*, 1929–1940.

Sotres-Bayon, F., Diaz-Mataix, L., Bush, D. E., & LeDoux, J. E. (2009). Dissociable roles for the ventromedial prefrontal cortex and amygdala in fear extinction: NR2B contribution. *Cerebral Cortex, 19*, 474–482.

Sullivan, G. M., Apergis, J., Bush, D. E., Johnson, L. R., Hou, M., & LeDoux, J. E. (2004). Lesions in the bed nucleus of the stria terminalis disrupt corticosterone and freezing responses elicited by a contextual but not by a specific cue-conditioned fear stimulus. *Neuroscience, 128*, 7–14.

Sullivan, G. M., Dębiec, J., Bush, D. E. A., Lyons, D. M., & LeDoux, J. E. (2009). The neurobiology of fear and anxiety: contributions of animal models to current understanding. In D. S. Charney, & E. J. Nestler (Eds.), *Neurobiology of mental illness* (pp. 603–626). Oxford: Oxford University Press.

Tronson, N. C., Wiseman, S. L., Olausson, P., & Taylor, J. R. (2006). Bidirectional behavioral plasticity of memory reconsolidation depends on amygdalar protein kinase A. *Nature Neuroscience, 9*, 167–169.

Tully, K., Li, Y., Tsvetkov, E., & Bolshakov, V. Y. (2007). Norepinephrine enables the induction of associative long-term potentiation at thalamo-amygdala synapses. *Proceedings of the National Academy of Sciences USA, 104*, 14146–14150.

Vaiva, G., Ducrocq, F., Jezequel, K., Averland, B., Lestavel, P., Brunet, A., & Marmar, C. R. (2003). Immediate treatment with propranolol decreases posttraumatic stress disorder two months after trauma. *Biological Psychiatry, 54*, 947–949.

Vuilleumier, P., Armony, J. L., Driver, J., & Dolan, R. J. (2001). Effects of attention and emotion on face processing in the human brain: an event-related fMRI study. *Neuron, 30,* 829–841.

Walker, D. L., Ressler, K. J., Lu, K. T., & Davis, M. (2002). Facilitation of conditioned fear extinction by systemic administration or intra-amygdala infusions of D-cycloserine as assessed with fear-potentiated startle in rats. *Journal of Neuroscience, 22,* 2343–2351.

Yehuda, R., Levengood, R. A., Schmeidler, J., Wilson, S., Guo, L. S., & Gerber, D. (1996). Increased pituitary activation following metyrapone administration in post-traumatic stress disorder. *Psychoneuroendocrinology, 21,* 1–16.

21

Stress and Glucocorticoid Effects on Memory
Implications for Anxiety Disorders
Dominique J.-F. de Quervain

Introduction

Stress activates the hypothalamic–pituitary–adrenal axis, which results in the release of glucocorticoid hormones (cortisol in humans, corticosterone in rodents) from the adrenal cortex. It has long been recognized that glucocorticoids readily enter the brain and affect cognition. Early reports on both enhancing and impairing properties of glucocorticoids on memory (Bohus and Lissak, 1968; Flood et al., 1978; Beckwith et al., 1986; Luine et al., 1993; Arbel et al., 1994) have indicated that these hormones have complex effects on cognitive functions. More recent studies investigating glucocorticoid effects on distinct memory phases and studies discerning acute from chronic effects helped to disentangle the multifaceted actions of these stress hormones. For example, acute elevations of glucocorticoids at levels known to enhance the consolidation of memory of emotionally arousing information have been shown to impair the retrieval of already stored emotionally arousing information (Roozendaal and McGaugh, 1996b; de Quervain et al., 1998; Roozendaal, 2000). Furthermore, growing evidence indicates that these acute glucocorticoid effects depend on emotional arousal-induced activation of noradrenergic transmission within the amygdala and on interactions of the amygdala with other brain regions (Roozendaal et al., 2008; de Quervain et al., 2009). Conditions with chronically elevated glucocorticoid levels are usually associated with impaired cognitive performance and these deficits are thought to result from a cumulative and long-lasting burden on hippocampal function and morphology (Sapolsky, 2000; McEwen, 2001; Conrad, 2008). Recently, however, evidence suggested that memory deficits observed under such chronic conditions can also result, at least in part, from acute and reversible glucocorticoid actions on memory retrieval processes (Coluccia et al., 2008).

This chapter briefly summarizes and discusses how glucocorticoids affect memory consolidation, retrieval and working memory and that these stress hormones specifically modulate memory of emotionally arousing experiences. Furthermore, because emotional memory plays a crucial role in the pathogenesis and symptomatology of anxiety disorders, such as posttraumatic stress disorder (PTSD) or phobias, it will be discussed to what extent the basic findings on glucocorticoid effects on emotional memory might have clinical implications. In this context, data will be reviewed suggesting that the administration of glucocorticoids might ameliorate chronic anxiety by reducing retrieval of aversive memories and enhancing fear extinction.

Glucocorticoid Effects on Memory Consolidation

Memory consolidation is the process by which a fragile short-term memory trace is transferred into stable long-term memory. However, not all information is equally well transferred into long-term storage. In fact, it is well recognized that especially emotionally arousing experiences are well remembered, even after decades (McGaugh et al., 2003). Successful memory consolidation depends on de novo protein synthesis and on long-term changes in synaptic plasticity (Kandel, 2001). There is extensive evidence that glucocorticoids, along with other components of the stress response, are critically involved in regulating memory consolidation of emotionally arousing experiences (McGaugh and Roozendaal, 2002). Blockade of glucocorticoid production with the synthesis inhibitor metyrapone impairs memory consolidation in both animals and humans (Roozendaal et al., 1996a; Maheu et al., 2004) and prevents stress- or epinephrine (adrenaline)-induced memory enhancement (Roozendaal et al., 1996b; Liu et al., 1999). Acute systemic administration of glucocorticoids dose-dependently enhances long-term memory consolidation when given either before or immediately after training in emotionally arousing learning tasks (Flood et al., 1978; Sandi and Rose, 1994; Roozendaal and McGaugh, 1996a; Roozendaal et al., 1999; Buchanan and Lovallo, 2001; Cordero et al., 2002; Abercrombie et al., 2003). Such glucocorticoid effects on memory consolidation follow an inverted U-shape dose–response relationship: moderate doses enhance memory, whereas higher doses are typically less effective or may even impair memory consolidation (Roozendaal et al., 1999).

Glucocorticoids also play a role in the consolidation of memory of extinction training in emotionally arousing learning tasks. Extinction occurs when conditioned responding to a stimulus decreases when the reinforcer is omitted (Quirk and Mueller, 2008). Like other forms of learning, extinction acquisition is followed by a consolidation phase and it has been found that the administration of glucocorticoids facilitates the consolidation of extinction memory, whereas a suppression of glucocorticoid function impairs such extinction processes (Bohus and Lissak, 1968;

Barrett and Gonzalez-Lima, 2004; Cai et al., 2006; Yang et al., 2006). Glucocorticoids have been shown to enhance memory consolidation and synaptic plasticity by influencing a wide variety of cellular functions, including cell signaling, ion-channel properties, and cell structure (Karst et al., 2002; Revest et al., 2005; Bisaz et al., 2008).

Furthermore, growing evidence indicates that acute glucocorticoid effects on memory consolidation depend on emotional arousal-induced activation of noradrenergic transmission within the amygdala and on interactions of the amygdala with other brain regions, such as the hippocampus and neocortical regions (Roozendaal et al., 2008; de Quervain et al., 2009).

Glucocorticoid Effects on Memory Retrieval

In contrast to the memory-consolidation process, during which new information is stabilized in memory, memory retrieval refers to the process of recollecting previously stored information. In the first study investigating the specific effects of stress and glucocorticoids on memory retrieval (de Quervain et al., 1998), we reported that 30 min after exposure to foot-shock stress, rats had impaired retrieval of spatial memory (i.e., memory for the location of a platform in a water-maze task), which they had acquired 24 hr earlier. Interestingly, memory performance was not impaired when rats were tested either 2 min or 4 hr after the foot shock. These time-dependent effects on retrieval processes corresponded to the circulating corticosterone levels at the time of testing, which suggested that the retrieval impairment was directly related to increased adrenocortical function. In support of this idea, we found that suppression of corticosterone synthesis with metyrapone blocked the stress-induced retention impairment. In addition, systemic corticosterone administered to non-stressed rats 30 min before retention testing induced dose-dependent retention impairment. Further control experiments indicated that glucocorticoids did not affect spatial navigation, motivation, or motor performance.

In a next step, we have translated these findings to healthy humans and found that a single administration of cortisone (at a dose resulting in high physiological levels) impaired the recall of words learned 24 hr earlier (de Quervain et al., 2000). Several further studies from different laboratories have indicated that glucocorticoids impair the retrieval of hippocampus-dependent memory in rats (spatial or contextual memory) and humans (declarative memory) (Wolf et al., 2001; de Quervain et al., 2003; Roozendaal et al., 2003, 2004b; Buss et al., 2004; Domes et al., 2004; Rashidy-Pour et al., 2004; Het et al., 2005; Kuhlmann et al., 2005a, 2005b; Buchanan et al., 2006; Sajadi et al., 2007; Coluccia et al., 2008; Wolf, 2008). Furthermore, recent evidence indicates that emotionally arousing information is especially sensitive to the impairing effects of glucocorticoids (de Quervain et al., 2009). Thus, the mechanisms of acute glucocorticoid effects on memory retrieval are highly comparable to those seen in studies investigating memory consolidation in that the effects depend on emotional arousal. Moreover, comparable to the glucocorticoid effects on memory consolidation, the amygdala interacts with the hippocampus in mediating glucocorticoid effects on the retrieval of hippocampus-dependent memory (Roozendaal et al., 2008; de Quervain et al., 2009).

The impairment in memory retrieval induced by a single administration of glucocorticoids appears to be of temporary nature. The acute impairing effect of corticosterone on the retrieval of previously acquired contextual fear memory in rats is no longer observed when these animals are tested again 24 hr later (Cai et al., 2006). However, one study reported that a single administration of glucocorticoids induces not only acute, but also prolonged, impairment of memory retention in humans (Tollenaar et al., 2009). In that study, subjects were asked to retrieve previously learned information (declarative memory task) after ingestion of cortisol or a placebo. The single administration of cortisol induced an acute impairment in memory recall, which, however, was still observed in an additional recall test after a 1-week washout period. The persistence of this retrieval impairment might be due to a reduced rehearsal during retrieval under treatment and hence a lower reencoding of the material. Alternatively, cortisol might have inhibited memory-reconsolidation processes (see discussion under the final section).

Glucocorticoid Effects on Working Memory

Working memory is a dynamic process whereby information is updated continuously, providing a temporary storage of information (Baddeley, 1992; Jones, 2002). Evidence from lesion, pharmacological, imaging, and clinical studies indicates that working memory depends on the integrity of the prefrontal cortex (Brito et al., 1982; Fuster, 1991; Owen et al., 2005). Stress exposure is known to impair performance of rats on a delayed alternation task, a task commonly used to assess working memory in rodents (Arnsten and Goldman-Rakic, 1998). Basal levels of endogenous glucocorticoids are required to maintain prefrontal cortical function (Mizoguchi et al., 2004), but systemic injections of stress doses of corticosterone or administration of the glucocorticoid receptor agonist RU28362 into the medial prefrontal cortex impair delayed alternation performance in rats (Roozendaal et al., 2004a). Additionally, stress or stress-level cortisol treatment is known to impair working memory performance in human subjects during demanding tasks that require a high level of arousal (Baddeley, 1992; Lupien et al., 1999; Young et al., 1999; Wolf et al., 2001; Schoofs et al., 2008). Like glucocorticoid effects on memory consolidation and retrieval, these hormones interact with noradrenergic mechanisms in inducing impairment of working memory (Roozendaal et al., 2004a).

Modulatory Effects of Glucocorticoids on Emotional Memory: Implications for Anxiety Disorders

The findings reviewed above indicate that glucocorticoids enhance memory consolidation but impair memory retrieval and working memory in emotionally

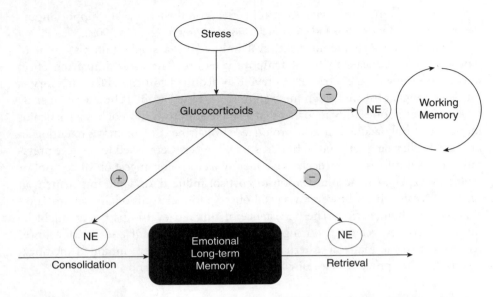

Figure 21.1 Effects of stress and glucocorticoids on memory functions. Whereas glucocorticoids enhance memory consolidation (initial memory consolidation as well as consolidation of extinction memory) they impair memory retrieval and working memory. All of these hormone effects depend on emotional arousal-induced activation of noradrenergic transmission. NE, norepinephrine. *Source:* From de Quervain et al. (2009). With permission from Elsevier.

arousing situations (Figure 21.1). Enhanced memory for emotional events is a well-recognized phenomenon, which helps us to remember important information. Although glucocorticoid-induced temporary impairments of memory retrieval and working memory are certainly unwanted in exam situations, these effects should not be regarded as maladaptive a priori. In fact, these effects may actually aid to an accurate storage of emotionally arousing information by blocking, for example, retroactive interference; that is, storage of important new information is not disturbed by recollected old information. However, whereas the enhanced memory for emotionally arousing events in most cases has a clear adaptive value, in certain circumstances extremely aversive experiences can also lead to highly emotional, traumatic or fearful memories, which contribute to the development and symptoms of anxiety disorders. Therefore, understanding the basic modulatory actions of glucocorticoids on different aspects of cognition may have important implications for understanding and, possibly, treating anxiety disorders. Although we focus in this chapter on the implications of memory-modulatory glucocorticoid effects for anxiety disorders, these glucocorticoid effects are likely to have important implications for other psychiatric disorders, such as depression or schizophrenia, as well (Starkman et al., 1981; Rubinow et al., 1984; Newcomer et al., 1998; Belanoff et al., 2001).

The role of aversive memories in anxiety disorders

Several lines of evidence indicate that after an aversive experience the formation of an aversive memory trace is an important pathogenic mechanism for the development of anxiety disorders, such as PTSD or phobias (Pitman, 1989; LeDoux, 2003; Phelps and LeDoux, 2005; Yehuda and LeDoux, 2007; Mineka and Oehlberg, 2008). PTSD is a chronic response to a traumatic event and characterized by the following features: reexperiencing of the traumatic event, avoidance of stimuli associated with the trauma, and hyperarousal. Reexperiencing symptoms include intrusive daytime recollections, traumatic nightmares, and flashbacks in which components of the event are relived (American Psychiatric Association, 1994; Yehuda, 2002a). Phobic disorders are characterized by marked and persistent fear that is excessive or unreasonable, cued by the presence or anticipation of a specific object or situation (Marks, 1987; American Psychiatric Association, 1994; Barlow et al., 1995).

Neuroimaging studies have shown that while the prefrontal cortex seems to be hyporesponsive, amygdala activity in response to viewing aversive information is exaggerated in patients with PTSD as compared to healthy controls and, importantly, correlates positively with later recall of the aversive information, and with PTSD symptom severity (Rauch et al., 2000; Armony et al., 2005; Shin et al., 2005, 2006; Francati et al., 2007; Dickie et al., 2008; Heim and Nemeroff, 2009). These findings are in line with the well-known role of the amygdala in the formation of emotional memory. Furthermore, some evidence indicates that the administration of a β-adrenoceptor blocker, which is known to reduce the consolidation of memory of emotionally arousing experiences, might be preventive with regard to the development of subsequent PTSD (Pitman et al., 2002). These findings underscore the important pathogenic role of aversive memory formation in the development of PTSD. However, the formation of a strong aversive memory trace is of course not sufficient to develop an anxiety disorder. In fact, building strong memories of an aversive event is a primarily adaptive mechanism and even intrusive thoughts (intrusive memory retrieval) and related symptoms are normal reactions in the first period after an aversive experience. In individuals who do not develop an anxiety disorder, which fortunately is mostly the case, intrusive memory retrieval declines over time, although the aversive memory can still be recalled voluntarily even after a long time. In contrast, in individuals who do develop a chronic anxiety disorder the aversive memory trace remains easily reactivated by an aversive cue (e.g., trauma cue or phobic stimulus), or even spontaneously, leading to uncontrollable aversive memory retrieval and related clinical symptoms (reexperiencing in PTSD, fear in phobia).

The reexperiencing symptoms in PTSD result from excessive retrieval of traumatic memories, which often retain their vividness and power to evoke distress for decades or even a lifetime. Importantly, traumatic reexperiencing phenomena are again consolidated (reconsolidated) into memory, which cements the traumatic memory trace (see the discussion of the concept of intrusions in the PTSD research literature, e.g., Brewin, 2001; Michael et al., 2005a, 2005b). Persistent retrieval, reexperiencing, and reconsolidation of traumatic memories is a process that keeps these memories vivid and thereby the disorder alive (see the final subsection on possible mode of action of glucocorticoids in the reduction of aversive memory).

In phobias, exposure to a phobic stimulus almost invariably provokes retrieval of stimulus-associated fear memory, which leads to the fear response (Lang et al., 1985; Foa and Kozak, 1986; Cuthbert et al., 2003). In addition, phobic individuals tend to construct highly negative images of a phobic situation, which substantially contribute to anticipatory anxiety as well as negative postevent processing. Such images are usually associated with explicit fearful memories of past phobic experiences which reinforce negative believes that are difficult to suppress and may strengthen the phobic response (Rapee and Heimberg, 1997; Fehm and Margraf, 2002). Thus, retrieval of aversive memories (traumatic memory in PTSD and fear memory in phobias) plays an important role in the symptomatology of these anxiety disorders.

Glucocorticoids and PTSD

Preventive effects of glucocorticoids with regard to the development of PTSD
From the basic studies discussed above, we have learned that acutely elevated glucocorticoids enhance the consolidation of emotional memories. Based on these findings, it can be assumed that elevated glucocorticoid levels at the time of an aversive experience may contribute to the formation of traumatic and fearful memories. This idea is supported by a recent study on traumatic memories in critically ill patients. These patients often report traumatic memories from intensive care treatment and have a relatively high incidence of chronic stress symptoms and PTSD during follow-up (Schelling et al., 2004a). The number of traumatic memories from the intensive care unit correlated positively with the amount of cortisol acutely administered to patients undergoing cardiac surgery (Schelling et al., 2003). Theoretically, it might therefore be useful to therapeutically block glucocorticoid signaling immediately after a traumatic incident, as has been proposed for adrenergic signaling (Pitman and Delahanty, 2005). However, to block initial consolidation of aversive memories, the anti-glucocorticoid treatment should be given shortly after the aversive event. This is usually not possible and therefore this approach seems difficult. Moreover, there is evidence suggesting that reduced cortisol excretion in response to a traumatic event is actually associated with an increased risk of developing subsequent PTSD (McFarlane et al., 1997; Yehuda et al., 1998; Delahanty et al., 2000). These findings suggest that elevated glucocorticoid levels after an aversive event might be preventive with regard to the development of PTSD. This idea is strongly supported by studies showing that prolonged (several days) administration of stress doses of cortisol during intensive care treatment reduces the risk for later PTSD (Schelling et al., 2001, 2004b, 2006; Weis et al., 2006). But how do such findings of preventive effects fit with the idea that glucocorticoids enhance the formation of traumatic memories? After initial

consolidation of traumatic experiences, which is likely to be enhanced by glucocorticoids, cortisol levels later on may play a crucial role in controlling the amount of retrieved traumatic memories. Specifically, by the known reducing effects of glucocorticoids on memory retrieval, high levels of these hormones may partly interrupt the vicious cycle of retrieving, reexperiencing, and reconsolidating aversive memories, thereby preventing a further cementation of the aversive memory trace. Studies showing that the preventive effects of glucocorticoid administration are also observed when the treatment started already at the time of the traumatic event (Schelling et al., 2004b; Weis et al., 2006) indicate that such an inhibitory effect of glucocorticoids on memory retrieval prevails the potentially enhancing effect on initial consolidation. Taken together, these findings suggest that elevated glucocorticoid levels (endogenously or pharmacologically) act preventively with regard to the development of PTSD.

Glucocorticoids reduce the retrieval of traumatic memories in chronic PTSD
In addition to individuals at risk for PTSD, patients with an established PTSD can also show low endogenous cortisol levels (Mason et al., 1986; Yehuda et al., 1995, 2007; Yehuda, 2002b; Bierer et al., 2006; Yehuda and Bierer, 2008), but see Pitman and Orr, 1990; Young and Breslau, 2004. A recent meta-analysis has shown that low cortisol levels depend on several factors, including gender and trauma type (Meewisse et al., 2007). Low cortisol levels may contribute to a hyper-retrieval of aversive memories. Based on the finding that glucocorticoids impair the retrieval of emotional information, we hypothesized that patients with chronic PTSD might benefit from glucocorticoid treatment. In an initial study, we tested this hypothesis in a small number of patients with chronic PTSD (Aerni et al., 2004). During a 3-month observation period, low-dose cortisol (10 mg per day) was administered orally for 1 month using a double-blind, placebo-controlled, crossover design. The administration of this low dose of cortisol for 1 month does not cause major side effects and does not suppress endogenous cortisol production (Cleare et al., 1999). The dose of hydrocortisone required to simulate the normal production of endogenous cortisol varies between 20 and 30 mg/day (Howlett, 1997). To assess possible treatment effects on the retrieval of traumatic memories, the patients rated daily the intensity and frequency of the feeling of reliving the traumatic event and the physiological distress felt in response to traumatic memories and nightmares (self-administered rating scales from questions on the Clinician Administered PTSD Scale (CAPS)). The results of this study indicated that low-dose cortisol treatment had beneficial effects with regard to reexperiencing symptoms and nightmares and we found evidence for cortisol effects that outlasted the treatment period (Aerni et al., 2004).

Glucocorticoids reduce fear in phobia

In recent clinical studies we found evidence that glucocorticoids may not only have beneficial effects in patients with PTSD but also in patients with phobias. We administered glucocorticoids to 40 subjects with social phobia and 20 subjects with spider phobia in two double-blind, placebo-controlled studies (Soravia et al., 2006). In the social phobia study, cortisone (25 mg) administered orally 1 hr before a socioevaluative stressor (Trier Social Stress Test; Kirschbaum et al., 1993; Dickerson and Kemeny, 2004) significantly reduced self-reported fear during the anticipation, exposure, and recovery phases of the stressor. Moreover, the stress-induced release of cortisol in placebo-treated subjects correlated negatively with fear ratings, suggesting that endogenously released cortisol in the context of a phobic situation buffers fear symptoms. This finding also indicates that reduced fear after glucocorticoid administration was not the result of a negative feedback on corticotropin-releasing hormone (CRH) release. In the spider phobia study, repeated oral administration of cortisol (10 mg), but not placebo, 1 hr before exposure to a spider photograph induced a progressive reduction of stimulus-induced fear. This effect was maintained when subjects were exposed to the stimulus again 2 days after the last cortisol administration, suggesting that cortisol also facilitated the extinction of phobic fear. In phobias the retrieval processes cannot be measured directly, so it cannot be ruled out that cortisol, perhaps in addition to influencing memory retrieval, may have reduced fear by exerting a direct anxiolytic effect or by modulating other systems involved in the expression of fear. For example, it has been found that acute cortisol administration can influence the startle reflex (Buchanan et al., 2001) and reduce preconscious attention to fear in anxious young men (Putman et al., 2007). However, in these studies cortisol did not affect subjective fear levels. In addition, in the phobia study, glucocorticoid administration did not affect phobia-unrelated anxiety, mood, wakefulness, or calmness, suggesting that glucocorticoids did not reduce phobic fear by general anxiolytic effects (Soravia et al., 2006). Moreover, recent findings indicating that acute cortisol elevations cause heightened arousal ratings of neutral stimuli (Abercrombie et al., 2005) make a general or direct anxiolytic effect of glucocorticoids unlikely.

Possible mode of action of glucocorticoids in the reduction of aversive memory

The results of our clinical studies suggest that elevated glucocorticoid administration have acute effects on clinical symptoms by reducing the retrieval of aversive memories, such as traumatic memory in PTSD (Aerni et al., 2004) and fear memory in phobia (Soravia et al., 2006). Additionally, in both studies we found evidence that symptoms were reduced even after cessation of the treatment period. What might be the underlying mechanism? Let's first review the processes which contribute to the persistence of these disorders. In PTSD, excessive retrieval of traumatic memory, which may be spontaneous or triggered by a trauma cue, leads to reexperiencing of the traumatic event (Michael and Ehlers, 2007). In phobia, retrieval of fear memory triggered by a fear cue (phobic situation or object) leads to a fear response. (Re) consolidation of such aversive experiences further cements the aversive memory trace and thereby contributes to the persistence of these disorders (Figure 21.2a). By inhibiting memory retrieval, cortisol may partly interrupt the vicious cycle of spontaneous retrieving, reexperiencing, and reconsolidating traumatic memories in PTSD and thereby promote forgetting, a spontaneous process that occurs when memory is not reactivated (Figure 21.2b). Furthermore, cortisol may facilitate the extinction of aversive memories, as evidenced by animal studies showing that glucocorticoid signaling promotes memory extinction processes (Bohus and Lissak, 1968; Barrett and Gonzalez-Lima, 2004; Yang et al., 2006). Glucocorticoids may facilitate extinction in two ways: (1) because of the cortisol-induced reduction of memory retrieval, an aversive cue is no longer followed by the usual aversive memory retrieval and related clinical symptoms but, instead, becomes associated with a non-aversive experience, which is stored as extinction memory and (2) because elevated glucocorticoid levels are known to enhance the long-term consolidation of memories (Kovacs et al., 1977; Flood et al., 1978; Roozendaal, 2000; Buchanan and Lovallo, 2001; Kuhlmann and Wolf, 2006) it is possible that glucocorticoids facilitate the storage of corrective experiences. This is supported by recent animal studies showing that postretrieval administration of glucocorticoids is able to enhance the consolidation of extinction memory (Cai et al., 2006; Abrari et al., 2008). Theoretically, such postretrieval (or postactivation) glucocorticoid effects may also be interpreted as an inhibition of reconsolidation (Tronson and Taylor, 2007; Wang et al., 2008). However, findings in animals suggest that reconsolidation of aversive memory is disrupted by blocking rather than by activating glucocorticoid signaling (Tronel and Alberini, 2007). Furthermore, in favor of the memory-extinction hypothesis it has been shown that postretrieval effects of glucocorticoids on memory are of transient nature and are reversed by a reminder (but see Wang et al., 2008), which should not occur after inhibited reconsolidation. Although the data currently available rather speak for a facilitating effect of glucocorticoids on memory extinction, it is possible that, perhaps under certain conditions, glucocorticoids may also inhibit memory-reconsolidation processes.

Conclusion

This chapter has reviewed evidence indicating that glucocorticoids at levels that enhance memory consolidation of emotionally arousing information impair memory retrieval and working memory (Figure 21.1). Importantly, these hormone effects depend on emotional arousal-induced activation of noradrenergic transmission within the amygdala and on interactions of the amygdala with other brain regions, such as the hippocampus and neocortical regions.

Enhanced consolidation for emotionally arousing information is an adaptive mechanism, which helps us to retain important information. Reduced memory retrieval and working memory should not be regarded a priori as maladaptive as they support this process of retaining important information. In addition, the reduction of memory retrieval may aid to suppressing behaviors that are no more

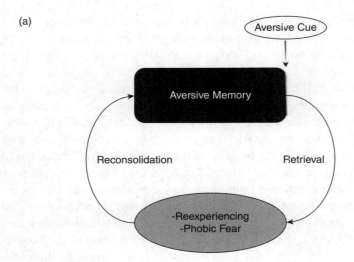

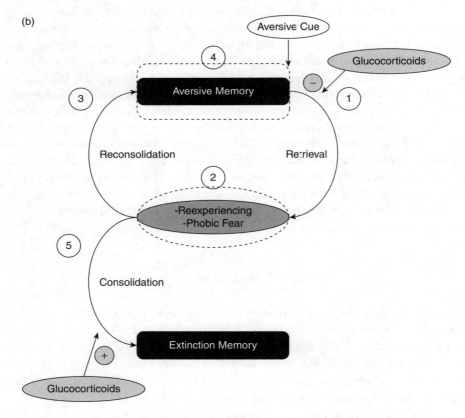

Figure 21.2   Model on the role of glucocorticoids in the reduction of aversive memory. (a) Excessive retrieval of aversive memories causes reexperiencing of symptoms in PTSD and phobic fear in phobia. Reconsolidation of such aversive experiences further cements the aversive memory trace. (b) Glucocorticoid-induced reduction of the aversive memory trace. By inhibiting memory retrieval, glucocorticoids partly interrupt this vicious cycle of retrieving (1), reexperiencing (2), and reconsolidating (3) aversive memories, which leads to a weakening of the aversive memory trace (4). Furthermore, because the aversive cue is no longer followed by the usual aversive memory retrieval and related clinical symptoms, the cue becomes associated with a nonaversive experience, which is stored as extinction memory (5). Based on the findings of animal studies, glucocorticoids are likely to enhance long-term consolidation of extinction memory. *Source:* From de Quervain et al. (2009). With permission from Elsevier.

←

---

relevant or even maladaptive. This mechanism is especially important in more chronic situations when the organism is forced to adapt to a changed environment (e.g., environmental disaster, war). Under such conditions, also the facilitating effects of glucocorticoids on extinction processes represent an adaptive response, which helps the organism to deal with stressful events (McEwen, 1998; de Kloet et al., 1999).

Because emotionally aversive memories play an important role in the development and symptomatology of anxiety disorders, we aimed to translate the basic findings on the effects of glucocorticoids on emotional memory in animals and healthy humans to clinical conditions. Specifically, the findings, which indicated that glucocorticoids reduce memory retrieval and enhance extinction of emotional memories led us to hypothesize that these stress hormones might be useful in the treatment of anxiety disorders. Clinical studies and studies in animal models of acquired fear indicate that glucocorticoid treatment indeed reduces the retrieval of traumatic memories and enhances extinction processes. These dual actions of glucocorticoids seem to be especially suited for the treatment of acquired fear. By inhibiting memory retrieval, glucocorticoids may partly interrupt the vicious cycle of spontaneous retrieving, reexperiencing, and (re)consolidating aversive memories. Furthermore, by enhancing extinction processes, glucocorticoids facilitate the storage of corrective experiences. Therefore, the combination of glucocorticoids with exposure techniques in cognitive-behavioral therapy may be a promising approach.

Future research should include large-scale clinical studies to evaluate the therapeutic efficacy of glucocorticoids in the treatment of anxiety disorders and to explore the efficacy of combining glucocorticoid treatment with psychotherapy. More research is also needed to better understand the molecular underpinnings of glucocorticoid actions on different memory processes as well as the role of (epi) genetic differences across individuals (de Quervain et al., 2007). Such research might further promote the understanding of why some individuals become vulnerable to anxiety disorders, whereas others are resilient or even gain strength from stressful experiences.

References

Abercrombie, H. C., Kalin, N. H., Thurow, M. E., Rosenkranz, M. A., & Davidson, R. J. (2003). Cortisol variation in humans affects memory for emotionally laden and neutral information. *Behavioral Neuroscience, 117*, 505–516.

Abercrombie, H. C., Kalin, N. H., & Davidson, R. J. (2005). Acute cortisol elevations cause heightened arousal ratings of objectively nonarousing stimuli. *Emotion, 5*, 354–359.

Abrari, K., Rashidy-Pour, A., Semnanian, S., & Fathollahi, Y. (2008). Administration of corticosterone after memory reactivation disrupts subsequent retrieval of a contextual conditioned fear memory: dependence upon training intensity. *Neurobiology of Learning and Memory, 89*, 178–184.

Aerni, A., Traber, R., Hock, C., Roozendaal, B., Schelling, G., Papassotiropoulos, A., Nitsch, R. M., Schnyder, U., & de Quervain, D. J. (2004). Low-dose cortisol for symptoms of posttraumatic stress disorder. *American Journal of Psychiatry, 161*, 1488–1490.

American Psychiatric Association (1994). *Diagnostic and statistical manual of mental disorders.* (4th ed.). Washington, DC: American Psychiatric Association.

Arbel, I., Kadar, T., Silbermann, M., & Levy, A. (1994). The effects of long-term corticosterone administration on hippocampal morphology and cognitive performance of middle-aged rats. *Brain Research, 657*, 227–235.

Armony, J. L., Corbo, V., Clement, M. H., & Brunet, A. (2005). Amygdala response in patients with acute PTSD to masked and unmasked emotional facial expressions. *American Journal of Psychiatry, 162*, 1961–1963.

Arnsten, A. F., & Goldman-Rakic, P. S. (1998). Noise stress impairs prefrontal cortical cognitive function in monkeys: evidence for a hyperdopaminergic mechanism. *Archives of General Psychiatry, 55*, 362–368.

Baddeley, A. (1992). Working memory. *Science, 255*, 556–559.

Barlow, D. H., Liebowitz, M. R., Kaplan, H. I., & Sadock, B. J. (1995). Specific and social phobias. In H. I. Kaplan, & B. J. Sadock (Eds.), *Comprehensive textbook of psychiatry* (vol. 6, pp. 1204–1218). New York: Williams and Wilkins.

Barrett, D., & Gonzalez-Lima, F. (2004). Behavioral effects of metyrapone on Pavlovian extinction. *Neuroscience Letters, 371*, 91–96.

Beckwith, B. E., Petros, T. V., Scaglione, C., & Nelson, J. (1986). Dose-dependent effects of hydrocortisone on memory in human males. *Physiology and Behavior, 36*, 283–286.

Belanoff, J. K., Kalehzan, M., Sund, B., Fleming Ficek, S. K., & Schatzberg, A. F. (2001). Cortisol activity and cognitive changes in psychotic major depression. *American Journal of Psychiatry, 158*, 1612–1616.

Bierer, L. M., Tischler, L., Labinsky, E., Cahill, S., Foa, E., & Yehuda, R. (2006). Clinical correlates of 24-h cortisol and norepinephrine excretion among subjects seeking treatment following the world trade center attacks on 9/11. *Annals of the New York Academy of Sciences, 1071*, 514–520.

Bisaz, R., Conboy, L., & Sandi, C. (2008). Learning under stress: A role for the neural cell adhesion molecule NCAM. *Neurobiology of Learning and Memory, 91*, 333–342.

Bohus, B., & Lissak, K. (1968). Adrenocortical hormones and avoidance behaviour of rats. *International Journal of Neuropharmacology, 7*, 301–306.

Brewin, C. R. (2001). A cognitive neuroscience account of posttraumatic stress disorder and its treatment. *Behaviour Research and Therapy, 39*, 373–393.

Brito, G. N., Thomas, G. J., Davis, B. J., & Gingold, S. I. (1982). Prelimbic cortex, mediodorsal thalamus, septum, and delayed alternation in rats. *Experimental Brain Research, 46,* 52–58.

Buchanan, T. W., & Lovallo, W. R. (2001). Enhanced memory for emotional material following stress-level cortisol treatment in humans. *Psychoneuroendocrinology, 26,* 307–317.

Buchanan, T. W., Brechtel, A., Sollers, J. J., & Lovallo, W. R. (2001). Exogenous cortisol exerts effects on the startle reflex independent of emotional modulation. *Pharmacology, Biochemistry, and Behavior, 68,* 203–210.

Buchanan, T. W., Tranel, D., & Adolphs, R. (2006). Impaired memory retrieval correlates with individual differences in cortisol response but not autonomic response. *Learning and Memory, 13,* 382–387.

Buss, C., Wolf, O. T., Witt, J., & Hellhammer, D. H. (2004). Autobiographic memory impairment following acute cortisol administration. *Psychoneuroendocrinology, 29,* 1093–1096.

Cai, W. H., Blundell, J., Han, J., Greene, R. W., & Powell, C. M. (2006). Postreactivation glucocorticoids impair recall of established fear memory. *Journal of Neuroscience, 26,* 9560–9566.

Cleare, A. J., Heap, E., Malhi, G. S., Wessely, S., O'Keane, V., & Miell, J. (1999). Low-dose hydrocortisone in chronic fatigue syndrome: a randomised crossover trial. *Lancet, 353,* 455–458.

Coluccia, D., Wolf, O. T., Kollias, S., Roozendaal, B., Forster, A., & de Quervain, D. J. (2008). Glucocorticoid therapy-induced memory deficits: acute versus chronic effects. *Journal of Neuroscience, 28,* 3474–3478.

Conrad, C. D. (2008). Chronic stress-induced hippocampal vulnerability: the glucocorticoid vulnerability hypothesis. *Reviews in Neuroscience, 19,* 395–411.

Cordero, M. I., Kruyt, N. D., Merino, J. J., & Sandi, C. (2002). Glucocorticoid involvement in memory formation in a rat model for traumatic memory. *Stress, 5,* 73–79.

Cuthbert, B. N., Lang, P. J., Strauss, C., Drobes, D., Patrick, C. J., & Bradley, M. M. (2003). The psychophysiology of anxiety disorder: fear memory imagery. *Psychophysiology, 40,* 407–422.

de Kloet, E. R., Oitzl, M. S., Joëls, M. (1999). Stress and cognition: are corticosteroids good or bad guys? *Trends in Neuroscience, 22,* 422–426.

de Quervain, D. J., Roozendaal, B., & McGaugh, J. L. (1998). Stress and glucocorticoids impair retrieval of long-term spatial memory. *Nature, 394,* 787–790.

de Quervain, D. J., Roozendaal, B., Nitsch, R. M., McGaugh, J. L., & Hock, C. (2000). Acute cortisone administration impairs retrieval of long-term declarative memory in humans. *Nature Neuroscience, 3,* 313–314.

de Quervain, D. J., Henke, K., Aerni, A., Treyer, V., McGaugh, J. L., Berthold, T., Nitsch, R. M., Buck, A., Roozendaal, B., & Hock, C. (2003). Glucocorticoid-induced impairment of declarative memory retrieval is associated with reduced blood flow in the medial temporal lobe. *European Journal of Neuroscience, 17,* 1296–1302.

de Quervain, D. J., Kolassa, I. T., Ertl, V., Onyut, P. L., Neuner, F., Elbert, T., & Papassotiropoulos, A. (2007). A deletion variant of the alpha2b-adrenoceptor is related to emotional memory in Europeans and Africans. *Nature Neuroscience, 10,* 1137–1139.

de Quervain, D. J., Aerni, A., Schelling, G., & Roozendaal, B. (2009). Glucocorticoids and the regulation of memory in health and disease. *Frontiers in Neuroendocrinology, 30,* 358–370.

Delahanty, D. L., Raimonde, A. J., & Spoonster, E. (2000). Initial posttraumatic urinary cortisol levels predict subsequent PTSD symptoms in motor vehicle accident victims. *Biological Psychiatry, 48*, 940–947.

Dickerson, S. S., & Kemeny, M. E. (2004). Acute stressors and cortisol responses: a theoretical integration and synthesis of laboratory research. *Psychological Bulletin, 130*, 355–391.

Dickie, E. W., Brunet, A., Akerib, V., & Armony, J. L. (2008). An fMRI investigation of memory encoding in PTSD: influence of symptom severity. *Neuropsychologia, 46*, 1522–1531.

Domes, G., Heinrichs, M., Rimmele, U., Reichwald, U., & Hautzinger, M. (2004). Acute stress impairs recognition for positive words–association with stress-induced cortisol secretion. *Stress, 7*, 173–181.

Fehm, L., & Margraf, J. (2002). Thought suppression: specificity in agoraphobia versus broad impairment in social phobia? *Behaviour Research and Therapy, 40*, 57–66.

Flood, J. F., Vidal, D., Bennett, E. L., Orme, A. E., Vasquez, S., & Jarvik, M. E. (1978). Memory facilitating and anti-amnesic effects of corticosteroids. *Pharmacology, Biochemistry, and Behavior, 8*, 81–87.

Foa, E. B., & Kozak, M. J. (1986). Emotional processing of fear: exposure to corrective information. *Psychological Bulletin, 99*, 20–35.

Francati, V., Vermetten, E., & Bremner, J. D. (2007). Functional neuroimaging studies in posttraumatic stress disorder: review of current methods and findings. *Depression and Anxiety, 24*, 202–218.

Fuster, J. M. (1991). The prefrontal cortex and its relation to behavior. *Progress in Brain Research, 87*, 201–211.

Heim, C., & Nemeroff, C. B. (2009). Neurobiology of posttraumatic stress disorder. *CNS Spectrums, 14*, 13–24.

Het, S., Ramlow, G., & Wolf, O. T. (2005). A meta-analytic review of the effects of acute cortisol administration on human memory. *Psychoneuroendocrinology, 30*, 771–784.

Howlett, T. A. (1997). An assessment of optimal hydrocortisone replacement therapy. *Clinical Endocrinology (Oxford), 46*, 263–268.

Jones, M. W. (2002). A comparative review of rodent prefrontal cortex and working memory. *Current Molecular Medicine, 2*, 639–647.

Kandel, E. R. (2001). The molecular biology of memory storage: a dialogue between genes and synapses. *Science, 294*, 1030–1038.

Karst, H., Nair, S., Velzing, E., Rumpff-van, E. L., Slagter, E., Shinnick-Gallagher, P., & Joels, M. (2002). Glucocorticoids alter calcium conductances and calcium channel subunit expression in basolateral amygdala neurons. *European Journal of Neuroscience, 16*, 1083–1089.

Kirschbaum, C., Pirke, K. M., & Hellhammer, D. H. (1993). The 'Trier Social Stress Test'–a tool for investigating psychobiological stress responses in a laboratory setting. *Neuropsychobiology, 28*, 76–81.

Kovacs, G. L., Telegdy, G., & Lissak, K. (1977). Dose-dependent action of corticosteroids on brain serotonin content and passive avoidance behavior. *Hormones and Behavoir, 8*, 155–165.

Kuhlmann, S., & Wolf, O. T. (2006). Arousal and cortisol interact in modulating memory consolidation in healthy young men. *Behavioral Neuroscience, 120*, 217–223.

Kuhlmann, S., Piel, M., & Wolf, O. T. (2005a). Impaired memory retrieval after psychosocial stress in healthy young men. *Journal of Neuroscience, 25*, 2977–2982.

Kuhlmann, S., Kirschbaum, C., & Wolf, O. T. (2005b). Effects of oral cortisol treatment in healthy young women on memory retrieval of negative and neutral words. *Neurobiology of Learning and Memory, 83*, 158–162.

Lang, P. J., Tuma, A. H., & Maser, J. D. (1985). The cognitive psychophysiology of emotion: fear and anxiety. In A. H. Tuma, & J. D. Maser (Eds.), *Anxiety and the anxiety disorders* (pp. 131–170). Hillsdale, NJ: Erlbaum.

LeDoux, J. (2003). The emotional brain, fear, and the amygdala. *Cellular and Molecular Neurobiology, 23*, 727–738.

Liu, L., Tsuji, M., Takeda, H., Takada, K., & Matsumiya, T. (1999). Adrenocortical suppression blocks the enhancement of memory storage produced by exposure to psychological stress in rats. *Brain Research, 821*, 134–140.

Luine, V. N., Spencer, R. L., & McEwen, B. S. (1993). Effects of chronic corticosterone ingestion on spatial memory performance and hippocampal serotonergic function. *Brain Research, 616*, 65–70.

Lupien, S. J., Gillin, C. J., & Hauger, R. L. (1999). Working memory is more sensitive than declarative memory to the acute effects of corticosteroids: a dose-response study in humans. *Behavioral Neuroscience, 113*, 420–430.

Maheu, F. S., Joober, R., Beaulieu, S., & Lupien, S. J. (2004). Differential effects of adrenergic and corticosteroid hormonal systems on human short- and long-term declarative memory for emotionally arousing material. *Behavioral Neuroscience, 118*, 420–428.

Marks, I. (1987). *Fears, phobias and rituals: Panic, anxiety, and their disorders.* New York: Oxford University Press.

Mason, J. W., Giller, E. L., Kosten, T. A., Ostroff, R. B., & Podd, L. (1986). Urinary free-cortisol levels in posttraumatic stress disorder patients. *Journal of Nervous and Mental Disease, 174*, 145–149.

McEwen, B. S. (1998). Protective and damaging effects of stress mediators. *New England Journal of Medicine, 338*, 171–179.

McEwen, B. S. (2001). Plasticity of the hippocampus: adaptation to chronic stress and allostatic load. *Annals of the New York Academy of Sciences, 933*, 265–277.

McFarlane, A. C., Atchison, M., & Yehuda, R. (1997). The acute stress response following motor vehicle accidents and its relation to PTSD. *Annals of the New York Academy of Sciences, 821*, 437–441.

McGaugh, J. L., & Roozendaal, B. (2002). Role of adrenal stress hormones in forming lasting memories in the brain. *Current Opinions in Neurobiology, 12*, 205–210.

McGaugh, J. L. (2003). *Memory and emotion: The making of lasting memory.* London: Weidenfeld and Nicolson.

Meewisse, M. L., Reitsma, J. B., de Vries, G. J., Gersons, B. P., & Olff, M. (2007). Cortisol and post-traumatic stress disorder in adults: systematic review and meta-analysis. *British Journal of Psychiatry, 191*, 387–392.

Michael, T., & Ehlers, A. (2007). Enhanced perceptual priming for neutral stimuli occurring in a traumatic context: two experimental investigations. *Behaviour Research and Therapy, 45*, 341–358.

Michael, T., Ehlers, A., & Halligan, S. L. (2005a). Enhanced priming for trauma-related material in posttraumatic stress disorder. *Emotion, 5*, 103–112.

Michael, T., Ehlers, A., Halligan, S. L., & Clark, D. M. (2005b). Unwanted memories of assault: what intrusion characteristics are associated with PTSD? *Behaviour Research and Therapy, 43*, 613–628.

Mineka, S., & Oehlberg, K. (2008). The relevance of recent developments in classical conditioning to understanding the etiology and maintenance of anxiety disorders. *Acta Psychologica, 127,* 567–580.

Mizoguchi, K., Ishige, A., Takeda, S., Aburada, M., & Tabira, T. (2004). Endogenous glucocorticoids are essential for maintaining prefrontal cortical cognitive function. *Journal of Neuroscience, 24,* 5492–5499.

Newcomer, J. W., Craft, S., Askins, K., Hershey, T., Bardgett, M. E., Csernansky, J. G., Gagliardi, A. E., & Vogler, G. (1998). Glucocorticoid interactions with memory function in schizophrenia. *Psychoneuroendocrinology, 23,* 65–72.

Owen, A. M., McMillan, K. M., Laird, A. R., & Bullmore, E. (2005). N-back working memory paradigm: a meta-analysis of normative functional neuroimaging studies. *Human Brain Mapping, 25,* 46–59.

Phelps, E. A., & LeDoux, J. E. (2005). Contributions of the amygdala to emotion processing: from animal models to human behavior. *Neuron, 48,* 175–187.

Pitman, R. K. (1989). Post-traumatic stress disorder, hormones, and memory. *Biological Psychiatry, 26,* 221–223.

Pitman, R. K., & Orr, S. P. (1990). Twenty-four hour urinary cortisol and catecholamine excretion in combat- related posttraumatic stress disorder. *Biological Psychiatry, 27,* 245–247.

Pitman, R. K., & Delahanty, D. L. (2005). Conceptually driven pharmacologic approaches to acute trauma. *CNS Spectrums, 10,* 99–106.

Pitman, R. K., Sanders, K. M., Zusman, R. M., Healy, A. R., Cheema, F., Lasko, N. B., Cahill, L., & Orr, S. P. (2002). Pilot study of secondary prevention of posttraumatic stress disorder with propranolol. *Biological Psychiatry, 51,* 189–192.

Putman, P., Hermans, E. J., Koppeschaar, H., van Schijndel, A., & van Honk, J. (2007). A single administration of cortisol acutely reduces preconscious attention for fear in anxious young men. *Psychoneuroendocrinology, 32,* 793–802.

Quirk, G. J., & Mueller, D. (2008). Neural mechanisms of extinction learning and retrieval. *Neuropsychopharmacology, 33,* 56–72.

Rapee, R. M., & Heimberg, R. G. (1997). A cognitive-behavioral model of anxiety in social phobia. *Behaviour Research and Therapy, 35,* 741–756.

Rashidy-Pour, A., Sadeghi, H., Taherain, A. A., Vafaei, A. A., & Fathollahi, Y. (2004). The effects of acute restraint stress and dexamethasone on retrieval of long-term memory in rats: an interaction with opiate system. *Behavioral Brain Research, 154,* 193–198.

Rauch, S. L., Whalen, P. J., Shin, L. M., McInerney, S. C., Macklin, M. L., Lasko, N. B., Orr, S. P., & Pitman, R. K. (2000). Exaggerated amygdala response to masked facial stimuli in posttraumatic stress disorder: a functional MRI study. *Biological Psychiatry, 47,* 769–776.

Revest, J. M., Di Blasi, F., Kitchener, P., Rouge-Pont, F., Desmedt, A., Turiault, M., Tronche, F., & Piazza, P. V. (2005). The MAPK pathway and Egr-1 mediate stress-related behavioral effects of glucocorticoids. *Nature Neuroscience, 8,* 664–672.

Roozendaal, B. (2000). 1999 Curt P. Richter award. Glucocorticoids and the regulation of memory consolidation. *Psychoneuroendocrinology, 25,* 213–238.

Roozendaal, B., & McGaugh, J. L. (1996a). Amygdaloid nuclei lesions differentially affect glucocorticoid-induced memory enhancement in an inhibitory avoidance task. *Neurobiology of Learning and Memory, 65,* 1–8.

Roozendaal, B., & McGaugh, J. L. (1996b). The memory-modulatory effects of glucocorticoids depend on an intact stria terminalis. *Brain Research, 709,* 243–250.

Roozendaal, B., Bohus, B., & McGaugh, J. L. (1996a). Dose-dependent suppression of adrenocortical activity with metyrapone: effects on emotion and memory. *Psychoneuroendocrinology, 21,* 681–693.

Roozendaal, B., Carmi, O., & McGaugh, J. L. (1996b). Adrenocortical suppression blocks the memory-enhancing effects of amphetamine and epinephrine. *Proceedings of the National Academy of Sciences USA, 93,* 1429–1433.

Roozendaal, B., Williams, C. L., & McGaugh, J. L. (1999). Glucocorticoid receptor activation in the rat nucleus of the solitary tract facilitates memory consolidation: involvement of the basolateral amygdala. *European Journal of Neuroscience, 11,* 1317–1323.

Roozendaal, B., Griffith, Q. K., Buranday, J., de Quervain, D. J., & McGaugh, J. L. (2003). The hippocampus mediates glucocorticoid-induced impairment of spatial memory retrieval: dependence on the basolateral amygdala. *Proceedings of the National Academy of Sciences USA, 100,* 1328–1333.

Roozendaal, B., McReynolds, J. R., & McGaugh, J. L. (2004a). The basolateral amygdala interacts with the medial prefrontal cortex in regulating glucocorticoid effects on working memory impairment. *Journal of Neuroscience, 24,* 1385–1392.

Roozendaal, B., Hahn, E. L., Nathan, S. V., de Quervain, D. J., & McGaugh, J. L. (2004b). Glucocorticoid effects on memory retrieval require concurrent noradrenergic activity in the hippocampus and basolateral amygdala. *Journal of Neuroscience, 24,* 8161–8169.

Roozendaal, B., Barsegyan, A., & Lee, S. (2008). Adrenal stress hormones, amygdala activation, and memory for emotionally arousing experiences. *Progress in Brain Research, 167,* 79–97.

Rubinow, D. R., Post, R. M., Savard, R., & Gold, P. W. (1984). Cortisol hypersecretion and cognitive impairment in depression. *Archives of General Psychiatry, 41,* 279–283.

Sajadi, A. A., Samaei, S. A., & Rashidy-Pour, A. (2007). Blocking effects of intra-hippocampal naltrexone microinjections on glucocorticoid-induced impairment of spatial memory retrieval in rats. *Neuropharmacology, 52,* 347–354.

Sandi, C., & Rose, S. P. (1994). Corticosterone enhances long-term retention in one-day-old chicks trained in a weak passive avoidance learning paradigm. *Brain Research, 647,* 106–112.

Sapolsky, R. M. (2000). Glucocorticoids and hippocampal atrophy in neuropsychiatric disorders. *Archives of General Psychiatry, 57,* 925–935.

Schelling, G., Briegel, J., Roozendaal, B., Stoll, C., Rothenhausler, H. B., & Kapfhammer, H. P. (2001). The effect of stress doses of hydrocortisone during septic shock on posttraumatic stress disorder in survivors. *Biological Psychiatry, 50,* 978–985.

Schelling, G., Richter, M., Roozendaal, B., Rothenhausler, H. B., Krauseneck, T., Stoll, C., Nollert, G., Schmidt, M., & Kapfhammer, H. P. (2003). Exposure to high stress in the intensive care unit may have negative effects on health-related quality-of-life outcomes after cardiac surgery. *Critical Care Medicine, 31,* 1971–1980.

Schelling, G., Roozendaal, B., & de Quervain, D. J. (2004a). Can posttraumatic stress disorder be prevented with glucocorticoids? *Annals of the New York Academy of Sciences, 1032,* 158–166.

Schelling, G., Kilger, E., Roozendaal, B., de Quervain, D. J., Briegel, J., Dagge, A., Rothenhausler, H. B., Krauseneck, T., Nollert, G., & Kapfhammer, H. P. (2004b). Stress doses of hydrocortisone, traumatic memories, and symptoms of posttraumatic stress disorder in patients after cardiac surgery: a randomized study. *Biological Psychiatry, 55,* 627–633.

Schelling, G., Roozendaal, B., Krauseneck, T., Schmoelz, M., de Quervain D. J., & Briegel, J. (2006). Efficacy of hydrocortisone in preventing posttraumatic stress disorder following critical illness and major surgery. *Annals of the New York Academy of Sciences*, *1071*, 46–53.

Schoofs, D., Preuss, D., & Wolf, O. T. (2008). Psychosocial stress induces working memory impairments in an n-back paradigm. *Psychoneuroendocrinology*, *33*, 643–653.

Shin, L. M., Wright, C. I., Cannistraro, P. A., Wedig, M. M., McMullin, K., Martis, B., Macklin, M. L., Lasko, N. B., Cavanagh, S. R., Krangel, T. S., Orr, S. P., Pitman, R. K., Whalen, P. J., & Rauch, S. L. (2005). A functional magnetic resonance imaging study of amygdala and medial prefrontal cortex responses to overtly presented fearful faces in posttraumatic stress disorder. *Archives of General Psychiatry*, *62*, 273–281.

Shin, L. M., Rauch, S. L., & Pitman, R. K. (2006). Amygdala, medial prefrontal cortex, and hippocampal function in PTSD. *Annals of the New York Academy of Sciences*, *1071*, 67–79.

Soravia, L. M., Heinrichs, M., Aerni, A., Maroni, C., Schelling, G., Ehlert, U., Roozendaal, B., & de Quervain, D. J. (2006). Glucocorticoids reduce phobic fear in humans. *Proceedings of the National Academy of Sciences USA*, *103*, 5585–5590.

Starkman, M. N., Schteingart, D. E., & Schork, M. A. (1981). Depressed mood and other psychiatric manifestations of Cushing's syndrome: relationship to hormone levels. *Psychosomatic Medicine*, *43*, 3–18.

Tollenaar, M. S., Elzinga, B. M., Spinhoven, P., & Everaerd, W. (2009). Immediate and prolonged effects of cortisol, but not propranolol, on memory retrieval in healthy young men. *Neurobiology of Learning and Memory*, *91*, 23–31.

Tronel, S., & Alberini, C. M. (2007). Persistent disruption of a traumatic memory by postretrieval inactivation of glucocorticoid receptors in the amygdala. *Biological Psychiatry*, *62*, 33–39.

Tronson, N. C., & Taylor, J. R. (2007). Molecular mechanisms of memory reconsolidation. *Nature Reviews Neuroscience*, *8*, 262–275.

Wang, X. Y., Zhao, M., Ghitza, U. E., Li, Y. Q., & Lu, L. (2008). Stress impairs reconsolidation of drug memory via glucocorticoid receptors in the basolateral amygdala. *Journal of Neuroscience*, *28*, 5602–5610.

Weis, F., Kilger, E., Roozendaal, B., de Quervain, D. J., Lamm, P., Schmidt, M., Schmolz, M., Briegel, J., & Schelling, G. (2006). Stress doses of hydrocortisone reduce chronic stress symptoms and improve health-related quality of life in high-risk patients after cardiac surgery: a randomized study. *Journal of Thoracic & Cardiovascular Surgery*, *131*, 277–282.

Wolf, O. T. (2008). The influence of stress hormones on emotional memory: relevance for psychopathology. *Acta Psychologica*, *127*, 513–531.

Wolf, O. T., Convit, A., McHugh, P. F., Kandil, E., Thorn, E. L., De Santi, S., McEwen, B. S., & de Leon, M. J. (2001). Cortisol differentially affects memory in young and elderly men. *Behavioral Neuroscience*, *115*, 1002–1011.

Yang, Y. L., Chao, P. K., & Lu, K. T. (2006). Systemic and intra-amygdala administration of glucocorticoid agonist and antagonist modulate extinction of conditioned fear. *Neuropsychopharmacology*, *31*, 912–924.

Yehuda, R. (2002a). Post-traumatic stress disorder. *New England Journal of Medicine*, *346*, 108–114.

Yehuda, R. (2002b). Current status of cortisol findings in post-traumatic stress disorder. *Psychiatric Clinics of North America*, *25*, 341–368, vii.

Yehuda, R., & LeDoux, J. (2007). Response variation following trauma: a translational neuroscience approach to understanding PTSD. *Neuron, 56,* 19–32.

Yehuda, R., & Bierer, L. M. (2008). Transgenerational transmission of cortisol and PTSD risk. *Progress in Brain Research, 167,* 121–135.

Yehuda, R., Kahana, B., Binder-Brynes, K., Southwick, S. M., Mason, J. W., & Giller, E. L. (1995). Low urinary cortisol excretion in Holocaust survivors with posttraumatic stress disorder. *American Journal of Psychiatry, 152,* 982–986.

Yehuda, R., McFarlane, A. C., & Shalev, A. Y. (1998). Predicting the development of posttraumatic stress disorder from the acute response to a traumatic event. *Biological Psychiatry, 44,* 1305–1313.

Yehuda, R., Teicher, M. H., Seckl, J. R., Grossman, R. A., Morris, A., & Bierer, L. M. (2007). Parental posttraumatic stress disorder as a vulnerability factor for low cortisol trait in offspring of holocaust survivors. *Archives of General Psychiatry, 64,* 1040–1048.

Young, A. H., Sahakian, B. J., Robbins, T. W., & Cowen, P. J. (1999). The effects of chronic administration of hydrocortisone on cognitive function in normal male volunteers. *Psychopharmacology (Berlin), 145,* 260–266.

Young, E. A., & Breslau, N. (2004). Cortisol and catecholamines in posttraumatic stress disorder: an epidemiologic community study. *Archives of General Psychiatry, 61,* 394–401.

22

Stress and Human
Neuroimaging Studies

J. Douglas Bremner

Lasting Effects of Traumatic Stress on the Brain and Behavior

Traumatic stressors can lead to several chronic psychiatric disorders, including post-traumatic stress disorder (PTSD), as well as depression (Franklin and Zimmerman, 2001; Prigerson et al., 2001), substance abuse (Bremner et al., 1996; Kessler et al., 1995), dissociative disorders (Putnam et al., 1986), and borderline personality disorder (Battle et al., 2004; Yen et al., 2002). For many trauma victims, PTSD, which affects about 8% of Americans at some time in their lives (Kessler et al., 1995), may be a lifelong problem (Saigh and Bremner, 1999). The past decade has seen an explosion of research using brain imaging to assess the effects of traumatic stress on the brain (Bremner, 2007; Bremner, 2005; Bremner et al., 2008). These studies have implicated the amygdala, hippocampus, and medial prefrontal cortex (including anterior cingulate) in PTSD and other stress-related psychiatric disorders. This chapter reviews brain-imaging studies looking at the effects of traumatic stress on the brain, and integrates them with basic science findings on the neuroscience of stress.

Neural Circuits of Trauma-spectrum Disorders

Psychiatric disorders linked to trauma have been termed *trauma-spectrum disorders* (Bremner, 2002a). Symptoms of PTSD and other trauma-spectrum disorders are hypothesized to represent the behavioral manifestation of stress-induced changes in brain structure and function. Stress results in acute and chronic changes in

The Handbook of Stress: Neuropsychological Effects on the Brain, First Edition.
Edited by Cheryl D. Conrad.

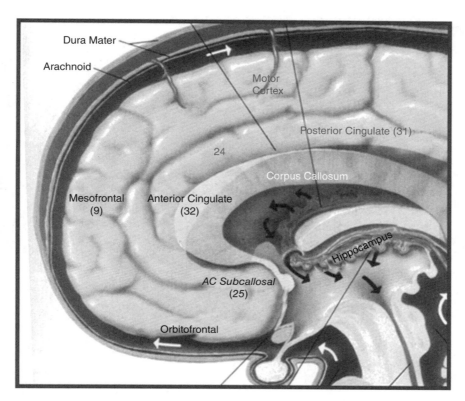

Figure 22.1 Brain and hippocampus. AC, anterior cingulate. Numbers refer to Brodmann's areas.

neurochemical systems and specific brain regions involved in the stress response, leading to long-term changes in brain *circuits* (Figure 22.1; Table 22.1) (Vermetten and Bremner, 2002b; Bremner, 2002a; Pitman, 2001; Vermetten and Bremner, 2002a).

Preclinical and clinical studies have shown alterations in memory function in PTSD patients (Elzinga and Bremner, 2002) as well as changes in a circuit of brain areas, including hippocampus, amygdala, and medial prefrontal cortex, that mediate alterations in memory (Bremner, 2003). The hippocampus, a brain area involved in verbal declarative memory, is very sensitive to the effects of stress. Declarative (or explicit) memory involves the remembrance of facts or lists (Squire, 2004). Stress in animals was associated with damage to neurons in the CA3 region of the hippocampus (which may be mediated by hypercortisolemia, decreased brain derived neurotrophic factor, and/or elevated glutamate levels; CA means cornu ammonis, a subregion of the hippocampus) and inhibition of neurogenesis (Gould et al., 1998; Magarinos et al., 1996; McEwen et al., 1992; Nibuya et al., 1995; Sapolsky et al., 1990; Sapolsky, 1996). These effects are reversible with antidepressant treatment (Nibuya et al., 1995; Malberg et al., 2000; Czeh et al., 2001; Santarelli et al., 2003; Lucassen et al., 2004).

Table 22.1   Changes in brain function in functional imaging studies in PTSD.

Brain region	Finding
Hippocampus	− − −/+
Parahippocampus	−/++++++++
Amygdala	−/+++++
mPFC/AC (32, 24, 25)	− − − − −/+
mPFC OBF (11)	− −/+
Anteromedial (9, 10)	−/+
Dorsolateral PFC (MFG; 6, 46)	− − − − −/+
Dorsolateral PFC (IFG)	− − − − −/+
Posterior cingulate (31)	−/++++++
Superior temporal (22)	−/+
Middle temporal (21)	− −/+
Inferior temporal/fusiform	− − −/+
Insula	−/+
Motor cortex	−/+
Sensory cortex	−/++
Visual association	− −/+
Precuneus/cuneus	−/+
Parietal (IPL)	− −/+
Parietal SMG (40)	− −/+
Cerebellum	−/++
Thalamus	− −

− indicates decreased function and + indicates increased function; the relative number of−and + symbols indicates the ratio of findings (not necessarily the number of studies). Numbers in parantheses indicate Brodmann areas. AC, anterior cingulate; mPFC, medial prefrontal cortex; OBF, orbitofrontal cortex; PFC, prefrontal cortex. MFG, middle frontal gyrus; IFG, inferior frontal gyrus; IPL, inferior parietal lobule; SMG, superior marginal gyrus.

In addition to the hippocampus, other brain structures have been implicated in a neural circuitry of stress including the amygdala and prefrontal cortex (McLaughlin et al., 2009). The amygdala is involved in memory for the emotional valence of events, and plays a critical role in the acquisition of fear responses (Davis, 1992). The medial prefrontal cortex includes the anterior cingulate gyrus (Brodmann's area 32) and subcallosal gyrus (area 25) as well as the orbitofrontal cortex. Lesion studies demonstrated that the medial prefrontal cortex modulates emotional responsiveness through inhibition of amygdala function (Morgan et al., 1993). Studies show that neurons of the medial prefrontal cortex play an active role in inhibition of fear responses that are mediated by the amygdala (Milad and Quirk, 2002; Milad et al., 2006). Conditioned fear responses are extinguished following repeated exposure to the conditioned stimulus (in the absence of the unconditioned stimulus (aversive; e.g., electric shock)). This inhibition appears to be mediated by medial prefrontal cortical inhibition of amygdala responsiveness. Animal studies also show that early stress is associated with a decrease in branching of neurons in the medial prefrontal cortex (Radley et al., 2004; Cook and Wellman, 2004; Brown et al., 2005).

Changes in Brain Structure in PTSD

Studies have shown changes in hippocampal volume in patients with PTSD (Plate 3). Veterans of the Vietnam War with PTSD were originally shown by us to have 8% smaller right hippocampal volume based on magnetic resonance imaging (MRI) relative to controls matched for a variety of factors such as alcohol abuse and education ($P < .05$); smaller volume was correlated with deficits in verbal declarative memory function as measured with the Wechsler memory scale (Bremner et al., 1995). In this study right hippocampal volume was compared between patients and controls. There was no significant interaction between side and diagnosis, consistent with a lack of difference in laterality between patients and controls. This study and the others reviewed below, however, did not look at measures such as the ratio of left to right hippocampal volume. A second study from our group showed a 12% reduction in left hippocampal volume in 17 patients with childhood-abuse-related PTSD compared to 17 case-matched controls that was significant after controlling for confounding factors (Bremner et al., 1997b). Smaller hippocampal volume was shown to be specific to PTSD within the anxiety disorders, and was not seen in panic disorder (Narayan et al., 1999).

Gurvits et al. (1996) showed bilateral hippocampal volume reductions in combat-related PTSD compared to combat veterans without PTSD and normal controls. Combat severity was correlated with volume reduction. Stein et al. (1997) found a 5% reduction in left hippocampal volume. Other studies in PTSD have found smaller hippocampal volume and/or reductions in N-acetyl-aspartate (NAA), a marker of neuronal integrity (Lindauer et al., 2004b; Bremner et al., 2003a; Freeman et al., 1998; Gilbertson et al., 2002; Schuff et al., 2001; Villarreal et al., 2002; Hedges et al., 2003; Shin et al., 2004b; Emdad et al., 2006; Lindauer et al., 2005, 2006; Mahmutyazicioglu et al., 2005; Irle et al., 2005; Li et al., 2006).

Some studies have found smaller hippocampal volume in PTSD subjects compared to trauma-exposed subjects without PTSD (Bremner et al., 2003a) while others have not, finding reductions in both trauma-exposed non-PTSD and trauma-exposed PTSD relative to non-trauma-exposed non-PTSD subjects (Winter and Irle, 2004). Studies in childhood (De Bellis et al., 1999, 2001; Carrion et al., 2001) PTSD did not find hippocampal volume reduction, although reduced NAA (indicating loss of neuronal integrity) was found in medial prefrontal cortex in childhood PTSD (De Bellis et al., 2000). Some studies of new-onset or recent PTSD did not find changes in hippocampal volume (Bonne et al., 2001; Notestine et al., 2002) while others showed a reduction (Wignall et al., 2004). In a recent meta-analysis we pooled data from all of the published studies and found smaller hippocampal volume for both the left and the right sides, equally in adult men and women with chronic PTSD, and no change in children (Kitayama et al., 2005).

Another recent meta-analysis had similar findings (Smith, 2005). More recent studies of holocaust survivors with PTSD did not find a reduction in hippocampal volume (Golier et al., 2005) although PTSD patients who developed PTSD in response to an initial trauma had smaller hippocampal volume compared to those who developed PTSD after repeated trauma, suggesting a possible vulnerability of smaller hippocampal volume (Yehuda et al., 2007). Several studies have looked specifically at neurochemical alterations in the hippocampus, most using magnetic-resonance spectroscopic measurement of NAA as a marker of neuronal integrity. Studies have found reduced NAA or NAA/creatine ratio in combat veterans with PTSD (Schuff et al., 1997, 2001, 2006; Freeman et al., 1998, 2006; Kimbrell et al., 2005), and patients with civilian-trauma-related PTSD (Villarreal et al., 2002; Lim et al., 2003; Mohanakrishnan Menon et al., 2003; Mahmutyazicioglu et al., 2005; Li et al., 2006).

Several studies have shown that PTSD patients have deficits in hippocampal activation while performing a verbal declarative memory task (Bremner et al., 2003a; Shin et al., 2004b) or a virtual water-maze task (Astur et al., 2006). Both hippocampal atrophy and hippocampal-based memory deficits reversed on treatment with the selective serotonin-reuptake inhibitor paroxetine, which has been shown to promote neurogenesis in the hippocampus in preclinical studies (Vermetten et al., 2003). We hypothesize that stress-induced hippocampal dysfunction may mediate many of the symptoms of PTSD which are related to memory dysregulation, including explicit memory deficits as well as fragmentation of memory in survivors of abuse. It is unclear at the current time whether these changes are specific to PTSD, whether certain common environmental events (e.g., stress) in different disorders lead to similar brain changes, or whether common genetic traits lead to similar outcomes.

Animal studies also show that early stress is associated with a decrease in branching of neurons in the medial prefrontal cortex (Radley et al., 2004). Several studies have found smaller anterior cingulate volume based on MRI measurements in PTSD (Rauch et al., 2003; Yamasue et al., 2003; Woodward et al., 2006) including women having suffered abuse and with PTSD (Kitayama et al., 2005). Some studies have found reduced anterior cingulate NAA (De Bellis et al., 2000; Mahmutyazicioglu et al., 2005) whereas others have not (Seedat et al., 2005). Other findings in PTSD include a decrease in gray-matter density (Corbo et al., 2005) and smaller volume of the corpus callosum in neglected children (Teicher et al., 2004) and adults with PTSD (Villarreal et al., 2004). One study showed a smaller volume of the insula with voxel-based morphometry (Chen et al., 2006). A study in twins found a smaller volume of the cavum septum pellucidum (May et al., 2004).

Functional Neuroimaging Studies in PTSD

Imaging studies of brain function in PTSD are consistent with dysfunction of the medial prefrontal cortex, amygdala, and hippocampus (Liberzon and Phan, 2003;

Liberzon and Martis, 2006; Liberzon et al., 2003; Pitman, 2001; Bremner, 1998, 2002b; Rauch et al., 2006; Cannistraro and Rauch, 2003). Studies of resting blood flow or metabolism with positron emission tomography (PET) and single-photon emission computed tomography (SPECT) showed alterations at rest in medial pre-frontal, temporal, and dorsolateral prefrontal cortex, cerebellum, and amygdala (Bonne et al., 2003; Chung et al., 2006; Bremner et al., 1997a). Stimulation of the noradrenergic system with yohimbine resulted in a failure of activation in dorsola-teral prefrontal, temporal, parietal, and orbitofrontal cortex, and decreased function in the hippocampus (Bremner et al., 1997a). Exposure to traumatic reminders in the form of traumatic slides and/or sounds or traumatic scripts was associated with an increase in PTSD symptoms, decreased blood flow, and/or failure of activation in the medial prefrontal cortex/anterior cingulate, including Brodmann's area 25, or subcallosal gyrus, areas 32 and 24, as measured with PET, SPECT, or functional MRI (Britton et al., 2005; Yang et al., 2004; Bremner et al., 1999a, 1999b; Lanius et al., 2001, 2003; Liberzon et al., 1999; Shin et al., 1997, 1999, 2004a, 2005; Semple et al., 2000; Lindauer et al., 2004a; Phan et al., 2006) (Plate 4). Other findings in studies of traumatic reminder exposure include decreased function in hippocampus (Bremner et al., 1999a), thalamus (Lanius et al., 2001, 2003), visual associa-tion cortex (Bremner et al., 1999a; Shin et al., 1997, 2004a; Lanius et al., 2003), parietal cortex (Rauch et al., 1996; Shin et al., 1997, 1999; Bremner et al., 1999a; Sakamoto et al., 2005), and inferior frontal gyrus (Shin et al., 1997, 1999, 2001; Rauch et al., 1996; Bremner et al., 1999a; Lanius et al., 2003; Sakamoto et al., 2005), and increased function in amygdala (Rauch et al., 1996; Shin et al., 2004a; Liberzon et al., 1999), posterior cingulate (Shin et al., 1997; Bremner et al., 1999a, 1999b; Lanius et al., 2001), and parahippocampal gyrus (Bremner et al., 1999a, 1999b; Liberzon et al., 1999). Shin and colleagues found a correlation between increased amygdala function and decreased medial prefrontal function with trau-matic reminders (Shin et al., 2004a), indicating that a failure of inhibition of the amygdala by the medial prefrontal cortex could account for increased PTSD symp-toms with traumatic reminders. Other studies found increased amygdala and parahippocampal function and decreased medial prefrontal function during perfor-mance of an attention task (Semple et al., 2000), and increased amygdala function at rest (Chung et al., 2006), during a working memory task (Bryant et al., 2005), during recall of traumatic words (Protopopescu et al., 2005), and with exposure to masked fearful faces (Rauch et al., 2000; Armony et al., 2005), overt fearful faces (Shin et al., 2005), traumatic sounds (Liberzon et al., 1999; Pissiota et al., 2002), and traumatic scripts (Rauch et al., 1996), and with classical fear conditioning (Bremner et al., 2005).

Several studies have examined neural correlates of cognitive tasks in PTSD. During working memory tasks patients showed decreased inferior frontal (Clark et al., 2003) and parietal function (Bryant et al., 2005; Clark et al., 2003). Retrieval of emotionally valenced words (Bremner et al., 2001; e.g., "rape-mutilate") in women with PTSD from early abuse resulted in decreases in blood flow in an exten-sive area which included the orbitofrontal cortex, anterior cingulate, and medial prefrontal cortex (Brodmann's areas 9, 25, 32), left hippocampus, and fusiform gyrus/inferior temporal gyrus (Bremner et al., 2003b). Another study found a failure of medial prefrontal cortical/anterior cingulate activation, and decreased visual association and parietal cortex function, in women having suffered abuse and with PTSD relative to women having suffered abuse without PTSD, during performance of the emotional Stroop task (i.e., naming the color of a word such as "rape") (Bremner et al., 2004). Shin and colleagues showed increased posterior cingulate and parahippocampal gyrus and decreased medial prefrontal and dorsolateral prefrontal during an emotional *counting* Stroop paradigm with functional MRI (Shin et al., 2001).

Neuroreceptor Studies in PTSD

Studies have begun to use PET and SPECT to measure neuroreceptors in PTSD. Reduced binding of benzodiazepine receptors has been found in combat veterans in the frontal cortex in some studies (Bremner et al., 2000; Geuze et al., 2008) but not others (Fujita et al., 2004). One study found no changes in binding of the 5-hydroxytryptamine 5-HT$_{1A}$ receptor (Bonne et al., 2005). Other studies found a reduction in anterior cingulate opiate receptor binding (Liberzon et al., 2007) and an increase in hippocampal β2 nicotinic acetylcholine receptor binding in PTSD (Czermak et al., 2008).

Brain-imaging Findings in Other Trauma-spectrum Disorders

We have tested the hypothesis that patients with trauma-related psychiatric disorders, which have been described as trauma-spectrum disorders (Bremner, 2002a), share in common abnormalities in specific brain areas, including the amygdala, medial prefrontal cortex, and hippocampus. These disorders include abuse-related PTSD, depression associated with early abuse, borderline personality disorder (BPD) associated with early abuse, and dissociative identity disorder with early abuse. To test this hypothesis, we exposed traumatized women with and without BPD to the stress of a script outlining a personally upsetting abandonment scene in conjunction with PET imaging of the brain (Schmahl et al., 2003a). Women with BPD exhibited a relative failure of medial prefrontal activation during abandonment scripts compared to non-BPD subjects. Women with BPD and who had suffered abuse had increased psychophysiological responses to abandonment scripts relative to trauma scripts, while women with PTSD and who had suffered abuse had the opposite pattern (Schmahl et al., 2002), indicating differential responses in these two disorders in spite of the common exposure to early abuse. Studies of structural MRI have also shown smaller hippocampal volume across several trauma-spectrum disorders, including abuse-related PTSD (Bremner et al., 1997b, 2003a), dissociative identity disorder with early abuse (Vermetten et al., 2006), BPD with early abuse (Schmahl et al., 2003b; Driessen et al., 2000), and depression with early abuse (Vythilingam et al., 2002).

Summary and Conclusions

Brain-imaging studies have shown that PTSD is associated with changes in brain function and structure. Brain areas implicated in the stress response include the amygdala, hippocampus, and prefrontal cortex. These brain areas also play a critical role in memory, highlighting the important interplay between memory and the traumatic stress response. Preclinical studies show that stress affects these brain areas. Furthermore, antidepressants have effects on the hippocampus that counteract the effects of stress. In fact, promotion of nerve growth (neurogenesis) in the hippocampus may be central to the efficacy of the antidepressants. Studies in patients with PTSD show alterations in brain areas implicated in animal studies, including the amygdala, hippocampus, and prefrontal cortex. Increased amygdala activation with acquisition of fear responses, and a failure of the medial prefrontal cortex to properly mediate extinction, are hypothesized to underlie symptoms of PTSD. Preliminary studies in patients with other trauma-spectrum disorders, including dissociative identity disorder and BPD, implicate a similar circuit as seen in PTSD.

References

Armony, J. L., Corbo, V., Clement, M. H., & Brunet, A. (2005). Amygdala response in patients with acute PTSD to masked and unmasked emotional facial expressions. *American Journal of Psychiatry*, *162*, 1961–1963.

Astur, R. S., St Germain, S. A., Tolin, D., Ford, J., Russell, D., & Stevens, M. (2006). Hippocampus function predicts severity of post-traumatic stress disorder. *Cyberpsychology Behavior*, *9*, 234–240.

Battle, C. L., Shea, M. T., Johnson, D. M., Yen, S., Zlotnick, C., Zanarini, M. C., Sanislow, C. A., Skodol, A. E., Gunderson, J. G., Grilo, C. M., Mcglashan, T. H., & Morey, L. C. (2004). Childhood maltreatment associated with adult personality disorders: findings from the Collaborative Longitudinal Personality Disorders Study. *Journal of Personality Disorders*, *18*, 193–211.

Bonne, O., Brandes, D., Gilboa, A., Gomori, J. M., Shenton, M. E., Pitman, R. K., & Shalev, A. Y. (2001). Longitudinal MRI study of hippocampal volume in trauma survivors with PTSD. *American Journal of Psychiatry*, *158*, 1248–1251.

Bonne, O., Gilboa, A., Louzoun, Y., Brandes, D., Yona, I., Lester, H., Barkai, G., Freedman, N., Chisin, R., & Shalev, A. Y. (2003). Resting regional cerebral perfusion in recent posttraumatic stress disorder. *Biological Psychiatry*, *54*, 1077–1086.

Bonne, O., Bain, E., Neumeister, A., Nugent, A. C., Vythilingam, M., Carson, R. E., Luckenbaugh, D. A., Eckelman, W., Herscovitch, P., Drevets, W. C., & Charney, D. S. (2005). No change in serotonin type 1A receptor binding in patients with posttraumatic stress disorder. *American Journal of Psychiatry*, *162*, 383–385.

Bremner, J. D. (1998). Neuroimaging of posttraumatic stress disorder. *Psychiatric Annals, 28,* 445–450.

Bremner, J. D. (2002a). *Does stress damage the brain? Understanding trauma-related disorders from a mind-body perspective.* New York: W.W. Norton.

Bremner, J. D. (2002b). Neuroimaging of childhood trauma. *Seminars in Clinical Neuropsychiatry, 7,* 104–112.

Bremner, J. D. (2003). Functional neuroanatomical correlates of traumatic stress revisited 7 years later, this time with data. *Psychopharmacology Bulletin, 37,* 6–25.

Bremner, J. D. (2005). *Brain imaging handbook.* New York: W.W. Norton.

Bremner, J. D. (2007). Neuroimaging in posttraumatic stress disorder and other stress-related disorders. *Neuroimaging Clinics of North America, 17,* 523–538.

Bremner, J. D., Randall, P. R., Scott, T. M., Bronen, R. A., Delaney, R. C., Seibyl, J. P., Southwick, S. M., McCarthy, G., Charney, D. S., & Innis, R. B. (1995). MRI-based measurement of hippocampal volume in patients with combat-related posttraumatic stress disorder. *American Journal of Psychiatry, 152,* 973–931.

Bremner, J. D., Southwick, S. M., Darnell, A., & Charney, D. S. (1996). Chronic PTSD in Vietnam combat veterans: Course of illness and substance abuse. *American Journal of Psychiatry, 153,* 369–375.

Bremner, J. D., Innis, R. B., Ng, C. K., Staib, L., Duncan, J., Bronen, R., Zubal, G., Rich, D., Krystal, J. H., Dey, H., Soufer, R., & Charney, D. S. (1997a). PET measurement of cerebral metabolic correlates of yohimbine administration in posttraumatic stress disorder. *Archives of General Psychiatry, 54,* 246–256.

Bremner, J. D., Randall, P. R., Vermetten, E., Staib, L., Bronen, R. A., Mazure, C. M., Capelli, S., Mccarthy, G., Innis, R. B., & Charney, D. S. (1997b). MRI-based measurement of hippocampal volume in posttraumatic stress disorder related to childhood physical and sexual abuse: A preliminary report. *Biological Psychiatry, 41,* 23–32.

Bremner, J. D., Narayan, M., Staib, L. H., Southwick, S. M., Mcglashan, T., & Charney, D. S. (1999a). Neural correlates of memories of childhood sexual abuse in women with and without posttraumatic stress disorder. *American Journal of Psychiatry, 156,* 1787–1795.

Bremner, J. D., Staib, L., Kaloupek, D., Southwick, S. M., Soufer, R., & Charney, D. S. (1999b). Neural correlates of exposure to traumatic pictures and sound in Vietnam combat veterans with and without posttraumatic stress disorder: A positron emission tomography study. *Biological Psychiatry, 45,* 806–816.

Bremner, J. D., Innis, R. B., White, T., Fujita, M., Silbersweig, D., Goddard, A. W., Staib, L., Stern, E., Cappiello, A., Woods, S., Baldwin, R., & Charney, D. S. (2000). SPECT [I-123] iomazenil measurement of the benzodiazepine receptor in panic disorder. *Biological Psychiatry, 47,* 96–106.

Bremner, J. D., Soufer, R., Mccarthy, G., Delaney, R. C., Staib, L. H., Duncan, J. S., & Charney, D. S. (2001). Gender differences in cognitive and neural correlates of remembrance of emotional words. *Psychopharmacology Bulletin, 35,* 55–87.

Bremner, J. D., Vythilingam, M., Vermetten, E., Southwick, S. M., Mcglashan, T., Nazeer, A., Khan, S., Vaccarino, L. V., Soufer, R., Garg, P., Ng, C. K., STAIB, L. H., Duncan, J. S., & Charney, D. S. (2003a). MRI and PET study of deficits in hippocampal structure and function in women with childhood sexual abuse and posttraumatic stress disorder (PTSD). *American Journal of Psychiatry, 160,* 924–932.

Bremner, J. D., Vythilingam, M., Vermetten, E., Southwick, S. M., Mcglashan, T., Staib, L., Soufer, R., & Charney, D. S. (2003b). Neural correlates of declarative memory for emotionally valenced words in women with posttraumatic stress disorder (PTSD) related to early childhood sexual abuse. *Biological Psychiatry, 53,* 289–299.

Bremner, J. D., Vermetten, E., Vythilingam, M., Afzal, N., Schmahl, C., Elzinga, B. M., & Charney, D. S. (2004). Neural correlates of the classical color and emotional Stroop in women with abuse-related posttraumatic stress disorder. *Biological Psychiatry, 55,* 612–620.

Bremner, J. D., Vermetten, E., Schmahl, C., Vaccarino, V., Vythilingam, M., Afzal, N., Grillon, C., & Charney, D. S. (2005). Positron emission tomographic imaging of neural correlates of a fear acquisition and extinction paradigm in women with childhood sexual abuse-related posttraumatic stress disorder. *Psychological Medicine, 35,* 791–806.

Bremner, J. D., Elzinga, B., Schmahl, C., & Vermetten, E. (2008). Structural and functional plasticity of the human brain in posttraumatic stress disorder. *Progress in Brain Research, 167,* 171–186.

Britton, J. C., Phan, K. L., Taylor, S. F., Fig, L. M., & Liberzon, I. (2005). Corticolimbic blood flow in posttraumatic stress disorder during script-driven imagery. *Biological Psychiatry, 57,* 832–840.

Brown, S. M., Henning, S., & Wellman, C. L. (2005). Mild, short-term stress alters dendritic morphology in rat medial prefrontal cortex. *Cerebral Cortex, 15,* 1714–1722.

Bryant, R. A., Felmingham, K. L., Kemp, A. H., Barton, M., Peduto, A. S., Rennie, C., Gordon, E., & Williams, L. M. (2005). Neural networks of information processing in posttraumatic stress disorder: a functional magnetic resonance imaging study. *Biological Psychiatry, 58,* 111–118.

Cannistraro, P. A., & Rauch, S. L. (2003). Neural circuitry of anxiety: evidence from structural and functional neuroimaging studies. *Psychopharmacology Bulletin, 37,* 8–25.

Carrion, V. G., Weems, C. F., Eliez, S., Patwardhan, A., Brown, W., Ray, R. D., & Reiss, A. L. (2001). Attenuation of frontal asymmetry in pediatric posttraumatic stress disorder. *Biological Psychiatry, 50,* 943–951.

Chen, S., Xia, W., Li, L., Liu, J., He, Z., Zhang, Z., Yan, L., Zhang, J., & Hu, D. (2006). Gray matter density reduction in the insula in fire survivors with posttraumatic stress disorder: a voxel-based morphometric study. *Psychiatry Research, 146,* 65–72.

Chung, Y. A., Kim, S. H., Chung, S. K., Chae, J. H., Yang, D. W., Sohn, H. S., & Jeong, J. (2006). Alterations in cerebral perfusion in posttraumatic stress disorder patients without re-exposure to accident-related stimuli. *Clinical Neurophysiology, 117,* 637–642.

Clark, C. R., Mcfarlane, A. C., Morris, P., Weber, D. L., Sonkkilla, C., Shaw, M., Marcina, J., Tochon-Danguy, H. J., & Egan, G. E. (2003). Cerebral function in posttraumatic stress disorder during verbal working memory updating: A positron emission tomography study. *Biological Psychiatry, 53,* 474–481.

Cook, S. C., & Wellman, C. L. (2004). Chronic stress alters dendritic morphology in rat medial prefrontal cortex. *Journal of Neurobiology, 60,* 236–248.

Corbo, V., Clement, M. H., Armony, J. L., Pruessner, J. C., & Brunet, A. (2005). Size versus shape differences: contrasting voxel-based and volumetric analyses of the anterior cingulate cortex in individuals with acute posttraumatic stress disorder. *Biological Psychiatry, 58,* 119–124.

Czeh, B., Michaelis, T., Watanabe, T., Frahm, J., De Biurrun, G., Van Kampen, M., Bartolomucci, A., & Fuchs, E. (2001). Stress-induced changes in cerebral metabolites, hippocampal volume, and cell proliferation are prevented by antidepressant treatment with tianeptine. *Proceedings of the National Academy of Sciences USA, 98,* 12796–12801.

Czermak, C., Staley, J. K., Kasserman, S., Bois, F., Young, T., Henry, S., Tamagnan, G. D., Seibyl, J. P., Krystal, J. H., & Neumeister, A. (2008). Beta-2 nicotinic acetylcholine receptor availability in post-traumatic stress disorder. *International Journal of Neuropsychopharmacology, 11*, 419–424.

Davis, M. (1992). The role of the amygdala in fear and anxiety. *Annual Review of Neuroscience, 15*, 353–375.

De Bellis, M. D., Keshavan, M. S., Clark, D. B., Casey, B. J., Giedd, J. N., Boring, A. M., Frustaci, K., & Ryan, N. D. (1999). A.E. Bennett Research Award: Developmental traumatology: Part II. Brain development. *Biological Psychiatry, 45*, 1271–1284.

De Bellis, M. D., Keshavan, M. S., Spencer, S., & Hall, J. (2000). N-acetylaspartate concentration in the anterior cingulate of maltreated children and adolescents with PTSD. *American Journal of Psychiatry, 157*, 1175–1177.

De Bellis, M. D., Hall, J., Boring, A. M., Frustaci, K., & Moritz, G. (2001). A pilot longitudinal study of hippocampal volumes in pediatric maltreatment-related posttraumatic stress disorder. *Biological Psychiatry, 50*, 305–309.

Driessen, M., Herrmann, J., Stahl, K., Zwaan, M., Meier, S., Hill, A., Osterheider, M., & Petersen, D. (2000). Magnetic resonance imaging volumes of the hippocampus and the amygdala in women with borderline personality disorder and early traumatization. *Archives of General Psychiatry, 57*, 1115–1122.

Elzinga, B. M., & Bremner, J. D. (2002). Are the neural substrates of memory the final common pathway in PTSD? *Journal of Affective Disorders, 70*, 1–17.

Emdad, R., Bonekamp, D., Sondergaard, H. P., Bjorklund, T., Agartz, I., Ingvar, M., & Theorell, T. (2006). Morphometric and psychometric comparisons between non-substance-abusing patients with posttraumatic stress disorder and normal controls. *Psychotherapy and Psychosomatics, 75*, 122–132.

Franklin, C. L., & Zimmerman, M. (2001). Posttraumatic stress disorder and major depressive disorder: Investigating the role of overlapping symptoms in diagnostic comorbidity. *Journal of Nervous and Mental Disease, 189*, 548–551.

Freeman, T. W., Cardwell, D., Karson, C. N., & Komoroski, R. A. (1998). In vivo proton magnetic resonance spectroscopy of the medial temporal lobes of subjects with combat-related posttraumatic stress disorder. *Magnetic Resonance in Medicine, 40*, 66–71.

Freeman, T., Kimbrell, T., Booe, L., Myers, M., Cardwell, D., Lindquist, D. M., Hart, J., & Komoroski, R. A. (2006). Evidence of resilience: neuroimaging in former prisoners of war. *Psychiatry Research, 146*, 59–64.

Fujita, M., Southwick, S. M., Denucci, C. C., Zoghbi, S. S., Dillon, M. S., Baldwin, R. M., Bozkurt, A., Kugaya, A., Verhoeff, N. P., Seibyl, J. P., & Innis, R. B. (2004). Central type benzodiazepine receptors in Gulf War veterans with posttraumatic stress disorder. *Biological Psychiatry, 56*, 95–100.

Geuze, E., Van Berckel, B. N., Lammertsma, A. A., Boellaard, R., de Kloet, C. S., Vermetten, E., & Westenberg, H. G. (2008). Reduced GABAA benzodiazepine receptor binding in veterans with post-traumatic stress disorder. *Molecular Psychiatry, 13*, 74–83, 3.

Gilbertson, M. W., Shenton, M. E., Ciszewski, A., Kasai, K., Lasko, N. B., Orr, S. P., & Pitman, R. K. (2002). Smaller hippocampal volume predicts pathologic vulnerability to psychological trauma. *Nature Neuroscience, 5*, 1242–1247.

Golier, J. A., Yehuda, R., De Santi, S., Segal, S., Dolan, S., & De Leon, M. J. (2005). Absence of hippocampal volume differences in survivors of the Nazi Holocaust with and without posttraumatic stress disorder. *Psychiatry Research, 139*, 53–64.

Gould, E., Tanapat, P., McEwen, B. S., Flugge, G., & Fuchs, E. (1998). Proliferation of granule cell precursors in the dentate gyrus of adult monkeys is diminished by stress. *Proceedings of the National Academy of Sciences USA, 95,* 3168–3171.

Gurvits, T. G., Shenton, M. R., Hokama, H., Ohta, H., Lasko, N. B., Gilbertson, M. B., Orr, S. P., Kikinis, R., & Lolesz, F. A. (1996). Magnetic resonance imaging study of hippocampal volume in chronic combat-related posttraumatic stress disorder. *Biological Psychiatry, 40,* 192–199.

Hedges, D. W., Allen, S., Tate, D. F., Thatcher, G. W., Miller, M. J., Rice, S. A., Cleavinger, H. B., Sood, S., & Bigler, E. D. (2003). Reduced hippocampal volume in alcohol and substance naive Vietnam combat veterans with posttraumatic stress disorder. *Cognitive and Behavioral Neurology, 16,* 219–224.

Irle, E., Lange, C., & Sachsse, U. (2005). Reduced size and abnormal asymmetry of parietal cortex in women with borderline personality disorder. *Biological Psychiatry, 57,* 173–182.

Kessler, R. C., Sonnega, A., Bromet, E., Hughes, M., & Nelson, C. B. (1995). Posttraumatic stress disorder in the national comorbidity survey. *Archives of General Psychiatry, 52,* 1048–1060.

Kimbrell, T., Leulf, C., Cardwell, D., Komoroski, R. A., & Freeman, T. W. (2005). Relationship of in vivo medial temporal lobe magnetic resonance spectroscopy to documented combat exposure in veterans with chronic posttraumatic stress disorder. *Psychiatry Research, 140,* 91–94.

Kitayama, N., Vaccarino, V., Kutner, M., Weiss, P., & Bremner, J. D. (2005). Magnetic resonance imaging (MRI) measurement of hippocampal volume in posttraumatic stress disorder: A meta-analysis. *Journal of Affective Disorders, 88,* 79–86.

Lanius, R. A., Williamson, P. C., Densmore, M., Boksman, K., Gupta, M. A., Neufeld, R. W., Gati, J. S., & Menon, R. S. (2001). Neural correlates of traumatic memories in posttraumatic stress disorder: A functional MRI investigation. *American Journal of Psychiatry, 158,* 1920–1922.

Lanius, R. A., Williamson, P. C., Hopper, J., Densmore, M., Boksman, K., Gupta, M. A., Neufeld, R. W. J., Gati, J. S., & Menon, R. S. (2003). Recall of emotional states in posttraumatic stress disorder: An fMRI investigation. *Biological Psychiatry, 53,* 204–210.

Li, L., Chen, S., Liu, J., Zhang, J., He, Z., & Lin, X. (2006). Magnetic resonance imaging and magnetic resonance spectroscopy study of deficits in hippocampal structure in fire victims with recent-onset posttraumatic stress disorder. *Canadian Journal of Psychiatry, 51,* 431–437.

Liberzon, I., & Phan, K. L. (2003). Brain-imaging studies of posttraumatic stress disorder. *CNS Spectrums, 8,* 641–650.

Liberzon, I., & Martis, B. (2006). Neuroimaging studies of emotional responses in PTSD. *Annals of the New York Academy of Sciences, 1071,* 87–109.

Liberzon, I., Taylor, S. F., Amdur, R., Jung, T. D., Chamberlain, K. R., Minoshima, S., Koeppe, R. A., & Fig, L. M. (1999). Brain activation in PTSD in response to trauma-related stimuli. *Biological Psychiatry, 45,* 817–826.

Liberzon, I., Britton, J. C., & Phan, K. L. (2003). Neural correlates of traumatic recall in posttraumatic stress disorder. *Stress, 6,* 151–156.

Liberzon, I., Taylor, S. F., Phan, K. L., Britton, J. C., Fig, L. M., Bueller, J. A., Koeppe, R. A., & Zubieta, J. K. (2007). Altered central micro-opioid receptor binding after psychological trauma. *Biological Psychiatry, 61,* 1030–1038.

Lim, M. K., Suh, C. H., Kim, H. J., Kim, S. T., Lee, J. S., Kang, M. H., Kim, J. H., & Lee, J. H. (2003). Fire-related post-traumatic stress disorder: brain 1H-MR spectroscopic findings. *Korean Journal of Radiology*, 4, 79–84.

Lindauer, R. J., Booij, J., Habraken, J. B., Uylings, H. B., Olff, M., Carlier, I. V., Den Heeten, G. J., Van Eck-Smit, B. L., & Gersons, B. P. (2004a). Cerebral blood flow changes during script-driven imagery in police officers with posttraumatic stress disorder. *Biological Psychiatry*, 56, 853–861.

Lindauer, R. J., Vlieger, E. J., Jalink, M., Olff, M., Carlier, I. V., Majoie, C. B., Den Heeten, G. J., & Gersons, B. P. (2004b). Smaller hippocampal volume in Dutch police officers with posttraumatic stress disorder. *Biological Psychiatry*, 56, 356–363.

Lindauer, R. J., Vlieger, E. J., Jalink, M., Olff, M., Carlier, I. V., Majoie, C. B., Den Heeten, G. J., & Gersons, B. P. (2005). Effects of psychotherapy on hippocampal volume in outpatients with post-traumatic stress disorder: a MRI investigation. *Psychological Medicine*, 35, 1421–1431.

Lindauer, R. J., Olff, M., Van Meijel, E. P., Carlier, I. V., & Gersons, B. P. (2006). Cortisol, learning, memory, and attention in relation to smaller hippocampal volume in police officers with posttraumatic stress disorder. *Biological Psychiatry*, 59, 171–177.

Lucassen, P. J., Fuchs, E., & Czeh, B. (2004). Antidepressant treatment with tianeptine reduces apoptosis in the hippocampal dentate gyrus and temporal cortex. *European Journal of Neuroscience*, 14, 161–166.

Magarinos, A. M., McEwen, B. S., Flugge, G., & Fluchs, E. (1996). Chronic psychosocial stress causes apical dendritic atrophy of hippocampal CA3 pyramidal neurons in subordinate tree shrews. *Journal of Neuroscience*, 16, 3534–3540.

Mahmutyazicioglu, K., Konuk, N., Ozdemir, H., Atasoy, N., Atik, L., & Gundogdu, S. (2005). Evaluation of the hippocampus and the anterior cingulate gyrus by proton MR spectroscopy in patients with post-traumatic stress disorder. *Diagnostic and Interventional Radiology*, 11, 125–129.

Malberg, J. E., Eisch, A. J., Nestler, E. J., & Duman, R. S. (2000). Chronic antidepressant treatment increases neurogenesis in adult rat hippocampus. *Journal of Neuroscience*, 20, 9104–9110.

May, F. S., Chen, Q. C., Gilbertson, M. W., Shenton, M. E., & Pitman, R. K. (2004). Cavum septum pellucidum in monozygotic twins discordant for combat exposure: relationship to posttraumatic stress disorder. *Biological Psychiatry*, 55, 656–658.

McEwen, B. S., Angulo, J., Cameron, H., Chao, H. M., Daniels, D., Gannon, M. N., Gould, E., Mendelson, S., Sakai, R., Spencer, R., & Woolley, C. S. (1992). Paradoxical effects of adrenal steroids on the brain: Protection versus degeneration. *Biological Psychiatry*, 31, 177–199.

Mclaughlin, K. J., Baran, S. E., & Conrad, C.D. (2009). Chronic stress- and sex-specific neuromorphological and functional changes in limbic structures. *Molecular Neurobiology*, 40, 166–182.

Milad, M. R., & Quirk, G. J. (2002). Neurons in medial prefrontal cortex signal memory for fear extinction. *Nature*, 420, 70–73.

Milad, M. R., Rauch, S. L., Pitman, R. K., & Quirk, G. J. (2006). Fear extinction in rats: implications for human brain imaging and anxiety disorders. *Biological Psychology*, 73, 61–71.

Mohanakrishnan Menon, P., Nasrallah, H. A., Lyons, J. A., Scott, M. F., & Liberto, V. (2003). Single-voxel proton MR spectroscopy of right versus left hippocampi in PTSD. *Psychiatry Research*, 123, 101–108.

Morgan, C. A., Romanski, L. M., & LeDoux, J. E. (1993). Extinction of emotional learning: Contribution of medial prefrontal cortex. *Neuroscience Letters, 163,* 109–113.

Narayan, M., Bremner, J. D., & Kumar, A. (1999). Neuroanatomical substrates of late-life mental disorders. *Journal of Geriatric Psychiatry and Neurology, 12,* 95–106.

Nibuya, M., Morinobu, S., & Duman, R. S. (1995). Regulation of BDNF and trkB mRNA in rat brain by chronic electroconvulsive seizure and antidepressant drug treatments. *Journal of Neuroscience, 15,* 7539–7547.

Notestine, C. F., Stein, M. B., Kennedy, C. M., Archibald, S. L., & Jernigan, T. L. (2002). Brain morphometry in female victims of intimate partner violence with and without post-traumatic stress disorder. *Biological Psychiatry, 51,* 1089–1101.

Phan, K. L., Britton, J. C., Taylor, S. F., Fig, L. M., & Liberzon, I. (2006). Corticolimbic blood flow during nontraumatic emotional processing in posttraumatic stress disorder. *Archives of General Psychiatry, 63,* 184–192.

Pissiota, A., Frans, O., Fernandez, M., Von Knorring, L., Fischer, H., & Fredrikson, M. (2002). Neurofunctional correlates of posttraumatic stress disorder: a PET symptom provocation study. *European Archives of Psychiatry & Clinical Neuroscience, 252,* 68–75.

Pitman, R. K. (2001). Investigating the pathogenesis of posttraumatic stress disorder with neuroimaging. *Journal of Clinical Psychiatry, 62,* 47–54.

Prigerson, H. G., Maciejewski, P. K., & Rosenheck, R. A. (2001). Combat trauma: Trauma with highest risk of delayed onset and unresolved posttraumatic stress disorder symptoms, unemployment, and abuse among men. *Journal of Nervous and Mental Disease, 189,* 99–108.

Protopopescu, X., Pan, H., Tuescher, O., Cloitre, M., Goldstein, M., Engelien, W., Epstein, J., Yang, Y., Gorman, J., LeDoux, J., Silbersweig, D., & Stern, E. (2005). Differential time courses and specificity of amygdala activity in posttraumatic stress disorder subjects and normal control subjects. *Biological Psychiatry, 57,* 464–473.

Putnam, F. W., Guroff, J. J., Silberman, E. K., Barban, L., & Post, R. M. (1986). The clinical phenomenology of multiple personality disorder: A review of 100 recent cases. *Journal of Clinical Psychiatry, 47,* 285–293.

Radley, J. J., Sisti, H. M., Hao, J., Rocher, A. B., Mccall, T., Hof, P. R., McEwen, B. S., & Morrison, J. H. (2004). Chronic behavioral stress induces apical dendritic reorganization in pyramidal neurons of the medial prefrontal cortex. *Neuroscience, 125,* 1–6.

Rauch, S. L., Van Der Kolk, B. A., Fisler, R. E., Alpert, N. M., Orr, S. P., Savage, C. R., Fischman, A. J., Jenike, M. A., & Pitman, R. K. (1996). A symptom provocation study of posttraumatic stress disorder using positron emission tomography and script driven imagery. *Archives of General Psychiatry, 53,* 380–387.

Rauch, S. L., Whalen, P. J., Shin, L. M., Mcinerney, S. C., Macklin, M. L., Lasko, N. B., Orr, S. P., & Pitman, R. K. (2000). Exaggerated amygdala response to masked facial stimuli in posttraumatic stress disorder: a functional MRI study. *Biological Psychiatry, 47,* 769–776.

Rauch, S. L., Shin, L. M., Segal, E., Pitman, R. K., Carson, M. A., Mcmullin, K., Whalen, P. J., & Makris, N. (2003). Selectively reduced regional cortical volumes in post-traumatic stress disorder. *Neuroreport, 14,* 913–916.

Rauch, S. L., Shin, L. M., & Phelps, E. A. (2006). Neurocircuitry models of posttraumatic stress disorder and extinction: human neuroimaging research–past, present, and future. *Biological Psychiatry, 60,* 376–382.

Saigh, P. A., & Bremner, J. D. (1999). *Posttraumatic stress disorder: A comprehensive text.* Needham Heights, MA: Allyn & Bacon.

Sakamoto, H., Fukuda, R., Okuaki, T., Rogers, M., Kasai, K., Machida, T., Shirouzu, I., Yamasue, H., Akiyama, T., & Kato, N. (2005). Parahippocampal activation evoked by masked traumatic images in posttraumatic stress disorder: a functional MRI study. *Neuroimage, 26*, 813–821.

Santarelli, L., Saxe, M., Gross, C., Surget, A., Battaglia, F., Dulawa, S., Weisstaub, N., Lee, J., Duman, R., Arancio, O., Belzung, C., & Hen, R. (2003). Requirement of hippocampal neurogenesis for the behavioral effects of antidepressants. *Science, 301*, 805–809.

Sapolsky, R. M. (1996). Why stress is bad for your brain. *Science, 273*, 749–750.

Sapolsky, R. M., Uno, H., Rebert, C. S., & Finch, C. E. (1990). Hippocampal damage associated with prolonged glucocorticoid exposure in primates. *Journal of Neuroscience, 10*, 2897–2902.

Schmahl, C. G., Elzinga, B. M., & Bremner, J. D. (2002). Individual differences in psychophysiological reactivity in adults with childhood abuse. *Clinical Psychology and Psychotherapy, 9*, 271–276.

Schmahl, C. G., Elzinga, B. M., Vermetten, E., Sanislow, C., Mcglashan, T. H., & Bremner, J. D. (2003a). Neural correlates of memories of abandonment in women with and without borderline personality disorder. *Biological Psychiatry, 54*, 42–51.

Schmahl, C. G., Vermetten, E., Elzinga, B. M., & Bremner, J. D. (2003b). *Magnetic resonance imaging* of hippocampal and amygdala volume in women with childhood abuse and borderline personality disorder. *Psychiatry Research: Neuroimaging, 122*, 193–198.

Schuff, N., Marmar, C. R., Weiss, D. S., Neylan, T. C., Schoenfeld, F., Fein, G., & Weiner, M. W. (1997). Reduced hippocampal volume and n-acetyl aspartate in posttraumatic stress disorder. *Annals of the New York Academy of Sciences, 821*, 516–520.

Schuff, N., Neylan, T. C., Lenoci, M. A., Du, A. T., Weiss, D. S., Marmar, C. R., & Weiner, M. W. (2001). Decreased hippocampal N-acetylaspartate in the absence of atrophy in posttraumatic stress disorder. *Biological Psychiatry, 50*, 952–959.

Schuff, N., Meyerhoff, D. J., Mueller, S., Chao, L., Sacrey, D. T., Laxer, K., & Weiner, M. W. (2006). N-acetylaspartate as a marker of neuronal injury in neurodegenerative disease. *Advances in Experimental Medicine and Biology, 576*, 241–262.

Seedat, S., Videen, J. S., Kennedy, C. M., & Stein, M. B. (2005). Single voxel proton magnetic resonance spectroscopy in women with and without intimate partner violence-related posttraumatic stress disorder. *Psychiatry Research, 139*, 249–258.

Semple, W. E., Goyer, P., Mccormick, R., Donovan, B., Muzic, R. F., Rugle, L., Mccutcheon, K., Lewis, C., Liebling, D., Kowaliw, S., Vapenik, K., Semple, M. A., Flener, C. R., & Schulz, S. C. (2000). Higher brain blood flow at amygdala and lower frontal cortex blood flow in PTSD patients with comorbid cocaine and alcohol abuse compared to controls. *Psychiatry, 63*, 65–74.

Shin, L. M., Kosslyn, S. M., Mcnally, R. J., Alpert, N. M., Thompson, W. L., Rauch, S. L., Macklin, M. L., & Pitman, R. K. (1997). Visual imagery and perception in posttraumatic stress disorder: A positron emission tomographic investigation. *Archives of General Psychiatry, 54*, 233–237.

Shin, L. M., Mcnally, R. J., Kosslyn, S. M., Thompson, W. L., Rauch, S. L., Alpert, N. M., Metzger, L. J., Lasko, N. B., Orr, S. P., & Pitman, R. K. (1999). Regional cerebral blood flow during script-driven imagery in childhood sexual abuse-related PTSD: A PET investigation. *American Journal of Psychiatry, 156*, 575–584.

Shin, L. M., Whalen, P. J., Pitman, R. K., Bush, G., Macklin, M. L., Lasko, N. B., Orr, S. P., Mcinerney, S. C., & Rauch, S. L. (2001). An fMRI study of anterior cingulate function in posttraumatic stress disorder. *Biological Psychiatry, 50*, 932–942.

Shin, L. M., Orr, S. P., Carson, M. A., Rauch, S. L., Macklin, M. L., Lasko, N. B., Peters, P. M., Metzger, L. J., Dougherty, D. D., Cannistraro, P. A., Alpert, N. M., Fischman, A. J., & Pitman, R. K. (2004a). Regional cerebral blood flow in the amygdala and medial prefrontal cortex during traumatic imagery in male and female Vietnam veterans with PTSD. *Archives of General Psychiatry, 61*, 168–176.

Shin, L. M., Shin, P. S., Heckers, S., Krangel, T. S., Macklin, M. L., Orr, S. P., Lasko, N., Segal, E., Makris, N., Richert, K., Levering, J., Schacter, D. L., Alpert, N. M., Fischman, A. J., Pitman, R. K., & Rauch, S. L. (2004b). Hippocampal function in posttraumatic stress disorder. *Hippocampus, 14*, 292–300.

Shin, L. M., Wright, C. I., Cannistraro, P. A., Wedig, M. M., Mcmullin, K., Martis, B., Macklin, M. L., Lasko, N. B., Cavanagh, S. R., Krangel, T. S., Orr, S. P., Pitman, R. K., Whalen, P. J., & Rauch, S. L. (2005). A functional magnetic resonance imaging study of amygdala and medial prefrontal cortex responses to overtly presented fearful faces in posttraumatic stress disorder. *Archives of General Psychiatry, 62*, 273–281.

Smith, M. E. (2005). Bilateral hippocampal volume reduction in adults with post-traumatic stress disorder: a meta-analysis of structural MRI studies. *Hippocampus, 15*, 798–807.

Squire, L. R. (2004). Memory systems of the brain: A brief history and current perspective. *Neurobiology of Learning and Memory, 82*, 171–177.

Stein, M. B., Koverola, C., Hanna, C., Torchia, M. G., & Mcclarty, B. (1997). Hippocampal volume in women victimized by childhood sexual abuse. *Psychological Medicine, 27*, 951–959.

Teicher, M. H., Dumont, N. L., Ito, Y., Vaituzis, C., Giedd, J. N., & Andersen, S. L. (2004). Childhood neglect is associated with reduced corpus callosum area. *Biological Psychiatry, 56*, 80–85.

Vermetten, E., & Bremner, J. D. (2002a). Circuits and systems in stress. I. Preclinical studies. *Depression & Anxiety, 15*, 126–147.

Vermetten, E., & Bremner, J. D. (2002b). Circuits and systems in stress. II. Applications to neurobiology and treatment of PTSD. *Depression & Anxiety, 16*, 14–38.

Vermetten, E., Vythilingam, M., Southwick, S. M., Charney, D. S., & Bremner, J. D. (2003). Long-term treatment with paroxetine increases verbal declarative memory and hippocampal volume in posttraumatic stress disorder. *Biological Psychiatry, 54*, 693–702.

Vermetten, E., Schmahl, C., Lindner, S., Loewenstein, R. J., & Bremner, J. D. (2006). Hippocampal and amygdalar volumes in Dissociative Identity Disorder. *American Journal of Psychiatry, 163*, 1–8.

Villarreal, G., Hamilton, D. A., Petropoulos, H., Driscoll, I., Rowland, L. M., Griego, J. A., Kodituwakku, P. W., Hart, B. L., Escalona, R., & Brooks, W. M. (2002). Reduced hippocampal volume and total white matter in posttraumatic stress disorder. *Biological Psychiatry, 52*, 119–125.

Villarreal, G., Hamilton, D. A., Graham, D. P., Driscoll, I., Qualls, C., Petropoulos, H., & Brooks, W. M. (2004). Reduced area of the corpus callosum in posttraumatic stress disorder. *Psychiatry Research: Neuroimaging, 131*, 227–235.

Vythilingam, M., Heim, C., Newport, C. D., Miller, A. H., Vermetten, E., Anderson, E., Bronen, R., Staib, L., Charney, D. S., Nemeroff, C. B., & Bremner, J. D. (2002). Childhood trauma associated with smaller hippocampal volume in women with major depression. *American Journal of Psychiatry, 159*, 2072–2080.

Wignall, E. L., Dickson, J. M., Vaughan, P., Farrow, T. F., Wilkinson, I. D., Hunter, M. D., & Woodruff, P. W. (2004). Smaller hippocampal volume in patients with recent-onset posttraumatic stress disorder. *Biological Psychiatry, 56*, 832–836.

Winter, H., & Irle, E. (2004). Hippocampal volume in adult burn patients with and without posttraumatic stress disorder. *American Journal of Psychiatry, 161*, 2194–2200.

Woodward, S. H., Kaloupek, D. G., Streeter, C. C., Martinez, C., Schaer, M., & Eliez, S. (2006). Decreased anterior cingulate volume in combat-related PTSD. *Biological Psychiatry, 59*, 582–587.

Yamasue, H., Kasai, K., Iwanami, A., Ohtani, T., Yamada, H., Abe, O., Kuroki, N., Fukuda, R., Tochigi, M., Furukawa, S., Sadamatsu, M., Sasaki, T., Aoki, S., Ohtomo, K., Asukai, N., & Kato, N. (2003). Voxel-based analysis of MRI reveals anterior cingulate gray-matter volume reduction in posttraumatic stress disorder due to terrorism. *Proceedings of the National Academy of Sciences USA, 100*, 9039–9043.

Yang, P., Wu, M. T., Hsu, C. C., & Ker, J. H. (2004). Evidence of early neurobiological alternations in adolescents with posttraumatic stress disorder: a functional MRI study. *Neuroscience Letters, 370*, 13–18.

Yehuda, R., Golier, J. A., Tischler, L., Harvey, P. D., Newmark, R., Yang, R. K., & Buchsbaum, M. S. (2007). Hippocampal volume in aging combat veterans with and without posttraumatic stress disorder: Relation to risk and resilience factors. *Journal of Psychiatric Research, 41*, 435–445.

Yen, S., Shea, M. T., Battle, C. L., Johnson, D. M., Zlotnick, C., Dolan-Sewell, R., Skodol, A. E., Grilo, C. M., Gunderson, J. G., Sanislow, C. A., Zanarini, M. C., Bender, D. S., Rettew, J. B., & Mcglashan, T. H. (2002). Traumatic exposure and posttraumatic stress disorder in borderline, schizotypal, avoidant, and obsessive-compulsive personality disorders: findings from the collaborative longitudinal personality disorders study. *Journal of Nervous and Mental Disease, 190*, 510–518.

23

Chronic Stress and Depression

Eberhard Fuchs and Gabriele Flügge

Introduction

Since the pioneering work of Cannon (1929) and Selye (1936), stress research has gradually shifted from physiologically oriented stimulus-response paradigms towards models in which the psychological impact of stress gained a central role. This shift was accompanied by an increasing awareness that traumatic life events, in combination with genetic, epigenetic, and environmental factors, play a central role in the etiology of various diseases. One conclusion from these diathesis–stress models is the hypothesis that stress is a primary factor in the development of depressive disorders. It has been shown in many patients that episodes of major depression are preceded by negative life events (Kessler, 1997) and, according to the classification of the symptoms of depression in the *Diagnostic and Statistical Manual of Mental Disorders* (DSM-IV), the subjective report of feeling stressed is one of the leading symptoms of depression. Cognitive biases, which are key symptoms of major depression, can be exacerbated by stressful experiences (Monroe et al., 2007).

Although it may happen that a single severe traumatic experience triggers a psychiatric disease (e.g., posttraumatic stress disorder, PTSD), it is often chronic stress that changes the emotional life of a vulnerable individual disastrously. When an individual cannot cope with a stressful stimulus that occurs repeatedly, hormonal and transmitter systems that are needed as defenses in life-threatening situations attack the neuronal network and impair proper functioning of the brain areas that generate emotions and enable cognition. This chronic activation may lead to the eventual exhaustion of these defense systems and to profound physiological imbalances in both the body and the brain. The present article aims at reviewing some

The Handbook of Stress: Neuropsychological Effects on the Brain, First Edition.
Edited by Cheryl D. Conrad.
© 2011 Blackwell Publishing Ltd. Published 2011 by Blackwell Publishing Ltd.

of the currently known processes of chronic stress that have the potential to induce depressive diseases. However, it should be kept in mind that major depression is a complex disorder that results not only from environmental factors but also from genetic influences (Sullivan et al., 2000).

Acute Versus Chronic Stress

Since Selye's original formulation of the stress theory, improvement in the methods of assessment and in research design have helped identify multiple hormonal and transmitter systems as stress mediators that prepare the body and the brain to deliver proper defense (alarm) reactions in dangerous or even life-threatening situations. The best studied of these systems is the hypothalamic–pituitary–adrenal (HPA) axis, which is responsible for the stress-induced rise in plasma glucocorticoids (cortisol in humans; corticosterone in rats) (Joëls and Baram, 2009; see also other chapters in this book). Elevated levels of glucocorticoids, which have numerous effects on the metabolism of carbohydrates, proteins, and lipids, guarantee enhanced energy supply to cells in the body and brain in alarming situations, when a *fight-or-flight response* (Cannon, 1929) is required. Another natural defense mechanism that evolved during vertebrate evolution is the activation of the peripheral sympathetic nervous system. Norepinephrine (noradrenaline) released from the terminals of the sympathetic nerves, together with epinephrine (adrenaline) released from the adrenal medulla, regulate the activity of many organs and the cardiovascular system. Among their diverse functions, these catecholaminergic transmitters ensure enhanced blood flow through skeletal muscles, which is an obvious physiological need in fight-or-flight situations. Also in the brain, norepinephrine regulates the activity of many cells that are necessary for proper defense reactions; for example, regulation of attention and vigilance by cortical neurons, and counteraction of the high blood pressure induced by the stress-mediated hyperactivity of the sympathetic nervous system by brainstem neurons. However, in the brain, stress activates a multitude of mediators and neurotransmitters, many of which exert a potentially harmful effect on neural cells (see below).

In most acute stress situations, the defense systems are only transiently activated; as soon as the stressful situation is terminated and the individual perceives it as safe, the activities of these systems return to baseline. As an example, social defeat in male rats leads to an immediate rise in heart rate, body temperature, and plasma corticosterone, which all decline gradually within 3–5 hr after the beginning of the social encounter (Koolhaas et al., 1997). In contrast, during chronic stress, the stimulus occurs repeatedly over a long period (in humans this could be weeks or months) and complete recovery of the affected systems between stress episodes is no longer possible; this means that the defense systems remain at elevated activity levels. After a few negative stress experiences, the system can still respond to an additional challenge, although often less effectively compared with the reaction to the first challenge. However, after many such stress exposures, the body and the

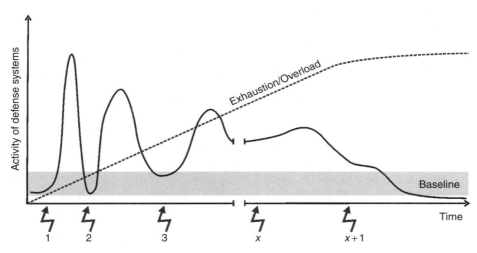

Figure 23.1 Schematic illustration of the temporal dynamics of the activation of defense systems (solid line) during chronic stress in a vulnerable individual. The abscissa represents a hypothetical period of weeks (for rats) to months (for humans). Note that a stressful experience (arrow 1) leads to immediate activation of defense systems; however, shortly after that acute challenge, the system returns to baseline. After several stressful events (arrows 2 and 3), the response of the defense system is blunted and, after many challenges (hypothetical number indicated by *X*), the system's activity cannot return to baseline. At this point, there is the risk of strong exhaustion and overload (dashed line) and upon a further challenge (arrow *X*+1) the system is no longer able to respond adequately. In this state, the activity of the defense system is in the range or even below the baseline.

brain become exhausted and activation of defense systems ceases to occur (Figure 23.1). In male rats, social defeat repeated every day for a period of up to 4 weeks induces a persistent depressive-like behavior (reduced sucrose preference), from the second week of the chronic-stress period onwards (Rygula et al., 2006). The extent and the temporal dynamics of the physiological reactions depend on the type of stressor, its intensity and duration, previous experiences of the affected individual, and the subject's vulnerability, which is determined partly by genetic predisposition. When a stressor is weak, there may be habituation. For instance, repeated occurrence of a *mild stimulus* leads to a gradual decrease in plasma catecholamine responses (McCarty and Pacak, 2007). In rats maintained at 5°C, the activity of tyrosine hydroxylase (the rate-limiting enzyme in the catecholamine biosynthesis pathway) in the locus coeruleus increased after 3 days spent in that cold environment; however, it decreased gradually thereafter, to reach almost basal levels after 2–3 weeks in that same environment (Nisenbaum et al., 1991). McLaughlin et al. (2007) reported that the apical dendrites of pyramidal neurons in the CA3 hippocampal region (where CA means cornu ammonis of the hippocampus) of rats change significantly after 3 weeks of restraint stress for 6 hr, whereas there was no significant stress effect on this neuronal parameter after only 10 days (McLaughlin et al., 2007). In humans, mobbing or workplace bullying may go on for several months before a strong reaction occurs, possibly presented as severe mental exhaustion or even a depressive episode.

Some stressors may even sensitize the organism in a way that subsequent stress reactions are stronger than the initial response; for example, painful stimuli often give rise to prior expectation of further pain experiences, leading to more pronounced subsequent stress responses (Koolhaas et al., 1997). A high activity of the HPA axis is a characteristic reaction to chronic aversive stressors, and it has been claimed that HPA axis hyperactivity is also a typical feature of major depression. However, a remarkable heterogeneity of neuroendocrine functions has been observed in depressed subjects, whereas the proportion of individuals demonstrating HPA axis abnormalities may be as low as 35% (Matthews et al., 2005). Moreover, hypercortisolism has also been described in patients with very distinct diagnoses, such as Alzheimer's disease or substance abuse (Martignoni et al., 1990; Contoreggi et al., 2003). In contrast, cortisol levels below the baseline (hypocortisolism) were detected in PTSD and burnout patients (Yehuda, 2007; Heim and Nater, 2007). Therefore, it appears that psychopathologies that are induced by chronic or traumatic stress can be accompanied by various levels of HPA axis activity.

A major factor that can render an individual sensitive to stress is age. It is a common observation that, compared with young subjects, old people perceive daily challenges as more stressful; for example, finding a ticket counter in a large, crowded railway station. After a cognitive task, blood-pressure elevation was more exaggerated in 75–80-year-old subjects with mild cognitive impairment than in old persons in full control of themselves (Kawashima et al., 2008). In an animal model of chronic social stress, the male tree shrew, the effects of daily social defeat on neurogenesis in the hippocampal formation were more pronounced in older individuals (21–30 months) than in young adults (less than 10 months) (Simon et al., 2005). This study also showed that hippocampal neurogenesis, which is regarded as a form of neuroplasticity, decreases with age. Thus, it appears that the age-related decline in processes of neuroplasticity is accompanied by enhanced stress susceptibility.

Animal Models of Chronic Stress

It has been claimed that it is difficult to develop a true animal model of depressive disorders, as mental illnesses may be uniquely human. In particular, the typical symptoms of depression in patients, such as recurring thoughts of suicide or excessive thoughts of guilt, are impossible to model in animals. Nevertheless, the fact that stress can lead to depressive diseases in humans stimulated the development of a number of animal models in which chronic stress induces depressive-like symptoms. In such experimental paradigms, many of the stress-induced behavioral symptoms of the animals show similarities with the behavior of human patients, and some of these symptoms in animals can be normalized by the administration of antidepressive drugs that are also effective in patients. This indicates that the stress-induced neurobiological mechanisms and the pathological processes that lead to depression have something in common.

The earliest experimental models of depression-like states in animals were based on maternal separation (see Jesberger and Richardson, 1985). Adult monkeys that had been separated from their mothers during infancy showed long-term alterations in social coping style, emotional and behavioral regulation, and in neuroendocrine responsiveness to stress (Coe et al., 1983; Sánchez et al., 2001). Another approach is the learned helplessness model, in which rats are sensitized to a painful stressor (foot shock), the recurrence of which they cannot control (Seligman, 1972). However, the results obtained with this experimental paradigm are difficult to replicate and ethical constraints speak against the wide use of such experiments (Nestler et al., 2002). The chronic mild stress model is based on exposure of animals (usually rats) to varying kinds of mild stressors, such as disrupted light/dark cycle, wet bedding, or frequent changing of the home cage (Willner, 2005). In female rats, the social-instability stress paradigm, which consists of alternating periods of crowding and social isolation, evokes stress responses (Haller et al., 1999; Herzog et al., 2009). In the chronic-restraint stress paradigm, rats are immobilized in a tube or wire mesh for a certain time daily for several weeks. This model was used successfully in many studies to elucidate the effects of chronic stress on the brain (McLaughlin et al., 2007).

In humans, loss of rank and/or social status is a very aversive experience associated with a great risk of depression. Therefore, social stress paradigms in animals are regarded as natural and ethologically relevant models for the study of the behavioral, endocrine, and neurobiological changes that may underlie stress-related disorders (Koolhaas et al., 1997). In the psychosocial stress paradigm in tree shrews, the stress that a subordinate male experiences over several weeks in the presence of a dominant counterpart has diverse hormonal and behavioral effects and induces changes in neurons and glial cells of the brain (Kramer et al., 1999; Fuchs and Flügge, 2002). Many of these stress effects are reversible and can be prevented by treatment with an antidepressant drug (Fuchs et al., 2004, 2006). In addition, a social stress paradigm in male rodents has been validated as a model of depression in which several of the social stress-induced behaviors of male rats can be normalized by the administration of antidepressants (Rygula et al., 2005).

One may argue that the above paradigms would be described more correctly as models of stress, rather than as models of depression, as not all responses to stress are pathological but may fulfill adaptive or protective functions. Therefore, to model depression truly, other factors, such as the genetic background causing a predisposition for the disease, should also be taken into consideration. However, in the case of major depression, genetic factors can only account for approximately 30% of the variance and environmental factors clearly play a major role in the manifestation of the illness (Sullivan et al., 2000). Nevertheless, animal models of depression based on the interaction between stress and genetic vulnerability can contribute to the understanding of processes that lead to the disease. Studies using knockout models with a mutation in a single gene may be of limited usefulness because of confounding factors, such as developmental adaptational processes. Conditional knockouts are probably an improvement compared with straight knockouts; however, they only provide information about the role of single genes. Therefore, more complex models involving the interaction of various genes with the environment may yield information that is more useful. For instance, this is the case in paradigms where an individual's reaction to social defeat is evaluated. Although the respective literature is constantly expanding, one can state that the current models of chronic stress greatly increased our understanding of the processes that take place in the brain during the depressive-like states of an individual.

Brain Cells Under Stress

The brain reacts to stressful events by modulating the activity of various neurotransmitter systems (Figure 23.2). Rapid neuronal responses to a stressful stimulus

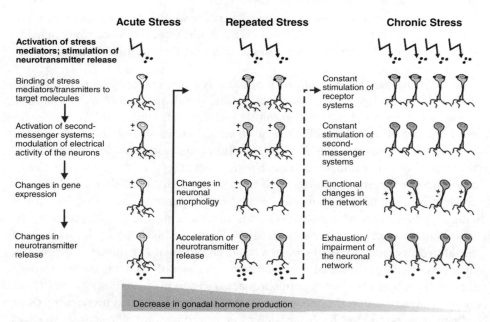

Figure 23.2   Schematic illustration summarizing the effects of chronic stress on neurons in the brain. An acute challenge (zigzag arrow, upper left) induces a transient rise in stress mediators (black dots), which bind to target molecules, stimulate second messenger systems, and modify electrical activity, gene expression, and neurotransmitter release. The repeated occurrence of stressful stimuli leads to the stimulation of additional neurons (middle). The synergistic actions of stress mediators and the lack of gonadal steroids stimulate the neurons further, which change their morphology subsequently. The repeated occurrence of the stressful stimuli over a long period (chronic stress; right) may lead to impairment of the integrity and function of the neuronal network and to the exhaustion of the self-repair capacities of the system.

are elicited by the excitatory neurotransmitter glutamate and by the inhibitory neurotransmitter γ-aminobutyric acid (GABA), which exert their effects within milliseconds by acting on specific receptors and ion channels in the plasma membrane of the target cells. Accordingly, the concentrations of glutamate and GABA are increased after a stressful challenge (Bagley and Moghaddam, 1997; de Groote and Linthorst, 2007). Other transmitters, such as the monoamines (e.g., dopamine, norepinephrine, epinephrine, and serotonin), have slower effects on numerous neurons and glial cells. Nevertheless, the activation of brain monoaminergic systems is a major component of the stress response and it is well known that the turnover of monoamines is increased during stressful experiences (Bliss et al., 1968; Nisenbaum et al., 1991; Stanford, 1995). Activation of these systems is regarded as the basis for stress-related behavior and the stress-mediated hyperactivity of catecholaminergic and serotonergic neurons induces imbalances between the different alarm systems that may finally lead to the emotional characteristics of chronically stressed subjects (Bremner et al., 1996; see also Flügge, 2000). Currently, a multitude of processes in neurons and glial cells are known that are due to overactivation of the brain neurotransmitter systems, as outlined below.

The components of monoaminergic systems in the brain undergo dynamic changes during stress. For example, in the locus coeruleus, a pontine nucleus which innervates many brain regions, stress-stimulated firing of norepinephrine neurons is accompanied by faster synthesis of the neurotransmitter itself and increased expression of the gene encoding tyrosine hydroxylase (Smith et al., 1991). In addition, reduced neurotransmitter degradation due to diminished activity of the metabolizing enzyme monoamine oxidase can occur (see Flügge, 2000). Furthermore, stress raises the activity of phenylethanolamine-N-methyltransferase, which is the enzyme that converts norepinephrine to epinephrine in brainstem areas that are involved in blood-pressure regulation (Saavedra and Torda, 1980). Altogether, these processes lead to fluctuations of transmitter concentrations in brain regions innervated by monoamine neurons. Concomitantly, high norepinephrine concentrations induce agonist-dependent downregulation of adrenergic receptors—for example, α_2-adrenoceptors—on target cells in brain areas known to be involved in emotional processing. In addition, the number of β_1-adrenoceptors changes as a function of agonist concentration (in the hippocampus, for example) (see Flügge et al., 2004). In the prefrontal cortex (PFC), which is important for the regulation of mood and behavior, α_2-adrenoceptors were transiently downregulated after 10 days of psychosocial stress in male tree shrews, but were upregulated after 4 weeks. Although the initial downregulation of the receptors indicates high norepinephrine concentrations, receptor upregulation is due most probably to low levels of the neurotransmitter. These results indicate that a prolonged stress period finally leads to a norepinephrine deficit in the PFC, as supply of this transmitter to the area distant from the locus coeruleus is insufficient after 4 weeks of social stress. In addition, the upregulation of α_2-adrenoceptors was detected in the neocortex of depressed patients (data from post mortem brain material), which supports the hypothesis that depression is caused by a deficit in norepinephrine in brain regions that regulate emotional behavior (see Flügge et al., 2004). Moreover, these findings imply that the neurochemical processes taking place in the brains of stressed animals are similar to those observed in patients in the course of the development of a depressive episode.

Reactions of the dopaminergic system to stress are particularly interesting because dopamine plays a prominent role in the regulation of motivation, and deficits in that system may contribute to anhedonia, which is a key symptom of depression. However, persistent stress-induced activation, as shown for the noradrenergic system, has not been demonstrated for the dopaminergic system. Under restraint stress, an initial increase in mesolimbic dopamine release was followed by a decrease, suggesting that repeated exposure to the same stressor results in inhibition, rather than activation, of dopaminergic neurons. Conflicting data on this issue indicate that the effects depend on the severity and controllability of the stressor, the genetic background of the animals, and their life history. In tree shrews, 4 weeks of psycho-social stress downregulated dopamine transporter expression in the striatum, and we found a correlation between locomotor activity (which was diminished in the stressed animals) and the total number of dopamine-transporter-binding sites. Low levels of dopamine transporter may reflect reduced extracellular dopamine concentrations. In accordance with these findings, social defeat in male rats decreased striatal dopamine-transporter-binding sites (see Flügge et al., 2004).

A stress-induced increase in neurotransmitter activity does not target all brain regions in the same way, as different neuronal circuits are affected according to the type of stressor. Prior to initiation or inhibition of the stress response, signals evoking emotional reactions require a central nervous processing of the information coming from the different sensory organs. This information processing involves limbic (e.g., hippocampus and amygdala) and cortical regions, and its outcome depends on previous experience. In contrast, mere physiological threats, such as exposure to ether, activate efferent visceral pathways directly. In this case, the rapid activation of the brainstem and hypothalamus circumvents cognitive/emotional processing via the *higher* brain regions (Herman and Cullinan, 1997).

Plasticity of the Mature Brain

One may regard the dynamic processes in neurotransmitter systems described above as neuroplasticity, which enables the brain to adapt to stressful environmental stimuli. Neuroplasticity is based on the capacity of neurons to change their biochemical, electrophysiological, and structural properties if they receive too much or too little input. The best-known phenomenon of neuroplasticity is long-term potentiation, a long-lasting enhancement in neuronal signal transduction in response to synchronous stimulation. Chronic stress in male rats reduced commissural/associational long-term potentiation in the hippocampus (Pavlides et al., 2002). In CA3 pyramidal neurons of male tree shrews, subthreshold excitability was diminished by chronic stress, with preservation of the efficacy of somatic excitability of the neurons (Kole et al., 2004). Such changes in membrane properties are accompanied by morphological alterations that are used by neurons to modify their cell surfaces. Thus, chronic stress induces a retraction of apical dendrites of the hippocampal pyramidal neurons and this morphological change may contribute to disturbances in spatial memory (see McLaughlin et al., 2009). Moreover, different kinds of chronic, but not acute, stress change the morphology of the mossy fiber synapses in the CA3 hippocampal area (Magariños et al., 1997). In addition to these stress effects on pyramidal neurons, there are also changes in the inhibitory neuronal network. In the dentate gyrus and CA3 area of the hippocampal formation, chronic psychosocial stress diminished the number of parvalbumin-immunoreactive cells, which represent a subset of GABAergic interneurons (Czéh et al., 2005). A recent electrophysiological study showed that stress changes GABAergic network functioning, at least in the rat hippocampus (Hu et al., 2010). In addition, neurons of the glutamatergic system are affected by stress, as a quantitative study showed that expression of the membrane glycoprotein M6a in glutamatergic axons is reduced by chronic stress (Cooper et al., 2009). Furthermore, stress induces changes in the cytoskeleton. α-Tubulin, a major component of microtubules, undergoes dynamic changes via posttranslational modification. Four days of daily restraint stress decreased the expression of tyrosinated α-tubulin and increased the expression of the acetylated form in the hippocampus (see Alfonso et al., 2005). Persistent chronic stress leads to morphological changes in an increasing number of neurons in the brain (Figure 23.2).

In parallel to these changes in the morphology of individual neurons, chronic stress reduces the entire volume of the hippocampal formation by about 5% (Czéh et al., 2001). The reasons for this shrinkage of the brain tissue remain unclear. However, among other processes, the effect may be related to reductions in dendritic, axonal, and synaptic material. Interestingly, the hippocampal volume is smaller in unmedicated patients with major depression compared with healthy controls (Neumeister et al., 2005), although one should keep in mind that a reduction in hippocampal volume does not only occur in depression but also in other psychiatric diseases such as schizophrenia.

Despite the popular view that stress induces neuronal death in the brain, this phenomenon was never observed under controlled experimental conditions (Fuchs et al., 2004). In addition, no neuronal loss was observed in depressed patients. In contrast, post mortem studies on hippocampi of patients with major depression have shown that the packaging density of neurons and glial cells in all hippocampal subfields was increased, an effect that may be related to the overall shrinkage of the tissue (Stockmeier et al., 2004). Another study on human post mortem brain material also reported that there are no indications for cell loss in the hippocampus after stress and/or depression (Bao et al., 2008). Furthermore, the tree shrew model of chronic social stress, which allows the exact counting of brain cells in defined brain regions, revealed an absence of hippocampal neuronal loss (Vollmann-Honsdorf et al., 1997). However, in addition to the above-mentioned retraction in neuronal dendrites, stress suppresses neurogenesis in the dentate gyrus, which is an intrinsic part of the hippocampal formation, and the blockage of certain glutamate receptors or the application of antidepressive drugs prevents this suppression

(Gould et al., 1997; Czéh et al., 2001). Whether restoration of normal neurogenesis is essential for the beneficial effects of antidepressive drugs remains controversial, in view of the fact that only a small number of neurons are generated in relatively small regions in the brain (e.g., dentate gyrus; Czéh and Lucassen, 2007). New neurons represent only a minute proportion of the total neuronal population; however, their continuous addition over an entire life span implies considerable structural changes within the neural network. Nevertheless, several of the stress-induced morphological changes in neurons—for example, the retraction of dendrites and the reduction in neurogenesis rate—were reversed by the administration of antidepressant drugs (McEwen et al., 2002). Based on these and other studies it was proposed that antidepressants induce processes of neuroplasticity that reorganize the central nervous neural networks, thus provoking the observed therapeutic effects (Fuchs et al., 2004). The specific serotonin-reuptake inhibitor fluoxetine even restored neuroplasticity in the adult visual cortex of rats with a deficit in cortical plasticity due to monocular deprivation (Maya-Vetencourt et al., 2008). As regulators of cell proliferation and differentiation, neurotrophic factors are probably essential within these processes of neural network reorganization (Castrén et al., 2007).

Many of the stress effects on brain cells known to date have been investigated in the hippocampal formation; however, other brain regions are also targeted by stress, in particular those of the limbic system. The growing number of publications on this subject reveals that stress effects are brain region-specific and that chronic stress does not always reduce neuronal components. Instead, 10 days of daily restraint stress stimulated the formation of new spines on certain dendrites in the basolateral nucleus of the rat amygdala (Mitra et al., 2005). Stress has multiple effects on dendrites of pyramidal neurons in the medial PFC (mPFC) (Cook and Wellman, 2004). Hemispheric differences indicate an involvement of monoamines in these morphological changes, as the chronic-stress-induced retraction of dendrites is stronger in the right hemisphere (where more dopamine is released) than in the left PFC (Perez-Cruz et al., 2009). Some alterations in the morphology of mPFC neurons are reversible or occur during the course of the normal diurnal rhythm (Radley et al., 2005; Perez-Cruz et al., 2009). These neuroplastic modifications may represent adaptational processes that are used by neurons to react to changing input from various neurotransmitter and hormonal systems. As long as such neuroplastic processes are reversible, they are probably not pathological; however, if the changes persist, pathological states such as depression may develop. In line with this idea, various differences between depressed and healthy subjects in several regions of the human PFC indicate that pathological changes in this brain region are correlated with major depression (Drevets et al., 2008).

Neuroplasticity at the Level of Gene Transcription

The stress-induced changes in neuronal structure imply that brain cells are able to adjust their biosynthetic pathways to new requirements. For example, concomitant with the retraction of dendrites, there is most probably a reduced need for certain membrane proteins, and related adaptational processes should in part take place at the level of gene transcription. In the hippocampal formation, expression of the transcripts of several genes was downregulated by chronic social stress; for example, mRNA for the gene encoding CDC-like kinase 1 and *GNAQ*, a gene encoding a distinct subunit of certain G-proteins (see Alfonso et al., 2005). Both of these proteins are involved in neurite outgrowth and neuronal differentiation, thus supporting the view that alterations in neuronal morphology and/or formation of neurons are primary effects of stress, at least in the hippocampal formation. Furthermore, the expression of the neural cell adhesion molecule (NCAM) was downregulated after chronic restraint stress in the hippocampus. NCAM regulates neurite outgrowth and neuronal target recognition in the developing nervous system by mediating cell adhesion and regulating signal transduction (Bisaz et al., 2009).

It was proposed that the beneficial effects of antidepressant drugs are due to restoration of "normal neuroplasticity" (Fuchs et al., 2004; Castrén et al., 2007). The mRNA for cAMP-response-element binding protein (CREB)-binding protein (CBP), which is a protein that interacts with the transcription factor CREB, was upregulated in the dorsal raphe nucleus of male rats, where chronic stress activates serotonergic neurons (Abumaria et al., 2007). CBP binds to DNA and unfolds chromatin to enable transcription. Treatment of the stressed rats with the specific selective serotonin-reuptake inhibitor (SSRI) and antidepressant drug citalopram prevented the upregulation of the CBP mRNA and, therefore, probably hindered transcription. Moreover, the mRNA for tryptophan hydroxylase, the enzyme that synthesizes serotonin, was also upregulated by chronic social stress, and citalopram prevented this upregulation. These data show that chronic blockade of serotonin reuptake has an impact on transcription, as it prevents some stress-induced changes in gene expression (Abumaria et al., 2007). Altogether, these data demonstrate that both stress and antidepressant drugs, when given chronically, modify gene transcription. Furthermore, citalopram blocked the stress-induced upregulation of the synaptic vesicle protein 2b, a protein localized to the terminal vesicles of many synapses. This demonstrates that chronic blockade of serotonin reuptake has an impact on neurotransmission in general, and not only on the serotonergic system. It appears that antidepressants restore neuroplasticity and thus support the self-healing capacities of the brain.

Sex-specific Differences in Reactions to Stress

Findings of gender differences in the response to stress, and especially in the reactivity to stress, may provide clues to explain the greater rates of depression in women (Kessler et al., 2005). Despite this knowledge, most of the abovementioned preclinical data are derived from studies performed using male animals. Gonadal steroids regulate gene transcription and, thus, the expression of neuronal components

(McLaughlin et al., 2009); consequently, the relationship between neuron morphology and function is very different between genders. For instance, female rats showed an estrogen-dependent, stress-induced increase in apical dendrites of mPFC neurons, whereas male rats displayed a decrease (Garrett and Wellman, 2009). This and other findings indicate that, in females, estrogens can have a protective effect on neurons, so that stress fails to exert a measurable influence. In male animals, it is the gonadal steroid testosterone that prevents certain stress effects. Chronic social stress in male tree shrews reduces testosterone production and downregulates serotonin-1A receptors in the hippocampus. This shows that the reduction in gonadal steroids contributes to the effects of stress on neuronal morphology (Figure 23.2). Substitution of testosterone restored the normal number of hippocampal serotonin-1A receptors and normal behavior in chronically stressed male tree shrews (Flügge et al., 1998).

Plasticity of Astrocytes

Most cells within the central nervous system are glia. In the adult mammalian brain there are 10–50 times more glial cells than neurons. One type of glial cell, the astrocytes, account for about one-third of brain mass. In addition to their housekeeping functions, these cells are dynamic regulators of synaptogenesis and synaptic strength and control neurogenesis, as measured in the adult dentate gyrus. Thus, abnormalities in glial functioning are likely to contribute to the impairment of structural plasticity in the brain. In line with these ideas, chronic stress reduced both the number and the volume of astroglial cell bodies in the hippocampus. The SSRI fluoxetine prevented the stress-induced decrease in the number of astrocytes, indicating that (1) fluoxetine targets glia and (2) restoration of glial functioning contributes to the beneficial antidepressive effects (Czéh et al., 2006). Weakened activity of astrocytes could change the levels of extracellular glutamate in the brain, thus leading to high concentrations of this excitatory neurotransmitter, which may result in excitotoxic effects. An upregulation of the glial glutamate transporter 1 (GLT1) was detected in the hippocampus after chronic restraint stress, and it has been suggested that this could be a compensatory mechanism to control for the increased extracellular glutamate concentrations caused by the stress (Reagan et al., 2004). Interestingly, the antidepressant drug tianeptine blocked this stress-induced upregulation. These changes in the structure and molecular plasticity of astroglia in response to stress and antidepressant treatment support the notion that disturbed glial functioning contributes to the pathophysiology of stress-related disorders, such as major depression, as well as to the cellular actions of antidepressants (Fuchs et al., 2004). Magnetic resonance spectroscopy of the human PFC showed that patients with major depression had abnormal levels of GABA and glutamate, which indicates reduced density of glial cells (Hasler et al., 2007).

Conclusions

Based on the data summarized above, one can conclude that insights into the central nervous system processes that are mediated and modified by stressful experiences in laboratory animals provide a basis for the understanding of the mechanisms that underlie the etiology of depressive disorders. The fact that some antidepressive drugs prevent or even reverse the effects of chronic stress indicates that the neurobiological processes of stress and depression have something in common. However, several challenges remain for further research: (1) some chronic stress effects may be reversible per se, (2) depression in human patients reveals itself in multiple forms (e.g., major depression, PTSD, and comorbidity with anxiety), and (3) a given antidepressive drug may be ineffective in a significant number of patients. Future studies should clarify whether, among the numerous molecular factors that are known currently to be changed in the brain of stressed and/or depressed subjects, there are molecules that play a key role in the etiology of stress-related diseases. Such molecules could potentially serve as targets for effective therapies.

References

Abumaria, N., Rygula, R., Hiemke, C., Fuchs, E., Havemann-Reinecke, U., Rüther, E., & Flügge, G. (2007). Effect of chronic citalopram on serotonin-related and stress-regulated genes in the dorsal raphe nucleus of the rat. *European Neuropsychopharmacology, 17,* 417–429.

Alfonso, J., Frasch, A. C., & Flügge, G. (2005). Chronic stress, depression and antidepressants: effects on gene transcription in the hippocampus. *Reviews in Neuroscience, 16,* 43–56.

Bagley, J., & Moghaddam, B. (1997). Temporal dynamics of glutamate efflux in the prefrontal cortex and in the hippocampus following repeated stress: effects of pretreatment with saline or diazepam. *Neuroscience, 77,* 65–73.

Bao, A. M., Meynen, G., & Swaab, D. F. (2008). The stress system in depression and neurodegeneration: focus on the human hypothalamus. *Brain Research Reviews, 57,* 531–553.

Bisaz, R., Conboy, L., & Sandi, C. (2009). Learning under stress: a role for the neural cell adhesion molecule NCAM. *Neurobiology of Learning and Memory, 91,* 333–342.

Bliss, E. L., Ailion, J., & Zwanziger, J. (1968). Metabolism of norepinephrine, serotonin and dopamine in rat brain with stress. *Journal of Pharmacology and Experimental Therapeutics, 164,* 122–134.

Bremner, J. D., Krystal, J. H., Southwick, S. M., & Charney, D. S. (1996). Noradrenergic mechanisms in stress and anxiety: I. Preclinical studies. *Synapse, 23,* 28–38.

Cannon, W. (1929). *Bodily changes in pain, hunger, fear, and rage.* New York: Appleton.

Castrén, E., Võikar, V., & Rantamäki, T. (2007). Role of neurotrophic factors in depression. *Current Opinions in Pharmacology, 7,* 18–21.

Coe, C. L., Glass, J. C., Wiener, S. G., & Levine, S. (1983). Behavioral, but not physiological, adaptation to repeated separation in mother and infant primates. *Psychoneuroendocrinology, 8,* 401–409.

Contoreggi, C., Herning R.I., Na, P., Gold, P. W., Chrousos, G., Negro, P. J., Better, W., & Cadet, J. L. (2003). Stress hormone responses to corticotropin-releasing hormone in substance abusers without severe comorbid psychiatric disease. *Biological Psychiatry*, 54, 873–878.

Cook, S. C., & Wellman, C. L. (2004). Chronic stress alters dendritic morphology in rat medial prefrontal cortex. *Journal of Neurobiology*, 60, 236–248.

Cooper, B., Fuchs, E., & Flügge, G. (2009). Expression of the axonal membrane glycoprotein M6a is regulated by chronic stress. *PLoS One*, 4(1), e3659.

Czéh, B., & Lucassen, P. J. (2007). What causes the hippocampal volume decrease in depression? Are neurogenesis, glial changes and apoptosis implicated? *European Archives of Psychiatry and Clinical Neuroscience*, 257, 250–260.

Czéh, B., Michaelis, T., Watanabe, T. Frahm, J., de Biurrun, G., van Kampen, M., Bartolomucci, A., & Fuchs, E. (2001). Stress-induced changes in cerebral metabolites, hippocampal volume, and cell proliferation are prevented by antidepressant treatment with tianeptine. *Proceedings of the National Academy of Sciences USA*, 98, 12796–12801.

Czéh, B., Simon, M., van der Hart, M. G., Schmelting, B., Hesselink, M. B., & Fuchs, E. (2005). Chronic stress decreases the number of parvalbumin-immunoreactive interneurons in the hippocampus: prevention by treatment with a substance P receptor (NK1) antagonist. *Neuropsychopharmacology*, 30 (Suppl. 1), 67–79.

Czéh, B., Simon, M., Schmelting, B., Hiemke, C., & Fuchs, E. (2006). Astroglial plasticity in the hippocampus is affected by chronic psychosocial stress and concomitant fluoxetine treatment. *Neuropsychopharmacology*, 31, 1616–1626.

de Groote, L., & Linthorst, A. C. (2007). Exposure to novelty and forced swimming evoke stressor-dependent changes in extracellular GABA in the rat hippocampus. *Neuroscience*, 148, 794–805.

Drevets, W. C., Price, J. L., & Furey, M. L. (2008). Brain structural and functional abnormalities in mood disorders: implications for neurocircuitry models of depression. *Brain Structure and Function*, 213, 93–118.

Flügge, G. (2000). Regulation of monoamine receptors in the brain: dynamic changes during stress. *International Review of Cytology*, 195, 145–213.

Flügge, G., Kramer, M., Rensing, S., & Fuchs, E. (1998). 5HT1A-receptors and behaviour under chronic stress: selective counteraction by testosterone. *European Journal of Neuroscience*, 10, 2685–2693.

Flügge, G., van Kampen, M., & Mijnster, M. J. (2004). Perturbations in brain monoamine systems during stress. *Cell and Tissue Research*, 315, 1–14.

Fuchs, E., & Flügge, G. (2002). Social stress in tree shrews: effects on physiology, brain function, and behavior of subordinate individuals. *Pharmacology, Biochemistry, and Behavior*, 73, 247–258.

Fuchs, E., Czéh, B., Kole, M. H., Michaelis, T., & Lucassen, P. J. (2004). Alterations of neuroplasticity in depression: the hippocampus and beyond. *European Neuropsychopharmacology*, 14 (Suppl. 5), 481–490.

Fuchs, E., Flügge, G., & Czéh, B. (2006). Remodeling of neuronal networks by stress. *Frontiers in Bioscience*, 11, 2746–2758.

Garrett, J. E., & Wellman, C. L. (2009). Chronic stress effects on dendritic morphology in medial prefrontal cortex: sex differences and estrogen dependence. *Neuroscience*, 162, 195–207.

Gould, E., McEwen, B. S., Tanapat, P., Galea, L. A., & Fuchs, E. (1997). Neurogenesis in the dentate gyrus of the adult tree shrew is regulated by psychosocial stress and NMDA receptor activation. *Journal of Neuroscience*, 17, 2492–2498.

Haller, J., Fuchs, E., Halász, J., & Makara, G. B. (1999). Defeat is a major stressor in males while social instability is stressful mainly in females: towards the development of a social stress model in female rats. *Brain Research Bulletin, 50*: 33–39.

Hasler, G., van der Veen, J. W., Tumonis, T., Meyers, N., Shen, J., & Drevets, W. C. (2007). Reduced prefrontal glutamate/glutamine and gamma-aminobutyric acid levels in major depression determined using proton magnetic resonance spectroscopy. *Archives of General Psychiatry, 64*, 193–200.

Heim, C. M., & Nater, U. M. (2007). Hypocortisolism and stress. In Fink, G. (Ed.), *Encyclopedia of stress* (2nd ed., Vol. 2., pp. 400–407). Amsterdam: Elsevier Academic Press.

Herman, J. P., & Cullinan, W. E. (1997). Neurocircuitry of stress: central control of the hypothalamo-pituitary-adrenocortical axis. *Trends in Neuroscience, 20*, 78–84.

Herzog, C. J., Czéh, B., Corbach, S., Wuttke, W., Schulte-Herbrüggen, O., Hellweg, R., Flügge, G., & Fuchs, E. (2009). Chronic social instability stress in female rats: a potential animal model for female depression. *Neuroscience, 159*, 982–992.

Hu W., Zhang, M., Czéh, B., Flügge, G., & Zhang, W. (2010). Stress impairs GABAergic network function in the hippocampus by activating nongenomic glucocorticoid receptors and affecting the integrity of the parvalbumin-expressing neuronal network. *Neuropsychopharmacology, 35*, 1693–1707.

Jesberger, J. A., & Richardson, J. S. (1985). Animal models depression: Parallels and correlates to serve depression in humans. *Biological Psychiatry, 20*, 764–784.

Joëls, M., & Baram, T. Z. (2009). The neuro-symphony of stress. *Nature Reviews Neuroscience, 10*, 459–66.

Kawashima, Y., Akishita, M., Hasegawa, H., Kozaki, K., & Toba, K. (2008). Stress-induced blood pressure elevation in subjects with mild cognitive impairment: effects of the dual-type calcium channel blocker, cilnidipine. *Geriatrics and Gerontology International, 8*, 278–283.

Kessler, R. C. (1997). The effects of stressful life events on depression. *Annual Review of Psychology, 48*, 191–214.

Kessler, R. C., Chiu, W. T., Demler, O., Merikangas, K. R., & Walters, E. E. (2005). Prevalence, severity, and comorbidity of 12-month DSM-IV disorders in the National Comorbidity Survey Replication. *Archives of General Psychiatry, 62*, 617–627.

Kole, M. H., Czéh, B., & Fuchs, E. (2004). Homeostatic maintenance in excitability of tree shrew hippocampal CA3 pyramidal neurons after chronic stress. *Hippocampus, 14*, 742–751.

Koolhaas, J. M., Meerlo, P., De Boer, S. F., Strubbe, J. H., & Bohus, B. (1997). The temporal dynamics of the stress response. *Neuroscience and Biobehavioral Reviews, 21*, 775–782.

Kramer, M., Hiemke, C., & Fuchs, E. (1999). Chronic psychosocial stress and antidepressant treatment in tree shrews: time-dependent behavioral and endocrine effects. *Neuroscience and Biobehavioral Reviews, 23*, 937–947.

Magariños, A. M., Verdugo, J. M., & McEwen, B. S. (1997). Chronic stress alters synaptic terminal structure in hippocampus. *Proceedings of the National Academy of Sciences USA, 94*, 14002–14008.

Martignoni, E., Petraglia, F., Costa, A., Monzani, A., Genazzani, A. R., & Nappi, G. (1990). Dementia of the Alzheimer type and hypothalamus–pituitary–adrenocortical axis: changes in cerebrospinal fluid corticotropin releasing factor and plasma cortisol levels. *Acta Neurologica Scandinavica, 81*, 452–456.

Matthews, K., Christmas, D., Swan, J., & Sorrell, E. (2005). Animal models of depression: navigating through the clinical fog. *Neuroscience and Biobehavioral Reviews, 29*, 503–513.

Maya Vetencourt, J. F., Sale, A., Viegi, A., Baroncelli, L., De Pasquale, R., O'Leary, O. F., Castrén, E., & Maffei, L. (2008). The antidepressant fluoxetine restores plasticity in the adult visual cortex. *Science, 320*, 385–388.

McCarty, R., & Pacak, K. (2007). Alarm phase and general adaptation syndrome. In Fink, G. (Ed.), *Encyclopedia of stress* (2nd ed., Vol. 2, pp. 119–123). Amsterdam: Elsevier Academic Press.

McEwen, B. S., Magariños, A. M., & Reagan, L. P. (2002). Structural plasticity and tianeptine: cellular and molecular targets. *European Psychiatry, 17* (suppl. 3), 318–330.

McLaughlin, K. J., Gomez, J. L., Baran, S. E., & Conrad, C. D. (2007). The effects of chronic stress on hippocampal morphology and function: an evaluation of chronic restraint paradigms. *Brain Research, 1161*, 56–64.

McLaughlin, K. J., Baran, S. E., & Conrad, C. D. (2009). Chronic stress- and sex-specific neuromorphological and functional changes in limbic structures. *Molecular Neurobiology, 40*, 166–182.

Mitra, R., Jadhav, S., McEwen, B. S., Vyas, A., & Chattarji, S. (2005). Stress duration modulates the spatiotemporal patterns of spine formation in the basolateral amygdala. *Proceedings of the National Academy of Sciences USA, 102*, 9371–9376.

Monroe, S. M., Slavich, G. M., Torres, L. D., & Gotlib, I. H. (2007). Severe life events predict specific patterns of change in cognitive biases in major depression. *Psychological Medicine, 37*, 863–871.

Nestler, E. J., Gould, E., Manji, H., Buncan, M., Duman, R. S., Greshenfeld, H. K., Hen, R., Koester, S., Lederhendler, I., Meaney, M., Robbins, T., Winsky, L., & Zalcman, S. (2002). Preclinical models: status of basic research in depression. *Biological Psychiatry, 52*, 503–528.

Neumeister, A., Wood, S., Bonne, O., Nugent, A. C., Luckenbaugh, D. A., Young, T., Bain, E. E., Charney, D. S., & Drevets, W. C. (2005). Reduced hippocampal volume in unmedicated, remitted patients with major depression versus control subjects. *Biological Psychiatry, 57*, 935–937.

Nisenbaum, L. K., Zigmond, M. J., Sved, A. F., & Abercrombie, E. D. (1991). Prior exposure to chronic stress results in enhanced synthesis and release of hippocampal norepinephrine in response to a novel stressor. *Journal of Neuroscience, 11*, 1478–1484.

Pavlides, C., Nivón, L. G., & McEwen, B. S. (2002). Effects of chronic stress on hippocampal long-term potentiation. *Hippocampus, 12*, 245–257.

Perez-Cruz, C., Simon, M., Czéh, B., Flügge, G., & Fuchs, E. (2009). Hemispheric differences in basilar dendrites and spines of pyramidal neurons in the rat prelimbic cortex: activity- and stress-induced changes. *European Journal of Neuroscience, 29*, 738–747.

Radley, J. J., Rocher, A. B., Janssen, W. G., Hof, P. R., McEwen, B. S., & Morrison, J. H. (2005). Reversibility of apical dendritic retraction in the rat medial prefrontal cortex following repeated stress. *Experimental Neurology, 196*, 199–203.

Reagan, L. P., Rosell, D. R., Wood, G. E., Spedding, M., Muñoz, C., Rothstein, J., & McEwen, B. S. (2004). Chronic restraint stress up-regulates GLT-1 mRNA and protein expression in the rat hippocampus: reversal by tianeptine. *Proceedings of the National Academy of Sciences USA, 101*, 2179–2184.

Rygula, R., Abumaria, N., Flügge, G., Fuchs, E., Rüther, E., & Havemann-Reinecke, U. (2005). Anhedonia and motivational deficits in rats: impact of chronic social stress. *Behavioral Brain Research, 162*, 127–134.

Rygula, R., Abumaria, N., Flügge, G., Hiemke, C., Fuchs, E., Rüther, E., & Havemann-Reinecke, U. (2006). Citalopram counteracts depressive symptoms evoked by chronic social stress in rats. *Behavioral Pharmacology, 17*, 19–29.

Saavedra, J. M., & Torda, T. (1980). Increased brain stem and decreased hypothalamic adrenaline-forming enzyme after acute and repeated immobilization stress in the rat. *Neuroendocrinology, 31*, 142–146.

Sánchez, M. M., Ladd, C. O., & Plotsky, P. M. (2001). Early adverse experience as a developmental risk factor for later psychopathology: evidence from rodent and primate models. *Developmental Psychopathology, 13*, 419–449.

Seligman, M. E. (1972). Learned helplessness. *Annual Review of Medicine, 23*, 407–412.

Selye, H. (1936). A syndrome produced by diverse nocuous agents. *Nature, 138*: 32.

Simon, M., Czéh, B., & Fuchs, E. (2005). Age-dependent susceptibility of adult hippocampal cell proliferation to chronic psychosocial stress. *Brain Research, 1049*, 244–248.

Smith, M. A., Brady, L. S., Glowa, J., Gold, P. W., & Herkenham, M. (1991). Effects of stress and adrenalectomy on tyrosine hydroxylase mRNA levels in the locus ceruleus by in situ hybridization. *Brain Research, 544*, 26–32.

Stanford, S. C. (1995). Central noradrenergic neurones and stress. *Pharmacology & Therapeutics, 68*, 297–242.

Stockmeier, C. A., Mahajan, G. J., Konick, L. C., Overholser, J. C., Jurjus, G. J., Meltzer, H. Y., Uylings, H. B., Friedman, L., & Rajkowska, G. (2004). Cellular changes in the postmortem hippocampus in major depression. *Biological Psychiatry, 56*, 640–650.

Sullivan, P. F., Neale, M. C., & Kendler, K. S. (2000). Genetic epidemiology of major depression: review and meta-analysis. *American Journal of Psychiatry, 157*, 1552–1562.

Vollmann-Honsdorf, G. K., Flügge, G., & Fuchs, E. (1997). Chronic psychosocial stress does not affect the number of pyramidal neurons in tree shrew hippocampus. *Neuroscience Letters, 233*, 121–124.

Willner, P. (2005). Chronic mild stress (CMS) revisited: consistency and behavioural-neurobiological concordance in the effects of CMS. *Neuropsychobiology, 52*, 90–110.

Yehuda, R. (2007). HPA alterations in PTSD. In Fink, G. (Ed.), *Encyclopedia of stress* (2nd ed., Vol. 2, pp. 359–364). Amsterdam: Elsevier Academic Press.

24

How Can Stress Alter Emotional Balance Through Its Interaction with the Serotonergic System?

Raymond Mongeau, Michel Hamon,
and Laurence Lanfumey

Introduction

Anxiety and depression are among the most common forms of the psychiatric disorders involving maladaptive stress responses. As originally defined by Hans Selye, the stress reaction is a normal and nonspecific response of the body to a demand or an environmental change that disturbs the maintenance of homeostasis (Sapolsky, 2003) and allostasis (McEwen and Wingfield, 2010). The stress response includes a series of physiological reactions such as endocrine activation (especially of the hypothalamic–pituitary–adrenal, or HPA, axis) and cardiovascular changes, which, per se, do not produce any psychopathological changes. However, when this response is repeatedly triggered by innocuous stimuli or when sustained stimulation produces excessive allostatic load, stress can produce sequelae. Exposure to repeated stressors has multiple consequences and can cause disease in the broad sense of the term. In particular, psychopathological symptoms can emerge after an acute reacting phase, encompassing anxiety, irritability, and a feeling of being unable to cope with stress, which can ultimately lead to depression.

Repeated stress per se is not sufficient to cause anxiety and depression. In some individuals, traits of *negativity bias*, which themselves result from interactions between genetic predispositions and environmental stressors, are believed to cause these diseases (Caspi and Moffitt, 2006). Furthermore, in addition to the HPA axis, the monoaminergic systems, and in particular the serotonergic (5-hydroxytryptamine, 5-HT) system, are clearly involved in stress-related disorders. Limbic brain regions, such as the amygdala, the septohippocampal complex, and the frontal cortex, which play crucial roles in fear and mood control, are abundantly innervated by seroto-

The Handbook of Stress: Neuropsychological Effects on the Brain, First Edition.
Edited by Cheryl D. Conrad.
© 2011 Blackwell Publishing Ltd. Published 2011 by Blackwell Publishing Ltd.

nergic projections and are particularly sensitive to glucocorticoids (Moore and Halaris, 1975). The HPA axis and the 5-HT system are closely cross-regulated under normal physiological conditions (Chaouloff, 1993) and these interactions are of particular relevance considering the large body of evidence implicating dysfunctions of stress mediators and the 5-HT system in depression and anxiety (Porter et al., 2004).

The serotonergic deficiency hypothesis of affective disorders has long been proposed, and some evidence supports this hypothesis, such as data concerning cerebrospinal fluid levels of the main 5-HT metabolite, 5-hydroxyindolacetic acid (5-HIAA), in suicide-depressed patients (Asberg et al., 1986). The most convincing arguments for 5-HT dysregulation came more recently, however, from 5-HT receptor studies. Positron emission tomography (PET) imaging studies revealed decreased 5-HT$_{1A}$ receptor binding in the brain (in both the raphe and hippocampus) of depressed patients (Drevets et al., 2007), while an increased density of cortical 5-HT$_{2A}$ receptors was associated with anxiety and increased risk of affective disorders (Frokjaer et al., 2008). In addition, the short variant of a polymorphism in the 5-HT transporter (5-HTT), which decreases 5-HTT expression and 5-HT reuptake, is associated with depression and anxiety-related traits (Lesch et al., 1996; Caspi et al., 2003), but discrepant results have recently been reported regarding this association (Uher and McGuffin, 2008, 2010).

Aside these changes in serotonergic system stands one of the most consistent findings in biological psychiatry, the increased tonic activity of the HPA axis associated with major depression, resulting from a deficit in the negative-feedback regulation of the HPA axis, as shown by the failure of glucocorticoid-receptor (GR) activation to decrease plasma levels of cortisol in the *dexamethasone suppression test* in depressed patients (Montgomery et al., 1988). In contrast, anxious patients do not generally show this specific deficit of HPA axis regulation, and in fact some patients suffering from posttraumatic stress disorder (PTSD) even show hypocortisolism and an increased suppression in the dexamethasone test (Arborelius et al., 1999).

The present review focuses on the reciprocal interactions between the 5-HT system and the HPA axis. Following a brief overview of the HPA axis and selected 5-HT receptors, (i.e., the 5-HT$_{1A}$, 5-HT$_{2A}$, and the 5-HT$_{2C}$ types long thought to be involved in anxiodepressive symptoms), we analyze various functional aspects of the HPA axis–5-HT system interactions, to finally examine how alterations in these interactions can underlie stress-related neurotrophic or neuroanatomical changes.

HPA Axis, Corticotropin-releasing Factor, and Corticosteroids

HPA axis

Several crucial processes are engaged in the central nervous system (CNS) when a situation is perceived as stressful, particularly in the paraventricular nucleus (PVN) of the hypothalamus. This region is responsible for the stress-induced release of corticotropin-releasing hormone (CRH) and its cosecretagogue arginine vasopressin (AVP), which reach, through local blood circulation, the anterior pituitary gland, where they cause the release of adrenocorticotropic hormone (ACTH) into the general circulation. In addition to the PVN, CRH cell bodies are also present in some other areas involved in fear and anxiety, such as the amygdala and the bed nucleus of the stria terminalis (Shekhar et al., 2005), but projections from these neurons do not directly act at the level of the pituitary gland. The ACTH released by the pituitary gland stimulates the cortical cells of the adrenal glands, which causes release of glucocorticoids into the blood; that is, cortisol in humans and corticosterone in rodents. These hormones exert numerous actions not only in the CNS but also in the periphery where they trigger lipolysis, glycogenolysis, and modulatory controls on the cardiovascular system, the immune system, bone and muscle growth, epithelial cell growth, and erythroid cell production (McEwen and Stellar, 1993).

CRH and corticosteroid receptors in the central nervous system

CRH exerts its various roles during the stress response, at the level of the anterior pituitary and in other brain areas, through its action at G-protein-coupled CRH_1 and CRH_2 receptors. The affinity of CRH for CRH_1 receptors is greater than that for CRH_2 receptors (Hauger et al., 2003), while the recently discovered CRH-related neuropeptides urocortin 2 and urocortin 3 have a higher affinity for CRH_2 receptors (Lewis et al., 2001). These receptors are found throughout the CNS in primates, with the highest expression in the prefrontal and the cingulate cortices, and the central nucleus of the amygdala (Sanchez et al., 1999). In rodents, although CRH_1 receptors are found throughout the CNS, CRH_2 receptors are concentrated in specific brain regions such as the lateral septum, the medial nucleus of the amygdala and the dorsal raphe nucleus (DRN). In the latter nucleus, CRH_2 receptors are found on 5-HT neurons at the middle level and in γ-aminobutyric acid (GABA)ergic neurons at the caudal level (Day et al., 2004). During acute stress, the increased 5-HT release in the central amygdaloid nucleus is under CRH_2 receptor-mediated control (Mo et al., 2008). Although stress, as well as intracerebral administration of high doses of CRH, increases the firing rate of 5-HT neurons and/or the release of 5-HT in several brain areas, small doses of CRH can, in contrast, inhibit the firing activity of 5-HT neurons and decrease 5-HT release (Kirby et al., 2000; Price and Lucki, 2001; Amat et al., 2004). CRH_1 receptors mediate these inhibitory effects of low doses of CRH, while CRH_2 receptors mediate those excitatory effects produced by either urocortin 2 or high doses of CRH (Amat et al., 2004).

Corticosteroid actions occur through two types of intracellular steroid receptors, the mineralocorticoid receptors (MRs) and the GRs, in various brain areas (de Kloet et al., 1998; Gass et al., 2001). Corticosteroid receptors belong to the superfamily of nuclear receptors (Beato and Sanchez-Pacheco, 1996; Tasker et al., 2006), which means that after crossing the cell membrane corticosteroids in the cytosol bind to and activate their intracellular receptors, which then translocate into the cell nucleus.

MR affinity for corticosterone is tenfold higher compared to that of GRs, which results in MRs being almost completely occupied (90%) by basal corticosterone levels, while GR are occupied at only about 10% under basal (*resting*) conditions (Reul and de Kloet, 1986). It is only when the level of corticosterone rises up to its circadian maximum or when an organism is under stress that GRs become substantially occupied by glucocorticoids (de Kloet et al., 1998). In view of this differential occupation of MRs and GRs under distinct physiological conditions, it has been hypothesized that MRs exert a tonic inhibitory regulatory function, while GRs would have a preponderant role in the negative-feedback control of HPA axis activity during stress or at circadian peak (de Kloet et al., 1998).

While MR is expressed mainly in limbic regions such as the hippocampus (Jacobson and Sapolsky, 1991), GR has a rather widespread distribution in the brain (Reul and de Kloet, 1986), with particularly high densities not only in the PVN but also in the hippocampus, in noradrenergic neurons of the locus coeruleus and in the DRN (Harfstrand et al., 1986; Reul and de Kloet, 1986). In the latter structure, both GR mRNA and protein are expressed exclusively by serotonergic neurons (Harfstrand et al., 1986; Reul and de Kloet, 1986), pointing to a potentially important role of circulating glucocorticoids in regulating gene expression in DRN 5-HT neurons.

Both MRs and GRs are coexpressed in hippocampal pyramidal neurons where they can influence gene expression. MRs are abundant in all layers of the hippocampus, compared to GRs, which are found principally in the CA1 and CA2 regions (CA means cornu ammonis, a subregion of the hippocampus), with low density in CA3, and intermediate levels in the dentate gyrus. The high levels of corticosteroid receptors in the hippocampus make this structure a key component of the HPA axis negative-feedback mechanism (de Kloet et al., 2008). Critical for pathologies such as depression, repeated stress is well known to decrease hippocampal GR mRNA and protein levels (Kitraki et al., 1999), which results in deficits in glucocorticoid negative-feedback regulation and, thereby, chronically elevated glucocorticoid levels.

Membrane-associated GRs

Several recent studies suggest that corticosteroids can also exert rapid nongenomic effects on neuronal function, in particular in the hippocampal CA1 region and the hypothalamus, via the activation of one or more membrane-associated receptors (de Kloet et al., 2008). This would account for the discrepancies between the rapid onset of some corticosteroid-induced effects and the mediation of such effects through a slow genomic process. Therefore, some acute physiological and behavioral effects of glucocorticoids would involve actions at molecular targets in the plasma membrane most likely through G-protein-dependent mechanisms (Tasker et al., 2006). For example, acute glucocorticoid application has been shown to enhance long-term potentiation in the hippocampus (Wiegert et al., 2006). On the other hand, Hinz and Hirschelmann (2000) demonstrated that in addition to their slow gene transcription-dependent actions, glucocorticoids can suppress CRH-induced ACTH secretion within minutes via a rapid, transcription-independent mechanism.

The 5-HT System and 5-HT Receptors Involved in Anxiety and Depression

Organization and functions of the 5-HT system

In the CNS, serotonin is a neurotransmitter synthesized from the essential amino acid L-tryptophan exclusively in 5-HT neurons located within the raphe nuclei. Raphe 5-HT neurons project to virtually all parts of the CNS, which makes the serotonergic network one of the most diffused neurochemical systems in the brain. However, specificity does exist in this anatomical organization because the hippocampus receives a dense projection of 5-HT fibers mainly from the median raphe nucleus, while the amygdala receives 5-HT fibers from the dorsal raphe (Jacobs and Azmitia, 1992). The widespread distribution of 5-HT fibers throughout the CNS accounts for the large variety of functions that can be controlled by 5-HT, such as food intake, sleep, learning/memory, thermoregulation, sexual behavior, cardiovascular function, nociception, locomotion, and endocrine secretions, in addition to regulating anxiety-like behaviors and the psychoaffective tone.

During the past two decades, numerous 5-HT receptor types have been cloned and extensively characterized. To date, molecular biology research has identified at least 15 distinct encoding genes, some of which giving rise to several proteins (up to 24, with discrete variations in amino acid sequence, through a pre-mRNA editing process in the case of 5-HT_{2C} receptors). With the exception of the 5-HT_3 receptor (a ligand-gated cation channel), all 5-HT receptor types are linked with specific G proteins in the plasma membrane through which they modulate various enzymes (adenylate cyclase, phospholipases A2 and C, and mitogen-activated protein-kinases, or MAPKs) and cation channels (especially K^+ and Ca^{2+} channels; Kushwaha and Albert, 2005). Among these receptors, numerous ones have been implicated in stress-related disorders, but those for which there is the most abundant literature are the 5-HT_{1A} receptor type coupled to its various effectors mainly via $G_{\alpha i}/G_{\alpha o}$ proteins (Raymond et al., 2001) and 5-HT_{2A} and 5-HT_{2C} receptor types coupled to phospholipases via $G_{\alpha q}$ protein (Berg et al., 2005). These receptors have been implicated in numerous functions and psychiatric diseases (Figure 24.1), and they are widely distributed in brain areas involved in the regulation of emotions and the stress response (Plate 5).

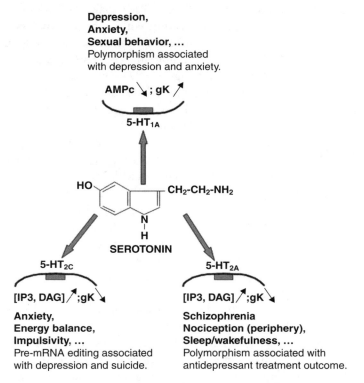

Figure 24.1   Overview of 5-HT$_{1A}$, 5-HT$_{2A}$, and 5-HT$_{2C}$ receptor functions, polymorphisms, and implications in psychiatric diseases. DAG, diacylglycerol; gK, potassium conductance; IP3, inositol trisphosphate.

Characteristics of 5-HT$_{1A}$ and 5-HT$_{2A/2C}$ receptors and their regulation by antidepressant drugs

Because they are expressed as both postsynaptic heteroreceptors in the limbic system and somatodendritic autoreceptors on serotonergic neurons in raphe nuclei (Plate 5), 5-HT$_{1A}$ receptors play an important dual role in central 5-HT neurotransmission (Hamon, 1997). Somatodendritic 5-HT$_{1A}$ autoreceptors determine— at least partly—brain 5-HT tone, by mediating the 5-HT-inhibitory feedback control of serotonergic neuron firing. Indeed, 5-HT$_{1A}$ receptor-knockout mice are characterized both by an increased rate of 5-HT neuron discharge (Richer et al., 2002) and by elevated baseline extracellular 5-HT levels in the frontal cortex and the hippocampus (Parsons et al., 2001). It is well established that long-term treatment with selective serotonin-reuptake inhibitors (SSRIs) as well as 5-HT transporter gene deletion (5-HTT$^{-/-}$) induce a functional desensitization of 5-HT$_{1A}$ autoreceptors in the DRN, but no change in postsynaptic 5-HT$_{1A}$ heteroreceptors in the hippocampus (Mongeau et al., 1997; Le Poul et al., 2000; Mannoury la Cour et al., 2001). This 5-HT$_{1A}$ adaptive regulation within the DRN is associated with decreased 5-HT$_{1A}$ agonist-induced [^{35}S]GTP-γ-S binding, suggesting an alteration of the 5-HT$_{1A}$ receptor/G-protein coupling in both SSRI-treated and 5-HTT-knockout animals. Importantly, this change in 5-HT$_{1A}$ receptor-mediated [^{35}S]GTP-γ-S binding is not observed in the hippocampus (Fabre et al., 2000; Hensler, 2002). A disparity in G-protein coupling could explain regional differences in adaptive regulation of brain 5-HT$_{1A}$ receptors (Mannoury la Cour et al., 2006). Although there is no adaptive change at the level of 5-HT$_{1A}$ heteroreceptors in the hippocampus, there is a clear increase in 5-HT input at the 5-HT$_{1A}$ receptors after treatment with various classes of antidepressant drugs (Haddjeri et al., 1998).

Recent evidence indicates that 5-HT$_{2A}$ and 5-HT$_{2C}$ receptors also exert an indirect modulatory effect on the firing rate of 5-HT neurons. In the DRN, 5-HT$_{2A}$ and 5-HT$_{2C}$ receptors are expressed by GABAergic interneurons (Liu et al., 2000; Boothman et al., 2006), and activation of these receptors by specific agonists decreases the firing activity of 5-HT neurons via GABA-dependent mechanisms (Boothman et al., 2006; Queree et al., 2009). Surprisingly, however, 5-HT$_{2A}$ and 5-HT$_{2C}$ receptor activation is without effects on basal 5-HT release (Gobert and Millan, 1999; Gobert et al., 2000). Nonetheless, an enhancing effect of 5-HT$_{2C}$, but not 5-HT$_{2A}$, receptor blockade on extracellular 5-HT in the frontal cortex and the hippocampus has been evidenced in conditions of elevated serotonergic tone after acute administration of high doses of SSRIs (Marek et al., 2005). This synergistic effect of 5-HT$_{2C}$ receptor antagonism on the SSRI-induced enhancement of extracellular 5-HT is indirectly mediated by local GABAergic interneurons and GABA$_B$ heteroreceptors (Cremers et al., 2004). In a recent study, 5-HT$_{2C}$ receptor activation was found to prevent the enhancement of 5-HT turnover induced by restraint stress in basal ganglia, the hippocampus and the frontal cortex, an effect also observed on the stress-induced increase in extracellular 5-HT measured by microdialysis (Mongeau et al., 2010). Because these inhibitory effects were not evidenced under basal conditions—that is, in absence of stress—it is conceivable that an indirect 5-HT$_{2C}$ receptor-mediated circuit exerting a negative regulation on 5-HT release plays a pivotal role on the modulation of serotonergic tone in stress conditions.

It has long been known that chronic treatment with various classes of antidepressant drugs decreases 5-HT$_{2A/2C}$ receptor binding (Peroutka and Snyder, 1980). 5-HT$_{2A}$ receptors autoradiographic labeling was found to be attenuated in 5-HTT-knockout mice (Rioux et al., 1999). Furthermore, repeated treatment with a 5-HT$_{2A/2C}$ agonist decreased 5-HT$_{2A}$ receptor-mediated phospholipase C signaling (Damjanoska et al., 2004). Recently, we have found a functional desensitization of those 5-HT$_{2C}$ receptors that exert an inhibitory regulation on stress-induced increase in 5-HT turnover after long-term SSRI treatment (Mongeau et al., 2010). The same adaptive change in 5-HT$_{2C}$ receptors was also observed in mice lacking the 5-HT transporter (Martin et al., 2010). Interestingly, many antidepressant drugs, including the recently introduced agomelatine, have 5-HT$_{2C}$ antagonist properties (Millan, 2005) and could, even after acute administration, produce overall effects on 5-HT transmission similar to those resulting from long-term antidepressant-induced 5-HT$_{2C}$ receptor desensitization.

5-HT$_{1A}$ and 5-HT$_{2A/2C}$ receptors in anxiety and affective disorders

Numerous studies have addressed the question as to whether or not 5-HT$_{1A}$ receptors are involved in depressive- and anxiety-like disorders. Indeed, some genetic polymorphism studies in humans have challenged the hypothesis that 5-HT$_{1A}$ receptor expression is altered in severe depression and suicide. Most of the studies concluded that no association exists between 5-HT$_{1A}$ receptor gene polymorphisms and major depression (Xie et al., 1995; Nishiguchi et al., 2002). However, an association of the C(−1019)G 5-HT$_{1A}$ promoter polymorphism, that could presumably lead to decreased serotonin signaling at forebrain postsynaptic target sites via increased autoreceptor expression, has been reported both with major depression and suicide (Lemonde et al., 2003), and with amygdala reactivity and trait anxiety (Fakra et al., 2009). Furthermore, gene polymorphism-associated changes in 5-HT$_{1A}$ receptor expression may influence the antipanic and antidepressant responses to SSRI treatments (Lemonde et al., 2004).

As explained above, the level of expression of somatodendritic 5-HT$_{1A}$ autoreceptors determines—at least partly—the brain 5-HT tone. Interestingly, the raised 5-HT tone in 5-HT$_{1A}^{-/-}$ mice (see Parsons et al., 2001) is associated with an anxiety-like phenotype in several behavioral models, and with an increased sensitivity to stress (Parks et al., 1998; Overstreet et al., 2003). Selective regional rescue of 5-HT$_{1A}$ receptors in 5-HT$_{1A}$-knockout mice indicated that postsynaptic 5-HT$_{1A}$ heteroreceptors are required for the antidepressant-like effect of SSRIs in the tail-suspension test (Overstreet et al., 2003).

On the other hand, the antidepressant-like effect of SSRIs in the tail-suspension test was shown to be increased in 5-HT$_{2C}$ receptor-knockout mice and in wild-type mice treated with a 5-HT$_{2C}$ antagonist (Cremers et al., 2004). In rats injected with a 5-HT$_{2A}$ receptor antisense oligodeoxynucleotide and in both 5-HT$_{2A}^{-/-}$ and 5-HT$_{2C}^{-/-}$ mice, anxiety-like behaviors are less than in paired controls (Cohen, 2005; Weisstaub et al., 2006; Heisler et al., 2007). This is consistent with the fact that the preferential 5-HT$_{2C}$ agonist m-chlorophenylpiperazine (mCPP) induces intense symptoms of anxiety and panic attack in humans (Charney et al., 1987). Interestingly, this effect of mCPP was increased in panic, but not social anxiety, disorder patients (Van Veen et al., 2007). However, although there are contradictions, evidence generally argues against a major role for promoter-associated 5-HT$_{2C}$ or 5-HT$_{2A}$ receptor polymorphisms in panic disorder (Deckert et al., 2000; Rothe et al., 2006). Nevertheless, variation in the gene encoding 5-HT$_{2A}$ receptors was associated with the response to antidepressant treatment (McMahon et al., 2006). Recent preclinical studies indicated that 5-HT$_{2C}$ receptor blockade not only enhances the increase in extracellular 5-HT induced by an SSRI in the hippocampus, but also restores the antidepressant-like effect of SSRIs in nonresponder mice (Calcagno et al., 2009). In addition, 5-HT_{2C} receptors are involved in the anxiolytic effect of long-term SSRIs treatment (Bristow et al., 2000) and this effect might become particularly important and alter 5-HT neurotransmission when animals are challenged with stress (Mongeau et al., 2010).

Regulation of the Serotonergic System via the HPA Axis

Interactions between the 5-HT system and the HPA axis

In accordance with the data reviewed above, marked changes in brain 5-HT turnover have been shown to occur in both rodents and humans upon activation of the HPA axis. For example, stressful conditions such as electrical foot shocks, cold environment, immobilization sessions, or tail pinches all induce significant increases in the synthesis and release of 5-HT in various brain areas (Clement et al., 1993). Corticosterone plays a critical role in these effects as shown by adrenalectomy (ADX) and exogenous corticosterone administration data demonstrating that the adrenal steroid hormone exerts a stimulatory influence on tryptophan hydroxylase activity and brain 5-HT turnover (Singh et al., 1990). Furthermore, stress increases DRN 5-HT neuronal activity as indicated by an increase in both c-Fos expression in 5-HT neurons (Greenwood et al., 2003) and 5-HT release in both the DRN (Maswood et al., 1998) and its projection areas (Bland et al., 2003). It is noteworthy that inescapable, but not escapable, stresses produce this increase in 5-HT outflow within the DRN and postsynaptic areas such as the hippocampus and the amygdala. Conversely, in the periaqueductal gray, escapable rather than inescapable stress increases 5-HT release (Maswood et al., 1998). Surprisingly, in the study of Takase et al. (2004), serotoninergic neurons in the DRN, in contrast to noradrenergic cells in the locus coeruleus, did not display an increased firing rate in response to acute stress even if that stress did increase c-Fos expression in the DRN. Therefore, acute stress-induced increase in 5-HT output might result from elevated 5-HT turnover and release rather than changes in DRN electrical activity (Takase et al., 2004).

Besides these data on the effects of stress and corticosteroids on serotonergic transmission, there is a large body of evidence showing that, conversely, the 5-HT system exerts marked influences on the secretion of corticosteroids. In particular, acute administration of 5-HT receptor ligands, such as the 5-HT_{1A} agonist ipsapirone, the preferential 5-HT_{2C} agonist mCPP, and the mixed $5\text{-HT}_{2A/2C}$ agonist MK-212, all produce marked increases in ACTH and glucocorticoid plasma levels in both animals and humans (Lowy and Meltzer, 1988; Wetzler et al., 1996; Klaassen et al., 2002). 5-HT_{1A} and $5\text{-HT}_{2A/2C}$ receptors located in brain areas involved in psychogenic stress, such as the amygdala, very probably mediate these effects. However, neuroanatomical studies also suggest a direct action of 5-HT through synaptic contacts between serotonergic terminals and CRH-containing cells in the PVN (Liposits et al., 1987). Indeed, local activation of 5-HT_{1A} receptors by microinjection of 8-hydroxy-*N,N*-dipropyl-2-aminotetralin (8-OH-DPAT) into the PVN triggers ACTH release (Osei-Owusu et al., 2005). As expected by the exclusive involvement of postsynaptic 5-HT$_{1A}$ heteroreceptors, notably those in the PVN, 5,7-dihydroxytryptamine-induced lesions of serotonergic neurons, which effectively eliminate somatodendritic 5-HT$_{1A}$ autoreceptors in raphe nuclei, do not prevent 8-OH-DPAT-induced ACTH release (Van de Kar et al., 1998).

Activation of 5-HT$_{2A}$ and 5-HT$_{2C}$ receptors in the PVN also induces ACTH release (Bagdy, 1996). Indeed, these receptors, rather than 5-HT$_{1A}$ receptors, are those which mediate the stimulatory effect of 5-HT on glucocorticoid secretion during emotional stress because 5-HT$_{2A/2C}$ receptor antagonists nearly abolish stress-induced ACTH release, whereas a selective 5-HT$_{1A}$ receptor antagonist is, at best, only partially effective in this respect (Jorgensen et al., 1998). A recent study using laser dissection of the PVN coupled with transcriptomic analyses indicated that the 5-HT$_{2C}$ receptor type is the most abundant among all 5-HT receptors expressed in this brain structure (Heisler et al., 2007). Genetic inactivation of 5-HT$_{2C}$ receptors abolished CRH surges induced by mCPP or the mixed 5-HT$_{2A/2C}$ agonist 1-(2,5-dimethoxy-4-iodophenyl)-2-aminopropane (DOI), and the enhancement of CRH secretion by the 5-HT releaser fenfluramine was completely blocked by a 5-HT$_{2C}$ antagonist (Heisler et al., 2007). In addition, the demonstration of CRH mRNA and c-Fos/IR coexpression combined with in vitro electrophysiological recordings clearly showed the existence of excitatory 5-HT$_{2C}$ receptors on CRH-containing neurons in the PVN. 5-HT$_{2C}$ receptors also appear to regulate the activity of CRH neurons at the level of the amygdala and the bed nucleus of the stria terminalis, and this action probably underlies—at least partially—anxiety-related behavior evoked by 5-HT$_{2C}$ agonists because CRH is a potent anxiogenic neuropeptide (Heisler et al., 2007).

Long-term effects of stress and corticosteroids on 5-HT$_{1A}$, 5-HT$_{2A}$ and 5-HT$_{2C}$ receptors

5-HT$_{1A}$ receptors

Several lines of evidence have demonstrated that 5-HT$_{1A}$ receptor function is under the influence of the HPA axis. In agreement with molecular biology data on the inhibitory effect of corticosteroids on 5-HT$_{1A}$ receptor gene transcription (Meijer et al., 2000; Wissink et al., 2000), chronic immobilization stress as well as severe acute stress raise circulating levels of corticosterone and consistently decrease hippocampal 5-HT$_{1A}$ receptor binding and mRNA levels (Mendelson and McEwen, 1991; Lopez et al., 1999). Furthermore, early life stress decreases 5-HT$_{1A}$ receptor signaling, although this is not necessarily linked to lower 5-HT$_{1A}$ mRNA expression (Van Riel et al., 2004).

In contrast, 5-HT$_{1A}$ receptor binding increases in the hippocampus following ADX-induced corticosteroid depletion (Kuroda et al., 1994). ADX induces a rapid (within hours) and marked increase of de novo 5-HT$_{1A}$ mRNA synthesis, total

5-HT$_{1A}$ mRNA levels, and 5-HT$_{1A}$ binding sites in the septohippocampal complex (Zhong and Ciaranello, 1995). Furthermore, electrophysiological studies in ADX rats showed that selective activation of MRs decreases the hyperpolarization of hippocampal CA1 pyramidal neurons in response to 5-HT$_{1A}$ receptor stimulation (Joels et al., 1991). Interestingly, this effect on MR activation can be reversed by concomitant activation of GRs, indicating that, in certain cases, there can be opposite action of GRs and MRs (Hesen and Joels, 1996). The ADX-induced hippocampal increases in 5-HT$_{1A}$ mRNA and protein are completely reversed by treatment with low doses of corticosterone that preferentially activate MRs (Meijer and de Kloet, 1994). However, pharmacological and gene-knockout studies provided evidence that both MRs and GRs are involved in the negative regulation of 5-HT$_{1A}$ gene expression by corticosterone (Meijer et al., 1997). Long-term changes in the MR/GR receptor ratio could also be important in determining hippocampal 5-HT$_{1A}$ receptor function since overexpression of MRs (which decreases GRs in the hippocampus) increased, rather than decreased, 5-HT$_{1A}$ receptor mRNA and protein levels in the mouse hippocampus (Rozeboom et al., 2007). In addition, mice bearing the latter mutation were less anxious than paired wild-type animals in validated paradigms which contrasts with the anxiogenic effect of overexpressing GRs (Rozeboom et al., 2007).

In the dorsal raphe nucleus, ADX induces no changes in the expression of somatodendritic 5-HT$_{1A}$ autoreceptors (Tejani-Butt and Labow, 1994). Nonetheless, repeated GR activation in the DRN generates a significant decrease in the potency of 5-HT$_{1A}$ receptor agonists to inhibit the firing of serotonergic neurons, as expected of a functional desensitization of 5-HT$_{1A}$ autoreceptors (Laaris et al., 1995). Similarly, various chronic stress procedures that lastingly raise serum corticosterone levels have been shown to decrease the potency of 5-HT$_{1A}$ agonists to inhibit the electrical activity of serotonergic neurons in the DRN (Laaris et al., 1999; Lanfumey et al., 1999). Recently, social defeat stress was shown to decrease 5-HT$_{1A}$ mRNA in the DRN, and possibly because of reduced autoreceptor-mediated inhibition, stress-induced DRN neuronal activity was particularly pronounced in this paradigm (Cooper et al., 2009).

In vivo electrophysiological studies indicated that long-term, but not acute, exposure to elevated corticosterone levels attenuated 5-HT$_{1A}$ autoreceptor function in the DRN (Judge et al., 2004). In another assay commonly used to assess mouse somatodendritic 5-HT$_{1A}$ autoreceptor function, 5-HT$_{1A}$ agonist-induced hypothermia, a decreased response was also found after repeated administration of corticosterone (Man et al., 2002). The decrease in the negative feedback exerted by somatodendritic 5-HT$_{1A}$ autoreceptors, by contributing to increase 5-HT neurotransmission, might be of physiological relevance for effective coping with stress.

5-HT$_{2A}$ and 5-HT$_{2C}$ receptors

Repeated stress and corticosterone treatment have been consistently found to increase 5-HT$_{2A}$ receptors in the frontal cortex, an effect prevented by chronic antidepressant treatment (Ossowska et al., 2002; Dwivedi et al., 2005). Early-life stress, which decreases 5-HT$_{1A}$ function (see above), increases in contrast with mRNA encoding 5-HT$_{2A}$ receptors in the hippocampus and the amygdala (Sumner et al., 2008). Transgenic mice studies also showed that enhanced GR signaling upregulates hippocampal 5-HT$_{2A}$ receptors, while the converse occurs when GR levels are low (Trajkovska et al., 2009), suggesting that 5-HT$_{2A}$ receptor density is governed—at least partly—by GRs. However, activation of PVN neurons by a 5-HT$_{2A/2C}$ agonist (DOI), as assessed using c-Fos immunoreactivity, is markedly reduced following repeated corticosterone administration (Lee et al., 2009). Knowing that 5-HT$_{2A/2C}$ receptors provide an excitatory tone over the HPA axis, the fact that HPA axis activation is blunted under conditions of chronically elevated cortisol in depressed patients might be accounted for by decreased 5-HT$_{2A/2C}$ receptor responsiveness at the level of the PVN (Lee et al., 2009). These data show that marked regional differences exist in the regulatory effects of glucocorticoids on 5-HT$_{2A/2C}$ receptor expression in the brain.

Specific studies on 5-HT$_{2C}$ receptor clearly demonstrated that this receptor type is also modulated by stress and glucocorticoids. Variations in basal and stress-induced corticosterone levels significantly correlate with changes in 5-HT$_{2C}$ mRNA expression in the hippocampus: thus, 5-HT$_{2C}$ mRNA levels were higher after an acute laparatomy stress and lower after chronic arthritis stress (Holmes et al., 1995). A microarray analysis study pointed to an overexpression of 5-HT$_{2C}$ mRNA in the amygdala following a single prolonged stress that enhances HPA axis negative feedback activity, like that occurring in anxiety disorders such as PTSD (Harada et al., 2008). Furthermore, an enhancement of 5-HT$_{2C}$ receptor-mediated corticosterone release (in response to mCPP administration) and higher levels of 5-HT$_{2C}$ receptor-like immunoreactivity in the hippocampus were observed in rats subjected to the social-isolation stress paradigm (Fone et al., 1996). In both the learned helplessness and the forced-swim tests, inescapable stress induces in some mouse strains a site-specific increase in 5-HT$_{2C}$ pre-mRNA editing (Englander et al., 2005; Iwamoto et al., 2005). This editing process is unique to the 5-HT$_{2C}$ receptor type among all 5-HT receptors, and in vitro studies indicated that editing decreases the coupling of the receptor with its signaling system downstream (McGrew et al., 2004). In contrast, however, a recent study on transgenic mice expressing only the fully edited receptor showed that these mice have increased 5-HT$_{2C}$ receptor-mediated behavioral responses (hypolocomotion, decreased feeding) and increased 5-HT$_{2C}$ receptor binding compared to paired wild-type mice and mice expressing only the nonedited isoform (Kawahara et al., 2008). Therefore, increased 5-HT$_{2C}$ pre-mRNA editing after depressiogenic stress might lead to enhanced 5-HT$_{2C}$ receptor functional activity, thereby contributing to exacerbated anxiety-related behaviors. The increased sensitivity of 5-HT$_{2C}$ receptor-mediated inhibition of accumbal dopamine release observed in the Flinders Sensitive Line (FSL) rat model of depression (Dremencov et al., 2005) is also in line with this view.

Beyond the HPA–5-HT Interactions: Stress-related Changes in Neurotrophic and Epigenetic Factors

Stress and elevated glucocorticoid levels do have effects beyond the mere interactions between the HPA axis and the serotonergic system. In particular, both stress and glucocorticoids are known to reduce the brain levels of neurotrophic factors, such as nerve growth factor, brain-derived neurotrophic factor (BDNF), and neurotrophin-3 (Duman and Monteggia, 2006). BDNF is a major neurotrophic factor required for the survival, differentiation and normal functioning of neurons in the brain. In rodents, a downregulation of both BDNF mRNA and protein was found in several brain regions following a period of stress (Smith et al., 1995; Gronli et al., 2006). Through activation of its tyrosine kinase TrkB receptor, BDNF can initiate a variety of intracellular signaling cascades, notably those involving the cAMP responsive-element binding protein (CREB), which is downregulated by stress (Alfonso et al., 2006; Gronli et al., 2006). Interestingly, the effects of stress on BDNF levels seem to depend, at least in part, on the serotonergic system: pretreatment with a selective 5-HT_{2A} receptor antagonist, but not selective 5-HT_{1A} or 5-HT_{2C} receptor antagonists, significantly attenuated stress-induced downregulation of BDNF mRNA in the hippocampus (Vaidya et al., 1999). On the other hand, different classes of antidepressant drugs, including SSRIs, increase the expression of BDNF in the hippocampus, in contrast to nonantidepressant psychotropic drugs, such as opiates, antipsychotics, and psychostimulants which are ineffective in this respect (Duman and Monteggia, 2006).

Although a decrease in BDNF levels in areas such as the amygdala is associated with anxiety-like behaviors (Pandey et al., 2006), increased levels of BDNF mRNA levels are nevertheless observed in the amygdala during acute stress (Aguilar-Valles et al., 2005), probably in relation with coping mechanisms. Long-term reduction in BDNF levels, such as that observed in depressed patients (Karege et al., 2002), can have deleterious effects in other areas known to play crucial roles in the 5-HT system–HPA axis interactions, such as the hippocampus. Indeed, brain-imaging studies have evidenced that depression and PTSD are frequently associated with a decrease of the hippocampal volume (Sheline et al., 1996). This reduction is probably caused by an atrophy of dendritic arborizations and a loss of hippocampal neurons as observed by Stockmeier et al. (2004) in the postmortem hippocampus of depressed patients. At least for some authors, the abnormality in hippocampal volume, observed in both PTSD and depressed patients, can be reversed by antidepressant treatments (Sheline et al., 2003; Vermetten et al., 2003).

Finally, a large body of data accumulated in various species indicate that chronic stress and high glucocorticoid levels exert a drastic negative effect on hippocampal neurogenesis at adulthood (see Warner-Schmidt and Duman, 2006). For example, repeated social stress in tree shrews and mice as well as repeated restraint stress in rats were all found to cause a significant depletion of dentate gyrus precursor cells (McKittrick et al., 2000; Czeh et al., 2001). Furthermore, in glucocorticoid negative-feedback-impaired mice (GR-i mice, with a constitutive GR downexpression), with a depression-like phenotype, both BDNF levels and granule cell proliferation are downregulated (Paizanis et al., 2010). The close relationship between depression-like behavior and impaired hippocampal neurogenesis in theses models is illustrated by convergent data showing that antidepressant treatments reverse both abnormalities in parallel (see Paizanis et al., 2010).

Recently, the implication of chromatin remodeling in the effects of stress and antidepressant treatment has been emphasized with regard to resulting consequences on BDNF production and action (Tsankova et al., 2006). It has notably been observed that social defeat stress in mice produced long-lasting methylation of histone-3 subunits around the *BDNF* gene-promoter region, thereby causing inhibition of *BDNF* gene transcription. Furthermore, chronic antidepressant treatment counteracted the reduction in *BDNF* gene transcription through acetylation of the same histone subunits. These data indicate that epigenetic mechanisms underlie the long-lasting repression on BDNF mRNA production by chronic stress and the opposite effect of antidepressant treatment. However, an antidepressant treatment that induced histone acetylation in mice previously exposed to social stress was without effect in nonstressed controls (Tsankova et al., 2006). The possibility therefore exists that increased BDNF signaling is required for the induction of the behavioral response to antidepressant drugs specifically in experimental—that is, stressed—animals (Castren et al., 2007). Indeed, BDNF signaling on its own appears to be sufficient for antidepressant-like effects, as direct infusion of BDNF into midbrain or hippocampal areas induces behavioral responses that are similar to those produced by antidepressants (Duman and Monteggia, 2006). However, in addition to BDNF, other neurotrophic factors seem to play a role in mood disorders and the action of antidepressant drugs (Duman and Monteggia, 2006). In particular, alterations in the levels of fibroblast growth factors and their receptors have been detected in the brain of patients with major depressive disorder, and expression of fibroblast growth factors can be modulated by antidepressant drugs. Similarly, brain concentrations of insulin-like growth factor and vascular endothelial growth factor were reported to be increased by chronic treatments with these drugs (Castren et al., 2007). These data strongly suggest that several factors with neurotrophic properties are involved in antidepressant therapy. Whether neuroplastic changes in response to such factors are important for mood regulation and adaptive behavioral responses to stress is an important question to be addressed in the future.

Overview

Dysfunctions of the HPA axis together with alterations in 5-HT$_{1A}$, 5-HT$_{2A}$, and 5-HT$_{2C}$ receptors have been consistently observed in anxious and depressed patients. The serotonergic system plays an important role in the regulation of endocrine responses to stressful stimuli, and conversely a sustained increase in glucocorticoid secretion can have numerous long-term effects on serotonergic neurotransmission. During stress, CRH is released in several areas such as the amygdala, which exerts excitatory effects on 5-HT neurons in the raphe. In the hypothalamus, PVN neurons release CRH from their terminals into pituitary portal circulation, thereby causing ACTH secretion from anterior pituitary and, in turn, corticosterone/cortisol secretion from adrenal cortex. This hormone, mainly through GRs, then induces modifications of gene expression and exerts rapid nongenomic effects.

Following sustained GR stimulation and in stress-related diseases, both 5-HT$_{1A}$ and 5-HT$_{2A/2C}$ receptor signaling mechanisms are strongly affected. Antidepressant treatments can overcome these effects of stress by increasing 5-HT input at 5-HT$_{1A}$ receptors and, in contrast, decreasing 5-HT$_{2A}$ and 5-HT$_{2C}$ receptor functioning. It seems overall that chronic stress decreases 5-HT$_{1A}$ versus 5-HT$_{2A/2C}$ receptor-mediated transmission at projection sites such as the hippocampus, the amygdala, or the frontal cortex, and that this imbalance would be corrected by chronic antidepressant treatment (Figure 24.2).

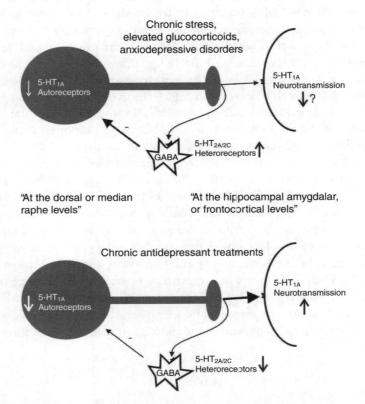

Figure 24.2 Contrasting effects of chronic stress or stress-related disorders versus antidepressant treatments on some components of serotonergic neurotransmission. Both chronic stress and chronic antidepressant treatments decrease the function of somatodendritic 5-HT$_{1A}$ autoreceptors. Postsynaptic 5-HT$_{1A}$ receptors are also downregulated by chronic stress in validated animal models and in patients suffering from anxiodepressive disorders. In contrast, 5-HT$_{2A/2C}$ receptor signaling is increased in these patients and by sustained stress-associated secretion of glucocorticoids. Long-term antidepressant treatments often produce opposite adaptive changes at these postsynaptic targets.

Following stress, hypersensitive 5-HT$_{2A}$ receptors might lead to a downregulation of neurotrophic factors, with concomitant neuroanatomical abnormalities affecting notably the hippocampus and the amygdala (Dranovsky and Hen, 2006). The contributions of the HPA axis and the 5-HT system to the respective negative/positive control of granule cell proliferation within the dentate gyrus of the hippocampus are probably of key importance for the understanding of pathophysiological mechanisms underlying affective diseases. By increasing 5-HT$_{1A}$ receptor signaling in the hippocampus, antidepressant therapies might work, at least in part, by promoting dentate-gyrus neurogenesis. Future studies in humans should allow us to assess whether alterations in hippocampal neurogenesis and/or neuroplasticity induced by stress are really involved in the etiology of affective diseases. In any case, the serotonergic system is profoundly embedded in these stress-related changes, including those related to epigenetic mechanisms which appear to be of major importance in stress-related disorders and relevant treatments.

References

Aguilar-Valles, A., Sanchez, E., de Gortari, P., Balderas, I., Ramirez-Amaya, V., Bermudez-Rattoni, F., & Joseph-Bravo, P. (2005). Analysis of the stress response in rats trained in the water-maze: differential expression of corticotropin-releasing hormone, CRH-R1, glucocorticoid receptors and brain-derived neurotrophic factor in limbic regions. *Neuroendocrinology, 82*, 306–319.

Alfonso, J., Frick, L. R., Silberman, D. M., Palumbo, M. L., Genaro, A. M., & Frasch, A. C. (2006). Regulation of hippocampal gene expression is conserved in two species subjected to different stressors and antidepressant treatments. *Biological Psychiatry, 59*, 244–251.

Amat, J., Tamblyn, J. P., Paul, E. D., Bland, S. T., Amat, P., Foster, A. C., Watkins, L. R., & Maier, S. F. (2004). Microinjection of urocortin 2 into the dorsal raphe nucleus activates serotonergic neurons and increases extracellular serotonin in the basolateral amygdala. *Neuroscience, 129*, 509–519.

Arborelius, L., Owens, M. J., Plotsky, P. M., & Nemeroff, C. B. (1999). The role of corticotropin-releasing factor in depression and anxiety disorders. *Journal of Endocrinology, 160*, 1–12.

Asberg, M., Nordstrom, P., & Traskman-Bendz, L. (1986). Cerebrospinal fluid studies in suicide. An overview. *Annals of the New York Academy of Sciences, 487*, 243–255.

Bagdy, G. (1996). Role of the hypothalamic paraventricular nucleus in 5-HT1A, 5-HT2A and 5-HT2C receptor-mediated oxytocin, prolactin and ACTH/corticosterone responses. *Behavioral Brain Research, 73*, 277–280.

Beato, M., & Sanchez-Pacheco, A. (1996). Interaction of steroid hormone receptors with the transcription initiation complex. *Endocrine Reviews, 17*, 587–609.

Berg, K. A., Harvey, J. A., Spampinato, U., & Clarke, W. P. (2005). Physiological relevance of constitutive activity of 5-HT2A and 5-HT2C receptors. *Trends in Pharmacological Sciences, 26*, 625–630.

Bland, S. T., Hargrave, D., Pepin, J. L., Amat, J., Watkins, L. R., & Maier, S. F. (2003). Stressor controllability modulates stress-induced dopamine and serotonin efflux and morphine-induced serotonin efflux in the medial prefrontal cortex. *Neuropsychopharmacology, 28*, 1589–1596.

Boothman, L., Raley, J., Denk, F., Hirani, E., & Sharp, T. (2006). In vivo evidence that 5-HT(2C) receptors inhibit 5-HT neuronal activity via a GABAergic mechanism. *British Journal of Pharmacology, 149*, 861–869.

Bristow, L. J., O'Connor, D., Watts, R., Duxon, M. S., & Hutson, P. H. (2000). Evidence for accelerated desensitisation of 5-HT(2C) receptors following combined treatment with fluoxetine and the 5-HT(1A) receptor antagonist, WAY 100,635, in the rat. *Neuropharmacology, 39*, 1222–1236.

Calcagno, E., Guzzetti, S., Canetta, A., Fracasso, C., Caccia, S., Cervo, L., & Invernizzi, R. W. (2009). Enhancement of cortical extracellular 5-HT by 5-HT1A and 5-HT2C receptor blockade restores the antidepressant-like effect of citalopram in non-responder mice. *International Journal of Neuropsychopharmacology, 12*, 793–803.

Caspi, A., & Moffitt, T. E. (2006). Gene-environment interactions in psychiatry: joining forces with neuroscience. *Nature Reviews Neuroscience, 7*, 583–590.

Caspi, A., Sugden, K., Moffitt, T. E., Taylor, A., Craig I.W., Harrington, H., McClay, J., Mill, J., Martin, J., Braithwaite, A., & Poulton, R. (2003). Influence of life stress on depression: moderation by a polymorphism in the 5-HTT gene. *Science, 301*, 386–389.

Castren, E., Voikar, V., & Rantamaki, T. (2007). Role of neurotrophic factors in depression. *Current Opinions in Pharmacology, 7*, 18–21.

Chaouloff, F. (1993). Physiopharmacological interactions between stress hormones and central serotoninergic systems. *Brain Research Reviews, 18*, 1–32.

Charney, D. S., Woods, S. W., Goodman, W. K., & Heninger, G. R. (1987). Serotonin function in anxiety. II. Effects of the serotonin agonist MCPP in panic disorder patients and healthy subjects. *Psychopharmacology (Berlin), 92*, 14–24.

Clement, H. W., Schafer, F., Ruwe, C., Gemsa, D., & Wesemann, W. (1993). Stress-induced changes of extracellular 5-hydroxyindoleacetic acid concentrations followed in the nucleus raphe dorsalis and the frontal cortex of the rat. *Brain Research, 614*, 117–124.

Cohen, H. (2005). Anxiolytic effect and memory improvement in rats by antisense oligodeoxynucleotide to 5-hydroxytryptamine-2A precursor protein. *Depression and Anxiety, 22*, 84–93.

Cooper, M. A., Grober, M. S., Nicholas, C. R., & Huhman, K. L. (2009). Aggressive encounters alter the activation of serotonergic neurons and the expression of 5-HT1A mRNA in the hamster dorsal raphe nucleus. *Neuroscience, 161*, 680–690.

Cremers, T. I., Giorgetti, M., Bosker, F. J., Hogg, S., Arnt, J., Mork, A., Honig, G., Bogeso, K. P., Westerink, B. H., den Boer, H., Wikstrom, H. V., & Tecott, L. H. (2004). Inactivation of 5-HT(2C) receptors potentiates consequences of serotonin reuptake blockade. *Neuropsychopharmacology, 29*, 1782–1789.

Czeh, B., Michaelis, T., Watanabe, T., Frahm, J., de Biurrun, G., van Kampen, M., Bartolomucci, A., & Fuchs, E. (2001). Stress-induced changes in cerebral metabolites, hippocampal volume, and cell proliferation are prevented by antidepressant treatment with tianeptine. *Proceedings of the National Academy of Sciences USA, 98*, 12796–12801.

Damjanoska, K. J., Heidenreich, B. A., Kindel, G. H., D'Souza, D. N., Zhang, Y., Garcia, F., Battaglia, G., Wolf, W. A., Van De Kar, L. D., & Muma, N. A. (2004). Agonist-induced serotonin 2A receptor desensitization in the rat frontal cortex and hypothalamus. *Journal of Pharmacology and Experimental Therapeutics, 309*, 1043–1050.

Day, H. E., Greenwood, B. N., Hammack, S. E., Watkins, L. R., Fleshner, M., Maier, S. F., & Campeau, S. (2004). Differential expression of 5-HT-1A, alpha 1b adrenergic, CRF-R1, and CRF-R2 receptor mRNA in serotonergic, gamma-aminobutyric acidergic, and catecholaminergic cells of the rat dorsal raphe nucleus. *Journal of Comparative Neurology, 474*, 364–378.

Deckert, J., Meyer, J., Catalano, M., Bosi, M., Sand, P., DiBella, D., Ortega, G., Stober, G., Franke, P., Nothen, M. M., Fritze, J., Maier, W., Beckmann, H., Propping, P., Bellodi, L., & Lesch, K. P. (2000). Novel 5'-regulatory region polymorphisms of the 5-HT2C receptor gene: association study with panic disorder. *International Journal of Neuropsychopharmacology, 3*, 321–325.

de Kloet, E. R., Vreugdenhil, E., Oitzl, M. S., & Joels, M. (1998). Brain corticosteroid receptor balance in health and disease. *Endocrine Reviews, 19*, 269–301.

de Kloet, E. R., Karst, H., & Joels, M. (2008). Corticosteroid hormones in the central stress response: Quick-and-slow. *Frontiers in Neuroendocrinology, 29*, 268–272.

Dranovsky, A., & Hen, R. (2006). Hippocampal neurogenesis: regulation by stress and anti-depressants. *Biological Psychiatry, 59*, 1136–1143.

Dremencov, E., Newman, M. E., Kinor, N., Blatman-Jan, G., Schindler, C. J., Overstreet, D. H., & Yadid, G. (2005). Hyperfunctionality of serotonin-2C receptor-mediated inhibition of accumbal dopamine release in an animal model of depression is reversed by antidepressant treatment. *Neuropharmacology, 48*, 34–42.

Drevets, W. C., Thase, M. E., Moses-Kolko, E. L., Price, J., Frank, E., Kupfer, D. J., & Mathis, C. (2007). Serotonin-1A receptor imaging in recurrent depression: replication and literature review. *Nuclear Medicine and Biology, 34*, 865–877.

Duman, R. S., & Monteggia, L. M. (2006). A neurotrophic model for stress-related mood disorders. *Biological Psychiatry, 59*, 1116–1127.

Dwivedi, Y., Mondal, A. C., Payappagoudar, G. V., & Rizavi, H. S. (2005). Differential regulation of serotonin (5HT)2A receptor mRNA and protein levels after single and repeated stress in rat brain: role in learned helplessness behavior. *Neuropharmacology, 48*, 204–214.

Englander, M. T., Dulawa, S. C., Bhansali, P., & Schmauss, C. (2005). How stress and fluoxet-ine modulate serotonin 2C receptor pre-mRNA editing. *Journal of Neuroscience, 25*, 648–651.

Fabre, V., Beaufour, C., Evrard, A., Rioux, A., Hanoun, N., Lesch, K. P., Murphy, D. L., Lanfumey, L., Hamon, M., & Martres M.P. (2000). Altered expression and functions of serotonin 5-HT1A and 5-HT1B receptors in knock-out mice lacking the 5-HT trans-porter. *European Journal of Neuroscience, 12*, 2299–2310.

Fakra, E., Hyde, L. W., Gorka, A., Fisher, P. M., Munoz, K. E., Kimak, M., Halder, I., Ferrell, R. E., Manuck, S. B., & Hariri, A. R. (2009). Effects of HTR1A C(-1019)G on amygdala reactivity and trait anxiety. *Archives of General Psychiatry, 66*, 33–40.

Fone, K. C., Shalders, K., Fox, Z. D., Arthur, R., & Marsden, C. A. (1996). Increased 5-HT2C receptor responsiveness occurs on rearing rats in social isolation. *Psychopharmacology (Berlin), 123*, 346–352.

Frokjaer, V. G., Mortensen, E. L., Nielsen, F. A., Haugbol, S., Pinborg, L. H., Adams, K. H., Svarer, C., Hasselbalch, S. G., Holm, S., Paulson, O. B., & Knudsen, G. M. (2008). Frontolimbic serotonin 2A receptor binding in healthy subjects is associated with per-sonality risk factors for affective disorder. *Biological Psychiatry, 63*, 569–576.

Gass, P., Reichardt, H. M., Strekalova, T., Henn, F., & Tronche, F. (2001). Mice with targeted mutations of glucocorticoid and mineralocorticoid receptors: models for depression and anxiety? *Physiology and Behavior, 73*, 811–825.

Gobert, A., & Millan, M. J. (1999). Serotonin (5-HT)2A receptor activation enhances dia-lysate levels of dopamine and noradrenaline, but not 5-HT, in the frontal cortex of freely-moving rats. *Neuropharmacology, 38*, 315–317.

Gobert, A., Rivet, J. M., Lejeune, F., Newman-Tancredi, A., Adhumeau-Auclair, A., Nicolas, J. P., Cistarelli, L., Melon, C., & Millan, M. J. (2000). Serotonin(2C) receptors tonically suppress the activity of mesocortical dopaminergic and adrenergic, but not serotonergic, pathways: a combined dialysis and electrophysiological analysis in the rat. *Synapse*, 36, 205–221.

Greenwood, B. N., Foley, T. E., Day, H. E., Campisi, J., Hammack, S. H., Campeau, S., Maier, S. F., & Fleshner, M. (2003). Freewheel running prevents learned helplessness/behavioral depression: role of dorsal raphe serotonergic neurons. *Journal of Neuroscience*, 23, 2889–2898.

Gronli, J., Bramham, C., Murison, R., Kanhema, T., Fiske, E., Bjorvatn, B., Ursin, R., & Portas, C. M. (2006). Chronic mild stress inhibits BDNF protein expression and CREB activation in the dentate gyrus but not in the hippocampus proper. *Pharmacology, Biochemistry, and Behavior*, 85, 842–849.

Haddjeri, N., Blier, P., & de Montigny, C. (1998). Long-term antidepressant treatments result in a tonic activation of forebrain 5-HT1A receptors. *Journal of Neuroscience*, 18, 10150–10156.

Hamon, M. (1997). The main features of central 5-HT$_{1A}$ receptors. In serotoninergic neurons and 5-HT receptors in the CNS. In H. G. Baumgarten, & M. Göthert (Eds.), *Handbook of experimental pharmacology* (Vol. 29, pp. 239–268). Berlin: Springer-Verlag.

Harada, K., Yamaji, T., & Matsuoka, N. (2008). Activation of the serotonin 5-HT2C receptor is involved in the enhanced anxiety in rats after single-prolonged stress. *Pharmacology, Biochemistry, and Behavior*, 89, 11–16.

Harfstrand, A., Fuxe, K., Cintra, A., Agnati, L. F., Zini, I., Wikstrom, A. C., Okret, S., Yu, Z. Y., Goldstein, M., Steinbusch, H., Verhofstad, A., & Gustafsson, J. A. (1986). Glucocorticoid receptor immunoreactivity in monoaminergic neurons of rat brain. *Proceedings of the National Academy of Sciences USA*, 83, 9779–9783.

Hauger, R. L., Grigoriadis, D. E., Dallman, M. F., Plotsky, P. M., Vale, W. W., & Dautzenberg, F. M. (2003). International Union of Pharmacology. XXXVI. Current status of the nomenclature for receptors for corticotropin-releasing factor and their ligands. *Pharmacological Reviews*, 55, 21–26.

Heisler, L. K., Zhou, L., Bajwa, P., Hsu, J., & Tecott, L. H. (2007). Serotonin 5-HT(2C) receptors regulate anxiety-like behavior. *Genes Brain & Behavior*, 6, 491–496.

Hensler, J. G. (2002). Differential regulation of 5-HT$_{1A}$ receptor-G protein interactions in brain following chronic antidepressant administration. *Neuropsychopharmacology*, 26, 565–573.

Hesen, W., & Joels, M. (1996). Modulation of 5-HT$_{1A}$ responsiveness in CA1 pyramidal neurons by in vivo activation of corticosteroid receptors. *Journal of Neuroendocrinology*, 8, 433–438.

Hinz, B., & Hirschelmann, R. (2000). Rapid non-genomic feedback effects of glucocorticoids on CRF-induced ACTH secretion in rats. *Pharmaceutical Research*, 17, 1273–1277.

Holmes, M. C., French, K. L., & Seckl, J. R. (1995). Modulation of serotonin and corticosteroid receptor gene expression in the rat hippocampus with circadian rhythm and stress. *Brain Research Molecular Brain Research*, 28, 186–192.

Iwamoto, K., Nakatani, N., Bundo, M., Yoshikawa, T., & Kato, T. (2005). Altered RNA editing of serotonin 2C receptor in a rat model of depression. *Neuroscience Research*, 53, 69–76.

Jacobs, B. L., & Azmitia, E. C. (1992). Structure and function of the brain serotonin system. *Physiological Reviews*, 72, 165–229.

Jacobson, L., & Sapolsky, R. (1991). The role of the hippocampus in feedback regulation of the hypothalamic-pituitary-adrenocortical axis. *Endocrine Reviews, 12,* 118–134.

Joels, M., Hesen, W., & de Kloet, E. R. (1991). Mineralocorticoid hormones suppress serotonin-induced hyperpolarization of rat hippocampal CA1 neurons. *Journal of Neuroscience, 11,* 2288–2294.

Jorgensen, H., Knigge, U., Kjaer, A., Vadsholt, T., & Warberg, J. (1998). Serotonergic involvement in stress-induced ACTH release. *Brain Research, 811,* 10–20.

Judge, S. J., Ingram, C. D., & Gartside, S. E. (2004). Moderate differences in circulating corticosterone alter receptor-mediated regulation of 5-hydroxytryptamine neuronal activity. *Journal of Psychopharmacology, 18,* 475–483.

Karege, F., Perret, G., Bondolfi, G., Schwald, M., Bertschy, G., & Aubry, J. M. (2002). Decreased serum brain-derived neurotrophic factor levels in major depressed patients. *Psychiatry Research, 109,* 143–148.

Kawahara, Y., Grimberg, A., Teegarden, S., Mombereau, C., Liu, S., Bale, T. L., Blendy, J. A., & Nishikura, K. (2008). Dysregulated editing of serotonin 2C receptor mRNAs results in energy dissipation and loss of fat mass. *Journal of Neuroscience, 28,* 12834–12844.

Kirby, L. G., Rice, K. C., & Valentino, R. J. (2000). Effects of corticotropin-releasing factor on neuronal activity in the serotonergic dorsal raphe nucleus. *Neuropsychopharmacology, 22,* 148–162.

Kitraki, E., Karandrea, D., & Kittas, C. (1999). Long-lasting effects of stress on glucocorticoid receptor gene expression in the rat brain. *Neuroendocrinology, 69,* 331–338.

Klaassen, T., Riedel, W. J., van Praag, H. M., Menheere, P. P., & Griez, E. (2002). Neuroendocrine response to meta-chlorophenylpiperazine and ipsapirone in relation to anxiety and aggression. *Psychiatry Research, 113,* 29–40.

Kuroda, Y., Watanabe, Y., Albeck, D. S., Hastings, N. B., & McEwen, B. S. (1994). Effects of adrenalectomy and type I or type II glucocorticoid receptor activation on 5-HT1A and 5-HT2 receptor binding and 5-HT transporter mRNA expression in rat brain. *Brain Research, 648,* 157–161.

Kushwaha, N., & Albert, P. R. (2005). Coupling of 5-HT$_{1A}$ autoreceptors to inhibition of mitogen-activated protein kinase activation via G beta gamma subunit signaling. *European Journal of Neuroscience, 21,* 721–732.

Laaris, N., Haj-Dahmane, S., Hamon, M., & Lanfumey, L. (1995). Glucocorticoid receptor-mediated inhibition by corticosterone of 5-HT$_{1A}$ autoreceptor functioning in the rat dorsal raphe nucleus. *Neuropharmacology, 34,* 1201–1210.

Laaris, N., Le Poul, E., Laporte, A. M., Hamon, M., & Lanfumey, L. (1999). Differential effects of stress on presynaptic and postsynaptic 5-hydroxytryptamine-1A receptors in the rat brain: an in vitro electrophysiological study. *Neuroscience, 91,* 947–958.

Lanfumey, L., Pardon, M. C., Laaris, N., Joubert, C., Hanoun, N., Hamon, M., & Cohen-Salmon, C. (1999). 5-HT$_{1A}$ autoreceptor desensitization by chronic ultramild stress in mice. *Neuroreport, 10,* 3369–3374.

Lee, T. T., Redila, V. A., Hill, M. N., & Gorzalka, B. B. (2009). 5-HT(2A) receptor mediated neuronal activation within the paraventricular nucleus of the hypothalamus is desensitized following prolonged glucocorticoid treatment. *European Journal of Pharmacology, 602,* 54–57.

Lemonde, S., Turecki, G., Bakish, D., Du, L., Hrdina, P. D., Bown, C. D., Sequeira, A., Kushwaha, N., Morris S.J., Basak, A., Ou, X. M., & Albert, P. R. (2003). Impaired repression at a 5-hydroxytryptamine 1A receptor gene polymorphism associated with major depression and suicide. *Journal of Neuroscience, 23,* 8788–8799.

Lemonde, S., Du, L., Bakish, D., Hrdina, P., & Albert, P. R. (2004). Association of the C(-1019) G 5-HT1A functional promoter polymorphism with antidepressant response. *International Journal of Neuropsychopharmacology*, 7, 501–506.

Le Poul, E., Boni, C., Hanoun, N., Laporte, A. M., Laaris, N., Chauveau, J., Hamon, M., & Lanfumey, L. (2000). Differential adaptation of brain 5-HT$_{1A}$ and 5-HT$_{1B}$ receptors and 5-HT transporter in rats treated chronically with fluoxetine. *Neuropharmacology*, 39, 110–122.

Lesch, K. P., Bengel, D., Heils, A., Sabol, S. Z., Greenberg, B. D., Petri, S., Benjamin, J., Muller, C. R., Hamer, D. H., & Murphy, D. L. (1996). Association of anxiety-related traits with a polymorphism in the serotonin transporter gene regulatory region. *Science*, 274, 1527–1531.

Lewis, K., Li, C., Perrin, M. H., Blount, A., Kunitake, K., Donaldson, C., Vaughan, J., Reyes, T. M., Gulyas, J., Fischer, W., Bilezikjian, L., Rivier, J., Sawchenko, P. E., & Vale, W. W. (2001). Identification of urocortin III, an additional member of the corticotropin-releasing factor (CRF) family with high affinity for the CRF2 receptor. *Proceedings of the National Academy of Sciences USA*, 98, 7570–7575.

Liposits, Z., Phelix, C., & Paull, W. K. (1987). Synaptic interaction of serotonergic axons and corticotropin releasing factor (CRF) synthesizing neurons in the hypothalamic paraventricular nucleus of the rat. A light and electron microscopic immunocytochemical study. *Histochemistry*, 86, 541–549.

Liu, R., Jolas, T., & Aghajanian, G. (2000). Serotonin 5-HT2 receptors activate local GABA inhibitory inputs to serotonergic neurons of the dorsal raphe nucleus. *Brain Research*, 873, 34–45.

Lopez, J. F., Liberzon, I., Vazquez, D. M., Young, E. A., & Watson, S. J. (1999). Serotonin 1A receptor messenger RNA regulation in the hippocampus after acute stress. *Biological Psychiatry*, 45, 934–937.

Lowy, M. T., & Meltzer, H. Y. (1988). Stimulation of serum cortisol and prolactin secretion in humans by MK-212, a centrally active serotonin agonist. *Biological Psychiatry*, 23, 818–828.

Man, M. S., Young, A. H., & McAllister-Williams, R. H. (2002). Corticosterone modulation of somatodendritic 5-HT1A receptor function in mice. *Journal of Psychopharmacology*, 16, 245–252.

Mannoury la Cour, C., Boni, C., Hanoun, N., Lesch, K. P., Hamon, M., & Lanfumey, L. (2001). Functional consequences of 5-HT transporter gene disruption on 5-HT(1a) receptor-mediated regulation of dorsal raphe and hippocampal cell activity. *Journal of Neuroscience*, 21, 2178–2185.

Mannoury la Cour, C., El Mestikawy, S., Hanoun, N., Hamon, M., & Lanfumey, L. (2006). Regional differences in the coupling of 5-hydroxytryptamine-1A receptors to G proteins in the rat brain. *Molecular Pharmacology*, 70, 1013–1021.

Marek, G. J., Martin-Ruiz, R., Abo, A., & Artigas, F. (2005). The selective 5-HT2A receptor antagonist M100907 enhances antidepressant-like behavioral effects of the SSRI fluoxetine. *Neuropsychopharmacology*, 30, 2205–2215.

Martin, C., Chevarin, C., Lesch, K. P., Hamon, M., Lanfumey, L., & Mongeau, R. (2010). Behavioral and neurochemical consequences of 5-HT transporter deletion on anxiety and 5-HT2C receptor functions. *European Neuropsychopharmacology*, 20, S44 suppl. 1.

Maswood, S., Barter, J. E., Watkins, L. R., & Maier, S. F. (1998). Exposure to inescapable but not escapable shock increases extracellular levels of 5-HT in the dorsal raphe nucleus of the rat. *Brain Research*, 783, 115–120.

McEwen, B. S., & Stellar, E. (1993). Stress and the individual. Mechanisms leading to disease. *Archives of Internal Medicine, 153,* 2093–2101.

McEwen, B. S., & Wingfield, J. C. (2010). What is in a name? Integrating homeostasis, allostasis and stress. *Hormones and Behavior, 57,* 105–111.

McGrew, L., Price, R. D., Hackler, E., Chang, M. S., & Sanders-Bush, E. (2004). RNA editing of the human serotonin 5-HT2C receptor disrupts transactivation of the small G-protein RhoA. *Molecular Pharmacology, 65,* 252–256.

McKittrick, C. R., Magarinos, A. M., Blanchard, D. C., Blanchard, R. J., McEwen, B. S., & Sakai, R. R. (2000). Chronic social stress reduces dendritic arbors in CA3 of hippocampus and decreases binding to serotonin transporter sites. *Synapse, 36,* 85–94.

McMahon, F. J., Buervenich, S., Charney, D., Lipsky, R., Rush, A. J., Wilson, A. F., Sorant, A. J., Papanicolaou, G. J., Laje, G., Fava, M., Trivedi, M. H., Wisniewski, S. R., & Manji, H. (2006). Variation in the gene encoding the serotonin 2A receptor is associated with outcome of antidepressant treatment. *American Journal of Human Genetics, 78,* 804–814.

Meijer, O. C., & de Kloet, E. R. (1994). Corticosterone suppresses the expression of 5-HT$_{1A}$ receptor mRNA in rat dentate gyrus. *European Journal of Pharmacology, 266,* 255–261.

Meijer, O. C., Cole, T. J., Schmid, W., Schutz, G., Joels, M., & De Kloet, E. R. (1997). Regulation of hippocampal 5-HT$_{1A}$ receptor mRNA and binding in transgenic mice with a targeted disruption of the glucocorticoid receptor. *Brain Research Molecular Brain Research, 46,* 290–296.

Meijer, O. C., Williamson, A., Dallman, M. F., & Pearce, D. (2000). Transcriptional repression of the 5-HT$_{1A}$ receptor promoter by corticosterone via mineralocorticoid receptors depends on the cellular context. *Journal of Neuroendocrinology, 12,* 245–254.

Mendelson, S. D., & McEwen, B. S. (1991). Autoradiographic analyses of the effects of restraint-induced stress on 5-HT$_{1A}$, 5-HT$_{1C}$ and 5-HT$_2$ receptors in the dorsal hippocampus of male and female rats. *Neuroendocrinology, 54,* 454–461.

Millan M J. (2005). Serotonin 5-HT2C receptors as a target for the treatment of depressive and anxious states: focus on novel therapeutic strategies. *Therapie, 60,* 441–460.

Mo, B., Feng, N., Renner, K., & Forster, G. (2008). Restraint stress increases serotonin release in the central nucleus of the amygdala via activation of corticotropin-releasing factor receptors. *Brain Research Bulletin, 76,* 493–498.

Mongeau, R., Blier, P., & de Montigny, C. (1997). The serotonergic and noradrenergic systems of the hippocampus: their interactions and the effects of antidepressant treatments. *Brain Research Brain Research Reviews, 23,* 145–195.

Mongeau, R., Martin, C., Chevarin, C., Maldonado, R., Hamon, M., Robledo, P., & Lanfumey, L. (2010). 5-HT$_{2C}$ receptor activation prevents stress-induced enhancement of brain 5-HT turnover and extracellular levels in the mouse brain—modulation by chronic paroxetine treatment. *Journal of Neurochemistry, 115,* 438–449.

Montgomery, S. A., Dufour, H., Brion, S., Gailledreau, J., Laqueille, X., Ferrey, G., Moron, P., Parant-Lucena, N., Singer, L., & Danion, J. M. (1988). The prophylactic efficacy of fluoxetine in unipolar depression. *British Journal of Psychiatry* (Suppl), *3,* 69–76.

Moore, R. Y., & Halaris A E. (1975). Hippocampal innervation by serotonin neurons of the midbrain raphe in the rat. *Journal of Comparative Neurology, 164,* 171–183.

Nishiguchi, N., Shirakawa, O., Ono, H., Nishimura, A., Nushida, H., Ueno, Y., & Maeda, K. (2002). Lack of an association between 5-HT$_{1A}$ receptor gene structural polymorphisms and suicide victims. *American Journal of Medical Genetics, 114,* 423–425.

Osei-Owusu, P., James, A., Crane, J., & Scrogin, K. E. (2005). 5-Hydroxytryptamine 1A receptors in the paraventricular nucleus of the hypothalamus mediate oxytocin and adrenocorticotropin hormone release and some behavioral components of the serotonin syndrome. *Journal of Pharmacology and Experimental Therapeutics, 313*, 1324–1330.

Ossowska, G., Nowak, G., Klenk-Majewska, B., Danilczuk, Z., & Zebrowska-Lupina, I. (2002). Effect of imipramine on brain D-1 and 5-HT-2A receptors in a chronic unpredictable stress model in rats. *Polish Journal of Pharmacology, 54*, 89–93.

Overstreet, D. H., Commissaris, R. C., De La Garza, R., File, S. E., Knapp, D. J., & Seiden, L. S. (2003). Involvement of 5-HT$_{1A}$ receptors in animal tests of anxiety and depression: evidence from genetic models. *Stress, 6*, 101–110.

Paizanis, E., Renoir, T., Lelievre, V., Saurini, F., Melfort, M., Gabriel, C., Barden, N., Mocaer, E., Hamon, M., & Lanfumey, L. (2010). Behavioural and neuroplastic effects of the new-generation antidepressant agomelatine compared to fluoxetine in glucocorticoid receptor-impaired mice. *International Journal of Neuropsychopharmacology, 13*, 759–777.

Pandey, S. C., Zhang, H., Roy, A., & Misra, K. (2006). Central and medial amygdaloid brain-derived neurotrophic factor signaling plays a critical role in alcohol-drinking and anxiety-like behaviors. *Journal of Neuroscience, 26*, 8320–8331.

Parks, C. L., Robinson, P. S., Sibille, E., Shenk, T., & Toth, M. (1998). Increased anxiety of mice lacking the serotonin1A receptor. *Proceedings of the National Academy of Sciences USA,95*, 10734–10739.

Parsons, L. H., Kerr, T. M., & Tecott, L. H. (2001). 5-HT(1A) receptor mutant mice exhibit enhanced tonic, stress-induced and fluoxetine-induced serotonergic neurotransmission. *Journal of Neurochemistry, 77*, 607–617.

Peroutka, S. J., & Snyder, S. H. (1980). Long-term antidepressant treatment decreases spiroperidol-labeled serotonin receptor binding. *Science, 210*, 88–90.

Porter, R. J., Gallagher, P., Watson, S., & Young, A. H. (2004). Corticosteroid-serotonin interactions in depression: a review of the human evidence. *Psychopharmacology (Berlin), 173*, 1–17.

Price, M. L., & Lucki, I. (2001). Regulation of serotonin release in the lateral septum and striatum by corticotropin-releasing factor. *Journal of Neuroscience, 21*, 2833–2841.

Queree, P., Peters, S., & Sharp, T. (2009). Further pharmacological characterization of 5-HT(2C). receptor agonist-induced inhibition of 5-HT neuronal activity in the dorsal raphe nucleus in vivo. *British Journal of Pharmacology, 158*, 1477–1485.

Raymond, J. R., Mukhin, Y. V., Gelasco, A., Turner, J., Collinsworth, G., Gettys, T. W., Grewal, J. S., & Garnovskaya, M. N. (2001). Multiplicity of mechanisms of serotonin receptor signal transduction. *Pharmacology & Therapeutics, 92*, 179–212.

Reul, J. M., & de Kloet, E. R. (1986). Anatomical resolution of two types of corticosterone receptor sites in rat brain with in vitro autoradiography and computerized image analysis. *Journal of Steroid Biochemistry, 24*, 269–272.

Richer, M., Hen, R., & Blier, P. (2002). Modification of serotonin neuron properties in mice lacking 5-HT$_{1A}$ receptors. *European Journal of Pharmacology, 435*, 195–203.

Rioux, A., Fabre, V., Lesch, K. P., Moessner, R., Murphy, D. L., Lanfumey, L., Hamon, M., & Martres, M. P. (1999). Adaptive changes of serotonin 5-HT2A receptors in mice lacking the serotonin transporter. *Neuroscience Letters, 262*, 113–116.

Rothe, C., Koszycki, D., Bradwejn, J., King, N., Deluca, V., Tharmalingam, S., & Kennedy, J. L. (2006). Association of the Val158Met catechol-O-methyltransferase genetic polymorphism with panic disorder. *Neuropsychopharmacology, 31*, 2237–2242.

Rozeboom, A. M., Akil, H., & Seasholtz, A. F. (2007). Mineralocorticoid receptor overexpression in forebrain decreases anxiety-like behavior and alters the stress response in mice. *Proceedings of the National Academy of Sciences USA, 104*, 4688–4693.

Sanchez, M. M., Young, L. J., Plotsky, P. M., & Insel, T. R. (1999). Autoradiographic and in situ hybridization localization of corticotropin-releasing factor 1 and 2 receptors in nonhuman primate brain. *Journal of Comparative Neurology, 408*, 365–377.

Sapolsky, R. M. (2003). Taming stress. *Scientific American, 289*, 86–95.

Shekhar, A., Truitt, W., Rainnie, D., & Sajdyk, T. (2005). Role of stress, corticotrophin releasing factor (CRF) and amygdala plasticity in chronic anxiety. *Stress, 8*, 209–219.

Sheline, Y. I., Wang, P. W., Gado, M. H., Csernansky, J. G., & Vannier, M. W. (1996). Hippocampal atrophy in recurrent major depression. *Proceedings of the National Academy of Sciences USA, 93*, 3908–3913.

Sheline, Y. I., Gado, M. H., & Kraemer, H. C. (2003). Untreated depression and hippocampal volume loss. *American Journal of Psychiatry, 160*, 1516–1518.

Singh, V. B., Corley, K. C., Phan, T. H., & Boadle-Biber, M. C. (1990). Increases in the activity of tryptophan hydroxylase from rat cortex and midbrain in response to acute or repeated sound stress are blocked by adrenalectomy and restored by dexamethasone treatment. *Brain Research, 516*, 66–76.

Smith, M. A., Makino, S., Kvetnansky, R., & Post, R. M. (1995). Stress and glucocorticoids affect the expression of brain-derived neurotrophic factor and neurotrophin-3 mRNAs in the hippocampus. *Journal of Neuroscience, 15*, 1768–1777.

Stockmeier, C. A., Mahajan, G. J., Konick, L. C., Overholser, J. C., Jurjus, G. J., Meltzer, H. Y., Uylings, H. B., Friedman, L., & Rajkowska, G. (2004). Cellular changes in the postmortem hippocampus in major depression. *Biological Psychiatry, 56*, 640–650.

Sumner, B. E., D'Eath, R. B., Farnworth, M. J., Robson, S., Russell, J. A., Lawrence, A. B., & Jarvis, S. (2008). Early weaning results in less active behaviour, accompanied by lower 5-HT1A and higher 5-HT2A receptor mRNA expression in specific brain regions of female pigs. *Psychoneuroendocrinology, 33*, 1077–1092.

Takase, L. F., Nogueira, M. I., Baratta, M., Bland, S. T., Watkins, L. R., Maier S. F., Fornal, C. A., & Jacobs, B. L. (2004). Inescapable shock activates serotonergic neurons in all raphe nuclei of rat. *Behavioral Brain Research, 153*, 233–239.

Tasker, J. G., Di, S., & Malcher-Lopes, R. (2006). Minireview: rapid glucocorticoid signaling via membrane-associated receptors. *Endocrinology, 147*, 5549–5556.

Tejani-Butt, S. M., & Labow, D. M. (1994). Time course of the effects of adrenalectomy and corticosterone replacement on 5-HT$_{1A}$ receptors and 5-HT uptake sites in the hippocampus and dorsal raphe nucleus of the rat brain: an autoradiographic analysis. *Psychopharmacology (Berlin), 113*, 481–486.

Trajkovska, V., Kirkegaard, L., Krey, G., Marcussen, A. B., Thomsen, M. S., Chourbaji, S., Brandwein, C., Ridder, S., Halldin, C., Gass, P., Knudsen, G. M., & Aznar, S. (2009). Activation of glucocorticoid receptors increases 5-HT2A receptor levels. *Experimental Neurology, 218*, 83–91.

Tsankova, N. M., Berton, O., Renthal, W., Kumar, A., Neve, R. L., & Nestler, E. J. (2006). Sustained hippocampal chromatin regulation in a mouse model of depression and antidepressant action. *Nature Neuroscience, 9*, 519–525.

Uher, R., & McGuffin, P. (2008). The moderation by the serotonin transporter gene of environmental adversity in the aetiology of mental illness: review and methodological analysis. *Molecular Psychiatry, 13*, 131–146.

Uher, R., & McGuffin, P.(2010). The moderation by the serotonin transporter gene of environmental adversity in the etiology of depression: 2009 update. *Molecular Psychiatry*,
15, 18–22.

Vaidya, V. A., Terwilliger, R. M., & Duman, R. S. (1999). Role of 5-HT2A receptors in the
stress-induced down-regulation of brain-derived neurotrophic factor expression in rat
hippocampus. *Neuroscience Letters*, *262*, 1–4.

Van de Kar, L. D., Li, Q. Cabrera, TM., Brownfield, M. S., & Battaglia, G. (1998). Alterations
in 8-hydroxy-2-(dipropylamino).tetralin-induced neuroendocrine responses after
5,7-dihydroxytryptamine-induced denervation of serotonergic neurons. *Journal of
Pharmacology and Experimental Therapeutics*, *286*, 256–262.

Van Riel, E., van Gemert, N. G., Meijer, O. C., & Joëls, M. (2004). Effect of early life stress
on serotonin responses in the hippocampus of young adult rats. *Synapse*, *53*, 11–19.

Van Veen, J. F., Van der Wee, N. J., Fiselier, J., Van Vliet, I. M., & Westenberg, H. G. (2007).
Behavioural effects of rapid intravenous administration of meta-chlorophenylpiperazine
(m-CPP) in patients with generalized social anxiety disorder, panic disorder and healthy
controls. *European Neuropsychopharmacology*, *17*, 637–642.

Vermetten, E., Vythilingam, M., Southwick, S. M., Charney, D. S., & Bremner, J. D. (2003).
Long-term treatment with paroxetine increases verbal declarative memory and hippocampal volume in posttraumatic stress disorder. *Biological Psychiatry*, *54*, 693–702.

Warner-Schmidt, J. L., & Duman, R. S. (2006). Hippocampal neurogenesis: opposing effects
of stress and antidepressant treatment. *Hippocampus*, *16*, 239–249.

Weisstaub, N. V., Zhou, M., Lira, A., Lambe, E., Gonzalez-Maeso, J., Hornung, J. P., Sibille,
E., Underwood, M., Itohara, S., Dauer, W. T., Ansorge, M. S., Morelli, E., Mann, J. J.,
Toth, M., Aghajanian, G., Sealfon, S. C., Hen, R., & Gingrich, J. A. (2006). Cortical
5-HT2A receptor signaling modulates anxiety-like behaviors in mice. *Science*, *313*,
536–540.

Wetzler, S., Asnis, G. M., DeLecuona, J. M., & Kalus, O. (1996). Serotonin function in panic
disorder: intravenous administration of meta-chlorophenylpiperazine. *Psychiatry
Research*, *64*, 77–82.

Wiegert, O., Joels, M., & Krugers, H. (2006). Timing is essential for rapid effects of corticosterone on synaptic potentiation in the mouse hippocampus. *Learning & Memory*, *13*,
110–113.

Wissink, S., Meijer, O., Pearce, D., van der Burg, B., & van der Saag, P. T. (2000). Regulation
of the rat serotonin-1A receptor gene by corticosteroids. *Journal of Biological Chemistry*,
275, 1321–1326.

Xie, D. W., Deng, Z. L., Ishigaki, T., Xie, D. W., Deng, Z. L., Ishigaki, T., Nakamura, Y., Suzuki,
Y., Miyasato, K., Ohara, K., & Ohara, K. (1995). The gene encoding the 5-HT$_{1A}$ receptor
is intact in mood disorders. *Neuropsychopharmacology*, *12*, 263–268.

Zhong, P., & Ciaranello, R. D. (1995). Transcriptional regulation of hippocampal 5-HT$_{1A}$
receptors by corticosteroid hormones. *Brain Research Molecular Brain Research*, *29*,
23–34.

25

Stress, Prefrontal Cortex Asymmetry, and Depression

Ron M. Sullivan and François Laplante

Overview of Prefrontal Cortical Involvement in Stress and Depression

The prefrontal cortex (PFC) is one of the most, if not the most, commonly implicated brain regions in the pathophysiology of depression (Brody et al., 2001; Pizzagalli et al., 2002). This should not be surprising given its roles in the highest levels of cognitive and emotional processing, and the fact that it is exquisitely sensitive to the detrimental effects of stress (Arnsten, 2009). Stress of course, is a major precipitating factor in the emergence and maintenance of depressive states. Suboptimal functioning of the hypothalamic–pituitary–adrenal (HPA) axis, induced by a combination of genetic, environmental, and social factors, has been suggested to play a substantial and even causal role in the development of depression and the expression of its symptomatology (Holsboer, 2001; Herbert et al., 2006). Circulating levels of glucocorticoids are frequently excessively high in depressed patients, particularly in the recovery phase after the experience of stress, suggesting impaired negative-feedback control over continued HPA axis activation (Burke et al., 2005). It is known from rodent studies that the (medial) PFC is a key (suprahypothalamic) brain region where corticosteroids act to exert negative-feedback control in times of stress (Diorio et al., 1993). In primates, the PFC contains an especially high density of glucocorticoid receptors (much more than hippocampus), suggesting a prominent role for the human PFC in the modulation of HPA axis function and in stress regulation generally (Sanchez et al., 2000).

Stress or excess glucocorticoids affect brain structure and function in many, complex ways, as have been reviewed previously by Arnsten (2009), Herbert et al.

The Handbook of Stress: Neuropsychological Effects on the Brain, First Edition.
Edited by Cheryl D. Conrad.
© 2011 Blackwell Publishing Ltd. Published 2011 by Blackwell Publishing Ltd.

(2006), Lupien et al. (2009), and in other chapters of this volume. The present discussion focuses more on the intrinsic role(s) of the PFC in stress and emotion regulation and how they may relate to depression. It is important to first note that any generalizations regarding the roles of the PFC in this capacity are complicated by the considerable functional heterogeneity of the frontal cortical subregions (for review, see Phillips et al., 2008). Broadly speaking however, depression tends to be associated with reduced cerebral metabolic rate or blood flow in the more medial and dorsolateral regions of the PFC, while increases are reported in more ventral and ventrolateral regions (Bivier et al., 1994; Brody et al., 2001; Buchsbaum et al., 1997; Drevets et al., 2002; Mayberg et al., 2000). Successful antidepressant treatment is associated with normalization of activity in these regions, as well as normalization of HPA axis function (Mayberg et al., 2000; Aihara et al., 2007).

The more ventral regions of the PFC, including the ventral (subgenual) anterior cingulate cortex, are part of a larger functional network involving the amygdala, insula, and ventral striatum. In contrast, the dorsal anterior cingulate cortex and dorsolateral PFC form a close functional network with the hippocampus. The major function of the ventral system has been described as identifying the emotional significance of a situation/stimulus and producing an appropriate affective state in response. The dorsal system regulates these affective states and is more effortful in its function, while the former is more automatic (Phillips et al., 2003a, 2003b). The ventromedial sector of the PFC has been similarly conceptualized as representing elementary positive and negative emotional states, while the dorsolateral PFC is involved in representing the goal states to which the elementary emotional states are directed (Davidson and Irwin, 1999). A dysregulated ventral system could thus compromise the initial ability to appropriately identify and respond to emotional or stressful situations, perhaps reflecting a hypersensitivity to otherwise manageable challenges. In addition, suboptimal activity in the dorsal system is consistent with deficits in both goal-oriented behavior and the effortful and appropriate regulation of emotional states which could lead to the impaired coping ability typical of depression (see Figure 25.1).

In the rat, a substantial body of evidence supports a similar notion of dorsal/ventral functional subdivisions in PFC from behavioral, autonomic, and neuroendocrine perspectives (reviewed in Sullivan, 2004). The ventromedial PFC or infralimbic (IL) cortex of the rat plays an important role in the assessment and perception of stressful situations and in mediating appropriately cautious or adaptive behavior necessary for dealing with potential threats. Selective lesions of this region result in a reduction of *normal* anxious behavior, such as open-arm avoidance in the elevated-plus maze (Lacroix et al., 2000; Sullivan and Gratton, 2002b) and reduced freezing behavior and ultrasonic vocalizations in response to a conditioned fear stimulus (Frysztak and Neafsey, 1991). In contrast, damage to more dorsal regions, namely prelimbic and dorsal anterior cingulate cortex, increases freezing behavior and fear reactivity (Holson, 1986; Morgan and LeDoux, 1995).

In terms of autonomic function, the IL cortex of the rat has been described as visceral motor cortex (Cechetto and Saper, 1990), necessary for the sympathetic

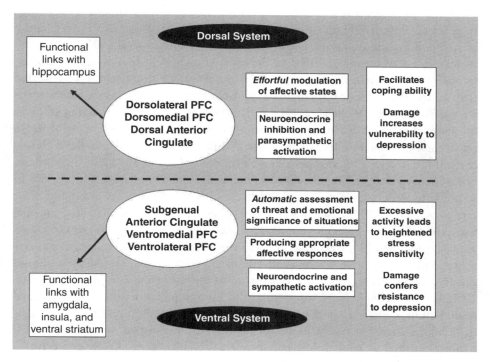

Figure 25.1 Simplified schematic representation of functional distinctions between dorsal and ventral prefrontal systems as relating to stress and emotion regulation and vulnerability to depression. In this schema, the ventral system is seen as more activational in responding to stress and producing affective responses, whereas dorsal regions play a more inhibitory, modulatory role in tempering the activity of the ventral system. Similar dorsal/ventral interactions are seen in the rat, where *dorsal* regions comprise prelimbic and anterior cingulate cortex, while the infralimbic cortex is homologous with the ventral system.

activation of cardiovascular and respiratory responses to stress (Frysztak and Neafsey, 1994). Lesions in this area also block the formation of stress-induced gastric ulcers (Sullivan and Gratton, 1999). In humans, damage to the ventromedial PFC results in failure to respond autonomically to emotional stimuli and impairments in decision-making and risk assessment (Damasio et al., 1990). Animal studies suggest, however, that while the ventromedial PFC is involved in sympathetic activation, prelimbic and anterior cingulate regions mediate parasympathetic effects (Frysztak and Neafsey, 1994; Powell et al., 1994), suggesting a reciprocal functional relationship between dorsal and ventral PFC regions, a pattern observed in both animals and humans.

HPA axis function is also modulated by the medial PFC in the rat where the ventral (IL) region appears to play a stimulatory role, while the more dorsal prelimbic and anterior cingulate regions are inhibitory (Herman et al., 2005). IL cortex lesions reduce stress-induced corticosterone secretion (Sullivan and Gratton, 1999), while the same measure is increased by more dorsal lesions (Diorio et al., 1993; Brake et al., 2000), although some stressor-specificity exists in the PFC regulation of neuroendocrine function (Diorio et al., 1993; Herman et al., 2005). Electrical stimulation of ventromedial PFC in the rat is known to increase plasma corticosterone levels (Feldman and Conforti, 1985) and an earlier study in humans reported that ventral frontal (but not cingulate) stimulation increased plasma adrenocorticotrophic hormone levels (Frankel and Jenkins, 1975). A recent imaging study in monkeys confirmed that heightened metabolism in subgenual PFC (analogous to rat IL cortex; Quirk and Beer, 2006) is consistently associated with increased plasma cortisol levels across various behavioral situations (Jahn et al., 2010). In humans, brain-imaging studies have shown sustained activation of ventral frontal regions in response to stress which correlated positively with salivary cortisol levels and heart rate (Wang et al., 2005). Kern et al. (2008) revealed that metabolic activity in the rostromedial (frontopolar) region near the cortical surface was *negatively* correlated with salivary cortisol in response to psychosocial stress. Moreover, human subjects responding to psychosocial stress with significant cortisol increases, show profound *deactivation* in certain limbic regions including anterior cingulate (Pruessner et al., 2008; Dedovic et al., 2009). Interestingly, in human patients which had sustained brain lesions, damage to dorsomedial and/or dorsolateral PFC resulted in substantially higher-than-normal incidence of depression. In contrast, ventromedial PFC damage resulted in a much lower-than-normal incidence, essentially conferring a resistance to depression (Koenigs et al., 2008).

Taken together, the PFC plays a significant and complex role in stress and emotion regulation, in many instances broadly suggestive of a reciprocal (or complementary) interaction between *dorsal* and *ventral* prefrontal systems, with the former exerting an inhibitory modulatory influence over the latter. Notwithstanding, many subregions of PFC may be uniquely involved in modulating specific aspects of stress and emotion processing, such as arousal level, appraisal mechanisms, integrating prior experience, cognitive coping strategies, and affective styles. In the remainder of this chapter we focus on one aspect of such regulation, particularly as it relates to stress and depression: namely the hemispheric asymmetry of prefrontal function.

Lateralization of Stress Regulatory Systems: Autonomic Function

The right hemisphere has been hypothesized to be preferentially associated with activities essential for survival, from basic autonomic and neuroendocrine regulation to vigilance, spatial orientation, and attention to external threats (Wittling, 1997). Geschwind and Galaburda (1987) advanced the concept of right hemisphere conservatism in this regard, and attributed this to the earlier development of the right hemisphere relative to the left. It was also suggested that gross anatomical asymmetries in organs such as the heart and stomach may contribute to a right-sided asymmetry in visceral sensory innervation.

Wittling et al. (1998), employing a lateralized film-presentation technique, showed that the right hemisphere exerts dominance in the sympathetic control of cardiac function, while the left controls parasympathetic function. In studies employing hemispheric inactivation (as a presurgical evaluation in epilepsy patients), the same conclusion was reached of a right sympathetic asymmetry and left parasympathetic bias (Hilz et al., 2001; Yoon et al., 1997). Meadows and Kaplan (1994) examined sympathetically mediated skin conductance responses in patients with left or right brain damage in response to emotional slides. Patients with right-hemisphere damage showed lower skin conductance responses than controls, while left-brain-damaged patients showed higher reactivity than controls, suggesting not only a right-hemisphere dominance for such activation, but that the left exerts tonic inhibitory control over the right, or provides a necessary balance of autonomic function. This is consistent with other findings that left brain damage results in heightened visceral-autonomic response to stimuli (Crucian et al., 2000).

More localized asymmetries in autonomic regulation have implicated frontal brain regions. Critchley et al. (2000) reported that cardiovascular arousal common to exercise and mental stress was associated with increased blood flow in the anterior cingulate and insula of the right hemisphere. In brain-damaged patients Hilz et al. (2006) reported that patients with right-sided damage to the ventromedial PFC showed greater alterations in cardiovascular reactivity than those with comparable damage in the left. Additionally, Tranel et al. (2002) employed a gambling task and reported that anticipatory skin conductance responses were absent in patients with damage to the right (but not left) ventromedial PFC.

Asymmetric Regulation of Neuroendocrine Function

In general the right hemisphere is also believed to be preferentially involved in activation of the HPA axis (Henry, 1997). Wittling and Pflüger (1990) showed that the majority of normal adults show greater increases in salivary cortisol when an aversive film is presented to the right hemisphere than to the left. This asymmetry may be advantageous, as subjects which exhibited the less common reversed asymmetry of cortisol regulation, reported substantially more physical complaints, which may have implications for a variety of somatic or psychosomatic conditions, as well as depression (Wittling and Schweiger, 1993).

Wang et al. (2005) reported that in normal humans cerebral metabolic activation by mental stress is lateralized selectively to the right ventral PFC and right orbitofrontal cortex and this activation is correlated with cortisol increases and perceived stress ratings. Kern et al. (2008) also reported that increases in cortisol induced by a psychosocial stressor were positively associated with increases in glucose metabolism in right prefrontal regions. MacLullich et al. (2006) performed a volumetric analysis of brain regions in two groups of healthy elderly men distinguished by their ability to show cortisol suppression following a low dose of the synthetic glucocorticoid dexamethasone. Such treatments normally suppress the secretion of endogenous cortisol by the activation of glucocorticoid receptors in the brain as a form of negative-feedback regulation. Nonsuppression is suggestive of impaired HPA feedback regulation and a vulnerability to depression, possibly due to chronically elevated levels of circulating glucocorticoids. In this study, nonsuppressors showed significantly reduced volume selectively in the left anterior cingulate cortex relative to suppressors. Indeed, the same selective reduction in left anterior cingulate volume has been reported in unmedicated bipolar-depressed patients (Sassi et al., 2004). Moreover, it has been shown in rats that artificially elevated levels of glucocorticoids lead to reduced volume of the anterior cingulate, particularly in the left hemisphere (Cerqueira et al., 2005). Taken together, such findings suggest that states of high cortisol activity may be associated with relatively greater activity of right prefrontal regions, or reduced functioning of left prefrontal regions.

In keeping with the above pattern, Lueken et al. (2009) recently examined groups of unilateral stroke patients to determine the effects of laterality on HPA axis regulation in both tonic (morning cortisol levels) and phasic conditions (a mentally challenging task). It was found that right hemispheric anterior lesions were most strongly associated with blunting of the phasic or stress-induced increases in cortisol, suggesting an excitatory role of this region in HPA axis activation. Conversely, morning cortisol levels were *increased* relative to controls in left-hemisphere stroke patients, suggesting that the left hemisphere normally exerts a tonic inhibitory control over cortisol secretion. An earlier, smaller study also reported that strokes (especially in PFC) resulted in elevated morning cortisol levels and although the small number of subjects precluded finding a laterality effect, the majority of patients had left-sided strokes (Tchiteya et al., 2003).

Brain-imaging Studies, Depression, and Laterality

Brain-imaging studies have contributed enormously to our understanding of the neuropathological features of the various forms of depression (for comprehensive review, see Savitz and Drevets, 2009). In many of these studies, lateralized abnormalities in prefrontal regions have been observed relative to normal controls.

One such early example showed that unmedicated depressed subjects had significantly lowered metabolism in the left dorsolateral prefrontal region relative to controls (Baxter et al., 1989). Antidepressant treatment increased metabolism in this region which correlated with clinical improvement. Left frontal hypometabolism was then confirmed in bipolar and unipolar depressed patients in resting-state cerebral metabolic rate (Martinot et al., 1990). In this case, the metabolic asymmetry in prefrontal metabolism was reduced by treatment with tricyclic antidepressants, resulting in a more normal balance of prefrontal activity. Others have reported that left prefrontal metabolism *decreased* with clinical remission, although a prefrontal metabolic asymmetry (left < right) was nonetheless present in patients both before and after treatment (Holthoff et al., 2004). Drevets et al. (1997) examined subjects with familial depression, both bipolar and unipolar, and reported a significant reduction in volume of the left subgenual C, associated with an overall reduction in metabolism in this region. Moreover, in a study of elderly subjects, Potter et al. (2007) suggested that white-matter lesions in the most anterior regions of the left PFC may underlie the neurocognitive deficits common in geriatric depression.

Finally, a study by Johnstone et al. (2007) employing a cognitive reappraisal task found that a normal inverse relationship in activity between the left ventral PFC and amygdala was absent in depressed subjects. They proposed that the lack of engagement of left ventral PFC regions to suppress amygdala responses to negative stimuli, in combination with the "counterproductive engagement" of right prefrontal regions, represent key features of the pathophysiology of depression.

Taken together, a number of findings are consistent with left prefrontal hypo-function and possibly a hemispheric imbalance of activity in prefrontal regions favoring the right side, as predisposing features in the development of depression (Figure 25.2).

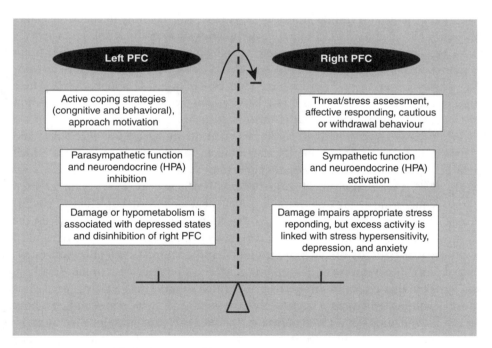

Figure 25.2 Simplified schematic of hemispheric specialization of prefrontal function. In this scenario, deficient left PFC function and/or excessive right PFC function can increase the vulnerability to, or expression of, stress-related psychopathology. The arrow indicates a tonic inhibitory modulation of right PFC function by the left. The seesaw suggests the need to maintain an optimal balance (or interhemispheric integration) between those processes mediated preferentially by the left and right PFC. This model also suggests that those processes generally mediated by more dorsal PFC regions (Figure 25.1) are left-lateralized, whereas more ventrally mediated functions are right-lateralized.

Brain Damage, Laterality, and Depression

For many years, the role of lesion location in the incidence and severity of poststroke depression has sparked interest and controversy. Robinson and Price (1982) reported that left-frontal-lobe infarctions within 2 years of stroke resulted in more frequent and severe depression than comparable damage in right-hemisphere regions or brainstem. Subsequent studies continued to find a strong association between development of depression and left anterior brain injury (even quite small lesions) involving left frontal and associated left basal ganglia circuits (eg. Morris et al., 1996). A meta-analysis of studies in this area concluded that a strong inverse relationship exists between severity of depression and distance of the lesion from the left frontal pole, with no such relationship in patients with right hemisphere stroke (Narushima et al., 2003). In contrast, right hemispheric strokes (particularly in the right frontal operculum) have been associated with a significantly increased incidence of mania, or "undue cheerfulness" (Starkstein et al., 1989). Even in trauma patients with closed head injury, transient depression was most common in patients with left dorsolateral frontal and/or basal ganglia damage only in the acute stages of injury (Jorge et al., 1993). In a long-term study of veterans of the Vietnam War who had sustained damage to the left or right prefrontal region (or other brain regions), no effect of lesion laterality was observed for the vulnerability to developing depression at 15 or 35 years postlesion (Koenigs and Grafman, 2009). These findings suggest that if there is a link between left frontal damage and depression it may only be evident in the early stages after the damage has occurred.

While some heterogeneity of findings remain in studies of lesion location and depression, several methodological and other factors have been identified which may account for much of this variation and guide future studies in this area (Bhogal et al., 2004). A particularly interesting study by Starkstein et al. (1991) again reported more frequent and severe depression in patients with left frontal or left basal ganglia lesions, but only in patients with a *typical* occipital asymmetry. In other words, the asymmetrical regulation of mood/depression by frontal regions is intimately linked with broader patterns of cerebral functional and anatomical lateralization established early in development. As a point of interest, *postmortem* human data have shown that this typical asymmetry in occipital volume (left > right), as well as frontal volume asymmetry (right > left), is present in 80% of individuals, both as adults and prenatally (Weinberger et al., 1982). It thus appears that in many instances compromised left frontal activity may be causally related to an increased vulnerability to developing depression.

Frontal Brain Asymmetry, Electroencephalographic Studies, and Depression

Electroencephalographic (EEG) studies of frontal brain asymmetry have generated considerable interest in the field of affective neuroscience, due largely to the pioneering studies of Davidson and colleagues (see Davidson, 2004). Initial findings were viewed largely within an affective valence framework, where left- and right-biased asymmetries were associated with positive and negative affect, respectively (Tomarken et al., 1992). Left frontal biases have been linked with behavioral activation or approach and right biases with behavioral inhibition or withdrawal (Sutton and Davidson, 1997). Conceptual views of frontal brain asymmetries continue to evolve, in part due to findings that the left PFC appears preferentially involved in processing aspects of anger, which while negative in valence, often evokes approach motivation (Harmon-Jones, 2004; van Honk and Schutter, 2006).

Concerning depression, EEG studies of this kind have been very useful and shown evidence of both left frontal hypoactivity and right frontal hyperactivity. Left frontal hypoactivity has been reported in both previously and currently depressed subjects, suggesting that this asymmetrical pattern is a stable trait marker for the vulnerability to depression (Henriques and Davidson, 1990; Gotlib et al., 1998). Tomarken and Davidson (1994), in a study of normal subjects distinguished by personality/coping styles, concluded that a relative left (greater than right) frontal asymmetry in activity, was associated with an "enhanced self-regulatory style" that reduced the risk of psychopathology.

Schaffer et al. (1983) also demonstrated that depressed subjects exhibited right-sided hyperactivation in frontal (but not parietal) cortex relative to nondepressed subjects. Bruder et al. (1997) found that increased right anterior activation was particularly pronounced in depressed patients who were also anxious. Using an EEG source-localization technique, Pizzagalli et al. (2002) observed that depressed patients exhibited greater right-sided activity in superior and inferior frontal regions than controls. This activity was most evident in severe depression and right frontal activity correlated positively with anxiety. Such findings are consistent with another EEG study by Davidson et al. (2000) who found that the marked increases in anxiety and autonomic reactivity seen in social phobics while anticipating making a public speech is associated with increased right-sided anterior cortical activity.

It therefore appears that while depression may be marked by left frontal hypoactivation alone, a right frontal hyperfunctional (or disinhibited) state may emerge over time in cases of more severe forms of depression, particularly when comorbid with anxiety.

Transcranial Magnetic Stimulation

Another line of evidence highlighting the importance of prefrontal asymmetry in depression comes from studies using repetitive transcranial magnetic stimulation (rTMS). In studies of major depression, the dorsolateral PFC is commonly targeted using either low-frequency rTMS (1 Hz) or higher frequencies in the 5–20 Hz range. The former appears to reduce neural activity in the underlying cortex while the latter stimulates neural activity and metabolism (Padberg and George, 2009). Initial studies reported antidepressant effects of either high-frequency stimulation over the left PFC (Pascual-Leone et al., 1996; George et al., 1997) or low-frequency rTMS of the right PFC (Klein et al., 1999; Menkes et al., 1999). Recent reviews and meta-analyses have confirmed that these approaches are effective, although the effects may not always be dramatic and uncertainty remains regarding optimal stimulation parameters (Mitchell and Loo, 2006; Padberg and George, 2009).

Importantly in the present context, antidepressant effects can be achieved by either enhancing left PFC activity or reducing right PFC activity, presumably restoring a more optimal functional hemispheric balance in prefrontal activity. Importantly, neural systems distal to the stimulation site are affected by rTMS. A recent brain-imaging study examining the effects of low-frequency rTMS over the right dorsolateral PFC found that regional cerebral blood flow was reduced not only in dorsal cortical regions as expected, but also orbitofrontal cortex and the ipsilateral subgenual anterior cingulate (Kito et al., 2008). Moreover, patients showing the best clinical response also showed *increased* blood flow at baseline in left prefrontal regions following rTMS treatments, again suggesting the restoration of a functional hemispheric balance.

Some Relevant Animal Findings on Prefrontal Lateralization

Although it is not the purpose of the present chapter to dwell on animal findings, it is important to note that a growing body of findings in rats is consistent with the general pattern of asymmetrical stress and emotion regulation described above in humans (reviewed in Sullivan, 2004). Of particular relevance are findings that the right ventromedial PFC (IL cortex) preferentially activates neuroendocrine, autonomic, and behavioral systems in times of stress (Sullivan and Gratton, 1999, 2002a). Also the mesocortical dopamine system plays an important adaptive role in this region by preventing excessive reactivity of these stress regulatory systems, protecting against stress-related pathologies (Sullivan and Szechtman, 1995; Sullivan and Dufresne, 2006). It is also now known that chronic stress or artificially elevated glucocorticoid levels affect neural plasticity and cytogenesis in prelimbic and IL cortex in a hemisphere-dependent manner, often reversing normal asymmetries (Czéh et al., 2007, 2008).

An important theme throughout this discussion is the notion of an optimal balance of activity, particularly between the left and right PFC. From the extensive early animal studies by Denenberg (1981) and Denenberg et al. (1986), it was confirmed not only that right cortical mechanisms mediate numerous forms of emotional behavior and aversion, but the left cortex is essential in modulating this expression by interhemispheric inhibition. Such functional integration between the hemispheres also appears to be clinically relevant in achieving an optimal balance between various forms of behavioral and neuroendocrine activation/inhibition, withdrawal/approach, and sympathetic/parasympathetic functions; in other words, optimal stress and emotion regulation and good mental health.

Denenberg (1981) also demonstrated that such patterns of right cortical lateralization are dependent upon early-life stimulation. This principle was recently demonstrated specifically in the IL cortex. In rats that had received early-life han-dling stimulation, unilateral dopaminergic receptor blockade in the right (but not left) IL cortex prior to stress caused an exaggerated HPA stress response, whereas in nonhandled rats this effect was not lateralized (Sullivan and Dufresne, 2006). As well, following repeated mild restraint stress as adults, early-handled rats showed a rightward shift in dopamine metabolism in the IL cortex associated with adaptation or habituation to mild stress, which nonhandled rats did not show. If such right-biased asymmetries represent an optimal pattern of stress regulation, it is also the case that adverse early-life events or stressful challenges can lead to altered and presumably less adaptive patterns of lateralized brain function, accounting for much of the individual variation on such measures in both rats and humans (Davidson, 1994; Zhang et al., 2005).

The Question of Gender

As just noted, despite the general (right-biased) pattern of stress and emotion regu-lation described herein, and its possible implications for depression, there remains considerable individual variation in the patterns of such functional asymmetries. In addition to the many genetic, developmental, and later epigenetic influences that shape individual brain asymmetries, sex/gender may be a particularly important determinant.

In terms of emotion processing, some imaging studies have suggested that women tend to be less strongly lateralized in regional brain activations than men (Wager et al., 2003). Others have shown distinctly right-sided regional activations in men, but left-sided activations in women (see Cahill et al., 2004; Cahill, 2006; Gasbarri et al., 2007). EEG studies of affective processing have also shown gender differences in the nature of frontal brain asymmetries (Davidson et al., 1976; Kline et al., 1998; Baving et al., 2002). The pronounced deficits in social and emotional functioning in patients with right ventromedial PFC damage have been found to hold true only in men, as left-sided damage appears to produce similar deficits in women (Tranel et al., 2005). Moreover, a magnetic resonance imaging study has shown that the volume of the right ventromedial PFC is predictive of a family history of psycho-pathology, but the direction of this association is opposite in males and females (Sharma et al., 2003). In response to psychological stress, Wang et al. (2007) reported that only men showed a right-biased increase in prefrontal blood flow (which cor-related with cortisol increases), while women's pattern of activation was distinctly different. In fact, in a study by Buchanan et al. (2010), damage to the medial PFC has been reported to increase the cortisol response to a social stressor in men, but reduce it in women (most of these patients had bilateral medial PFC damage, pre-cluding the finding of lateralized gender differences on this measure). Additionally, the interhemispheric regulation of blood pressure in emotionally laden situations reportedly shows clear sex differences (Wittling, 1990).

Such examples indicate the urgent need for careful examination of gender differ-ences, not only where functional asymmetries are specifically examined, but in the study of stress, emotion, and depression generally. Many of the human studies cited throughout this chapter, particularly those dealing with depression, certainly involved female subjects/patients and nonetheless fit the general pattern of (right-biased) asymmetrical brain function. Yet others clearly do not. It is tempting to speculate, based on the above examples, that at least some of the hemispheric specializations described here may be more consistently applicable to men than women. The issue is an important one. If certain patterns of functional asymmetry are advantageous in stress regulation or confer a resistance to depression, then fundamental sex differences in the nature of functional brain asymmetry may be significantly related to the unusually high incidence of depression and anxiety seen in women (Linzer et al., 1996; Kendler et al., 2001). It will be important to dissect more accurately the ways in which functional lateralization differs in men and women and to study how such differences may be relevant to stress-related psychopathology.

Summary

The present chapter briefly summarizes findings of the distinct but complementary roles of ventral and dorsal prefrontal systems in stress and emotion regulation, the former being more activational in nature and the latter more modulatory. Superimposed on this basic organization, a similar functional interaction is suggested to exist between the two hemispheres, with right prefrontal regions being essentially activational in nature, while the left plays a more inhibitory, modulatory role to complement or balance right brain stress processing strategies. Depression is associated with deficits in dorsal prefrontal systems or hyperfunction of ventral PFC regions. Similarly, depression is linked to left prefrontal deficits or right prefrontal hyperfunction. While much data support this general framework, much individual variation exists, particularly in the nature of functional brain asymmetry. It is suggested that this pattern of lateralized stress and emotion regulation, while influenced by many factors, may be more typical of males than females. It is urged that future studies in the area of stress and/or depression, particularly those incorporating brain asymmetry, will systematically examine sex/gender differences in this regard. The results will not only better elucidate the role of functional asymmetries in stress and depression, but may further our understanding of sex differences in the incidence, neuropathology, and potential treatments of depressive disorders.

References

Aihara, M., Ida, I., Yuuki, N., Oshima, A., Kumano, H., Takahashi, K., Fukuda, M., Oriuchi, N., Endo, K., Matsuda, H., & Mikuni, M. (2007). HPA axis dysfunction in unmedicated major depressive disorder and its normalization by pharmacotherapy correlates with alteration of neural activity in prefrontal cortex and limbic/paralimbic regions. *Psychiatry Research, 155*(3), 245–256.

Arnsten, A. F. (2009). Stress signalling pathways that impair prefrontal cortex structure and function. *Nature Reviews Neuroscience, 10*(6), 410–422.

Baving, L., Laucht, M., & Schmidt, M. H. (2002). Frontal brain activation in anxious school children. *Journal of Child Psychology and Psychiatry, 43*(2), 265–274.

Baxter, Jr., L. R., Schwartz, J. M., Phelps, M. E., Mazziotta, J. C., Guze, B. H., Selin, C. E., Gerner, R. H., & Sumida, R. M. (1989). Reduction of prefrontal cortex glucose metabolism common to three types of depression. *Archives of General Psychiatry, 46*(3), 243–250.

Bhogal, S. K., Teasell, R., Foley, N., & Speechley, M. (2004). Lesion location and poststroke depression: systematic review of the methodological limitations in the literature. *Stroke, 35*(3), 794–802.

Biver, F., Goldman, S., Delvenne, V., Luxen, A., De, M., V, Hubain, P., Mendlewicz, J., & Lotstra, F. (1994). Frontal and parietal metabolic disturbances in unipolar depression. *Biological Psychiatry, 36*(6), 381–388.

Brake, W. G., Flores, G., Francis, D., Meaney, M. J., Srivastava, L. K., & Gratton, A. (2000). Enhanced nucleus accumbens dopamine and plasma corticosterone stress responses in adult rats with neonatal excitotoxic lesions to the medial prefrontal cortex. *Neuroscience, 96*(4), 687–695.

Brody, A. L., Barsom, M. W., Bota, R. G., & Saxena, S. (2001). Prefrontal-subcortical and limbic circuit mediation of major depressive disorder. *Seminars in Clinical Neuropsychiatry, 6*(2), 102–112.

Bruder, G. E., Fong, R., Tenke, C. E., Leite, P., Towey, J. P., Stewart, J. E., McGrath, P. J., & Quitkin, F. M. (1997). Regional brain asymmetries in major depression with or without an anxiety disorder: a quantitative electroencephalographic study. *Biological Psychiatry, 41*(9), 939–948.

Buchanan, T. W., Driscoll, D., Mowrer, S. M., Sollers, J. J., III, Thayer, J. F., Kirschbaum, C., & Tranel, D. (2010). Medial prefrontal cortex damage affects physiological and psychological stress responses differently in men and women. *Psychoneuroendocrinology, 35*(1), 56–66.

Buchsbaum, M. S., Wu, J., Siegel, B. V., Hackett, E., Trenary, M., Abel, L., & Reynolds, C. (1997). Effect of sertraline on regional metabolic rate in patients with affective disorder. *Biological Psychiatry, 41*(1), 15–22.

Burke, H. M., Davis, M. C., Otte, C., & Mohr, D. C. (2005). Depression and cortisol responses to psychological stress: a meta-analysis. *Psychoneuroendocrinology, 30*(9), 846–856.

Cahill, L. (2006). Why sex matters for neuroscience. *Nature Reviews Neuroscience, 7*(6), 477–484.

Cahill, L., Uncapher, M., Kilpatrick, L., Alkire, M. T., & Turner, J. (2004). Sex-related hemispheric lateralization of amygdala function in emotionally influenced memory: an FMRI investigation. *Learning & Memory, 11*(3), 261–266.

Cechetto, D. F., & Saper, C. B. (1990). Role of the cerebral cortex in autonomic function. In A. D. Loewy, & K. M. Spyer (Eds.), *Central regulation of autonomic functions* (pp. 208–223). Oxford: Oxford University Press.

Cerqueira, J. J., Catania, C., Sotiropoulos, I., Schubert, M., Kalisch, R., Almeida, O. F., Auer, D. P., & Sousa, N. (2005). Corticosteroid status influences the volume of the rat cingulate cortex—a magnetic resonance imaging study. *Journal of Psychiatric Research, 39*(5), 451–60.

Critchley, H. D., Corfield, D. R., Chandler, M. P., Mathias, C. J., & Dolan, R. J. (2000). Cerebral correlates of autonomic cardiovascular arousal: a functional neuroimaging investigation in humans. *Journal of Physiology, 523*(1), 259–270.

Crucian, G. P., Hughes, J. D., Barrett, A. M., Williamson, D. J., Bauer, R. M., Bowers, D., & Heilman, K. M. (2000). Emotional and physiological responses to false feedback. *Cortex, 36*(5), 623–647.

Czeh, B., Muller-Keuker, J. I., Rygula, R., Abumaria, N., Hiemke, C., Domenici, E., & Fuchs, E. (2007). Chronic social stress inhibits cell proliferation in the adult medial prefrontal cortex: hemispheric asymmetry and reversal by fluoxetine treatment. *Neuropsychopharmacology, 32*(7), 1490–1503.

Czeh, B., Perez-Cruz, C., Fuchs, E., & Flugge, G. (2008). Chronic stress-induced cellular changes in the medial prefrontal cortex and their potential clinical implications: does hemisphere location matter? *Behavioral Brain Research, 190*(1), 1–13.

Damasio, A. R., Tranel, D., & Damasio, H. (1990). Individuals with sociopathic behavior caused by frontal damage fail to respond autonomically to social stimuli. *Behavioral Brain Research, 41*(2), 81–94.

Davidson, R. J. (1994). Asymmetric brain-function, affective style, and psychopathology—the role of early experience and plasticity. *Development and Psychopathology, 6*(4), 741–758.

Davidson, R. J. (2004). What does the prefrontal cortex do in affect: perspectives on frontal EEG asymmetry research. *Biological Psychology, 67*(1–2), 219–233.

Davidson, R. J., & Irwin, W. (1999). The functional neuroanatomy of emotion and affective style. *Trends in Cognitive Science, 3*(1), 11–21.

Davidson, R. J., Schwartz, G. E., Pugash, E., & Bromfield, E. (1976). Sex differences in patterns of EEG asymmetry. *Biological Psychology, 4*(2), 119–138.

Davidson, R. J., Marshall, J. R., Tomarken, A. J., & Henriques, J. B. (2000). While a phobic waits: regional brain electrical and autonomic activity in social phobics during anticipation of public speaking. *Biological Psychiatry, 47*(2), 85–95.

Dedovic, K., Duchesne, A., Andrews, J., Engert, V., & Pruessner, J. C. (2009). The brain and the stress axis: the neural correlates of cortisol regulation in response to stress. *Neuroimage, 47*(3), 864–871.

Denenberg, V. H. (1981). Hemispheric laterality in animals and the effects of early experience. *Behavioral and Brain Sciences, 4*(1), 1–21.

Denenberg, V. H., Gall, J. S., Berrebi, A., & Yutzey, D. A. (1986). Callosal mediation of cortical inhibition in the lateralized rat brain. *Brain Research, 397*(2), 327–332.

Diorio, D., Viau, V., & Meaney, M. J. (1993). The role of the medial prefrontal cortex (cingulate gyrus) in the regulation of hypothalamic-pituitary-adrenal responses to stress. *Journal of Neuroscience, 13*(9), 3839–3847.

Drevets, W. C., Price, J. L., Simpson, Jr., J. R., Todd, R. D., Reich, T., Vannier, M., & Raichle, M. E. (1997). Subgenual prefrontal cortex abnormalities in mood disorders. *Nature, 386*(6627), 824–827.

Drevets, W. C., Bogers, W., & Raichle, M. E. (2002). Functional anatomical correlates of antidepressant drug treatment assessed using PET measures of regional glucose metabolism. *European Neuropsychopharmacology, 12*(6), 527–544.

Feldman, S., & Conforti, N. (1985). Modifications of adrenocortical responses following frontal cortex simulation in rats with hypothalamic deafferentations and medial forebrain bundle lesions. *Neuroscience, 15*(4), 1045–1047.

Frankel, R. J., & Jenkins, J. S. (1975). Pituitary hormone response to brain stimulation in man. *Journal of Endocrinology, 67*(1), 113–117.

Frysztak, R. J., & Neafsey, E. J. (1991). The effect of medial frontal cortex lesions on respiration, freezing, and ultrasonic vocalizations during conditioned emotional responses in rats. *Cerebral Cortex, 1*(5), 418–425.

Frysztak, R. J., & Neafsey, E. J. (1994). The effect of medial frontal cortex lesions on cardiovascular conditioned emotional responses in the rat. *Brain Research*, *643*(1–2), 181–193.

Gasbarri, A., Arnone, B., Pompili, A., Pacitti, F., Pacitti, C., & Cahill, L. (2007). Sex-related hemispheric lateralization of electrical potentials evoked by arousing negative stimuli. *Brain Research*, *1138*, 178–186.

George, M. S., Wassermann, E. M., Kimbrell, T. A., Little, J. T., Williams, W. E., Danielson, A. L., Greenberg, B. D., Hallett, M., & Post, R. M. (1997). Mood improvement following daily left prefrontal repetitive transcranial magnetic stimulation in patients with depression: a placebo-controlled crossover trial. *American Journal of Psychiatry*, *154*(12), 1752–1756.

Geschwind, N., & Galaburda, A. M. (1987). *Cerebral lateralization: Biological mechanisms, associations, and pathology*. Cambridge, MA: The MIT Press.

Gotlib, I. H., Ranganath, C., & Rosenfeld, J. P. (1998). Frontal EEG alpha asymmetry, depression, and cognitive functioning. *Cognition & Emotion*, *12*(3), 449–478.

Harmon-Jones, E. (2004). Contributions from research on anger and cognitive dissonance to understanding the motivational functions of asymmetrical frontal brain activity. *Biological Psychology*, *67*(1–2), 51–76.

Henriques, J. B., & Davidson, R. J. (1990). Regional brain electrical asymmetries discriminate between previously depressed and healthy control subjects. *Journal of Abnormal Psychology*, *99*(1), 22–31.

Henry, J. P. (1997). Psychological and physiological responses to stress: the right hemisphere and the hypothalamo-pituitary-adrenal axis, an inquiry into problems of human bonding. *Acta Physiologica Scandinavica Supplement*, *640*, 10–25.

Herbert, J., Goodyer, I. M., Grossman, A. B., Hastings, M. H., de Kloet, E. R., Lightman, S. L., Lupien, S. J., Roozendaal, B., & Seckl, J. R. (2006). Do corticosteroids damage the brain? *Journal of Neuroendocrinology*, *18*(6), 393–411.

Herman, J. P., Ostrander, M. M., Mueller, N. K., & Figueiredo, H. (2005). Limbic system mechanisms of stress regulation: hypothalamo-pituitary-adrenocortical axis. *Progress in Neuro-psychopharmacology & Biological Psychiatry*, *29*(8), 1201–1213.

Hilz, M. J., Dutsch, M., Perrine, K., Nelson, P. K., Rauhut, U., & Devinsky, O. (2001). Hemispheric influence on autonomic modulation and baroreflex sensitivity. *Annals of Neurology*, *49*(5), 575–584.

Hilz, M. J., Devinsky, O., Szczepanska, H., Borod, J. C., Marthol, H., & Tutaj, M. (2006). Right ventromedial prefrontal lesions result in paradoxical cardiovascular activation with emotional stimuli. *Brain*, *129*(12), 3343–3355.

Holsboer, F. (2001). Stress, hypercortisolism and corticosteroid receptors in depression: implications for therapy. *Journal of Affective Disorders*, *62*(1–2), 77–91.

Holson, R. R. (1986). Mesial prefrontal cortical lesions and timidity in rats. I. Reactivity to aversive stimuli. *Physiology and Behavior*, *37*(2), 221–230.

Holthoff, V. A., Beuthien-Baumann, B., Zundorf, G., Triemer, A., Ludecke, S., Winiecki, P., Koch, R., Fuchtner, F., & Herholz, K. (2004). Changes in brain metabolism associated with remission in unipolar major depression. *Acta Physiologica Scandinavica*, *110*(3), 184–194.

Jahn, A. L., Fox, A. S., Abercrombie, H. C., Shelton, S. E., Oakes, T. R., Davidson, R. J., & Kalin, N. H. (2010). Subgenual prefrontal cortex activity predicts individual differences in hypothalamic-pituitary-adrenal activity across different contexts. *Biological Psychiatry*, *67*(2), 175–181.

Johnstone, T., van Reekum, C. M., Urry, H. L., Kalin, N. H., & Davidson, R. J. (2007). Failure to regulate: counterproductive recruitment of top-down prefrontal-subcortical circuitry in major depression. *Journal of Neuroscience, 27*(33), 8877–8884.

Jorge, R. E., Robinson, R. G., Arndt, S. V., Starkstein, S. E., Forrester, A. W., & Geisler, F. (1993). Depression following traumatic brain injury: a 1 year longitudinal study. *Journal of Affective Disorders, 27*(4), 233–243.

Kendler, K. S., Thornton, L. M., & Prescott, C. A. (2001). Gender differences in the rates of exposure to stressful life events and sensitivity to their depressogenic effects. *American Journal of Psychiatry, 158*(4), 587–593.

Kern, S., Oakes, T. R., Stone, C. K., McAuliff, E. M., Kirschbaum, C., & Davidson, R. J. (2008). Glucose metabolic changes in the prefrontal cortex are associated with HPA axis response to a psychosocial stressor. *Psychoneuroendocrinology, 33*(4), 517–529.

Kito, S., Fujita, K., & Koga, Y. (2008). Regional cerebral blood flow changes after low-frequency transcranial magnetic stimulation of the right dorsolateral prefrontal cortex in treatment-resistant depression. *Neuropsychobiology, 58*(1), 29–36.

Klein, E., Kreinin, I., Chistyakov, A., Koren, D., Mecz, L., Marmur, S., Ben-Shachar, D., & Feinsod, M. (1999). Therapeutic efficacy of right prefrontal slow repetitive transcranial magnetic stimulation in major depression: a double-blind controlled study. *Archives of General Psychiatry, 56*(4), 315–320.

Kline, J. P., Allen, J. J., & Schwartz, G. E. (1998). Is left frontal brain activation in defensiveness gender specific? *Journal of Abnormal Psychology, 107*(1), 149–153.

Koenigs, M., & Grafman, J. (2009). Prefrontal asymmetry in depression? The long-term effect of unilateral brain lesions. *Neuroscience Letters, 459*(2), 88–90.

Koenigs, M., Huey, E. D., Calamia, M., Raymont, V., Tranel, D., & Grafman, J. (2008). Distinct regions of prefrontal cortex mediate resistance and vulnerability to depression. *Journal of Neuroscience, 28*(47), 12341–12348.

Lacroix, L., Spinelli, S., Heidbreder, C. A., & Feldon, J. (2000). Differential role of the medial and lateral prefrontal cortices in fear and anxiety. *Behavioral Neuroscience, 114*(6), 1119–1130.

Linzer, M., Spitzer, R., Kroenke, K., Williams, J. B., Hahn, S., Brody, D., & deGruy, F. (1996). Gender, quality of life, and mental disorders in primary care: results from the PRIME-MD 1000 study. *American Journal of Medicine, 101*(5), 526–533.

Lueken, U., Leisse, M., Mattes, K., Naumann, D., Wittling, W., & Schweiger, E. (2009). Altered tonic and phasic cortisol secretion following unilateral stroke. *Psychoneuroendocrinology, 34*(3), 402–412.

Lupien, S. J., McEwen, B. S., Gunnar, M. R., & Heim, C. (2009). Effects of stress throughout the lifespan on the brain, behaviour and cognition. *Nature Reviews Neuroscience, 10*(6), 434–445.

MacLullich, A. M., Ferguson, K. J., Wardlaw, J. M., Starr, J. M., Deary, I. J., & Seckl, J. R. (2006). Smaller left anterior cingulate cortex volumes are associated with impaired hypothalamic-pituitary-adrenal axis regulation in healthy elderly men. *Journal of Clinical Endocrinology and Metabolism, 91*(4), 1591–1594.

Martinot, J. L., Hardy, P., Feline, A., Huret, J. D., Mazoyer, B., Attar-Levy, D., Pappata, S., & Syrota, A. (1990). Left prefrontal glucose hypometabolism in the depressed state: a confirmation. *American Journal of Psychiatry, 147*(10), 1313–1317.

Mayberg, H. S., Brannan, S. K., Tekell, J. L., Silva, J. A., Mahurin, R. K., McGinnis, S., & Jerabek, P. A. (2000). Regional metabolic effects of fluoxetine in major depression: serial changes and relationship to clinical response. *Biological Psychiatry, 48*(8), 830–843.

Meadows, M. E., & Kaplan, R. F. (1994). Dissociation of autonomic and subjective responses to emotional slides in right hemisphere damaged patients. *Neuropsychologia, 32*(7), 847–856.

Menkes, D. L., Bodnar, P., Ballesteros, R. A., & Swenson, M. R. (1999). Right frontal lobe slow frequency repetitive transcranial magnetic stimulation (SF r-TMS) is an effective treatment for depression: a case-control pilot study of safety and efficacy. *Journal of Neurology, Neurosurgery, and Psychiatry, 67*(1), 113–115.

Mitchell, P. B., & Loo, C. K. (2006). Transcranial magnetic stimulation for depression. *Australian and New Zealand Journal of Psychiatry, 40*(5), 406–413.

Morgan, M. A., & LeDoux, J. E. (1995). Differential contribution of dorsal and ventral medial prefrontal cortex to the acquisition and extinction of conditioned fear in rats. *Behavioral Neuroscience, 109*(4), 681–688.

Morris, P. L., Robinson, R. G., Raphael, B., & Hopwood, M. J. (1996). Lesion location and poststroke depression. *Journal of Neuropsychiatry and Clinical Neuroscience, 8*(4), 399–403.

Narushima, K., Kosier, J. T., & Robinson, R. G. (2003). A reappraisal of poststroke depression, intra- and inter-hemispheric lesion location using meta-analysis. *Journal of Neuropsychiatry and Clinical Neuroscience, 15*(4), 422–430.

Padberg, F., & George, M. S. (2009). Repetitive transcranial magnetic stimulation of the prefrontal cortex in depression. *Experimental Neurology, 219*(1), 2–13.

Pascual-Leone, A., Rubio, B., Pallardo, F., & Catala, M. D. (1996). Rapid-rate transcranial magnetic stimulation of left dorsolateral prefrontal cortex in drug-resistant depression. *Lancet, 348*(9022), 233–237.

Phillips, M. L., Drevets, W. C., Rauch, S. L., & Lane, R. (2003a). Neurobiology of emotion perception II: Implications for major psychiatric disorders. *Biological Psychiatry, 54*(5), 515–528.

Phillips, M. L., Drevets, W. C., Rauch, S. L., & Lane, R. (2003b). Neurobiology of emotion perception I: The neural basis of normal emotion perception. *Biological Psychiatry, 54*(5), 504–514.

Phillips, M. L., Ladouceur, C. D., & Drevets, W. C. (2008). A neural model of voluntary and automatic emotion regulation: implications for understanding the pathophysiology and neurodevelopment of bipolar disorder. *Molecular Psychiatry, 13*(9), 829, 833–857.

Pizzagalli, D. A., Nitschke, J. B., Oakes, T. R., Hendrick, A. M., Horras, K. A., Larson, C. L., Abercrombie, H. C., Schaefer, S. M., Koger, J. V., Benca, R. M., Pascual-Marqui, R. D., & Davidson, R. J. (2002). Brain electrical tomography in depression: the importance of symptom severity, anxiety, and melancholic features. *Biological Psychiatry, 52*(2), 73–85.

Potter, G. G., Blackwell, A. D., McQuoid, D. R., Payne, M. E., Steffens, D. C., Sahakian, B. J., Welsh-Bohmer, K. A., & Krishnan, K. R. (2007). Prefrontal white matter lesions and prefrontal task impersistence in depressed and nondepressed elders. *Neuropsychopharmacology, 32*(10), 2135–2142.

Powell, D. A., Watson, K., & Maxwell, B. (1994). Involvement of subdivisions of the medial prefrontal cortex in learned cardiac adjustments in rabbits. *Behavioral Neuroscience, 108*(2), 294–307.

Pruessner, J. C., Dedovic, K., Khalili-Mahani, N., Engert, V., Pruessner, M., Buss, C., Renwick, R., Dagher, A., Meaney, M. J., & Lupien, S. (2008). Deactivation of the limbic system during acute psychosocial stress: evidence from positron emission tomography and functional magnetic resonance imaging studies. *Biological Psychiatry, 63*(2), 234–240.

Quirk, G. J., & Beer, J. S. (2006). Prefrontal involvement in the regulation of emotion: convergence of rat and human studies. *Current Opinions in Neurobiology, 16*(6), 723–727.

Robinson, R. G., & Price, T. R. (1982). Post-stroke depressive disorders: a follow-up study of 103 patients. *Stroke, 13*(5), 635–641.

Sanchez, M. M., Young, L. J., Plotsky, P. M., & Insel, T. R. (2000). Distribution of corticosteroid receptors in the rhesus brain: relative absence of glucocorticoid receptors in the hippocampal formation. *Journal of Neuroscience, 20*(12), 4657–4668.

Sassi, R. B., Brambilla, P., Hatch, J. P., Nicoletti, M. A., Mallinger, A. G., Frank, E., Kupfer, D. J., Keshavan, M. S., & Soares, J. C. (2004). Reduced left anterior cingulate volumes in untreated bipolar patients. *Biological Psychiatry, 56*(7), 467–475.

Savitz, J., & Drevets, W. C. (2009). Bipolar and major depressive disorder: neuroimaging the developmental-degenerative divide. *Neuroscience and Biobehavioral Reviews, 33*(5), 699–771.

Schaffer, C. E., Davidson, R. J., & Saron, C. (1983). Frontal and parietal electroencephalogram asymmetry in depressed and nondepressed subjects. *Biological Psychiatry, 18*(7), 753–762.

Sharma, V., Menon, R., Carr, T. J., Densmore, M., Mazmanian, D., & Williamson, P. C. (2003). An MRI study of subgenual prefrontal cortex in patients with familial and non-familial bipolar I disorder. *Journal of Affective Disorders, 77*(2), 167–171.

Starkstein, S. E., Robinson, R. G., Honig, M. A., Parikh, R. M., Joselyn, J., & Price, T. R. (1989). Mood changes after right-hemisphere lesions. *British Journal of Psychiatry, 155*, 79–85.

Starkstein, S. E., Bryer, J. B., Berthier, M. L., Cohen, B., Price, T. R., & Robinson, R. G. (1991). Depression after stroke: the importance of cerebral hemisphere asymmetries. *Journal of Neuropsychiatry and Clinical Neuroscience, 3*(3), 276–285.

Sullivan, R. M. (2004). Hemispheric asymmetry in stress processing in rat prefrontal cortex and the role of mesocortical dopamine. *Stress, 7*(2), 131–143.

Sullivan, R. M., & Szechtman, H. (1995). Asymmetrical influence of mesocortical dopamine depletion on stress ulcer development and subcortical dopamine systems in rats: implications for psychopathology. *Neuroscience, 65*(3), 757–766.

Sullivan, R. M., & Gratton, A. (1999). Lateralized effects of medial prefrontal cortex lesions on neuroendocrine and autonomic stress responses in rats. *Journal of Neuroscience, 19*(7), 2834–2840.

Sullivan, R. M., & Gratton, A. (2002a). Prefrontal cortical regulation of hypothalamic-pituitary-adrenal function in the rat and implications for psychopathology: side matters. *Psychoneuroendocrinology, 27*(1–2), 99–114.

Sullivan, R. M., & Gratton, A. (2002b). Behavioral effects of excitotoxic lesions of ventral medial prefrontal cortex in the rat are hemisphere-dependent. *Brain Research, 927*(1), 69–79.

Sullivan, R. M., & Dufresne, M. M. (2006). Mesocortical dopamine and HPA axis regulation: role of laterality and early environment. *Brain Research, 1076*(1), 49–59.

Sutton, S. K., & Davidson, R. J. (1997). Prefrontal brain asymmetry: A biological substrate of the behavioral approach and inhibition systems. *Psychological Science, 8*(3), 204–210.

Tchiteya, B. M., Lecours, A. R., Elie, R., & Lupien, S. J. (2003). Impact of a unilateral brain lesion on cortisol secretion and emotional state: anterior/posterior dissociation in humans. *Psychoneuroendocrinology, 28*(5), 674–686.

Tomarken, A. J., & Davidson, R. J. (1994). Frontal brain activation in repressors and nonre-pressors. *Journal of Abnormal Psychology, 103*(2), 339–349.

Tomarken, A. J., Davidson, R. J., Wheeler, R. E., & Doss, R. C. (1992). Individual differences in anterior brain asymmetry and fundamental dimensions of emotion. *Journal of Personality and Social Psychology, 62*(4), 676–687.

Tranel, D., Bechara, A., & Denburg, N. L. (2002). Asymmetric functional roles of right and left ventromedial prefrontal cortices in social conduct, decision-making, and emotional processing. *Cortex, 38*(4), 589–612.

Tranel, D., Damasio, H., Denburg, N. L., & Bechara, A. (2005). Does gender play a role in functional asymmetry of ventromedial prefrontal cortex?. *Brain, 128*(12), 2872–2881.

van Honk. J., & Schutter, D. J. (2006). From affective valence to motivational direction: the frontal asymmetry of emotion revised. *Psychological Science, 17*(11), 963–965.

Wager, T. D., Phan, K. L., Liberzon, I., & Taylor, S. F. (2003). Valence, gender, and lateraliza-tion of functional brain anatomy in emotion: a meta-analysis of findings from neuroimaging. *Neuroimage, 19*(3), 513–531.

Wang, J., Rao, H., Wetmore, G. S., Furlan, P. M., Korczykowski, M., Dinges, D. F., & Detre, J. A. (2005). Perfusion functional MRI reveals cerebral blood flow pattern under psy-chological stress. *Proceedings of the National Academy of Sciences USA, 102*(49), 17804–17809.

Wang, J., Korczykowski, M., Rao, H., Fan, Y., Pluta, J., Gur, R. C., McEwen, B. S., & Detre, J. A. (2007). Gender difference in neural response to psychological stress. *Social Cognitive & Affective Neuroscience, 2*(3), 227–239.

Weinberger, D. R., Luchins, D. J., Morihisa, J., & Wyatt, R. J. (1982). Asymmetrical volumes of the right and left frontal and occipital regions of the human brain. *Annals of Neurology, 11*(1), 97–100.

Wittling, W. (1990). Psychophysiological correlates of human brain asymmetry: blood pressure changes during lateralized presentation of an emotionally laden film. *Neuropsychologia, 28*(5), 457–470.

Wittling, W. (1997). The right hemisphere and the human stress response. *Acta Physiologica Scandinavica Supplement, 640*, 55–59.

Wittling, W., & Pflüger, M. (1990). Neuroendocrine hemisphere asymmetries: salivary cortisol secretion during lateralized viewing of emotion-related and neutral films. *Brain and Cognition, 14*(2), 243–265.

Wittling, W., & Schweiger, E. (1993). Alterations of neuroendocrine brain asymmetry: a neural risk factor affecting physical health. *Neuropsychobiology, 28*(1–2), 25–29.

Wittling, W., Block, A., Genzel, S., & Schweiger, E. (1998). Hemisphere asymmetry in para-sympathetic control of the heart. *Neuropsychologia, 36*(5), 461–468.

Yoon, B. W., Morillo, C. A., Cechetto, D. F., & Hachinski, V. (1997). Cerebral hemispheric lateralization in cardiac autonomic control. *Archives in Neurology, 54*(6), 741–744.

Zhang, T. Y., Chretien, P., Meaney, M. J., & Gratton, A. (2005). Influence of naturally occur-ring variations in maternal care on prepulse inhibition of acoustic startle and the medial prefrontal cortical dopamine response to stress in adult rats. *Journal of Neuroscience, 25*(6), 1493–1502.

Part V

Stress, Coping, Predisposition, and Sex Differences

26

Chronic Stress and Sex Differences on Cognition
Animal Studies
Victoria N. Luine

Introduction

Research during the past 20 years has documented the debilitating effects of chronic stress on physiological function and described stress-related changes in systems ranging from neural cells in culture to laboratory rodents, subhuman primates, and humans. While there is general agreement on the adaptive properties of acute stress versus the deleterious nature of chronic stress (Selye, 1976), it is remarkable to note that the vast majority of studies were conducted in only males of these species, especially in nonhuman animals. Thus, it is only quite recently that the response of females to stress has been investigated, especially in relation to cognitive function. Surprising to some researchers, but not to most neuroendocrinologists, responses in females can be dramatically different than in males, especially in the cognitive realm (Luine et al., 2007; Luine, 2008). These sexually differentiated responses to stress appear early in development, become somewhat larger through adolescence and adulthood, and then abate at advanced ages.

The importance of determining the nature and extent of sex differences in stress responses is that such differences may provide information for understanding why some stress-related diseases have different incidence rates between the sexes. For example, depression and posttraumatic stress disorder are more prevalent in females than males, and stress often precipitates drug and alcohol use, two dependencies that show sex-related differences. Finally, stress can be an antecedent to some diseases such as schizophrenic episodes. While there is no sex difference in schizophrenic incidence, symptoms and severity are differentiated by sex (for further discussion and pertinent references on these issues, see Becker et al., 2008). Thus,

The Handbook of Stress: Neuropsychological Effects on the Brain, First Edition.
Edited by Cheryl D. Conrad.

it can be hypothesized that better therapies for some psychological disorders might be dependent on different treatment courses for each sex depending on the nature of stress-induced changes. This review describes current knowledge about sex differences in cognitive responses to chronic stress in animal models over the life span and possible neurobiological and psychological bases for the responses.

Chronic Stress: Daily Restraint Model

A variety of stressors have been applied to rats and mice in order to assess the physiological consequences of stress. As previously discussed in Luine (2002), stressors have two main categories: systemic and processive (Anisman et al., 2001; see also Chapters 1 and 2 in this volume). Systemic stressors constitute an immediate physiological threat to homeostasis and include immunologic challenge, hemorrhage, excess alcohol, ether, and hypoglycemia. These stresses are relayed to the paraventricular nucleus via brainstem monoaminergic projections. Processive stressors, used in more recent experiments, require integration at higher brain centers before relay to the paraventricular nucleus through limbic forebrain circuits in prefrontal cortex (PFC), hippocampus, and amygdala (Herman and Cullinan, 1997) and are further delineated as either psychogenic, which are mainly psychological and include exposure to a predator or a novel open field, or neurogenic, which are mainly physical but have psychological impact like foot shock, cold swim, and immobilization. Some processive stressors, like restraint stress (see below for description) and overcrowding have elements of both types of processive stressor. For example, because subjects are trapped, restraint has a psychological character, but it is also physical because the response/defensive style of the subject is limited physically (McIntyre et al., 1999). Since restraint combines both processive stressor types, it might result in widespread morphological and neurochemical effects in brain, and ultimately to behavioral changes. Thus, restraint stress was adopted by a number of laboratories to investigate stress effects. While restraint stress has been shown to cause numerous behavioral and neural changes, it remains unclear whether it, or other stressors, best models human stressors or whether specific stressors might be associated with specific behavioral outcomes, such as depression, posttraumatic stress disorder, or psychotic episodes. As evidenced by circulating cortisol or corticosterone (CORT) levels, a common denominator of the stress response, major differences in the effects of various stressors are not present. Anisman et al. (2001) reported more similarities than differences in serum CORT levels in mice after exposures to different stressors such as a rat, fox odor, restraint, foot shock, cold swim, acoustic startle, or open field. However, an important consideration for current studies is whether different stressors might impact males and females differently, but little information is available on this subject. Following acute stress (chronic stress was not investigated) using a predator, a cat, Park et al. (2008) reported that performance of both male and female rats declined on the radial-arm water maze, but, interestingly, the stressed males performed at the same level as chance whereas the stressed females still performed better than chance. Acute application of a psychophysical (foot shock) in contrast to psychological (social defeat) stress also had different effects on anxiety- and depression-related behaviors (Kavushansky et al., 2009). Thus, further research needs to examine chronic stressors.

This review, which compares the responses of the sexes to stress, focuses primarily on restraint stress because this is the paradigm where both sexes have been consistently tested. With most other chronic stressors, only males were examined, but where information on both sexes is extant, it will be presented. Restraint stress consists of placing subjects in small plastic or mesh containers where they have limited movement (but they are not immobilized). This technique has been utilized by a number of laboratories because it reliably activates the stress response, and subjects, male or female, stressed for up to 6 hr daily for up to 4 weeks remain generally active and healthy without adverse physical symptoms that are present in paradigms like shock (see Luine et al., 2007). Such considerations are critical when evaluating cognitive function; subjects cannot be debilitated or physically compromised when undergoing learning and memory tests. In relation to females, daily restraint stress for up to 1 month, unlike extended periods with neurogenic stressors, does not alter estrus cyclicity in rats (Bowman et al., 2001; Conrad et al., 2003). The restraint stress model is also advantageous because it has been well characterized in terms of CORT secretion patterns and morphological, neurochemical, and functional consequences. Moreover, information is also available in females including CORT release (Galea et al., 1997), morphological changes (Galea et al., 1997; McLaughlin et al., 2005, 2010), and neurochemistry (Bowman et al., 2002, 2003, 2009).

Spatial Memory Tasks in Rodents

Spatial memory, dependent on an intact hippocampus, has been widely assessed in rodents using both the Morris water-maze task (Morris, 1984) and the radial-arm maze developed by Olton (Olton and Samuelson, 1976), and more recently by recognition memory tasks (Ennaceur and Aggleton, 1994; Ennaceur et al., 1997; Conrad et al., 1996). In these tasks, rats construct a cognitive map of an environment or room by remembering the location of landmarks, and this information, which is processed by the hippocampus, allows them to solve/complete various tasks which depend on finding a positive reward or avoiding an aversive stimulus in a specific location in the environment. In the radial-arm maze each of the eight arms has a food reward, and, because the rats are food-deprived (90% of normal weight), they readily enter the arms and eat the reward after habituation and training. During training, rats learn the locations of arms in relation to cues in the room, and rats that learn and remember best make the fewest errors; that is, entering an arm which they previously visited and ate a reward from. The Morris water maze uses a similar spatial context but an aversive stimulus for motivation. In a water-filled pool, subjects must swim to learn the location of a submerged, invisible escape platform using landmarks/cues present in the area around the pool. In a more recently developed task, spatial recognition memory is tested by allowing rats to explore two objects, and then during an intertrial delay of minutes to hours, one object is moved to a new location. Rats are exploratory in nature and seek novelty; thus more time spent with the object in the new location than in the old location suggests better spatial memory. Finally, the Y maze also utilizes rodents' novelty-seeking propensity. Subjects are placed in one arm (start arm) and are only allowed to explore the start arm and one of the other arms. After an intertrial delay, they are allowed to explore all three arms. Like the object-placement task, more time spent in the novel arm indicates better spatial memory.

The performance of males, both animal and human, is usually better than females on spatial memory tasks. Yet, however, both sexes reach the same level of steady-state performance over time. This sex difference has been ascribed to both organizational and activational effects of gonadal hormones as well as to differences in learning strategies and various environmental contingencies. For further discussion see Luine and Dohanich (2008).

Spatial memory is impaired in males following chronic stress

My laboratory was the first to report that 21 days of restraint stress for 6 hr/day impairs the performance of male rats on the radial-arm maze (Luine et al., 1994). Stressed males made significantly more errors (see Figure 26.1a), fewer correct choices, and earlier mistakes in completing the eight arm choices than unstressed males. While significant, stress-dependent impairments are smaller than impairments seen in aged male rats (Luine and Rodriguez, 1994; Bowman et al., 2006). In addition, impairments are reversible because if stressed males are trained and tested beginning at 18 days poststress, no impairments are present (Luine et al., 1994). Stress-dependent impairments in this and many other spatial memory tasks in males have now been reported (see Conrad 2010 for review). For example, Beck and Luine (1999) showed that memory in the object-placement task was impaired (Figure 26.1b) and Conrad et al. (1996) reported that 21 days of restraint stress impaired spatial memory on the Y maze (Figure 26.1c). Finally, Kitraki et al. (2004) demonstrated that male rats were impaired on the water maze following 21 days of daily restraint (Figure 26.1d). It is notable that, consistent with Selye's model of physiological effects of stress, shorter periods of chronic restraint stress are not impairing in males: 1 week of daily restraint does not affect performance of radial-arm maze (Luine et al., 1996) or object placement (Bowman et al., 2009). The majority of stress-related studies have utilized spatial learning and memory tasks, but some information on nonspatial memory is extant. In an object recognition task, a new object is placed on the field instead of moving an object to a new location. Daily restraint for 21 days impairs male memory (Beck and Luine, 2002; Bisagno et al., 2004).

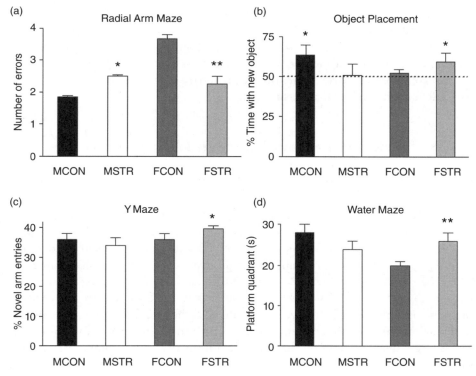

Figure 26.1 Sex differences in chronic stress effects on spatial memory tasks. Adult male and female rats received 21 days of daily (6 hr) restraint stress. (a) Radial-arm maze. Data pooled from Luine et al. (1994) for males and from Bowman et al. (2001) for females. The number of errors to complete the task significantly increased in stressed males and decreased in stressed females. (b) Object placement. Data from Beck and Luine (2002). The percentage of time exploring objects in the new location is shown. Control males and stressed females could significantly discriminate the old from new location but stressed males and control females could not. (c) Y maze. Data from Conrad et al. (2003). The percentage of entries into the novel arms is shown. Stressed females entered the novel arm more than the start and other arms, indicating enhanced memory. (d) Morris water maze. Data from Kitraki et al. (2004). Time spent in the target quadrant (platform location) during the probe trial. Stress enhanced female time in the target quadrant. Not shown is that stressed males spent significantly more time in the opposite quadrant than control males. $*P < 0.05$; $**P < 0.01$. MCON, control males; MSTR, stressed males; FCON, control females; FSTR, stressed females. *Source:* From Becker et al. (2008), p. 239, fig. 12.3. By permission of Oxford University Press.

Thus, it is established that chronic restraint stress impairs performance of spatial learning and memory tasks in males. An extensive discussion of this topic can be found in Conrad (2010), where stress effects on cognition in males are reviewed in relation to acquisition or memory and the nature of the tasks utilized. Conclusions are similar to ones reported here: the vast majority of studies show chronic stress dependent cognitive impairments in males.

Spatial memory is enhanced in females following chronic stress

Based on observations that the female gonadal hormone, estradiol, was neuro-trophic, antioxidant, antiapoptotic, and promoted some aspects of cognitive function (Garcia-Segura et al., 2001), we hypothesized that female rats might be less sensitive to the cognition-impairing effects of chronic stress than male rats because of these neuroprotective effects of estradiol. Thus, females were subjected to the same 21 days of daily 6-hr restraint and cognitive testing as males (Bowman et al., 2001, 2003; Beck and Luine, 2002; Luine, 2002; Bisagno et al., 2004). To our surprise, females were not only less sensitive to the impairing effects of stress on spatial memory, but this chronic stress regimen enhanced their performance on the radial-arm maze and in object placement (Figure 26.1a and b). In females, the number of errors to complete the task on the radial-arm maze decreased from approximately four to two, while in stressed males errors increased from less than two to more than two. In object placement, control females did not significantly discriminate between the old and new location of the object but stressed females did. The opposite pattern is seen in males, control males can significantly discriminate between old and new locations but stressed males cannot. Shortly after our report of better performance of spatial memory tasks after stress in females, Conrad et al. (2003) reported that the 21-day restraint paradigm also enhanced some aspects of performance in females on the Y-maze, and Kitraki et al. (2004) reported a similar finding in the water maze task. In these spatial memory tasks, previously reported better performance of control males than control females was also seen, and stress appears to mitigate the sex differences. For object recognition, stress does not impair female memory (Beck and Luine, 2002; Bisagno et al., 2004), but males are impaired by stress on this task (see above).

Sex differences in response to stress, impairments in males and enhancements in females, is also maintained at shorter stress intervals (Luine et al., 1996; Conrad et al., 2003; Bowman, 2005; Bowman et al., 2009). In addition, estradiol appears to be important for the enhancement in stressed females since ovariectomized rats failed to show enhanced radial-arm maze performance following 21 days of daily restraint stress, but ovariectomized females receiving estradiol did show enhanced performance (Bowman et al., 2002). In contrast, McLaughlin et al. (2005) found that chronically stressed, ovariectomized rats still showed some improvements on the Y maze compared to nonstressed subjects. More recently, it was shown that estradiol administration to ovariectomized females blocked the CA3 dendritic retractions (where CA means cornu ammonis, a subregion of the hippocampus; McLaughlin et al., 2010). Interactions between the hypothalamic–pituitary–gonadal and the hypothalamic–pituitary–adrenal (HPA) axis following chronic stress in females have not generally been investigated (see Carey et al. 1995 for further information). However, there are also sex-related differences in stress effects on morphology and neurochemistry of neurons in the hippocampus and frontal cortex which may underlie the behavioral differences, and estrogen–stress interactions appear to influence some of these changes (see below).

Thus, current evidence supports the hypothesis that chronic stress affects cognitive function differently in male and female rats. However, this conclusion is based on only a few studies which applied mainly restraint stress and investigated a limited number of learning and memory tasks. Thus, further investigation and validation is required. The influence of age on sexually dimorphic responses to chronic restraint stress will be reviewed next followed by a discussion of possible psychological/behavioral parameters contributing to the differences. Finally, a brief summary of some neural changes engendered by stress in the sexes will be presented.

Age Affects Cognitive Responses to Stress in a Sex-dependent Manner

Prenatal chronic stress effects

Stress experienced during the prenatal developmental stage permanently effects neural functioning; that is, at adulthood prenatally stressed subjects show differences from nonstressed subjects in neural functions and behavior. This permanent effect on the brain is unlike stress experienced at adulthood, which is generally reversible/transitory. Very few studies have examined prenatal stress effects on adult cognitive function in both sexes. Experiments in my laboratory exposed pregnant rat dams to three sessions of 45 min of daily restraint stress from days 14 to 21 of pregnancy (Bowman et al., 2004) and then examined behavioral and neural functions in the offspring of the stressed dams and offspring of unstressed dams at adulthood (2 months of age). In the radial-arm maze, prenatally stressed males performed less well than unstressed males, and prenatally stressed females performed better than unstressed females. Thus, prenatal stress mitigated the usual better performance of males in this spatial memory task. Object recognition was not affected by prenatal stress, unlike stress effects in adulthood. Thus, stress experienced in utero has effects which last until adulthood. Whether these prenatal stress effects persist throughout all of adulthood has not been examined. Similar to these results, Zagron and Weinstock (2006) found once daily restraint of dams for 30 min on days 14–21 of gestation led to impaired water-maze performance in males but not females at adulthood. Hosseini-Sharifabad and Hadinedoushan (2007) also reported that prenatal stress impaired Morris water-maze performance in adult males, but females were not tested. Thus, prenatal stress, like adult stress, appears to cause sex-specific changes in cognitive function, but these results need further verification since few developmental studies of stress have investigated cognitive function and even fewer have included females.

Periadolescent/adolescent chronic stress effects

While many recent studies show the increased vulnerability of the adolescent compared to the adult brain after stress, drugs, and alcohol (Romeo, 2010; see also Chapter 14 in this volume), most have focused on effects on anxiety, mood, and risk-taking. However, Isgor et al. (2004) stressed 28-day-old males (no females) for 4 weeks and found that 3 weeks following the stress, Morris water-maze performance was impaired. This persistent impairment in adolescent rats should be viewed in the context that adults given a comparable stress displayed no impairments in radial-arm maze performance approximately 10 days following stress (Luine et al., 1994). Thus, this single study suggests that effects of stress on cognition may be more long-lasting in adolescents than in adults, but this observation clearly warrants further investigation in this age group and also in females.

Aging and chronic stress effects

Few studies have assessed effects of chronic stress in aged subjects. Since aged rats, like primates, show a general decline in physiological functions, it could be envisioned that chronic stress might exert even greater impairments in aged as compared to young subjects or that the transition from adaptive to maladaptive effects of stress might be faster in aged subjects. In addition, aged male rats show prolonged elevations in corticosterone following stress (Di Nicola et al., 2006) which might contribute to greater stress-dependent impairments than in young adult males (females have not been investigated).

When 21-month-old rats were given 21 days of daily restraint stress, sex differences in their cognitive responses were no longer present (Bowman et al., 2006). For object recognition, stressed males and females both performed better than nonstressed control rats. In the spatial memory task, object placement, sex differences in performance of control males and females were no longer present, and stress did not alter performance in either sex. By contrast, in young rats, stress impaired male, but not female, object recognition and object placement was impaired in stressed males and enhanced in stressed females. It should be noted that overall performance of aged rats on the tasks was well below that of young rats, a usual finding for aged subjects. Thus, stress in aged rats caused a different pattern of change in recognition memory tasks than in adults, and, more importantly, sex differences in the stress response were no longer present. Similar to its effects in adult rats, estradiol may contribute to the sex differences in response in aged rats, in this case the lack of sex differences in both control rats and in rats receiving stress.

Circulating estradiol decreases in aged females, but males show a fivefold increase in estradiol (Figure 26.2a; Luine et al., 2007). In fact, estradiol levels in aged males are equivalent to young females in diestrus. The increase in estradiol in aged males may protect against the impairing effects of stress, just like in adult females, while the decrease in estradiol in aged females may render them more sensitive to stress effects, just like adult males. In support of our findings in aged rats, estrogen treatments to 20-month-old male rats reversed some aging effects on the HPA axis (females were not examined; Di Nicola et al., 2006). Interactions between androgens and the HPA axis during aging have not been examined, but as shown in other studies and in Figure 26.2b, testosterone levels do not decrease as drastically in males

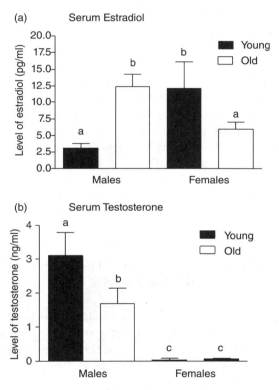

Figure 26.2 Levels of gonadal hormones in young and aged, male and female rats. (a) Serum estradiol: levels of estradiol in young, 2.5-month-old, male and female (solid bars, $n = 6$ for each sex) and aged, 21.5-month-old, male ($n = 7$) and female ($n = 8$) rats. Entries are means±SEM. Data were analyzed by two-way ANOVA, sex × age, and showed a significant interaction, $P < 0.01$ where bars with different superscripts (a, b) are significantly different from each other, $P < 0.05$. (b) Serum testosterone, levels of testosterone in young, 2.5-month-old, male and female (solid bars, $n = 6$ for each sex) and aged, 21.5-month-old, male ($n = 7$) and female ($n = 8$) rats. Entries are means±SEM. Data were analyzed as for panel (a) and showed a significant sex effect, $P < 0.00001$, and an interaction trend, $P < 0.08$, where bars with different superscripts (a, b, c) are significantly different from each other, $P < 0.05$. *Source:* From Luine et al. (2007) by permission of John Wiley and Sons.

as estradiol levels do in females. There is an approximately 30% reduction in testo-sterone levels in 21.5-month-old as compared to 2.5-month-old male rats. Thus, the maintenance of testosterone levels with aging may provide a *buffering effect* against cognitive impairments by stress.

The results of our studies on stress during aging await investigation and confir-mation by others. However, it is notable that Hodes and Shors (2007) found a similar pattern of results for stress effects during aging in that acute stress, brief tail shocks for 1 hr, to 17–18-month-old male and female rats did not affect acquisition of eyeblink conditioning. In contrast, this acute stress to adult rats enhances male, but impairs female, eyeblink conditioning.

Thus, mounting evidence shows that chronic stress causes sexually differen-tiated effects on learning and memory in rats. Moreover, the nature of the sex differences appears to change somewhat over the life cycle. Briefly, sexually differentiated responses to stress occur early in development (in utero) and are permanent (present at adulthood). At adulthood these sexually differentiated changes are larger, but the changes are not permanent. The effects of chronic stress on cognitive function during adolescence has received little attention, but stress effects on other neural functions last longer than when the stress is given at adult-hood, but whether they are permanent, as with prenatal stress, is unknown. At advanced ages, limited studies suggest that sex differences to stress are mitigated. Thus, these observations raise the question of whether the classic formulation of Selye that stress responses change from being adaptive at short intervals to maladap-tive at longer intervals needs reconsideration (Selye, 1976). From this prospective, updating should include information as to both the age and sex of the subject.

Influence of Psychological and Performance Parameters on Cognitive Responses to Stress

A critical question for the body of work presented here is whether the sex differences found in learning and memory following stress are changes in actual mnemonic processes or instead reflect sex differences in various other parameters that could influence performance of the cognitive tasks. Parameters which might be sexually dimorphic and influence/obscure the outcome of cognitive testing include (1) sensory-perceptive properties like olfaction, vision, audition, touch, and noci-ception, (2) regulatory processes including thirst, hunger, and body weight/composition, (3) motor considerations such as activity and skill, and, importantly, (4) affective parameters like arousal, anxiety, and motivation. Detailed discussion of these factors is beyond the scope of this review, but a short consideration follows.

First, it is important to note that when behavioral psychologists develop tasks, extensive control experiments are completed to determine contingencies that influ-ence task performance and to identify other miscellaneous parameters that might indirectly affect performance (see Olton and Samuelson 1976, for example). Not surprisingly, male rodents were the target subjects for these tasks. Thus, most tasks currently in use that mitigate the effects of nonmnemonic variables and enhance the effects of mnemonic variables are biased toward males. Therefore, it is possible that stress could be affecting mnemonic variables in males but nonmnemonic variables in females leading to an erroneous conclusion that stress enhances female cognition. Somewhat abrogating this notion, similar stress effects were found using five different tasks, and these tasks have different bases for their performance. The water maze has an aversive-stimulus component (possibility of drowning) whereas the radial-arm maze uses a positive stimulus (food reward) in order to promote completion of the task. Recognition memory tasks and the Y maze do not depend on reinforcement of any variety (aversive or positive) but rely on exploratory drive of the subjects to complete the task. The demonstration of sex differences in stress effects across these differently motivated tasks provides some support that nonmnemonic factors in category 1 may not be primary in causing the sexually dimorphic changes.

In relation to category 2, regulatory processes, stress elicits decreases in weight gain across 21 days in both males and females, but losses are present earlier in males, at 7 days of stress, than in females (Beck and Luine, 2002; Bowman et al., 2009). Females have more body fat which could also influence results in the radial-arm maze wherein subjects are food-deprived. While regulatory differences by stress in the sexes might contribute to enhanced performance of stressed females on the radial-arm maze, they would not contribute to enhancements in recognition memory tasks or in the water maze. For category 3, motor considerations, female rats are generally more active than males, and 21 days of daily restraint did not alter activity in either sex at adulthood or at an advanced age (Beck and Luine, 2002; Bowman et al., 2006). Thus, changes in overall activity do not appear to have influenced the cognitive effects in these studies. Similarly, prenatal stress did not alter activity at adulthood but did change cognitive profiles (Bowman et al., 2004). In contrast, 7 days of daily restraint decreased male and increased female activity (Bowman et al., 2009), and the stressed males showed decreased object-recognition memory (but not object-placement memory) and the stressed females showed increased object-placement memory (but not object-recognition memory). Thus, activity changes may have had some impact on the cognitive testing following the 7-day stress regimen but not at longer stress intervals.

Of the affective parameters in category 4, little is known about chronic stress effects on arousal; however, it has been extensively studied following acute stress. In contrast, anxiety has been frequently assessed following chronic stress, and increases in this behavior could adversely affect learning and memory, especially in tests relying on exploration like recognition-memory tasks. Adult males are generally more anxious and less active than females when assessed on the open field or in elevated-plus maze (Zimmerberg and Farley,1993; Imhof et al., 1993; Beck and Luine, 2002; Bowman et al., 2009).

Following 21 days of daily restraint, sex differences in anxiety are largely eliminated; stressed males become less anxious (able to perform better?), and stressed females become more anxious (perform worse?) as indexed by latency to enter the field or center visits (Beck and Luine, 2002). Thus, stress decreases in male memory (radial-arm maze, object placement, object recognition) and increases in female memory (radial-arm maze and object placement) suggest that the anxiety changes are not causing the memory changes. Moreover, there were no differences in exploration time in the recognition-memory tasks due to either sex or stress, suggesting no differences in anxiety for objects. In support of these findings, Wright and Conrad (2005), using the Y maze, showed that 21 days of chronic restraint in males impaired their performance on a spatial version of the maze, but the rats performed well in an intramaze cue version which indicates the cognitive deficit was not attributable to neophobia. In aged rats, stress caused a different effect on anxiety; males became more anxious and females became less anxious as indexed by open-arm entries on the elevated-plus maze (Bowman et al., 2004; Luine et al., 2007). Since both sexes showed improved object recognition following stress, changes in anxiety do not appear critical for this age group. At a shorter stress interval (7 days), testing in the elevated-plus maze showed that stressed males were more anxious than controls but females were not affected (Bowman et al., 2009). Males were impaired on object recognition and females were enhanced on object placement so anxiety could have influenced the stressed-male performance. However, the stressed subjects explored the objects more than controls suggesting anxiety on the plus maze may not have carried over to exploration of the objects in the cognitive test. Overall, no apparent relationship emerges between stress-induced changes in anxiety and stress-induced changes in cognitive performance.

While changes in nonmnemonic parameters may contribute to the sex differences in stress effects on spatial memory, the preponderance of current evidence does not support a major role for nonmnemonic factors in chronic stress effects on learning and memory nor in the sex differences in stress responses. However, further research is necessary to substantiate this view.

Stress-induced Changes in Neural Processing/ Strategies by the Sexes

Another factor which may contribute to sex differences in cognitive responses to stress is the use of different learning strategies in relation to sex, stress, or both. Both humans and rodents use multiple learning and memory systems in the brain which can be "switched on or off" (White and McDonald, 2002). One system involves the hippocampus which processes associative relations from spatial-contextual representations and another involves the caudate nucleus which uses a stimulus-response procedural representation. Most simply, the hippocampal system forms memories of where things are in space (item A is in northeast area of the room) and the caudate system uses procedural relations (item A is located to the right of item B). Important for the current discussion is that the sexes may rely differently on these systems and that stress may impact use of these systems.

The T-maze task has been utilized to test learning strategies for solving spatial tasks, and rats can use a hippocampus-based place strategy (go to a specific place-arm) or a caudate-based response strategy (always turn right). Packard and McGaugh (1996) reported that 90% of males use a place strategy. On the other hand, Korol (2004) reported that females use both strategies with high gonadal hormone levels biasing toward a place strategy (71%) while low levels change the bias toward a response strategy. Thus, females shift their strategies over the estrus cycle, and this change could account for the poorer acquisition of spatial tasks in females as their strategies change over days when learning a task.

Based mainly on human studies and some animal research, it has been hypothesized that stress may cause a uniform shift in neural processing which leads to altered cognitive function from a place to a response-based strategy (Schwabe et al., 2008). We (Beck and Luine, 2010) further speculated that sex differences in ability to shift strategies may contribute to sex differences in stress effects on cognition in both humans and rodents. Thus, males may be impaired in spatial memory tasks following stress because stress (most likely through corticosterone actions in the hippocampus) forces a shift to a response strategy which is new for them. Females, on the other hand, cope better with stress because they already shift strategies between place and response, and, additionally, stress may stabilize female rats to one strategy. Shifts in processing style rely on activity of monoaminergic systems in the amygdala which in turn interacts with PFC and hippocampal areas (Packard et al., 1994). We have previously documented sex differences in stress effects on monoaminergic systems, and the next section presents data in stressed males and females relevant to this hypothesis. Further discussion of these speculative concepts can be found in Beck and Luine (2010) and Luine and Dohanich (2008).

Sex-dependent Neural Changes Following Chronic Stress

Almost 20 years have elapsed since it was first demonstrated that 21 days of stress causes a retraction/pruning of apical dendrites and dendritic spine loss in pyramidal neurons in hippocampal (Watanabe et al., 1992) and PFC areas (Radley et al. 2004, 2006) of male rats. Yet, the mechanisms for sex differences in responses to stress are still largely unknown. Consistent with the different pattern of behavioral changes between the sexes, chronically stressed females show different morphological changes, no retraction in apical CA3 dendrites but pruning in basal dendrites and increased spines in CA1 (Galea et al., 1997; McLaughlin et al., 2009, 2010). Consistent with the maladaptive cascade of effects in males, glucocorticoid receptors are downregulated in hippocampus of males but are upregulated in females (Kitraki et al., 2004).

An important candidate for mediating sex differences to stress is brain-derived neurotrophic factor (BDNF) because 3 weeks of restraint decreases hippocampal BDNF in males (Luo et al., 2004), and BDNF infusion into the hippocampus protects against stress-induced impairments in the water-maze task (Radecki, 2005).

Females were not investigated, but Lin et al. (2009) reported that 43 days of daily foot shock decreased BDNF in prelimbic cortex of females but not males, and no changes were found in the dentate gyrus. The hormone oxytocin is also a potential target for modulating stress responses because it is higher in females, is important for social recognition, and may enhance spatial memory; however, little information is currently available.

Monoaminergic systems are among important responders/mediators to stress, and following 21 days of restraint stress, decreased norepinephrine (noradrenaline), dopamine, and serotonin (5-hydroxytryptamine, or 5-HT) levels are found in the hippocampus of males (Sunanda and Raju, 2000; Beck and Luine, 2002; Luine, 2002), but opposite changes in these monoamines are found in females (Beck and Luine, 2002; Luine, 2002; Bowman et al., 2006). Moreover, dopamine activity in the PFC decreases in males and increases in females following chronic stress (Bowman et al., 2003). In contrast, chronic mild stress for 6 weeks increased dopamine activity in PFC and hippocampus of males and decreased dopamine activity in PFC, but not hippocampus, of females (Dalla et al., 2008). Recently, we examined effects of restraint for a shorter period, 1 week, and like behavioral responses, monoaminergic systems showed sex differences (Bowman et al., 2009). Activity of monoamines was indexed by ratios of metabolite to monoamine. In the PFC, norepinephrine activity was unaltered by stress in males but increased in females, and 5-HT activity increased in males but decreased in females. As shown in Figure 26.3, hippocampal areas showed sexually dimorphic responses: in CA1 of males norepinephrine activity increased threefold and 5-HT activity also increased while dopamine activity decreased. In contrast, activity of 5-HT and dopamine did not change in females, and norepinephrine activity decreased. In CA3, norepinephrine activity did not change in either sex following stress while stressed males showed increased 5-HT and dopamine activity while both transmitter activities decreased in activity in

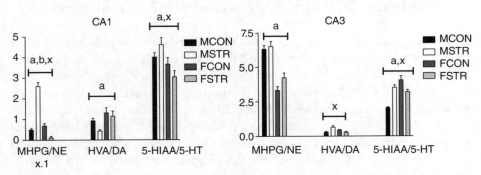

Figure 26.3 Effect of 7 days of daily restraint stress on monoaminergic activities in the hippocampus. Entries are ratio of metabolite to monoamine. Data were analyzed by two-way ANOVA (sex × treatment) where a indicates main effect of sex (male, female), b is main effect of treatment (control, stress) and x indicates a sex × treatment interaction. *P* values are at least 0.05. DA, dopamine; 5-HIAA, 5-hydroxyindole acetic acid; 5-HT, 5-hydroxytryptamine; HVA, homovanillic acid; MHPG, 3-methoxy-4-hydroxyphenylglycol; NE, norepinephrine. *Source:* Based on Bowman et al. (2009).

females. These remarkably different patterns in monoaminergic activity in the hippocampus of males and females following stress may be critically important in mediating spatial memory changes. Prenatal stress also led to sexually differentiated changes in monoamines at adulthood (Bowman et al., 2004). Thus, monoaminergic activities may be important contributors to sex differences in stress responses in developing and adult rats but duration of stress appears critical in the responses.

Conclusion

A limited, but compelling and growing, body of data shows that chronic stress causes sexually differentiated cognitive and neural responses in rats. In general, females are not cognitively impaired like males following chronic stress. These sex differences appear early in development and continue across the life span but appear to abate in aged rats. Underlying mechanisms for the responses are mainly not determined but monoamines may be important neural mediators.

References

Anisman, H., Hayley, S., Kelly, O., Borowski, T., & Merali, Z. (2001). Psychogenic, neurogenic, and systemic stressor effects on plasma corticosterone and behavior: mouse strain-dependent outcomes. *Behavioral Neuroscience, 115*, 443–454.

Beck, K., & Luine, V. N. (2010). Evidence for sex specific shifting of neural processes underlying learning and memory following stress. *Physiology & Behavior, 99*, 204–211.

Beck, K. D., & Luine, V. N. (1999). Food deprivation modulates chronic stress effects on object recognition in male rats: role of monoamines and amino acids. *Brain Research, 830*, 56–71.

Beck, K. D., & Luine, V. N. (2002). Sex differences in behavioral and neurochemical profiles after chronic stress: role of housing conditions. *Physiology & Behavior, 75*(5), 661–673.

Becker, J. B., Berkley, K. J., Geary, N., Hampson, E., Herman, J. P., & Young, E. A. (2008). *Sex differences in the brain: From genes to behavior.* New York: Oxford University Press.

Bisagno, V., Grillo, C. A., Piroli, G. G., Giraldo, P., McEwen, B. S., & Luine, V. N. (2004). Chronic stress alters the behavioral and neural effects of amphetamine. *Pharmacology, Biochemistry & Behavior, 78*, 541–550.

Bowman, E., Ferguson, D., & Luine, V. N. (2002). Effects of chronic restraint stress and estradiol on open field activity, spatial memory, and monoaminergic neurotransmitters in ovariectomized rats. *Neuroscience, 113*, 401–410.

Bowman, R. E. (2005). Stress-induced changes in spatial memory are sexually differentiated and vary across the lifespan. *Journal of Neuroendocrinology, 17*, 526–535.

Bowman, R. E., Zrull, M. C., & Luine, V. N. (2001). Chronic restraint stress enhances radial arm maze performance in female rats. *Brain Research, 904*, 279–289.

Bowman, R. E., Beck, K. D., & Luine, V. N. (2003). Chronic stress effects on memory: Sex differences in performance and monoamines. *Hormones and Behavior, 43*, 48–59.

Bowman, R., MacLusky, N. J., Sarmiento, Y., Frankfurt, M., Gordon, M., & Luine, V. N. (2004). Sexually dimorphic effects of prenatal stress on cognition, hormonal responses and central neurotransmitters. *Endocrinology, 145*, 3778–3787.

Bowman, R. E., Maclusky, N. J., Zrull, M. C., Diaz, S. E., & Luine, V. N. (2006). Sex differences in aged rats: behavioral and physiological responses to chronic stress. *Brain Research, 1126*, 156–166.

Bowman, R. E., Micik, R., Gautreaux, C., Fernandez, L., & Luine, V. N. (2009). Sex dependent changes in anxiety, memory, and monoamines following one week of stress. *Physiology & Behavior, 97*, 21–29.

Carey, M. P., Deterd, C. H., de Koning, J., Helmerhorst, F., & de Kloet, E. R. (1995). The influence of ovarian steroids on hypothalamic–pituitary– adrenal regulation in the female rat. *Journal of Endocrinology, 144*, 311–321.

Conrad, C. D. (2010). A critical review of chronic stress effects on spatial learning and memory. *Progress in Neuro-psychopharmacology & Biological Psychiatry, 34*, 742–755.

Conrad, C. D., Galea, L. A., Kuroda, Y., & McEwen, B. S. (1996). Chronic stress impairs rat spatial memory on the Y maze, and this effect is blocked by tianeptine pretreatment. *Behavioral Neuroscience, 110*, 1321–1334.

Conrad, C. D., Grote, K. D., Hobbs, R. J., & Ferayorni, A. (2003). Sex differences in spatial and non-spatial Y-maze performance after chronic stress. *Neurobiology of Learning and Memory, 79*, 32–40.

Dalla, C., Antoniou, K., Kokras, N., Drossopoulou, G., Papathansious, G., Bekris, S., Daskas, S., & Papadopoulou-Daifoti, Z. (2008). Sex differences in the effects of two stress paradigms on dopaminergic neurotransmission. *Physiology & Behavior, 93*, 595–605.

Di Nicola, A. F., Saravia, F. E., Beauquis, J., Pietranera, L., & Ferrini, M. G. (2006). Estrogens and neuroendocrine hypothalamic-pituitary-adrenal axis function. *Frontiers in Hormone Research, 35*, 157–168.

Ennaceur, A., & Aggleton, J. P. (1994). Spontaneous recognition of object configurations in rats: effects of fornix lesions. *Experimental Brain Research, 100*, 85–92.

Ennaceur, A., Neave, N., & Aggleton, J. P. (1997). Spontaneous object recognition and object location memory in rats: the effects of lesions in the cingulate cortices, the medial prefrontal cortex, the cingulum bundle and the fornix. *Experimental Brain Research, 113*, 509–519.

Galea, L. A., McEwen, B. S., Tanapat, P., Deak, T., Spencer, R. L., & Dhabhar, F. S. (1997). Sex differences in dendritic atrophy of CA3 pyramidal neurons in response to chronic restraint stress. *Neuroscience, 81*, 689–697.

Garcia-Segura, L. M., Azcortia, I., & DonCarlos, L. C. (2001). Neuroprotection by estrogen. *Progress in Neurobiology, 63*, 29–60.

Herman, J. P., & Cullinan, W. E. (1997). Neurocircuitry of stress: central control of the hypothalamo-pituitary-adrenocortical axis. *Trends in Neuroscience, 20*, 78–84.

Hodes, G. E., & Shors, T. J. (2007). Learning during middle age: a resistance to stress? *Neurobiology of Aging, 28*, 1783–1788.

Hosseini-Sharifabad, M., & Hadinedoushan, H. (2007). Prenatal stress induces learning deficits and is associated with a decrease in granules and CA3 cell dendritic tree size in rat hippocampus. *Anatomical Science International, 82*, 211–217.

Imhof, J. T., Coelho, Z. M. I., Schmitt, M. L., Morato, G. S., & Carobrez, A. P. (1993). Influence of gender and age on performance of rats in the elevated plus maze apparatus. *Behavioral Brain Research, 56*, 177–180.

Isgor, C., Kabbaj, M., Akil, H., & Watson, S. J. (2004). Delayed effects of chronic variable stress during peripubertal-juvenile period on Hippocampal morphology and on cognitive and stress axis functions in rats. *Hippocampus, 14*, 636–648.

Kavushansky, A., Ben-Shachar, D., Richter-Levin, G., & Klein, E. (2009). Physical stress differs from psychosocial stress in the pattern and time-course of behavioral responses, serum corticosterone and expression of plasticity-related genes in the rat. *Stress, 12*, 412–425.

Kitraki, E., Kremmyda, O., Youlatos, D., Alexis, M. N., & Kittas, C. (2004). Gender-dependent alterations in corticosteroid receptor status and spatial performance following 21 days of restraint stress. *Neuroscience, 125*, 47–55.

Korol, D. L. (2004). Role of estrogen in balancing contributions from multiple memory systems. *Neurobiology of Learning and Memory, 82*, 309–323.

Lin, Y., Ter Horst, G. J., Wichmann, R., Bakker, P., Liu, A., Li, X., & Westenbroek, C. (2009). Sex differences in the effects of acute and chronic stress and recovery after long-term stress on stress-related brain regions of rats. *Cerebral Cortex, 19*, 1978–1989.

Luine, V. N. (2002). Sex differences in chronic stress effects on memory in rats. *Stress 5*, 205–216.

Luine, V. N. (2008). Sex steroids and cognitive function. *Journal of Neuroendocrinology, 20*, 866–872.

Luine, V., & Rodriguez, M. (1994). Effects of estradiol on radial arm maze performance of young and aged rats. *Behavioral and Neural Biology, 62*, 230–236.

Luine, V. N., & Dohanich, G. (2008). Sex differences in cognitive function in rodents. In J. B. Becker, K. J. Berkley, N. Geary, E. Hampson, J. P. Herman, & E. A. Young (Eds.), *Sex differences in the brain: From genes to behavior* (pp. 227–252). Oxford: Oxford University Press.

Luine, V., Villegas, M., Martinez, C., & McEwen, B. S. (1994). Repeated stress causes reversible impairments of spatial memory performance. *Brain Research, 639*, 167–170.

Luine, V., Martinez, C., Villegas, M., Magarinos, A. M., & McEwen, B. S. (1996). Restraint stress reversibly enhances spatial memory performance, *Physiology & Behavior, 59*, 27–32.

Luine, V. N., Beck, K. D., Bowman, R. E., Frankfurt, M., & MacLusky, N. J. (2007). Stress and neural function – Accounting for sex and age. *Journal of Neuroendocrinology, 19*, 743–751.

Luo, C., Xu, H., & Li, X. M. (2004). Post-stress changes in BDNF and Bcl-2 immunoreactivities in hippocampal neurons: effect of chronic administration of olanzapine. *Brain Research, 1025*, 194–202.

McIntyre, D. C., Kent, P., Hayley, S., Merali, Z., & Anisman, H. (1999). Influence of psychogenic and neurogenic stressors on neuroendocrine and central monoamine activity in fast and slow kindling rats. *Brain Research, 840*, 65–74.

McLaughlin, K. J., Baran, S. E., Wright, R. L., & Conrad, C. D. (2005). Chronic stress enhances spatial memory in ovariectomized female rats despite CA3 dendritic retraction: Possible involvement of CA1 neurons. *Neuroscience, 135*, 1045–1054.

McLaughlin, K. J., Baran, S. E., & Conrad, C. D. (2009). Chronic stress-and sex-specific neuromorphological and functional changes in limbic structures. *Molecular Neurobiology, 40*, 166–182.

McLaughlin, K. J., Wilson, J. O., Harman, J., Wright, R. L., Wieczorek, L., Gomez, J., Korol, D. L., & Conrad, C. D. (2010). Chronic 17β-estradiol or cholesterol prevents stress-induced hippocampal CA3 dendritic retraction in ovariectomized female rats: possible correspondence between CA1 spine properties and spatial acquisition. *Hippocampus, 20*, 768–786.

Morris, R. G. M. (1984). Development of a water-maze procedure for studying spatial learning in the rat. *Journal of Neuroscience Methods, 11*, 47–60.

Olton, D. S., & Samuelson, R. J. (1976). Remberance of places passed: spatial memory in rats. *Journal of Experimental Psychology Animal Behavior Proceedings, 2*, 97–116.

Packard, G., & McGaugh, J. L. (1996). Inactivation of hippocampus or caudate nucleus with lidocaine differentially affects expression of place and response learning. *Neurobiology of Learning and Memory, 65*, 65–72.

Packard, M. G., Cahill, L., & McGaugh, J. L. (1994). Amygdala modulation of hippocampal-dependent and caudate nucleus-dependent memory processes. *Proceedings of the National Academy of Sciences USA, 91*, 8477–8481.

Park, C. R., Zoladz, P. R., Conrad, C. D., Fleshner, M., & Diamond, D. M. (2008). Acute predator stress impairs the consolidation and retrieval of hippocampus-dependent memory in male and female rats. *Learning & Memory, 15*, 271–280.

Radecki, D. T., Brown, L. M., Martinez, J., & Teyler, T. J. (2005). BDNF protects against stress-induced impairments in spatial learning and memory and LTP. *Hippocampus, 15*, 246–253.

Radley, J. J., Sisti, H. M., Hao J, Rocher, A. B., McCall, T., Hof, P. R., McEwen, B. S., & Morrison, J. H. (2004). Chronic behavioral stress induces apical dendritic reorganization in pyramidal neurons of the medial prefrontal cortex. *Neuroscience, 125*, 1–6.

Radley, J. J., Rjocher, A. B., Miller M, Janssen, W. G., Listen C, Hof, P. R., McEwen, B. S., & Morrison, J. H. (2006). Repeated stress induces dendritic spine loss in the rat medial prefrontal cortex. *Cerebral Cortex, 16*, 313–320.

Romeo, R. D. (2010). Adolescence: A central event in shaping stress reactivity. *Developmental Psychobiology, 52*, 62–70.

Schwabe, L., Dalm, S., Schachinger, H., & Oitzl, M. S. (2008). Chronic stress modulates the use of spatial and stimulus-response learning strategies in mice and man. *Neurobiology of Learning and Memory, 90*, 495–503.

Selye, H. (1976). *The stress of life.* New York: McGraw Hill.

Sunanda, R. B. S., & Raju, T. R. (2000). Restraint stress-induced alterations in the levels of biogenic amines, amino acids, and AchE activity in the hippocampus. *Neurochemical Research, 25*, 1547–1552.

Watanabe, Y., Gould, E., & McEwen, B. S. (1992). Stress induces atrophy of apical dendrites of hippocampal CA3 pyramidal neurons. *Brain Research, 588*, 341–345.

White, N. M., & McDonald, R. B. (2002). Theoretical review: multiple parallel memory systems in the brain of the rat. *Neurobiology of Learning and Memory, 77*, 125–184.

Wright, R. L., & Conrad, C. D. (2005). Chronic stress leaves novelty-seeking behavior intact while impairing spatial recognition memory in the Y-maze. *Stress, 8*, 151–154.

Zagron, G., & Weinstock, M. (2006). Maternal adrenal hormone secretion mediates behavioural alterations induced by prenatal stress in male and female rats. *Behavioural Brain Research, 175*, 323–328.

Zimmerberg, B., & Farley, M. J. (1993) Sex differences in anxiety behavior in rats: role of gonadal hormones. *Physiology & Behavior, 54*, 1119–1124.

27

Effects of Stress on Learning and Memory
Evidence for Sex Differences in Humans
Oliver T. Wolf

Introduction

There is good evidence that women and men differ in how they respond to stressors, based upon endocrinological and behavioral responses (Taylor et al., 2000). These differences might translate into vulnerabilities for dissimilar stress-associated psychiatric disorders. Compared to men, women have, for example, a higher risk for major depression, posttraumatic stress disorder, and several anxiety disorders (Nemeroff et al., 2006; Yehuda, 2002), but lower prevalence in conduct disorders, psychopathy, substance abuse, and autism (Zahn-Waxler et al., 2008).

When discussing possible sex differences in how stressors affect learning and memory, two possible scenarios should be considered. On the one hand, sex differences might occur because the two sexes differ in their endocrinological response to a stressor. Alternatively or additionally sex differences might reflect a different responsivity of the brain to the same neuroendocrine stress signal (e.g., glucocorticoids).

Endocrinologically, both sexes respond to stressors with the activation of the hypothalamic–pituitary–adrenal (HPA) axis, leading to a rise in cortisol (the most prominent glucocorticoid in humans). The magnitude of the HPA axis response is modulated by gondal steroids (Kajantie and Phillips, 2006; Kudielka and Kirschbaum, 2005; Taylor et al., 2000). Experimental studies in humans using psychosocial laboratory stressors often observed that men showed a stronger HPA axis response to a stressor than women (Kajantie and Phillips, 2006; Kudielka and Kirschbaum, 2005). However, this might depend on the specific paradigm used (Stroud et al., 2002) and no strong overall influence of sex on the cortisol response to laboratory stressors

The Handbook of Stress: Neuropsychological Effects on the Brain, First Edition.
Edited by Cheryl D. Conrad.
© 2011 Blackwell Publishing Ltd. Published 2011 by Blackwell Publishing Ltd.

was detected in a recent large meta-analysis, which however did not further investigate a possible influence of menstrual cycle (Dickerson and Kemeny, 2004). Moreover, in a real-life stress study (oral exam at the university), no sex differences in stress-induced cortisol elevations were detected (Schoofs et al., 2008a).

In women, fluctuations of gonadal steroids during the menstrual phase seem to further modulate the HPA axis response. A more pronounced HPA axis response to stressors is observed during the luteal phase (Kajantie and Phillips, 2006; Kudielka and Kirschbaum, 2005), which is characterized by elevated progesterone and estradiol levels. The situation in humans is further complicated by the fact that oral hormonal contraceptives appear to dampen the free (unbound; i.e., biologically active) cortisol stress response, possibly by increasing cortisol-binding globulin (Kirschbaum et al., 1999).

To conclude, sex and gonadal steroids impact HPA axis reactivity in humans, with the magnitude of this influence being moderate and the variance of the reported results large. Nevertheless, as a result of the complex interaction between the HPA axis and the hypothalamic–pituitary–gonadal axis, a lot of experimental human studies are conducted exclusively with men. Moreover, in studies with women, information about menstrual cycle phase and/or hormonal contraception are often not taken into account in the experimental design (e.g., Beckner et al., 2006; Smeets et al., 2008). Similarly, most rodent studies focus exclusively on males when conducting stress effects on memory (Diamond et al., 2007; Joels et al., 2006; Sandi and Pinelo-Nava, 2007).

For the current chapter, the focus is on possible differences in sensitivities of the brains of men and women for stress and stress hormones. I will review evidence for sex differences in the impact of acute experimentally induced stress on episodic long-term memory, working memory, and two forms of classical conditioning (eyeblink and fear conditioning).

Effects of Stress on Episodic Memory: Evidence for Sex Differences?

Episodic long-term memory refers to the conscious and voluntary storage of specific events that are connected to a spatial and temporal context. Together with semantic memory (the knowledge of facts and rules about the world) it is referred to as declarative or explicit memory. Episodic memory relies on the hippocampus, a brain structure within the medial temporal lobe (LaBar and Cabeza, 2006; Nadel and Moscovitch, 1997). Long-term memory processes can be further divided according to specific memory phases (encoding or acquisition), consolidation, and retrieval (see Roozendaal et al., 2006, Wolf, 2008, 2009).

Experiments in rodents and humans have established that stress influences episodic long-term memory (see Chapters 8, 9, 11, and 12 in this volume). It has been reported that stress within the learning context (i.e., when the learning condition is stressful) enhances memory consolidation (Joels et al., 2006; Roozendaal et al.,

2006). In contrast, memory retrieval of previously learned information is impaired when we are stressed (Roozendaal et al., 2006; Wolf, 2008, 2009). The beneficial effects on consolidation as well as the impairing effects on retrieval are more pronounced for emotionally arousing stimuli (e.g., emotional pictures or word; Wolf, 2009). Animal studies illustrate that these effects are mediated by an interactive effect of glucocorticoids with noradrenergic arousal (induced by a concurrent activation of the sympathetic nervous system). The basolateral nucleus of the amygdala influences the hippocampus, thereby creating a state where memory consolidation is enhanced, but memory retrieval is impaired (Roozendaal et al., 2006, 2009). Human behavioral, pharmacological, as well as neuroimaging studies demonstrate that similar results occur in humans (de Quervain et al., 2009; Wolf, 2008, 2009).

With respect to possible sex differences, studies in rodents report that acute (Conrad et al., 2004) as well as chronic (Bowman et al., 2001; Luine, 2002) stress impairs spatial (hippocampal-dependent) memory in male rats. In contrast to males, stress in females enhances memory, thus leading to truly opposing effects of stress on memory in the two sexes (Conrad et al., 2004; Bowman et al., 2001; Luine, 2002). However it has to be mentioned that not all studies observed strong sexual dimorphic response to stress (Park et al., 2008, see also Chapter 26 for more information on sex differences in rodents).

In a first study on the issue of sex differences in humans (Wolf et al., 2001b), it was investigated whether men and women differ in the association between the stress-induced cortisol response and its effect on episodic memory. A previous study from our laboratory (Kirschbaum et al., 1996) as well as findings from others (Takahashi et al., 2004) had reported that a more pronounced stress-induced cortisol rise was associated with impaired memory afterwards (encoding and immediate retrieval). Stress was induced prior to encoding with the use of the Trier Social Stress Test (TSST; Kirschbaum et al., 1993), a well-established human laboratory stressor combining a free-speech and a mental-arithmetic task in front of an audience, which leads to robust HPA axis activation. It is the combination of motivated performance, uncontrollability, and social-evaluative threat makes TSST so powerful (Dickerson and Kemeny, 2004). Overall no effects of stress on memory were found; however, the cortisol response within the stress group was strongly associated with poorer memory in men ($r = -.82$), while no such association was observed in women. In this study all women were tested in the luteal phase of their menstrual cycle to assure a similar HPA axis response to the stressor in both sexes (Kirschbaum et al., 1999). This suggests that women (at least in the luteal phase) are less sensitive to the memory-impairing effect of stress on immediate recall (Wolf et al., 2001b). The situation might be different for the beneficial effects of cortisol on memory consolidation. Here studies reported a significant positive correlation between cortisol and memory consolidation for women in the luteal phase (Andreano et al., 2008) or for women not stratified for menstrual cycle phase (Preuß and Wolf, 2009).

Additional studies on the topic of sex differences focused on stress or cortisol effects on memory retrieval. Using a pharmacological approach it had been shown that cortisol administered prior to memory retrieval had impairing effects in men (Wolf et al., 2001a). This finding was extended later on to women (Kuhlmann et al., 2005a). In order to characterize the influence of gonadal steroids further, three groups of women were investigated: (1) women in the early follicular phase (low estradiol and progesterone), (2) women in the luteal phase (high estradiol and progesterone), and (3) women using oral contraceptives (low endogenous but high exogenous estrogens and progestins). Both groups of freely cycling women showed memory-retrieval impairment after cortisol treatment. In contrast, no effect was observed in the oral-contraceptive group (Kuhlmann and Wolf, 2005). This indicated that the exogenous synthetic sex steroids directly or indirectly reduced the sensitivity of the central nervous system to glucocorticoids.

Most recently, the effects of stress on memory retrieval in women in the luteal phase were tested using a psychosocial stress protocol (TSST). These women failed to show evidence for stress-induced retrieval impairment (Schoofs and Wolf, 2009), which was in contrast to results obtained in men (Kuhlmann et al., 2005b) and also in contrast to the results from the aforementioned pharmacological study (Kuhlmann and Wolf, 2005). Those data suggest that women in the luteal phase of the menstrual cycle are less susceptible to stress induced memory impairment (but not to pharmacological cortisol-induced memory impairments). There is good evidence to hypothesize that this effect is mediated by progesterone, since progesterone (among other ways of action) can bind to the glucocorticoid receptor (Schoofs and Wolf, 2009).

Taken together, research in humans provides evidence that the effects of stress on episodic long-term memory are sometimes less pronounced in women compared to men. This appears to be the case for encoding, consolidation, as well as retrieval. However, stress effects in women are by no means absent for this domain. Most importantly, an opposing pattern (as has been reported in rats; see Conrad et al., 2004, but see also Diamond et al., 2007) has so far not been reported. The conclusions to be drawn are so far limited by the fact that several studies tested only one sex and/or did not report possible sex differences. Finally specific menstrual-cycle phases have only be investigated in very few studies on this issue (Andreano et al., 2008; Kuhlmann and Wolf, 2005).

Effects of Stress on Working Memory: Evidence for Sex Differences?

Working memory refers to a short-term storage and manipulation system thought to be situated within the prefrontal cortex. Studies in rodents have reported that females are more susceptible to the acute effects of stress on working memory. This enhanced stress susceptibility was mediated by estradiol (Shansky et al., 2004, 2006; Shansky, 2009). In humans, the effects of stress (or cortisol treatment) on working memory have not been investigated very often. In addition, results are quite heterogeneous. Several recent studies, however, observed that stress impaired working memory at least when difficult and challenging working memory tasks are used (Luethi et al., 2008; Oei et al., 2006; Schoofs et al., 2008b, 2009). However, those studies were all conducted in healthy young men, so that no information is available on the presence of sex differences. Along these lines, previous pharmacological studies investigating the effects of cortisol on working memory have also been conducted almost exclusively in men (Lupien et al., 1999; Wolf et al., 2001a). Thus additional studies are needed to test the hypothesis derived from studies with rodents that the female prefrontal cortex is more susceptible to stress.

Effects of Stress on Classical Conditioning: Evidence for Sex Differences?

Rodent studies on the topic of stress and learning have often used classical conditioning paradigms, with eyeblink conditioning and fear conditioning being used the most. In these studies the animal learns that a previously neutral stimulus (the conditioned stimulus, CS; e.g., a tone) predicts an aversive event (the unconditioned stimulus, US; e.g., an air puff to the eye, or a foot shock). Several conditioning paradigms need to be differentiated. Delay conditioning (CS coterminates with the US) has to be differentiated from trace conditioning (there is a short interval or *trace* between the CS and the US). Only the latter is thought to depend on hippocampal functioning (Christian and Thompson, 2003). In addition, simple conditioning paradigms (a single CS predicts the US) can be contrasted with discriminative tasks (a CS+ predicts the US, while in contrast a CS− predicts the absence of the US).

Eyeblink conditioning

The most impressive and consistent sex differences in rodents have been reported for the domain of eyeblink conditioning. Shors and colleagues observed that in the no-stress control condition female rats outperform their male counterparts in simple conditioning. This sex difference is reversed following acute stress, when males outperform females (Dalla and Shors, 2009; Shors, 2004). Several stressors produce this effect and it occurs in delay, as well as trace conditioning paradigms. Of note, the sex difference pattern differs (is a mirror image) from that observed with spatial tasks (Conrad et al., 2004). However, both describe scenarios whereby sex differences under nonstressed conditions are reversed following acute stress.

Surprisingly, few studies have investigated the effects of acute stress on eyeblink conditioning in humans. Of the few studies, one observed that a mild version of the Cold Pressor Test enhanced hippocampal-dependent trace conditioning in men, but females were not tested (Duncko et al., 2007). In addition, the stressor failed to activate the HPA axis, indicative of a failure to truly induce stress. This study suggests a beneficial effects of ardrenergic arousal on eyeblink conditioning while permitting a strong conclusion about HPA-mediated effects.

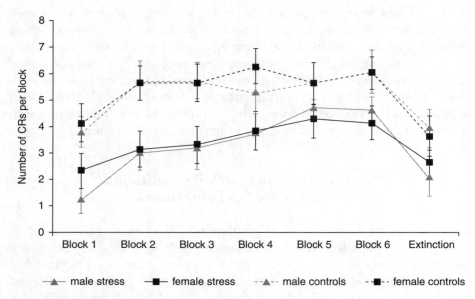

Figure 27.1 Effects of acute psychosocial stress on acquisition and extinction of delay eyeblink conditioning. Stress led to slower acquisition in men and women, but had no effect on extinction. CR, conditioned response. *Source:* Reprinted from Wolf et al. (2009). With permission from Elsevier.

Recently, the impact of a psychosocial stressor (TSST) on delay conditioning in healthy men and women was tested, representing the only study published, as of today, that tested acute stress effects on simple delay eyeblink conditioning (Wolf et al., 2009). In contrast to the observations made in rats, men and women performed similarly in their eyeblink conditioning in the control condition. In both sexes stress impaired eyeblink conditioning (Figure 27.1). Moreover, higher cortisol levels were associated with impaired conditioning (Wolf et al., 2009). Taken together this study indicates that stress induced cortisol elevations impair the acquisition of eyeblink conditioning in men and women.

The idea that stress-induced cortisol elevations cause impaired eyeblink conditioning in humans is supported by recent pharmacological studies (Vythilingam et al., 2006), as well as by studies in patients with endogenous hyppercortisolemia (Grillon et al., 2004). Why our study in humans failed to find the striking sex differences observed in rats (see Dalla and Shors, 2009; Shors, 2004) is perplexing. There are at least three possible explanations. First, Wolf et al. (2009) did not observe any a priori sex differences before acute stress was applied in the nonstressed controls, which contrasts with the work using rats (Dalla and Shors, 2009; Shors, 2004). Second, a psychosocial laboratory stressor was used in the human study, while Shors used physical stressors. Physical and psychological stressors differ with respect to activated brain regions (Ulrich-Lai and Herman, 2009). Third, the conditioning procedure used is quite invasive in rats (the electrodes are implanted into the eyelid, whereas it is noninvasive in humans: we used special goggles for the assessment of the eyelid reflex). Rodent studies have repeatedly observed that task aversiveness is an important mediator in determining the effects of stress on memory (Conrad, 2005; Sandi and Pinelo-Nava, 2007). A fourth explanation would simply state that humans and rodents differ in how stress influences their eyelid-conditioning abilities. Additional studies in humans on this topic are needed, but this example illustrates that current extrapolation from animal studies to the human situation needs to be made with caution.

Fear conditioning

Surprisingly little information is available on possible sex differences in fear conditioning in rodents. The impressive sexual dimorphic acute stress effects observed with eyelid conditioning have not been reported for this amygdala-dependent form of emotional learning, making the evaluation of this topic difficult. Either it has not been tried or the results have been nonsignificant and therefore were not published. However, at least for chronic stress sexual dimorphic responses in rats have been studied and reported (Baran et al., 2009).

In human stress research, several studies report fear conditioning effects with sex differences consistently found. Stress or cortisol exerts sex-dependent effects on this form of emotional learning, which depends upon the amygdala and other brain regions (LaBar and Cabeza, 2006). Three previous studies related basal and/or stress-induced cortisol levels to fear conditioning performance in men and women. Stress exposure or elevated/rising cortisol levels were associated with enhanced fear conditioning in men, but not women (Jackson et al., 2006; Zorawski et al., 2005, 2006).

Recently an alternative approach was implemented to investigate the effect of stress hormones on fear conditioning. Cortisol levels were experimentally manipulated using a placebo-controlled design. In this neuroimaging study (functional magnetic resonance imaging, fMRI) fear conditioning was conducted inside the scanner using a discriminative fear-conditioning paradigm (CS+ compared to CS–) with neutral (geometric symbols) stimuli as the CS and a mild electric shock as the UC. In the first study on this topic, cortisol impaired peripheral as well as neural correlates of fear conditioning in men, yet enhanced them in women (Stark et al., 2006). Under placebo women showed poorer fear conditioning, while under cortisol the opposite pattern was observed (Stark et al., 2006). The same sex-dependent effects of cortisol administration were observed in three frontal regions; namely the anterior cingulate gyrus, the lateral orbitofrontal cortex, and the medial prefrontal cortex. In all three regions cortisol enhanced neuronal activity (the contrast CS+ minus CS–) in women, while reducing it in men.

In a second study (Plate 6) these opposing effects of cortisol on neural correlates of fear conditioning in men and women were replicated. This time an implicit (without contingency awareness) fear-conditioning paradigm was administered (Merz et al., 2010). Contingency awareness is known to influence the peripheral as well as neural correlates of classical conditioning. By interleaving the presentation of the CS stimuli with a second demanding task (an n-back working-memory task) participants can be successfully prevented from becoming aware of the contingencies between the CS+ and the US. Previous studies have established that a lack of contingency awareness causes an abolishment of some peripheral indices of fear conditioning (electrodermal response; Hamm and Weike, 2005). In contrast, clear evidence for fear conditioning can be detected at the neural levels using fMRI (Tabbert et al., 2006). Using the just-described paradigm the effects of cortisol on implicit fear conditioning were tested, focusing on possible sex differences (Merz et al., 2010). Again opposing effects of cortisol administration in men and women occurred. Due to the implicit nature of the fear-conditioning paradigm the location of the effects had shifted from prefrontal regions towards subcortical regions. It was observed that cortisol reduced activity in the thalamus, insula, and hippocampus in men. In contrast in women (who showed lower activity under placebo than men) cortisol enhanced activity in these regions (Merz et al., 2010). This second study again indicates that cortisol enhances the neuronal correlates of fear learning in women, while impairing them in men.

The direction of the observed effects in our pharmacological study (impairing effect of cortisol on fear conditioning in men) contrasts to those observed after psychosocial stress (Jackson et al., 2006; Zorawski et al., 2006). At least two explanations are plausible. Nonlinear dose–response relationships might underlie an enhancement of fear conditioning in men after stress, while a substantial increase in cortisol in response to pharmacological cortisol treatment might impair fear conditioning. A second explanation could focus on the timing and/or on the neuroendocrine mediators involved. An increase in cortisol levels due to stress is preceded by a rise in hypothalamic (and extrathalamic) corticotropin-releasing hormone, which could enhance fear conditioning directly (Croiset et al., 2000). In contrast, cortisol treatment reduces corticotropin-releasing hormone via its negative feedback on the HPA axis (Joels and Baram, 2009). In addition, other stress mediators (e.g., the sympathetic nervous system) might be responsible for the difference between experimental stress studies and cortisol-administration studies. Future studies are needed to test these hypotheses and to create a more detailed picture on the effects of stress on fear conditioning in humans.

Despite some of the unresolved issues discussed, one can conclude that our pharmacological studies (Merz et al., 2010; Stark et al., 2006) observed substantial and opposing effects of the stress hormone cortisol on neural correlates of fear conditioning. Together with the studies investigating the effects of stress-induced alterations on peripheral fear conditioning (see summary above; Jackson et al., 2006; Zorawski et al., 2005, 2006) they illustrate evidence that sex differences in the response to stressors or stress hormones in fear conditioning can be substantial.

Summary

In this chapter, evidence was reviewed for sex differences in the influence of stress and cortisol on learning and memory processes. For episodic memory, some evidence exists that women compared to men are sometimes less susceptible to stress or cortisol treatment (Kuhlmann and Wolf, 2005; Schoofs and Wolf, 2009; Wolf et al., 2001b). However, the empirical situation is quite heterogeneous. Truly opposing effects of stress on episodic memory in men and women have not been observed in humans as of today, as found in rodents (Conrad et al., 2004).

Possible sex differences have not been investigated sufficiently for the area of human working memory. Thus it awaits to be determined, whether the enhanced stress susceptibility observed in female rats (Shansky et al., 2004, 2006; Shansky, 2009) translates into a higher stress sensitivity in women (with respect to working memory).

For eyeblink conditioning stress impaired performance in men and women (Wolf et al., 2009). Thus, for this form of classical conditioning the strong and opposing sex differences observed in rodents (Dalla and Shors, 2009; Shors, 2004) could so far not be found in humans. Possible reasons for these discrepancies have been discussed above and additional empirical work is needed to decide which of the possible explanations are true.

In contrast sex differences have been repeatedly shown in the domain of fear conditioning. Studies observed that the effects of stress were more pronounced in men, while being blunted or absent in women (Jackson et al., 2006; Zorawski et al., 2005, 2006). Research using a pharmacological approach demonstrated that cortisol impaired the neuronal correlates of fear conditioning in men, while enhancing them in women (Merz et al., 2010; Stark et al., 2006). Thus, cortisol treatment during fear conditioning led to opposing results in men and women, similarly to those reported in rodents using spatial tasks (Conrad et al., 2004) or eyeblink conditioning (Dalla and Shors, 2009; Shors, 2004).

At the very least, the empirical evidence supports the notion that sex has to be taken into account when investigating the effects of stress on learning and memory (in all species). At the same time, the complex picture argues against any global conclusions that argue that "women are more (or less) susceptible to stress." The results appear to be mediated by numerous factors, among them type (and duration) of the stressor, and memory domain assessed. It is conceivable that the effects of psychological stressors might differ from those of more physical stressors so a systematic comparison would be of interest. In addition the memory phase investigated (acquisition, consolidation, and retrieval) needs to be taken into account. High estradiol levels in women might make them more stress-susceptible in some cognitive domains but not others. In addition, it is important to emphasize that activational effects of gonadal steroids might not be the source of sex differences, as organization, genetic or other events could be important.

The topic of human aging has not been addressed in this review. Due to the substantial changes in sex steroid levels after the menopause (and to a lesser degree in aging men as well) the topic of sex steroids and memory after stress exposure is of substantial relevance for aging individuals (Wolf and Kudielka, 2008). The empirical evidence for antistress effects of sex steroid treatment in older women is so far sparse (Wolf and Kudielka, 2008). While basic science studies conducted in rodents are somewhat promising more research is needed before clinical trials can be initiated.

When Do We See Sex Differences? Some Hypotheses

Despite the somewhat unsatisfying empirical situation, it has become obvious that sex differences are not omnipresent in this field. Thus, the challenging theoretical question is to understand the conditions leading to sex differences (in the effects of stress on learning and memory). The fear-conditioning results could be interpreted in a way suggesting that sex differences occur most likely in tasks relying heavily on the amygdala. Studies on the topic of emotional memory have repeatedly observed sex differences (Andreano and Cahill, 2009; Cahill, 2006) and this has been in part attributed to a sexually dimorphic response of the amygdala. Thus, highly emotional learning and memory task might show sexually dimorphic stress effects.

Another broader and not mutually exclusive explanation focuses on baseline sex differences. Based on the human fear conditioning findings, as well as on some of the behavioral studies in rodents (Conrad et al., 2004; Dalla and Shors, 2009; Shors, 2004), one could hypothesize that sex differences under stress free control conditions predict a sexually dimorphic response after stress. Thus, stress might abolish or even reverse sex differences, which are present prior to stress and therefore might reflect sex differences in cerebral organization. Along these lines, there might be a sex-specific shift in neural processes underlying spatial memory after stress, which reflect in part sex differences prior to stress (Beck and Luine, 2010). This hypothesis focused on the observation that stress appears to induce a shift away from hippocampal (cognitive) forms of memory towards caudate-based (habit or stimulus response) forms of memory (Dias-Ferreira et al., 2009; Schwabe et al., 2010). While this hypothesis is quite attractive from a conceptual point of view, human studies on this topic have not observed strong sex differences (Schwabe et al., 2007; Schwabe and Wolf, 2009). The more global hypothesis that sex differences occurring in a stress-free control condition predict sex differences after stress could still be accurate and should be tested in future human studies using memory measures with known sex differences.

Outlook

The above summary indicates that there is some evidence for sex differences in how stress affects learning and memory, but clearly more research in this area is needed. Of course the inclusion of women into a psychoneuroendocrine study comes with a whole package of additional issues. Should one differentiate menstrual cycle phases and if yes, then how many phases should be considered? What about hormonal contraceptives (which again come in hundreds of different varieties)? Depending on how detailed one would like to tease apart possible interactions between gonadal hormones and stress hormones, three or four groups need to be studied (Andreano et al., 2008; Kuhlmann and Wolf, 2005), which will substantially increase running costs and time for data collection. A feasible initial approach might be to first study women, without taking into account their current sex steroid status and depending on the initial findings, pay attention to the menstrual cycle issue in a follow-up study (e.g., Andreano and Cahill, 2006; Andreano et al., 2008). While the decision to study males only can be understood from a pragmatic point of view, it leads to an unsatisfactory empirical situation. It is clearly unacceptable when half of the population is ignored. Moreover, the inclusion of both sexes often leads to quite exciting results thus rewarding those scientists who take the extra effort to study both sexes in parallel.

References

Andreano, J. M., & Cahill, L. (2006). Glucocorticoid release and memory consolidation in men and women. *Psychological Science, 17,* 466–470.

Andreano, J. M., & Cahill, L. (2009). Sex influences on the neurobiology of learning and memory. *Learning & Memory, 16,* 248–266.

Andreano, J. M., Arjomandi, H., & Cahill, L. (2008). Menstrual cycle modulation of the relationship between cortisol and long-term memory. *Psychoneuroendocrinology, 33,* 874–882.

Baran, S. E., Armstrong, C. E., Niren, D. C., Hanna, J. J., & Conrad, C. D. (2009). Chronic stress and sex differences on the recall of fear conditioning and extinction. *Neurobiology of Learning and Memory, 91,* 323–332.

Beck, K. D., & Luine, V. N. (2010). Evidence for sex-specific shifting of neural processes underlying learning and memory following stress. *Physiology & Behavior, 99,* 204–211.

Beckner, V. E., Tucker, D. M., Delville, Y., & Mohr, D. C. (2006). Stress facilitates consolidation of verbal memory for a film but does not affect retrieval. *Behavioral Neuroscience, 120,* 518–527.

Bowman, R. E., Zrull, M. C., & Luine, V. N. (2001). Chronic restraint stress enhances radial arm maze performance in female rats. *Brain Research, 904,* 279–289.

Cahill, L. (2006). Why sex matters for neuroscience. *Nature Reviews Neuroscience, 7,* 477–484.

Christian, K. M., & Thompson, R. F. (2003). Neural substrates of eyeblink conditioning: acquisition and retention. *Learning & Memory, 10,* 427–455.

Conrad, C. D. (2005). The relationship between acute glucocorticoid levels and hippocampal function depends upon task aversiveness and memory processing stage. *Nonlinearity in Biology, Toxicology and Medicine, 3,* 57–78.

Conrad, C. D., Jackson, J. L., Wieczorek, L., Baran, S. E., Harman, J. S., Wright, R. L., & Korol, D. L. (2004). Acute stress impairs spatial memory in male but not female rats: influence of estrous cycle. *Pharmacology, Biochemistry, and Behavior, 78,* 569–579.

Croiset, G., Nijsen, M. J., & Kamphuis, P. J. (2000). Role of corticotropin-releasing factor, vasopressin and the autonomic nervous system in learning and memory. *European Journal of Pharmacology, 405*, 225–234.

Dalla, C., & Shors, T. J. (2009). Sex differences in learning processes of classical and operant conditioning. *Physiology & Behavior, 97*, 229–238.

de Quervain, D. J., Aerni, A., Schelling, G., & Roozendaal, B. (2009). Glucocorticoids and the regulation of emotional memory in health and disease. *Frontiers in Neuroendocrinology, 30*, 358–370.

Diamond, D. M., Campbell, A. M., Park, C. R., Haloren, J., & Zoladz, P. R. (2007). The temporal dynamics model of emotional memory processing: a synthesis on the neurobiological basis of stress-induced amnesia, flashbulb and traumatic memories, and the Yerkes-Dodson law. *Neural Plasticity*, 60803.

Dias-Ferreira, E., Sousa, J. C., Melo, I., Morgado, P., Mesquita, A. R., Cerqueira, J. J., & Costa, R. M. (2009). Chronic stress causes frontostriatal reorganization and affects decision-making. *Science, 325*, 621–625.

Dickerson, S. S., & Kemeny, M. E. (2004). Acute stressors and cortisol responses: a theoretical integration and synthesis of laboratory research. *Psychological Bulletin, 130*, 355–391.

Duncko, R., Cornwell, B., Cui, L., Merikangas, K. R., & Grillon, C. (2007). Acute exposure to stress improves performance in trace eyeblink conditioning and spatial learning tasks in healthy men. *Learning & Memory, 14*, 329–335.

Grillon, C., Smith, K., Haynos, A., & Nieman, L. K. (2004). Deficits in hippocampus-mediated pavlovian conditioning in endogenous hypercortisolism. *Biological Psychiatry, 56*, 837–843.

Hamm, A. O., & Weike, A. I. (2005). The neuropsychology of fear learning and fear regulation. *International Journal of Psychophysiology, 57*, 5–14.

Jackson, E. D., Payne, J. D., Nadel, L., & Jacobs, W. J. (2006). Stress differentially modulates fear conditioning in healthy men and women. *Biological Psychiatry, 59*, 516–522.

Joels, M., & Baram, T. Z. (2009). The neuro-symphony of stress. *Nature Reviews Neuroscience, 10*, 459–466.

Joels, M., Pu, Z., Wiegert, O., Oitzl, M. S., & Krugers, H. J. (2006). Learning under stress: how does it work? *Trends in Cognitive Science, 10*, 152–158.

Kajantie, E., & Phillips, D. I. (2006). The effects of sex and hormonal status on the physiological response to acute psychosocial stress. *Psychoneuroendocrinology, 31*, 151–178.

Kirschbaum, C., Pirke, K. M., & Hellhammer, D. H. (1993). The "Trier Social Stress Test"–a tool for investigating psychobiological stress responses in a laboratory setting. *Neuropsychobiology, 28*, 76–81.

Kirschbaum, C., Wolf, O. T., May, M., Wippich, W., & Hellhammer, D. H. (1996). Stress- and treatment-induced elevations of cortisol levels associated with impaired declarative memory in healthy adults. *Life Sciences, 58*, 1475–1483.

Kirschbaum, C., Kudielka, B. M., Gaab, J., Schommer, N. C., & Hellhammer, D. H. (1999). Impact of gender, menstrual cycle phase, and oral contraceptives on the activity of the hypothalamus-pituitary-adrenal axis. *Psychosomatic Medicine, 61*, 154–162.

Kudielka, B. M., & Kirschbaum, C. (2005). Sex differences in HPA axis responses to stress: a review. *Biological Psychiatry, 69*, 113–132.

Kuhlmann, S., & Wolf, O. T. (2005). Cortisol and memory retrieval in women: influence of menstrual cycle and oral contraceptives. *Psychopharmacology, 183*, 65–71.

Kuhlmann, S., Kirschbaum, C., & Wolf, O. T. (2005a). Effects of oral cortisol treatment in healthy young women on memory retrieval of negative and neutral words. *Neurobiology of Learning and Memory, 83*, 158–162.

Kuhlmann, S., Piel, M., & Wolf, O. T. (2005b). Impaired memory retrieval after psychosocial stress in healthy young men. *Journal of Neuroscience, 25*, 2977–2982.

LaBar, K. S., & Cabeza, R. (2006). Cognitive neuroscience of emotional memory. *Nature Reviews Neuroscience, 7*, 54–64.

Luethi, M., Meier, B., & Sandi, C. (2008). Stress effects on working memory, explicit memory, and implicit memory for neutral and emotional stimuli in healthy men. *Frontiers in Behavioral Neuroscience, 2*, 5.

Luine, V. (2002). Sex differences in chronic stress effects on memory in rats. *Stress, 5*, 205–216.

Lupien, S. J., Gillin, C. J., & Hauger, R. L. (1999). Working memory is more sensitive than declarative memory to the acute effects of corticosteroids: a dose-response study in humans. *Behavioral Neuroscience, 113*, 420–430.

Merz, C. J., Wolf, O. T., Tabbert, K., Schweckendiek, J., Klucken, T., Vaitl, D., & Stark, R. (2010). Investigating the impact of sex and cortisol on implicit fear conditioning with fMRI. *Psychoneuroendocrinology, 35*, 33–46.

Nadel, L., & Moscovitch, M. (1997). Memory consolidation, retrograde amnesia and the hippocampal complex. *Current Opinions in Neurobiology, 7*, 217–227.

Nemeroff, C. B., Bremner, J. D., Foa, E. B., Mayberg, H. S., North, C. S., & Stein, M. B. (2006). Posttraumatic stress disorder: a state-of-the-science review. *Journal of Psychiatric Research, 40*, 1–21.

Oei, N. Y., Everaerd, W. T., Elzinga, B. M., van Well, S., & Bermond, B. (2006). Psychosocial stress impairs working memory at high loads: An association with cortisol levels and memory retrieval. *Stress, 9*, 133–141.

Park, C. R., Zoladz, P. R., Conrad, C. D., Fleshner, M., & Diamond, D. M. (2008). Acute predator stress impairs the consolidation and retrieval of hippocampus-dependent memory in male and female rats. *Learning & Memory, 15*, 271–280.

Preuß, D., & Wolf, O. T. (2009). Post-learning psychosocial stress enhances consolidation of neutral stimuli. *Neurobiology of Learning and Memory, 92*, 318–326.

Roozendaal, B., Okuda, S., de Quervain, D. J., & McGaugh, J. L. (2006). Glucocorticoids interact with emotion-induced noradrenergic activation in influencing different memory functions. *Neuroscience, 138*, 901–910.

Roozendaal, B., McEwen, B. S., & Chattarji, S. (2009). Stress, memory and the amygdala. *Nature Reviews Neuroscience, 10*, 423–433.

Sandi, C., & Pinelo-Nava, M. T. (2007). Stress and memory: behavioral effects and neuro-biological mechanisms. *Neural Plasticity, 2007*, 78970.

Schoofs, D., & Wolf, O. T. (2009). Stress and memory retrieval in women: No strong impairing effect during the luteal phase. *Behavioral Neuroscience, 123*, 547–554.

Schoofs, D., Hartmann, R., & Wolf, O. T. (2008a). Neuroendocrine stress responses to an oral academic examination: No strong influence of sex, repeated participation and personality traits. *Stress, 11*, 52–61.

Schoofs, D., Preuss, D., & Wolf, O. T. (2008b). Psychosocial stress induces working memory impairments in an n-back paradigm. *Psychoneuroendocrinology, 33*, 643–653.

Schoofs, D., Wolf, O. T., & Smeets, T. (2009). Cold pressor stress impairs performance on working memory tasks requiring executive functions in healthy young men. *Behavioral Neuroscience, 123*, 1066–1075.

Schwabe, L., & Wolf, O. T. (2009). Stress prompts habit behavior in humans. *Journal of Neuroscience, 29*, 7191–7198.

Schwabe, L., Oitzl, M. S., Philippsen, C., Richter, S., Bohringer, A., Wippich, W., & Oitzl, M. S. (2007). Stress modulates the use of spatial versus stimulus-response learning strategies in humans. *Learning & Memory, 14*, 109–116.

Schwabe, L., Wolf, O. T., & Oitzl, M. S. (2010). Memory formation under stress: quantity and quality. *Neuroscience and Biobehavioral Reviews, 34*, 584–591.

Shansky, R. M. (2009). Estrogen, stress and the brain: progress toward unraveling gender discrepancies in major depressive disorder. *Expert Review of Neurotherapeutics, 9*, 967–973.

Shansky, R. M., Glavis-Bloom, C., Lerman, D., McRae, P., Benson, C., Miller, K., Cosand, L., Horvath, T. L., & Arnsten, A. F. T. (2004). Estrogen mediates sex differences in stress-induced prefrontal cortex dysfunction. *Molecular Psychiatry, 9*, 531–538.

Shansky, R. M., Rubinow, K., Brennan, A., & Arnsten, A. F. (2006). The effects of sex and hormonal status on restraint-stress-induced working memory impairment. *Behavioural Brain Function, 2*, 8.

Shors, T. J. (2004). Learning during stressful times. *Learning & Memory, 11*, 137–144.

Smeets, T., Otgaar, H., Candel, I., & Wolf, O. T. (2008). True or false? Memory is differentially affected by stress-induced cortisol elevations and sympathetic activity at consolidation and retrieval. *Psychoneuroendocrinology, 33*, 1378–1386.

Stark, R., Wolf, O. T., Tabbert, K., Kagerer, S., Zimmermann, M., Kirsch, P., Schienle, A., & Vaitl, D. (2006). Influence of the stress hormone cortisol on fear conditioning in humans: evidence for sex differences in the response of the prefrontal cortex. *Neuroimage, 32*, 1290–1298.

Stroud, L., Salovey, P., & Epel, E. (2002). Sex differences in stress responses: social rejection versus achievement stress. *Biological Psychiatry, 52*, 318–327.

Tabbert, K., Stark, R., Kirsch, P., & Vaitl, D. (2006). Dissociation of neural responses and skin conductance reactions during fear conditioning with and without awareness of stimulus contingencies. *Neuroimage, 32*, 761–770.

Takahashi, T., Ikeda, K., Ishikawa, M., Tsukasaki, T., Nakama, D., Tanida, S., & Kameda, T. (2004). Social stress-induced cortisol elevation acutely impairs social memory in humans. *Neuroscience Letters, 363*, 125–130.

Taylor, S. E., Klein, L. C., Lewis, B. P., Gruenewald, T. L., Gurung, R. A., & Updegraff, J. A. (2000). Biobehavioral responses to stress in females: tend-and-befriend, not fight-or-flight. *Psychological Review, 107*, 411–429.

Ulrich-Lai, Y. M., & Herman, J. P. (2009). Neural regulation of endocrine and autonomic stress responses. *Nature Reviews Neuroscience, 10*, 397–409.

Vythilingam, M., Lawley, M., Collin, C., Bonne, O., Agarwal, R., Hadd, K., Charney, D. S., & Grillon, C. (2006). Hydrocortisone impairs hippocampal-dependent trace eyeblink conditioning in post-traumatic stress disorder. *Neuropsychopharmacology, 31*, 182–188.

Wolf, O. T. (2008). The influence of stress hormones on emotional memory: Relevance for psychopathology. *Acta Psychologica (Amsterdam), 127*, 513–531.

Wolf, O. T. (2009). Stress and memory in humans: twelve years of progress? *Brain Research, 1293*, 142–154.

Wolf, O. T., & Kudielka, B. M. (2008). Stress, health and ageing: a focus on postmenopausal women. *Menopause International, 14*, 129–133.

Wolf, O. T., Convit, A., McHugh, P. F., Kandil, E., Thorn, E. L., De Santi, S., McEwen, B. S., & de Leon, M. J. (2001a). Cortisol differentially affects memory in young and elderly men. *Behavioral Neuroscience*, *105*, 1002–1011.

Wolf, O. T., Schommer, N. C., Hellhammer, D. H., McEwen, B. S., & Kirschbaum, C. (2001b). The relationship between stress induced cortisol levels and memory differs between men and women. *Psychoneuroendocrinology*, *26*, 711–720.

Wolf, O. T., Minnebusch, D., & Daum, I. (2009). Stress impairs acquisition of delay eyeblink conditioning in men and women. *Neurobiology of Learning and Memory*, *91*, 431–436.

Yehuda, R. (2002). Post-traumatic stress disorder. *New England Journal of Medicine*, *346*, 108–114.

Zahn-Waxler, C., Shirtcliff, E. A., & Marceau, K. (2008). Disorders of childhood and adolescence: gender and psychopathology. *Annual Review of Clinical Psychology*, *4*, 275–303.

Zorawski, M., Cook, C. A., Kuhn, C. M., & LaBar, K. S. (2005). Sex, stress, and fear: individual differences in conditioned learning. *Cognitive, Affective, & Behavioral Neuroscience*, *5*, 191–201.

Zorawski, M., Blanding, N. Q., Kuhn, C. M., & LaBar, K. S. (2006). Effects of stress and sex on acquisition and consolidation of human fear conditioning. *Learning & Memory*, *13*, 441–450.

28

Influence of Diet on Stress Response and Behavior

Efthymia Kitraki

Introduction

Glucocorticoids are important players in critical homeostatic mechanisms, conferring adaptation to environmental challenges of a physical, emotional, immune, or metabolic nature. Excess or depletion of glucocorticoid release or signaling in the brain endangers neuronal survival and leads to deregulation in stress responsiveness, cognitive function, and energy management. Interventions in normal feeding, such as excessive consumption of calorie-dense foods, enriched in fat, sugar, or both, are sensed as a metabolic *threat* and can modify the activity of the hypothalamic–pituitary–adrenal (HPA) axis. However, not all nutrients have the same impact. High-fat foods usually exaggerate the basal and stress HPA axis response, whereas palatable foods highly enriched in sucrose can attenuate this response (Strack et al., 1997). It should be also noted that it is not simply the calories that account for the dampening of the stress response in animal models, but also the provision of choice (Warne, 2009).

Consumption of fatty meals is contributing significantly to the obesity epidemic. Food-related obesity, often characterized by dislipidemia and high blood pressure and glucose levels, subsequently leads to a number of pathologies, including cardiovascular aberrations, mood disorders, and type 2 diabetes (a form of diabetes owing to insulin resistance rather than to insulin depletion). Observations in humans as well as animal studies suggest the existence of a bidirectional causative link between obesity and stress (Bornstein et al., 2006; Reagan et al., 2008). Obesity-related pathologies, such as those aforementioned, are also met in the metabolic syndrome, a stress-associated disorder characterized mainly by visceral fat accumulation,

The Handbook of Stress: Neuropsychological Effects on the Brain, First Edition.
Edited by Cheryl D. Conrad.
© 2011 Blackwell Publishing Ltd. Published 2011 by Blackwell Publishing Ltd.

hypertension, cardiovascular dysfunction, and insulin resistance. Other symptoms include chronic fatigue, depression, and mood disorders, also met in chronic stress. Due to the escalating levels of everyday stress, metabolic syndrome affects an increasing number of individuals in Western societies. Individuals at stress frequently overeat comfort or rewarding foods to minimize the emotional load of the adverse situation. Indeed, palatable foods temporarily exert an anxiolytic effect (Macht, 2008; Pecoraro et al., 2004). However, in the long run this practice has detrimental metabolic effects, as it can lead to obesity and related diseases. In several instances a fatty dietary milieu even enhances the effect of chronic stress in the appearance of obesity (Tamashiro et al., 2006). In this vicious cycle, obesity impairs brain physiology by affecting neuronal survival, cognitive ability, and stress reactivity (Gómez-Pinilla, 2008).

Chronic overconsumption of fat-enriched foods is needed for the manifestation of obesity. However, many of the effects of dietary fat on brain physiology and behavior precede and are independent of the appearance of obesity. It appears that there are immediate (homeostatic) responses to fat feeding, in both the periphery and the brain, some of which may be transient (Legendre and Harris, 2006), whereas the obese state is probably governed by additional and/or distinct mechanisms. These initial fat-diet-induced disturbances merit further attention as they may represent early signs of future pathologies related to obesity.

In this chapter we will discuss evidence from rodents addressing the influence of high-fat diets on the neuroendocrine and behavioral stress response and concomitant cognitive ability. Whenever possible the underlying mechanisms will be referred to, including the implication of important energy regulators, such as insulin and leptin. Given the substantial sex differences existing in the above functions, evidence for the involvement of gender in the effects of fat diet will be also provided.

Effects of Fat Diets on the Neuroendocrine Stress Response

Over the past few decades evidence has accumulated for a possible association between dietary fat and activation of the HPA axis. The studies described below have used several variations in the percentage and/or source of fat and also vary in the balance of micronutrients and proteins in the regime compared to the control diet. Although it is generally believed that fat accumulation in the adrenals, irrespective of fat origin, is able to augment stress reaction, and probably less fat is needed in the case of saturated fat to reach the same effect, this information is included as it may contribute to the variation of the reported impact. Additionally, the type of stressor used varies among the different studies (restraint, swimming, and social stress are mostly in use) and this may also affect the final diet impact, particularly between the sexes.

In 1978, Hülsmann, based on corticosterone measurements, suggested that diets enriched in fat (40% fat from rapeseed oil) can elicit abnormal stress responses in male rats upon adrenocorticotrophic hormone (ACTH) administration (Hülsmann,

1978). Brindley et al. (1981) showed that rats maintained on high-fat diets (the fat provided from lard or corn oil) increased their corticosterone levels more after a metabolic challenge. By providing 59% of calories from fat, Pascoe et al. (1991) reported that besides corticosterone, noradrenergic activity in the hypothalamus was also enhanced in high-fat-fed male rats following swimming stress at two different temperatures. A positive-feedback loop between the concentration of free fatty acids that are increased upon fat feeding (Ruderman et al., 1969) and the levels of corticosterone and ACTH was first reported by Widmaier et al. (1992).

In a detailed study Tannenbaum et al. (1997) examined the effect of a high-fat diet (20% from corn oil and balanced for protein and micronutrients) on the HPA axis activity of male rats, by measuring corticosterone and ACTH responses throughout the day. Following restraint stress, both corticosterone and ACTH levels increased more in high-fat-fed animals, compared to chow fed. In the same study, basal corticosterone levels were increased and the number of glucocorticoid receptors (GRs) in the hypothalamus was decreased due to fat diet. The authors concluded that the pattern of effects of the high-fat diet on the HPA axis is similar to that observed after chronic stress.

Shortly afterwards Kamara and colleagues (1998) further verified the effect of a fat diet on the enhancement of corticosterone response following restraint stress. These authors exposed rats to diets of differing fat composition (soybean oil, fish oil, corn oil, and olive oil; each contributing 54% of calories from fat) and measured the basal and stress-induced corticosterone levels of these animals after 2 and 10 weeks on the diets. All diets were similarly effective in augmenting corticosterone release following stress in the second week. When the same stress was applied again in the tenth week on the diet, the initial response of corticosterone was not affected. However, the recovery from stress was significantly delayed by the fat diet, pointing to impaired HPA axis negative feedback.

By providing a diet 20% enriched in corn oil (and proportionally lower in protein and carbohydrates) for 1 week we showed that even a short-term exposure to fat excess was able to reduce GR mRNA levels in the hypothalamus of male rats following acute swimming stress (Kitraki et al., 2004). Although the diet used was not exactly the same as those applied previously and was not equally effective in modifying basal or stress-induced corticosterone release, at least in males, it could impair stress response, in line with the previous reports, by lowering the GR-mediated negative feedback.

In obese Zucker rats, a model for type 2 diabetes, exhibiting increased basal and poststress corticosterone release, reduced mineralocorticoid receptor (MR) mRNA levels were detected in all hippocampal regions and in the frontal cortex, without changes in GR mRNA levels (Mattsson et al., 2003). However, the impaired negative feedback in these animals may rely on deficient corticosterone signaling, as they have an impaired local regeneration of corticosterone by 11β-hydroxysteroid dehydrogenase type 1 (an enzyme converting inactive corticosteroid compounds to active corticosterone). These findings provide another possible mechanism for the impaired axis feedback at the obese state. However, more studies are needed to clarify the implicated mechanism(s) of HPA axis deregulation in preobese and genetically obese animals, particularly since most studies in preobese fat-fed rats have failed to detect changes in hippocampal MR levels (Lee et al., 2000; Han et al., 1995).

Interestingly, the effect of short-term fat exposure on HPA axis appears sexually dimorphic. Under basal conditions, adult females, but not males, exposed for a week to a 20% fat diet showed increased plasma corticosterone and reduced GR mRNA levels in the hippocampus (Soulis et al., 2005), implying that females experienced the diet as a metabolic stress earlier than males. Furthermore, following acute swimming stress, the response was also sexually dimorphic, with females showing a blunted corticosterone and GR response.

The aforementioned findings were the first indication that the impact of fat diets on HPA axis responsiveness can differ between the sexes. The sexually dimorphic effect of fat diet on the endocrine response to stress was further verified in a later study (Soulis et al., 2007), where both males and females, fed the same fat diet as above, were sampled upon exposure to one or two sequential mild stressors (swimming and open field). In fat-fed males, corticosterone response was exaggerated in both instances, in accordance with previous studies (Tannenbaum et al., 1997; Legendre and Harris, 2006). In contrast, fat-fed females failed to show an exaggerated corticosterone response to the stressors used. Notably, in both sexes fat feeding abolished the facilitation in corticosterone release that normally occurs when a stressed animal is exposed to a subsequent stress (Akana et al., 1992; Martí et al., 1994), implying a fat-induced impairment of a prompt neuroendocrine stress response. On the other hand, this neuroendocrine impairment may result to a more passive behavioral response, translated to a more effective coping, of fat-fed animals at stress (discussed below).

More recent studies from our group—using a balanced fat diet (45% of calories from lard)—provide additional support for a differential effect of fat diets on the female HPA axis. In these studies, the temporal effect of fat feeding was studied by including groups of animals fed the fat diet from weaning to puberty (3-week feeding period) or to adulthood (10-week feeding period), as well as groups that crossed their diets (from fat to chow and vice versa) at puberty onset. None of the groups had increased body weight at death, denoting that animals were still at a preobese state. Under basal conditions, the *stress-like* effect of fat feeding on female HPA axis was witnessed already at puberty onset, by means of enlarged adrenals, increased plasma corticosterone, and reduced hypothalamic GR levels. In adult females fed the diet for 10 weeks, the adrenal hypertrophy was no longer detected; however, basal corticosterone levels and hypothalamic GRs were similarly modified. In addition, GR levels in the hippocampus were reduced by the fat diet. In adult female rats, switching from fat to normal chow at puberty onset restored the levels of corticosterone and GR in the hypothalamus, but not in the hippocampus (Boukouvalas et al., 2010b). Remarkable differences were observed in the neuroendocrine response of the respective male groups. The fat diet used did not alter basal corticosterone levels or brain receptors in pubertal males, while it led to a reduction of basal GR levels in the adult male hippocampus that was restored upon crossing the fat diet with normal chow at puberty onset (Boukouvalas et al., 2010a).

Overall, the data presented so far clearly show that fat diets, even short-term ones, impair the basal and stress neuroedocrine response in a sexually dimorphic manner: they exaggerate basal and stress corticosterone response in males and can impair their axis negative feedback at stress. Females appear more sensitive to diet-induced HPA dysfunction under basal conditions but show a blunted corticosterone response to stress. Accordingly, males on fat diets may be exposed to increased corticosteroids for longer periods following stress, as they cannot properly terminate stress response due to the reduced brain GR levels. However, the decrease in GR could also confer neuroprotection from the deleterious effects of stress, by reducing corticosterone signaling in vulnerable brain regions like the hippocampus. On the other hand, females on a fat diet experience under basal conditions a neuroendocrine state of chronic stress, characterized by increased corticosterone levels in the periphery and downregulated brain receptors. This diet-induced dysfunction of HPA axis appears at an earlier age in females than in males and it could render them more vulnerable to stress-related mood disorders, like *depression*.

The sex differences detected in the impact of fat diet on HPA axis may reside on the sexually dimorphic actions of female hormones in the brain. Estrogen is known to potentiate corticosterone levels (Kitay et al., 1965). Plasma estrogen levels increase proportionally to the fat content of diet in adult female rats (Leibowitz et al., 2007). Accordingly, increased estradiol levels in fat-fed females could have potentiated the observed corticosterone increase and subsequent reduction of GR levels under basal conditions. In this case, the previously described competition between estrogen and GRs (Patchev et al., 1995; Weiser and Handa, 2009) could also contribute to the observed HPA axis impairment.

Effects of Fat Diets on Behavioral Stress Response

Although high-fat diets enhance HPA axis activity, there is a consensus from behavioral observations, conducted mainly in males, that they reduce anxiety levels. Diet-induced obese rats show reduced anxiety in a chronic unpredictable stress paradigm, compared to obesity-resistant rats (Levin et al., 2000). Very-high-fat diets consisting of more than 60% fat (ketogenic diets) are known to reduce anxiety in rats and have been used in the treatment of epilepsy that is refractory to drugs (Murphy, 2005). Prasad and Prasad (1996) used a 90% fat diet for 7 days to treat high-anxiety male rats and succeeded in reducing their anxiety, as determined by the performance of the animals in the elevated-plus maze. Buwalda et al. (2001) provided a 61% fat diet (fat mostly from beef tallow) in male rats for 4 months and studied their physiological and behavioral responses upon exposure to a psychological (social defeat) or immunological (lipopolysaccharide administration) stress. They reported that fat-fed males had a faster recovery following social defeat or immune challenge (in terms of body temperature increase/fever response and body weight gain) compared to similarly stressed chow-fed males. Behaviorally, fat-fed males exhibited reduced suppression of locomotion following social defeat. However, in another social-stress paradigm, fat feeding (40% calories from fat) did not affect social behavior (Tamashiro et al., 2006), indicating that the effects of the fat diet on a certain behavior may be also influenced by the paradigm used and the duration of feeding, as well as the percentage of fat.

Diets moderately enriched in fat can also modify the activity of adult rats in behavioral tests. Adult rats of both sexes fed with a 20% fat diet for 1 week adopted a less-active coping strategy when forced to swim in a cylinder filled with water (Soulis et al., 2007). In addition, fat-fed males were more active and explorative in the open-field test, an indication of reduced anxiety, in agreement with the previous studies using diets with a higher fat content. In opposition to males, however, fat-fed females were less explorative and active in the open field, implying that these animals were at a state of increased *anxiety* that often suppresses reactivity in a new environment (Faraday, 2002). Given that anxiety is related to the hyperactivation of HPA axis (Greaves-Lord et al., 2007) the reduced locomotion of fat-fed females may reside in their enhanced basal corticosterone levels.

The impact of dietary fat on behavior does not seem to be significantly altered from juvenility to adulthood. We have examined the impact of postweaning high-fat feeding on the behavioral responses of male and female rats at the onset of puberty (Boukouvalas et al., 2008). Overall their behavioral responses in the forced swimming and the open-field tests were similar to those observed in adult animals (Soulis et al., 2007), with males being less *anxious* and more active than females.

Taken together, the above data from rodents support the linkage between high fat consumption and positive emotional behavior, often reported in humans (Macht, 2008). These data also reveal the existence of sexually distinct effects of dietary fat on behavioral stress coping and suggest that comfort diets are probably more effective in ameliorating stress in males. A possible mechanism for the fat diet anxiolytic effect could implicate the melanocortin system (α-melanocortin-stimulating hormone, α-MSH). Activation of melanocortin signaling by acute glucocorticoid rise following stress leads to increased anxiety and reduced food intake (Liu et al., 2007). Conversely, in fat-fed animals exhibiting an impaired stress response system, an inefficient activation of the melanocortin pathway by the glucocorticoids could lower the anxiety load and at the same time enhance food intake. In support to this hypothesis, melanocortin-4 receptor antagonists are used to treat depression and eliminate anxiety (Chaki and Okubo, 2007)

Implication of Metabolic Regulators

The brain's stress-response system and that controlling energy homeostasis share neuroanatomical substrates that converge in the hypothalamus. Circulating nutrients (such as free fatty acids and glucose) modulate the secretion of peripheral metabolic regulators such as leptin, insulin, and other gut peptides proportionally to body energy stores. Leptin, a key sensor of the status of fat stores, in concert with insulin regulate energy homeostasis and glucose availability. These signals reach the brain, where neuronal systems sense the inputs and respond by adaptive changes in energy intake, energy expenditure, and hepatic glucose production. Leptin and insulin, through their receptors in the arcuate nucleus of the hypothalamus, integrate peripheral signals to central energy homeostasis (Figure 28.1). According to the adiposity negative-feedback hypothesis, leptin and insulin in the arcuate nucleus reduce food intake by stimulating anorexigenic neuropeptides (including proopiomelanocortin, α-MSH, corticotropin-releasing hormone (CRH), and brain-derived neurotrophic factor (BDNF)) and downregulating the orexigenic ones (including neuropeptide Y, orexin, and agouti-related peptide). The anabolic and

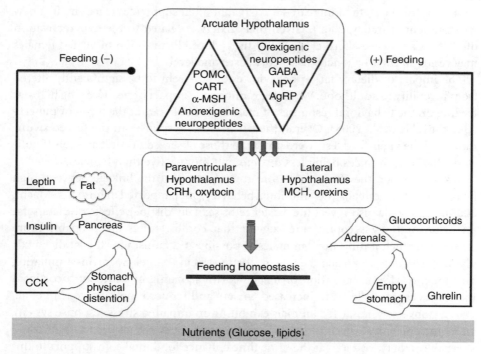

Figure 28.1 Homeostatic mechanisms of feeding within the hypothalamus. Leptin and insulin in the periphery increase proportionally to the fat content and act in the arcuate nucleus of the hypothalamus to reduce food intake by stimulating anorexigenic neuropeptides (corticotropin-releasing hormone (CRH), proopiomelanocortin (POMC), cocaine-and amphetamine-regulated transcript (CART), α-MSH) and downregulating orexigenic mediators (γ-aminobutyric acid (GABA), neuropeptide Y (NPY), agouti-related peptide (AgRP), and melanin-concentrating hormone (MCH)). The anabolic and catabolic pathways originating in the arcuate project to the paraventricular nucleus and lateral hypothalamic nucleus. Signals from stomach and duodenum may be either anorexigenic (like cholecystokinin (CCK) following a meal) or orexigenic (as in the case of ghrelin, which is released from an empty stomach). Glucocorticoids promote feeding, except in the acute phase of a stress response.

catabolic pathways originating in the arcuate project to the paraventricular nucleus (PVN) and lateral hypothalamic nucleus. From there, they connect to other pathways projecting to hind brain centers of satiety regulation (Fehm et al., 2006). Additional satiety signals from the liver and gut reach the brain via the vagus nerve and sympathetic fibers and integrate with the descending hypothalamic afferents in the hindbrain. These signals can either inhibit or stimulate food intake, like cholecystokinin and ghrelin, respectively.

Glucocorticoids are critically involved in glucose homeostasis and energy expenditure and PVN is a central neuroanatomical substrate for both metabolic and stress-related glucocorticoid actions. Free fatty acids from fat consumption stimulate glucocorticoid release from the adrenals, similarly to acute stress. In the acute phase of a stress response, as well as in response to a fat diet, CRH is released in the PVN. This molecule is a major component of both the HPA axis (see Chapter 1 in this volume) and of the central anorexigenic pathways activated by leptin and insulin. Thus, increased glucocorticoids transiently reduce feeding in synergy with leptin and insulin, conferring to the adiposity negative feedback (Figure 28.2). Upon chronic fat consumption, the prolonged elevation of free fatty acids and glucose levels often lead to leptin or insulin resistance, hence reducing the central anorexigenic tone. At the same time, chronically elevated glucocorticoids and HPA axis activation exert a negative feedback on CRH release through GRs and instead promote the increase of orexigenic signals in the brain that lead to enhanced food intake (Nieuwenhuizen and Rutters, 2008). The interplay between satiety signals like leptin or insulin and the glucocorticoids appears biphasic and is bidirectional, as leptin inhibits glucocorticoid production by the adrenal gland (Spinedi and Gaillard, 1998) and exerts an inhibitory effect on HPA axis response to various stress stimuli (Heiman et al., 1997; Giovambattista et al., 2000). Early compensatory alterations in the levels of these adiposity signals influence the action of stress mediators and can modify the stress response and behavior. When the dietary manipulation/imbalance is prolonged, as in cases of chronic fat consumption, persistent changes in the energy-sensing molecules are established (including brain resistance to insulin or leptin) that lead to the development of a central metabolic syndrome and further deterioration of the neuroendocrine stress response.

Among the signs of high-fat-diet-induced metabolic disturbance that proceed with obesity is the appearance of central insulin and/or leptin resistance (van Dijk et al., 2003; Gerozissis, 2008). Elevated glucocorticoid levels are among the key factors promoting central insulin insensitivity. One of the main mechanisms for this glucocorticoid-induced insulin resistance involves the inhibition of translocation of the GLUT4 glucose transporter from the interior of cells to the cell surface and subsequent glucose entry to the cells (Piroli et al., 2007). The reduction of leptin sensitivity in the hypothalamus is often attributed to the downregulation of its receptor (Martin et al., 2000; Boukouvalas et al., 2010a, 2010b). Elimination of the anorexigenic leptin actions in the hypothalamus promotes the emergence of a central metabolic syndrome that can consequently lead to reduced α-MSH activity and hyperinsulinemia (Huang et al., 2004). As mentioned above, the attenuated response of glucocorticoids to stress in fat-fed animals could also reduce α-MSH

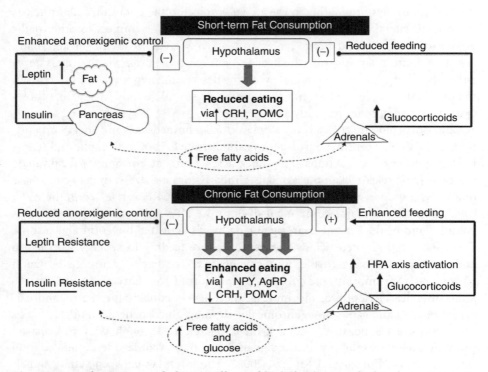

Figure 28.2 Short-term and chronic effects of high-fat diets on feeding homeostasis. In cases of short-term fat consumption, an adiposity negative-feedback loop driven by leptin and insulin reduce food intake and body weight through increasing anorexigenic neuropeptides (CRH, proopiomelanocortin (POMC), etc.) and downregulating orexigenic signals. Free fatty acids stimulate glucocorticoid release from the adrenals that, similarly to acute stress, transiently reduce food intake by increasing CRH levels. Upon long-term fat consumption, the prolonged elevation of free fatty acids and glucose levels often lead to leptin or insulin resistance, thus reducing the central anorexigenic control. At the same time, chronically elevated glucocorticoids and HPA axis activation promote the increase of orexigenic signals in the brain that lead to enhanced food intake. AgRP, agouti-related peptide; NPY, neuropeptide Y.

activity, thus further diminishing the anorexigenic control. In this framework, van Dijk and Buwalda (2008) have proposed that high fat consumption can aggravate the metabolic load of a stressful experience. At the same time, the reduced α-MSH tone confers amelioration of the anxiety load (Larsen and Mau, 1994; Chaki and Okubo, 2007) in fat-fed animals. Furthermore, a downregulated leptin receptor in the hypothalamus could also participate in the relief of anxiety symptoms in the obese state by lowering the tone of the sympathetic nervous system (Haynes et al., 1997).

As already mentioned glucocorticoids exert anabolic actions in the brain, counterbalancing the anorexigenic actions of leptin and insulin. In the hypothalamus of adult males fed with fat diet from weaning onwards, we detected increased levels of GRs and reduced levels of leptin receptors (Boukouvalas et al., 2010a). This combination suggests an increased orexigenic to anorexigenic signal that is considered crucial for the development of the metabolic syndrome (Zakrzewska et al., 1997). Given that the metabolic disequilibrium caused by fat feeding is initially affecting the brain and in the second place the periphery, these data suggest that males on fat diet are more vulnerable than females to the metabolic consequences of this dietary manipulation. In line with this, estrogens appear to protect the brain from the deleterious effects of fat feeding that lead to central resistance in insulin or leptin (Riant et al., 2009; Matyšková et al., 2010).

Based on the above evidence, we can assume that gut peptides represent another potential source of stress-response modifiers in cases of dietary imbalance. Furthermore, these molecules through their nonmetabolic actions can possibly aggravate or ameliorate the impact of a fat diet on behavior and cognitive ability. Lu et al. (2006) evaluated the antidepressant-like properties of leptin in male rats by measuring its effects on anhedonia and despair-like behaviors, caused by chronic unpredictable stress and forced swimming, respectively. Leptin administration improved behavioral deficits, similarly to the antidepressants targeting the serotonergic system. It is thus possible that the increased leptinemia often observed in rats following a high-fat diet (Cha et al., 2000; Kitraki et al., 2004; Banas et al., 2009) may contribute to the lightening of the emotional load following stress. A permissive role of insulin signaling pathways in the hippocampal control of eating behavior and cognitive function has also been reported. A potential role of insulin in cognitive enhancement is of particular interest not only in the context of type 2 diabetes, which is characterized by systemic hyperglycemia, insulin resistance, and memory deficits (McNay and Cotero, 2010), but also at a preobese state, often accompanied by analogous symptoms.

Effect of Dietary Fat in Cognitive Function

There are many reports associating obesity and diabetes with cognitive decline. Recent work suggests that cognitive function can be adversely affected by obesity. Subjects on high-fat or high-sucrose diets are at higher risk of developing type 2 diabetes and the neurological symptoms of the disease, including cognitive impairment. However, the magnitude of deficit is still a matter of debate (Reagan et al., 2008). Genetically obese Zucker rats, which exhibit insulin resistance, are cognitively deficient (Winocur et al., 2005).

Even prior to the appearance of obesity, however, consumption of fat or/ and sucrose-enriched foods has been shown to severely impact brain plasticity and cognitive performance in a number of animal studies. Winocur and Greenwood (2005), by using a battery of learning and memory tests, have shown that chronic consumption of a moderate level of fat by young adult rats, similar to the current upper limit of human consumption, results in cognitive impairment. The cognitive deficit was more severe in cases of saturated fat and adverse effects of fat diets were substantially ameliorated by housing the animals in an enriched environment.

Two months' exposure of rats to a diet rich in saturated fat and refined sugar could reduce spatial performance, as well as BDNF levels and its downstream effectors synapsin I and cAMP-response-element-binding protein (CREB) selectively in the hippocampus (Molteni et al., 2002). Given the well-established role of BDNF in synaptic plasticity, its reduction drastically diminishes cognitive performance. The increased amount of dietary lipids and subsequent oxidations, leading to oxidative damage of hippocampal neurons (Mattson, 2007), could account for this BDNF decrease. Indeed the use of an antioxidant factor in fat-fed rats restored the diet-induced impairment on BDNF and cognition (Wu et al., 2004), suggesting that there is a causative link between increased lipid content, oxidative stress, and BDNF reduction. In another study with a combined high-fat and -sucrose diet for 8 months, the spatial learning impairment was accompanied by reduced dentritic spine density and long-term potentiation (LTP) in the hippocampus (Stranahan et al., 2008a). Sucrose appears more effective in reducing learning ability, compared to fat, at least in young rats (Jurdak et al., 2008).

Given the direct influence of dietary sugars on glucose levels and insulin sensitivity in the brain, another possible mechanism for cognitive disturbances could relay on the destruction of glucoregulation. Blockade of insulin actions or signaling in the brain and particularly within the hippocampus have been implicated in diet-induced cognitive impairment (Park, 2001). Hippocampal insulin receptors are involved in the maintenance of synaptic plasticity, LTP, and memory processing (Zhao et al., 1999). Insulin administration in cognitively deficient animals can significantly restore their performance (De Castro and Balagura, 1976; Moosavi et al., 2006). The same holds true for glucose administration in young adult rats (Winocur and Greenwood, 2005).

Stress levels of glucocorticoids negatively impact learning and memory (de Kloet et al., 1999). The increased corticosterone due to fat diet can disrupt N-methyl-D-aspartate (NMDA) homeostasis, glutamatergic tone, and conversely reduce LTP in the hippocampus (Farr et al., 2008). When chronic stress is experienced in parallel with a high-fat diet, these two factors act in synergy to cause a retraction of CA3 hippocampal dendrites (where CA means cornu ammonis, a subregion of the hippocampus) that are essential in hippocampus-dependent learning and memory (Baran et al., 2005, see also Chapter 10).

In addition, stress hormones are often behind insulin resistance in the periphery (Amatruda et al., 1985), but also in the brain. One week's exposure to stress levels of corticosterone is able to impair insulin signaling and glucose utilization in the hippocampus of rats (Piroli et al., 2007). Accordingly, the elevated glucocorticoids due to fat diet could have participated in insulin imbalance at this area and the concomitant reduction in cognitive function. In a glucose-independent pathway, glucocorticoids could also impinge the outcome of cognitive performance during a fat diet, by reducing synaptic plasticity and hippocampal neurogenesis (Stranahan et al., 2008b).

Closing Remarks

Consumption of fat-enriched diets elicits an array of responses that range from early compensatory reactions to pathology-related dysfunctions, depending primarily on the duration of fat exposure. The brain circuits involved in food intake and metabolic balance share a common neuroanatomical basis and molecular mediators with those controlling stress response. For this reason, metabolic manipulations reflect neuroendocrine and behavioral stress responses, and vice versa.

Early homeostatic responses in fat-fed rodents include increased levels of leptin and corticosterone, reduced brain GR levels, and concomitant reduced feeding under basal conditions (Figure 28.3). At the behavioral level, male rats benefit more from the anxiolytic effects of fat feeding, showing enhanced exploration attitude and reduced anxiety. When an acute stress is exerted during the fat feeding period, the HPA axis response is deregulated in a sexually dimorphic manner. Males exhibit an exaggerated corticosterone and ACTH response, and an impaired negative feedback, as deduced by the decreased GR levels in the limbic system. Females exhibit a blunted response with no further increase in corticosterone or decrease in GRs. Behavioral coping following stress is also less active, supporting the hypothesis of an anxiolytic effect of fat diets. On the other hand, metabolic disturbance is

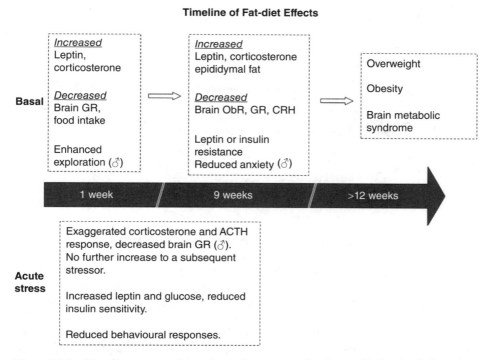

Figure 28.3 Timeline summarizing the major neuroendocrine and behavioral alterations detected in adult rodents exposed to fat diets for 1 week or more (up to 9 and more than 12 weeks) under basal conditions or following an acute stress. The sex symbol in parentheses denotes a male selective effect. ObR, leptin receptor.

augmented in short-term fat-fed animals after stress, as shown by the increased leptin and glucose levels and the reduced insulin sensitivity detected in these animals.

Prolonged fat feeding dampens metabolic deregulation through the appearance of leptin and/or insulin resistance within the brain, before the appearance of overweight or obesity. HPA axis is permanently activated through the increase of free fatty acids and further enhances food intake. Elevated glucocorticoid levels are among the key factors promoting central insulin and leptin resistance. Brain insensitivity to these two energy sensors facilitates the appearance of a central metabolic syndrome (Figure 28.4). This positive feedback loop ultimately leads to the appear-

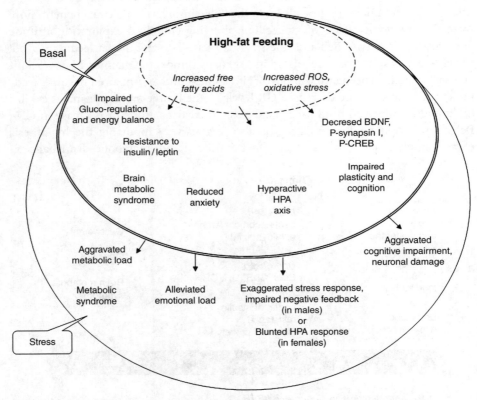

Figure 28.4 Effect of high-fat feeding on stress response, energy balance, and cognitive function. Excess fat intake increases free fatty acids and subsequently the levels of glucocorticoids. Increased glucocorticoids affect both basal HPA axis and glucose homeostasis leading to axis hyperactivation and leptin/insulin resistance, respectively. The impaired leptin/melanocortin system and probably additional factors lower anxiety levels in fat-fed animals. Increased formation of reactive oxygen species (ROS) through excess energy production decreases the levels of BDNF and downstream effectors, compromising cognitive ability. Stress potentiates the effects of a fat diet on the above brain functions, leading to aggravated metabolic and cognitive load, sexually dimorphic impairment of the neuroendocrine stress response, and alleviated emotional load. pCREB, phosphorylated CREB; pSynapsin I, phosphorylated synapsin I.

ance of obesity. Prolonged fat feeding not only affects metabolic and stress response but has also pronounced effects on cognitive function. Brain networks that are associated with stress response and energy homeostasis are intimately related with those involved in cognition. Fat intake reduces synaptic plasticity and endangers cognitive ability. Several mechanisms have been proposed including the reduction of synaptic proteins and neurotrophins by fat diet-enhanced oxidative stress, as well as direct and indirect actions of increased glucocorticoids. A stressful situation experienced in parallel with a fat diet potentiates the diet's effects, leading to aggravated metabolic and cognitive load. At the same time, the impaired leptin/melanocortin signaling confers alleviation of the emotional load by lowering anxiety levels in fat-fed animals.

These observations can explain how stress works as a potential feed-forward factor to the obesity epidemic. Stressful situations promote comfort fat feeding to relieve anxiety and emotional distress; at the same time the palatable meal further aggravates the neuroendocrine, metabolic, and cognitive impact of stress. Managing emotional eating under stress could help to reduce the high number of people reaching obesity in Western societies.

References

Akana, S. F., Dallman, M. F., Bradbury, M. J., Scribner, K. A., Strack, A. M., & Walker, C. D. (1992). Feedback and facilitation in the adrenocortical system: unmasking facilitation by partial inhibition of the glucocorticoid response to prior stress. *Endocrinology*, *131*(1), 57–68.

Amatruda, J. M., Livingston, J. N., & Lockwood, D. H. (1985) Cellular mechanisms in selected states of insulin resistance: human obesity, glucocorticoid excess and chronic renal failure. *Diabetes/Metabolism Reviews*, *1*(3), 293–317.

Banas, S. M., Rouch, C., Kassis, N., Markaki, E. M., & Gerozissis, K. (2009). A dietary fat excess alters metabolic and neuroendocrine responses before the onset of metabolic diseases. *Cellular and Molecular Neurobiology*, *29*(2), 157–168.

Baran, S. E., Campbell, A. M., Kleen, J. K., Foltz, C. H., Wright, R. L., Diamond, D. M., & Conrad, C. D. (2005) Combination of high fat diet and chronic stress retracts hippocampal dendrites. *Neuroreport*, *16*(1), 39–43.

Bornstein, S. R., Schuppenies, A., Wong, M. L., & Licinio, J. (2006). Approaching the shared biology of obesity and depression: the stress axis as the locus of gene-environment interactions. *Molecular Psychiatry*, *11*(10), 892–902.

Boukouvalas, G., Antoniou, K., Papalexi, E., & Kitraki, E. (2008). Post weaning high fat feeding affects rats' behavior and hypothalamic pituitary adrenal axis at the onset of puberty in a sexually dimorphic manner. *Neuroscience*, *153*(2), 373–382.

Boukouvalas, G., Gerozissis, K., & Kitraki, E. (2010a). Fat feeding of rats during pubertal growth leads to neuroendocrine alterations in adulthood. *Cellular and Molecular Neurobiology*, *30*(1), 91–99.

Boukouvalas, G., Gerozissis, K., & Kitraki, E. (2010b). Adult consequences of post-weaning high fat feeding on the limbic-HPA axis of female rats. *Cellular and Molecular Neurobiology*, *30*, 91–99.

Brindley, D. N., Cooling, J., Glenny, H. P., Burditt, S. L., & McKechnie, I. S. (1981). Effects of chronic modification of dietary fat and carbohydrate on the insulin, corticosterone and metabolic responses of rats fed acutely with glucose, fructose or ethanol. *Biochemical Journal*, *200*(2), 275–283.

Buwalda, B., Blom, W. A., Koolhaas, J. M., & van Dijk, G. (2001). Behavioral and physiological responses to stress are affected by high-fat feeding in male rats. *Physiology & Behavior*, *73*(3), 371–377.

Cha, M. C., Chou, C. J., & Boozer, C. N. (2000). High-fat diet feeding reduces the diurnal variation of plasma leptin concentration in rats. *Metabolism*, *49*(4), 503–507.

Chaki, S., & Okubo, T. (2007). Melanocortin-4 receptor antagonists for the treatment of depression and anxiety disorders. *Current Topics in Medical Chemistry*, *7*(11), 1145–1151.

De Castro, J. M., & Balagura, S. (1976). Insulin pretreatment facilitates recovery after dorsal hippocampal lesions. *Physiology & Behavior*, *16*(5), 517–520.

de Kloet, E. R., Oitzl, M. S., & Joëls, M. (1999). Stress and cognition: are corticosteroids good or bad guys? *Trends in Neuroscience*, *22*(10), 422–426.

Faraday, M. M. (2002). Rat sex and strain differences in responses to stress. *Physiology & Behavior*, *75*(4), 507–522.

Farr, S. A., Yamada, K. A., Butterfield, D. A., Abdul, H. M., Xu, L., Miller, N. E., Banks, W. A., & Morley, J. E. (2008). Obesity and hypertriglyceridemia produce cognitive impairment. *Endocrinology*, *149*(5), 2628–2636.

Fehm, H. L., Kern, W., & Peters, A. (2006). The selfish brain: competition for energy resources. *Progress in Brain Research*, *153*, 129–140.

Gerozissis, K. (2008). Brain insulin, energy and glucose homeostasis; genes, environment and metabolic pathologies. *European Journal of Pharmacology*, *585*(1), 38–49.

Giovambattista, A., Chisari, A. N., Gaillard, R. C., & Spinedi, E. (2000). Food intake-induced leptin secretion modulates hypothalamo-pituitary-adrenal axis response and hypothalamic Ob-Rb expression to insulin administration. *Neuroendocrinology*, *72*(6), 341–349.

Gómez-Pinilla, F. (2008). Brain foods: the effects of nutrients on brain function. *Nature Reviews Neuroscience*, *9*(7), 568–578.

Greaves-Lord, K., Ferdinand, R. F., Oldehinkel, A. J., Sondeijker, F. E., Ormel, J., & Verhulst, F. C. (2007). Higher cortisol awakening response in young adolescents with persistent anxiety problems. *Acta Psychiatrica Scandinavica*, *116*(2), 137–144.

Han, E. S., Levin, N., Bengani, N., Roberts, J. L., Suh, Y., Karelus, K., & Nelson, J. F. (1995). Hyperadrenocorticism and food restriction-induced life extension in the rat: evidence for divergent regulation of pituitary proopiomelanocortin RNA and adrenocorticotropic hormone biosynthesis. *Journals of Gerontology. Series A, Biological Sciences and Medical Sciences*, *50*(5), B288–B294.

Haynes, W. G., Morgan, D. A., Walsh, S. A., Mark, A. L., & Sivitz, W. I. (1997). Receptor-mediated regional sympathetic nerve activation by leptin. *Journal of Clinical Investigation*, *100*(2), 270–278.

Heiman, M. L., Ahima, R. S., Craft, L. S., Schoner, B., Stephens, T. W., & Flier, J. S. (1997). Leptin inhibition of the hypothalamic-pituitary-adrenal axis in response to stress. *Endocrinology*, *138*(9), 3859–3863.

Huang, X. F., Xin, X., McLennan, P., & Storlien, L. (2004). Role of fat amount and type in ameliorating diet-induced obesity: insights at the level of hypothalamic arcuate nucleus leptin receptor, neuropeptide Y and pro-opiomelanocortin mRNA expression. *Diabetes Obesity & Metabolism*, 6(1), 35–44.

Hülsmann, W. C. (1978). Abnormal stress reactions after feeding diets rich in (very) long-chain fatty acids: high levels of corticosterone and testosterone. *Molecular and Cellular Endocrinology*, 12(1), 1–8.

Jurdak, N., Lichtenstein, A. H., & Kanarek, RB. (2008). Diet-induced obesity and spatial cognition in young male rats. *Nutrition & Neuroscience*, 11(2), 48–54.

Kamara, K., Eskay, R., & Castonguay, T. (1998). High-fat diets and stress responsivity. *Physiology & Behavior*, 64, 1–6.

Kitay, J. I., Coyne, M. D., Newsom, W., & Nelson, R. (1965). Relation of the ovary to adrenal corticosterone production and adrenal enzyme activity in the rat. *Endocrinology*, 77(5), 902–908.

Kitraki, E., Soulis, G., & Gerozissis, K. (2004). Impaired neuroendocrine response to stress following a short-term fat-enriched diet. *Neuroendocrinology*, 79(6), 338–345.

Larsen, P. J., & Mau, S. E. (1994). Effect of acute stress on the expression of hypothalamic messenger ribonucleic acids encoding the endogenous opioid precursors pre-proenkephalin A and proopiomelanocortin. *Peptides*, 15(5), 783–790.

Lee, J., Herman, J. P., & Mattson, M. P. (2000). Dietary restriction selectively decreases glucocorticoid receptor expression in the hippocampus and cerebral cortex of rats. *Experimental Neurology*, 166(2), 435–441.

Legendre, A., & Harris, R. B. (2006). Exaggerated response to mild stress in rats fed high-fat diet. *American Journal of Physiology Regulatory, Integrative and Comparative Physiology*, 291(5), R1288–R1294.

Leibowitz, S. F., Akabayashi, A., Wang, J., Alexander, J. T., Dourmashkin, J. T., & Chang, G. Q. (2007). Increased caloric intake on a fat-rich diet: role of ovarian steroids and galanin in the medial preoptic and paraventricular nuclei and anterior pituitary of female rats. *Journal of Neuroendocrinology*, 19(10), 753–766.

Levin, B. E., Richard, D., Michel, C., Servatius, R. (2000). Differential stress responsivity in diet-induced obese and resistant rats. *American Journal of Physiology Regulatory, Integrative and Comparative Physiology*, 279(4), R1357–R1364.

Liu, J., Garza, J. C., Truong, H. V., Henschel, J., Zhang, W., & Lu, X. Y. (2007). The melano-cortinergic pathway is rapidly recruited by emotional stress and contributes to stress-induced anorexia and anxiety-like behaviour. *Endocrinology*, 148(11), 5531–5540.

Lu, X. Y., Kim, C. S., Frazer, A., & Zhang, W. (2006). Leptin: a potential novel antidepressant. *Proceedings of the National Academy of Sciences USA*, 103(5), 1593–1598.

Macht, M. (2008) How emotions affect eating: a five-way model. *Appetite*, 50(1), 1–11.

Martí, O., Gavaldà, A., Gómez, F., & Armario, A. (1994). Direct evidence for chronic stress-induced facilitation of the adrenocorticotropin response to a novel acute stressor. *Neuroendocrinology*, 60(1), 1–7.

Martin, R. L., Perez, E., He, Y. J., Dawson, R Jr & Millard, W. J. (2000). Leptin resistance is associated with hypothalamic leptin receptor mRNA and protein downregulation. *Metabolism*, 49(11), 1479–1484.

Mattson, M. P. (2007). Calcium and neurodegeneration. *Aging Cell*, 6(3), 337–350.

Mattsson, C., Lai, M., Noble, J., McKinney, E., Yau, J. L., Seckl, J. R., & Walker, B. R. (2003). Obese Zucker rats have reduced mineralocorticoid receptor and 11beta-hydroxysteroid dehydrogenase type 1 expression in hippocampus-implications for dysregulation of the hypothalamic-pituitary-adrenal axis in obesity. *Endocrinology*, 144(7), 2997–3003.

Matyšková, R., Zelezná, B., Maixnerová, J., Koutová, D., Haluzík, M., & Maletínská, L. (2010). Estradiol supplementation helps overcome central leptin resistance of ovariectomized mice on a high fat diet. *Hormone and Metabolic Research, 42*(3), 182–186.

McNay, E. C., & Cotero, V. E. (2010). Mini-review: Impact of recurrent hypoglycemia on cognitive and brain function. *Physiology & Behavior, 100*(3), 234–238.

Molteni, R., Barnard, R. J., Ying, Z., Roberts, C. K., & Gómez-Pinilla, F. (2002). A high-fat, refined sugar diet reduces hippocampal brain-derived neurotrophic factor, neuronal plasticity, and learning. *Neuroscience, 112*(4), 803–814.

Moosavi, M., Naghdi, N., Maghsoudi, N., & Zahedi, Asl. S. (2007). Insulin protects against stress-induced impairments in water maze performance. *Behavioral Brain Research, 176*(2), 230–236.

Murphy, P. (2005) Use of the ketogenic diet as a treatment for epilepsy refractory to drug treatment. *Expert Review of Neurotherapeutics, 5*(6), 769–775.

Nieuwenhuizen, A. G., & Rutters F. 2008). The hypothalamic-pituitary-adrenal-axis in the regulation of energy balance. *Physiology & Behavior, 94*(2), 169–177.

Park, C. R. (2001). Cognitive effects of insulin in the central nervous system. *Neuroscience and Biobehavioral Reviews, 25*(4), 311–323.

Pascoe, W. S., Smythe, G. A., & Storlien, L. H. (1991). Enhanced responses to stress induced by fat-feeding in rats: relationship between hypothalamic noradrenaline and blood glucose. *Brain Research, 550*(2), 192–196.

Patchev, V. K., Hayashi, S., Orikasa, C., & Almeida, O. F. (1995). Implications of estrogen-dependent brain organization for gender differences in hypothalamo-pituitary-adrenal regulation. *FASEB Journal, 9*(5), 419–423.

Pecoraro, N., Reyes, F., Gómez, F., Bhargava, A., & Dallman, M. F. (2004). Chronic stress promotes palatable feeding, which reduces signs of stress: feedforward and feedback effects of chronic stress. *Endocrinology, 145*(8), 3754–3762.

Piroli, G. G., Grillo, C. A., Reznikov, L. R., Adams, S., McEwen, B. S., Charron, M. J., & Reagan, L. P. (2007). Corticosterone impairs insulin-stimulated translocation of GLUT4 in the rat hippocampus. *Neuroendocrinology, 85*(2), 71–80

Prasad, A., & Prasad, C. (1996). Short-term consumption of a diet rich in fat decreases anxiety response in adult male rats. *Physiology & Behavior* 60: 1039–1042.

Reagan, L. P., Grillo, C. A., & Piroli, G. G. (2008). The As and Ds of stress: metabolic, morphological and behavioral consequences. *European Journal of Pharmacology, 585*(1), 64–75.

Riant E., Waget A., Cogo H., Arnal, J. F., Burcelin R., & Gourdy P. 2009). Estrogens protect against high-fat diet-induced insulin resistance and glucose intolerance in mice. *Endocrinology, 150*(5), 2109–2117.

Ruderman, N. B., Toews, C. J., & Shafrir, E. (1969). Role of free fatty acids in glucose homeostasis. *Archives of Internal Medicine, 123*(3), 299–313.

Soulis, G., Kitraki, E., & Gerozissis, K. (2005). Early neuroendocrine alterations in female rats following a diet moderately enriched in fat. *Cellular and Molecular Neurobiology, 25*(5), 869–880.

Soulis, G., Papalexi, E., Kittas, C., & Kitraki, E. (2007). Early impact of a fat-enriched diet on behavioral responses of male and female rats. *Behavioral Neuroscience, 121*(3), 483–490.

Spinedi, E., & Gaillard, R. C. (1998). A regulatory loop between the hypothalamo-pituitary-adrenal (HPA) axis and circulating leptin: a physiological role of ACTH. *Endocrinology, 139*(9), 4016–4020.

Strack, A. M., Akana, S. F., Horsley, C. J., & Dallman, M. F. (1997). A hypercaloric load induces thermogenesis but inhibits stress responses in the SNS and HPA system. *American Journal of Physiology Regulatory, Integrative and Comparative Physiology, 272*(3 Pt 2), R840–R848.

Stranahan, A. M., Norman, E. D., Lee, K., Cutler, R. G., Telljohann, R. S., Egan, J. M., & Mattson, M. P. (2008a). Diet-induced insulin resistance impairs hippocampal synaptic plasticity and cognition in middle-aged rats. *Hippocampus, 18*(11), 1085–1088.

Stranahan, A. M., Arumugam, T. V., Cutler, R. G., Lee, K., Egan, J. M., & Mattson, M. P. (2008b). Diabetes impairs hippocampal function through glucocorticoid-mediated effects on new and mature neurons. *Nature Neuroscience, 11*(3), 309–317.

Tamashiro, K. L., Hegeman, M. A., & Sakai, R. R. (2006). Chronic social stress in a changing dietary environment. *Physiology & Behavior, 89*(4), 536–542.

Tannenbaum, B. M., Brindley, D. N., Tannenbaum, G. S., Dallman, M. F., McArthur, M. D., & Meaney, M. J. (1997). High-fat feeding alters both basal and stress-induced hypothalamic-pituitary-adrenal activity in the rat. *American Journal of Physiology Endocrinology and Metabolism, 273*, E1168–E1177.

van Dijk, G., & Buwalda, B. (2008). Neurobiology of the metabolic syndrome: an allostatic perspective. *European Journal of Pharmacology, 585*(1), 137–146.

van Dijk, G., de Vries, K., Benthem, L., Nyakas, C., Buwalda, B., & Scheurink, A. J. (2003). Neuroendocrinology of insulin resistance: metabolic and endocrine aspects of adiposity. *European Journal of Pharmacology, 480*(1–3), 31–42.

Warne, J. P. (2009). Shaping the stress response: interplay of palatable food choices, glucocorticoids, insulin and abdominal obesity. *Molecular and Cellular Endocrinology, 300*(1–2), 137–146.

Weiser, M. J., & Handa, R. J. (2009). Estrogen impairs glucocorticoid dependent negative feedback on the hypothalamic-pituitary-adrenal axis via estrogen receptor alpha within the hypothalamus. *Neuroscience, 159*(2), 883–895.

Widmaier, E. P., Rosen, K., & Abbott, B. (1992). Free fatty acids activate the hypothalamic-pituitary-adrenocortical axis in rats. *Endocrinology, 131*(5), 2313–2318.

Winocur, G., & Greenwood, C. E. (2005). Studies of the effects of high fat diets on cognitive function in a rat model. *Neurobiology of Aging, 1*, 46–49.

Winocur, G., Greenwood, C. E., Piroli, G. G., Grillo, C. A., Reznikov, L. R., Reagan, L. P., & McEwen, B. S. (2005). Memory impairment in obese Zucker rats: an investigation of cognitive function in an animal model of insulin resistance and obesity. *Behavioral Neuroscience, 119*(5), 1389–1395.

Wu, A., Ying, Z., & Gómez-Pinilla, F. (2004). The interplay between oxidative stress and brain-derived neurotrophic factor modulates the outcome of a saturated fat diet on synaptic plasticity and cognition. *European Journal of Neuroscience, 19*(7), 1699–1707.

Zakrzewska, K. E., Cusin, I., Sainsbury, A., Rohner-Jeanrenaud, F., & Jeanrenaud, B. (1997) Glucocorticoids as counterregulatory hormones of leptin: toward an understanding of leptin resistance. *Diabetes, 46*(4), 717–719.

Zhao, W., Chen, H., Xu, H., Moore, E., Meiri, N., Quon, M. J., & Alkon, D. L. (1999). Brain insulin receptors and spatial memory. Correlated changes in gene expression, tyrosine phosphorylation, and signaling molecules in the hippocampus of water maze trained rats. *Journal of Biological Chemistry, 274*(49), 34893–34902.

29

Influence of Appraisal and Coping Following Extreme Stress

Miranda Olff

Introduction

Although many people are exposed to extreme stress, only some of them develop (mental) health problems. Most people manage extremely stressful experiences with minimal to no impact on their daily functioning. In some cases, however, acute or chronic stress leads to psychiatric disorders for which help may be sought. One of the most extreme types of stressor involves that of psychological trauma which may give rise to posttraumatic stress disorder (PTSD) or other posttrauma psychopathology. It is yet unclear why some people show extreme psychobiological dysregulation due to stressful events whereas others do not, or why people develop different types of psychopathology following extreme stress. This chapter describes that it is not the stressor per se but individual differences in types of psychological appraisal and coping that play a crucial role in the relationships between stressors and mental and physical health.

Individual Differences in the Stress Response

There is clear evidence that not everyone copes with life stressors, including extremely stressful events, in the same way (e.g., see Aldwin and Yancura, 2004; Bonanno and Mancini, 2008). Research has indicated that most individuals exposed to extreme stressors cope very well and do not develop adjustment problems or psychiatric or physical disorders. Up to 50–80% of people experience a traumatic event during their life, of whom about 10% develop PTSD (Kessler et al., 1995; de Vries and Olff, 2009). How can we explain why only a relatively small subset of

The Handbook of Stress: Neuropsychological Effects on the Brain, First Edition.
Edited by Cheryl D. Conrad.
© 2011 Blackwell Publishing Ltd. Published 2011 by Blackwell Publishing Ltd.

people show psychobiological dysregulation due to exposure to trauma and may develop (chronic) psychopathology?

Adverse health consequences of stressors depend to a large extent on the individual's ability to cope with these stressors. How individuals cope with stressors does have an effect on their physiology (Biondi and Picardi, 1999; Aldwin and Yancura, 2004), and subsequently on stress-related mental and physical disorders (Olff et al., 1993; Schnurr and Green, 2004). More specifically, individual differences in the specific appraisal of the stressful event and in subsequent coping behaviors are crucial in determining outcome. In the stress literature cognitive theories do identify appraisal and coping as critical mediators of stressful person–environment relations and their psychobiological outcomes (Olff et al., 1993, 2005; Ursin and Olff, 1993; Lazarus, 1996; McEwen, 1998; Biondi and Picardi, 1999; Ursin, 2009). Findings in stress research can be summarized according to the type of coping strategy used and their consequences (Vickers, 1988; Ehlert and Straub, 1998; Biondi and Picardi, 1999; Cramer, 2003; Aldwin and Yancura, 2004). A wide variety of coping behaviors or strategies have been described, ranging from actively attacking the stressful situation (facing the fear), to trying to remain calm or denying the adversity. There is an abundance of terms and concepts for such coping behaviors, and a corresponding large number of instruments to operationalize these terms.

A Model of Stress Coping

It is a complex route from stressor to different health outcomes, including a cascade of responses. In short, as shown in Figure 29.1, the stressor first has to be perceived, interpreted, and evaluated. The appraisal process, reflecting the person's subjective perception, interpretation, and evaluation of the event, is the crucial first step in the cascade eventually leading to symptoms (Frazier, 2002). The subsequent emotional behavioral and biological response is determined by the subject's specific coping strategies. Once a situation is perceived as threatening, a person decides how dangerous or problematic it is and what kind of coping strategy to use to reduce the potential harm to his mental and/or physical well-being. Coping moderates the appraisal of the stressor as well as the following emotional and/or biological responses, which, if sustained, may cause both somatic and emotional health problems (Olff et al., 1993; Ursin and Olff, 1993).

Below, the conceptualization of appraisal and coping processes are described in more detail. The following section describes the findings in the stress literature on appraisal and coping in relationship to biological responses, in particular neuroendocrine responses and health outcomes.

Conceptualization of Appraisal and Coping Processes

Before any type of coping behavior can occur, the stressful situation has to be perceived, appraised, and evaluated. Lazarus and Folkman (1984) perceive the

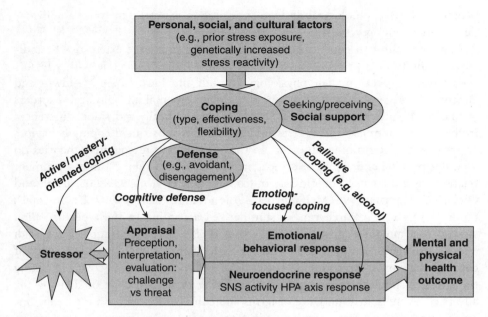

Figure 29.1   Stress coping model. HPA, hypothalamic–pituitary–adrenal; SNS, sympathetic nervous system. *Source:* From Olff et al. (2005). Reproduced by permission of Wiley-Blackwell Publishing.

processes of appraisal and coping that occur between stressors and outcome as follows: during the appraisal process, the individual perceives whether the situation implies potential harm or negative consequences and subsequently the individual asks what can be done to reduce the emotional and physiological tension (the coping response). After *coping* (i.e., the process of executing that response) there is reappraisal, in which the efficacy of the coping strategy is evaluated. Coping is defined as all types of cognitive and behavioral efforts made to master, tolerate, or reduce external and internal demands and conflicts created by stressors. The term *coping style* refers to the use of similar behaviors across situations.

Furthermore, it is important to note that there are gender differences in appraisal and coping, eventually explaining gender differences in prevalence rates of stress disorders, particularly PTSD (Olff et al, 2007a). For example, differences in neuroendocrine responses to extreme stressors may be explained by differences in threat appraisal between men and women (Rasmusson and Friedman, 2002) or in subjectively reported arousal (Wallbott and Scherer, 1991). Appraisals of threat refer to the degree to which individuals experience events as unpredictable, uncontrollable, or overwhelming. Women are more likely than men to overestimate the probability of danger (Menzies and Clarke, 1995). Compared to men, women are also more likely to expect harm and to anticipate poor coping ability (Thorpe and Salkovskis, 1995). In addition, in a brain-imaging study gender differences in the activation of neural structures thought to mediate attention to threat have been observed (McClure et al., 2004). Women showed greater activation in the orbitofrontal cortex and amygdala than men when presented with threat cues.

Appraisal

Subjective appraisals of events include perceived threat, harm, or controllability. These different appraisals do explain differences in risk for negative consequences like PTSD. As McNally (2003) describes, these variables help to explain surprising findings in the PTSD literature, as for instance, why someone develops PTSD after stressful, but seemingly noncatastrophic, events (e.g., a divorce), whereas others never develop PTSD after a seemingly horrific trauma (e.g., capture and torture). Consistent evidence has accumulated that greater levels of perceived loss, threat, and harm and lower perceptions of controllability of the event or situation are associated with higher levels of posttrauma symptoms, including (current) PTSD symptoms or diagnosis (see Norris et al., 2002; Ozer et al., 2003).

Specific appraisals have been related to the development of PTSD (Ehlers et al., 1998; McNally, 2003; Aldwin and Yancura, 2004; Olff et al., 2005), as well as to the persistence of PTSD through negative beliefs and appraisals of ongoing threat (Foa et al., 1989; Ehlers and Steil, 1995). For example, central in cognitive models of PTSD is the assumption that perception of a stressful situation or event as a threat may be at least as important as trauma severity and variation in pretrauma experience in the development and maintenance of PTSD (Janoff-Bulman, 1985; Horowitz, 1986; Foa et al., 1989; Ehlers and Clark, 2000). In addition to appraisal of the traumatic event, a link between (negative) appraisals of acute symptoms and PTSD has been postulated (Foa et al., 1993; Ehlers and Steil, 1995), mainly because this leads to a sense of serious, current threat (Ehlers and Clark, 2000). These factors may indirectly contribute to both the development of PTSD and its persistence by motivating coping processes involving a choice of cognitive and behavioral strategies that prevent recovery, such as cognitive avoidance and attempts to suppress thoughts about the trauma (Ehlers et al., 1998; Fedoroff et al., 2000; Steil and Ehlers, 2000; Engelhard et al., 2001, 2002; Halligan et al., 2003). Negative appraisal of initial PTSD symptoms may maintain PTSD by directly producing negative emotions and by encouraging individuals to engage in dysfunctional coping strategies that have the paradoxical effect of enhancing PTSD symptoms (Ehlers and Clark, 2000). For example, studies examining links between PTSD and anxiety sensitivity suggest that trauma-exposed individuals who develop unmanageable PTSD (anxiety) symptoms and who catastrophize about the consequences of such symptoms are particularly likely to cope with these symptoms by using psychoactive substances that have arousal- and anxiety-reducing properties (Stewart et al., 2000).

Several other factors may be important in the appraisal phase—for example, peritraumatic dissociation and specific acute physiological reactions—which are implicated in the development of PTSD or depression (Shalev et al., 1998a, 1998b,

2000; Bryant and Harvey, 2003). Panic and its physiological symptoms may mediate the relation between traumatic fear and peritraumatic dissociation (i.e., at the time of a traumatic event or in its immediate aftermath) (Bernat et al., 1998) and the core cognitions of panic (i.e., fear of death, fear of losing control) may act as mediators of the relation between peritraumatic dissociation and PTSD severity (Gershuny et al., 2003). Finally, associations have been reported between the tendency to interpret distressing intrusions themselves as evidence that danger is impending (*intrusion-based reasoning*) and PTSD, regardless of objective danger information, in veterans of the Vietnam War (Engelhard et al., 2001) and in exposed residents to a train disaster (Engelhard et al., 2002).

Coping

The function of a healthy or adaptive coping strategy encompasses the adequate management of life stress and negative emotional states. Generally, two major coping strategies are defined: *problem-focused coping*, including strategies that are aimed to solve the problem such as active or instrumental coping; and, *emotion-focused coping*, including strategies that are aimed at reducing the (potentially) experienced distress like cognitive/defensive strategies, palliative coping, or seeking emotional support.

Problem-focused coping/instrumental mastery-oriented coping

These more instrumental coping strategies typically involve the individual trying to attack the stressor in an active way and the subject experiences control over the situation. For example, problem-focused coping can be broken down into planning, taking action, seeking assistance, and solving the problem. These strategies may be more effective in the long term, but not always possible in extreme situations. Problem-focused coping may reduce activation of the emotional behavioral and biological response by eliminating the source of stress and attenuate the mental and/or physiological response to the stressor.

Emotion-focused coping

Emotion-focused coping can involve responses such as seeking (instrumental or emotional) social support and ventilation of emotions. Women tend to use this coping style much more frequently than men (Luckow et al., 1998). When perceived as successful, emotion-focused coping may attenuate the mental and/or physiological response to the stressor. Lack of (perceived) social support on the other hand is a risk factor for the development of PTSD (e.g., Ozer et al., 2003).

Recent findings on the significant role of negative network orientation in the relationship between social support and PTSD are of interest (Clapp and Beck, 2009). Network orientation is conceptualized as an individual's attitudes and expectations regarding the usefulness of support networks in coping with stress.

Palliative coping styles

Palliative coping styles are aimed at reducing the arousal provoked by the stressor, for instance by relaxation and alcohol or tobacco use; some are more adaptive than others (e.g., Olff et al., 2006). Compared to men, women tend to use palliative coping styles, in particular drinking, more often than men during (extreme) stressful situations (see Ouimette and Brown, 2003).

Defensive coping

Of specific interest are defensive coping strategies like dissociation and emotional disengagement. These strategies are often considered as a form of emotion-focused coping. However, some authors regard defense as a kind of behavior that not only should be identified as something quite different from coping, but also as a kind of behavior that may actually be harmful or counterproductive (e.g., Haan, 1977; Vaillant, 1986). Defensive coping strategies will by definition affect the way the situation is perceived. The distorted perception of reality serves to keep the threatening character of the stressful encounter unconscious or at least minimizes the negative affective response to the stressor. This may be beneficial in the short term, but may be dangerous in situations where reality testing is important (Vaernes et al., 1982). Highly defensive coping may shield individuals psychologically from threat, minimizing the negative affective response to the stressor; however, in the long term these strategies may not always be adaptive (see below).

The early stress-coping phase has also been described as being characterized by *antecedent-focused strategies*, which modulate emotional response tendencies early on, before they give rise to full-fledged responses (e.g., cognitive reappraisal), compared with *response-focused strategies*, which modulate the emotional responses themselves later on once they have arisen (e.g., expressive suppression). These strategies differentially influence negative emotion experience, behavior, and physiological responses (Gross, 1998). In an interesting study, Goldin et al. (2009) showed that reappraisal, in terms of cognitive-linguistic strategies to reinterpret the meaning of a situation, for example "This does not influence me" or "This does not impact me," have an effect on brain activation in regions that have been implicated in modulating the trajectory of an emotional response, the limbic-cortical network. Reappraisal resulted in early (0–4.5 s) prefrontal cortical responses, decreased negative emotion experience, and decreased amygdala and insular responses. The idea is that reappraisal can intervene relatively early in the emotion-generative process, recruiting executive cognitive control processes downregulating negative emotion (Goldin et al., 2009). When functioning optimally, the limbic-cortical network confers psychological resilience, flexibility, and well-being. This means that successful acute negative emotion induction may prevent exaggerated emotional reactivity and affective dysregulation that are thought to be core features of many psychiatric problems.

Suppression of emotions, on the other hand, produced late (10.5–15 s) prefrontal cortical responses, decreased negative emotion behavior and experience, but increased amygdala and insula responses (Goldin et al., 2009). Emotion suppression is a strategy directed towards inhibiting behaviors associated with emotional responding (e.g., facial expressions, verbal utterances, gestures) known to produce decreased expressive behavior and increase sympathetic activation of the cardiovascular system (Gross, 2002). Reappraisal reduced while suppression enhanced or maintained elevated neural signals encoding a potential threat in bilateral dorsal amygdala and anterior insula, a network of ventral emotion-detection/generation-related limbic regions. Amygdala and insula signal reduction result in a reduction of anxiety symptoms.

Positive outcomes of stress coping

Until quite recently, the stress, appraisal, and coping literature nearly exclusively emphasized the negative sequelae of stressful events. It was assumed that the enduring absence of psychopathology after exposure to (extreme) stress was a sign of exceptional emotional strength (e.g., McFarlane and Yehuda, 1996). There has been a growing recognition that, in addition to negative outcomes, there are positive outcomes of stress coping (e.g., Park et al., 1996; Folkman and Moskowitz, 2000). In line with these developments, a range of novel concepts have been explored, including, among others, stress-related growth (Park et al., 1996), meaning-based coping (Folkman and Moskowitz, 2000), benefit-finding (Tennen and Affleck, 1999), and benefit appraisals (Lazarus, 1999). These concepts are collectively referred to as positive changes; that is, changes that may arise after struggling with adversity that propel the individual to a higher level of functioning than that which existed prior to the event (see Linley and Joseph, 2004). Accordingly, there has been a growing publication of reports on positive outcomes or growth resulting from coping efforts following stress (Linley and Joseph, 2004; see also Mancini and Bonanno, 2009).

Paradoxically, greater levels of perceived threat and harm, and particularly appraisal of awareness and controllability of the event, have also been associated with higher perception of positive growth in the longitudinal course of adaptation (see Park, 1998; Davis and Macdonald, 2004; Linley and Joseph, 2004). This might be due to positive reappraisal, a cognitive coping strategy for reframing a situation to see it in a positive light with a resulting reduction in emotional response, that has been associated with positive affect in stressful events (for a review, see Aldwin et al., 1994; Epel et al., 1998) and posttrauma adaptation (Dohrenwend et al., 2004). Besides, strong global, religious, spiritual, or political belief systems and practices (e.g., appraisal of self and the world) may be a protective factor in development of psychopathology, in particular PTSD (e.g., Basoglu et al., 1996). Evidently, coping responses, which enhance positive effects and promote health-related quality of life, merit greater attention from researchers.

There is some evidence linking positive appraisal and perception of control with resilient neuroendocrine functioning. Women who have grown psychologically from trauma showed quicker cortisol habituation to other stressors, demonstrating greater flexibility in their hypothalamic–pituitary–adrenal (HPA) axis, probably through positive affect (Epel et al., 1998). Changing one's perception of an extreme stressor (positive reappraisal) can be effective in terms of serving as a protector of PTSD, as has been shown for example in rescue workers after an earthquake (Chang et al., 2003). A study among combat veterans indicated that the cognitive appraisal of being able to cope mediated the observed association between heart-rate recovery and PTSD (Kibler and Lyons, 2004).

Neuroendocrine Consequences of Appraisal and Coping

Two neuroendocrine response systems have been described for specific stress-coping patterns (Henry and Stephens, 1977; Frankenhaeuser, 1980, 1983; Henry, 1986). In the event the subject has to have a *fight-or-flight response* or has to make an effort to control the situation, the sympathetic adrenal medullary system (sympathetic nervous system, SNS) is activated. It responds immediately to threatened homeostasis with the release of catecholamines. Where efficient coping is not possible, as with severe prolonged stress and the experience of negative affect, the HPA system plays an important role: the *conservation-withdrawal* or *distress* reaction. Cortisol inhibits the SNS to maintain physiological homeostasis in stress situations (Ursin and Murison, 1983; Munck et al., 1984; Kvetnansky et al., 1995; see also Chapter 1 in this volume).

Taylor et al. (2000) argued that the familiar fight-or-flight characterization of the human stress response does not accurately describe the behavioral response of women. In contrast, the female response may be marked by a pattern of behavior which the authors termed tend-and-befriend. Through hypervigilance to threat and prioritizing social networks, the oxytocin-mediated tend-and-befriend response may lower women's perceived coping ability and encourage avoidance (for more detailed reviews of gender and PTSD see Olff et al., 2007b, 2010).

Appraisal and its neuroendocrine consequences

Negative appraisals of stressors lead to the release of cortisol (Buchanan et al., 1999). Given that cortisol is not released until the situation is perceived as noxious, the cognitive ability to evaluate events is the key in the body's response to threat (Chrousos and Gold, 1998; Ehlert and Straub, 1998; Biondi and Picardi, 1999). Most studies about stressor appraisal demonstrate an effect on physiological reactivity (Tomaka et al., 1993, 1997; Peters et al., 1998; Maier et al., 2003; Dickerson and Kemeny, 2004).

The magnitude of neuroendocrine stress response depends on whether the stressor is appraised as threatening (possibility of damage/harm) or as challenging (opportunity for gain) (Nicolson, 1992; Tomaka et al., 1993, 1997; Al'Absi et al.,

1997; Epel et al., 1998; Peters et al., 2003). In terms of adaptation, the threat-response pattern serves to protect the individual from attack, whereas the challenge response pattern is associated with increased energy mobilization for coping (Dienstbier, 1989). Whether the stressor is appraised as threatening versus challenging is associated with different profiles of endocrine and sympathetic arousal. Threat appraisals are more strongly associated with demands exceeding perceived coping abilities, high negative emotion, and poorer coping, and may lead to increased peripheral vascular resistance (Tomaka et al., 1993, 1997) and higher reactive levels of cortisol (Lundberg and Frankenhauser, 1980; Vaernes et al., 1982). Peripheral vascular resistance was measured as total peripheral resistance, which is a summary index of systemic vascular resistance derived from blood pressure and impedance cardiographic recordings using the formula of Sherwood et al. (1990) (mean arterial pressure/cardiac output × 80). The literature on traumatic stress describes appraisal of threat as an important peritraumatic predictor of PTSD (McNally, 2003). Appraisal of a stressful situation as a threat might contribute to pathology because it directs coping towards excessive emotional regulation and diverts it from problem-solving. Relatively few studies have related appraisals of traumatic stressors to physiological reactivity. A study among combat veterans indicated that cognitive appraisal (i.e., perceived coping ability, but not perceived threat) mediated the observed association between heart-rate recovery and PTSD (Kibler and Lyons, 2004).

Challenge appraisals are more strongly associated with response patterns characterized by short-term increases in catecholamines and, probably strong anabolic counterregulatory responses and cortisol adaptation, when faced with similar stressors over time (Epel et al., 1998). The challenge response is more strongly associated with perceived coping ability, low negative emotion, and enhanced coping, and may lead to relatively strong cardiac activation coupled with decreased peripheral vascular resistance (Tomaka et al., 1993). Challenge appraisals indicating a shift to perceived positive arousal and perceived controllability can moderate biological stress responses (Brosschot et al., 1998; Epel et al., 1998) (Figure 29.2).

Some trauma studies have focused on alcohol's impairment or disruption of an initial appraisal of threat (Levenson et al., 1980; Sayette, 1993), resulting in the physiological stress response dampening. Study findings do suggest that diminished threat appraisal through alcohol use just before or during a traumatic event gives rise to attenuated peritraumatic physiological arousal reactions; that is, lower SNS activity (heart rate, blood pressure) at the time of the traumatic event or in its immediate aftermath (Koss et al., 1996; Maes et al., 2001; Clum et al., 2002). An association between reported alcohol use/intoxication and reduced risk for developing PTSD has been found in these studies (Mellman et al., 1998). Also of interest in this respect is that individuals with cerebral damage or who were unconscious in the direct aftermath of trauma also show a reduced risk of PTSD (Chemtob et al., 1998; O'Brien and Nutt, 1998; Bryant, 2001). Apparently, a conscious threat perception is necessary to dysregulate the stress-response system. Even in healthy volunteers only following higher doses of alcohol both the spontaneous memories following a trauma film as well as explicit memory for the film were decreased

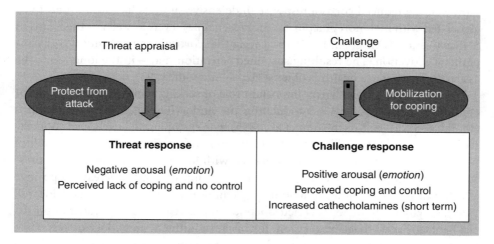

Figure 29.2 Appraisal and its psychobiological consequences.

(Bisby et al., 2009). In a similar vein, the literature suggests that awareness or perception of life threat during a cardiac arrest increases the risk of developing PTSD (van Driel and Op den Velde, 1995), whereas sedation during a cardiac arrest reduced the risk of developing PTSD fivefold (Ladwig et al., 1999). More general, nonawareness of threat or diminished threat appraisal may dampen the neuroendocrine reactivity in stressful situations which may—in the long term—be associated with fewer health problems.

Coping and the neuroendocrine responses

With regard to coping and neuroendocrine responses, the type of coping strategy used determines the neuroendocrine response. For example, subjects with high levels of active or mastery-oriented coping show little stress response, in both the SNS and the HPA axis (Levine and Ursin, 1991; Bonanno et al., 2003). Also, palliative coping such as use of alcohol or other sedatives has been shown to reduce physiological arousal. Additionally, coping including positive emotions produces a faster return to baseline levels of cardiovascular activation following negative emotional arousal and prompts toward a flexible use of a wider range of coping strategies (Fredrickson et al., 2000, 2003).

In particular regarding defensive coping, the effectiveness of defenses in warding of negative emotions may be crucial for the neuroendocrine reactivity in stressful situations. The effective use of defense mechanisms may dampen the endocrine stress response: individuals using effective defense strategies protect themselves by not getting overwhelmed by negative affect which allows them to maintain an adequate level of functioning. They show lower cortisol levels (Olff et al., 1995; Brown et al., 1996; see also Vickers, 1988) which in the short term may be adaptive.

However, the reduced cortisol response in defensive subjects has been found to be associated with high norepinephrine (noradrenaline) levels as well as other signs of SNS activation (Olff et al., 1995), indicating that cortisol may not shut down sympathetic activation. The resulting sustained activation may—in the long term—be associated with more health problems (Ursin and Olff, 1993).

Stress research has shown an important role of seeking social support (as part of emotion-focused coping) in modulating the endocrine reaction to acute stress (Biondi et al., 1986; Kirschbaum et al., 1995). For example, effective social support-seeking—that is, availability of and satisfaction with social support—may reduce neuroendocrine reactivity as it is associated with lower heart rate and blood pressure, lower catecholamine levels, use of more coping strategies, increase in positive affect, and better immune functioning (Uchino et al., 1996; Biondi and Picardi, 1999). Oxytocin, an interesting neuropeptide in this regard, is implicated in prosocial behavior and anxiety regulation, for instance in the neuroendocrine responses to stress. Social support and oxytocin seem to interact to suppress cortisol and subjective responses to psychosocial stress (Heinrichs et al., 2003). The stress literature emphasizes a key role of oxytocin as an underlying biological mechanism for stress-protective effects of positive social interactions (Uvnas-Moberg, 1998; Neumann, 2002; Charney, 2004), and potentially also important for the development of PTSD (Olff et al., 2010). If this mechanism also holds true for traumatic stress, it could explain the protective effect of social support in developing PTSD (Olff et al., 2007a).

Clinical Implications

Knowing more about the interrelationships between stressors, appraisal and coping processes, biological stress responses, and mental health problems may have important implications for psychosocial and pharmacological interventions designed to alleviate stress-related symptoms. In particular, an understanding of effective methods of coping close to the time of the extreme stressful events may be quite useful for preventing symptoms and informing treatment interventions, respectively. Findings as such would be helpful in designing coping effectiveness training in the acute symptom phase or interventions to support coping processes.

It has already been shown that certain forms of psychotherapy can enhance optimism and facilitate reappraisal of extreme stressful events in a more positive light (Lee et al., 2004). Therefore, understanding a victim's appraisals and coping efforts are important in trauma therapy (reappraisal of the trauma, redirecting coping efforts towards more adaptive ways of dealing with the memories of trauma).

More recent formulations of cognitive-behavioral interventions have explicitly incorporated modules that address training in emotion regulation by using more effective coping strategies (e.g., Cloitre et al., 2004). It could be hypothesized that if effective psychological interventions increase effective coping abilities, they may alter neuroendocrine disturbances associated with exposure to extreme stress as well. However, until now, very little is known about the effects of treatment—psychological or pharmacological—on hormone levels in PTSD. Olff et al. (2007b) showed that with effective psychotherapy low cortisol levels increase during treatment. Effective psychotherapy for PTSD may thus alter dysregulations in the HPA axis. But few studies have specifically investigated the impact of the effects of enhancing effective coping styles on neuroendocrine parameters in traumatized patients or other stress-related disorders.

Acknowledging the important implication of appraisal and coping for interventions designed to alleviate (posttraumatic) stress (Saakvine et al., 1998; Ehlers and Clark, 2000), because these variables are more amenable to change than neuroendocrine response, further research focusing on these variables is warranted. The reviewed findings give some direction to psychological rehabilitation with regard to the pliable nature of appraisals and coping and their potential to facilitate adaptive adjustment.

References

Al'Absi, M., Bongard, S., Buchanan, T., Pincomb, G. A., Licinio, J., & Lovallo, W. R. (1997). Cardiovascular and neuroendocrine adjustment to public speaking and mental arithmetic stressors. *Psychophysiology, 34*(3), 266–275.

Aldwin, C. M., & Yancura, L. A. (2004). Coping and health: a comparison of the stress and trauma literatures. In P. P. Schnurr, & B. L. Green, (Eds.), *Trauma and health. Physical health consequences of exposure to extreme stress* (pp. 99–125). Washington DC: American Psychological Association.

Aldwin, C. M., Levenson, M. R., & Spiro, A., III (1994). Vulnerability and resilience to combat exposure: can stress have lifelong effects? *Psychology and Aging, 9*(1), 34–44.

Basoglu, M., Ozmen, E., Sahin, D., Paker, M., Tasdemir, O., Ceyhanli, A., Incesu, C., & Sarimurat, N. (1996). Appraisal of self, social environment, and state authority as a possible mediator of posttraumatic stress disorder in tortured political activists. *Journal of Abnormal Psychology, 105*(2), 232–236.

Bernat, J. A., Ronfeldt, H. M., Calhoun, K. S., & Arias, I. (1998). Prevalence of traumatic events and peritraumatic predictors of posttraumatic stress symptoms in a nonclinical sample of college students. *Journal of Trauma and Stress, 11*(4), 645–664.

Biondi, M., & Picardi, A. (1999). Psychological stress and neuroendocrine function in humans: the last two decades of research. *Psychotherapy and Psychosomatics, 68*(3), 114–150.

Biondi, M., Pancheri, P., Falaschi, D., Teodori, A., Paga, G., Delle Chiaie, R., DiCasare, G., & Proietti, A. (1986). Social support as a moderator of the psychobiological stress response. *New Trends in Experimental and Clinical Psychiatry, 2*, 173–183

Bisby, J. A., Brewin, C. R., Leitz, J. R., & Valerie, C. H. (2009). Acute effects of alcohol on the development of intrusive memories. *Psychopharmacology (Berlin), 204*(4), 655–666.

Bonanno, G. A., & Mancini, A. D. (2008). The human capacity to thrive in the face of potential trauma. *Pediatrics, 121*(2), 369–375.

Bonanno, G. A., Noll, J. G., Putnam, F. W., O'Neill, M., & Trickett, P. K. (2003). Predicting the willingness to disclose childhood sexual abuse from measures of repressive coping and dissociative tendencies. *Child Maltreatment*, 8(4), 302–318.

Brosschot, J. F., Godaert, G. L., Benschop, R. J., Olff, M., Ballieux, R. E., & Heijnen, C. J. (1998). Experimental stress and immunological reactivity: a closer look at perceived uncontrollability. *Journal of Psychosomatic Research*, 60(3), 359–361.

Brown, L. L., Tomarken, A. J., Orth, D. N., Loosen, P. T., Kalin, N. H., & Davidson, R. J. (1996). Individual differences in repressive-defensiveness predict basal salivary cortisol levels. *Journal of Personality and Social Psychology*, 70(2), 362–371.

Bryant, R. A. (2001). Posttraumatic stress disorder and traumatic brain injury: can they co-exist? *Clinical Psychology Review*, 21(6), 931–948.

Bryant, R. A., & Harvey, A. G. (2003). Gender differences in the relationship between acute stress disorder and posttraumatic stress disorder following motor vehicle accidents. *Australian and New Zealand Journal of Psychiatry*, 37(2), 226–229.

Buchanan, T. W., Al'Absi, M., & Lovallo, W. R. (1999). Cortisol fluctuates with increases and decreases in negative affect. *Psychoneuroendocrinology*, 24(2), 227–241.

Chang, C. M., Lee, L. C., Connor, K. M., Davidson, J. R., Jeffries, K., & Lai, T. J. (2003). Posttraumatic distress and coping strategies among rescue workers after an earthquake. *Journal of Nervous and Mental Disorders*, 191(6), 391–398.

Charney, D. S. (2004). Psychobiological mechanisms of resilience and vulnerability: implications for successful adaptation to extreme stress. *American Journal of Psychiatry*, 161(2), 195–216.

Chemtob, C. M., Muraoka, M. Y., Wu-Holt, P., Fairbank, J. A., Hamada, R. S., & Keane, T. M. (1998). Head injury and combat-related posttraumatic stress disorder. *Journal of Nervous and Mental Disorders*, 186(11). 701–708.

Chrousos, G. P., & Gold, P. W. (1998). A healthy body in a healthy mind–and vice versa–the damaging power of "uncontrollable" stress. *Journal of Clinical Endocrinology and Metabolism*, 83(6), 1842–1845.

Clapp, J. D., & Gayle, B. J. (2009). Understanding the relationship between PTSD and social support: the role of negative network orientation. *Behavioral Research and Therapy*, 47(3), 237–244.

Cloitre, M., Stovall-McClough, K. C., Miranda, R., & Chemtob, C. M. (2004). Therapeutic alliance, negative mood regulation, and treatment outcome in child abuse-related post-traumatic stress disorder. *Journal of Consulting and Clinical Psychology*, 72(3), 411–416.

Clum, G. A., Nishith, P., & Calhoun, K. S. (2002). A preliminary investigation of alcohol use during trauma and peritraumatic reactions in female sexual assault victims. *Journal of Trauma and Stress*, 15(4), 321–328.

Cramer, P. (2003). Defense mechanisms and physiological reactivity to stress. *Journal of Personality*, 71(2), 221–244.

Davis, C. G., & Macdonald, S. L. (2004). Threat appraisals, distress and the development of positive life changes after September 11th in a Canadian sample. *Cognitive and Behavioral Therapy*, 33(2), 68–78.

de Vries, G. J., & Olff, M. (2009). The lifetime prevalence of traumatic events and posttraumatic stress disorder in the Netherlands. *Journal of Trauma and Stress*, 22(4), 259–267.

Dickerson, S. S., & Kemeny, M. E. (2004). Acute stressors and cortisol responses: a theoretical integration and synthesis of laboratory research. *Psychological Bulletin*, 130(3), 355–391.

Dienstbier, R. A. (1989). Arousal and physiological toughness: implications for mental and physical health. *Psychology Review, 96*(1), 84–100.

Dohrenwend, B. P., Neria, Y., Turner, J. B., Turse, N., Marshall, R., Lewis-Fernandez, R., & Koenen, K. C. (2004). Positive tertiary appraisals and posttraumatic stress disorder in U.S. male veterans of the war in Vietnam: the roles of positive affirmation, positive reformulation, and defensive denial. *Journal of Consulting and Clinical Psychology, 72*(3), 417–433.

Ehlers, A., & Steil, R. (1995). Maintenance of intrusive memories in post-traumatic stressdisorder: a cognitive approach. *Behavioural and Cognitive Psychotherapy, 23*, 217–249.

Ehlers, A., & Clark, D. M. (2000). A cognitive model of posttraumatic stress disorder. *Behavioral Research and Therapy, 38*(4), 319–345.

Ehlers, A., Mayou, R. A., & Bryant, B. (1998). Psychological predictors of chronic posttraumatic stress disorder after motor vehicle accidents. *Journal of Abnormal Psychology, 107*(3), 508–519.

Ehlert, U., & Straub, R. (1998). Physiological and emotional response to psychological stressors in psychiatric and psychosomatic disorders. *Annals of the New York Academy of Science, 851*, 477–486.

Engelhard, I. M., Macklin, M. L., McNally, R. J., van den Hout, M. A., & Arntz, A. (2001). Emotion- and intrusion-based reasoning in Vietnam veterans with and without chronic posttraumatic stress disorder. *Behavioral Research and Therapy, 39*(11), 1339–1348.

Engelhard, I. M., van den Hout, M. A., Arntz, A., & McNally, R. J. (2002). A longitudinal study of "intrusion-based reasoning" and posttraumatic stress disorder after exposure to a train disaster. *Behavioral Research and Therapy, 40*(12), 1415–1424.

Epel, E. S., McEwen, B. S., & Ickovics, J. R. (1998). Embodying psychological thriving: physical thriving in response to threat. *Journal of Social Issues, 54*(2), 301–322.

Fedoroff, I. C., Taylor, S., Asmundson, G. J.G., & Koch, W. J. (2000). Cognitive factors in traumatic stress reactions: predicting PTSD symptoms from anxiety sensitivity and beliefs about harmful events. *Behavioural and Cognitive Psychotherapy, 28*, 5–15

Foa, E. B., Steketee, G., & Rothbaum, B. O. (1989). Behavioral/cognitive conceptualizations of post-traumatic stress disorder. *Behavioral Therapy, 20*(2), 155–176

Foa, E. B., Riggs, D. S., Dancu, C. V., & Rothbaum, B. O. (1993). Reliability and validity of a brief instrument for assessing post-traumatic stress. *Journal of Traumatic Stress, 6*, 459–473.

Folkman, S., & Moskowitz, J. T. (2000). Positive affect and the other side of coping. *American Psychologist, 55*(6), 647–654.

Frankenhaeuser, M. (1980). Psychobiological aspects of life stress. In S. Levine, & H. Ursin (Eds.), *Coping and health* (pp. 203–224). New York: Plenum Press.

Frankenhaeuser, M. (1983). The sympathetic-adrenal and pituitary-adrenal response to challenge: comparison between the sexes. In T. M. Dembroski, T. H. Schmidt, & G. Bluemchen (Eds.), *Biobehavioral bases of coronary heart diseases* (pp. 91–105). Basel: Kärger.

Frazier, L. D. (2002). Stability and change in patterns of coping with Parkinson's disease. *International Journal of Aging and Human Development, 55*(3), 207–231.

Fredrickson, B. L., Mancuso, R. A., Branigan, C., & Tugade, M. M. (2000). The undoing effect of positive emotions. *Motivation and Emotion, 24*, 237–258

Fredrickson, B. L., Tugade, M. M., Waugh, C. E., & Larkin, G. R. (2003). What good are positive emotions in crises? A prospective study of resilience and emotions following the terrorist attacks on the United States on September 11th, 2001. *Journal of Personality and Social Psychology, 84*(2), 365–376.

Gershuny, B. S., Cloitre, M., & Otto, M. W. (2003). Peritraumatic dissociation and PTSD severity: do event-related fears about death and control mediate their relation? *Behavioral Research and Therapy, 41*(2), 157–166.

Goldin, P. R., Manber, T., Hakimi, S., Canli, T., & Gross, J. J. (2009). Neural bases of social anxiety disorder: emotional reactivity and cognitive regulation during social and physical threat. *Archives of General Psychiatry, 66*(2), 170–180.

Gross, J. J. (1998). Antecedent- and response-focused emotion regulation: Divergent consequences for experience, expression, and physiology. *Journal of Personality and Social Psychology, 74*, 224–237.

Gross, J. J. (2002). Emotion regulation: affective, cognitive, and social consequences. *Psychophysiology, 39*(3), 281–291.

Haan, N. (1977). *Coping and defending: Processes of self-environment organization.* New York: Academic Press.

Halligan, S. L., Michael, T., Clark, D. M., & Ehlers, A. (2003). Posttraumatic stress disorder following assault: the role of cognitive processing, trauma memory, and appraisals. *Journal of Consulting and Clinical Psychology, 71*(3), 419–431.

Heinrichs, M., Baumgartner, T., Kirschbaum, C., & Ehlert, U. (2003). Social support and oxytocin interact to suppress cortisol and subjective responses to psychosocial stress. *Biological Psychiatry, 54*(12), 1389–1398.

Henry, J. P. (1986). Stress, neuroendocrine patterns, and emotional response. In J. D. Noshpitz, & R. D. Coddington (Eds.), *Stressors and adjustment disorders.* Wiley Series in General and Clinical Psychiatry (pp. 477–496). New York: John Wiley and Sons.

Henry, J. P., & Stephens, P. M. (1977). *Stress, health and the social environment. A sociobiological approach to medicine.* New York, Springer Verlag.

Horowitz, M. J. (1986). Stress-response syndromes: a review of posttraumatic and adjustment disorders. *Hospital and Community Psychiatry, 37*(3), 241–249.

Janoff-Bulman, R. (1985). The aftermath of victimization: rebuilding shattered assumptions. In C. R. Figley (Ed.), *Trauma and its wake. The study and treatment of post-traumatic stress disorder* (pp. 15–35). Bristol: Brunner/Mazel

Kessler, R. C., Sonnega, A., Bromet, E., Hughes, M., & Nelson, C. B. (1995). Posttraumatic stress disorder in the National Comorbidity Survey. *Archives of General Psychiatry, 52*(12), 1048–1060.

Kibler, J. L., & Lyons, J. A. (2004). Perceived coping ability mediates the relationship between PTSD severity and heart rate recovery in veterans. *Journal of Trauma and Stress, 17*(1), 23–29.

Kirschbaum, C., Klauer, T., Filipp, S. H., & Hellhammer, D. H. (1995). Sex-specific effects of social support on cortisol and subjective responses to acute psychological stress. *Psychosomatic Medicine, 57*(1), 23–31.

Koss, M. P., Figueredo, A. J., Bell, I., Tharan, M., & Tromp, S. (1996). Traumatic memory characteristics: a cross-validated mediational model of response to rape among employed women. *Journal of Abnormal Psychology, 105*(3), 421–432.

Kvetnansky, K., Pacak, K., Fukuhara, K., Viskupic, E., Hiremagalur, B., Nankova, B., Goldstein, D. S., Sabban, E. L., & Kopin, I. J. (1995). Sympathoadrenal system in stress. Interaction with the hypothalamic-pituitary-adrenocortical system. *Annals of the New York Academy of Science, 771*, 131–158

Ladwig, K. H., Schoefinius, A., Dammann, G., Danner, R., Gurtler, R., & Herrmann, R. (1999). Long-acting psychotraumatic properties of a cardiac arrest experience. *American Journal of Psychiatry, 156*(6), 912–919.

Lazarus, R. S. (1996). The role of coping in the emotions and how coping changes over the life course. In C. Magai, & S. H. McFadden (Eds.), *Handbook of emotion, adult development, and aging* (pp. 289–306), San Diego, CA: Academic Press.

Lazarus, R. S. (1999). *Stress and emotion: A new synthesis.* New York: Springer.

Lazarus, R. S., & Folkman, S. (1984). *Stress, appraisal and coping.* New York: Springer.

Lee, V., Cohen, S. R., Edgar, L., Laizner, A. M., & Gagno, A. J. (2004). Clarifying "meaning" in the context of cancer research: a systematic literature review. *Palliative Support, 2,* 291–303.

Levenson, R. W., Sher, K. J., Grossman, L. M., Newman, J., & Newlin, D. B. (1980). Alcohol and stress response dampening: pharmacological effects, expectancy, and tension reduction. *Journal of Abnormal Psychology, 89*(4), 528–538.

Levine, S., & Ursin, H. (1991). What is stress? In M. R. Brown, G. F. Koob, & C. River (Eds.), *Stress-neurobiology and neuroendocrinology* (pp. 3–21). New York: Marcel Dekker.

Linley, P. A., & Joseph, S. (2004). Positive change following trauma and adversity: a review. *Journal of Trauma and Stress, 17*(1), 11–21.

Luckow, A., Reifman, A., & McIntosh, D. N. (1988). *Gender differences in coping: A meta-analysis.* San Francisco, CA: Annual Meetings of the American Psychological Association.

Lundberg, U., & Frankenhaeuser, M. (1980). Pituitary-adrenal and sympathetic-adrenal correlates of distress and effort. *Journal of Psychosomatic Research, 24*(3–4), 125–130.

Maes, M., Delmeire, L., Mylle, J., & Altamura, C. (2001). Risk and preventive factors of posttraumatic stress disorder (PTSD): alcohol consumption and intoxication prior to a traumatic event diminishes the relative risk to develop PTSD in response to that trauma. *Journal of Affective Disorders, 63*(1–3), 113–121.

Maier, K. J., Waldstein, S. R., & Synowski, S. J. (2003). Relation of cognitive appraisal to cardiovascular reactivity, affect, and task engagement. *Annals of Behavioral Medicine, 26*(1), 32–41.

Mancini, A. D., & Bonanno, G. A. (2009). Predictors and parameters of resilience to loss: toward an individual differences model. *Journal of Personality, 77*(6), 1805–1832.

McClure, E. B., Monk, C. S., Nelson, E. E., Zarahn, E., Leibenluft, E., Bilder, R. M., Charney, D. S., Ernst, M., & Pine, D. S. (2004). A developmental examination of gender differences in brain engagement during evaluation of threat. *Biological Psychiatry, 55*(11), 1047–1055.

McEwen, B. S. (1998). Protective and damaging effects of stress mediators. *New England Journal of Medicine, 338*(3), 171–179.

McFarlane, A. C., & Yehuda, R. (1996). Resilience, vulnerability, and the course of posttraumatic reactions. In B. van der Kolk, A. C. McFarlane, & L. Weisaeth (Eds.), *Traumatic stress: The effects of overwhelming experience on mind, body, and society* (pp. 155–181). New York: Guilford Press.

McNally, R. J. (2003). Psychological mechanisms in acute response to trauma. *Biological Psychiatry, 53*(9), 779–788.

Mellman, T. A., Ramos, J., David, D., Williams, L., & Augenstein, J. S. (1998). Possible inhibition of family PTSD symptoms by alcohol intoxication. *Depression and Anxiety, 7*(3), 145.

Menzies, R. G., & Clarke, J. C. (1995). The etiology of phobias: A non-associative account. *Clinical Psychology Review, 15*, 23–48.

Munck, A., Guyre, P. M., & Holbrook, N. J. (1984). Physiological functions of gluco-corticoids in stress and their relation to pharmacological actions. *Endocrine Review*, *5*(1), 25–44.

Neumann, I. D. (2002). Involvement of the brain oxytocin system in stress coping: interactions with the hypothalamo-pituitary-adrenal axis. *Progress in Brain Research*, *139*, 147–162.

Nicolson, N. A. (1992). Stress, coping and cortisol dynamics in daily life. In M. W. de Vries (Ed.), *The experience of psychopathology: Investigating mental disorders in their natural settings* (pp. 219–232). New York: Cambridge University Press.

Norris, F. H., Friedman, M. J., Watson, P. J., Byrne, C. M., Diaz, E., & Kaniasty, K. (2002). 60,000 disaster victims speak: Part I. An empirical review of the empirical literature, 1981–2001. *Psychiatry*, *65*(3), 207–239.

O'Brien, M., & Nutt, D. (1998). Loss of consciousness and post-traumatic stress disorder. A clue to aetiology and treatment. *British Journal of Psychiatry*, *173*, 102–104.

Olff, M., Brosschot, J. F., & Godaert, G. (1993). Coping styles and health. *Personality and Individual Difference*, *15*, 81–90.

Olff, M., Brosschot, J. F., Godaert, G., Benschop, R. J., Ballieux, R. E., Heijnen, C. J., de Smet, M. B., & Ursin, H. (1995). Modulatory effects of defense and coping on stress-induced changes in endocrine and immune parameters. *International Journal of Behavioral Medicine*, *2*(2), 85–103.

Olff, M., Langeland, W., & Gersons, B. P. (2005). Effects of appraisal and coping on the neuroendocrine response to extreme stress. *Neuroscience Biobehavioral Review*, *29*(3), 457–467.

Olff, M., Meewisse, M. L., Kleber, R. J., Van, D. V., Drogendijk, A. N., van Amsterdam, J. G., Opperhuizen, A., & Gersons, B. P. (2006). Tobacco usage interacts with postdisaster psychopathology on circadian salivary cortisol. *International Journal of Psychophysiology*, *59*(3), 251–258.

Olff, M., Langeland, W., Draijer, N., & Gersons, B. P. (2007a). Gender differences in post-traumatic stress disorder. *Psychological Bulletin*, *133*(2), 183–204.

Olff, M., de Vries, G. J., Guzelcan, Y., Assies, J., & Gersons, B. P. (2007b). Changes in cortisol and DHEA plasma levels after psychotherapy for PTSD. *Psychoneuroendocrinology*, *32*(6), 619–626.

Olff, M., Langeland, W., Witteveen, A. B., & DeNys, D. (2010). A psychobiological rationale for oxytocin in the treatment of PTSD. *CNS Spectrums*, *15*, 522–530.

Ouimette, P., & Brown, P. J. (Eds.). (2003). *Trauma and substance abuse. Causes, consequences, and treatment of comorbid disorders*. Washington, DC: American Psychological Association.

Ozer, E. J., Best, S. R., Lipsey, T. L., & Weiss, D. S. (2003). Predictors of posttraumatic stress disorder and symptoms in adults: a meta-analysis. *Psychological Bulletin*, *129*(1), 52–73.

Park, C. L. (1998). Implications of posttraumatic growth for individuals. In R. G. Tedeschi, C. L. Park, & L. G. Calhoun (Eds.), *Posttraumatic growth: On change in the aftermath of crisis* (pp. 153–177). Mahwah, NJ: Lawrence Erlbaum.

Park, C. L., Cohen, L. H., & Murch, R. L. (1996). Assessment and prediction of stress-related growth. *Journal of Personality*, *64*(1), 71–105.

Peters, M. L., Godaert, G. L., Ballieux, R. E., van, V. M., Willemsen, J. J., Sweep, F. C., & Heijnen, C. J. (1998). Cardiovascular and endocrine responses to experimental stress: effects of mental effort and controllability. *Psychoneuroendocrinology*, *23*(1), 1–17.

Peters, M. L., Godaert, G. L., Ballieux, R. E., & Heijnen, C. J. (2003). Moderation of physiological stress responses by personality traits and daily hassles: less flexibility of immune system responses. *Biological Psychology, 65*(1), 21–48.

Rasmusson, A. M., & Friedman, M. J. (2002). The neurobiology of PTSD in women. In R. Kimerling, P. C. Ouimette, & J. Wolfe (Eds.), *Gender and PTSD* (pp. 43–75). New York: Guilford Press.

Saakvine, K. W., Tennen, H., & Affleck, G. (1998). Exploring thriving in the context of clinical trauma theory: constructivist self-development theory. *Journal of Social Issues, 54,* 279–299.

Sayette, M. A. (1993). An appraisal-disruption model of alcohol's effects on stress responses in social drinkers. *Psychological Bulletin, 114*(3), 459–476.

Schnurr, P. P., & Green, B. L. (Eds.). (2004). *Trauma and health. Physical health consequences of exposure to extreme stress.* Washington DC: American Psychological Association.

Shalev, A. Y., Freedman, S., Peri, T., Brandes, D., Sahar, T., Orr, S. P., & Pitman, R. K. (1998a). Prospective study of posttraumatic stress disorder and depression following trauma. *American Journal of Psychiatry, 155*(5), 630–637.

Shalev, A. Y., Sahar, T., Freedman, S., Peri, T., Glick, N., Brandes, D., Orr, S. P., & Pitman, R. K. (1998b). A prospective study of heart rate response following trauma and the subsequent development of posttraumatic stress disorder. *Archives of General Psychiatry, 55*(6), 553–559.

Shalev, A. Y., Peri, T., Brandes, D., Freedman, S., Orr, S. P., & Pitman, R. K. (2000). Auditory startle response in trauma survivors with posttraumatic stress disorder: a prospective study. *American Journal of Psychiatry, 157*(2), 255–261.

Sherwood, A., Allen, M. T., Fahrenberg, J., Kelsey, R. M., Lovallo, W. R., & van Doornen, L. J. P. (1990). Methodological guideliness for impedance cardiography. *Psychophysiology, 27,* 1–23.

Steil, R., & Ehlers, A. (2000). Dysfunctional meaning of posttraumatic intrusions in chronic PTSD. *Behavioral Research and Therapy, 38*(6), 537–558.

Stewart, S. H., Conrod, P. J., Samoluk, S. B., Pihl, R. O., & Dongier, M. (2000). Posttraumatic stress disorder symptoms and situation-specific drinking in women substance abusers. *Alcoholism Treatment Quarterly, 18,* 31–47.

Taylor, S. E., Klein, L. C., Lewis, B. P., Gruenewald, T. L., Gurung, R. A., & Updegraff, J. A. (2000). Biobehavioral responses to stress in females: tend-and-befriend, not fight-or-flight. *Psychology Review, 107*(3), 411–429.

Tennen, H., & Affleck, G. (1999). Finding benefits in adversity. In C. R. Snyder (Ed.), *Coping: the psychology of what works* (pp. 279–304). New York: University Press.

Thorpe, S. J., & Salkovskis, P. M. (1995). Phobic beliefs: do cognitive factors play a role in specific phobias? *Behavioral Research and Therapy, 33,* 805–816.

Tomaka, J., Blascovich, J., & Kelsey, R. (1993). Subjective, physiological, and behavioral effects of threat and challenge appraisal. *Journal of Personality and Social Psychology, 65*(248), 260.

Tomaka, J., Blascovich, J., Kibler, J., & Ernst, J. M. (1997). Cognitive and physiological antecedents of threat and challenge appraisal. *Journal of Personality and Social Psychology, 73*(1), 63–72.

Uchino, B. N., Cacioppo, J. T., & Kiecolt-Glaser, J. K. (1996). The relationship between social support and physiological processes: a review with emphasis on underlying mechanisms and implications for health. *Psychological Bulletin, 119*(3), 488–531.

Ursin, H. (2009). The development of a Cognitive Activation Theory of Stress: from limbic structures to behavioral medicine. *Scandinavian Journal of Psychology, 50*(6), 639–644.

Ursin, H., & Murison, R. (1983). *Biological and psychological basis of psychosomatic disease*. Oxford: Pergamon Press.

Ursin, H., & Olff, M. (1993). Psychobiology of coping and defence strategies. *Neuropsychobiology, 28*(1–2), 66–71.

Uvnas-Moberg, K. (1998). Oxytocin may mediate the benefits of positive social interaction and emotions. *Psychoneuroendocrinology, 23*(8), 819–835.

Vaernes, R., Ursin, H., Darragh, A., & Lambe, R. (1982). Endocrine response patterns and psychological correlates. *Journal of Psychosomatic Research, 26*(2), 123–131.

Vaillant, G. E. (1986). *Empirical studies of ego mechanisms of defense*. Washington DC: American Psychiatric Press.

van Driel, R. C., & Op den Velde, W. (1995). Myocardial infarction and post-traumatic stress disorder. *Journal of Trauma and Stress, 8*(1), 151–159.

Vickers, Jr., R. R. (1988). Effectiveness of defenses: a significant predictor of cortisol excretion under stress. *Journal of Psychosomatic Research, 32*(1), 21–29.

Wallbott, H. G., & Scherer, K. R. (1991). Stress specificities: differential effectsof coping style, gender, and type of stressor on autonomic arousal, facialexpression, and subjective feeling. *Journal of Personality and Social Psychology, 61*(1), 147–156.

Name Index

Abbott, B. 562
Abbott, D. H. 380
Abdi, A. 184, 187
Abdul–Razzak, K. K. 330
Abdul, H. M. 570
Abe, K. 271
Abe, O. 450
Abel, L. 506
Abel, S. 325
Abercrombie, E. D. 291, 465, 469
Abercrombie, H. C. 181, 255, 427, 434,
    505, 508, 513
Aberg, M. A. 147
Aberg, N. D. 147
Abner, J. L. 308
Abo, A. 486
Abraham, I. 337
Abrari, K. 435
Abrous, D. N. 356
Abumaria, N. 141, 465, 467, 473, 514
Aburada, M. 38, 429
Acconcia, F. 86–7
Acker, J. D. 337
Acsady, L. 191
Adachi, M. 124
Adamec, R. 391
Adams, D. 38–9
Adams, S. 567, 570

Adcock, I. M. 122
Adhumeau-Aucair, A. 486
Adlard, P. A. 214, 359
Adler, N. E. 353
Adolphs, R. 184, 256, 426
Aerni, A. 159, 179–81, 426, 428–30, 433–4,
    436–7, 547
Affleck, G. 584, 589
Afzal, N. 452
Agartz, I. 449
Agarwal, R. 550
Aggleton, J. P. 529
Aghajamian, G. K. 210–11, 213–14, 217,
    219, 486–7
Agid, O. 310
Agnati, L. F. 295, 483
Aguado, F. 292–3
Aguerre, S. 376
Aguilar-Valles, A. 492
Aguilera, G. 15, 37, 64
Agullana, R. 373
Aguzzi, A. 57
Ahima, R. S. 31–3, 567
Ahlenius, S. 293
Ahmat, A. 139
Ahmed, S. H. 209
Ahmed, T. 157
Ahn, S. M. 354

The Handbook of Stress: Neuropsychological Effects on the Brain, First Edition.
Edited by Cheryl D. Conrad.
© 2011 Blackwell Publishing Ltd. Published 2011 by Blackwell Publishing Ltd.

Subject Index

The Handbook of Stress: Neuropsychological Effects on the Brain, First Edition.
Edited by Cheryl D. Conrad.
© 2011 Blackwell Publishing Ltd. Published 2011 by Blackwell Publishing Ltd.